SEVENTH EDITION

Information Systems Today

Managing in the Digital World

Joseph Valacich
University of Arizona

Christoph Schneider
City University of Hong Kong

PEARSON

Boston Columbus Indianapolis New York San Francisco Amsterdam
Cape Town Dubai London Madrid Milan Munich Paris Montréal Toronto
Delhi Mexico City São Paulo Sydney Hong Kong Seoul Singapore Taipei Tokyo

Editor-in-Chief: Stephanie Wall
Acquisitions Editor: Nicole Sam
Program Manager Team Lead: Ashley Santora
Program Manager: Denise Vaughn
Editorial Assistant: Daniel Petrino
Vice President, Product Marketing: Maggie Moylan
Director of Marketing, Digital Services and Products: Jeanette Koskinas
Executive Product Marketing Manager: Anne Fahlgren
Field Marketing Manager: Lenny Ann Raper
Senior Strategic Marketing Manager: Erin Gardner
Project Manager Team Lead: Judy Leale
Project Manager: Karalyn Holland
Operations Specialist: Diane Peirano
Creative Director: Blair Brown
Senior Art Director: Janet Slowik
Interior and Cover Designer: S4Carlisle Publishing Services
Cover Image: VKA/Shutterstock
Vice President, Director of Digital Strategy & Assessment: Paul Gentile
Manager of Learning Applications: Paul Deluca
Digital Editor: Brian Surette
Digital Studio Manager: Diane Lombardo
Digital Studio Project Manager: Robin Lazrus
Digital Studio Project Manager: Alana Coles
Digital Studio Project Manager: Monique Lawrence
Digital Studio Project Manager: Regina DaSilva
Full-Service Project Management and Composition: S4Carlisle Publishing Services
Printer/Binder: LSC Communications
Cover Printer: LSC Communications
Text Font: Times LT Std, 10/12

Library of Congress Cataloging-in-Publication Data

Valacich, Joseph S.,
Information systems today: managing in the digital world. — Seventh edition/Joe Valacich, University of Arizona, Christoph Schneider, City University of Hong Kong.
pages cm
First through 3rd ed. by Leonard M. Jessup, Joseph S. Valacich.
Includes bibliographical references and indexes.
ISBN 978-0-13-394030-5 — ISBN 0-13-394030-6 1. Information technology. 2. Information storage and retrieval systems—Business. I. Schneider, Christoph, 1976- II. Jessup, Leonard M., 1961- Information systems today. III. Title.
T58.5.J47 2016
658.4'038011—dc23

2014030569

6 17

ISBN 10: 0-13-394030-6
ISBN 13: 978-0-13-394030-5

MyMISLab™: Improves Student Engagement Before, During, and After Class

- **Video exercises** – engaging videos that bring business concepts to life and explore business topics related to the theory students are learning in class. Quizzes then assess students' comprehension of the concepts covered in each video.
- **Learning Catalytics** – a "bring your own device" student engagement, assessment, and classroom intelligence system helps instructors analyze students' critical-thinking skills during lecture.
- **Dynamic Study Modules (DSMs)** – through adaptive learning, students get personalized guidance where and when they need it most, creating greater engagement, improving knowledge retention, and supporting subject-matter mastery. Also available on mobile devices.
- **Business Today** – bring current events alive in your classroom with videos, discussion questions, and author blogs. Be sure to check back often, this section changes daily.
- **Decision-making simulations** – place your students in the role of a key decision-maker. The simulation will change and branch based on the decisions students make, providing a variation of scenario paths. Upon completion of each simulation, students receive a grade, as well as a detailed report of the choices they made during the simulation and the associated consequences of those decisions.

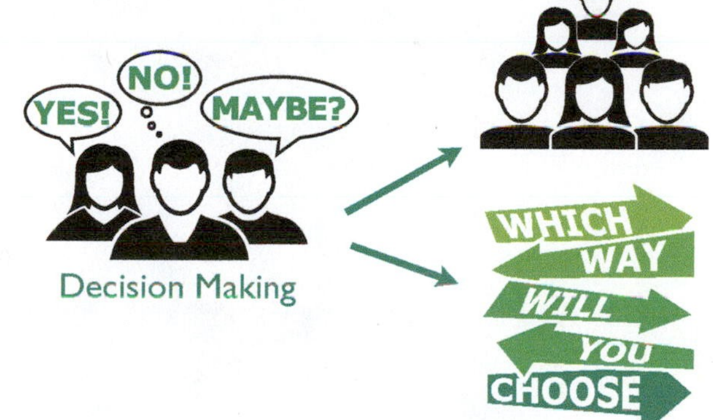

- **Writing Space** – better writers make great learners—who perform better in their courses. Providing a single location to develop and assess concept mastery and critical thinking, the Writing Space offers automatic graded, assisted graded, and create your own writing assignments, allowing you to exchange personalized feedback with students quickly and easily.

  Writing Space can also check students' work for improper citation or plagiarism by comparing it against the world's most accurate text comparison database available from **Turnitin**.

- **Additional Features** – included with the MyLab are a powerful homework and test manager, robust gradebook tracking, comprehensive online course content, and easily scalable and shareable content.

Dedication

To my mother Mary, you are the best.
—Joe

To Birgit for your love and support.
—Christoph

About the Authors

Joe Valacich is an Eller Professor at the University of Arizona, Eller College of Management. He was previously on the faculty at Indiana University, Bloomington, and Washington State University, Pullman. He has had visiting faculty appointments at City University of Hong Kong, Buskerud College (Norway), the Helsinki School of Economics and Business, and the Norwegian University of Life Sciences. He currently teaches in a program for Riga Technical University (Latvia). He received a PhD degree from the University of Arizona (MIS) and MBA and BS (Computer Science) degrees from the University of Montana. Prior to his academic career, Dr. Valacich worked in the software industry in Seattle in both large and startup organizations.

Dr. Valacich has served on various national task forces designing model curricula for the information systems discipline, including *IS '97*, *IS 2002*, and *IS 2010: The Model Curriculum and Guidelines for Undergraduate Degree Programs in Information Systems,* where he was co-chairperson. He also served on the task force that designed *MSIS 2000* and *2006: The Master of Science in Information Systems Model Curriculum.* He served on the executive committee, funded by the National Science Foundation, to define the *IS Program Accreditation Standards* and served on the board of directors for CSAB (formally, the Computing Sciences Accreditation Board) representing the Association for Information Systems (AIS). He was the general conference co-chair for the 2003 International Conference on Information Systems (ICIS) and the 2012 Americas Conference on Information Systems (AMCIS); both were held in Seattle.

Dr. Valacich has conducted numerous corporate training and executive development programs for organizations, including AT&T, Boeing, Dow Chemical, EDS, Exxon, FedEx, General Motors, Microsoft, and Xerox. He is currently co-editor-in-chief of the Association for Information Systems journals *Transactions on Human-Computer Interaction* and *Transactions on Replication Research.* His primary research interests include human–computer interaction, deception detection, technology-mediated collaboration, mobile and emerging technologies, e-business, and distance education. He has published more than 100 scholarly articles in numerous prestigious journals, including *MIS Quarterly, Information Systems Research, Management Science, Academy of Management Journal, Journal of MIS, Decision Sciences, Journal of the AIS, Communications of the ACM, Organizational Behavior and Human Decision Processes,* and *Journal of Applied Psychology*. He is a coauthor of the leading textbooks *Modern Systems Analysis and Design* (7th ed.) and *Essentials of Systems Analysis and Design* (6th ed.), both published by Prentice Hall.

Dr. Valacich was awarded the 2012 Distinguished Alumnus Award from the University of Montana Alumni Association and the 2009 Outstanding Alumnus Award from the University of Montana's School of Business Administration. Dr. Valacich is also ranked as one of most prolific scholars in the history of *MIS Quarterly* over the life of the journal (1977–2014) (see www.misq.org). In 2009, he was named a Fellow of the Association for Information Systems. Throughout his career, he has won numerous teaching, service, and research awards.

Christoph Schneider is an assistant professor in the Department of Information Systems at City University of Hong Kong and previously held a visiting faculty appointment at Boise State University. He earned a Swiss Higher Diploma in Hotel Management at the University Centre César Ritz in Brig, Switzerland, and a BA in Hotel and Restaurant Administration at Washington State University. Following extensive experience in the international hospitality industry, he studied information systems at the Martin Luther University in Halle, Germany, before joining the information systems department at Washington State University to earn his PhD degree. His teaching interests include the management of information systems and Web design.

Dr. Schneider is an active researcher. His primary research interests include human–computer interaction, electronic commerce, and computer-mediated collaboration. His research has appeared in peer-reviewed journals, such as *Information Systems Research, Management Information Systems Quarterly, Management Science,* and *IEEE Transactions on Professional Communication*; further, he has presented his research at various national and international conferences, such as the International Conference on Information Systems, the European Conference on Information Systems, and the Hawaii International Conference on System Sciences. He serves as a member of the International Steering Committee of the International Conference on Information Systems Development (ISD) and as senior editor at *Information Systems Journal.*

Brief Contents

Contents

Preface

APPROACH

Information systems have become *pervasive*. *Mobile devices, social media,* and *cloud computing* have transformed organizations and society. Organizations see the possibilities of the *Internet of Things*, in that not only computers, but various sensors, motors, actuators, or even cameras can generate a wealth of potentially useful data. Businesses face unprecedented opportunities, but also challenges, through the ability to utilize *Big Data*. What does all this mean? What are the catalysts of these concepts and of all this change? More important, how can organizations thrive in this dynamic and highly competitive marketplace? The answer to these and many similar questions is that information systems and related information technologies are driving globalization, new business models, and hypercompetition. It is little wonder that teaching an introductory course on information systems has never been more crucial—or more challenging.

One of the greatest challenges that we face in teaching information systems courses is how to keep pace in the classroom with what is happening out in the real world. Being relevant to students while at the same time providing the necessary foundation for understanding the breadth, depth, and complexity of information systems has never been more difficult. We wrote *Information Systems Today,* Seventh Edition, with this overarching goal in mind, to be both rigorous *and* relevant. To accomplish this, we want students not only to learn about information systems, but also to clearly understand the importance of information systems for individuals, organizations, and society. Additionally, we do not want to simply spoon-feed students with technical terms and the history of information systems. Instead, students must understand exactly what innovative organizations are doing with contemporary information systems and, more important, where things are heading. Finally, we want to empower students with the essential knowledge needed to be successful in the use and understanding of information systems in their careers.

To this end, we wrote *Information Systems Today,* Seventh Edition, so that it is contemporary, fun to read, and useful, focusing on what business students need to know about information systems to survive and thrive in the digital world.

AUDIENCE

Information Systems Today, Seventh Edition, is primarily for the undergraduate introductory information systems course required of all business students. The introductory information systems course typically has a diverse audience of students majoring in many different areas, such as accounting, economics, finance, marketing, general management, human resource management, production and operations, international business, entrepreneurship, and information systems. This book was also written for students studying topics outside of business, especially in the growing and broad area of information sciences. Given the range of students taking this type of course, we have written this book so that it is a valuable guide to all students, providing them with the essential information they need to know. Therefore, this book has been written to appeal to a diverse audience.

Information Systems Today, Seventh Edition, can also be used for the introductory course offered at the graduate level—for example, in the first year of an MBA program. Such usage would be especially appropriate if the course heavily focused on the diverse set of cases provided in each chapter.

WHAT'S NEW TO THE SEVENTH EDITION

Our primary goal for *Information Systems Today,* Seventh Edition, was to emphasize the importance of information systems to all business students as the role of information technology and systems continues to expand within organizations and society. Most notably, we extensively examine how five big megatrends—mobile, social media, the Internet of Things, cloud computing, and Big Data—are transforming how individuals and organizations use information systems. Given this clear focus, we are better able to identify those topics most critical to students and future business professionals. Consequently, we have made substantial revisions to the basic content of the chapters and pedagogical elements that we believe achieve this goal. New or expanded chapter topics include the following:

- A revised chapter—Chapter 1, "Managing in the Digital World"—focuses on not only on defining what an information system consists of but also provides an update on the role of the five big megatrends as catalysts for tremendous change, as evidenced by the rise of globalization and emerging ethical issues.
- An extensively revised chapter—Chapter 2, "Gaining Competitive Advantage Through Information Systems"—provides new content describing how information systems play a key part in the business and revenue models of most organizations.
- A revised chapter—Chapter 3, "Managing the Information Systems Infrastructure and Services"—provides a stronger focus on the need for a reliable, adaptable, and scalable infrastructure to support the needs of today's organizations. Chapter 3 also covers essential infrastructure concepts related to hardware, software, storage, networking and the Internet, and data centers, and provides an extended discussion on cloud computing and related concepts and their role in supporting an organization's information systems infrastructure.
- A revised chapter—Chapter 4, "Enabling Business-to-Consumer Electronic Commerce"—focuses primarily on topics related to e-commerce involving the end consumer, with expanded coverage of mobile commerce and payment and related issues.
- A revised chapter—Chapter 5, "Enhancing Organizational Communication and Collaboration Using Social Media"—centers around various topics related to the need for organizational communication, and discusses how organizations use both traditional communication and collaboration tools and social media for communication, collaboration, cooperation, and connection.
- A revised chapter—Chapter 6, "Enhancing Business Intelligence Using Information Systems"—provides extended coverage on databases to include Big Data and organizations' use of non-relational databases for handling and analyzing the ever-increasing amount of data.
- An extensively revised chapter—Chapter 8, "Strengthening Business-to-Business Relationships Via Supply Chain and Customer Relationship Management"—greatly expands the coverage of supply chain management by including foundational topics of business-to-business electronic commerce. This chapter further provides extended coverage of customer relationship management (CRM) by including evolving topics such as social CRM.
- An extensively revised chapter—Chapter 10, "Securing Information Systems"—provides extended coverage on pertinent topics such as IS risk management.
- A revised Technology Briefing covers foundational concepts related to various information technologies. The Technology Briefing provides the foundations for a deeper understanding of the topics introduced in Chapter 3 and is intended for use in more technically oriented courses. Each section of this briefing was designed to stand alone—it can be read with or without the other sections.

Beyond the chapter content and features, we have also made substantial changes and refinements to the end of each chapter. First, we carefully revised many of the end-of-chapter problems and exercises to reflect content changes and new material. Second, we have carefully updated the end-of-chapter cases about contemporary organizations and issues to illustrate the complexities of the digital world. Each case mirrors the primary content of its chapter to better emphasize its relevancy within the context of a real organization. Third, we have updated the Team Work Exercises based on interesting, important trends related to Internet usage within a variety of contexts; these exercises encourage students to keep up to date on these topics, discuss the significance of changes brought about by the Internet, and visualize and present the most pertinent findings. All these elements are discussed more thoroughly next.

Our goal has always been to provide only the information that is relevant to all business students, nothing more and nothing less. We believe that we have again achieved this goal with *Information Systems Today,* Seventh Edition. We hope you agree.

KEY FEATURES

As authors, teachers, developers, and managers of information systems, we understand that in order for students to best learn about information systems with this book, they must be motivated to learn. To this end, we have included a number of unique features to help students quickly and easily assess the true value of information systems and their impact on everyday life. We show how today's professionals are using information systems to help modern organizations become more efficient and competitive. Our focus is on the application of technology to real-world, contemporary situations. Next, we describe each of the features that contribute to that focus.

A Multitiered Approach

Each chapter utilizes cases in a variety of ways to emphasize and highlight how contemporary organizations are utilizing information systems to gain competitive advantage, streamline organizational processes, or improve customer relationships.

OPENING CASE—MANAGING IN THE DIGITAL WORLD. All chapters begin with an opening case describing a real-world company, technology, and/or issue to spark students' interest in the chapter topic. We have chosen engaging cases that relate to students' interests and concerns by highlighting why information systems have become central for managing in the digital world. Each opening case includes a series of associated questions the students will be able to answer after reading the chapter contents. The organizations, technologies, or issues highlighted in these cases include the following:

- Apple's rise, fall, and reemergence as a global technology giant
- How Groupon achieved a first-mover advantage by reinventing the business model of group buying
- Google's meteoric rise and the challenges associated with maintaining its success
- How Chinese e-commerce company Taobao became a leader in the world of e-commerce
- How Facebook has emerged as one of the most successful and powerful social media sites
- Intelligence agencies' use of social media to gather intelligence about changes in worldwide public sentiment
- Amazon.com's use of its sophisticated infrastructure to automate the supply chain for both large and small customers
- How Walmart became a leader in managing its global supply chains
- How Microsoft's Xbox rose to the top with the help of an ecosystem of devices and apps
- How the hacking group "Anonymous" uses various tactics to further its ideological goals

BRIEF CASE. Each chapter also includes a brief case that discusses important issues related to companies, technologies, or society. These are embedded in the text of the chapter and highlight concepts from the surrounding chapter material. Discussion questions are provided to seed critical thinking assignments or class discussions. The organizations, trends, and products highlighted in these cases include the following:

- How Starbuck's CIO is turning the organizational IS-ship around by introducing various internal and external IS-based innovations
- How broadband Internet access in airplanes has overcome its teething problems
- How domainers—those who buy and sell lucrative domain names on the Internet—have grown into a multibillion-dollar industry
- How organizations such as CrowdSpring enable the crowdsourcing of services
- How crowdfunding is transforming startup companies
- How companies such as eLoyalty use business intelligence to identify hotline callers' personality types
- How Amazon Studios crowdsources movie ideas and scripts, allowing aspiring screenwriters to bypass Hollywood production companies
- How Demand Media creates a supply chain for content published on sites such as eHow, Livestrong.com, and Trails.com
- How hardware and software companies are fighting a global patent war
- How law enforcement uses 3D technology to re-create crime scenes

END-OF-CHAPTER CASE. To test and reinforce chapter content, we present two current real-world cases at the end of each chapter. Sources for these cases include *BusinessWeek, CIO* magazine, *InformationWeek, Wired,* and various Web sites. Like the Brief Cases within the chapter, these cases are taken from the news and are contemporary. However, these are longer and more substantive than the Brief Cases. They too are followed by discussion questions that help the student apply and master the chapter content. The organizations, products, and issues highlighted in these cases include the following:

- How the One Laptop per Child program is attempting to bridge the digital divide
- How YouTube has grown into a mainstream Web marvel
- How LinkedIn, a social networking site for professionals, can help people find jobs, useful business contacts, and business opportunities
- How streaming video is disrupting the movie rental and TV broadcasting industries
- How creators of social games like FarmVille and Candy Crush Sage struggle to overcome infrastructure challenges
- How the deep Web fuels legal and illegal activities
- How Bitcoin created a shadow currency
- How PayPal created a global currency to enable worldwide collaboration and commerce
- How social media giants have joined the world's most valuable companies
- How Wikipedia has become both a useful and a sometimes controversial Web resource
- How the National Security Agency, or NSA, is being viewed as the National *Surveillance* Agency
- How web analytics are providing unprecedented insights into consumer behavior on the Internet
- How Software as a Service has enabled small and medium-sized organizations to utilize enterprise resource planning (ERP) systems
- How Bridgestone's ERP failure turned into a blame game
- How natural disasters disrupt global supply chains
- How customer relationship management is evolving to include social media capabilities
- How the Federal Bureau of Investigation and Department of Homeland Security joined forces in developing a comprehensive database of biometric information to better track and apprehend criminals
- How the rise of open source software systems, such as the Linux operating system, Apache Web server, and Firefox Web browser, is transforming the software industry
- How the National Security Agency is attempting to stop insider leaks
- How China limits information exchange within its society through its "great firewall"

COMMON CHAPTER FEATURES

Throughout every chapter, various short pedagogical elements are presented to highlight key information systems issues and concepts in a variety of contexts. These elements help to show students the broader organizational and societal implications of various topics.

Industry Analysis

Every industry is being transformed by the Internet and the increasing use of information systems by individuals and organizations. To give you a feel for just how pervasive and profound these changes are, each chapter presents an analysis of a specific industry to highlight the new rules for operating in the digital world. Given that no industry or profession is immune from these changes, each Industry Analysis highlights the importance of understanding information systems for *every* business student, not only for information systems majors. Discussion questions help students better understand the rapidly changing opportunities and risks of operating in the digital world. Chapter 1 examines how the digital world is transforming the opportunities for virtually all business professions. Subsequent chapters examine how globalization and the digital world have forever transformed various industries, including education, entertainment, retail, travel, health care, automobile, manufacturing, broadcasting, and law enforcement. Clearly, we are in a time of tremendous change, and understanding this evolution will better equip students to not only survive but also thrive in the digital world.

Coming Attractions

We worked to ensure that this book is contemporary. We cover literally hundreds of different current and emerging technologies throughout the book. This feature, however, focuses on innovations that are likely to soon have an impact on organizations or society. Topics include the following:

- Wearable electronics saving lives
- Google's augmented reality glasses
- Google's Project Loon
- Carbon nanocomputers
- Dissolvable electronics to fight bacteria
- Intelligence through drones
- Combating counterfeits using liquid crystal lasers
- Saving lives through 3D bioprinting
- IBM's predictions for the future
- Speeding security screening using the AVATAR kiosk

When Things Go Wrong

Textbooks don't usually describe what not to do, but this can be very helpful to students. This feature enables students to learn about a real-world situation in which information systems did not work or were not built or used well. Topics include the following:

- Apple's numerous product and strategy failures
- Groupon and the dangers of miscalculating coupons
- Dirty data centers and the environmental impact of cloud computing
- How companies are trying to rig "likes" and reputation on social networking sites
- JP Morgan's social media fiasco
- How Twitter can quickly disseminate *mis*information, with unforeseen consequences
- Avon's not-so-beautiful implementation
- How supply chain issues exacerbated GM's problems with faulty ignition switches
- How an Internet security startup couldn't fight fire with fire
- How the "heartbleed" bug almost killed the Internet

Who's Going Mobile

Mobile technologies have become pervasive throughout society. New opportunities and issues have emerged with the growing importance of mobile devices, such as smartphones and tablets, which are in people's immediate reach 24/7. Related to each chapter's content, this feature examines topics related to the growth in mobile device usage throughout the world. Topics include the following:

- The rise of wearable technologies
- The battle of mobile phone platforms
- How mobile phones have transformed developing countries
- The rise of mobile payments
- Going SoLoMo: Yelp
- The location-based service AroundMe
- Managing businesses on the road using mobile ERP
- The power of mobile CRM
- How to succeed in mobile app development
- Mobile security threats

Ethical Dilemma

Ethical business practices are now a predominant part of contemporary management education and practice. This feature examines contemporary dilemmas related to the chapter content and highlights the implications of these dilemmas for managers, organizations, and society. Topics include the following:

- The human cost of the newest gadgets
- An underground gaming industry selling virtual goods for "real" money

- The ethics of publishing street photography on the Web
- The ethics of reputation management
- The negative impacts of social media use
- Tracking shoppers using mobile phone signals
- Privacy of radio-frequency identification
- Using CRM systems to target or exploit consumers
- Ethical app development
- Industrial espionage

Key Players

A variety of key companies have shaped the information technology industry. While there are countless companies that have contributed to today's digital world, this feature presents some of the more prominent organizations that have significantly advanced technologies or are the leaders in their respective markets. These key players include the following:

- Wipro and Infosys, the global outsourcing leaders
- Huawei, Foxconn, et al.: The global technology elite
- Dell, IBM, Rackspace, and other giants of the infrastructure
- Amazon, GoDaddy, Shopify, and other players behind online storefronts
- The "other" social networking giants
- SAS, MicroStrategy, and other business intelligence leaders
- SAP, Oracle, and Microsoft: The titans of ERP
- Salesforce.com, an SaaS pioneer
- Activision Blizzard, Electronics Arts, and other players in game development
- TrendMicro, McAfee, and other white knights of the Internet Age

End-of-Chapter Material

Our end-of-chapter material is designed to accommodate various teaching and learning styles. It promotes learning beyond the book and the classroom. Elements include the following:

- ***Key Terms***—Highlight key concepts within the chapter.
- ***Review Questions***—Test students' understanding of basic content.
- ***Self-Study Questions***—Enable students to assess whether they are ready for a test.
- ***Matching Questions***—Check quickly to see if students understand basic terms.
- ***Problems and Exercises***—Push students deeper into the material and encourage them to synthesize and apply it.
- ***Application Exercises***—Challenge students to solve two real-world management problems using spreadsheet and database applications from a running case centered on a university travel agency. Student data files referenced within the exercises are available on the book's Web site: www.pearsonhighered.com/valacich.
- ***Team Work Exercise***—Encourage students to keep up with, discuss, visualize, and present interesting, important trends and forecasts related to Internet usage within a variety of contexts.

We have extensively updated these elements to reflect new chapter content and the natural evolution of the material.

Pedagogy

In addition to the features described above, we provide a list of learning objectives to lay the foundation for each chapter. At the end of the chapter, the Key Points Review repeats these learning objectives and describes how each objective was achieved. A list of references appears at the end of each chapter.

Organization

The content and organization of this book are based on our own teaching as well as on feedback from reviewers and colleagues throughout the field. Each chapter builds on the others to reinforce key concepts and allow for a seamless learning experience. Essentially, the book has been structured to answer three fundamental questions:

1. What are contemporary information systems, and how are they being used in innovative ways?
2. Why are information systems so important and interesting?
3. How best can we build, acquire, manage, and safeguard information systems?

The ordering and content of our chapters were also significantly influenced by the "IS 2010 Curriculum Guidelines for Undergraduate Degree Programs in Information Systems," with a particular focus on "What Every Business Student Needs to Know About Information Systems."[1] These articles, written by prominent information systems scholars, define the information systems core body of knowledge for all business students. By design, the content of *Information Systems Today,* Seventh Edition, carefully follows the guidance of these articles. We are, therefore, very confident that our book provides a solid and widely agreed-on foundation for any introductory information systems course.

The chapters are organized as follows:

- ***Chapter 1: Managing in the Digital World***—This chapter helps the student understand what information systems are, how the big five megatrends—mobile, social media, the Internet of Things, cloud computing, and Big Data—influence organizations and society, and how information systems have become a vital part of modern organizations. We walk the student through the technology, people, and organizational components of an information system, and lay out types of jobs and career opportunities in information systems and in related fields. We also focus on how technology is driving globalization and creating countless ethical concerns. We use a number of cases and examples, such as that of Apple, to show the student the types of systems being used and to point out common "best practices" in information systems use and management.
- ***Chapter 2: Gaining Competitive Advantage Through Information Systems***—In this extensively updated chapter, we discuss how companies such as Groupon can use information systems for automation, organizational learning, and strategic advantage by creating new and innovative business models. Given the rapid advancement of new technologies, we explain why and how companies are continually looking for innovative ways to use information systems for competitive advantage, and how information systems support organizations' international business strategies.
- ***Chapter 3: Managing the Information Systems Infrastructure and Services***—Here, we provide an overview of the essential information systems infrastructure components and describe why they are necessary for satisfying an organization's informational needs. With the ever-increasing complexity of maintaining a solid information systems infrastructure, it becomes increasingly important for organizations such as Google to design a reliable, robust, and secure infrastructure. We also examine the rapid evolution toward the delivery of infrastructure capabilities through a variety of cloud-based services.
- ***Chapter 4: Enabling Business-to-Consumer Electronic Commerce***—Perhaps nothing has changed the landscape of business more than the use of the Internet for electronic commerce. In this extensively updated chapter, we describe how firms such as Taobao, Travelocity, or Timbuk2, and also governments, use the Internet to conduct commerce in cyberspace. Further, we describe the requirements for successful e-commerce Web sites and discuss Internet marketing and mobile commerce, as well as consumer-to-consumer and consumer-to-business e-commerce. Finally, we discuss payment and legal issues in e-commerce.

---

[1] Topi, H., Valacich, J., Wright, R. T., Kaiser, K., Nunamaker Jr., J. F., Sipior, J. C., & de Vreede, G. J. (2010). IS 2010: Curriculum guidelines for undergraduate degree programs in information systems. *Communications of the Association for Information Systems,* 26(18); Ives, B., Valacich, J., Watson, R., & Zmud, R. (2002). What every business student needs to know about information systems. *Communications of the Association for Information Systems,* 9(30). Other contributing scholars to this article include Maryam Alavi, Richard Baskerville, Jack J. Baroudi, Cynthia Beath, Thomas Clark, Eric K. Clemons, Gordon B. Davis, Fred Davis, Alan R. Dennis, Omar A. El Sawy, Jane Fedorowicz, Robert D. Galliers, Joey George, Michael Ginzberg, Paul Gray, Rudy Hirschheim, Sirkka Jarvenpaa, Len Jessup, Chris F. Kemerer, John L. King, Benn Konsynski, Ken Kraemer, Jerry N. Luftman, Salvatore T. March, M. Lynne Markus, Richard O. Mason, F. Warren McFarlan, Ephraim R. McLean, Lorne Olfman, Margrethe H. Olson, John Rockart, V. Sambamurthy, Peter Todd, Michael Vitale, Ron Weber, and Andrew B. Whinston.

- ***Chapter 5: Enhancing Organizational Communication and Collaboration Using Social Media***—Social media have forever changed how people interact. In addition to enabling various business opportunities, social media have also enabled companies to better harness the power and creativity of their workforce. In this extensively updated chapter, we provide an overview of traditional communication and collaboration tools, and examine how different social media can enhance communication, collaboration, cooperation, and connection within organizations but also between organizations and their customers. Further, we discuss the importance of carefully managing an Enterprise 2.0 strategy. Finally, using examples such as Twitter and Facebook, we describe how companies can deal with potential pitfalls associated with social media.
- ***Chapter 6: Enhancing Business Intelligence Using Information Systems***—Given how many different types of information systems organizations use to run their businesses and gain business intelligence, in this chapter we describe key business intelligence concepts and explain how databases serve as a foundation for gaining business intelligence. Further, we discuss three components of business intelligence: information and knowledge discovery, business analytics, and information visualization.
- ***Chapter 7: Enhancing Business Processes Using Enterprise Information Systems***—In this updated chapter, we focus on enterprise systems, which are a popular type of information system used to integrate information and span organizations' boundaries to better connect a firm with customers, suppliers, and other partners. We walk students through various core business processes and then examine how enterprise resource planning systems can be applied to improve these processes and organizational performance.
- ***Chapter 8: Strengthening Business-to-Business Relationships via Supply Chain and Customer Relationship Management***—In this extensively updated chapter, we continue our focus on enterprise systems by examining the complexities of supply networks and the rise of business-to-business electronic commerce, before examining how supply chain management systems can support the effective management of supply networks. Additionally, we examine customer relationship management systems and their role in attracting and retaining customers, and, using examples from companies such as Dell, discuss how organizations can integrate social media in their CRM efforts.
- ***Chapter 9: Developing and Acquiring Information Systems***—In this chapter, we begin by describing how to formulate and present the business case to build or acquire a new information system. We then walk the student through the traditional systems development approach and explain how numerous other approaches, such as prototyping, rapid application development, and object-oriented analysis and design, can be utilized depending on the situation. Finally, we examine the steps followed when acquiring an information system from an outside vendor.
- ***Chapter 10: Securing Information Systems***—With the pervasive use of information systems, new dangers have arisen for organizations, and the interplay between threats, vulnerabilities, and potential impacts has become a paramount issue within the context of global information management. In this extensively updated chapter, we define computer crime and contrast several types of computer crime, and discuss the growing significance of cyberwar and cyberterrorism. We then highlight the primary threats to information systems security and explain how systems can be compromised and safeguarded. We conclude this chapter with a discussion of the role of auditing, information systems controls, and the Sarbanes–Oxley Act. Note that some instructors may choose to introduce this chapter prior to the discussion of the information systems infrastructure in Chapter 3.
- ***Technology Briefing***—In addition to these 10 chapters, we include a Technology Briefing that focuses on foundational concepts regarding hardware, software, networking and the Internet, and databases. While Chapter 3, "Managing the Information Systems Infrastructure and Services," provides a more managerial focus to these enabling technologies, this foundational material is intended to provide a more in-depth examination of these topics. By delivering this material as a Technology Briefing, we provide instructors the greatest flexibility in how and when they can apply it.

Instructor Resources

At the Instructor Resource Center, www.pearsonhighered.com/irc, instructors can easily register to gain access to a variety of instructor resources available with this text in downloadable format. If assistance is needed, our dedicated technical support team is ready to help with the media supplements that accompany this text. Visit http://247.pearsoned.com for answers to frequently asked questions and toll-free user support phone numbers.

The following supplements are available with this text:

- Instructor's Resource Manual
- Test Bank
- TestGen® Computerized Test Bank
- PowerPoint Presentation
- Image Library

Reviewers

We wish to thank the following faculty who participated in reviews for this and previous editions:

Lawrence L. Andrew, *Western Illinois University*
Karin A. Bast, *University of Wisconsin–La Crosse*
David Bradbard, *Winthrop University*
Rochelle Brooks, *Viterbo University*
Brian Carpani, *Southwestern College*
Amita Chin, *Virginia Commonwealth University*
Jon D. Clark, *Colorado State University*
Paul Clay, *Fort Lewis College*
Khaled Deeb, *Barry University*
Thomas Engler, *Florida Institute of Technology*
Badie Farah, *Eastern Michigan University*
Roy H. Farmer, *California Lutheran University*
Mauricio Featherman, *Washington State University*
David Firth, *University of Montana*
Frederick Fisher, *Florida State University*
Jonathan Frank, *Suffolk University*
James Frost, *Idaho State University*
Frederick Gallegos, *California State Polytechnic University–Pomona*
Dale Gust, *Central Michigan University*
Peter Haried, *University of Wisconsin–La Crosse*
Albert Harris, *Appalachian State University*
Michelle Hepner, *University of Central Oklahoma*
Traci Hess, *University of Massachusetts*
Bruce Hunt, *California State University–Fullerton*
Carol Jensen, *Southwestern College*
Bhushan Kapoor, *California State University–Fullerton*
Elizabeth Kemm, *Central Michigan University*
Beth Kiggins, *University of Indianapolis*
Chang E. Koh, *University of North Texas*
Brian R. Kovar, *Kansas State University*
Kapil Ladha, *Drexel University*
Linda K. Lau, *Longwood University*
Amy Lavin, *Temple University*
Cameron Lawrence, *University of Montana*
Martha Leva, *Penn State University–Abington*
Weiqi Li, *University of Michigan–Flint*
Clayton Looney, *University of Montana*
Dana L. McCann, *Central Michigan University*
Richard McCarthy, *Quinnipiac University*
Patricia McQuaid, *California State Polytechnic University, San Louis Obispo*
Michael Newby, *California State University–Fullerton*
Kathleen Noce, *Penn State University–Erie*
W. J. Patterson, *Sullivan University*
Timothy Peterson, *University of Minnesota–Duluth*
Lara Preiser-Houy, *California State Polytechnic University, Pomona*
Sridhar Ramachandran, *Indiana University Southeast*
Eugene Rathswohl, *University of San Diego*
Rene F. Reitsma, *Oregon State University*
Jose Rodriguez, *Barry University*
Bonnie Rohde, *Albright College*
Kenneth Rowe, *Purdue University*
Dana Schwieger, *Southeast Missouri State University*
G. Shankaranarayanan, *Boston University*
James Sneeringer, *St. Edward's University*
Cheri Speier, *Michigan State University*
Bill Turnquist, *Central Washington University*
Craig K. Tyran, *Western Washington University*
William Wagner, *Villanova University*
Minhua Wang, *State University of New York–Canton*
John Wells, *University of Massachusetts*
Nilmini Wickramasinghe, *Cleveland State University*
Yue Zhang, *California State University–Northridge*

ACKNOWLEDGMENTS

Although only our two names are listed as the authors for this book, this was truly a team effort that went well beyond the two of us. Pearson Prentice Hall has been an outstanding publishing company to work with. Pearson Prentice Hall is innovative, has high standards, and is as competitive as we are.

Among the many amazingly helpful people at Pearson, there are a handful of people we wish to thank specifically. First, Karalyn Holland, our project manager, helped to whip us and this book into shape and get it finished on time. Additionally, Vinolia Benedict Fernando from S4 Carlisle helped in getting approval for photos, figures, Web sites, and other graphics, as well as coordinating refinements as the book moved through the stages of production. Finally, we want to thank our editor, Nicole Sam. In addition to our current Pearson team, we would also like to thank our former editor, Bob Horan, who took a well-earned retirement in early 2014. Bob worked with us for the past decade, always challenging us to build the best book possible. Thanks Bob!

In addition to our colleagues at Pearson Prentice Hall, several individuals have been particularly instrumental in making the seventh edition the best ever. First, Dave Wilson, PhD candidate at the University Arizona, did an outstanding job on creating and revising several of our case elements. Also, a special thanks goes out to Catherine Chan from Hong Kong Baptist University, who has been instrumental in drafting earlier chapter elements. Thanks team! We could not have done it without you.

Most important, we thank our families for their patience and assistance in helping us to complete this book. Joe's wife Jackie, daughter Jordan, and son James were a constant inspiration, as was Christoph's wife Birgit. This one is for all of you.

1

Managing in the Digital World

After reading this chapter, you will be able to do the following:

1. Describe the characteristics of the digital world and the advent of the Information Age.
2. Define globalization, describe how it evolved over time, and describe the key drivers of globalization.
3. Explain what an information system is, contrasting its data, technology, people, and organizational components.
4. Describe the dual nature of information systems in the success and failure of modern organizations.
5. Describe how computer ethics impact the use of information systems and discuss the ethical concerns associated with information privacy and intellectual property.

Preview

Today, organizations from Apple to Zales Jewelers use information systems to better manage their organizations in the digital world. These organizations use information systems to provide high-quality goods and services as well as to gain or sustain competitive advantage over rivals. In addition to helping organizations to be competitive, information systems have contributed to tremendous societal changes. Our objective for this chapter is to help you understand the role of information systems as we continue to move further into the digital world, and how they have helped fuel globalization. We then highlight what information systems are, how they have evolved to become a vital part of modern organizations, and why this understanding is necessary for you to become an effective manager in the digital world. We conclude by discussing ethical issues associated with the use of information systems.

Managing in the Digital World: **Apple**

Apple is one of the largest, most profitable technology companies in world. Each year, Apple sells hundreds of millions of its popular iMacs, MacBooks, iPods, iPads, and iPhones. Apple's products—and the technology that supports them—have influenced the way people behave and interact. Think how waiting in line at the grocery store or waiting for the next train is more productive, or at least no longer tedious, when you get to check your inbox or play a round of Angry Birds (Figure 1.1). Now remember how insecure you felt the last time you left your smartphone sitting on your living room sofa. Whichever way you look at it, the Apple craze is certainly here to stay, with people camping out for days to get their hands on the latest Apple gadgets.

Over the course of its history, Apple had its ups and downs, with Steve Wozniak and Steve Jobs, the company's founders, leaving Apple in the 1980s. After Steve Jobs' return to Apple in 1997, Apple has had an impressive run of successful products, including the iMac, the PowerBook, the iPod, and iTunes. Building on its success with the iPod, Apple introduced the iPhone in 2007 and, shortly thereafter, the "App Store," revolutionizing the way we purchase and use applications on mobile devices. The era of iPhones continued as successive updates to the iPhone line were introduced year after year, each garnering wider adoption than the last. In 2010, Apple introduced the revolutionary iPad, touted as a "third-category" device between smartphones and laptop personal computers (PCs). Clearly, innovations fueled by Apple have changed the lives of many people all over the world, and have contributed to the move into the post-PC era.

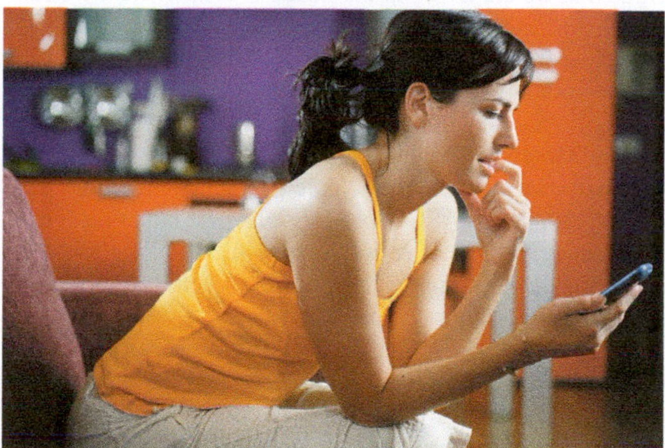

FIGURE 1.1

Smartphones have taken the dreadfulness out of waiting.
Source: Diego Cervo/Fotolia.

Because of this wild success, Apple has managed to become not only a hardware vendor, but also a keeper of people's (often private) information. As it is being stored in the cloud, personal information can easily be (ab)used to predict future behavior, potential trends, music tastes, and more. Connected as we may be to the rest of the world, salient concerns are warranted regarding issues of privacy and information property—that is, who has access to what and how private information is being used. Certainly, there are potential risks associated with being an active participant in the digital world, so the next time you purchase an app, think about how much you reveal about yourself with the swipe of your finger.

After reading this chapter, you will be able to answer the following:

1. Given the pace at which technology is converging (e.g., phones, music players, cameras, and so on), what do you think is next in the post-PC era?
2. How have Apple's products influenced the way we work and socialize?
3. What are the ethical concerns associated with storing and analyzing user data?

Based on:
Apple Inc. (2014, May 2). In *Wikipedia, The Free Encyclopedia*. Retrieved May 7, 2014, from http://en.wikipedia.org/w/index.php?title=Apple_Inc.&oldid=606715547.

INFORMATION SYSTEMS TODAY

Today, computers—the core components of information systems (IS)—are ubiquitous: Be it e-book readers, laptop computers, digital cameras, smartphones, etc., you name it; computers are all around us, whether you see them or not. Companies such as FedEx and UPS use information systems to route trucks and track packages. Retailers such as Walgreens and Walmart use information systems for everything from optimizing supply chains to recording purchases and analyzing customer tastes and preferences. Cities use information systems for adaptive traffic control systems or variable speed limits. Cars use computers for everything from ignition control to airbags to distance control and park assist systems; in fact, U.S. automaker Ford now considers itself a technology company, pioneering, for example, applications that allow accessing smartphone apps from an in-dash touchscreen. Alternatively, just look around your school or place of work. At your school, you register for classes online; use e-mail, Twitter, or Facebook to communicate with fellow students and your instructors; access e-books from your library; and complete or submit assignments on online learning platforms such as BlackBoard, Moodle, or Sakai. At work, you may use a PC for e-mail and many other tasks. Your paychecks are probably generated by computer and automatically deposited in your banking account via high-speed networks. Even in your spare time, information technology is ubiquitous: You use social networking sites like Facebook to stay connected with your friends and family, you watch videos on YouTube, you upload pictures taken with your cell phone or digital camera to picture-sharing sites like Flickr, and you use your smartphone for playing games, sending e-mails, or even reading books. Chances are that each year you see more information technology than you did the year before, and this technology is a more fundamental and important part of your social, learning, and work life than ever before.

Over the past decades, the advent of powerful, relatively inexpensive, easy-to-use computers has had a major impact on business. When you stop and think about it, it is easy to see why information technology is important. Increasing global competitiveness has forced companies to find ways to be better and to do things less expensively. The answer for many firms continues to be to use information systems to do things better, faster, and cheaper. Using global telecommunications networks, companies can more easily integrate their operations to access new markets for their products and services as well as access a large pool of talented labor in countries with lower wages.

Clearly, we are living in a digital world. Given the proliferation of new form factors, such as tablets or smartphones, some even argue that we are living in the **post-PC era**, where wireless, mobile devices allow for novel ways of interacting with information systems. In fact, already in 2011, the majority of Apple's revenues came from "post-PC devices," and in the last quarter of 2011, Apple sold more iPads than HP (traditionally one of the world's leading PC makers) sold PCs. With Apple's introduction of the latest iPads in late 2013, this trend is likely to continue; analysts estimate 285 million name-brand tablets worldwide. Forrester research predicts that by 2016, one in every three U.S. adults will own a tablet, be it Apple's iPad; a tablet manufactured by electronics manufacturers such as Samsung, ASUS, or Motorola; or a tablet designed by the online bookseller Amazon.com (Kindle) or Barnes & Noble (Nook). Initially created as consumer devices, tablets have already made their way into various business settings, including warehouses, showrooms, airplane cockpits, and hospitals (Figure 1.2).

Yet, desktop PCs and laptops are unlikely to go away. Rather, devices with newer form factors will work in tandem with older form factors to provide truly ubiquitous experiences, and the changes we've seen so far will give rise to future developments, including wearable computers, augmented reality devices, or surface computers (Epps, Gownder, Golvin, Bodine, & Corbett, 2011).

Changes in technology have enabled new ways of working and socializing; whereas traditionally, people were bound to a stationary PC to do essential tasks, they can now perform such tasks from almost anywhere they have a cell phone signal. At the same time, workdays traditionally had a clear beginning and a clear end—from when you power your computer on to when you turn it off at night. Today, many tasks (especially more casual tasks such as reading or sending e-mails) can be done at any time, often in small chunks in between other tasks, such as when waiting in line at the supermarket cashier.

Computing has changed from an activity primarily focused on automating work to encompass various social and casual activities. Devices such as smartphones or tablets, paired with mobile broadband networks, allow for instant-on computing experiences, whenever and wherever; advances

FIGURE 1.2

Post-PC devices are increasingly being used in various business settings.
Source: Minerva Studio/Fotolia.

in *cloud computing* (think Gmail, Office Online, or DropBox) allow for accessing e-mails, files, notes, and the like from different devices, further enhancing portability and mobility.

In effect, we are in a virtuous cycle (or in a vicious cycle, considering the creep of work life into people's leisure time, and the increasing fixation on being permanently "on call"), where changes in technology enable social changes, and social changes shape technological changes. For example, communication, social networking, and online investing almost necessitate mobility and connectivity, as people have grown accustomed to checking e-mails, posting status updates, or checking on real-time stock quotes while on the go. In addition, the boundaries between work and leisure time are blurring, so that employees increasingly demand devices that can support both, often bringing their own devices into the workplace. In fact, a study conducted by research firm Forrester in 2011 found that 54 percent of online consumers in the United States and 70 percent of iPad owners believe that technology helps them to optimize both work and personal life.

In 1959, Peter Drucker predicted that information and information technology (IT) would become increasingly important, and at that point, over half a century ago, he coined the term **knowledge worker**. Knowledge workers are typically professionals who are relatively well educated and who create, modify, and/or synthesize knowledge as a fundamental part of their jobs.

Drucker's predictions about knowledge workers were accurate. As he predicted, they are generally paid better than their prior agricultural and industrial counterparts; they rely on and are empowered by formal education, yet they often also possess valuable real-world skills; they are continually learning how to do their jobs better; they have much better career opportunities and far more bargaining power than workers ever had before; they make up about a quarter of the workforce in the United States and in other developed nations; and their numbers are rising quickly.

Drucker also predicted that, with the growth in the number of knowledge workers and with their rise in importance and leadership, a **knowledge society** would emerge. He reasoned that, given the importance of education and learning to knowledge workers and the firms that need them, education would become the cornerstone of the knowledge society. Possessing knowledge, he argued, would be as important as possessing land, labor, or capital (if not more so) (Figure 1.3). Indeed, research shows that people equipped to prosper in the knowledge society, such as those with a college education, earn far more on average than people without a college education, and that gap is increasing. In fact, the most recent data from the American Community Survey (2012 data) reinforce the value of a college education: Median earnings for workers 18 and over with a bachelor's degree were US$49,157 a year, while those for workers with a high school diploma were US$27,024. Median earnings for workers with a graduate or professional degree were US$65,164, and of those without a high school diploma US$19,404. These data suggest that a bachelor's degree is worth about US$1 million in additional lifetime earnings compared to a worker with only a high school diploma. Additionally, getting a college degree will qualify you for many jobs that would not be available to you otherwise and will distinguish

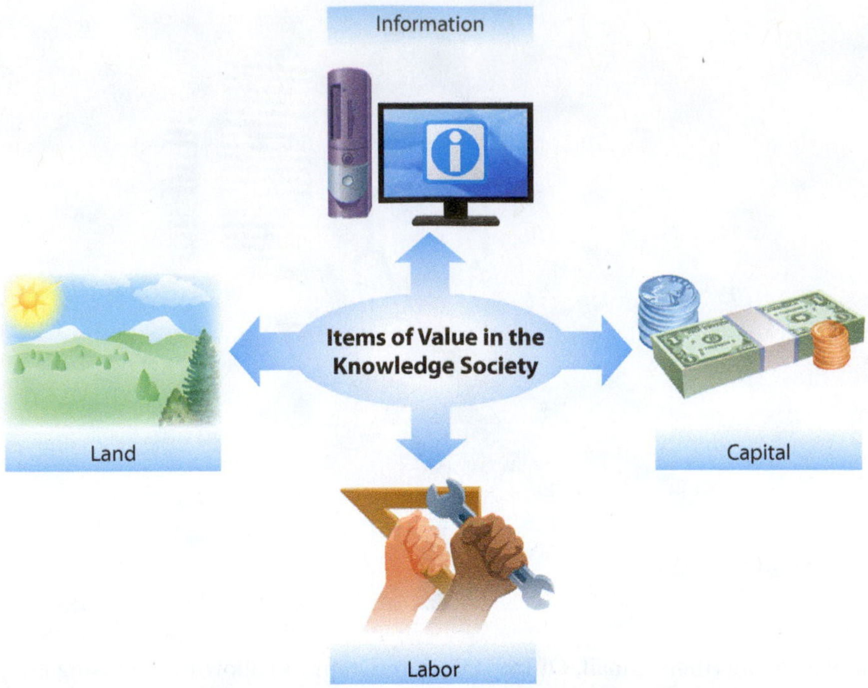

FIGURE 1.3

In the knowledge society, information has become as important as—and many feel more important than—land, labor, and capital resources.

you from other job candidates. Finally, a college degree is often a requirement to qualify for career advancement and promotion opportunities once you do get that job.

People generally agree that Drucker was accurate about knowledge workers and the evolution of society. While people have settled on Drucker's term "knowledge worker," there are many alternatives to the term "knowledge society." Others have referred to this phenomenon as the knowledge economy, new economy, the digital society, the network era, the Internet era, and other names. We simply refer to this as the *digital world*. All these ideas have in common the premise that information and related technologies and systems have become very important to us and that knowledge workers are vital.

Similarly, many "traditional" occupations now increasingly use information technologies—from the UPS package delivery person using global positioning system (GPS) technology to plan the best route to deliver parcels, to the farmer in Iowa who uses precision agriculture to plan the use of fertilizers to increase crop yield. In essence, (almost) every organization can now be considered an e-business. Like the term "e-commerce," "e-business" refers to the use of information technologies and systems to support the business. Whereas "e-commerce" generally means the use of the Internet and related technologies to support commerce, **e-business** has a broader meaning: the use of nearly any information technologies or systems to support every part of the business. The lines between "knowledge workers" and "manual workers" are blurring, to the point that some argue that "every worker is a knowledge worker" (Rosen, 2011). The people at the front lines typically have a very good understanding of how certain business processes work, and can provide valuable input for improving or optimizing those processes; further, knowing how their work contributes to business results can foster commitment, leading to higher job performance.

Some have argued, however, that there is a downside to being a knowledge worker and to living in the digital world. For example, some have argued that knowledge workers will be the first to be replaced by automation with information technology. Others have argued that in the new economy there is a **digital divide**, where those with access to information technology have great advantages over those without access to information technology. The digital divide is one of the major ethical challenges facing society today when you consider the strong linkage between computer literacy and a person's ability to compete in the Information Age. For example, access to raw materials and money fueled the Industrial Revolution, "but in the informational society, the fuel, the power, is knowledge," emphasized John Kenneth Galbraith, an American economist who specialized in emerging trends in the U.S. economy. "One has now come to see a new class structure divided by those who have information and those who must function out of ignorance. This new class has its power not from money, not from land, but from knowledge" (Galbraith, 1987).

The good news is that the digital divide in America is rapidly shrinking, but there are still major challenges to overcome. In particular, people in rural communities, the elderly, people with disabilities, and minorities lag behind national averages for Internet access and computer literacy. Outside the United States and other developed countries, the gap gets even wider and the obstacles get much more difficult to overcome, particularly in the developing countries where infrastructure and financial resources are lacking (see also Case 1 at the end of this chapter). For example, most developing countries are lacking modern informational resources such as affordable Internet access or efficient electronic payment methods like credit cards.

To be sure, there is a downside to overreliance on information technology, but one thing is for certain: Knowledge workers and information technologies are now critical to the success of modern organizations, economies, and societies. How did information systems become so pervasive throughout our lives and society? This is examined next.

The Rise of the Information Age

In his book *The Third Wave*, futurist Alvin Toffler describes three distinct phases, or "waves of change," that have taken place in the past or are presently taking place within the world's civilizations (Figure 1.4). The first wave—a civilization based on agriculture and handwork—was a comparatively primitive stage that replaced hunter-gatherer cultures and lasted for thousands of years. The second wave of change—the Industrial Revolution—overlapped with the first wave. The Industrial Revolution began in Great Britain toward the end of the eighteenth century and

BRIEF CASE Technology at Starbucks

Since its founding in Seattle in the early 1970s, Starbucks has opened nearly 20,000 stores in 58 countries; most Starbucks' stores attract a loyal crowd of customers, not only by offering a variety of coffees and related drinks, but also by providing a comfortable place to meet, study, work, or just hang out. In 2008, Starbucks hired Steve Gillett (named "Chief Information Officer, or CIO, of the Year" by *InformationWeek* in 2011) to improve the company's information systems to better support its operations. Blending marketing with technology, Gillett started a number of initiatives, with a focus on both the customers and Starbucks' employees. Here are just a few examples of how technology is being used at Starbucks:

1. Connecting with Customers—A key component of the Starbucks coffeehouse atmosphere is connectivity. In addition to free Wi-Fi access, customers can enjoy free access to premium content from the *Wall Street Journal* and other sources. Another way to connect with customers is "My Starbucks Idea," where customers can post ideas and suggestions, as well as vote on or discuss others' ideas. Hundreds of customer-generated ideas have been launched over the years. The company's Facebook page, which has more than 37 million "likes," serves as another avenue for customers to stay connected.
2. Mobile Payments—Starbucks is a leader in mobile payments. A smartphone app tied to the customer's loyalty and payment can be used to make transactions, while at the same time generating a wealth of information about Starbucks' loyal customers. By late 2013, over 10 percent of all Starbucks sales were made using the mobile apps.
3. Virtual Talent—A new addition to Starbucks' headquarters is the "Tech Cafe." Resembling Apple's "Genius Bars," this IS help desk allows employees to get help with IS-related problems, choose technologies they need for their own workplace, and discuss needs and suggestions. Having recognized the increasing IS-related knowledge of its employees, Starbucks hopes to obtain valuable new ideas and suggestions from each employee.
4. Contextual Retailing—Starbucks strives to offer an individualized experience for every customer. For example, using mobile technologies, the baristas at Starbucks can be alerted if a regular customer enters the store, know the customer's preferred drinks, or suggest new alternatives based on the customer's history. Even further, the music played within a store could be based on the collective preferences of the customers sitting in the store.

These are but some examples that show that in today's highly competitive world, successful companies have to do more than just brew a good cup of coffee.

Questions

1. What are other ways in which Starbucks could use technology to connect with its customers?
2. To what extent do such innovations influence your choice of coffee shops? What would make you switch to another store? Why?

Based on:

Murphy, C. (2011, December 12). Starbucks' Stephen Gillett: Information-Week's IT Chief of The Year. *InformationWeek*. Retrieved May 10, 2014, from http://www.informationweek.com/news/global-cio/interviews/232200549.

Starbucks. (2014, May 9). In *Wikipedia, The Free Encyclopedia*. Retrieved May 10, 2014, from http://en.wikipedia.org/w/index.php?title=Starbucks&oldid=607798080.

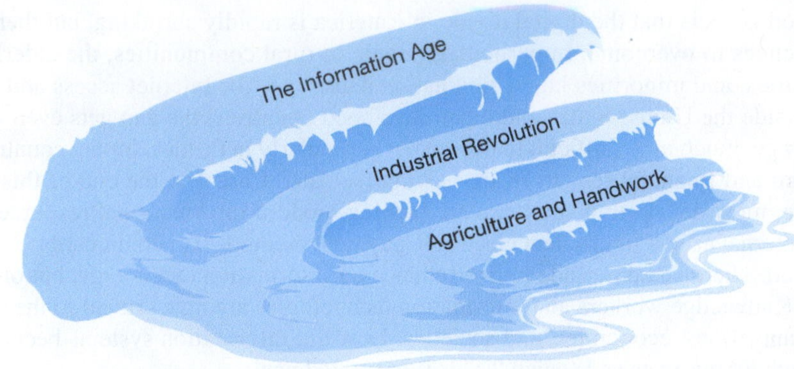

FIGURE 1.4

The Information Age is the biggest wave of change.

continued over the next 150 years, moving society from a predominantly agrarian culture to the urbanized machine age. Where once families supported themselves by working the land or handcrafting items for sale or trade, now mothers, fathers, and children left home to work in factories. Steel mills, textile factories, and eventually automobile assembly lines replaced farming and handwork as the principal source of family income.

As the Industrial Revolution progressed, not only did occupations change to accommodate the mechanized society, but so did educational, business, social, and religious institutions. On an individual level, punctuality, obedience, and the ability to perform repetitive tasks became qualities to be instilled and valued in children in public schools and, ultimately, in workers.

In a much shorter period of time than it took for civilization to progress past the first wave, societies worldwide moved from the machine age into the **Information Age**—a period of change Toffler has dubbed the "third wave." As the third wave gained speed, information became the currency of the realm. For thousands of years, from primitive times through the Middle Ages, information, or the body of knowledge known to that point, was limited. It was transmitted verbally within families, clans, and villages, from person to person and generation to generation. Then came Johannes Gutenberg's invention of the printing press with movable type in the middle of the fifteenth century, and a tremendous acceleration occurred in the amount and kinds of information available to populations (Figure 1.5). Now knowledge could be imparted in written form and sometimes came from distant locations. Information could be saved, absorbed, debated, and written about in publications, thus adding to the exploding data pool.

FIGURE 1.5

The printing press gave birth to the Information Age.
Source: ChipPix/Shutterstock.

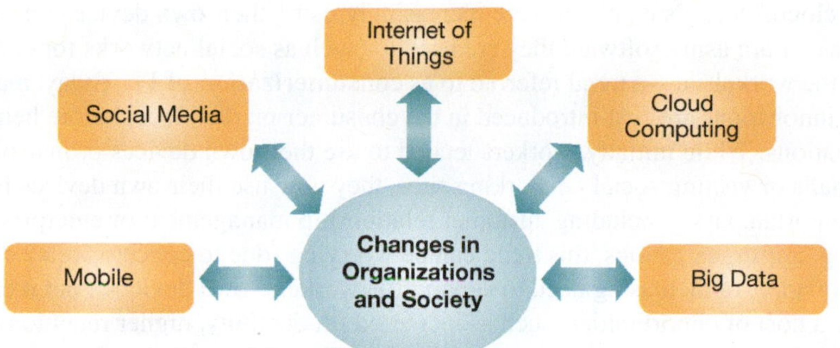

FIGURE 1.6

Five IT megatrends.

Five IT Megatrends in the Information Age

Today, in most developed societies, information technologies have become pervasive—information technologies are in fact used throughout society. The development of sophisticated Web technologies has brought about a fundamental shift in types of information technologies that are being used, and we're seeing five (intertwined) "megatrends" that shape organizations and society (Figure 1.6). Knowing about the influence of these megatrends will be increasingly important for both your work life and your personal life.

- ***Mobile.*** Many believe that we're living in a post-PC era, and one of the biggest trends we're seeing today is the move toward mobile devices, as indicated in the opening section of this chapter. In most developed countries, the vast majority of adults has a mobile phone, and typically, people have their mobile phones within their reach 24/7. Compare that with the access to your laptop or PC. In the developing world, mobile devices are frequently seen leapfrogging traditional PCs, often owing to the lack of stable, reliable power or lacking landline telephone infrastructures, making mobile devices the primary means of accessing the Internet. For organizations, this increase in mobility has a wide range of implications, from increased collaboration to the ability to manage a business in real time—at any time, from anywhere—to changes in the way new (or existing) customers can be reached (Figure 1.7). With the increase in mobile devices, organizations not only have to create mobile-device-friendly versions of their Web sites, but often build mobile **apps** (software programs designed to perform a particular, well-defined function) to market their products or services. In addition, fueled by advances in consumer-oriented mobile devices (such as smartphones and tablets) and the ability to access data and applications

FIGURE 1.7

Mobile devices allow running business in real time—at any time, from anywhere.

"in the cloud," today's employees are increasingly using their own devices for work-related purposes, or are using software they are used to (such as social networks for communicating) in the workplace—a trend referred to as **consumerization of IT**. Today, many technological innovations are first introduced in the consumer marketplace, before being used by organizations. While initially, workers tended to use their own devices primarily for checking e-mails or visiting social networking sites, they now use their own devices for various other important tasks, including customer relationship management or enterprise resource planning. For organizations, this trend can be worrying (due to concerns related to security or compliance, or increasing need to support the workers' own devices), but it can also provide a host of opportunities, such as increased productivity, higher retention rates of talented employees, or higher customer satisfaction (TrendMicro, 2011). Managing this trend of "bring your own device" (**BYOD**) is clearly a major concern of business and IT managers alike. Throughout the text, we will introduce issues and new developments associated with increases in mobility.

- ***Social Media.*** A second megatrend, as you have undoubtedly noticed, is social media. You may be one of the over 1.28 billion (and growing) Facebook users who share status updates or pictures with friends and family, or you may use a social network such as Google+ to stay informed about the activities of your social "circles." University professors use social networks to provide students with updates about course-related topics, and organizations use social media to encourage employee collaboration or to connect with their customers (Figure 1.8). In addition, companies can harness the power of the crowd, by using social media to get people to participate in innovation and other activities. Another example of the power of social media is Wikipedia, the online encyclopedia that everyone can contribute to. As you can imagine, social media are here to stay; while we will touch on social media–related aspects throughout the book, we will devote Chapter 5, "Enhancing Organizational Communication and Collaboration Using Social Media," to social media and related topics.
- ***The Internet of Things.*** A third megatrend is the **Internet of Things**—a broad range of physical objects (such as computer, sensors, or motors) that are interconnected and automatically share data over the Internet. Already in 2008, more devices were connected to the Internet than there were people living on earth. Fueled by advances in chips and wireless radios and decreasing costs of sensors, in the not-too-distant future everything that can generate useful information will be equipped with sensors and wireless radios (Figure 1.9). In other words, anything that can generate data or uses data can be connected, accessed, or controlled via the Internet. With the ability to connect "things" such as sensors, meters, signals, motors, or cameras, the potential for gathering useful data is almost limitless. For example, one can monitor home temperatures when on vacation, and remotely adjust the air-conditioning; likewise, sensors integrated in a road's surface could monitor temperatures and trigger dynamic speed limits in case there is the risk of ice or snow. Similarly, sensors could monitor availability of parking spaces or traffic flow, alerting drivers of changes in conditions. Millions of sensors connected to the Internet could monitor weather conditions, helping to generate more accurate local weather predictions, or could monitor soil moisture in golf courses, reducing the need for watering. Cardiac monitors can alert physicians of patients' health risks. Various types of sensors can be used in factories to monitor machinery, making production more efficient. In sum, the applications of sensor technology for home automation, smart cities, smart metering, smart farming, e-health, and

FIGURE 1.8

Social media are used in various personal and business settings.

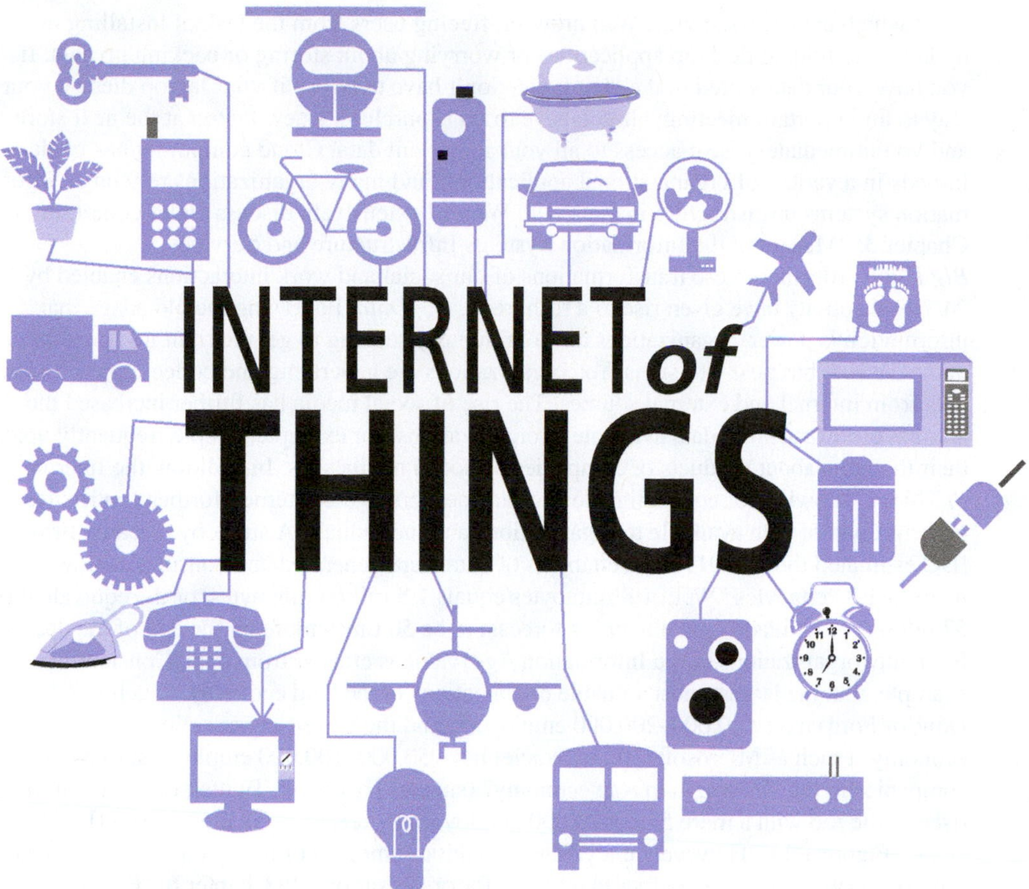

FIGURE 1.9

The Internet of Things.

other areas are limitless. As the number of sensors and devices connected to the Internet grows, the Internet of Things will evolve to become the Internet of Everything, where just about any device's functionality is enhanced through connectivity and intelligence.

- ***Cloud Computing.*** The fourth megatrend is **cloud computing**. Whereas traditionally each user would install applications for various tasks—from creating documents to listening to music—as well as store documents, pictures, and other data on his or her computer, Web technologies enable using the Internet as the platform for applications and data. Now, much of the functionality previously offered by applications installed on each individual computer is offered by applications "in the cloud," accessed via your Web browser (Figure 1.10). In fact, many regard cloud computing as the beginning of the "fourth wave" of change, where not only the applications but also the data reside in the cloud, to be accessed at any time from anywhere. A good example of cloud computing is the various services offered by Google, such as Gmail (e-mail), Google docs (word processing), and Google Calendar,

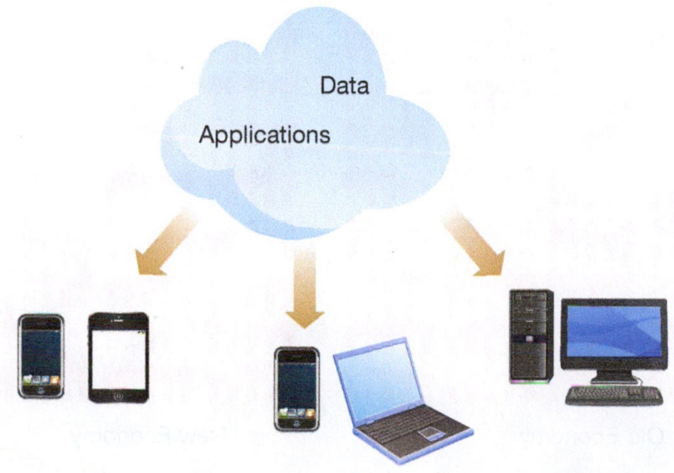

FIGURE 1.10

Applications and data stored in the cloud can be accessed from different devices.

all of which are accessed via a Web browser, freeing users from the task of installing or updating traditional desktop applications or worrying about storing or backing up data. If you have your data stored in the cloud, you don't have to worry if your laptop dies on your way to an important meeting; all you have to do is purchase a new laptop at the next store, and you immediately have access to all your important data. Cloud computing has made inroads in a variety of organizational applications, and many organizations rely on an information systems infrastructure in the cloud. We will extensively discuss cloud computing in Chapter 3, "Managing the Information Systems Infrastructure and Services."

- ***Big Data.*** Together, these transformations of our social and work interactions enabled by 24/7 connectivity have given rise to a fifth trend, *Big Data*. Following the old adage that information is power, organizations are continuously seeking to get the right information to make the best business decisions. Yet, organizations are generating and collecting ever more data from internal and external sources. The rise of social media has further increased the amount of unstructured data available to organizations; for example, people frequently voice their thoughts about products or companies on social media sites. In addition, the Internet of Things, allowing for connecting devices and sensors to the Internet, further contributes to the growth of data available to organizations and individuals. A study by research firm IDC estimated that in 2011, 1.8 zettabytes of data were generated and consumed. How much is 1.8 zettabytes? Well, 1.8 zettabytes equals 1.8 trillion gigabytes, or the equivalent of 57 billion 32GB iPads. The number is forecast to be 50 times more by the end of the decade. For many organizations in the Information Age, value is created from data. Consider, for example, that the largest/most valuable organizations in the "old economy" (such as GE, Dow, or Ford) have 100,000–200,000 employees, and the largest organizations in the "new economy" (such as Microsoft, HP, or Oracle) have 50,000–100,000 employees; in contrast, companies in the "Information Age economy" (such as Facebook, Twitter, or Groupon) have risen to the top with a mere 5,000–20,000 employees by creating value from data (Hofmann, 2011) (Figure 1.11). However, analyzing tremendous amounts of (often unstructured) data (i.e., Big Data) poses tremendous challenges for organizations. In Chapter 6, "Enhancing Business Intelligence Using Information Systems," we will discuss how organizations can harness Big Data to gain business intelligence and make better business decisions.

The success of these megatrends is largely based on the **network effect**. The network effect refers to the notion that the value of a network (or tool or application based on a network) increases with the number of other users. In other words, if a network has few users, it has little or no value. For example, how useful would social media be if none of your friends or family members had access to it? Likewise, eBay would not be an effective auction Web site if only a few bidders were present: In order for eBay auctions to be valued, there must be a large number of users who are involved in the auctions. As more users hear about eBay and then become active buyers and sellers, the value of eBay continues to grow.

What do these megatrends mean for today's workforce? On a most basic level, it implies that being able to use information systems, to assess the impacts of new technologies on one's work or private life, and to learn new technologies as they come along will be increasingly important skills.

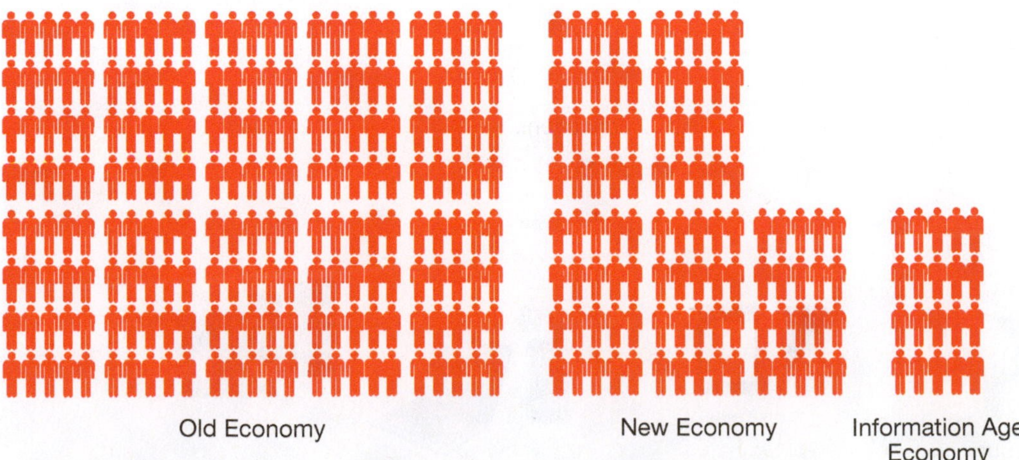

FIGURE 1.11

Companies in the Information Age economy are creating value not from people, but from data.

WHO'S GOING MOBILE

Wearable Technology

Consumer electronics companies continually seek to create the next big thing that will capture the attention (and purchasing dollars) of millions of consumers. Current trends suggest that so-called wearable technology is a product category that will see rapid growth in the near future. The term **wearable technology** refers to clothing or accessories that incorporate electronic technologies. Many such technologies, such as smart watches or fitness trackers like the Fitbit, are designed to be worn and passively used on a regular basis, supporting the "quantified self" to improve one's daily life. Others are intended for special-use cases—as in the "Climbax," a rock-climbing device that tracks your climbing technique.

Many large companies are investing heavily in wearable technologies. Perhaps the most visible example of wearable technology is Google's Glass—a pair of glasses equipped with a camera, microphone, inductive speaker, and novel display capabilities—which people can use to check Web-based information, receive notifications, and take pictures and video, among other uses. Samsung recently developed its Galaxy Gear smart watch, designed as a companion device to Samsung smartphones and tablets, which can display notifications from the phone or tablet devices, monitor various fitness activities, and provide quick access to a few of the phone's or tablet's functions without the need to pull them out of your pocket or bag. In 2014, Facebook spent over US$2 billion to purchase Oculus VR, a virtual reality technology company that has been exciting gamers with prototypes of virtual gaming experiences through head-mounted display devices. There has also been wide speculation that Apple has been developing wearable watchlike technologies as a fitness and notification extension to its popular iOS mobile platform.

Many of these technologies are both exciting and futuristic, but there remain privacy, infrastructure, and other issues to resolve. For example, people may be uncomfortable with the idea of everyone around them wearing a glasses-mounted camera that can be activated without their knowledge. There is also broad concern about the potential distractions to automobile drivers or students in classrooms from such wearable devices. Assuming that these devices are being developed by companies hoping for wide adoption, there are also risks of the Internet infrastructure in certain areas of the world not being able to handle the traffic generated by millions of additional connected devices. These exciting technologies will require adjustments and compromises if they are to obtain the extensive adoption their manufacturers are aiming for.

Based on:

Green, C. (2014, May 12). Wearable technology creates $50 billion investment frenzy. *Information Age*. Retrieved May 12, 2014, from http://www.information-age.com/technology/mobile-and-networking/123457988/wearable-technology-creates-50-billion-investment-frenzy.

Wearable Technology. (2014, May 10). In *Wikipedia, The Free Encyclopedia*. Retrieved May 12, 2014, from http://en.wikipedia.org/w/index.php?title=Wearable_technology&oldid=607910942.

Most modern-day high school and university students have grown up in a computerized world. If by some chance they do not know how to operate a computer by the time they graduate from high school, they soon acquire computer skills, because in today's work world, knowing how to use a computer—called **computer literacy** (or information literacy)—can not only open up myriad sources of information, but can also mean the difference between being employed and being unemployed. In fact, some fear that the Information Age will not provide the same advantages to "information haves"—those computer-literate individuals who have unlimited access to information—and "information have-nots"—those with limited or no computer access or skills.

Computer-related occupations have evolved as computers have become more sophisticated and more widely used. Where once we thought of computer workers as primarily programmers, data entry clerks, systems analysts, or computer repairpersons, today many more job categories in virtually all industries, from accounting to the medical field, involve the use of computers. In fact, today there are few occupations where computers are not somehow in use. Computers manage air traffic, perform medical tests, monitor investment portfolios, control construction machinery, and more. Since they are especially adept at processing large amounts of data, they are used extensively by universities and public schools, in businesses of all sizes, and in all levels and departments of government. Engineers, architects, interior designers, and artists use special purpose computer-aided design programs. Musicians play computerized instruments, and they write and record songs with the help of computers. Professionals in the medical industry use **healthcare IS** to support everything from patient diagnosis and treatment to analyzing patient and disease data to running doctors' offices and hospitals. Not only do we use computers at work, we also use them in our personal lives. We teach our children on them, manage our finances, do our taxes, compose letters and term papers, create greeting cards, send and receive electronic mail, surf the Internet, purchase products, and play games on them. With the increasing use of computers in all areas of society, many argue that being computer literate—knowing how to use a computer and use certain applications—is not sufficient in today's world; rather, **computer fluency**—the ability to independently learn new technologies as they emerge and assess their impact on one's work and life—is what will set you apart in the future.

In addition to changing the way people work and interact, information technology has also enabled *globalization*, the integration of economies throughout the world, fundamentally changing how not only people but also organizations and countries interact. In the next section, we examine the evolution of globalization and the effects on our daily lives.

EVOLUTION OF GLOBALIZATION

You can see the effects of globalization in many ways, such as the greater international movement of commodities, money, information, and labor, as well as the development of technologies, standards, and processes to facilitate this movement (Figure 1.12). Specifically, a more global and competitive world spurs visible economic, cultural, and technological changes, including the following:

- ***Economic Changes.*** Increases in international trade, in the development of global financial systems and currency, and in the outsourcing of labor.
- ***Cultural Changes.*** Increases in the availability of multiculturalism through television and movies; the frequency of international travel, tourism, and immigration; the availability of ethnic foods and restaurants; and the frequency of worldwide fads and phenomena such as Facebook, Groupon, Twitter, and YouTube.
- ***Technological Changes.*** The development of low-cost computing platforms and communication technologies; the availability of low-cost communication systems such as e-mail, Skype, and instant messaging; the ubiquitous nature of a low-cost global telecommunications infrastructure like the Internet; and the enforcement of global patent and copyright laws to spur further innovation.

Through economic and cultural changes, fueled by a rapidly evolving global technology infrastructure, the world has forever changed.

Over the past centuries, **globalization**—the integration of economies throughout the world, enabled by innovation and technological progress (International Monetary Fund, 2002)—has come a long way, from separate nation-states on different continents to what we see today, a world where people and companies can enjoy worldwide communication and collaboration, with increasingly fewer barriers. What is driving globalization? One of the key drivers of globalization is the evolution of technology, which led not only to a tremendous increase in processing power, but at the same time to a tremendous decrease in prices for computing devices. In addition, falling telecommunications costs have provided billions of people with access to the Internet, opening up opportunities for organizations operating on a global scale. Finally, the opening up of China has given organizations huge markets for their goods and services, and has allowed organizations

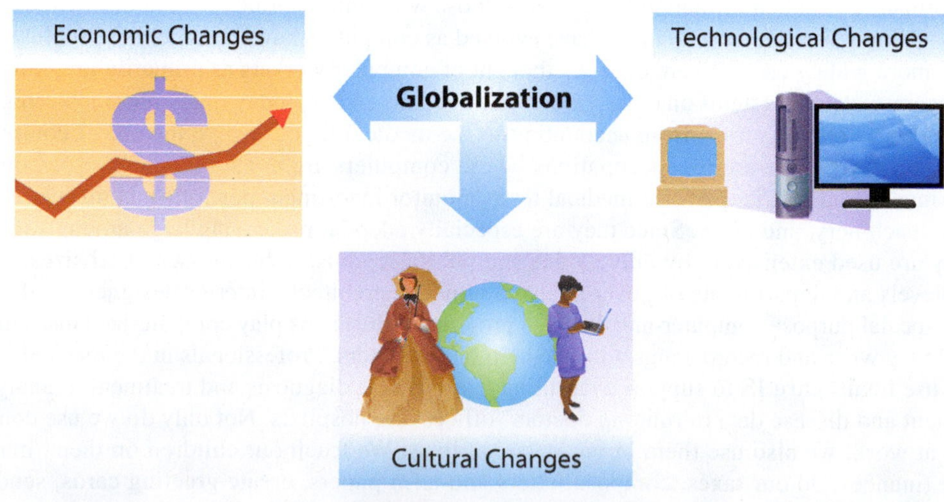

FIGURE 1.12

Globalization can be seen in visible economic, cultural, and technological changes.

to outsource the manufacturing of everything from clothing to smartphones. Outsourcing is discussed next.

The Rise of Outsourcing

Outsourcing is the moving of business processes or tasks (such as accounting, manufacturing, or security) to another company, either onshore (domestically) and offshore. Traditionally, organizations (domestically) outsourced many of the more routine jobs or entire business functions, such as accounting, to other companies. The tremendous decrease in communication costs has added another dimension to outsourcing, as now companies can outsource business processes on a global scale. For example, companies commonly outsource customer service functions (such as call centers) or accounting to companies specializing in these services. Often, companies located in countries such as India can provide these services much cheaper because of lower labor costs. Sometimes, companies also perform certain functions in a different country to reduce costs or harness skilled labor. For example, aircraft manufacturer Boeing offshored design work (such as computational fluid dynamics) for its new 787 Dreamliner aircraft to Russia, making use of the availability of highly skilled aeronautical engineers.

When China officially joined the World Trade Organization in 2001, it agreed to follow certain accepted standards of trade and fair business practices. Now, companies can set up entire factories in emerging countries in order to mass-produce goods at a fraction of the price it would cost to produce these goods in the United States, Canada, or even in Mexico (Figure 1.13).

Companies are choosing to outsource business activities for a variety of reasons; the most important reasons include the following (King, 2003):

- To reduce or control costs
- To free up internal resources
- To gain access to world-class capabilities
- To increase the revenue potential of the organization
- To reduce time to market
- To increase process efficiencies
- To be able to focus on core activities
- To compensate for a lack of specific capabilities or skills

Early examples of offshore outsourcing in the United States included the manufacturing of goods in countries such as Mexico to take advantage of lower wages and less stringent regulations. Then, companies started to introduce offshore outsourcing of *services,* starting with the development of computer software and the staffing of customer support and telemarketing call centers. Today, a wide variety of services—ranging from telephone support to tax returns—are candidates for offshore outsourcing to different countries, be it Ireland, China, or India. Even highly specialized services, such as reading of X-rays by skilled radiologists, are outsourced by U.S. hospitals to doctors around the globe, often while doctors in the United States are sleeping. However, companies operating in the digital world have to carefully choose offshore outsourcing locations, considering factors such as English proficiency, salaries, or geopolitical risk. While

FIGURE 1.13

Companies are offshoring production to overseas countries (such as China) to utilize talented workers or reduce costs.
Source: Lianxun Zhang/fotolia.

TABLE 1.1 Examples of Outsourcing

Industry	Examples
Airlines	British Airways moves customer relations and passenger revenue accounting to India.
	Delta outsources reservation functions to India.
Airplane design	Parts of Airbus and Boeing airplanes are designed and engineered in Moscow, Russia.
Consulting	McKinsey moves global research division to India.
	Ernst & Young moves part of its tax preparation to India.
Insurance	British firm Prudential PLC moves call center operations to India.
Investment banking	J.P. Morgan moves investment research to India.
Retail banking	Worldwide banking group HSBC moves back-office operations to China and India.
Credit card operations	American Express moves a variety of services to India.
Government	The Greater London Authority outsources the development of a road toll system to India.
Telecommunications	T-Mobile outsources part of its content development and portal configuration to India.

Source: Based on http://www.ebstrategy.com (2006).

countries such as India remain popular for offshore outsourcing, other formerly popular countries (such as Singapore, Canada, or Ireland) are declining because of rising salaries. With these shifts, outsourcers are constantly looking at nascent and emerging countries such as Bulgaria, Egypt, Ghana, Bangladesh, or Vietnam. Obviously, organizations have to weigh the potential benefits (e.g., cost savings) and drawbacks (e.g., higher geopolitical risk or less experienced workers) of outsourcing to a particular country.

As you can see, outsourcing is now a fact of life, and no matter which industry you're in, you will likely feel the effects of outsourcing (see Table 1.1). Today, individuals will have to ask themselves how they can seize the global opportunities and how they will be able to compete with individuals from all over the world who might be able to do their job at the same quality but at a lower cost.

However, offshore outsourcing does not always prove to be the best approach for an organization. For example, only about a decade ago, German companies manufacturing highly specialized products such as large crankshafts, ship cranes, or road-paving equipment offshored parts of their operations to Eastern European countries in order to cut costs. However, the cost savings have turned out to be negligible because of added overhead, such as customs, shipping, or training, and quality problems ran rampant, leading to a reversal of this trend. Today, many companies are moving production back to Germany in order to better control production quality and costs. Similarly, *InformationWeek*, a leading publication targeting business IT users, found that 20 percent of the 500 most innovative companies in terms of using IT took back previously offshored projects. The noted technology author Nicholas Carr recently suggested that cloud computing may contribute to a decline in outsourcing; because much of an IT outsourcer's business is built around managing complex internal systems, a shift to a simpler cloud-based IT infrastructure (see Chapter 3) should reduce the need for outsourcing (Heath, 2009). Nevertheless, IT outsourcing is big business: Research firm Gartner estimated that the market for IT outsourcing reached $288 billion in 2013 (Rivera & van der Meulen, 2013).

The next sections will outline some opportunities and challenges made possible by increasing globalization.

Opportunities and Challenges of Operating in the Digital World

Clearly, globalization has opened up many opportunities, brought about by falling transportation and telecommunication costs. Today, shipping a bottle of wine from Australia to Europe merely costs a few cents, and using the Internet, people can make PC-to-PC phone calls around the globe for free. To a large extent fueled by television and other forms of media, the increasing globalization has moved cultures closer together—to the point where people now talk about a "global village." Customers in all corners of the world can receive television programming from other countries or watch movies produced in Hollywood, Munich, or Mumbai (sometimes called "Bollywood"), helping to create a shared understanding about forms of behavior or interaction, desirable goods or services, or even forms of government. Over the past decades, the world has seen a democratization of many nations, enabling millions of people to enjoy freedoms never experienced before. All this makes operating and living in the digital world much easier than ever before.

OPPORTUNITIES FOR REACHING NEW MARKETS. After the fall of communism, new markets opened up for countless companies. The fall of communism in Eastern bloc countries, as well as the rise of a new middle class in China, enabled the sales of products to literally millions of new customers.

OPPORTUNITIES OF A GLOBAL WORKFORCE. With the decrease in communication costs, companies can now draw on a large pool of skilled professionals from all over the globe. Many countries, such as Russia, China, and India, offer high-quality education, leading to an ample supply of well-trained people at low cost. Some countries are even building entire industries around certain competencies, such as software development or tax preparation in India and call centers in Ireland. For companies operating in the digital world, this can be a huge opportunity, as they can "shop" for qualified, low-cost labor all over the world.

These factors translate into a number of direct opportunities for companies, including greater and larger markets to sell products and larger pools of qualified labor. Nevertheless, while globalization has brought tremendous opportunities to companies, they also face a number of daunting challenges when operating in the global marketplace.

CHALLENGES OF OPERATING IN THE DIGITAL WORLD. Traditionally, companies acquired resources and produced and sold goods or services all within the same country. Such domestic businesses did not have to deal with any challenges posed by globalization but also could not leverage the host of opportunities. The challenges faced can be broadly classified into governmental, geoeconomic, and cultural challenges. See Table 1.2 for a summary of the challenges of operating in the digital world.

TABLE 1.2 Challenges of Operating in the Digital World

Broad Challenges	Specific Challenges	Examples
Governmental	Political system	Market versus planned economy; political instability
	Regulatory	Taxes and tariffs; embargoes; import and export regulations
	Data sharing	European Union Data Protection Directive
	Standards	Differences in measurement units, bar code standards, address conventions, academic degrees
	Internet access and individual freedom	Internet censorship in various countries
Geoeconomic	Time zone differences	Videoconferences across different time zones
	Infrastructure-related reliability	Differences in network infrastructures throughout the world
	Differences in welfare	Migration and political instability caused by welfare differences between rich and poor countries
	Demographic	Aging population in the United States and Western Europe; younger workforce in other countries
	Expertise	Availability of labor force and salary differences
Cultural	Working with different cultures	Differences in power distance, uncertainty avoidance, individualism/collectivism, masculinity/femininity, concept of time, and life focus; differences in languages, perceptions of aesthetics, beliefs, attitudes, religion, or social organizations
	Challenges of offering products or services in different cultures	Naming and advertising for products; intellectual property

KEY PLAYERS

Wipro and Infosys—The Global Outsourcing Leaders

For students majoring in any business discipline, it is important to be aware of the key players in the information systems area. Infosys and Wipro are two global giants to remember; both companies work to improve business efficiency by providing consulting and IT services, bringing offshore outsourcing to another level with their fast-expanding networks and growing patronage.

Infosys Limited, founded in Pune, India, in 1981 with only seven people and US$250, was one of the pioneers of offshore outsourcing. Rather than companies trying to hire the best talents, and trying to get these talents to relocate to where the work should be done, Infosys helped introduce the "global delivery model," taking the work to where the talent is, where it is most economical, and where the potential risk involved is minimized. Now headquartered in Bangalore, India, Infosys uses this approach to provide services from business and technology consulting to product engineering, IT infrastructure services, testing and validation services, and others to Global 2000 companies. Based on the rationale of making the most out of location and talent at the lowest risk, Infosys has thus far expanded to 73 offices and 94 development centers in more than a dozen countries, and employs well over 160,000 people from 85 nationalities.

One of its closest competitors, Wipro, also found success in providing IS development and technical support to businesses. Initially incorporated in 1945 as a producer of vegetable oil, Wipro has emerged as one of the biggest players in the IT outsourcing business, with now over 140,000 employees. Headquartered in Bangalore, India, Wipro has produced many innovations in the IT area, including large-scale projects such as India's most powerful supercomputer. Due to the growing influence of technology in enabling and improving business processes, Wipro has grown from its humble beginnings in pre-independent India to become a service provider for 150 global Fortune 500 clients in fields like financial services, manufacturing, telecommunications, and media.

In today's digital world, information systems are crucial in developing successful business models. Yet, for many companies, hiring the best employees to get the job done is close to impossible; global outsourcing giants such as Infosys and Wipro help to take the jobs to where the talent needed to get the job done is located. No matter which discipline you are in, chances are that someday, you will find yourself working together with someone who introduces herself as coming from Infosys, Wipro, or some other company focusing on providing outsourcing services.

Based on:

Infosys. (n.d.). What we do. *Infosys.com*. Retrieved May 12, 2014, from http://www.infosys.com/about/pages/index.aspx.

Wipro. (n.d.). About Wipro. *Wipro.com*. Retrieved May 12, 2014, from http://www.wipro.com/about-wipro.

INFORMATION SYSTEMS DEFINED

Information systems use information technology to collect, create, and distribute useful data. **Information technology** includes **hardware**, **software**, and **telecommunications networks**. Hardware refers to physical computer equipment, such as a computer, tablet, or printer, as well as components like a computer monitor or keyboard. Software refers to a program or set of programs that tell the computer to perform certain tasks. Telecommunications networks refer to a group of two or more computer systems linked together with communications equipment. Although we discuss the design, implementation, use, and implications of hardware, software, and telecommunications throughout the text, the specifics on hardware, software, and telecommunications are discussed in Chapter 3 and the Technology Briefing. While traditionally the term *information technology* referred to the hardware, software, and networking components of an information system, the difference is shrinking, with many using the terms IS and IT synonymously. In Figure 1.14, we show the relationships among these IS components.

People in organizations use information systems to process sales transactions, manage loan applications, or help financial analysts decide where, when, and how to invest. Product managers also use them to help decide where, when, and how to market their products and related services, and production managers use them to help decide when and how to manufacture products. Information systems also enable us to get cash from ATMs, communicate by live video with people in other parts of the world, or buy concert or airline tickets. (Note that the term "information systems" is also used to describe the field comprising people who develop, use, manage, and study information systems in organizations.)

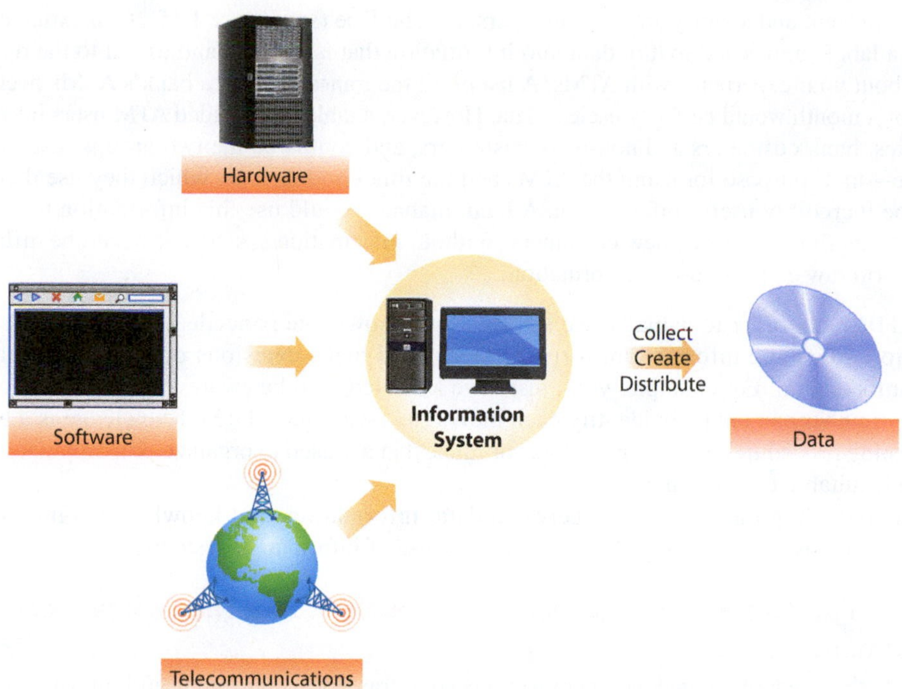

FIGURE 1.14

Information systems use information technology to collect, create, and distribute useful data.

It is important to note that people use various terms to describe the field of information systems, such as management information systems, business information systems, computer information systems, and simply "systems." Next, we more thoroughly examine each of the key components of the IS definition.

Data: The Root and Purpose of Information Systems

Earlier, we defined information systems as the use of information technology to collect, create, and distribute useful data. We begin by talking about data, the most basic element of any information system.

DATA. Before you can understand how information systems work, it is important to distinguish between raw, unformatted data and information. Unformatted data, or simply **data**, are raw symbols, such as words and numbers. Data have no meaning in and of themselves, and are of little value until processed (Ackoff, 1989). For example, if we asked you what 465889727 meant or stood for, you could not tell us (Figure 1.15). However, if we presented the same data as 465-88-9727 and told you it was located in a certain database, in John Doe's record, in a field labeled "SSN," you might rightly surmise that the number was actually the Social Security number of someone named John Doe. While data have no inherent meaning, the old adage "garbage in, garbage out" applies to data as well; thus, a key consideration of assessing whether data are reliable for making decisions is data quality, consisting of completeness, accuracy, timeliness, validity, and consistency.

INFORMATION. Data can be formatted, organized, or processed to be *useful*; it is transformed into **information**, which can be defined as a representation of reality, and can help to answer questions about who, what, where, and when (Ackoff, 1989). In the previous example, 465-88-9727 was

Data	Information	Knowledge
465889727	465-88-9727	465-88-9727 → John Doe
Raw Symbols	Formatted Data	Data Relationships
Meaning: ------------ ???	Meaning: ------------ SSN	Meaning: ------------ SSN → Unique Person

FIGURE 1.15

Data, information, and knowledge.

used to represent and identify an individual person, John Doe (see Figure 1.15). Contextual cues, such as a label, are needed to turn data into information that is familiar and useful to the reader. Think about your experience with ATMs. A list of all the transactions at a bank's ATMs over the course of a month would be fairly useless data. However, a table that divided ATM users into two categories, bank customers and non-bank customers, and compared the two groups' use of the machine—their purpose for using the ATMs and the times and days on which they use them—would be incredibly useful information. A bank manager could use this information to create marketing mailings to attract new customers. Without information systems, it would be difficult to transform raw data into useful information.

KNOWLEDGE. In order to actually use information, knowledge is needed. **Knowledge** is the ability to understand information, form opinions, and make decisions or predictions based on the information. For example, you must have knowledge to be aware that only one Social Security number can uniquely identify each individual (see Figure 1.15). Knowledge is a body of governing procedures, such as guidelines or rules, that are used to organize or manipulate data to make it suitable for a given task.

Understanding the distinctions between data, information, and knowledge is important because all are used in the study, development, and use of information systems.

Hardware, Software, and Telecommunications Networks: The Components of Information Systems

Ever since the dawn of humankind, there was a need to transform data into useful information for people, and people have invented various calculating devices, such as the abacus or the slide rule. Before the introduction of the first computers (which worked on a mechanical basis using punch cards), almost all business and government information systems consisted of file folders, filing cabinets, and document repositories. Computer hardware has replaced these physical artifacts, providing the technologies to input and process data and output useful information; software enables organizations to utilize the hardware to execute their business processes and competitive strategy by providing the computer hardware with instructions on what processing functions to perform. Finally, the telecommunications networks allow computers to share information and services, enabling the global collaboration, communication, and commerce we see today.

People: The Builders, Managers, and Users of Information Systems

The IS field includes a vast collection of people who develop, maintain, manage, and study information systems. Yet, an information system does not exist in a vacuum, and is of little use if it weren't for you—the user. We will begin by discussing the IS profession, and then talk about why knowing about fundamental concepts of information systems is of crucial importance in your personal and professional life.

If you are choosing a career in the IS field, you will find countless opportunities. With the growing value of data for competitive advantage, every company can now be considered a technology company, needing people with the right skill set to help optimize its business processes. The career opportunities for a person with IS training continue to be strong, and they are expected to continue to improve over the next 10 years. For example, the 2014–15 edition of the *Occupational Outlook Handbook* published by the U.S. Bureau of Labor Statistics predicted that employment for computer and IS managers will grow 15 percent through 2022, faster than the average for all occupations (http://www.bls.gov/ooh/management/computer-and-information-systems-managers.htm). This boost in employment will occur in nearly every industry, not just computer hardware and software companies, as more and more organizations rely more heavily on IS professionals. Likewise, *Money* magazine (http://money.cnn.com/pf/best-jobs/) ranked software developers, software architects, and IT configuration managers as three of its top 10 best jobs in America (Table 1.3); also, *U.S. News* magazine (http://money.usnews.com/careers/best-jobs/rankings/the-100-best-jobs) rated software developers, computer systems analysts, and Web developers as being among the top 10 jobs, stressing that the industry is looking for people who can balance business and technology.

In addition to an ample supply of jobs, earnings for IS professionals will remain strong. According to the U.S. Bureau of Labor Statistics, median annual earnings of these managers in May 2012 were US$120,950, with the top 10 percent earning more than US$187,200. Also, according to Salary.com, the median salary in 2014 for IT managers was US$109,039. According

TABLE 1.3 Best Jobs in America

Rank	Career	Job Growth (10-year forecast)	Median Pay (in US$)
1	Biomedical engineer	62%	87,000
2	Clinical nurse specialist	26%	86,500
3	Software architect	28%	121,000
4	General surgeon	24%	288,000
5	Management consultant	29%	110,000
6	Petroleum geologist	21%	183,000
7	Software developer	28%	88,700
8	IT configuration manager	29%	95,800
9	Clinical research associate	36%	95,100
10	Reservoir engineer	17%	179,000

Source: Based on http://money.cnn.com/pf/best-jobs.

to a 2014 survey by the National Association of Colleges and Employers, starting salary offers for IS majors, with one year or less of experience, averaged US$62,100, making it one of the 10 top-paid bachelor's degrees. Finally, computer and IS managers, especially those at higher levels, often receive more employment-related benefits—such as expense accounts, stock option plans, and bonuses—than do non-managerial workers in their organizations (a study by Payscale .com found that IS majors were—post-graduation—among the most satisfied with their careers).

As you can see, even with some lower-level, highly technical jobs (such as systems programmers) being outsourced to organizations in other countries, there continues to be a very strong need for people with IS knowledge, skills, and abilities—in particular, people with advanced IS skills, as we describe here. In fact, IS careers are regularly selected as not only one of the fastest growing but also a career with far-above-average opportunities for greater personal growth, stability, and advancement. Although technology continues to become easier to use, there is still and is likely to continue to be an acute need for people within the organization who have the responsibility of planning for, designing, developing, maintaining, and managing technologies. Much of this will happen within the business units and will be done by those with primarily business duties and tasks as opposed to systems duties and tasks. However, we are a long way from the day when technology is so easy to deploy that a need no longer exists for people with advanced IS knowledge and skills. In fact, many people believe that this day may never come. Although increasing numbers of people will incorporate systems responsibilities within their nonsystems jobs, there will continue to be a need for people with primarily systems responsibilities. In short, IS staffs and departments will likely continue to exist and play an important role in the foreseeable future.

Given that information systems continue to be a critical tool for business success, it is not likely that IS departments will go away or even shrink significantly. Indeed, all projections are for long-term growth of information systems in both scale and scope. Also, as is the case in any area of business, those people who are continually learning, continuing to grow, and continuing to find new ways to add value and who have advanced and/or unique skills will always be sought after, whether in information systems or in any area of the firm.

The future opportunities in the IS field are likely to be found in a variety of areas, which is good news for everyone. Diversity in the technology area can embrace us all. It really does not matter much which area of information systems you choose to pursue—there will likely be a promising future there for you. Even if your career interests are outside information systems, being a well-informed and capable user of information technologies will greatly enhance your career prospects.

CAREERS IN INFORMATION SYSTEMS. The field of information systems includes those people in organizations who design and build systems, those who use these systems, and those responsible for managing these systems. The people who help develop and manage systems in organizations include systems analysts, systems programmers, systems operators, network administrators, database administrators, systems designers, systems managers, and chief information officers.

TABLE 1.4 Some IS Management Job Titles and Brief Job Descriptions

IS Activities	Job Title	Job Description	Salary Ranges, in US$, in Percentiles (25%–75%)
Develop	Systems analyst	Analyze business requirements and select information systems that meet those needs	61,000–80,000
	Software developer	Code, test, debug, and install programs	68,000–87,000
	Systems consultant	Provide IS knowledge to external clients	66,000–80,000
Maintain	IS auditor	Audit information systems and operating procedures for compliance with internal and external standards	60,000–79,000
	Database administrator	Manage database and database management software use	77,000–100,000
	Webmaster	Manage the firm's Web site	60,000–81,000
Manage	IS manager	Manage existing information systems	95,000–125,000
	IS security manager	Manage security measures and disaster recovery	95,000–117,000
	Chief information officer (CIO)	Highest-ranking IS manager; oversee strategic planning and IS use throughout the firm	195,000–303,000
	Chief digital officer (CDO)	Executive focused on converting traditional "analog" businesses to digital; oversee operations in rapidly changing digital sectors like mobile apps and social media	150,000–200,000
Study	University professor	Teach undergraduate and graduate students; study the use of information systems in organizations and society	70,000–180,000
	Government scientist	Perform research and development of information systems for homeland security, intelligence, and other related applications	60,000–200,000

Source: Based on http://www.salary.com.

(In Table 1.4 we describe some of these careers.) This list is not exhaustive; rather, it is intended to provide a sampling of IS management positions. Furthermore, many firms will use the same job title, but each is likely to define it in a different way, or companies will have different titles for the same basic function. As you can see from Table 1.4, the range of career opportunities for IS managers is broad, and salary expectations are high.

WHAT MAKES IS PERSONNEL SO VALUABLE? In addition to the growing importance of people in the IS field, there have been changes in the nature of this type of work. No longer are IS departments in organizations filled only with nerdy men with pocket protectors. Many more women are in IS positions now. Also, it is now more common for an IS professional to be a polished, professional systems analyst who can speak fluently about both business and technology. IS personnel are now well-trained, highly skilled, valuable professionals who garner high wages and prestige and who play a pivotal role in helping firms be successful.

Many studies have been aimed at helping us understand what knowledge and skills are necessary for a person in the IS area to be successful. Interestingly, these studies also point out just what it is about IS personnel that makes them so valuable to their organizations. In a nutshell, good IS personnel possess valuable, integrated knowledge and skills in three areas—technical, business, and systems—as outlined in Table 1.5 (see also Figure 1.16).

Technical Competency The technical competency area includes knowledge and skills in hardware, software, networking, and security. In a sense, this is the "nuts and bolts" of information systems. This is not to say that the IS professional must be a technical expert in these areas. On the contrary, the IS professional must know just enough about these areas to understand how they work, what they can do for an organization, and how they can and should be applied. Typically, the IS professional manages or directs those who have deeper, more detailed technical knowledge.

The technical area of competency is, perhaps, the most difficult to maintain because of the rapid pace of technological innovation in the digital world. With the economy rebounding, organizations are starting new projects or are reviving projects put on hold during the economic

TABLE 1.5 IS Professional Core Competencies

Domain	Description
Technical Knowledge and Skills	
Hardware	Hardware platforms, infrastructure, cloud computing, virtualization, peripherals, mobile devices
Software	Operating systems, application software, mobile apps
Networking	Network administration, cabling and network interface cards, wireless, Internet, security
Business Knowledge and Skills	
Business integration, industry	Business processes, functional areas of business and their integration, industry characteristics
Managing people and projects	Planning, organizing, leading, controlling, managing people and projects
Social	Interpersonal, group dynamics, political
Communication	Verbal, written, and technological communication and presentation
Systems Knowledge and Skills	
Systems integration	Connectivity, compatibility, integrating subsystems and systems
Development methodologies	Steps in systems analysis and design, systems development life cycle, alternative development methodologies
Critical thinking	Challenging one's and others' assumptions and ideas
Problem solving	Information gathering and synthesis, problem identification, solution formulation, comparison, choice

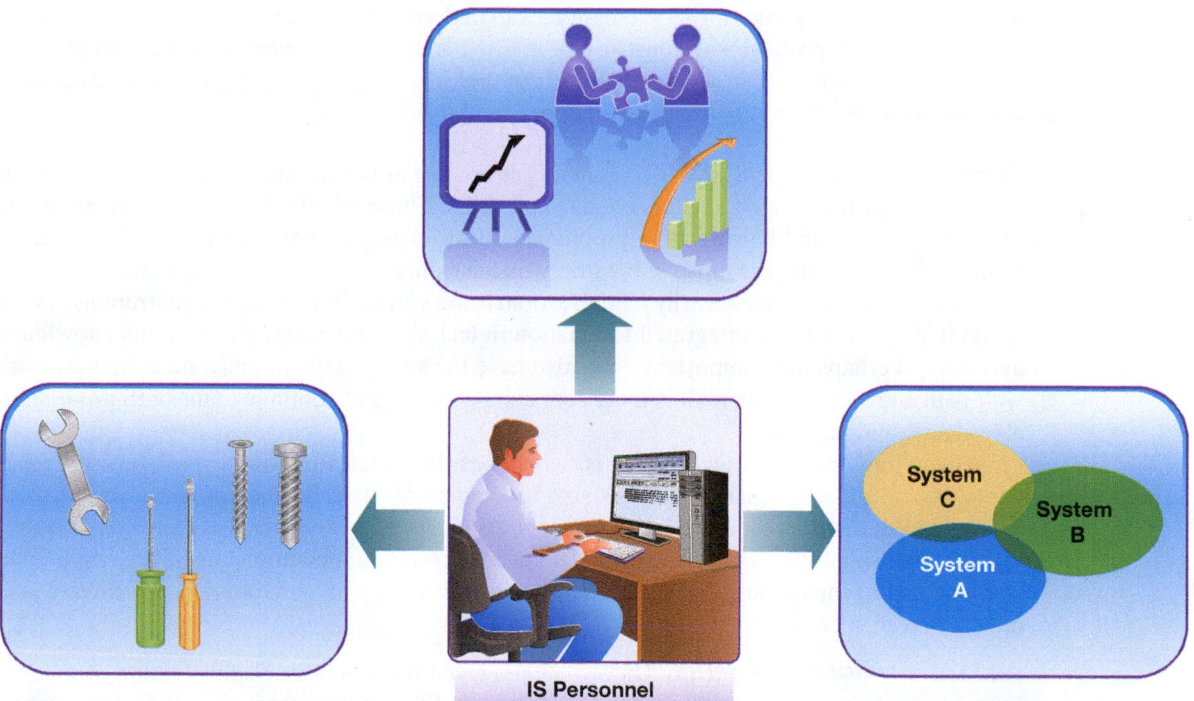

FIGURE 1.16

Good IS personnel possess valuable, integrated knowledge and skills in three areas—technical, business, and systems.

downturn; hence, while it once appeared as if most programming jobs or support jobs would be outsourced to third-party providers abroad, there is an increased demand in many companies for people with application development skills, especially in combination with sound business analysis and project management skills (Brandel, 2013). In fact, many of the hot skills listed in Table 1.6 are focused on the business domain, which is discussed next.

TABLE 1.6 Hot Skills for the Next Decade

Domain	Hot Skills
Business	Business–IT alignment; business analysis; enterprise solutions; business process modeling; project management; third-party provider management; Enterprise 2.0 and social media
Technology infrastructure and services	Virtualization; cloud computing/infrastructure as a service; systems analysis and design; network design; systems auditing; wireless; telecommunications/VoIP (Voice over Internet Protocol); data center
Security	IT security planning and management; BYOD; governance, risk, and compliance
Applications	Customer-facing application development; mobile app development; Web development; open source; portal technologies; cloud computing; user experience; legacy systems integration
Internet	Social media; customer-facing Web applications; mobile apps; search engine optimization; artificial intelligence; Web mining; Internet of Things
Business intelligence	Business intelligence; data warehousing; data mining; Big Data

Source: Based on Brandel (2014), Connolly (2014), Leung (2009), and Veritude (2009).

Business Competency The business competency area is one that sets the IS professional apart from others who have only technical knowledge and skills, and in an era of increased outsourcing, it may well save a person's job. For example, even though some low-level technology jobs may be outsourced, the Bureau of Labor Statistics recently reported that there is an increased need for IS managers as organizations embrace mobility and cloud computing (http://www.bls.gov/ooh/management/computer-and-information-systems-managers.htm). As a result, it is absolutely vital for IS professionals to understand the technical areas *and* the nature of the business. IS professionals must also be able to understand and manage people and projects, not just the technology. These business skills propel IS professionals into project management and, ultimately, high-paying middle- and upper-level management positions.

Systems Competency Systems competency is another area that sets the IS professional apart from others with only technical knowledge and skills. Those who understand how to build and integrate systems and how to solve problems will ultimately manage large, complex systems projects as well as manage those in the firm who have only technical knowledge and skills.

Perhaps now you can see why IS professionals are so valuable to their organizations. These individuals have a solid, integrated foundation in technical, business, and systems knowledge and skills. Perhaps most important, they also have the social skills to understand how to work well with and motivate others. It is these core competencies that continue to make IS professionals valuable employees.

Given how important technology is, what does this mean for your career? Technology is being used to radically change how business is conducted—from the way products and services are produced, distributed, and accounted for to the ways they are marketed and sold. Whether you are majoring in information systems, finance, accounting, operations management, human resource management, business law, or marketing, knowledge of technology is critical to a successful career in business.

FINDING QUALIFIED PERSONNEL. Unfortunately, given the increased sophistication of modern information systems, organizations can often have a difficult time finding qualified personnel, and attracting the right people with the right skills is not possible in some areas. Consequently, many technology-focused organizations tend to cluster in areas where talented workers are available. Such areas are often characterized by a high quality of life for the people living there, and it is no surprise that many companies in the IT sector within the United States are headquartered in Silicon Valley, California; Boston, Massachusetts; Austin, Texas; or Seattle, Washington. With increasing globalization, other regions throughout the world are boasting about their highly skilled personnel. One such example is the Indian city of Bangalore, where, over a century ago, Maharajas started to lure talented technology-oriented people to the region, building a world-class human resource infrastructure that attracted companies from around the world. In other areas, organizations may have to find creative ways to attract and retain people, such as by offering favorable benefits packages that include educational grants or expense-matching programs to encourage employees to improve their education and skills. Other human resource policies, such as telecommuting, flextime, and creative benefit packages, can also help to attract and retain the best employees.

YOU—THE USER. Clearly, the field of information systems offers a wide variety of interesting career choices, and you will likely find a career that offers a host of opportunities for lifelong learning and advancement. Yet, understanding fundamental concepts related to information systems will be critical in almost any career, as well as in your private life. In almost any business-related field, you will be extensively using information systems, and you will likely be involved in various information systems–related decisions within your organization. Understanding what information systems are capable of doing (as well as what they cannot do), being able to communicate with the "techies," and being able to make educated IS-related decisions is likely to set you apart from your competition. Especially in smaller organizations (that may not have dedicated IS departments), you are likely to be involved in IS-related investment decisions, and lacking a basic understanding of fundamental issues associated with topics such as IS infrastructure, systems analysis and design, or information systems security will put you at the mercy of outside consultants or (worse yet) vendors who are likely to act out of their own interests, often trying to sell you their "technology of the week/month/year."

In addition, as you have undoubtedly noticed, you are facing a number of IS-related decisions in your private life. Examples of such decisions abound; for example, you may face the question of what mobile phone to purchase next: an iPhone, a phone using some version of the Android operating system, or a phone sporting Microsoft's Windows Phone operating system. Such decisions are likely to include your own preferences or influence by your peers, but there are a number of critical differences in terms of privacy, security, applications, and the like. Likewise, you may face the problem of how to best secure your wireless network at home, or may wonder how to best keep your various files in sync across different computers or mobile devices. Throughout this text, we will touch on those issues, and hope that you will gain valuable knowledge to understand the trade-offs involved when selecting new information systems.

Organizations: The Context of Information Systems

We have talked about data versus information, the technology side of information systems, and the people side of information systems. Information systems do not exist in a vacuum; they are built and/or used within a certain context. Organizations use information systems to become more productive and profitable, to gain competitive advantage, to reach more customers, or to improve customer service. This holds true for all types of organizations—professional, social, religious, educational, and governmental—and for all types of industries—medical, legal, and business. In fact, the U.S. Internal Revenue Service launched its own Web site for the reasons just described (Figure 1.17). The Web site was so popular that approximately 220,000 users visited it during the first 24 hours and more than 1 million visited it in its first week—even before the Web address for the site was officially announced. Today, popular Web sites like Facebook.com and WSJ.com receive millions of visitors every day.

TYPES OF INFORMATION SYSTEMS. Throughout this text, we explore various types of information systems commonly used in organizations. It makes sense, however, for us to describe briefly here the various types of systems used so that you will better understand what we mean by the term "information system" as we use it throughout the rest of the book. Table 1.7 provides a list of the major categories of information systems used in organizations.

Topping the list in the table are some of the more traditional, major categories that are used to describe information systems. For example, **transaction processing systems (TPS)** are used by a broad range of organizations to not only more efficiently process customer transactions, but also generate a tremendous amount of data that can be used by the organization to learn about customers or ever-changing product trends. Your local grocery store uses a TPS at the checkout that scans bar codes on products; as this occurs, many stores will print discount coupons on the backs of receipts for products related to current purchases. Every hour, online retailer Amazon.com's Web site processes thousands of transactions from around the world. This massive amount of data is fed

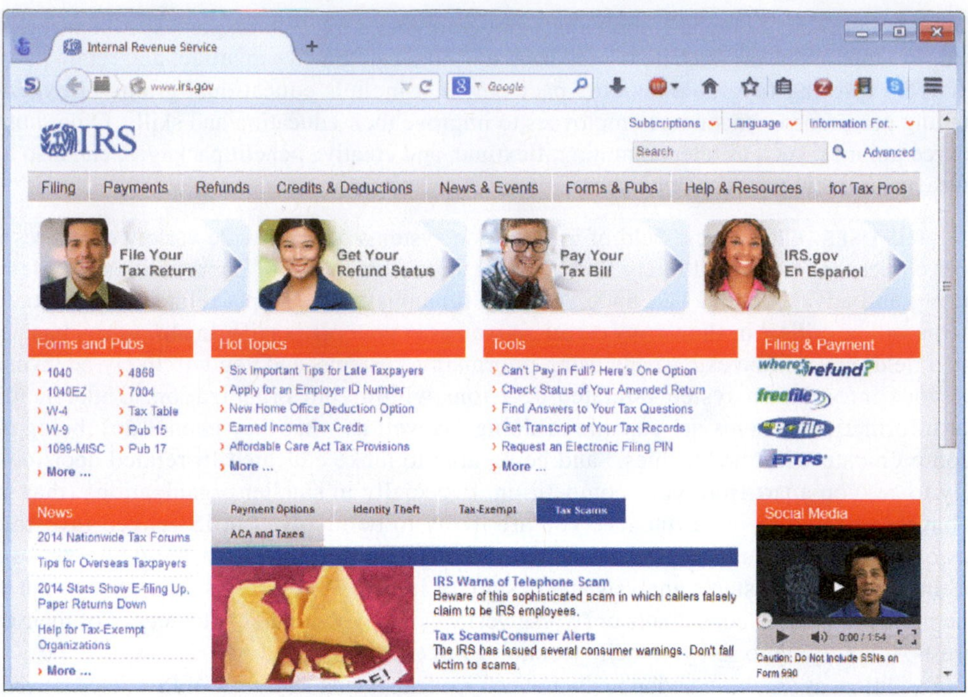

FIGURE 1.17

Web site of the U.S. Department of the Treasury, Internal Revenue Service, http://www.irs.gov.

Source: Courtesy of the United States Department of the Treasury.

into large data warehouses and is then analyzed to provide purchase recommendations to future customers. In addition, TPS data are sorted and organized to support a broad range of managerial decision making using a variety of systems; the most common of these is generally referred to as a **management information system**. TPS data also provide input into a variety of information systems within organizations, including *decision support systems, intelligent systems, data mining and visualization systems, knowledge management systems, social software, geographic information systems*, and *functional area information systems*. Five to 10 years ago, it would have been typical to see systems that fell cleanly into one of these categories. Today, many organizations have replaced standalone systems with *enterprise systems* that span the entire organization. Likewise, with **internetworking**—connecting host computers and their networks together to form even larger networks like the Internet—and **systems integration**—connecting separate information systems and data to improve business processes and decision making—it is difficult to say that any given information system fits into only one of these categories (e.g., that a system is a management information system only and nothing else). In addition, many of these systems are not housed within organizations any more, but are located "in the cloud," and accessed via the user's browser when needed. Modern-day information systems tend to span several of these categories of information systems, helping not only to collect data from throughout the firm and from customers but also to integrate data from diverse sources and present it to busy decision makers, along with tools to manipulate and analyze those data. *Customer relationship management*, *supply chain management*, and *enterprise resource planning* systems are good examples of these types of systems that encompass many features and types of data and cannot easily be categorized.

Office automation systems such as Microsoft Office and the OpenOffice.org Productivity Suite provide word processing, spreadsheet, and other personal productivity tools, enabling knowledge workers to accomplish their tasks; *collaboration systems*, such as Microsoft's Exchange/Outlook, Lotus Notes, or Google Apps, provide people with e-mail, automated calendaring, and online, threaded discussions, enabling close collaboration with others, regardless of their location.

Systems for electronic commerce, such as corporate Web sites, are also popular and important. These systems enable (1) consumers to find information about and to purchase goods and services from each other and from business firms and (2) business firms to electronically exchange products, services, and information. In Chapter 4, "Enabling Business-to-Consumer Electronic Commerce," we talk about different forms of electronic commerce involving the end consumer; in Chapter 8, "Strengthening Business-to-Business Relationships Via Supply Chain and Customer Relationship Management," we discuss how organizations use the Internet to enable or facilitate business-to-business transactions.

TABLE 1.7 Categories of Information Systems Used in Organizations

Category of System	Purpose	Sample Application(s)
Transaction processing system	Process day-to-day business event data at the operational level of the organization	Grocery store checkout cash register with connection to network, student registration system
Management information system	Produce detailed information to help manage a firm or part of a firm	Inventory management and planning system, student enrollment by major and by course
Decision support system	Provide analysis tools and access to databases in order to support quantitative decision making	Product demand forecasting system, loan and investment analysis
Intelligent system	Emulate or enhance human capabilities	Automated system for analyzing bank loan applications, evaluate complex medical data
Business intelligence system	Methods and systems for analyzing data warehouses to better understand various aspects of a business	Online Analytical Processing (OLAP) system
Office automation system (personal productivity software)	Support a wide range of predefined day-to-day work activities of individuals and small groups	Word processor, spreadsheet, presentation software, electronic mail client
Collaboration system	Enable people to communicate, collaborate, and coordinate with each other	Electronic mail system with automated, shared calendar
Knowledge management system	Collection of technology-based tools to enable the generation, storage, sharing, and management of knowledge assets	Knowledge portal for finding answers to common questions
Social software	Facilitates collaboration and knowledge sharing	Social network, connecting colleagues and friends
Geographic information system	Create, store, analyze, and manage spatial data	Site selection for new shopping mall
Functional area information system	Support the activities within a specific functional area of the firm	Planning system for personnel training and work assignments
Customer relationship management system	Support interaction between the firm and its customers	Sales force automation, lead generation
Enterprise resource planning system	Support and integrate all facets of the business, including planning, manufacturing, sales, marketing, and so on	Financial, operations, and human resource management
Supply chain management system	Support the coordination of suppliers, product or service production, and distribution	Procurement planning
Electronic commerce system	Enable customers to buy goods and services from a firm's Web site	Amazon.com, eBay.com, Nordstrom.com

While many modern-day information systems span several of these IS categories, it is still useful to understand these categories. Doing so enables you to better understand the myriad approaches, goals, features, and functions of modern information systems.

We have talked about each of the parts of our definition of information systems, and we have talked about different types of information systems. In the next section, we focus on how information systems can be managed within organizations.

ORGANIZING THE IS FUNCTION. Old-school IS personnel believed that they owned and controlled the computing resources, that they knew better than users did, and that they should tell users what they could and could not do with the computing resources; in addition, early IS departments typically had huge project backlogs, and IS personnel would often deliver systems that were over budget, were completed much too late, were difficult to use, and did not always work well. The increasing pervasiveness of technology in businesses and societies has led to a shifting mindset about information systems within organizations. Increasingly fast-paced competition is forcing businesses to regard IS as an enabler, so as to streamline business processes, provide better customer service, and better connect and collaborate with various stakeholders inside and outside the organization. Many organizations, for example, have realized that some of the best ideas for solving business problems come from the employees using the system; as a result, personnel within many IS units have taken on more of a consulting relationship with their users, helping the users solve problems, implement ideas, and be more productive. As shown in the example of Starbucks' Tech Cafe (see the Brief Case earlier in this chapter), IS personnel are increasingly reaching out to their internal customers and proactively seek their input and needs rather than waiting for customers to come in with systems complaints. They modify the systems at a moment's notice just to meet customer needs quickly and effectively. They celebrate the customers' new systems ideas rather than putting up roadblocks and giving reasons that the new ideas cannot or will not work. They fundamentally believe that the customers own the technology and the information and that the technology and information are there for the customers, not for the systems personnel. They create help desks, hotlines, information centers, and training centers to support customers. These service-oriented IS units structure the IS function so that it can better serve the customer.

The implications of this new service mentality for the IS function are staggering. It is simply amazing how unproductive a company can be when the IS personnel and other people within the firm are at odds with one another. On the other hand, it is even more amazing how productive and enjoyable work can be when people in the IS function work hand in hand with people throughout the organization. Technology is, potentially, the great lever, but it works best when people work together, not against each other, to use it.

THE SPREAD OF TECHNOLOGY IN ORGANIZATIONS. Another phenomenon that shows how integral and vital information systems and their proper management have become to organizations is the extent to which the technology is firmly integrated and entrenched within the various business units (such as accounting, sales, and marketing).

In many organizations today, you will find that the builders and managers of a particular information system or subsystem spend most of their time out in the business unit, along with the users of that particular system. Many times, these systems personnel are permanently placed—with an office, desk, phone, and PC—in the business unit along with the users.

In addition, it is not uncommon for systems personnel to have formal education, training, and work experience in information systems as well as in the functional area that the system supports, such as finance. It is becoming increasingly more difficult to separate the technology from the business or the systems staff from the other people in the organization. For this reason, how information systems are managed is important to you, no matter what career option you pursue.

As information systems are used more broadly throughout organizations, IS personnel often have dual-reporting relationships—reporting both to the central IS group and to the business function they serve. Therefore, at least some need for centralized IS planning, deployment, and management continues—particularly with respect to achieving economies of scale in systems acquisition and development and in optimizing systems integration, enterprise networking, and the like. Even in organizations that are decentralizing technology and related decisions, a need to coordinate technology and related decisions across the firm still persists. This coordination is likely to continue to happen through some form of a centralized (or, at least, centrally coordinated) IS staff. Organizations are likely to continue to want to reap the benefits of IS decentralization (flexibility, adaptability, and systems responsiveness), but it is equally likely that they will not want to—and will not be able to—forgo the benefits of IS centralization (coordination, economies of scale, compatibility, and connectivity).

Given the trend toward pushing people from the IS staff out into the various business units of the firm and given the need for people within each of the functional areas of the business to have technology skills, there is clearly a need for people who know both the technology side *and* the business side of the business. This is becoming increasingly important due to ever faster IT cycles: Where traditionally, IS departments thought in time frames of about five years, nowadays, new devices (such as new versions of Apple's iPad) come out every 6–18 months, and organizations wanting to harness the opportunities brought about by new devices have to adjust to this change in pace.

THE DUAL NATURE OF INFORMATION SYSTEMS

Given how important and expensive information systems have become, information technology is like a sword—you can use it effectively as a competitive weapon, but, as the old saying goes, those who live by the sword sometimes die by the sword. The two following cases illustrate this dual nature of information systems.

FIGURE 1.18

A computer glitch in AA's reservation systems left thousands of passenger stranded.
Source: Nmcandre/Fotolia.

Case in Point: An Information System Gone Awry: Computer Glitch Grounds Flights

Founded in 1930, American Airlines (AA) has flown through turbulent times, oscillating between being on the verge of bankruptcy and becoming the largest airline in the world (following a merger with U.S. Airways). As compared to the early days of flying, computerized reservation systems are now a strategic necessity for airlines, and any problems with such systems can lead to consequences ranging from dissatisfied customers to lost revenues—in extreme cases, even to flight disruptions. In April 2013, this worst nightmare came true, and a glitch in the airline's computerized reservation system grounded flights across the United States. Not being able to check in passengers, or make or change reservations, the airline was left with no choice but to ask the Federal Aviation Administration (FAA) to halt all flights while it attempted to fix the problem (Figure 1.18). Ultimately, the glitch resulted in over 700 delayed flights, 125,000 affected passengers, and a public apology by the airline's CEO, posted on YouTube.

Case in Point: An Information System That Works: FedEx

Just as there are examples of information systems gone wrong, there are many examples of information systems gone right. FedEx, a US$40 billion family of companies (2012 data), is the world's largest express transportation company and delivers millions of packages and millions of pounds of freight to 220 countries and territories each business day. FedEx uses extensive, interconnected information systems to coordinate more than 290,000 employees, hundreds of aircraft, and tens of thousands of ground vehicles worldwide. To improve its services and sustain a competitive advantage, FedEx continuously updates and fine-tunes its systems. For example, FedEx.com has more than 15 million unique visitors per month and over 3 million tracking requests per day, and FedEx strives to provide the most accurate tracking information to each visitor. Similarly, in FedEx's ground hubs, automation is another enabler of competitive advantage. En route to its destination, each package typically travels through at least one sorting facility, where it is routed to its intermediate and final destinations (Figure 1.19). Traveling through an extensive network of conveyor belts, each package is scanned multiple times, and can be rerouted as needed. Once a package passes an overhead scanner, there is between one and two seconds of time to divert a package, so decisions have to be made in a few hundred milliseconds (King, 2011). On average, FedEx reengineers and improves the performance twice a year, and now manages to deliver a quarter of all daily packages handled within one business day. These and other information systems have positioned FedEx as the global leader in express transportation.

FIGURE 1.19

Packages travel through an extensive network of conveyor belts, where they are routed to their intermediate and final destinations.
Source: Stephen Mahar/Shutterstock.

Information Systems for Competitive Advantage

The American Airlines and FedEx systems are typical of systems that are pervasive in today's life or used in large, complex organizations. These systems are so large in scale and scope that they are difficult to build. It is important to handle the development of such systems the right way the first time around. These examples also show that as we rely more and more on information systems, the capabilities of these systems are paramount to business success.

Not only were these systems large and complicated, but they were—and continue to be—critical to the success of the organizations that built them. The choices made in developing the systems at American Airlines and FedEx were **strategic** in their intent. For airlines, computerized reservation systems are a strategic necessity; the systems developed by FedEx are developed and continuously updated to help gain or sustain some **competitive advantage** (Porter, 1985; Porter & Millar, 1985) over its rivals. Let us not let this notion slip by us—while the use of technology can enable efficiency and while information systems must provide a return on investment, technology use can also be strategic and a powerful enabler of competitive advantage.

Although we described the use of information systems at two very large organizations, firms of all types and sizes can use information systems to gain or sustain a competitive advantage over their rivals. Whether it is a small mom-and-pop boutique or a large government agency, every organization can find a way to use information technology to beat its rivals.

Some argue that as information systems have become standardized and ubiquitous, they are now more of a commodity that is absolutely necessary for every company, and companies should focus information technology strictly on cost reduction and risk mitigation and that investing in information technology for differentiation or for competitive advantage is futile. Yet, as evidenced by the advances in smartphones, emergence of social networks, or changes in various creative industries, IT is changing rapidly, and many companies have gained competitive advantage by innovatively using the potential of new technologies. Specifically, companies from Amazon.com to Zynga created competitive advantage by combining certain commoditized technologies with proprietary systems and business processes. Companies with bad business models tend to fail regardless of whether they use information technology or not, but companies that have good business models and use information technology successfully to carry out those business models tend to be very successful. For companies such as Google or Facebook, data generated by the customers create value, and how data are being gathered, processed, and used can be a source of sustained competitive advantage (Vellante, 2011); companies such as Amazon.com use their IT expertise to sell cloud computing services to other businesses, directly generating revenue from their IT investments.

In sum, we believe that information systems are a necessary part of doing business and that they can be used to create efficiencies, but that they can also be used as an enabler of competitive advantage. Organizations should also note, however, that the competitive advantage from the use of information systems can be fleeting, as competitors can eventually do the same thing.

WHEN THINGS GO WRONG

Failure: The Path to Success?

Management consultant Tom Peters, author and coauthor of 10 international best-selling business books, often tells business managers that a company's survival may depend upon those employees who fail over and over again as they try new ideas. There's little that is more important to tomorrow's managers than failure, Peters maintains. Apparently, Apple lives by Peters' philosophy. In January 2008, to help celebrate 24 years of the Mac, first introduced to consumers in 1984, *Wired* magazine recalled some of Apple's more infamous failures.

One of Apple's most visible flops was the Newton, actually the name of a newly conceived operating system that stuck to the product as a whole. The Newton, which Apple promised would "reinvent personal computing," fell far short of its hype when it was introduced in 1993 as a not-so-revolutionary personal digital assistant (PDA). The Newton was on the market for six years—a relatively long time for an unsuccessful product—but one of Steve Jobs' first acts when he returned to Apple's helm in 1997 was to cut the Newton Systems Group.

Other Apple product failures include: The Pippin (1993), a gaming device that couldn't compete with Nintendo's 64 or the Sony PlayStation; the Macintosh television (1993), which only sold 10,000 units; the PowerMac G4 Cube (2000), an 8″ × 8″ × 8″ designer machine that was widely regarded as overpriced; the puck mouse included with the iMac G3 (1998), a too-small, awkward-to-control device that users often mistakenly used upside down; and the Lisa (1983), whose whopping US$9,995 price tag (over US$20,000 in current dollars) made it too expensive for most businesses.

In recent years, Apple has introduced a large variety of new products, all with remarkable success. Innovative products that consumers stand in line to get include the Macbook Air, a line of iPods, iPhones, and iPads. Time will tell if Apple's current success streak continues, or if, at some point, Apple will yet again introduce a product that is "too innovative" for the consumers. Although Apple's failures are often cited by its competitors, the company has proved Peters right time and time again: Any company without an interesting list of failures probably isn't trying hard enough.

Based on:

Gardiner, B. (2008, January 24). Learning from failure: Apple's most notorious flops. *Wired*. Retrieved May 12, 2014, from http://archive.wired.com/gadgets/mac/multimedia/2008/01/gallery_apple_flops.

IS ETHICS

A broad range of ethical issues have emerged through the use and proliferation of computers. Especially with the rise of companies such as Google, which generate tremendous profits by collecting, analyzing, and using their customers' data, and the emergence of social networks such as Facebook, many people fear negative impacts such as social decay, increased consumerism, or loss of privacy. **Computer ethics** is used to describe moral issues and standards of conduct as they pertain to the use of information systems. In 1986, Richard O. Mason wrote a classic and very insightful article on the issues central to this debate—information privacy, accuracy, property, and accessibility (aka, "PAPA"). These issues focus on what information an individual should have to reveal to others in the workplace or through other transactions, such as online shopping, ensuring the authenticity and fidelity of information, who owns information about individuals and how that information can be sold and exchanged, and what information a person or organization has the right to obtain about others and how this information can be accessed and used.

With the societal changes brought about by information systems, the issues surrounding privacy have moved to the forefront of public concern; in addition, the ease of digitally duplicating and sharing information has raised not only privacy concerns, but also issues related to intellectual property. Next, we examine these issues.

Information Privacy

If you use the Internet regularly, sending e-mail messages, posting status updates on Facebook, or just visiting Web sites, you may have felt that your personal privacy is at risk. Several e-commerce Web sites where you like to shop greet you by name and seem to know which products you are most likely to buy (Figure 1.20); other Web sites provide you with advertising that appears to be targeted accurately at you. As a result, you may feel as though eyes are on you every time you go online. **Information privacy** is concerned with what information an individual should have to reveal to others in the workplace or through other transactions, such as online shopping.

COMING ATTRACTIONS

Smart Shirts Saving Lives

In the coming decades, it is predicted that many everyday objects will be infused with networking capabilities and connected to the Internet, creating the "Internet of Things." One class of such connectable things that is being actively developed is so-called smart clothes, which contain technology sensors and connectivity so that they can be used for a number of innovative solutions. One such solution, being developed at City University of Hong Kong, has the potential to save lives.

Researchers at City University have developed a smart shirt that is equipped with 10-inch silicon sensor pads that detect the heart's electrical activity and transmit this information to a receiver via Bluetooth. The shirt is able to detect a range of heart problems before and when they arise. The developers believe that this shirt will save lives, allowing medical professionals to constantly monitor the heart activity of their patients. Still in development, the prototypes of the shirt and associated sensors weigh 3–5 kilograms and cost over US$2,500 per shirt to manufacture. In its current form, the shirt would have to be custom made for each potential patient. Despite these resource demands, the technology and others like it show strong potential to have a major impact on the lives of many individuals.

These wearable medical devices are only a subset of the many technologies being developed to contribute to the Internet of Things. Many other types of Internet-connected technology are being developed, from refrigerators to automobiles to bodyweight scales. Clearly, our lives will become increasingly infused with technology in the coming years.

Based on:
Choi, C. (2014, April 2). City University researchers develop life-saving "smart" shirt that can detect heart problems. *South China Morning Post*. Retrieved May 12, 2014, from http://www.scmp.com/news/hong-kong/article/1463212/city-university-researchers-develop-life-saving-smart-shirt-can.

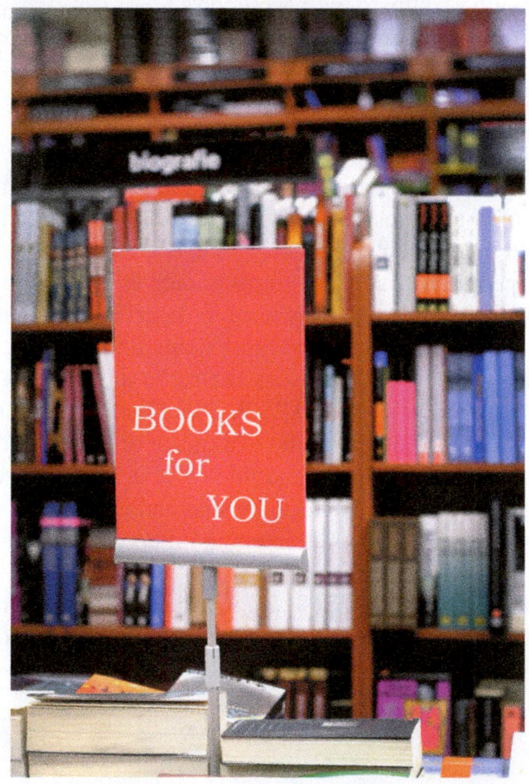

FIGURE 1.20
Just like the owners of your neighborhood bookstore, online merchants such as Amazon.com greet you by name and personalize their Web sites to individual customers.
Source: Jurgita Genyte/Shutterstock.

Although the Information Age has brought widespread access to information, the downside is that others may now have access to personal information that you would prefer to keep private. Personal information, such as Social Security numbers, credit card numbers, medical histories, and even family histories, is now available on the Internet. Using search engines, your friends, coworkers, current or future employers, or even your spouse can find out almost anything that has been posted by or about you on the Internet. For example, it is very easy to locate your personal blog, your most recent party pictures posted on Facebook, or even sensitive questions you asked in a public discussion forum about drug use or mental health. Moreover, many of these pages are stored in the search engines' long-term cache, so they remain accessible for a long time even after they have been taken off the Web. Yet, come countries are seeking to protect their citizens from this. In 2014, the European Court of Justice ruled that individuals have the "Right to be Forgotten," and that search engines may have to remove links with personal information, if the "information is inaccurate, inadequate, irrelevant or excessive for the purposes of the data processing" (European Commission, n.d.). In order to uphold freedom of expression and freedom of the media, such requests are handled on a case-by-case basis.

INFORMATION PROPERTY ON THE WEB. It happens to all of us. Nearly every day in our physical or virtual mailboxes, we receive unwanted solicitations from credit card companies, department stores, magazines, or charitable organizations. Many of these items are never opened. We ask the same question over and over again: "How did I get on another mailing list?" Our names, addresses, and other personal information were most likely sold from one company to another for use in mass mailings.

Who owns the computerized information about people—the information that is stored in thousands of databases by retailers, credit card companies, and marketing research companies? The answer is, the company that maintains the database of customers or subscribers legally owns the information and is free to sell it. Your name, address, and other information are all legally kept in a company database to be used for the company's future mailings and solicitations, and the company can sell its customer list or parts of it to other companies who want to send similar mailings.

There are limits, however, to what a company can do with such data. For example, if a company stated at one time that its collection of marketing data was to be used strictly internally as a gauge of its own customer base and then sold that data to a second company years later, it would be unethically and illegally breaking its original promise. Companies collect data from credit card purchases (by using a credit card, you indirectly allow this) or from surveys and questionnaires you fill out when applying for a card. They also collect data when you fill in a survey at a bar, restaurant, supermarket, or the mall about the quality of the service or product preferences. By providing this information, you implicitly agree that the data can be used as the company wishes (within legal limits, of course).

What is even more problematic is the combination of survey data with transaction data from your credit card purchases. As information systems are becoming more powerful it becomes easier to collect and analyze various types of information about people. For example, using demographic data (Who am I, and where do I live?) and psychographic data (What do I like, what are my tastes and preferences?), companies can piece together bits of information about people, creating highly accurate profiles of their customers or users, with each additional bit helping to create a more accurate picture. Such pictures, sometimes referred to as "the Database of Intentions" (Battelle, 2010), can contain information about what people want, purchase, like, are interested in, are doing, where they are, who they are, and whom they know (Figure 1.21).

Needless to say, just because people provide data at different points does not mean that they agree for the data to be combined to create a holistic picture. Companies are often walking a fine line, as information about customers is becoming increasingly valuable; Facebook founder Mark Zuckerberg, for example, is known for stretching people's privacy expectations. Throughout its existence, Facebook has pushed the boundaries of people's privacy expectations, maintaining that privacy would no longer be a social norm, and unilaterally changing default privacy settings; this has gone so far that in 2011 the U.S. Federal Trade Commission (FTC) ordered Facebook to perform regular independent privacy audits for the following two years. In early 2012, Google similarly pushed the privacy boundary by combining the data gathered at Google's different services (be it Google, Gmail, or YouTube) into one database, enabling the company to create an even more complete picture of any user of Google's services.

How do you know who is accessing these databases? This is an issue that each company must address at both a strategic/ethical level (Is this something that we should be doing?) and a tactical level (If we do this, what can we do to ensure the security and integrity of the data?). The company needs to ensure proper hiring, training, and supervision of employees who have access to the data and implement the necessary software and hardware security safeguards.

In today's interconnected world, there are even more dangers to information privacy. Although more and more people are concerned about their privacy settings on social networks

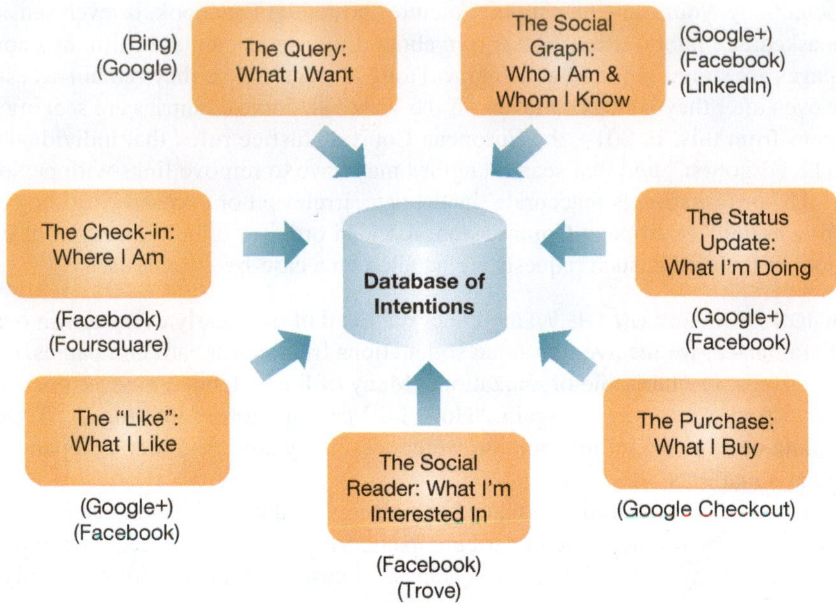

FIGURE 1.21

The database of intentions.
Source: Based on Batelle (2010).

such as Facebook, there are things that you may not be able to control. For example, if one of your friends (or even a stranger) posts a photo of you on Facebook, it will be there for many others to view, whether you like it or not. By the time you realize it, most of your friends, coworkers, and family members may have already seen it. At other times, you may divulge sensitive information (such as your address or date of birth) when signing up for yet another social network; as newer, more exciting applications come up, you abandon your profile, but your information stays out there. Sometimes, you may forget who's following your activities at the various social networking sites, and you may tell people things you never wanted them to know. As these examples show, there are many more threats to your privacy than you may have thought.

E-MAIL PRIVACY. The use of e-mail raises further privacy issues, as nowadays, almost everyone sends and receives electronic mail, whether or not they have a PC. All that is needed to participate is access to the Internet, whether through a home PC, a school's computer lab, a smartphone, or any other device that provides Internet access. Although it is slowly being supplanted by social networking services and text messages, e-mail is still one of the most popular software applications of all time, having contributed greatly to a steady decline of physical mail. However, recent court cases have not supported computer privacy for employee e-mail transmissions and Internet usage. For example, although most companies provide employees with access to the Internet and other outside e-mail systems, many periodically monitor the e-mail messages that employees send and receive. Monitoring employee behavior is nothing new, and for many businesses it was a natural extension to monitor employee e-mail messages.

Surprisingly, there is little legal recourse for those who support e-mail privacy. In 1986, Congress passed the Electronic Communications Privacy Act (ECPA), but it offered far stronger support for voice mail than it did for e-mail communications. This act made it much more difficult for anyone (including the government) to eavesdrop on phone conversations. E-mail privacy is, therefore, much harder to protect. In addition, no other laws at the federal or state levels protect e-mail privacy. However, some states, most notably California, have passed laws that define how companies should inform their employees of this situation and in which situations monitoring is legal. Even so, this law is more of a guideline for ethical practice than a protection of privacy (Sipior & Ward, 1995).

Fortunately, the ECPA and the court case judgments thus far on e-mail monitoring suggest that companies must be prudent and open about their monitoring of e-mail messages and Internet usage. Companies should use good judgment in monitoring e-mail and should make public their policy about monitoring messages. One primary reason that employees perceive their e-mail to be private is the fact that they are never told otherwise (Weisband & Reinig, 1995). In addition, employees should use e-mail only as appropriate, based on their company's policy and their own ethical standards. Given recent actions and rulings on the capture and usage of e-mail messages over the Internet, it appears that online privacy is in jeopardy both in and out of business organizations. As a general rule, we all need to realize that what we type and send via e-mail in and out of the workplace is likely to be read by others for whom the messages were not intended. It is wise to write only those e-mail messages that would not embarrass us if they were made public.

HOW TO MAINTAIN YOUR PRIVACY ONLINE. In general, companies operating in the online world are not required by law to respect your privacy. In other words, a vendor can track what pages you look at, what products you examine in detail, which products you choose to buy, what method of payment you choose to use, and where you have the product delivered. After collecting all that information, unscrupulous vendors can sell it to others, resulting in more direct-mail advertising, electronic spam in your e-mail inbox, or calls from telemarketers.

When surveyed about concerns related to Internet use, most consumers list issues of information privacy as a top concern. As a result, governments have pressured businesses to post their privacy policies on their Web sites. As outlined in the U.S. Federal Trade Commission's "Fair Information Practice Principles" (http://www.ftc.gov/reports/privacy3/fairinfo.shtm, see also Figure 1.22), widely accepted fair information practices include:

- ***Notice/Awareness.*** Providing information about what data are gathered, what the data are used for, who will have access to the data, whether provision of the data is required or voluntary, and how confidentiality will be ensured. Such information is typically contained in **data privacy statements** on a Web site.
- ***Choice/Consent.*** Providing options about what will be done with the data (e.g., subscription to mailing lists after a purchase). Typically, consumers are given a choice to **opt-in** (i.e., signal agreement to the collection/further use of the data, e.g., by checking a box) or **opt-out** (i.e., signal that data cannot be collected/used in other ways).
- ***Access/Participation.*** Providing customers with means to access data collected about them, check for accuracy, and request correction of inaccuracies.
- ***Integrity/Security.*** Ensuring integrity of the data (e.g., by using only reputable sources of data), as well as implementing controls against unauthorized access, disclosure, or destruction of data (we will discuss these controls in Chapter 10, "Securing Information Systems").
- ***Enforcement/Redress.*** Providing means to enforce these practices, and/or for customers to receive remedies, for example, through self-regulation or appropriate laws and regulations.

Unfortunately, while data privacy statements provide information about, for example, how data will be used, they often do not *protect* the privacy of consumers. To protect yourself, you should always review the privacy policy of all companies you do business with and refuse to do business with those that do not have a clear policy or do not respect your privacy. To make sure your shopping experience is a good one, you can take a few additional steps to maintain your privacy:

- ***Choose Web Sites That Are Monitored by Independent Organizations.*** Several independent organizations monitor the privacy and business practices of Web sites (e.g., www.truste.com).

FIGURE 1.22

Fair Information Practice Principles.

Source: Courtesy of the Federal Trade Commission, http://www.ftc.gov/reports/privacy3/fairinfo.shtm.

- ***Avoid Having "Cookies" Left on Your Machine.*** Many commercial Web sites leave cookies on your machine so that the owner of the site can monitor where you go and what you do on the site. To enhance your privacy, you should carefully manage your browser's cookie settings or get special "cookie management" software (see Chapter 10 for more on cookies).
- ***Visit Sites Anonymously.*** There are ways to visit Web sites anonymously. Using services provided by companies such as Anonymizer (www.anonymizer.com), you have a high degree of privacy from marketers, identity thieves, or even coworkers when surfing the Web.
- ***Use Caution When Requesting Confirmation E-Mail.*** When you buy products online, many companies will send you a confirming e-mail message to let you know that the order was received correctly. A good strategy is to use a separate e-mail account, such as one that is available for viewing via a Web browser, when making online purchases.
- ***Beware What You Post or Say Online.*** As an old adage goes, "the Internet never forgets"; anything from status updates to Twitter messages to blog posts can be stored forever, and most information remains somewhere on the Web, even after the original page has long been taken down. It is safe to say that probably almost everybody engages in some regrettable activities at some point in time. Yet, having such activities appear on the Web can be devastating for one's career, so use common sense before you post that drunken party pic on Facebook, or tweet that you are so bored on your job.

Of course, there are no guarantees that all your online experiences will be problem free, but if you follow the advice provided here, you are much more likely to maintain your privacy.

Intellectual Property

Another set of ethical issues centers around **intellectual property** (i.e., creations of the mind that have commercial value), and the ability to easily download, copy (and potentially modify), and share or distribute digital information. For example, back in the days of analog music, it was all but impossible to create a copy of a song without sacrificing quality. Nowadays, you can almost effortlessly copy your friend's entire digital music library without any quality loss (Figure 1.23); with just a little more effort, you can share it with your friends, or even strangers using peer-to-peer networks. Alternatively, you may come across a great photograph or article on the Web, and share it on Facebook or Google+, without asking for permission from the creator.

Similarly, your school may have licensing agreements with certain vendors, allowing you to install and use certain software while you are a student; yet, you never uninstall the software after graduating, or you may lend the software to some friend or family member for personal use. In other cases, you may not be able to afford certain programs, and download a pirated version from the Web.

Just as digital technology enables lossless duplication of files, **3D printing** enables creating physical three-dimensional objects from digital models. When building prototypes or

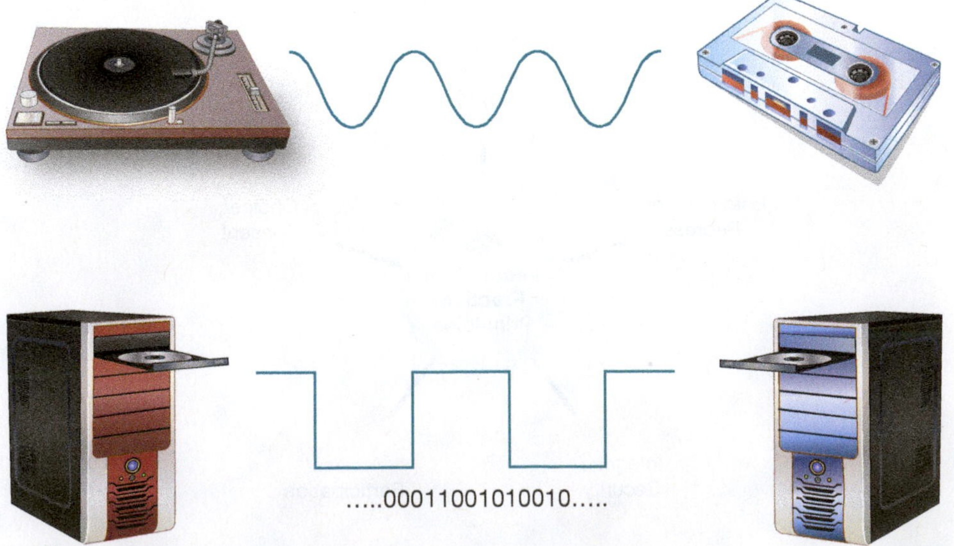

FIGURE 1.23

Digital media allows for lossless duplication.

manufacturing parts, companies have traditionally used machine tools to drill, cut, or mill the part out of a solid piece of material, leaving up to 90 percent of a slab of material ready to go in the recycling or garbage bin. Instead of removing material, 3D printing successively adds thin layers of material to produce the final object. As 3D printers are becoming better, faster, and more affordable, however, they also open up new avenues for quickly and inexpensively producing counterfeit goods. Obviously, this causes problems for consumers expecting to purchase the original product, but also leads to tremendous losses in intellectual property, when tools are widely available that enable anyone to manufacture their own copy of a product.

Obviously, there are legal issues associated with each of these scenarios. However, there are also ethical issues associated with such behaviors. You may argue that there was no real loss involved for the creator of the files or software, as otherwise, you would have gone for a free alternative or chosen not to purchase the product at all, or you may argue that students do not have the funds to purchase expensive software. These issues become even more complex when viewed

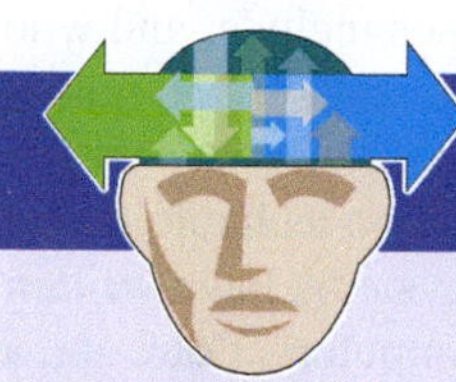

ETHICAL DILEMMA

The Human Cost of the Newest Gadgets

We all face ethical dilemmas. Such situations, sometimes called moral dilemmas, occur when one has to choose between two different options, each of which involves breaking a moral imperative. Throughout this book, we will present situations that involve ethical dilemmas for the players involved. For most (if not all) of these situations, there are no definite solutions. In trying to resolve ethical dilemmas, decision makers should take into consideration both the consequences of and the actions involved in each approach: First, consider the *consequences* of each potential course of action, in terms of benefits and harms (considering degree and time horizon), so as to identify the option that maximizes benefits while minimizing harms. The second step is to consider the *actions* involved (irrespective of the consequences), and to evaluate which actions are least problematic from a moral standpoint (in terms of honesty, fairness, respect, etc.). While you may not arrive at a perfect solution, taking these two factors into account should give you some guidance on how to arrive at a decision.

There are various ethical dilemmas surrounding the production, use, and disposal of electronic devices, and Apple is no exception. For example, tiny silver letters printed on the back of an iPhone say: "Designed by Apple in California—Assembled in China." Globalization has enabled Apple to focus on designing electronics consumers crave, while outsourcing the manufacturing of components and assembling of the devices to contract manufacturers on a global scale. However, while Apple keeps tight control over the designs of its devices, it does not always have complete control over *how* its suppliers build the components.

As a case in point, Foxconn, one of Apple's primary Chinese assembly partners, was recently scrutinized following a series of complaints of poor working conditions. The pressures of huge production volumes and tight deadlines resulted in pushing workers to their limit, causing twitching hands, uncontrollable mimicking of the motion after work, and a rapid burnout rate causing the resignation of 50,000 workers each month, and even resulted in up to 14 suicides. In light of these issues, the company has gradually attempted to improve the working conditions by reducing overtime or offering counseling services. In addition, Apple has asked the nonprofit Fair Labor Association to conduct an independent audit at various factories; this audit, among other things, confirmed that laborers worked excessive overtime and faced health and safety issues. Apple has agreed to address these issues, but they remind us that increasing consumerism and a focus on having the latest technologies carries a human cost.

Apple's CEO Tim Cook faces a number of dilemmas. For its shareholders, Apple pursues a goal of profit maximization. In pursuing this goal, Apple introduces gadgets consumers crave at an ever-increasing pace, creating a hype around each new device, which, in turn, creates huge demand. There are few suppliers worldwide who can, on relatively short notice, produce the numbers needed to meet the demand for Apple's products, so shifting suppliers is not easy for Apple. At the same time, reducing working hours, raising salaries, or offering other fringe benefits negatively impacts Apple's profit margin. Further, for many young Chinese, working at Foxconn for a few months is better than the alternative of tilling the fields on their families' small farming operations, or not working at all, as evidenced by the thousands of workers lining up for Foxconn's recruiting sessions every week. If you were in Tim Cook's shoes, what would you do? As a consumer, what are your ethical dilemmas associated with the ever-increasing desire for new gadgets?

Based on:

Anonymous. (2012, March 29). Apple addresses China Foxconn factory report. *BBC News*. Retrieved May 12, 2014, from http://www.bbc.com/news/technology-17557630.

Moore, M. (2012, January 11). "Mass suicide" protest at Apple manufacturer Foxconn factory. *Telegraph.co.uk*. Retrieved May 12, 2014, from http://www.telegraph.co.uk/news/worldnews/asia/china/9006988/Mass-suicide-protest-at-Apple-manufacturer-Foxconn-factory.html.

from a global perspective. In many non-Western societies, using someone else's work is considered praise for the creator, and it is perfectly alright to use a famous song as background music in a YouTube video, or to include another person's writing in one's personal blog (or term paper).

In either case, you are using someone else's intellectual property without permission (and often without attribution), and without compensating the creator.

The Need for a Code of Ethical Conduct

Not only has the Internet age found governments playing catch-up to pass legislation pertaining to computer crime, privacy, and security, but it has also created an ethical conundrum. For instance, the technology exists to rearrange and otherwise change photographs, but is the practice ethical? If you can use a computer at your school or workplace for professional purposes but "steal" computer time to do personal business, is this ethical? Is it ethical for companies to compile information about your shopping habits, credit history, and other aspects of your life for the purpose of selling such data to others? Should guidelines be in place to dictate how businesses and others use information and computers? If so, what should the guidelines include, and who should write them? Should there be penalties imposed for those who violate established guidelines? If so, who should enforce such penalties?

Many businesses have devised guidelines for the ethical use of information technology and computer systems; similarly, most universities and many public school systems have written guidelines for students, faculty, and employees about the ethical use of computers. EduCom, a non-profit organization of colleges and universities, has developed a policy for ethics in information technology that many universities endorse. In part, the EduCom statement concerning software and intellectual rights says,

> Because electronic information is volatile and easily reproduced, respect for the work and personal expression of others is especially critical in computer environments. Violations of authorial integrity, including plagiarism, invasion of privacy, unauthorized access, and trade secret and copyright violations, may be grounds for sanctions against members of the academic community. (Courtesy of EduCom)

Most organization and school guidelines encourage all system users to act responsibly, ethically, and legally when using computers and to follow accepted rules of online etiquette as well as federal and state laws.

RESPONSIBLE COMPUTER USE. The Computer Ethics Institute is a research, education, and policy study organization that studies how advances in information technology have impacted ethics and corporate and public policy. The institute has issued widely quoted guidelines for the ethical use of computers. The guidelines prohibit the following:

- Using a computer to harm others
- Interfering with other people's computer work
- Snooping in other people's files
- Using a computer to steal
- Using a computer to bear false witness
- Copying or using proprietary software without paying for it
- Using other people's computer resources without authorization or compensation
- Appropriating other people's intellectual output

In addition, the guidelines recommend the following:

- Thinking about social consequences of programs you write and systems you design
- Using a computer in ways that show consideration and respect for others

Responsible computer use in the Information Age includes following the guidelines mentioned here. As a computer user, when in doubt, you should review the ethical guidelines published by your school, place of employment, and/or professional organization. Some users bent on illegal or unethical behavior are attracted by the anonymity they believe the Internet affords. But the fact is that we leave electronic tracks as we wander through the Web, and many perpetrators have been traced and successfully prosecuted when they thought they had hidden their trails. The fact is, too, that if you post objectionable material on the Internet and people complain about it, your Internet service provider can ask you to remove the material or remove yourself from the service.

INDUSTRY ANALYSIS

Business Career Outlook

Today, organizations are increasingly moving away from focusing exclusively on local markets. For example, PriceWaterhouseCoopers is focusing on forming overseas partnerships to increase its client base and to better serve the regions located away from its U.S. home. This means that it is not only more likely that you will need to travel overseas in your career or even take an overseas assignment, but it is also extremely likely that you will have to work with customers, suppliers, or colleagues from other parts of the world. Given this globalization trend, there is a shortage of business professionals with the necessary "global skills" for operating in the digital world. Three strategies for improving your skills include the following:

1. **Gain International Experience.** The first strategy is straightforward. Simply put, by gaining international experiences, you will more likely possess the necessary cultural sensitivity to empathize with other cultures and, more important, you will be a valuable asset to any global organization.
2. **Learn More Than One Language.** A second strategy is to learn more than your native language. Language problems within global organizations are often hidden beneath the surface. Many people are embarrassed to admit when they don't completely understand a foreign colleague. Unfortunately, the miscommunication of important information can have disastrous effects on the business.
3. **Sensitize Yourself to Global Cultural and Political Issues.** A third strategy focuses on developing greater sensitivity to the various cultural and political differences within the world. Such sensitivity and awareness can be developed through coursework, seminars, and international travel. Understanding current events and the political climate of international colleagues will enhance communication, cohesiveness, and job performance.

In addition to these strategies, prior to making an international visit or taking an international assignment, there are many things you can do to improve your effectiveness as well as enhance your chances of having fun, including the following:

1. Read books, newspapers, magazines, and Web sites about the country.
2. Talk to people who already know the country and its culture.
3. Avoid literal translations of work materials, brochures, memos, and other important documents.
4. Watch locally produced television as well as follow the local news through international news stations and Web sites.
5. After arriving in the new country, take time to tour local parks, monuments, museums, entertainment locations, and other cultural venues.
6. Share meals and breaks with local workers and discuss more than just work-related issues, such as current local events and issues.
7. Learn several words and phrases in the local languages.

Regardless of what business profession you choose, globalization is a reality within the digital world. In addition to globalization, the proliferation of information systems is having specific ramifications for all careers. For example, managers use enterprise resource planning systems to manage business operations, doctors use healthcare information systems to analyze patient data and diagnose conditions, law enforcement officers use databases to identify gang members by their tattoos, and farmers use geographical information systems to reduce the application of fertilizers and optimize plant yields. In other words, no matter what your career focus is, information systems will be an important part of your job.

Based on:

Berdan, M. (2014, January 23). Preparing our children for the global economy. *Huffington Post*. Retrieved May 14, 2014, from http://www.huffingtonpost.com/marshall-s-berdan/preparing-our-children-for-the-global-economy_b_4652835.html.

Sophie. (2013, August 19). Global studies programs: Preparing students for a globalized world. *Nerdwallet.com*. Retrieved May 14, 2014, from http://www.nerdwallet.com/blog/nerdscholar/2013/global-studies-programs.

Key Points Review

1. ***Describe the characteristics of the digital world and the advent of the Information Age.*** Today, we live in a knowledge society, and information systems have become pervasive throughout our organizational and personal lives. Technological advances have enabled a move into the post-PC era, where mobility, social media, the Internet of Things, cloud computing, and Big Data shape the way we work and interact. Being successful in many careers today requires that people be computer literate, because the ability to access and effectively operate computing technology is a key part of many careers.

2. ***Define globalization, describe how it evolved over time, and describe the key drivers of globalization.*** A more global and competitive world includes visible economic, cultural, and technological changes. Globalization is the integration of economies throughout the world, fueled by technological progress and innovation, and has, among other changes, led to a rise in outsourcing and has helped to shape the world as we know it today. Companies operating in the digital world see a number of opportunities, but operating in the digital world also poses a number of challenges to companies.
3. ***Explain what an information system is, contrasting its data, technology, people, and organizational components.*** Information systems use information technology to collect, create, and distribute useful data. Information technology includes hardware, software, and telecommunications networks. When data are organized in a way that is useful to people, these data are defined as information. The field of information systems is huge, diverse, and growing, and encompasses many different people, purposes, systems, and technologies. The people who build, manage, use, and study information systems make up the people component. They include systems analysts, systems programmers, IS professors, and many others. Finally, information systems are used by all organizations, in all industries, so they are said to have an organizational component.
4. ***Describe the dual nature of information systems in the success and failure of modern organizations.*** If information systems are conceived, designed, used, and managed effectively and strategically, then together with a sound business model they can enable organizations to be more effective, to be more productive, to expand their reach, and to gain or sustain competitive advantage over rivals. Modern organizations that embrace and manage information systems effectively and strategically and combine that with sound business models tend to be the organizations that are successful and competitive.
5. ***Describe how computer ethics impact the use of information systems and discuss the ethical concerns associated with information privacy and intellectual property.*** Information privacy is concerned with what information an individual should have to reveal to others through the course of employment or through other transactions, such as online shopping. In the Information Age, others may have access to personal information that you would prefer to keep private. This becomes especially problematic as organizations are increasingly able to piece together information about you, forming an ever more complete picture. With the ease of duplicating, manipulating, and sharing digital information, intellectual property becomes an increasingly important issue.

Key Terms

3D printing 36
apps 9
BYOD 10
cloud computing 11
competitive advantage 30
computer ethics 31
computer fluency 14
computer literacy 13
consumerization of IT 10
data 19
data privacy statement 35
digital divide 6
e-business 6
globalization 14
hardware 18
healthcare IS 13
information 19
Information Age 8
information privacy 31
information system 18
information technology 18
intellectual property 36
Internet of Things 10
internetworking 26
knowledge 20
knowledge society 5
knowledge worker 5
management information system 26
network effect 12
office automation system 26
opt-in 35
opt-out 35
outsourcing 15
post-PC era 4
software 18
strategic 30
systems integration 26
telecommunications network 18
transaction processing system (TPS) 25
wearable technologies 13

Go to **mymislab.com** to complete the problems marked with this icon ✪.

Review Questions

1-1. What is the "post-PC era"?

1-2. Define the term "knowledge worker." Who coined the term?

1-3. Name your two favorite mobile devices. For each device, discuss how it has influenced your work or personal life.

1-4. Describe how cloud computing can improve your personal productivity.

1-5. List and describe several reasons why companies are choosing to outsource business activities.

1-6. List and contrast several challenges of operating in the digital world.

1-7. Define and contrast data, information, and knowledge.

1-8. Describe three or four types of jobs and career opportunities in information systems and in related fields.

1-9. List and define four of the systems knowledge and/or skills core competencies.

1-10. List and define five types of information systems used in organizations.

1-11. Discuss the issues surrounding information privacy, and how you can protect yourself.

1-12. How are the digital divide and computer literacy related?

Self-Study Questions

1-13. Information systems today are _______.
A. slower than in the past
B. ubiquitous
C. utilized by only a few select individuals
D. stable and should not change

1-14. Whereas data are raw unformatted symbols or lists of words or numbers, information is _______.
A. data that have been organized in a form that is useful
B. accumulated knowledge
C. what you put in your computer
D. what your computer prints out for you

1-15. Information systems were described in this chapter as _______.
A. any complicated technology that requires expert use
B. the use of information technology to collect, create, and distribute data
C. any technology (mechanical or electronic) used to supplement, extend, or replace human, manual labor
D. any technology used to leverage human capital

1-16. Other terms that can be used to represent the knowledge society include _______.
A. the new economy
B. the network era
C. the digital world
D. all of the above

1-17. Which of the following was *not* discussed as a common type, or category, of information system used in organizations?
A. transaction processing
B. decision support
C. enterprise resource planning
D. Web graphics

1-18. What is meant by BYOD?
A. the increased focus of hardware companies on the mass market
B. the phenomenon that devices are becoming increasingly playful
C. the use of personal devices and applications for work-related purposes
D. the increase of technology in people's households

1-19. A Web site asking you for permission to send you a weekly newsletter is an example of _______.
A. opt-in
B. permissions
C. opt-out
D. data privacy

1-20. Which of the following is *not* considered an intellectual property violation?
A. giving software licensed to your school or workplace to friends or family members
B. downloading pirated movies or music
C. making copies of music for your friends
D. all of the above are considered intellectual property violations

1-21. Being _______, or knowing how to use the computer as a device to gather, store, organize, and process information, can open up myriad sources of information.
A. technology literate
B. digitally divided
C. computer literate
D. computer illiterate

Answers are on page 44.

Problems and Exercises

1-22. Match the following terms with the appropriate definitions:

i. Information
ii. Internet of Things
iii. Information systems
iv. Information privacy
v. Computer fluency
vi. Globalization
vii. Outsourcing
viii. Digital divide
ix. Intellectual property
x. Computer ethics

a. The issues and standards of conduct as they pertain to the use of information systems
b. Data that have been formatted in a way that is useful
c. The integration of economies around the world, enabled by innovation and technological progress
d. The ability to independently learn new technologies as they emerge and assess their impact on one's work and life
e. A broad range of physical objects (such as computer, sensors, or motors) that are interconnected and automatically share data over the Internet
f. Systems that use information technology to collect, create, and distribute data
g. The moving of routine jobs and/or tasks to people in another firm to reduce costs
h. An area concerned with what information an individual should have to reveal to others through the course of employment or through other transactions, such as online shopping
i. The gap between those individuals in our society who are computer literate and have access to information resources, such as the Internet, and those who do not
j. Creations of the mind that have commercial value

1-23. Of the several information systems listed in the chapter, how many do you have experience with? What systems would you like to work with? What types of systems do you encounter at the university you are attending? The Web is also a good source for additional information.

1-24. Identify someone who works within the field of information systems as an IS instructor, professor, or practitioner (e.g., as a systems analyst or systems manager). Find out why this individual got into this field and what this person likes and dislikes about working within the field of information systems. What advice can this person offer to someone entering the field?

1-25. As a small group, conduct a search on the Web for job placement services. Pick at least four of these services and find as many IS job titles as you can. You may want to try monster.com or careerbuilder.com. How many did you find? Were any of them different from those presented in this chapter? Could you determine the responsibilities of these positions based on the information given to you?

1-26. Visit Walmart China (www.wal-martchina.com/english/index.htm). Compare and contrast www.walmart.com with Walmart China's site. What is the focus of Walmart China's Web site? Discuss how the focus differs from www.walmart.com. What are possible reasons for the differences?

1-27. What are potential costs and benefits of using your own devices in the workplace? How can organizations balance costs and benefits?

1-28. What is the impact of mobility and social networks on your personal life? On the Web, find statistics about these topics. How does your own behavior compare to the statistics you found?

1-29. As a small group, brainstorm what different types of data make up "Big Data" for a company like Amazon.com. What data are easiest/hardest to analyze? What data are least/most important? Justify your answers.

1-30. Compare and contrast the data privacy statements of three different e-commerce Web sites. What are the similarities and differences? Which business would you be least/most willing to do business with? Why?

1-31. Global outsourcing appears to be here to stay. Use the Web to identify a company that is providing low-cost labor from some less developed part of the world. Provide a short report that explains who the company is, where it is located, who its customers are, what services and capabilities it provides, how long it has been in business, and any other interesting information you can find in your research.

1-32. The Electronic Frontier Foundation (www.eff.org) has a mission of protecting rights and promoting freedom in the "electronic frontier." The organization provides additional advice on how to protect your online privacy. Review its suggestions and provide a summary of what you can do to protect yourself.

1-33. Find your school's guidelines for ethical computer use on the Internet and answer the following questions: Are there limitations as to the type of Web sites and material that can be viewed (e.g., pornography)? Are students allowed to change the programs on the hard drives of the lab computers or download software for their own use? Are there rules governing personal use of computers and e-mail?

Application Exercises

Note: The existing data files referenced in these exercises are available on the book's Web site: www.pearsonhighered.com/valacich.

Spreadsheet Application: Ticket Sales at Campus Travel

1-34. The local travel center, Campus Travel, has been losing sales. The presence of online ticketing Web sites, such as Travelocity.com and Expedia.com, has lured many students away. However, given the complexity of making international travel arrangements, Campus Travel could have a thriving and profitable business if it concentrated its efforts in this area. You have been asked by the director of sales and marketing to help with analyzing prior sales data in order to design better marketing strategies. Looking at these data, you realize that it is nearly impossible to perform a detailed analysis of ticket sales given that the data are not summarized or organized in a useful way to inform business decision making. The spreadsheet TicketSales.csv contains the ticket sales data for a three-month period. Your director has asked you for the following information regarding ticket sales. Modify the TicketSales.csv spreadsheet to provide the following information for your director:

- The total number of tickets sold.
  a. Select the data from the "tickets sold" column.
  b. Then select the "autosum" function.
- The largest amount of tickets sold by a certain salesperson to any one location.
  a. Select the appropriate cell.
  b. Use the "MAX" function to calculate each salesperson's highest ticket total in one transaction.
- The least amount of tickets sold by a certain salesperson to any one location.
  a. Select the appropriate cells.
  b. Use the "MIN" function to calculate the "least tickets sold."
- The average number of tickets sold.
  a. Select the cells.
  b. Use the "AVERAGE" function to calculate the "average number of tickets sold" using the same data you had selected in the previous steps.

Database Application: Tracking Frequent-Flier Miles at the Campus Travel Agency

1-35. The director of sales and marketing at the travel agency would like to increase the efficiency of handling those who have frequent-flier accounts. Often, frequent fliers have regular travel routes and a preferred seating area or meal category. In previous years, the data have been manually entered into a three-ring binder. In order to handle the frequent fliers' requests more efficiently, your director has asked you to build an Access database containing the traveler's name (first and last name), address, phone number, frequent-flier number, frequent-flier airline, meal category, and preferred seating area.

To do this, you will need to do the following:

- Create an empty database named "Frequent Flier."
- Import the data contained in the file FrequentFliers.txt. Use "Text File" under "Import" in the "External Data" tab. Hint: Use tab delimiters when importing the data; note that the first row contains field names.

After importing the data, create a report displaying the names and addresses of all frequent fliers by doing the following:

- Select "Report Wizard" under "Report" in the "Create" tab.
- Include the fields "first name," "last name," and "address" in the report.
- Save the report as "Frequent Fliers."

Team Work Exercise

Net Stats: Worldwide Internet Usage

In May 2014, there were almost 2.9 billion people worldwide who had access to the Internet at home (i.e., Internet users). Since its inception, the number of users has grown tremendously, from only around 14 million users in 1993 to 1 billion users in 2005, 2 billion users in 2010, and 3 billion users by the end of 2014 (forecast). Having grown exponentially in the early years, the growth in user numbers has slowed to less than 10 percent per year, as worldwide Internet penetration has surpassed 40 percent. In July 2013, almost 10 percent of the world's Internet users were located in the United States, with an Internet penetration of 84 percent. However, other countries are catching up. In 2013, China, with an Internet penetration of 46 percent (and much room to grow) accounted for over 23 percent of worldwide Internet users; similarly, only 16 percent of India's population had access to the Internet, accounting for 7 percent of worldwide Internet users (Table 1.8).

TABLE 1.8 Countries with Largest Number of Internet Users

Country	Population	Internet Access	% Population (penetration)	Usage (% of world)
China	1.4 billion	642 million	46	22.0
United States	323 million	280 million	87	9.6
India	1.3 billion	243 million	19	8.3
Japan	127 million	109 million	86	3.7
Brazil	202 million	109 million	53	3.7
Russia	142 million	84 million	59	2.9
Germany	83 million	72 million	87	2.5
Nigeria	179 million	67 million	38	2.3
U.K.	63 million	57 million	90	2.0
France	65 million	55 million	86	1.9

Note: Internet usage and population statistics were updated for July 1, 2014.

Source: Based on http://www.internetlivestats.com/internet-users-by-country.

Questions and Exercises

1-36. Search the Web for the most up-to-date statistics.

1-37. As a team, interpret these numbers. What is striking/ important about these statistics?

1-38. As a team, discuss how these numbers will look like in 5 years and 10 years. What will the changes mean for globalization? What issues/opportunities do you see arising?

1-39. Using your spreadsheet software of choice, create a graph/figure most effectively visualizing the statistics/ changes you consider most important.

Based on:

Anonymous. (n.d.). Internet users. Retrieved May 14, 2014, from http://www.internetlivestats.com/internet-users.

Answers to the Self-Study Questions

1-13. B, p. 4 **1-14.** A, p. 19 **1-15.** B, p. 18 **1-16.** D, p. 6 **1-17.** D, p. 25

1-18. C, p. 10 **1-19.** A, p. 35 **1-20.** D, p. 36 **1-21.** C, p. 13

CASE 1 Bridging the Digital Divide

An important ethical issue related to computer use is the *digital divide*, which refers to the unequal access to computer technology within various populations. The digital divide occurs on several levels: socioeconomic (rich/poor), racial (majority/minority), and geographical (urban/rural and developed/undeveloped countries). Studies have shown that as the Information Age progresses, those individuals who have access to computer technology and to opportunities for learning computer skills generally have an educational edge.

To bridge the divide, Nicholas Negroponte, an architect and computer scientist who founded the Massachusetts Institute of Technology's Media Lab, announced the creation of One Laptop per Child (OLPC), a non-profit organization, in 2005 at the World Economic Forum in Davos, Switzerland. As part of the project, the XO-1, a US$100 computer, was designed expressly for child use. With US$2 million startup contributions, OLPC intended to distribute the computers to children around the world, including locations within the United States. The computers were to be given to children at an early age, were designed for child ownership and use, had built-in Internet access, were intended to accompany children from school to homes, and were designed for free and open programming access.

The project's goal was to close the digital divide and transform education by providing access to computers for children who would otherwise not have the opportunity to fully participate in the Information Age. Yet, the project was off to a slow start, as OLPC was not able to produce the laptop at the price initially envisioned; the XO-1 shipped for US$200, double the envisioned price.

In 2007, the project received a boost when the "Give 1 Get 1" program was launched. For US$399, a shopper could buy the XO laptop for themselves, and an additional XO laptop was given to the project. In six weeks, over 80,000 laptops were given to children through this initiative. Owing to this success, the program was relaunched in 2008, this time with online retail giant Amazon.com. After the end of the program on December 31, 2008, Amazon.com offered the XO-1 laptop for US$199, this time to be donated to a child in a developing country. In October 2009, every child in the country of Uruguay received a laptop (through Uruguay's official "Plan Ceibal" project), making Uruguay the first country to fulfill the mission of the OLPC program. The program has since delivered laptops to Rwanda, Afghanistan, Uganda, Mongolia, Nicaragua, and Peru, among others. In total, OLPC has distributed over 2.4 million of the US$200 laptops to children all over the world.

Since the development of the first model, OLPC has continued evolving the design of the XO-1 series, with a focus on significantly reducing power consumption, while increasing processing power. At the 2012 Consumer Electronics Show (CES) in Las Vegas, Nevada, OLPC presented the XO-3: a tablet that would bring costs significantly lower. Today, you can buy the XO-780 tablet at various stores for around US$100. The project has thus finally reached its original target price point.

A recent study by the Inter-American Development Bank, however, revealed that the educational benefits from handing out these devices to children are far from given: In Peru, which spent US$225 million for 850,000 laptops (the largest number for any single country), there were no significant differences in math skills or literacy between children who received a laptop and those who did not. This is partially attributed to lack of training of teachers, who often do not know how to harness the potential of using these laptops in the classrooms. In addition, one of the main goals of the program in Peru was to give children a feeling of inclusion and self-esteem, rather than just improving learning.

Despite criticisms, the OLPC campaign continues to provide computing devices to children around the world. Still, access to the Internet and digital information remains elusive for much of the human population, especially on the African continent. In light of this, the OLPC program continues to innovate and find ways to bring technology to children around the world. With every device delivered, the digital divide is shrinking.

Questions

1-40. Why does the digital divide matter to children and their families?

1-41. What will the rise in mobile devices in the developing world mean for the OLPC project?

1-42. Identify and discuss what you feel is the major challenge for making the OLPC a success. How can this challenge be overcome?

Based on:

Negroponte, N. (n.d.). Retrieved May 12, 2014, from http://web.media.mit.edu/~nicholas.

Osborne, C. (2012, April 9). One Laptop per Child: Disappointing results? *ZDNet*. Retrieved May 12, 2014, from http://www.zdnet.com/blog/igeneration/one-laptop-per-child-disappointing-results/15920.

One Laptop per Child. (2014, May 11). In *Wikipedia, The Free Encyclopedia*. Retrieved May 13, 2014, from http://en.wikipedia.org/w/index.php?title=One_Laptop_per_Child&oldid=608063102.

CASE 2 YouTube

It's the website everyone visits at least once, and most surfers come back again and again: the ubiquitous YouTube. Where else can you watch a video of a cat swimming contentedly in a bathtub, a 12-year-old rendering a professional performance of the "The Star Spangled Banner" at a small-town basketball game, or a public political debate where candidates answer questions visitors to the site have submitted?

YouTube, a video-sharing Web site, went online in 2005. Two former PayPal employees, Steve Chen and Chad Hurley, created the site, and it was practically an overnight success. The San Bruno, California–based service displays a wide variety of user-generated video content, including movie and TV clips, music videos, video blogs, and short original videos. In July 2006, YouTube reported that visitors to the site were viewing more than 100 million video clips a day—a fact that compelled Google Inc. to buy the site that year for US$1.76 billion in stock. As of 2014, YouTube continues to be a successful video site and a top destination for Web surfers, who watch over 1 billion unique visitors each month. According to the site, over 6 billion hours of videos are watched each month, and 100 hours of video are uploaded every minute.

All of that video requires YouTube to have access to tremendous bandwidth. In 2013, the viewing of videos on YouTube consumed about 17 percent of global Internet bandwidth. In fact, in 2007 the British publication *The Telegraph* expressed fears that the Internet could "grind to a halt within two years" without massive upgrades to the Internet infrastructure. Fortunately for YouTube fans and Internet users in general, that didn't happen. Bandwidth issues aside, YouTube continues to try to draw in more viewers.

As YouTube has gained popularity, police forces around the country have used the service to help catch criminals. In April 2010, for example, homicide investigators in Vancouver, British Columbia, posted a video about a victim in an unsolved but high-profile murder case. Although the case was being actively investigated, the investigative team had exhausted its list of leads. The posted video included photos of the woman who had been killed and a recap of what the investigators had pieced together up to that point. Their hope was that by using social media and getting the story in front of viewers, it might help jog a memory of someone who might have seen something pertinent to the case. Some police departments, however, such as St. George County in Virginia, said they would not use YouTube for catching criminals because posting police videos next to those with "crazy" content would be "bad publicity" for the police.

Regardless of the propensity for catching criminals or lack thereof, YouTube has had its share of legal issues as well. After several lawsuits were filed alleging copyright violations over copyrighted material posted on YouTube, the company agreed to remove copyrighted material on request. In addition, YouTube installed software intended to automatically detect and remove copyrighted clips. In order to function correctly, however, the software needed to compare clips of copyrighted material to YouTube content, which meant that music, movie, and television companies would have to send decades of clips of copyrighted material to YouTube so that comparisons could be made.

In March 2010, the entertainment corporation Viacom entered into a US$1 billion lawsuit against YouTube alleging that the video site knowingly made a financial gain from 62,637 Viacom video clips that were viewed over 507 million times. YouTube has countered by alleging that Viacom was covertly uploading clips of its content in an attempt to sabotage YouTube's efforts to remove copyrighted material. Later that year, a U.S. district court ruled in favor of YouTube, a decision that Viacom was unlikely to accept; in April 2012, a judge at a U.S. federal appeals court sent the case back to a district court, asking the lower court to determine to what extent YouTube was aware of the copyright infringements. In April 2013, a district judge again granted summary judgment in favor of YouTube. An appeal was begun, but the parties settled in March 2014. Whatever YouTube's future, it's not likely that Internet users will soon lose interest in video sharing.

Questions

1-43. Do you use YouTube? If so, what is your favorite type of content? If not, why not? What other video-sharing sites do you use? Why?

1-44. How can businesses use YouTube to promote a good brand image? Have you seen any "good" campaigns on YouTube? If so, what made them appealing?

1-45. What potential dangers for a business's reputation can arise from user-generated content posted on sites such as YouTube? How can a business react to such dangers?

Based on:

Anonymous. (n.d.). Statistics. *YouTube*. Retrieved May 12, 2014, from http://www.youtube.com/yt/press/statistics.html.

Bolan, K. (2010, April 1). Police enlist YouTube in hunt for a killer. *Vancouver Sun*. Retrieved June 13, 2014, from http://www.canada.com/vancouversun/news/westcoastnews/story.html?id=acf3b299-6086-4e24-b68f-ede6543e3ed1.

Viacom International Inc. v. YouTube, Inc. (2014, March 18). In *Wikipedia, The Free Encyclopedia*. Retrieved May 13, 2014, from http://en.wikipedia.org/w/index.php?title=Viacom_International_Inc._v._YouTube,_Inc.&oldid=600224157.

Kafka, P. (2013, November 11). Netflix + YouTube = Half your broadband diet. *AllThingsD*. Retrieved May 12, 2014, from http://allthingsd.com/20131111/netflix-youtube-half-your-broadband-diet.

Go to **mymislab.com** for Auto-graded writing questions as well as the following Assisted-graded writing questions:

1-46. How do the five megatrends influence how people work and interact?

1-47. Describe and contrast the economic, cultural, and technological changes occurring in the digital world.

References

Ackoff, R. L. (1989). From data to wisdom. *Journal of Applied Systems Analysis*, 16, 3–9.

American Fact Finder. (2012). Educational attainment: 2012 American Community Survey 1-year estimates. *United States Census Bureau.* Retrieved May 27, 2014, from http://factfinder2.census.gov/faces/tableservices/jsf/pages/productview.xhtml?pid=ACS_12_1YR_S1501.

Anonymous. (2014, May). Information technology manager salary. *Salary.com.* Retrieved May 29, 2014, from http://www1.salary.com/Information-Technology-Manager-salary.html.

Battelle, J. (2010, March 5). The database of intentions is far larger than I thought. *Searchblog.* Retrieved May 29, 2014, from http://battellemedia.com/archives/2010/03/the_database_of_intentions_is_far_larger_than_i_thought.php.

Berdan, M. S. (2014, January 23). Preparing our children for the global economy. *HuffPost Education.* Retrieved May 27, 2014, from http://www.huffingtonpost.com/marshall-s-berdan/preparing-our-children-for-the-global-economy_b_4652835.html.

Brandel, M. (2013, September 23). 8 hot IT skills for 2014. *Computerworld.* Retrieved May 27, 2014, from http://www.computerworld.com/s/article/9242548/8_hot_IT_skills_for_2014.

Bureau of Labor Statistics. (2013, May). Occupational employment and wages, May 2013: Computer and information systems managers. *BLS.gov.* Retrieved May 28, 2014, from http://www.bls.gov/oes/current/oes113021.htm.

Bureau of Labor Statistics. (2014, January 8). Occupational outlook handbook: Computer and information systems managers. *BLS.gov.* Retrieved May 27, 2014, from http://www.bls.gov/ooh/management/computer-and-information-systems-managers.htm.

Carr, N. (2003). IT doesn't matter. *Harvard Business Review, 81*(5), 41–49.

Carr, N. (2004). *Does IT matter? Information technology and the corrosion of competitive advantage*. Boston: Harvard Business School Press.

Collett, S. (2014, April 7). IT Salary Survey 2014: Who's hot, who's not. *Computerworld.* Retrieved May 29, 2014, from http://www.computerworld.com/s/article/9247252/IT_Salary_Survey_2014_Who_s_hot_who_s_not.

Connolly, B. (2014, January 16). Hot tech skills in 2014. *CIO.com.* Retrieved May 27, 2014, from http://www.cio.com.au/article/536059/hot_tech_skills_2014.

De La Mora, R. (2014, March 26). Internet of Things: More than a trend, a real business opportunity. *Cisco Blogs.* Retrieved May 27, 2014, from http://blogs.cisco.com/ioe/internet-of-things-more-than-a-trend-a-real-business-opportunity.

Drucker, P. (1959). *Landmarks of tomorrow*. New York: Harper.

Elgan, M. (2010, February 20). Mike Elgan: How Buzz, Facebook and Twitter create "social insecurity." *Computerworld.* Retrieved May 29, 2014, from http://www.computerworld.com/s/article/9159679/Mike_Elgan_How_Buzz_Facebook_and_Twitter_create_social_insecurity.

Epps, S. R., Gownder, J. P., Golvin, C. S., Bodine, K., & Corbett, A. E. (2011, May 17). *What the post-PC era really means*. Cambridge, MA: Forrest Research.

European Commission (n.d.). Factsheet on the "Right to be Forgotten" ruling (C-131/12). Retrieved July 16, 2014, from http://ec.europa.eu/justice/data-protection/files/factsheets/factsheet_data_protection_en.pdf.

Galbraith, J. K. (1987). *The affluent society*. New York: Houghton Mifflin.

Heath, N. (2009, November 19). Outsourcers to fall victim to cloud computing rush? *ZDNet.* Retrieved May 29, 2014, from http://www.zdnet.com/outsourcers-to-fall-victim-to-cloud-computing-rush-3040153103.

Hinchcliffe, D. (2011, October 2). The "Big Five" IT trends of the next half decade: Mobile, social, cloud, consumerization, and big data. *ZDNet.* Retrieved May 29, 2014, from http://www.zdnet.com/blog/hinchcliffe/the-big-five-it-trends-of-the-next-half-decade-mobile-social-cloud-consumerization-and-big-data/1811.

Hofmann, P. (2011, October 15). The big five IT megatrends. *Slideshare.* Retrieved July 15, 2014, from http://www.slideshare.net/paulhofmann/the-big-five-it-mega-trends.

International Monetary Fund. (2002). Globalization: Threat or opportunity? Retrieved May 29, 2014, from http://www.imf.org/external/np/exr/ib/2000/041200to.htm.

King, J. (2003, September 15). IT's global itinerary: Offshore outsourcing is inevitable. *Computerworld.* Retrieved May 29, 2014, from http://www.computerworld.com/managementtopics/outsourcing/story/0,10801,84861,00.html.

King, J. (2011, June 6). Extreme automation: FedEx Ground hubs speed deliveries. *Computerworld.* Retrieved May 29, 2014, from http://www.computerworld.com/s/article/356328/Extreme_automation_FedEx_Ground_hubs_speed_deliveries.

Kirschner, B. (2014, February 13). Who art thou, chief digital officer? *Entrepreneur.com.* Retrieved May 27, 2014, from http://www.entrepreneur.com/article/231484.

Leung, L. (2009). 10 hot skills for 2009. *Global Knowledge.* Retrieved May 29, 2014, from http://www.globalknowledge.com/training/generic.asp?pageid=2321.

Mason, R. O. (1986). Four ethical issues of the information age. *MIS Quarterly, 10*(1), 5–12.

Michaeli, R. (2009). *Competitive intelligence: Competitive advantage through analysis of competition, markets and technologies*. New York: Springer.

NACE. (2014, April 16). Top-paid majors for the class of 2014. *Naceweb.org.* Retrieved May 27, 2014, from http://www.naceweb.org/s04162014/top-paid-majors-class-of-2014.aspx.

Pettey, C. (2011, November 8). Gartner says consumerization will drive at least four mobile management styles. *Gartner.* Retrieved May 29, 2014, from http://www.gartner.com/it/page.jsp?id=1842615.

Porter, M. E. (1985). *Competitive advantage: Creating and sustaining superior performance*. New York: Free Press.

Porter, M. E., & Millar, V. (1985). How information gives you competitive advantage. *Harvard Business Review, 63*(4), 149–161.

Rivera, J., & van der Meulen, R. (2013, July 17). Gartner says worldwide IT outsourcing market to reach $288 billion in 2013. *Gartner.com.* Retrieved May 27, 2014, from http://www.gartner.com/newsroom/id/2550615.

Rosen, E. (2011, January 11). Every worker is a knowledge worker. *BusinessWeek.* Retrieved May 29, 2014, from http://www.businessweek.com/managing/content/jan2011/ca20110110_985915.htm.

Savitz, E. (2012, February 20). Consumerization of IT: Getting beyond the myths. *Forbes.* Retrieved May 29, 2014, from http://www.forbes.com/sites/ciocentral/2012/02/20/consumerization-of-it-getting-beyond-the-myths.

Sipior, J. C., & Ward, B. T. (1995). The ethical and legal quandary of e-mail privacy. *Communications of the ACM, 38*(12), 48–54.

Suh, C. (2014, January 31). Is 2014 the year of the chief digital officer? *Wired.com.* Retrieved May 27, 2014, from http://www.wired.com/2014/01/2014-year-chief-digital-officer.

Tapscott, D. (2004, May 1). The engine that drives success: The best companies have the best business models because they have the best IT strategies. *CIO.com.* Retrieved May 29, 2014, from http://www.cio.com/article/32265/IT_The_Engine_That_Drives_Success.

Todd, P., McKeen, J., & Gallupe, R. (1995). The evolution of IS job skills: A content analysis of IS jobs. *MIS Quarterly, 19*(1), 1–27.

TrendMicro. (2011). Consumerization of IT. Retrieved May 29, 2014, from http://www.trendmicro.com/cloud-content/us/pdfs/business/reports/rpt_consumerization-of-it.pdf.

United States Census. (2011, September). Education and synthetic work-life earnings estimates. Retrieved May 29, 2014, from http://www.census.gov/prod/2011pubs/acs-14.pdf.

Vandervoorn, R. (2014, May 13). The state of the tablet market. *Tabtimes.com.* Retrieved May 27, 2014, from http://tabtimes.com/resources/the-state-of-the-tablet-market.

Vellante, D. (2011, November 14). When IT consumers become technology providers. *Cliff Davies.* Retrieved May 29, 2014, from http://cliffdavies.com/blog/cloudcomputing/when-it-consumers-become-technology-providers.

Veritude (2009). 2009 IT hiring outlook. Retrieved July 20, 2012, from https://www.vtrenz.net/imaeds/ownerassets/1010/Ver_WP_2009%20IT%20Outlook%20Report_FINAL.pdf.

Weisband, S. P., & Reinig, B. A. (1995, December). Managing user perceptions of e-mail privacy. *Communications of the ACM, 38*(12), 40–47.

2 Gaining Competitive Advantage Through Information Systems

After reading this chapter, you will be able to do the following:

1. Discuss how information systems can be used for automation, organizational learning, and strategic advantage.
2. Describe how information systems support business models used by companies operating in the digital world.
3. Explain why and how companies are continually looking for innovative ways to use information systems for competitive advantage.

MyMISLab™

Over 10 million students improved their results using the Pearson MyLabs. Visit **mymislab.com** for simulations, tutorials, and end-of-chapter problems.

Preview

This chapter examines how organizations can use information systems (IS) strategically, enabling them to gain or sustain competitive advantage over their rivals. As described in Chapter 1, "Managing in the Digital World," a firm has competitive advantage over rival firms when it can do something better, faster, more economically, or uniquely. In this chapter, we begin by examining the role of information systems at different levels of the organization. We then examine international business strategies that shape how information systems can be designed to support how data and controls flow across national borders. Finally, we talk about the continual need to find innovative ways to succeed with and through information systems.

Managing in the Digital World: **The Business of Merging "Groups" and "Coupons"**

It comes as no surprise that the Internet has not only helped advance traditional business models, but also enabled entirely new kinds of business models. The Web is more flexible than real-life society in many ways, changing how we communicate with friends and family, changing how we work, and clearly changing the way we shop for products and services. This flexibility is a catalyst for the creation of a seemingly endless array of new types of businesses or the reinvention of tried-and-true business models of the past.

One example is the highly popular Web site Groupon, which prompts consumers to get together with their friends and family, to shop in groups, and buy in volume, in order to benefit from higher discounts from national and local businesses. Groupon's business model is to partner with established merchants looking to clear out seasonal stocks or excessive supply, or to work with newer businesses looking to build a customer base. As the merchants sell higher volume, the cost per unit decreases (at least up to some point). This is where the "group" in Groupon comes in: A deal only goes through when a certain, predetermined number of Groupon subscribers sign up for it; once this number is reached, everyone who signed up for the deal enjoys the lower price. Groupon took the old-fashioned business model of using coupons to attract customers, marrying the network effects and economies of scale capabilities of the Internet to create a new and highly successful business model (Figure 2.1).

Being an early player in the group-buying market, and rapidly gaining market share, Groupon enjoyed a first-mover advantage, but due to its success, Groupon has been cloned by numerous other "impersonators" around the globe. In 2010, the company decided to buy up its "clones" to reclaim its identity and, most important, fast-track its expansion into foreign markets in Europe and Asia. Thanks to the expansion facilitated by buying its "wannabe" clones, Groupon now has over 45 million active customers and over 200 million subscribers worldwide. Over 650,000 different merchants have been featured with Groupon promotions.

FIGURE 2.1

The network effect is central to many innovative business models.

Unfortunately, Groupon's inability to distinguish itself from others has so far resulted in lackluster financial performance. While it is certain that high-volume group couponing will continue to exist on the Internet, it is clear that the current instantiation of Groupon's business model does not provide a sustainable competitive advantage. Time will tell whether Groupon will be able to fine-tune its business model in order to have a lasting presence on the Web, or be another infamous Internet failure like Pets.com, Webvan.com, MVP.com, Kozmo.com, eToys.com, and countless others.

After reading this chapter, you will be able to answer the following:

1. How have information systems enabled new, interesting business models like that of Groupon?
2. What are the key components of Groupon's current business model?
3. How might Groupon leverage technology to strategically create a competitive advantage?

Based on:

Anonymous. (n.d.). Benefits-Groupon. *Groupon*. Retrieved May 15, 2014, from https://www.grouponworks.com/benefits-of-advertising-with-groupon.

Groupon. (2014, April 29). In *Wikipedia, The Free Encyclopedia*. Retrieved May 16, 2014, from http://en.wikipedia.org/w/index.php?title=Groupon&oldid=606284237.

ENABLING ORGANIZATIONAL STRATEGY THROUGH INFORMATION SYSTEMS

In Chapter 1, we introduced the notion that information systems can have strategic value to an organization. Because organizations are composed of different levels and functions, a broad range of information is needed to support an organization's business processes. **Business processes** are the activities organizations perform in order to reach their business goals, including core activities that transform inputs and produce outputs, and supporting activities that enable the core activities to take place. As a review, we briefly describe how organizations are generally structured as well as the common functional areas of most modern organizations. Understanding how organizations are structured helps to illustrate how different types of information systems can support various business processes and provide different levels of value to the organization.

Organizational Decision-Making Levels

Every organization is composed of decision-making levels, as illustrated in Figure 2.2. Each level of an organization has different responsibilities and, therefore, different informational needs.

OPERATIONAL LEVEL. At the **operational level** of a firm, the routine, day-to-day business processes and interactions with customers occur. Information systems at this level are designed to automate repetitive activities, such as sales transaction processing, and to improve the efficiency of business processes at the customer interface. A **transaction** refers to anything that occurs as part of a firm's daily business of which it must keep a record. Operational planning typically has a time frame of a few hours or days, and the managers at the operational level, such as foremen or supervisors, make day-to-day decisions that are highly structured and recurring. **Structured decisions** are those in which the procedures to follow for a given situation can be specified in advance. Because structured decisions are relatively straightforward, they can be programmed directly into operational information systems so that they can be made with little or no human intervention. For example, an inventory management system for a shoe store in the mall could keep track of inventory and issue an order for additional inventory when levels drop below a specified level. Operational managers within the store would simply need to confirm with the inventory management system that the order for additional shoes was needed. At the operational level, information systems are typically used to increase **efficiency** (i.e., the extent to which goals are accomplished faster, at lower cost, or with relatively little time and effort) by optimizing processes and better understanding the underlying causes of any performance problems. Using information systems to optimize processes at the operational level can offer quick returns on the IS investment, as activities at this level are clearly delineated and well focused. Figure 2.3 summarizes the general characteristics of the operational level.

MANAGERIAL/TACTICAL LEVEL. At the **managerial level** (or tactical level) of the organization, functional managers (e.g., marketing managers, finance managers, manufacturing managers,

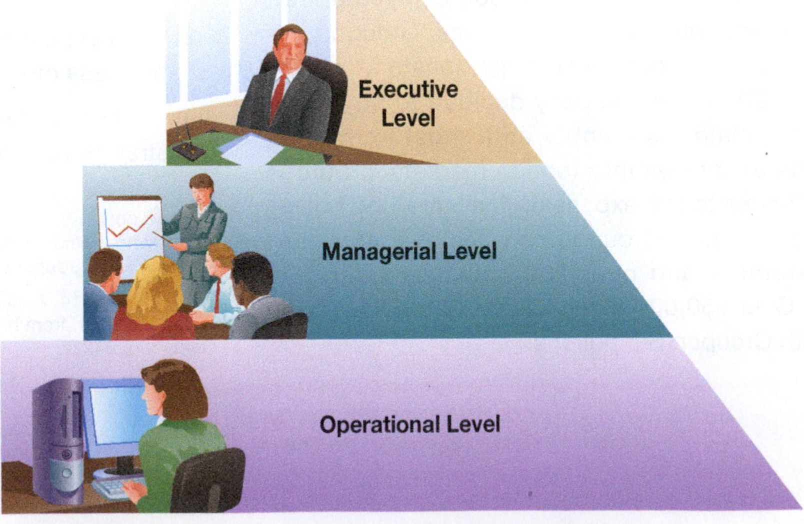

FIGURE 2.2

Organizations are composed of different decision-making levels.

FIGURE 2.3

Information systems at the operational level of an organization help to improve efficiency by automating routine and repetitive activities.

FIGURE 2.4

Information systems at the managerial level of an organization help to improve effectiveness by automating the monitoring and controlling of operational activities.

human resource managers) focus on monitoring and controlling operational-level activities and providing information to higher levels of the organization (Figure 2.4). Managers at this level, referred to as midlevel managers, focus on effectively utilizing and deploying organizational resources to increase **effectiveness** (i.e., the extent to which goals or tasks are accomplished well) to achieve the strategic objectives of the organization. Midlevel managers typically focus on problems within a specific business function, such as marketing or finance. Here, the scope of the decision usually is contained within the business function, is moderately complex, and has a time horizon of a few days to a few months (also referred to as tactical planning). For example, a marketing manager at Nike may decide how to allocate the advertising budget for the next business quarter or some other fixed time period.

Managerial-level decision making is not nearly as structured or routine as operational-level decision making. Managerial-level decision making is referred to as semistructured decision making because solutions and problems are not clear-cut and often require judgment and expertise. For **semistructured decisions**, some procedures to follow for a given situation can be specified in advance, but not to the extent where a specific recommendation can be made. For example, an information system could provide a production manager at Nike with performance analytics and forecasts about sales for multiple product lines, inventory levels, and overall production capacity. The metrics deemed most critical to assessing progress toward a certain goal (referred to as **key performance indicators [KPIs]**) are displayed on performance *dashboards* (described later in Chapter 6, "Enhancing Business Intelligence Using Information Systems"). The manager could use this information to create multiple hypothetical production schedules. With these schedules, the manager could then perform predictive analyses to examine inventory

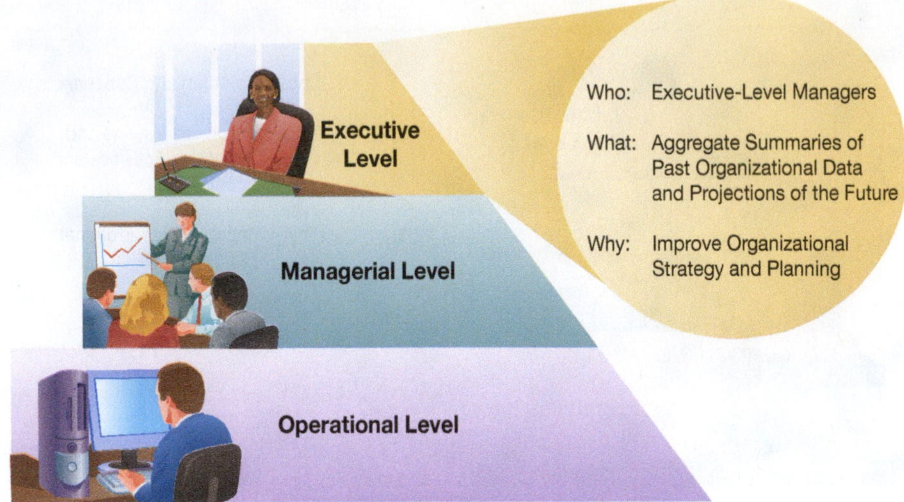

FIGURE 2.5

Information systems at the executive level of an organization help to improve strategy and planning by providing summaries of past data and projections of the future.

levels and potential sales profitability, depending on the order in which manufacturing resources were used to produce each type of product.

EXECUTIVE/STRATEGIC LEVEL. At the **executive level** (or strategic level) of the organization, managers focus on long-term strategic questions facing the organization, such as which products to produce, which countries to compete in, and what organizational strategy to follow (Figure 2.5). Below we will examine various strategic decisions that executives need to address. Managers at this level include the president and chief executive officer, chief information officer, vice presidents, and possibly the board of directors; they are referred to as "executives." Executive-level decisions deal with complex problems with broad and long-term ramifications for the organization. Executive-level decisions are referred to as unstructured decisions because the problems are relatively complex and non-routine. In addition, executives must consider the ramifications of their decisions in terms of the overall organization. For **unstructured decisions**, few or no procedures to follow for a given situation can be specified in advance. For example, top managers may decide to develop a new product or discontinue an existing one. Such a decision may have vast, long-term effects on the organization's levels of employment and profitability. To assist executive-level decision making, information systems are used to obtain aggregate summaries of trends and projections of the future. At the executive level, information systems provide KPIs that are focused on balancing performance across the organization, such that, for example, product launches are staggered to smooth out the effects of spikes in demand on the supply chain. Other KPIs are used to benchmark the organization's performance against its competitors.

In summary, most organizations have three general decision-making levels: operational, managerial, and executive. Each level has unique activities and business processes, each requiring different types of information. In other words, it is common that each decision-making level is supported by different types of information systems.

Organizational Functional Areas

In addition to different decision-making levels within an organization, there are also different functional areas. A functional area represents a discrete area of an organization that focuses on a specific set of activities. For example, people in the marketing function focus on the activities that promote the organization and its products in a way that attracts and retains customers; people in the accounting and finance functions focus on managing and controlling capital assets and financial resources of the organization. Table 2.1 lists various organizational functions and lists examples of the types of information systems that are commonly used. These **functional area information systems** are designed to support the unique business processes of specific functional areas (Figure 2.6).

When deploying information systems across organizational levels and functions, there are three general ways the information system can provide value: to automate, to learn, and to execute organizational strategy (Figure 2.7). These three ways are not necessarily mutually exclusive, but we believe that each is progressively more useful to the firm and thus adds more value to the business. This is examined next.

TABLE 2.1 Organizational Functions and Representative Information Systems

Functional Area	Information System	Examples of Typical Systems
Accounting and finance	Systems used for managing, controlling, and auditing the financial resources of the organization	■ Accounts payable ■ Expense accounts ■ Cash management ■ Payroll processing
Human resources	Systems used for managing, controlling, and auditing the human resources of the organization	■ Recruiting and hiring ■ Education and training ■ Benefits management ■ Employee termination ■ Workforce planning
Marketing	Systems used for managing new product development, distribution, pricing, promotional effectiveness, and sales forecasting of the products and services offered by the organization	■ Market research and analysis ■ New product development ■ Promotion and advertising ■ Pricing and sales analysis ■ Product location analysis
Production and operations	Systems used for managing, controlling, and auditing the production and operations resources of the organization	■ Inventory management ■ Cost and quality tracking ■ Materials and resource planning ■ Job costing ■ Resource utilization

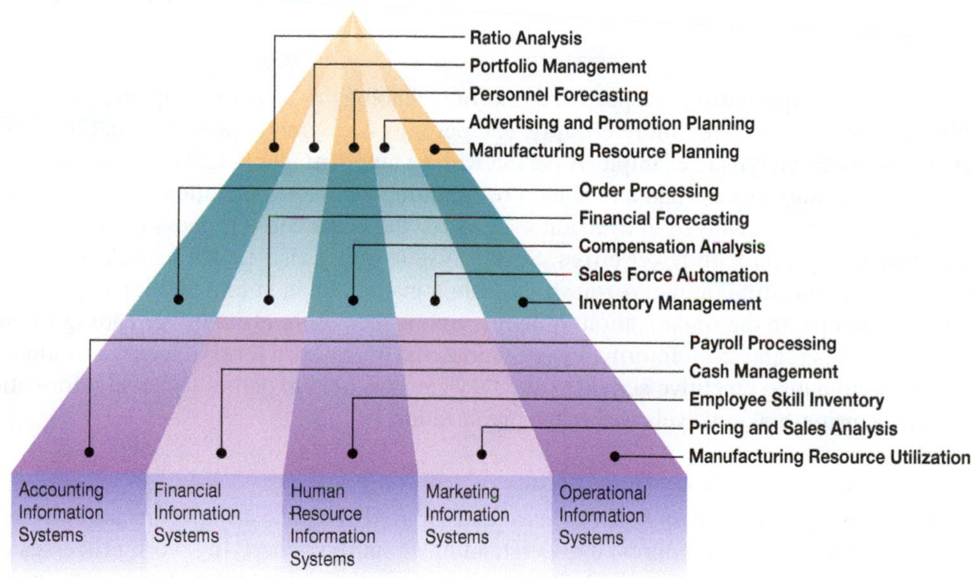

FIGURE 2.6

Business processes supported by various functional area information systems.

FIGURE 2.7

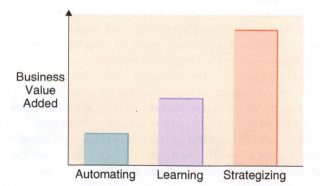

The business value added from automating, learning, and strategizing with information systems.

TABLE 2.2 Activities Involved Under Three Different Loan Application Processes and the Average Time for Each Activity

Primary Activities of Loan Processing	Manual Loan Process (Time)	Technology-Supported Process (Time)	Fully Automated Process (Time)
1. Complete and submit loan application	Customer takes the application home, completes it, and returns it (1.5 days)	Customer takes the application home, completes it, and returns it (1.5 days)	Customer fills out application from home via the Web (15 minutes)
2. Check application for errors	Employee does this in batches (2.5 days)	Employee does this in batches (2.5 days)	Computer does this as it is being completed (1 second)
3. Input data from application into the information system	Applications are kept in paper form, although there is handling time involved (1 hour)	Employee does this in batches (2.5 days)	Done as part of the online application process (no extra time needed)
4. Assess loan applications under $250,000 to determine whether to fund them	Employee does this completely by hand (15 days)	Employee does this with the help of the computer (1 hour)	Computer does this automatically (1 second)
5. Committee decides on any loan over $250,000	(15 days)	(15 days)	(15 days)
6. Applicant notified	Employee generates letters manually in batches (1 week)	Employee generates letters with the help of a computer (1 day)	System notifies applicant via e-mail (1 second)
Total time	Anywhere from 25–40 days, depending on size of loan	Anywhere from 5–20 days, depending on size of loan	Anywhere from 15 minutes to 15 days, depending on size of loan

Note: Many online loan application services can now give you instant "tentative" approval pending verification of data you report in your online application. Also, only some of the activities within the manual and technology-supported processes can occur in parallel.

Information Systems for Automating: Doing Things Faster

Someone with an **automating** perspective thinks of technology as a way to help complete a task within an organization faster, more cheaply, and perhaps with greater accuracy and/or consistency. Let us look at a typical example. A person with an automating mentality would take a loan application screening process and automate it by inputting the loan applications into a computer database so that those involved in decision making for the loans could process the applications faster, more easily, and with fewer errors. Such a system might also enable customers to complete the loan application online. A transition from a manual to an automated loan application process might enable the organization to deploy employees more efficiently, leading to even more cost savings (Table 2.2). Information systems at the operational level of an organization often help in automating repetitive activities, but they can also help to gather valuable information for higher decision-making levels within the organization.

Information Systems for Organizational Learning: Doing Things Better

We can also use information systems to learn and improve. By analyzing information created when automating a process, improved understanding about the underlying work processes can be developed. The learning mentality builds on the automating mentality because it recognizes that information systems can be used as a vehicle for **organizational learning**—the ability of an organization to use past behavior and information to improve its business processes—and for change as well as for automation.

To illustrate a learning mentality, let us think again about our loan processing example. Figure 2.8 shows how a computer-based loan processing system tracks types of loan applications by date, month, and season. The manager easily sees the trends and can plan for the timely staffing and training of personnel in the loan department. The manager can also more efficiently manage the funds used to fulfill loans. This computer-based loan processing system, focusing on learning, is an example of an information system used at the managerial level of an organization.

A learning approach allows managers to track and learn about the types of applications filed by certain types of people at certain times of the year (e.g., more auto loan applications in the fall, mostly from men in their 20s and 30s), the patterns of the loan decisions made, or the subsequent performance of those loans. This new system creates data about the underlying business process that can be used to better monitor, control, and change that process. In other words, you

Winter	Spring	Summer	Fall
Home Mortgage, Auto Loan, Holiday Credit Line	Home Mortgage, Auto Loan, RV and Boat Loan	Home Mortgage, Auto Loan, RV and Boat Loan	Home Mortgage, Auto Loan

FIGURE 2.8

A computer-based loan processing system enables the bank manager to identify trends in loan applications.

learn from this information system about loan applications and approvals; as a result, you can do a better job at evaluating loan applications.

A combined automating and learning approach, in the long run, is more effective than an automating approach alone. If the underlying business process supported by technology is inherently flawed, a learning use of the technology might help you detect problems with the process and change it. For instance, in our loan processing example, a learning use of technology may help us uncover a pattern among the accepted loans that enables us to distinguish between low- and high-performing loans over their lives and subsequently to change the criteria for loan acceptance.

If, however, the underlying business process is bad and you are using technology only for automating (i.e., you would not uncover the data that would tell you this process is bad), you are more likely to continue with a flawed or less-than-optimal business process. In fact, such an automating use of technology may mask the process problems.

With a bad underlying set of loan acceptance criteria (e.g., rules that would allow you to approve a loan for someone who had a high level of debt as long as he or she had not been late on any payments recently), a person might manually review four applications in a day and, because of the problematic criteria used, inadvertently accept on average two "bad" applications per week. If you automated the same faulty process, with no learning aspects built in, the system might help a person review 12 applications per day, with six "bad" applications accepted per week on average. The technology would serve only to magnify the existing business problems (Figure 2.9). Without learning, it is more difficult to uncover bad business processes underlying the information system.

Information Systems for Supporting Strategy: Doing Things Smarter

Using information systems to automate or improve processes has advantages, as described previously. In most cases, however, the best way to use an information system is to support the organization's strategy in a way that enables the firm to gain or sustain competitive advantage over rivals. To understand why, think about **organizational strategy**—a firm's plan to accomplish its mission and goals as well as to gain or sustain competitive advantage over rivals—and how it relates to information systems. When senior managers—at the executive level of the organization—conduct **strategic planning**, they form a vision of where the organization needs to head, convert that vision into measurable objectives and performance targets, and craft a strategy to achieve the desired results. In Figure 2.10, we show some common organizational strategies. An organization might decide to pursue a **low-cost leadership strategy**, as does Walmart, by which it offers the best prices in its industry on its goods and/or services. Alternatively, an organization might decide to pursue a **differentiation strategy**, as do Porsche, Nordstrom, and IBM, by which it tries to provide better products or services than its competitors. A company

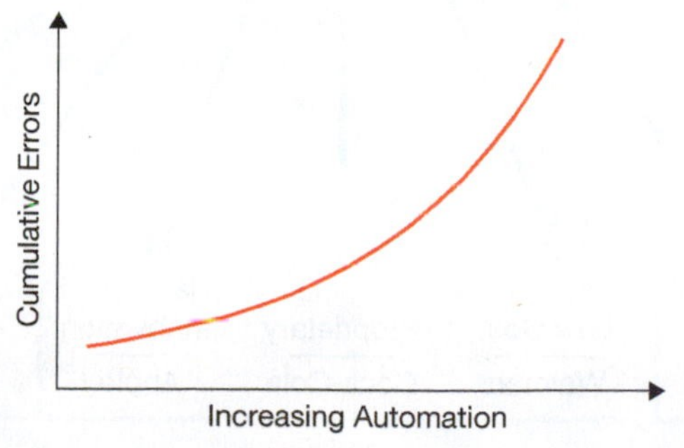

FIGURE 2.9

Automating a loan processing system requires sound underlying business processes, or errors will rapidly increase.

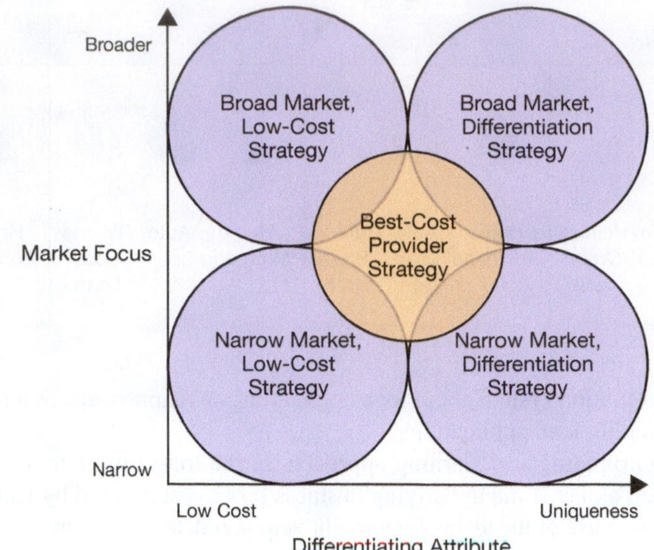

FIGURE 2.10

Five general types of organizational strategy: broad differentiation, focused differentiation, focused low-cost leadership, overall low-cost leadership, and best-cost provider.

might aim that differentiation broadly at many different types of consumers, or it might focus on a particular segment of consumers, as Apple did for many years with its focus on high-quality computers for home and educational markets. Still other organizations might pursue a middle-of-the-road strategy, following a **best-cost provider strategy**, offering products or services of reasonably good quality at competitive prices, as does Dell.

A person with a strategic mentality toward information systems goes beyond mere automating and learning and instead tries to find ways to use information systems to achieve the organization's chosen strategy, such as by streamlining operations, optimizing the supply chain, or better understanding customers. This person wants the benefits of automating and learning but also looks for some strategic, competitive advantage from the system. In fact, in today's business environment, if a proposed information system isn't going to clearly deliver some strategic value (i.e., help to improve the business so that it can compete better) while also helping people to work smarter and save money in the process, then it isn't likely to be funded.

Sources of Competitive Advantage

How do business firms typically get a competitive advantage? An organization has competitive advantage whenever it has an edge over rivals in attracting customers and defending against competitive forces (Porter, 1985, 2001). In order to be successful, a business must have a clear vision, one that focuses investments in resources such as information systems and technologies to help achieve a competitive advantage. Some sources of competitive advantage include the following (Figure 2.11):

- Being the first to enter a market (i.e., having a **first-mover advantage**)
- Having the best-made product on the market
- Delivering superior customer service

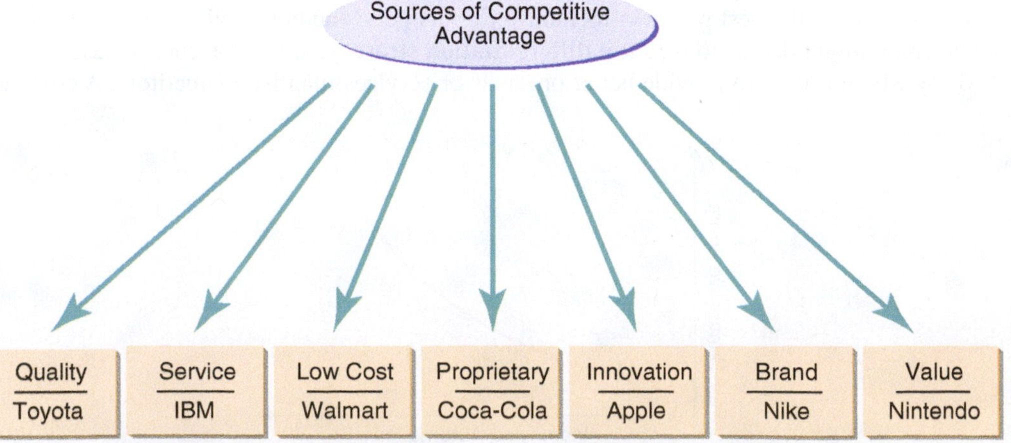

FIGURE 2.11

Sources of competitive advantage.

BRIEF CASE Wi-Fi in the Sky

Broadband connectivity is fast becoming a competitive area in the airline industry. Since many passengers on long flights don't want to be deprived of their Wi-Fi-enabled digital devices, the industry is rushing to comply. Wi-Fi in the sky has become common among many airlines and is one of the key battlegrounds for attracting new passengers and keeping them loyal.

Aircell's cellular ground-based "GoGo" service has been installed on over 2,000 aircraft and is being used by most domestic airlines in the United States. Likewise, Row 44's satellite service is currently being installed in Southwest's entire fleet of aircraft. Today, passengers on airlines all over the world can enjoy access to the Internet on a variety of routes (except over the airspace of countries such as China or Iran). While some airlines offer Internet access for free, other airlines charge customers by flight hour, or offer 24-hour or monthly passes.

Near the end of 2013, the Federal Aviation Administration (FAA) lifted the infamous ban on the use of small personal electronic devices during take-off and landing. While devices' cellular connectivity must still be disabled (i.e., put in "airplane mode"), these devices can be used during all phases of flight. The Federal Communications Commission (FCC) recently announced that it would review the (separate) ban on in-flight voice communications, though this has been met with considerably more resistance. Although it has been determined that cell phone signals don't interfere with a plane's instrumentation, their use is prohibited in the United States while planes are in flight because of possible annoyance of other passengers. The subject of allowing in-flight voice calls has met fierce resistance from frequent fliers and the largest flight attendants' union. In early 2014, a U.S. congressional committee proposed a bill that would keep in-flight calls off-limits.

Airline Wi-Fi services will undoubtedly continue to improve as mobile devices become more ubiquitous, and now that these devices are allowed during all phases of flight, busy commuters, bored passengers, and parents with small children are able to happily make use of their technology. Whether voice services for airline passengers will come to North America remains to be seen.

Questions

1. How do you feel about cell phone use during a flight? Would you switch to or abandon carriers if cell phone use were allowed on one but not the other? Why or why not?
2. Do you think that using the Internet or cell phones creates any security problems on a flight? Why or why not?

Based on:

Mobile phones on aircraft. (2014, March 30). In *Wikipedia, The Free Encyclopedia*. Retrieved May 17, 2014, from http://en.wikipedia.org/w/index.php?title=Mobile_phones_on_aircraft&oldid=602033055.

Martin, A. (2014, February 2014). Committee approves bill that would ban in-flight calls. *The Ripon Advance*. Retrieved May 17, 2014, from http://riponadvance.com/news/committee-approves-bill-ban-flight-calls/6583.

- Achieving lower costs than rivals
- Having a proprietary manufacturing technology, formula, or algorithm
- Having shorter lead times in developing and testing new products
- Having a well-known brand name and reputation
- Giving customers more value for their money

To develop and sustain a competitive advantage, organizations must have resources and/or capabilities that are superior to those of their competitors. **Resources** reflect the organization's specific assets that are utilized to create cost or product differentiation from their competitors. Examples of resources might include proprietary technology, brand equity, or a loyal and established customer base. **Capabilities** reflect the organization's ability to leverage these resources in the marketplace. For example, design quality or efficient operations could be capabilities that help a firm effectively utilize its resources. Together, the resources and capabilities provide the organization with **distinctive competencies**—such as innovation, agility, quality, or low cost—in the marketplace. These competencies help to pursue the organizational strategy (low-cost leadership, differentiation, etc.) and make the organization's product valuable to its customers relative to its competitors; superior **value creation** occurs when an organization can provide products at a lower cost or with superior (differentiated) benefits to the customer (Figure 2.12). This is how organizations gain a competitive advantage.

Companies can gain or sustain each of these sources of competitive advantage by effectively using information systems. Returning to our loan example, a person with a strategic view of information systems would choose a computer-based loan application process because it can help achieve the organization's strategic plan to process loan applications faster and better than rivals and to improve the selection criteria for loans. This process and the supporting information system add value to the organization and match the organization's strategy. It is, therefore, essential to the long-term survival of the organization. If, on the other hand, managers determine

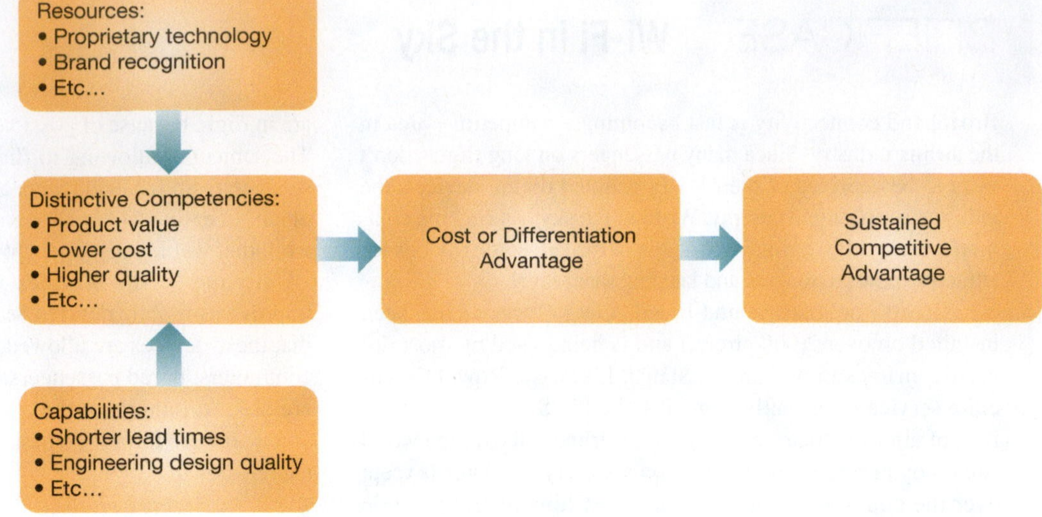

FIGURE 2.12

Distinctive competencies lead to value creation and a sustained competitive advantage.

Source: Based on http://www.quickmba.com/strategy/competitive-advantage.

that the organization's strategy is to grow and generate new products and services, the computer-based loan application process and the underlying system might not be an efficient, effective use of resources, even though the system could provide automating and learning benefits.

Identifying Where to Compete: Analyzing Competitive Forces

Organizations struggle with identifying the best uses of their resources to execute their strategy. Given that every industry is different, organizations can better understand where to focus their resources by analyzing the competitive forces within their industry. One framework often used to analyze the competition within an industry is Porter's (1979) notion of the five primary competitive forces: (1) the rivalry among competing sellers in your industry, (2) the threat of potential new entrants into your industry, (3) the bargaining power that customers have within your industry, (4) the bargaining power that suppliers have within your industry, and (5) the potential for substitute products from other industries (Figure 2.13). Table 2.3 provides examples of how the Internet has influenced the various competitive forces in an industry. Porter's five-forces model of competition can help you determine which forces may be most important, and which specific technologies could be used to address these forces. You can then use this knowledge as the basis for identifying particular investments.

Identifying How to Compete: Analyzing the Value Chain

Managers use value chain analysis to identify opportunities where information systems can be used to develop a competitive advantage (Porter, 1985, 2001; Shank & Govindarajan, 1993). Think

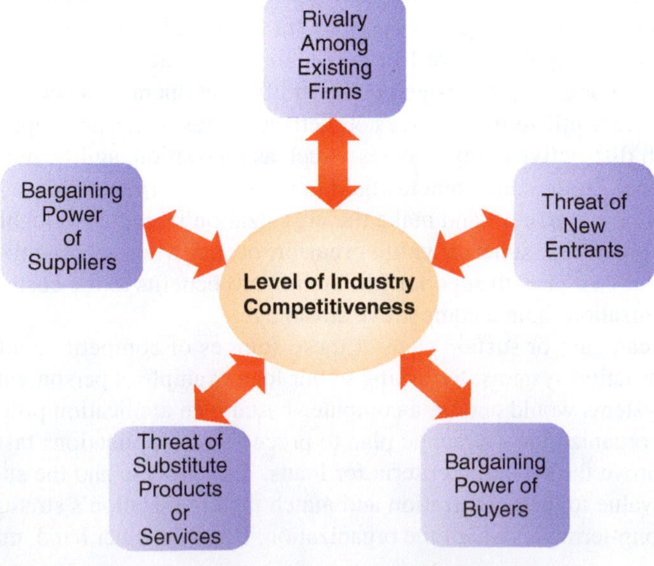

FIGURE 2.13

Five forces influence the level of competitiveness in an industry.

TABLE 2.3 The Influence of the Internet on the Competitive Forces

Competitive Force	Implication for Firm	How the Internet Has Influenced Competitive Force
Traditional rivals within your industry	Competition in price, product distribution, and service	Increase of competitors due to wider geographic reach; customers can more easily compare products, so competition focuses more on price.
Threat of new entrants into your market	Increased capacity in the industry, reduced prices, and decreased market share	Reduced barriers to entry, as the Internet reduces the difficulty of obtaining critical resources.
Customers' bargaining power	Reduced prices, need for increased quality, and demand for more services	Wider choices for customers lead to lower switching costs and higher bargaining power of customers.
Suppliers' bargaining power	Increased costs and reduced quality	Companies have equal access to suppliers; at the same time, suppliers have access to more potential buyers.
Threat of substitute products from other industries	Product returns from customers, decreased market share, and losing customers for life	New substitutes are created by the Internet and other information technologies.

Source: Based on Applegate, Austin, & Soule (2009).

of an organization as a big input/output process. At one end, supplies are purchased and brought into the organization (Figure 2.14). The organization integrates those supplies to create products and services that it markets, sells, and then distributes to customers. The organization also provides customer service after the sale of these products and services. Throughout this process, opportunities arise for employees to add value to the product or service by acquiring supplies in a more effective manner, improving products, and selling more products. This set of activities that add value throughout the organization is known as the **value chain** within an organization.

Value chain analysis is the process of analyzing an organization's activities to determine where value is added to products and/or services and what costs are incurred for doing so. Because information systems can automate many activities along the value chain, value chain analysis has become a popular tool for applying information systems for competitive advantage. In value chain analysis, you first draw the value chain for your organization by fleshing out each of the activities, functions, and processes where value is or should be added, and where performance can be improved. Next, you determine the costs—and the factors that drive costs or cause them to fluctuate—within each of the areas in your value chain diagram. You then determine which activities need to be optimized, so as to improve performance, cut costs, and ultimately gain or sustain competitive advantage.

The Role of Information Systems in Value Chain Analysis

The use of information systems has become one of the primary ways that organizations improve their value chains. In Figure 2.14, we show a sample value chain and some ways that information

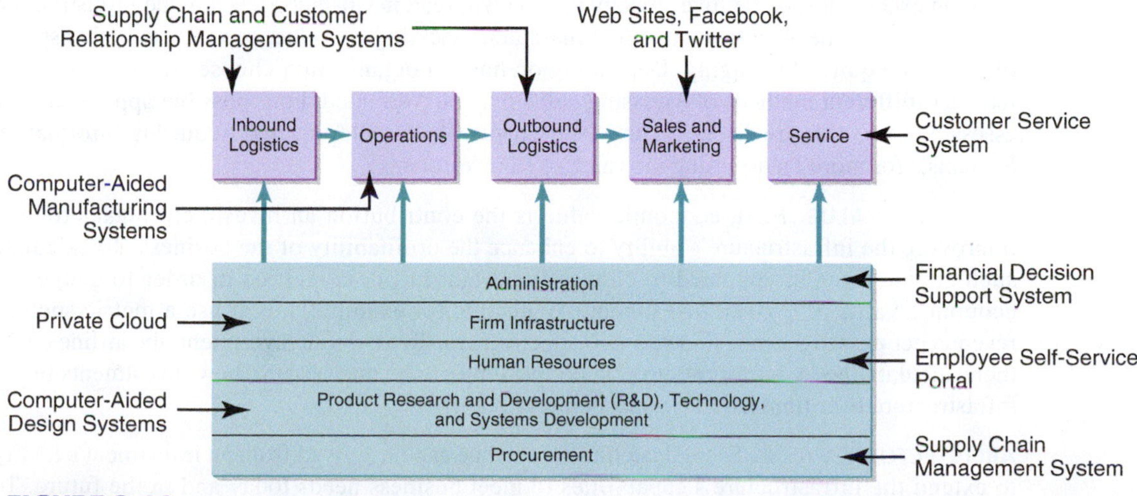

FIGURE 2.14

Information systems can improve an organization's value chain.

systems can improve productivity within it. For example, many organizations use the Internet to connect businesses with one another electronically so that they can exchange orders, invoices, and receipts online in real time. Likewise, organizations use various social media such as blogs, Twitter, or Facebook to connect with their customers.

The Technology/Strategy Fit

You might be asking, if any information system helps do things faster and better and helps save money, who cares whether it matches the company's strategy? Good question. If money grew on trees, you probably would build and use just about every information system you could imagine. Organizations could build or acquire many different valuable systems, but they are constrained by time and money to build or acquire only those that add the most value: those that help automate and learn as well as have strategic value. The old way for managers to think about information systems was that they were a necessary service, a necessary evil, and a necessary, distasteful expense that was to be minimized. Managers cannot afford to think this way anymore. Successful managers now think of information systems as a competitive asset to be nurtured and invested in, and think of them as an enabler of opportunities and mechanism for supporting or executing their business model. In other words, organizations are trying to maximize **business/IT alignment**, and in most cases, you do not want systems that do not match the strategy, even if they offer automating and learning benefits. Further, while spending on information systems is rising, most companies are willing to spend money on projects only when they can see clear, significant value. Often, however, organizations have no choice in making some types of investments that may or may not coincide with their overall strategy. Such investments are called a **strategic necessity**—something the organization must do in order to survive.

Given this focus on the value that the system will add, you probably do not want a system that helps differentiate your products based on high quality when the organizational strategy is to be the overall industry low-cost leader. In other words, if a firm were pursuing a strategy for low-cost leadership, investments to help drive costs down would be valued over those that didn't. Throughout this book, we introduce various technologies, infrastructures, and services that can help to support an organization's competitive strategy.

We should also caution that merely choosing and implementing an emerging information system is not sufficient to gain or sustain competitive advantage. In any significant IS implementation, there must be commensurate, significant organizational change. This typically comes in the form of *business process management* and other similar methods of improving the functioning of the organization, as opposed to merely dropping in an information system with no attempts at changing and improving the organization. We will talk more in Chapter 7, "Enhancing Business Processes Using Enterprise Information Systems," about the role of business process management for transforming organizational business processes.

Assessing Value for the IS Infrastructure

The IS infrastructure is a complex collection of technologies and capabilities that helps an organization execute its competitive strategy (as you will read in Chapter 3). While the infrastructure is critical and expensive to acquire and maintain, assessing its value, or some specific aspects of it, can be quite challenging. Depending on how an organization chooses to compete in its industry, different methods of assessing value may be warranted. Four possible approaches for assessing this value are discussed next (see Chapter 9, "Developing and Acquiring Information Systems," for more on assessing the value of IS investments).

ECONOMIC VALUE. First, economic value is the contribution an investment makes toward improving the infrastructure's ability to enhance the profitability of the business. To calculate such enhancements, you need to choose important business metrics in order to gauge the economic value of a given investment. An airline, for example, might use a metric such as revenue per passenger mile to determine effectiveness. To assess an investment, the airline could then calculate the IS infrastructure cost per passenger mile and observe how investments in the infrastructure over time have an impact on profitability.

ARCHITECTURAL VALUE. Second, architectural value can be derived from an investment's ability to extend the infrastructure's capabilities to meet business needs today and in the future. To measure architectural value, "before-and-after" assessments of infrastructure characteristics such as interoperability, portability, scalability, recoverability, and compatibility can be taken.

Such assessments can be taken for each area of the business, where various infrastructure characteristics are rated as to how well various investments influence the infrastructure's ability to meet those needs.

OPERATIONAL VALUE. Third, operational value is derived from assessing an investment's impact on enabling the infrastructure to better meet business processing requirements. To assess this, you could measure the impact of not investing in a particular project. For example, what would be the cost of not investing in a new customer relationship management system in terms of lost staff productivity, lost business revenue, or even lost customers?

WHO'S GOING MOBILE

Mobile Platforms

Today, more and more people are enjoying the power and convenience of smartphones like Apple's iPhone or the Samsung Galaxy S series. These mobile devices are having a significant impact on our lives, and are in fact redefining the way we access information and communicate with others. To make these gadgets "smart" they must have great hardware, useful apps, and a powerful operating system, all working together seamlessly.

Depending on the type of computer you own, it runs a particular type of operating system. If you have a Dell computer, you probably run some version of Windows (e.g., Windows 7 or 8). If you have a Mac, you run some version of the Mac OS X (e.g., Lion, Mountain Lion, or Mavericks). In a similar way, smartphones run a specific operating system they were designed for: In general, an Android mobile device will only work with some version of Android and an iPhone will only run some version of iOS.

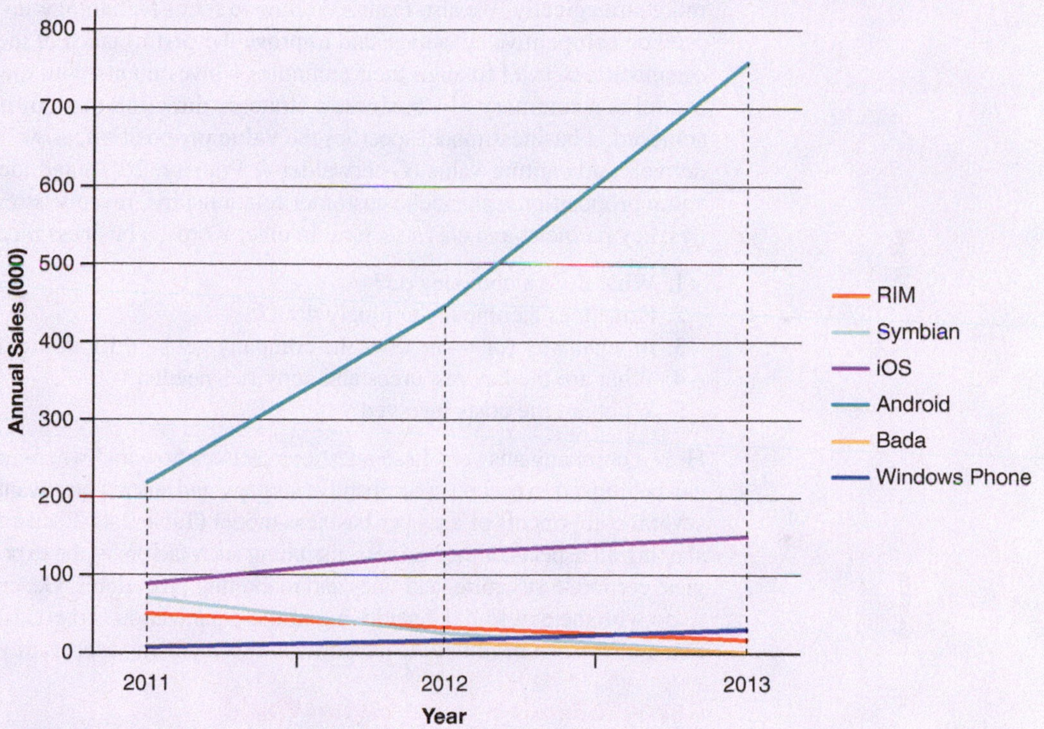

FIGURE 2.15
Worldwide smartphone sales by operating system.

Google's Android and Apple's iOS continue to dominate the mobile operating system market share war. In late 2012, Microsoft released its widely anticipated Windows Phone 8 operating system, but a lack of broad adoption has discouraged application developers from producing many key mobile apps for the platform. Despite widely acclaimed hardware (in particular from its recently acquired hardware partner Nokia), the Windows Phone 8 operating system has yet to garner more than 5 percent of the worldwide smartphone market share (Figure 2.15).

It used to be that people chose their phones only by their carriers and what brands they offered. Today, many choose their phones based on the manufacturer, its operating system's features, and the ecosystem of apps developed for the operating system.

Based on:

Anonymous. (2014, February 13). Gartner says annual smartphone sales surpassed sales of feature phones for the first time in 2013. *Gartner*. Retrieved May 15, 2014, from http://www.gartner.com/newsroom/id/2665715.

Mobile operating system. (2014, May 14). In *Wikipedia, The Free Encyclopedia*. Retrieved 04:51, May 16, 2014, from http://en.wikipedia.org/w/index.php?title=Mobile_operating_system&oldid=608557531.

REGULATORY AND COMPLIANCE VALUE. Fourth, regulatory and compliance value is derived from assessing the extent to which an investment helps to meet requirements for control, security, and integrity as required by a governing body or a key customer. For example, what is the impact of, say, noncompliance with government reporting requirements necessitated by the Sarbanes-Oxley Act?

Finally, where possible, all evaluation measures should be compared with external benchmarks such as industry averages or your key competitors. All of these assessment metrics can be significantly impacted by the cloud computing megatrend. For instance, prior to cloud computing, making sure new technologies worked well on the existing technological architecture was critical. By using a cloud-based architecture, this concern is reduced because virtually any architecture is available within the cloud. In any event, these provide a useful framework for more broadly evaluating a particular investment.

BUSINESS MODELS IN THE DIGITAL WORLD

We have examined how organizations can leverage technology investments faster, smarter, and more strategically. We also examined how to focus technology investments toward activities that provide competitive advantage and improve the performance of their value chain. Taken together, organizations need to align their technology investments with their business model. A **business model** is a summary of a business's strategic direction that outlines how the objectives will be achieved; a business model specifies the **value proposition**, as well as how a company will create, deliver, and capture value (Osterwalder & Pigneur, 2010) and identifies its customer segments, value propositions, channels, customer relationships, revenue streams, key resources, key activities, key partners, and cost structure. In other words, a business model reflects the following:

1. What does a company do?
2. How does a company uniquely do it?
3. In what way (or ways) does the company get paid for doing it?
4. What are the key resources and activities needed?
5. What are the costs involved?

How a company answers these questions dictates how and where information systems investments can be utilized to execute a competitive strategy and sustain an advantage over competitors. There are several components of a proper business model (Table 2.4). Each component plays a critical role in shaping all aspects of the business, including such factors as the expenses, revenues, operating strategies, corporate structure, and sales and marketing procedures. Generally speaking, anything that has to do with the day-to-day functioning of the organization is part of its business model, and information systems can be utilized to support and execute many aspects of your business model.

Revenue Models in the Digital World

Perhaps the most important ingredient for any organization is determining how to generate revenue. A **revenue model** describes how the firm will earn revenue, generate profits, and produce a superior return on invested capital (even non-profit organizations need a revenue model). In addition to sales, transaction fees, and advertising-based business models common in the offline world, the Internet has enabled or enhanced other revenue models, such as **affiliate marketing** (Table 2.5). Many companies selling products or services (such as Amazon.com) use the Web as an economic medium to reach a large customer base; large numbers of customers allow these companies to turn over their inventory quickly, thus enabling the company to offer low prices while still making a profit. Other companies (such as Netflix.com) generate revenue using a subscription model where customers pay a monthly or annual fee for using the product or service. In addition, the Internet has provided large and small companies alike with the ability to generate revenues in various other ways. Traditionally, revenue models based on advertising, referrals, or transaction fees were difficult to sustain. For example, free newspapers have to set their rates for advertising space sufficiently high so as to offset the paper's production costs; in contrast, advertising on the Web is typically rather inexpensive, and the advertiser is charged based on how many people view or click on an ad (see Chapter 4, "Enabling Business-to-Consumer E-Commerce"). The Web site on which the ad is placed generates it revenue by serving cheap ads to large numbers of visitors. Using such revenue models, Web sites like Google or Facebook, as well as companies such as Zynga (the maker of games such as FarmVille), make millions of dollars in revenue.

TABLE 2.4 Components of a Business Model

Component	Description	Questions to Ask
Customer segments	The customers targeted with the product/service offering	Who will be our target customers? Who are the most important customers?
Value proposition	The utility that the product/service has to offer to customers	Why do customers need our product/service? What problems will our product/service solve? Why would customers choose our product/service over our competitors' products/services?
Channels	The ways in which the product/service offerings reach the target customers	How will our customers be reached? Which channels are best in terms of cost and convenience for the customers?
Customer relationships	The relationships formed with the target customers	What types of relationships do we build with our customers? How do we maintain these relationships?
Revenue streams	The way a firm generates income	How do we generate income? What are we selling? What are customers willing to pay for?
Key resources	The most important assets needed to make the business model work	What key resources are needed to enable our value proposition, channels, customer relationships, and revenue streams?
Key activities	The most important activities needed to make the business model work	What key activities are needed to enable our value proposition, channels, customer relationships, and revenue streams?
Key partners	The network of partners and suppliers needed to make the business model work	Who are our key partners and suppliers? What resources do they offer, and what activities do they perform?
Cost structure	The costs incurred when operating the business model	What are the costs incurred when operating the business model? Which resources and activities are most expensive?

Source: Based on Osterwalder & Pigneur (2010).

TABLE 2.5 Typical Revenue Models for E-Businesses

Revenue Type	Description	Who Is Doing This?
Affiliate marketing	Paying businesses that bring or refer customers to another business. Revenue sharing is typically used.	Amazon.com's Associates program
Subscription	Users pay a monthly or yearly recurring fee for the use of the product/service.	Netflix.com, World of Warcraft
Licensing	Users pay a fee for using protected intellectual property (e.g., software)	Symantec, Norton
Transaction fees/ Brokerage	A commission is paid to the business for aiding in the transaction.	PayPal.com, eBay.com, Groupon.com, Scottrade.com
Traditional sales	A consumer buys a product/service from the Web site.	Nordstrom.com, iTunes.com
Web advertising	A free service/product is supported by advertising displayed on the Web site.	Facebook.com, Answers.com

Freeconomics: Why Free Products Are the Future of the Digital World

Chris Anderson (2009), editor in chief of *Wired Magazine*, has put forth a provocative idea that the revenue model of the future in the digital world will be charging customers nothing for products and services. In fact, he argues that this strategy is a viable approach for making a fortune in virtually any industry. Obvious examples include Google making billions from its free search engine or Yahoo! making millions from its free Web e-mail service. While these examples are not likely to be easily replicated, Anderson convincingly argues that such moneymaking principles are not limited to Google and Yahoo!, but can be applied to countless industries. Here we examine how **freeconomics**—the leveraging of digital technologies to provide *free* goods and services to customers as a business strategy for gaining a competitive advantage—can be utilized by organizations from virtually any industry in the highly competitive digital world.

HOW FREECONOMICS WORKS. According to basic economics within a competitive marketplace, the price of something is set by its marginal cost—the cost of producing an additional unit of output. Given the push toward globalization, the world has never been more competitive (see Chapter 1). Likewise, given the exponential increases in processing power (see Moore's law in Chapter 3), along with even greater increases in storage and networking capacity, the prices of computer processing, storage, and bandwidth are in a free fall. For

WHEN THINGS GO WRONG

The Pains of Miscalculating Groupon

For customers and businesses alike, the Groupon coupon service is certainly a hot attraction. Imagine a perfect outcome where business owners boost profits and attract and satisfy a vast number of new customers. A closer look at Groupon's business partners, however, reveals that this doesn't always happen. Out of the 150 small to midsize businesses surveyed by Rice University in 2010, 32 percent found using Groupon unprofitable and 40 percent swore to never again use the service. So, what is the problem?

The buying frenzy that may result from coupon purchases is a tricky matter that should not be underestimated. For instance, judging from the experience of an Oregon-based coffee shop called Posies Café, the owner eventually lost more than US$8,000, thanks to unexpected increases in customer volume and the stress of hiring additional manpower, from a Groupon-enabled tidalwave of customers. Most small businesses are not capable of coping with a sudden flood of hundreds, or even thousands, of new customers. Think of the logistics of juggling overwhelming customer traffic and associated service quality issues. In addition, if a deal offers a 50 percent discount, Groupon takes about a 40 percent share of the deal's price (the numbers depend on factors such as size of the deal), leaving the merchant with 30 percent of the original price. Many businesses forget (or are not advised) to cap the number of deals, so that they end up having more business than they can handle, and may not be able to limit the losses incurred. Thus, businesses that miscalculate the impact of a Groupon campaign usually end up either suffering huge losses or garnering a crushed reputation as service quality goes down the drain.

Aside from miscalculating the capacity of one's business to handle a rush of new clients, businesses often overestimate the long-term impact of a deal on the business. Many customers are looking for a one-time deal, and never visit the business afterward. (How often would you repeat that helicopter trip if you had to pay full price, or how often do you need Lasik eye surgery?) Thus, businesses are advised to make the most out of the publicity brought about by Groupon's coupon campaign. Instead of relying solely on the one-time increase of buyers, which does not always generate profits, business owners should use the opportunity to sell additional products to customers. Likewise, service-oriented businesses should consider offering incentives for customers to come back by signing up for additional appointments. E-mail addresses and other personal information should be collected for future promotional needs. If Groupon is perceived more as an advertising strategy that requires careful management, business owners may, after all, achieve the ends of boosting their reputation and generating enhanced revenue.

Based on:

Hall, J. (2011, November 22). Groupon demand almost finishes cupcake-maker. *The Telegraph*. Retrieved May 15, 2014, from http://www.telegraph.co.uk/finance/newsbysector/retailandconsumer/8904653/Groupon-demand-almost-finishes-cupcake-maker.html.

Purewal, S. J. (2010, December 5). Groupon nightmares (and how to avoid them). *PCWorld*. Retrieved May 15, 2014, from http://www.pcworld.com/article/212328/how_to_avoid_groupon_nightmares.html.

example, now that Yahoo! has built its Web e-mail environment, the cost to provide this service for each additional person (i.e., the marginal cost) is nearly zero. At the same time, huge profits are made giving away this service to more and more customers, as Yahoo! receives payments for every additional customer who views or clicks on advertisements placed by companies on pages within Yahoo!'s Web e-mail service (Figure 2.16).

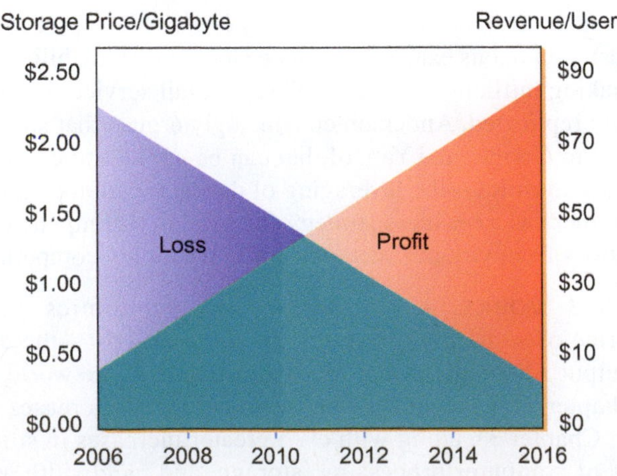

FIGURE 2.16

How Yahoo! makes millions of dollars from its ***free*** Web-based e-mail service—as the cost of storage has dropped, revenue per user has increased.

It is important to note that *any* industry that utilizes digital technologies (not just those like Google or Yahoo!) is on a path toward increasingly lower costs, ultimately toward a price of free—or at least "free" for consumers. As digital technologies increase in capabilities and at the same time decrease in cost, the industry as a whole will see rapid cost reductions. As costs are reduced, prices for consumers will drop. Moreover, as that industry relies more and more on digital technologies to further reduce costs and to further increase efficiencies, the competitiveness of the industry will further increase, pushing the price closer and closer toward its marginal cost. In other words, as an industry relies more and more on digital technologies, free becomes the inevitable price.

THE FREECONOMICS VALUE PROPOSITION. Within freeconomics, just because products are free to consumers doesn't mean that someone, somewhere, isn't paying for it and, most important, that someone else isn't also making a lot of money. For example, Google earns revenue from companies when someone performing a Google search clicks on a sponsored link. Here the value proposition—what a business provides to a customer and what that customer is willing to pay for that product or service—is larger than simply buyers and sellers. For Google, the value proposition includes a broad ecosystem of many participants, only some of whom exchange payments (Figure 2.17). This value proposition is very similar to that of the radio and television broadcast industries, where consumers receive free content, while advertisers make payments to stations to broadcast commercials. Freeconomics is therefore an extension of this basic advertising model and can be applied to virtually any industry. Additionally, this basic model can be applied in a variety of creative ways beyond advertising.

APPLYING FREECONOMICS IN THE DIGITAL WORLD. To demonstrate how freeconomics can be applied to a variety of industries beyond Web e-mail or online searches, Anderson explains how cable TV giant Comcast gave a free DVR to millions of its customers, leading to huge profits for the company. The DVRs cost Comcast around US$250 each, so giving them away needed to stimulate some other type of revenue. Specifically, once consumers had the DVR, they were charged a monthly subscription fee to utilize its capabilities. Comcast was also able to create a stronger relationship with its customers, leading to other revenue streams, including high-speed Internet access, digital telephony services, and pay-per-view movies. In the end, this free DVR generated tremendous revenue and profits for Comcast.

In another example, the music icon Prince gave away 2.8 million copies of his 2007 CD *Planet Earth,* retail value US$19, inside the Sunday edition of London's *Daily Mail.* Although Prince lost money on the giveaway—he received 36 cents per disc from the newspaper while the cost to produce each disc was around US$2—he more than made up for this loss through the sale of concert tickets. After the giveaway, he sold out a record-breaking 21 shows in the O_2 Arena in London, netting the entertainer nearly US$19 million in profits. Indeed, there are many approaches for making money by giving things away.

Table 2.6 outlines six general approaches for applying the concepts of freeconomics to a broad range of industries. For example, the online photo-sharing application Flickr (owned by Yahoo!) allows users to store, share, organize, and tag a limited number of pictures for free; applying the **freemium** approach, users can upgrade to a paid "pro account," providing additional features, such as unlimited storage and advertisement-free browsing, or can use other paid services, such as printing through Hewlett-Packard's print services, creating photo gifts, or creating

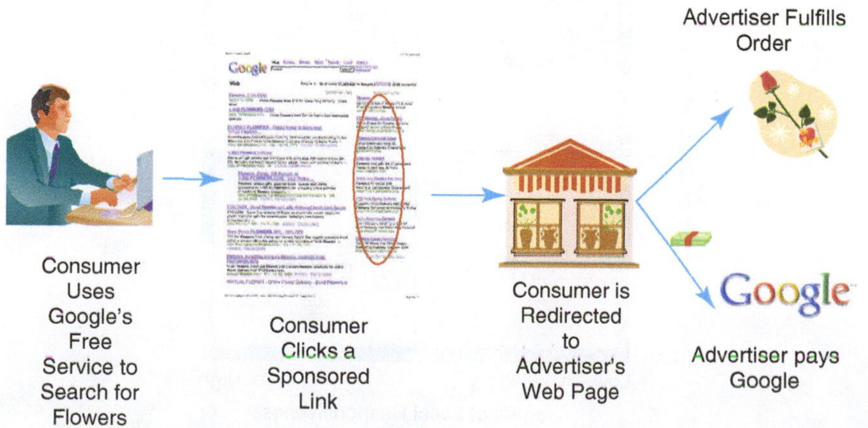
Consumer Uses Google's Free Service to Search for Flowers
Consumer Clicks a Sponsored Link
Consumer is Redirected to Advertiser's Web Page
Advertiser Fulfills Order
Advertiser pays Google
Google

FIGURE 2.17

Google uses a value proposition similar to that of television and radio broadcast advertising.

Source: Based on www.google.com.

TABLE 2.6 General Approaches for Applying Freeconomics to Various Industries

Approach	What It Means	Examples
Advertising	Free services are provided to customers and paid for by a third party.	Yahoo!'s banner ads; Google's pay-per-click; Amazon's pay-per-transaction "affiliate ads"
Freemium	Basic services are offered for free, but a premium is charged for special features.	Flickr; Skype; Dropbox.com; giving away an app for free but having to buy paid upgrades to get full usage and benefit of the app
Cross subsidies	Sale price of one item is reduced in order to sell something else of value.	Comcast DVR; free theater ticket for those willing to buy a large popcorn and beverage; free cell phone with two-year contract
Zero marginal cost	Products are distributed to customers without an appreciable cost to anyone.	Online music distribution at iTunes; software distribution; video content on YouTube
Labor exchange	Services are provided to customers; the act of using the services creates value for the company.	Yahoo! Answers; Answers.com
Gift economy	Environments are created that allow people to participate and collaborate to create something of value for everyone.	Open source software development; Wikipedia; Freecycle—free secondhand goods to anyone willing to haul them away

Source: Based on Anderson (2009).

books using blurb.com. Understanding how to leverage the value of IS investments is fundamental to thriving in the digital world.

International Business Strategies in the Digital World

Before the era of globalization, most companies were solely operating in the domestic arena, conducting their activities exclusively in one country, starting from the acquisition of raw materials to the selling of final products. Although such businesses are likely to benefit from easier access to raw materials or other resources, many **domestic companies** also feel some negative effects brought about by globalization.

In today's digital world, the number of exclusively domestic companies is continually shrinking, with most domestic companies being relatively small (often local) businesses, such as local service providers, restaurants, farms, or independent grocery stores (and even those have international customers, suppliers, or products). Most of today's large companies, no matter if they are in car manufacturing (such as General Motors [GM], Toyota, or Daimler), insurance (Allianz or Munich Re), or consumer goods (Nestlé or Procter & Gamble), have some **international business strategy** for competing in different global markets.

Such companies pursue either a home replication, multidomestic, global, or transnational strategy, depending on the degree of supply chain integration and necessary local customer responsiveness (Figure 2.18; Hitt, Ireland, & Hoskisson, 2015; Prahalad & Doz, 1987). For example, organizations pursuing a **home-replication strategy** (such as the German automaker Porsche) view

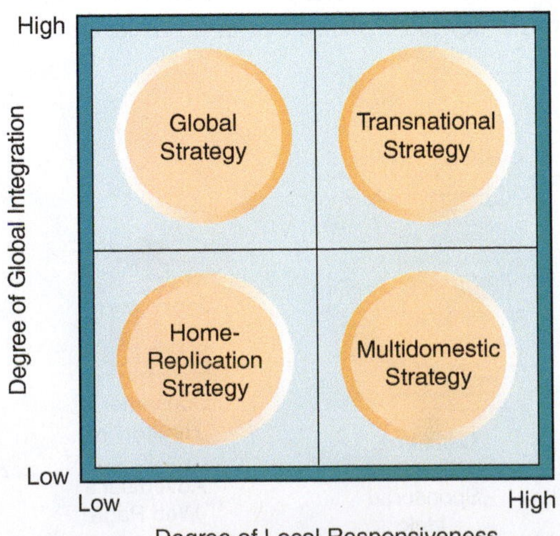

FIGURE 2.18

International business strategies.

international operations as secondary to their home operations, focusing on their domestic customers' needs and wants and merely exporting their products to generate additional sales; this allows companies to focus on their core competencies in their respective domestic markets. Companies pursuing a **global business strategy** (such as Sony) attempt to achieve economies of scale by developing products for the global market, which can be sold in large quantities. Companies pursuing a **multidomestic business strategy** (such as GM) attempt to be extremely flexible and responsive to the needs and demands of local markets by using a loose federation of associated business units, each of which is rather independent in its strategic decisions, so that they can respond quickly to their respective market demands. Finally, companies pursuing a **transnational business strategy** (such as Unilever or Nestlé) attempt to leverage the flexibility offered by a decentralized organization (to be more responsive to local conditions) while at the same time reaping economies of scale enjoyed by centralization, and selectively decide which aspects of the organization should be under central control and which should be decentralized. Different international business strategies are suited better for different situations (Figure 2.19 and Table 2.7).

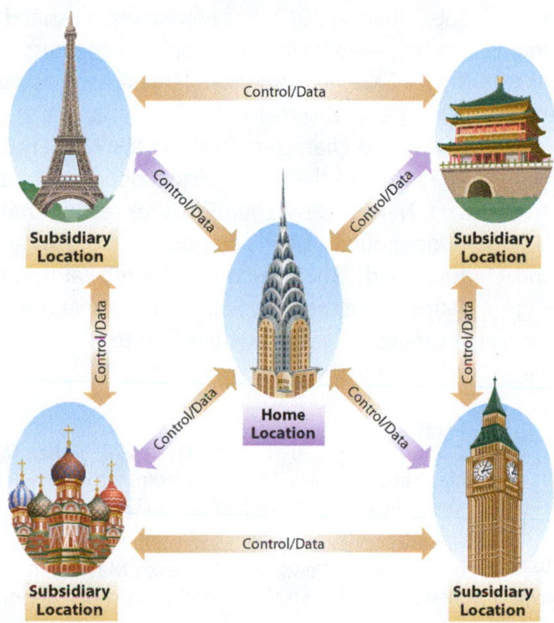

FIGURE 2.19

Potential control and data flows in businesses operating in the digital world.

TABLE 2.7 When to Use International Business Strategies

Strategy	Description	Strengths/Weaknesses	Systems and Communication
Home replication	International business seen as extension of home business; used in homogeneous markets	■ Focus on core competencies in home market ■ Inability to react to local market conditions	■ Domestic systems with limited communications ■ Local databases
Global	Centralized organization with standardized offerings across markets; used in homogeneous markets	■ Standardized product offerings allow achieving economies of scale ■ Inability to react to local market conditions	■ Centralized systems with multiple networks between home office and subsidiaries ■ Data sharing between home office and subsidiaries
Multidomestic	Federation of associated business units; decentralized; used in very heterogeneous markets	■ Ability to quickly react to local conditions ■ Differing product offerings limit economies of scale, and limited inter-unit communication limits knowledge sharing	■ Decentralized systems with bi-directional communication between home office and subsidiaries ■ Local databases
Transnational	Some aspects centralized, others decentralized; integrated network; used in integrated global markets	■ Can achieve benefits of multidomestic and global strategies ■ Difficult to manage; very complex	■ Distributed/shared systems with enterprise-wide linkages ■ Common global data resources

Source: Based on Alavi & Young (1992), Karimi & Konsynski (1991), and Ramarapu & Lado (1995).

ETHICAL DILEMMA

Underground Gaming Economy

Entropia Universe is one of many massively multiplayer online role-playing games (MMORPGs). Other online role-playing games include but are not limited to Sony's Everquest, EA's Star Wars: The Old Republic, and Blizzard's World of Warcraft. Players pay monthly subscription fees and assume virtual identities called avatars. The total virtual goods market in the United States is expected to climb to US$5 billion by 2016, up from US$500 million in 2008.

In most MMORPGs, gamers slay enemies, build houses and businesses, choose professions, pick up mystical attributes, and fill their virtual bank accounts with gold and cash. Each player's avatar "lives" in the game's virtual community. A recent trend, however, is for serious players to play to collect virtual tools, gold, or cash and then sell the booty for real cash. Given the opportunity to earn real money in a virtual environment, the practice of buying and selling assets from MMORPGs has become widespread. These virtual moguls of the MMORPG world often employ "gold farmers" to build their empires. Farming has become especially popular in China, where companies employ rows of gamers who play for up to 12 hours at a time, collecting virtual assets and ascending to the highest levels of a game—all of which the companies will sell. Items for sale range from characters that have advanced to higher levels of a game to weapons, gold, and other items captured in a game.

As you might expect, gold farming is highly controversial. In addition to the human rights issues, critics of this new virtual economy say that buying gold on the virtual market penalizes gamers who play strictly for fun but allows those with cash to spend to advance through levels of a game they have not mastered. Others say there is nothing wrong with players buying advantages that let them play at higher levels without putting in large amounts of time.

Some game companies have banned farmers from the playing field. For example, Blizzard Entertainment, the makers of World of Warcraft, a game that boasted more than 10 million subscribers in 2012, has permanently banned thousands of users following its investigation into cheaters and farmers. Similarly, *PC Gamer*, America's largest gaming magazine, stopped taking advertisements from companies that trade in virtual goods and characters from MMORPGs; and as early as 2007, eBay banned the sale of virtual goods such as currency or avatars. Nevertheless, countless sites remain that explain how the underground markets operate for the buying and selling of virtual goods. The companies cite ethical reasons for penalizing farmers, but they also realize that farmers can eventually impact revenues, as gamers who refuse to buy and sell attributes may refuse to play with those who do.

Based on:

Gold farming. (2014, April 1). In *Wikipedia, The Free Encyclopedia*. Retrieved May 16, 2014, from http://en.wikipedia.org/w/index.php?title=Gold_farming&oldid=602251077.

Holisky, Lyons, D. (2010, March 29). Why behavioral economists love online games. *Newsweek*. Retrieved May 16, 2014, from http://www.newsweek.com/why-behavioral-economists-love-online-games-69323.

VALUING INNOVATIONS

To differentiate itself, an organization often must deploy new, state-of-the-art technologies to do things even better, faster, and more cheaply than rivals that are using older technologies. Although firms can choose to continually upgrade older systems rather than investing in new systems, these improvements can at best give only a short-lived competitive edge. To gain and sustain significant competitive advantage, firms must often deploy the latest technologies or redeploy and reinvest in existing technologies in clever, new ways.

But with the plethora of new information technologies and systems available, how can you possibly choose winners? Indeed, how can you even keep track of all the new breakthroughs, new products, new versions, and new ways of using technologies? For example, in Figure 2.20 we present a small subset of some new information technologies and systems, ranging from some that are here now and currently being used to some that are easily a decade away from being a reality. Which one is important for you? Which one will make or break your business? Does this list even include the one that you need to be concerned about?

The Need for Constant IS Innovation

Sir John Maddox, a physicist and the editor of the influential scientific journal *Nature* for 22 years, was quoted in *Scientific American* in 1999 as saying, "The most important discoveries of the next 50 years are likely to be ones of which we cannot now even conceive" (John Maddox. Reprinted from *Scientific American*, 1999). Think about that for a moment. Most of the important discoveries of the next 50 years are likely to be things that, at present, we have no

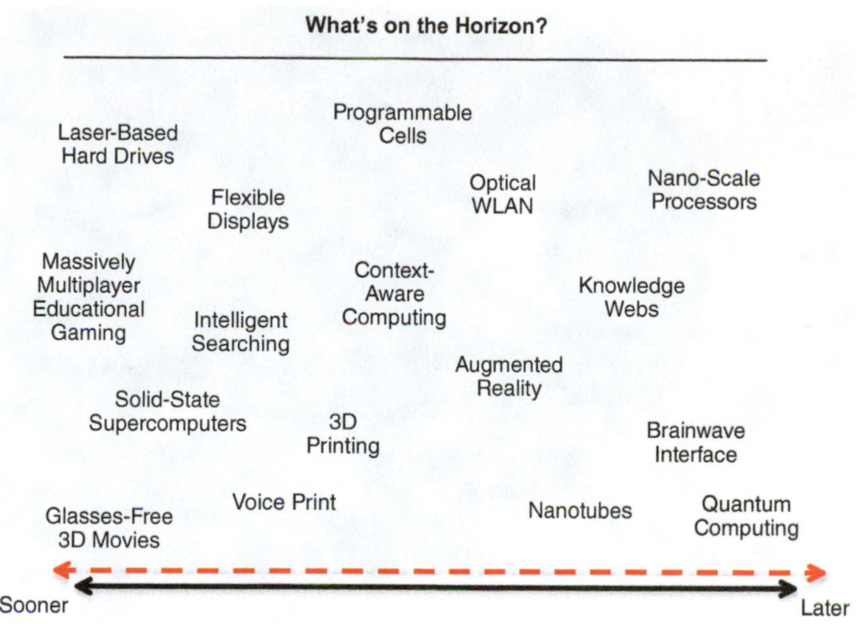

FIGURE 2.20

Some enabling technologies on the horizon.

clue about. To illustrate that point, think back to what the state of the Internet was back in 1999. Then, the Internet was not on the radar screens of many business organizations. Those that had Web sites were mostly providing an electronic brochure to customers and weren't exploiting the technology to streamline business processes as is the norm today. Look now at how the Internet has transformed modern business. How could something so transformational not have been easier for businesses to imagine or predict a decade earlier? It is difficult to see these things coming. Next, we examine how you can improve your ability to spot and exploit new innovations.

Successful Innovation Is Difficult

As we hinted at previously, there are limits to using emerging information systems to gain or sustain a competitive advantage. Information systems are often bought from or built by someone else. They are often either purchased from a vendor or developed by a consultant or outsourcing partner. In these situations, the information systems are usually not proprietary technologies owned by the organization. For example, although a soft-drink company can patent the formula of a cola or a pharmaceutical company can patent a new drug, an organization typically cannot patent its use of an information system, particularly if someone else developed it. The data in the system may be proprietary, but the information system typically is not. One classic counterexample, however, is Amazon.com's patented "one-click" ordering process that has been successfully defended in the courts.

INNOVATION IS OFTEN FLEETING. Given the pace of change in the digital world, advantages gained by innovations often have a limited life span. For example, even in situations where an organization has developed an innovative information system in-house, it usually did so with hardware, software, and networking components that others can purchase. In short, rivals can copy emerging information systems, so this form of competitive advantage can be short-lived. Indeed, if use of the new system causes one organization to gain a significant advantage over others, smart rivals are quick to duplicate or improve on that use of the system.

INNOVATION IS OFTEN RISKY. Developing innovative information systems always entails risk. The classic example from consumer electronics is the choice of a videocassette recorder (VCR) in the early days of that technology and the competing Betamax (developed by Sony) and VHS (developed by JVC) formats. Most experts agreed that the Betamax had superior recording and playback quality, but VHS ultimately won the battle in the marketplace. People who made the "smart" choice at the time probably would have chosen a VCR with the Betamax format. Ultimately, however, that turned out to be an unfortunate choice. Recently, consumers again had to choose between two competing formats, namely, for high-definition (HD) DVD players, where the Blu-ray and HD DVD formats competed to become the industry standard. In this battle, Microsoft, Toshiba, and many others backed the HD DVD format, while Sony led the

FIGURE 2.21

Blu-ray has become the industry standard for high-definition DVD players.
Source: Matthew Jacques/Shutterstock.

fight for Blu-ray (and even incorporated it into its PlayStation 3 gaming console). This time around, Sony (and the Blu-ray format) won the "format war," with the dissolution of the HD DVD Promotion Group in early 2008, effectively making Blu-ray the dominant format for HD video discs (Figure 2.21).

INNOVATION CHOICES ARE OFTEN DIFFICULT. Choosing among innovative IS-related investments is just as difficult as choosing consumer electronics. In fact, for organizations, choosing among the plethora of available innovative technologies is far more difficult, given the size and often mission-critical nature of the investment. Choosing a suboptimal DVD player, although disappointing, is usually not devastating.

Choosing new technologies in the IS area is like trying to hit one of several equally attractive fast-moving targets. You can find examples of the difficulty of forecasting emerging technologies in the experiences that many organizations have had in forecasting the growth, use, and importance of the Internet. The 1994 Technology Forecast prepared by the major consulting firm Price Waterhouse (now PriceWaterhouseCoopers) mentioned the word "Internet" on only five pages of the 750-page document. The next year, more than 75 pages addressed the Internet. Only three years later, in the 1997 briefing, the Internet was a pervasive topic throughout. Back in 1994, it would have been difficult, perhaps even foolish, to forecast such pervasive, rapidly growing business use of the Internet today. Table 2.8 illustrates how many people and organizations have had difficulty making technology-related predictions.

Given the pace of research and development in the IS and components area, staying current has been nearly impossible. Probably one of the most famous metrics of computer evolution has been "Moore's law." Intel founder Gordon Moore predicted that the number of transistors that could be squeezed onto a silicon chip would double every 24 months (this number is now often reduced to 18 months), and this prediction has proven itself over the past 40 years (see Chapter 3). In fact, some computer hardware and software firms roll out new versions of their products every three months. Keeping up with this pace of change can be difficult for any organization.

Organizational Requirements for Innovation

Certain types of competitive environments require that organizations remain at the cutting edge in their use of information systems. For example, consider an organization that operates within an environment with strong competitive forces (Porter, 1979). The organization has competitive pressures coming from existing rival firms or from the threat of entry of new rivals. It is critical for these organizations to do things better, faster, and more cheaply than rivals. These organizations are driven to deploy innovative information systems.

These environmental characteristics alone, however, are not enough to determine whether an organization should deploy a particular information system. Before an organization can deploy any new system well, its processes, resources, and risk tolerance must be capable of adapting to and sustaining the development and implementation processes.

TABLE 2.8 Some Predictions About Technology That Were Not Quite Correct

Year	Source	Quote
1876	Western Union, internal memo	"This 'telephone' has too many shortcomings to be seriously considered as a means of communication. The device is inherently of no value to us."
1895	Lord Kelvin, president, British Royal Society	"Radio has no future. Heavier-than-air flying machines are impossible. X-rays will prove to be a hoax."
1899	C. H. Duell, commissioner, U.S. Office of Patents	"Everything that can be invented has been invented."
1927	H. M. Warner, Warner Brothers	"Who the hell wants to hear actors talk?"
1943	Thomas Watson, chairman, IBM	"I think there is a world market for maybe five computers."
1949	*Popular Mechanics*	"Where a calculator on the ENIAC is equipped with 18,000 vacuum tubes and weighs 30 tons, computers in the future may have only 1,000 vacuum tubes and weigh only 1.5 tons."
1957	Editor, business books, Prentice Hall	"I have traveled the length and breadth of this country and talked with the best people, and I can assure you that data processing is a fad that won't last out the year."
1968	*BusinessWeek*	"With over 50 foreign cars already on sale here, the Japanese auto industry isn't likely to carve out a big slice of the U.S. market."
1977	Ken Olsen, president, Digital Equipment Corporation	"There is no reason anyone would want a computer in their home."
1989	Bill Gates, Microsoft	"We will never make a 32-bit operating system."
2004	Bill Gates, Microsoft	"Spam will be a thing of the past in two years' time."
2005	Sir Alan Sugar	"Next Christmas the iPod will be dead, finished, gone, kaput."
2010	Steve Jobs, Apple	"This size is useless unless you include sandpaper so users can sand their fingers down to a quarter of their size." (speaking about 7-inch tablets)

PROCESS REQUIREMENTS. To deploy innovative information systems well, people in the organization must be willing to do whatever they can to bypass and eliminate internal bureaucracy, set aside political squabbles, and pull together for the common good. Can you imagine, for example, a firm trying to deploy a Web-based order entry system that enables customers to access inventory information directly, when people in that firm do not even share such information with each other?

RESOURCE REQUIREMENTS. Organizations deploying innovative information systems must also have the human capital necessary to deploy the new systems. The organization must have enough employees available with the proper systems knowledge, skills, time, and other resources to deploy these systems. Alternatively, the organization must have resources and able systems partners available to outsource the development of such systems if necessary.

RISK TOLERANCE REQUIREMENTS. The last characteristic of an organization ready for the deployment of innovative information systems is that its members must have the appropriate tolerance for risk and uncertainty as well as the willingness to deploy and use new systems that may not be as proven and pervasive as more traditional technologies. If people within the organization desire low risk in their use of information systems, then gambling on cutting-edge systems will probably not be desirable or tolerable for them.

Predicting the Next New Thing

As you can see, using information systems as a strategic innovation will be difficult to identify, implement, and sustain. As Bakos and Treacy (1986) and others have argued, if you are using information systems to gain a competitive advantage in the area of operating efficiencies, it is likely that your rivals can just as easily adopt the same types of information systems and achieve the same gains. For example, in the early days of online shopping, some progressive online retailers set up Web sites that enabled customers to check on the status of their order without requiring help from a customer service representative, which helped the retailers to cut costs and increase customer satisfaction. Rivals, however, quickly copied this approach, matching cost reductions and service improvements. Thus, the competitive advantage achieved with clever use of information systems did not last long, and the systems turned into strategic necessity for anyone in this industry.

COMING ATTRACTIONS

Google's Project Glass: A Pair of Glasses

It's an early Monday morning, and you're running late. Your friend from 5,000 miles away initiates a video-call so you can have a quick chat, but you simultaneously need to check the weather and find your way to where the meeting will be held in less than half an hour. There is no doubt that your smartphone usefully pops out to help, but researchers at Google's secretive Google X Lab have come up with an even more convenient answer—Google Glass.

At first glance, Google Glass looks like an ultramodern pair of glasses, but a closer look reveals a lot of innovation that seems closer to science fiction than science fact. These glasses augment reality by providing an embedded microphone and a partly transparent (and very tiny) screen slightly above the user's right eye. This screen enables displaying information about the wearer's surroundings, communicating with other people, browsing the Web, listening to music, and taking photos or recording video. In sum, these shades squeeze the various functions of a smartphone and a computer into a pair of glasses, including global positioning system (GPS) location-tracking capabilities. These are certainly not just another pair of geeky glasses!

As if living in a real-life sci-fi movie, users immediately see 14 different services displayed on the video screen once the glasses are put on, gliding between information about the weather, their location, or their appointment schedule. For instance, when you look out the window on a cloudy day, Glass reminds you that there is an 80 percent chance of rain. When you stare at a blank wall, the screen displays that it is bowling night. When a friend sends a text message, an alert pops up to which a reply could be sent through voice command, courtesy of the built-in microphone.

Google Glass, originally restricted to an invitation-only beta program, officially became available to the public in May 2014 at a price of US$1,500. At such a relatively high price, it is unclear if Google Glass will be commercially successful. In addition, people are increasingly becoming concerned with the privacy implications of someone being able to take pictures or record video without informing others; this has gone so far that wearers of Google Glass are sometimes referred to as "Glassholes." However, many of the capabilities of Google Glass will surely arrive in the mainstream soon, whether in Google Glass or in other wearable technologies. Such innovative capabilities will augment our day, reducing inefficiency and enriching our lives. While you should not be a "Glasshole," you can certainly expect some useful features in innovative wearable technologies.

Based on:

Google Glass. (2014, May 15). In *Wikipedia, The Free Encyclopedia*. Retrieved May 16, 2014, from http://en.wikipedia.org/w/index.php?title=Google_Glass&oldid=608716927.

There are certainly ways to use information systems to gain a longer lasting, sustainable competitive advantage; Bakos and Treacy (1986) argued that if you can use information systems to make your products or services unique or to cause your customers to invest so heavily in you that their switching costs are high (i.e., if switching to a competitor's product involves significant investment in terms of time and/or money for the customer), then you are better able to develop a competitive advantage that is sustainable over the long haul. For example, you might combine heavy investments in computer-aided design systems with very bright engineers in order to perfect your product and make it unique and something relatively difficult to copy. Alternatively, you might use a customer relationship management system to build an extensive database containing the entire history of your interaction with each of your customers, and then use that system to provide very high-quality, intimate, rapid, and customized service that would convince customers that if they switched to a rival, it would take them years to build up that kind of relationship with the other firm.

The Innovator's Dilemma

Deciding which innovations to adopt and pursue has never been easy. In fact, there are many classic examples where so-called industry leaders failed to see the changing opportunities introduced by new innovations (see Table 2.8). In his influential book *Diffusion of Innovations*, Everett Rogers (2003) theorized that the adoption of innovations usually follows an S-shaped curve (Figure 2.22). When an innovation is brought to market, initially only a small group of "innovators" will adopt that innovation. After some time, sales pick up as the innovators are followed by the "early adopters" and the "early majority," and the increase in sales is strongest. Then sales slowly level off when the "late majority" starts adopting the innovation. Finally, sales stay level as only the "laggards" are left to adopt the innovation.

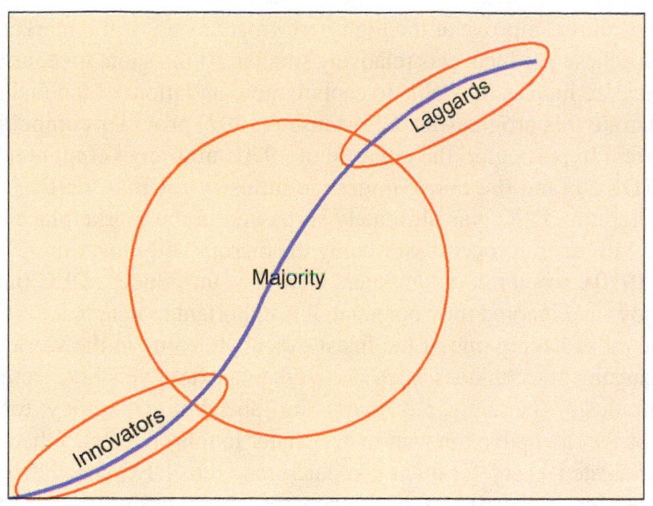

FIGURE 2.22

Diffusion of innovations.

Source: Based on Rogers, E. (2003). Diffusion of innovations (5th ed.). New York: Free Press.

However, some innovations are more disruptive, turning entire industries upside down. Clayton Christensen's (1997) *The Innovator's Dilemma* outlines how *disruptive innovations* undermine effective management practices, often leading to the demise of an organization or an industry. **Disruptive innovations** are new technologies, products, or services that eventually surpass the existing dominant technology or product in a market (Table 2.9). For example, retail giant Sears nearly failed in the early 1990s when it did not recognize the transformational power of the disruptive innovation discount retailing; today, discounters like Walmart and segment-specific stores like Home Depot dominate retailing.

Within every market, there are customers who have relatively high, moderate, or low performance requirements from the existing product offerings. For example, within the mobile phone industry today, some low-performance customers demand very basic phones and services (e.g., no camera, touchscreen, or data services), whereas high-performance customers use devices and services that rival the capabilities of some personal computers with high-speed Internet connections. Over time, as disruptive innovations and incremental improvements are introduced into an industry, the capabilities of the products in all segments (i.e., low to high performance) improve; as

TABLE 2.9 Examples of Disruptive Innovations and Their Associated Displaced or Marginalized Technology

Disruptive Innovation	Displaced or Marginalized Technology
Digital photography	Chemical photography
Desktop publishing	Traditional publishing
Online stock brokerage	Full-service stock brokerage
Online retailing	Brick-and-mortar retailing
Free, downloadable greeting cards	Printed greeting cards
Distance education	Classroom education
Unmanned aircraft	Manned aircraft
Nurse practitioners	Medical doctors
Semiconductors	Vacuum tubes
Automobiles	Horses
Airplanes	Trains
Compact discs	Cassettes and records
MP3 players, music downloading, streaming	Compact discs and music stores
Smartphones	MP3 players, dedicated GPS navigation
Mobile telephony	Wire-line telephony
Tablets	Notebook computers
Xbox, PlayStation, Smartphones	Desktop computers

product capabilities improve at the high-performance end of the market, the number of potential customers for these products gets relatively smaller. At the same time, as the low-end products also improve, they are increasingly able to capture more and more of the mainstream marketplace.

To illustrate this progression, Christensen (1997) provides compelling examples within several industries. In particular, the collapse of 1970s midrange computer giant Digital Equipment Company (DEC) (and the entire midrange industry for that matter) clearly illustrates the innovator's dilemma. DEC was ultimately surpassed in the marketplace by microprocessor-based computers, with the microprocessor being the disruptive innovation.

In the 1970s, when microcomputers were first introduced, DEC (and its customers) deemed them to be toys and ignored their potential. It is important to note that DEC was a well-run company and was touted as having one of the finest executive teams in the world. Additionally, DEC used leading management techniques, such as conducting extensive market research with its existing customers and industry (i.e., DEC put "marketing" ahead of technology; for a divergent view, see the discussion of the disruptive innovation cycle later in this chapter). When surveyed, none of DEC's customers indicated a need for microcomputers, and thus DEC concluded that developing improved capabilities within its *existing* midrange computer product line is where they should focus. At this time, DEC's goal was to serve the needs of high- and mid-performance users, which made up the largest part of the total market for computers (Figure 2.23). The increasing performance of DEC's products started meeting the needs of customers who would traditionally purchase mainframe computers, so DEC could try to "upsell" to mainframe customers of IBM, Burroughs, and Honeywell, where the margins were even greater than in the midrange computer industry.

Initially, there were virtually no competitive product offerings serving the needs of the low-performance users; in other words, current product offerings by established computer manufacturers, such as DEC, were either too powerful or too expensive (or both) for these low-end customers. In the 1980s, the microcomputer industry was launched by Apple, and the (disruptive) microprocessor, developed in the 1970s, was now being turned into a product that had the right capabilities and price for users in the low-performance category of the marketplace. DEC was not alone in ignoring the introduction of microcomputers; virtually all established players in the computing industry continued to focus on their existing customers and existing product lines, incrementally improving their products over time. Meanwhile, in just a few years, the microcomputer industry grew and matured, going from toy to office automation device (e.g., a replacement for the typewriter or adding machine) to a multipurpose business computer for many small and medium-sized businesses that could never before afford a computer. As the low end of the market took shape in the 1980s, DEC continued to focus on its existing customers and business model (e.g., direct selling, personal service). Rapidly, the capabilities of the

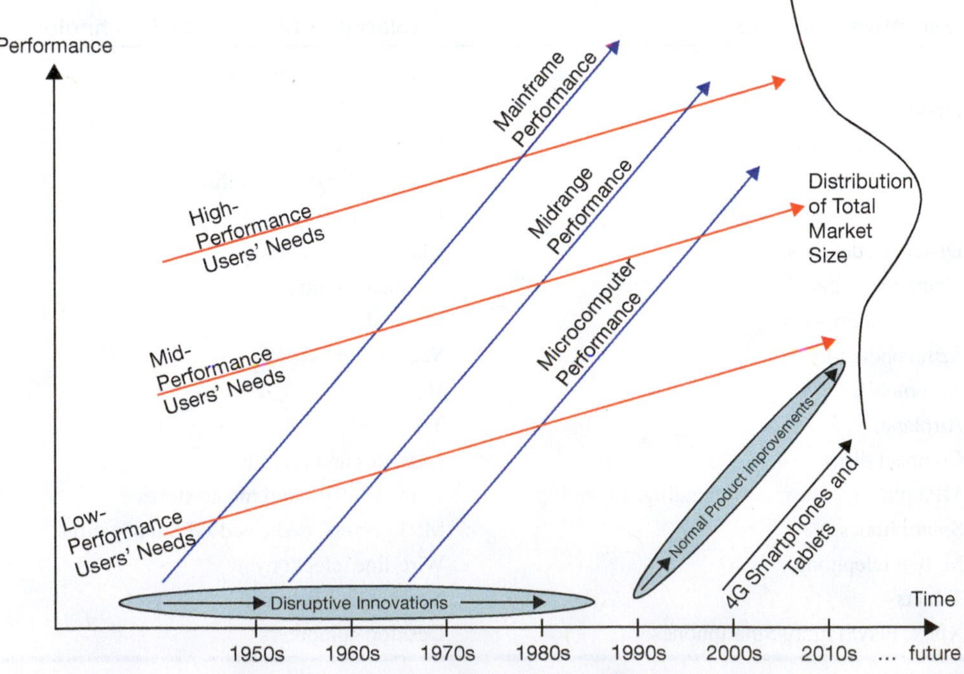

FIGURE 2.23

Innovator's dilemma view of the evolution of the computing industry.

"disruptive" microcomputers improved, meeting the needs of not only the low end but also the mid-performance range of the marketplace, which was traditionally served by DEC's midrange computers. Being far more inexpensive than DEC's products, the microcomputers took over the bulk of the market. Sadly, DEC continued to ignore the microcomputer industry until it was too late, and DEC could do nothing but watch the loss of its biggest traditional market segment. By January 26, 1998, what was left of DEC was sold to Compaq Computers; in 2002, Compaq was acquired by Hewlett-Packard.

Today, microprocessor-based computers from Dell, HP, Apple, and others meet or exceed the needs of much of the *entire* marketplace; additionally, only a handful of high-end computer manufacturers remain. So what is next for this industry? Many believe that 4G smartphones and tablets from companies like Apple and Samsung are disrupting traditional PCs and laptops, and cheap smartphones using Android or the Firefox operating system will disrupt high-end mobile devices. So, the **innovator's dilemma** refers to how disruptive innovations, typically ignored by established market leaders, cause these established firms or industries to lose market dominance, often leading to failure. What DEC experienced, so too have countless other companies in numerous industries. Table 2.10 summarizes the typical progression and effects of a disruptive innovation on an industry.

ORGANIZING TO MAKE INNOVATION CHOICES. Given the evolution of industries outlined in the innovator's dilemma, how do organizations make decisions on which innovations to embrace and which to ignore? In the follow-up book, *The Innovator's Solution*, Christensen and Raynor (2003) outline a process called the *disruptive growth engine*, which all organizations can follow to more effectively respond to disruptive innovations in their industry. This process has the following steps:

1. ***Start Early.*** To gain the greatest opportunities, become a leader in identifying, tracking, and adopting disruptive innovations by making these processes a formal part of the organization (budgets, personnel, and so on).
2. ***Display Executive Leadership.*** To gain credibility as well as to bridge sustaining and disruptive product development, visible and credible leadership is required.
3. ***Build a Team of Expert Innovators.*** To most effectively identify and evaluate potential disruptive innovations, build a competent team of expert innovators.
4. ***Educate the Organization.*** To see opportunities, those closest to customers and competitors (e.g., marketing, customer support, and engineering) need to understand how to identify disruptive innovations.

In addition to formalizing the identification of innovations within the organization, shifts in business processes and fundamental thinking about disruptive innovations are needed. Next, we examine how to implement the innovation identification process.

IMPLEMENTING THE INNOVATION PROCESS. Executives today who are serious about using information technology in innovative ways have made it a point to have their people be

TABLE 2.10 Typical Progression and Effects of Disruptive Innovations on an Industry

1. The first mover introduces a new technology. It is expensive, focusing on a small number of high-performance, high-margin customers.
2. Over time, the first mover focuses on improving product capabilities to meet the needs of higher-performance customers in order to continue to reap the highest margins.
3. Later entrants, using a disruptive innovation, have an inferior market position, focusing on lower-performance, lower-margin customers.
4. Over time, later entrants focus on incremental product improvements to serve the needs of more lower-performance customers, also focusing on cost efficiencies to offset the lack of margins with economies of scale.
5. As the market matures, all products improve, competition increases, and margins diminish; the first mover rarely learns the efficiencies of the later entrants and is entrenched in high-margin business practices; the first mover's market share rapidly erodes as that of the later entrants rapidly grows.
6. Ultimately, the later entrants' products meet or exceed the requirements for the vast majority of the marketplace; they "win" with efficient, low-cost business processes demanded by the majority of the marketplace.

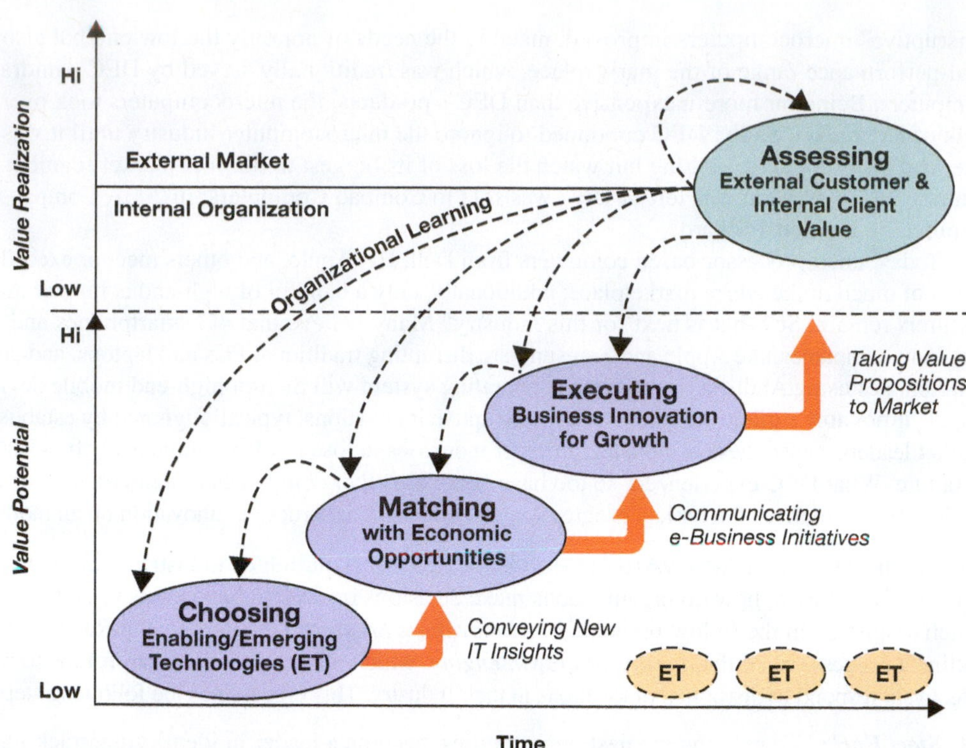

FIGURE 2.24

The disruptive innovation cycle.
Source: Based on Wheeler (2002).

continually on the lookout for new disruptive innovations that will have a significant impact on their business. Wheeler (2002) has summarized this process nicely as the **disruptive innovation cycle** (Figure 2.24). The model essentially holds that the key to success for modern organizations is the extent to which they use information technologies and systems in timely, innovative ways. The vertical dimension of the disruptive innovation cycle shows the extent to which an organization derives value from a particular information technology, and the horizontal dimension shows time. Next, we examine the cycle.

Choosing Enabling/Emerging Technologies The first bubble left of the graph shows that successful organizations first create jobs, groups, and processes that are all devoted to scanning the environment for new emerging and **enabling technologies** (i.e., information technologies that enable a firm to accomplish a task or goal or to gain or sustain competitive advantage in some way; also called disruptive innovations) that appear to be relevant for the organization. For example, an organization might designate a small group within the IS department as the "Emerging Technologies" unit and charge the group with looking for new technologies that will have an impact on the business. As part of its job, this group will pore over current technology magazines, participate in Internet discussion forums on technology topics, go to technology conferences and conventions, and have strong, active relationships with technology researchers at universities and technology companies.

Matching Technologies to Opportunities Next, in the second bubble, the organization matches the most promising new technologies with current **economic opportunities**. For example, the Emerging Technologies group might have identified advances in 3D printing as a key enabling technology that now makes faster and cheaper prototyping feasible. In addition, managers within the marketing function of the firm have recognized that competitors have not release new models recently, and reducing product development cycle times can provide an opportunity to gain customers and market share.

Executing Business Innovation for Growth The third bubble represents the process of selecting—among myriad opportunities to take advantage of—those emerging technologies that have the biggest potential to address the current opportunities. The organization decides to acquire 3D printers that enable it to create prototypes much faster, helping the company to release new product models at shorter intervals, in order to attract new customers.

KEY PLAYERS

The Global Elite

Throughout the world, there are technology giants that provide us with gadgets and innovations that touch every aspect of our lives. For the U.S.-based companies, you probably can recognize their names, and maybe their primary markets. Companies like Hewlett-Packard, AT&T, Apple, IBM, Verizon, Microsoft, and Dell are just some of the global giants based in the United States. What about the non-U.S.-based giants? Who are they, where are they from, and what are their primary markets? We will briefly highlight a few of the non-U.S. technology firms. While you may not know all of their names, locations, or products, they are indeed key players in the global tech industry.

Huawei Technologies is a Chinese networking and telecommunications equipment company. It is the largest telecommunications equipment manufacturer in the world, with over US$38.5 billion in revenue in 2013. Huawei has partnered with many large mobile technologies firms, including 3Com, Siemens, Nokia, and Motorola, to develop various wireless technologies and standards that are in wide use around the world.

Foxconn Technology Group, the world's largest electronics manufacturer, is headquartered in Taiwan, but primarily produces products in China, in addition to countries such as Brazil, Mexico, Malaysia, and the United States. Foxconn is the primary manufacturer for many of the electronic devices you may use every day. The list of products Foxconn manufactures includes the Xbox One, Wii U, Playstation 4, Amazon Kindle, and Apple's iPad and iPhone. Many of the companies designing and marketing these various products compete aggressively against each other, but most of the leading products in these categories all originate from the same Foxconn factory complex in China.

A final example is ZTE, a Chinese company specializing in mobile phones and telecommunications equipment such as network switches, routers, and mobile phone base stations. Measured by revenues, ZTE was the fifth largest manufacturer of telecommunications equipment. With its focus on low-end smartphones, ZTE managed to become the fifth largest smartphone vendor in the United States.

These technology giants, and many more, do not receive as much attention as Apple, Samsung, or Microsoft. But they play a major role in the technology industry and you would do well to become familiar with them.

Based on:

Foxconn. (2014, May 14). In *Wikipedia, The Free Encyclopedia*. Retrieved May 16, 2014, from http://en.wikipedia.org/w/index.php?title=Foxconn&oldid=608587084.

Huawei. (2014, May 15). In *Wikipedia, The Free Encyclopedia*. Retrieved May 16, 2014, from http://en.wikipedia.org/w/index.php?title=Huawei&oldid=608709918.

ZTE. (2014, May 15). In *Wikipedia, The Free Encyclopedia*. Retrieved May 17, 2014, from http://en.wikipedia.org/w/index.php?title=ZTE&oldid=608646386.

Assessing Value The fourth bubble represents the process of assessing the value of that use of technology, not only to customers but also to internal clients (sales representatives, marketing managers, the chief operating officer, and so on).

THINKING ABOUT INVESTMENTS IN DISRUPTIVE INNOVATIONS. The disruptive innovation cycle suggests three new ways to think about investments in disruptive innovations:

1. ***Put Technology Ahead of Strategy.*** This approach says that technology is so important to strategy and to success that you have to begin with technology. Notice that the first bubble involves understanding, identifying, and choosing technologies that are important. The first bubble does not begin with strategy, as a traditional approach to running a business organization would suggest. In fact, many would argue that given how important technology is today and how fast it changes, if you start with a strategy and then try to retrofit technology into your aging strategy, you are doomed. This approach argues that you begin by understanding technology and develop a strategy from there. This approach is admittedly very uncomfortable for people who think in traditional ways and/or who are not comfortable with technology. We believe, however, that for many modern organizations, thinking about technology in this way is key.
2. ***Put Technology Ahead of Marketing.*** The second way that this approach turns conventional wisdom on its head is that, like strategy, marketing also takes a backseat to technology. Think about it carefully, and you will see that marketing does not come into play until later in this model. A very traditional marketing-oriented approach would be to go first to your customers and find out from them what their needs are and what you ought to be

doing with technology (as did DEC). The trouble with this approach is that, given the rapid evolution of technology, your customers are not likely to know about new technologies and their capabilities. In some sense, they are the last place you ought to be looking for ideas about new technologies and their impact on your business. Indeed, if they know about the new technology, then chances are your competitors already do too, meaning that this technology is not the one to rest your competitive advantage on. As Steve Jobs of Apple put it, "You can't just ask people what they want and then try to give that to them. By the time you get it built, they'll want something new."

3. ***Innovation is Continuous.*** The third way that this approach is interesting—and potentially troubling—is that the process has to be ongoing. As shown along the time dimension at the bottom of the graph, the first bubble repeats over and over again as the Emerging Technologies group is constantly on the lookout for the "next new thing" that will revolutionize the business. The rate of information technology evolution is not likely to slow down, and innovative organizations truly cannot—and do not—ever rest.

Today, dealing with rapid change caused by disruptive innovations is a reality for most industries. If you are a leader in an industry, you must continually learn to embrace and exploit disruptive innovations, potentially *destroying* your existing core business while at the same time building a new business around the disruptive innovation. If you fail to do this, your competition may do it for you.

INDUSTRY ANALYSIS

Education

For decades, the cost of higher education in the United States has steadily increased (an average increase of 16 percent every five years for the past four decades), and the average college graduate enters the workforce with around US$30,000 in student loans. Several emerging changes in the education industry hold the promise of bringing those costs down. Information systems are at the core of these exciting developments.

One way education is changing is through globalization. Universities increasingly partner with other universities around the world, encouraging collaboration among researchers, consistency in curriculum design, and cross-border movement of students, graduates, and faculty. Many countries outside of the United States and other Western countries are investing heavily in their education systems, and there are now many universities in less developed parts of the world that can compete with the best of the "old-school" Ivy League universities. The global economy has produced an equally global education system.

Along with the trend of globalization, many universities are extending their reach by implementing online courses or, in many cases, whole degrees that can be obtained via remote, self-directed courses via the Internet. These programs are typically far less expensive to administer because once the materials are produced and refined, they can be used repeatedly by large groups of (paying) students. Some argue that such courses are less engaging and/or less effective, and there may be some truth to that. Regardless, universities continue to forge ahead in finding new ways to reach more students.

Another recent trend in education is the proliferation of so-called massively open online courses (MOOCs). These courses, which are freely available to the public, are able to effectively reach millions of students. Some very prestigious schools participate in providing these free courses, including Stanford, Wharton School of Business, UC Berkley, MIT, and Harvard. While the course content is provided free of charge, many of these institutions generate revenue by charging students for certifications or tutoring services.

Clearly, higher education is changing rapidly and in very significant ways and technology has enabled each of these changes.

Questions

1. Are online courses better or worse as compared to traditional, face-to-face courses? Why?
2. In what ways could technology be used to improve on the deficiencies of online courses?

Based on:
Massive open online course. (2014, May 16). In *Wikipedia, The Free Encyclopedia*. Retrieved May 16, 2014, from http://en.wikipedia.org/w/index.php?title=Massive_open_online_course&oldid=608884395.

Belkin, D. (2014, May 11). Can MOOCs and universities co-exist? *The Wall Street Journal*. Retrieved May 16, 2014, from http://online.wsj.com/news/articles/SB10001424052702303825604579515521328500810.

Key Points Review

1. ***Discuss how information systems can be used for automation, organizational learning, and strategic advantage.*** Information systems are used at different levels of an organization to support automating and organizational learning, and to support strategy. To apply information systems strategically, you must understand the organization's competitive landscape as well as the value chain and be able to identify opportunities in which you can use information systems to make changes or improvements in the value chain to gain or sustain a competitive advantage.
2. ***Describe how information systems support business models used by companies operating in the digital world.*** Organizations utilize information systems investments as a central component for executing their business models and delivering the value proposition. Common revenue models include affiliate marketing, subscriptions, licensing, transactions fees, sales, and Web advertising revenue. Freeconomics refers to the leveraging of digital technologies to provide *free* goods and services to customers as a business strategy for gaining a competitive advantage. Companies operating in the digital world can use different international business strategies, such as a home-replication strategy, global business strategy, multidomestic business strategy, or transnational business strategy.
3. ***Explain why and how companies are continually looking for innovative ways to use information systems for competitive advantage.*** Given that new technologies are not as stable as traditional ones, being at the technological cutting edge has its disadvantages and is typically quite difficult to execute. Those organizations that find themselves in highly competitive environments probably most need to deploy new technologies to stay ahead of rivals. To best deploy these new technologies, organizations must be ready for the business process changes that will ensue, have the resources necessary to deploy new technologies successfully, and be tolerant of the risk and problems involved in being at the cutting edge. Deploying emerging information systems is an ongoing process in which organizations should continuously scan the environment for emerging and enabling (and potentially disruptive) technologies, narrow down the list to those technologies that match with the challenges the firm faces or that create economic opportunities, choose a particular technology, implement it in a way that enables them to gain or sustain a competitive advantage, and assess the value of the technology.

Key Terms

affiliate marketing 64
automating 56
best-cost provider strategy 58
business/IT alignment 62
business model 64
business process 52
capabilities 59
differentiation strategy 57
disruptive innovation 75
disruptive innovation cycle 78
distinctive competency 59
domestic company 68
economic opportunities 78
effectiveness 53
efficiency 52
enabling technology 78
executive level 54
first-mover advantage 58
freeconomics 65
freemium 68
functional area information system 54
global business strategy 69
home-replication strategy 68
innovator's dilemma 77
international business strategy 68
key performance indicator (KPI) 53
low-cost leadership strategy 57
managerial level 52
multidomestic business strategy 69
operational level 52
organizational learning 56
organizational strategy 57
resources 59
revenue model 64
semistructured decision 53
strategic necessity 62
strategic planning 57
structured decision 52
transaction 52
transnational business strategy 69
unstructured decision 54
value chain 61
value chain analysis 61
value creation 59
value proposition 64

Go to **mymislab.com** to complete the problems marked with this icon.

Review Questions

2-1. Compare and contrast the characteristics of the operational, managerial, and executive levels of an organization.

2-2. Compare and contrast automating and learning.

2-3. Describe competitive advantage and list six sources.

2-4. How do an organization's resources and capabilities result in a competitive advantage?

2-5. Describe the four international business strategies.

2-6. What is freeconomics, and what are several approaches for applying its concepts to various industries?

2-7. Why is successful application of innovative technologies and systems often difficult?

2-8. What is the "innovator's dilemma"?

2-9. Using past examples, explain what is meant by a disruptive innovation.

2-10. Describe the disruptive innovation cycle.

Self-Study Questions

2-11. _____________ is using technology as a way to help complete a task within an organization faster and, perhaps, more cheaply.
A. Automating
B. Learning
C. Strategizing
D. Processing

2-12. What are new technologies, products, or services that eventually surpass the existing dominant technology or product in a market called?
A. surpassing event
B. disruptive innovation
C. innovative technology
D. technology change

2-13. Which of the following is *not* improving the value chain?
A. improving procurement processes
B. increasing operating costs
C. minimizing marketing expenditures
D. streamlining production processes

2-14. A company is said to have _____________ when it has gained an edge over its rivals.
A. monopoly
B. profitability
C. competitive advantage
D. computer advantage

2-15. Each of the following was described in this chapter as a source of competitive advantage *except* for _____________.
A. delivering superior customer service
B. achieving lower cost than rivals
C. being the subject of a hostile takeover
D. having shorter lead times in developing and testing new products

2-16. _____________ refers to the emergence of disruptive innovations that undermine effective management practices, often leading to the demise of an organization or an industry.
A. Moore's law
B. Technological obsolescence
C. Life-cycle analysis
D. Innovator's dilemma

2-17. What is the process of choosing, matching, executing, and assessing innovative technologies called?
A. environmental scanning
B. disruptive innovation cycle
C. strategic planning
D. none of the above

2-18. The revenue model involving the referring of customers to another business is called _____________.
A. referral marketing
B. Internet marketing
C. affiliate marketing
D. ad marketing

2-19. At the _____________ level of the organization, functional managers (e.g., marketing managers, finance managers, manufacturing managers, and human resource managers) focus on monitoring and controlling operational-level activities and providing information to higher levels of the organization.
A. operational
B. managerial
C. organizational
D. executive

2-20. A supervisor's having to decide when to reorder supplies or how best to allocate personnel for the completion of a project is an example of a(n) _____________ decision.
A. structured
B. unstructured
C. automated
D. delegated

Answers are on page 84.

Problems and Exercises

2-21. Match the following terms with the appropriate definitions:

i. value chain analysis
ii. freeconomics
iii. managerial level
iv. value chain
v. disruptive innovation cycle
vi. disruptive innovations
vii. innovator's dilemma
viii. transnational business strategy
ix. multidomestic business strategy
x. operational level

a. The notion that disruptive innovations can cause established firms or industries to lose market dominance, often leading to failure
b. The process of analyzing an organization's activities to determine where value is added to products and/or services and the costs that are incurred for doing so
c. New technologies, products, or services that eventually surpass the existing dominant technology or product in a market
d. The middle level of the organization, where functional managers focus on monitoring and controlling operational-level activities and providing information to higher levels of the organization
e. A model suggesting that the extent to which modern organizations use information technologies and systems in timely, innovative ways is the key to success
f. The leveraging of digital technologies to provide free goods and services to customers as a business strategy for gaining competitive advantage
g. The set of primary and support activities in an organization where value is added to a product or service
h. An international business strategy employed to be flexible and responsive to the needs and demands of heterogeneous local markets
i. An international business strategy that allows companies to leverage the flexibility offered by a decentralized organization (to be more responsive to local conditions) while at the same time reaping economies of scale enjoyed by centralization
j. The bottom level of an organization, where the routine day-to-day interactions with customers occur

2-22. Using a business or organization that you are familiar with, contrast the operational, managerial, and executive levels by contrasting each level's typical activities, types of decisions, and information needs.

2-23. Using your own life, contrast several structured versus unstructured decisions that you regularly have to make.

2-24. Identify a company utilizing the distinct competitive strategies shown in Figure 2.10; provide evidence to support your selections.

2-25. Of the five industry forces presented in the chapter (Porter's model), which is the most significant for an organization in terms of making IS investment decisions? Why? Which is the least significant? Why?

2-26. Using a company or organization that you are familiar with, map its various business processes into a value chain.

2-27. Using a business or organization that you are familiar with, analyze the organization's business model, including its customer segments, value proposition, channels, customer relationships, revenue streams, key resources, key activities, key partners, and cost structure.

2-28. Go to Amazon.com's affiliate site. How does affiliate marketing at Amazon.com work? How do Amazon .com's business partners get paid? Who can sign up for this service?

2-29. Find and describe an example not discussed in this chapter that demonstrates the freeconomics concept of freemium.

2-30. Find and describe an example not discussed in this chapter that demonstrates the freeconomics concept of cross-subsidy.

2-31. Find and describe an example not discussed in this chapter that demonstrates the freeconomics concept of zero marginal cost.

2-32. Find and describe an example not discussed in this chapter that demonstrates the freeconomics concept of labor exchange.

2-33. Why shouldn't every organization deploy innovative information systems? What are some of the recommended characteristics of an organization that are necessary for that organization to successfully deploy innovative technologies?

2-34. Identify examples not discussed in the chapter of disruptive innovations that successfully displaced or marginalized an industry or technology.

2-35. Apply the progression and effects of disruptive innovation on an industry (see Table 2.9), describing the evolution of a disruptive technology to a product or industry.

Application Exercises

Note: The existing data files referenced in these exercises are available on the book's Web site: www.pearsonhighered.com/valacich.

Spreadsheet Application: Valuing Information Systems

2-36. The cost of maintaining information systems is high for Campus Travel. You have been assigned to evaluate the total cost of ownership (TCO) of a few systems that are currently in use by Campus Travel employees. Take a look at the TCO.csv file to obtain the list of systems that are in use and the costs associated with maintaining the software, hardware, and the associated personnel for each type of system. Calculate the following for your operations manager:

- The costs for server hardware by adding a new row to include Web servers. This includes US$4,500 for the main campus and US$2,200 for the other campuses.
- The TCO for the entire information system in Campus Travel. Hint: Sum all the values for all the systems together.
- The TCO for servers and network components of the information system.
- Make sure that you format the table, including using the currency format, in a professional manner.

Database Application: Building a System Usage Database

2-37. To understand the assets in Campus Travel, the IS manager has asked you to design a database that would be able to store all the assets. Your manager asks you to do the following:

- Create a new blank database called asset.mdb.
- Create a new table called "assets" in the asset database with the following fields:
  a. Item ID (Text field)
  b. Item Name (Text field)
  c. Description (Memo field)
  d. Category (hardware, software, other)
  e. Condition (new, good, fair, poor)
  f. Acquisition Date (Date field)
  g. Purchase Price (Currency field)
  h. Current Value (Currency field)

Team Work Exercise

Net Stats: Online Searching

The Google search engine has become so popular with Internet users that the word "Google" is often used as a verb ("I 'Googled' the restaurant to see its reviews"), but there are other well-known search engines, such as Yahoo! and Microsoft's Bing. Table 2.11 shows the percentage of Internet surfers who used each search engine (i.e., the search engines' market share) in April 2014 as compared to April 2012.

Questions and Exercises

2-38. Search the Web for the most up-to-date statistics about the search engine market.

2-39. As a team, interpret these numbers. What is striking/important about these statistics? How do the numbers compare to your own search behavior?

2-40. How have the numbers changed? Will there be other important players in the search engine market?

2-41. Using your spreadsheet software of choice, create a graph/figure most effectively visualizing the statistics/changes you consider most important.

TABLE 2.11 Top Search Engines by Market Share, April 2014 Compared with April 2012

Search Engine	April 2014 Market Share (%)	April 2012 Market Share (%)	Change (percentage points)
Google	72.8	79.7	−6.9
Baidu	13.8	5.7	8.1
Yahoo!	6.2	6.5	0.3
Bing	5.6	4.5	1.1
Other	1.6	3.6	−2.0

Source: Based on http://marketshare.hitslink.com/search-engine-market-share.aspx?qprid=5.

Answers to the Self-Study Questions

2-11. A, p. 56 **2-12.** B, p. 26 **2-13.** B, p. 61 **2-14.** C, p. 58 **2-15.** C, p. 58
2-16. D, p. 74 **2-17.** B, p. 78 **2-18.** C, p. 64 **2-19.** B, p. 50 **2-20.** A, p. 52

CASE 1 LinkedIn

YouTube is for video entertainment; iTunes services is for music lovers; Facebook is primarily for socializing; Flickr is for photo exchange; World of Warcraft is for participating in virtual communities; Gamezone is for gamesters; and so on and so on. It would seem that the Web has anticipated all of our needs and responded. But wait, what's out there for those of us who want to further our professional lives—to visit with others in our field of expertise, to look at jobs that are available in other parts of the world, to find out what's happening in the business world outside our own familiar circle, and to garner introductions to those who might help us succeed? LinkedIn is an online service that fills this niche. LinkedIn advertises itself as "an interconnected network of experienced professionals from around the world, representing 150 industries and 200 countries. You can find, be introduced to, and collaborate with qualified professionals that you need to work with to accomplish your goals." As of 2014, LinkedIn had over 300 million members, with 61 percent from countries outside the United States, and has executives from all Fortune 500 companies in its ranks. In addition to access via a Web browser, LinkedIn is also available on various smartphones and tablets using customized apps.

Reid Hoffman, a former executive vice president of PayPal, founded LinkedIn in 2002; the service was launched in May 2003. Hoffman remains chairman of the board at LinkedIn, which is based in Mountain View, California, but also has offices in Omaha, New York, and London. His LinkedIn profile is available at http://www.linkedin.com/in/reidhoffman.

LinkedIn uses a freemium approach, where joining is free, with the option of upgrading to a paid account with additional functionality. Newcomers to LinkedIn create a profile, listing professional accomplishments. Each newcomer then links trusted colleagues, contacts, and clients—called *connections*—by inviting them to join and linking to him or her. In this way, LinkedIn participants create their own professional networks, where contacts may number in the thousands. Connections can be used in many ways:

- Users list trusted contacts, who then list their contacts, called second-degree connections. Second-degree connections list their trusted contacts, called third-degree connections. In this way, the original LinkedIn user brings together thousands of professionals, gaining many valuable contacts.
- Users can then find jobs, people, and business opportunities recommended by someone in the network.
- Employers using the network can list jobs and search for available candidates to fill job openings.
- Job seekers can search the connections of potential employers and find mutual connections who might introduce them.

A free feature called "LinkedIn Answers" lets users ask business-related questions for the community to answer. LinkedIn Groups is another free feature that allows users to make additional contacts by joining alumni, professional, or other job-related groups.

There are ways to enhance one's use of professional profile sites such as LinkedIn, writes Kevin Donlin for the *Minneapolis–St. Paul Star Tribune*. First, enhance your profile. One way to do this is to jazz up your profile with a few pertinent details and statements from colleagues. For example, staff members at LinkedIn advised Guy Kawasaki, managing director of Garage Technology Ventures in San Francisco, California, to add the following statement from a former colleague at Apple, where Guy said he was "chief evangelist." "Spirited and exceptionally bright with a highly developed sense of humor, Guy continues to be one of the most gifted marketing executives I know."

Enhance your profile, Donlin advises, but "keep your dirt to yourself. According to NBC News, 77 percent of employers will search the Internet to check your background, and 35 percent of employers have eliminated a candidate for consideration after finding 'digital dirt' about them online." So don't post that video of yourself imbibing too much at a party on Facebook, and remember that potential employers may not appreciate the video of the tasteless practical joke you played on a friend, so keep it off YouTube.

Like some other social media sites, LinkedIn has come under recent criticism for its threats to business and corporate security. According to a recent Security Threat Report by Sophos, an information security firm, LinkedIn is increasingly being used as a conduit for hackers and other malicious entities to develop "road maps" attacks. According to the report, LinkedIn is providing what amounts to a corporate directory of who works at a firm and what their responsibilities are as well as corporate e-mail addresses. In June 2012, 6.5 million LinkedIn passwords were posted on a hacker site. Armed with this type of information, hackers can easily set up a fake LinkedIn account or devise a social engineering attack—the act of manipulating people into divulging confidential information—and target who and what they want to attack to effectively meet their sinister goals. Security concerns aside, LinkedIn is clearly a valuable technological tool for Internet users and entrepreneurs alike who are looking for better ways to network.

Questions

2-42. Do you think it is ethical for employers to search the Internet for information on potential employees?

2-43. Do you believe that you can gain a competitive advantage by joining a network such as LinkedIn? Why or why not?

2-44. Have you joined or do you plan to join LinkedIn (or a similar type of site)? Why or why not?

Based on:

Donlin, K. (2008, April 9). Three ways to get found and hired. *Star Tribune*. Retrieved May 16, 2014, from http://www.startribune.com/jobs/15116626.html.

LinkedIn. (2014, May 15). In *Wikipedia, The Free Encyclopedia*. Retrieved May 16, 2014, from http://en.wikipedia.org/w/index.php?title=LinkedIn&oldid=497074823.

Linkedin.com. (n.d.) Retrieved May 16, 2014, http://www.linkedin.com/about-us.

Robertson, J. (2012, June 12). Stolen LinkedIn passwords can sell for as low as $1. *BusinessWeek*. Retrieved June 12, 2012, from http://www.businessweek.com/news/2012-06-12/stolen-linkedin-passwords-can-sell-for-as-low-as-1.

CASE 2 Streaming Video

Remember the old brick-and-mortar movie rental services? You drove to the physical location, scanned shelves for your movie of choice (too frequently, it wasn't in), paid the clerk, and left. The flick was due back in 24 hours (or, at most, three to five days later), or you were billed a hefty late fee. In some cases, forgetful customers answered the door to find a police officer asking why they hadn't returned a rental movie.

Movie rental stores still exist, but in quickly dwindling numbers. Many alternatives have spawned, beginning with Netflix, the first and now the world's largest online movie service. Though originally started as a mail-order DVD rental service, Netflix has rapidly embraced the streaming video market. As of December 2013, Netflix offers its 40 million subscribers tens of thousands of movie and television titles, and is responsible for 34 percent of all downstream Web traffic during prime-time hours. Though Netflix continues to battle rising costs as movie and TV studios raise their licensing fees, the company continues to dominate in the streaming market.

Other competitors have entered the market as well. Amazon's Prime subscription service, in addition to providing discounts on fast shipping for all products, provides subscribers access to a vast library of movie and TV content. This content is available to users via Amazon's mobile devices, like the Kindle Fire, as well as the recently released Amazon FireTV, a US$99 set-top box that also supports gaming.

Apple and Google also compete in this space, though currently with a slightly different approach. iTunes has long been the leader in digital music distribution, and Apple moved seamlessly to movie and TV distribution as those became popular. The distinction from the Netflix and Amazon models is that iTunes provides a rental and purchasing marketplace, where customers can pay for temporary rights to a movie (rental), or may pay a higher price to purchase the movie for indefinite ownership. The Google Play store uses a similar rental/purchase model. The advantage of this model is that movie and TV studios are much more willing to participate in this type of distribution (which mirrors physical movie and TV distribution and the accompanying revenues). As a result, these marketplaces typically provide the latest, most popular movies. In contrast, a drawback of Netflix and Amazon's streaming services is their limited selection of popular or recent titles; their streaming libraries are dependent on content deals they have made with individual studios.

One of the major advantages to these digital video distribution services is their ability to personalize a customer's experience to a degree previously not possible. These personalized services learn about a user's preferences according to the movies they frequently watch. From this information, the company creates a profile of each customer and a list of recommended movies. If, for example, a customer liked the movie *Prometheus*, he or she may also like the 1979 sci-fi classic *Alien*, and that movie will be included in a list of suggested movies. Customers can refine the recommendations by rating titles according to their preferences. These systems allow customers to tap large databases of movies, many of which they may not have been aware of at all.

Consider how fast things are changing. Just a few years ago, the only way to watch a movie other than paying to purchase it was to drive to a movie rental store like Blockbuster or Hollywood Video and pay to borrow a DVD for a few days. Today, that same entertainment can be obtained via any computer or mobile device, or through an increasing number of "connected" TVs, Blu-ray players, or small video-streaming devices like the Amazon FireTV, AppleTV, or Google's Chromecast. These services and devices have completely disrupted the movie rental business. Hollywood Video, once a major competitor to Blockbuster Video with stores all over the country, declared bankruptcy in 2010 and closed all of its stores. Blockbuster Video slowly bled customers until it too declared bankruptcy in 2010. Some stores remained open for a few years, but by the end of 2013, the company announced that it would be closing its remaining 300 stores.

Questions

2-45. In what ways has technology enabled the transformation and destruction of the traditional video rental industry?

2-46. Paid programming from cable companies still largely follows the model it has been following for the past few decades. How will technology and the public's appetite for on-demand, streaming video change the cable television industry in the coming years?

2-47. Discuss whether and how Netflix or Amazon can continue to grow their business and revenues in the streaming video market.

Based on:

Atkinson, C. (2014, May 14). Netflix is a prime-time bandwidth hog. *The New York Post*. Retrieved May 16, 2014, from http://nypost.com/2014/05/14/netflix-is-a-prime-time-bandwidth-hog.

Blockbuster LLC. (2014, May 16). In *Wikipedia, The Free Encyclopedia*. Retrieved May 16, 2014, from http://en.wikipedia.org/w/index.php?title=Blockbuster_LLC&oldid=608850633.

Netflix. (2014, May 12). In *Wikipedia, The Free Encyclopedia*. Retrieved May 16, 2014, from http://en.wikipedia.org/w/index.php?title=Netflix&oldid=608180091.

MyMISLab™

Go to **mymislab.com** for Auto-graded writing questions as well as the following Assisted-graded writing questions.

2-48. List and describe five general types of organizational strategy.

2-49. What is a business model and what are its primary components?

References

Alavi, M., & Young, G. (1992). Information technologies in international enterprise: An organizing framework. In S. Palvia, P. Palvia, & R. Zigli (Eds.), *Global issues in information technology management* (pp. 495–516). Harrisburg, PA: Idea Group.

Anderson, C. (2009). *Free: The future of a radical price*. New York: Hyperion.

Applegate, L. M., Austin, R. D., & Soule, D. L. (2009). *Corporate information strategy and management* (8th ed.). New York: McGraw-Hill.

Bakos, J. Y., & Treacy, M. E. (1986). Information technology and corporate strategy: A research perspective. *MIS Quarterly, 10*(2), 107–120.

Bartlett, C., & Ghoshal, S. (1998). *Managing across borders: The transnational solution*. Boston: Harvard Business School Press.

Christensen, C. M. (1997). *The innovator's dilemma*. Boston: Harvard Business School Press.

Christensen, C. M., & Raynor, M. E. (2003). *The innovator's solution: Creating and sustaining successful growth*. Boston: Harvard Business School Press.

Christensen, C. M., Roth, E. A., & Anthony, S. D. (2004). *Seeing what's next: Using theories of innovation to predict industry change*. Boston: Harvard Business School Press.

Garvin, D. A. (1993). Building a learning organization. *Harvard Business Review, 71*(4), 78–91.

Ghoshal, S. (1987). Global strategy: An organizing framework. *Strategic Management Journal, 8*(5), 425–440.

Hitt, M. A., Ireland, R. D., & Hoskisson, R. E. (2015). *Strategic management: Competitiveness and globalization* (11th ed.). Boston: South-Western.

Karimi, J., & Konsynski, B. R. (1991). Globalization and information management strategies. *Journal of Management Information Systems, 7*(4), 7–26.

Maddox, J. (1999, December). The unexpected science to come. *Scientific American, 281*, 62–67.

McKeen, J. D., Guimaraes, T., & Wetherbe, J. C. (1994). A comparative analysis of MIS project selection mechanisms. *Database, 25*(2), 43–59.

Osterwalder, A., & Pigneur, Y. (2010). *Business model generation*. Hoboken, NJ: Wiley.

Porter, M. E. (1979, March–April). How competitive forces shape strategy. *Harvard Business Review, 57*, 137–145.

Porter, M. E. (1985). *Competitive advantage: Creating and sustaining superior performance*. New York: Free Press.

Porter, M. E. (2001). Strategy and the internet. *Harvard Business Review, 79*(3), 62–78.

Prahalad, C. K., & Doz, Y. L. (1987). *The multinational mission: Balancing local demands and global vision*. New York: Free Press.

Ramarapu, N. K., & Lado, A. A. (1995). Linking information technology to global business strategy to gain competitive advantage: An integrative model. *Journal of Information Technology, 10*, 115–124.

Rogers, E. (2003). *Diffusion of innovations* (5th ed.). New York: Free Press.

Rubin, H. (2004, June 1). Real value: The elusive value of infrastructure. *CIO.com*. Retrieved May 29, 2014, from http://www.cio.com/article/32321/Real_Value_The_Elusive_Value_of_Infrastructure.

Shank, J., & Govindarajan, V. (1993). *Strategic cost management: Three key themes for managing costs effectively*. New York: Free Press.

Wheeler, B. C. (2002). NeBIC: A dynamic capabilities theory for assessing net-enablement. *Information Systems Research, 13*(2), 125–146.

Zuboff, S. (1988). *In the age of the smart machine: The future of work and power*. New York: Basic Books.

3 Managing the Information Systems Infrastructure and Services

After reading this chapter, you will be able to do the following:

1. Describe how changes in businesses' competitive landscape influence changing IS infrastructure needs.
2. Describe the essential components of an organization's IS infrastructure.
3. Discuss managerial issues associated with managing an organization's IS infrastructure.
4. Describe cloud computing and other current trends that can help an organization address IS infrastructure–related challenges.

Preview

Just as any city depends on a functioning infrastructure, companies operating in the digital world are relying on a comprehensive information systems (IS) infrastructure to support their business processes and competitive strategy. Transactions are conducted with ever-increasing speed; likewise, with ever-increasing amounts of data to be captured, analyzed, and stored, companies have to thoroughly plan and manage their infrastructure needs in order to gain the greatest returns on their IS investments. When planning and managing their IS architectures, organizations must answer many important and difficult questions. For example, how will we utilize information systems to enable our competitive strategy? What technologies and systems best support our core business processes? Which vendors should we partner with, which technologies do we adopt, and which do we avoid? What hardware, software, or services do we buy, build, or have managed by an outside service provider? How can we use cloud computing to increase our agility? How can we get the most out of the data captured from internal and external sources? Clearly, effectively managing an organization's IS infrastructure is a complex but necessary activity in today's digital world.

This chapter focuses on helping managers understand the key components of a comprehensive IS infrastructure and why its careful management is necessary. With the increasing complexity of an organization's information needs and the increasing complexity of the systems needed to satisfy these requirements, the topic of infrastructure management is fundamental for managing in the digital world.

Managing in the Digital World: "I Googled You!"

"Supercalifragilisticexpialidocious." Not sure what that means? Google it. This search engine has become so associated with our daily lives that the *Oxford English Dictionary* officially incorporated *Google* as a verb in June 2006. More than any other American multinational Internet and software corporation, Google, best known for its search platform, has branched out to develop a number of Internet-based services and products. No matter what you are searching for, one of Google's products is likely to have the answer. Another popular service is Gmail, a free e-mail service that is also available as an enterprise solution to businesses and universities. The video-sharing Web site YouTube has operated as a subsidiary of Google since 2006. Google is, in fact, in every corner of the World Wide Web, and the different technologies it offers have been incorporated into our everyday lives.

The biggest revenue generator for Google is its AdSense program, which allows any Web site to publish advertisements on its pages. The Web site publisher is paid every time someone clicks on an ad originating from that page; using AdSense, the Web site publisher can tailor the types of ads that are placed on a Web site, including the function of blocking competitor ads and the freedom to eliminate unwanted ads regarding death, war, or explicit materials. The advertisers, in turn, can specifically target their ads using various metrics provided by AdSense, including how many people look at the site, the cost per click, click-through rates, and more.

Building on the success of its advertising programs, the company has single-handedly expanded into a global empire. Simply google "Google" to see how many hits you come up with—Google News, Google Scholar, Google Finance, Google Translate, and Google Images, to name a handful. In 2008, Android was released as an open source operating system for mobile phones that directly and successfully competed against Apple's iPhone, Research in Motion's BlackBerry, and Microsoft's Windows Phone. That same year Google introduced Chrome, a Web browser lauded for its speed and unique features, thus attacking established companies such as Microsoft on yet another front (Figure 3.1).

From e-mail to mobile devices, it may look as if Google's services have become so broad that it is impossible to find a common link, but this is not so. Many of these services are cloud-based, offering heavenly convenience and cloud-nine centralization. Do you remember the last time you had to download something to update your Gmail? Did you have to install an application to watch Madonna's Super Bowl half-time performance on YouTube? Of course not. In short, that is what Google is all about; no installation required. The magic begins and ends in Google's servers.

After reading this chapter, you will be able to answer the following:

1. How does Google benefit from a well-functioning infrastructure?
2. What are the major components of Google's infrastructure?
3. How and why does Google's success rely on the cloud-computing model?

Based on:
Anonymous. (n.d.). Our history in depth. Retrieved May 16, 2014, from http://www.google.com/about/company/history.

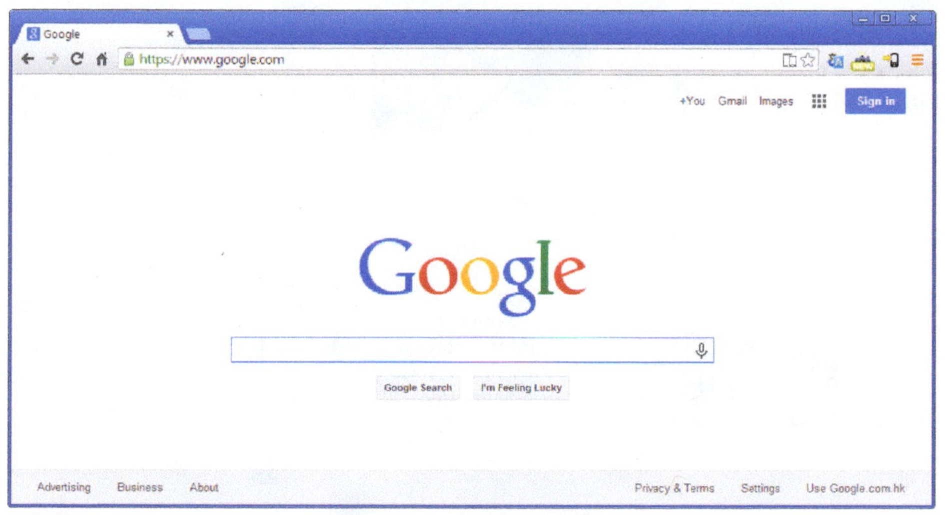

FIGURE 3.1

Google search page inside Google's Chrome browser.
Source: Courtesy of Google, Inc.

THE IS INFRASTRUCTURE

Most people expect a variety of basic municipal services, such as sanitation, security, transportation, provision of energy and water, and so on, to be provided by the city they live in. Any area where people live or work needs a supporting **infrastructure**, which entails the technical structures enabling the provision of services (Figure 3.2); many infrastructure components, such as power, telephone, water, and sewage lines, are "invisible" to the users, meaning that the users typically do not know (or even care) where, for example, their water comes from, as long as it flows when they open their faucets. Other, more visible, infrastructure components include streets, schools, retail stores, and law enforcement. Both the area's inhabitants and businesses depend on the services provided by that infrastructure, and cities with a good infrastructure are considered more livable than cities with poorer infrastructure and are much more likely to attract businesses and residents.

For organizations, many decisions are based on the provision of such services, such as when choosing a site for a new manufacturing plant or company headquarters. Indeed, many municipalities attempt to attract new businesses and industries by setting up new commercial zones with a well-planned infrastructure. In some cases, specific infrastructure components are of special importance, such as access to freeways or rail tracks, or sufficient availability of cheap energy. Just as an aluminum smelter needs access to rail tracks or an ample supply of energy, the data centers powering much of the digital world need connectivity to the Internet backbone and energy for powering and cooling the computers. With rising costs of energy, companies such as Google, Apple, and Facebook are not only looking for technological advances to increase the efficiency of their data centers, but also try to find geographical locations where energy efficiency can be optimized (Figure 3.3). One such example is search engine giant Google, which built a data center in an abandoned paper mill in Hamina, Finland, where the cool climate reduced the needs for cooling. This location also provided the necessary connectivity and allowed for using sea water for cooling. Likewise, Apple and Facebook built data centers in the high desert in Oregon, where power is cheap, and the cool climate significantly reduces the need for cooling.

For organizations operating globally, local differences in infrastructure pose additional challenges, particularly when operating in developing nations. For example, in many parts of the world, organizations cannot count on an uninterrupted supply of water or electricity. Consequently, many of the large call centers in India that support customers around the world for companies like Dell Computers or Citibank have installed massive power generators to minimize the effects of frequent power outages, or have set up their own satellite links to be independent from the local, unreliable communications networks.

Just as people and companies rely on basic municipal services to function, businesses rely on an **information systems infrastructure** (consisting of hardware, system software, storage,

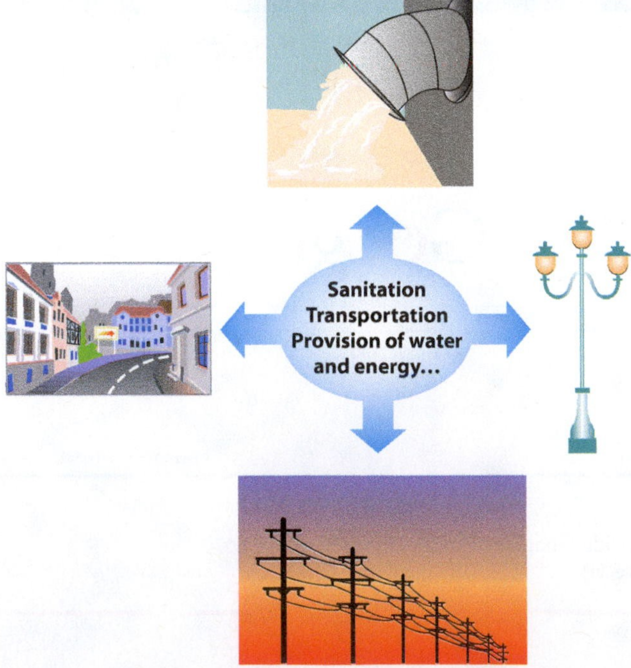

FIGURE 3.2

Infrastructure components of a city enable the provision of basic services.

FIGURE 3.3

Google uses solar energy to power its main campus in Mountain View, California.
Source: REUTERS/Kimberly White

networking, and data centers) to support their decision making, business processes, and competitive strategy. Earlier, we defined business processes as the activities organizations perform in order to reach their business goals, including core activities that transform inputs and produce outputs, and supporting activities that enable the core activities to take place. To enable such processes, organizations rely on three basic capabilities supported by information systems: processing, storage, and transmission of data (Figure 3.4). Hence, almost all of an organization's business processes depend on the underlying IS infrastructure, albeit to different degrees.

Organizations nowadays are facing continuously changing business environments. Traditionally, companies were operating in relatively stable markets, and could gain or sustain competitive advantage from relatively few innovations. Advances in information and communication technologies have leveled the playing field, allowing even small companies from all over the world to compete on a global scale. As new competitors can literally come out of nowhere, any competitive advantage will be increasingly short-lived, forcing organizations to keep innovating.

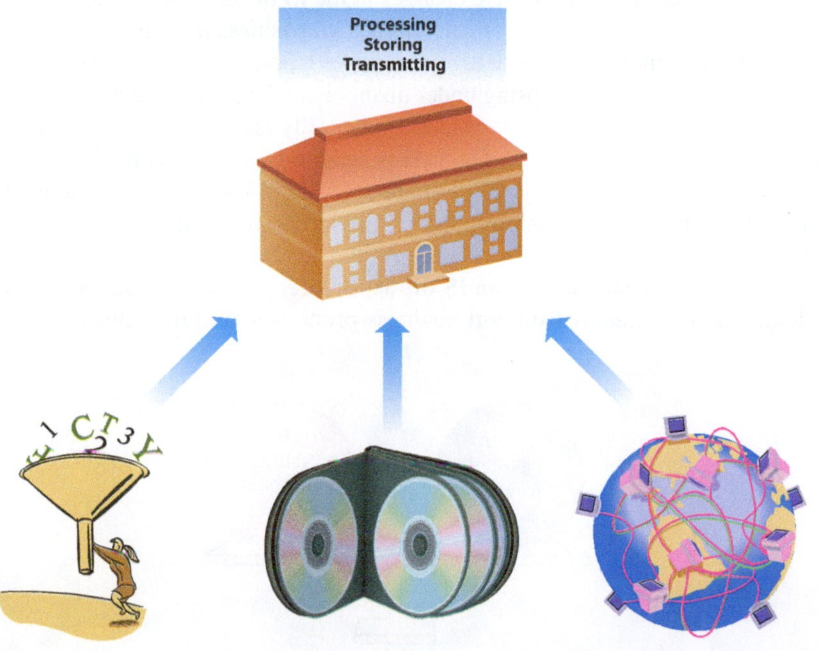

FIGURE 3.4

The information systems infrastructure enables processing, storing, and transmitting of data.

WHO'S GOING MOBILE

Mobile Developments in Developing Countries

In a relatively short period of time, mobile technologies have transformed the technology scene in many developing countries. These countries have historically had poor infrastructure for communications technologies such as telephone lines. With the comparatively low cost of cellular communications technologies, however, citizens of developing nations have rapidly adopted cell phones and, increasingly, smartphones. These devices are, for many people in developing countries, the only point of connection to the Internet and worldwide communications. But these devices have not only allowed for their users to connect with the worldwide economy, they have also transformed whole economies.

In the United States and other Western countries, there is frequent talk of mobile payment systems using cell phones. Many payment platforms have been developed, but none has obtained wide enough adoption for the service to be very useful. But care to make a guess where the largest of such mobile payment platforms is located? M-Pesa, located in Kenya, has revolutionized mobile technology for millions. In Kenya, it is easier to pay for a cab ride with your mobile phone than it is just about anywhere else in the world. Nearly 80 percent of Kenyans with cell phones use them for mobile payment and banking, primarily through the M-Pesa system. Half of all mobile money transactions in the world take place in Kenya, where annual transfers have reached US$10 billion, as of March 2014. M-Pesa provides the majority of the country's citizens with banking access, no matter how isolated they are, a key consideration given Kenya's spread-out populace.

Smartphones are still relatively rare in these countries, though adoption continues to accelerate. As smartphone proliferation continues, individuals in developing countries will have access to increasingly powerful technologies and Internet services.

Based on:

Anonymous. (2014, February 13). Emerging nations embrace internet, mobile technology. Pew Research. Retrieved May 16, 2014, from http://www.pewglobal.org/2014/02/13/emerging-nations-embrace-internet-mobile-technology.

Gilpin, L. (2014, March 12). The world's unlikely leader in mobile payments: Kenya. *Tech Republic*. Retrieved May 16, 2014, from http://www.techrepublic.com/article/the-worlds-unlikely-leader-in-mobile-payments-kenya.

Facing this situation, organizations have to adapt, or will sooner or later go out of business. Quickly adapting to a constantly changing competitive environment necessitates that businesses are increasingly flexible and agile. To achieve this flexibility and agility, organizations seek an alignment of their organizational strategy and business processes with the information systems architecture. As discussed in Chapter 2, "Gaining Competitive Advantage Through Information Systems," Business–IT alignment is a continuous process of adjusting business goals and the information systems infrastructure to achieve business objectives (Figure 3.5). To achieve alignment, changing business conditions drive changes in the IS infrastructure. Likewise, changes and enhancements in the IS infrastructure enable innovative business models and processes. In addition, any *lack* of availability, performance, or security (e.g., the news of an organization's Web site being attacked by hackers, or collapsing under unanticipated customer demand) is often immediately visible to customers or other stakeholders, potentially leading to loss of business, trust, and goodwill. Thus, organizations' business processes need to be supported by the right applications and the right data, which in turn rely on a solid underlying IS infrastructure (Figure 3.6). In sum, organizations rely on a complex, interrelated IS infrastructure to thrive in the ever-increasingly competitive digital world.

To get a better understanding of an IS infrastructure, we first provide a brief overview of how applications and databases support business processes, and then discuss how hardware,

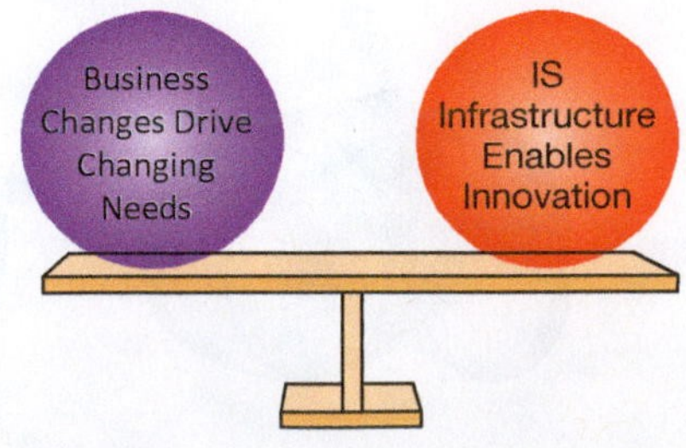

FIGURE 3.5

Business–IT alignment drives IS infrastructure changes, to enable innovative business models and processes.

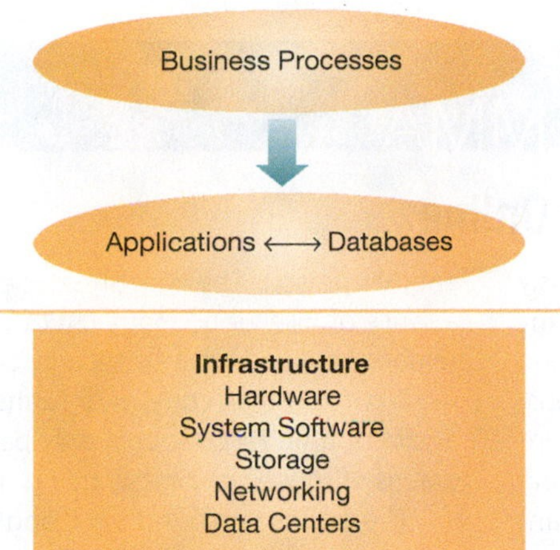

FIGURE 3.6

A solid IS infrastructure is needed to support an organization's business processes.

system software, storage, networking, and data centers interact to form an organization's IS infrastructure. Note that in this chapter, we will primarily focus on these components from a business perspective. For more technical details, please refer to the Technology Briefing.

Applications and Databases Supporting Business Processes

Data are probably among the most important assets an organization has, as data are essential for both executing business processes and gaining business intelligence. No matter what the business process is, data are used, processed, or generated along the way. For example, business processes associated with manufacturing products need data about inventory levels of raw materials, production capacities, and demand forecasts; likewise, back-office business processes associated with accounts receivable need data about customers, sales, receipts, and so on. In addition, increasing amounts of data are used for gaining business intelligence. Data once taken for granted or never collected at all are now used to make organizations more productive and competitive. Stock prices in the market, potential customers who meet a company's criteria for its products' target audiences, as well as the credit rating of wholesalers and customers are all types of data that organizations collect and analyze to turn into useful information. Yet, just having access to data is not sufficient; it is through applications that the data can be used effectively. Next, we briefly describe the role of application software in supporting an organization's business processes.

APPLICATION SOFTWARE. Organizations are continuously looking for ways to streamline and automate business processes, so as to generate more revenue or reduce costs, thus making the organization more profitable. **Application software** helps to automate business processes, and enables processes that would otherwise not even be possible. Accountants have for centuries used thick books for maintaining the accounting records of a business; automating the associated tasks using accounting software applications not only has helped to make the tasks less effortful and reduce error rates, but in addition allows quick analysis of accounting records, so as to examine sales trends, delinquencies, profit margins, and the like. Similarly, automating inventory management functions using specialized inventory management software not only helps keep a more accurate and up-to-date inventory, but can also generate a wealth of data that can be used to optimize inventory levels, taking into account the costs of keeping inventory and the potential costs of stockouts. E-commerce Web sites such as Amazon.com would not be possible without the applications needed for automatically processing transactions.

In addition to various types of application software for different business functions, other types of application software let users perform tasks such as writing business letters, managing stock portfolios, or manipulating forecasts to come up with the most efficient allocation of resources for a project. Application software also includes personal productivity software such as Microsoft Office; supply chain management systems to support the coordination of suppliers as well as the production and distribution of products or services; or customer relationship management (CRM) systems to help companies win and retain customers, gain marketing and customer insight, and focus on customer service (as discussed in Chapter 1, "Managing in the Digital World").

Many types of application software supporting business processes interact with databases, so as to efficiently retrieve and store the data needed for executing business processes and gaining business intelligence. Databases are discussed next.

ETHICAL DILEMMA

Putting People's Lives Online

Is that a man breaking into an apartment? There's obviously a house on fire. The lady in this picture looks exactly like my next-door neighbor, and those are obviously my clothes drying in my backyard. Search a random location on Google Maps, and you may find—via the Street View feature—the most unexpected candid shots of people walking on the street, waiting for a bus, or even hanging out in places they may not want others to know about. Without doubt, Google Maps can be tremendously useful; combining traditional maps, information from the Web, and innovative technology, the application is a helpful assistant for planning trips, locating businesses, and so on. However, Google Maps has been under fire since the introduction of the Street View feature, with many questioning whether a strict line has been unnecessarily crossed in the invasion of public privacy.

The biggest argument behind the dilemma is the collective sense of intrusion that has stimulated concerns of losing one's privacy—parents are worried pictures of their children could possibly make them targets of child predators, and people visiting adult shops simply do not find it essential for the entire world to know where they went last Saturday afternoon. Although Google has so far attempted to ease public concern by blurring the faces of people, license plate numbers, and house numbers, it still is rather awkward to find, say, a good shot of your underclothes hanging on the clothesline and be informed about it by another person. The way Street View operates indeed creates a sense of insecurity; many critics believe that Street View resembles having a gigantic security camera capturing their every move without their consent or further, even without their being aware of it (in fact, Google only periodically takes still photographs of streets, and these are quickly outdated).

The issues surrounding Google's Street View highlight an even broader issue: With ever more (often very personal) information being stored, shared, and exchanged in the cloud, companies such as Google, Facebook, and Apple effectively become the custodians of data that have the potential to ruin millions of people's lives. Having access to vast amounts of data provides the potential of monetizing the data in some way. Where can a company draw the line between the responsibility that comes with having access to the data and the responsibility toward the company's shareholders to maximize profits?

Based on:

Anonymous. (2014, May 17). Cut that link. *The Economist*. Retrieved May 16, 2014, from http://www.economist.com/news/business/21602239-european-court-justice-forces-google-remove-links-some-personal-information-cut.

Snyder, S. J. (2007, June 12) Google Maps: An invasion of privacy? *Time.com*. Retrieved May 16, 2014, from http://www.time.com/time/business/article/0,8599,1631957,00.html.

DATABASES. **Databases**, which are collections of related data organized in a way that facilitates data searches, are vital to an organization's operations and often are vital to competitive advantage and success. In organizations, databases are performing various important functions. On the most fundamental level, databases are used to store data and to make the data accessible where and when needed. More specifically, the use of databases to store organizational data ranging from inventory to demand forecasts to customer data enables applications from across an organization to access the data needed. Typically, various business processes throughout an organization make use of the same data, and providing the associated applications with quick and easy access to the data can help streamline and optimize these processes. For example, if a salesperson has access to inventory levels, she can quickly give precise estimates of delivery times, which may help close the sale. Similarly, if business processes associated with inbound logistics or operations have access to order forecasts, this can help to streamline procurement and production processes, helping to avoid stockouts and minimize money tied up in excess inventory. Well-managed databases can help to provide organization-wide access to the data needed for different business processes.

Additionally, database technology fuels electronic commerce, from helping to track available products for sale to providing customer service. For example, any product information you see on e-commerce sites such as Amazon.com is dynamically retrieved from a database; any changes to product information, pricing, or shipping estimates do not require changes to the product's Web page itself, but can be accomplished by simply changing the associated entry in the database. In order to harness the power of the data contained in the databases, organizations use **database management systems**, which are a type of software that allows organizations to more easily store, retrieve, and analyze data.

Finally, databases support storing and analyzing Big Data from a variety of sources. Gaining insights from internal and external sources (such as social media) can provide valuable business intelligence for organizations.

How these data are collected, stored, and manipulated is a significant factor influencing the success of modern organizations. As databases have become a critical component for most organizations, they rely on a solid underlying IS infrastructure (note that sometimes, databases are considered part of the infrastructure; given their importance and role in an organization's business processes, we do not consider them infrastructure). In Chapter 6, we talk more about the benefits of effectively and efficiently collecting, storing, and manipulating data stored in databases.

IS INFRASTRUCTURE COMPONENTS

Computing, storage, and networking technologies can create value by enabling efficiency, effectiveness, and agility. In recent times, fueled by globalization, e-commerce, and advances in technology, a well-functioning IS infrastructure has become increasingly important for organizations, leading to the need for making informed infrastructure decisions. In this section, we will introduce hardware, system software, storage, networking, and data centers, and discuss how making the right choices about the IS infrastructure can contribute to business success.

Hardware

A fundamental component of the IS infrastructure is the hardware—that is, the computers that run the applications and databases necessary for processing transactions or analyzing business data. As organizations need to carry out hundreds or thousands of different activities belonging to various business processes, they need different types of computers to support these processes. The five general classes of computers are supercomputer, mainframe, server, workstation, and personal computer (Table 3.1). A **supercomputer** is the most expensive and most powerful kind of computer; typically not used by business organizations, it is used primarily to assist in solving massive scientific problems. In contrast, large **mainframe** computers are used primarily as the main, central computing system for major corporations; optimized for high availability, resource utilization, and security, mainframes are typically used for mission-critical applications, such as transaction processing. A **server** is any computer on a network that makes access to files, printing, communications, and other services available to users of the network. Servers are used to provide services to users within large organizations or to Web users. Servers are optimized for access by many concurrent users and therefore have more advanced microprocessors, more memory, a larger cache, and more disk storage than single-user computers; servers also boast high reliability and fast network connectivity. To support different business processes, organizations often have many different servers in different configurations. For example, whereas some Web servers display the same static Web pages for every visitor (as is the case with many informational Web sites), others are designed to dynamically create Web pages based on user requests (e.g., Facebook displays content based on each individual user's network of friends); such servers have different requirements (e.g., in terms of processing power, network connectivity, or software) than e-mail servers, print servers, or other types of servers.

In contrast to mainframes and servers, which are designed for multiple concurrent users, workstations and personal computers are typically used by one user at a time. **Workstations**, designed for medical, engineering, architectural, or animation and graphics design uses, are optimized for visualization and rendering of 3D models, and typically have fast processors, large memory, and advanced video cards. **Personal computers (PCs)** are used for personal computing and small business computing. Over the past few years, portable computers—notebook computers, netbooks, tablets, and smartphones—have increasingly become part of an organization's information systems infrastructure. In contrast to general-purpose computers, **embedded systems** are optimized to perform a well-defined set of tasks, ranging from playing MP3 music files to controlling engine performance, traffic lights, or DVD players. In addition to the processing components, IS hardware also encompasses input devices (such as computer mice, touch screens, or cameras) and output devices (such as monitors, printers, or speakers). With the advent of the Internet of Things, various single-purpose, non-traditional computing devices are used to provide valuable data as input to these different processing technologies.

TABLE 3.1 Characteristics of Computers Currently Being Used in Organizations

Type of Computer	Number of Simultaneous Users	Physical Size	Typical Use	Memory	Possible Cost (in US$)
Supercomputer	One to many	Like an automobile to as large as multiple rooms	Scientific research	5,000+ GB	Up to $20 million
Mainframe	1,000+	Like a refrigerator	Transaction processing, enterprise-wide applications	Up to 3,000+ GB	Up to $10 million
Server	10,000+	Like a DVD player and mounted in a rack to fitting on a desktop	Providing Web sites or access to databases, applications, or files	Up to 512 GB	Up to $50,000
Workstation	Typically one	Fitting on a desktop to the size of a file cabinet	Engineering, medical, graphic design	Up to 512 GB	Up to $100,000
Personal computer	One	Fitting on a desktop	Personal productivity	512 MB to 32 GB	Up to $5,000

The application software used for various business processes cannot directly interact with these various types of hardware. Rather, the application software interacts with the system software, which, in turn, interacts with the computer hardware.

System Software

System software is the collection of programs that control the basic operations of computer hardware. The most prominent type of system software, the **operating system** (e.g., Windows 8, OS X, Ubuntu Linux), coordinates the interaction between hardware components (e.g., the CPU and the monitor), **peripherals** (e.g., printers), application software (e.g., office programs), and users, as shown in Figure 3.7. Operating systems are often written in assembly language, a very

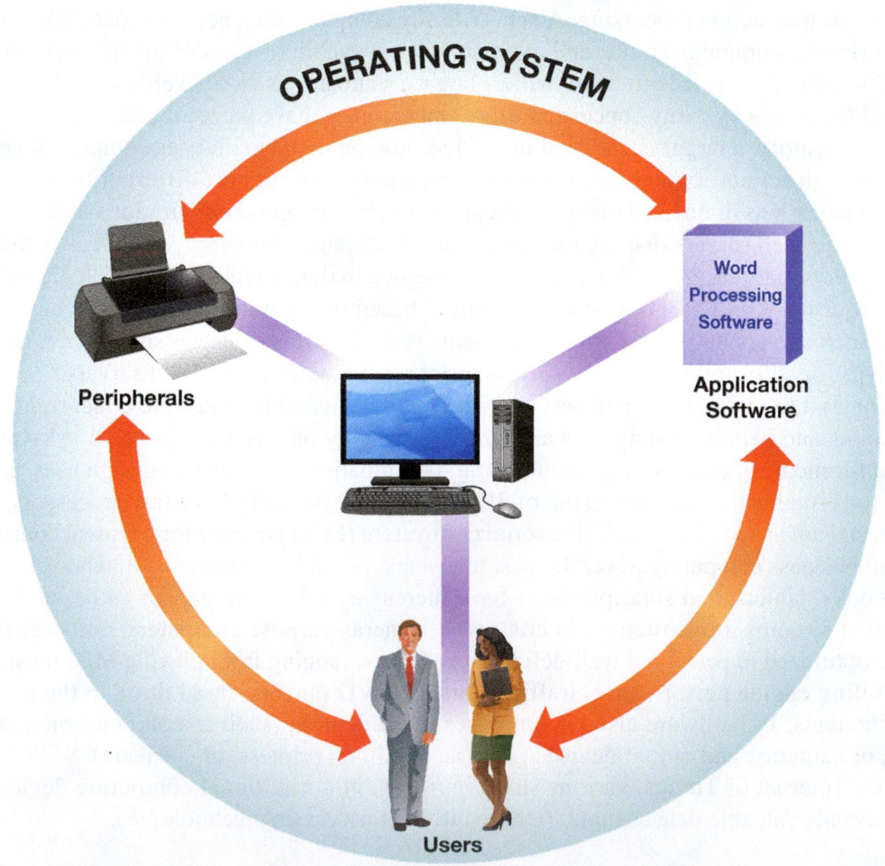

FIGURE 3.7

Operating systems coordinate the interaction between users, application software, hardware, and peripherals.

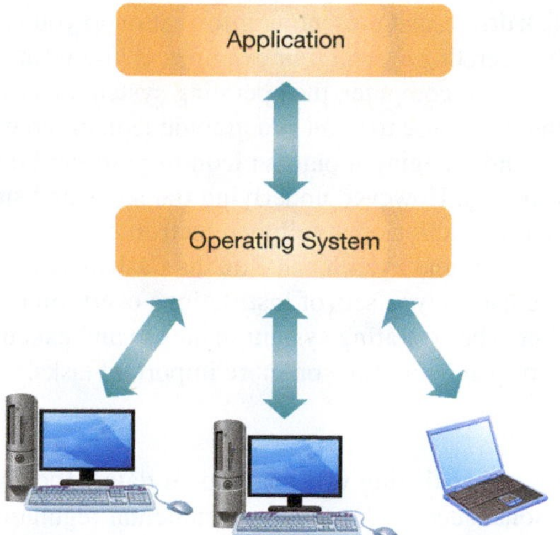

FIGURE 3.8

The operating system provides a common layer for different underlying devices, so that applications only have to be developed for different operating systems, rather than for each different computer model.

low-level computer programming language that allows the computer to operate quickly and efficiently. The operating system is designed to insulate you from this low-level language and make computer operations unobtrusive. Further, the operating system provides a common layer for different underlying devices, so that applications only have to be developed for different operating systems, rather than for each different computer model (Figure 3.8); **device drivers** allow the computer to communicate with various different hardware devices. The operating system performs all of the day-to-day operations that we often take for granted when using a computer, such as updating the system clock, printing documents, or saving data to a disk. Just as our brain and nervous system control our body's breathing, heartbeat, and senses without our conscious realization, the system software transparently controls the computer's basic operations.

COMMON OPERATING SYSTEM FUNCTIONS. Many tasks are common to almost all computers. These include getting input from a keyboard or mouse, reading from and/or writing to a storage

COMING ATTRACTIONS

Internet for Everyone

Billions of people around the world, especially in developing nations and in rural areas, do not have reliable access to the Internet. Someone who is not connected to the Internet is at a significant disadvantage in our globalized economy. If the Internet was made available to people in remote and developing locations, these people would be provided immense benefits. In addition, large Internet companies like Google and Facebook, which derive more value as more people use the Internet more often, are deeply interested in gaining access to the billions of people around the world currently unconnected. To this end, several companies are developing some innovative ways to bring the Internet to the remote areas of the world.

One such initiative is Google's Project Loon—an Internet delivery system that uses balloons designed to float around the world for up to 100 days at a time. Each balloon flies at an altitude of around 20 miles (32 km), is capable of raising and lowering itself automatically to access winds blowing in the desired direction, and is equipped with solar-powered wireless transmitters capable of delivering Internet at speeds similar to 3G cell phone data speeds. The balloons communicate with each other in a chain-linked network back to a land-based access point that connects the balloon network to the global Internet. Though still in testing phases, Project Loon has the potential to change the lives of many millions of currently unconnected people.

A similar effort from Facebook uses a different approach to accomplish the same goal. Facebook's project uses high-altitude, long-endurance drones, which can stay in the air for months at a time, to broadcast Wi-Fi signals to receivers on the ground below. These drones are intended to provide more densely populated areas with Internet connectivity. Facebook's team is also exploring the use of low-Earth-orbit satellites that can beam Internet access to the ground. Whether these or other, similar projects ultimately succeed, it is clear that companies are working hard to bring the Internet to the unconnected masses.

Based on:

Johnston, C. (2014, March 28). Facebook's solar-powered planes will provide Wi-Fi to the 'burbs. *Arstechnica*. Retrieved May 17, 2014, from http://arstechnica.com/information-technology/2014/03/facebook-to-provide-internet-connectivity-from-solar-powered-planes.

Google. (n.d.). Project Loon. *Google.com*. Retrieved July 16, 2014, from http://www.google.com/loon.

device (such as a hard disk drive), and presenting information to you via a monitor. Each of these tasks is performed by the operating system. For example, if you want to copy a word processing file from a flash drive onto your computer, the operating system makes this very easy for you, as all it takes is simply using the mouse to point at a graphic icon of the word processing file on the flash drive, then clicking and dragging it onto an icon of your hard disk. The operating system makes this process appear easy. However, underlying the icons and simple dragging operations is a complex set of coded instructions that tell the electronic components of the computer that you are transferring a set of bits and bytes located on the flash drive to a location on your internal hard disk. Imagine if you had to type sets of instructions every time you wanted to copy a file from one place to another. The operating system manages and executes these types of system operations so that you can spend your time on more important tasks.

Storage

In addition to processing and analyzing vast amounts of data, efficiently storing and retrieving data is key for organizational success. Further, governmental regulations such as the Sarbanes–Oxley Act mandate archiving business documents and relevant internal communication, including e-mail and instant messages. Hence, organizations are faced with the need to reliably process and store tremendous amounts of data, and this storage requirement is growing at an increasing rate. Earlier, we discussed the role of databases in supporting organization-wide business processes. To enable efficient storage and retrieval of the content of such databases (as well as digital content not stored in databases), organizations need to have a solid storage infrastructure. Typically, organizations store data for three distinct purposes, each with distinct requirements in terms of timeliness, access speed, and life span (Figure 3.9):

- Operational—for example, for processing transactions or for data analysis
- Backup—short-term copies of organizational data, used to recover from system-related disaster (Backup data are frequently overwritten with newer backups.)
- Archival—long-term copies of organizational data, often used for compliance and reporting purposes

These different uses of organizational data call for different physical storage technologies. For example, operational data are typically stored in databases (e.g., data from transaction processing systems or customer data) or files (e.g., business documents, images, or company brochures) using disk-based storage media such as hard drives. Hard drives offer high access speeds and are thus preferred for data that are frequently accessed or where response time is of the essence (as in an e-commerce Web site); in addition, flash-based storage is increasingly used for situations where access speed is of crucial importance. To ensure continuous business operations in case disaster strikes, organizations periodically back up their data to a secure location; often, companies have completely redundant systems so as to be able to seamlessly continue business

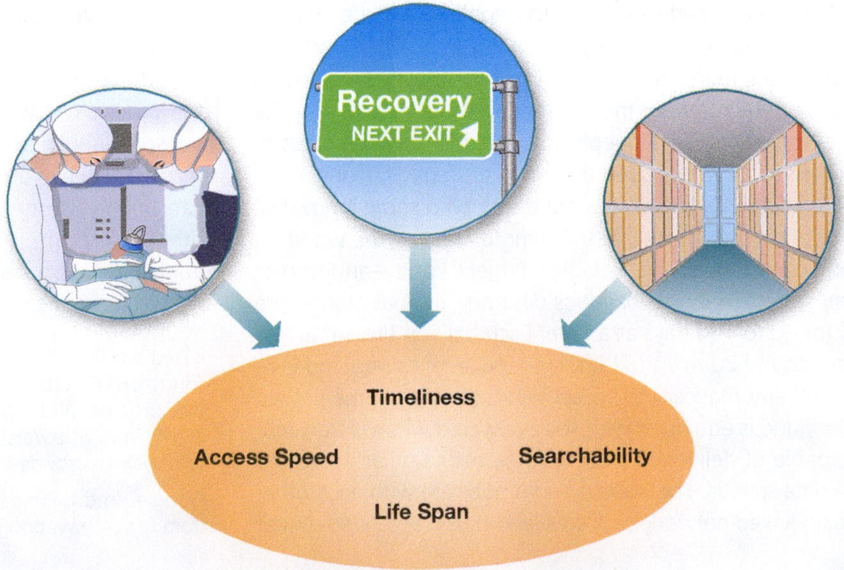

FIGURE 3.9

Operational, backup, and archival data have different requirements.

if the primary systems fail (see Chapter 10, "Securing Information Systems"). Storing backup data on hard drives enables quick recovery without slowing the company's operations. Data that are no longer used for operational purposes (such as old internal e-mails) are archived for long-term storage, typically on magnetic tapes. As data are stored sequentially on magnetic tapes, access speed can be very slow; however, magnetic tape has a shelf life of up to 30 years, is very low cost as compared to other storage media, and is removable, meaning that it is highly expandable and tapes can be easily stored in a secure, remote location (see the Technology Briefing for more on different storage technologies).

Networking

As you have seen, organizations depend on a variety of different applications, hardware, and storage technologies to support their business processes: Organizations have servers, mainframes, personal computers, storage devices, mobile devices, environmental control systems, and various other devices. Yet, taken alone, each individual piece of technology has little value; it is through connecting the different pieces that business value can be realized: For example, the best-performing database would be useless if it could not be accessed by those people or applications throughout the organization that depend on the data. Further, one of the reasons why information systems have become so powerful and important is the ability to interconnect, allowing internal and external constituents to communicate and collaborate with each other. The infrastructure supporting this consists of a variety of components, such as the networking hardware and software that facilitate the interconnection of different computers, enabling collaboration within organizations, across organizations, and literally around the world.

HUMAN COMMUNICATION AND COMPUTER NETWORKING. Human communication involves the sharing of information and messages between senders and receivers. The sender of a message formulates the message in his brain and codes the message into a form that can be communicated to the receiver—through voice, for example. The message is then transmitted along a communication pathway to the receiver. The receiver, using her ears and brain, then attempts to decode the message, as shown in Figure 3.10. This basic model of human communication helps us to understand telecommunications or computer networking. **Computer networking** is the sharing of data or services. The information source produces a message, which is encoded so that it can be transmitted via a communication channel; a receiver then decodes the message so that it can be understood by the destination. Thus, analogous to human communication, computer networks require three things:

- A sender (source) and a receiver (destination) that have something to share (a message)
- A pathway or transmission medium, such as a cable, to send the message
- Rules or protocols dictating communication between senders and receivers

The easiest way to understand computer networking is through the human communication model. Suppose you are applying for a job in France after graduation. You need information about different employers. The first requirement for a network—information to share—has now been met. After contacting a few potential employers, a company sends you information about its hiring process (the encoded message) via e-mail. This is the second requirement: a means of transmitting the coded message. The Internet is the pathway or transmission medium used to contact

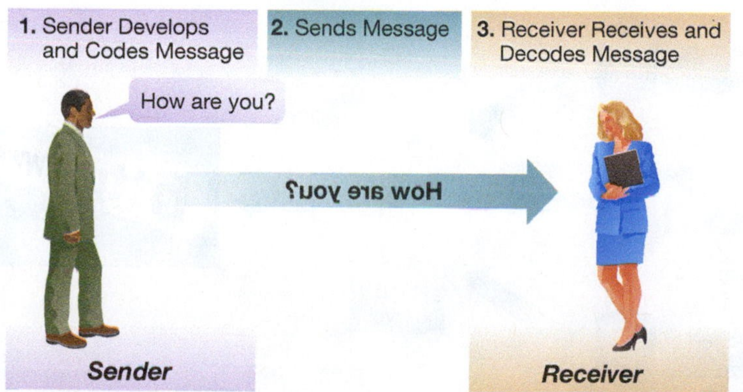
1. Sender Develops and Codes Message
2. Sends Message
3. Receiver Receives and Decodes Message
How are you?
How are you?
Sender
Receiver

FIGURE 3.10

Communication requires senders, a message to share, and receivers.

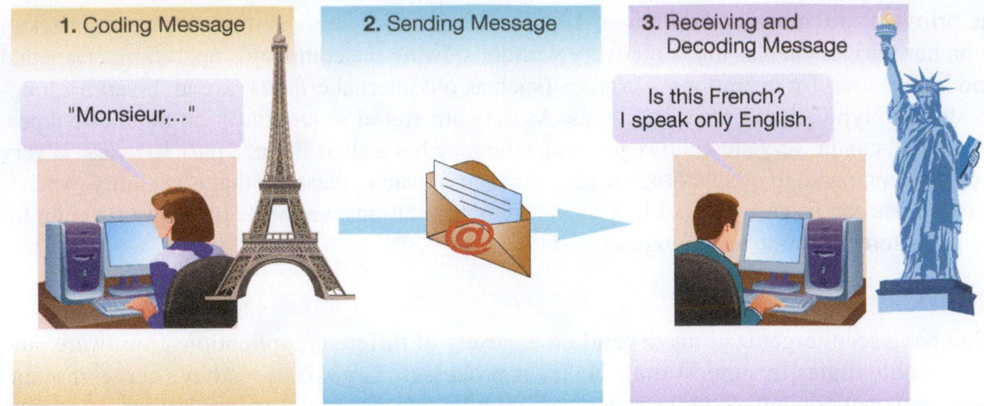

FIGURE 3.11

Coding, sending, and decoding a message.

the receiver. **Transmission media** refers to the physical pathway—cable(s) and wireless—used to carry network information. At this point, you may run into some difficulties. If the potential employer has sent you information in French, you may not understand what they have written—that is, decode their message—if you don't speak French; if the message is not understood by the receiver, there is no communication. Although you have contacted the receiver, you and the receiver of your message must meet the third requirement for successful communication: You must establish a language of communication—the rules or protocols governing your communication. **Protocols** define the procedures that different computers follow when they transmit and receive data. You both might decide that one communication protocol will be that you communicate in English. This communication session is illustrated in Figure 3.11.

COMPUTER NETWORKS. A fundamental difference between human and computer communication is that human communication consists of words, whereas computer communication consists of bits, the fundamental information units of computers. Virtually all types of information can be transmitted on a computer network—documents, art, music, or film—although each type of information has vastly different requirements for effective transmission. For example, a page of text is approximately 14 KB of data, whereas a publication-quality photograph could be larger than 200 MB of data. Similarly, to support different business processes, vast amounts of data have to be transmitted. For example, a customer viewing a product on Amazon.com receives a Web page that is assembled by a Web server using data coming from different databases (e.g., containing data about products, inventory, pricing, or customer reviews), a content server (e.g., for product images), and other sources (Figure 3.12); the actual transaction then involves product data, inventory data, customer data, payment data, confirmation e-mails, and so on. To transmit such vast amounts of data in a timely manner from one location to another, adequate bandwidth is needed. **Bandwidth** is the transmission capacity of a computer or communications channel, measured in bits per second (bps) or multiples thereof, and represents how much binary data can be reliably transmitted over the medium in one second. To appreciate the importance of bandwidth for speed, consider how long it would take to download a 45-minute TV show (about 200 megabytes) from iTunes. It would take about six minutes at 1 megabit per second (Mbps) (regular cable or DSL connection) and 2 minutes at 15 Mbps (high-speed cable or DSL connection). In contrast, using an old-fashioned PC modem that transmits data at a rate of 56 kilobits per second (Kbps), it would almost nine hours

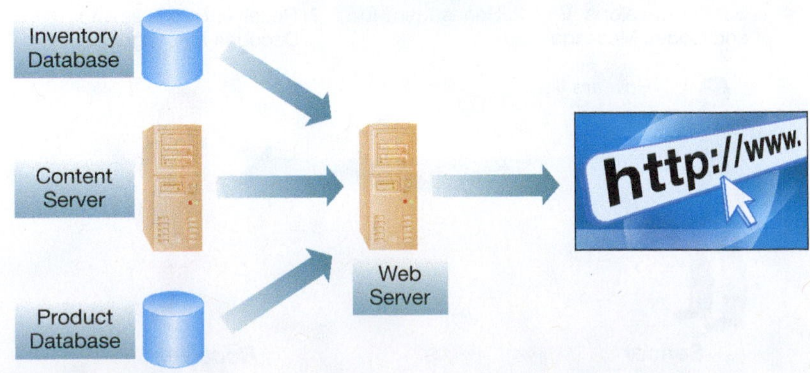

FIGURE 3.12

Dynamic Web pages are assembled using data from various data sources.

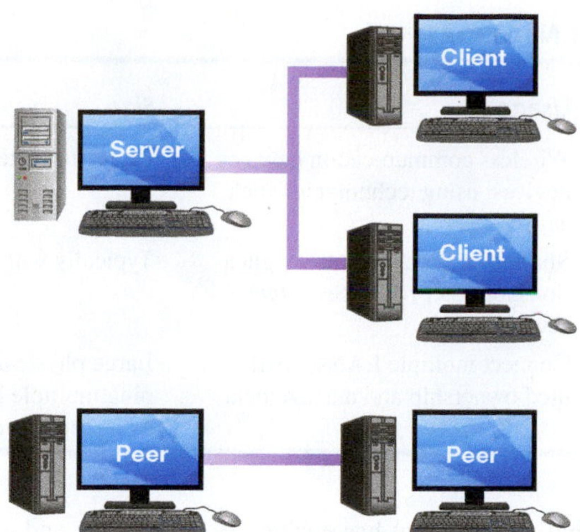

FIGURE 3.13

A server is a computer on the network that enables multiple computers (or "clients") to access data. A peer is a computer that may both request and provide services.

to transmit the same TV show. Hence, different types of information have different communication bandwidth requirements (see www.numion.com/Calculators/Time.html for a tool that helps you calculate download times). Typical local area networks have a bandwidth of 10 Mbps to 1 Gbps.

Telecommunications advances have enabled individual computer networks—constructed with different hardware and software—to connect together in what appears to be a single network. Networks are increasingly being used to dynamically exchange relevant, value-adding information and knowledge throughout global organizations and institutions. The following sections take a closer look at the fundamental building blocks of these complex networks and the services they provide.

Servers, Clients, and Peers Computers in a **network** typically have one of three distinct roles—servers, clients, and peers—as depicted in Figure 3.13. A server is any computer on the network that makes access to files, printing, communications, and other services available to users of the network. Servers only provide services. A **client** is any computer, such as a user's PC or laptop, on the network, or any software application, such as Microsoft's Outlook e-mail client, that uses the services provided by the server. Clients only request services. A client usually has only one user, whereas many different users share the server. So-called **thin clients**—microcomputers with minimal memory, storage, and processing capabilities—use **desktop virtualization** to provide workers with a virtual desktop environment, helping to reduce costs for software licensing or maintenance and to comply with stringent privacy and data protection laws. A **peer** is any computer that may both request and provide services. The trend in business is to use **client-server networks**, in which servers and clients have defined roles. With ubiquitous access to company local area networks (LANs) and the Internet, almost everyone works in a client-server environment today. In contrast, **peer-to-peer networks** (often abbreviated as P2P) enable any computer or device on the network to provide and request services; these networks can be found in small offices and homes. In P2P networks, all peers have equivalent capabilities and responsibilities; this is the network architecture behind the Internet telephony service Skype and popular file-sharing protocols such as BitTorrent, which allow peers to connect directly to the hard drives of other peers on the Internet that are utilizing the software.

Types of Networks Computing networks are commonly classified by size, distance covered, and structure. The most commonly used classifications are a **personal area network**, **local area network**, and **wide area network** (Table 3.2). These networks are typically used to connect devices within an organization, or across organizational subunits. Wide area networks can range from spanning multiple buildings (sometimes called a **campus area network**) to covering the area of a city (sometimes called a **metropolitan area network**) to worldwide (the Internet). To enable the connection of mobile devices, or to install a network where running cables is infeasible, organizations install **wireless local area networks (WLANs)** using high-frequency radio-wave technology; WLANs are also referred to as **Wi-Fi networks (wireless fidelity)**. The ease of installation has made WLANs popular for business and home use, and public WLANs can be found in many coffee shops, airports, or university campuses. For more on the different types of networks, see the Technology Briefing.

TABLE 3.2 Types of Networks

Type	Usage	Size
Personal area network (PAN)	Wireless communication between devices, using technologies such as Bluetooth	Under 10 meters
Local area network (LAN)	Sharing of data, software applications, or other resources between several users	Typically within a building
Wide area network (WAN)	Connect multiple LANs, distributed ownership and management	Large physical distance, from spanning multiple buildings or the area of a city, up to worldwide (Internet)

THE INTERNET. One global network that has enabled organizations and individuals to interconnect in a variety of ways is the **Internet**, a large worldwide collection of networks that use a common protocol to communicate with each other. The name "Internet" is derived from the concept of internetworking, which means connecting host computers and their networks together to form even larger networks.

WORLD WIDE WEB. One of the most powerful uses of the Internet is something that you probably use almost every day—the World Wide Web. The **World Wide Web** is a system of interlinked documents on the Internet, or a graphical user interface to the Internet that provides users with a simple, consistent interface to access a wide variety of information. A **Web browser** is a software application that can be used to locate and display Web pages, including text, graphics, and multimedia content.

A key feature of the Web is **hypertext**. A hypertext document, otherwise known as a **Web page**, contains not only information but also **hyperlinks**, which are references or links to other documents. The standard method of specifying the structure and content of Web pages is called **Hypertext Markup Language (HTML)**. Specific content within each Web page is enclosed within codes, or markup tags, that stipulate how the content should appear to the user. These Web pages are stored on **Web servers**, which process user requests for pages using the **Hypertext Transfer Protocol (HTTP)**. Web servers typically host a collection of interlinked Web pages (called a **Web site**) that are owned by the same organization or by an individual. Web sites and specific Web pages within those sites have a unique Internet address. A user who wants to access a Web page enters the address, and the Web server hosting the Web site retrieves the desired page from its hard drive and delivers it to the user.

Web Domain Names and Addresses A **Uniform Resource Locator (URL)** is used to identify and locate a particular Web page. For example, www.google.com is the URL used to find the main Google Web server. The URL has three distinct parts: the domain, the top-level domain, and the host name (Figure 3.14).

The **domain name** is a term that helps people recognize the company or person that the domain name represents. For example, Google's domain name is google.com. The prefix *google* lets you know that it is very likely that this domain name will lead you to the Web site of Google. Domain names also have a suffix that indicates which **top-level domain** they belong to.

FIGURE 3.14
Dissecting a URL.

For example, the ".com" suffix is reserved for commercial organizations. Some other popular suffixes are listed here:

- .edu—educational institutions
- .org—organizations (non-profit)
- .gov—U.S. government entity
- .net—network organizations
- .de—Germany (there are over 240 two-letter "country code top-level domains")

Domain names can be registered through many different companies (known as registrars) that compete with one another. Given the proliferation of domain names, more generic top-level domains (gTLDs) have been added, such as .aero for the air transport industry, .name for individuals, .coop for business industry cooperatives, and .museum for museums. Recently, the ICANN (Internet Corporation for Assigned Names and Numbers—the organization that coordinates the domain name system) relaxed the strict rules for gTLDs, so that regions, businesses, or other entities can apply for their own gTLD. For example, new gTLDs include .bike, .club, .tips, and .cab, as well as many other gTLDs coming soon.

The host name is the particular Web server or group of Web servers (if it is a larger Web site) that will respond to the request. In most cases, the "www" host name refers to the default Web site including the home page of the particular domain. Other host names can be used. For example, drive.google.com will take you to the group of Web servers that are responsible for serving up Google's cloud-based storage for documents. Larger companies have several host names for their different functions. Some examples used by Google are the following:

- mail.google.com (Google's free e-mail service)
- picasa.google.com (Google's application for organizing and editing photos)
- maps.google.com (Google's mapping application)

All the domain names and the host names are associated with one or more Internet protocol (IP) addresses. For example, the domain name google.com represents about a dozen underlying **IP addresses**. IP addresses serve to identify all the computers or devices on the Internet. The IP address serves as the destination address of that computer or device and enables the network to route messages to the proper destination. Traditionally, the format of an IP address (version 4) is a 32-bit numeric address written as four numbers separated by periods (the latest version, IPv6 uses 128-bit addresses, enabling more devices to be connected to the Internet). Each of the four numbers can be any number between 0 and 255. For example, 128.196.134.37 is an underlying IP address of www.arizona.edu, the University of Arizona's main Web page.

IP addresses can also be used instead of URLs to navigate to particular Web addresses. This practice is not done regularly, as IP addresses are far more difficult to remember than domain names, and an organization may assign their domain name to a server with a different IP address; for example, whereas the IP address behind google.com may change, the domain name stays the same.

In addition to specifying the address of the Web server, URLs typically also include the path to the requested resource, such as a particular page located in a particular directory (e.g., http://mis.eller.arizona.edu/faculty/index.asp).

World Wide Web Architecture The Web consists of a large number of interconnected Web servers, which host the sites users access with their Web browsers. The Internet uses the **Transmission Control Protocol/Internet Protocol (TCP/IP)** to facilitate the transmission of Web pages and other information. Users can access Web pages by entering the URL of the Web page into their Web browser. Once the user enters the URL into the address bar of the Web browser, TCP/IP breaks the request into packets and routes them over the Internet to the Web server where the requested Web page is stored. When the packets reach their destination, TCP/IP reassembles them and passes the request to the Web server. The Web server understands that the user is requesting a Web page (indicated by the http:// prefix in the URL) and retrieves the Web page, which is packetized by TCP/IP and transmitted over the Internet back to the user's computer. TCP/IP reassembles the packets at the destination and delivers the Web page to the Web browser. In turn, the Web browser translates the HTML code contained in the Web page, formats its physical appearance, and displays the results. If the Web page contains a hyperlink, the user can click on it and the process repeats.

INTRANETS AND EXTRANETS. As organizations have realized the advantage of using the Internet and Web to communicate public information outside corporate boundaries, they can

BRIEF CASE For Sale by Owner: Your Company's Name.com

They don't sell houses or land, but they do deal in Internet real estate, and most turn a handsome profit. "They" are called domainers, and the real estate they buy and sell consists of domain names on the Web (such as www.cellphones.com). Although they keep a low profile and usually don't flaunt their success, domainers participated in a virtual land grab worth US$23 billion in 2009, with no end in sight. In January 2012, there were over 220 million registered domain names. In 2014, the first of what will eventually be 1,000 new "generic top-level domains" were put up for sale, including .bike, .clothing, and .guru. This new expansion beyond the regular .com and .edu domains gave domainers an even larger market to work with.

Domainers trade on the fact that many businesses, organizations, and celebrities want domain names for their Web sites that clearly identify the site's owner and are, therefore, easy for Web surfers to find. A domainer might buy the domain names "adidas.clothing," for instance, and then try to sell it to Adidas; that is exactly how the domain-buying business operated in the 1990s: buy a name, hold it, and wait for a buyer who wanted it to make an offer. But when pay-per-click advertising was developed, the game changed. Currently, domainers can profit most by renting advertising space on the domain names they hold to marketers. Here is how the domainer makes a profit from renting ad space: (1) Buy and hold a general domain name, such as "cellphones.com"; (2) direct Web traffic to a middleman, called an aggregator, who designs a Web site and then taps into Yahoo!, Google, or Microsoft's advertising networks and lists the best-paying clients; (3) each time a searcher clicks on one of the URLs listed on the domain name's page, the search engine owner (Yahoo!, Google, or Microsoft) or advertiser pays the domainer a fee.

In March 2008, the U.S. Congress proposed the Anti-Phishing Consumer Protection Act, but this bill has stalled. In addition to its fight against phishing, the bill was intended to levy heavy fines on domainers that violated company trademarks. While formal legislation has stalled, some actions have been taken to curb domainers. For instance, a number of large international corporations including Dell, DIRECTV, Hilton, Nike, and Wells Fargo joined together and formed the Coalition Against Domain Name Abuse, Inc. (CADNA), which aims to build awareness and stop this practice.

Questions

1. How do you feel about domainers? Is it an ethical business?
2. Discuss the pros and cons of having Google, Yahoo!, Bing, and others "cut out" domainers as middlemen in the Web search process.

Based on:

Fisher, D. (2014, February 27). Cybersquatters rush to claim brands in the new GTLD territories. *Forbes*. Retrieved May 15, 2014, from http://www.forbes.com/sites/danielfisher/2014/02/27/cybersquatters-rush-to-claim-brands-in-the-new-gtld-territories.

Anonymous. (2014). CADNA—The Coalition Against Domain Name Abuse. Retrieved May 15, 2014, from http://www.cadna.org.

also leverage Web-based technologies to support proprietary, internal communications through the implementation of an **intranet**. An intranet looks and acts just like a publicly accessible Web site and uses the same software, hardware, and networking technologies to communicate information. All intranet pages are behind the company's *firewall*, which secures proprietary information stored within the corporate local area network and/or wide area network so that the information can be viewed only by authorized users.

In the simplest form of an intranet, communications take place only within the confines of organizational boundaries and do not travel across the Internet. Organizations can use intranets for disseminating corporate information, employee training, project management, collaboration, or enabling employee self-service for administering benefits, managing retirement plans, or other human resources–based applications through *employee portals*.

Increases in employees' mobility necessitate that an intranet be accessible from anywhere. Thus, most companies allow their employees to use *virtual private networks (VPNs)* to securely connect to the company's intranet while on the road or working from home (i.e., telecommuting). Figure 3.15 depicts a typical intranet system architecture (see Chapter 10 for more on firewalls and VPNs).

Similar to an intranet, an **extranet**, which can be regarded as a private part of the Internet that is cordoned off from ordinary users, enables two or more firms to use the Internet to do business together. Although the content is "on the Web," only authorized users can access it after logging on to the company's extranet Web site. As an extranet uses the public (and normally insecure) Internet infrastructure to connect two or more business partners, it often uses VPNs to ensure the secured transmission of proprietary information between business partners (Figure 3.16). To access information on an extranet, authorized business partners access their business partner's main extranet Web page using their Web browsers. Table 3.3 summarizes the similarities and differences between intranets, extranets, and the Internet.

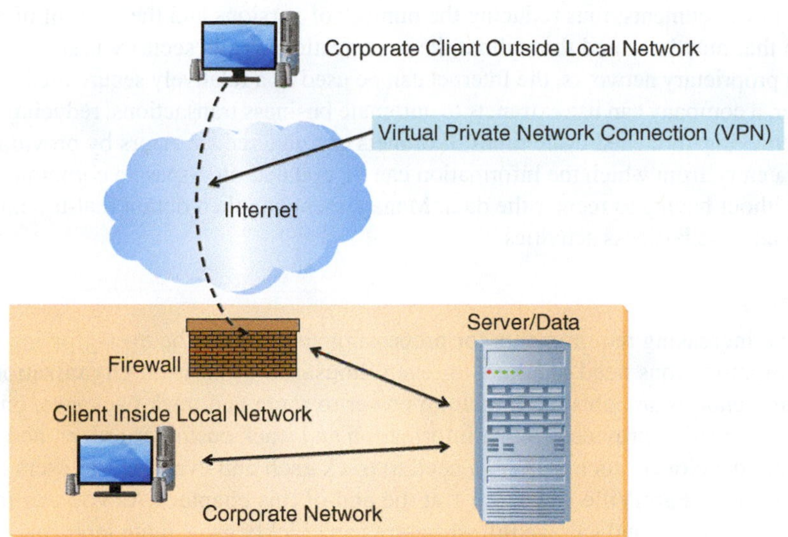

FIGURE 3.15
Typical intranet system architecture.

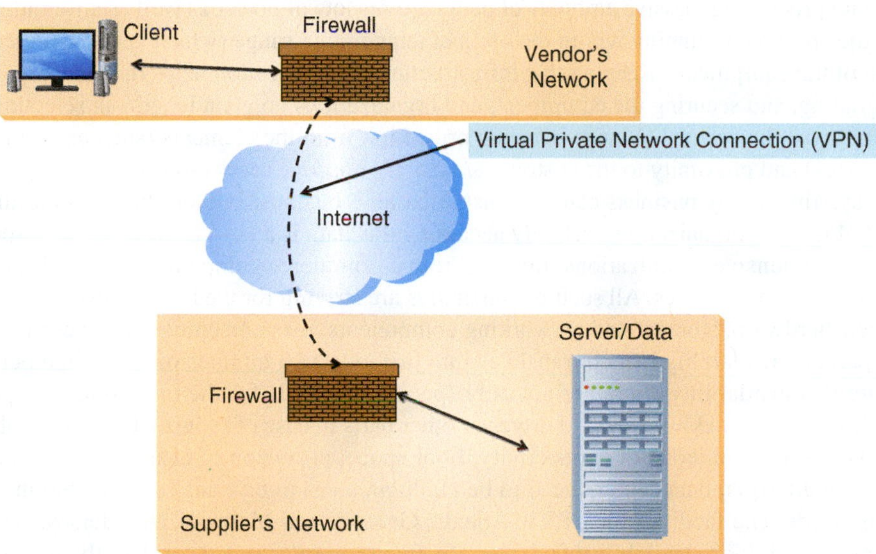

FIGURE 3.16
Typical extranet system architecture.

TABLE 3.3 Characteristics of the Internet, Intranet, and Extranet

	Focus	Type of Information	Users	Access
Internet	External communications	General, public, and "advertorial" information	Any user with an Internet connection	Public and not restricted
Intranet	Internal communications	Specific, corporate, and proprietary information	Authorized employees	Private and restricted
Extranet	External communications	Communications between business partners	Authorized business partners	Private and restricted

Source: Based on Szuprowicz (1998) and Turban, King, Lee, Liang, and Turban (2012).

Extranets benefit corporations in a number of ways. For example, extranets can dramatically improve the timeliness and accuracy of communications, reducing the potential for misunderstandings within the organization as well as with business partners and customers. In the business world, very little information is static; therefore, information must be continually updated and disseminated as it changes. Extranets facilitate this process by providing a cost-effective, global medium over which proprietary information can be distributed. Furthermore, they allow central management of documents, thus reducing the number of versions and the amount of out-of-date information that may be stored throughout the organization. While security is still considered to be better on proprietary networks, the Internet can be used as a relatively secure medium for business. Further, a company can use extranets to automate business transactions, reducing processing costs and achieving shortened cycle times. Extranets can also reduce errors by providing a single point of data entry from which the information can be updated on disparate corporate computing platforms without having to reenter the data. Management can then obtain real-time information to track and analyze business activities.

Data Centers

To satisfy the increasing requirements for processing and storing the ever-growing volume of data, large organizations need hundreds or even thousands of servers. Organizations such as UPS need tremendous amounts of computing power to route and track packages, online stores such as Zappos need to provide product information and track customer orders, and social networking game developers such as Zynga need to track each and every action users take on the once-popular game FarmVille (see Case 1 at the end of this chapter). As you can imagine, an organization's hardware and storage infrastructure can quickly grow quite large, and companies typically set aside dedicated space for their infrastructure components (such data centers can range in size from a single dedicated server room to buildings the size of a large warehouse). Storing and processing massive amounts of data requires lots of power as well as air-conditioning to keep the equipment running within the optimal temperature range (which helps to increase the life span of the equipment). Keeping this infrastructure in one location helps in managing, repairing, upgrading, and securing the equipment, and organizations go great lengths in selecting locations that strike the optimal balance between protection from the elements (such as earthquakes or hurricanes) and proximity to the customers/users (to improve access speeds).

Today, almost any business can be considered an e-business. Given that data are the lifeblood of almost all organizations, reliably accessing this data is a key concern. This is especially true for data-intensive organizations, ranging from e-commerce companies to logistics companies to government agencies. All such organizations are striving for the highest level of availability of their hardware, storage, and networking components, often reaching for "five-nines" (i.e., 99.999 percent availability, which translates into just over five minutes of downtime per year). To ensure this availability, there are not only specific demands for the individual components (e.g., being able to quickly swap hard drives or other parts in case of failure), but also for the data center overall (e.g., in terms of connectivity, floor space, provision of energy and cooling, and security). In addition, data centers need to be modular, so as to be easily expandable in case of changing needs. The facilities for UPS in Atlanta, Georgia, and Mahwah, New Jersey, are prime examples of such high-availability facilities. To ensure uninterrupted service, the data centers are self-sufficient, and each can operate for up to two days on self-generated power. The power is needed not only for the computers but also for air-conditioning, as each facility needs air-conditioning capacity equaling that of or more than 2,000 homes. In case power fails, the cooling is provided using more than 600,000 gallons of chilled water, and the UPS facilities even have backup wells in case the municipal water supply should fail. Other protective measures include raised floors (to protect from floods) and buildings designed to withstand winds of 200 miles per hour. Alternatively, organizations can rent space for their servers in collocation facilities, which are data centers managed by a third party that rents out space to multiple organizational customers (see Chapter 10 for more on securing data centers and collocation facilities).

ISSUES ASSOCIATED WITH MANAGING THE IS INFRASTRUCTURE

Needless to say, for organizations, obtaining, operating, maintaining, and upgrading the information systems infrastructure can be a tremendous challenge, especially when this is not part of their core business.

As you have undoubtedly noticed, computing technology has evolved rapidly and will most likely continue to evolve rapidly in the future. In general, because of the increasing pace of change with modern technologies, most organizations face accelerating obsolescence of their hardware and software investments as well as increasing storage and space constraints, demand

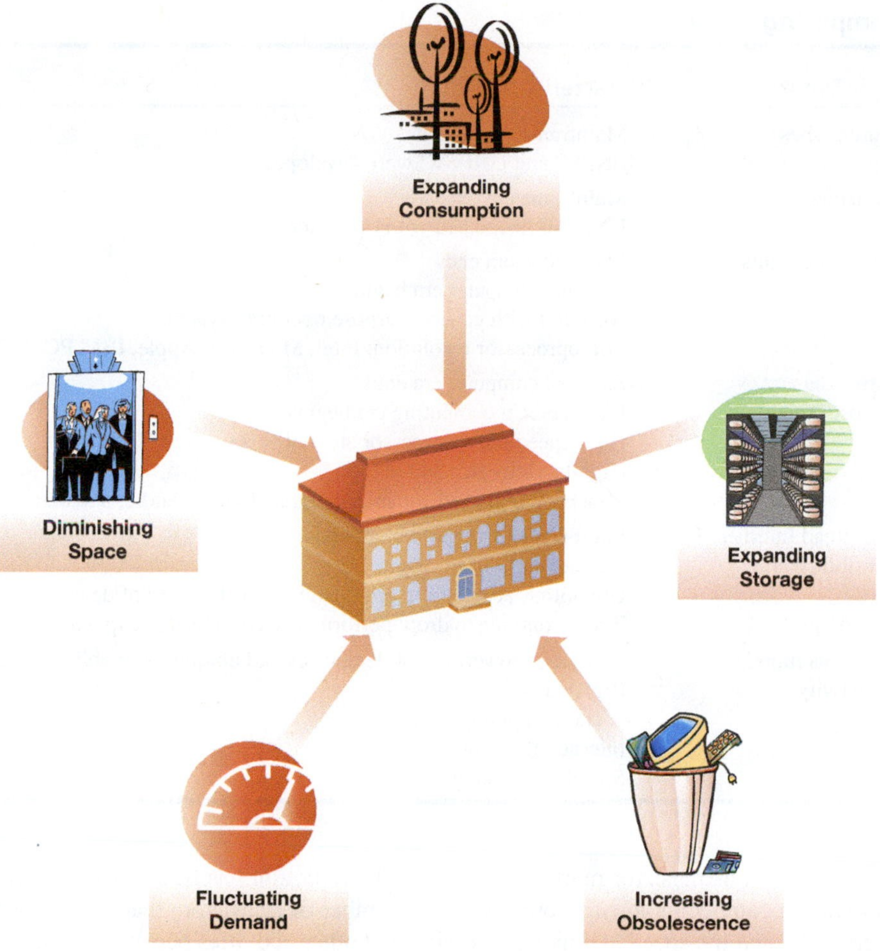

FIGURE 3.17
Information systems infrastructure challenges for modern organizations.

fluctuations, and increasing energy costs (Figure 3.17). In the following section, we discuss how the interplay between the different infrastructure components both encourages and necessitates continuous upgrading of the infrastructure.

Rapid Obsolescence and Shorter IT Cycles

Over the past 75 years, information systems have gone through many radical changes. Rapid advances in both hardware and software capabilities have enabled or facilitated many business processes, and organizations are continuously faced with the need to upgrade the IS infrastructure so as to gain or maintain competitive advantage. In this section, we discuss the history of computing, as well as the effects of rapid advances in technology.

BRIEF HISTORY OF COMPUTING. When the Zuse Z1 Computer (a mechanical computer using program punch cards) was introduced in 1936, almost all business and government information systems consisted of file folders, filing cabinets, and document repositories. Huge rooms were dedicated to the storage of these records. Information was often difficult to find, and corporate knowledge and history were difficult to maintain. Only certain employees knew specific information. When these employees left the firm, so did all their knowledge about the organization. The computer provided the solution to the information storage and retrieval problems facing organizations up to the 1940s. Shifts in computing eras were facilitated by fundamental changes in the way computing technologies worked. Each of these fundamental changes is referred to as a distinct generation of computing. Table 3.4 highlights the technology that defined the six generations of computing.

MOORE'S LAW. In 1965, Intel cofounder Dr. Gordon Moore hypothesized that the number of transistors on a chip would double about every two years. When Moore made this bold prediction, he did not limit it to any specified period of time. This prediction became known as **Moore's law**. Interestingly, whereas the first CPU had 2,200 transistors, the newest models have

TABLE 3.4 Six Generations of Computing

Generation	Time Line	Major Event	Characteristics
1	1946–1958	Vacuum tubes	■ Mainframe era begins ■ ENIAC and UNIVAC were developed
2	1958–1964	Transistors	■ Mainframe era expands ■ UNIVAC is updated with transistors
3	1964–1990s	Integrated circuits	■ Mainframe era ends ■ Personal computer era begins ■ IBM 360 with general purpose operating system ■ Microprocessor revolution: Intel, Microsoft, Apple, IBM PC, MS-DOS
4	1990s–2000	Multimedia and low-cost PCs	■ Personal computer era ends ■ Interpersonal computing era begins ■ High-speed microprocessor and networks ■ High-capacity storage ■ Low-cost, high-performance integrated video, audio, and data
5	2000–2010	Widespread Internet accessibility	■ Interpersonal computing era ends ■ Internetworking era begins ■ Ubiquitous access to Internet with a broad variety of devices ■ Prices continue to drop; performance continues to expand
6	2010–present	Ubiquitous mobile connectivity	■ Advent of powerful mobile devices and ubiquitous mobile connectivity ■ Big data ■ Cloud computing ■ Internet of Things ■ Social networking

broken the 5-billion-transistor mark, so Dr. Moore's prediction has been fairly accurate so far (see www.intel.com/technology/mooreslaw). The number of transistors that can be packed into a modern CPU and the speed at which processing and other activities occur are remarkable. For example, the Intel Core i7 Extreme CPU can complete hundreds of millions of operations every second. Given technological and economic limitations, today, gains in computing power are increasingly being realized by adding more computing cores that can perform tasks in parallel.

FASTER IT CYCLES AND CONSUMERIZATION. For organizations, this increase in capabilities is both a blessing and a curse. On the one hand, increases in processing power enable applications that were previously not possible; on the other hand, managers have to continuously think about when to upgrade the hardware components of the IS infrastructure. Beyond Moore's law, there are two other factors exacerbating this problem. First, IT cycles are becoming increasingly faster, with manufacturers releasing new devices at an ever-increasing pace. Whereas traditionally, IS managers would think in terms of 5 years, nowadays new versions of devices are released every 6–12 months. Second, with the increasing trends toward consumerization of IT, managers have to consider how to integrate their users' various mobile devices into the organization's IS infrastructure.

SOFTWARE OBSOLESCENCE. In addition to constant increases in hardware capabilities, companies such as Microsoft are continuously developing new and improved software that uses this power to help people be more productive. New operating systems such as Windows 8 can use new processor architectures and offer a richer set of features than older operating systems such as Windows XP. However, these new operating systems often require new hardware, and older-generation application software may not be compatible with the new operating system (Figure 3.18). Further, new generations of application software promise better performance and more (or improved) features, enabling higher productivity. One example is Microsoft Office 2007 (and its most recent successor Office 2013); when developing Office 2007, Microsoft conducted many usability studies to improve the human–computer interface (see Chapter 9, "Developing and Acquiring Information Systems") so as to facilitate the execution of common tasks and, as a result, introduced the so-called "Ribbon" interface. Although people used to the "old" interface were initially reluctant to switch—because of the associated learning curve—many have now realized the benefits this new feature brings. Manufacturers of hardware and

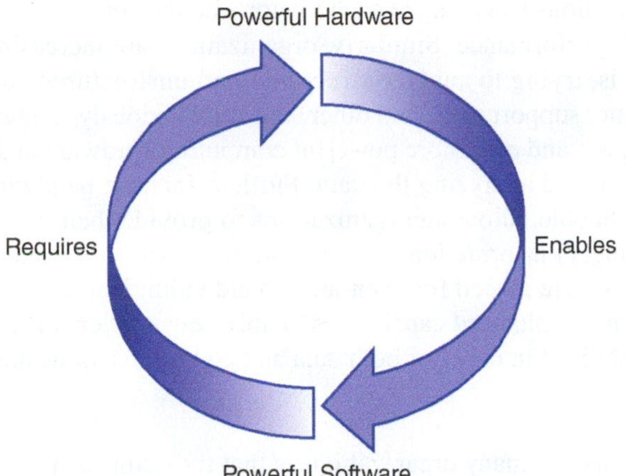

FIGURE 3.18

New hardware enables more powerful software; more powerful software often requires new hardware.

software often apply the concept of **planned obsolescence**, meaning that the product is designed to last only for a certain life span. For hardware, this can mean that certain components are not built to be serviceable, and the device has to be replaced once one of these components breaks down; similarly, older versions of software may not be able to open newer file formats, or a company may cease support for a product (mainstream support for the Windows XP operating system ended in 2009, and paid support as well as critical security updates ended in 2014), effectively forcing users to switch to newer versions. Hence, organizations are constantly faced with the decision of when and how to upgrade their current information systems infrastructure. Although such upgrades may increase productivity, often they do not but are still a large cost factor, both in terms of costs for hardware and software, and in terms of the time and resources needed for upgrading tens, hundreds, or thousands of computers. Further, the rapid obsolescence of computer hardware carries a high price tag for the environment in terms of resources needed both to manufacture the new systems and to dispose of the old ones (Figure 3.19).

Big Data and Rapidly Increasing Storage Needs

Another issue organizations face is the amount of data available and the amount of data needed to stay ahead of the competition. Today, organizations can collect and analyze vast amounts of data for *business intelligence* (see Chapter 6) and other purposes (such as compliance).

FIGURE 3.19

The rapid obsolescence of computer hardware carries a high price tag for the environment.
Source: Tonis Valing/Shutterstock

For example, organizations can analyze each visitor's actions on the company Web site in order to improve the site's performance. Similarly, organizations are increasingly trying to make use of "Big Data," that is, trying to analyze structured and unstructured data from media reports, social media, customer support calls, and other sources. Obviously, capturing more data requires ever more storage space and ever more powerful computing hardware and database management systems for managing and analyzing the data. Further, Internet bandwidth grew tremendously during the dot-com bubble, allowing organizations to provide their customers with richer (and more bandwidth-hungry) information. At the same time, services such as YouTube and videos streamed by Netflix create a need for even more bandwidth. Hence, this is another example of a "vicious circle" where enhanced capabilities enable new applications, which in turn require a certain level of capabilities in terms of both data and communications infrastructure.

Demand Fluctuations

An additional challenge for many organizations is that the demands for computing resources are often fluctuating, leading to either having too few resources at some times or having too many idle resources most of the time (according to estimates, up to 70 percent of organizations' IS infrastructure is utilized at only 20 percent of its capacity). Companies engaged in (or supporting) business-to-consumer electronic commerce (such as Amazon.com or FedEx; see Chapter 4, "Enabling Business-to-Consumer Electronic Commerce"), for instance, face large spikes in demand during the pre-holiday season in December; consequently, increased capacity is needed to handle this demand. While it is relatively easy to hire temporary staff to handle an increase in orders, it is typically not that easy to make quick changes to the IS infrastructure based on changing needs. Just a few years ago, launching a startup involved purchasing lots of hardware and installing Web servers in one's basement, with no real idea of how much demand would need to be met; fluctuation in demand for computing resources is especially difficult to cope with for new entrants who are not able to forecast demand and may not have the resources to quickly expand their IS infrastructure to meet increases in demand for their products or services.

For organizations with an increasing customer (or user) base, the facilities infrastructure has to grow along with any increase in computing needs (as Google grew, they eventually had to move their equipment out of their friend's garage; now Google is said to have more than 30 major data centers). This can be especially problematic for fast-growing companies, as renting (let alone building) additional facilities is expensive and significant time is needed for locating the right facilities, contract negotiations, and setup of the hard- and software; further, long-term contracts limit the companies' flexibility to scale the infrastructure down in times of lower demand.

Increasing Energy Needs

Finally, the worldwide increase in demand for energy has become another concern for organizations. As computers process data, they consume electricity; further, various components (such as the CPU and the power supply) generate heat, and most computers have multiple fans to control the temperature. More powerful hardware needs more energy to enable the increase in computing power; at the same time, having more powerful hardware requires more energy for cooling. A typical desktop uses between 40 and 170 watts when idling and can use up to 300 watts or more under full load. A typical server rack (holding multiple servers) in a data center can easily consume 15–17 kilowatts, the equivalent of power needed for more than 10 homes. Although you may not feel the impact of your personal computer usage on your home energy bill, for organizations having hundreds or thousands of computers, rising energy costs are becoming a major issue. Further, power consumption and heat emissions continue to rise as hardware manufacturers pack more and more processing power into servers, often without providing much improvement in energy efficiency. Thus, power and cooling can be a significant cost factor for companies. Google has invested many resources into developing more efficient data centers. Google now uses modular data centers that use specially equipped shipping containers for housing servers so as to be able to maximize efficiency by optimizing airflow, cooling, and power transformation (we will talk more about another trend, "green computing," later in the chapter).

Given these issues, organizations have been looking for ways to better manage their IS infrastructure so as to enhance flexibility and agility while reducing costs. In the following section, we will discuss cloud computing, and how it can address some of these infrastructure-related challenges.

WHEN THINGS GO WRONG

Dirty Data Centers

A 2011 report conducted by Greenpeace allowed a sneak peek into the environmental impact of data storage and transmission. The report, entitled "How Dirty Is Your Data?" measured the energy consumption of data centers owned by top technology companies to assess the environmental impacts of actions as simple as sending and receiving e-mail messages or posting status updates.

According to the study, Apple's data centers turned out to be the dirtiest of all companies, followed closely by HP, IBM, and Oracle. It was Apple's use of "dirtier" energy sources like coal and nuclear power, as opposed to solar or wind power, that had the company landing in the top spot. Apple's 500,000 square-foot facility in Maiden, North Carolina (used to power Apple's iCloud), was estimated to consume energy that could provide for 80,000 homes in the United States—only 5 percent of this was considered clean energy. In years since the Greenpeace report, Apple has made significant strides to combat this negative image; as of May 2014, Apple's data centers are now powered by 100 percent renewable energy sources.

Although Facebook came in fifth on the list of dirty data centers, the giant has since put much effort into going green with its data center located in Oregon's high desert—Prineville. Sitting on a plateau of about 2,800 feet above sea level gives Facebook's data center the advantage of using outside air to cool its servers; heating is done by using hot air that is produced by the servers themselves. Inside the data center, found water is used to run toilets, and the lighting system is controlled via Ethernet. Facebook put even more effort into designing highly efficient servers. For example, Facebook's servers have custom power supplies that reduce power loss by eliminating the need to transform power; similarly, the servers' fans spin slower, reducing energy consumption.

With environmental awareness fast on the rise, Google also claims to run its data center without chillers and is investing in wind and solar power. Similarly, Yahoo! has already located most of its data centers near sources of renewable energy. It is speculated that more technology companies will duly follow suit. As an encouraging step to clean up its dirty data center, Apple has confirmed plans to build a data center in Prineville; sources have further disclosed that the giant company is looking to take after Facebook's energy-conscious design to improve its record and make an effort to go environmental-friendly.

Based on:

Apple. (n.d.). Apple—environmental responsibility. *Apple, Inc.* Retrieved May 16, 2014, from http://www.apple.com/environment.

Greenpeace. (2011, April 20). How dirty is your data?. Retrieved May 16, 2014, from http://www.greenpeace.org/international/en/publications/reports/How-dirty-is-your-data.

CLOUD COMPUTING

Managing the IS infrastructure can be a challenge for many organizations, due to the evolution of hardware and software, the demand for more storage and networking bandwidth, and the rising costs of energy. Further, organizations need dedicated staff to support their infrastructure, which incurs further costs; often, managing the IS infrastructure is not among the organization's core competencies, so others may be better at managing the infrastructure for them.

In many organizations, the infrastructure has grown over the years, leading to a fragmented infrastructure that tends to be difficult to consolidate. However, efficiency, effectiveness, and agility are key for successfully competing in the digital world, and organizations require a flexible, scalable infrastructure for their applications and databases. As a result, over the past decades, there has been a shift away from thinking about developing and maintaining the IS infrastructure toward thinking about what *services* the infrastructure should deliver. For example, people and organizations want to use e-mail rather than having to think about purchasing an e-mail server and dealing with associated issues such as administration, maintenance, storage, energy consumption, and so on. In addition, organizations increasingly buy or rent, rather than build, applications (except for highly specialized systems that help gain or sustain competitive advantage, as is the case with Amazon.com or Dell) to support their business processes; in other words, organizations leave the building of applications to other parties, and assume that these applications will work. Given this trend, a solid infrastructure is important, as the infrastructure determines how quickly new systems can be implemented, and how well they will function; turning over the responsibility for the lower levels of the infrastructure to other organizations allows a business to focus on developing and implementing those applications that help to gain or sustain competitive advantage. This becomes even more important as any lack of robustness or

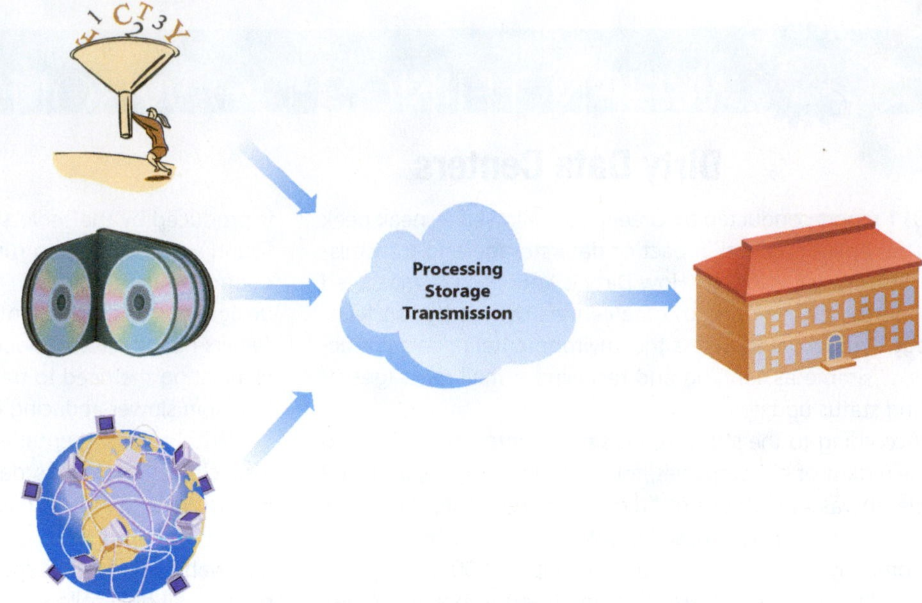

FIGURE 3.20

Processing, storage, and transmission of data taking place in the cloud.

integration of an organization's infrastructure will be immediately noticed by customers or other stakeholders, potentially leading to loss of business, trust, or goodwill.

What Is Cloud Computing?

Technological advances such as increasing Internet bandwidth and advances in virtualization have given rise to cloud computing (the "cloud" is a metaphor for the Internet; see Figure 3.20). As defined by the National Institute of Standards and Technology (NIST), "Cloud computing is a model for enabling ubiquitous, convenient, on-demand network access to a shared pool of configurable computing resources (e.g., networks, servers, storage, applications, and services) that can be rapidly provisioned and released with minimal management effort or service provider interaction" (http://csrc.nist.gov/publications/nistpubs/800-145/SP800-145.pdf). Using a **utility computing** model (i.e., organizations "renting" resources such as processing, data storage, or networking from an external provider on an as-needed basis, and pay only for what is actually used), cloud computing thus helps to transform IT infrastructure costs from a capital expenditure to an operational expenditure (Figure 3.21). One prime example of a cloud computing provider

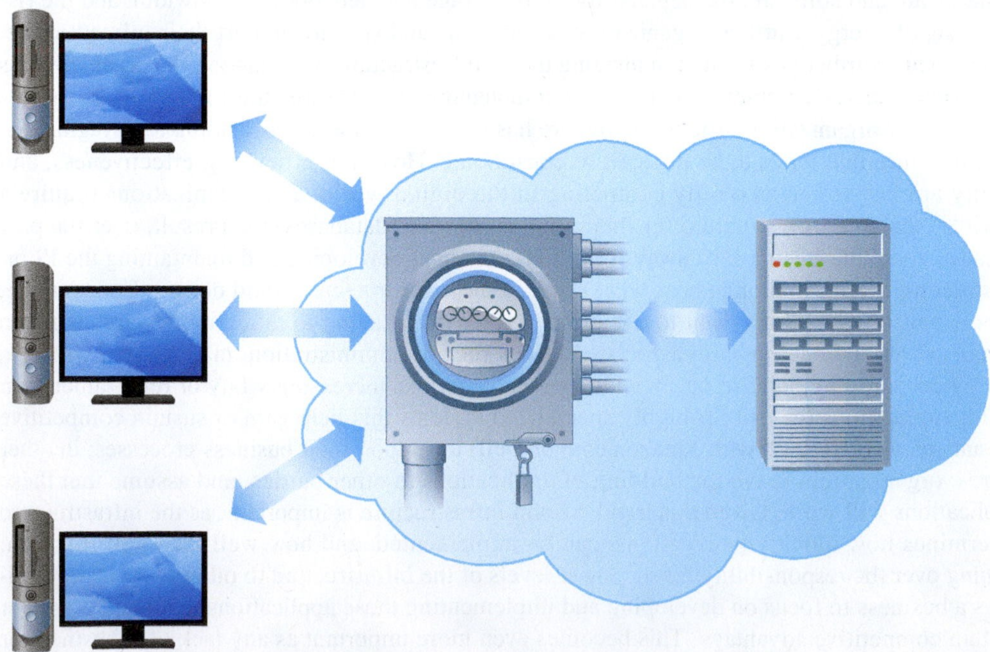

FIGURE 3.21

Cloud computing uses a utility computing model, allowing companies to pay for computing resources on an as-needed basis.

is Amazon Web Services; having built an immense infrastructure (in terms of both information technology and logistics) for supporting its online store, Amazon.com has decided to use these resources to generate additional revenue streams. For example, individuals and organizations can rent storage space on Amazon's Simple Storage Service (S3) or computing time on Amazon's Elastic Compute Cloud (EC2), all on an as-needed basis. The ability to create an entire infrastructure by combining Amazon's various services has facilitated many successful startup companies, such as the social scrapbooking site Pinterest or the community travel marketplace Airbnb. As Airbnb grew in popularity with travelers all over the globe, the company found itself being limited by challenges and constraints imposed by their original service provider. Moving to Amazon Web Services allowed Airbnb to quickly obtain 200 servers without needing to negotiate service contracts or commit to minimum usage. Flexibly scaling the infrastructure would have been close to impossible were Airbnb using its own data center because of both the time and the money needed to acquire this number of servers; and, at the time, who knew whether Airbnb's business would actually take off? With a traditional in-house infrastructure, Airbnb would have had to add capacity in "chunks," leading to either having too many unused resources or not being able to satisfy its users' demand; using a cloud infrastructure, Airbnb can elastically scale the resources to be just above what is needed to keep the users satisfied (Figure 3.22).

CLOUD CHARACTERISTICS. The cloud computing model has several unique and essential characteristics that distinguish cloud computing from an in-house infrastructure and provide various benefits to users (NIST, 2011). These characteristics are discussed next.

On-Demand Self-Service To allow for most flexibility, users can access cloud resources in a buffet-style fashion on an as-needed basis without the need for lengthy negotiations with the service provider; in many cases, resources in the cloud are accessible by the customer with no need for human interaction with the provider. In the case of Amazon Web Services, a customer needs only a credit card (for billing purposes) and can set up server instances or expand storage space via a Web-based control panel. For businesses, whose needs may rapidly change, this allows for unprecedented flexibility, as it greatly facilitates scaling the infrastructure up or down as needed.

Rapid Elasticity Typically, servers and other elements of an IS infrastructure take several weeks to be delivered and days or weeks to be configured (as a company's IS personnel has to install and configure system software, databases, and application software, depending on the organization's needs); in contrast, in a cloud environment, computing resources can be scaled up or down almost instantaneously and often automatically, based on user needs. Hence, there is no need to purchase expensive equipment to prepare for an anticipated surge in demand (which ultimately may not materialize) during the holiday season. If, however, the surge in demand does materialize, businesses can access the required resources instantaneously at almost any quantity.

Broad Network Access As cloud services are accessed via the Internet, they are accessible from almost anywhere and from almost any Web-enabled device. For organizations, this enables real-time management of business processes, as applications hosted in the cloud can be accessed whenever needed, from any location, be it from one's desktop or laptop, or using an iPhone, iPad, or Android smartphone app. Thus, knowledge workers can swiftly respond to anything that may require their immediate attention, without having to be physically in their office.

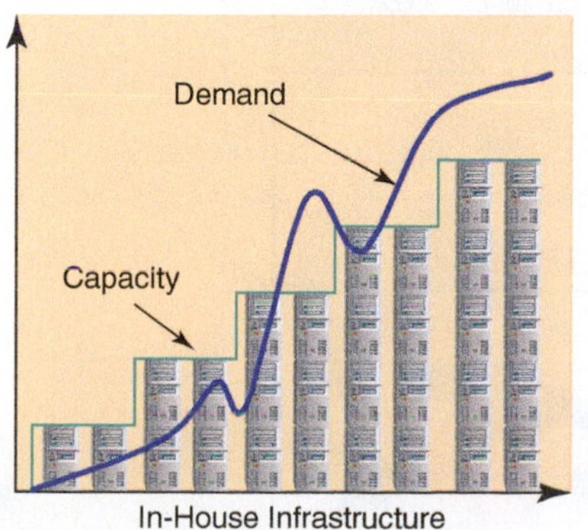

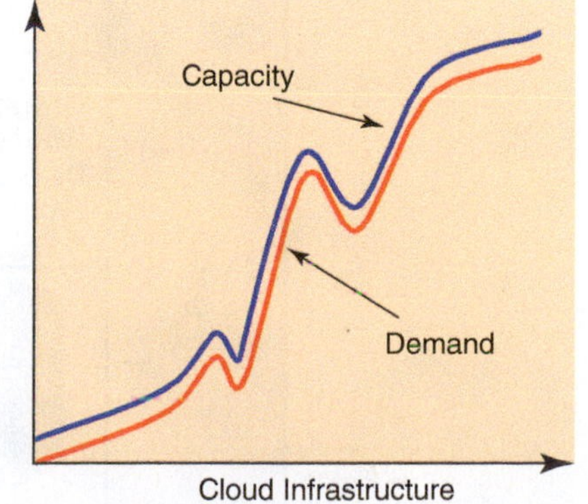

FIGURE 3.22

It is difficult to match demand using an in-house infrastructure; with a cloud infrastructure, resources can be added incrementally, on an as-needed basis.

Resource Pooling Rather than renting out space or time to each customer on one specific, physical machine, cloud providers manage multiple distributed resources that are dynamically assigned to multiple customers based on their needs. Hence, the customer only rents a resource, with no knowledge or control over how it is provided or where it is located. In some cases, however, service providers allow for specifying particular geographic areas of the resources; for example, a California company may want to rent resources located in California (close to its customers) so as to reduce response latency, or a European company may need to rent storage space on servers located in Europe so as to comply with data protection directives.

Measured Service Service is typically provided using a utility computing model, where customers pay only for what they use, and the metering depends on type of resource. For example, customers are charged on an hourly basis for the use of server instances (the price typically depends on the instance's computing power, memory, and operating system), based on volume of data stored, and/or based on the volume of data transferred into or out of the cloud. For customers, the fixed costs associated with the IS infrastructure are thus transformed into variable costs, which are very easy to track and monitor.

SERVICE MODELS. As can be seen from the previously mentioned examples, various services are provided in the cloud. Whereas some users require access only to certain software, others want to have more control, being able to run the software of their choice on a server in the cloud (Figure 3.23). Different cloud computing service models (NIST, 2011) are discussed next.

Infrastructure as a Service In the **infrastructure as a service (IaaS)** model, only the basic capabilities of processing, storage, and networking are provided. Hence, the customer has the most control over the resources. For example, using Amazon Web Services, customers can choose computing power, memory, operating system, and storage based on individual needs and requirements, thus being able to build (almost) their entire infrastructure in the cloud. Using such infrastructure, Netflix migrated its own IT infrastructure to Amazon Web Services to transcode movies into various formats, power its customer-focused Web site, and host other mission-critical applications. The IaaS model provides the customer with the greatest flexibility; on the other hand, while the infrastructure is provided, managing software licenses is still the responsibility of the customer, and setup costs are relatively high.

Platform as a Service In the **platform as a service (PaaS)** model, customers can run their own applications, which are typically designed using tools provided by the service provider. In this model, the user has control over the applications but has limited or no control over the underlying infrastructure. One example is Microsoft's Windows Azure, which acts as a cloud services operating system that customers can use to deploy custom applications. Using this platform, Outback Steakhouse launched a viral marketing campaign when it first introduced its Facebook Fan Page. To support the spikes in demand, Outback developed and deployed an e-mail marketing campaign using Windows Azure. As the underlying computing platform is

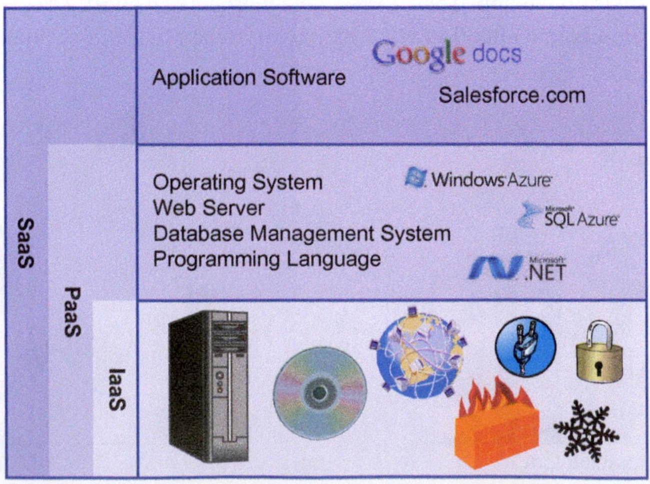

FIGURE 3.23

Services by SaaS, PaaS, and IaaS providers.

provided, the customer does not have to worry about purchasing software licenses, for example, for the Web servers' operating systems or for database management systems, and the service provider manages the functioning and updating of the platform provided.

Software as a Service In the **software as a service (SaaS)** model, the customer uses only applications provided via a cloud infrastructure. Typically, such applications include Web-based e-mail services (e.g., Google's Gmail) and Web-based productivity suites (such as Zoho or Google Docs), but also advanced applications such as CRM systems, as provided by salesforce .com (see Chapter 8, "Strengthening Business-to-Business Relationships Via Supply Chain and Customer Relationship Management"). Typically, the customer cares only about the application, with no knowledge or control over the underlying infrastructure, and typically has only limited ability to control or configure application-specific settings. Applications under the SaaS model are typically easiest to deploy, because the customer does not have to worry about maintaining or updating the software, the underlying platform, or the hardware infrastructure.

TYPES OF CLOUDS. Cloud service providers such as Amazon.com offer what is referred to as a **public cloud**. Services in a public cloud can be used by any interested party on a pay-per-use basis; hence, they are often used for applications that need rapid **scalability** (i.e., the ability to adapt to increases or decreases in demand for processing or data storage), or in cases where there is insufficient capital or other resources to build or expand an IT infrastructure. In contrast, a **private cloud** (or internal cloud) is internal to an organization and can help the organization to balance demand and supply of computing resources within the organization; similar to a public cloud, a private cloud provides self-service access to resources, allowing business users to provision resources on-demand using a utility computing model. A private cloud does not free an organization from the issues associated with managing the cloud infrastructure, but it does give the organization a high degree of customizability, flexibility, and control over their data and applications (Figure 3.24).

Managing the Cloud

Because of its various benefits, cloud computing has gained much popularity, especially among executives who try to harness the potential of scalability and increase the business' agility. However, there are also various issues management should consider when moving their infrastructure to the public cloud. The first consideration is which applications, services, or data to move to the cloud. Typically, there is no single cloud computing provider that can meet all needs of an organization. Rather, organizations often have to partner with different service providers, selecting IaaS, PaaS, and SaaS models based on the business' needs, often combining public and private clouds; as there is not one solution that fits all, organizations have to carefully weigh the benefits and downsides of cloud computing. In addition, organizations must carefully consider which cloud services provider to choose. Some of the long-term, strategic issues that management should consider when evaluating different public cloud service providers include availability,

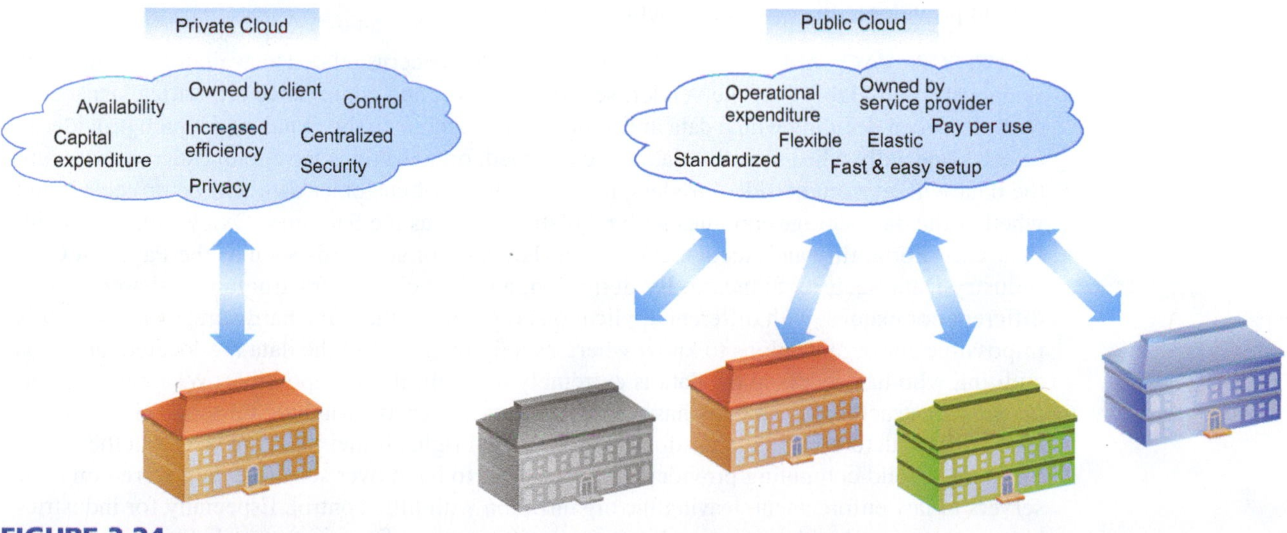

FIGURE 3.24

Public clouds versus private clouds.

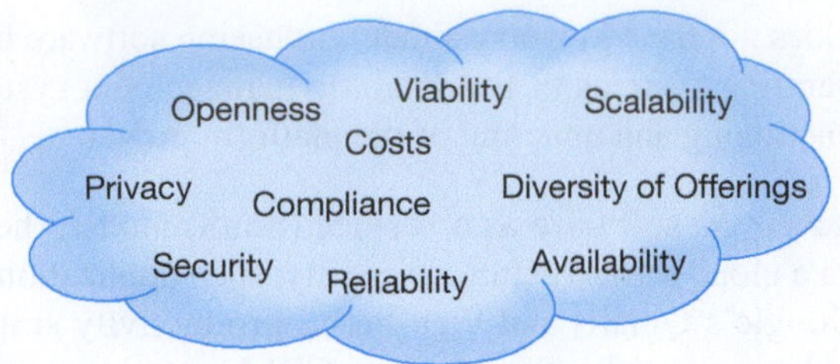

FIGURE 3.25

Organizations have to consider various issues when managing their cloud infrastructure.

reliability, scalability, viability, security, privacy, compliance, diversity of offerings, openness, and, not least, cost (Figure 3.25). These are discussed next (see also Hofmann and Woods, 2010).

AVAILABILITY/RELIABILITY. The availability of the service is a primary concern for most organizations. As shown by examples from Google, Amazon, and Microsoft, not even the largest public cloud computing providers are immune from failures, be it hardware failures, programming errors, or some network outage. Organizations thus have to evaluate which applications to move to the cloud, and how to ensure the availability of cloud-based applications. In addition to examining what the promised uptime of the application/system is, what backups are made to the servers and storage, or whether sufficient bandwidth will be provided to access large amounts of data, organizations have to implement their own precautionary measures. As it is often too costly (e.g., in terms of lost business or goodwill) to be affected by negative events, organizations should plan ahead and replicate their cloud-based infrastructure in different locations. Related to this, an important criterion to consider is the provider's support policies. In case something does not work as promised, how will issues be resolved? One of the advantages of cloud computing is self-service, allowing clients to provision resources as needed. At the same time, this can be a potential downside, as there is not always the guarantee of having help available, if needed. Thus, organizations must ensure that acceptable support capabilities and personnel are available, especially for mission-critical applications, to rapidly solve technical issues when they arise.

SCALABILITY. One of the biggest promises of cloud computing is scalability, such that organizations can scale up or down their infrastructure as needed. Yet, not every provider will be able to meet every organization's demands. Thus, organizations have to carefully evaluate to what extent the provider will be able to meet current and future business needs in terms of data storage, transaction volumes, and so on.

VIABILITY. Another important issue is associated with the viability and stability of the provider in the long run. As an organization moves to a public cloud infrastructure, it puts much data and processing capabilities into the hands of an outside entity. If this outside entity happens to go out of business, this can have many repercussions for the organization, such as costs and efforts involved in setting up a new infrastructure, migrating applications, or transferring the data from the old provider to the new infrastructure.

SECURITY, PRIVACY, AND COMPLIANCE. In addition to concerns related to availability, reliability, scalability, and viability of the vendor, security, privacy, and compliance are critical aspects to consider when deciding which data and applications to move to the cloud, and which provider to select. Especially when sensitive data are concerned, organizations have to question how secure the data will be from outside intruders, how the privacy of customer data will be protected, and whether the data storage complies with regulations such as the Sarbanes–Oxley Act, the Health Insurance Portability and Accountability Act (HIPAA), or standards such as the Payment Card Industry Data Security Standard. By definition, a public cloud infrastructure is shared among different companies, with different applications running on the same hardware; as a result, it is impossible for organizations to know where exactly (physically) the data are located, and thus auditing who has access to the data is extremely difficult, if not impossible. Whereas in an in-house infrastructure, a company has complete control over its own data, this control is lost in a cloud infrastructure, and organizations have less legal rights if their data are stored in the cloud. Similarly, cloud computing providers may be asked to hand over sensitive data stored on their servers to law enforcement, leaving the organization with little control. Especially for industries heavily concerned with privacy and data protection, such as firms in the medical or legal fields, these issues are of critical importance. On the other hand, public cloud computing providers are certainly aware of these issues, and organizations have to weigh which applications or data to move to the cloud, and which to keep in-house.

Issues such as availability, reliability, and security are normally covered in **service-level agreements**, or SLAs, which are contracts specifying the level of service provided in terms of performance (e.g., as measured by uptime), warranties, disaster recovery, and so on. A big caveat is that such service-level agreements do not *guarantee* the availability of resources; rather, they only promise certain service levels and provide for refunds or discounts if these promises are not met, and can thus be regarded mostly as a vehicle for resolving conflicts in case of problems.

For businesses, this poses a serious dilemma, as such refunds and discounts only cover the costs paid for the service, but can never offset the opportunity costs arising from lost business. On the other hand, when evaluating the benefits and drawbacks of moving the infrastructure to the public cloud, organizations also have to critically evaluate how they would be able to maintain certain uptime using an in-house infrastructure, and at what costs; often, organizations realize that even though certain SLAs may not be met by the provider, the provider can still offer better uptime than a poorly managed in-house infrastructure. In evaluating their options, organizations often choose a hybrid approach, having certain mission-critical applications in-house, while moving other, less demanding applications (in terms of uptime, etc.) to the public cloud.

DIVERSITY OF OFFERINGS. As discussed earlier, there are various providers of cloud computing services, ranging from IaaS to SaaS. As a larger number and diversity of providers is more difficult to manage, many organizations prefer to deal with fewer providers that can meet all needs. Thus, an important question to ask is which provider can offer the services needed both presently and in the future.

OPENNESS. A related question organizations face is the issue of interoperability. Most cloud providers use different infrastructures, different ways to store data, and so on. This, however, makes migrating data between providers extremely difficult, and can lead a company to be locked in by a certain provider. In addition to different infrastructures and storage models, existing network bandwidth (and data transmission costs) poses an additional limitation to interoperability, as moving terabytes of data from one provider to another, even using very high-speed networks, can prove extremely time consuming and expensive (as cloud computing providers often charge for transferring data into or out of their infrastructure).

COSTS. A final issue to consider when moving to a public cloud infrastructure is costs. The utility computing model used by cloud computing providers gives organizations control over the resources used and paid for—the organization only pays for the resources used, and can scale the resources up or down when needed. Thus, this provides the organization with much transparency over the cost of the resources. Yet, there is considerable disagreement over whether moving to the public cloud is cheaper than maintaining an in-house infrastructure. For example, the online game developer Zynga recently moved from a public cloud infrastructure to an in-house private cloud, and decided to own, rather than rent, its infrastructure. Comparing the costs of owning versus renting is not an easy feat. Whereas it is easy to calculate the costs per month of a server in Amazon's EC2 cloud, many organizations do not know how much exactly it costs to run a comparable server in an in-house infrastructure, including the costs of the server itself, the fees for software licenses, the electricity, the data center, the staff, and so on. Thus, organizations have to carefully balance the benefits and costs of the flexibility and scalability the cloud offers, such as by using a cloud infrastructure only for periods of peak demand; needless to say, this adds another layer of complexity to the IT operations.

In sum, there are various issues to consider when moving to a cloud infrastructure, and each organization has to make various informed choices about how to harness the opportunities the cloud offers while minimizing potential drawbacks. In the next section, we will provide a brief discussion of various other applications enabled by the cloud.

Advanced Cloud Applications

Clearly, the cloud offers many ways for businesses to solve their IT infrastructure–related issues. In addition to the different cloud services models, the cloud has enabled other trends, such as using a *service-oriented architecture* for flexibly deploying new applications, *grid computing* to help solve large-scale computing problems, *content delivery networks* for increasing Web application performance, and *IP convergence* for transmitting voice and video communication over the Internet. These applications are discussed next.

SERVICE-ORIENTED ARCHITECTURE. In order to achieve greater flexibility and agility, organizations have tried to move away from deploying large, monolithic applications in favor of a **service-oriented architecture (SOA)**. Using SOA, business processes are broken down into individual components (or **services**) that are designed to achieve the desired results for the service consumer (which can either be an application, another service, or a person). To illustrate this concept, think about the next oil change for your car. As you can't be expert in everything, it is probably more effective to have someone change the oil for you. You may take your car to the dealership, you may go to an independent garage or oil change service, or you may ask your friend to do it for you. For you, all that matters is that the service will be provided at the expected level of quality and cost, but you typically do not care if different service providers do things differently or use different tools.

By breaking down business processes into individual services, organizations can more swiftly react to changing business needs. For example, using an SOA approach, multiple services (such as "check inventory" or "order supplies") would be orchestrated to handle the individual tasks associated with processing customer orders and could be changed relatively easily if the business process changes.

To facilitate online collaboration with suppliers, business partners, and customers, SOA uses and reuses individual services as "building blocks," so that systems can be easily built and reconfigured as requirements change. To achieve these benefits, services have to follow three main principles:

1. ***Reusability.*** A service should be usable in many different applications.
2. ***Interoperability.*** A service should work with any other service.
3. ***Componentization.*** A service should be simple and modular.

Following these principles, multiple applications can invoke the same services. For example, both an organization's point-of-sale system and e-commerce Web site could invoke the service "process credit card," and the executive dashboard could invoke the services "display products," "display inventory," and "display sales" (Figure 3.26). Hosting and deploying such services in the cloud can help in building applications using SOA. In addition, various services an organization may need are available in the cloud, eliminating the need to "reinvent the wheel." However, whereas an SOA approach appears to be appealing for many companies, it requires tremendous effort and expertise to plan the architecture, select the right services from hundreds or thousands of available services, and orchestrate and deploy the services. Hence, while an SOA approach helps to increase flexibility, the integration of various services can be extremely complex and can be well beyond the means of small enterprises.

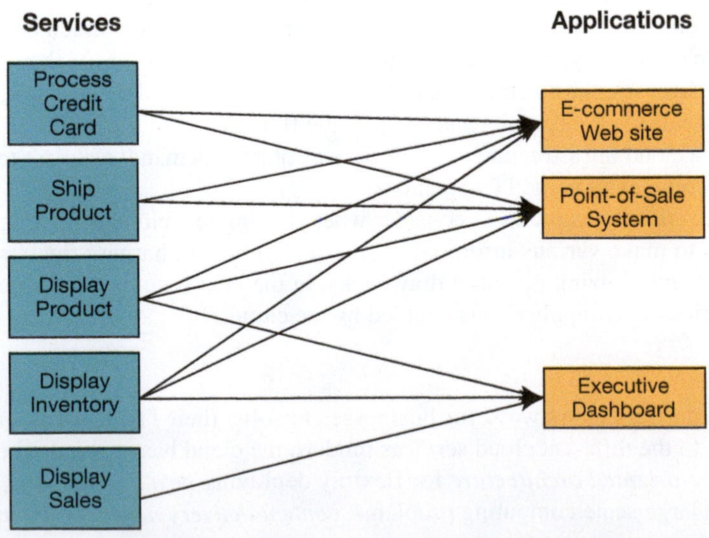

FIGURE 3.26

Using SOA, multiple applications can invoke multiple services.

FIGURE 3.27

The Titan supercomputer can perform more than 20,000 trillion calculations per second.

Source: Courtesy of Oak Ridge National Laboratory, U.S. Dept. of Energy.

GRID COMPUTING. Businesses and public organizations heavily involved in research and development face an ever-increasing need for computing performance. For example, auto manufacturers, such as the GM German subsidiary Opel or Japanese Toyota, use large supercomputers to simulate automobile crashes and to evaluate design changes for vibrations and wind noise. Research facilities such as the Oak Ridge National Laboratory use supercomputers to model neutron transport in nuclear reactors or to study climate change scenarios (Figure 3.27), while others simulate earthquakes using supercomputers; such research sites have a tremendously complex hardware infrastructure.

Although today's supercomputers have tremendous computing power, some tasks are even beyond the capacity of a supercomputer. Indeed, some complex simulations can take a year or longer to calculate even on a supercomputer. Sometimes an organization or a research facility would have the need for a supercomputer but may not be able to afford one because of the extremely high cost. For example, the fastest supercomputers can cost more than US$200 million, and this does not represent the "total cost of ownership," which also includes all the other related costs for making the system operational (e.g., personnel, facilities, storage, software, and so on; see Chapter 9). Additionally, the organization may not be able to justify the costs because the supercomputer may be needed only occasionally to solve a few complex problems. In these situations, organizations either have had to rent time on a supercomputer or have decided simply not to solve the problem.

One way for overcoming cost or use limitations is to utilize **grid computing**. Grid computing refers to combining the computing power of a large number of smaller, independent, networked computers (often regular desktop PCs) into a cohesive system in order to solve problems that only supercomputers were previously capable of solving. Similar to cloud computing, grid computing makes use of distributed resources; however, in contrast to cloud computing, the resources in a grid are typically applied to a single large problem (in fact, Amazon.com recently created the 42nd-fastest supercomputer in the world using its cloud infrastructure). To make grid computing work, large computing tasks are broken into small chunks, which can then be completed by individual computers (Figure 3.28). However, as the individual computers are also in regular use, the individual calculations are performed during the computers' idle time so as to maximize the use of existing resources. For example, when writing this book, we used only minimal resources on our computers (i.e., we typically used only a word processor, the Internet, and e-mail); if our computers were part of a grid, the unused resources could be utilized to solve large-scale computing problems. This is especially useful for companies operating on a global scale. In each country, many of the resources are idle during the night hours, often more than 12 hours per day. Because of time zone differences, grid computing helps utilize those resources constructively. One way to put these resources into use would be to join the Berkeley Open

KEY PLAYERS

Giants of the Infrastructure

In the world of information systems, there are a few crucial names that claim the center stage in infrastructure. In the game of hardware, three particular companies tend to stand out from the crowd:

1. **Dell**—This multinational technology corporation occupies the 41st spot in the Fortune 500 list. Being the third-largest PC maker in the world, Dell has become known for its innovative supply chain and its built-to-order model, building customized computers for consumers. Dell has since shifted focus to higher-margin business customers, offering servers, storage, and networking infrastructure components to enterprises, along with services ranging from cloud computing to IT consulting.
2. **IBM**—This company operates both as a multinational technology corporation and a consulting firm, covering hardware, software, and services. IBM is one of the market leaders in the area of servers and mainframe computers.
3. **HP**—This company has become one of the most important players in the IS infrastructure market. Aside from its well-known printers, HP is known for its personal computing devices, networking products, and servers that are sold to a broad range of clients from small households to enterprises through online distribution, retailers, software partners, and major technology vendors.

In the now indispensable field of networking infrastructure, Cisco stands at the top. Cisco serves several different markets, ranging from networking hardware and software to various services, including WebEx collaboration solutions, as well as security services, data center services, and others.

In the area of cloud hosting, Rackspace is the big name. Rackspace offers public and private cloud hosting to its customers, ranging from Carlsberg and Wendy's to Skechers, the blogging site Posterous, and the University of British Columbia.

Without doubt, Dell, IBM, HP, Cisco, and Rackspace are some of the biggest players in the area of providing IS infrastructure solutions. With cross-partnerships growing and multiple acquisitions going around, it is hard to tell who will come out as the long-standing survivor.

Based on:

Cisco. (n.d.). Retrieved May 17, 2014, from http://www.cisco.com.

Dell. (n.d.). Retrieved May 17, 2014, from http://www.dell.com.

HP. (n.d.). Retrieved May 17, 2014, from http://www.hp.com.

IBM. (n.d.). Retrieved May 17, 2014, from http://www.ibm.com.

Rackspace Hosting. (n.d.). Retrieved May 17, 2014, from http://www.rackspace.com.

FIGURE 3.28

Grid computing: Computers located around the world work on parts of a large, complex problem.

Infrastructure for Network Computing (http://boinc.berkeley.edu), which lets individuals "donate" computing time for various research projects, such as searching for extraterrestrial intelligence (SETI@home) or running climate change simulations.

However, as you can imagine, grid computing poses a number of demands in terms of the underlying network infrastructure or the software managing the distribution of the tasks. Further, the slowest computer often creates a bottleneck, thus slowing down the entire grid. A **dedicated grid**, consisting of a large number of homogeneous computers (and not relying on underutilized

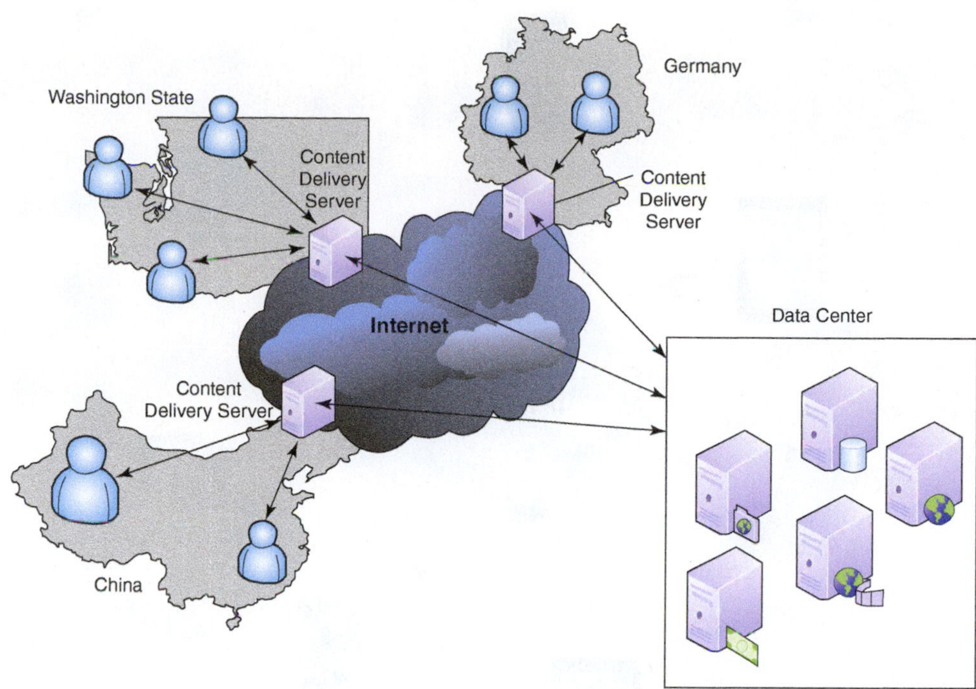

FIGURE 3.29

Content delivery networks store copies of content closer to the end user.

resources), can help overcome these problems. A dedicated grid is easier to set up and manage and, for many companies, much more cost effective than purchasing a supercomputer.

CONTENT DELIVERY NETWORKS. Another recent trend in IS hardware infrastructure management is the use of **content delivery networks** to increase performance of websites. Typically, the larger the geographical distance between a user and the Web server hosting certain content, the longer it takes to transmit the content; this can be especially noticeable for content such as streaming media, but also for other content presented on a Web page. Content delivery networks help reduce this latency by providing a network of servers in various physical locations, which store copies of particular Web sites. If a user in a particular geographic location requests a certain Web page, the content delivery server closest to the user's location delivers the content, significantly speeding up the delivery of the content (Figure 3.29), a process that is normally transparent to the user. This process not only saves valuable resources such as bandwidth but also offers superior performance that would otherwise be too expensive for organizations to offer.

CONVERGENCE OF COMPUTING AND TELECOMMUNICATIONS. Today, much of an organization's communication and collaboration needs are supported by Internet technologies; for example, e-mail has become the communications medium of choice for many people. However, for some topics, other forms of communication are more suited, so managers turn to the telephone, instant messaging, meetings, or videoconferences. One recent trend to satisfy such diverse communication and collaboration needs is the growing convergence of computing and telecommunications. The computing industry is experiencing an ever-increasing convergence of functionality of various devices. Whereas just a few years ago a cell phone was just capable of making phone calls and people used personal digital assistants to support mobile computing needs, such devices are now converging such that the boundaries between devices are becoming increasingly blurred. Today, smartphones, such as the iPhone or Samsung's Galaxy S5, offer a variety of different functionalities—formerly often available only on separate dedicated devices—to address differing needs of knowledge workers and consumers alike (e.g., phone, e-mail, Web browser, navigation system, camera, music player, and so on).

In addition to a convergence of capabilities of devices, there is also increasing convergence within the underlying infrastructures. For example, in the past, the backbone networks for the telephone and Internet were distinct. Today, increasingly, voice and data traffic share a common network infrastructure. To facilitate this convergence, also termed **IP convergence**, the use of the *Internet protocol (IP)* for transporting voice, video, fax, and data traffic has allowed enterprises to make use of new forms of communication and collaboration (e.g., instant messaging

FIGURE 3.30

IP convergence allows various devices to communicate using IP technologies.

and online whiteboard collaboration) as well as traditional forms of communication (such as phone and fax) at much lower costs (Figure 3.30). In the following sections, we discuss two uses of IP for communication: voice over IP and videoconferencing over IP.

Voice over IP Voice over IP (**VoIP**) (or IP telephony) refers to the use of Internet technologies for placing telephone calls (Figure 3.31). Whereas just a few years ago the quality of VoIP calls was substandard, recent technological advances now allow the quality of calls to equal or even surpass the quality of traditional calls over (wired) telephone lines. In addition to the

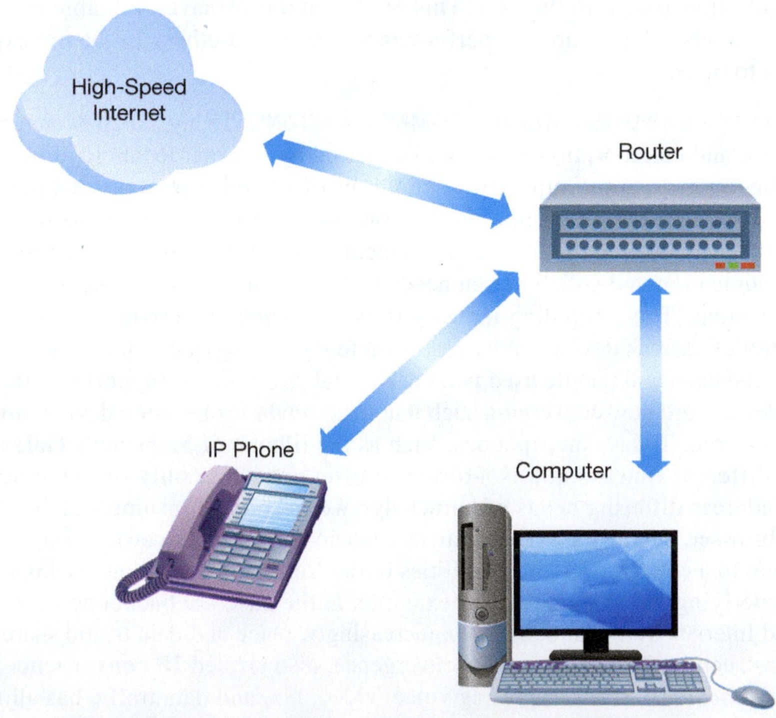

FIGURE 3.31

VoIP technology enables organizations and individuals to reduce their telecommunications costs.

quality, VoIP offers a number of other benefits; for example, users can receive calls from almost anywhere they connect to the Internet. In other words, knowledge workers are not bound to their desk to receive VoIP calls; instead, using IP routing, their telephone number "follows" them to wherever they connect to the Internet. For example, Christoph, who lives in Hong Kong, has VoIP telephone numbers in the United States and Germany so that friends and family members living in these countries can call him at local rates. Organizations can also benefit from tremendous cost savings, as often there is little cost incurred over and above the costs for a broadband Internet connection (e.g., VoIP software such as Skype allows users to make Skype-to-Skype calls for free).

Videoconferencing over IP In addition to voice communications, IP can also be used to transmit video data. Traditionally, videoconferences were held either via traditional phone lines, which were not made to handle the transfer of data needed for high-quality videoconferencing, or via dedicated digital lines, which was a very costly option. Similar to VoIP, the Internet also helped to significantly reduce costs and enhance the versatility of videoconferences by enabling **videoconferencing over IP**.

For some videoconferences, desktop videoconferencing equipment (consisting of a webcam, a microphone, speakers, and software such as Google Hangouts or Skype) may be sufficient; for others, higher-end equipment may be needed. Such infrastructure can include specific videoconferencing hardware, or it can be a dedicated virtual meeting room featuring life-sized images allowing people from across the globe to meet as if they were sitting in the same room. We discuss videoconferencing in more detail in Chapter 5, "Enhancing Organizational Communication and Collaboration Using Social Media."

Green Computing

Fueled by the rapid advances of developing nations, the world has seen a tremendous increase in demand for and cost of energy. You may not feel the impact of your personal computer usage on your home energy bill; however, for organizations having hundreds or thousands of computers, rising energy costs are becoming a major issue. Further, organizations are being increasingly scrutinized for their contribution to societal issues such as global warming; more and more organizations are trying to portray a "greener" image when it comes to the use of energy and natural resources, as company executives have realized that they cannot afford the consequences of inaction on the company's reputation. As "green" efforts can save money on energy and water use, waste disposal, and carbon taxes, and can be subsidized by grants, rebates, or free technical advice, they can also have positive impacts on a company's bottom line.

Green computing can contribute to these efforts by helping to use computers more efficiently, doing the same (or more) with less. For example, organizations can save large amounts of money for power and cooling by using virtualization to replace hundreds of individual servers with just a few powerful mainframe computers. As studies have shown, computing resources in organizations are often very much underutilized, and using virtualization can help lower an organization's energy bill and carbon footprint. Similarly, cloud computing has been argued to contribute to reduced energy consumption, as the service provider's infrastructure is shared by many users. Installing sophisticated power management software on individual desktops can save much energy that is wasted by leaving computers idling or on standby overnight; for instance, General Electric saved US$6.5 million in electricity annually by simply changing the power saving settings for its computers (Wheeland, 2007). Further, discouraging employees from printing out e-mails or business documents can help to reduce the waste of paper—an average office worker prints more than a tree's worth of paper each year.

A related issue is the retiring of obsolete hardware. Today, companies cannot just send retired equipment to a landfill. Rather, companies as well as individuals have to evaluate how to best dispose of unwanted computers, monitors, and parts. Whereas the first step is to make the decision *when* to retire equipment, the next steps are equally important. Needless to say, it has to be ensured that old computers are wiped of all user data. Many third-party outsourcers ("IT asset disposition" vendors) offer services including wiping all computer hard drives, and either refurbishing and selling usable equipment, or dismantling the components to recycle valuable raw materials and properly dispose of hazardous waste.

INDUSTRY ANALYSIS

Movie Industry

Do you remember the original *Star Wars* movies or movies such as *King Kong* (1976) or *Godzilla* (1954)? Compare these to recent box office hits such as the *Lord of the Rings Trilogy* (2001–2003), *Rise of the Planet of the Apes* (2011), *Avatar* (2009), *The Hobbit* (2012–2014) and *Transformers: Age of Extinction* (2014), or animated movies such as *Ice Age* (2002–2012), *Despicable Me* (2010–2013), and *Frozen* (2013). The tremendous increase in computing power has enabled film studios such as Dreamworks and Universal Studios or special effects studios such as Weta Digital and Pixar to create animations and special effects of hitherto unimaginable quality using specialized powerful software and hardware for computer-generated imagery (CGI, also known as computer graphics).

As for major studios, rapidly evolving digital technology (specifically, recording hardware and sophisticated yet easy-to-use digital editing software) has opened vast opportunities for independent filmmakers who are producing studio-quality films without having to rely on expensive lighting, film development, and postproduction facilities. Thus, people who could never afford all the necessary equipment can now produce movies digitally. Further, digital cameras and projectors and advances in software have made the transition from celluloid to digital more attainable for filmmakers who until recently used traditional technology. In fact, over 30 percent of the submissions to the Sundance Film Festival (the primary film festival for independent movies, comparable to festivals in Cannes or Berlin for mainstream movies) are now in digital format.

The impact of technology on the movie industry does not stop with movie production. Many movie theaters across the world have shifted to digital projection technologies, reducing the need for duplicating and shipping large reels of film, reducing distribution costs by up to 90 percent, while speeding up the time from the studio to the theater. Rather than shipping reels of film (that are susceptible to out-of-focus projection, scratches, or "pops"), the movies are stored on central servers, from which they are accessed and downloaded via the Internet by individual theaters. Theater owners can much more swiftly react to fluctuating demand and easily show movies on more than one screen in case of high demand. Clearly, the use of information systems has tremendously changed the movie industry.

Questions

1. Can digital technologies help movie theaters compete with the increasing trend toward more sophisticated home theaters? If so, how?
2. What are the ethical issues associated with special effects becoming more and more realistic with the help of digital technologies?
3. From the perspective of movie studios and theaters, list the pros and cons of using digital distribution technologies.

Based on:

Jardin, X. (2005, July 28). Hollywood plots end of film reels. *Wired*. Retrieved May 17, 2014, http://archive.wired.com/entertainment/music/news/2005/07/68332.

Meyers, M. (2006, January 18). Tech plays supporting role at Sundance festival. *CNET News.com*. Retrieved May 17, 2014, from http://news.cnet.com/Tech-plays-supporting-role-at-Sundance-festival/2100-1025_3-6028354.html.

Key Points Review

1. ***Describe how changes in businesses' competitive landscape influence changing IS infrastructure needs.*** Organizations are facing continuously changing business environments, and quickly adapting to a constantly changing competitive environment necessitates that businesses are increasingly flexible and agile. Modern organizations use various applications and databases to support their business processes; these applications and databases rely on a solid underlying IS infrastructure, consisting of hardware, system software, storage, networking, and data.
2. ***Describe the essential components of an organization's IS infrastructure.*** Organizations use various types of IS hardware to meet their diverse computing needs. The most prominent type of system software, the operating system, coordinates the interaction between hardware devices, peripherals, application software, and users. Further, organizations need to store massive amounts of data for operational, backup, and archival purposes. Networking is one of the reasons why information systems have become so powerful and important to modern organizations. Finally, organizations use data centers to house the different infrastructure components, so as to ensure security and availability.
3. ***Discuss managerial issues associated with managing an organization's IS infrastructure.*** Radical advances in information technology have opened many opportunities for organizations but have also brought about challenges. Advances in hardware have

enabled advances in software. Hardware and software obsolescence, faster IT cycles, and consumerization present issues such as when and how to upgrade the current infrastructure. Further, organizations' storage needs are growing at an ever-increasing pace, and organizations also have to deal with fluctuations in demand for computing power while often being unable to quickly scale the IS infrastructure accordingly. The increasing need for both computing power and storage fuels an increasing demand for energy, which can affect a company's image as well as its bottom line.

4. ***Describe cloud computing and other current trends that can help an organization address IS infrastructure–related challenges.*** Cloud computing uses a utility computing business model, where customers can draw on a variety of computing resources that can be accessed on demand, with minimal human interaction. Characteristics of cloud computing include on-demand self-service, rapid elasticity, broad network access, resource pooling, and measured service. Typical cloud computing service models are infrastructure as a service, platform as a service, and software as a service. When considering the move to a public cloud-based infrastructure, organizations have to weigh issues such as availability, reliability, scalability, viability, security, privacy, compliance, openness, diversity of offerings, and, not least, cost. Other applications in the cloud include SOA, grid computing, content delivery networks, voice over IP, and videoconferencing over IP. Finally, a recent trend is green computing, as companies realize potential cost savings and a positive effect on the company's image by implementing ways to reduce energy consumption and waste.

Key Terms

application software 93
bandwidth 100
campus area network 101
client 101
client-server network 101
computer networking 99
content delivery network 121
database 94
database management system 94
dedicated grid 120
desktop virtualization 101
device driver 97
domain name 102
embedded system 95
extranet 104
green computing 123
grid computing 119
hyperlink 102
hypertext 102
Hypertext Markup Language (HTML) 102
Hypertext Transfer Protocol (HTTP) 102
information systems infrastructure 90
infrastructure 90
infrastructure as a service (IaaS) 114
Internet 102
intranet 104
IP address 103
IP convergence 121
local area network 101
mainframe 95
metropolitan area network 101
Moore's law 107
network 101
operating system 96
peer 101
peer-to-peer network 101
peripherals 96
personal area network 101
personal computer (PC) 95
planned obsolescence 109
platform as a service (PaaS) 114
private cloud 115
protocols 100
public cloud 115
scalability 115
server 95
service 118
service-level agreement 117
service-oriented architecture (SOA) 118
software as a service (SaaS) 115
supercomputer 95
system software 96
thin client 101
top-level domain 102
Transmission Control Protocol/Internet Protocol (TCP/IP) 103
transmission media 100
Uniform Resource Locator (URL) 102
utility computing 112
videoconferencing over IP 123
Voice over IP (VoIP) 122
Web browser 102
Web page 102
Web server 102
Web site 102
wide area network 101
Wi-Fi network (wireless fidelity) 101
wireless local area network (WLAN) 101
workstation 95
World Wide Web 102

Go to **mymislab.com** to complete the problems marked with this icon ✪.

Review Questions

3-1. How do applications support organizational business processes?

3-2. How do databases support organizational business processes?

3-3. Describe the key functions of system software.

3-4. For which purposes are data stored in organizations?

3-5. What are the distinguishing characteristics of different storage media?

3-6. How does computer networking work?

3-7. What are the major types of networks?

3-8. What is the World Wide Web, and what is its relationship to the Internet?

3-9. What are URLs, and why are they important to the World Wide Web?

3-10. What are the problems associated with software obsolescence?

3-11. Describe the characteristics of the cloud computing model.

3-12. Define grid computing and describe its advantages and disadvantages.

3-13. Describe what is meant by the term "IP convergence."

3-14. Describe why green computing has become so important to modern organizations.

Self-Study Questions

3-15. All of the following are examples of infrastructure components except ______________.
A. hardware
B. system software
C. data centers
D. applications

3-16. Which of the following is *not* a consequence of lack of availability, performance, or security?
A. loss of managerial oversight
B. loss of business
C. loss of trust
D. loss of goodwill

3-17. Engineering drawings are typically prepared using ______________.
A. mainframes
B. servers
C. personal computers
D. workstations

3-18. Tape drives are typically used for ______________.
A. storing operational data
B. backing up critical data
C. maintaining customer records
D. archiving data

3-19. Which of the following is the protocol of the Internet?
A. URL
B. HTML
C. TCP/IP
D. ARPA

3-20. All of the following are correct domain suffixes except
A. edu—educational institutions
B. gov—U.S. government
C. neo—network organizations
D. com—commercial businesses

3-21. The ability to adapt to increases or decreases in demand for processing or storage is referred to as ______________.
A. adaptability
B. flexibility
C. scalability
D. agility

3-22. In cloud computing, services are typically offered using ______________.
A. private clouds
B. heterogeneous grids
C. a utility computing model
D. edge computing

3-23. For the most flexibility in the use of computing resources, companies choose a (n) ______________ provider.
A. utility computing
B. software as a service
C. platform as a service
D. infrastructure as a service

3-24. Large-scale computing problems can be solved using ______________ computing.
A. grid
B. utility
C. cloud
D. edge

Answers are on page 128.

Problems and Exercises

3-25. Match the following terms with the appropriate definitions:

i. Utility computing
ii. Service-level agreement
iii. System software
iv. Software as a service
v. Voice over IP
vi. Cloud computing
vii. Bandwidth
viii. Server
ix. Planned obsolescence
x. Scalability

a. The incorporation of a life span into the design of a product
b. The use of Internet technology for placing telephone calls
c. A cloud computing model in which the customer uses an application provided via a cloud infrastructure
d. A model for enabling convenient, on-demand network access to a shared pool of configurable computing resources
e. Any computer on a network that makes access to files, printing, communications, and other services available to users of the network
f. The transmission capacity of a computer or communications channel
g. A business model where computing resources are rented on an as-needed basis
h. Contracts specifying the level of service provided in terms of performance, warranties, disaster recovery, and so on
i. The collection of programs that control the basic operations of computer hardware
j. The ability to adapt to increases or decreases in demand for processing or data storage

3-26. Take a look at the Web site of an online retailer. Which pieces of information are likely coming from information stored in databases?

3-27. Which applications are mission-critical for an online retailer? For a bank? Justify your assessment.

3-28. How do software programs affect your life? Give examples of software from areas other than desktop computers. Are the uses for software increasing over time?

3-29. Interview an IS professional about IS infrastructure. Which infrastructure components does this professional regard as most important? Why?

3-30. Using the Web, find information about archiving your data. What options are available? What are the advantages and disadvantages of each option?

3-31. Scan the popular press and/or the Web for clues concerning emerging technologies for computer networking. This may include new uses for current technologies or new technologies altogether. Discuss as a group the "hot" issues. Do you feel they will become a reality in the near future? Why or why not? Prepare a 10-minute presentation of your findings to be given to the class.

3-32. Do you have your own Web site with a specific domain name? How did you decide on the domain name? If you don't have your own domain, research the possibilities of obtaining one. Would your preferred name be available? Why might your preferred name not be available?

3-33. How does hardware and software obsolescence affect your life? Give examples of experiences with outdated hardware or software. How did you deal with these situations?

3-34. Using information on the Web, find (or try to estimate) your computer's energy consumption. What are ways to decrease your computer's energy consumption?

3-35. Research the Web for an example of a startup using a cloud infrastructure. What were the main reasons for choosing a cloud infrastructure? What alternatives did the startup have?

3-36. Are you using any services offered in the cloud? If so, what service model is offered by your provider? If not, what are your primary reasons for not using services offered in the cloud?

3-37. Interview an IS professional about cloud computing. Does this professional have a preference for public versus private clouds? Additionally, find out what data he or she would most likely entrust to a public cloud.

3-38. Research the Web for service-level agreements of two different providers of cloud services and compare these based on availability, security, and privacy. How do the agreements differ? Are the agreements reasonable? Which provider would you select for your cloud infrastructure if you were to start a company?

3-39. Using a search engine, enter the key phrase "voice over IP providers." Who are the large vendors in this industry? What type of solutions do they offer to their clients? Does any vendor suit your communication needs?

Application Exercises

Note: The existing data files referenced in these exercises are available on the book's Web site: www.pearsonhighered.com/valacich.

Spreadsheet Application: Tracking Frequent-Flier Mileage

3-40. You have recently landed a part-time job as a business analyst for Campus Travel. In your first meeting, the operations manager learned that you are taking an introductory MIS class. As the manager is not very proficient in using office software tools, he is doing all frequent-flier mileage in two separate Excel workbooks. One is the customer's contact information, and the second is the miles flown. Being familiar with the possibilities of spreadsheet applications, you suggest setting up one workbook to handle both functions. To complete this, you must do the following:

- Open the spreadsheet frequentflier2.csv. You will see a tab for customers and a tab labeled "miles flown."
- Use the vlookup function to enter the miles flown column by looking up the frequent-flier number. (Hint: If done correctly with absolute references, you should be able to enter the vlookup formula in the first cell in the "miles flown" column and copy it down for all the cells.)
- Use conditional formatting to highlight all frequent fliers who have less than 4,000 total miles.
- Finally, sort the frequent fliers by total miles in descending order and print out the spreadsheet.

Database Application: Building a Knowledge Database

3-41. Campus Travel seems to be growing quite rapidly. Now it has franchises in three different states, totaling 16 locations. As the company has grown tremendously over the past few years, it has become increasingly difficult to keep track of the areas of expertise of each travel consultant; often, consultants waste valuable time trying to find out who in the company possesses the knowledge about a particular region. Impressed with your skills, the general manager of Campus Travel has asked you to add, modify, and delete the following records from its employee database:

- Open employeedata.mdb.
- Select the "employee" tab.
- Add the following records:
  a. Eric Tang, Spokane Office, Expert in Southwest, Phone (509)555-2311
  b. Janna Connell, Spokane Office, Expert in Delta, Phone (509)555-1144
- Delete the following record:
  a. Carl Looney from the Pullman office
- Modify the following:
  a. Change Frank Herman from the Pullman office to the Spokane office
  b. Change Ramon Sanchez's home number to (208)549-2544

Team Work Exercise

Net Stats: Broadband Access Increases

Reports show that broadband penetration in the United States is growing steadily. In late 2013, 70 percent of the U.S. population had access to broadband connections at home, and the gap between different population segments is shrinking. Still, a higher percentage of people with higher household income and higher educational attainment tend to have access to broadband Internet. Further, in terms of average connection speed, the United States is back in eighth place, not only behind South Korea and Hong Kong, but also behind countries like Latvia and the Czech Republic.

Questions and Exercises

3-42. Search the Web for the most up-to-date statistics.

3-43. As a team, interpret these numbers. What is striking/important about these statistics?

3-44. As a team, discuss how these numbers may look in 5 years and 10 years. What changes have to be made to the global networking infrastructure? What issues/opportunities do you see arising?

3-45. Using your spreadsheet software of choice, create a graph/figure most effectively visualizing the statistics/changes you consider most important.

Based on:

Belson, D. (2013). The state of the Internet, 2nd quarter, 2013. *Akamai.com*. Retrieved May 17, 2014, from http://www.akamai.com/dl/documents/akamai_soti_q213.pdf.

Anonymous. (n.d.). Broadband technology fact sheet. *Pew Research*. Retrieved May 17, 2014, from http://www.pewinternet.org/fact-sheets/broadband-technology-fact-sheet.

Answers to the Self-Study Questions

3-15. D, p. 90	**3-16.** A, p. 92	**3-17.** D, p. 95	**3-18.** D, p. 99	**3-19.** C, p. 103
3-20. C, p. 103	**3-21.** C, p. 115	**3-22.** C, p. 112	**3-23.** D, p. 114	**3-24.** A, p. 119

CASE 1 Building Farms and Crushing Candy: The Infrastructure Behind Social Games

Since its initial launch in 2004, Facebook has become the world's largest social network, helping people to communicate with friends, family members, and coworkers. In addition to communication capabilities (such as features that allow posting "status updates," a chat system, or photo albums), users can access a variety of third-party applications developed using Facebook's own development platform. Interestingly, a category of applications that has become hugely popular is social network games, such as FarmVille, CastleVille, or Candy Crush Saga. Social network games are typically asynchronous, multiplayer games, where users play while interacting with their online social network.

San Francisco–based game developer Zynga was once one of the most important players in this market, having developed games such as Mafia Wars, FarmVille, and Bubble Safari; in fact, six out of the seven most popular social games were developed by Zynga. Though Zynga enjoyed early success and massive gains in stock price, the company has declined fairly steadily, consistently losing money and putting the company's business model in question. Though the company's market worth reached over US$10 billion shortly following its initial public offering (IPO) in 2012, it is currently worth just under US$3 billion.

Zynga's flagship game, FarmVille, grew from 1 million daily users after four days to 10 million daily users after just 60 days; nine months after launch, 75 million people logged in to FarmVille each month. On FarmVille, users can grow crops and trees, raise animals, build barns and fences, and so on. Fields need to be plowed and crops sowed and harvested before they wither, forcing the user to log in to the game frequently. A successor, FarmVille 2, was released near the end of 2012, at which point the FarmVille games were in the top 10 most popular social games on Facebook. As of January 2014, their popularity had declined somewhat, and the game only remains among the top 50.

In April 2012, a new game developer, King Digital Entertainment, released Candy Crush Saga, which quickly rose in popularity and, in March 2013, surpassed FarmVille in active users with 46 million monthly users. Shortly after the launch the game developer also released a version for the iOS and Android mobile platforms. The addition of these mobile apps has helped Candy Crush Saga become an international superstar. Across the three platforms (Facebook, iOS, and Android), Candy Crush Saga has been installed over 500 million times, and 97 million people play the game every day. It is the most popular game on Facebook, and ranks very high in both the Apple and Google app marketplaces.

A key advantage that Candy Crush Saga has had over FarmVille is its ability to monetize the gameplay. Though the game is free to download and play, players can purchase "boosts" that provide assistance during difficult levels. The ease with which these boosts can be purchased (and used) means that some players spend large amounts of money in small increments without really knowing it. This business model has been very effective for King, to the tune of US$850,000 per day from in-game purchases. In March 2014, King completed an IPO, which valued the company at over US$7 billion, the largest ever for a mobile/social gaming company in the United States, just slightly higher than Zynga's initial valuation.

Compared to other applications, response time is critical for these types of games, as time lags in the game's response can quickly kill a player's gaming experience. Further, the introduction of new features (such as new game tokens being offered) often cause spikes in user activity. Hence, supporting a successful social network game requires an IS infrastructure that is solid, responsive, and highly scalable. In addition, social games place further demands on an IS infrastructure; most Web sites primarily serve content to the user and are thus very "read intensive." In contrast, social network games are "write intensive"; that is, large amounts of data are written to the games' underlying databases. For example, whenever a player plants a new crop, builds a windmill, or moves a fence on Farmville, an object changes its state or a new object is created; all these actions have to be properly stored so as to avoid objects colliding or other "illegal" maneuvers. Overall, FarmVille's read-to-write ratio is 3 to 1, which is considered incredibly high.

To support this demand, Zynga early on started using a cloud computing architecture. Using Amazon EC2, Zynga deployed more than a thousand servers for FarmVille alone. To flexibly deal with changes in demand, Zynga uses a cloud management platform that automatically adds or removes servers based on predetermined parameters, such as when to start scaling or how fast to add or remove resources

Realizing that the company was paying huge amounts of money to rent Amazon's infrastructure, Zynga decided to launch its own private cloud. This move allowed Zynga to fine-tune its infrastructure for gaming purposes, which was not possible using Amazon's all-purpose servers. Yet, Zynga maintains a hybrid cloud model, using Amazon's public cloud infrastructure as a fallback for times of unexpected spikes in demand. Likewise, building an infrastructure that supports the growth of Candy Crush Saga is key for King Digital in the coming years. Clearly, mobility has fueled the popularity of social games, and companies have to find innovative ways to keep their infrastructure running and maximize user experience.

Questions

3-46. What infrastructure components are most critical for Zynga and King?

3-47. Compare and contrast the business models of Zynga and King Digital. Why has King been more successful so far?

3-48. Discuss the advantages and disadvantages for social game developers choosing to develop for multiple platforms.

Based on:

Candy Crush Saga. (2014, May 16). In *Wikipedia, The Free Encyclopedia*. Retrieved May 17, 2014, from http://en.wikipedia.org/w/index.php?title=Candy_Crush_Saga&oldid=608805336.

Zynga. (2014, May 6). In *Wikipedia, The Free Encyclopedia*. Retrieved May 17, 2014, from http://en.wikipedia.org/w/index.php?title=Zynga&oldid=607273191.

King (company). (2014, May 11). In *Wikipedia, The Free Encyclopedia*. Retrieved May 17, 2014, from http://en.wikipedia.org/w/index.php?title=King_(company)&oldid=608023171.

Day, E. (2014, May 10). Candy Crush Saga: Sweet success for global flavour of the moment. *The Guardian*. Retrieved May 17, 2014, from http://www.theguardian.com/technology/2014/may/11/candy-crush-saga-games.

CASE 2 The Deep Web

What we commonly call "the Web" is really just the tip of the iceberg. The common Web that you know and use every day—sites like Facebook, Google, Wikipedia, and news agencies—comprise as little as 1 percent of the total size of the Web. Beyond this surface, the "deep Web" is comprised of tens of trillions of Web pages that most people have never seen.

Researchers refer to the portion of the Internet that is indexed by search engines like Google and Bing as the "surface Web." The surface Web is constantly scanned (or "crawled") by computers whose sole purpose is to traverse the billions of interconnected Web pages that are publicly available on the Internet. These "Web crawlers" create an index that is much more quickly searched than a full search of the Web. So when you type in a search on Google.com, the reason you are provided millions of results in a fraction of a second is that Google has a very efficient algorithm that uses its indexes to provide you highly relevant results. The size of the surface Web (i.e., that which has been indexed) is difficult to estimate accurately, since it is constantly and quickly expanding, but it is only a small *fraction* of the total size of the Web.

The deep Web, otherwise called the invisible Web or hidden Web, is a completely different animal. It consists of the portions of the Web that are not indexed by search engines, including private areas requiring authentication, dynamic Web pages created from connected databases, and static Web pages that are not connected to other pages via hyperlinks.

For these reasons, the deep Web is difficult to traverse, and it is therefore difficult to know exactly what it contains. The deep Web has, however, been the object of study by several researchers. It is estimated that around 54 percent of websites are nonindexable databases. Some of these are public, such as the U.S. National Oceanic and Atmospheric Administration, NASA, the Patent and Trademark Office, and the Securities and Exchange Commission's EDGAR search system. Search engines cannot traverse these databases because their contents are dynamically generated from the database and displayed on-demand based on database queries. Other databases are private or behind a paywall, such as the government documents on Lexis-Nexis and Westlaw or the academic journals on Elsevier. Organizations that maintain these databases charge users and institutions for access, and their contents are thus not freely available for search engine indexing.

Another 13 percent of pages lie hidden because they are only found on internal networks, such as at corporations or universities. Such internal networks have access to message boards, personnel files, or industrial control panels that can flip a light switch or shut down a power plant, but are not accessible to search engines.

In addition to these innocuous portions of the deep Web are an uncountable number of secret Web pages that require special software to access. The most popular software for traversing this "dark corner of the Web" is called Tor. Tor directs Internet traffic through a worldwide volunteer network of relays (rather than the usual channels of the Internet). These relays allow users to conceal their location or usage from anyone conducting network surveillance or traffic analysis, and are intended to protect the personal privacy of users. The privacy also provides the ability to conduct confidential business by keeping Internet activities from being monitored. An National Security Agency (NSA) report once characterized Tor as "the King of high secure, low latency Internet anonymity" with "no contenders for the throne in waiting." Some use it for sensitive communications, including political dissent. But in the last decade, it's also become a hub for black markets that sell or distribute weapons, drugs, stolen credit cards, illegal pornography, pirated media, and more. You can even hire assassins.

Because of the noted difficulties in searching and accessing the deep Web, very little has been done to make the deep Web more accessible to the general public. Given the tremendous infrastructure resources required to search just the surface Web, it is difficult to imagine the technologies, hardware, and software that would be required to allow the same search capabilities in the deep Web. And, given the nefarious nature of the dark corners of the Web, perhaps it is better for us to leave it down in the deep.

Questions

3-49. What infrastructure components are most important for providing the surface Web to the public users of the Internet?

3-50. Should more effort be expended to enable wider access to the deep Web? Why or why not?

3-51. What are the implications of the deep Web for individuals? Companies? Governments?

Based on:

Pagliery, J. (2014, March 10). The Deep Web you don't know about. *CNN Money*. Retrieved May 17, 2014, from http://money.cnn.com/2014/03/10/technology/deep-web/index.html.

Deep Web. (2014, May 14). In *Wikipedia, The Free Encyclopedia*. Retrieved May 18, 2014, from http://en.wikipedia.org/w/index.php?title=Deep_Web&oldid=608491527.

Tor (anonymity network). (2014, May 13). In *Wikipedia, The Free Encyclopedia*. Retrieved May 18, 2014, from http://en.wikipedia.org/w/index.php?title=Tor_(anonymity_network)&oldid=608333807.

Go to **mymislab.com** for Auto-graded writing questions as well as the following Assisted-graded writing questions:

3-52. Describe the difference between SaaS, PaaS, and IaaS.

3-53. Describe the different types of computers and their key distinguishing characteristics.

References

Amazon. (2014). Amazon Web services. *Amazon.com.* Retrieved May 29, 2014, from http://aws.amazon.com.

Belson, D. (2014). The state of the Internet. 4th quarter, 2013 report. *Akamai.* Retrieved May 29, 2014, from http://akamai.com/stateoftheinternet.

Berghel, H. (1996). U.S. technology policy in the information age. *Communications of the ACM, 39*(6), 15–18.

Golden, B. (2009, January 22). The case against cloud computing, part one. *CIO.com.* Retrieved May 29, 2014, from http://www.cio.com/article/477473/The_Case_Against_Cloud_Computing_Part_One.

Google. (2014). Google green. *Google.com.* Retrieved May 29, 2014, from http://www.google.com/green.

Hoffer, J., Ramesh, V., & Topi, H. (2013). *Modern database management* (11th ed.). Upper Saddle River, NJ: Pearson Prentice Hall.

Hoffer, J. A., George, J. F., & Valacich, J. S. (2014). *Modern systems analysis and design* (7th ed.). Upper Saddle River, NJ: Pearson Prentice Hall.

Hofmann, P., & Woods, D. (2010, November/December). Cloud computing: The limits of public clouds for business applications. *IEEE Internet Computing*, 90–93.

Laberta, C. (2012). *Computers are your future* (12th ed.). Upper Saddle River, NJ: Pearson Prentice Hall.

National Institute of Standards and Technology. (2011, September). The NIST definition of cloud computing. Retrieved May 29, 2014, from http://csrc.nist.gov/publications/nistpubs/800-145/SP800-145.pdf.

Netcraft. (2014, May 7). May 2014 Web server survey. *Netcraft.com.* Retrieved May 29, 2014, from http://news.netcraft.com/archives/2014/05/07/may-2014-web-server-survey.html.

Panko, R., & Panko, J. (2013). *Business data networks and security* (9th ed.). Upper Saddle River, NJ: Pearson Prentice Hall.

Stallings, W. (2014). *Network security essentials: Principles and practice* (5th ed.). Upper Saddle River, NJ: Pearson Prentice Hall.

Szuprowicz, B. O. (1998). *Extranets and intranets: E-Commerce business strategies for the future.* Charleston, SC: Computer Technology Research.

Tebutt, D. (2010, February 9). Ten green issues for CIOs. *Techworld.* Retrieved May 29, 2014, from http://features.techworld.com/green-it/3212282/ten-green-issues-for-cios.

Te'eni, D., Carey, J. M., & Zhang, P. (2007). *Human-computer interaction: Developing effective organizational information systems.* New York: Wiley.

Top 500. (2014, June). Retrieved July 21, 2014, from http://www.top500.org/lists/2014/06/.

Turban, E., King, D., Lee, J., Liang, T.-P., Turban, D. (2012). *Electronic commerce 2012: Managerial and social networks perspectives* (7th ed.). Upper Saddle River, NJ: Pearson.

Violino, B. (2011, December 5). Preparing for the real cost of cloud computing. *Computerworld.* Retrieved May 29, 2014, from http://www.computerworld.com/s/article/359383/The_Real_Costs_of_Cloud_Computing.

Wheeland, M. (2007, May 2). Green computing at Google. Retrieved May 29, 2014, from http://www.greenbiz.com/news/2007/05/02/green-computing-google.

4 Enabling Business-to-Consumer Electronic Commerce

After reading this chapter, you will be able to do the following:

1. Describe different business models used to compete in cyberspace as well as different forms of electronic government.
2. Describe business-to-consumer electronic commerce strategies.
3. Understand the keys to successful electronic commerce Web sites, and explain the different forms of Internet marketing.
4. Describe mobile commerce, consumer-to-consumer electronic commerce, and consumer-to-business electronic commerce.
5. Describe how to conduct financial transactions and navigate the legal issues of electronic commerce.

Preview

This chapter focuses on electronic commerce (e-commerce, or EC), explaining how companies conduct business with customers over the Internet. The Internet and World Wide Web are extremely well suited for conducting business electronically on a global basis. Web-based e-commerce has introduced unprecedented opportunities for the marketing of products and services, accompanied by features, functionality, and innovative methods to serve and support consumers. With e-commerce representing a growing proportion of overall retail sales, an understanding of e-commerce can be a powerful tool in your arsenal. People with e-commerce skills are in high demand in the marketplace; therefore, the more you know about e-commerce, the more valuable you will become.

Managing in the Digital World: **Taobao and the World of e-Commerce**

Most people in this world have heard of eBay and Amazon.com, two U.S.-based online retail sites where one can typically find any desired product. The online shopping fever has spread to China in the form of companies like Taobao and JD.com. Taobao, owned by Alibaba, was founded in 2003 and only eight years later had 370 million registered users, more than the entire population of the United States. If you have tried any of Taobao's services, you know that it has various branches. There's Taobao Marketplace, China's eBay, which dominates the country's online consumer-to-consumer (C2C) e-commerce business with its 90 percent market share. Then there's Taobao Mall, a separate site where renowned brands sell directly to consumers in a business-to-consumer (B2C) manner. In fact, Taobao has fostered such a holistic shopping experience that international names like Gap, Adidas, and Levi's, just to name a few, decided to launch their own official online retail storefronts in the virtual mall. By 2011, Taobao had become the 3rd-most visited site in China, and the 15th-most visited site in the entire world, holding a gross merchandise volume of an estimated US$60 billion. For the year 2013, the combined gross merchandise volume of Taobao Marketplace and Taobao Mall exceeded US$160 billion.

However, shoppers should beware. Taobao might be the talk of the town, but it is also known as a notorious market for piracy and counterfeit goods. You may want to try out JD.com instead (short for Jingdong Mall, formerly 360Buy) which has not made it to the list of notorious markets. The company is expanding fast, with an ambitious plan of solving logistics and delivery troubles that are a hallmark of the Chinese market, given the country's size and differences in population density (Figure 4.1). JD.com hopes to build a trucking fleet of close to 300 trucks and enter the logistics and distribution market, specifically to get rid of long-distance transport headaches. The greatest barrier to online shopping in China remains trust; within China, people fear being defrauded or receiving substandard products. Outside China, potential customers often face language barriers when attempting to communicate with the suppliers. While low-priced offers directly from Chinese suppliers may seem tempting, these factors can easily convince overseas consumers to turn to the more familiar Amazon.com or eBay.

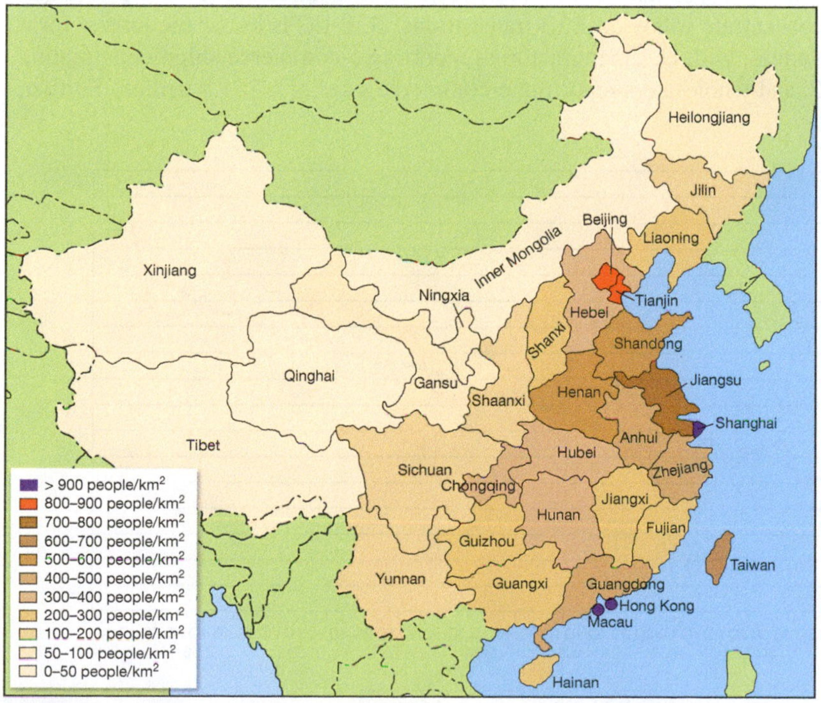

FIGURE 4.1

Companies serving the Chinese market face huge logistics problems.

After reading this chapter, you will be able to answer the following:

1. How have Taobao and JD.com evolved their e-commerce strategies to remain competitive in the global marketplace?
2. How does the proliferation of mobile devices change the competitive landscape for these companies?
3. How can these companies address issues related to trust and fraud?

Based on:

JD.com. (2014, April 30). In *Wikipedia, The Free Encyclopedia*. Retrieved May 21, 2014, from http://en.wikipedia.org/w/index.php?title=JD.com&oldid=606440789.

Taobao. (2014, May 5). In *Wikipedia, The Free Encyclopedia*. Retrieved May 21, 2014, from http://en.wikipedia.org/w/index.php?title=Taobao&oldid=607208999.

ELECTRONIC BUSINESS: E-COMMERCE AND E-GOVERNMENT

The Internet provides a set of interconnected networks for individuals and businesses to complete transactions electronically. We define **electronic commerce (EC)** very broadly as the exchange of goods, services, and money[1] among firms, between firms and their customers, and between customers, supported by communication technologies and, in particular, the Internet. The Census Bureau of the Department of Commerce reported that while total U.S. annual retail sales in 2013 increased by 4 percent from 2012, online retail sales were up by 17 percent and that EC accounted for 5.8 percent of total retail sales, resulting in sales of more than US$263.6 billion (Figure 4.2). Research firm eMarketer forecasts steady growth, anticipating global business-to-consumer e-commerce sales to reach US$1.5 trillion in 2014 and to exceed US$2.3 trillion by 2017. Considering all online markets, it is clear that online transactions have become a major segment of the global economy. With this much money at stake, it is little wonder that no other information systems (IS) issue has captured as much attention as has EC. Already during the Berlin airlift in 1948, the foundations for EC transactions between businesses were laid, as the Military Air Transport Service of the U.S. Air Force in Europe realized that not only the airlifted cargo was important, but that *information* about the cargo was equally important, and devised standard universal codes for transmitting these data via teletype (Seideman, 1996). The emergence of the Internet and Web further facilitated EC and, in addition, paved the way for marketing and selling products and services to individual consumers. This has led to the creation of an electronic marketplace where a virtually limitless array of services, features, and functionality can be offered. As a result, a presence on the Web has become a strategic necessity for most companies.

Electronic Commerce Business Models

Contrary to popular belief, EC goes beyond consumers merely buying and selling products online. EC can involve the events leading up to the purchase of a product as well as customer service after the sale. Furthermore, EC is not limited to transactions between businesses and consumers, which is known as **business-to-consumer (B2C)** EC. EC is also used by organizations to conduct business with business partners such as suppliers and intermediaries. This form of EC, not involving the end consumer, is commonly referred to as **business-to-business (B2B)** EC. As many firms concentrate solely on B2B transactions, B2B EC is by far the largest form of EC in terms of revenues, with U.S manufacturers reporting e-commerce shipments totaling US$3 trillion in 2012, and wholesalers reporting e-commerce sales of US$1.8 trillion. Further,

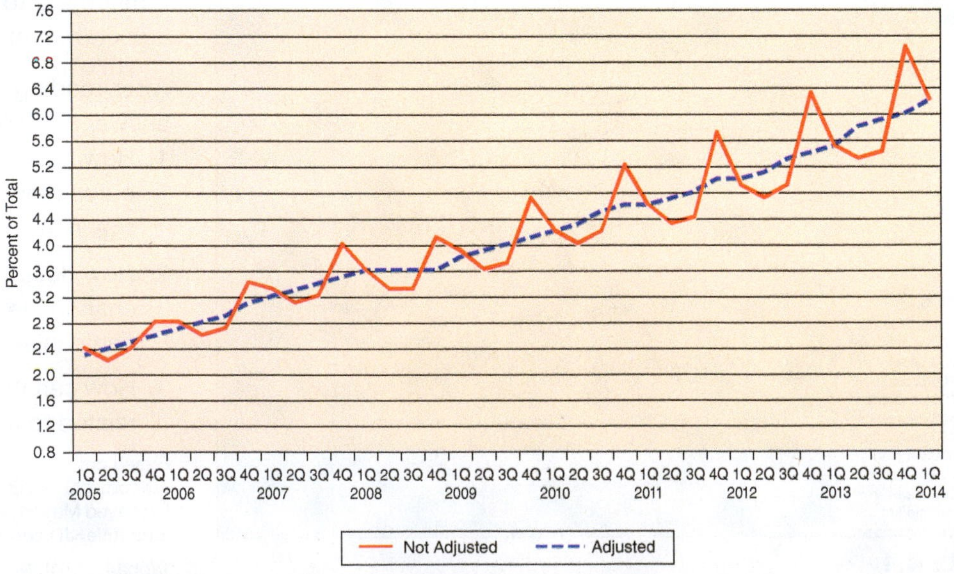

FIGURE 4.2

Online retailing continues to grow rapidly.

Source: U.S. Census Bureau News. "Table 3: Estimated Quarterly U.S. Retail Sales (Adjusted): Total and E-commerce". U.S. Department of Commerce. http://www2.census.gov/retail/releases/historical/ecomm/14q1.pdf

[1]EC can also include the distribution of digital products, such as software, music, movies, and digital images.

TABLE 4.1 Types of EC

Types of EC	Description	Example
Business-to-consumer (B2C)	Transactions between businesses and their customers	A person buys a book from Amazon.com.
Business-to-business (B2B)	Transactions among businesses	A manufacturer conducts business over the Web with its suppliers.
Consumer-to-business (C2B)	Transactions between customers and businesses	A person offers his photography at shutterstock.com.
Consumer-to-consumer (C2C)	Transactions between people not necessarily working together	A person purchases some memorabilia from another person via eBay.com.

almost all companies focusing on the B2C arena, such as the clothing and home furnishing retailer Eddie Bauer, also engage in B2B EC. In the process of producing goods and services, a business typically sources its raw materials from a variety of specialized suppliers (in B2B transactions); after the production, the business sells each finished product to a distributor or wholesaler (in a B2B transaction) or directly to the end consumer (in a B2C transaction). We will discuss B2B EC in Chapter 8, "Strengthening Business-to-Business Relationships Via Supply Chain and Customer Relationship Management."

Some forms of EC do not even involve business firms, as would be the case with an online auction site such as eBay; these forms of EC are referred to as **consumer-to-consumer (C2C)** EC. An emerging EC model, referred to as **consumer-to-business (C2B)** EC, where consumers offer products, labor, and services to companies, is a complete reversal of the traditional B2C model. These basic types of EC are summarized in Table 4.1.

The five megatrends mobile, social, cloud computing, the Internet of Things, and Big Data have influenced various aspects of the digital world, and e-commerce is no exception. The tremendous increase in the use of mobile devices has given rise to **m-commerce (mobile commerce)**—that is, any electronic transaction or information interaction conducted using a wireless, mobile device and mobile networks (wireless or switched public network) that leads to the transfer of real or perceived value in exchange for information, services, or goods (MobileInfo, 2014). Researchers estimate that B2C m-commerce sales will exceed US$56 billion in 2014, accounting for 19 percent of retail e-commerce sales; in addition, B2B transactions will increasingly take place on mobile platforms. Fueled by the rise of social media, organizations are trying to leverage their visitors' social networks to build lasting relationships, advertise products, or otherwise create value—a trend referred to as *social commerce*. Digital products and services are provided through the cloud (think iTunes, Dropbox, or Gmail). The Internet of Things enables companies to offer various innovative products and services that go beyond the initial purchase (such as the Nest thermostat that not only can be controlled from one's smartphone, but also learns the user's schedules and habits, optimizing home energy use). Together, these megatrends generate a wealth of data, allowing companies to obtain an in-depth understanding of each individual customer, so as to deliver individualized value propositions and build long-lasting customer relationships. In the following section, we examine the use of information systems for interactions with and between governments.

e-Government

e-Government is the use of information systems to provide citizens, organizations, and other governmental agencies with information about public services and to allow for interaction with the government. Similar to the EC business models, e-government involves three distinct relationships (Figure 4.3).

GOVERNMENT-TO-CITIZENS. **Government-to-citizen (G2C)** EC allows for interactions between federal, state, and local governments and their constituents. The Internal Revenue Service's Internet tax filing, or *e-filing*, is one of the more recognizable G2C tools, saving resources in terms of time and paper. Some states have begun working on e-voting initiatives, allowing citizens to vote online. However, concerns over security and protection from manipulation have thus far slowed the adoption of e-voting.

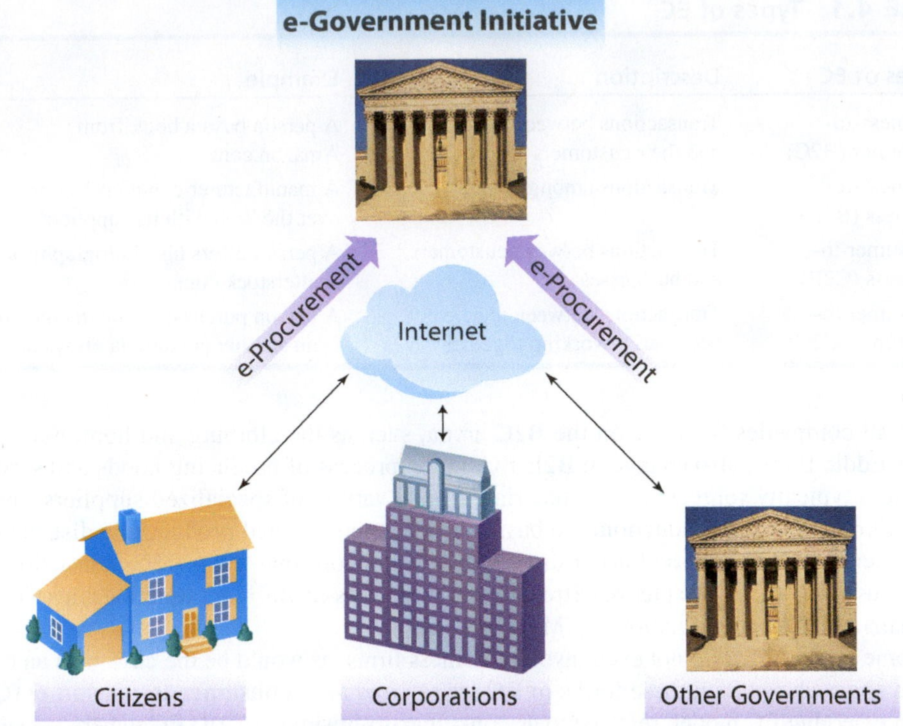

FIGURE 4.3
e-Government initiatives include interaction with citizens, corporations, and other governments.

GOVERNMENT-TO-BUSINESS. **Government-to-business (G2B)** is similar to G2C, but this form of EC involves businesses' relationships with all levels of government. This includes e-procurement, in which the government streamlines its supply chain by purchasing materials directly from suppliers using its proprietary Internet-enabled procurement system. Also included in G2B initiatives are forward auctions that allow businesses to buy seized and surplus government equipment. Other G2B services include online applications for export licenses, verification of employees' Social Security numbers, and online tax filing.

GOVERNMENT-TO-GOVERNMENT. Finally, **government-to-government (G2G)** EC is used for electronic interactions that take place between countries or between different levels of government within a country. Since 2002, the U.S. government has provided comprehensive e-government tools that allow foreign entities to find government-wide information related to business topics. Other G2G transactions relate to the intergovernmental collaboration at the local, state, federal, and tribal levels.

BUSINESS-TO-CONSUMER E-COMMERCE

Technological forces are driving business, lowering barriers to entry and leveling the playing field, allowing small and large businesses from around the globe to sell products to a global customer base. For small companies, this opens up vast opportunities. Unlike in international sports tournaments such as the Ironman World Championship, where athletes first have to compete locally to qualify for the big event, online businesses can "participate in the world championships" (i.e., compete on a global scale) right from the start. Companies are exploiting the capabilities of the Web to reach a wider customer base, offer a broader range of products, and develop closer relationships with customers by striving to meet their unique needs (Valacich, Parboteeah, & Wells, 2007).

While it is beneficial for many small companies to access a global marketplace, this also means that every company participating in a market faces increased competition, and companies must strategically position themselves to compete in the EC environment. The online sales of goods and services, or **e-tailing**, can take many forms. At one extreme, companies following a **brick-and-mortar business strategy** choose to operate solely in the traditional physical markets. These companies approach business activities in a traditional manner by operating physical locations such as retail stores, and not offering their products or services online. In contrast,

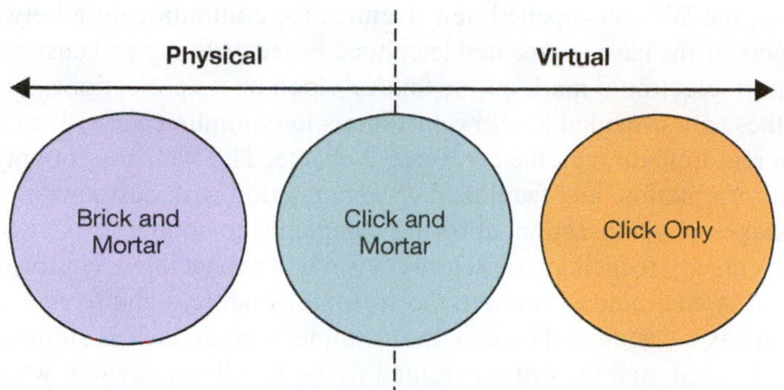

FIGURE 4.4
General approaches to EC.

companies following a **click-only business strategy** (i.e., **virtual companies**) conduct business electronically in cyberspace. These firms have no physical store locations, allowing them to focus purely on EC. An example of a click-only company is the online retailer Amazon.com, which does not have a physical storefront in the classic sense. In e-business terminology, click-only companies are sometimes called "pure play companies," focusing on one very distinct way of doing business; other firms, such as the bookseller Barnes & Noble, choose to utilize the Internet to extend their traditional offline retail channels. These firms employ a **click-and-mortar business strategy** approach (also referred to as the **bricks-and-clicks business strategy**). The three general approaches are depicted in Figure 4.4.

THE CLICK-AND-MORTAR STRATEGY. The greatest impact of the Web-based EC revolution has occurred in companies adopting the click-and-mortar approach. Click-and-mortars continue to operate their physical locations (often a reduced number of physical locations) and have added the EC component to their business activities. With transactions occurring in both physical and virtual environments, it is imperative that click-and-mortars learn how to fully maximize commercial opportunities in both domains. Conducting physical and virtual operations presents special challenges for these firms, as business activities must be tailored to each of these different environments in order for the firms to compete effectively (e.g., differential pricing or shipping and inventory management can suddenly become huge concerns for companies selling physical products).

Another challenge for click-and-mortars involves increasing IS complexity. Design and development of complex computing systems are required to support each aspect of the click-and-mortar approach. Furthermore, different skills are necessary to support Web-based computing, requiring substantial resource investments.

THE CLICK-ONLY STRATEGY. Click-only companies can often compete more effectively on price since they do not need to support the physical aspects of the click-and-mortar approach. Thus, these companies can reduce prices to rock-bottom levels (although a relatively small click-only firm may not sell enough products and/or may not order enough from suppliers to be able to realize economies of scale and thus reduce prices). Click-only firms, such as Amazon.com or eBay.com, also tend to be highly adept with technology and can innovate very rapidly as new technologies become available. This can enable them to stay one step ahead of their competition. However, conducting business in cyberspace has some problematic aspects. For example, it is more difficult for a customer to return a product to a purely online company than simply to return it to a local department store. In addition, some consumers may not be comfortable making purchases online. Individuals may be leery about the security of giving credit card numbers to a virtual company. We will discuss these potential drawbacks later in this chapter.

e-Tailing: Capabilities and Benefits

Powerful Web technologies have given rise to a global platform where firms from across the world can effectively compete for customers and gain access to new markets. Global customers do not have to rely on old information from printed catalogs or account statements that arrive in the mail once a month, but can access Web sites that are linked to corporate databases to provide real-time access to personalized information. Likewise, companies in the travel industries, such as airlines, can dynamically adjust fares based on availability, booking time, current and historical demand, forecast demand, and other factors to maximize revenues (a practice referred to as yield management), and disseminate the most current fares in real-time on the company's

Web site. Further, the Web has opened new avenues for communication between companies and their customers; firms have augmented telephone-based ordering and customer support with Web-based support, electronic mail, online text or video chat applications, and social media. In many cases, these are provided to allow customers to communicate with a customer service representative in real-time through the corporate Web site. The Web has not only facilitated the dissemination of information, and facilitated communication with customers, but is often used to facilitate all stages of a transaction, allowing companies to conduct business online without human assistance, greatly reducing transaction costs while enhancing operational efficiency. For example, once a customer places an order, the customer's address and payment information is stored in the company's customer database, the customer's credit card is automatically charged, the inventory is checked, and the order is routed to the fulfillment center, where the shipping label is automatically generated. Aside from picking and packing the actual product, most of the transaction requires little to no human interaction. For the business, this tremendously reduces the costs associated with the transactions by reducing the demand for phone representatives taking the order or back-office staff handling the orders. In addition, the Internet has enabled various new business and revenue models. These are discussed next.

MASS CUSTOMIZATION. Web technologies have been key in enabling various business models based on mass customization. **Mass customization** helps firms tailor their products and services to meet a customer's particular needs on a large scale. Linking online product configuration systems with just-in-time production allows companies to assemble each individual product based on the customers' specifications, so that companies are able to provide individualized products, while at the same time reaping the economies of scale provided by mass production. For instance, Dell Computer Corporation allows customers to customize their computers based on their specific performance needs. Likewise, customers can design personalized tennis shoes at Nike.com, customize their Mini at miniusa.com, or even have their personalized cookies baked at kekswerkstatt.de. While manufacturing a customized product tends to be more expensive than traditional mass production, the product's value for the customer increases, allowing the producer to charge a higher price, leading to higher profit margins (Figure 4.5).

DISINTERMEDIATION. Another disruption enabled by the Web is the ability to sell products directly to the end customers, without the need for distributors or retailers. This phenomenon of cutting out the "middleman" and reaching customers more directly and efficiently is known as **disintermediation**. Disintermediation creates both opportunities and challenges. While disintermediation allows producers or service providers to offer products at lower prices (or reap greater profits), they also have to take on those activities previously performed by the middleman. For example, when airlines started selling tickets online and dealing directly with customers, they disintermediated travel agents (and thus directly had to deal with upset travelers in case of delays or cancellations). To make up for this lost revenue, travel agents now charge

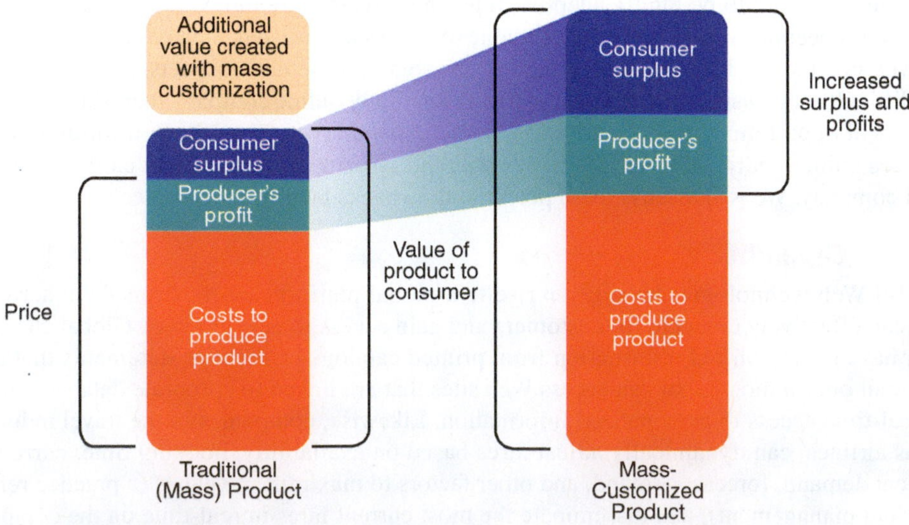

FIGURE 4.5

Mass customization generates additional value for customers and profits for producers.

booking fees when arranging a person's travel. In contrast, **reintermediation** refers to the design of business models that reintroduce middlemen in order to reduce the chaos brought on by disintermediation. For example, without middlemen like Travelocity.com, Orbitz.com, and other travel Web sites, a consumer would have to check all airline Web sites in order to find the flight with the best connection or lowest price.

GROUP BUYING. An innovative business model enabled by the Internet is **group buying**. Companies such as Groupon or Livingsocial negotiate special volume discounts with local businesses and offer them to their members in the form of "daily deals"; if enough people agree to purchase the product or service, the customers typically get significant discounts over the original purchase price. The business offering the product or service uses these deals to either reduce unsold inventory, or to get new customers "into the door"; yet, local businesses face the danger of making significant losses on these deals, as the group purchasing site typically takes a hefty share of the deal's price (often around 50 percent), or they may not be able to cope with the sudden increase in demand (see Chapter 2, "Gaining Competitive Advantage Through Information Systems," for more on Groupon's business model).

NEW REVENUE AND PRICING MODELS. The Internet has enabled or facilitated various revenue models, with companies earning revenues not only through traditional sales, but also through subscription, licensing, or transaction fees (refer to Chapter 2). Further, organizations and individuals alike can generate revenues through Web advertisement or affiliate marketing programs (see Chapter 2 for more on revenue models). In addition, companies have come up with innovative pricing models that transcend traditional **menu-driven pricing**, in which companies set the prices that consumers pay for products. For example, Priceline.com offers consumers discounts on airline tickets, hotel rooms, rental cars, new cars, home financing, and long-distance telephone service. The revolutionary aspect of the Priceline.com Web site lies in its **reverse pricing** model called *Name Your Own Price*. Customers specify the product they are looking for and how much they are willing to pay for it and Priceline.com matches the customers' bids with offers from companies (who often use Priceline.com to get rid of excess inventory). After a user searches for a service and submits a bid on Priceline.com, the system routes the information to appropriate brand-name companies, such as United Airlines and Avis Rent-a-Car, which either accept or reject the consumer's offer (Figure 4.6).

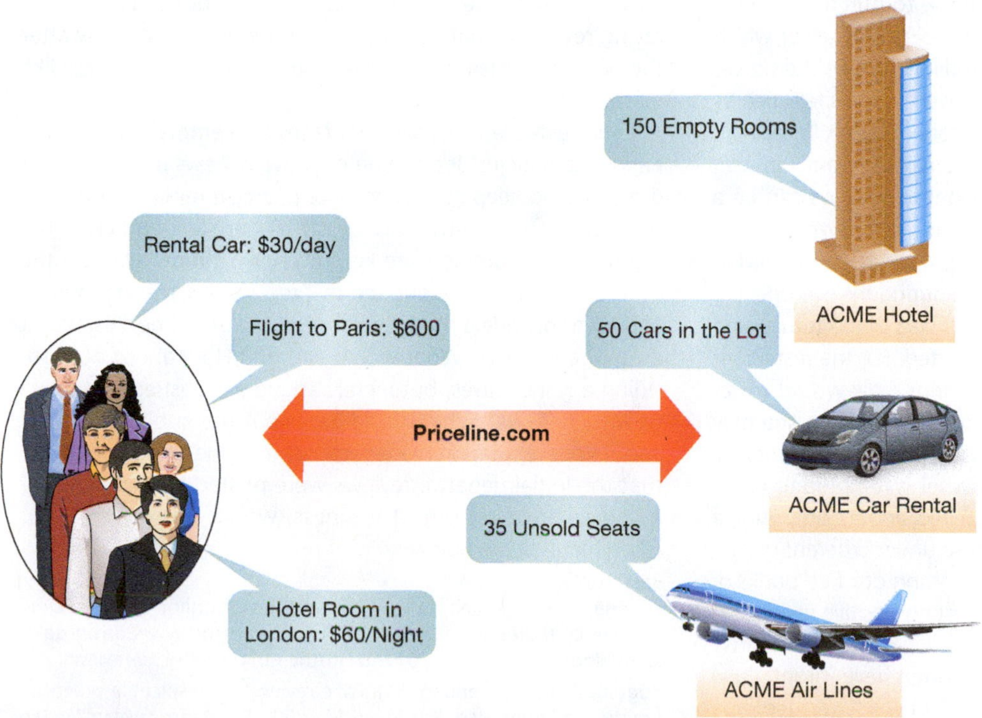

FIGURE 4.6
Priceline.com lets consumers name their own price for travel-related services.

SOCIAL COMMERCE. Increasingly, companies operating in the digital world are attempting to move away from merely using the Web as a medium for facilitating quick and painless transactions. Rather, organizations are trying to leverage their visitors' social networks to build lasting relationships, advertise products, or otherwise create value. This relatively new phenomenon, termed **social commerce**, encompasses various aspects. For example, Amazon presents recommendations based on what other shoppers with similar tastes have viewed or purchased, and encourages shoppers to share their recent purchases on social networking sites. Consumers-to-consumer marketplaces such as eBay or Etsy allow individuals to sell products to other individuals. Group buying sites such as Groupon use the network effect to increase buying power and obtain deals and discounts. Shopping discovery sites such as Fancy allow users to suggest novel and exciting products, and let merchants sell these products on the site (or app). Sites such as Motile attempt to replicate offline shopping experiences by offering users second opinions and style advice about anything related to fashion. Some new forms of social commerce are even bypassing traditional retail channels; recently, people have started forming buying co-ops on social networks such as Facebook, in order to purchase goods at wholesale prices. Clearly, while social commerce has various facets, it is certain that social aspects will play an ever-increasing role in e-commerce interactions.

Benefits of e-Tailing

e-Tailing can provide many benefits over traditional brick-and-mortar retailing in terms of the marketing concepts of product, place, and price. These are discussed next.

PRODUCT. Web sites can offer a virtually unlimited number and variety of products because e-tailing is not limited by physical store and shelf space restrictions. For instance, e-tailer Amazon.com offers

ETHICAL DILEMMA

The Ethics of Reputation Management

If you're trying to decide on which book to purchase, which movie to watch at the theater, which hotel to stay at, or which restaurant to go to for dinner, you are likely to use the power of the crowd—that is, you probably consult Web sites such as Amazon.com (books), Rottentomatoes.com (movies), Tripadvisor .com or Booking.com (hotels), or Yelp.com (restaurants) to read reviews from others. For consumers, online reviews can be a valuable decision aid. On the other hand, online reviews can make or break a business. For example, a restaurant receiving just a few negative reviews on Yelp.com during the pre-opening phase will be much less likely to attract diners in the future, and the restaurant may fail before it even started. For the restaurant owner, who has invested her life's savings, this would mean that she would have to declare bankruptcy; further, she may have to lay off the chef, the wait staff, and the dishwasher, all of whom have families to feed. The owner is tempted to boost the reputation of the restaurant, and thinks about composing a few reviews herself, and publishing those under different pseudonyms. Alternatively, she is considering giving out free drinks or desserts to diners, as an incentive for posting positive reviews.

Needless to say, Web sites that publish customer reviews want to provide unbiased reviews, and often have (proprietary) mechanisms in place to minimize (or at least reduce) the potential of biased reviews. In addition, under rules of the U.S. Federal Trade Commission, paying someone to post reviews may actually be illegal. Yet, you may have noticed extensive, raving reviews about a 500-page book posted just a day after the book was released, or reviews that sound suspiciously like marketing copy.

The restaurant owner thus faces a dilemma. On the one hand, she may just ignore the negative reviews and hope that diners would keep coming in spite of these reviews; however, this may result in having to lay off all her staff and close the restaurant if customers are kept away by the reviews. On the other hand, she may engage in "reputation management" and try to provide a more "balanced" picture of her restaurant on the review site. What would you do? How about not providing any incentives, but merely asking all satisfied customers to write reviews? What would happen if the public found out about your reputation management? Imagine the owner knew that the initial negative reviews were posted by a competitor trying to drive her out of business, would this change your assessment? If so, how?

Based on:

Tijerina, A. (2011, February 11). The ethics of online reviews. *Drivingsales.com*. Retrieved May 21, 2014, from http://www.drivingsales .com/blogs/arnoldtijerina/2011/02/11/the-ethics-of-online-reviews.

Roggio, A. (2012, January 31). Fake reviews, a despicable practice? *Practical eCommerce*. Retrieved May 21, 2014, from http://www .practicalecommerce.com/articles/3330-Fake-Reviews-a-Despicable -Practice-.

millions of book titles on the Web, compared to a local brick-and-mortar–only book retailer, which can offer "only" a few thousand titles in a store because of the restricted physical space.

For online customers, comparison shopping is much easier on the Web. In particular, numerous comparison shopping services that focus on aggregating content are available to consumers. Some companies fulfilling this niche are Google Shopping (focusing on a wide range of products), AllBookstores.com (books), and Booking.com (hotel rooms). These comparison shopping sites can literally force sellers to focus on relatively low prices in order to be successful. If sellers do not have the lowest price, they must be able to offer better quality, better service, or some other advantage. These comparison shopping sites generate revenue by charging a small commission on transactions, by charging usage fees to sellers, and/or through advertising on their site.

PLACE. As company storefronts can (virtually) exist on every computer that is connected to the Web, e-tailers can compete more effectively for customers, giving e-tailers an advantage. Whereas traditional retailers are bound to physical store locations and open hours, e-tailers can conduct business anywhere at any time.

The ubiquity of the Internet has enabled companies to sell goods and services on a global scale. Consumers looking for a particular product are not limited to merchants from their own city or country; rather, they can search for the product where they are most likely to get it or where they may get the best quality. For example, if you're looking for fine wines from France, you can order directly from the French site Chateau Online (www.chateauonline.fr).

PRICE. e-Tailers can also compete on price effectively since they can turn their inventory more often because of the sheer volume of products and customers who purchase them. Companies can sell more products, reducing prices for consumers while at the same time enhancing profits for the company. Further, virtual companies have no need to rent expensive retail space or employ sales clerks, allowing them to further reduce prices.

THE LONG TAIL. Together, these benefits of e-tailing have enabled a form of business model centered on the "Long Tails." Coined by Chris Anderson (2004, 2006), the concept of the **Long Tail** refers to catering to niche markets in addition to (or instead of) purely selling mainstream products. The distribution of consumers' needs and wants can be compared to a statistical normal distribution: The center of the distribution reflects the "mass market," characterized by relatively similar "mainstream" needs and wants shared by many people; the tails are the niche markets, catering to very diverse needs and wants (but very few of these people share the same needs and wants) (Figure 4.7). Because of high storage and distribution costs, most traditional brick-and-mortar retailers and service providers are forced to limit their product offerings to serving the needs and wants of the mainstream customers in the center of the distribution. For example, most independent movie productions are not shown at local cinemas, as they are unlikely to draw a large enough audience to cover the movie theater's costs to show the movie; in contrast, large mainstream productions typically draw a huge audience. Similarly, record stores carry only CDs of which a certain number of copies will be sold each year to cover the costs for shelf space, sales personnel, and so on. Given the limited local reach of brick-and-mortar stores, this ultimately limits the stores' product selection.

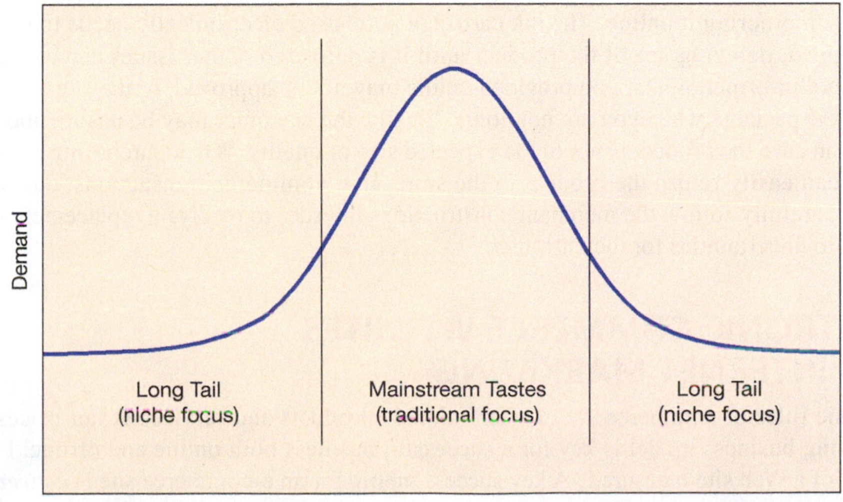

FIGURE 4.7

The Long Tails.

In contrast, enabled by their extended reach, many e-tailers can focus on the Long Tails, that is, on products outside the mainstream tastes. Whereas a local Blockbuster video rental store is unlikely to have a large selection of documentaries (because of a lack of local demand), Netflix can afford to have a very large selection of rather unpopular movies and still make a profit with it. Rather than renting a few "blockbusters" to many people, many (often outside the mainstream) titles are rented to a large number of people spread out on the Long Tails. Similarly, online bookseller Amazon.com can carry a tremendous selection of (often obscure) titles, as the costs for storage are far lower than those of their offline competitors. In fact, more than half of Amazon.com's book sales are titles that are *not* carried by the average physical bookstore, not even by megastores such as Barnes & Noble. In other words, focusing on those titles that are on the Long Tails of the distribution of consumers' wants can lead to a very successful business model in the digital world. A similar strategy is the mass-customization strategy pursued by Dell, which offers customized computers based on people's diverse needs and wants.

Drawbacks of e-Tailing

Despite all the recent hype associated with e-tailing, there are some downsides to this approach, in particular, issues associated with trust.

TRUST. One of the main factors keeping many consumers from purchasing goods and services online is trust. Especially for new online businesses, this tends to be challenging, as customers may be hesitant to purchase from companies they have never heard of. Often, trust becomes an issue due to the customer's inability to adequately experience the capabilities and characteristics of a product prior to purchase, as well as due to uncertainties surrounding product delivery and returns.

Direct Product Experience For many products, customers desire not only information about product characteristics, but also sensory information, such as taste, smell, and feel. When shopping for clothes at Lands' End, how can you be sure that you will like the feel of the material? Or what if you discover that the pair of size 9 EE hockey skates you just purchased online fits you like an 8 D? Likewise, products such as fragrances and foods can also be difficult for consumers to assess via the Web. Does the strawberry cheesecake offered online actually taste as good as it looks? How do you know if you will really like the smell of a perfume without actually sampling it? Finally, e-tailing eliminates the social aspects of the purchase. Although growing in popularity, e-tailers won't soon replace the local shopping mall, because going to the mall with some friends or interacting with a knowledgeable salesperson cannot be replicated online. On the other hand, online shopping provides certain anonymity, allowing people to shop for products they may not feel comfortable buying in an offline retail store.

Product Delivery and Returns Except for products that you can download directly, such as music, games, or electronic magazines, e-tailing requires additional time for products to be delivered. If you have run out of ink for your printer and your research paper is due this afternoon, chances are that you will visit your local office supply store to purchase a new ink cartridge rather than ordering it online. The ink cartridge purchased electronically needs to be packaged and shipped, delaying use of the product until it is delivered. Other issues can also arise. The credit card information that you provided online may not be approved, or the shipper may try to deliver the package when you are not home. Finally, the customer may be unsure about product returns, in case the product is not of the expected size or quality. When purchasing goods offline, people can easily return the product to the store. In e-commerce transactions, customers will have to carefully follow the merchant's instructions in order to receive a replacement or refund, leading to uncertainties for the customer.

ELECTRONIC COMMERCE WEBSITES AND INTERNET MARKETING

The basic rules of commerce are to offer valuable products and services at fair prices; a sound underlying business model is key for a successful business both online and offline. How is the success of a Web site measured? A key success metric for an e-commerce site is *conversion rate*, defined as the percentage of visitors who perform the desired action, be it to make a purchase, sign up for a newsletter, watch a video, and so on. In order to increase conversion rate, e-tailers should keep in mind a few recommendations:

RECOMMENDATION 1—THE WEB SITE SHOULD OFFER SOMETHING UNIQUE. Providing visitors with information or products that they can find nowhere else leads to EC profitability. Many small firms have found success on the Web by offering hard-to-find goods to a global audience at reasonable prices. Such niche markets can be in almost any category, be it elk meat, art supplies, or hard-to-find auto parts.

RECOMMENDATION 2—THE WEB SITE MUST MOTIVATE PEOPLE TO VISIT, TO STAY, AND TO RETURN. Given the pervasiveness of e-tailing, online consumers can choose from a multitude of vendors for any (mainstream) product they are looking for and are thus less likely to be loyal to a particular e-tailer. Rather, people go to the Web sites that offer the lowest prices, or they visit Web sites with which they have built a relationship, such as one that provides useful information, product ratings, and customer reviews, or offers free goods and services that they value. These sites help to establish an online community where members can build relationships, help each other, and feel at home. Likewise, e-tailers such as Amazon.com try to "learn" about their customers' interests in order to provide customized recommendations and strengthen virtual relationships.

RECOMMENDATION 3—YOU MUST ADVERTISE YOUR PRESENCE ON THE WEB. Like any other business, a Web site cannot be successful without customers. Companies must attract visitors to their site and away from the thousands of other sites they could be visiting. One method of attracting visitors involves advertising the Web site. The first way to advertise your firm's presence on the Web is to include the Web site address on all company materials, from business cards and letterheads to advertising copy. It is now common to see a company's URL listed at the end of its television commercials, and more and more companies integrate **QR codes** into their offline ads. QR codes are two-dimensional barcodes with a high storage capacity. In a consumer context, such bar codes are typically used to point the consumer to a particular Web page when he or she scans the barcode with a mobile device's camera (Figure 4.8). Alternatively, QR codes can trigger certain actions, such as initiating a phone call to a sales representative or sending a text message to a prespecified number.

FIGURE 4.8

Scanning a QR code can trigger certain actions, such as launching a Web site.

Source: Oleksiy Mark/Shutterstock.

RECOMMENDATION 4—YOU SHOULD LEARN FROM YOUR WEB SITE. Smart companies learn from their Web sites. A firm can track the path that visitors take through the many pages of its Web site and record the length of the visits, page views, common entry pages, a page's bounce rate and exit rate, and even the user's region, browser, or Internet service provider, among other statistics. **Exit rate** is defined as the percentage of visitors who leave the Web site (i.e., terminate the session) after viewing that page; in other words, it is the last page that users view before moving on to a different site, or closing their browser window. In contrast, **bounce rate** is defined as the percentage of single-page visits; in other words, it reflects the percentage of users for whom a particular page is the only page visited on the Web site during a session. As the different metrics can be affected by the page itself as well as by the quality of the traffic being attracted, the company can use this information to improve its Web site, or attempt to attract higher quality traffic. If the exit rate for a particular page is 75 percent, the company can try to find out why this occurs and redesign the page to entice the users to stay. Similarly, pages that go unused can be eliminated from the site, reducing maintenance and upkeep. This process of analyzing Web surfers' behavior in order to improve Web site performance (and, ultimately, maximize sales) is known as **Web analytics** (for more on this topic, see Chapter 6, "Enhancing Business Intelligence Using Information Systems").

Designing Web Sites to Meet Online Consumers' Needs

In addition to these recommendations, successful companies design their Web sites to enhance their online customers' experience when interacting with the Web site. Valacich, Parboteeah, and Wells (2007) found that online consumers' needs can be categorized in terms of the site's **structural firmness** (characteristics that influence the Web site's security and performance),

KEY PLAYERS

Behind the Online Storefront: How e-Commerce Giants Help Small Businesses Flourish

As numerous examples show, the Web allows almost anyone to set up an online store. The first step in starting your B2C e-commerce business is to set up an online storefront that is easy to use, fast, reliable, and aesthetically pleasing. Luckily, you don't have to start from scratch, and there are numerous options to choose from, depending on your needs. If you want to benefit from being associated with large, successful e-businesses, and want to minimize your effort in setting up a storefront, you can simply turn to the e-commerce giants eBay or Amazon, which let you sell products on their sites on a large scale. Alternatively, you can set up your own storefront, complete with your own domain name, giving you the most flexibility in how to present your store and your products to your customers.

As a fledgling online merchant, you can choose from literally hundreds of providers, ranging from commercial providers such as Intuit, GoDaddy, Shopify, or Yahoo! to open source solutions such as osCommerce or PrestaShop. Typically, such providers offer various templates for your storefront, an integrated shopping cart, and so on. Setting up your own storefront requires various decisions about the features you need; in addition to basic features such as product images, reviews, or search functionality, you may desire additional features such as reward programs, membership, coupons, and so on. Further, the online stores differ in features such as checkout/payment options, shipping calculation, or tracking integration; different options come at different price points, and you will not only have to decide what your current needs are, but also how your business will grow and what your future needs will be.

If your online shop is successful, your inventory will likely soon outgrow your living room, and to pick, pack, and ship the orders consumes considerable time. At this point you may consider outsourcing your order fulfillment. Many companies offer e-commerce order fulfillment services; all you have to do is ship your products (in bulk) to their warehouses, where the products will be stored until an order is received. Employees from the fulfillment service then pick, pack, and ship the order for you, so you can concentrate on managing your online business. Not surprisingly, one of the biggest players offering such services is Amazon.com. Having built a state-of-the-art warehouse and information systems infrastructure, Fulfillment by Amazon "rents out" these services to anyone wanting to run a successful online business. With the help of these big players, you should be able quickly get up and running with your new online business.

Based on:
Amazon.com (2012). Fulfillment by Amazon. *Amazon.com.* Retrieved June 13, 2012, from http://www.amazonservices.com/content/fulfillment-by-amazon.htm.

functional convenience (characteristics that make the interaction with the Web site easier or more convenient), and **representational delight** (characteristics that stimulate a consumer's senses). These are discussed next.

Structural Firmness For Web sites to be successful, structural firmness is a must. Online customers are unlikely to trust and revisit a Web site (let alone make a transaction) if the Web site does not function well (at least reasonably well). For example, the Web site should not have (or at least minimize) bad links, it should provide understandable error messages should something go wrong, and it should ensure privacy and security of the customers' data (EC Web sites often use trust seals to signal that privacy and security is ensured). Further, the Web site should be fast; if online customers have to wait for screens to download, they are not apt to stay at the site long or to return. In fact, studies suggest that the average length of time that a Web surfer will wait for a Web page to download on his or her screen is only a couple of seconds.

Functional Convenience The Web site must be easy to use. As with nearly all software, Web sites that are easy to use are more popular. If visitors have trouble finding things at the site or navigating through the site's links, they are unlikely to make a transaction or return to the site. Thus, Web sites should provide easy navigation for users to find their way (and back), should provide feedback about where the users are on the site, and offer help features. Further, features such as one-click ordering, offering a variety of payment methods, or order tracking can increase the perceived functional convenience of a Web site.

Representational Delight Finally, the Web site must be aesthetically pleasing. Successful firms on the Web have sites that are nice to look at. People are more likely to visit, stay at, and return to a Web site that looks good, as the design of a Web site can signal other characteristics of an online business, such as professionalism (Wells, Valacich, & Hess, 2011). Creating a unique look and feel can separate a Web site from its competition. Aesthetics can include the use of color schemes, fonts, backgrounds, and high-quality images. Furthermore, Web sites should have a clear, concise, and consistent layout, taking care to avoid unnecessary clutter. Nowadays, online businesses can choose from various (often freely available) e-commerce solutions that offer numerous well-designed store templates.

THE ONLINE CONSUMERS' HIERARCHY OF NEEDS. In a perfect world, an organization would strive to maximize all three sets of characteristics. In reality, businesses constantly have to make trade-offs between complexity, resource limitations, and other factors; thus, it is important to understand online consumers' *relative* needs. Valacich and colleagues' (2007) "online consumer's hierarchy of needs" suggests that overall, a site's structural firmness is most critical; once visitors' needs for structural firmness have been met, functional convenience is the next most important set of characteristics, followed by representational delight. In other words, if a Web site is only nice to look at, but difficult to navigate or appears not secure, visitors are unlikely to stay or make a purchase.

Needless to say, a basic level of structural firmness, functional convenience, and representational delight should be provided by any Web site (in other words, online visitors have a "zone of intolerance"). Beyond this basic level, the importance of the different sets of characteristics depends on the objective of a particular page on a Web site (Figure 4.9). For example, for a very utilitarian Web page, such as the login page of your online banking site, structural firmness should be emphasized to the user (though both functional convenience and representational delight should not be neglected). In contrast, for a relatively more hedonic Web page, such as a page designed to engage a visitor into considering a new home loan, representational delight should be emphasized (again, not neglecting the other factors). Hybrid pages, offering both hedonic and utilitarian value, such as those within Amazon.com or eBay.com, should balance the different factors.

Internet Marketing

One fundamental mistake companies can make when taking a current business online or creating an online business is assuming that if you build it, they will come. As with an offline business, marketing is a critical activity in any online endeavor.

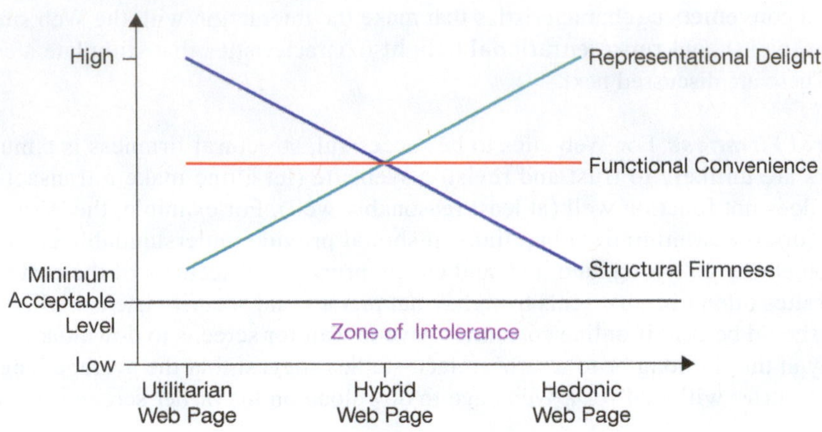

FIGURE 4.9

Different Web sites (pages) must focus on different design features.
Source: Based on Valacich et al. (2007).

Historically, companies' advertising budgets were mostly spent on noninteractive advertising campaigns, such as billboards, newspaper, radio, or television ads. However, by 2013, 42 percent of U.S. online adults were accessing the Internet multiple times a day from multiple devices and locations (Parrish et al., 2013). In response to these changes, companies are reallocating their advertising budgets; in 2011, organizations spent 19 percent of their advertising budget on Internet marketing; research firm Forrester estimates that by 2016, companies will spend 35 percent of their advertising budget on Internet marketing, including search marketing, display ads, e-mail marketing, social media, and mobile marketing (VanBoskirk, 2011). All of these are discussed next.

SEARCH MARKETING. Whereas people would traditionally obtain information about products or companies from offline sources, many Web surfers now just enter the name of a product into a search engine such as Google or Bing and then visit the resulting pages. Given this trend, it is not surprising that search marketing is now big business. Research firm Forrester reports that by 2016, companies in the United States will spend US$33.3 billion on search marketing (Figure 4.10). Included in search marketing are paid search and search engine optimization, both of which are discussed next.

Paid Search The results presented by search engines such as Google or Bing are typically separated into organic results (i.e., based on the page's content) and sponsored results. A way to ensure that your company's page appears on the first page users see when searching for a specific term is using **search advertising** (or **sponsored search**). For example, using Google's "AdWords," a company can bid for being listed in the sponsored search results for the term "LCD Monitor" (Figure 4.11). In order to present the most relevant ads to its users, Google then determines the relevance of the ad's and the page's content to the search term, and, depending on the amount of the bid, the company's Web page is listed in the sponsored results;

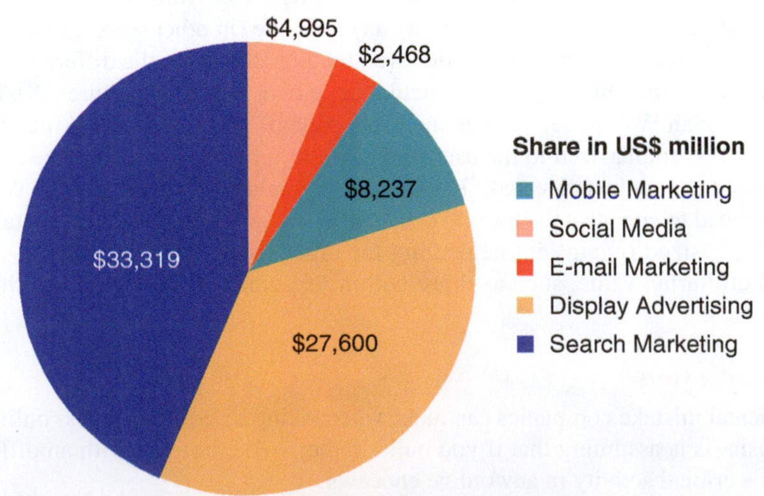

FIGURE 4.10

Search marketing is forecasted to have the largest share of interactive marketing by 2016.
Source: Based on VanBoskirk, S. (2011, August 24). US interactice marketing foercast, 2011–2016. Cambridge, MA: Forrester Research.

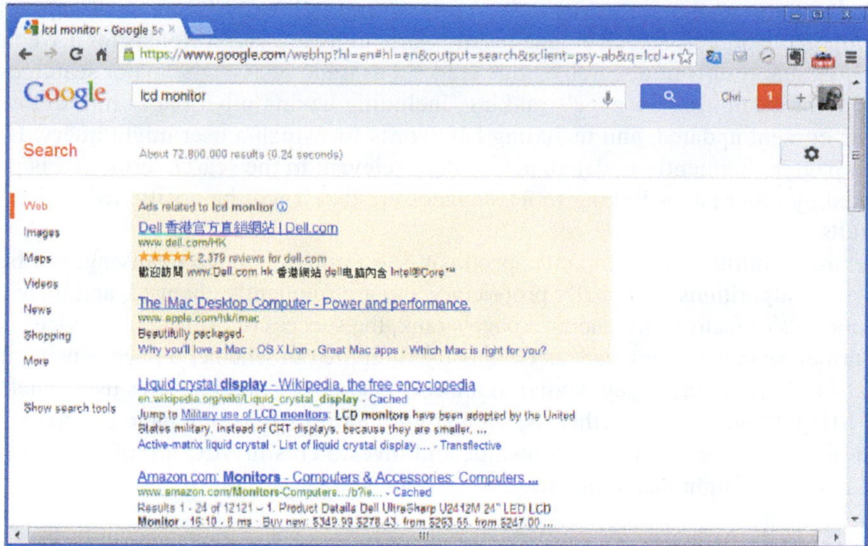

FIGURE 4.11

Companies pay per click for being included in the sponsored listings.
Source: Courtesy of Google, Inc.

Google is paid on a pay-per-click basis (see the following discussion of pricing models). As you can imagine, this can quickly become very expensive for advertisers, especially when the sponsored link is associated with a popular search term, and the advertiser has to bid against many competitors. On the other hand, a system such as Google's AdWords ensures high-quality leads, as the ads are presented only to users actually searching for a specific key word (in contrast to traditional ads, which are presented to anyone). As programs such as AdWords can be tweaked in myriad ways (such as by key words, negative key words, region, time of day, and so on), many companies turn to professional consultants who help to optimize sponsored search campaigns. Alternatively, some search engines offer to elevate a page's position in the organic results after paying a fee (**paid inclusion**). Many search engines that pride themselves on offering unbiased results (such as Google), however, do not offer paid inclusion. Overall, Forrester Research estimates that spending on paid search will increase from US$16.5 billion to US$29 billion between 2011 and 2016.

Search Engine Optimization Internet search engines such as Google, Yahoo!, and Bing order the organic results of a user's search according to complex, proprietary formulas, and the ranking (position of the link to a particular page) in the search results is largely outside the control of the Web site's owner (Figure 4.12). Given the incredible numbers of results that are returned for common searches such as "apparel," "sportswear," or "digital camera," most surfers visit only the first few links that are presented and rarely go beyond the first page of the

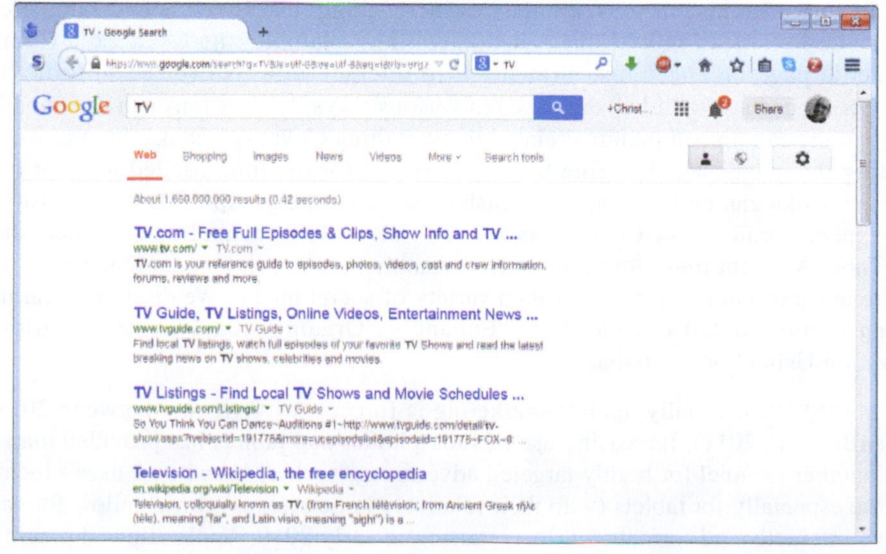

FIGURE 4.12

It is hard to influence the ranking of your company's page in the organic search results.
Source: Courtesy of Google, Inc.

search results; thus, companies use **search engine optimization (SEO)** in an attempt to boost their ranking in the organic search engine results. Although the exact formulas for a Web page's rank in the organic results of a search engine are kept as trade secrets, the major search engines give tips on how to optimize a page's ranking, including having other pages link to the page, keeping the content updated, and including key words for which a user might query. In other words, if a page is frequently updated, has content relevant to the search term, and is popular (as indicated by other pages linking to it), chances are that it will be positioned higher in the search results.

There are a multitude of companies promising to improve a page's ranking, but because search engines' algorithms are usually proprietary and are frequently changed, and there can be literally hundreds of factors influencing a page's rank, the success of using such services is often limited. Further, search engines such as Google try to figure out whether a page is using unethical "tricks" (such as "hidden" key words) to improve its ranking and ban sites using such tricks from the listing altogether. Nevertheless, even slight modifications to a page can have a large impact on the site's ranking in search results, and investments in SEO are often worthwhile, especially in times of tight marketing budgets.

DISPLAY ADS. In the early days of the Web, display advertising was the prevalent form of online advertising. Similar to traditional newspaper ads, companies would advertise their presence on other popular Web sites, such as nytimes.com, using static banner ads, video ads, or interactive banner ads, where users can interact with the advertisement. A recent trend in display advertising has been contextual advertising, where the ads placed on a page are in some way related to the content of that page. If, for example, you are reading tournament results from a PGA golf event at a popular sports Web site such as espn.com, you will also likely see an advertisement to buy new golf equipment or to visit a golf resort. A variety of interactive features, rich media ads, the ability to place ads in online videos, as well as the ability to accurately measure an ad's impact, contribute to display advertising's increasing popularity.

E-MAIL MARKETING. E-mail marketing has been, and continues to be, very popular among advertisers, with over 95 percent of marketers using e-mail marketing in their overall interactive marketing mix (VanBoskirk, 2011). Given the low cost of less than US$0.01 per e-mail, advertisers are increasingly trying to move away from direct-mail advertising and replace it with e-mail advertising. In addition to low cost, the effectiveness of e-mail advertising campaigns can be measured directly (such as by including special links or images in the e-mail that allow tracking which e-mails the customers have opened or reacted to). Further, e-mail marketing saves tremendous amounts of paper over direct marketing, allowing a company to build a positive green image.

SOCIAL MEDIA MARKETING. One relatively recent trend in Internet marketing is harnessing the power of social media, such as the social networking site Facebook. More and more people rely on social media to stay in contact with their friends or business associates, so including such sites in the interactive marketing mix is a natural move for companies. In addition to placing display ads on such sites, companies increasingly use social networking sites for interactive communication with their customers. For example, the Coca-Cola Company has created a page on Facebook, allowing it to interact with its over 82 million "fans" (i.e., Facebook users who "like" the page) in various ways; Coke's fans can download free virtual goodies, can upload pictures related to everything Coke, or can use interactive apps. By creating this page (which is free for Coke, except for the time needed to set it up and maintain it), Coke can build strong relationships with a large group of its target customers. Similarly, people can follow Coke on Twitter or visit Coke's channel on the video-sharing site YouTube. A recent trend for companies is establishing "social media listening centers" to feel the pulse of public opinion across a variety of social media. We discuss social media marketing in more detail in Chapter 5, "Enhancing Organizational Communication and Collaboration Using Social Media."

MOBILE MARKETING. Finally, mobile marketing is forecast to skyrocket between 2011 and 2016 (VanBoskirk, 2011). Increasing use of smartphones and tablets has provided marketers with yet another channel for highly targeted advertising (such as based on a user's location). This is true especially for tablets (with their relatively large screens), which allow for various innovative interactive ad formats. Further, starting in early 2010, Apple allowed placing ads

WHEN THINGS GO WRONG

Buying Likes

We've all seen them in our social network feeds: "Like this page for a chance to win a cash prize," or "Share this link to help John Doe get a backstage pass to the concert!" Social media sites like Facebook are a great platform for businesses to generate buzz and, with a well-executed marketing campaign, get noticed by millions of users. Many businesses entice users to "like" their business page for some reward—a discount or chance to win a prize—and in turn, the users who "like" the business spread the word to each of their network connections automatically. Users of Twitter and Instagram can also promote topics or businesses using hashtags (keywords denoted with a "#" symbol, see Chapter 5). These campaigns can be very effective. For example, AT&T promoted its "Be The Fan" campaign during the U.S. college football season in 2013, providing "Fan Challenges" to football fans and encouraging individuals to share their results via social media and include the hashtag #BeTheFan. Users sharing the hashtag were then randomly selected for weekly prizes, including trips to big games. Over 200 million users engaged in the program across all social networks, and there was a 400 percent increase in contest entries over a similar promotion held the previous year.

Sometimes, however, these campaigns and contests can be deeply biased by automated "likes" and votes, giving unfair advantage to users who game the system. There are many services that offer "like buying," and other forms of electronic voting fraud. One such company, based in Chennai, India, employs 54 people whose job is to use a multitude of social media accounts to "like," follow, vote for, or otherwise promote whatever campaign their clients hire them to promote. Some of these companies use special software to spoof and rapidly change their IP address, preventing filtering from contest sponsors who try to prevent multiple votes from the same IP address, or who limit valid entries to only those within a specified geographical region.

Social media platforms try to suppress this type of devious behavior, but, as with many such practices, it turns into a cat-and-mouse game with both the social networks and the fraudsters constantly finding new ways to outsmart the other. Do a search for "vote buying services" online and see who is currently ahead.

Based on:

Cassenelli, A. (2013, December 31). 13 best social media campaigns of 2013. *Postano*. Retrieved May 22, 2014, from http://www.postano.com/blog/13-best-social-media-campaigns-of-2013.

Permenter, C. (2013, June 6). Buying likes and rigging votes: Facebook's seedy underworld. *The Daily Dot*. Retrieved May 21, 2014, from http://www.dailydot.com/business/facebook-buy-votes-rig-contests-likes.

into iPhone apps, which allowed app developers to offer apps for lower prices (or free, under the freeconomics model; see Chapter 2) and gave marketers another opportunity to reach their target audience through their favorite channels. Finally, the growth in mobile commerce further contributes to the growth of mobile marketing, as companies are trying to reach their customers wherever, whenever.

ASSESSING PERFORMANCE OF INTERNET MARKETING. The performance of Internet marketing can be assessed by metrics such as **click-through rate**, reflecting the number of surfers who click on an ad (i.e., clicks) divided by the number of times it was displayed (i.e., impressions), or **conversion rate**, reflecting the percentage of visitors who actually perform the marketer's desired action (such as making a purchase). Targeting a well-defined audience with an ad campaign can help to attract high-quality leads, ultimately resulting in higher conversion rates.

One common pricing model for online advertising is impression based—that is, based on the number of times the page containing an ad is viewed, typically expressed in cost per thousand impressions (i.e., cost per mille, or CPM). Depending on advertising volume and the popularity of the site where the ad is placed, costs can range from US$8 to US$40 per thousand impressions. Given the fact that many Web surfers do not even look at the online ads (and Web browsers such as Firefox offer the option to block certain ads), the trend in Web advertising is moving toward performance-based pricing models, where the return on investment is more direct, such as **pay-per-click** models. Under this type of pricing model, the firm running the advertisement pays only when a Web surfer actually clicks on the advertisement; the cost per click is typically between US$0.01 and US$0.50 per click, depending on the site, its viewers, and so on.

Click Fraud One drawback, however, of pay-per-click models is the possibility of abuse by repeatedly clicking on a link to inflate revenue to the host or increase the costs for the advertiser; this is known as **click fraud**. Click fraud has become increasingly problematic; research firms estimate that between 30 and 60 percent of Web site visits may be generated by non-human traffic. However, this is primarily a problem for impression-based pricing models, and companies such as Google are constantly monitoring clicks to detect potentially fraudulent activity.

MOBILE COMMERCE, CONSUMER-TO-CONSUMER EC, AND CONSUMER-TO-BUSINESS EC

Fueled by the megatrends, mobile commerce has seen tremendous growth in the past few years. As defined earlier in the chapter, m-commerce is any electronic transaction or information interaction conducted using a wireless, mobile device and mobile networks (wireless or switched public network) that leads to the transfer of real or perceived value in exchange for information, services, or goods (MobileInfo, 2014).

Powerful mobile devices such as Apple's iPhone and iPad or Samsung's Galaxy, supporting high-speed data transfer and "always-on" connectivity, provide a wide variety of services and capabilities in addition to voice communication, such as multimedia data transfer, video streaming, video telephony, a sheer unlimited number of useful apps, and full Internet access, allowing consumers to access information or make transactions on the go. Indeed, research firm eMarketer forecasts the m-commerce market in the United States to grow from US$41 billion to US$113 billion from 2013 to 2017. Relatedly, Goldman Sachs predicts worldwide m-commerce sales to reach US$626 billion, with over 70 percent of transactions being made using tablets.

The increasing use of tablets is seen as a major driver of mobile commerce. Although providing for mobility, tablets are often used in people's living rooms as "couch computers"; thus, tablets allow people to shop from the comfort of their homes, without being tied to a desk and a computer screen (Figure 4.13). In addition, tablets provide larger screen sizes, allowing for better product presentation. An analysis of 16.2 billion transactions from 150 online retailers showed that tablet users tend to spend significantly more per order than shoppers using smartphones or personal computers (Adobe, 2012); given that tablet users tend to have above-average incomes, tablets may be an Internet marketer's dream. For companies operating in the digital world, this means that in order to harness the opportunities of mobile commerce, they have to ensure to provide their content in formats suited for the different devices' form factors.

LOCATION-BASED M-COMMERCE. Another key driver for m-commerce is **location-based services**, which are highly personalized mobile services based on a user's location. Location-based services are implemented via the cellular network, Wi-Fi networks, and global positioning

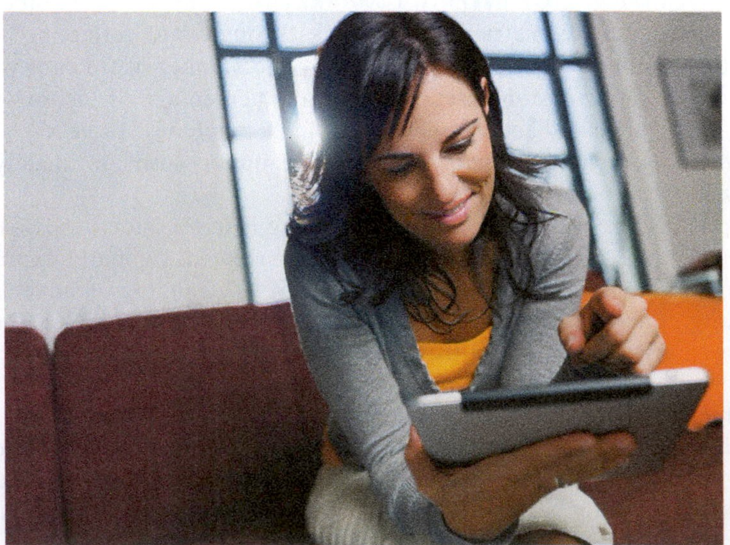

FIGURE 4.13

Tablets are often used as "couch computers."
Source: Diego Cervo/Shutterstock.

TABLE 4.2 GPS-Enabled Location-Based Services

Service	Example
Location	Determining the basic geographic position of the cell phone
Mapping	Capturing specific locations to be viewed on the phone
Navigation	The ability to give route directions from one point to another
Tracking	The ability to see another person's location

system (GPS) functionality, now built into most modern cell phones. Location-based services allow the service provider to offer information or services tailored to the consumers' needs, depending on their location. For example, search engines can provide specific information about attractions or restaurants located in the user's vicinity, retail stores can enhance store locators with navigation instructions, or users can receive real-time traffic or public transport information (Table 4.2).

INFORMATION ON THE GO. In the digital world, people have become increasingly used to having tremendous amounts of information available. Mobile devices have taken this to the next level, in that people now have the information available whenever, wherever (Figure 4.14). For instance, when deciding on whether or not to enter a particular restaurant, people can get further information or customer reviews from sites such as yelp.com using their mobile devices; similarly, when standing in a retail store, customers can easily retrieve a host of information and reviews about particular products. For customers, this capability can help tremendously when making purchase decisions; for companies operating in the offline world, this has turned into a mixed blessing. On the one hand, they can augment the offline shopping experience by being able to provide much more information than they would typically be able to. On the other hand, the rise in smartphone use has led to **showrooming**—that is, shoppers coming into a store to evaluate the look and feel of a product, just to then purchase it online or at a competitor's store. Obviously, click-only companies benefit from this practice; online retailer Amazon.com even offers an app that lets the user scan a product's barcode with the smartphone's camera, and then displays the product information and price offered by Amazon.com.

In addition to providing information on the go, service providers have started to offer mobile tickets or even mobile boarding passes; typically a QR barcode is sent to the smartphone of the user, who then just has to present the code to a barcode reader to verify the ticket or boarding pass. This adds convenience for the user, who does not have to keep track of paper tickets, physical boarding passes, and the like. In addition, the service provider can offer additional information and services, such as automatic notifications of delays or gate changes for passengers.

FIGURE 4.14

Using mobile devices, information is always at your fingertips.

Source: Courtesy of Google, Inc.

FIGURE 4.15

Businesses have to decide whether to build apps for different platforms and form factors.
Source: Scanrail/Fotolia.

Mobile social networking is another trend fueled by the increasing penetration and increasing capabilities of mobile devices. With the success of social networking sites such as Facebook, many innovators are looking to social networks and mobile technologies. Social networks such as Foursquare are offering various features supporting mobile social networking, such as allowing people to "check in" at places like restaurants or attractions using their mobile devices, letting their friends know about their location or activities, and uploading pictures directly from the mobile phone. We will discuss more about (mobile) social networking in Chapter 5.

PRODUCT AND CONTENT SALES. Mobile users increasingly use their mobile devices to make purchases of products or content on the go. In an attempt to harness this trend, many online retailers designed mobile versions of their Web sites, so as to facilitate the shopping process on mobile devices. With the increasing popularity of mobile commerce, companies have to strategically decide whether to go beyond mobile versions of their Web sites and create a focused mobile app. While mobile apps can offer many interactive features, they are typically costly to develop as they have to be tailored to different platforms (e.g., Apple's iOS vs. Android) and device form factors (such as different screen sizes of smartphones and tablets) (Figure 4.15). Recently, Home plus, the Korean subsidiary of the British grocery giant Tesco, built a "virtual supermarket" in a subway station. Using billboard-sized posters, Home plus displayed pictures of all products that could be ordered; customers just had to scan the QR code beneath a product to make a purchase, which would then be delivered to the customer's home or office.

Especially among commuters, accessing content from mobile devices is extremely popular. Content providers ranging from newspapers to TV stations are now offering various ways to access their content from mobile devices. The increasing field of mobile content is obviously an important part of many companies' mobile marketing mix, as it allows reaching people in more places, and provides for extremely targeted marketing efforts (such as based on a user's location).

C2C EC

C2C commerce has been with us since the start of commerce itself. Whether it was bartering, auctions, or tendering, commerce has always included C2C economics. According to the American Life Project, 17 percent of online American adults, or 25 million people, have used the Internet to sell things. Electronically facilitated interactions create unique opportunities (such as a large pool of potential buyers) and unique problems (such as the potential of being defrauded; see Table 4.3). This section discusses *e-auctions* and *online classifieds*, two of the most popular mechanisms consumers use to buy, sell, and trade with other consumers.

COMING ATTRACTIONS

Carbon Nanocomputers

For over 50 years, advances in computing capabilities have progressed at a steady pace. The first transistors were developed around 1950, and electronic components have become increasingly powerful and compact since that time. A modern smartphone carries a microprocessor with well over 1 billion tiny transistors; these pocketable processors are roughly 15,000 times more powerful than the first personal computers introduced in the 1980s. Impressive as these advances in computing power are, manufacturers of these processors are constantly battling the limits of silicon—the material used to create nearly all electronic components. Microprocessor manufacturers must constantly develop new ways to cram more computing power into increasingly smaller silicon chips, and the possibility that we will eventually reach the limit of what silicon can do has led some researchers to explore alternative computing paradigms.

The leading contender for heir to silicon's throne is the carbon nanotube. Carbon nanotubes are hollow cylinders composed of a single sheet of carbon atoms. Numerous features of nanotubes make them ideal as the basis of tomorrow's electronic components. The nanotubes are so small that it takes relatively little energy to power a nanotube transistor—only a fraction of the energy required by transistors made of silicon—which could be a major boon to the legions of battery-powered mobile and wearable devices predicted in the future. Nanotubes' small size also makes them easier to pack into small places. Nanotubes are also much more heat efficient, a key consideration, as excess heat severely decreases the effectiveness of computing devices. In short, nanotube-based processors could do a whole lot more useful work while using a whole lot less power.

Scientists at Stanford University recently announced that they had successfully created the first functioning nanotube-based computer. The computer operates with just one "bit" of information, and can only count to 32. The researchers' progress, however, lays the groundwork for computing devices that are essentially limitless in computational power. Such technologies could fuel a computing paradigm that causes a monumental leap forward in computing technology.

Based on:

Morgan, J. (2013, September 25). First computer made of carbon nanotubes is unveiled. *BBC*. Retrieved May 27, 2014, from http://www.bbc.com/news/science-environment-24232896.

Gaudin, Sharon. (2013, September 30). Replacing silicon with nanotubes could revolutionize tech. *Computer World*. Retrieved May 27, 2014, from http://www.computerworld.com/s/article/9242812/Replacing_silicon_with_nanotubes_could_revolutionize_tech.

E-AUCTIONS. As seen throughout this text, the Internet has provided the possibility to disseminate information and services that were previously unavailable in many locations. This dissemination can be seen clearly in the emergence of electronic auctions, or **e-auctions**. e-Auctions provide a place where sellers can post goods and services for sale and buyers can bid on these items. Relatedly, bartering typically takes place on a one-on-one basis, but Web sites such as swap.com bring together many people listing items to swap.

The largest e-auction site, as you probably know, is eBay (www.ebay.com). eBay's revenue model is based on small fees that are associated with posting items, but these small fees quickly add up, so that in 2013 eBay's net revenues exceeded US$16 billion. Whereas eBay is hugely popular, there continue to be cases of fraud. According to the Internet Crime Complaint Center, e-auctions are marred with fraud (ic3.gov, 2014), with e-auction fraud being among the

TABLE 4.3 Opportunities and Threats of C2C EC

Opportunities	Threats
Consumers can buy and sell to broader markets	No quality control
Eliminates the middleman that increases the final price of products and services	Higher possibility of fraud
Always available for consumers, 24/7/365	Harder to use traditional payment methods (checks, cash, ATM cards)
Market demand is an efficient mechanism for setting prices in the electronic environment	
Increases the numbers of buyers and sellers who can find each other	

FIGURE 4.16

Amateur and professional photographers can sell their creations through microstock photo sites such as shutterstock.com.

top five most common crime types filed with the center. From a buyer's standpoint, counterfeit items tend to be the biggest problem; with the proliferation of fake goods ranging from handbags to brake pads, air bags, and chain saws, using counterfeit goods can not only lead to legal complications, but can potentially have dangerous or even deadly consequences. For sellers, bid shielding (sometimes called "shill bidding") continues to be a problem: Using two different accounts, a shopper places a low followed by a very high bid on a desired item, leading other bidders to drop out of the auction, to then retract the high bid, and win the item at the low bid. Needless to say, online auction sites warn users to exercise caution when purchasing goods; in addition, e-auction providers such as eBay offer swift conflict resolution mechanisms to preserve people's trust in the marketplace, and use sophisticated business intelligence applications (see Chapter 6) to detect and minimize e-auction fraud, attempting to make C2C EC a safer shopping experience.

ONLINE CLASSIFIEDS. Another type of C2C e-commerce is online classifieds. Although online classifieds sites such as craigslist.com are enabled by Web capabilities, no transactions take place online. Yet, online classifieds have flourished in recent years, enabling people to sell anything from flowers to furniture. A related concept that has gained popularity is "freecycling," that is, giving away goods for free to anyone who is willing to pick them up. Likewise, C2C marketplaces such as Etsy allow individuals to sell vintage or handmade products to other consumers.

C2B EC

Just as the Web has enabled small businesses to participate in global EC, it has also enabled consumers to sell goods or services to businesses, reversing the more typical B2C model. As a relatively new phenomenon, consumer-to-business (C2B) EC has seen a few implementations. One prime example is microstock photo sites such as www.shutterstock.com, which sells pictures, videos, or artwork to publishers, newspapers, Web designers, or advertising agencies; however, in contrast to traditional stock photo agencies, such as Getty Images, Shutterstock sources much of its content not from professionals but from amateur photographers (Figure 4.16). Similarly, companies use crowdsourcing on micro-task marketplaces such as Amazon's Mechanical Turk (see Chapter 5) in order to have small, well-defined tasks (such as tagging pictures or describing products) completed by a scalable ad hoc workforce of everyday people. However, it can be argued that consumers who regularly engage in C2B transactions and make parts of their living with such transactions can be considered businesses; hence, the line between C2B and B2B transactions is somewhat blurry.

MANAGING FINANCES AND NAVIGATING LEGAL ISSUES IN EC

Within a short period of time, radical developments in technology and systems have brought EC from a fringe economic activity to one of the most prevalent in today's global economy. This innovation has not slowed down and has opened some promising new areas within EC. This section outlines Web-based financial transactions and legal issues related to engaging in EC.

BRIEF CASE CrowdSpring—The Graphic Designers' Marketplace

Ever wanted a new logo or flier or website, but lack the expertise to make it great? It used to be that a business would have to hire or train a graphic designer to take care of creative work like that, which tends to be expensive and impractical for many individuals or small businesses. CrowdSpring and its competitors seek to solve this problem with their popular graphic designers' marketplaces.

CrowdSpring is a large marketplace designed to connect businesses with creative professionals in a mutually beneficial relationship. Using this marketplace, businesses create a description of the design project they would like accomplished, including anything from logos to business cards to presentation slides to mobile app designs. The business sets a deadline and a price it is willing to pay, and the project is posted to the marketplace for designers to see. Designers who are willing to create the design for the offered price submit design ideas (a typical project received over 100 ideas from designers around the world), and then the business can choose a design and work with the designer to perfect the design. And if none of the submitted designs was quite what the business was looking for, it receives a full refund of its listing fees in a 100 percent money-back guarantee.

Such marketplaces provide tremendous value for all parties involved. Businesses are able to access designers and other creative professionals at a fraction of the cost of hiring a designer or contracting with a design firm. Designers, who often do design work on the side separately from their day job, have the opportunity to use their design skills to get paid. Both of these parties have access to a much more global marketplace than in decades past—a designer in the Philippines can create designs for a small business in New Jersey. In return for providing a trusted platform that hosts transactions and connects these two parties, CrowdSpring is rewarded with transaction fees for every successful match it makes. It's a clear win-win-win.

Questions

1. What are the drawbacks of using sites such as CrowdSpring for designers? What are the drawbacks of using sites such as CrowdSpring for businesses?
2. What other innovative business models can you think of that could use the crowds as labor force?

Based on:

Anonymous. (n.d.). How CrowdSpring works. *CrowdSpring*. Retrieved May 21, 2014, from http://www.crowdspring.com/how-it-works.

e-Banking

One special form of services frequently offered online is managing financial transactions. Whereas traditionally consumers had to visit their bank to conduct financial transactions, they can now manage credit card, checking, or savings accounts online using **online banking** or pay their bills using **electronic bill pay** services. However, concerns about the security of online transactions have worried many online users, with 41 percent of the respondents to a survey by research firm Entersekt worrying about their account being compromised (Li, 2012).

In addition to online banking, **online investing** has seen steady growth over the past several years. The Internet has changed the investment landscape considerably; now, people use the Internet to get information about stock quotes or to manage their portfolios. For example, many consumers turn to sites such as MSN Money, Yahoo! Finance, or CNN Money to get the latest information about stock prices, firm performance, or mortgage rates. Then they can use online brokerage firms to buy or sell stocks. Increasingly, financial service providers offer ways for their customers to use their mobile devices for conducting banking transactions. For example, many banks created **mobile banking** apps for checking account balances, or initiating transactions. Similarly, most large online brokerage services offer trading apps for various smartphone platforms. Large banks like Chase, Citibank, USAA, ING direct, and Charles Schwab offer mobile check deposit apps, allowing customers to deposit a check by simply taking a picture of the check with a smartphone's camera.

Securing Payments in the Digital World

One of the biggest impediments to B2C EC, C2C EC, and m-commerce is ensuring that consumers can make secure transactions on the Web site. Although the transfer of money is a critical factor in online shopping, online banking, and online investing, security researchers and software companies are lamenting that people are often reluctant to change their habits when surfing the Web and carelessly reveal sensitive information to unknown or fraudulent sites. In fact, more than 11.6 million consumers in the United States (or 4.9 percent of U.S. adults) became victims of *identity theft* in 2011 (see Chapter 10, "Securing Information Systems").

WHO'S GOING MOBILE

Mobile Payments

The advent of the credit card and electronic funds transfer (EFT) mechanisms have paved the way for cashless societies. Indeed, in the United States, only 7 percent of all transactions are made in cash, and in Sweden, the number is only 3 percent. Yet, even though the number of cash transactions seems to be on the decline, there are still various scenarios in which using EFT or credit cards is cumbersome or downright impossible. For example, many offline retailers resist accepting credit cards for small purchases, mainly due to the high costs involved, and many small amounts (such as paying at the parking meter) cannot be paid using credit cards. Similarly, the friend who covered the bill for dinner is unlikely to accept credit cards, and paying for online purchases on your mobile phone (e.g., for movie tickets) is very cumbersome.

With increasing mobility in the digital world, the smartphone appears to be a natural payment companion: Just like a wallet, most people carry their phone with them at all times. To harness this opportunity, companies have devised various ways to use a smartphone as a payment device. Many companies are innovating to incorporate mobile payment systems within their operations. For example, near-field communication (NFC) allows for simply waving an NFC-enabled phone in front of a reading device; the payment amount is typically billed to a linked credit card. Similarly, the American coffee giant Starbucks developed an app that lets users pay for their coffee by having the barista scan a barcode generated by the app, and PayPal developed an app that allows for sending money to friends or for ordering products by simply scanning a QR code. McDonalds is piloting a new mobile ordering and payment system in Austria that allows customers to order their food while en route to the restaurant, pay automatically via one of several payment options, and pick up their order by simply verifying their payment with the cashier.

Mobile payment appears to be here to stay. However, it is not without problems. For example, critics cite the lack of accessibility for older generations, as well as costs involved for the merchants, and, last but not least, privacy concerns: unlike cash, mobile transactions are always stored somewhere, and may put people's privacy at risk when making purchases or even donations. On the other hand, mobile payments offer a host of opportunities for retailers, enabling them to build ever closer relationships with their customers.

Based on:

Cave, A. (2012, April 10). Is mobile the way we'll all be paying? *Telegraph.co.uk*.. Retrieved May 27, 2014, from http://www.telegraph.co.uk/finance/festival-of-business/9195540/Is-mobile-the-way-well-all-be-paying.html.

Gahran, A. (2011, November 22). Why mobile payments haven't gone mainstream. *CNN*. Retrieved May 27, 2014, from http://www.cnn.com/2011/11/22/tech/mobile/google-wallet-payment/index.html.

Boden, R. (2014, May 22). McDonald's launches Quick Mac mobile payments in Austria. *NFC World*. Retrieved May 27, 2014, from http://www.nfcworld.com/2014/05/22/329315/mcdonalds-launches-quick-mac-mobile-payments-austria.

Security concerns and other factors (such as impatience, lengthy checkout procedures, or comparison shopping) lead shoppers to frequently abandon their shopping carts and to not follow through with a purchase—reports show that more than half of the online shopping carts are abandoned. Traditionally, paying for goods and services was limited to using credit and debit cards, but now different companies offer payment services for buying and selling goods or services online. Issues related to different forms of online payment are discussed next.

CREDIT AND DEBIT CARDS. Credit and debit cards are still among the most accepted forms of payment in B2C EC. For customers, paying online using a credit card is easy; all the customer needs to do is to enter his or her name, billing address, credit card number, expiration date, and the so-called **Card Verification Value (CVV2)**, a three-digit code located on the back of the card, to authorize a transaction. However, for each transaction, an online customer has to transmit much personal information to a (sometimes unknown) merchant, and many Internet users (sometimes rightfully) fear being defrauded by an untrustworthy seller or falling victim to some other form of computer crime (see Table 4.4 for guidelines on how to conduct safe transactions on the Internet; see also Chapter 10). For online merchants, the risk of people using fraudulent credit card data may be equally high. This is discussed next.

MANAGING RISK IN B2C TRANSACTIONS. As in offline transactions, online consumers at times dispute transactions for various reasons. In such cases, the merchant is financially responsible for the transactions, and credit card issuers typically charge back transactions that

TABLE 4.4 Ways to Protect Yourself When Shopping Online

Tip	Example
Use a secure browser	Make sure that your browser has the latest encryption capabilities; also, always look for the padlock icon in your browser's status bar before transmitting sensitive information
Check the site's privacy policy	Make sure that the company you're about to do business with does not share any information you would prefer not to be shared
Read and understand the refund and shipping policies	Make sure that you can return unwanted/defective products for a refund
Keep your personal information private	Make sure that you don't give out information, such as your Social Security number, unless you know what the other entity is going to do with it
Give payment information only to businesses you know and trust	Make sure that you don't provide your payment information to fly-by-night operations
Keep records of your online transactions and check your e-mail	Make sure that you don't miss important information about your purchases
Review your monthly credit card and bank statements	Make sure to check for any erroneous or unauthorized transactions

Source: Based on Federal Trade Commission (2010).

are disputed by cardholders. For the merchants, such chargebacks normally result in the loss of the transaction amount, loss of the merchandise, processing costs, and chargeback fees; in addition, the merchant's bank may charge higher fees or even close the merchant account if the chargeback rate is excessively high. Thus, minimizing chargebacks is of prime concern for online merchants. Some of the reasons for chargebacks, such as unclear store policies, product descriptions, shipping terms, or transaction currencies, can be minimized through good Web store design; other reasons, such as stolen credit cards, require different safeguards (Visa, 2008).

Any credit card transactions must be authorized by the issuer of the credit card. However, this authorization merely assures that the credit card was not reported as lost or stolen, but does not assure that the person making the transaction is the actual cardholder. In e-commerce transactions, there is no imprint of the physical card and no cardholder signature, so online merchants have to be especially careful when deciding whether or not to make a transaction. While online customers demand a quick checkout process, leaving the merchant with little time to authenticate whether the customer is indeed the cardholder, the transaction date is the date the merchandise is shipped; thus, online merchants typically have one or several days to verify the identity of the cardholder. To minimize risk, online merchants often use automated fraud screening services that provide the merchants with a risk score based on a number of variables such as match between shipping address, billing address, and phone number; the time of the order and the customer's time zone; transaction volume; and the customer's IP address and its geographic location. Based on the risk score, merchants can then decide whether or not to let the transaction go through. For such screening services to be most effective, the merchant should collect as much data as possible during the checkout process, which may lead some customers to abandon their shopping carts. In addition, online merchants can assess orders based on various fraud indicators (Figure 4.17); Visa recommends looking for fraud indicators such as:

- ***E-mail addresses.*** Legitimate e-mail addresses often contain some parts of the customer's name; in contrast, fraudsters often set up e-mail addresses consisting of meaningless character combinations with free email providers.
- ***Shipping and billing addresses.*** Fraudsters often have the merchandise shipped to foreign, high-risk countries. Thus, merchants may require billing and shipping addresses to be the same. In addition, as many fraudsters come from foreign countries, misspellings of common words or street names may serve as a potential fraud indicator.

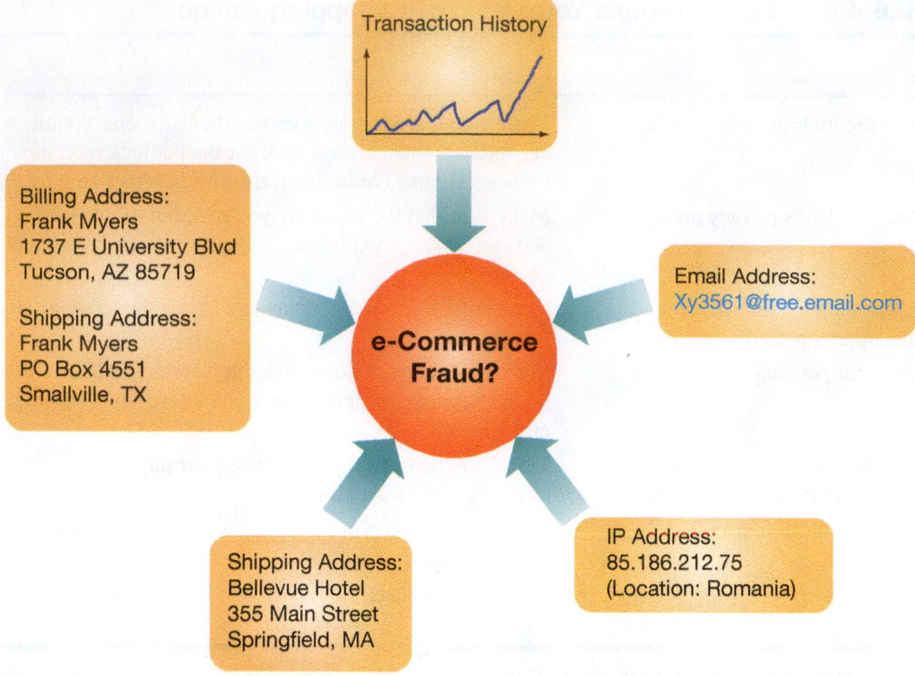

FIGURE 4.17
Various indicators can signal potential e-commerce fraud.

- ***Transaction patterns.*** Fraudulent transactions often show very distinct patterns. For example, the orders may be larger than normal, may consist of multiple items of the same type, or may consist largely of big-ticket items. Similarly, fraudulent transactions often consist of multiple orders using the same credit card in a short period, or multiple orders using different cards shipped to the same address. Further, fraudsters often use overnight shipping, so as to reduce the merchant's time for verification checks, and to be able to quickly resell the merchandise.

Being alert for such fraud indicators can help an online merchant to reduce the risk of fraudulent transactions. Often, it is prudent to either call the customer for verification of the order (though this may be problematic for privacy reasons) or outright reject the transaction.

In contrast to merchants, ordinary people can only *make* payments by using credit cards—to receive payments, one has to open up a merchant account to accept credit card payments. For people who sell things online only once in a while (such as on the online auction site eBay), this is not a good option. To combat these problems, online shoppers (and sellers) are increasingly using third-party payment services. These are discussed next.

PAYMENT SERVICES. Concerns for security have led to the inception of independent payment services such as PayPal (owned by eBay) or Google Checkout. These services allow online customers to purchase goods online without having to give much private information to the actual sellers. Rather than paying a seller by providing credit card information, an online shopper can simply pay by using his or her account with the payment service. Thus, the customer has to provide the (sensitive) payment information only to the payment service, which keeps this information secure (along with other information such as e-mail address or purchase history) and does not share it with the online merchant. Google linked its payment service to the search results so that Internet users looking for a specific product can immediately see whether a merchant offers this payment option; this is intended to ease the online shopping experience for consumers, thus reducing the number of people abandoning their shopping carts. Another payment service, PayPal, goes a step further by allowing anyone with an e-mail address to send and receive money. In other words, using this service, you can send money to your friends or family members, or you can receive money for anything you're selling. This easy way to transfer money has been instrumental in the success of eBay, where anyone can sell or buy goods from other eBay users.

Legal Issues in EC

Although EC is now a viable and well-established business practice, there are issues that have changed the landscape for businesses and consumers and continue to do so. Two of the most important issues for EC businesses are taxation of online purchases and the protection of intellectual property, especially as it pertains to digital products, both of which are outlined next.

TAXATION. Although this issue is a relatively old one, it remains controversial within the American legal system. With EC global transactions increasing at an exponential rate, many governments are concerned that sales made via electronic sales channels have to be taxed in order to make up for the lost revenue in traditional sales methods. As people shop less in local retail stores, cities, states, and even countries are now seeing a decrease in their sales tax income because of EC. Table 4.5 highlights issues associated with taxation of EC transactions.

According to tax laws such as the **Internet Tax Freedom Act**, sales on the Internet are treated the same way as mail-order sales, and a company is required to collect sales tax only from customers residing in a state where the business had substantial presence. In other words, only if an EC business had office facilities or a shipping warehouse in a certain state (say, California), it would have to collect sales tax on sales to customers from that state (in that case, California). Many EC businesses thus strategically selected their home bases to offer "tax-free shopping" to most customers. For example, Amazon.com tended to be very selective in where it located shipping facilities and warehouses, to offer favorable tax conditions for most customers while still being able to offer fast delivery. Walmart.com, on the other hand, collects taxes on all of its U.S. EC transactions, as it is physically present in every U.S. state. Note that even if the EC business does not *collect* sales tax on goods or services you may have purchased, you are still liable for *paying* "use tax" (usually equal to your state's sales tax) on those goods and services. Currently, Amazon has negotiated tax agreements with various states, and the U.S. legislation has proposed the Marketplace Fairness Act to simplify taxation issues surrounding e-commerce, and to allow states to require e-tailers to collect sales tax, even if the e-tailer had no physical presence. No matter whether (or when) this act is passed, taxation will remain a difficult issue.

On an international level, taxation is even more difficult. A customer ordering from a U.S. seller would not have to pay U.S. sales tax, but may be liable for paying tax (and/or import duty) in his or her home country on the shipment's arrival. For digital products (such as software or music downloads), the movement of the product is difficult to track, and the tax revenue is easily lost. Obviously, e-businesses actively doing business in other countries have to comply with the various different tax laws in different countries.

OTHER LEGAL CONSIDERATIONS. In addition to taxation, companies selling goods or services on the Web face a myriad of other issues. For example, companies should ensure to have explicit, enforceable terms of contract, terms of sale, and/or terms of Web site use; such terms may also cover questions surrounding the liability for content and its accuracy. Further, ownership of content and trademarks can be a virtual minefield. When posting content on one's site, one has to ensure not to infringe on others' copyrights or trademarks (e.g., by posting product photographs without permission, or even by having trademarked names in one's domain name). Likewise, care has to be taken if third parties develop content for one's site: Who will own the copyright for that material? However, online businesses should not

TABLE 4.5 Arguments For and Against Taxation of EC Transactions

For	Against
Increases tax income of local, state, and federal governments	Slows EC growth and opportunity Creates additional compliance burden for e-tailers
Removes unfair advantage for e-tailers over brick-and-mortar stores	e-Tailers located in one state would subsidize other states or jurisdictions
Increases accountability for e-tailers	Drives EC businesses to other countries

only ensure not to infringe on others' intellectual property, but also make sure to protect their own intellectual property, such as by displaying copyright notices and the like. Finally, it is important to clearly state the jurisdiction, and ensure to comply with the laws and regulations of that jurisdiction.

DIGITAL RIGHTS MANAGEMENT. With consumers increasingly using EC as a viable alternative for traditional commerce, the entertainment industry has no choice but to embrace the Internet as a distribution medium. At the same time, digital media are easily copied and shared by many people, as the entertainment industry has painfully learned after the introduction of the compact disc. Hence, the entertainment industry has turned to **digital rights management (DRM)**, which is a technological solution that allows publishers to control their digital media (music, movies, and so on) to discourage, limit, or prevent illegal copying and distribution. DRM restrictions include which devices will play the media, how many devices the media will play on, and even how many times the media can be played. The entertainment industry argues that DRM allows copyright holders to minimize sales losses by preventing unauthorized duplication.

To prevent illegal sharing of DRM-free content, it is often watermarked so that any illegal copy can be traced to the original purchaser (e.g., content purchased on iTunes contains the e-mail address used for the purchase) (Figure 4.18). A digital **watermark** is an electronic version of physical watermarks placed on paper currency to prevent counterfeiting. Likewise, to prevent counterfeiting of currency, most color laser printers print nearly invisible yellow dots uniquely identifying the originating printer on each page; privacy advocates argue that this could potentially be used to identify or persecute dissidents (EFF, 2010).

Critics refer to DRM as "digital restriction management," stating that publishers are arbitrary on how they enforce DRM. Further, critics argue that DRM enables publishers to infringe on existing consumer rights and to stifle innovation; for example, restrictions and limitations such as limiting the number of times a game can be activated, or limiting on which devices media can be accessed cause much inconvenience to users (such as when purchasing a new computer), and can thus breed piracy. Finally, critics argue that examples such as Amazon.com or Apple's iTunes show that businesses can be very successful with DRM-free content (CNet, 2012).

NET NEUTRALITY. The Internet was designed as an open network, which means that every Web site, every application, and every type of data (e.g., a game, Skype call, or YouTube video) is treated the same. Because of this openness, virtually anyone or any business, well known or unknown, can access and be found on the Web. For example, unknown bloggers can compete with large news providers like CNN for readers. Many believe that this openness has been the primary catalyst for countless innovations and some of the Information Age's most successful companies, like eBay and Google. Without net neutrality, many fear that startups and entrepreneurs will be muscled out of the marketplace by big corporations that have the money to control what people are able to see or do on the Web.

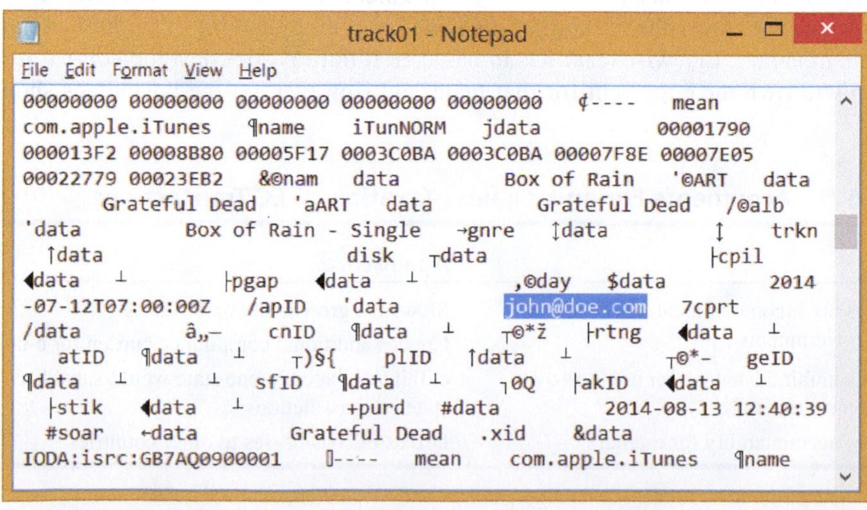

FIGURE 4.18

Digital watermarks are used to trace illegal copies of digital media to the original purchaser.
Source: Microsoft Notepad, Courtesy of Microsoft Corporation.

In general, **net neutrality** is the principle that all Internet data should be treated the same. Proponents of net neutrality believe that the Internet should forward all data packets on a first-come, first-served basis, allowing anyone to freely communicate with any application or content without interference from a third party. Proponents are worried that without strong laws to protect the Internet, governments, providers, and large corporations will be able to block Internet applications and content, and even block out competitors.

Many large corporations and telecommunications providers, however, would like to change the way information is accessed and prioritized on the Web. Large telecommunication providers would like to charge differing rates to access different Web sites, to have adequate speed to run certain applications, or even to have permission to plug in certain types of devices. Here, larger and more established companies will have tremendous power over smaller and startup firms. Without legal protection, consumers could find that a network operator has blocked the Web site of a competitor, or slowed the delivery of content from companies unwilling to pay additional fees.

Many believe that retaining net neutrality is critical to preserve current freedoms. It guarantees a level playing field for all Web sites and Internet technologies. Without net neutrality, many of the next generation of innovations may be shut out.

While electronic commerce has now existed for nearly two decades, it continues to evolve and mature. Each year, innovative strategies continue to emerge in virtually all sectors of business and government. Technologies evolve as well as how and where people conduct electronic commerce, from desktops, to laptops, to tablets, and to smartphones. At home, and while on the road. New capabilities often create unforeseen issues that require new laws and regulations. The best prediction about the future is that change will continue in this rapidly evolving space.

INDUSTRY ANALYSIS

Retailing

You may make many purchases online in order to benefit from greater convenience or lower prices, but you will likely set foot in a brick-and-mortar retail store at least occasionally and you may have noticed some changes brought by technology. A few decades ago, large retail chains started introducing computerized point-of-sale inventory systems consisting of checkout computers and an inventory control system. A simple barcode scan captures a sale, and the item is automatically deducted from the store's inventory, allowing real-time tracking of purchases so that the retailer knows when to reorder merchandise or restock shelves. In addition to a speedier checkout process, such systems help to reduce stockouts, increasing customer satisfaction. In many grocery stores, this system has been taken a step further, allowing the customers to conduct the checkout process themselves, saving time and labor costs.

In the near future, many items may be equipped with radio frequency identification (RFID) tags (see Chapter 8), eliminating the need to scan every individual item, so that the total price for a cart full of merchandise can be calculated within a second, saving even more time and adding convenience for the customer. Imagine the time you'll save when all you have to do is pass with your cart through an RFID reader and swipe your credit card.

Payment systems are also changing. A new "Pay by Fingerprint" system allows customers to complete a purchase by placing a finger onto a fingerprint scanner, without the need to sign a sales slip or enter a personal identification number (PIN); this makes the checkout process extremely convenient and secure. Another innovative way to pay for a purchase is via mobile phone. Using a technology called Near Field Communication (NFC; similar to Bluetooth), the customer's mobile phone communicates with the retailer's payment terminal, and the payment amount is automatically debited from the customer's bank account. NFC-based payment systems have already begun to be implemented; major smartphone manufacturers such as Samsung, Nokia, Motorola, and HTC actively support this new technology by integrating it into new handsets.

Further, many brick-and-mortar retailers have had to respond to the phenomenon of showrooming, in which, as discussed earlier, customers examine products in person at a store and then leave to order the same product online for less. Retailers invest billions to build and maintain their storefronts, and online retailers can often undercut physical stores' prices; when a customer takes advantage of this, the brick-and-mortar retailer fails to recoup the cost of the storefront. Some retailers like Best Buy and Target are embracing this trend, however, by encouraging consumers to browse their shelves and compare prices online. By providing perks such as superior, personal customer service and instituting price-matching policies, these retailers prevent loss of customers due to price, while benefiting by selling additional products.

(continued)

As you can see, information systems have had a huge impact on retailing, and many more changes are yet to hit the shelves.

Questions

1. How can technology help brick-and-mortar retailers compete against e-tailers?
2. Privacy advocates criticize the use of RFID, as it allows better tracking of purchasing habits. How can brick-and-mortar retailers alleviate these concerns?
3. As you have read, part of the "human element" in retailing is being replaced by technology. How can brick-and-mortar stores avoid becoming too "sterile" when using information systems to compete against e-tailers?

Based on:

Fitzgerald, D. (2013, November 3). Fear of "showrooming" fades. *The Wall Street Journal*. Retrieved May 27, 2014, from http://online.wsj.com/news/articles/SB10001424052702303661404579175690690126298.

Anonymous. (n.d.). *METRO Group Future Store Initiative*. Retrieved May 27, 2014, from http://www.future-store.org/internet/site/ts_fsi/node/25216/Len/index.html.

Voerste, A., & von Truchsess, A. (2008, May 28). METRO Group and Real open the store of the future. *METRO Group Future Store Initiative*. Retrieved May 27, 2014, from http://www.metrogroup.de/internet/site/metrogroup/node/150792/Len/index.html.

Key Points Review

1. ***Describe different business models used to compete in cyberspace as well as different forms of electronic government.*** EC is the online exchange of goods, services, and money between firms and between firms and their customers. Companies and individuals are engaging in business-to-business, business-to-consumer, consumer-to-consumer, or consumer-to-business e-commerce. In addition, e-government is a government's use of IS to provide a variety of services to citizens (government-to-citizens), businesses (government-to-business), and other governmental agencies (either within a country or between countries; government-to-government).
2. ***Describe business-to-consumer electronic commerce strategies.*** Companies must strategically position themselves to compete in the EC environment, and choose between operating as brick-and-mortar companies, click-and-mortar (or bricks-and-clicks) companies, or click-only (or virtual) companies. Capabilities of the Web have enabled new business models based on mass customization, disintermediation, or group buying. In addition, companies are trying to harness users' social networks. e-Tailers can benefit from being able to offer a wider variety of goods to more people at lower prices. On the other hand, a major drawback is customers' lack of trust.
3. ***Understand the keys to successful electronic commerce Web sites, and explain the different forms of Internet marketing.*** Successful B2C companies have a Web site that offers something unique, is aesthetically pleasing, is easy to use, and is fast, and that motivates people to visit, to stay, and to return. A company should also advertise its presence on the Web (e.g., using search engine marketing) and should try to learn from its Web site (using Web analytics). Popular ways to advertise products or services on the Web are search marketing, display ads, e-mail marketing, social media, and mobile marketing. Advertisers pay for these types of Internet marketing on the basis of either the number of impressions or pay-per-click.
4. ***Describe mobile commerce, consumer-to-consumer electronic commerce, and consumer-to-business electronic commerce.*** M-commerce is rapidly expanding with the continued evolution of faster cellular networks, more powerful handheld devices, and more sophisticated applications. Location-based services, based on GPS technology, are a key driver enabling even more innovative m-commerce applications. As mobile consumers not only use their devices to obtain timely information on the go, but also increasingly purchase products or content in mobile settings, businesses have to consider the specific settings and devices of their target customers. Further, the Internet has fueled the development of a variety of ways people can trade goods, socialize, or voice their thoughts and opinions. Specifically, e-auctions allow private people to sell goods to large markets. One emerging topic in EC is C2B EC, where individuals offer products or services to businesses.
5. ***Describe how to conduct financial transactions and navigate legal issues of electronic commerce.*** The Internet has enabled obtaining real-time financial information as well as making transactions online. Yet, securing payments in the digital world is still of concern, both for customers and for merchants, who have to minimize their risk arising from potentially fraudulent credit card transactions; as a result, many (especially smaller) retailers use online payment services. Finally, legal issues surrounding Web site content, contracts, taxation, transactions, protecting intellectual property, and net neutrality continue to be major issues and impediments to EC.

Key Terms

brick-and-mortar business strategy 136
bricks-and-clicks business strategy 137
bounce rate 144
business-to-business (B2B) 134
business-to-consumer (B2C) 134
Card Verification Value (CVV2) 156
click fraud 150
click-and-mortar business strategy 137
click-only business strategy 137
click-through rate 149
consumer-to-business (C2B) 135
consumer-to-consumer (C2C) 135
conversion rate 149
digital rights management (DRM) 160
disintermediation 138
e-auction 153
e-government 135
electronic bill pay 155
electronic commerce (EC) 134
e-tailing 136
exit rate 144
functional convenience 145
government-to-business (G2B) 136
government-to-citizen (G2C) 135
government-to-government (G2G) 136
group buying 139
Internet Tax Freedom Act 159
location-based services 150
Long Tail 141
mass customization 138
m-commerce (mobile commerce) 135
menu-driven pricing 139
mobile banking 155
net neutrality 161
online banking 155
online investing 155
paid inclusion 147
pay-per-click 149
QR code 143
reintermediation 139
representational delight 145
reverse pricing 139
search advertising 146
search engine optimization (SEO) 148
showrooming 151
social commerce 140
sponsored search 146
structural firmness 144
virtual company 137
watermark 160
Web analytics 144

Go to **mymislab.com** to complete the problems marked with this icon .

Review Questions

4-1. What is EC, and what different business models do companies use to compete in cyberspace?

4-2. What are the primary forms of e-government? Provide examples for each.

4-3. Compare and contrast two EC business strategies.

4-4. Describe the effects of disintermediation.

4-5. Describe social commerce and explain how companies can leverage consumers' social networks.

4-6. Describe the benefits and drawbacks of e-tailing.

4-7. What is the online consumer's hierarchy of needs, and why is it important for e-tailers?

 **4-8.** Describe the differences between SEO, search marketing, and sponsored search.

4-9. Describe m-commerce and explain how it is different from regular EC.

4-10. What is showrooming, and how has it affected offline retailers?

4-11. Explain the different forms of online auctions.

4-12. How does taxation pose a threat to EC?

4-13. How does net neutrality pose a threat to EC?

Self-Study Questions

4-14. EC is the online exchange of ______________ among firms, between firms and their customers, and between customers, supported by communication technologies and, in particular, the Internet.
A. goods
B. services
C. money
D. all of the above

4-15. ______________ are those companies that operate in the traditional, physical markets and do not conduct business electronically in cyberspace.
A. Brick-and-mortars
B. Click-onlys
C. Both A and B
D. Dot-coms

4-16. The ability to sell products directly to the end customers, without the need for distributors or retailers, is called ______________.
A. disintermediation
B. disintegration
C. reintegration
D. reintermediation

4-17. Business models based on catering to niche markets in addition to (or instead of) purely selling mainstream products are said to center on the ______________.
A. far ends
B. long ends
C. niches
D. Long Tails

4-18. ______________ reflects the percentage of users for whom a particular page is the only page visited on the Web site.
A. Bounce rate
B. Exit rate
C. Click-through rate
D. Conversion rate

4-19. A Web site should ______________.
A. be easy to use and fast
B. offer something unique and be aesthetically pleasing
C. motivate people to visit, to stay, and to return
D. be all of the above

4-20. Trying to "outsmart" a search engine to improve a page's ranking is known as ______________.
A. rank enhancement
B. SEO
C. search engine hacking
D. Google fooling

4-21. In order to minimize fraud, e-tailers look for anomalies in ______________.
A. e-mail addresses provided
B. shipping and billing addresses
C. transaction patterns
D. all of the above

4-22. According to the Internet Tax Freedom Act, e-tailers ______________.
A. have to collect sales tax from all customers, regardless of their location
B. have to collect sales tax based on the place of the customer's residence
C. have to collect sales tax based on the prevalent tax rate at the e-tailer's headquarters
D. have to collect sales tax only from customers residing in a state where the business has substantial presence

Answers are on page 166.

Problems and Exercises

4-23. Match the following terms with the appropriate definitions:
i. Click-through rate
ii. Reintermediation
iii. Web analytics
iv. Paid inclusion
v. Conversion rate
vi. Long Tails
vii. Click fraud
viii. Search engine optimization
ix. e-Government
x. Group buying

a. Special volume discounts negotiated with local businesses and offered to people in the form of "daily deals"
b. The design of business models that reintroduce middlemen in order to reduce the chaos brought on by disintermediation
c. The large parts of consumer demand that are outside the relatively small number of mainstream tastes
d. The percentage of visitors who actually perform the marketer's desired action
e. The number of surfers who click on an ad divided by the number of times it was displayed
f. The use of information systems to provide citizens and organizations with handy information about public services
g. Methods used to improve a site's ranking
h. The analysis of Web surfers' behavior in order to improve a site's performance
i. The practice of paying a fee to be included in a search engine's listing
j. The abuse of pay-per-click advertising models by repeatedly clicking on a link to inflate revenue to the host or increase the costs for the advertiser

4-24. Visit www.firstgov.gov. What kind of services do you see that would help you? What services would you use? What areas are missing?

4-25. Visit Alaska Airlines' Web site (www.alaskaair.com) for real-time pricing and test the custom messenger bag builder at www.timbuk2.com. How have Internet technologies improved over the years?

4-26. Search the Web for a company that is purely Web-based. Next, find the Web site of a company that is a hybrid (i.e., the company has a traditional brick-and-mortar business plus a presence on the Web). What are the pros and cons of dealing with each type of company?

4-27. Are the advertisements you receive through e-mail directed toward any specific audience or product category? Which ads seem to be most prevalent? Do you pay much attention or just delete them? How much work is it to get off an advertising list? Why would or wouldn't you try to get off the list?

4-28. What is it about a company's Web site that draws you to it, keeps you there on the site longer, and keeps you coming back for more? If you could summarize these answers into a set of criteria for Web sites, what would those criteria be?

4-29. Visit the following services for comparison shopping: BestBookBuys (www.bestwebbuys.com/books), Bizrate (www.bizrate.com), and mySimon (www.mysimon.com). These companies focus on aggregating content for consumers. What are the advantages of these Web sites? What does the existence of such sites mean for the online merchants?

4-30. Compare three different search engines. What tips do they provide to improve a page's rankings? How much does it cost to advertise a page on their results pages? If you were a company, could you think of any situation where you would pay almost any amount to have the first listing on the first results page?

4-31. Describe your experiences in online shopping. How did you pay for your purchases? What information did you have to reveal to the merchant? Did you feel comfortable giving out that information?

4-32. Have you ever used a mobile, wireless device such as a smartphone for online shopping? If so, what do you like or dislike about it? In what ways could your shopping experience be made better? If you have not used a mobile device for shopping, what prevented you from doing so? What would have to happen before you would begin using a mobile device for shopping?

4-33. When you shop online, is sales tax a criterion for you? Do you try to purchase goods where you do not have to pay sales tax? If you would have to pay sales tax for everything you buy online, would that change your online shopping behavior?

Application Exercises

Note: The existing data files referenced in these exercises are available on the book's Web site: www.pearsonhighered.com/valacich.

Spreadsheet Application: Analyzing Server Traffic

4-34. Campus Travel has recently found that its Internet connections between offices are becoming slow, especially during certain periods of the day. Since all the online traffic is maintained by another company, an increase in bandwidth requires a formal approval from the general manager. The IS manager has proposed to increase the bandwidth of the company's network; in a few days, he has to present the business case for this proposal at the weekly meeting of the department heads. You are asked to prepare graphs for the presentation to support the IS manager's business case. In the file ServerLogs.csv, you will find information about the network traffic for a one-week period. Prepare the following graphs:

- Total bandwidth used for each day (line graph)
- Bandwidth used per day, by time period (line graph)
- Average bandwidth used in each two-hour period (line graph)

Format the graphs in a professional manner and print out each graph on a separate page. (Hint: If you are using Microsoft Excel's Chart Wizard, select "Place chart: As New Sheet.")

Database Application: Tracking Network Hardware

4-35. As Campus Travel is new to EC, the management suggests following a stepwise approach for using the Internet to conduct business. Before using the Internet for conducting transactions, the managers recommend setting up a site that provides information to customers. Part of this informational site is an agency locator that shows the services each agency has. You have been asked to create a new database. This includes creating relationships between entities. To create this new database, do the following:

- Create a database called "agency."
- Create a table called "agencies" and include fields for agency ID, street address, city, state, ZIP code, phone number, number of service agents, and working hours.
- Create a table called "services" that includes service ID, name (i.e., type of service), and description.
- Create a third table called "agency_services" that includes the agency ID field from the agencies table and the service ID field from the services table.
- Once these tables are created, go to the relationship view and connect the agencies (one side) and agency_services (many side) tables and the services (one side) and agencyservices (many side) tables using two one-to-many relationships (i.e., each agency can offer many services; each service can be offered by many agencies).

Team Work Exercise

Net Stats: Who Is Subsidizing Web Content?

When you subscribe to cable television, you typically have to decide between different packages, each offering various channels focusing on sports, movies, cartoons, and so on. In addition, you have the option of subscribing to other channels that interest you. Hence, the charges on your monthly cable bill are for your subscribed services. In contrast, the charges on your Internet bill are for connecting to the Internet rather than for the content on the Web. Hence, content providers on the Internet are typically dependent on other ways to generate revenue. Companies such as CNN, the Washington Post, Google, or Yahoo!, which provide content for free, subsidize their expenses by advertising revenue. One of the most common forms of advertising on the Web is display ads, which have moved from simple static images to rich, interactive advertisements. Although the cost per thousand views may be only between US$5 and US$20, display ads are big business.

Where do people visit most often on the Web? Research firm comScore regularly provides rankings of the Web's most popular "web properties," based on the number of unique monthly visitors. The top five properties in the year 2014 are:

- Google Sites: 187.0 million unique visitors
- Yahoo Sites: 183.1 million unique visitors
- Microsoft Sites: 162.8 million unique visitors
- Facebook: 133.6 million unique visitors
- AOL, Inc.: 109.6 million unique visitors

Questions and Exercises

4-36. Search the Web for the most up-to-date statistics.

4-37. As a team, interpret these numbers. What is striking/important about these statistics?

4-38. How have the numbers changed? Which industries seem to be most interested in online advertising? Why?

4-39. Using your spreadsheet software of choice, create a graph/figure most effectively visualizing the statistics/changes you consider most important.

Based on:

ComScore (2014, March 25). comScore Media Metrix ranks top 50 U.S. desktop Web properties for February 2014. *comScore*. Retrieved May 27, 2014, from https://www.comscore.com/Insights/Press_Releases/2014/3/comScore_Media_Metrix_Ranks_Top_50_US_Desktop_Web_Properties_for_February_2014.

Wojcicki, S. (2010, March 15). The future of display advertising. *Google Blog*. Retrieved May 27, 2014, from http://googleblog.blogspot.com/2010/03/future-of-display-advertising.html.

Answers to the Self-Study Questions

4-14. D, p. 134	**4-15.** A, p. 136	**4-16.** A, p. 138	**4-17.** D, p. 141	**4-18.** A, p. 144
4-19. D, p. 143	**4-20.** B, p. 147	**4-21.** D, p. 157	**4-22.** D, p. 159	

CASE 1 Bitcoin

Have you ever purchased something you found posted in a classified ad in the newspaper? Or in a listing on Craigslist.org? Mostly likely, the seller would accept nothing other than cold, hard cash in exchange for the item you purchased, and you were probably only willing to provide the cash after personally examining the item. Financial transactions in the physical world have been happening for thousands of years, and still you take such precautions in order to ensure that you are taking as little financial risk as possible during the transaction. Of course, the Internet has enabled an entirely new set of buying and selling opportunities, and many of these take place virtually—where you don't have the opportunity to personally inspect or experience a product or service before paying for it.

Most of us are comfortable with providing credit card information to a reputable online retailer such as Amazon.com or NewEgg.com. Likewise, many of us have purchased things from other individuals or small companies using a payment service like PayPal. Credit card companies and payment services like PayPal provide consumers a safety net, giving them the confidence that their purchase will produce the desired good or service, and ensuring that their personal financial information remains confidential. These services, however, come at a fairly significant cost. Credit card companies charge vendors between 1 and 3 percent of the purchase amount of every transaction, a cost that is typically passed on to the consumer in the form of higher prices. Payment services such as PayPal also charge fees, ranging up to several percentage points of the total price. For many of us, these fees are simply a cost of doing business electronically. For a small group of forward-thinking developers, however, the relatively high cost of electronic transactions represents an opportunity to change the way the world does business.

Bitcoin was launched around the year 2008 by an anonymous developer pseudonamed Satoshi Nakamoto. Bitcoins are so-called digital currency, a form of value storage and payment that is completely electronic. Bitcoins are transferred as payment within a completely decentralized peer-to-peer payment network—the payment processing is handled by thousands of computers around the world, each running the open-source bitcoin software. When someone pays for something using bitcoin, the payment is broadcast within the bitcoin network, and the transaction is stored on a secure, public ledger that is accessible to any computer that wants to verify the transaction. The authenticity of each transaction is ensured by digital signatures corresponding to the sending address of the payer and payee. The public ledger is constantly verified and maintained by the bitcoin network, and is thus "open for business" 24 hours a day, 7 days a week, and is not subject to any national holidays. In addition, since there is no regulatory body or central clearinghouse as in the modern banking system, the transaction fees associated with any bitcoin transaction are very small. Though the concept is still quite new, a number of businesses are accepting bitcoin as a valid form of payment. Such companies include Wordpress, TigerDirect.com, Overstock.com, and a growing number of restaurants, apartments, and even law firms.

There remains substantial public concern about the bitcoin payment platform, however. Its anonymity lends itself well to illicit transactions. In 2013, for example, the Federal Bureau of Investigation (FBI) seized and shut down the notorious Silk Road trading site, which used the bitcoin payment system to allow purchases of illegal drugs, fraudulent documents, and even hitmen. As a part of the takedown, the FBI seized over US$28.5 million worth of bitcoins. Other, less dramatic issues include price volatility, occasional software bugs, and a low degree of acceptance by most mainstream retailers. These issues have led many to pan the payment platform as a trend that will quickly die.

Still, many aspects of the platform are intriguing. Use of bitcoins solves a number of problems that we currently deal with in the electronic marketplace: reducing fees, granting full control and (if desired) anonymity, and freeing consumers from geographical or temporal constraints common to physical payment systems. If some of the weaknesses of bitcoin can be addressed, the platform may be the perfect solution for an increasingly global and digital economy.

Questions

4-40. Is a service like bitcoin needed? Why or why not?

4-41. If you were able to institute changes in bitcoin's policy, what would you change and why?

4-42. Would you use bitcoin if Amazon.com accepted it as a form of payment? Why or why not?

Based on:

Anonymous. (n.d.). Bitcoin—Frequently asked questions. *Bitcoin.org*. Retrieved May 27, 2014, from https://bitcoin.org/en/faq.

Bitcoin. (2014, May 27). In *Wikipedia, The Free Encyclopedia*. Retrieved May 28, 2014, from http://en.wikipedia.org/w/index.php?title=Bitcoin&oldid=610399007.

Hall, B. (2014, May 27). How bitcoin can go mainstream. *CIO.com*. Retrieved May 27, 2014, from http://www.cio.com/article/753261/How_Bitcoin_Can_Go_Mainstream.

CASE 2 Enabling Global Payments at PayPal

If you have used eBay (and who hasn't?), you know how easy it is to pay for items you buy and to receive payment for items you have sold. Checks, credit card charges, and money orders are unnecessary. Instead of these traditional methods of payment, digital money is easily and effortlessly zapped to and from accounts at PayPal, the most frequently used digital money transfer service online.

Peter Thiel, a hedge fund manager, and Max Levchin, an online security specialist, founded what was to become PayPal—it was first named Field Link, then Confinity, and finally, in 2001, PayPal. The company went online rather naively in 1999. The founders' vision was to create a digital currency exchange service free of government controls; however, hackers, con artists, and organized crime groups quickly realized the potential of using the site for scams and money laundering. After implementing tighter security measures to stop criminal activity and assuage customer complaints, the next hurdle to overcome was government regulators. Attorneys general in several states investigated PayPal's business practices, and New York and California levied fines for violations. Louisiana banned the company from operating in that state (the ban has since been lifted).

When PayPal began, payment for Web products could only be made through credit card charges at the purchase site and via checks and money orders sent through the U.S. Postal Service. Other companies, such as Beenz.com and Flooz.com, had tried to establish electronic payment systems based on a special digital currency, but merchants, banks, and customers were hesitant to accept "money" that wasn't based on real dollars. Thiel and Levchin saw the need for an electronic payment system that relied on real currency, especially when eBay became popular, and PayPal filled that niche.

After PayPal solved its security and customer support problems, customers liked the convenience and ease of using the service, and its client base grew. Buyers like not having to reveal their credit card numbers to every online merchant, and merchants appreciate having PayPal handle payment collection. New PayPal clients establish an account with a user name and password and fund the account by giving PayPal a credit card number or bank account transaction information. Although PayPal prefers the latter (because bank account transactions are cheaper than credit card transactions), half of PayPal's accounts are funded via credit cards.

eBay bought PayPal in 2002 for US$1.5 billion and since then has also been a major source of income for the money transfer site. At the same time, PayPal has expanded its client base both in the United States and abroad and is generating much of its revenue by charging fees for payment processing for a wide variety of online vendors, auction sites, and corporations. Services to buyers are free, but sellers are charged a fee, which is generally lower than fees charged by major credit card companies. PayPal now offers special merchant accounts for transferring larger amounts of money and also offers a donation box feature for blogs and other Web sites where visitors can make donations.

PayPal spawned many rivals after its initial launch, but most have since died, including Citigroup's C2it and Bank One's E-mail Money. As of 2014, the company operated in 193 worldwide markets, had localized Web sites in 80 countries, and managed over 143 million active accounts. It also allows customers to send, receive, and hold funds in 26 currencies worldwide, having handled over US$180 billion in transactions during the year 2013 alone.

Another key element of PayPal's business is mobile payments. In 2013, PayPal's mobile transactions topped US$27 billion, nearly a 100 percent increase from its 2012 mobile transaction figures. According to many analysts, the increasing number of smartphone applications is responsible for the increase. More and more mobile users are conducting business on eBay using their smartphones. With PayPal's mobile apps, sending money on the winning bid is easy and can be handled from nearly anywhere. PayPal's app for the iPhone and Android phones allows users to "bump" their phones together to transfer money between one another. The app also allows a user to request money from a group of people for things like a going-away gift at the office, a fundraiser, or any other event where money needs to be pooled. Additionally, the app gives users the ability to "split the ticket" at a restaurant and send their portion of the check total to whoever paid the bill—including tax and tip!

While the company has had its share of problems with fraud and phishers (scamsters who send fraudulent e-mail messages and duplicate legitimate Web sites), PayPal continues to innovate and be the number-one method of payment for the world's buyers and sellers.

Questions

4-43. Why do you think PayPal has been so successful throughout the world?

4-44. What other opportunities will megatrends such as mobility and social networking provide for PayPal?

4-45. Do you use PayPal? Why or why not?

Based on:

Anonymous. (n.d.). PayPal—About us. Retrieved May 27, 2014, from https://www.paypal-media.com/about.

PayPal. (2014, May 25). In *Wikipedia, The Free Encyclopedia*. Retrieved May 28, 2014, from http://en.wikipedia.org/w/index.php?title=PayPal&oldid=610122867.

Walker, L. (2005, May 19). PayPal looks to evolve beyond its auction roots. *Washingtonpost.com*. Retrieved May 27, 2014, from http://www.washingtonpost.com/wp-dyn/content/article/2005/05/18/AR2005051802187.html.

Walsh, M. (2010, February 18). Facebook and PayPal become payment pals. *Online Media Daily*. Retrieved May 10, 2012, from http://www.mediapost.com/publications/?fa=Articles.showArticle&art_aid=122775.

Go to **mymislab.com** for Auto-graded writing questions as well as the following Assisted-graded writing questions:

4-46. Describe mass customization and explain how companies can reap higher profits despite higher production costs for manufacturing customized products.

4-47. How can online retailers minimize the risk associated with credit card transactions?

References

Adobe.com. (2012). The impact of tablet visitors on retail websites. *Adobe.com.* Retrieved May 29, 2014, from http://success.adobe.com/assets/en/downloads/whitepaper/13926_digital_index_tablet_report.pdf.

Alipay. (2014). About Alipay. Retrieved May 29, 2014, from https://www.alipay.com/static/aboutalipay/englishabout.htm.

Anderson, C. (2004). The Long Tail. *Wired.* Retrieved May 29, 2014, from http://www.wired.com/wired/archive/12.10/tail.html.

Anderson, C. (2006). *The Long Tail: Why the future of business is selling less of more*. New York: Hyperion.

California Office of the Attorney General. (2014, May 29). Identity theft. Retrieved May 29, 2014, from http://oag.ca.gov/idtheft.

CNet Australia. (2012, June 13). Do we really need DRM? *CNet.com.au.* Retrieved May 29, 2014, from http://www.cnet.com.au/do-we-really-need-drm-339339633.htm.

EFF. (2010). Is your printer spying on you? *Electronic Frontier Foundation*. Retrieved May 29, 2014, from http://www.eff.org/issues/printers.

eMarketer. (2014, February 3). Global B2C ecommerce sales to hit $1.5 trillion this year driven by growth in emerging markets. *eMarketer.com.* Retrieved May 27, 2014, from http://www.emarketer.com/Article/Global-B2C-Ecommerce-Sales-Hit-15-Trillion-This-Year-Driven-by-Growth-Emerging-Markets/1010575.

Evan, P., & Wurster, T. (1999). *Blown to bits: How the new economics of information transforms strategy*. Boston: Harvard Business School Press.

Google. (2007). Marketing and advertising using Google. Retrieved May 29, 2014, from books.google.com/intl/en/googlebooks/pdf/MarketingAndAdvertisingUsingGoogle.pdf.

Internet Crime Complaint Center. (2014). 2013 IC3 annual report. Retrieved May 29, 2014, from https://www.ic3.gov/media/annualreport/2013_IC3Report.pdf.

Jayaraman, K., & Blank, P. (2012, February). 2012 Identity fraud report: Consumers taking control to reduce their risk of fraud. *Javelinstrategy.com.* Retrieved June 15, 2012, from https://www.javelinstrategy.com/uploads/web_brochure/1201.R_2012%20Identity%20Fraud%20Consumer%20Report.pdf.

Jones, C. (2013, October 2). Ecommerce is growing nicely while mcommerce is on a tear. *Forbes.* Retrieved May 27, 2014, from http://www.forbes.com/sites/chuckjones/2013/10/02/ecommerce-is-growing-nicely-while-mcommerce-is-on-a-tear.

Kalakota, R., Oliva, R. A., & Donath, E. (1999). Move over, e-commerce. *Marketing Management, 8*(3), 23–32.

Laudon, K., & Guercio Traver, C. (2014). *E-commerce 2015* (11th ed.). Upper Saddle River, NJ: Pearson Prentice Hall.

Lee, M., & Lin, D. (2009, November 24). Alipay to become world's no. 1 e-payment firm. *Reuters.* Retrieved May 29, 2014, from http://www.reuters.com/article/idUS-SHA32192420091124.

Li, S. (2012, April 12). Many people see risks in online banking and shopping, survey says. *Los Angeles Times.* Retrieved May 29, 2014, from http://articles.latimes.com/2012/apr/12/business/la-fi-mo-banking-shopping-online-20120411.

MacMillan, D. (2009, August 31). Can Hulu's high prices hold? *BusinessWeek.* Retrieved May 29, 2014, from http://www.businessweek.com/the_thread/techbeat/archives/2009/08/can_hulus_high.html.

MobileInfo. (2014). M-commerce. *MobileInfo.com.* Retrieved May 29, 2014, from http://www.mobileinfo.com/Mcommerce/index.htm.

Nystedt, D. (2009, October 12). Researchers advise cyber self defense in the cloud. *PCWorld.* Retrieved May 29, 2014, from http://www.pcworld.com/businesscenter/article/173467/researchers_advise_cyber_self_defense_in_the_cloud.html.

Parrish, M., Elliott, N., Mullen, A., Nail, J., O'Connell, J., VanBoskirk, S., & Wise, J. (2013, February 11). 2013 Interactive Marketing Predictions. *Forrester.* Retrieved July 17, 2014, from http://www.forrester.com/2013+Interactive+Marketing+Predictions/fulltext/-/E-RES90761.

Priceline. (2014). 2013 annual report. Retrieved May 29, 2014, from http://ir.pricelinegroup.com/common/download/download.cfm?companyid=PCLN&fileid=740730&filekey=DBC9F395-7E6C-4B20-A4D6-9F94343B46AF&filename=PCLN_2013_Annual_Report.pdf.

Quelch, J. A., & Klein, L. R. (1996, Spring). The Internet and international marketing. *Sloan Management Review, 63,* 60–75.

Seideman, T. (1996) What Sam Walton learned from the Berlin airlift. *Audacity: The Magazine of Business Experience*, Spring, 52–61.

Siwicki, B. (2014, March 10). Mobile commerce will be nearly half of e-commerce by 2018. *Internetretailer.com.* Retrieved May 28, 2014, from http://www.internetretailer.com/2014/03/10/mobile-commerce-will-be-nearly-half-e-commerce-2018.

Turban, E., King, D., Lee, J., Liang, T.-P., & Turban, D. (2012). *Electronic commerce 2012: Managerial and social networks perspectives* (7th ed.). Upper Saddle River, NJ: Pearson.

U.S. Census Bureau. (2014, May 22). 2012 e-stats. Retrieved May 27, 2014, from http://www.census.gov/econ/estats/2012_e-stats_report.pdf.

U.S. Census Bureau News. (2014, May 15). Quarterly retail e-commerce sales 1st quarter 2014. Retrieved May 27, 2014, from http://www.census.gov/retail/mrts/www/data/pdf/ec_current.pdf.

Valacich, J. S., Parboteeah, D. V., & Wells, J. D. (2007). The online consumer's hierarchy of needs. *Communications of the ACM, 50*(9), 84–90.

VanBoskirk, S. (2011, August 24). *US interactive marketing forecast, 2011 to 2016*. Cambridge, MA: Forrester Research.

Visa (2008). Visa e-commerce merchants' guide to risk management. Retrieved May 29, 2014, from http://usa.visa.com/download/merchants/visa_risk_management_guide_ecommerce.pdf.

Wells, J., & Gobeli, D. (2003). The three R framework: Improving e-strategy across reach, richness and range. *Business Horizons, 46*(2), 5–14.

Wells, J. D., Valacich, J. S., & Hess, T. J. (2011). What signals are you sending? How website quality influences perceptions of product quality and purchase intentions. *MIS Quarterly, 35*(2), 373–396.

Worstall, T. (2013, December 13). Over 60% of all website visits are bot traffic. *Forbes.* Retrieved May 27, 2014, from http://www.forbes.com/sites/timworstall/2013/12/13/over-60-of-all-website-visits-are-bot-traffic.

Yang, A., & Birge, J. (2013). How inventory is (should be) financed. Trade credit in supply chains with demand uncertainty and costs of financial distress. Retrieved May 29, 2014, from http://papers.ssrn.com/sol3/papers.cfm?abstract_id=1734682.

Zottola, A.J., & Parr, R.F. (2014, April 14). Legal considerations for e-commerce businesses. *Lexology.* Retrieved May 27, 2014, from http://www.lexology.com/library/detail.aspx?g=0de245fb-3ae2-4291-84aa-3872904edb58.

Zwass, V. (1996). Electronic commerce: Structures and issues. *International Journal of Electronic Commerce, 1*(1), 3–23.

5 Enhancing Organizational Communication and Collaboration Using Social Media

After reading this chapter, you will be able to do the following:

1. Explain organizations' needs for communication and collaboration.
2. Explain social media and evolving Web capabilities.
3. Describe various social media applications, and explain their role in enhancing communication, collaboration, cooperation, and connection.
4. Describe how companies can manage their Enterprise 2.0 strategy and deal with potential pitfalls associated with social media.

Preview

This chapter focuses on social media, and how social media can enhance organizational communication and collaboration. Most likely, you are actively using various social media applications such as Facebook or Wikipedia, and you may ask, "Why do we need to have a chapter on this?" Social media introduce unprecedented ways to connect to friends, share knowledge with your colleagues, or collaborate with a team of engineers 5,000 miles away, and many of today's companies cannot afford to miss this trend. Most young people entering the workforce have grown accustomed to using Facebook or Twitter for their communication needs (and some even regard e-mail as an outmoded communication medium); if a company doesn't allow the use of these tools, some employees may leave and work for another company. Additionally, you may have noticed your parents' generation joining sites such as Facebook, as the masses are more and more taking those tools for granted.

With social media providing a new set of capabilities for individuals and businesses, an understanding of how they can be applied can be very helpful. Being able to understand and apply these emerging capabilities and strategies that are associated with social media is a highly valued skill.

Managing in the Digital World: Facebook.com

Managing our lives in the modern, digital world seems to be far more complex than it was in the past. The same is true for companies. Interactions with customers were limited to one-way communication using TV ads, billboards, posters, or radio broadcasts. In return, people showed affinity to a particular brand by displaying bumper stickers, wearing t-shirts, or refusing to even try alternative brands. Marketers played their own game in promoting products and consumers spread the word around their circle of friends whenever they found something they loved. All in all, no real interaction could be recorded between customers and brands; the two parties led separate lives and acted their own respective parts.

Things have changed since then. In early 2014, a mere 10 years after its launch and 8 years after it was opened to the public, Facebook reports impressive usage statistics (Figure 5.1). Each month, more than 1.28 billion users access the site, and over 1 billion of those users access the service via a mobile device. On average, Facebook users upload over 350 million photos per day, and users have collectively uploaded over 350 billion photos in total.

Many companies have also joined Facebook, creating pages to extend their reach and promote new products.

FIGURE 5.1

Facebook is the most popular social network, with over 1 billion active users.
Source: Thomas Pajot/Fotolia

In addition, celebrities, musicians, public figures, movies, and almost any other product or service you can think of now appears to have a Facebook page. Facebook has become another get-together space for people who have acquaintances, friends, or beliefs in common. Businesses use it to build and track customer loyalty, and connections are made even tighter with the help of "Like" buttons that seem to be on almost every site on the Web. Facebook has changed the scope of social interactions, as consumer preferences, collective tastes, and future demands are now more easily analyzed and predicted through the number of "likes" or the comments left by consumers responding to photos regarding the latest smartphone or that new movie premiering next Thursday. Through this social media platform, companies can interact with customers like never before.

Yet, while Facebook's tremendous success appears to continue, it received a bit of a setback when it decided to go public in May 2012. The company, originally valued at US$104 billion, lost over half its value as investors expressed concerns regarding the financial viability of such a high-value company that earned just US$32 million in income during all of 2012. The company's stock has since recovered, as advertising revenues, particularly from mobile users, have grown quickly. As of early 2014, the company was valued at over US$163 billion, with revenues continuing to grow. Facebook remains a social networking behemoth, and has clearly changed the way we interact with friends, acquaintances, and companies.

After reading this chapter, you will be able to answer the following:

1. How can a social networking site such as Facebook become a part of everyday life?
2. Besides pure social interaction, what are some other ways Facebook can be used?
3. What are the pros and cons of using a social networking site in a business setting?

Based on:

Anonymous. (2014, April 23). Facebook reports first quarter 2014 results. Retrieved May 28, 2014, from http://investor.fb.com/releasedetail.cfm?ReleaseID=842071.

Facebook. (2014, May 26). In *Wikipedia, The Free Encyclopedia*. Retrieved May 28, 2014, from http://en.wikipedia.org/w/index.php?title=Facebook&oldid=610251825.

THE NEED FOR COMMUNICATION AND COLLABORATION

Just as you communicate with your friends when planning a vacation or organizing a party, or collaborate with your teammates on a class project, organizations rely on effective communication and **collaboration** (i.e., two or more people working together to achieve a common goal), both within and outside organizational boundaries. Most organizational business processes require communication and collaboration between employees of different departments, as well as with outside business partners (such as suppliers), customers, and other external stakeholders. Many organizations operate on a national or global scale, and rely on effective and efficient communication between various locations or subsidiaries, and even small, local companies need to communicate with suppliers or promote their products or services to customers. Further, globalization has enabled companies to source raw materials, parts, or components on a global scale, or manufacture products wherever they can find the lowest cost, best quality, or most qualified workforce. In all of these scenarios, effective and efficient communication is essential to convey specifications, coordinate production or delivery schedules, and so on. Similarly, salespeople rely on efficient communication with the customers and with other departments within the organization. With the increased global reach of organizations, the needs for *internal* communication have also changed tremendously.

Virtual Teams

To be competitive, organizations constantly need to bring together the right combinations of people who have the appropriate set of knowledge, skills, information, and authority to solve problems quickly and easily. Traditionally, organizations have used task forces, which are temporary work groups with a finite task and life cycle, to solve problems that cannot be solved well by existing work groups. Unfortunately, traditional task forces, like traditional organizational structures, cannot always solve problems quickly. Structure and logistical problems often get in the way of people trying to get things done quickly. Thus, organizations routinely need flexible teams that can be assembled quickly and can solve problems effectively and efficiently. Time is of the essence, and organizations are increasingly trying to harness the expertise of highly specialized team members, regardless of their location. With increasing globalization and increasing use of the Internet, collaborators on projects or teams do not have to be colocated; rather, businesses increasingly form **virtual teams**, comprised of members from different geographic areas, assembled as needed to collaborate on a certain project (Figure 5.2). Membership on these virtual teams is fluid, with teams forming and disbanding as needed, with team size fluctuating as necessary, and with team members coming and going as they are needed.

FIGURE 5.2

Members of highly specialized virtual teams are often not colocated.

Source: Toria/Shutterstock

Employees may, at times, find themselves on multiple teams, and the life of a team may be very short. In addition, team members must have easy, flexible access to other team members, meeting contexts, and information. Think of these virtual teams as highly dynamic task forces. Virtual teams are commonly used for tasks such as developing systems and software; for example, the programmers are located in India, the project managers are in the United States, and the testers are in Europe. However, systems development is not the only place you will find virtual teams. For instance, the healthcare industry has embraced the idea of using technology to create superior care for patients by creating virtual teams that may include dieticians, physicians, surgeons, pharmacists, and social workers from different cities, all of whom can coordinate care of the patients using various Web technologies to collaborate, so as to provide the best healthcare professionals regardless of where the patients reside.

If you have ever worked on a team project for your class (and you probably have), you have noticed that there are many different communication needs, such as talking, sharing documents, and making decisions. Just as there are many things to discuss within your team project, there are also many ways that you can communicate and collaborate, and different time horizons. One key distinction is between the need for **synchronous** (i.e., at the same time) and **asynchronous** (i.e., not coordinated in time) communication. For example, chatting online or making a telephone call are examples of synchronous communication, whereas e-mail is an example of asynchronous communication. Likewise, meetings of virtual teams typically take the form of **virtual meetings** using an online environment; such meetings can be done synchronously, like a teleconference, or asynchronously, using technologies such as online discussion boards. If time is of the essence, such as when attempting to meet deadlines or resolve urgent customer problems, synchronous media may be best suited, as delays can create process inefficiencies or dissatisfied customers, and can thus be costly for the organization. Thus, over the years, different tools have emerged to support various communication and collaboration needs (Table 5.1).

Groupware

The term **groupware** refers to a class of software that enables people to work together more effectively. Groupware and other collaboration technologies are often distinguished along two dimensions:

1. Whether the system supports synchronous or asynchronous collaboration and communication
2. Whether the system supports groups working together face-to-face or distributed

Using these two dimensions, groupware systems can be categorized as being able to support four types of group interaction methods, as shown in Figure 5.3. With the increased use of group-based problem solving and virtual teams, there are many potential benefits of utilizing groupware systems.

TABLE 5.1 Categories of Collaborative Tools

Title	Description	Instances	Examples
Electronic communication tools	Tools allowing users to send files, documents, and pictures to each other and share information	Fax, e-mail, voice mail, blogs, wikis, static Web sites	MS Outlook, Blogger, Wikipedia
Electronic conferencing tools	Tools allowing information sharing and rich interactions between users	Internet forums, instant messaging, application sharing, videoconferencing	Apple FaceTime, Skype, Google Hangouts, WebEx
Collaboration management tools	Tools used to facilitate virtual or collocated meetings and manage group activities	Electronic calendars, knowledge management systems, intranets, online document systems	Google Docs, MS Office Online, MS SharePoint

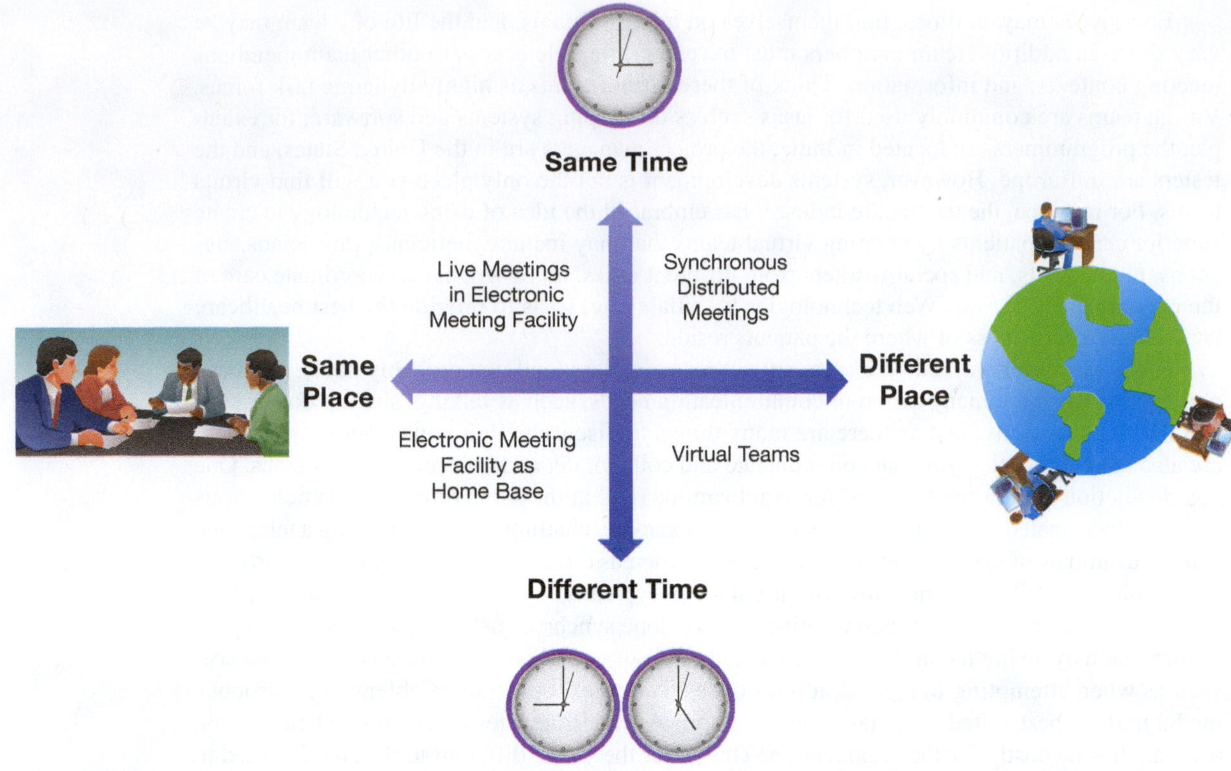

FIGURE 5.3

Groupware supports various modes of group interaction.

Large numbers of asynchronous groupware tools are becoming common in organizations, including e-mail, mailing lists, workflow automation systems, intranets (see upcoming discussion), group calendars, and collaborative writing tools. One widely used tool for group communication is discussion forums. Predating the Web 2.0 era, **discussion forums** (also known as discussion boards or online forums) emulate traditional bulletin boards and allow for threaded discussions between participants. Typically, discussion forums are dedicated to specific topics, and users can start new threads (Figure 5.4). Depending on the owner or host of the forum, the discussion forum may be moderated so that new postings appear only after they have been vetted by a moderator; further, some discussion forums may only allow posts from registered users, whereas others allow anyone to contribute. As the purpose of such forums is to enable discussion, there are usually multiple participants exchanging (typically rather short) thoughts.

Like asynchronous groupware, there are also many forms of synchronous groupware available to support a wide variety of activities, including shared whiteboards, online chat, electronic meeting systems, and, of course, video communication systems (discussed in the following section). An **electronic meeting system (EMS)** is a sophisticated software tool used to help

FIGURE 5.4

Microsoft offers discussion forums for questions and feedback related to its various products and services.

Source: Courtesy of Microsoft, Inc.

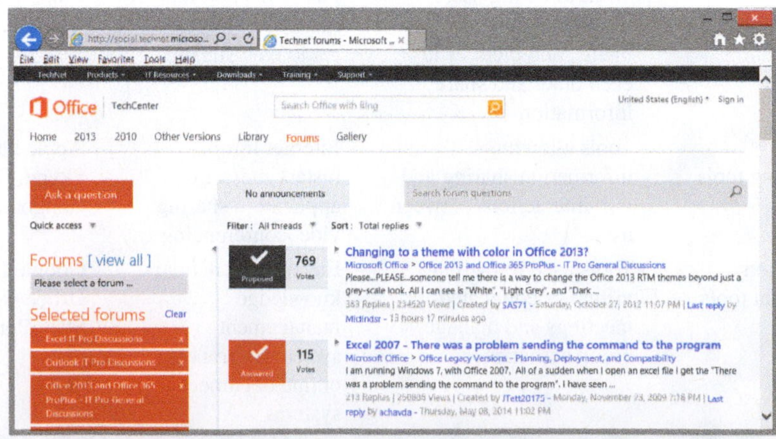

FIGURE 5.5

An electronic meeting system utilizes networked computers and sophisticated software to support various group tasks.
Source: Konstantinos Kokkinis/Shutterstock

group members solve problems and make decisions through interactive structured processes such as electronic idea generation, idea evaluation, and voting (Figure 5.5). These structured processes help groups stay on track and avoid costly diversions that regularly occur in meetings. EMSs have traditionally been housed within a dedicated meeting facility; increasingly, Web-based implementations support team members around the globe. Many groupware systems used by organizations combine a variety of tools supporting both synchronous and asynchronous communication and collaboration.

Videoconferencing

In the 1960s, at Disneyland and other theme parks and special events, the picturephone was first being demonstrated to large audiences. It took another 30 years to take off, but today, organizations are routinely conducting videoconferencing to replace traditional meetings, using either desktop videoconferencing or dedicated videoconferencing systems that can cost from a few thousand dollars up to US$500,000.

Desktop videoconferencing has been enabled by the growing power of processors powering personal computers and faster Internet connections. For desktop videoconferencing, all that is needed is a **webcam** (i.e., a small video camera that is connected directly to a PC), a speaker telephone or separate microphone, videoconferencing software (e.g., Skype, Google+, or Apple FaceTime), and a high-speed Internet connection. Similarly, people can now use various apps on their mobile devices, enabling them to make video calls on the go.

Dedicated videoconferencing systems are typically located within organizational conference rooms, facilitating meetings with customers or project team members across town or around the world. These systems can be highly realistic—as if you are almost colocated with your colleagues—but high-end systems can be extremely expensive. No matter what type of videoconferencing system utilized by an organization, this collaboration technology has come a long way from the demonstration at Disneyland in the 1960s, becoming mainstream in most modern organizations.

Intranets and Employee Portals

Internet technologies have given rise to another widely used tool for communicating and collaborating within organizational boundaries. Specifically, many large organizations have intranet-based employee portals. As discussed in Chapter 3, "Managing the Information Systems Infrastructure and Services," an intranet is a private network using Web technologies, used to facilitate the secured transmission of proprietary information within an organization. Intranets take advantage of standard Internet and Web protocols to communicate information to and from authorized employees. An intranet looks and acts just like a publicly accessible Web site, and uses the same software, hardware, and networking technologies to communicate information.

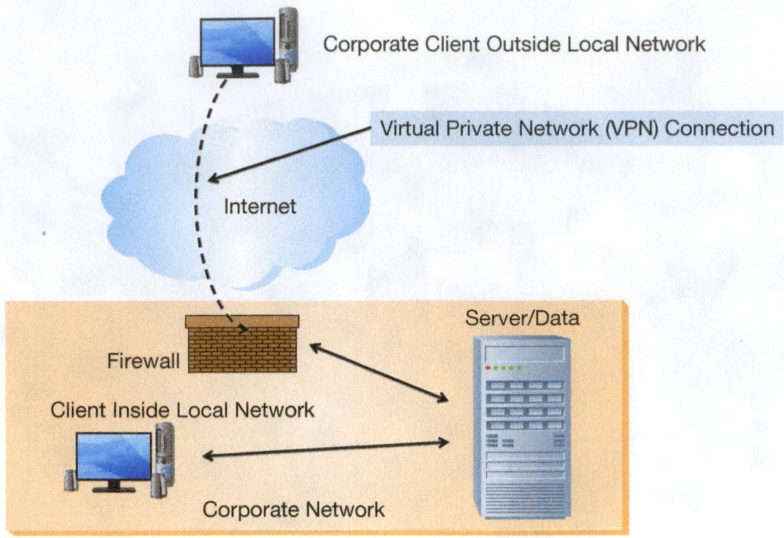

FIGURE 5.6

Typical intranet system architecture.

Thus, users access their company's intranet using their Web browser. Many companies such as Boeing provide customized intranet pages for each employee depending on job functions or even geographical location. Whereas all pages have the same look and feel and draw on the same underlying data, each employee can access only the information needed to perform his or her job function. For example, if an employee from human resources logs on to the employee portal, he or she would see only content that pertains to his or her job, such as payroll information or hiring statistics.

All intranet pages are behind the company's firewall, and in the simplest form of an intranet, communications take place only within the confines of organizational boundaries and do not travel across the Internet. However, increases in employees' mobility necessitate that an intranet be accessible from anywhere. Thus, most companies allow their employees to use virtual private networks (VPNs) to connect to the company's intranet while on the road or working from home (i.e., telecommuting). Figure 5.6 depicts a typical intranet system architecture (see Chapter 10, "Securing Information Systems," for more on firewalls and VPNs).

REAL-TIME ACCESS TO INFORMATION. A major benefit of corporate intranets is the ability to increase the efficiency and effectiveness of collaboration by providing real-time access to information. Unlike paper-based documents, which need to be continually updated and distributed to employees when changes occur, intranets make it less complicated to manage, update, distribute, and access corporate information. For instance, Boeing disseminates corporate news using multimedia files distributed over the company's intranet, allowing employees to view digital copies of company news releases as they occur, from the convenience of their desktops.

With intranet-based solutions such as those deployed at Boeing, up-to-date, accurate information can be easily accessed on a company-wide basis from a single source that is both efficient and user friendly. Companies can become more flexible with resources required to create, maintain, and distribute corporate documents, while in the process employees become more knowledgeable and current about the information that is important to them. Employees develop a sense of confidence and become self-reliant, reducing time spent dealing with employment-related issues and allowing them to focus on their work responsibilities.

ENTERPRISE SEARCH. Another component supporting employee productivity by providing real-time access to information is the integration of enterprise search functionality. As more and more content is accessible via a company's intranet, relevant information becomes increasingly difficult to locate, especially if the information is in different languages and located on different servers or databases, as is the case in many large global organizations such as Nestlé. Hence, the requirements for enterprise search engines are very different from those of Internet search engines such as Google or Bing. Enterprise search engines such as Microsoft's Enterprise Search or the Google Search Appliance are designed to retrieve content from various internal data sources, including documents, databases, or applications linked to the company's intranet. Such capabilities allow organizations to easily share millions of documents located throughout the organization. Thus, providing enterprise search functionality can enhance productivity and be an important factor contributing to users' satisfaction with the company's intranet.

COLLABORATION. One of the most common problems occurring in large corporations relates to the coordination of and collaboration on business activities in a timely fashion across divisions or functional areas. For instance, Boeing uses its intranet to facilitate collaborative efforts, such as in the process of designing new aircraft components. In this process, three-dimensional digital models of aircraft designs frequently need to be shared between aerospace engineers. Using Boeing's intranet, an engineer can share a drawing with another engineer at a remote location; the second engineer revises the drawing as necessary and uploads the updated drawing to a shared folder on the intranet. The Boeing intranet provides the company with the capability of reducing product development cycle times as well as the ability to stay abreast of current project, corporate, and market conditions. Likewise, intranets are being used to poll staff about current issues or by employees to communicate with each other and executives in a secure non-public forum.

EMPLOYEE PORTALS. In addition to being used for communication and collaboration, organizational intranets are widely used to provide **employee portals** that enable **employee self-service** for administering benefits, managing retirement plans, or other human resources–based applications. For example, for large companies, processing human resources–related forms can be a large cost factor. Depending on the complexity of the form, processing a paper-based form can cost US$20 to US$30, according to benefits administration solutions provider Workscape, Inc. Whereas interactive voice response–based telephone applications can cut these costs to US$2 to US$4, using intranet-based employee self-service applications can reduce this further, to a mere 5 to 10 cents per form (Wagner, 2002). Considering that an employee, on average, conducts 15 human resources–related transactions per year, the savings can be significant. Using the intranet, report templates can be centrally managed, and modifications can be made instantaneously as conditions change; thus, employees can submit the appropriate template electronically with the assurance that they have used the correct version. Further, using online forms can help to significantly reduce error rates, as the entries can be checked for accuracy when the data are entered, thus preventing the user from inputting incorrect or illogical entries.

THE EVOLVING WEB

The traditional collaboration tools previously introduced are based on Internet technologies. However, up until a few years ago, the Web was regarded as a one-way medium, with a relatively strict distinction between content creators and content consumers (sometimes referred to as "Web 1.0"). Some entities would create content (say, a Web site), and others would consume this content. However, changes in technology have enabled new uses of the Web; dynamic Web applications, often referred to as **Web 2.0** applications, allow people to collaborate and share information online, shifting the users' role from the passive consumer of content to its creator (Figure 5.7). In contrast to the TV network ABC's site, where content is provided by ABC, the Web 2.0 application YouTube depends on content created and uploaded by other users; similarly, whereas *Encyclopaedia Britannica* invests large sums in professionally researched articles, the

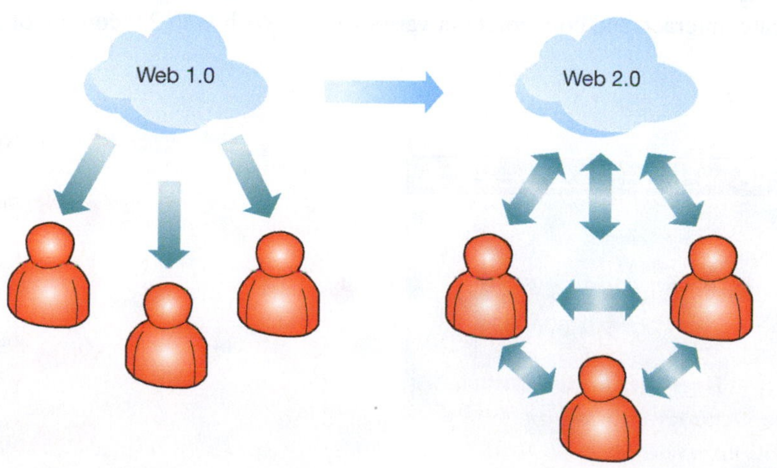

FIGURE 5.7
Web 2.0 applications shift a Web user's role from a passive consumer of content to its creator.

articles in the online encyclopedia Wikipedia are jointly written and edited by the online community (owing to societal changes and competition from Wikipedia, *Encyclopaedia Britannica* decided to stop producing printed encyclopedias in 2012, instead focusing on its online offerings). In addition to these applications, many organizations have successfully incorporated Web 2.0 concepts into their business models. For example, Amazon.com adds value to its site by incorporating book reviews from its customers. This way, it gives customers a channel to voice their thoughts; at the same time, a larger number of reviews can help other customers make better decisions, thus attracting more visitors to Amazon.com's site. In the following sections, we will discuss technological and societal changes that both enable and necessitate changes in the way many organizations do business.

Evolving Web Capabilities

Many successful Web 2.0 applications rely on the network effect. The network effect (as defined in Chapter 1, "Managing in the Digital World") refers to the notion that the value of a network (or tool or application based on a network) increases with the number of other users. In other words, if a network has few users, it has little or no value. In addition, new Web capabilities allow Web sites or service providers (such as Google) to make parts of their functionality or data (such as mapping data) available for other Web sites to use, and thus enable creating unique and dynamic applications, or **mashups**, quickly and easily.

The idea of mashups came from popular music where many songs are produced by mixing two or more existing songs together; in Web 2.0 terminology, a mashup is a new application (or Web site) that uses data from one or more service providers. For example, a mashup could combine mapping data, photos, reference information, hotel prices, and weather information to provide a comprehensive overview of travel destinations. Rather than having to collect or generate all of this information single-handedly, the creator of the mashup could simply draw on services provided by Google Maps, Flickr, Wikipedia, Expedia, and AccuWeather (Figure 5.8). The online itinerary planner Tripomatic integrates data from Google maps, hotel booking services, and other services to let users plan their next holiday. Likewise, users and companies can create mobile apps by combining various services and data sources. The local search app AroundMe uses data from services such as Booking.com, Opentable.com, or Foursquare to display information, reviews, or driving directions about businesses, restaurants, or medical facilities near a given location. Other Web sites and mobile apps use information from airlines, radio stations, recommendation services, or any other sources of useful information.

Many organizations have recognized the power and benefits of allowing other sites and apps to incorporate their services and data into mashups. Why are companies doing this? By providing access to useful services and data, organizations extend their reach and build and strengthen customer relationships, providing a base for revenue-generating services (e.g., Google offers mapping services for free for low-volume usage, but offers the services as a paid version for high-volume commercial usage, such as integration in a hotel booking site).

Evolving Social Interaction

Many successful Web 2.0 applications embody core Web 2.0 values such as collaboration and social sharing; these can be classified as **social media** (or **social software**), allowing people to communicate, interact, and collaborate in various ways. With Web 2.0 coming of age, people's

FIGURE 5.8

A mashup is a new application (or Web site) that uses data from one or more service providers.

TABLE 5.2 Shifting Perspectives from Web 1.0 to Web 2.0

Web 1.0	Web 2.0
Me	Me and you
Read	Read and write
Connect ideas	Connect ideas and people
Search	Receive and give recommendations to friends and others
Find	Share
Techies rule	Users rule
Organizations	Individuals

Source: Based on Sessums (2009).

behaviors as well as societies' have undergone rapid changes. For example, many people have changed the ways they search for information. Whereas in the past people turned to paper encyclopedias as sources of unbiased information, people now increasingly turn to Web sites such as Wikipedia, or ask their friends and acquaintances on social networks such as Facebook or Google+ for personalized information. Similarly, there has been a marked shift in the way people view privacy and share information; although criticized by privacy advocates, people are sharing more personal information online than ever before. Repeatedly, you can read about people posting the most private information, without thinking about the consequences; as Facebook and other social Web sites have become pervasive in many people's lives, you have information about your friend's recent drinking escapades leading to a driving under the influence (DUI) arrest, your coworker's breaking up with his girlfriend, and other things you may or may not want to know, all at your fingertips. Clearly, social software has strongly influenced the lives of many people. Table 5.2 highlights the shift in perspectives from the Web 1.0 to the Web 2.0 era.

The Evolving Workspace

The "millennials," or "Generation Y," who grew up being tied to social software such as MySpace, YouTube, or Facebook, are joining the workforce and have much different expectations for their workplace than prior generations, and some fundamental shifts are taking place in employer–employee relationships (see Smythe, 2007). For example, employees are now looking for a portfolio career rather than a cradle-to-grave job, tend to view themselves as citizens rather than employees, and "loan their talent" to the employer rather than being a "human resource." A global study by Accenture revealed that for 37 percent of 18- to 27-year-olds, state-of-the-art technology is a vital consideration in the choice of workplace; of the working millennials, 55 percent use instant messaging, and 45 percent use social networking sites for work-related activities (Francis & Harrigan, 2010). The millennials bring with them many new and valuable skills, but also attitudes that may be difficult to integrate with more traditional business environments: Over 19 percent of businesses worldwide ban social networking sites at work (Clearswift, 2011), but many millennials are skilled at finding creative work-arounds to circumvent such policies (which may result in increases in security breaches). A recent survey showed that 29 percent of college students would not join a company that bans social media applications, and 71 percent do not obey policies related to social media use in the workplace (Cisco, 2011, 2012). As a result, companies are increasingly starting to embrace social media to enhance communication, cooperation, collaboration, and connection (Cook, 2008).

Future Web Capabilities

Web technologies and collaboration are ever-evolving topics, and many developments have yet to be fully realized. This section briefly forecasts future capabilities of the Web, in particular, focusing on efforts to create the semantic Web and characteristics of Web 3.0.

THE SEMANTIC WEB. Since the Web opened up for public use, the number of Web pages and sites has grown exponentially. Although this increase in Web pages should mean that we have ever more information at our fingertips, it also means that the information is increasingly harder to find. What if the information on the Web was organized in a way that users could more easily find information or relevant content? Traditionally, Web pages were designed to be understood by people but not by computers, and search engines were examining pages for the existence of key terms; for example, when searching for "what eats penguins," a search engine would

BRIEF CASE Crowdfunding

Ever have a great idea for a product that you just know would sell well? Maybe you have a great solution to a problem that everyone seems to have. Inventing such a solution, developing the product designs and the manufacturing processes, and then manufacturing enough stock to meet your planned initial demand could take tens or even hundreds of thousands of dollars. And then there's the problem that you don't know how many people will be initially interested in the product, and you may be left with large overstocks of items that you can't sell to recoup your costs. New product design used to follow this paradigm, which is expensive and risky for any aspiring inventor. In 2009, Kickstarter.com launched with ambitious plans to change all that.

Kickstarter is one of several popular crowdfunding platforms. **Crowdfunding** is the securing of business financing from individuals in the marketplace—the "crowd"—to fund an initiative. Individuals who support a given initiative—called "backers"—pledge a certain amount of financial support to the project in return for certain benefits. In the case of Kickstarter, a funding campaign usually centers around a product—such as a smartphone case, a belt, an electronic gadget, or even a board game. Interested backers pledge money in support of the product, generally above a minimum amount in return for one count of the item being backed. If (and only if) the campaign reaches its funding goal, the backers are charged the amount they pledged and the product goes into production. If too few backers are interested and the goal is not met, the campaign fails and no backers are charged any money. Kickstarter in particular has been very successful and has helped many campaigns get funded, totaling over 135,000 projects with over US$1 billion generated in pledges.

Backing a project with a pledge is not without risks. Kickstarter leaves the campaign creator responsible for completing successfully funded projects. It is up to the backers to determine the viability of the projects they support. Kickstarter provides a rating and feedback system that aids backers in making these determinations, but there remains a risk that your pledge will go to waste if the project was ill-conceived or otherwise fails after successful funding.

Even with these risks, crowdfunding platforms like Kickstarter have provided a compelling opportunity for people with good ideas to get the funding required to develop and manufacture their products.

Questions

1. Who should bear the responsibility for ensuring that Kickstarter projects deliver the products their campaigners promise?
2. What other benefits do crowdfunding platforms like Kickstarter provide society?

Based on:

Anonymous. (2014). Kickstarter basics: Kickstarter 101. *Kickstarter*. Retrieved May 28, 2014, from https://www.kickstarter.com/help/faq/kickstarter+basics?ref=faq_subcategory#Kick.

Kickstarter. (2014, May 23). In *Wikipedia, The Free Encyclopedia*. Retrieved May 28, 2014, from http://en.wikipedia.org/w/index.php?title=Kickstarter&oldid=609822889.

return Web pages that may have this information, but would have been more likely that the pages just have the words or key terms "what" and "eats" and "penguins," as search engines were not sophisticated enough to be able to find, understand, and integrate information presented on Web pages. The **semantic Web**, originally envisioned by Tim Berners-Lee, one of the inventors of the World Wide Web, is a set of design principles that will allow computers to be able to better index Web pages, topics, and subjects. When Web pages are designed using semantic principles, computers will be able to understand the meaning of the content, and search engines will be able to give richer and more accurate answers. The major search engines encourage webmasters to integrate so-called microdata into their pages' HTML markup to help search engines understand the *meaning* of content on the pages; for example, the markup of a business' address can be enhanced by specifying the meaning of the different parts of an address. In 2012, Google has started making strides toward implementing concepts related to the semantic Web in its "knowledge graph." When searching for terms in Google, the search engine now attempts to foresee what the user may mean; for example, when searching for "kings," the search engine not only provides a list of pages containing the keyword "kings," but also displays a box containing links to search results specific to the *Los Angeles Kings*, the *Sacramento Kings*, and the NBC TV series *Kings*. Similarly, when searching for "Los Angeles Kings," Google not only returns a list of Web pages, but also a summary of relevant information about the hockey team, culled from various Web sources. Although the semantic Web is largely unrealized, Google's efforts show that the semantic Web experience is getting closer.

WEB 3.0. In many ways, Web 2.0 has already replaced Web 1.0, and the question is "What will replace Web 2.0?" For some, Web 2.0 is just a short transitional period before the next wave of Internet technologies, which is predicted to last until 2020. There are several ideas on what this next wave, Web 3.0, will entail. Some, such as *Forbes* contributor Eric Jackson, envision the next wave of the Web to be centered around mobility, almost announcing the demise of the Web as we know it. Others see Web 3.0 as the "contextual Web," where the immense amounts of content available to users will be filtered by contextual factors such as time, location, social activities, and so on. You may have already seen some of these emerging technologies in practice, especially regarding the context of a user's location, and we may only know what Web 3.0 really is when we see it; it may even forever remain a buzzword. Nevertheless, we can see exciting new developments on the horizon, and the coming trends will likely involve true integration of devices and connectivity to create powerful, socially aware Internet applications. Stay tuned to see what the future holds.

Enterprise 2.0

Having realized the opportunities brought about by these profound changes, many business organizations are continuously looking for ways to use social media to support their existing business processes; many organizations have built successful business models entirely based on core Web 2.0 values such as social sharing or collaboration (see Chapter 4, "Enabling Business-to-Consumer Electronic Commerce," for a discussion on social commerce). The use of social media within a company's boundaries or between a company and its customers or stakeholders (often referred to as **Enterprise 2.0**) can help in sharing organizational knowledge, making businesses more innovative and productive, and helping them to effectively connect with their customers and the wider public (McAfee, 2006a). In the following section, we will introduce various social media applications used by individual Web users as well as organizations.

SOCIAL MEDIA AND THE ENTERPRISE

You were likely familiar with many of the tools discussed previously, but there may have been some that you were not aware of. You are probably more comfortable or find more value using some tools over others. Similarly, organizations are increasingly trying to find the right tools for their different needs. In the following sections, we will discuss how different social media applications enable or support communication, cooperation, collaboration, or connection; needless to say, many of these applications cannot be neatly categorized, fitting into more than one category.

Enhancing Communication Using Social Media

A prime application of Enterprise 2.0 is facilitating and enhancing the communication within an organization as well as between an organization and its stakeholders. For organizations, social media have opened up a vast array of opportunities for presenting themselves to their (potential) customers; at the same time, these applications have opened up literally thousands of channels for customers to voice their opinions about an organization. In this section, we introduce various social media tools used for communication.

BLOGS. Blogging originally started out as a way for novices to express themselves using very simple Web pages. **Blogging** is the process of creating an online text diary (i.e., a **blog**, or Web log) made up of chronological entries that comment on everything from one's everyday life to wine and food, or even computer problems (Figure 5.9). Rather than trying to produce

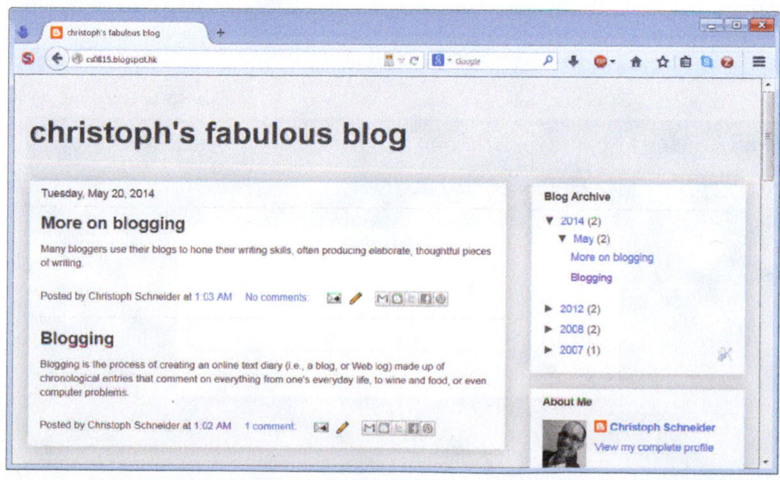

FIGURE 5.9

Blogging is the process of creating an online text diary (i.e., a blog, or Web log) made up of chronological entries.

Source: Blogspot/Google, Inc.

physical books to sell or use as gifts, bloggers (i.e., the people maintaining blogs) merely want to share stories about their lives or voice their opinions (although feedback is often encouraged through associated threaded discussions). Many bloggers use their blogs to hone their writing skills, often producing elaborate, thoughtful pieces of writing. Others write blogs with the aim of attracting large audiences, so as to monetize their efforts using online advertising or affiliate marketing programs.

However, blogs are not without controversy. Nicholas Carr, noted technology journalist (and active blogger himself), classifies blogging as the **"amateurization" of journalism**. Often the value of blogging is the ability to bring breaking news to the public in the fastest possible way. By doing so, some bloggers cut journalistic corners, rendering some of the posts on the blogs less than accurate, and blogs have been criticized for frequently providing the biased opinions of the writers, particularly because many of the authors' sources cannot or have not been verified.

Nevertheless, blogs have massively influenced the way in which people gather and consume information, and have become important voices that can sway public opinion. In fact, turning to free information from blogs and other online sources, many readers have cancelled newspaper subscriptions. In turn, diminishing readership in traditional newspapers has enticed advertisers to begin to withdraw from this traditional medium, leading to budget cuts and layoffs at reputable newspapers such as the *San Francisco Chronicle, The New York Times,* the *Washington Times,* and many others. Unfortunately—and ironically—this may erode the very sources that many bloggers base their information on.

In addition to blogs created by and/or for individual readers, blogs are being used by small, medium-sized, and large organizations for connecting with their employees or customers. For example, IBM's business-oriented social software suite IBM Connections includes blogs, helping people to voice ideas and obtain feedback from others. Similarly, companies such as Google maintain official company blogs (e.g., http://googleblog.blogspot.com) to inform their stakeholders about news, rumors, or current thoughts.

MICROBLOGGING TOOLS. **Microblogging tools** (sometimes called **social presence tools**), similar to blogging, enable people to voice their thoughts; however, in contrast to blogs, which often contain lengthy posts, social presence tools are designed for broadcasting relatively short "status updates." In contrast to social networks, where a user can choose who can or cannot receive his or her status updates, typically, anyone can follow another person's microblog. A popular social presence tool is Twitter, which allows users to post short (up to 140 characters of text) "tweets" that are delivered to the author's followers or subscribers via mobile phone or Twitter applications (Figure 5.10). The recipient can "retweet" (i.e., re-broadcast) interesting tweets to his or her followers. With many people broadcasting everything they find interesting, Twitter has become a source for breaking news. Many social networking sites (discussed later) also have social presence functionality built in; for example, users can update their status on Facebook, letting their friends know about their current thoughts and allowing them to post replies.

Many organizations have used this trend and created accounts on Twitter. For example, Coca-Cola has an official Twitter account used to post news or interact with its (as of mid-2014) over 2.7 million followers; Coca-Cola follows more than 67,000 Twitter accounts and actively replies to and retweets Twitter messages. This way, Coca-Cola signals that it cares about its

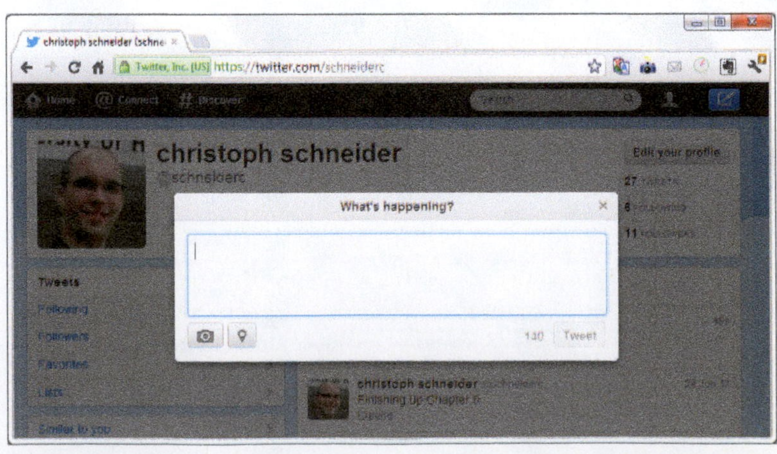

FIGURE 5.10

Twitter allows posting short "tweets" that are delivered to the author's followers or subscribers via mobile phone or Twitter applications.

Source: Christoph Schneider

followers, trying to increase its customers' brand loyalty. When posting a tweet, users can tag words or phrases with a "#"—called a **hashtag** (e.g., #openhappiness, #Ukraine or #street fashion). A word phrase or topic that is tagged at a greater rate than others is said to be **trending**. A trending topic becomes popular because of a concerted effort by users, or because of an event (e.g., a new winner of the Super Bowl) that prompts people to tweet about the topic. Tumblr, another popular microblogging tool, takes the concept a step further by allowing users to go beyond the 140-character limit and share any kind of digital content, including text, music, and videos, and allows companies to communicate and connect with their customers. For example, in May 2014, AMC premiered a full-episode sneak preview of its new TV series, *Halt and Catch Fire,* on Tumblr.

INSTANT MESSAGING. In contrast to asynchronous discussion forums, blogs, and status updates, **instant messaging** (or online chat) enables real-time written conversations. Using instant messaging, multiple participants can have conversations and enjoy immediate feedback from their conversation partners. Some social networking sites such as Facebook have integrated instant messaging functionality. In addition, the increase in smartphone usage has merged instant messaging with cell phone–based text messaging by enabling cloud-based messaging services such as WhatsApp or Line, allowing for group chat, free text messages (even internationally), and even the exchange of multimedia content between different devices, using the smartphone users' data plan or Wi-Fi connection. New instant messaging apps such as Snapchat allow users to set a time limit specifying for how long the recipient can view the message before it is automatically deleted. Many organizations have adopted Web-based instant messaging for internal communications, and also use live chat for sales and customer support functions. For example, the Chinese business-to-business marketplace Alibaba.com includes a chat interface so that interested buyers can immediately contact potential sellers.

VIRTUAL WORLDS. **Virtual worlds** have taken the concept of real-time communication a step further by allowing people to communicate using avatars. These worlds promised to become a channel for rich, interactive communication, as well as for education-related activities, employee training, or medical uses. After the initial hype, the popularity of virtual worlds for business use has currently faded, and virtual world–based games are now primarily used for entertainment purposes. However, the interactions taking place in games such as World of Warcraft remain in the focus of researchers studying various forms of group behaviors. In addition, Facebook is betting on the future of virtual reality, having acquired Oculus, the creators of a virtual reality headset, for US$2 billion in 2014.

Enhancing Cooperation with Social Media

In addition to communication, companies and individuals can benefit from social media applications that enable cooperation. Cooperation between individuals or organizations creates win-win situations such that one participant's success improves the chances of success of other participants. Social media applications facilitating such cooperation rely on the network effect to provide the greatest benefits for users.

MEDIA SHARING. One example of cooperative social media applications making use of the network effect is media sharing. The sharing of pictures, videos, audio, and even presentations has become immensely popular on the Web, using applications such as Flickr or Instagram (images), Vimeo or YouTube (videos), or SlideShare (presentations); using sites such as Pandora, users can even create their favorite music stream and share it with others who may have similar interests. Typically, the shared content is hosted on media sharing sites; however, the content can also be embedded into other sites, creating a win-win situation for the content creator and the site embedding the content. For example, embedding an interesting and relevant YouTube video into a blog post helps to increase the attractiveness of the blog while at the same time increasing the viewership of the video, thus creating positive returns for both parties.

Similarly, webcasting is increasingly used for media sharing. **Webcasting** (or **podcasting**) is the distribution of digital media, such as audio or video files for on-demand playback on digital media players. The increase in mobile devices such as smartphones and tablets has contributed to the tremendous growth of webcasts, as the consumption can be time shifted and place shifted; in other words, webcasts allow media content to be viewed at one's convenience, whenever or wherever. The term "podcasting," derived from combining the terms "broadcasting" and "iPod,"

COMING ATTRACTIONS

Dissolvable Electronics

The pharmaceutical industry is fighting a constant battle against various bacteria that can quickly evolve to become resistant to antibiotic treatments. Drug researchers can spend months or years developing a new treatment, only to have that treatment lose effectiveness when the bacteria it was designed to kill become resistant. New antibiotics must then be developed, and these cunning bacteria keep pharmaceutical companies on their toes. It is not known whether researchers will be able to stay ahead of the bacteria indefinitely and keep the population healthy. But some researchers are developing alternative methods of killing bacteria that are not susceptible to the mutations of bacteria.

Researchers at the University of Illinois are developing specialized electronic devices with the ability to perform short-term therapeutic tasks without active treatment from a medical professional. The key characteristic of these devices is their ability to disappear—to dissolve after a time and be absorbed by the person they were helping to heal. For example, after a surgery in which a large incision is made, a key risk for recovering patients is that of bacterial infection. A dissolvable electronic device could be embedded in the incision, designed to use just enough heat to kill bacteria. After the risk of infection has passed, the device, which is made of "biocompatible" materials, would then dissolve and be incorporated or excreted through the normal biological processes of the body.

This scenario is not quite a reality yet; researchers have thus far merely demonstrated the creation of dissolvable electronic circuits. But perhaps the technology will soon develop into something that will help the human race further reduce disease and sickness that still afflicts many around the world.

Based on:
Drake, N. (2013, May 24). New wireless electronics could heal wounds and then dissolve. *Wired*. Retrieved May 28, 2014, from http://www.wired.com/2013/05/remote-controlled-dissolvable-electronics.

is a misnomer, as **webcasts** (or **podcasts**) can be played on a variety of devices in addition to Apple's iPods. As with blogging, webcasting has grown substantially, with traditional media organizations now webcasting everything from shows on National Public Radio to Fox's *Family Guy* to the *Oprah Winfrey Show*. In addition to media organizations and independent webcasters, the educational sector uses webcasts for providing students access to lectures, lab demonstrations, or sports events; this allows students to review lectures or prepare for class during their morning and evening commutes. In 2007, Apple launched iTunes U, which offers free content provided by major U.S. universities, such as Stanford, Berkeley, and the Massachusetts Institute of Technology (Figure 5.11). As webcasts can be enriched by allowing for interactive Q&A sessions or by embedding PowerPoint presentations, organizations increasingly use webcasts to provide access to shareholder meetings, online training, road shows, or other applications.

To receive the most current content, users can subscribe to blogs, webcasts, videos, and news stories through Apple's iTunes, or via **Real Simple Syndication (RSS)** feeds. RSS feeds are provided by content publishers so that the users get notified of updates to the content.

FIGURE 5.11

A student listens to a podcast on iTunes U.

Source: Courtesy of Christoph Schneider

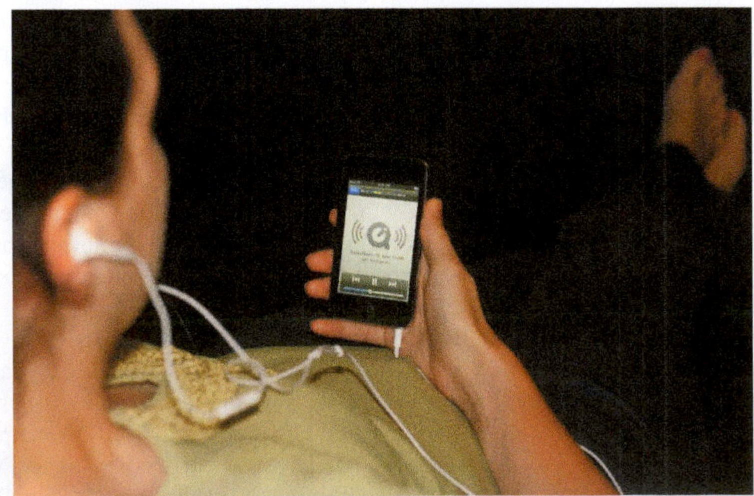

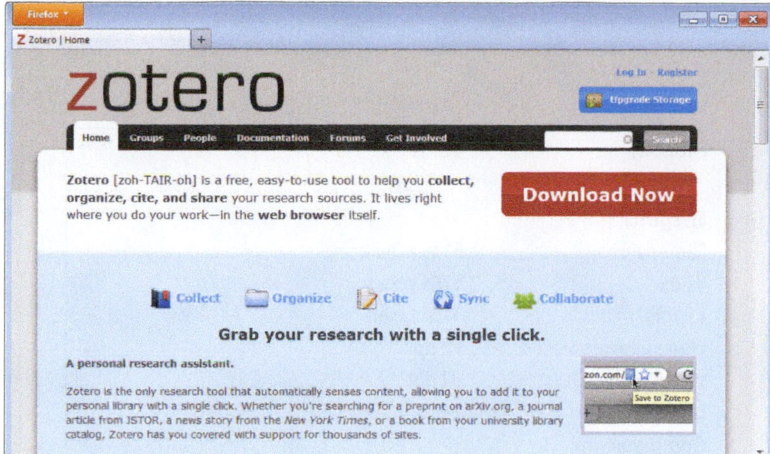

FIGURE 5.12

Zotero helps in organizing citations and research resources.

Source: Courtesy of Center for History and New Media, George Mason University.

Rather than users actively having to check multiple sources for updated content, RSS readers automatically check the feeds for updates, and provide a synopsis of a document or the full text.

SOCIAL BOOKMARKING. Another category of social media applications relying on the network effect is social bookmarking. For many Web surfers, key challenges are finding information and then finding it *again* at a later time; hence, people often keep long lists of bookmarks to sites they find interesting or visit frequently. Although this is useful for individuals, users may miss a plethora of other, related, and potentially interesting Web sites. **Social bookmarking** helps to address this by allowing users to share Internet bookmarks and to create categorization systems (referred to as **folksonomies**). As more people participate in social bookmarking, the value for each user grows as the bookmarks become more complete and more relevant to each user. Widely used public social bookmarking tools include reddit, StumbleUpon, and Delicious. Likewise, Pinterest allows users to "pin" everything they find interesting, and media Web sites such as CNN.com provide sharing links, so as to increase the reach of their content. For organizations, social bookmarking can be extremely valuable for knowledge management and harnessing the collective intelligence of employees. Using enterprise-oriented social bookmarking tools, it is easy to map "islands" of knowledge within an organization, thus helping to easily find experts on a given topic.

SOCIAL CATALOGING. Similar to social bookmarking, **social cataloging** is the creation of a categorization system by users. Contributors build up catalogs regarding specific topics such as academic citations, wireless networks, books and music, and so on. For example, users can create virtual bookshelves with goodreads, organize their collections, write reviews, and then share this bookshelf with others on the Web. Similarly, students and researchers can use free tools such as Mendeley or Zotero (Figure 5.12) to manage their citations, thus facilitating the creation of reference lists for research papers. Organizations are typically dealing with tremendous amounts of information, ranging from supplier information to frequent customer complaints, and can use social cataloging for structuring this information and making it more accessible and useful.

TAGGING. Social cataloging relies on the concept of **tagging**, or manually adding metadata to media or other content. **Metadata** can be simply thought of as data about data. In essence, metadata describe data in terms of who, where, when, why, and so on. For example, metadata about a Word document include the author, the time the document was created, and when it was last saved; metadata about a digital photo include date and time, focal length, shutter speed, aperture value, and so on (Figure 5.13).

Whereas certain metadata about documents or media files are captured automatically (e.g., when saving a document in a word processor, or when taking a picture with a digital camera), there are various other important pieces of information that are not automatically captured, such as keywords about a document or the names of people in a picture. Tagging is the process of adding such metadata to pieces of information. Tags are commonly added to pictures and videos on Web sites such as Flickr, a picture and video-hosting Web site that allows users to upload their content. Likewise, social media applications such as Twitter, Tumblr, and Instagram have

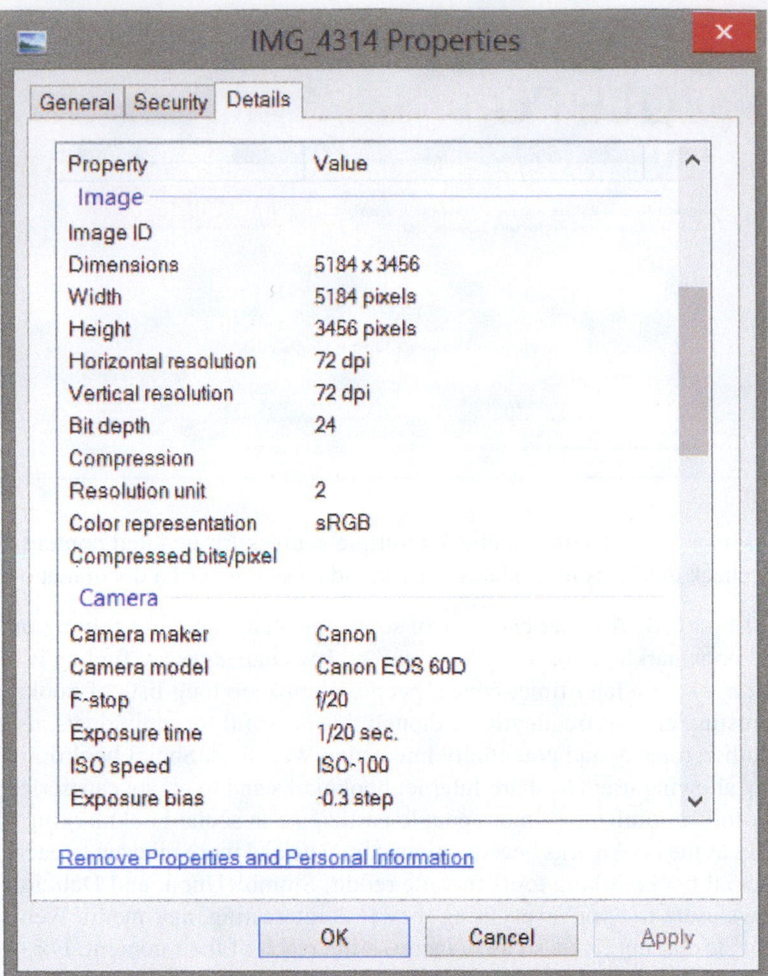

FIGURE 5.13

Metadata about a photo.
Source: Microsoft Windows 8 dialog browser, Courtesy of Microsoft Corporation.

FIGURE 5.14

A tag cloud representing words and concepts that are key to social media.
Source: Shutterstock.

popularized the use of hashtags, which are used to add metadata to messages posted on these services, allowing users to search for content related to a certain topic. A way to visualize user-generated tags or content on a site is through **tag clouds** (Figure 5.14). The size of a word in a tag cloud represents its importance or frequency, so that it is easy to spot the most important or frequent words or tags.

KEY PLAYERS

The "Other" Social Networking Giants

Anyone who is a part of modern society has likely heard of the big social networks like Facebook, Google+, Twitter, and LinkedIn. These networks boast impressive usage statistics and have affected our lives in many ways. Facebook is the worldwide leader in user base, with nearly 1.3 billion users (roughly half of the world's 2.5 billion Internet users). But what you may not know is that between Facebook and the next widely known social network, Google+, there are three social platforms that you may have never heard of or used. These platforms have large user bases in Asian, European, and African regions, and you would do well to be familiar with them and their services.

One of the biggest players in the Asian social platform space is Tencent Holdings, a Chinese conglomerate that provides e-commerce, gaming, social networking, and microblogging services. Tencent is responsible for four of the top 10 social and messaging platforms in the world. The second largest social platform in the world, second only to Facebook, is QQ, an instant messaging service with a strong user base in China. First released in 1999 as a basic instant messaging service, the platform has evolved into a huge service (with over 816 million users) that provides a range of services, including social games, music, group and voice chat, and even a mobile payment platform. In 2005, Tencent created QZone, a social network and blogging platform similar to Blogspot or Tumblr. The platform has grown very quickly, and now boasts over 630 million users, mostly in China. Acknowledging the exponential growth of mobile Internet users, Tencent developed a new mobile messaging and networking service called WeChat. The service was introduced in 2010, and has quickly grown to be larger than LinkedIn, Twitter, or Tumblr in number of users, with over 400 million users; the WeChat mobile app is the fifth most used smartphone app in the world. Rounding out Tencent's varied offerings is the Tencent Weibo service, a microblogging platform patterned after Twitter, launched in 2010, which has grown to be nearly the same size as Twitter, despite Twitter's four-year lead in the marketplace.

One final key player is one that you may have heard of. The WhatsApp messaging platform was created in 2009, and has quickly risen to broad popularity. Though the platform is relatively popular in the North American markets with which you may be familiar, we highlight the platform here because of its significance in international markets. In particular, WhatsApp has a strong presence in many countries, including India, Russia, Brazil, and Australia among others. WhatsApp has grown to become the fourth largest platform in the world, with over 500 million active users. Recognizing the success of the platform, Facebook announced in early 2014 that it would acquire the platform for a whopping US$19 billion.

Based on:

Kemp, S. (2014, January 9). Social, digital, & mobile worldwide in 2014. *We Are Social*. Retrieved May 28, 2014, from http://wearesocial.net/blog/2014/01/social-digital-mobile-worldwide-2014.

Tencent. (2014, May 26). In *Wikipedia, The Free Encyclopedia*. Retrieved May 28, 2014, from http://en.wikipedia.org/w/index.php?title=Tencent&oldid=610189512.

WhatsApp. (2014, May 28). In *Wikipedia, The Free Encyclopedia*. Retrieved May 28, 2014, from http://en.wikipedia.org/w/index.php?title=WhatsApp&oldid=610526463.

GEOTAGGING. Another type of metadata about media such as photos, videos, or even blogs or tweets is of geospatial nature; knowing where exactly a photo was taken and in what direction the camera was pointing, or knowing the location of a person sending out a breaking news update on Twitter, can be extremely valuable. Adding geospatial metadata (such as latitude, longitude, or altitude) to media is referred to as **geotagging**. Once the geographical coordinates of an item are known, it can easily be visualized on a map. For example, Google Maps can display various types of geotagged information, such as Wikipedia articles about places or landmarks, photos, webcams, or even Twitter posts. Thus, Google can offer a map experience containing pictures of attractions, reviews, and things to do without having to take a single picture or write a single review itself.

Enhancing Collaboration with Social Media

Traditional office technologies, such as telephones or e-mail, are very useful to organizations; yet, such technologies are not well suited to support rich, rapid, multiple-person team collaboration. For example, the telephone is best suited for person-to-person communication; e-mail is a useful technology for teams, but it does not provide the structure needed for effective multiperson, interactive problem solving. Modern organizations need technologies that enable team members to interact through a set of media either at the same place and time or at different times and in different locations, with structure to aid in interactive problem solving and access

TABLE 5.3 Benefits and Risks of Cloud-Based Collaboration Tools

Domain	Benefit	Risk
Information technology	Reduced costs and risks when using preexisting, easily deployed, and low-cost Web-based tools (versus in-house developed tools).	Loss of control regarding data and service quality (data and tools will likely reside on the provider's server).
Organization	Tools are easy to use, facilitating widespread adoption throughout an organization.	Little or no documentation, training, or support for system complexities or problems.
Competition	More efficient and effective than e-mail, FTP, or legacy collaboration tools, potentially speeding up product development cycles and enabling quick responses to competitors' actions.	Security and compliance policies are nearly impossible to enforce, which may increase the possibility of exposing sensitive corporate data; increased threat of industrial espionage.
Upgrade cycles	No need to purchase software upgrades.	Tools and features in the collaboration environment can change without notice, potentially causing problems with users and corporate IT strategy.

to real-time information. The Internet and various social media applications, described next, provide many capabilities that have forever transformed the way individuals and teams can work together.

CLOUD-BASED COLLABORATION TOOLS. One key trend that has greatly facilitated collaboration is the rise of cloud computing. Traditionally, sharing and collaborating on documents was cumbersome; users typically had to e-mail documents back and forth, or had to worry about having the latest version of the software installed. **Cloud-based collaboration tools** have greatly facilitated collaboration; for example, cloud-based collaboration tools allow for easy access and easy transfer of documents or other files from one person to another; using services such as Dropbox, documents are not only stored on a user's computer, but also synced to other computers or devices via a copy of the document stored in the cloud. This way, a user can access a file from multiple devices, always having the latest version at his or her fingertips, or collaborators can work on documents without needing to e-mail documents. Similarly, tools such as Evernote, Wunderlist, or Microsoft OneNote allow for synchronizing and sharing of notes, task lists, and the like. Cloud-based productivity suites take this concept a step further by not only storing the files in the cloud, but also enabling the access of office productivity tools from any computer (or even mobile device) with a Web browser and Internet connectivity. While this frees the user from having to locally install productivity software, using cloud-based collaboration tools requires a live Internet connection to work on shared documents, and thus users may not be able to work when traveling or when having Internet connectivity problems. Also, the applications are limited in what they can do. For example, many online spreadsheets can do only basic formulas. Table 5.3 outlines various benefits and risks of cloud-based collaboration tools.

Organizations and individuals can choose from different options for using cloud-based collaboration tools. On the one hand, companies offer single-purpose tools for everything from creating presentations to managing projects. On the other end of the spectrum, cloud-based collaboration tools such as Google Apps or Microsoft Office 365 integrate everything from document sharing to videoconferencing, thereby mirroring (or even surpassing) the capabilities of traditional offline office suites (Table 5.4).

CONTENT MANAGEMENT SYSTEMS. A **content management system** allows users to publish, edit, version track, and retrieve digital content, such as documents, images, audio files, videos, or anything else that can be digitized. For example, organizations use open source content management systems such as WordPress, Joomla, or Drupal to create blogs or Web sites; Carnival Cruise Lines uses WordPress for publishing company news, the French subsidiary of

TABLE 5.4 Web-Based Collaboration Tools

Type	Names
Spreadsheets	Bad Blue, Google Drive, Zoho Sheet, Microsoft Office 365
Word processors	Adobe Buzzword, ThinkFree, Zoho Writer, Google Drive, ZCubes, Microsoft Office 365
Presentation	Google Drive, Zoho Show, Microsoft Office 365, Prezi
Office suites	Zoho, Google Apps, Microsoft Office 365
Project	Trac, Redmine, eGroupWare, Collabtive
Notes/task management	Evernote, Wunderlist, Microsoft OneNote Web
Cloud storage/sharing	Dropbox, Google Drive, Microsoft SkyDrive, SugarSync, iCloud

cereal manufacturer Kellogg's uses Joomla for its company Web site, and Turner Entertainment's Belgian site uses Drupal. Whereas traditionally, webmasters would have the task of adding, modifying, or deleting content on a company's Web site, content management systems provide easy-to-use interfaces that allow the *creators* of content to make necessary changes; thus, a member of the marketing team may edit a product's description, without having to ask the IS department to make the changes. Typically, such content management systems facilitate the creation and management of Web content by allowing the assignment of different roles to different users, such that some users can create and edit content, others can edit but not create, and yet others can only view content contained in the system. Many open source content management systems can even be used for building e-commerce sites, by incorporating functionality such as inventory management or shopping cart functionality. Yet, content management systems, also known by several other names, including digital asset management systems, document management systems, and enterprise content systems, can be used for collaboration beyond the creation and management of Web sites. For example, Microsoft SharePoint is a document management platform that can be used to host intranet sites, extranet sites, or public Web sites that enable shared workspaces and integrate other collaborative applications such as document sharing, *wikis* (see upcoming discussion), and blogs. SharePoint also includes workflow functionality such as to-do lists, discussion boards, and messaging alerts (Figure 5.15). Because SharePoint has been designed to be easily customizable, it has been installed in a variety of businesses, which can personalize the collaborative SharePoint Web sites to meet their needs.

Learning Management Systems Similar to content management systems used for communication and collaboration, learning management systems such as BlackBoard, Sakai, and Moodle have facilitated business processes in educational settings. Typically, learning management systems enable uploading and viewing content, administering of exams, and self-service functions such as registering for courses or viewing grades. Increasingly, learning management systems offer additional tools for enabling team collaboration, class discussions, and the like.

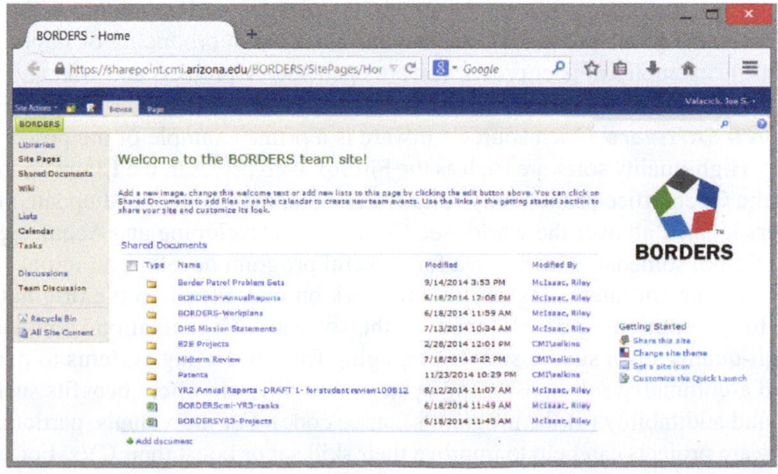

FIGURE 5.15

Researchers at the University of Arizona use the Microsoft SharePoint content management system to assist in project collaboration.

Source: Microsoft SharePoint, Microsoft Corporation, Courtesy University of Arizona.

WHO'S GOING MOBILE

Going SoLoMo: Yelp

If you're looking for a good restaurant, tailor, or pest control service in town, it is difficult to know which of the many options will provide the best service. Luckily, there's Yelp .com. You've probably heard of Yelp.com, the review and rating platform where you can find valuable information on local businesses from previous customers. The company began in 2004 as a way for friends to exchange local service recommendations via e-mail. The service quickly evolved to include social networking services and has expanded its operations to many countries around the world. Yelp has also been a pioneer in developing mobile, location-based services. It tends to come up as an example whenever people talk about the intersection of social, local, and mobile services (sometimes called **SoLoMo**, for short). And the service has become valuable to many users. A recent Nielsen study revealed that 93 percent of Yelp users say that they consult Yelp ratings and reviews prior to making a purchase from a local business.

Yelp has embraced the rising trends in mobile device usage. Shortly after the iOS app store launched the mobile app craze in 2008, Yelp released its first app for the iPhone. Apps for other platforms followed. With Apple's release of iOS 6 in September 2012, Yelp's rating and review content was integrated into the mapping and directions app of the iOS operating system. By November 2013, Yelp reported that 45 percent of its traffic came from mobile devices. Part of the reason for Yelp's mobile success is the fact that a smartphone with a Yelp app installed is "location-aware," meaning that users can use a phone's global positioning system (GPS) capabilities to find Yelp reviews of locations in the area. This is very useful if you are in an unfamiliar area and would like to go eat somewhere with positive reviews. You can simply search for restaurants and choose from among the highest-rated restaurants within walking distance.

Yelp has leveraged its dominating mobile presence to its advantage. The company began allowing local businesses to advertise to local users, and the advertising technique has proven quite powerful. If you open the Yelp app and are searching for restaurants, Yelp can be pretty confident that you're hungry and about to make a purchase. A cleverly placed ad offering a discount from a local pizza place may be just the thing that convinces you to buy a pizza instead of the Big Mac offered next door. Yelp is seeing rapid growth of its mobile advertising platform, and in late 2013, local advertisements constituted 40 percent of Yelp's overall local ad revenue.

Based on:

Danova, T. (2013, September 4). Yelp's local-mobile success shows how consumers are using mobile to drive local purchases. *Business Insider*. Retrieved May 28, 2014, from http://www.businessinsider.com/yelp-and-its-local-mobile-strategy-2013-9.

Yelp. (2014, May 26). In *Wikipedia, The Free Encyclopedia*. Retrieved May 28, 2014, from http://en.wikipedia.org/w/index.php?title=Yelp&oldid=610272441.

COLLECTIVE INTELLIGENCE. One major benefit of social software is the ability to harness the "wisdom of crowds," or collective intelligence (Surowiecki, 2004). The concept of **collective intelligence** is based on the notion that distributed groups of people with a divergent range of information and expertise will be able to outperform the capabilities of individual experts. For organizations, making effective use of the collective intelligence of their employees, customers, and other stakeholders can prove extremely valuable. Based on the concept of collective intelligence, **peer production** is the creation of goods or services by self-organizing communities. In peer production, the creation of the goods or services is dependent on the incremental contributions of the participants such that anyone can help in producing or improving the final outcome. Prime examples of peer production are open source projects and wikis.

Open Source Software Open source software is a prime example of the power of collective intelligence. High-quality software such as the Firefox Web browser, the Linux operating system, or the Apache OpenOffice productivity suite are created, maintained, and updated by thousands of volunteers located all over the world (see Chapter 9, "Developing and Acquiring Information Systems"). Often, someone with an idea for a useful program develops an initial version; other developers looking for interesting projects to work on may then join the original creator, and contribute to the continuing development of the software. Organizations now have access to various high-quality open source software, ranging from operating systems to databases, Web servers, and e-commerce solutions; using open source software offers benefits such as security, flexibility, and auditability (of the program's source code). For individuals, participating in open source software projects can help to improve their skill set or boost their CVs. For organizations,

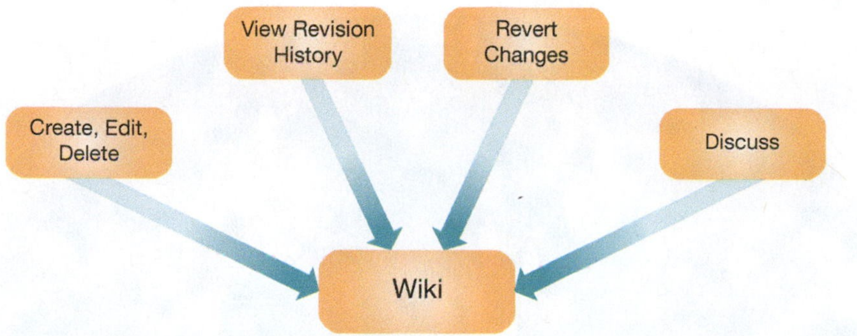

FIGURE 5.16

The ability to create, edit, or delete content, view prior versions, revert any changes, and discuss article content and suggested changes are key to the creation of high quality content by a community.

participating in open source projects can be a way to influence the direction the software's development may take and to build goodwill by giving back to the community.

Wikis Also based on the concept of collective intelligence, wikis are used for a variety of collaboration tasks. A **wiki** is a Web site allowing people to create, edit, or delete content, as well as discuss article content or suggested changes with other members of the community. In contrast to a regular Web site, a wiki is linked to a database keeping a history of all prior versions and changes, and thus a wiki allows viewing prior versions of the pages, as well as reverting any changes made to the content. The idea behind wikis is that they allow anyone to contribute information or edit others' contributions; this collaborative work performed by the community helps to minimize vandalism and ensure high-quality content (Figure 5.16). For example, Wikipedia articles are created by Wikipedia users, and almost any of these articles can be edited by either anonymous or registered users. By allowing easy access, Wikipedia has grown exponentially in a short amount of time. However, Wikipedia is not without its critics. Some argue that by allowing anyone to create and edit articles, a systematic bias in the content can occur. This includes the ability for users to add misinformation that is hard to verify. For example, recent news show that politicians, companies, and other entities of interest frequently edit their Wikipedia pages to portray a more positive image. Sometimes, so-called "wiki wars" arise, where contributors continuously edit or delete each others' posts. Also, Wikipedia has been found to have a significant cultural bias, as most contributors are males from either North America or Europe. Since the information is often not backed by verifiable sources, Wikipedia is not considered a credible source, and many universities discourage students from citing Wikipedia. In fact, in some instances professors have been failing students for using Wikipedia as their primary (or only) source. While a Wikipedia article may be a good starting point for researching about a topic, it is good practice to evaluate the sources used within the article, and to consult other sources as well. Wikipedia openly acknowledges this situation and encourages users to check the facts against multiple sources.

Wikis have been used for many more things than just an online encyclopedia. The ability for users to contribute and edit content has a wide variety of applications, such as designing software, helping people find media, and even helping people play video games. In fact, many organizations are using wiki technology to create internal knowledge repositories.

HUMAN-BASED COMPUTING (CROWDSOURCING). Another way companies are using the collective intelligence of individuals is through crowdsourcing. When companies look for cheap labor, many immediately think about outsourcing work to *companies* in different countries, such as India, China, or Russia (see Chapter 1, "Managing in the Digital World"). However, companies have now found a way to use *everyday people* as a cheap labor force, a phenomenon called **crowdsourcing** (Figure 5.17; see also Chapter 4 for more on consumer-to-business business models).

For example, up until a few years ago, book publishers such as Pearson Prentice Hall had to rely on so-called stock photography for many of a book's images; in other words, publishers had to pay large sums for pictures taken by professional photographers. Clearinghouses for stock photography had to charge high fees just to cover their expenses, as they had to purchase pictures from professional photographers. Today, high-quality digital cameras can be had for far less than US$1,000, and, with the right editing software, amateur photographers can create images that almost match those of professional photographers. Amateur photographers can upload their pictures to image-sharing sites such as iStockphoto.com, where interested parties can

FIGURE 5.17

Crowdsourcing uses everyday people from all over the world as a cheap labor force.

Source: Medioimages/Photodisc/ Thinkstock Royalty Free

license and download the images for US$1 to US$5 per image, which is a fraction of the price of a regular stock photo. Given that overhead costs are almost negligible, iStockphoto can make a profit while still sharing part of the revenue with the pictures' creators.

Similarly, companies are increasingly realizing that **open innovation**, or the process of integrating external stakeholders into the innovation process, can prove very beneficial. For example, pharmaceutical giant Eli Lilly created a site called InnoCentive, where companies can post scientific problems, and everybody can take a shot at solving the problem. Usually, a reward is paid to a successful solver. This way, an ad hoc research-and-development network is created, and companies have to rely less on a dedicated research-and-development department or on hiring specialists to solve a certain problem. At the same time, people can use their spare time and expertise to solve problems and earn rewards for their contributions.

Amazon.com took crowdsourcing mainstream with its micro-task marketplace called Mechanical Turk. Using this marketplace, requesters can crowdsource so-called human intelligence tasks (HITs), which are small, self-contained tasks that humans can solve easily but would be difficult for a computer to solve. Examples of HITs include tagging images, generating potential search key words for a product, fixing product titles on e-commerce sites, and so on. Users can find HITs that are of interest to them, solve the tasks, and earn money that is credited to their Amazon.com account. As you can see, for companies, crowdsourcing is an innovative way to reduce costs by using the expertise of the crowds. Similar to grid computing (see Chapter 3), a person's "idle time" is used for a certain business task, and many people are willing to provide their resources in exchange for a relatively small amount of money. Just imagine that you could pay for your textbooks using the money you earned from the collection of digital pictures you've taken, all for almost no extra effort.

Enhancing Connection with Social Media

Social media applications also aid in connecting people with each other, companies with their customers or stakeholders, or people with content. Without a doubt, social networking has become the most popular type of application in this category; we explore social networking and other, lesser-known applications in the following sections.

SOCIAL NETWORKING. In addition to direct collaboration, **social networking** has become one of the most popular uses of the Internet over the past few years. Social networking sites create **social online communities** where individuals with a broad and diverse set of interests meet, communicate, and collaborate (Figure 5.18). Facebook exemplifies this trend, being the second most popular site on the Web (and being surpassed only by Google), according to Alexa.com. Facebook took the spot as the most frequented social network from MySpace.com, which originally was designed to be a social network based on musical interests, but then changed to a general interest social network used primarily by teens and young adults; over time, the importance of MySpace has declined tremendously, and in May 2014, Myspace was barely ranked in the top 1,000 sites on the Web. Because of the network effect, as Facebook grew, it

FIGURE 5.18

Individuals with a broad and diverse set of interests meet and communicate using social networks.

Source: Sean Nel/Shutterstock

became ever more attractive for other people to join. In May 2014, Facebook announced that it had 1.28 billion users, and it is still growing. Other social networks are built on the tremendous increase in mobile devices. For example, the location-based social network Foursquare is built around the idea of people using their mobile devices to "check in" at places.

Social networks were initially largely popular among preteens, teens, and young adults, but social networking demographics have slowly shifted. Although in 2014 about 57 percent of U.S. Facebook's users were between 18 and 34 years old, 46 percent of the users were 35 years or older (onlinemba.com, 2012). In addition to general interest social networks, several social online communities are targeted at professional audiences, allowing users to meet business contacts, post career profiles, present themselves in a professional context, ask for expert advice, or be contacted regarding job opportunities. For example, LinkedIn has more than 300 million members, and Xing (which is widely popular in Europe) has around 12 million members. Further, enterprise-oriented social software such as IBM Connections features social networking tools, allowing people within organizations to connect to one another; similarly, Yammer, part of Microsoft, is designed as a private social network for communication and collaboration within organizations. Designed to mirror consumer-oriented social media apps people are used to, applications such as Yammer are but one example of increasing consumerization of IT, where technologies and applications are first designed for the consumer marketplace and then make inroads into organizational settings.

Organizations also increasingly use social networks to connect to their customers. Numerous companies have their own Facebook pages to interact with their customers, get feedback on new products or services, or in general portray a positive brand image (similar to mobile phone applications developed by companies; see Chapter 4).

Social Search As the Web has grown explosively since its early days (in the first 6 years, the growth rate was 850 percent, and after only 15 years, the number of Web sites was larger than 100 million; Nielsen, 2006), finding relevant information has become increasingly difficult. Early search engines such as Altavista were based on key words embedded within pages, and often tried to assemble "directories" of the Web (see http://dir.yahoo.com). In 1996, Sergey Brin and Larry Page, the founders of Google, came up with a new algorithm for Internet search. Called BackRub, the algorithm used the number of *other* pages linking to a Web page so as to return more relevant results to users. Yet, returning the most relevant results to each user remains the holy grail for search engines. Given that people tend to trust recommendations from their networks of friends, search engines and social networks are trying to capitalize on the fact that content posted by friends is typically more relevant than content posted by complete strangers. **Social search** attempts to increase the relevance of search results by including content

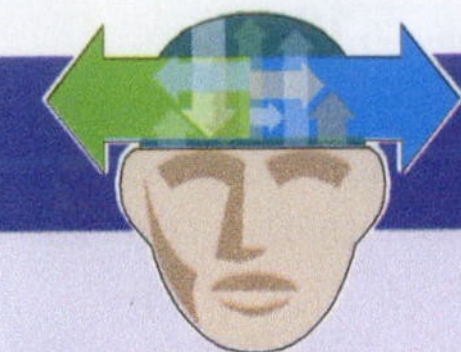

ETHICAL DILEMMA

Negative Impacts of Social Media Use

As you're sitting in front of your most incredible lunch, you take a picture of your meal and upload it to Facebook. As you scroll through the news feed, you see that your friend just got his driver's license and someone else invites you to join a house party on Saturday. Almost every aspect of our lives has become intertwined with Facebook. Although the social networking site works well for keeping in touch with people, concerns have been voiced over the possibility that Facebook is stealing the innocence from our generation.

As many people now spend more time interacting with virtual friends than interacting with people in the "real world," for many, there has been a shift in identity from the "real world" to a virtual world where the sense of self is closely linked to social media presence. In other words, as people define themselves by what others in the social media universe think of them (and how many friends they have on Facebook), they lose the sense of self. Traditionally, solitude was considered a driving force to nurturing good relationships; now, the social media world fills in that solitary absence with endless online updates, weakening our sense of self. In addition to losing that "human touch," social media can lead to narcissism and increase the need to be vain; instead of feeling good about oneself, confidence is built in status updates and picture posts. However, people should know better than to base self-assurance on such vulnerable grounds; professionals have warned that this leads to a vicious cycle: As pointed out by entrepreneur and "professional skeptic" Andrew Keen, "The more we self-broadcast, the emptier we become and the emptier we become, the more we need to self-broadcast."

Making things worse is that with social networks becoming ubiquitous, it becomes increasingly challenging for children to grow up without being in danger of virtually exposing themselves to the entire world. In your childhood days, there was limited potential for losing your privacy (except for your "friends" revealing embarrassing secrets to others). Today, children risk losing their privacy to "Facebook parenting" (i.e., parents documenting their kids' every move during the infant and early childhood phases on Facebook) and later grow up assuming that it isn't a problem to reveal everything about themselves to the vast world of social networking. If one day Facebook becomes a normal means of attaining one's identity, and people lose their sense of what privacy entails, then our sense of self is no doubt facing the greatest crisis humankind has ever seen. Next time you feel an urge to post a picture of what your significant other just prepared for breakfast, consider this: Is it more important to inform the virtual and transparent world of your every move than to enjoy quality time with the person who prepared the breakfast for you?

Based on:

Keen, A. (2012, May 30). Facebook threatens to "Zuck up" the human race. *CNN*. Retrieved May 28, 2014, from http://www.cnn.com/2012/05/30/tech/keen-technology-facebook-privacy.

from social networks, blogs, or microblogging services. For example, Facebook implemented graph search, where a user can search for terms such as "Restaurants in Austin, Texas visited by my friends" to return relevant and useful information. Other social search approaches let users annotate or tag search results, making it easier for others to find relevant information; this is especially valuable for enterprise search applications, where other users within an organization can tag internal documents, making it easier to find information as well as to find people who have certain information within the organization.

VIRAL MARKETING. In the offline world, marketing one's products or services is one of the most important aspects of successfully running a business. In an online context, marketing Web sites, products, and services is equally important, and business organizations use techniques such as search marketing, paid inclusion, and banner advertisements to promote their Web sites (see Chapter 4). Building on the foundations of social networking, advertisers are now using **viral marketing** to promote their Web sites, products, or services. Viral marketing is using the network effect to increase brand awareness. The term *viral marketing* was coined by Harvard business professor Jeffrey Rayport to describe how good marketing techniques can be driven by word-of-mouth or person-to-person communication, similar to how real viruses are transmitted through offline social networks. Rather than creating traditional banner ads or sending out massive amounts of spam, businesses create advertisements in a way that entices the viewers to share the message with their friends through e-mail or social networks so that the message will spread like a virus. Viral marketing can take many forms, such as video clips, e-books, flash games, and even text messages.

The power of viral marketing can be a great tool, and there are several techniques that are critical to making a successful viral marketing campaign. Writer and interaction designer

Thomas Baekdal (2006) has outlined some critical factors in viral marketing, including the following:

1. Do something unexpected
2. Make people feel something
3. Make sequels
4. Allow sharing and easy distribution
5. Never restrict access to the viral content

Following these principles entices users to view content, share it with their friends, and revisit the site to look for new content. For example, Turkish Airlines' "Kobe vs. Messi Selfie Shootout" video quickly went viral. Likewise, Volvo Trucks' "Epic Split" video featuring Jean-Claude van Damme became one of the most successful viral videos (and triggered a large number of parodies created by Web users).

One of the earliest viral marketing campaigns was used during the launch of the free Hotmail e-mail service. One of the techniques involved adding a footer to every outbound message. This footer gave a short message about Hotmail.com's free e-mail service, and the message about the service was spread with every e-mail sent through the service. This campaign proved very effective (Hotmail spent only US$500,000 to get 12 million subscribers), and Microsoft later bought Hotmail.

MANAGING THE ENTERPRISE 2.0 STRATEGY

As you have seen, mobile social, the cloud, and Big Data have enabled various tools that organizations can use for communicating with external stakeholders as well as for enhancing collaboration and connection of employees within the enterprise. In the following sections, we discuss factors to be examined when considering the use of Enterprise 2.0 tools within an organization. Then we highlight potential pitfalls brought about by these tools, when used by people within and outside an organization.

Organizational Issues

In previous discussions, you have learned that in many cases, technology can be an important enabler of strategic advantage, if implemented and managed carefully. Similarly, with internal Enterprise 2.0 tools, the technology is a critical success factor, but it is not the only component, and change management can be critical for success or failure of such initiatives. Just providing the tools in the hope that employees will use them for the intended purpose is not enough; rather, management has to ensure that employees are aware of the tools, their purpose, and rules or policies surrounding the use of these tools. Given that social media applications are based on close social interaction, information sharing, and network effects, corporate culture is key to successful Enterprise 2.0 implementations. Specifically, a corporate culture of knowledge sharing, trust, and honest feedback is conducive to Enterprise 2.0 implementations. In addition to culture, various other caveats have to be taken into consideration for any Enterprise 2.0 application (Khan, 2008) (Figure 5.19).

ENTERPRISE≠WEB. While reading this chapter, you have learned about many Web-based technologies you are familiar with from your daily life. Although many of those technologies are hugely successful in a consumer environment, this success does not always translate to success in a corporate environment. On the Web, sites such as YouTube, Wikipedia, and Facebook have evolved over the years to become as successful as they are today, and examples such as MySpace show that success at one point in time is not guaranteed to continue. Further, what appears as seamless "magic" collaboration is sometimes based on intricate processes. For example, good articles in Wikipedia are based not only on the contributions of many editors, but also on many behind-the-scenes discussions over controversial issues or over how to improve an article. In contrast, many open source software projects closely guard changes to the software's programming code such that only a limited number of "committers" can actually implement suggested changes.

CULTURE. As highlighted earlier, organizational culture is a critical Enterprise 2.0 success factor, and many proposed projects face strong cultural resistance. Enterprise 2.0 applications, based on the premise of open communication, do not always do well within traditional top-down organizational structures based on rigid hierarchies and control. Further, social media applications

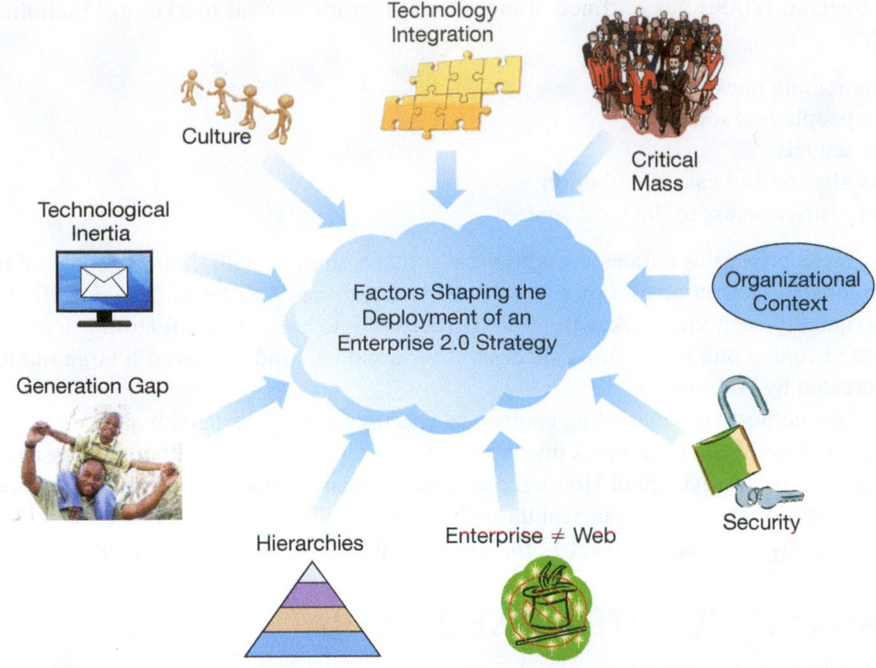

FIGURE 5.19
Various factors have to be taken into account for successful Enterprise 2.0 applications.

base their success on user-driven self-expression (if no one were willing to update his or her status on Facebook, people would eventually stop visiting the site); on the Web, people participate by choice, but people in organizations cannot be forced to participate. Hence, organizations have to understand the multiple stakeholders, personalities, and perspectives of future users and ensure that any Enterprise 2.0 initiative will appeal to the organization's members.

WHEN THINGS GO WRONG

Social Media Meltdown

Many businesses have embraced social media as a fantastic way to connect with their customers. For example, CEO of popular online retailer Zappos.com, Tony Hsieh, is famous for frequently and directly interacting with customers via his Twitter account. Customers can ask questions or raise concerns and Tony will openly address the customers and try to resolve issues. This seems like a great strategy for any company to try to emulate. But sometimes such interactions can quickly escape the control of the company with dire consequences. One recent gaffe from JP Morgan Chase shows what can happen when social media melts down.

In late 2013, JP Morgan Chase announced that it would be hosting a live Q&A session on Twitter with one of its top executives. The session promised to provide customers an opportunity to interact with the executive-level leadership of the company. Customers wanting to join the discussion simply had to include the hashtag #AskJPM in their tweets. Shortly after the session began, however, things got out of hand, and the bank got far more than it bargained for. Disgruntled consumers began posting jokes and complaining about JP Morgan Chase's business practices. Tweets related to mortgage foreclosures that were perceived to be unfair, or jokes about sending credit card applications to former customers who have lost their homes to foreclosure, were the norm. Word got around on Twitter that a fairly humorous bit of poor public relations was happening, and many more Twitter users happily joined the hijacking of the session. JP Morgan realized its mistake and announced that the session had been cancelled, but the damage had already been done. The topic trended popularly for days after the incident, drawing substantial negative publicity for the bank.

The story is a lesson in the power of social media for all would-be public relations professionals and organizations. The global reach and lightning speed of these media allow messages, whether bitter or sweet, to spread like wildfire. Social media marketing can be a two-edged sword and must be carefully managed.

Based on:

Rawlings, N. (2013, November 14). JPMorgan cancels Twitter Q&A after an epic #fail. *Time*. Retrieved May 28, 2014, from http://business.time.com/2013/11/14/jpmorgan-cancels-twitter-qa-after-an-epic-fail.

Morrissey, B. (2008, April 14). Zappos CEO really enjoys this Twitter thing. *Adweek*. Retrieved May 28, 2014, from http://www.adweek.com/adfreak/zappos-ceo-really-enjoys-twitter-thing-16007.

ORGANIZATIONAL CONTEXT. Any implementation of Enterprise 2.0 applications should be driven by a specific usage context. Just as users choose popular social media applications such as YouTube or Wikipedia to fulfill a particular need, the work-related context should drive the choice of Enterprise 2.0 tools. In other words, organizations should always ask what objective is to be accomplished with the tool and only then decide which type of tool to implement. Merely setting up a wiki site and hoping that the employees will use it for the "right" purpose most likely will not lead to the intended results.

ORGANIZATIONAL HIERARCHIES. Often, Enterprise 2.0 initiatives are driven by user departments, and small-scale pilot implementations appear to work quite well. However, organization-wide Enterprise 2.0 implementations typically need changes in terms of organizational culture and processes, and often the flattening of organizational hierarchies. Therefore, to be successful, Enterprise 2.0 implementations need the support and active involvement of senior management so as to cope with the large magnitude of changes.

NETWORK EFFECTS AND CRITICAL MASS. Successful social media applications such as Wikipedia base their success on network effects and the Long Tail (see Chapter 4), and have needed some time to achieve a critical mass. For example, although Wikipedia enjoys millions of page views per day, there is only a small number of people who choose to actively participate in the creation of content. Within organizations, achieving the critical mass needed for an Enterprise 2.0 application is often difficult and takes considerable time and patience. Although for many smaller organizations collaborative Enterprise 2.0 tools can be beneficial, they will most likely not be able to harness the network effects that can be achieved with a larger user base.

GENERATION GAP. The success of an Enterprise 2.0 initiative is also heavily dependent on the composition of the organization's workforce. In organizations with high numbers of millennials, who have grown accustomed to highly interactive and communicative online social environments, Enterprise 2.0 initiatives have a higher likelihood of success; in contrast, many baby boomers are used to rigid hierarchies and organizational structures and are less likely to fully embrace the capabilities of Enterprise 2.0 tools. Further, senior organizational members may not fully grasp the potential and implications of social media applications in organizational settings.

TECHNOLOGICAL INERTIA. One factor hindering the adoption of many new technologies is technological inertia. In many cases, people are not willing to switch to new applications unless they see real, tangible benefits. This can be especially a hindrance with social media applications, many of which incorporate a variety of other tools (such as chat or message interfaces within social networking sites).

TECHNOLOGICAL INTEGRATION. Organizations will have to ensure that any Enterprise 2.0 applications are integrated well with the organization's existing information systems infrastructure so as to reap the greatest benefits from connecting people and connecting people with information. Typically, organizations choose systems provided by outside vendors such as Ning or Yammer, which allows the organization to create its own private social network. However, organizational users will use the tools they are used to as a benchmark, and public domain tools such as Facebook often create high expectations of usability for any internal tool.

SECURITY. A final issue is related to security and intellectual property. For organizations, securing their information systems infrastructure is of paramount concern (see Chapter 10). Any application that allows closer collaboration by increasing data sharing will necessarily incur greater risks of security breaches. Companies thus have to balance their desire for enhancing collaboration with the need to protect intellectual property and compliance with rules and regulations such as the Sarbanes–Oxley Act.

Pitfalls of Web 2.0 Marketing

Many organizations (and individuals) have learned painful lessons from public relations blunders and from not considering the fundamental rule: The Internet never forgets. Another fundamental rule brought about by social media applications is to constantly monitor social media and quickly and appropriately react to emerging issues. In this section, we highlight potential pitfalls of marketing using social media applications.

ONLINE PRODUCT REVIEWS. Online as well as offline consumers increasingly consult the Web before making a purchase decision. When making a purchase on Amazon.com, many potential buyers first consult the user reviews; relatedly, people read other travelers' reviews of hotels or restaurants on Tripadvisor.com, or consult Web sites dedicated to providing expert reviews. Unfortunately, such reviews are not always as unbiased as they seem; and sometimes, companies hire people to deliberately spread positive word-of-mouth across a variety of sites. The act of posting fake product reviews is unethical, to say the least. For companies operating globally, this is becoming even more problematic. For example, in China, where reviews are often posted by the millions, consulting the Web for advice is even more common, especially among online shoppers. As with the products being offered, fakes are a problem with product reviews as well, and Chinese Internet marketing companies employ legions of people who do nothing but post positive comments about a client—and negative comments about competitors. Further, a number of Internet marketing companies specialize in removing negative posts, usually by bribing forum managers or administrators, with fees being as high as US$1,500, depending on how urgent the request is or how popular the Web site or post is; for many companies, this is considered a regular advertising expense (Jiao, 2010). Companies operating globally should certainly be aware of such practices, and adjust their strategies accordingly.

MICROBLOGGING. Whereas **microblogging** can be very valuable for corporate communications, it has to be used carefully and is not without controversy. For example, in early 2014, New York City's police department (NYPD), attempting to boost the department's image, encouraged people to tweet images with police officers, using the hashtag #myNYPD. Unfortunately, the response was not what the NYPD had hoped for. Rather than tweeting positive photos, the department's critics soon used the hashtag for pictures depicting police brutality and racial discrimination.

For individuals, posting the wrong "tweets" can also have serious consequences, as they are more likely than not to reach the wrong readers—sooner or later. A Chicago woman was recently sued by her landlord for posting a tweet complaining about the management company's reaction to mold in her apartment. The management company sued her for defamation, arguing that the tweet was published on a global scale. Whereas the lady had a mere 22 followers on Twitter, the landlord's lawsuit was covered in major news outlets, online and offline, including the *Chicago Tribune*, the Associated Press, and the *New York Times*.

SOCIAL NETWORKS. While free to host, having a page on a social network is not free for organizations—the company should take great care to monitor what is happening on the page and take appropriate action. For example, Starbucks lets its customers upload their favorite Starbucks-related pictures to its Facebook page. However, people frequently post unrelated pictures, play pranks with the company logo, or post otherwise inappropriate content. A company then has to walk the fine line of removing inappropriate content to preserve the company's image while not alienating its fans. Starbucks chooses to liberally allow unrelated content.

As with most social software, posting the "wrong" content can quickly get you in trouble. Companies routinely check social networking sites before making hiring decisions, and many applicants have lost a job offer they almost had secured. Similarly, your posts may make it farther than you think; stories abound of people getting laid off after ranting about their jobs and their bosses in Facebook status updates—unfortunately, the boss was in the employee's contacts list and could immediately see the post. Further, many people never bother to adjust their accounts' privacy settings and inadvertently shout things out for the whole world to read.

BAD VIBES GOING VIRAL. As with other social media, viral marketing can be a blessing or a nightmare (see also "When Things Go Wrong: Social Media Meltdown"). One of the most infamous examples happened back in 2008, when a musician on a tour witnessed from his airplane window how baggage handlers mishandled—and broke—his US$3,500 guitar. After not getting a satisfying response from the airline, the musician decided to write a song and post it on YouTube in 2009. The video quickly went viral, and the airline rushed to "make things right" for the musician. For the airline, however, the damage was done, and as of mid-2014, the video had almost 14 million views. Likewise, a Ryanair passenger's complaint letter posted on Facebook was shared over 68,000 times in less than 10 days. Whereas traditional phone complaints were a one-to-one conversation between the customer and a call center agent, the balance of power has shifted toward the customer, necessitating swift, effective responses by the companies. A case in point is the response of Domino's Pizza, where two employees posted videos on YouTube displaying them playing not-so-harmless pranks and preparing sandwiches with disgusting ingredients; the videos quickly went viral and attracted more than a million viewers in just a few days. Domino's was initially slow in responding and decided not to respond to the crisis, fearing that a reaction may draw even more interest. After 48 hours, however, Domino's changed its strategy, opened a Twitter account to interact with concerned customers, and posted a video response by the president of Domino's on YouTube assuring that the culprits had been found, that the entire store had been closed and sanitized, and that everything would be done to avoid hiring the "wrong" people in the future. A nationwide survey by a media research company has found the response to be fairly successful, with over 90 percent of the respondents indicating that the response video was effective in restoring trust in the brand.

LESSONS LEARNED. As you probably know from your own experience and have seen from these stories, news travels fast in social media. For the companies in question, this is an enormous threat, as negative publicity can quickly reach millions of people. At the same time, the company's reaction is equally critical, as it can reach people just as fast and thus has to be carefully crafted. Richard Levick, president of Levick Strategic Communications, has provided some tips on how to prepare for and deal with such crises:

1. Identify a crisis team including members from within your organization (e.g., public relations or executive team) and from the outside (e.g., lawyers).
2. Identify your worst social media nightmare (and make sure to know the signs to look for, such as search engine key terms your opposition could use).
3. Monitor your social media environment (such as YouTube, Facebook, and Twitter) and be connected and responsive.
4. Act fast. The first 24 hours count.

As in the offline world, companies should try to avoid such crises in the first place, but being prepared for a public relations disaster is crucial in today's fast-paced world. Many organizations have realized the need for social media monitoring; for example, Dell recently opened its "Social Media Listening Command Center" as a key part of its overall marketing efforts. Monitoring social media posts mentioning Dell in about a dozen languages enables Dell not only to respond to customers' problems before they go viral, but also serves as an effective means to gather business intelligence. We will discuss more about the role of social media monitoring and business intelligence in Chapter 8, "Strengthening Business-to-Business Relationships Via Supply Chain and Customer Relationship Management."

INDUSTRY ANALYSIS

Online Travel

Spring break is coming, and you've decided to go to Puerto Vallarta this year. Chances are that your first step will be to check the Web sites of Expedia, Priceline, Travelocity, and Orbitz for flights to and hotels in your chosen destination. We all know the big four online travel agencies; in today's digital world, they dominate the travel industry. They took the old brick-and-mortar travel industry and turned it into an online service where you can click to book flights and hotel reservations, change or cancel flights, reserve rental cars—even plan a vacation. In Internet terms, you can think of the big four as still being in Online Travel 1.0. But technology marches relentlessly on, and Online Travel 2.0 is in the works.

A new crop of travel sites has popped up, offering several benefits over the big online travel agencies. These travel sites are very different from typical online travel services, however. The first, and arguably the most prominent, example is airbnb.com. Airbnb allows people to offer houses, condos, apartments, and rooms (private or shared) to anyone who happens to be traveling through the area. If you're planning a vacation, you can always use a travel service to book a hotel. Alternatively, you can usually rent a house or apartment from someone for a fraction of the cost. Property owners benefit by generating income from unused living space, and Airbnb handles the processing of all rent payments. The site also offers an extensive rating and review platform that motivates property owners to provide excellent service to attract future renters. Airbnb has been fairly successful so far, and as of April 2014 is valued at approximately US$10 billion. If renting a house from a stranger worries you, there will always be hotels for you to use. But if you trust the ratings and experiences from "the crowd," you can save a bundle in many popular locations to which you might travel.

Once you get to your location, however, you'll need a way to get around. Again, you can book a rental car through a traditional travel service. Or you can save some more cash and use a social taxi service like Uber. This service provides a platform through which individuals can request and pay for a "taxi" service from qualified drivers in many cities in 36 countries around the world. Using the Uber mobile app, riders can request a ride at the tap of a button, then monitor the location of the reserved car in real time. Upon completion of the trip, the Uber app allows the driver to collect payment. Uber requires that drivers submit to an insurance and background check, and has typically targeted a higher-end market of users. The first Uber drivers had such cars as Cadillac Escalades, BMW 7 Series, and Mercedes-Benz S550 sedans. The company has since expanded to a wider selection of cars to appeal to more riders, and has recently implemented a ridesharing system that allows riders to quickly request to "ride along" with someone to a specific destination. Similar to Airbnb, Uber encourages the use of a rating and review system to incentivize drivers to provide excellent service.

So next time you go on a trip, consider the benefits available through these social travel platforms. You might save a few bucks, and maybe even make a friend in the process.

Questions

1. Do you use online travel agencies for assisting you with travel plans? If so, which service provider do you use, and why did you make this choice? If not, why not?
2. What features would you identify as crucial to the success of social travel services such as Airbnb and Uber?

Based on:

Airbnb. (2014, May 20). In *Wikipedia, The Free Encyclopedia*. Retrieved May 29, 2014, from http://en.wikipedia.org/w/index.php?title=Airbnb&oldid=609331519.

Uber (company). (2014, May 28). In *Wikipedia, The Free Encyclopedia*. Retrieved May 29, 2014, from http://en.wikipedia.org/w/index.php?title=Uber_(company)&oldid=610541696.

Key Points Review

1. ***Explain organizations' needs for communication and collaboration.*** In today's increasingly competitive world, organizations need to communicate and collaborate effectively and efficiently within and outside organizational boundaries. For example, virtual teams, composed of team members located around the globe that are forming and disbanding as needed, have communication needs that often cannot be met by traditional communication media. Traditionally, organizations used tools such as groupware, videoconferencing, or intranets for their communication and collaboration needs.
2. ***Explain social media and evolving Web capabilities.*** In contrast to traditional Web 1.0 sites, Web 2.0 applications allow people to collaborate and share information online, with a shift in the users' role from passive consumer of content to creator. Many successful Web 2.0 applications can be classified as social software that people widely use for communicating and socializing. Owing to societal changes, using social media can be an important factor in being able to attract or retain employees as younger generations are joining the workforce. Future Web capabilities extending Web 2.0 are the semantic Web, as well as the "contextual Web," which is characterized by devices providing the information and content needed depending on the user's specific context. To harness the opportunities brought about by these changes, organizations are increasingly using social software to connect with customers and internal or external stakeholders in order to become more innovative or productive.
3. ***Describe various social media applications, and explain their role in enhancing communication, collaboration, cooperation, and connection.*** Social software can enhance communication within organizations as well as between an organization and its stakeholders. Blogs, microblogging tools, and instant messaging are widely used by individuals and organizations to communicate with internal and external stakeholders. Social media applications such as media sharing, social bookmarking, or social cataloguing applications facilitate cooperation by using the network effect to provide the greatest benefit to users. Further, social media applications have enabled new forms of collaboration for organizations and individuals. These and other technologies have enabled cloud-based collaboration tools, content management systems, wikis, as well as the use of collective intelligence and crowdsourcing. Finally, social media applications aid in connecting people with each other. For individuals, social networking has become an important way to meet new friends, connect with family members, or meet new colleagues and business partners. The reach of social networks is also used by business organizations to market their products or services through viral marketing, which resembles offline word-of-mouth communication, in which advertising messages are spread like viruses through social networks.

4. ***Describe how companies can manage their Enterprise 2.0 strategy and deal with potential pitfalls associated with social media.*** Organizations have to take into account that success in a consumer environment does not necessarily translate into corporate environment success. Further, organizations have to take into account issues associated with culture, organizational context, and organizational hierarchies; in addition, lack of critical mass, the generation gap, and technological inertia can hinder the success of Enterprise 2.0 initiatives. Finally, in organizational contexts, integration with existing technologies and security are of primary concern. Further, an organization's opponents can use social media to spread damaging content or information to people all over the world within a very short time. Organizations should therefore carefully prepare for such incidents.

Key Terms

"amateurization" of journalism 182
asynchronous 173
blog 181
blogging 181
cloud-based collaboration tools 188
collaboration 172
collective intelligence 190
content management system 188
crowdfunding 180
crowdsourcing 191
desktop videoconferencing 175
discussion forum 174
electronic meeting system (EMS) 174
employee portal 177
employee self-service 177
Enterprise 2.0 181
folksonomy 185
geotagging 187
groupware 173
hashtag 183
instant messaging 183
mashup 178
metadata 185
microblogging 198
microblogging tools 182
open innovation 192
peer production 190
podcast 184
podcasting 183
Real Simple Syndication (RSS) 184
semantic Web 180
social bookmarking 185
social cataloging 185
social media 178
social networking 192
social online communities 192
social presence tools 182
social search 193
social software 178
SoLoMo 190
synchronous 173
tag cloud 186
tagging 185
trending 183
viral marketing 194
virtual meeting 173
virtual team 172
virtual world 183
Web 2.0 177
webcam 175
webcast 184
webcasting 183
wiki 191

Go to **mymislab.com** to complete the problems marked with this icon .

Review Questions

5-1. What are virtual teams, and how do they help to improve an organization's capabilities?

5-2. What are mashups? How do they enable social media applications?

5-3. What capabilities will define the Web of the future?

5-4. How can social software help harness the wisdom of the crowd?

5-5. Why is using social media an important factor for attracting and retaining employees?

5-6. How can social software enhance communication?

5-7. How can social bookmarking and social cataloging help in an organization's knowledge management efforts?

5-8. What is a wiki? Why would an organization want to implement a wiki?

5-9. Explain what is meant by crowdsourcing and how the Web is enabling this form of collaboration.

5-10. How can organizations use social networking to connect with their customers?

5-11. Why is organizational culture an important factor in Enterprise 2.0 initiatives?

5-12. Why can social media be both a blessing and a threat for organizations?

5-13. How can organizations plan for social media disasters?

Self-Study Questions

5-14. Collective intelligence is based on the notion that distributed groups of people with a divergent range of information and expertise will be able to outperform the capabilities of _______.
A. crowds
B. customers
C. individual experts
D. virtual teams

5-15. Microblogging tools are used for _______.
A. creating an online text diary
B. providing location information
C. short status updates
D. customer support functions

5-16. Tagging is adding _______ to a piece of information such as a map, picture, or Web page.
A. metadata
B. comments
C. blogs
D. knowledge

5-17. The process of adding information such as latitude and longitude to pictures, videos, or other information is called _______.
A. flagging
B. posting
C. geotagging
D. tagging

5-18. Successful Enterprise 2.0 implementations consider _______.
A. organizational culture
B. organizational hierarchies
C. technological inertia
D. all of the above

5-19. _______ is the process of creating an online diary made up of chronological entries.
A. Wikiing
B. Tagging
C. Blogging
D. None of the above

5-20. Webcasts are also known as _______.
A. podcasts
B. blogcasts
C. radiocasts
D. blogging

5-21. A wiki _______.
A. allows users to add content
B. allows users to revert edits
C. allows anyone to read content
D. allows all of the above

5-22. _______ is using the network effect to increase brand awareness.
A. Brand marketing
B. Shared marketing
C. Social marketing
D. Viral marketing

5-23. _______ communication is when people are all meeting at the same time or in real time.
A. Synchronous
B. Asynchronous
C. Collaboration
D. None of the above

Answers are on page 204.

Problems and Exercises

5-24. Match the following terms with the appropriate definitions:

i. Microblogging tools
ii. Asynchronous
iii. Metadata
iv. Social networking
v. Peer production
vi. Social software
vii. Webcasts
viii. Folksonomy
ix. Network effect
x. Blogging

a. Web 2.0 applications allowing people to communicate, interact, and collaborate in various ways
b. Digital media streams that can be distributed to and played by digital media players
c. The creation of goods or services by self-organizing communities
d. The notion that the value of a network (or tool or application based on a network) is dependent on the number of other users
e. User-created categorization system
f. The process of creating an online text diary made up of chronological entries
g. Data about data
h. Tools enabling people to voice their thoughts using relatively short "status updates"
i. Using Web-based services to link friends or colleagues
j. Not coordinated in time

5-25. Visit popular social online communities (such as Facebook). What features entice you to visit such sites repeatedly? Do you have an account in an online community? If yes, why? If no, what is keeping you from having such account? Is there any content you definitely would or would not post on such a page?

5-26. Go to the Web site Programmable Web (www.programmableweb.com). List some interesting mashups you find. What factors do you think make a good mashup Web site?

5-27. Go to Amazon's Mechanical Turk Web site (www.mturk.com). Which of the HITs do you think could be completed using a computer, and which could not? Why?

5-28. Search the Web for a social networking site that you have not heard about before. Describe the users of this social online community. Are the features of this site different from those you are familiar with? If so, describe those features. If not, describe common features.

5-29. Visit Google Drive (drive.google.com) and Microsoft Office Online (http://office.microsoft.com/en-001/online). Compare and contrast the features of each productivity suite. Which suite would you choose to use, and why?

5-30. Have you ever blogged? If so, what did you like or dislike about the experience? What do you see for the future in blogs?

5-31. Find an article you can contribute to on a wiki page. What do you like or dislike about this process? What would encourage you to contribute more to the wiki? Why?

5-32. Envision and describe general features of Web 3.0 applications. Describe a feature you would like to see in the next version of the Web.

5-33. Describe an application or service you would like to be able to use on the Web today that is not yet available. Describe the potential market for this application or service. Forecast how long you believe it will take before this will occur.

5-34. Search the Web for public relations blunders involving social software. How did the companies in question react? In your opinion, were the reactions effective? Why or why not?

5-35. Have you listened to or watched a webcast (or podcast)? If so, describe your experience. If not, why?

5-36. Describe the pros and cons of collaborating with colleagues over the Web. What is useful about this form of collaboration? What is difficult?

5-37. Describe an example of viral marketing that you have experienced.

Application Exercises

Note: The existing data files referenced in these exercises are available on the book's Web site: www.pearsonhighered.com/valacich.

Spreadsheet Application: Online Versus Traditional Spreadsheets

5-38. Campus Travel is currently evaluating the possibility of using an online spreadsheet as opposed to the traditional locally installed spreadsheet. There are a variety of issues involved in this decision. The company wants you to investigate the possibilities that are currently available while also paying special attention to the company requirements. Campus Travel has the following requirements: (1) the ability to share spreadsheets easily, (2) the ability to secure this information, (3) the ability to save the spreadsheets into other forms (i.e., CSV files), and (4) the ability to do work from anywhere in the world. Prepare the following information:

- On the Internet, find different options for online and traditional spreadsheets and list the available options.
- Using the company requirements, list the pros and cons for each spreadsheet option.
- Using an online spreadsheet, summarize the findings and provide a recommendation to the company. Present your findings with tables and/or graphs, if available.

Database Application: Tracking Web Site Visits

5-39. As Campus Travel expands its Web presence, the importance of tracking what the competitors are doing has become very important. This includes making sure Campus Travel tracks the prices of packages and services that its closest competitor offers. To do so, a database must be created to track this information. Follow these steps to create the database:

- Create a database called "tracking."
- Create a table called "company_info." In this table, create fields for company_name and company_URL.
- Create a table called "products." In this table, create fields for the company_name, product_name, product_description, product_price, and date_retrieved.
- Create a table called "services." In this table, create fields for company_name, service_name, service description, service_price, and date_retrieved.
- Once these tables are created, go to the relationship view (select "Relationships" under the "Database Tools" tab) and connect the company_info (one side) and products (many side) tables and the company_info (one side) and service (many side) tables.
- Make sure that when you create the relationships, the referential integrity option is selected. (This will make sure that when you delete a company, the products associated with the company are also deleted.)
- Test the referential integrity by adding data to the tables and make sure that when a company is deleted in the company table, the products table is updated, too.

Team Work Exercise

Net Stats: Most Popular Facebook Fan Pages

More and more organizations have discovered Facebook as a way to connect with their customers and drive word-of-mouth advertising. Any company can create a Facebook page containing basic information about the business, a "wall" to share content, a space for uploading photos or pictures (many organizations use this to show "behind-the-scenes" content), and so on. Further, businesses can add apps (such as an app that allows customers to make a reservation at a restaurant) to further engage with their customers.

Facebook users who "like" a page automatically receive the business's status updates in their news feeds. As the liking of a page is announced to others in the user's news feed and his or her profile, the liking of the page can spread throughout the user's network of friends. Further, each business's page has a listing of all Facebook users who like the page. What businesses are liked by most Facebook users? As of May 28, 2014, the top 10 most-liked product pages were the following:

Rank	Page	Likes
1	Facebook for Every Phone	445,362,537
2	Facebook	149,200,000
3	Shakira	95,924,940
4	Coca-Cola	95,924,940
5	YouTube	80,430,825
6	Michael Jackson	74,549,411
7	The Simpsons	73,461,758
8	Vin Diesel	76,250,441
9	Texas HoldEm Poker	70,389,014
10	Harry Potter	71,912,936

Questions and Exercises

5-40. Search the Web for the most up-to-date statistics. Try to find the number of "likes" for pages that interest you most.

5-41. As a team, interpret these numbers. What is striking/important about these statistics?

5-42. How have the numbers changed since May 2014? Which categories seem to draw most attention in social networks? Why?

5-43. Using your spreadsheet software of choice, create a graph/figure most effectively visualizing the statistics/changes you consider most important.

Based on:
Facebook: Browse pages. Retrieved May 28, 2014, from https://www.facebook.com/directory/pages/.

Answers to the Self-Study Questions

5-14. C, p. 190 **5-15.** C, p. 198 **5-16.** A, p. 185 **5-17.** C, p. 187 **5-18.** D, p. 195
5-19. C, p. 181 **5-20.** A, p. 184 **5-21.** D, p. 191 **5-22.** D, p. 191 **5-23.** A, p. 173

CASE 1 The Value of Social Media Giants

In May 2012, Facebook held its initial public offering, setting a new record as the biggest in Internet history. At its peak, the company's initial offering produced a market capitalization of over US$104 billion. Although the company lost over half its value in the months that followed, the stock has since rebounded and as of May 2014, the company has a market capitalization of over US$160 billion. With so much value in the marketplace, one might expect Facebook to generate substantial revenue to create value for its investors. Not so; in 2013, Facebook generated just US$1.5 billion in net income on US$7.8 billion in revenue. By way of comparison, when Facebook went public, another technology company, Samsung Electronics, had a market capitalization of about US$163 billion. During that same year, Samsung generated US$22 billion in net income on US$69.5 billion in gross revenues (which excludes the high cost of goods sold that Samsung's hardware business requires). Obviously investors are counting on Facebook's revenue to grow in the future, and Samsung has been around for much longer in a different industry than Facebook. But the fact remains that both are technology companies that at different points in their histories have been worth similar amounts to investors, despite a huge difference in the amount of profit being produced for shareholders.

Early in 2014, Facebook announced that it would acquire the popular mobile messaging platform WhatsApp for US$19 billion. With over 500 million users (and a million more joining every day), WhatsApp certainly attracted an impressive user base in the short five years since its creation. WhatsApp's business model relies on its users paying US$1 per year for the service, and the first year of service is free. While the company was acquired before it was publicly traded, we can still infer that yearly revenues are no larger than about US$500 million, which is less than 3 percent of the company's total valuation.

Why is Facebook valued so highly in the marketplace? And why would Facebook be willing to pay US$19 billion for a platform that generates relatively little revenue? The list goes on. Twitter went public in 2013, garnering a valuation of US$25 billion, despite never having turned a profit. Snapchat, a messaging service that has not yet found a way to monetize its service, was recently valued at over US$4 billion. Airbnb and Uber, discussed in an earlier case, are valued at US$2.5 billion and US$3.5 billion, respectively. Just how much value is there embedded in these social platforms? Is it possible that the market is repeating some of the mistakes that led to the dot-com bubble and subsequent recession? Some researchers argue that some of these valuations are a form of delusion. Others argue that there is great value in the vast user bases of these services. Thus far, the market seems to agree with the latter position.

Perhaps the biggest reason supporting these large valuations is the direct access that these companies have to their tens or hundreds of millions of users. These vast audiences actively use these services, and the service providers thus have a "captive audience" to which they can market products and services. In addition, many social platforms can gather large amounts of valuable information about their users. Consider as an example the social platform Pinterest, recently valued at over US$3.8 billion. Pinterest has tens of millions of active users who "pin" items in which they are interested to "pinboards" that can be viewed and followed by friends within the network. Aside from the tens of millions of people to whom Pinterest and future business partners can market products and services, Pinterest is constantly and explicitly informed regarding what its users are interested in. Armed with such detailed information about users' preferences, a company can very specifically target users who will be most responsive to the product or service being offered. Female users who post many items relating to the latest fashion trends, for example, are sure to be much more susceptible to a marketing campaign from Chanel or Gucci than middle-aged male users who frequently pin items about sports cars. Thus, these social networks, with their huge numbers of users providing very detailed information about demographics and interests, can offer marketing companies a degree of market segmentation that was previously unattainable.

Of course, not every social media company with a multibillion-dollar valuation will ultimately succeed. As we have seen with the likes of MySpace and Apple's social music service Ping, even services with huge user bases or substantial financial resources are not immune from failure. Some investors are likely to be disappointed when the company they chose as the winner ultimately loses steam and joins MySpace in the cyber graveyard. Business models will continue to evolve as these platforms find new ways of deriving value from their massive numbers of users. It will be an exciting battle to watch.

Questions

5-44. Do you think that the huge valuations for these companies are justified? Why or why not?

5-45. What factors will be key to the success of the budding social platforms mentioned in the case?

5-46. Do you think that Facebook will be replaced by a successor? What social media service would be the most likely candidate?

Based on:

Guynn, J. (2013, November 16). Social media startups' value is enormous—if you trust investors. *The Los Angeles Times*. Retrieved May 28, 2014, from http://articles.latimes.com/2013/nov/16/business/la-fi-tech-values-boom-20131116.

Heuer, C. (2012, October 25). Measuring—and capturing—the value of social media. *The Wall Street Journal*. Retrieved May 28, 2014, from http://deloitte.wsj.com/cio/2012/10/25/measuring-and-capturing-the-value-of-social-media-investments.

CASE 2 Wikipedia: Who Is Editing?

Research almost any topic on the Web, and a URL for a Wikipedia entry will likely appear on the list of resources. Wikipedia is a free, online encyclopedia that gets its entries from users—be they amateurs, professionals, or pranksters with nothing better to do. ("Wiki wiki" is the Hawaiian term for "quick.") As of 2014, Wikipedia had over 32 million article pages in 285 languages and 21 million registered users. It is the world's ninth most popular Web site, with over 500 million monthly visitors looking to read and edit its pages. Since Wikipedia's start in January 2001, there have been over 2.1 billion edits of content entries. Anybody is able to edit entries (although editing of more controversial articles is limited to registered users), but the Wikipedia site keeps detailed logs of the sources (IP addresses) of all changes. Users/editors are anonymous in that only their user names are known, but IP addresses can be traced back to the source.

Cal Tech computation and neural systems graduate student Virgil Griffith got curious about Wikipedia's anonymous editors in 2007 when he read that congressional aides had been editing entries about their employers—the senators and representatives of the U.S. Congress. Griffith wondered if other companies and organizations were doing the same thing, so he created a program to find out. Griffith created a database of all Wikipedia entries and changes, including the information logged each time an anonymous editor made a change. Griffith isolated the XML-based records of changes and IP addresses, then identified the owners of the IP addresses using public net-address lookup services, such as ARIN, as well as private domain name data obtained through http://IP2location.com.

Griffith's system revealed the following information about the editors:

- Someone on a computer at voting-machine maker Diebold Election Systems deleted 15 paragraphs from a Wikipedia article about electronic voting that were critical of Diebold's machines.
- Walmart made changes to improve its image.
- Politicians are frequent editors. For instance, a former U.S. senator from Montana made changes to indicate that he was a voice for farmers in his state.
- ExxonMobil deleted information about its nonpayment of damages to 32,000 Alaska fishermen after the *Exxon Valdez* oil spill.
- A computer registered to Disney deleted information critical of the company's digital rights management software.

Griffith emphasizes that his system, WikiScanner, cannot identify Wikipedia editors as agents of certain companies or organizations. It can only identify IP addresses that come from networks registered by a company or organization.

Since Wikipedia entries can be written and edited by any user registered at the site, its accuracy should obviously not be completely trusted. If one uses other reputable sources in addition to Wikipedia, however, it can often be a starting point for further research on a topic. Just don't depend on it exclusively when researching a topic, and be sure to verify content read there before quoting it as fact.

Inaccuracies aside, the ability for anyone to contribute and edit entries has been seen as the main strength of Wikipedia, allowing knowledge to be built on, refined, and policed. The number of editors peaked in 2007. By the end of 2009, however, there had been a steep dropoff in the number of volunteers editing Wikipedia's pages. According to Spanish researcher Felipe Ortega, who analyzed the site's editing activities, Wikipedia's English-language pages lost over 49,000 editors compared to around 5,000 only a year earlier.

What is causing the plunge in editor activity? Some observers think that the perception that most of the relevant information is now on the site, leaving little to be done but maintain what is there, is driving down the number of those willing to contribute and edit. Others point to the inaccuracies that plague the site and the amount of time it takes to police the information. Although editors try to maintain factual articles, anyone is free to go in and change the information. At times, a back-and-forth battle begins between two legitimate editors over what the article contains (such battles are sometimes called "wiki wars"). At other times, mischievous pranksters revert legitimate edits to their original format, insert offensive content, or otherwise deface the article, forcing editors to go back in and make corrections. Still other explanations focus on the rules and protocols surrounding the actual editing of the content. Making changes to content requires navigating a complex interface and coding scheme.

Hoping to stop the exodus of volunteers from the site, Wikipedia got its first facelift in the spring of 2010. Besides some cosmetic and layout updates to the site, site navigation has been improved, making it easier for users to find essential functions. In addition, the editing system has gotten a major overhaul. Users can now make changes to data in tables and information boxes through simple forms. The edit page has been "decluttered" and rewritten in simpler language. An outline tool has also been added, making it easy to navigate longer articles.

Clearly, Wikipedia has plenty to offer when you need some quick information on a subject. Although editors have been in decline, Wikipedia clearly is aware of the problem and has made strides to correct the issue.

Questions

5-47. Do you use Wikipedia for your research? Why or why not?

5-48. Have you ever made a change to a Wikipedia entry? If you were to see an obvious mistake (in your opinion), would you take the time to change it? Why or why not?

5-49. Anyone can edit entries on Wikipedia. Do you see this as a curse or as a blessing? Explain.

Based on:

Anonymous. (2011, December 13). Seeing things. *The Economist*. Retrieved May 28, 2014, from http://www.economist.com/blogs/babbage/2011/12/changes-wikipedia.

Borland, J. (2007, August 14). See who's editing Wikipedia—Diebold, the CIA, a campaign. *Wired.com*. Retrieved May 28, 2014, from http://archive.wired.com/politics/onlinerights/news/2007/08/wiki_tracker.

Wikipedia:About. (2014, May 28). In *Wikipedia, The Free Encyclopedia*. Retrieved May 28, 2014, from http://en.wikipedia.org/w/index.php?title=Wikipedia:About&oldid=609294101.

Wikipedia:Statistics. (2014, May 28). In *Wikipedia, The Free Encyclopedia*. Retrieved May 28, 2014, from http://en.wikipedia.org/w/index.php?title=Wikipedia:Statistics&oldid=610367399.

Go to **mymislab.com** for auto-graded writing questions as well as the following assisted-graded writing questions:

5-50. What is blogging, and why are blogs sometimes controversial?

5-51. What is viral marketing? What capabilities of the Web help to spread the virus?

References

Anonymous. (2014, May 29). Facebook.com site info. *Alexa.com.* Retrieved May 29, 2014, from http://www.alexa.com/siteinfo/facebook.com.

Baekdal, T. (2006, November 23). 7 tricks to viral Web marketing. *Baekdal.com.* Retrieved May 29, 2014, from http://www.baekdal.com/media/viral-marketing-tricks.

Batty, D. (2009, July 29). Lettings agent sues ex-tenant over Twitter complaint. *The Guardian.* Retrieved May 29, 2014, from http://www.theguardian.com/technology/2009/jul/29/horizon-group-management-twitter-lawsuit.

Carr, N. (2005). The amorality of Web 2.0. Retrieved May 29, 2014, from http://www.roughtype.com/archives/2005/10/the_amorality_o.php.

Cisco. (2011). 2011 Cisco connected world technology report. Retrieved July 12, 2012, from http://www.cisco.com/en/US/solutions/ns341/ns525/ns537/ns705/ns1120/2011-CCWTR-Chapter-3-All-Finding.pdf.

Cisco. (2012). 2012 Cisco connected world technology report. Retrieved May 29, 2014, from http://www.cisco.com/c/dam/en/us/solutions/enterprise/connected-world-technology-report/2012-CCWTR-Chapter1-Global-Results.pdf.

Clearswift. (2011, September 6). Worldwide clampdown on technology as businesses overreact to high profile data breaches. Retrieved July 12, 2012, from http://www.clearswift.com/news/press-releases/worldwide-clampdown-on-technology-as-businesses-overreact-to-high-profile-data-breaches.

Cook, N. (2008). *Enterprise 2.0: How social software will change the future of work.* Burlington, VT: Gower.

Flandez, R. (2009, April 20). Domino's response offers lesson in crisis management. *Wall Street Journal.* Retrieved May 29, 2014, from http://blogs.wsj.com/independentstreet/2009/04/20/dominos-response-offers-lessons-in-crisis-management.

Francis, J. A., & Harrigan, G. M. (2010). Jumping the boundaries of corporate IT: Accenture global research on millennials' use of technology. Retrieved May 29, 2014, from http://nstore.accenture.com/technology/millennials/global_millennial_generation_research.pdf.

Gaudin, S. (2009, October 6). Study: 54% of companies ban Facebook, Twitter at work. *Computerworld.* Retrieved May 29, 2014, from http://www.computerworld.com/s/article/9139020/Study_54_of_companies_ban_Facebook_Twitter_at_work.

Hinchcliffe, D. (2010, April 14). Enterprise 2.0 and improved business performance. *ZDNet.* Retrieved May 29, 2014, from http://www.zdnet.com/blog/hinchcliffe/enterprise-20-and-improved-business-performance/1355.

Jackson, E. (2012, April 30). Here's why Google and Facebook might completely disappear in the next 5 years. *Forbes.com.* Retrieved May 29, 2014, from http://www.forbes.com/sites/ericjackson/2012/04/30/heres-why-google-and-facebook-might-completely-disappear-in-the-next-5-years.

Jiao, P. (2010, August 17). The traits that separate China's Net from rest. *South China Morning Post.* Retrieved May 29, 2014, from http://www.scmp.com.

Keen, W. (2007). *The cult of the amateur: How today's Internet is killing our culture.* New York: Doubleday.

Khan, S. (2008, June 24). Enterprise 2.0—Giving the hype a second thought. *CIOUpdate.com.* Retrieved May 29, 2014, from http://www.cioupdate.com/reports/article.php/11050_3755056_1/Enterprise-20---Giving-the-Hype-a-Second-Thought.htm.

MacManus, R. (2007, August 7). Eric Schmidt defines Web 3.0. Retrieved May 29, 2014, from http://www.readwriteweb.com/archives/eric_schmidt_defines_web_30.php.

Madden, M., & Zickuhr, K. (2011, August 26). 65% of online adults use social networking sites. *Pew Research.* Retrieved May 29, 2014, from http://pewinternet.org/Reports/2011/Social-Networking-Sites.aspx.

McAfee, A. (2006a, April 1). Enterprise 2.0: The dawn of emergent collaboration. *MIT Sloan Management Review, 47*(3), 21–28.

McAfee, A. (2006b, May 27). Enterprise 2.0, version 2.0. Retrieved May 29, 2014, from http://andrewmcafee.org/2006/05/enterprise_20_version_20.

Nielsen. (2012). State of the media: Social media report 2012. *Nielsen.com.* Retrieved May 29, 2014, from http://www.nielsen.com/us/en/reports/2012/state-of-the-media-the-social-media-report-2012.html.

Nielsen, J. (2006, November 6). 100 million websites. *Jacob Nielsen's Alertbox.* Retrieved July 20, 2012, from http://www.useit.com/alertbox/web-growth.html.

Prescott, L. (2010, February 10). 54% of US Internet users on Facebook, 27% on MySpace. *SocialBeat.* Retrieved May 29, 2014, from http://venturebeat.com/2010/02/10/54-of-us-internet-users-on-facebook-27-on-myspace.

Rayport, J. (1996, December 31). The virus of marketing. *FastCompany.com.* Retrieved May 29, 2014, from http://www.fastcompany.com/magazine/06/virus.html.

Reynolds, C. (2009, July 7). Smashed guitar, YouTube song—United is listening now. *Los Angeles Times.* Retrieved May 29, 2012, from http://articles.latimes.com/2009/jul/07/travel/la-tr-smash-guitar-united-07072009.

Salesforce.com. (2012). The little blue book of social enterprise transformation. *Salesforce.com.* Retrieved May 29, 2014, from https://www.salesforce.com/form/pdf/social-enterprise-bluebook.jsp.

Sarker, S., & Sahay, S. (2002). Understanding virtual team development: An interpretive study. *Journal of the AIS, 3,* 247–285.

Saul, D.J. (2014, January 15). 3 million teens leave Facebook in 3 years: The 2014 Facebook demographic report. *Istrategylabs.* Retrieved May 28, 2014, from http://istrategylabs.com/2014/01/3-million-teens-leave-facebook-in-3-years-the-2014-facebook-demographic-report.

Sessums, C. D. (2009, December 17). A simple definition: Web 2.0. Retrieved July 20, 2012, from http://www.csessums.com/2009/12/a-simple-definition-web-2-0.

Smythe, J. (2007). *The CEO: The chief engagement officer: Turning hierarchy upside down to drive performance.* Burlington, VT: Gower.

Socialbakers. (2014, May 29). Facebook marketing statistics, demographics, reports, and news. Retrieved May 29, 2014, from http://www.socialbakers.com/facebook-overview-statistics.

Surowiecki, J. (2004). *The wisdom of crowds.* New York: Doubleday.

Twentyman, J. (2014, February 26). The secret to viral video marketing. *Guardian.* Retrieved May 28, 2014, from http://www.theguardian.com/technology/2014/feb/26/secret-to-viral-video-marketing.

Wagner, M. (2002, May 23). Saving trees and serving up benefits. *Internet Retailer.* Retrieved May 29, 2014, from http://www.internetretailer.com/2002/05/23/saving-trees-and-serving-up-benefits.

Wikipedia:About. (2014, May 19). In *Wikipedia, The Free Encyclopedia.* Retrieved May 29, 2014, from http://en.wikipedia.org/w/index.php?title=Wikipedia:About&oldid=609294101.

6 Enhancing Business Intelligence Using Information Systems

After reading this chapter, you will be able to do the following:

1. Describe the concept of business intelligence and how databases serve as a foundation for gaining business intelligence.
2. Explain the three components of business intelligence: information and knowledge discovery, business analytics, and information visualization.

Preview

Today, organizations operate in a global, highly competitive, and rapidly changing environment. A key to effective management is high-quality and timely information to support decision making. This high-quality and timely information, or business intelligence, can be provided from a variety of information systems (IS). Here, we first describe business intelligence, followed by a description of databases and data warehouses, two fundamental components for gaining business intelligence. Then we describe the primary IS components utilized by organizations to gain business intelligence. In Chapter 2, "Gaining Competitive Advantage Through Information Systems," you learned about general types of information systems supporting organizations' different decision-making levels and business functions that execute various business processes in order to realize the strategic goals of the organization. Here, we also introduce different technologies utilized at various decision-making levels of modern organizations to gain business intelligence.

Managing in the Digital World: Gathering Intelligence Using Social Media

In recent years, social media has become pervasive throughout society. No one can deny that social media have completely changed the context of privacy, shaping and reshaping relationships, exaggerating ideals of sharing, and reconstructing daily routines in order to visit your online friends at least once a day. Thanks to social media, people can now share every detail about the most mundane things in life. Updating where you are at any given moment alerts your friends to what you are up to, but also allows enterprises to learn how to better market products and promote celebrities.

Responding to the growing influence of social media and, in turn, demonstrating another crucial function of the phenomenon, all types of organizations are finding value in monitoring and digesting the nonstop flow of posts in the social media world (Figure 6.1). For instance, Dell's Radian 6 monitoring and management tools record an enormous 25,000 social media events each day, responding within 24 hours to tweets, Facebook posts, or other messages that deserve the attention of Dell.

Social media has not only become an important source of up-to-date information for businesses, but it is also emerging as a valuable resource for police and other first responders. Social media users have demonstrated that information about crises can travel at a rate that rivals 911 services. Indeed, analyzing public information is not unusual in the world of intelligence gathering either. Today, social media have people racing to express who they are and what they think, information that has never been this vast and openly accessible. Using such information, the U.S. government is developing tools to forecast everything from revolutions to upheavals to economic changes. Recently released documents also reveal that the U.S. National Security Agency uses Facebook and other social media profiles to create maps of social connections. From business corporations to government agencies, insights about what is happening, or about to happen, can be gleaned from social media where people are compelled to share what they know or think with just about anyone.

Have you checked your Facebook news feed today? Or, more accurately, how many times have you been on Facebook this morning? It is astonishing to see what a large part of our lives social media have become. By just keeping an eye on the number of posts your feed gets in an hour, you can easily imagine how analyzing these massive numbers of posts can quickly become a Big Data problem.

After reading this chapter, you will be able to answer the following:

1. How will organizations know what to look for when using social media for business intelligence?
2. How can government organizations analyze social media activities to predict social upheavals?
3. Given the speed and volume of activity on social media, what business analytics and visualization tools could be used to make sense of the information?

Based on:

Simpson, D. (2013, September 30). NSA mines Facebook for connections, including Americans' profiles. *CNN*. Retrieved May 29, 2014, from http://www.cnn.com/2013/09/30/us/nsa-social-networks.

Tittel, E. (2011, July 21), How Dell really listens to its customers. *ReadWriteWeb*. Retrieved May 29, 2014, from http://www.readwriteweb.com/enterprise/2011/07/how-dell-really-listens-to-its.

Wohlsen, M. (2012, February 12). FBI seeks digital tool to mine entire universe of social media. *Chicago Sun-Times*. Retrieved July 17, 2012, from http://www.suntimes.com/news/nation/10605702-418/fbi-seeks-digital-tool-to-mine-entire-universe-of-social-media.html.

FIGURE 6.1

Organizations are analyzing social media content of various types.

BUSINESS INTELLIGENCE

In Chapter 2, you learned about the importance of strategic planning for gaining and sustaining competitive advantage. To stay ahead of the competition, organizations have turned to **business intelligence**, or the use of information systems to gather and analyze data and information from internal and external sources in order to make better business decisions. To improve organizational performance, business executives are seeking answers to questions such as, "How effective is this year's promotion as compared to last year's?" "Which customer segments should we focus on?" "Which customers are most likely to switch to a competitor if we raise prices by X percent?" or, even more important, "Do we care if those customers switch?" Business intelligence also refers to the information gained from the use of such systems. Next, the need for business intelligence is examined.

Why Organizations Need Business Intelligence

Although a company's overall direction is decided on at the strategic level, business processes span all organizational levels and are highly interconnected. As discussed in Chapter 2, all business processes refer to the activities that organizations perform in order to reach their business goals. Unfortunately, the business processes outlined within strategic plans are often not implemented as envisioned at the managerial and operational levels of the organization because the information needed to effectively monitor and control these processes is simply not available. This "missing" information, in fact, often exists but resides in disconnected spreadsheets, reports, or databases.

To realize the goals of their strategic plans, organizations must have up-to-date, accurate, and *integrated* information to monitor and fine-tune a broad range of business processes. Consequently, information systems that provide business intelligence—by collecting and analyzing data and delivering needed information to the right decision maker at the right time—facilitate the effective management of modern organizations. Such organizations are being referred to as **data-driven organizations**—those that make decisions that can be backed up with verifiable data—and are measurably more productive and profitable than those that are not (McAfee & Brynjolfsson, 2012). Also, by letting data drive decisions, through a variety of business intelligence systems, decision making can be pushed lower into the organization, freeing up senior management time for more important decisions (Redman, 2013). In data-driven organizations, familiarity with data analysis is not only the responsibility of data analysts, but is a skill required of every business user. Additionally, business intelligence allows organizations to better respond to ongoing threats and opportunities as well as to better plan for the future.

RESPONDING TO THREATS AND OPPORTUNITIES. External factors such as globalization, competitive pressures, consumer demands, societal changes, and governmental regulations can create opportunities as well as threats for modern organizations. For example, globalization provides opportunities to compete in new markets, but it also creates the challenge of gaining new types of information in order to effectively manage these opportunities. Globalization can also lead to the threat of increased competition from developing countries, forcing organizations to rethink strategies or to further improve business processes. Thus, as the world becomes increasingly interconnected, market opportunities will expand, but, at the same time, markets will become increasingly more competitive, forcing companies to develop new products at an ever-increasing rate. Similarly, today's consumers have increasing access to information via social media and mobile devices, and can much more easily switch to a competitor's products or services. Further, large corporate and banking failures have brought about more stringent rules and regulations (such as the Sarbanes–Oxley Act; see Chapter 10, "Securing Information Systems"), and organizations have to comply with ever-increasing government reporting requirements. In sum, today's business environment is characterized by factors such as unstable market conditions, fierce competition, shorter product life cycles, more stringent regulations, and wider choices for customers than ever before. Business intelligence can help organizations make better decisions in this increasingly complex, fast-changing, and competitive environment by more effectively collecting and analyzing both internal and external data (Figure 6.2).

With increasing pressure to reduce costs, organizations have to focus on investing in systems that provide the greatest returns. Business intelligence solutions can provide quick returns, as they help to quickly react to problems by providing the right information at the right time. Further, business intelligence helps to leverage existing systems (such as enterprise-wide

FIGURE 6.2

Business intelligence helps organizations swiftly respond to external threats and opportunities.

information systems; see Chapter 7, "Enhancing Business Processes Using Enterprise Information Systems") by enabling decision makers to extract and analyze data provided by those systems. Finally, focusing on customer satisfaction can provide quick returns by helping to retain the most profitable customers.

BIG DATA. One significant opportunity for organizations is the abundance of data available for decision making. While research has demonstrated a strong linkage between effective data management and organizational performance, many organizations are unable to harness the value of **Big Data**. Organizations have long tried to collect, analyze, and use internal and external data to gain and sustain competitive advantage. Yet, the megatrends mobile and social, as well as the Internet of Things, have led to a tremendous increase in potentially useful data; the increase in mobile devices, social media, automated sensors, and other devices generates unprecedented amounts of *structured* and *unstructured data*. Big Data is typically characterized as being of high *volume*, *variety*, and *velocity*. One of the biggest opportunities is the sheer volume of data, which, for example, enables organizations to make business decisions based on more factors; at the same time, storing, analyzing, and managing increasing amounts of data pose tremendous challenges. The second characteristic is variety; useful data can come in the form of **structured data** (such as transaction data), which fit neatly into spreadsheets or databases, **semistructured data**, such as clickstreams and sensor data, or **unstructured data**, such as audio and video data, comments on social networks, and so on. Finally, Big Data is characterized based on its high velocity. On the one hand, data flow into organizations at increasingly higher rates; on the other hand, organizations have to process and use the data ever more quickly, such as when online retailer Amazon.com is providing recommendations for additional products. Thus, Big Data, ranging from geospatial data to customer sentiments, can prove invaluable for formulating and executing an organization's strategy. As data are becoming increasingly abundant, many organizations find themselves unable to use this data to make sound business decisions; being able to ask the right questions and successfully utilize Big Data remains elusive for many organizations. Realizing the opportunities and challenges brought about by Big Data and its management, high-level company executives are increasingly focusing on designing an organization-wide data management strategy.

EFFECTIVE PLANNING IS CONTINUOUS. In the past, organizations lacked the necessary information and tools to continuously plan for their future. Typically, organizations would first develop a strategic plan for some planning cycle (say, a year); then, once a strategic plan was agreed on, managers of various business units would prepare budgets for executing their portion of the plan. These budgets were often "backward looking" because they were typically based on historical data rather than being based on a clear understanding of current conditions and forecasts of future trends. Over time, managers would then execute their portion of the plan.

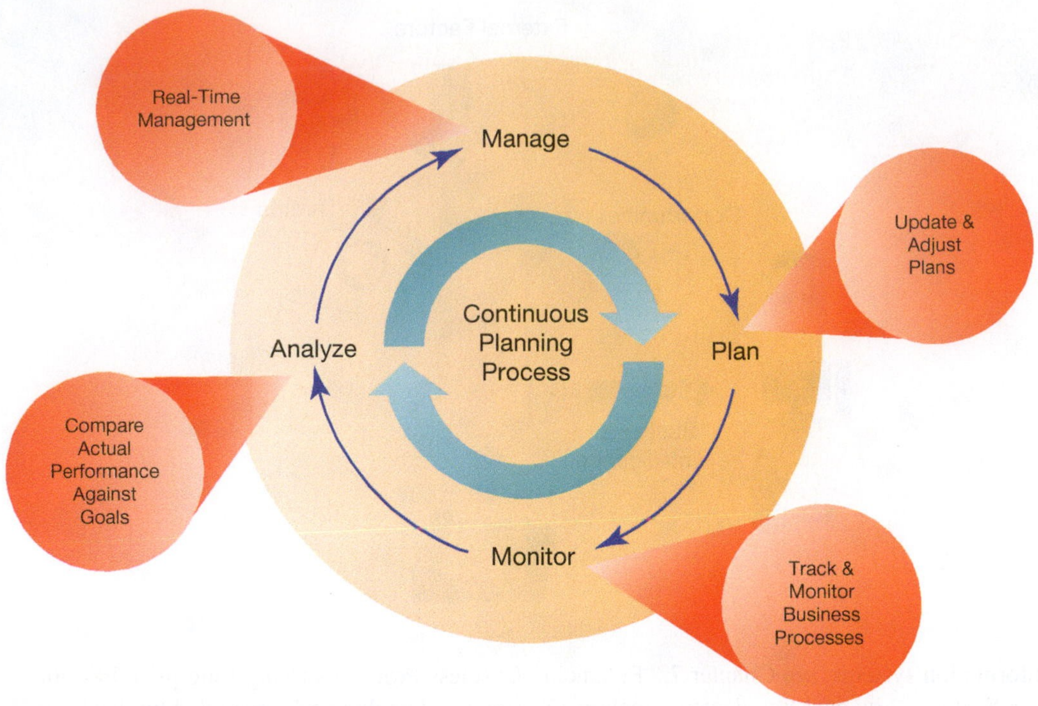

FIGURE 6.3
Effective business planning is continuous.

For many organizations, this method of planning and managing was adequate given the relatively slow pace of change.

Today, however, given the need to swiftly respond to a highly competitive and rapidly changing environment, organizations must implement new ways of planning. In fact, successful organizations are utilizing a **continuous planning process** (Figure 6.3). In a continuous planning process, organizations *continuously* monitor and analyze data and business processes; the results lead to ongoing adjustments to how the organization is managed, but these results are also reflected in ongoing updates to the organizational plans. It is only through timely and accurate business intelligence that continuous planning can be executed.

Responding to threats and opportunities and continuous planning are based on analyzing internal data (primarily from the operational level of the organization) as well as external data. In the next section, we describe how databases can be used to provide the necessary inputs to business intelligence applications.

Databases: Providing Inputs into Business Intelligence Applications

Data and knowledge are probably among the most important assets an organization has, as both are essential for executing business processes and gaining business intelligence. Databases, which are collections of related data organized in a way that facilitates data searches, are vital to an organization's success.

For instance, databases are essential for maintaining customer records and supporting business processes such as sales transactions and tracking inventory, but are also needed for marketing purposes, such as identifying target customers for personalized marketing communications. Additionally, database technology fuels electronic commerce on the Web, from tracking available products for sale to providing customer service.

ENABLING INTERACTIVE WEB SITES USING DATABASES. In today's highly dynamic digital world, any organization engaged in e-commerce makes extensive use of databases to provide dynamic and customized information on their Web pages. For example, many companies are enabling users of their Web sites to view product catalogs, check inventory, and place orders—all actions that ultimately read from and write to organizations' databases. Similarly, information about products (name, description, dimensions, shipping weight, and so on) is stored in databases and dynamically inserted into a Web page, freeing the company from having to develop a separate Web page for each individual product. For example, companies such as Amazon.com need only a few page templates for different product categories. Depending on what the user is looking for, these templates are then populated dynamically with the relevant product data that are pulled

WHEN THINGS GO WRONG

Twitter Fever—Where Good Conscience Meets Bad Intelligence

Over the past few years, Twitter has successfully transformed both the ways of information transmission and the pulse of pop culture. Serving as a source of news for growing numbers of people, Twitter also works as a gathering place for expressing compassion, sharing grief, and supporting disaster relief efforts. When Hurricane Sandy devastated entire neighborhoods of New York City in late 2012, Twitter became a sounding board for individuals and groups trying to offer support and relief. For example, Andy Wandilak, the owner of a pizza parlor in Brooklyn, offered to feed and shelter the family of a musician who plays at his restaurant. Upon hearing of the devastation of the storm's aftermath, Andy decided to try to provide food and shelter to as many victims as he could. He used Facebook and Twitter to ask the restaurant's patrons for support. By the weekend, he was serving up roughly 1,500 cups of soup daily.

Indeed, Twitter's ability to post thoughts in small snippets allows quick and easy dissemination of information to a broad audience. Thanks to the network effect, Twitter has become capable of gathering momentum so quickly that it is sometimes difficult to differentiate between truth and falsity. A tweet cannot exceed 140 characters, and can thus easily be read out of context; the sheer number of tweets, appearing at a rapid pace and often with little context, can easily result in endless confusion. In 2011, for instance, the phrase "RIP Jackie Chan" appeared for days on Twitter's Trending Topics list. The tweet's life cycle started with initial expressions of sadness, continued with spammers hoping to profit by hopping on the bandwagon, and ended with annoyance and people becoming irritated as it became apparent that the rumor of Jackie Chan's death was a hoax, but the topic would not stop trending.

In a more serious problem, Twitter raises questions over the legitimacy of a growing number of charity campaigns. Fueled by social media like Twitter and Facebook, *Kony 2012*, a short film about a Ugandan war criminal recruiting child soldiers, went viral. Initially, 77 percent of Twitter discussions concerning the campaign were positive, and many people supported the cause of Invisible Children, Inc., the creators of the video. Yet, when questions about exaggerated facts and criticisms of the organization arose, the tone immediately shifted. The sudden change of reaction opens up various other questions, but most important: How many people who sent out the tweet actually really understood the message behind *Kony 2012* (or even watched the video)?

When properly used for good, Twitter is undoubtedly a meaningful platform for reaching out to people. Sometimes, however, people seem to retweet first and ask questions later; yet, it may be better to do "due diligence" and try to Google first and retweet later, after establishing the veracity of some of the tweets that are circulating.

Based on:

Hempel, J. (2012, November 23). How Facebook and Twitter changed disaster relief. *CNN*. Retrieved May 29, 2014, from http://tech.fortune.cnn.com/2012/11/23/social-media-sandy.

Fox, Z. (2012, March 16). Kony 2012: How social media fueled the most viral video of all time. *Mashable*. Retrieved May 29, 2014, from http://mashable.com/2012/03/16/kony-2012-pew-study.

from a database; similarly, whenever a registered user places an order, the customer's billing and shipping information is retrieved from a database and displayed to the user for confirmation.

Some electronic commerce applications can receive and process millions of transactions per day. To ensure adequate system performance for customers, as well as to gain the greatest understanding of customer behavior, organizations must manage online data effectively. For example, Amazon.com, the world's largest bookstore, is open 24 hours a day, 365 days a year, and its servers log millions of transactions per day, with dozens of database reads and writes for every single transaction. This is but one example that shows that the key to effectively designing an online electronic commerce business is the effective management of online data. Beyond Web sites and e-commerce, it is important to stress that database management systems are at the heart of your university's student registration system, the inventory system at the local grocery store, Apple's iTunes store, and virtually anything else you can think of that requires recording and analyzing large amounts of data. Next we examine some basic concepts, advantages of the database approach, and database management.

DATABASES: FOUNDATION CONCEPTS. The database approach dominates nearly all computer-based information systems used today. To understand databases, we must familiarize ourselves with some terminology. In Figure 6.4, we compare database terminology (middle column) with equivalents in a library (left column) and a business office (right column). We use database management systems (DBMSs) to interact with the data in databases. A DBMS is a software

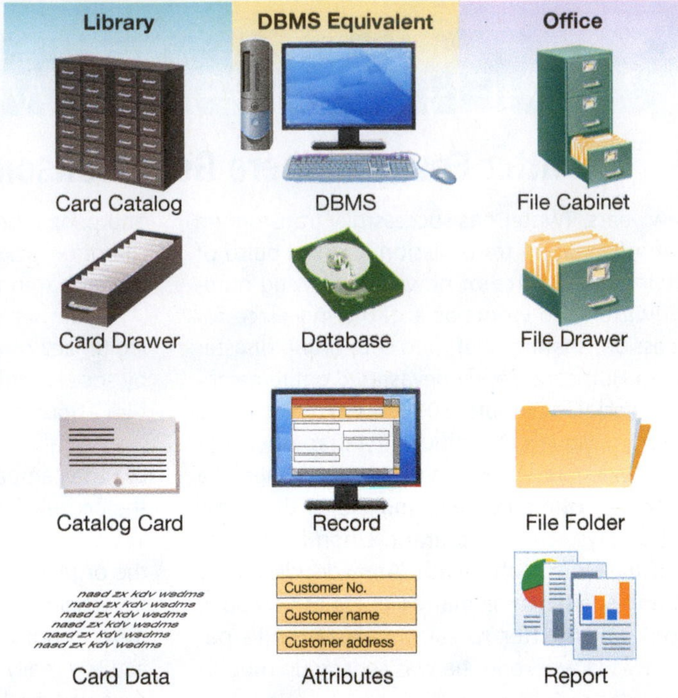

FIGURE 6.4

Computers make the process of storing and managing data much easier.

application with which you create, store, organize, and retrieve data from a single database or several databases. Microsoft Access is an example of a popular DBMS for personal computers. In the DBMS, the individual database is a collection of related attributes about entities. An **entity** is something you collect data about, such as people or classes (Figure 6.5). We often think of entities as **tables**, where each row is a **record** and each column is an **attribute** (also referred to as field). A record is a collection of related attributes about a single instance of an entity. Each record typically consists of many attributes, which are individual pieces of information. For example, a name and a Social Security number are attributes of a particular person.

DATABASES: ADVANTAGES. Before the advent of DBMS, organizations used the file processing approach to store and manipulate data electronically. As data were usually kept in long, sequential computer files that were often stored on tape, information about entities often appeared in several different places throughout the information system; further, the data were stored along with and sometimes embedded within the programming code that used the data. People had not yet envisioned the concept of separately storing information about entities in non-redundant databases, so different files frequently contained repetitive data about a customer, a supplier, or another entity. When someone's address changed, it had to be changed in every file where it occurred, a tedious process. Similarly, if programmers changed the code, they had to change the corresponding data along with it. Further, the programmer would have had to

FIGURE 6.5

This sample data table for the entity *Student* includes 7 attributes and 10 records.
Source: Microsoft Access

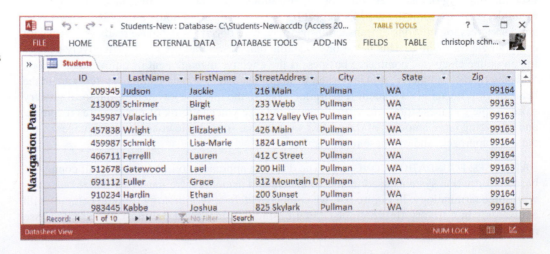

Students-New : Database- C:\Students-New.accdb (Access 20...

Students

ID	LastName	FirstName	StreetAddres	City	State	Zip
209345	Judson	Jackie	216 Main	Pullman	WA	99164
213009	Schirmer	Birgit	233 Webb	Pullman	WA	99163
345987	Valacich	James	1212 Valley Vie	Pullman	WA	99163
457838	Wright	Elizabeth	426 Main	Pullman	WA	99163
459987	Schmidt	Lisa-Marie	1824 Lamont	Pullman	WA	99164
466711	Ferrelll	Lauren	412 C Street	Pullman	WA	99164
512678	Gatewood	Lael	200 Hill	Pullman	WA	99163
691112	Fuller	Grace	312 Mountain D	Pullman	WA	99164
910234	Hardin	Ethan	200 Sunset	Pullman	WA	99164
983445	Kabbe	Joshua	825 Skylark	Pullman	WA	99163

Record: 1 of 10

TABLE 6.1 Advantages of the Database Approach

Advantages	Description
Program–data independence	It is much easier to evolve and alter software to changing business needs when data and programs are independent.
Minimal data redundancy	A single copy of data ensures that storage requirements are minimized.
Improved data consistency	Eliminating redundancy greatly reduces the possibilities of inconsistency.
Improved data sharing	It is easier to deploy and control data access using a centralized system.
Increased productivity of application development	Data standards make it easier to build and modify applications.
Enforcement of standards	A centralized system makes it much easier to enforce standards and rules for data creation, modification, naming, and deletion.
Increased security	A centralized system makes it easier to enforce access restrictions.
Improved data quality	Centralized control, minimized redundancy, and improved data consistency help to enhance the quality of data.
Improved data accessibility	A centralized system makes it easier to provide access for personnel within or outside organizational boundaries.
Reduced program maintenance	Information changed in the central database is replicated seamlessly throughout all applications.

know *how* the data were stored in order to make any changes. This was often no better than a pen-and-paper approach to storing data.

It is possible for a database to consist of only a single file or table. However, most databases managed under a DBMS consist of multiple tables or entities, often organized in several files. A DBMS can manage hundreds or even thousands of tables simultaneously by linking the tables as part of a single system. The DBMS helps us manage the tremendous volume and complexity of interrelated data so that we can be sure that the right data are accessed, changed, or deleted. For example, if a student or customer address is changed, that change is made through all the parts of the system where that data might occur. Using a database approach prevents unnecessary and problematic redundancies of the data, and the data are kept separate from the applications' programming code. This means that the database does not need to be changed if a change is made to an application. Consequently, there are numerous advantages to using a database approach to managing organizational data; these are summarized in Table 6.1. Of course, moving to the database approach comes with some costs and risks that must be recognized and managed (Table 6.2). Nonetheless, most organizations have embraced the database approach because most feel that the advantages far exceed the risks or costs.

TABLE 6.2 Costs and Risks of the Database Approach

Cost or Risk	Description
Need for new, specialized personnel	Conversion to the database approach may require hiring additional personnel.
Installation and management cost and complexity	The database approach has higher up-front costs and complexity in order to gain long-term benefits.
Conversion costs	Extensive costs are common when converting existing systems, often referred to as *legacy systems,* to the database approach.
Need for explicit backup and recovery	A shared corporate data resource must be accurate and available at all times.
Organizational conflict	Ownership—creation, naming, modification, and deletion—of data can cause organizational conflict.

DATABASES: TYPES. Traditionally, organizations have used relational database management systems (RDBMS) to support their business processes. An **RDBMS** attempts to balance efficiency of storage needs, ease of retrieval, and other factors by storing data in tables linked via relationships. However, RDBMSs are not easily scalable in response to peaks in demand, as is often the case in data-intensive applications such as e-commerce and social media, and traditional RDBMSs may simply not be able to handle massive volumes of often unstructured "Big Data." Further, as RDBMSs tend to be highly complex, any changes need to be carefully planned and managed, potentially reducing the agility of a business. To overcome these limitations, a new breed of database management systems, called "NoSQL," is increasingly becoming popular. **NoSQL** databases such as Amazon.com's SimpleDB are highly scalable, as they can be distributed across multiple machines, which works especially well in a cloud computing infrastructure. Further, NoSQL databases often offer much flexibility in the types of data they handle (such as comments of various lengths made by Facebook users, or audio or video data). However, implementing NoSQL databases comes at a cost, as they are still in their early stages of development; thus, some needed features may be lacking, and it may be difficult to find experienced NoSQL developers. Key in handling and processing Big Data is the ability to use not only a single computer, but also a distributed computing environment, and splitting the processing tasks among hundreds or thousands of machines, using frameworks such as Apache Hadoop.

DATABASES: EFFECTIVE MANAGEMENT. Now that we have outlined why databases are important to organizations, we can talk about how organizational databases can be managed effectively. The best database in the world is no better than the data it holds. Conversely, all the data in the world will do you no good if they are not organized in a manner in which there are few or no redundancies and in which you can retrieve, analyze, and understand them. The two key elements of an organizational database are the data and the structure of those data. The structure of the data is typically captured in a **data model**, that is, a map or diagram that represents entities and their relationships. Further, the structure of the data is documented to facilitate management of the database.

Each attribute in the database needs to be of a certain type. For example, an attribute may contain text, numbers, or dates. This **data type** helps the DBMS organize and sort the data, complete calculations, and allocate storage space. If tables are designed correctly, they will be easier to update and it will be faster to extract vital information to improve an organization's business intelligence capabilities.

Once the data model is created, the format of the data is documented in a **data dictionary**. The data dictionary (or metadata repository) is a document explaining several pieces of information for each attribute, such as its name, the type of data expected (dates, alphanumeric, numbers, and so on), and valid values. Data dictionaries can include information such as why the data item is needed, how often it should be updated, and on which forms and reports the data appears.

Data dictionaries often include **business rules**—that is, the policies by which a business runs—which help to prevent illegal or illogical entries from entering the database. For example, designers of a warehouse database could capture a rule in the data dictionary to prevent the entry of an invalid ship date for a future order from being entered into the database. Although NoSQL databases may not be as rigid as RDMBSs, or may not enforce business rules at all (leaving the enforcing to applications), it is wise to create data models and to consider what data will be captured, how the data will be related, and what rules should be enforced.

ENTERING AND QUERYING DATA. At some point, data must be entered into the database. Traditionally, a clerk or other data entry professional would create records in the database by entering data. These data may come from telephone conversations, preprinted forms that must be filled out, historical records, or electronic files. Today, much organizational data are captured automatically, as is the case with transactional data from a point-of-sale terminal or a user's input in a Web form; whenever you place an order on the Web, sign up for a newsletter, or respond to an online survey, your input is directly stored in a database. A **form** (Figure 6.6) typically has blanks where the user can enter information or make choices, each of which represents an attribute within a database record (such as the user's first name, last name, gender, and so on). This form presents the information to the user in an intuitive way so that the user can easily see the required items and enter the data. Forms are often used to capture data to be added, modified, or deleted from the database (e.g., modifying your password or removing an item from your shopping cart on Amazon.com).

COMING ATTRACTIONS

Intelligence Through Drones

In the robotics lab at the University of Pennsylvania, researchers are hard at work creating flying robots that can sense each other and features of the environment, giving the impression that they have a mind of their own. In one demonstration, a group of eight flying devices—called quadcopters—rise from the ground in unison and fly around the room in a carefully orchestrated formation. They then fly through a small window, one by one, and form up on the other side. What is particularly impressive about the devices is they are autonomous, meaning that aside from receiving instructions about going from point A to point B in the room, the devices get to decide where to move and how fast to get there, and are responsible for avoiding collisions. These devices are the precursor to drones that could be used in the real world for various uses, ranging from package delivery to surveillance to search and rescue operations.

Amazon.com recently announced its work on a drone delivery system that would allow a package ordered online to be delivered within 30 minutes by a small flying drone. In Amazon .com's ideal future, each city would have a local warehouse and a small task force of delivery drones, ready at a moment's notice to pick up and deliver thousands of small packages to Amazon.com's happy customers.

Another implementation of drone technology is in gathering geographic data to help farmers find and plant in plots of soil that are most suitable for crop growth. For example, researchers at the University of Aberdeen are developing drones with advanced imaging capabilities. These drones can be sent out to survey vineyards to find soil that is most optimal for grape growth. This could be especially valuable for growers given that soil content and area humidity tends to vary from year to year.

The technology described here is still several years away from being ready for widespread use. However, with relatively inexpensive drones, varied applications of these technologies may soon benefit society in a number of different ways.

Based on:

Bradley, J. (2013, May 1). Tiny flying robots! Meet the quadroter. *CNN*. Retrieved May 29, 2014, from http://edition.cnn.com/2013/05/01/tech/innovation/flying-robots-quadrotors.

Kleinman, Z. (2012, November 12). Cheers! How drones are helping the wine industry. *BBC*. Retrieved May 29, 2014, from http://www.bbc.com/news/business-20200856.

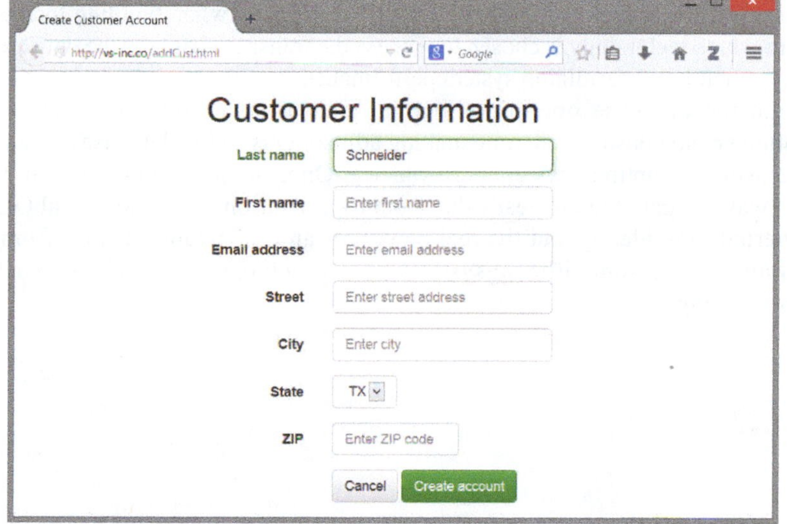

FIGURE 6.6

A computer-based form used for entering customer information.

In addition to transaction support, data stored in a database are extensively used for analysis and reporting. A **report** is a compilation of data from the database that is organized and produced in printed format (either electronic or on paper). Sophisticated **report generators** and analysis tools such as Crystal Reports or Tableau can help users to quickly build interactive reports and visualizations to present data in a useful format. To retrieve data from a database, we use a **query**. In fact, whenever a Web page is dynamically populated with content, a query is executed to retrieve the data from a database. The most common language used to interface with RDBMSs is **Structured Query Language (SQL)**. Figure 6.7 is an example of an SQL statement that an online bookstore would use to retrieve the information needed to populate a summary

FIGURE 6.7

This sample SQL statement would be used to retrieve the information needed to populate a summary Web page containing all books written by the first author of this textbook, sorted by publication date.

```
SELECT AUTHOR, TITLE, PUBLICATION_DATE, PRICE
FROM BOOKS
WHERE AUTHOR="VALACICH"
ORDER BY PUBLICATION_DATE;
```

page containing all books written by the first author of this textbook, sorted by publication date. Writing SQL statements requires time and practice, especially when you are dealing with complex databases with many entities, or when you are writing complex queries with multiple integrated criteria—such as adding numbers while sorting on two different attributes. Many desktop DBMS packages provide graphical user interfaces, where the user can pick the desired data from the database, to create queries quickly and easily (Figure 6.8).

ONLINE TRANSACTION PROCESSING. The systems that are used to interact with customers and run a business in real time are called **operational systems**. Examples of operational systems are sales order processing and reservation systems. As fast customer response is fundamental to having a successful Internet-based business, immediate automated responses to the requests of users are required. **Online transaction processing (OLTP)** systems provide this, and are designed to handle multiple concurrent transactions from customers. Typically, these transactions have a fixed number of inputs, such as order items, payment data, and customer name and address, and a specified output, such as total order price or order tracking number. In other words, the primary use of OLTP systems is gathering new data, transforming that data, and updating data in the system. Common transactions include receiving user information, processing orders, and generating sales receipts. Consequently, OLTP is a big part of interactive electronic commerce applications on the Internet. Since customers can be located virtually anywhere in the world, it is critical that transactions be processed efficiently. The speed with which DBMSs can process transactions is, therefore, an important design decision when building Internet systems. In addition to which technology is chosen to process the transactions, how the data are organized is also a major factor in determining system performance.

Although the database operations behind most transactions are relatively simple, designers often spend considerable time making adjustments to the database design in order to "tune" processing for optimal system performance. Once an organization has all this data, it must design ways to gain the greatest value from its collection; each individual OLTP system could be queried individually, but the real power for an organization comes from analyzing the aggregation of data from different systems, or *data mining*, using methods such as online analytical processing.

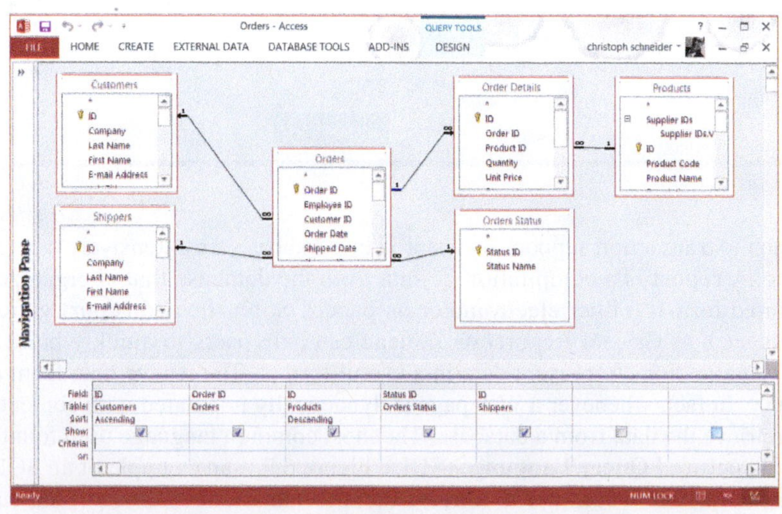

FIGURE 6.8

Microsoft Access provides a graphical user interface to let users select the required data.

Source: Courtesy of Microsoft Corporation

TABLE 6.3 Comparison of Operational and Informational Systems

Characteristic	Operational System	Informational System
Primary purpose	Run the business on a current basis	Support managerial decision making
Type of data	Current representation of state of the business	Historical or point-in-time (snapshot)
Primary users	Online customers, clerks, salespersons, administrators	Managers, business analysts, and customers (checking status and history)
Scope of usage	Narrow and simple updates and queries	Broad and complex queries and analyses
Design goal	Performance	Ease of access and use

OPERATIONAL SYSTEMS AND BUSINESS INTELLIGENCE. Operational systems can generate a wealth of data that can serve as useful inputs into business intelligence applications. For example, a grocery checkout system processes a specific transaction (the purchase) that can be linked to an inventory system (for reordering purposes), but it can also capture valuable data such as time of the purchase, items purchased together, form of payment, or loyalty program details. Coupled with external data (such as store location, weather data, or competitor information), these data can be analyzed for spending patterns, effectiveness of sales promotions, or customer profiling.

Systems designed to support decision making based on stable point-in-time or historical data are called **informational systems**. The requirements for designing and supporting operational and informational systems are quite different (Table 6.3). In a distributed online environment, performing real-time analytical processing diminishes the performance of transaction processing. For example, complex analytical queries require the locking of data resources for extended periods of execution time, whereas transactional events—data insertions and simple queries from customers—are fast and can often occur simultaneously; further, the operational databases typically only contain current data. Thus, a well-tuned and responsive transaction processing system may have uneven performance for customers while analytical processing occurs. As a result, many organizations replicate all transactions on a second database server so that analytical processing does not slow customer transaction processing performance. This replication typically occurs in batches during off-peak hours, when site traffic volumes are at a minimum.

MASTER DATA MANAGEMENT. To make sound operational, tactical, and strategic business decisions, it is imperative that decisions made in different departments are based on the same underlying data, definitions, and assumptions—that is, there is a "single version of the truth." For example, do the marketing and accounting departments have the same definitions of a customer or a sale? Does a "customer" entail anyone who may be interested in the company's product or service (marketing view) or only those who actually made a purchase (accounting view)? Part of creating a single version of the truth is **master data management. Master data** are the data deemed most important in the operation of a business. Typically shared among multiple organizational units, master data include data about customers, suppliers, inventory, employees, and the like. You can think of master data as the "actors" in an organization's transactions; for example, a *customer* purchases something, an *employee* is paid, and so on. Given the importance of an organization's master data, master data management is a management- rather than a technology-focused issue, as different business units and different corporate levels have to come to consensus on the meaning of master data items or on how to deal with duplicates. Especially for large organizations, arriving at a single version of the truth can be a challenge, as master data often have to be integrated from multiple systems. Likewise, after mergers or acquisitions, organizations have to try to consolidate the master data from two or more companies. Once the meaning and format of the master data have been agreed on, business intelligence applications can base their analyses on the single version of the truth by accessing multiple databases or by using a *data warehouse* that integrates data from various operational systems.

DATA WAREHOUSES. Large organizations, such as Walmart, UPS, and Alaska Airlines, have built **data warehouses** that integrate multiple large databases and other information sources into a single repository. Such repository, containing both historic and (almost) current data

TABLE 6.4 Sample Industry Uses of Data Warehousing

Uses of Data Warehousing	Representative Companies
Analysis of scanner checkout data	Safeway
Tracking, analysis, and tuning of sales promotions and coupons	Costco, CVS Corporation
Frequent buyer program management	Target, T-Mobile
Profitability analysis and market segmentation	Walgreens, Toyota
Product promotions for focused market segments	Walmart, Williams-Sonoma
Cross-segment marketing	Citigroup
Risk and credit analysis	HSBC
Customer profiling	Morgan Stanley

for analysis and reporting, is suitable for direct querying, analysis, or processing. Much like a physical warehouse for products and components, a data warehouse stores and distributes data on computer-based information systems. A data warehouse is a company's virtual storehouse of valuable data from the organization's disparate information systems and external sources. It supports the online analysis of sales, inventory, and other vital business data that have been culled from operational systems. The purpose of a data warehouse is to put key business information into the hands of more decision makers, and an organization that successfully deploys a data warehouse has committed to pulling together, integrating, and sharing critical corporate data throughout the firm. Table 6.4 lists sample industry uses of data warehouses. Data warehouses can take up hundreds of gigabytes (even terabytes) of data. They usually run on fairly powerful mainframe computers and can cost millions of dollars.

While no changes to the existing, historical data contained in the data warehouse are made, the data in a data warehouse are periodically appended with "new" data from operational systems. Consequently, a crucial process for consolidating data from operational systems with other organizational data (to facilitate the use of data mining techniques to gain the greatest and broadest understanding from the data) is **extraction, transformation, and loading**. First, the data need to be extracted from various different systems. In the transformation stage, data are being cleansed and manipulated to fit the needs of the analysis (such as by creating new calculated fields or summary values). **Data cleansing** refers to the process of detecting, correcting (e.g., standardizing the format), or removing corrupt or inaccurate data retrieved from different systems (such as differences in the way dates or ZIP codes are stored). Finally, the transformed data are loaded into the data warehouse and are ready for being used for complex analyses (Figure 6.9).

DATA MARTS. Rather than storing all enterprise data in one data warehouse, many organizations have created multiple data marts, each containing a subset of the data for a single aspect of a company's business, such as finance, inventory, or personnel. A **data mart** is a data warehouse that is limited in scope. It contains selected data from the data warehouse such that each separate data mart is customized for the decision support needs of a particular end-user group. Data marts have been popular among small and medium-sized businesses and among departments within larger organizations, all of which were previously prohibited from developing their own data warehouses because of the high costs involved.

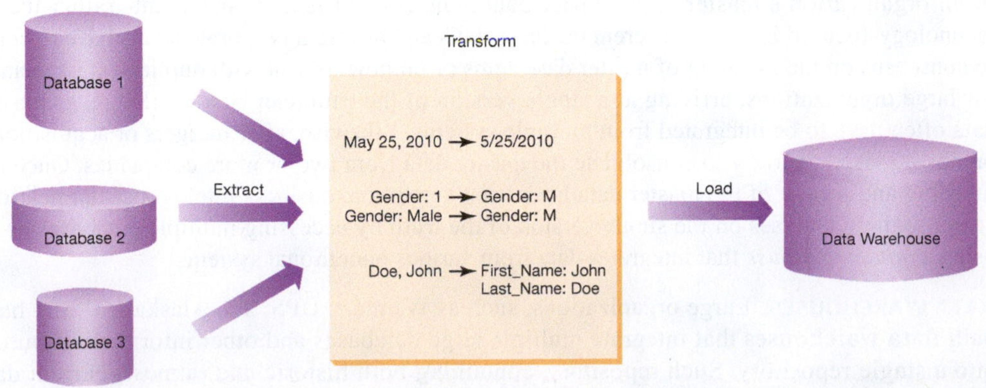

FIGURE 6.9

Extraction, transformation, and loading are used to consolidate data from operational systems into a data warehouse.

Data marts typically contain tens of gigabytes of data as opposed to the hundreds of gigabytes in data warehouses. Therefore, data marts can be deployed on less powerful hardware. The difference in costs between different types of data marts and data warehouses can be significant. The cost to develop a data mart is typically less than US$1 million, while the cost for a data warehouse can exceed US$10 million. However, with the advent of cloud computing, several vendors are offering data warehousing as a service, which can help to significantly lower the company's initial investment (see Chapter 3, "Managing the Information Systems Infrastructure and Services"); similarly, companies such as SAP are offering on-demand business intelligence as a service.

BUSINESS INTELLIGENCE COMPONENTS

Various different vendors offer a wide variety of tools as business intelligence applications. In general, however, there are three categories of business intelligence tools: tools for aiding information and knowledge discovery, tools for analyzing data to improve decision making, and tools for visualizing complex data relationships. Although each type of application by itself can be valuable to an organization, it is their convergence that enables organizations to gain and sustain competitive advantage through enhanced business intelligence. In the following sections, we discuss each of these categories as well as the various systems and technologies that each encompasses.

Information and Knowledge Discovery

Information and knowledge discovery tools are used primarily to extract information from existing data. Sometimes, information and knowledge discovery is completely atheoretical, and companies use business intelligence tools to search for hidden relationships between data, akin to panning for gold. In other cases, business users formulate hypotheses (such as "customers with a household income of $150,000 are twice as likely to respond to our marketing campaigns as customers with an income of $60,000 or less"), and these hypotheses are tested against existing data. Business intelligence tools can support both forms of information and knowledge discovery; yet, being able to ask the right questions is the most crucial skill, and should come before jumping into technological solutions. In the following sections, we describe some of the applications used for discovering new and unexpected relationships and for testing hypotheses.

AD HOC QUERIES AND REPORTS. Business users across an organization need the right information at the right time. Such information is typically presented as reports based on data stored in organizational databases and can take the form of **scheduled reports**, **drill-down reports**, **exception reports**, and **key-indicator reports** (Table 6.5). These reports are either produced at prespecified intervals or created whenever a prespecified event happens. However, decision makers frequently have information needs that are unforeseen and may never arise again. In such instances, the users need to run **ad hoc queries** (i.e., queries created because of unplanned information needs that are typically not saved for later use). Ad hoc query tools provide an easy-to-use interface, allowing managers to run queries and reports themselves without having to know query languages or the structure of the underlying data. Installed on a

TABLE 6.5 Common Reports and Queries

Report/Query	Description
Scheduled reports	Reports produced at predefined intervals—daily, weekly, or monthly—to support routine decisions
Key-indicator reports	Reports that provide a summary of critical information on a recurring schedule
Exception reports	Reports that highlight situations that are out of the normal range
Drill-down reports	Reports that provide greater detail, so as to help analyze why a key indicator is not at an appropriate level or why an exception occurred
Ad hoc queries	Queries answering unplanned information requests to support a non-routine decision; typically not saved to be run again

person's desktop, notebook computer, or mobile device, these tools can be used to run queries and reports whenever an unplanned information need arises without having to resort to calling the IS department for help in creating a complex query or a special report.

ONLINE ANALYTICAL PROCESSING. **Online analytical processing (OLAP)** refers to the process of quickly conducting complex, multidimensional analyses of data stored in a database that is optimized for retrieval, typically using graphical software tools. OLAP tools enable users to analyze different dimensions of data beyond simple data summaries and data aggregations of normal database queries. A typical question asked would be, "What were the profits for each week in 2016 by sales region and customer type?" In contrast to relatively simple ad hoc queries, running such multidimensional queries requires a deeper understanding of the underlying data. Given the high volume of transactions within Internet-based systems and the potential business value in the data, analysts must provide extensive OLAP capabilities to managers. The chief component of an OLAP system is the **OLAP server**, which understands how data are organized in the database and has special functions for analyzing the data. The use of dedicated databases allows for tremendous increases in retrieval speed. In the past, multidimensional queries against large transactional databases could take hours to run; in contrast, OLAP systems preaggregate data so that only the subset of the data necessary for the queries is extracted, greatly improving performance. Given the decrease in cost of random access memory (RAM, see the Technology Briefing), a recent trend is **in-memory computing**, where the data are stored in a computer's main memory, rather than on a comparatively slow hard drive, removing the bottlenecks associated with reading and writing data. Further, using in-memory computing for both transaction and analytical processing can help provide answers to questions as they arise, and enable making business decisions based on real-time data.

Measures and Dimensions Whenever a business transaction occurs, associated data can be stored and then analyzed from a variety of perspectives. To facilitate efficient processing of transactions, databases supporting online transaction processing systems treat all data in similar ways. In contrast, OLAP systems are designed for efficient retrieval of data and categorize data as measures and dimensions. **Measures** (or sometimes called **facts**) are the values or numbers the user wants to analyze, such as the sum of sales or the number of orders placed. **Dimensions** provide a way to summarize the data, such as region, time, or product line. Thus, sales (a measure) could be analyzed by product, time (year, quarter, or week), geographical region, or distributor (the dimensions). To enable the analysis of data at more or less detailed levels, the dimensions are organized as hierarchies (such as in year, quarter, month, or day). For example, when analyzing sales by geographical regions, a user can **drill down** from state, to county, to city, or to the individual store location, or **roll up** from state to sales region (northwest, south, southeast, and so on), to country, or to continent.

Cubes, Slicing, and Dicing To enable such multidimensional analyses, OLAP arranges the data in so-called cubes. An **OLAP cube** is a data structure allowing for multiple dimensions to be added to a traditional two-dimensional table (Figure 6.10). Although the figure only shows three dimensions, data can be analyzed in more than three dimensions. Analyzing the data on subsets of the dimensions is referred to as **slicing and dicing**. For example, a slice may show

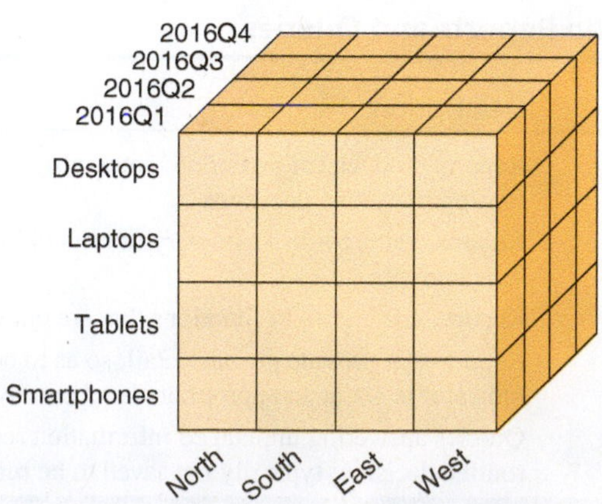

FIGURE 6.10

An OLAP cube allows for analyzing data by multiple dimensions.

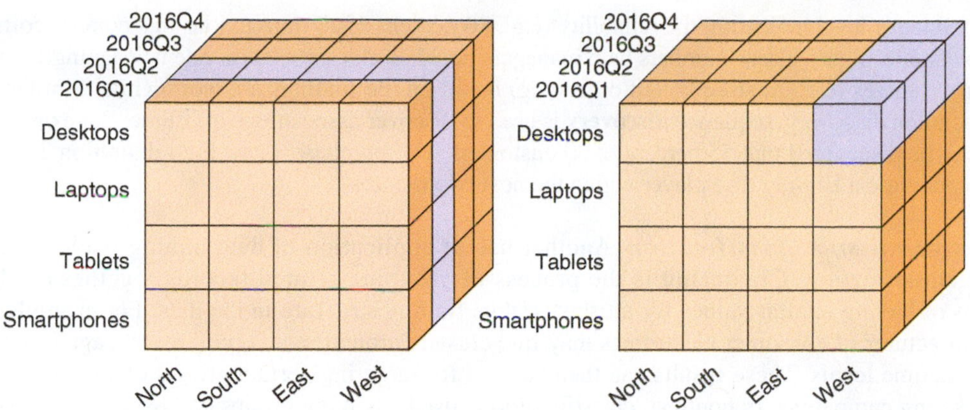

FIGURE 6.11

Slicing and dicing allows for analyzing subsets of the dimensions.

sales by product type and region only for the second quarter of 2016. Another slice may only show sales for desktops in the western region (Figure 6.11).

DATA MINING. **Data mining** complements OLAP in that it provides capabilities for discovering "hidden" predictive relationships in the data. Using complicated algorithms on powerful multiprocessor computers or cloud computing architectures, data mining applications can analyze massive amounts of data to identify characteristics of profitable customers, purchasing patterns, or even fraudulent credit card transactions. An **algorithm** refers to the step-by-step procedures used in a computer program to make a calculation or perform some type of computer-based process. Typically, data mining algorithms search for patterns, trends, or rules that are hidden in the data, so as to develop predictive models. Results from a data mining exercise (such as the characteristics of customers most likely to respond to a marketing campaign for a specific new product) can then be used in an ad hoc query (e.g., to identify customers sharing those characteristics so as to target them in the next campaign). It is important to note that any interesting predictive model derived from data mining should be tested against "fresh" data to determine if the model actually holds what it promises.

In order to increase predictive power, data mining algorithms are run against large data warehouses. Depending on the size of the data warehouse (large data warehouses often contain many terabytes of data), data mining algorithms can take a long time to run; thus, an important preparatory step to running data mining algorithms is **data reduction**, which reduces the complexity of the data to be analyzed. This can be achieved by rolling up a data cube to the smallest level of aggregation needed, reducing the dimensionality, or dividing continuous measures into discrete intervals.

Association Discovery One frequently used application of data mining is association discovery. **Association discovery** is a technique used to find associations or correlations among sets of items. For example, a supermarket chain wants to find out which items are typically purchased together in order to redesign the store's layout and optimize the customers' "navigational path" through the store, or to launch a new promotion. Mining sales transactions over the past five years may reveal that 80 percent of the time, people who purchase coffee also purchase sugar (Figure 6.12). Association rules typically contain two numbers: a percentage indicating support (e.g., the combination of coffee and sugar occurs in 20 percent of all transactions analyzed) and

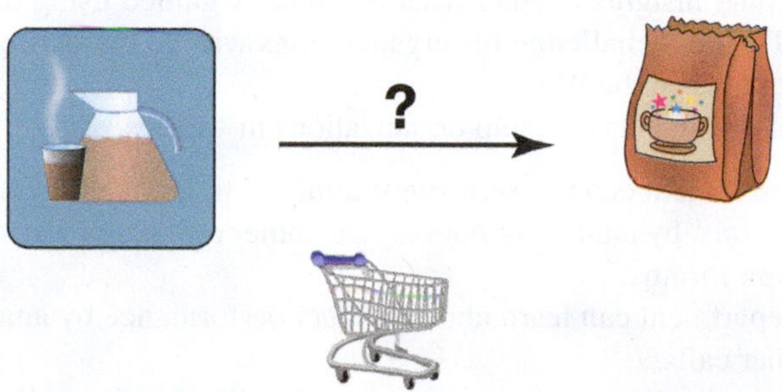

FIGURE 6.12

Association rules symbolize associations among sets of items.

a confidence level indicating the reliability (e.g., 80 percent of all transactions that contain coffee also contain sugar). These numbers help managers decide if the association rule is meaningful and if any changes (e.g., to store layout or pricing) based on the findings are worthwhile. Similar to association discovery, **sequence discovery** is used to discover associations over time. For example, it may be discovered that 55 percent of all customers who purchase a new high-definition TV set also purchase a Blu-ray disc player within the next two months.

Clustering and Classification Another useful application of data mining is clustering and classification. **Clustering** is the process of grouping related records together on the basis of having similar values for attributes, thus finding structure in the data. For example, a manufacturer of consumer electronics may find clusters around model preferences, age groups, and income levels. These results can then be used for targeting certain groups of customers in marketing campaigns. In contrast, **classification** is used when the groups ("classes") are known beforehand, and records are segmented into these classes. For example, a bank may have found that there are different classes of customers who differ in their likelihood of defaulting on a loan. As such, all customers can be classified into different (known) risk categories in order to ensure that the bank does not exceed a desired level of risk within its loan portfolio. Typically, classification would use a decision tree to classify the records.

UNSTRUCTURED DATA ANALYSIS. Although the quantitative methods just described can help decision makers get a better view of their organization's performance or their customers' behavior, they only provide a partial picture. By focusing purely on structured data (such as transactions, credit lines, and so on), a wealth of unstructured data (such as customer sentiments voiced in online forums, letters, or service-related call center records) is left untapped; in fact, researchers estimate that 80 percent of all enterprise data consist of unstructured or semistructured data (Stewart, 2013), and with the tremendous increase of user-generated content on the Web, this figure is likely to increase further. Therefore, making important business decisions purely based on structured data can be dangerous, as the massive amounts of unstructured data could either strengthen or contradict findings derived from analyzing only structured data. Hence, organizations are trying not only to reach a single version of the truth, but also to get the whole truth by analyzing unstructured data using *text mining, Web content mining,* or *Web usage mining*.

Text Mining and Web Content Mining **Text mining** refers to the use of analytical techniques for extracting information from textual documents. For organizations, the analysis of textual documents can provide extremely valuable insights into business performance, competitors' activities, or regulatory compliance. Such textual documents can include internal data such as letters or e-mails from customers, customer calls, internal communications, or external data such as blog posts, wikis, Twitter messages, and Facebook posts, as well as competitor's Web pages, marketing materials, patent filings, and so on. Text mining systems analyze a document's linguistic structures to extract data such as places, companies, concepts, or dates. Most systems can easily extract a wide range of content and can be customized to meet an organization's needs by adding specific key words related to competitors, product names, persons of interest, and the like.

Web content mining refers to extracting textual information from Web documents. To extract information from the overall Internet (or from some subset of Web sites), a document collection spider, or *Web crawler* (discussed later), would gather Web pages and documents that match some prespecified criteria and place this information in a massive document warehouse. Once collected, the text mining system would apply a variety of analytical techniques to produce reports that can be used to gain additional insights beyond what is typically gained using data mining analytics alone (Figure 6.13). The next challenge for organizations will be extracting useful information from audio or video streams on the Web.

Analyzing textual documents can help organizations in various ways:

- The marketing department can use **sentiment analysis** to learn about customers' thoughts, feelings, and emotions, by analyzing not only customer e-mails or letters but also blogs, wikis, or discussion forums.
- The operations department can learn about product performance by analyzing service records or customer calls.
- Strategic decision makers can gather **competitive intelligence** by analyzing press releases, news articles, or customer-generated Web content about competitors' products.

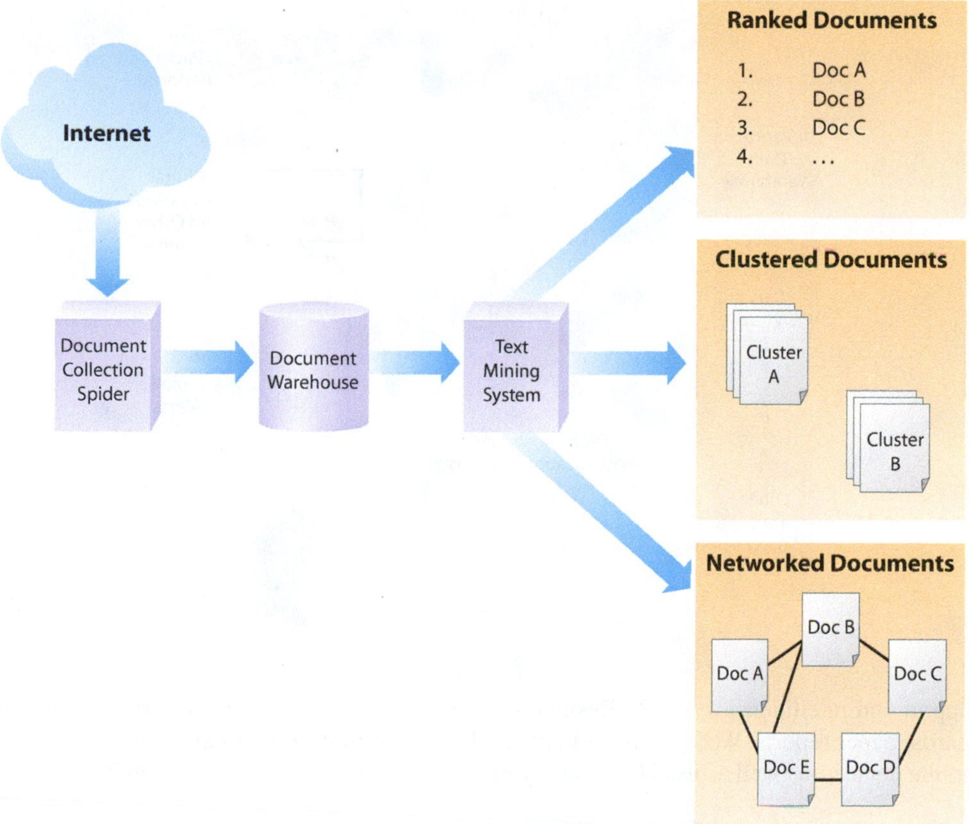

FIGURE 6.13

Text mining the Internet.

- The sales department can learn about major accounts by analyzing news coverage.
- The human resources department can monitor employee satisfaction or compliance to company policies by analyzing internal communications (this is especially important in order to comply with regulations such as the Sarbanes–Oxley Act; see Chapter 10).
- News reporters or intelligence agencies can find out what topics are trending when trying to understand public sentiments in unstable countries.
- Investigators can identify possible instances of noncompliance and fraud by analyzing e-mail communication within a company in a regulated industry.

Many major companies, including Capital One, Marriott International, United Airlines, and Walmart, use text mining solutions to assess customer sentiments and increase customer satisfaction. Similarly, raveable.com provides hotel ratings by aggregating information from sources such as tripadvisor.com, expedia.com, and travelocity.com as well as individual travel blogs; in addition to aggregating numerical ratings given for aspects such as cleanliness, value, or location, raveable.com uses text mining to analyze review comments based on key words such as "earplugs," "noise," or "clean" and the associated sentiments so as to categorize the reviews and classify them as positive or negative. We will further discuss social media monitoring and sentiment analysis and their role in customer relationship management in Chapter 8, "Strengthening Business-to-Business Relationships Via Supply Chain and Customer Relationship Management."

Web Usage Mining **Web usage mining** is used by organizations such as Amazon.com to determine patterns in customers' usage data, such as how users navigate through the site or how much time they spend on different pages. By analyzing users' **clickstream data** (i.e., a recording of a user's path through a Web site), a business such as Amazon.com can assess its pages' **stickiness** (i.e., the ability to attract and keep visitors) and how customers navigate through different item categories, ultimately helping Amazon.com to optimize the structure of its Web site. In addition, organizations can monitor users' mouse cursor movements to infer which areas of a Web page get most attention by the visitors.

The tools used for information and knowledge discovery can be embedded into a broad range of managerial, executive, and functional area information systems, as well as into decision

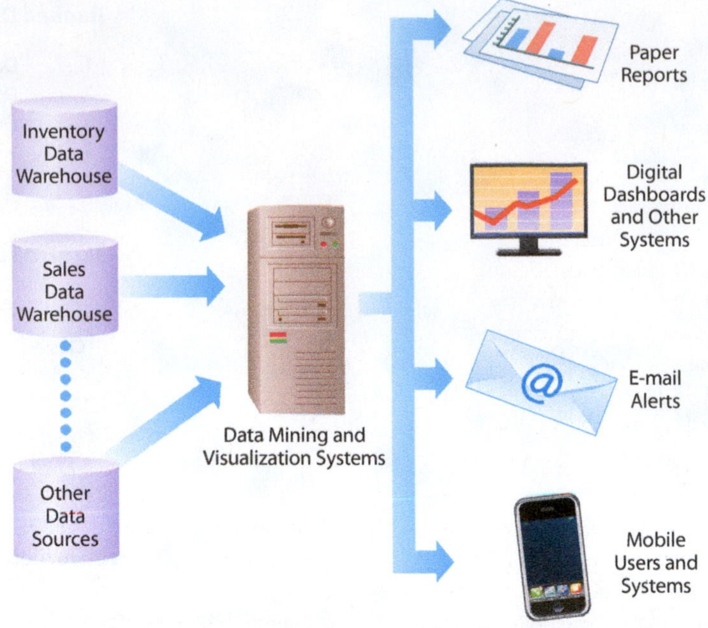

FIGURE 6.14

Data mining results can be delivered to users in a variety of ways.

support and intelligence systems. Results from these analyses can be provided on digital dashboards, paper reports, Web portals, e-mail alerts (using monitoring or data mining agents), and mobile devices, as well as used by a variety of other information systems (Figure 6.14).

Business Analytics to Support Decision Making

The second class of business intelligence applications comprises systems to support human and automated decision making. We first discuss applications designed to help predict future outcomes, followed by applications that support human decision makers in making unstructured decisions. Then we provide an overview of intelligent systems, which are designed to take some of these decisions out of the hands of the human decision makers, thus freeing up valuable resources. Finally, we examine various tools for managing organizational knowledge.

BUSINESS ANALYTICS. Traditional business intelligence applications for information and knowledge discovery are designed to focus on past and current performance, thus helping decision makers to get a detailed picture about the current state of a business. **Business analytics** augments business intelligence by using statistical analysis and **predictive modeling** to build explanatory models, help understand the data, identify trends, or predict business outcomes; whereas business intelligence is good for knowing what *is*, business analytics helps in understanding *why* something is a certain way and foreseeing what *will be*. For example, predictive modeling can help in understanding how a certain customer segment would respond to targeted promotions or help in determining measures to retain the most valuable customers (Business Objects, n.d.). However, predictive modeling is heavily dependent on statistical models and their underlying assumptions. Traditionally, such analyses were quite difficult for business users; in contrast, many of today's business analytics solutions offered by companies such as SAS or SAP guide the users through the process of conducting the desired analyses, selecting the right data, models, and so on, thus enabling "self-service business intelligence" and allowing business users to get self-service answers to the questions they have without relying on support staff.

DECISION SUPPORT SYSTEMS. A **decision support system (DSS)** is a special-purpose information system designed to support organizational decision making related to a particular recurring problem. DSSs are typically used by managerial-level employees to help them solve semistructured problems such as sales and resource forecasting, yet DSSs can be used to support decisions at virtually all levels of the organization. A DSS augments human decision-making performance and problem solving by enabling managers to examine alternative solutions to a problem. One common approach is performing "what-if" analyses. A **what-if analysis** allows you to make hypothetical changes to the data associated with a problem (e.g., loan duration or interest rate) and observe how these changes influence the results. For

BRIEF CASE Quality Assurance Through Call Recording

Call recording may be one of the most random, unnoticed aspects of our busy lives. What exactly goes on after the automated message says "This call is being recorded for quality assurance"? Certainly, it's more than just pushing the little red button. Call recording company ELoyalty was built on a US$50 million foundation, and it took a total of six years to perfect its complex software algorithms that work not only to define specific complaints, but also to decode a caller's personality.

Founder and CEO Kelly Conway says that the technology categorizes people into one of six personality types—Spock, Princess Diana, Rush Limbaugh, Robin Williams, Donald Trump, and Yoda. For example, if you are rational and go directly for the facts, then you are Spock. For those who are opinion-based and tend to hold strong beliefs, Rush Limbaugh may be your personality type. People like Limbaugh tend to be more formal, and are most likely to lay out the reason for their call at the beginning of a conversation, looking in turn for concrete explanations rather than apologies. In contrast, emotions-based people look for a connection and will try to joke around or ask personal questions of the customer service representative. Expressions of sympathy work well in gaining control when interacting with such callers.

In addition, ELoyalty's algorithms use past experience and call analysis to come up with patterns that advise customer service representatives on how to handle particular customers and calls in the future. If a customer has called in the past, call center computers quickly flag his personality for the assessment of chances that he may call again to cancel his account; other hints of dealing with him are also provided by the computer. The software further syncs with company accounts to calculate how valuable a caller is—for example, the higher the caller's credit card limits, the greater priority he gets.

After using 1,000 servers, an algorithm utilized by Wall Street firms, and methodologies created by well-known psychologist Taibi Kahler to analyze 2 million speech patterns and 600 million conversations (totaling 600 terabytes of customer data), ELoyalty is able to work wonders in a business where time means money. If a minute usually costs around US$1–US$1.50, ELoyalty successfully lowers call center operating expenses by 20 percent because of more productive calls. The company claims that its services generate 3 to 10 times the returns for its customers.

Questions

1. How do you feel about having your calls recorded and analyzed? Do you feel it is an invasion of privacy? Why or why not?
2. What personality type do you think you are? Which personality type do you think would be most and least difficult to deal with? Explain why.

Based on:

Singel, R. (2011, February 14). Meet the company that records your call for quality assurance. *Wired*. Retrieved May 29, 2014, from http://www.wired.com/2011/02/eloyalty-call-recording/all/1.

Anonymous. (2014). Frequently asked questions. *Mattersight*. Retrieved May 29, 2014, from http://www.mattersight.com/faqs.

example, a cash manager for a bank could examine what-if scenarios of the effect of various interest rates on cash availability. Some types of problems utilize a variety of input variables that each may have a different likelihood of occurring (e.g., there is a 25 percent likelihood that inflation will stay the same and a 75 percent likelihood that inflation will increase). Sensitivity analysis allows you to understand how different input values and their probability of occurring (e.g., rate of inflation and its probability of occurring) will impact the results of a model. Similarly, goal-seeking analyses help in determining how input parameters need to be changed to achieve a desired end state. Finally, optimization models allow finding the best balance between certain parameters within given constraints. With a DSS, the manager uses decision analysis tools such as Microsoft Excel—a widely used DSS environment—to either analyze or create meaningful information to support the decision making related to non-routine problems. In contrast to systems that primarily present the outputs in a passive way, a DSS is designed to be an "interactive" decision aid. The results from any analysis are displayed in both textual and graphical formats.

Architecture of a DSS Like the architecture of all systems, a DSS consists of input, process, and output components as illustrated in Figure 6.15 (Sprague, 1980). Specifically, a DSS uses **models** to manipulate data. For example, if you have some historic sales data, you can use many different types of models to create a forecast of future sales. One technique is to take an average of past sales, and adjust it for seasonal changes. The formula you would use to calculate and adjust the average is the model. A more complicated forecasting model might use time-series analysis or linear regression. See Table 6.6 for a summary of the ways organizations can use DSS to support decision making in organizations. Data for the DSS primarily come from transaction processing systems but can come from other sources as well.

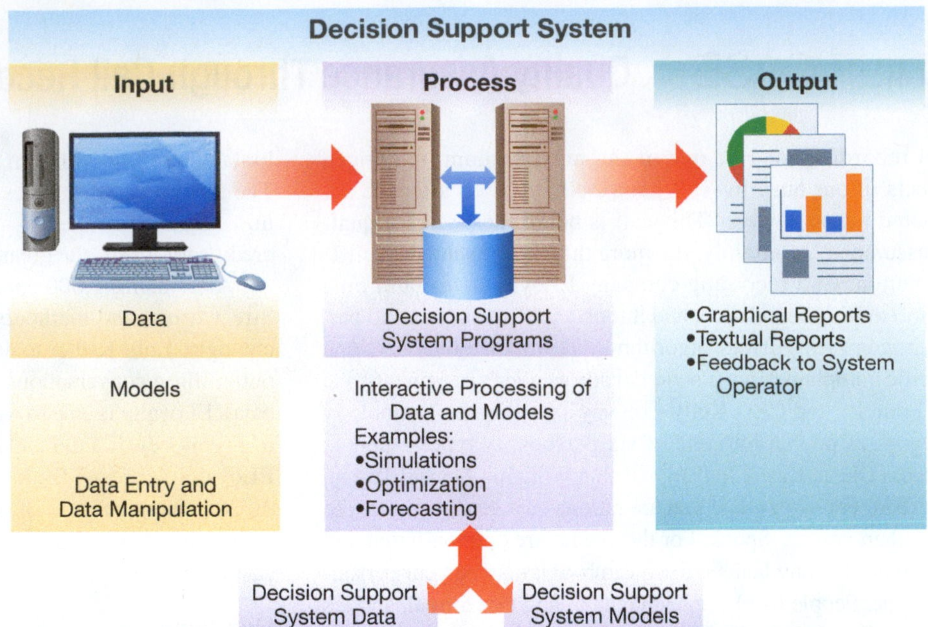

FIGURE 6.15
Architecture of a DSS using the basic systems model.

TABLE 6.6 Common DSS Uses for Specific Organizational Areas

Area	Common DSS Uses
Corporate level	Corporate planning, venture analysis, mergers and acquisitions
Accounting	Cost analysis, discriminant analysis, breakeven analysis, auditing, tax computation and analysis, depreciation methods, budgeting
Finance	Discounted cash flow analysis, return on investment, buy or lease, capital budgeting, bond refinancing, stock portfolio management, compound interest, after-tax yield, foreign exchange values
Marketing	Product demand forecast, advertising strategy analysis, pricing strategies, market share analysis, sales growth evaluation, sales performance
Human resources	Labor negotiations, labor market analysis, personnel skills assessment, employee business expenses, fringe benefit computations, payroll and deductions
Production	Product design, production scheduling, transportation analysis, product mix, inventory levels, quality control, plant location, material allocation, maintenance analysis, machine replacement, job assignment, material requirements planning
Management science	Linear programming, decision trees, simulation, project planning and evaluation, queuing, dynamic programming, network analysis

Table 6.7 summarizes the characteristics of a DSS. Inputs are data and models. Processing supports the merging of data with models so that decision makers can examine alternative solution scenarios. Outputs are graphs and textual reports.

INTELLIGENT SYSTEMS. **Artificial intelligence (AI)** is the science of enabling information technologies—software, hardware, networks, and so on—to simulate human intelligence, such as reasoning and learning, as well as gaining sensing capabilities, such as seeing, hearing, walking, talking, and feeling. AI has had a strong connection to science fiction writers, who have written stories about AI-enabled technologies aiding humans (e.g., Mr. Data in *Star Trek: The Next Generation*), attempting world domination (e.g., *The Matrix*), or enabling humans to exist on an alien planet (e.g., *Avatar*). The current reality of AI is that it is lagging far behind the imagination of most science fiction writers; nevertheless, great strides have been made.

Machine Learning Whereas "conventional" computers are very adept at processing large amounts of data by rapidly executing a program's instructions, they cannot easily adapt

TABLE 6.7 Characteristics of a DSS

Inputs	Data and models; data entry and data manipulation commands
Processing	Interactive processing of data and models; simulations, optimization, forecasts
Outputs	Graphs and textual reports; feedback to system user
Typical users	Midlevel managers (although a DSS could be used at any level of the organization)

to different circumstances or deal with noisy data. If a conventional computer is presented with a novel problem that it is not programmed to solve, it cannot deal with this situation. **Machine learning** is a branch of artificial intelligence that allows systems to learn by identifying meaningful patterns when processing massive amounts of data. Machine learning has enabled great advances in various fields; intelligent systems (discussed below) such as Google's self-driving cars, but also speech recognition, natural language processing, computer vision, Web searching, or image recognition, are based on improvements in machine learning algorithms. Recently, Netflix started applying machine learning algorithms to improve movie recommendations. One frequently used approach to machine learning is the use of artificial neural networks; **neural networks**, composed of a network of processing elements (i.e., artificial "neurons") that work in parallel to complete a task, attempt to approximate the functioning of the human brain and can learn by example. Typically, a neural network is *trained* by having it categorize a large database of past information (e.g., a database of handwritten digits) for common patterns, so as to infer rules (e.g., what features differentiate the digit 1 from a 7). These rules can then be applied to new data and conclusions drawn. For example, many financial institutions use neural network systems to analyze loan applications. These systems compare a person's loan application data with the neural network containing the *intelligence* of the success and failure of countless prior loans, ultimately recommending loan acceptance (or rejection) (Figure 6.16).

Machine learning is the basis for the development of several types of intelligent systems. **Intelligent systems**—comprised of sensors, software, and computers embedded in machines and devices—emulate and enhance human capabilities. Intelligent systems are having a tremendous impact in a variety of areas, including banking and financial management, medicine, engineering, and the military. Two types of intelligent systems—expert systems and intelligent agents—are particularly relevant in business contexts and are discussed next.

Expert Systems An **expert system (ES)** is a type of intelligent system that uses reasoning methods based on knowledge about a specific problem domain in order to provide advice, much like a human expert. ESs are used to mimic human expertise by manipulating knowledge

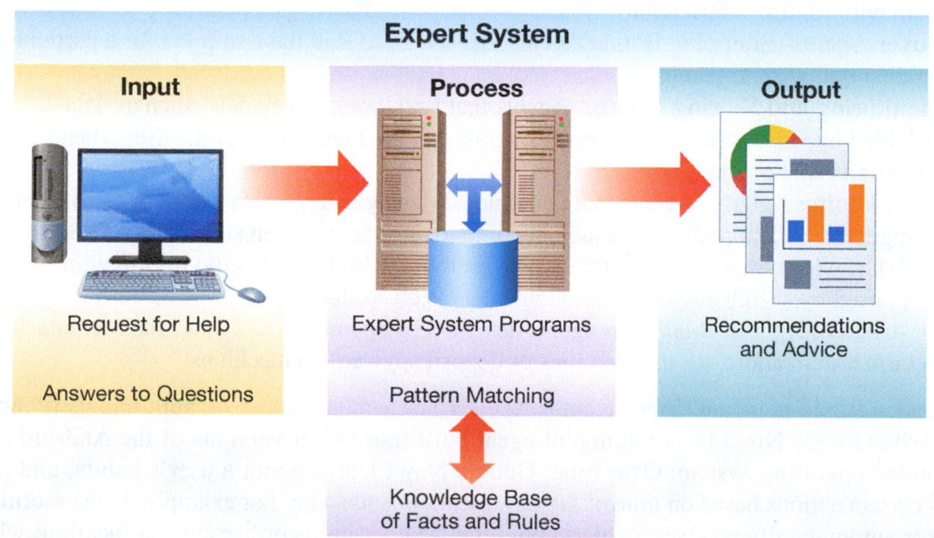

FIGURE 6.16

Architecture of an ES using the basic systems model.

(understanding acquired through experience and extensive learning) rather than simply manipulating data (for more information, see Sharda, Delen, & Turban, 2015). Human knowledge can be represented in an ES by facts and rules about a problem coded in a form that can be manipulated by a computer. When you use an ES, the system asks you a series of questions, much as a human expert would. It continues to ask questions, and each new question is determined by your response to the preceding question. The ES matches the responses with the defined facts and rules until the responses point the system to a solution. A **rule** is a way of encoding knowledge, such as a recommendation, after collecting information from a user. Rules are typically expressed using an "if–then" format. For example, a rule in an ES for assisting with decisions related to the approval of automobile loans for individuals could be represented as follows: *If* personal income is US$50,000 or more, *then* approve the loan.

Given that most experts make decisions with limited information as well as use general categories of information when making judgments, researchers have developed **fuzzy logic** to broaden the capabilities of ESs and other intelligent systems. Specifically, fuzzy logic allows ES rules to be represented using approximations or subjective values in order to handle situations where information about a problem is incomplete. For example, a loan officer, when assessing a customer's loan application, may generally categorize some of the customer's financial information, such as income and debt level, as high, moderate, or low rather than using precise amounts. In addition to numerous business applications, fuzzy logic is used to better control antilock braking systems and household appliances as well as when making medical diagnoses or filtering offensive language in chat rooms.

The most difficult part of building an ES is acquiring the knowledge from the experts and gathering and compiling it into a consistent and complete form useful for making recommendations. ESs are used when expertise for a particular problem is rare or expensive, such as in the case of a complex machine repair or medical diagnosis. Using fuzzy logic, ESs are also utilized when knowledge about a problem is incomplete.

As with other information systems, the architecture of an ES (and other intelligent systems) can be described using the basic systems model (Figure 6.17). Inputs to the system are questions and answers from the user. Processing is the matching of user questions and answers to information in the knowledge base. The processing in an ES is called **inferencing**, which consists of matching facts and rules, determining the sequence of questions presented to the user, and drawing a conclusion. The output from an ES is a recommendation. The general characteristics of an ES are summarized in Table 6.8.

Intelligent Agent Systems An **intelligent agent**, or simply an *agent* (also called a **bot**—short for "software robot"), is a program that works in the background to provide some service when a specific event occurs. There are several types of agents for use in a broad range of contexts, including the following:

- **User Agents.** Agents that automatically perform a task for a user, such as automatically sending a report at the first of the month, assembling customized news, or filling out a Web form with routine information.
- **Buyer Agents (Shopping Bots).** Agents that search to find the best price for a particular product you wish to purchase.
- **Monitoring and Sensing Agents.** Agents that keep track of key data, such as data provided by various sensors, meters, cameras, and the like, notifying the user when conditions change.
- **Data Mining Agents.** Agents that continuously analyze large data warehouses to detect changes deemed important by a user, sending a notification when such changes occur.
- **Web Crawlers.** Agents that continuously browse the Web for specific information (e.g., used by search engines)—also known as **Web spiders**.
- **Destructive Agents.** Malicious agents designed by spammers and other Internet attackers to farm e-mail addresses off Web sites or deposit spyware on machines.

One example of an intelligent agent is Apple's Siri personal assistant, built into its iPhones. Similarly, Google Now! is an intelligent agent built into newer versions of the Android mobile phone operating system. Over time, Google Now! learns about a user's habits, and performs certain actions based on time of the day, location, and so on. For example, in the morning, the user automatically receives an alert about the weather in his or her current location; when

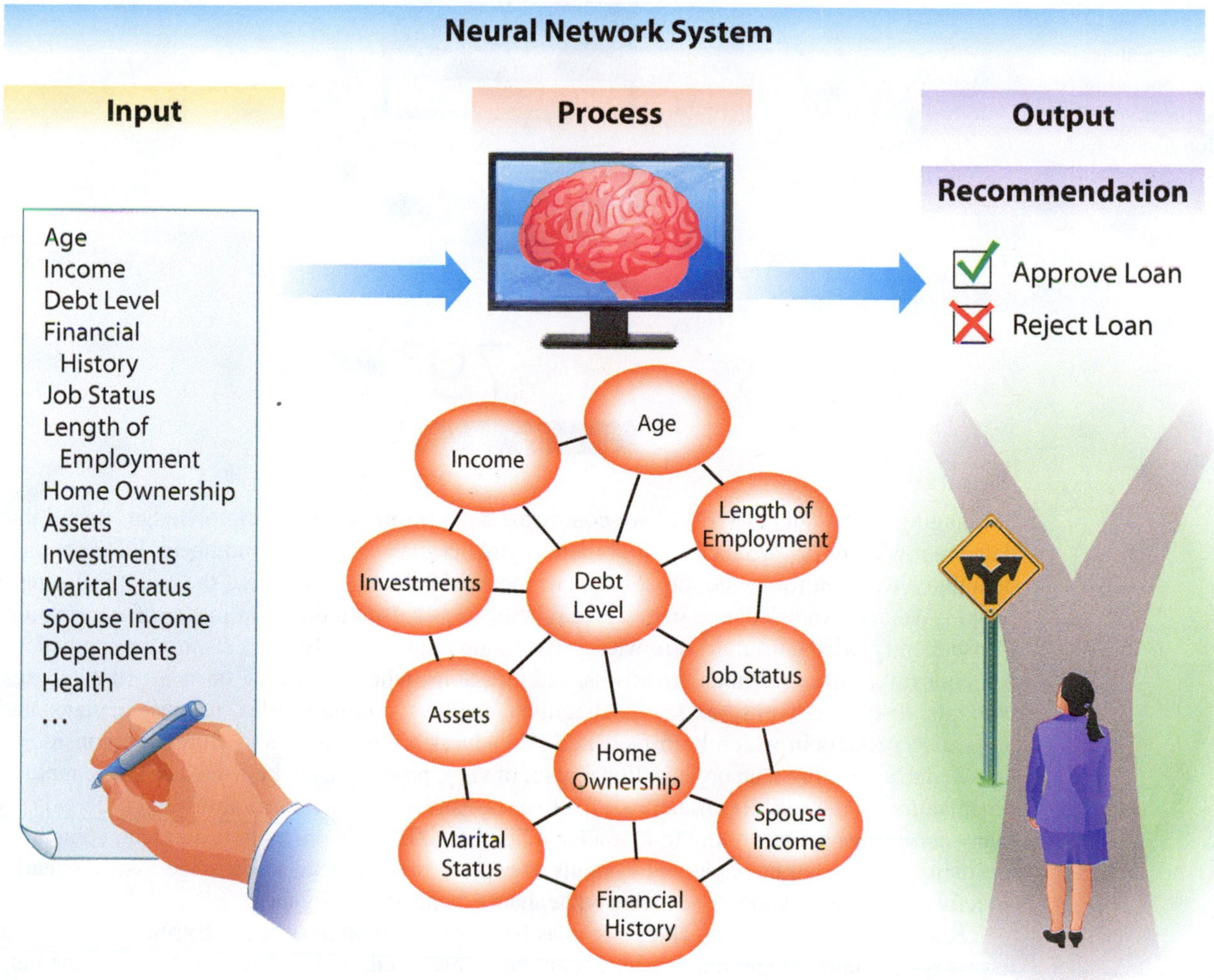

FIGURE 6.17

Neural networks approximate the functioning of the brain by creating common patterns in data and then comparing new data to learned patterns to make a recommendation.

TABLE 6.8 Characteristics of an ES

Inputs	Request for help, users' answers to questions posed by the ES
Processing	Pattern matching and inferencing
Outputs	Recommendation or advice or further questions
Typical users	Midlevel managers (although an ES could be used at any level of the organization)

passing by a subway station, public transport information is presented; when on a trip, the time to travel back home is automatically calculated (taking into consideration factors such as traffic situation); and so on (Figure 6.18). Google also developed intelligent agents for its **augmented reality** applications built into Google Glass, eyeglasses with a tiny embedded screen, which augments reality by displaying information about the wearer's surroundings, including weather information, public transportation schedules, reviews about a restaurant the wearer is looking at, and other useful information (see Chapter 2).

In sum, there are ongoing developments to make information systems *smarter* so that organizational decision makers gain business intelligence. Although systems such as ESs, neural networks, and intelligent agents have yet to realize the imagination of science fiction writers, they have taken great strides in helping information systems support business intelligence.

KNOWLEDGE MANAGEMENT SYSTEMS. There is no universal agreement on what exactly is meant by the term "knowledge management." In general, however, **knowledge management** refers to the processes an organization uses to gain the greatest value from its knowledge assets. In Chapter 1

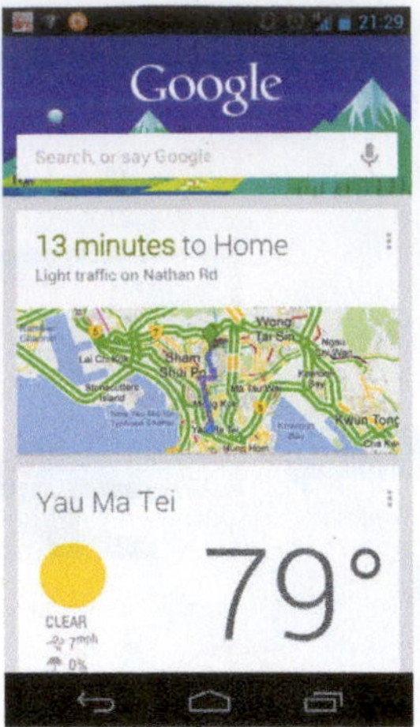

FIGURE 6.18

Google Now!, an intelligent agent built into the Android operating system, presents pertinent information based on factors such as the user's habits, location, and time of day.
Source: Courtesy of Google, Inc.

"Managing in the Digital World," we contrasted data, information, and knowledge. Recall that data are raw material—recorded, unformatted symbols such as words or numbers. Information is data that have been formatted, organized, or processed in some way so that the result is useful to people. We need knowledge to understand relationships between different pieces of information. Consequently, what constitutes **knowledge assets** are all the underlying skills, routines, practices, principles, formulas, methods, heuristics, and intuitions, whether explicit or tacit. All databases, manuals, reference works, textbooks, diagrams, displays, computer files, proposals, plans, and any other artifacts in which both facts and procedures are recorded and stored are considered knowledge assets. From an organizational point of view, properly used knowledge assets enable an organization to improve its efficiency, effectiveness, and, of course, profitability. Additionally, as many companies are beginning to lose a large number of baby boomers to retirement, companies are using knowledge management systems to capture these crucial knowledge assets. Clearly, effectively managing knowledge assets will enhance business intelligence.

Knowledge assets can be categorized as being either explicit or tacit. **Explicit knowledge assets** reflect knowledge that can be documented, archived, and codified, often with the help of information systems. Explicit knowledge assets reflect much of what is typically stored in a DBMS. In contrast, **tacit knowledge assets** reflect the processes and procedures that are located in a person's mind on how to effectively perform a particular task (Figure 6.19). Identifying key tacit knowledge assets and managing these assets so that they are accurate and available to people throughout the organization remains a significant challenge.

Tacit knowledge assets often reflect an organization's *best practices*—procedures and processes that are widely accepted as being among the most effective and/or efficient. Identifying how

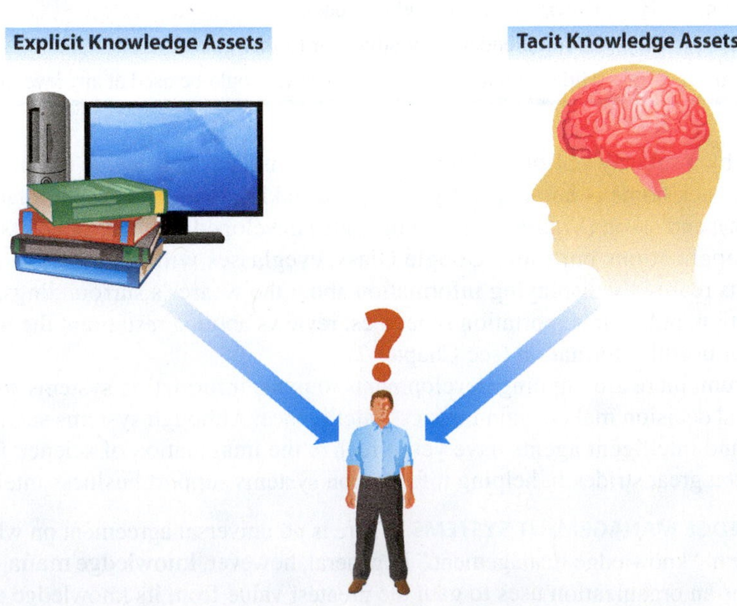

FIGURE 6.19

Explicit knowledge assets can easily be documented, archived, and codified, whereas tacit knowledge assets are located in a person's mind.

ETHICAL DILEMMA

Are You Being Tracked?

Consumer preference has always served as an important source for decisions about what to produce, or how to present, promote, or price products, and companies are always attempting to determine and/or influence buyer behavior. A recent legal debate sheds light on an innovative way of inferring individual shoppers' tastes simply by tracking them as they walk from store to store, tapping into shopping patterns and observing their behavior, all through the use of monitoring sensors that track mobile phone signals.

The technology, known as Footpath, was made possible by UK-based Path Intelligence. With the help of antennas that detect the Temporary Mobile Subscriber Identifier (TMSI) of mobile phones in the vicinity, Footpath senses the movement of customers by triangulation, thus following buyers as they stroll through the mall. To an extent, the system resembles Web usage mining, or the tracking of Web site visitors' paths when they are exploring the site or making a purchase, in that it allows brick-and-mortar retailers to track customers in an "offline" environment. Although Footpath was initially sold as an innovative method of collecting consumer information to boost revenue, two malls in the United States that carried the technology ended up receiving letters from a New York senator warning of privacy violation and potential abuse of the tracking service.

How could online tracking have gone on for years without getting caught in legal complications when Footpath swiftly came face-to-face with ethical questioning? The fact is, in order to prevent Web sites and advertisers from tracking Web visitors without their consent, the United States and the European Union have so far recommended consumers be given the "do-not-track" and "right-to-be-forgotten" options for the sake of privacy protection. Sans the consent of either Web visitors or mall shoppers to track their preferences and compile data off the record, both online and offline tracking actually do raise a number of privacy red flags.

As businesses boom, competition has gotten stiffer and technology has become an important tool for boosting revenue. However, privacy has simultaneously evolved as a crucial matter that requires further attention. If the only way to avoid being tracked by Footpath is to switch off one's mobile phone (which is rather vague considering it is not much of an option, especially when shoppers are not aware of the act), then it is up to corporate ethics and legal aid to ensure the protection of our privacy.

Based on:

Gallagher, S. (2011, November 26). We're watching: Malls track shopper's cell phone signals to gather marketing data. *Ars Technica*. Retrieved May 29, 2014, from http://arstechnica.com/business/2011/11/were-watching-malls-track-shoppers-cell-phone-signals-to-gather-marketing-data.

Anonymous. (2014). About—Path Intelligence. *Path Intelligence*. Retrieved May 29, 2014, from http://www.pathintelligence.com/about/.

to recognize, generate, store, share, and manage this tacit knowledge is the primary objective for deploying a knowledge management system. Consequently, a **knowledge management system** is typically not a single technology but rather a collection of technology-based tools that include communication technologies—such as e-mail, groupware, instant messaging, and the like—as well as information storage and retrieval systems, such as wikis or DBMSs, to enable the generation, storage, sharing, and management of tacit and explicit knowledge assets (Malhotra, 2005).

Benefits and Challenges of Knowledge Management Systems Many potential benefits can come from organizations' effectively capturing and utilizing their tacit knowledge assets (Levinson, 2010) (Table 6.9). Although there are many potential benefits for organizations that effectively deploy knowledge management systems, to do so requires that several substantial challenges be overcome.

First, effective deployment requires employees to agree to share their personal tacit knowledge assets and to take extra steps to utilize the system for identifying best practices. Therefore, organizations must create a culture that values and rewards widespread participation.

Second, experience has shown that a successful deployment must first identify what knowledge is needed, why it is needed, and who is likely to have this knowledge. Once an organization understands "why, what, and who," identifying the best technologies for facilitating knowledge exchange is a much easier task.

Third, the successful deployment of a knowledge management system must be linked to a specific business objective (e.g., increase innovativeness); and fourth, the knowledge management system must be easy to use, not only for entering, but also for retrieving knowledge. Similarly, the system cannot overload users with too much information or with information that

TABLE 6.9 Benefits and Challenges of Knowledge Management Systems

Benefits	Challenges
Enhanced innovation and creativity	Getting employee buy-in
Improved customer service, shorter product development, and streamlined operations	Focusing too much on technology Forgetting the goal
Enhanced employee retention	Dealing with knowledge overload and obsolescence
Improved organizational performance	

is obsolete. Just as physical assets can erode over time, knowledge can also become stale and irrelevant. Therefore, an ongoing process of updating, amending, and removing obsolete or irrelevant knowledge must occur, or the system will fall into disarray and will not be used.

How Organizations Utilize Knowledge Management Systems The people using a knowledge management system will be working in different departments within the organization, doing different functions, and will likely be located in different locations around the building, city, or even the world. Each person—or group of people—can be thought of as a separate island that is set apart from others by geography, job focus, expertise, age, and gender. Often, a person on one island is trying to solve a problem that has already been solved by another person located on some other island. Finding this "other" person is often a significant challenge. The goal of a successful knowledge management system is to facilitate the exchange of needed knowledge between these separate islands. To find and connect such separate islands, organizations use **social network analysis**, a technique that maps people's contacts to discover connections or missing links (sometimes called structural holes) within the organization (Figure 6.20); thus, social network analysis can be used to attempt to find groups of people who work together, to find people who don't collaborate but should, or to find experts in particular subject areas. In addition to social network analysis, organizations use social bookmarking and social cataloging to capture and structure employees' knowledge and harness their collective intelligence (see Chapter 5, "Enhancing Organizational Communication and Collaboration Using Social Media").

Once organizations have collected their knowledge into a repository, they must find an easy way to share it with employees (often using an intranet), customers, suppliers (often using an extranet), or the general public (often using the Internet). These **knowledge portals** can be customized to meet the unique needs of their intended users. For example, the U.S. Food and Drug Administration (FDA) uses a Web-based knowledge portal for keeping the public (e.g., citizens, researchers, and industry) informed on the most up-to-date information related to food (e.g., information on mad cow disease or product recalls) and drugs (e.g., the status of a drug trial) (Figure 6.21).

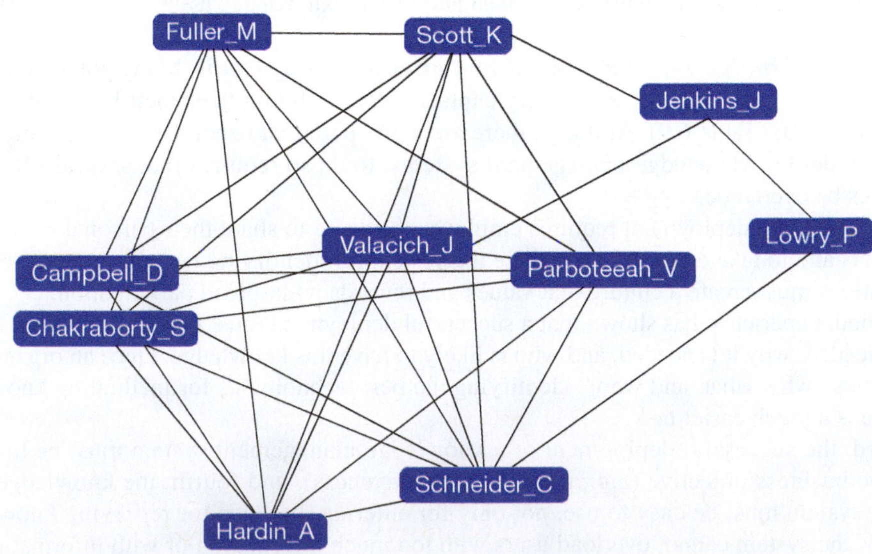

FIGURE 6.20

Social network analysis can help to analyze collaboration patterns.

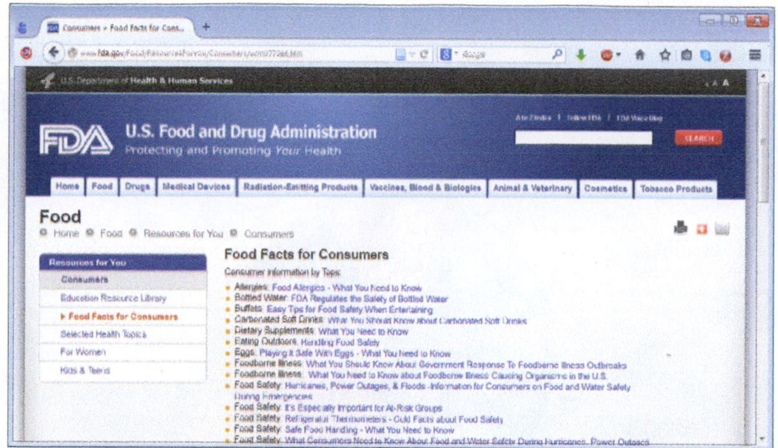

FIGURE 6.21

Countless organizations are using Web-based knowledge portals to provide information to employees, customers, and partners.
Source: Courtesy of the Food and Drug Administration

In addition to the FDA, countless other organizations, such as Ford Motor Company, Eli Lilly, Walmart, and Dell Computers, are also rapidly deploying knowledge management systems. We are learning from these deployments that all organizations, whether for-profit or nonprofit, struggle to get the right information to the right person at the right time. Through the use of a comprehensive strategy for managing knowledge assets, organizations are much more likely to gain a competitive advantage and a positive return on their IS investments.

Information Visualization

The third pillar of business intelligence applications is information visualization. **Visualization** refers to the display of complex data relationships using a variety of graphical methods, enabling managers to quickly grasp the results of the analysis. For example, Figure 6.22 shows the visualization of a hurricane as it is gaining strength. The image shows towering thunderclouds (in red), called hot towers, that were spotted just before the hurricane intensified to a Category 5 hurricane. Once represented visually, analysts can view changes over time and perform what-if analyses to better understand the behavior of hurricanes. In similar ways, organizations around the world are utilizing visualization technologies to enhance business intelligence.

DASHBOARDS. **Digital dashboards** are commonly used to present key performance indicators and other summary information used by managers and executives to make decisions. To provide

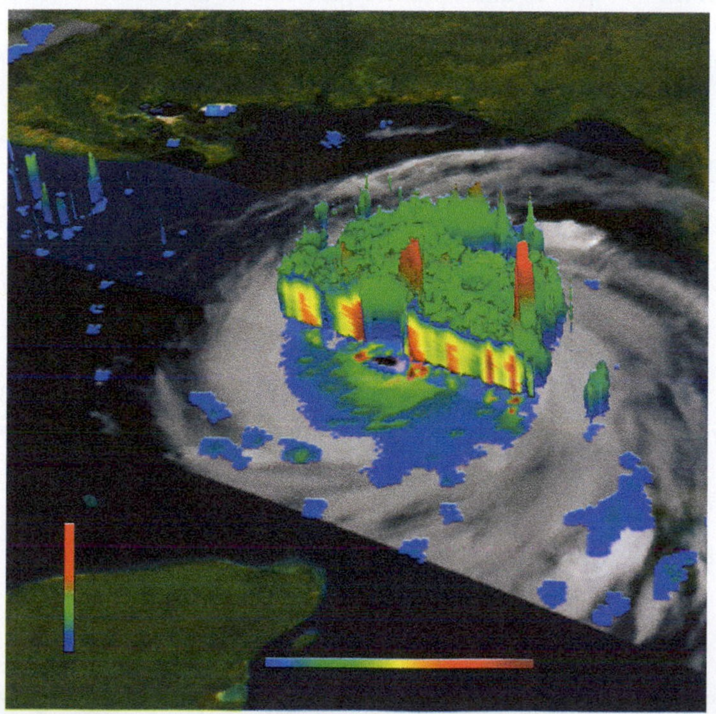

FIGURE 6.22

Visualization is the display of complex data relationships using a variety of graphical methods.
Source: NASA Headquarters

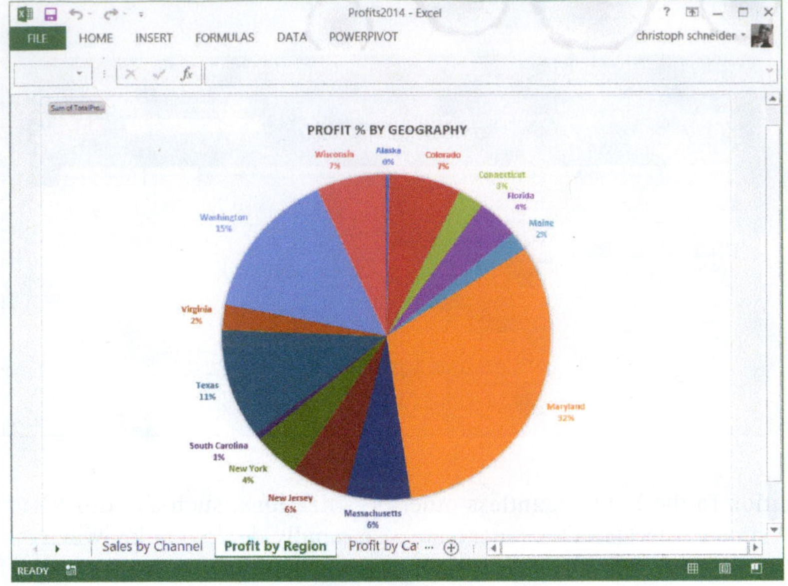

FIGURE 6.23

A digital dashboard showing profits by sales region.
Source: Courtesy of Microsoft Corporation

the greatest benefits for decision makers, digital dashboards typically support three usage models: push reporting, exception reporting and alerts, and pull reporting. Digital dashboards not only provide the decision makers with a quick, visual overview of key performance indicators and other key operational statistics and trends (i.e., push reporting), but also alert the user of any items that require immediate attention (i.e., exception reporting and alerts); if the user wants to analyze the root causes of an exception or perform other analyses, he or she can drill down or perform self-service ad hoc queries (i.e., pull reporting).

Digital dashboards (sometimes called executive dashboards) evolved from executive information systems designed to provide top-level managers with the needed information to support business processes, such as cash and investment management, resource allocation, and contract negotiation. Typically, executives require information presented in a highly aggregated form so that they can scan information quickly for trends and anomalies.

Although data are typically provided in a highly aggregated form, the executive also has the capability to drill down and see the details if necessary. For example, suppose a digital dashboard summarizes profits by states, as illustrated in Figure 6.23. If the executive wants to get a deeper understanding about a particular state, a selection on the screen can provide the details behind the aggregate numbers, as shown in Figure 6.24. By drilling down into the data, the executive can see

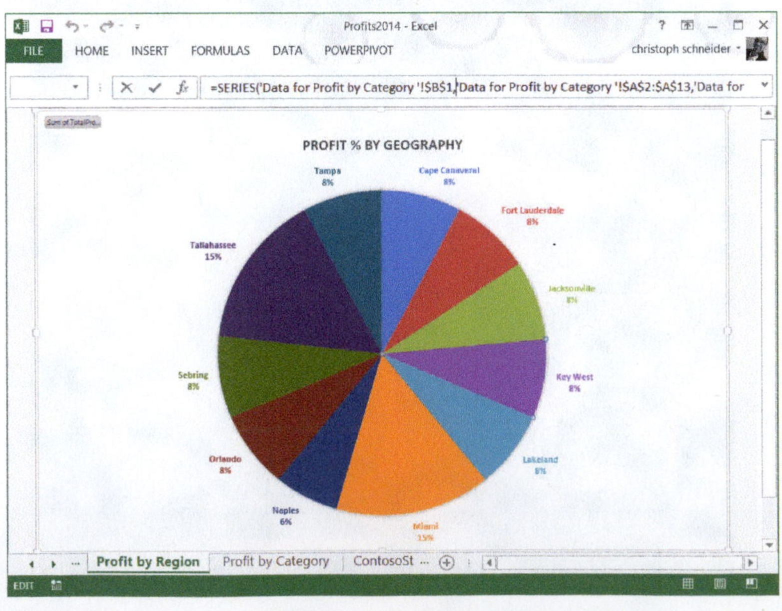

FIGURE 6.24

Drill-down numbers for profits by sales region.
Source: Courtesy of Microsoft Corporation

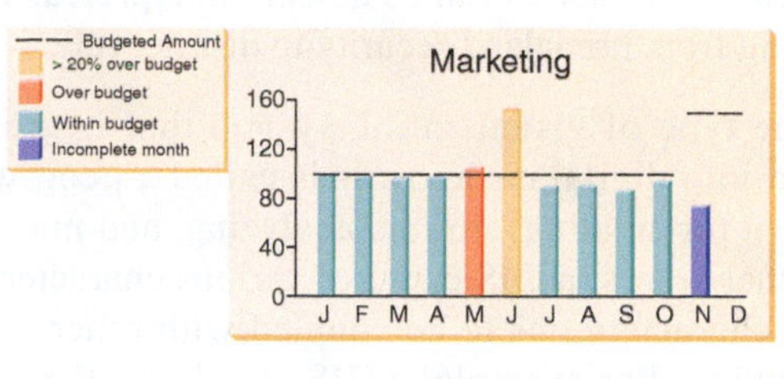

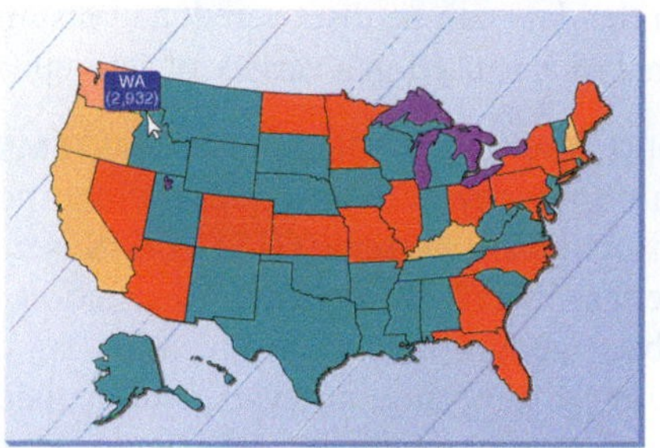

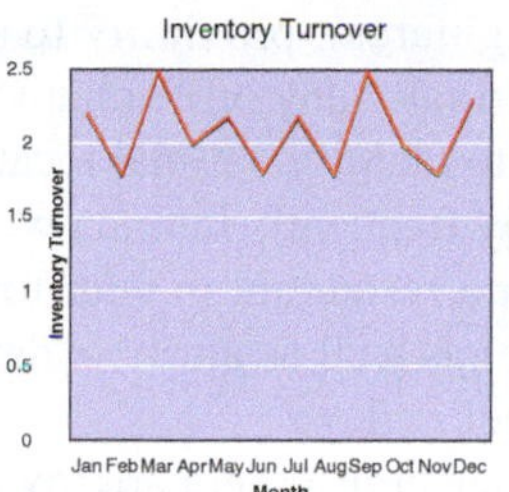

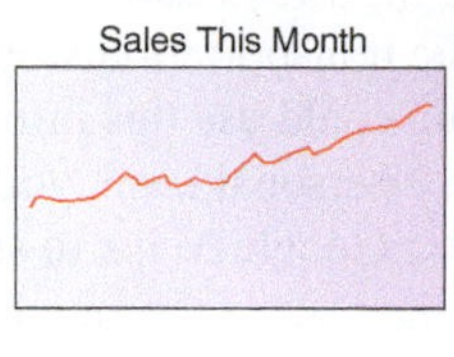

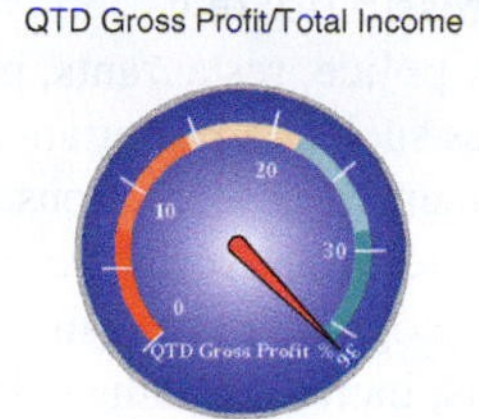

FIGURE 6.25

Dashboards use various graphical elements to highlight important information.

that the majority of the profits were made in a particular region, or city, or even store. Also, the digital dashboard can connect the data in the system to the organization's internal communication systems (e.g., electronic or voice mail) so that the executive can quickly send a message to the appropriate managers to discuss solutions to the problem discovered in the drill-down.

Dashboards make use of a variety of design elements to present the data in the most user-friendly way. To highlight deviations that need to be addressed or to symbolize changes over time, dashboards use maps, charts, spark lines, or graphics symbolizing traffic lights, thermometers, or speedometers (Figure 6.25); conditional formatting is often used to highlight exceptions and draw the user's attention to deviations from the normal course of business. Many dashboards now combine business intelligence with technologies typically used to deliver rich Web applications (such as Adobe Flash) in order to provide the level of interactivity desired by users at different levels of an organization.

One recent trend influencing the design of dashboards is mobile business intelligence. With the advances in mobile communication technology, today's executives want to be in touch with their organizational performance anytime, anywhere. Further, most of today's knowledge workers are increasingly mobile in terms of the device they're using—during a workday, one may use a desktop computer, a laptop, a smartphone, or an iPad. Hence, dashboard vendors are offering solutions for multiple devices and screen sizes so that the user can get the same information regardless of location and device used to access the most current information, facilitating business decisions based on real-time data.

One of the growing trends of mobile business intelligence (BI) is the coupling of location information that can easily be gained from GPS or Wi-Fi networks. This capability can be an important part of an innovative BI solution, since location-relevant information can be delivered to the device based on its location. For example, details about particular people, such as customers, colleagues, and staff, within a particular vicinity can be sent to the device in addition to location-specific reports. With such capabilities, the mobile device uses its data generation capabilities to enhance the intelligence of the user.

VISUAL ANALYTICS. As discussed in previous sections, business intelligence systems can provide business decision makers with a wide variety of analyses to support decision making. However, in the end, it is still the humans who have to interpret the output from these systems. With the growing complexity of the underlying data (such as multiple dimensions, including spatial dimensions), interpreting the outputs becomes extremely challenging. **Visual analytics** (sometimes called **visual data discovery**) is the combination of various analysis techniques and interactive visualization to solve complex problems. By combining human intelligence and reasoning capabilities with technology's retrieval and analysis capabilities, visual analytics can help in decision making, as the strengths of both the human and the machine are merged. With the humans' ability to make sense of "noisy" data, unexpected patterns or relationships in the data can be discovered, and results of complex queries can be quickly interpreted. Visual analytics is used in a variety of settings, ranging from homeland security to disaster relief.

GEOGRAPHIC INFORMATION SYSTEMS. One type of visualization system that is growing in popularity and is frequently incorporated into digital dashboards is called a **geographic information system (GIS)**. A GIS is a system for creating, storing, analyzing, and managing geographically referenced information. In other words, a GIS captures various characteristics about geographic locations, allowing these characteristics to be coupled with other data to support querying, analysis, and decision making. For example, a GIS could link the square footage of commercial real estate to its exact location in terms of latitude and longitude. These data could be paired with population density, average incomes of people living within an area, travel accessibility (e.g., interstate highways and major thoroughfares), proximity to services (e.g., fire, police, restaurants, public transportation stops), or virtually any other characteristic. A business such as a restaurant chain could use this information to identify optimal locations for the placement of new locations. On a personal level, you probably frequently interact with GISs. For example, when you're accessing Google Maps to search for a restaurant in your town, you can view geographic data (such as the map or the satellite image) as well as attribute data about restaurants, including name, address, opening hours, and customer reviews.

Businesses typically face many decisions with a spatial dimension: Where are my customers located? Where is the best location to open a new store? Which areas should be included in the next mailing? How far are my customers willing to drive? A GIS can help to create models used to answer questions such as where a company such as Levi Strauss should add authorized resellers, or how, where, and what kinds of fertilizers farmers should apply, enabling precision farming (see Table 6.10 for various industry uses of GISs).

Using GISs, analysts can combine geographic, demographic, and other data for locating target customers, finding optimal site locations, or determining the right product mix at different locations; additionally, GISs can perform a variety of analyses, such as market share analysis and competitor analysis. Cities, counties, and states also use GISs for aiding in infrastructure design and zoning issues (e.g., where should the new elementary school be located?). For the various geospatial aspects you can map with GISs, refer to Table 6.11. How does a GIS help in analyzing geospatial and related data? Typically, a GIS provides a user with a blank map of an area. The user can then add information stored in different **layers**, each resembling a transparency containing different information about the area; for example, one layer may contain all roads, another

TABLE 6.10 Various Industry Uses of GISs

Industry	Sample Uses
Agriculture	Analyze crop yield by location, soil erosion, or differences in fertilizer needs (precision farming)
Banking	Identify lucrative areas for marketing campaigns
Disaster response	Analyze historical events, set up evacuation plans, and identify areas most likely to be affected by disasters
Environment and conservation	Analyze wildlife behaviors or influences of climate change
Insurance	Risk analysis (e.g., earthquake insurance)
Government	Urban planning, zoning, and census planning
Law enforcement	Analyze high-crime areas
Marine biology	Track movements of fish swarms
Media	Create maps to visualize locations of events and analyze circulation
Mining and drilling	Locate potential areas for extraction of natural resources
Real estate	Create maps to visualize locations of properties
Retail	Analyze sales, inventory, customers, and so on by location; identify new retail locations; and visualize and present business data
Transportation and logistics	Route planning

Source: Based on ESRI, http://www.esri.com/what-is-gis/who-uses-gis.

KEY PLAYERS

SAS, MicroStrategy, and Other Business Intelligence Leaders

With business intelligence, as with many other applications, the old mantra "garbage in, garbage out" applies, and any output from business intelligence applications is only as good as the inputs the applications are working with. Thus, it comes as no surprise that, in addition to "pure play" business intelligence (BI) vendors, those companies that support collection and storage of the data also venture into providing business intelligence applications. Whereas pure plays such as SAS and MicroStrategy are independent companies, companies such as SAP, IBM, Oracle, and Microsoft have gained prominence in the BI market through acquisitions.

Beginning as a project to analyze agricultural research data at North Carolina State University, SAS expanded into various other industries and geographic regions. SAS now has more than 13,000 employees and provides a variety of solutions related to business intelligence, including customer intelligence, financial intelligence, and supply chain intelligence, for industries ranging from casinos to utilities.

MicroStrategy, the other major independent player in the BI arena, started out as a company offering data mining tools for businesses. Its innovativeness led to MicroStrategy becoming one of the first companies offering mobile BI solutions. Today, MicroStrategy is used by major companies ranging from McDonald's to the U.S. Postal Service.

Given organizations' increasing interest in business intelligence solutions, other players in the enterprise software market started a shopping frenzy, so as to be able to offer end-to-end solutions to their customers. For example, as much input into business intelligence applications comes from enterprise systems (see Chapter 7), the German enterprise software company SAP purchased BI vendor Business Objects to provide self-service BI functionality to its users. Similarly, one of SAP's biggest contenders in the enterprise systems market, Oracle, is complementing its enterprise systems offerings with BI solutions after having acquired Hyperion in 2007.

IBM was traditionally known as a hardware company, but has since morphed into a provider of a variety of systems supporting diverse business processes and industries. Similar to SAP and Oracle, IBM jumped on the BI bandwagon by acquiring an independent BI vendor, Cognos. Like IBM, software behemoth Microsoft has nearly uncountable product offerings focusing on diverse markets. Microsoft's BI solutions are designed with the end user in mind, and provide a familiar environment for many office workers.

Beyond these intelligent giants, various other companies focus on specific aspects related to business intelligence. While the companies presented here have emerged to become leaders in the overall business intelligence market, various specialized vendors should nevertheless remain on companies' watch lists.

Based on:
IBM. (n.d.). Business intelligence. Retrieved May 29, 2014, from http://www-03.ibm.com/software/products/en/category/business-intelligence.

Microsoft. (n.d.). Microsoft Business Intelligence. Retrieved May 29, 2014, from http://www.microsoft.com/en-us/server-cloud/solutions/business-intelligence/default.aspx.

MicroStrategy. (n.d.). About MicroStrategy. Retrieved May 29, 2014, from http://www.microstrategy.com/us/about-us/overview.

Oracle. (n.d.). Oracle Business Analytics. Retrieved May 29, 2014, from http://www.oracle.com/us/solutions/business-analytics/overview/index.htm.

SAP. (n.d.). Business intelligence. Retrieved May 29, 2014, from http://www.sap.com/pc/analytics/business-intelligence.html.

SAS. (n.d.). Business intelligence software. Retrieved May 29, 2014, from http://www.sas.com/en_us/software/business-intelligence.html.

TABLE 6.11 Various Ways of Representing Geospatial Data

Mapping	Example
Features and patterns (i.e., distribution of features)	Earthquake epicenters (features) and areas where the hazard may be highest (patterns)
Quantities	The number of young families with a high income in a census district
Densities	Number of high-income families per square mile in a census district
What's inside	Does a luxury real estate development fall within a 15-minute driving radius of a store?
What's nearby	How many Starbucks stores are within 5 miles of my new coffee shop?
Change	How have store sales changed after a large ad campaign?

Source: Based on ESRI, http://www.esri.com/what-is-gis/overview.

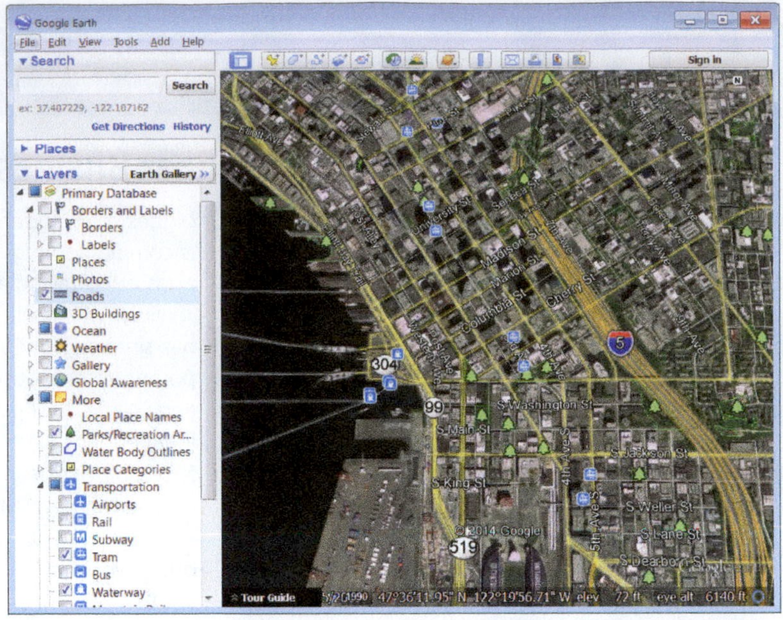

FIGURE 6.26

Google Earth uses layers to display information related to a specific geographical area.
Source: Courtesy of Google, Inc.

layer may contain ZIP code boundaries, and yet other layers may contain floodplains, average household sizes, locations of coffee shops, or other information of interest (in Google Earth, you can view various layers, such as roads, traffic patterns, weather, earthquakes, golf courses, and so on; see Figure 6.26). Adding or removing those layers helps to view the relevant information needed to answer questions that have a spatial dimension.

WHO'S GOING MOBILE

AroundMe

Mobile devices and location are a perfect match for each other; most people carry their smartphones wherever they go, enabling them to receive useful information specific to their current location. Search engines such as Google or Bing provide users with information on nearby restaurants, ATMs, post offices, attractions, and so on. Review sites such as Yelp help users to find restaurants located in their vicinity. Online mapping services help users locate their position, and provide directions to wherever they want to go. These and other services make smartphones an ever-more-useful companion when being away from home or the office.

One of the most popular location-based services is a mobile app called AroundMe. Launched in 2008, in the dawn of smartphone-enabled location apps, AroundMe has become a leader in providing local, location-based search results of all kinds. The app allows users to quickly find points of interest, including restaurants, hotels, theaters, parking, hospitals, and many more. The app pinpoints the user's location using the smartphone's global positioning system (GPS) capabilities, and a list of local businesses matching the user's search is displayed, along with options to get directions or find out more information.

From a business perspective, the real power of these services is in their ability to detect and leverage users' exact geographic location, along with having a pretty good idea regarding what the user is currently interested in. A user doing a search for "hotels" using the AroundMe app, for example, is likely looking for a place to stay. Using this information, businesses can use very targeted marketing to their advantage—providing this user a discount for choosing a certain hotel chain, for example. AroundMe was the first mobile app to make use of such an ad platform, called Google Dynamic Mobile Advertisement. These and other innovations have allowed AroundMe to expand its user base, and the company now offers apps on the iOS, Android, and Windows Phone platforms.

Based on:

Anonymous. (2014). About us—AroundMe. *AroundMe*. Retrieved May 29, 2014, from http://www.aroundmeapp.com/about-us.

One question that organizations often face is where the customers come from. In order to answer this question, organizations typically use data from survey respondents (or the cashier asks for customers' ZIP codes); this data is then geocoded (i.e., transformed into coordinates) to create a layer containing customer information that can then be added to a map. Comparing customers' locations with the location of one's business can help in deciding whether the store has the optimal location or whether opening a new store would be warranted. Relatedly, trade area analysis helps to assess where customers are coming from by combining location information with, for example, drive time information to determine if certain areas are underserved or if two stores' trade areas overlap. Another way to visualize geospatial data is by using thematic maps. Thematic maps color code data that are aggregated for specific geographic regions. For example, a thematic map could display the median household income in different blocks, or it could display average household sizes, helping a business to identify areas with the most promising target population; similarly, an insurance company could use GISs to determine where certain crimes (such as car theft) most frequently occur.

In addition to helping in analysis, GISs are also increasingly used by governments and organizations to effectively communicate with stakeholders. For example, many retail chains such as Best Buy and Walmart incorporate map-based store locators into their Web sites. When searching for a store by city, state, or ZIP code, the Web site returns a map showing the store's location (geographic data), along with attribute data such as distance, street address, phone number, and opening hours. Similarly, organizations use output from GISs to communicate to their stockholders about expansion plans, retail store density, and the like.

Clearly, GISs, like all the systems described here, are providing organizations with business intelligence to better compete in the digital world.

INDUSTRY ANALYSIS

Healthcare

Do you remember the times when your doctor wrote a prescription and the handwriting was worse than your professor's, making you wonder how the pharmacist could ever decipher it and dispense the correct drugs? If you recently went to a doctor, you may have noticed that information systems have had a huge impact on the healthcare field; indeed, health informatics has become a key focus of healthcare providers, insurance companies, and governments. Now, many doctors carry laptops or tablets, allowing them to digitally store any diagnosis, facilitating the sharing of information between the physician, nurses, and even your medical insurance provider. In addition to providing access to electronic patient records, the laptop or tablet provides your physician access to medical and drug information, as offered by the *Physician's Desk Reference* Web site (www.pdr.net), where your physician can obtain the latest information about drugs and clinical guidelines or check interactions between different drugs.

Information systems have also tremendously changed the diagnosis and monitoring of patients. For example, modern electroencephalogram (EEG) and electrocardiogram (EKG) devices heavily depend on computer technology, and, as the name implies, computed tomography (used to produce images of internal organs) could not be performed without computer technology. Even diagnostic tests such as X-rays now use digital technology, allowing the doctor to digitally enhance the image for improved diagnosis or to electronically transmit the image to a remote specialist. Following the diagnosis of a serious condition, technology can even help in the operating room. For example, many modern clinics use surgical robots and endoscopes for delicate procedures such as neurosurgery or gastrointestinal surgery. Taken a step further, such systems can be used for what is referred to as telemedicine, including remote diagnosis and remote surgery. Whereas traditionally a patient had to travel thousands of miles to visit a specialized surgeon, many surgeries can now be performed remotely, reducing the strain on the patient and potentially saving precious time. Further, telemedicine applications can be used for remote locations, battlefields, or even prisons, reducing costs for transporting patients and improving care.

Just as physicians, insurance companies, and healthcare providers are turning to information systems to improve business processes and better serve patients' needs, consumers are increasingly using the Internet for health information. For example, WebMD is one of the most popular Web sites providing health-related information, priding itself on having high-quality, timely, and unbiased information. In addition to objective information, people use social media to obtain information beyond what's published by the experts. Specifically, people seeking physician and hospital rankings or recommendations frequent blogs, health-related discussion forums, or review sites such as ratemd.com or Angie's List (angieslist.com). Further, major search engines such as Microsoft's Bing are constantly refining their search algorithms to provide the most relevant information to health-related queries. Regardless of whether you're visiting your doctor about a condition or for a routine checkup, or if you need more information about what your doctor is telling you, various information systems are likely to play a major role.

Questions

1. Discuss the benefits and drawbacks of online medical records.
2. Computer-aided diagnosis can replace years of experience, providing opportunities for young, inexperienced physicians. Contrast the benefits and drawbacks for the patients and the physicians.
3. Will there be a place for physicians without computer skills in the future? Why or why not?

Based on:

Anonymous. (n.d.). What is telemedicine? *American Telemedicine Association*. Retrieved May 29, 2014, from http://www.americantelemed.org/about-telemedicine/what-is-telemedicine.

Anonymous. (2010, April 15). Consumers increasingly turning to Internet, social media for health care information. *iHealthBeat*. Retrieved May 29, 2014, from http://www.ihealthbeat.org/insight/2010/consumers-increasingly-turning-to-internet-social-media-for-health-care-information.

Key Points Review

1. ***Describe the concept of business intelligence and how databases serve as a foundation for gaining business intelligence.*** Businesses need business intelligence to quickly respond to external threats and opportunities arising from unstable market conditions, fierce competition, short product life cycles, government regulation, fickle customers, and Big Data. Organizations use databases to capture and manage the data that can later be used as input to business intelligence applications. A database is a collection of related data organized in a way that facilitates data searches, and contains entities, attributes, records, and tables. A DBMS is a software application with which you create, store, organize, and retrieve data from a single database or several databases. The data within a database must be adequately organized so that it is possible to store and retrieve information effectively. To support more effective business processes, businesses use online transaction processing. Data from operational systems serve as an input to informational systems. Master data management helps organizations to arrive at a "single version of the truth" to gather business intelligence; data warehouses and data marts support the integration and analysis of large data sets.
2. ***Explain the three components of business intelligence: information and knowledge discovery, business analytics, and information visualization.*** Information and knowledge discovery tools are used to discover "hidden" relationships in data. Ad hoc query tools allow decision makers to run queries whenever needed. OLAP tools offer the ability to perform complex multidimensional queries. Data mining is used for association discovery and clustering and classification. Unstructured data analysis is used to extract information from textual documents. Business analytics augments business intelligence by using statistical analysis and predictive modelling to identify trends or predict business outcomes. Decision support and intelligent systems are used to support human and automated decision making. A DSS is designed to be an interactive decision aid. Intelligent systems such as expert systems, neural networks, and intelligent agents work to emulate and enhance human capabilities. Knowledge management systems are a collection of technology-based tools that enable the generation, storage, sharing, and management of knowledge assets. Visualization refers to the display of complex data relationships using a variety of graphical methods. Results of complex analyses as well as key performance indicators are displayed on digital dashboards, which are often used to provide decision makers with the right information in an easy-to-understand way. Visual analytics combines the human visual system and analysis techniques to aid in the analysis of complex relationships and make sense of "noisy" data. GISs aid in storing, analyzing, and managing geographically referenced information, such as for locating target customers or finding optimal store locations.

Key Terms

ad hoc query 221
algorithm 229
artificial intelligence (AI) 228
association discovery 223
attribute 214
augmented reality 231
Big Data 211
bot 230
business analytics 226
business intelligence 210
business rules 216
buyer agent 230
classification 224
clickstream data 225
clustering 224
competitive intelligence 224
continuous planning process 212
data cleansing 220
data dictionary 216
data-driven organizations 210
data mart 220
data mining 223
data mining agent 230
data model 216
data reduction 223
data type 216
data warehouse 219
decision support system (DSS) 226
destructive agent 230
digital dashboard 235
dimension 222
drill down 222
drill-down report 221
entity 214
exception report 221
expert system (ES) 229
explicit knowledge asset 232
extraction, transformation, and loading 220
fact 222
form 216
fuzzy logic 230
geographic information system (GIS) 238
in-memory computing 222
inferencing 230
informational system 219
intelligent agent 230
intelligent system 229
key-indicator report 221
knowledge assets 232
knowledge management 231
knowledge management system 233
knowledge portal 234
layer 238
machine learning 229
master data 219
master data management 219
measure 222
model 227
monitoring and sensing agent 230
neural network 229
NoSQL 216
OLAP cube 222
OLAP server 222
online analytical processing (OLAP) 222
online transaction processing (OLTP) 218
operational system 218
predictive modeling 226
query 217
RDBMS 216
record 214
report 217
report generator 217
roll up 222
rule 230
scheduled report 221
semistructured data 211
sentiment analysis 224
sequence discovery 224
shopping bot 230
slicing and dicing 222
social network analysis 234
stickiness 225
structured data 211
Structured Query Language (SQL) 217
table 214
tacit knowledge asset 232
text mining 224
unstructured data 211
user agent 230
visual analytics 237
visual data discovery 237
visualization 235
Web content mining 224
Web crawler 230
Web spider 230
Web usage mining 225
what-if analysis 226

MyMISLab™

Go to **mymislab.com** to complete the problems marked with this icon .

Review Questions

6-1. How can a continuous planning process help businesses respond to external threats and opportunities?

6-2. Describe the differences between entities, tables, rows, and attributes in a database.

6-3. What is the importance of master data management?

6-4. What are the advantages of a DBMS?

6-5. Explain the differences between OLAP and OLTP.

6-6. Describe how OLAP enables a user to conduct multidimensional queries.

6-7. Explain the difference between clustering and classification.

6-8. What is the relationship between measures and dimensions?

6-9. Describe and give examples of two types of Web mining.

6-10. What is a Web site's stickiness, and why is it important?

6-11. Explain the purpose of a model within a DSS.

6-12. Describe four types of intelligent agents. How can they be used to benefit organizations?

6-13. What is a knowledge management system, and what types of technologies make up a comprehensive system?

6-14. How can visual analytics be used to gain business intelligence and improve decision making?

6-15. What is the purpose of using layers in GIS applications?

Self-Study Questions

6-16. In an RDBMS, an entity is represented as a(n) ______________.
A. attribute
B. table
C. row
D. association

6-17. A(n) ______________ report provides a summary of critical information on a recurring schedule.
A. scheduled
B. exception
C. key indicator
D. drill-down

6-18. In order to swiftly respond to a highly competitive and rapidly changing environment, organizations utilize a ______________.
A. continuous planning process
B. structured decision-making process
C. decision support process
D. decision-making process

6-19. To determine the likelihood of new customers to default on a loan, a manager in a bank would typically use ______________.
A. association discovery
B. sequence discovery
C. classification
D. clustering

6-20. Web usage mining entails analyzing ______________.
A. clickstream data
B. page content
C. associations among sets of items
D. unstructured data

6-21. Market share analysis is typically used by the ______________ function of an organization.
A. marketing
B. accounting
C. production
D. management science

6-22. Examples of the types of activities that can be supported by ESs include all of the following except ______________.
A. payroll calculations
B. financial planning
C. machine configuration
D. medical diagnosis

6-23. ______________ agents keep track of key information such as inventory levels, notifying the users when conditions change.
A. User
B. Buyer
C. Monitoring and sensing
D. Data mining

6-24. What is true about knowledge management?
A. As baby boomers retire at an increasing rate, knowledge management is helping organizations capture their knowledge.
B. A knowledge management system is not a single technology but a collection of technology-based tools.
C. Finding the right technology to manage knowledge assets is much easier than identifying what knowledge is needed, why it is needed, and who has this knowledge.
D. All of the above are true.

6-25. Which of the following is an example of attribute data commonly used in GIS applications?
A. structured data
B. longitude
C. trade area
D. annual sales

Answers are on page 246.

Problems and Exercises

6-26. Match the following terms with the appropriate definitions:

i. Social network analysis
ii. Measures
iii. Master data
iv. Web content mining
v. Continuous planning process
vi. Data mining
vii. Expert system
viii. Digital dashboard
ix. Geographic information system
x. DSS

a. An information system designed to analyze and store spatially referenced data
b. A special-purpose information system designed to mimic human expertise by manipulating knowledge (understanding acquired through experience and extensive learning) rather than simply information
c. A technique that attempts to find groups of people who work together, to find people who don't collaborate but should, or to find experts in particular subject areas
d. A set of methods used to find hidden predictive relationships in a data set
e. A strategic business planning process involving continuous monitoring and adjusting of business processes to enable rapid reaction to changing business conditions
f. The values or numbers a user wants to analyze
g. A special-purpose information system designed to support organizational decision making primarily at the managerial level of an organization
h. Extracting textual information from Web documents

i. A user interface visually representing summary information about a business's health, often from multiple sources
j. The data that are deemed most important in the operation of a business

6-27. Interview a top-level executive within an organization with which you are familiar and find out the organization's most important external threats. Can business intelligence help to respond to these threats? If so, how; if not, why not?

6-28. Visit www.amazon.com and search for a product of interest to you. What attributes are likely stored in Amazon.com's database?

6-29. Using a search engine, enter the key word "data warehousing." Who are the large vendors in this industry? What type of solutions do they offer to their clients? Do you see any common trends in data warehousing?

6-30. Visit CNN Money (http://money.cnn.com/calculator/retirement/retirement-need) on the Web to plan your retirement using a DSS. What did you learn? To what extent is the DSS useful in planning your retirement? If you browse through CNN Money, what other interesting stuff do you find?

6-31. Interview a top-level executive within an organization with which you are familiar and determine the extent to which the organization utilizes tools for information visualization or digital dashboards. Does this individual utilize these tools in any way? Why or why not? Which executives do utilize such tools?

6-32. Think about the junk mail you receive every day in your postal mail. Which mailings do you believe to be a result of data mining? How have the companies chosen you for their targeted mailings?

6-33. Using any program you choose, find or create a template that you could use in the future to determine monthly payments on a car loan. Compare your template with the one at www.bankrate.com/brm/auto-loan-calculator.asp. Would you have categorized the program you used to create this template as a DSS before doing this exercise?

6-34. Describe your experiences with ESs or go to www.exsys.com or www.easydiagnosis.com on the Web and spend some time interacting with their demonstration systems. Now choose a problem that you know a lot about and would like to build your own ES for. Describe the problem and list the questions you would need to ask someone in order to make a recommendation.

6-35. Go out onto the Web and compare three shopping bots for a product you are interested in (e.g., www.mysimon.com, www.shopzilla.com, www.shopping.com, or www.pricegrabber.com). Did the different agents find the same information, or were there any differences? Did you prefer one over the others? If so, why?

6-36. Have you seen or used ad hoc, exception, key-indicator, and/or drill-down reports? What is the purpose of each report? Who produces and who uses the reports? Do any of these reports look or sound familiar from your work experience?

6-37. Interview an IS manager within an organization. What types of information and knowledge discovery tools does the organization use? Was there an increase or decrease in the past few years? What predictions does this manager have regarding the future of these systems? Do you agree? Prepare a 10-minute presentation to the class on your findings.

6-38. For your university, identify several examples of various knowledge assets and rate these assets on their value to the university on a 10-point scale (1 = low value to 10 = high value).

6-39. Examine your university's Web site to identify examples where a knowledge management system could be used or is being used to help provide improved services to students.

6-40. How do you prefer your desired information to be presented? Do you use any type of visualization tools? If so, which ones?

6-41. Visit Google maps (http://maps.google.com) and try out the different layers provided. What other information would you like to see? Are there any publicly available mashups that offer this information as layers on top of Google Maps?

Application Exercises

Note: The existing data files referenced in these exercises are available on the book's Web site: www.pearsonhighered.com/valacich.

Spreadsheet Application: Travel Loan Facility

6-42. A new aspect of the business has been added to Campus Travel. Students can apply for a loan to help pay for their travels. However, loans for travel are available only to students who are traveling outside the country for at least two weeks. Since the costs for this type of international travel differ depending on how you travel, where you stay, and what you do at the destination, different loan packages are available. For a month in Europe, you have decided to take out a loan. You have already taken a look at several offers but are unsure whether you can afford it. Set up a spreadsheet to calculate the payments per month for the following situations:

- Two weeks in Eastern Europe; Price: $2,000; Interest Rate: 5.5%; Time: one year
- Two weeks in Western Europe; Price: $3,000; Interest Rate: 6.0%; Time: one year
- Three weeks in Eastern Europe; Price: $3,000; Interest Rate: 6.5%; Time: two years

- Three weeks in Western Europe; Price: $3,500; Interest Rate: 5.5%; Time: two years
- Four weeks in Eastern Europe; Price: $4,000; Interest Rate: 6.0%; Time: two years
- Four weeks in Western Europe; Price: $5,000; Interest Rate: 6.5%; Time: three years

Once you have calculated the payments, calculate the total amount to be paid for each option as well as the total interest you would pay over the course of the loan. Make sure to use formulas for all calculations and print out a professionally formatted page displaying the results and a page displaying the formulas. (Hint: In Microsoft Excel, use the "PMT" function in the category "Financial" to calculate the payments. Use Ctrl+` [grave accent] to switch between formula and data views; calculate the number of payments before using the formula.)

Database Application: Tracking Regional Office Performance at Campus Travel

6-43. The general manager wants to know which offices were most profitable during the previous year and asks you to prepare several reports. In the file FY2012.mdb, you find information about the offices, sales agents, and destinations. Use the report wizard to generate the following reports:

- List of all sales agents grouped by office (including total number of agents per office)
- List of all sales agents for each destination (grouped by destination, including total number of agents)
- Destinations sold by each sales agent (including total number of destinations)

Hint: You will need to generate the necessary queries before creating the reports.

Team Work Exercise

Net Stats: The Demise of Broadcast TV

Recent studies of the TV industry indicate that it is in trouble. More and more people are choosing not to watch TV in the conventional "appointment" way. According to Nielsen, in 2011, 288 million people in the United States watched TV/video content via their TV set, compared with 143 million who watched content on the Internet, 111 million who watched time-shifted content, and 30 million who watched content on their mobile devices. A late 2013 survey by Nielson revealed that these numbers had shifted, in general moving from traditional TV to Internet and mobile TV viewing: 286 million watched TV via a TV set, 174 million watched time-shifted TV, and 101 million watched content using a mobile device. These changes tend to be especially strong in young people, with 18- to 24-year-olds' broadcast TV consumption dropping steadily from 2011 to 2013.

Questions and Exercises

6-44. Search the Web for the most up-to-date statistics. Try to find the statistics for other countries as well.

6-45. As a team, interpret these numbers. What is striking/important about these statistics? What may be the reason for differences between countries?

6-46. How have the numbers changed since 2013?

6-47. Using your spreadsheet software of choice, create a graph/figure most effectively visualizing the statistics/changes you consider most important.

Based on:

Anonymous. (2014, March 10). Are young people watching less TV? *MarketingCharts.com.* Retrieved May 29, 2014, from http://www.marketingcharts.com/wp/television/are-young-people-watching-less-tv-24817/.

Anonymous. (2014, March 5). An era of growth: The cross-platform report. *Nielsen.* Retrieved May 29, 2014, from http://www.nielsen.com/us/en/reports/2014/an-era-of-growth-the-cross-platform-report.html.

Answers to the Self-Study Questions

6-16. B, p. 216	**6-17.** C, p. 221	**6-18.** A, p. 212	**6-19.** C, p. 224	**6-20.** A, p. 225
6-21. A, p. 228	**6-22.** A, p. 229	**6-23.** C, p. 230	**6-24.** D, p. 232	**6-25.** D, p. 238

CASE 1 NSA: National Surveillance Agency?

In the 1950s, shortly after the end of World War II, President Harry S. Truman oversaw the organization of a secret security and intelligence organization, tasked with gathering and analyzing intelligence data in defense of the interests and operations of the United States and its government. The organization—named the National Security Agency (NSA)—has since grown to become one of the largest intelligence organizations in the world, with an estimated workforce of around 40,000 employees and annual budget of nearly US$11 billion (these types of information about the NSA are classified). The NSA has been involved in gathering intelligence on a wide range of issues and individuals, from the Vietnam War to Martin Luther King, Jr. to the post-9/11 War on Terror. By design, many of the NSA's successes are classified and not known to the general public, but the agency has been credited with providing key intelligence in support of major military and investigatory operations over the past several decades.

In its relentless pursuit of intelligence to defend U.S. national interests, the NSA has embraced technology and the vast amounts of digital information available across the globe. In late 2013, a series of disclosures of classified internal NSA documents revealed the extent of the NSA's spying activities. Most of these disclosures were provided by a former NSA contractor named Edward Snowden. These documents revealed that the NSA regularly intercepts the telephone and Internet communications of over a billion people worldwide. The NSA tracks the locations of hundreds of millions of cell phones per day. The organization reportedly has access to at least some communications made via services provided by AOL, Google, Microsoft, Facebook, and Yahoo, and collects hundreds of millions of contacts lists from personal e-mail and instant messaging accounts every year. The NSA also collects and stores cell phone call records from major cell phone providers. These surveillance activities have not been limited to countries considered to be enemies of the United States—they include longtime friendly countries such as France, Germany, and Spain. Perhaps most unsettling for U.S. citizens is the fact that NSA surveillance has also been targeted at U.S. citizens within U.S. borders, which appears to many as a clear violation of the Foreign Intelligence Surveillance Act of 1978—a law designed to limit the practice of mass surveillance in the United States.

Given that much of the NSA's activities are classified, it is hard to know how effective these massive surveillance practices have been in defending U.S. national interests and U.S. citizens. To some extent, many citizens likely expect the government to engage in spying and other intelligence-gathering practices to protect the public against terrorism, crime, or other dangers. To this end, the NSA reportedly provides foreign intelligence to the Central Intelligence Agency (CIA) regarding terrorist activities, and domestic intelligence to the Drug Enforcement Administration (DEA) and Federal Bureau of Investigation (FBI) regarding drug and other criminal activities. But just how much intelligence-gathering the NSA should engage in, and from whom, is a matter that has come under strong debate. Judging by the public outcry in response to the revelations from Edward Snowden's leaked documents, many people, both within and outside of the United States, believe that the NSA has gone too far.

In some sense, the NSA surveillance activities are little more than advanced business intelligence initiatives. In the modern world, we leave digital footprints in nearly all of our daily activities, from e-mail to text messages to phone calls to social media. The NSA has developed methods to collect and store this data, much to the consternation of many people now learning of these practices. But many large businesses engage in similar activities, perhaps not on the same scale, but with equal disregard for the privacy of the people being tracked. Google, Facebook, and many online advertising networks that you have likely never heard of go to great lengths to record where we go and what we are watching, listening to, and reading. These activities provide powerful business opportunities for segmented marketing, and they are the revenue source supporting many of the online services that we enjoy for free.

So how do we balance the privacy issues caused by surveillance—both by governments and online companies—with the valid purposes that these organizations use to justify their activities? Would you rather that the U.S. government miss the opportunity to stop a terrorist organization before it strikes because the NSA stopped monitoring electronic communications? Would you be willing to pay a yearly subscription fee to Google in order to use its search engine or e-mail services? Would you be willing to pay a fee each time you "friended" someone or posted a new photo album on Facebook? These are extreme examples, but they highlight the conflict inherent to any discussion that tries to weigh privacy against business intelligence practices. For governments and companies to succeed and provide the services we expect, we may need to become more comfortable with giving up some of our privacy.

Questions

6-48. Do you think that the NSA has gone too far in its surveillance activities? Why or why not?

6-49. What are the pros and cons inherent to data collection for business or national intelligence?

6-50. Propose a set of guidelines for the NSA to direct its surveillance activities in the future.

Based on:

National Security Agency. (2014, May 27). In *Wikipedia, The Free Encyclopedia*. Retrieved May 30, 2014, from http://en.wikipedia.org/w/index.php?title=National_Security_Agency&oldid=610317412.

Shane, S. (2013, November 2). No morsel too minuscule for all-consuming N.S.A. *The New York Times*. Retrieved May 29, 2014, from http://www.nytimes.com/2013/11/03/world/no-morsel-too-minuscule-for-all-consuming-nsa.html.

CASE 2 Web Analytics

In the 1990s, Josh James enrolled in an information systems class as part of his business management and entrepreneurship degree program. Being not particularly excited about the topic, Josh sat near the back of the room. During the first class period, Josh noticed a student near the front of the class who was easily answering all of the questions, and he decided he wanted to get to know him. His name was John Pestana and they quickly became friends. John—a technology whiz with a knack for spinning Web code—suggested that he and Josh start building Web sites for companies, and a partnership was born. As their student-run business grew amidst the dot-com craze of the late 1990s, their clients began to ask about whether their fancy new Web sites were drawing any more Web traffic. The two young entrepreneurs immediately recognized a compelling business opportunity, and they soon founded Omniture, a Web analytics company that quickly grew to dominate the Web analytics market. With innovative analytics tools, Omniture attracted many large companies, including Walmart, Comcast, NBC Universal, and Hyatt. In 2006, Omniture went public, and was the number-two performing technology initial public offering (IPO) that year. Three years later, Omniture was acquired by technology giant Adobe Systems for US$1.8 billion. Adobe continues to develop the Web analytics tools, which have since been integrated into the company's suite of online marketing solutions, the Adobe Marketing Cloud.

Web analytics is the measurement, collection, analysis, and reporting of Web traffic data, with the goal of understanding and optimizing Web usage. The key features of most Web analytics tools are enabled by a small bit of programming code that is embedded in each of the pages of a Web site. As a user navigates from page to page, various pieces of information about the user are collected. These include metadata such as the type of browser (Safari vs. Chrome vs. Internet Explorer), the type of device (mobile vs. desktop), or the viewable resolution of the user's screen; browsing data such as how long the user stays on each page or where the user clicks; and navigation path data, such as which page the user came from or how many total pages the user has viewed within the Web site. The data are collected anonymously and aggregated for later analysis. For popular sites like Walmart.com or Comcast .net, Web analytics software can collect millions of points of data within a relatively short amount of time.

Many companies employ entire teams whose sole purpose is to analyze Web analytics data. These analytics data can be a goldmine of valuable information that a company can use to inform strategic decisions regarding its own Web site. Consider the value of such information to a major online retailer like Zappos.com. Using analytics data, Zappos' analysts could study the browsing behaviors of thousands of different users to identify potential improvements to their Web site. They might find that users get stuck on a certain type of page and identify changes to the menu structure to improve the navigation. They may find that many users add items to their cart but exit the site without completing their order when they are prompted to create a user account. This discovery could lead them to move the account creation process to a different point in the checkout flow, or perhaps even make account creation optional. These are only a few of the nearly infinite potential discoveries that Web analytics data can help discover.

Given the large mass of Web analytics data collected by a site like Walmart.com, there is a high potential for information overload. Thus, a key feature of successful Web analytics solutions is the ability for business users to filter data in helpful ways, allowing them to drill down into items of interest. Another way in which analytics platforms reduce information overload is through the use of easy-to-interpret graphical representations of the data. These range from simple bar charts and line graphs to shaded geographical maps and complex charts depicting users' flow through a navigational structure. These and many other information summarization methods make the vast amount of Web analytic data digestible so that business leaders can make informed, strategic decisions.

Web analytics is a prime example of business analytics in the digital age. For companies that conduct the majority of their business online, and in particular for retailers, entertainment hubs, and news providers, Web analytics data provide invaluable insight into the behavior of their users. Those companies that learn to effectively leverage those data can make significant changes that directly affect their bottom line.

Questions

6-51. Why do you think Omniture services were so popular, given the time period in which the company was founded?

6-52. Think of an online service (not retail) that you use frequently. How could this company use Web analytics data to improve its Web site and positively impact its business?

6-53. Do you think that Web analytics data capture is an invasion of privacy? Why or why not?

Based on:

Omniture. (2014, May 21). In *Wikipedia, The Free Encyclopedia*. Retrieved May 30, 2014, from http://en.wikipedia.org/w/index.php?title=Omniture&oldid=609554331.

Anonymous. (n.d.). Adobe Marketing Cloud. *Adobe*. Retrieved May 29, 2014, from http://www.adobe.com/solutions/digital-marketing.html.

Web analytics. (2014, May 28). In *Wikipedia, The Free Encyclopedia*. Retrieved May 30, 2014, from http://en.wikipedia.org/w/index.php?title=Web_analytics&oldid=610475657.

MyMISLab™

Go to **mymislab.com** for auto-graded writing questions as well as the following assisted-graded writing questions:

6-54. What is the meaning of support and confidence in the context of data mining?

6-55. Explain the difference between explicit and tacit knowledge.

References

Alavi, M., & Leidner, D. (1999). Knowledge management systems: Issues, challenges, and benefits. *Communications of the AIS, 1* (Article 7).

Awad, E. M., & Ghaziri, H. M. (2004). *Knowledge management.* Upper Saddle River, NJ: Pearson Prentice Hall.

Blumberg, R., & Atre, S. (2003, February 1). The problem with unstructured data. *Information Management Magazine*. Retrieved May 29, 2014, from http://www.information-management.com/issues/20030201/6287-1.html.

Business Objects. (2008). Business intelligence—Now more than ever. Retrieved May 29, 2014, from http://www.clariba.com/pdf/bi_nowmorethanever.pdf.

Business Objects. (n.d.). Expanding BI's role by including predictive analytics. Retrieved May 29, 2014 from http://www.infoworld.com/t/business-intelligenceanalytics/wp/expanding-bi%E2%80%99s-role-including-predictive-analytics-638.

Checkland, P. B. (1981). *Systems thinking, systems practice.* Chichester, UK: Wiley.

Clarke, K. C. (2011). *Getting started with geographic information systems* (5th ed.). Upper Saddle River, NJ: Pearson Prentice Hall.

Dumbill, E. (2012, January 19). Volume, velocity, variety: What you need to know about Big Data. *Forbes.* Retrieved May 29, 2014, from http://www.forbes.com/sites/oreillymedia/2012/01/19/volume-velocity-variety-what-you-need-to-know-about-big-data.

Economist Intelligence Unit. (2007). In search of clarity: Unravelling the complexities of executive decision-making. Retrieved May 29, 2014, from http://graphics.eiu.com/upload/EIU_In_search_of_clarity.pdf.

Economist Intelligence Unit. (2011). Big Data: Harnessing a game-changing asset. Retrieved May 29, 2014, from http://www.sas.com/resources/asset/SAS_BigData_final.pdf.

Harrison, G. (2010, August 26). 10 things you should know about NoSQL databases. *Techrepublic.* Retrieved May 29, 2014, from http://www.techrepublic.com/blog/10things/10-things-you-should-know-about-nosql-databases/1772.

Larose, D. T. (2006). *Data mining methods and models.* New York: Wiley.

Leonard, D. (2006, January 30). How to salvage your company's deep smarts. *CIO.com.* Retrieved May 29, 2014, from http://www.cio.com.au/article/182425/how_salvage_your_company_deep_smarts.

Levinson, M. (2010). Knowledge management definition and solutions. *CIO.com.* Retrieved May 29, 2014, from http://www.cio.com/article/40343/Knowledge_Management_Definition_and_Solutions.

Lo, C. P., & Yeung, A. K. W. (2007). *Concepts and techniques of geographic information systems* (2nd ed.). Upper Saddle River, NJ: Pearson Prentice Hall.

Malhotra, Y. (2005). Integrating knowledge management technologies in organizational business processes: Getting real time enterprises to deliver real business performance. *Journal of Knowledge Management, 9*(1), 7–28.

Markoff, J. (2012, June 25). How many computers to identify a cat? 16,000. *The New York Times.* Retrieved May 29, 2014, from http://www.nytimes.com/2012/06/26/technology/in-a-big-network-of-computers-evidence-of-machine-learning.html.

McAfee, A., & Brynjolfsson, E. (2012, October). Big Data: The management revolution. *HBR.org.* Retrieved May 28, 2014, from http://hbr.org/2012/10/big-data-the-management-revolution/ar/1.

Myatt, G. J., & Johnson, W. P. (2009). *Making sense of data: A practical guide to data visualization, advanced data mining methods, and applications.* New York: Wiley.

Nielsen, M (2014, April). Neural networks and deep learning. Retrieved May 28, 2014, from http://neuralnetworksanddeeplearning.com/index.html.

Pettey, C., & Stevens, H. (2009, January 15). Gartner reveals five business intelligence predictions for 2009 and beyond. *Gartner.* Retrieved May 29, 2014, from http://www.gartner.com/it/page.jsp?id=856714.

Redman, T. C. (2013, July 11). Are you data driven? Take a hard look in the mirror. *HBR.org.* Retrieved May 28, 2014, from http://blogs.hbr.org/2013/07/are-you-data-driven-take-a-har.

Saarenvirta, G. (2004). The untapped value of geographic information. *Business Intelligence Journal, 9*(1), 58–63.

Savitz, E. (2013, February 4). Big Data: Big hype? *Forbes.* Retrieved May 28, 2014, from http://www.forbes.com/sites/ciocentral/2013/02/04/big-data-big-hype.

Sharda, R., Delen, D., & Turban, E. (2014). *Business intelligence: A managerial perspective on analytics* (3rd ed.). Upper Saddle River, NJ: Pearson Prentice Hall.

Sharda, R., Delen, D., & Turban, E. (2015). *Business intelligence and analytics: Systems for decision support* (10th ed.). Upper Saddle River, NJ: Pearson Prentice Hall.

Sprague, R. H., Jr. (1980). A framework for the development of decision support systems. *MIS Quarterly, 4*(4), 1–26.

Stewart, D. (2013, May 1). Big content: The unstructured side of big data. *Gartner.* Retrieved May 28, 2014, from http://blogs.gartner.com/darin-stewart/2013/05/01/big-content-the-unstructured-side-of-big-data.

Stubbs, E. (2011). *The value of business analytics.* New York: Wiley.

Swoyer, S. (2007, September 5). Unstructured data: Attacking a myth. *TDWI.* Retrieved May 29, 2014, from http://tdwi.org/articles/2007/09/05/unstructured-data-attacking-a-myth.aspx.

Tapscott, D. (2008). Actionable insights for business decision makers. Retrieved May 29, 2014, from http://www.businessobjects.com/campaigns/forms/q109/apj/everyone/tapscott/BI_for_Decision_Makers.pdf.

7

Enhancing Business Processes Using Enterprise Information Systems

After reading this chapter, you will be able to do the following:

1. Explain core business processes that are common in organizations.
2. Describe what enterprise systems are and how they have evolved.
3. Describe enterprise resource planning systems and how they help to improve internal business processes.
4. Understand and utilize the keys to successfully implementing enterprise systems.

Preview

This chapter describes how companies are deploying enterprise-wide information systems to support and enable core business processes. Enterprise systems help to integrate various business activities, to increase coordination among various business departments and partners, to streamline and better manage interactions with customers, and to coordinate better with suppliers in order to more efficiently and effectively meet rapidly changing customer demands.

Companies continue to find that they need systems that span their entire organization to tie everything together. As a result, an understanding of enterprise systems is needed to succeed in today's competitive and ever-changing digital world. This chapter focuses on how organizations are utilizing enterprise-wide information systems to best support internal business processes. In Chapter 8, "Strengthening Business-to-Business Relationships Via Supply Chain and Customer Relationship Management," we focus on systems that support business processes spanning multiple organizations, critical in today's competitive global environment.

Managing in the Digital World: **Amazon.com**

Amazon.com has transformed how we shop. Having started as an online bookseller, Amazon.com now retails nearly everything, from kitchen appliances, to garden furniture, and even groceries. Amazon.com strives to provide superior product selection well beyond the biggest mall and big-box stores paired with the convenience of allowing customers to purchase the products with one click from their computer or mobile devices.

Founded and headed by Jeff Bezos, Amazon.com started in 1994 with a commitment to be "customer-centric." Amazon.com custom-tailors its home page with recommendations for books, music, and other products that may entice you; these recommendations are provided by analyzing your prior purchases and comparing them to those of millions of other customers with similar tastes. Amazon.com offers free shipping when you place orders over US$35. In certain cities, Amazon.com offers same-day delivery on items placed before a cutoff time. Amazon.com recently announced that it is working on a package delivery system that uses small, unmanned drones to deliver small packages within 30 minutes of placing the order.

In order to keep its competitive advantages, Amazon.com uses enterprise-wide information systems to optimize its business processes, ranging from acquiring and receiving the right goods at the right time from its suppliers to efficiently shipping physical goods to its customers. Amazon.com has built not only a network of dozens of North American and international fulfillment centers for its physical products, but also a number of sophisticated data centers to support its operations and offer various digital products and services. Now, Amazon.com even manages online stores and sales fulfillment for small and large companies, including Target.com, creating a win–win situation: For small, independent retailers, warehousing becomes a variable cost, and for Amazon.com, this creates additional revenue streams and helps to utilize excess capacity (Figure 7.1). Using its information systems (IS) infrastructure, Amazon.com offers Amazon Web Services (AWS), a solid and reliable IS infrastructure that allows companies to rent computing resources or storage space on an as-needed basis, or even deploy enterprise resource planning systems in the cloud.

FIGURE 7.1

Companies can rent Amazon.com's warehouse infrastructure on an as-needed basis.

Source: Bombaert Patrick/Fotolia.

Clearly, Amazon.com is more than a vibrant online store. Having designed an impressive IS infrastructure, Amazon.com is constantly developing new and innovative products and services that utilize this infrastructure. The AWS infrastructure has become so pervasive that researchers estimate that one-third of North American Web users visit a site hosted by AWS at least once per day, and that 1 percent of consumer Internet traffic in North America is sent or received by Amazon.com's servers. What the future holds for Amazon.com is inconceivable, given its current rate of innovation and growth.

After reading this chapter, you will be able to answer the following:

1. How do the core business processes differ for Amazon.com's various product and service offerings?
2. How do enterprise-wide information systems enable Amazon.com's strategy?
3. What benefits would an organization realize by running its enterprise resource planning system on Amazon.com's cloud computing infrastructure?

Based on:

Amazon.com. (2014, May 4). In *Wikipedia, The Free Encyclopedia*. Retrieved May 4, 2014, from http://en.wikipedia.org/w/index.php?title=Amazon.com&oldid=607043615.

Darrow, B. (2013, June 4). Amazon's cloud is how big again? *Gigaom.com*. Retrieved May 3, 2014, from http://gigaom.com/2013/06/04/amazons-cloud-is-how-big-again.

Stone, B. (2007, April 27). Sold on eBay, shipped by Amazon.com. *The New York Times*. Retrieved May 3, 2014, from http://www.nytimes.com/2007/04/27/technology/27amazon.html.

CORE BUSINESS PROCESSES AND ORGANIZATIONAL VALUE CHAINS

Traditionally, companies are organized around five distinct functional areas: marketing and sales, supply chain management, manufacturing and operations, accounting and finance, and human resources. Each of these functional areas is responsible for various well-defined business functions, such as marketing a product; sales forecasting; procuring raw materials and components; manufacturing goods; planning and budgeting; or recruiting, hiring, and training. Although this model suggests that a company can be regarded as being comprised of distinct independent silos, the different functional areas are highly interrelated to perform value-added activities (Figure 7.2). In fact, most business processes cross the boundaries of business functions, so it is helpful for managers to think in terms of business processes from a customer's (both internal and external) point of view.

Core Business Processes

In most cases, customers do not care about how things are being done; they care only that things are being done to their satisfaction. When you buy a book at Amazon.com, you typically do not care which functional areas are involved in the transaction; you care only about quickly getting the right book for the right price. Buying a book at Amazon.com can help to illustrate one of the core business processes, namely, *order-to-cash.* Similarly, *procure-to-pay* and *make-to-stock* are core business processes also common to most business organizations. Other important business processes are related to tracking a firm's revenues and expenses, managing employees, and so on. Next, we discuss the core business processes involved in generating revenue.

ORDER-TO-CASH. For business organizations, selling products or services is the main way of generating revenue. In the example of Amazon.com, you need to create an account and add items to your shopping cart. You then need to complete your order by entering shipping and billing information and submitting the order. Amazon.com will then confirm that your address is valid and will check your credit card information. Your order will then be put together and

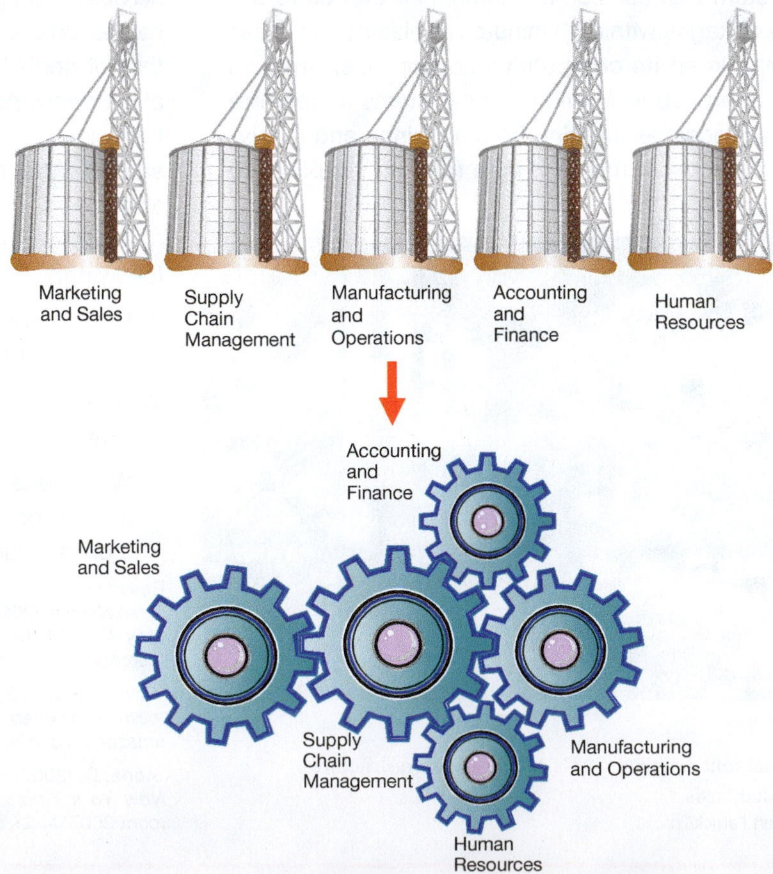

FIGURE 7.2

A company's functional areas should be interrelated.

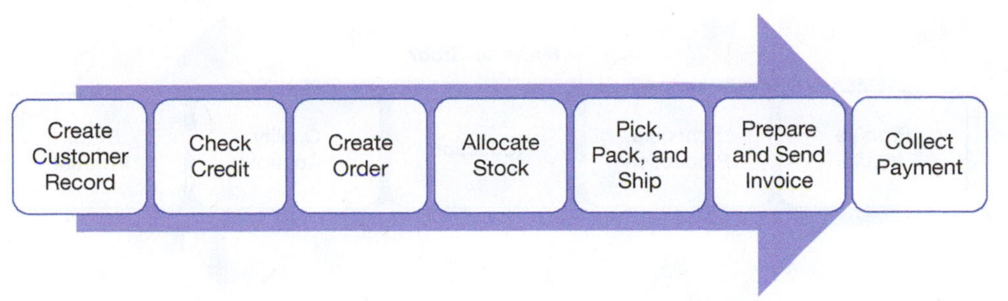

FIGURE 7.3

The order-to-cash process.

shipped, and your credit card will be charged. Together, the processes associated with selling a product or service are referred to as the **order-to-cash process** (Figure 7.3). As with all business processes, the order-to-cash process can be broken down into multiple subprocesses (most of which are common across organizations). For most businesses, the order-to-cash process entails subprocesses such as creating a customer record; checking the customer's creditworthiness; creating an order; checking and allocating stock; picking, packing, and shipping; invoicing; and collecting the payment. Depending on the nature of the transaction, the individual subprocesses and the time in which these are completed can differ considerably. For example, a sale in a convenience store may take only several seconds, and many of the subprocesses mentioned (such as creating a customer record) are not needed (although many stores now try to gather information such as customers' ZIP codes for business intelligence). In contrast, sales of many big-ticket items (such as commercial aircraft or specialized manufacturing machinery) may take months or years to complete and may involve many more steps. The subprocesses can be further broken down to a more granular level.

Obviously, an ineffective order-to-cash process can have various negative effects for organizations; for example, the manual input of order information often causes errors, as do suboptimal picking and shipping processes. Together, such errors can lead to a high rate of disputes that have to be resolved, ineffective collection processes, and, ultimately, defecting customers. In contrast, an effective order-to-cash process can create customer satisfaction, speed up the collection process, and serve to provide valuable inputs into business intelligence and customer relationship management applications (see Chapter 8).

PROCURE-TO-PAY. In order to be able to sell books and other products, Amazon.com needs to acquire these from its suppliers. Amazon.com needs to manage literally thousands of suppliers, place purchase orders, receive the products, allocate warehouse space, receive and pay invoices, and handle potential disputes. These processes associated with procuring goods from external vendors are together referred to as the **procure-to-pay process** (Figure 7.4). Subprocesses of the procure-to-pay process include price and terms negotiations, issuing of the purchase order, receiving the goods, and receiving and paying the invoice.

An ineffective procure-to-pay process can increase error rates in purchase order and invoice processing; further, it inhibits a company from developing close relationships with preferred vendors. Together, this can increase the cost per transaction, lead to an increase in disputes to be resolved, and prevent the company from obtaining the most favorable conditions from its vendors. In contrast, an effective procure-to-pay process can help to obtain favorable conditions, reduce transaction costs, and, ultimately, create customer goodwill as it helps to efficiently fulfill customer orders.

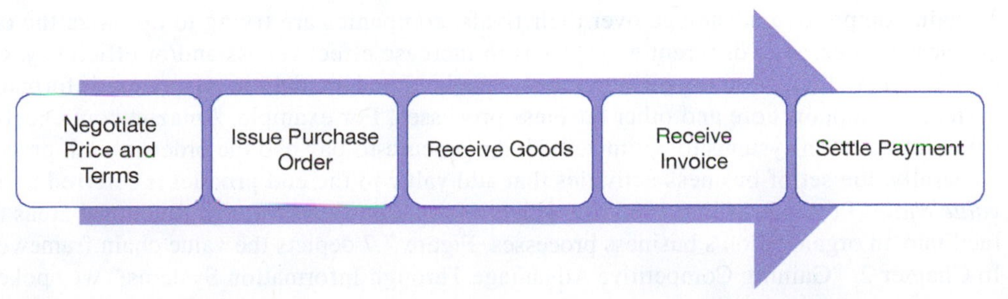

FIGURE 7.4

The procure-to-pay process.

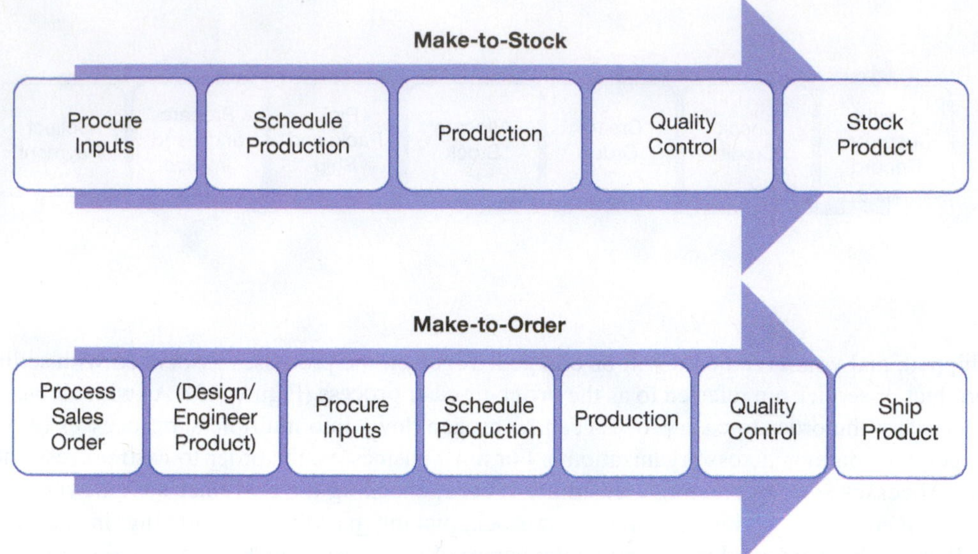

FIGURE 7.5
The make-to-stock versus the make-to-order process.

MAKE-TO-STOCK/MAKE-TO-ORDER. A third set of core business processes is associated with producing goods (such as Amazon.com's Kindle e-book reader), and entails make-to-stock and make-to-order. In the **make-to-stock process**, goods are produced based on forecasts and are stocked in a warehouse (i.e., a push-based approach); customers' orders are then fulfilled from inventory. In contrast, in the **make-to-order process**, raw materials, subcomponents, and accessories are procured based on forecasts, but actual manufacturing does not start until an order is received (a pull-based approach); in extreme cases, even design and engineering start only when an order is received. For example, mass-produced goods, such as television sets or home appliances, are typically produced under a make-to-stock approach. Here, the organization stocks the produced goods, *pushing* the products out to customers after orders are received. In contrast, highly customizable or very expensive low-volume goods are often produced under a make-to-order approach, as is the case with Dell computers or with commercial aircraft, where the assembly starts only after a customer has placed an order. Here, the organization waits for an order, allowing it to initiate a *pulling* sequence to move the order through the production process. The processes associated with making products are comprised of processing customers' orders, procuring the inputs to the manufacturing process, scheduling production, production, quality control, packaging, and stocking or shipping the product. Figure 7.5 illustrates the make-to-stock and make-to-order processes.

Together, these core business processes enable the creation of supply chains that are involved in transforming raw materials into products sold to the end consumer. A typical supply chain resembles a river, where the raw materials start out at the source and move downstream toward the end customer; at each step, the goods are transformed to make the end product. To meet the needs for various different inputs, each organization typically has multiple upstream suppliers; similarly, each organization typically sells to multiple downstream customers. Figure 7.6 shows the supply chain of a book. Within this supply chain, one company's sales-related processes overlap with the downstream company's procurement-related processes (supply chains are discussed in detail in Chapter 8).

Organizational Activities Along the Value Chain

To gain competitive advantage over their rivals, companies are trying to optimize the core business processes in different ways, so as to increase effectiveness and/or efficiency. One of the first challenges an organization must face is to understand how it can use information systems to support core and other business processes. For example, Amazon.com excels at using information systems to optimize both the procure-to-pay and the order-to-cash process. Generally, the set of business activities that add value to the end product is referred to as a *value chain* (Porter & Millar, 1985), in which information flows through functional areas that facilitate an organization's business processes. Figure 7.7 depicts the value chain framework. In Chapter 2, "Gaining Competitive Advantage Through Information Systems," we spoke of

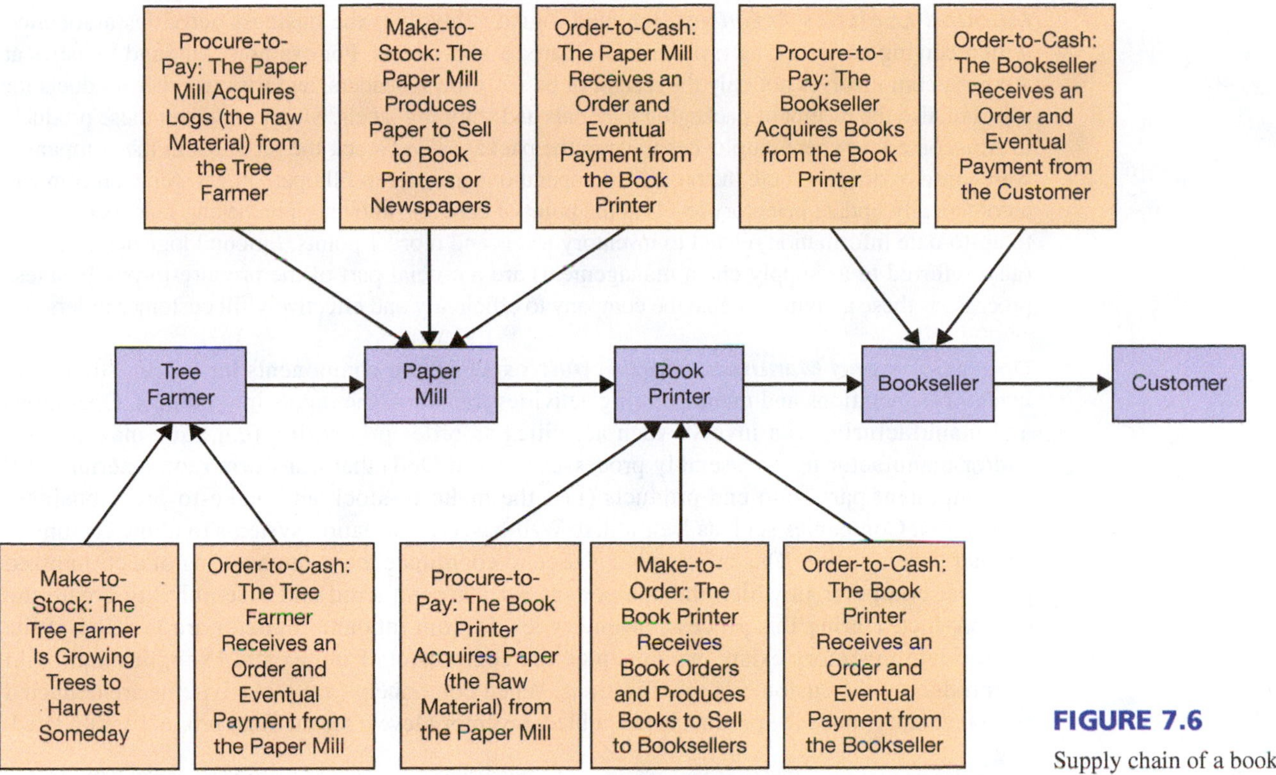

FIGURE 7.6

Supply chain of a book.

the strategic value of analyzing a value chain. Here, we show you how the activities along the value chain support business processes.

Many business processes depend on activities performed by various functional areas within an organization; for example, Amazon.com's order-to-cash process involves activities performed by sales, shipping, accounting, and other functional areas. The functional areas directly involved in the process are responsible for the core activities, whereas other functional areas are performing support activities. In other words, *core activities* are performed by the functional areas that process inputs and produce outputs, and *support activities* are those activities that enable core activities to take place. In the following sections, we focus on core activities and then turn our attention to the support activities that make them possible.

CORE ACTIVITIES. **Core activities** include inbound logistics (receiving), operations and manufacturing, outbound logistics (shipping), marketing and sales, and customer service. These activities may differ widely, depending on the unique requirements of the industry in which a company operates, although the basic concepts hold in most organizations.

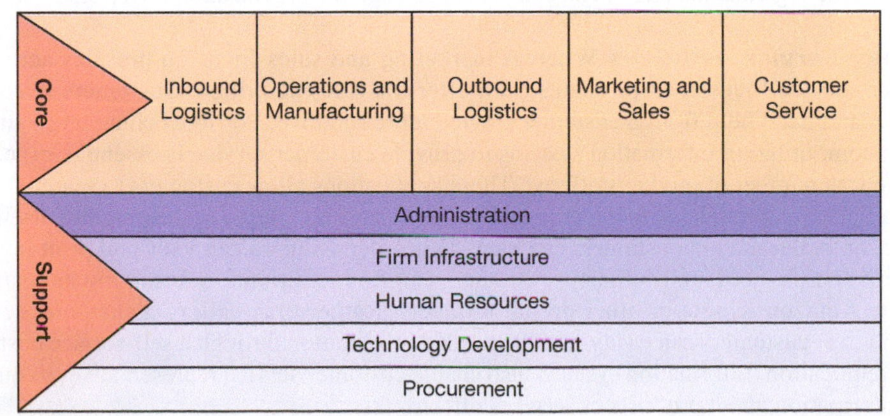

FIGURE 7.7

Value chain framework.

Source: Based on Porter and Millar (1985).

Inbound Logistics Activities Inbound logistics involves the business activities associated with receiving and stocking raw materials, parts, and products. For example, inbound logistics at Amazon.com involves not only the receipt of books, e-book readers, and various other products for sale, but also the receipt of packaging materials and shipping labels. Shippers deliver these products to Amazon.com, where employees unwrap the packages and stock the products in the company's warehouse or directly route the products to operations in order to fill open orders. Amazon.com can automatically update inventory levels at the point of delivery, allowing purchasing managers access to up-to-date information related to inventory levels and reorder points. Inbound logistics activities (also referred to as supply chain management) are a crucial part of the procure-to-pay business process, as these activities enable the company to efficiently and effectively fill customer orders.

Operations and Manufacturing Activities Once the components have been stocked in inventory, operations and manufacturing activities transform the inputs into outputs. Operations and manufacturing can involve such activities as order processing (e.g., at Amazon.com) and/or manufacturing or assembly processes (e.g., at Dell) that transform raw materials and/or component parts into end products (i.e., the make-to-stock and make-to-order business processes). Companies such as Dell utilize Web-based information systems to allow customers to enter orders online. This information is used to coordinate the manufacturing of a customized personal computer in which the component parts are gathered and assembled to create the end product. During this process, inventory levels from inbound logistics are verified; if the appropriate inventory exists, workers pick the components from existing supplies and build the product to the customer's specifications. When components are picked, items are deducted from inventory; once the product is assembled, inventory levels for the final product are updated.

Outbound Logistics Activities The activities associated with outbound logistics mirror those of inbound logistics. Instead of involving the receipt of raw materials, parts, and products, outbound logistics focuses on the distribution of end products within the order-to-cash business process. For example, outbound logistics at Amazon.com involves the shipping of books that customers have ordered. Orders that have been processed by operations are forwarded to outbound logistics, which picks the products from inventory and coordinates shipment to the customer. At that point, items are packaged and deducted from the company's inventory, and an invoice is created that will be sent to the customer. Amazon.com can automatically update sales information at the point of distribution, allowing managers to view inventory and revenue information in real time.

Marketing and Sales Activities Marketing and sales activities are associated primarily with the presales (i.e., before the sale) activities of the company. These activities include the creation of marketing literature, communication with potential and existing customers, and pricing of goods and services. Most companies support the business activity of marketing and sales by creating e-brochures, building pages on Facebook, or communicating on other social media such as Twitter (for further discussion, see Chapter 4, "Enabling Business-to-Consumer Electronic Commerce"). Many companies, especially those focused on selling products or services to the end consumer (e.g., passenger airlines such as United or online retailers such as Amazon.com), use information systems to update pricing information and/or schedules. This information is entered directly into the pricing and scheduling systems, allowing the information to become immediately accessible throughout the organization and to end consumers through the organization's Web site.

Customer Service Activities Whereas marketing and sales focus on presales activities, customer service focuses on postsales (i.e., after the sale) activities. Customers may have questions and need help from a customer service representative. For most companies, such as Amazon.com, utilizing information systems to provide customer service is essential, especially given the vast number of products offered. These applications allow customers to search for and download information related to the products that they have purchased or the purchase itself. For example, on Amazon.com customers can view their order status or can view and print invoices of current and past orders. Similarly, customers can find additional information and support about the Amazon Kindle or other digital products. Rather than calling a customer service representative, customers can easily find the needed information through a self-service customer support application. Information systems also enable customer service representatives to quickly locate information about products or services offered.

BRIEF CASE Crowdsourcing Cinema at Amazon Studios

It is an online bookstore, a producer of consumer electronics, and the world's largest online retailer. Every year, it seems like Amazon.com finds new ways to innovate and add to its legendary success. Take Amazon Studios, an innovative film production venture that is radically different from your typical Hollywood studio. In contrast to traditional studios, Amazon Studios crowdsources ideas and scripts for movies, meaning that anyone interested is free to jump on the ride to Hollywood fame and fortune.

Amazon Studios aims to discover voices and talents as it accepts submissions from screenwriters and filmmakers who have yet to make it into the big league, and even connects the makers of top projects with Warner Bros. development executives. Aspiring filmmakers are encouraged to upload a screenplay, make improvements to someone else's screenplay, or turn submitted screenplays into a test movie.

The notion of crowdsourcing entertainment has been gaining more recognition and getting more exposure in different venues. Attempting to challenge Netflix, Amazon.com now even creates pilots of comedies or drama series. This original content, at times featuring big-name stars such as Adam Brody or Ron Perlman, is "aired" on Amazon Instant Video; after receiving feedback from the audience, Amazon Studios then decides whether a full season will be produced. Series such as *Alpha House* and *Mozart in the Jungle* made it past the pilot stage and demonstrate that crowdsourcing can be an effective way to evaluate the success potential of series before producing a full season. Indeed, it appears that true creativity can be crowdsourced, with or without million-dollar budgets or a shot at Hollywood fame.

Questions:

1. How do business processes for creating content differ from those for selling products?
2. How can Amazon.com leverage its IS infrastructure for Amazon Studios?

Based on:

Amazon Studios. (n.d.). *Amazon Studios*. Retrieved May 3, 2014, from http://studios.amazon.com.

Ray, A. (2014, April 9). Amazon greenlights new pilot "The Cosmopolitans," starring Adam Brody and Chloe Seveigny. *Entertainment Weekly*. Retrieved May 3, 2014, from http://insidetv.ew.com/2014/04/09/amazon-the-cosmopolitans-hand-of-god.

Soalsman, J. E. (2013, November 14). How Amazon Studios went from grassroots idealist to Hollywood threat. *CNet.com*. Retrieved May 3, 2014, from http://www.cnet.com/news/how-amazon-studios-went-from-grassroots-idealist-to-hollywood-threat.

Companies can also use information systems to track service requests. When a customer calls in for repairs to a product, customer service representatives can access a bevy of information related to the customer. For instance, an agent can access technical information concerning the specific product as well as review any problems the customer has encountered in the past. This enables customer service representatives to react quickly to customer concerns, improving the customer service experience.

SUPPORT ACTIVITIES. **Support activities** are business activities that enable the primary activities to take place. Support activities include administrative activities, infrastructure, human resources, technology development, and procurement.

Administrative Activities Administrative activities focus on the processes and decision making that orchestrate the day-to-day operations of an organization, particularly those processes that span organizational functions and levels. Administration includes systems and processes from virtually all functional areas—accounting, finance, marketing, operations, and so on—at all levels of an organization.

Infrastructure Activities Infrastructure refers to the hardware and software that must be implemented to provide the necessary components that facilitate both primary and support activities (see Chapter 3, "Managing the Information Systems Infrastructure and Services"). For example, an order entry application requires that employees who enter orders have a computer and the necessary software to accomplish their business objectives. In turn, the computer must be connected via the network to a database containing the order information so that the order can be saved and recalled later for processing.

Human Resource Activities Human resource activities encompass all business activities associated with employee management, such as hiring, interview scheduling, payroll, and benefits management. Human resource activities are classified as support activities since the primary activities cannot be accomplished without the employees to perform them. In other words, all the primary activities rely on human resource–related business activities.

Technology Development Activities Technology development includes the design and development of applications that support the primary business activities, so as to improve products and/or services. If you are planning on pursuing a career in the management information systems (MIS) field, you will frequently participate in activities related to the development or acquisition of new applications and systems. Technology development can involve a wide array of responsibilities, such as the selection of packaged software or the design and development of custom software to meet a particular business need. Many companies are leveraging the technology development business activity to build Internet, intranet, extranet, or mobile applications to support a wide variety of primary business activities.

Procurement Activities Procurement refers to the purchasing of goods and services that are required as inputs to the primary activities. Procurement receives, approves, and processes requests for goods and services from the primary activities and coordinates the purchase of those items. Allowing each functional area to send out purchase orders can create problems for companies, such as maintaining relationships with more suppliers than necessary and not taking advantage of volume discounts. The procurement business activity can leverage information systems by accumulating purchase orders from the different functional areas within the organization and combining multiple purchase orders containing the same item into a single purchase order. This facilitates negotiating volume discounts and allows the primary activities to concentrate on running the business rather than adding to their workload.

VALUE CHAIN ACTIVITIES IN SERVICE INDUSTRIES. Originally, the value chain framework was developed for analyzing the value-adding activities of manufacturing industries, but it can also be used to understand service-based industries. Many of the processes within service industries are similar to processes performed in manufacturing industries (e.g., customer service, sales, and support). However, whereas manufacturing industries deal with physical products, service industries deal primarily with information-based products. As a result, activities such as inbound logistics and outbound logistics are often less important in the service sector. Likewise, in the manufacturing sector, operations include the physical handling of goods when transforming them from raw materials or components to finished products; in contrast, operations in the service sector typically encompass the manipulation of data and information. For example, in the service sector, a finished product equates to a closed file such as a bank loan that has been issued, an insurance claim that has been filed, or an investment that has been made. As a result, optimizing the value-adding activities in the services sector does typically not include eliminating physical bottlenecks or improving inventory management, but enhancing the flow of information.

Value Systems: Connecting Multiple Organizational Value Chains

The flow of information can be streamlined not only within a company but outside organizational boundaries as well. A company can create additional value by integrating internal applications with suppliers, business partners, and customers. Companies accomplish this by connecting their internal value chains to form a **value system** (Porter & Millar, 1985), in which information flows from one company's value chain to another company's value chain. Figure 7.8 depicts the value system framework. In this diagram, three companies are aligning their value chains to form a value system. First, Company A processes information through its value chain and forwards the information along to its customer, Company B, which processes the information through its value chain and sends the information along to its customer, Company C, which processes the information through its value chain. Adding additional suppliers, business partners, and customers can create complex value systems. However, for our purposes, we simply view an organization's information systems as a value chain that interacts with the value chains of other organizations.

As information systems can be used to streamline an organization's internal value chain, they can also be used to coordinate a company's value chain with another company's value chain or with consumers (such as in business-to-consumer electronic commerce). Any information that feeds into a company's value chain, whether its source is another company's value chain or an end consumer, is considered part of the value system.

A supply chain can be viewed as a river, where physical goods "flow" from a source to an ultimate destination. Like a river, at any particular point there is a flow coming from upstream and progressing downstream. In a similar way, a value system can be viewed as a river of information, comprising upstream and downstream information flows. An **upstream information flow**

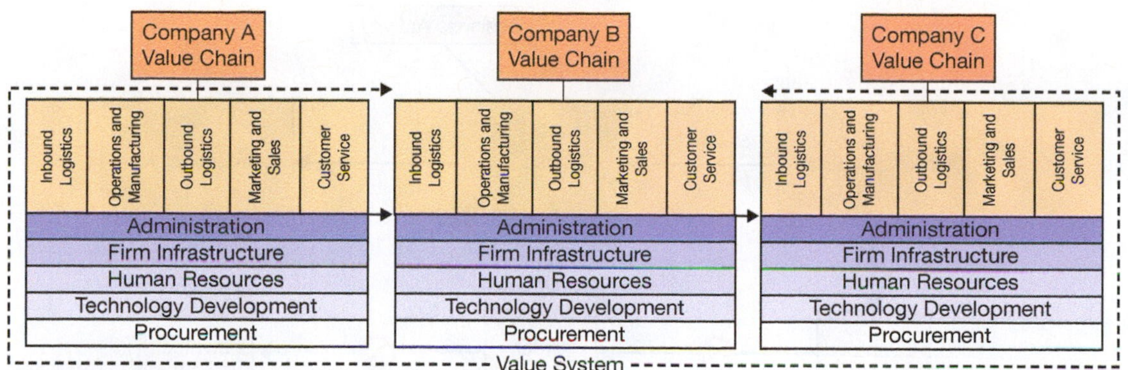

FIGURE 7.8

Three companies combine their value chains, forming a value system.
Source: Based on Porter and Millar (1985); Christensen (1997).

consists of information that is received from another organization, whereas a **downstream information flow** relates to the information that is produced by a company and sent along to another organization. For instance, in the value system depicted in Figure 7.8, the upstream and downstream information flows for Company B become quite evident. In this case, Company B receives information from its upstream supplier, processes the information through its internal value chain, and subsequently passes information downstream to its distributors and/or customers (see Chapter 8 for a discussion of product and information flows in the opposite direction). These flows of external information into and from a company can be leveraged to create additional value and gain competitive advantage.

ENTERPRISE SYSTEMS

Businesses have leveraged information systems to support business processes for decades, beginning with the installation of individual, separate applications to assist companies with specific business tasks, such as issuing paychecks. However, in order to efficiently and effectively conduct the core business processes (as well as other business processes), the different functional areas within a company need to share data. For example, data about your book order need to be shared between accounting (for billing purposes), marketing and sales (e.g., to feed into product recommendations for other customers), and operations and supply chain management (e.g., to fulfill the order and replenish the inventory).

The Rise of Enterprise Systems

As companies began to leverage IS applications, they typically started out by fulfilling the needs of particular business activities in a particular department within the organization, and purchased a variety of proprietary software systems from different software vendors or developed department-specific software (e.g., accounting) to support specific business processes. Systems that focus on the specific needs of individual departments are typically not designed to communicate with other systems in the organization (essentially, they are "speaking different languages") and are therefore referred to as **standalone applications**. Although such systems enable departments to conduct their daily business activities efficiently and effectively, these systems often are not very helpful when people from one part of the firm need information from another part of the firm. For example, if the applications for inbound logistics and operations are not integrated, companies will lose valuable time in accessing information related to inventory levels. When an order is placed through operations, personnel may have to access two separate applications to verify that the components are available in inventory before the order can be processed. Figure 7.9 provides an example of how information flows through standalone systems within an organization. As the diagram depicts, information is generated by the inbound logistics business activity, but it does not flow through to the next business activity, in this case operations; in other words, there are too many "rocks" in the river, impeding the flow of information. Since the inbound logistics and operations departments use different standalone systems, information cannot readily flow from one business activity to another.

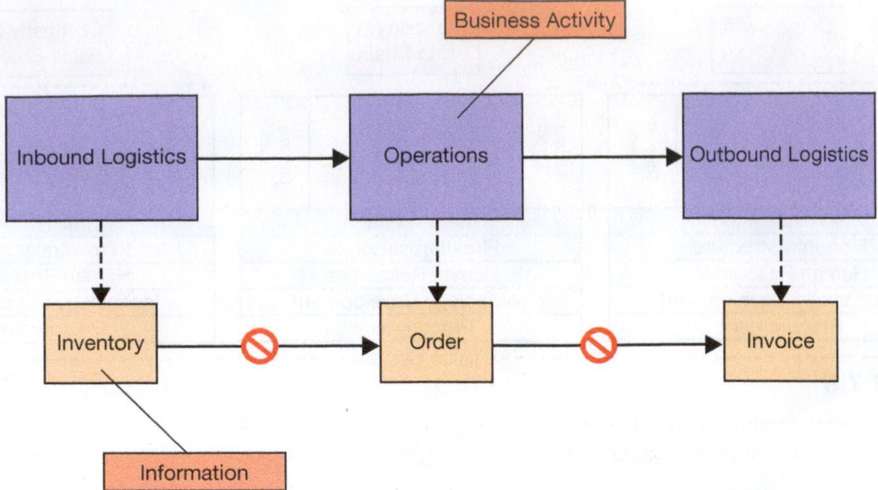

FIGURE 7.9
Information flows using standalone systems.

Understandably, this creates a highly inefficient process for operations personnel, who must have access to two systems or a common interface that pulls information together in order to get both the order entry and the inventory information. This can be challenging, as applications running on different computing platforms are difficult to integrate, and IS managers are faced with the problem of "knitting together" a hodgepodge portfolio of discordant proprietary applications into a system that shares information; often, custom interfaces are required in order for one system to communicate with another, and such integration is typically very costly. In some cases, information may be stored on both systems, creating redundancy. Should data be updated in one system but not the other, the data become inconsistent. In addition, there are further unnecessary costs associated with entering, storing, and updating data redundantly. As a result, many standalone applications are typically either fast approaching or beyond the end of their useful life within the organization; such systems are referred to as **legacy systems**.

To utilize data stored in separate standalone systems to facilitate business processes and decision making, information must be reentered from one system to the next (by either manual typing, copying and pasting, or even downloads to Excel) or be consolidated by a third system. Further, the same data may also be stored in several (sometimes conflicting) versions throughout the organization, making the information harder to consolidate, often causing the business to lose money because of inefficiencies or missed business opportunities. In addition, organizations need integrated data to demonstrate compliance with standards, rules, or government regulations. To address these challenges, organizations have turned to enterprise-wide information systems. An **enterprise-wide information system** (or **enterprise system**) is an integrated suite of business applications for virtually every business process, allowing companies to integrate information across operations on a company-wide basis. Rather than storing information in separate places throughout the organization, enterprise systems use an integrated database to provide a central repository common to all users. The central database alleviates the problems associated with multiple computing platforms by providing a single place where all information relevant to the company and particular departments can be stored and accessed. This, along with a common user interface, allows personnel to share information seamlessly, no matter where the user is located or who is using the application (Figure 7.10).

Enterprise systems come in a variety of shapes and sizes, each providing a unique set of features and functionality. When deciding to implement enterprise solutions, managers need to be aware of a number of issues. One of the most important involves selecting and implementing applications that meet the requirements of the business as well as of its customers and suppliers. In the following sections, we examine the ways in which information systems can be leveraged to support business processes and how companies are using these systems to support their internal and external operations.

Supporting Business Processes

As discussed previously, information systems can be used to gain and sustain competitive advantage by supporting and/or streamlining activities along the value chain. For example, an information system could be used to support a billing process in such a way that it reduces the

ETHICAL DILEMMA

Too Much Intelligence? RFID and Privacy

Radio frequency identification (RFID) tags have become increasingly popular for tracking physical objects. Each tag contains unique identification information that can be accessed by an RFID reader. The identification is then sent to the information system that can identify the product that was tagged. For example, the pharmaceutical industry tags certain drugs in large quantities, such as 100-pill bottles of Viagra and Oxycontin, in order to track them as they move through the supply chain and thus prevent counterfeits from reaching the public.

As is true with all electronic tracking devices, privacy advocates are concerned about misuse. Since RFID tags can be read by anyone who has an RFID reader, the tags have the potential of revealing private consumer information. For example, if you buy a product that has an RFID tag, someone with an RFID reader could possibly identify where you bought the product and how much you paid for it. The amount of information imprinted on an RFID tag is limited, however, and since few retail businesses have purchased RFID writers, readers, or the erasers that can clear information from the tags before they leave the store, the likelihood of privacy abuse is currently slim.

In addition to tracking products, RFID technologies can be embedded within people. For example, Mexico's attorney general and senior members of his staff have been implanted with security chips from a company called VeriChip that give them access to secure areas of their headquarters. VeriChip has been actively working to promote its chips to be used in older patients with Alzheimer's or patients with diabetes to aid medical staff in tracking their care, and recently announced a partnership with the National Foundation for the Investigation of Lost and Kidnapped Children to promote embedding VeriChips in children to help prevent kidnappings. These efforts, however, have received severe public opposition. Using RFID implants to speed up medical assistance may be a good thing, but what if crackers manage to access a person's medical conditions? Would you want someone with the right equipment to be able to track your child? Clearly, while RFID has become well accepted for tracking valuable products, many ethical questions will remain.

Based on:

Gillespie, I. (2014, April 17). Human microchipping: I've got you under my skin. *The Sydney Morning Herald*. Retrieved May 3, 2014, from http://www.smh.com.au/digital-life/digital-life-news/human-microchipping-ive-got-you-under-my-skin-20140416-zqvho.html.

Foster, K.R., & Jaeger, J. (2007). RFID Inside: The murky ethics of implanted chips. *IEEE Spectrum*, *44*(3), 24–29.

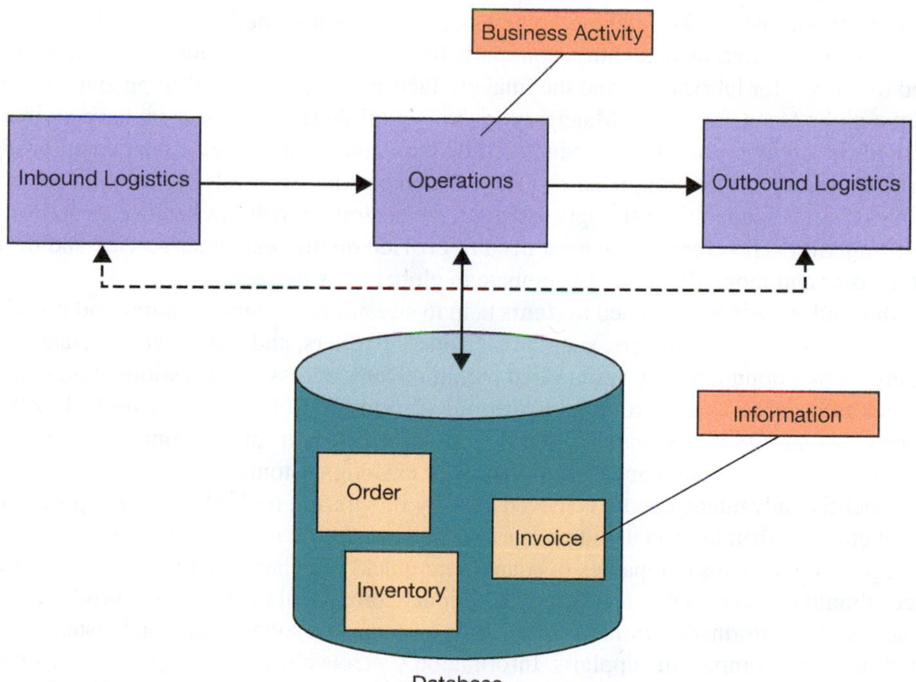

FIGURE 7.10

Enterprise systems allow companies to integrate information on a company-wide basis.

use of paper and, more important, the handling of paper, thus reducing material and labor costs. This system can help managers keep track of that same billing process more effectively because they will have more accurate, up-to-date information about the billing process, enabling them to make smart, timely business decisions.

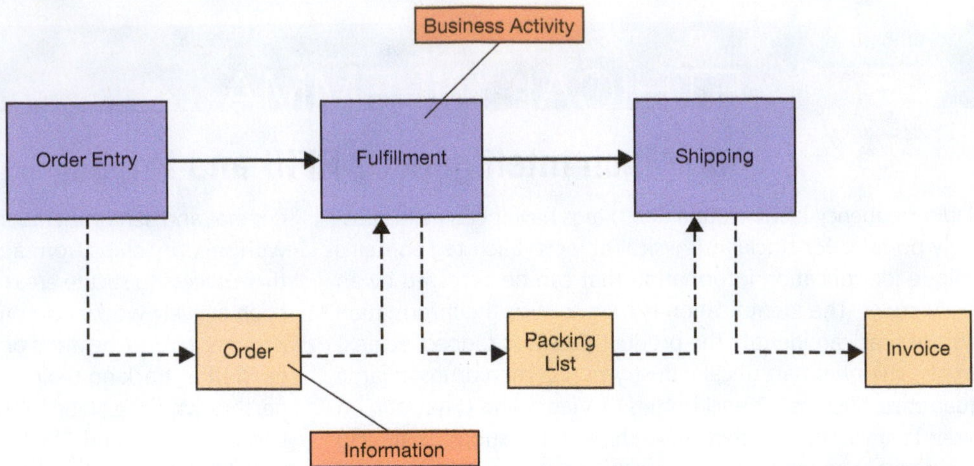

FIGURE 7.11

Information flow for a typical order.

Information systems can be used to support either internally or externally focused business processes. **Internally focused systems** support functional areas, business processes, and decision making *within* an organization. These activities can be viewed as a series of links in a chain along which information flows within the organization. At each stage (or link) in the process, value is added in the form of the work performed by people associated with that process, and new, useful information is generated. Information begins to accumulate at the point of entry and flows through the various links, or business processes, within the organization, progressing through the organization with new, useful information being added every step of the way (Figure 7.11).

Companies can gain several advantages by integrating and converting legacy systems so that information stored on separate computing platforms can be consolidated to provide a centralized point of access. However, although internally focused systems do an excellent job of serving the needs of internal business operations on an organization-wide basis, they are not necessarily designed to completely accommodate the communication of information outside the organization's boundaries. The emergence of the Internet and the Web has resulted in the globalization of customer and supplier networks, opening up new opportunities and methods to conduct business. For example, raw materials and component parts for a computer may come from China and be shipped to Europe for fabrication, and the final products are assembled and shipped to customers across the globe (see Chapter 1, "Managing in the Digital World"). Customers have an increasing number of options available to them, so they are demanding more sophisticated products that are customized to their unique needs. They also expect higher levels of customer service. If companies cannot keep their customers satisfied, the customers will not hesitate to do business with a competitor. Therefore, companies need to provide quality customer service and develop products faster and more efficiently to compete in global markets.

To this end, **externally focused systems** help to streamline communications and coordinate business processes with customers, suppliers, business partners, and others who operate *outside* an organization's boundaries. A system that communicates across organizational boundaries is sometimes referred to as an **interorganizational system (IOS)** (Kumar & Crook, 1999). The key purpose of an IOS is to streamline the flow of information from one company's operations to another's (e.g., from a company to its potential or existing customers).

Competitive advantage can be achieved here by integrating multiple business processes in ways that enable a firm to meet a wide range of unique customer needs. Sharing information between organizations helps companies to adapt more quickly to changing market conditions. For instance, should consumers demand that an additional component be added to a product, a company can gain this information from its information systems that support sales and instantaneously pass it along to its component suppliers. Information systems allow the company and its suppliers to satisfy the needs of customers efficiently since changes can be identified and managed immediately, creating a competitive advantage for companies that can respond quickly. In addition, streamlining the information flows can help companies find innovative ways to increase accurate on-time shipments, avoid (or at least anticipate) surprises (such as shortages in raw materials or weather problems), minimize costs, and ultimately increase customer satisfaction and the overall profitability of the company. We can view processes and information flows across organizations

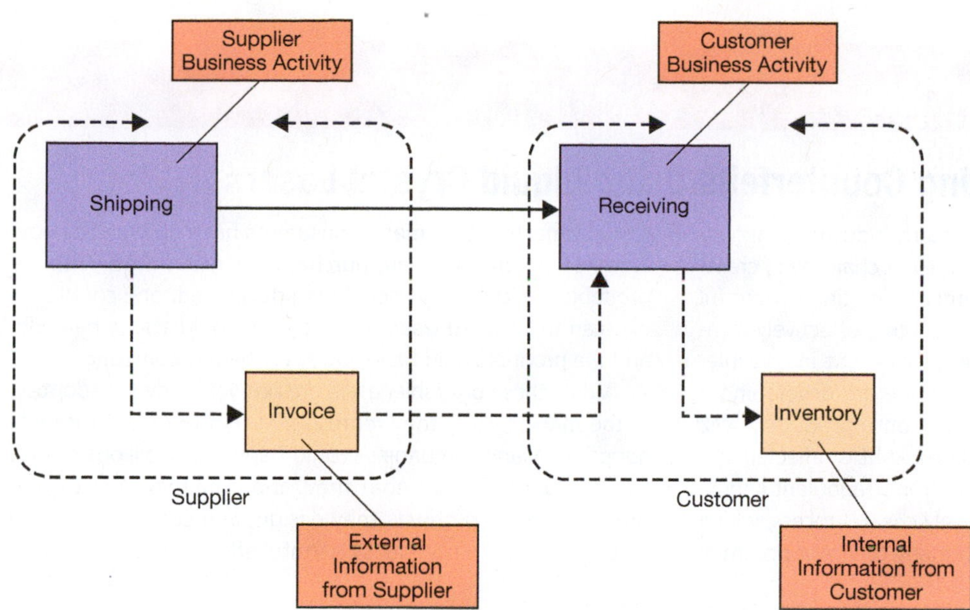

FIGURE 7.12

Information flow for a typical shipment across organizational boundaries.

just as we previously viewed the processes and information flows within an organization. At each stage (or link) in the process, value is added by the work performed, and new, useful information is generated and exchanged between organizations (Figure 7.12). Using an IOS, one company can create information and transmit it electronically to another company.

Systems that facilitate interorganizational communications focus on the upstream and downstream information flows. On the upstream side, *supply chain management* applications integrate the value chains of business partners within a supply chain, improving the coordination of suppliers, product or service production, and distribution. On the downstream side, *customer relationship management* applications concentrate on the activities involved in promoting and selling products to the customers as well as providing customer service and nourishing long-term relationships (both types of applications are discussed in Chapter 8). Integrating internally focused and externally focused applications can be extremely valuable for companies operating in global markets.

IMPROVING BUSINESS PROCESSES THROUGH ENTERPRISE SYSTEMS. Software programs come in two forms—packaged and custom. **Packaged software**, sometimes referred to as **off-the-shelf software**, is written by third-party vendors for the needs of many different users and organizations, supporting standardized, repetitive tasks, such as word processing, payroll processing, or preparing taxes. These programs can be quite cost effective since the vendor that builds the application can spread out development costs through selling to a large number of users.

Yet, packaged software may not be well suited for tasks that are unique to a particular business. In these cases, companies may prefer to develop (or have developed for them) **custom software**, which is designed and developed exclusively for specific organizations (see Chapter 9, "Developing and Acquiring Information Systems") and can accommodate their particular business needs. However, obtaining custom software is much more expensive because the organization has to bear all costs (in terms of time, money, and other resources) associated with designing and developing the software. Furthermore, applications need to be maintained internally when changes are required. With packaged software, the vendor makes the changes and distributes new versions to its customers. In all, there are trade-offs when choosing between the packaged and custom software routes. Managers must consider whether packaged software can meet the business requirements and, if not, conduct a cost–benefit analysis to ensure that taking the custom software approach will prove worthwhile to the company.

Because no two companies are alike, no packaged software application will exactly fit the unique requirements of a particular business. Thus, enterprise systems are designed around **modules**, which are components that can be selected and implemented as needed. In essence, each module is designed to replace a legacy system, be it a finance, human resources, or manufacturing system; after the conversion to an enterprise system, each business function has access to various modules that serve its needs, but the modules (and the underlying data) are tightly integrated and share the same look and feel (Figure 7.13).

COMING ATTRACTIONS

Combating Counterfeits Using Liquid Crystal Lasers

Counterfeit products are a problem in many industries, ranging from clothing to pharmaceuticals, and even chainsaws, creating losses for organizations, and potentially resulting in harmful consequences for the end users. Unfortunately, effectively combating knock-offs is cost-prohibitive, or outright impossible. Researchers at the University of Cambridge are developing a way to print a liquid crystal laser pattern onto product labels; when pointing a second laser to the label, light is reflected in a way that can distinguish a real product from fraudulent knock-offs. The laser is printed using a relatively cheap process, which means it could potentially be used in many different potential applications.

One such application is the pharmaceutical industry. Every year, hundreds of thousands of people are sold counterfeit drugs, and many of these sales take place in developing countries. These drugs are advertised as real, and their packaging and the actual capsules look real, but they are filled with a cheap substitute like sugar instead of the drug they purport to be. Unfortunately, many consumers have no way to know whether the drug they are purchasing is real or not. With the printable liquid crystal lasers being developed, one could simply scan the printed laser, just like one would scan a barcode, and the product could be instantly verified as authentic.

While these printable lasers are not yet ready for adoption in the marketplace, they represent strong potential for wide adoption. Many companies would happily pay billions of dollars in order to ensure that they, and only they, are reaping profits from the products they design, and consumers would be protected from potentially harmful effects of fake products.

Based on:

Drake, N. (2013, November 7). These printable liquid crystal lasers could be the future of anti-counterfeit technology. *Wired*. Retrieved May 3, 2014, from http://www.wired.com/2013/11/printed-liquid-crystal-lasers.

Liquid-crystal laser. (2014, January 8). In *Wikipedia, The Free Encyclopedia*. Retrieved May 3, 2014, from http://en.wikipedia.org/w/index.php?title=Liquid-crystal_laser&oldid=589826718.

Vanilla Versus Customized Software The features and modules that an enterprise system comes with out of the box are referred to as the **vanilla version**. If the vanilla version does not support a certain business process, the company may require a customized version. **Customization** provides either additional software that is integrated with the enterprise system or consists of direct changes to the vanilla application itself. Most enterprise systems include literally thousands of elements that can be customized. Companies must take special care when dealing with customization, as customization can be extremely costly, and maintaining and upgrading customizations can be troublesome. For example, a customization made to the vanilla version will need to be reprogrammed when a new release of the system is implemented because subsequent releases of the software will not include the previous customizations. In other words, new vanilla versions must be continually upgraded to accommodate the company-specific customizations. This process can involve a substantial investment of time and resources, diverting attention away from other key business activities and reducing company profits.

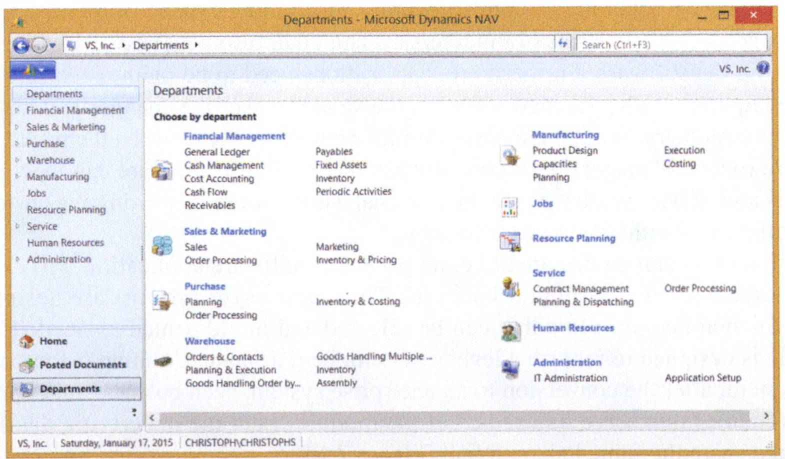

FIGURE 7.13

Each module in an enterprise system is designed to replace a standalone legacy system.
Source: Courtesy of Microsoft Corporation

Best Practices–Based Software One of the major hurdles facing companies that implement enterprise systems involves changing business processes to accommodate the manner in which the software works. Enterprise system implementations are often used as a catalyst for overall improvement of underlying business processes. As a result, most enterprise systems are designed to operate according to industry-standard business processes, or **best practices**, and vendors offer many industry-specific versions that have already been customized for particular industries based on best practices. Best practices reflect the techniques and processes, identified through experience and research, that have consistently shown results superior to those achieved with other means. In fact, because they have proven to consistently lead to superior performance, most enterprise system vendors build best practices into their applications to provide guidelines for management to identify business activities within their organizations that need to be streamlined. Implementations and future upgrades to the system will go more smoothly when companies change their business processes to fit the way the enterprise system operates, and companies that reject these best practices are in for a long and time-consuming implementation (although the vendors and external consultants typically offer help in the process).

However, many organizations have spent years developing business processes that provide them with a competitive advantage in the marketplace. Adopting their industry's best practices may force these companies to abandon their unique ways of doing business, putting them on par with their industry competitors. In other words, companies can potentially lose their competitive advantages by adopting the best practices within their industry. Given the importance and difficulty of changing business processes with enterprise and other systems implementations, we now briefly describe business process management.

Business Process Management Optimizing business processes is key for organizational efficiency, effectiveness, and agility, and over the years, various approaches for improving business processes have been developed. Given the magnitude of change that an enterprise system can impose on an organization's business processes, understanding the role of business process management in the implementation of an enterprise system is necessary. **Business process management (BPM)** is a systematic, structured improvement approach by all or part of an organization whereby people critically examine, rethink, and redesign business processes in order to achieve dramatic improvements in one or more performance measures, such as quality, cycle time, or cost.

BPM, which became very popular in the 1990s (and was then called **business process reengineering [BPR]**), is based on the notion that radical redesign of an organization is sometimes necessary in order to lower costs and increase quality, and that information systems are the key enabler for that radical change. The basic steps in BPM can be summarized as follows (Figure 7.14):

1. Develop a vision for the organization that specifies business objectives, such as reducing costs, shortening the time it takes to get products to market, improving quality of products and/or services, and so on.
2. Identify the critical processes that are to be redesigned.
3. Understand and measure the existing processes as a baseline for future improvements.
4. Identify ways that information systems can be used to improve processes.
5. Design and implement a prototype of the new processes.

At the heart of BPM initiatives are information systems that enable the streamlining of business processes. Given the importance of information systems in such endeavors, organizations are increasingly hiring IS consultants and business analysts who have a sound understanding of the business but who are also well versed in technology. In fact, business analysts and systems analysts are often listed among the hottest jobs because of good job prospects, high salaries, and the diversity of work. In enterprise systems projects, business analysts are deeply involved in analyzing and improving business processes and mapping the processes to the different enterprise systems modules.

BPM is similar to quality improvement approaches such as *total quality management* and *continuous process improvement* in that they are intended to be cross-functional approaches to improve an organization. BPM differs from these quality improvement approaches, however, in one fundamental way. These quality improvement approaches tend to focus on incremental change and gradual improvement of processes, while the intention behind BPM is radical redesign and drastic improvement of processes.

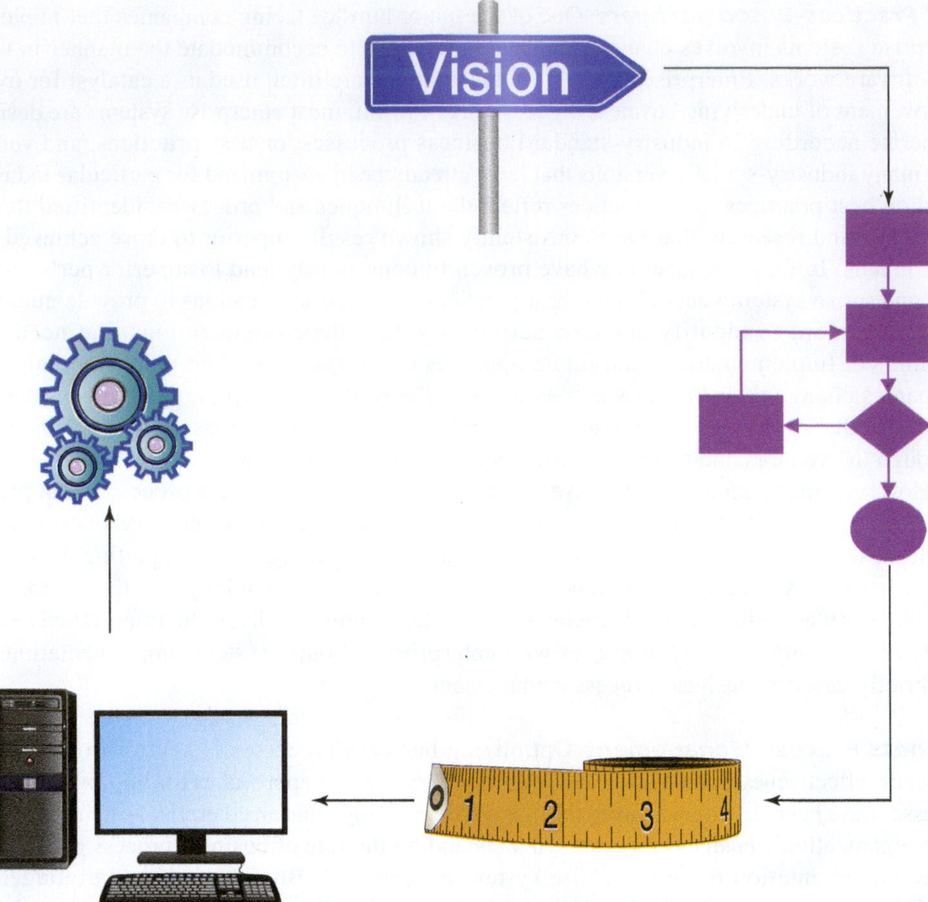

FIGURE 7.14

The basic steps of BPM include developing a vision, identifying the critical processes that are to be redesigned, understanding and measuring the existing processes, identifying ways that information systems can be used to improve processes, and designing and implementing the new processes.

When BPR was introduced in the 1990s, many efforts were reported to have failed. These failures occurred for a variety of reasons, including the lack of sustained management commitment and leadership, unrealistic scope and expectations, and resistance to change. In fact, BPR gained the reputation of being a nice way of saying "downsizing."

Nevertheless, BPR (and its successors such as BPM) lives on today and is still a popular approach to improving organizations. No matter what it is called, the conditions that appear to lead to a successful business process improvement effort include the following:

- Support by senior management
- Shared vision by all organizational members
- Realistic expectations
- Participants empowered to make changes
- The right people participating
- Sound management practices
- Appropriate funding

In any event, it is clear that successful business process change, especially involving enterprise systems, requires a broad range of organizational factors to converge that are far beyond the technical implementation issues.

Benefits and Costs of Enterprise Systems Beyond the improvements in critical business processes, there are various types of benefits and costs associated with the acquisition and development of enterprise systems. According to industry research, implementation costs run over budget 56 percent of the time (Panorama, 2012). On average, projects costs were around US$10 million, but running nearly US$2 million over budget. Top reasons cited for budget overruns are that the initial project scope was expanded, and that unanticipated technical or organizational change management issues resulted in additional costs.

Gaining a better understanding of both project benefits and costs can help to develop an improved understanding of the project's total cost of ownership, and help make the business case for a particular investment decision (see Chapter 9). Benefits of enterprise systems that can be used to make the business case include:

- Improved availability of information
- Increased interaction throughout the organization
- Improved (reduced) lead times for manufacturing
- Improved customer interaction
- Reduced operating expenses
- Reduced inventory
- Reduced IS costs
- Improved supplier integration
- Improved compliance with standards, rules, and regulations

The two mostly likely benefits realized from utilizing enterprise systems are improvements in information availability and increased interaction across the organization as a result of streamlining business processes.

Just as there are many possible benefits that can be realized when implementing an enterprise system, there are also many potential costs that can impact the total cost of ownership of these large and complex systems. Many companies underestimate these costs and, as a result, ultimately go over budget. Understanding all of the items that make up the total cost of ownership will help guide organizations into making better financial projections and project approval decisions. Beyond the system acquisition costs—for example, software licenses and maintenance costs, technical implementation, and hardware costs—other costs that are often overlooked when estimating project costs include:

- Travel and training costs for personnel
- Ongoing customization and integration costs
- Business process studies
- Project governance costs

If all costs are not considered, it can result in unexpected budget increases, delayed project timelines, and angry management. Next, we examine enterprise resource planning systems.

ENTERPRISE RESOURCE PLANNING

Today, most enterprise-wide information systems come in the form of **enterprise resource planning (ERP)** systems. In the 1990s, we witnessed companies' initial push to implement integrated applications, as exhibited by skyrocketing ERP sales at that time. Be aware that the terms "resource" and "planning" are somewhat misnomers, meaning that they only partially describe the purpose of ERP, since these applications do much more than just planning or managing resources. The reason for the term "enterprise resource planning" is that these systems evolved in part during the 1990s from material requirements planning and manufacturing resource planning packages. Do not get hung up on the words "resource" and "planning." The key word to remember from the acronym ERP is "enterprise."

ERP systems replace standalone applications by providing various modules based on a common database and similar application interfaces that serve the entire enterprise rather than portions of it. Information stored on legacy systems is converted into a large, centralized database that stores information related to the various business activities of an organization. Thus, ERP applications make accessing information easier by providing a central information repository, giving personnel access to accurate, up-to-date information throughout the organization. For example, inventory information is accessible not only to inbound logistics and operations, but also to accounting, sales, and customer service personnel. If a customer calls to inquire about the status of an order, customer service representatives can find out all

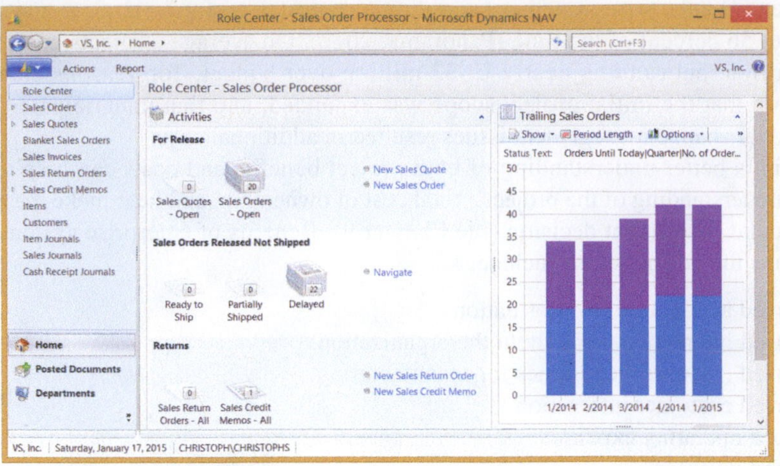

FIGURE 7.15

An ERP system can provide employees with relevant up-to-date information.

Source: Courtesy of Microsoft Corporation

necessary information through the ERP application (Figure 7.15). Storing data in a single place and making it available to everyone within the organization empowers everyone in the organization to be aware of the current state of business and to perform their jobs better. In addition, many ERP systems support business processes of globally operating organizations. For example, the ERP systems of SAP, the German enterprise systems pioneer, have multilingual interfaces and automatically convert measurement units (e.g., kilograms to pounds or centimeters to inches) and currencies. This way, engineers in Germany, Spain, or Italy can input the bill of materials, manufacturing engineers and factory specialists can buy the parts and set up the production run, and marketing and sales staff in the United States can easily communicate with their clients.

ERP modules that access the database are designed to have the same look and feel regardless of the unique needs of a particular department. Inbound logistics and operations personnel will use a common user interface to access the same pieces of information from the shared database. Although the inbound logistics module and the operations module will have different features tailored to the unique needs of the business functions, the screens will look comparable, with similar designs, screen layouts, menu options, and so on. The Microsoft Office products provide a useful analogy. Microsoft Word and Microsoft Excel are designed to provide different functions (word processing and spreadsheets, respectively), but overall the products look and feel very similar to one another. Word and Excel have similar user interfaces but differ vastly in the purpose, features, and functionality that each application offers. Likewise, the look and feel of Microsoft Dynamics (Microsoft's suite of enterprise-wide information systems) resembles that of Microsoft Office so as to reduce the learning curve for new users.

Responding to Compliance and Regulatory Demands

In addition to helping improve business processes, ERP systems improve and ease an organization's ability to implement audit controls and comply with government-imposed regulations. Compliance with far-reaching government mandates like the Sarbanes–Oxley Act and other evolving and emerging regulatory standards is based on the implementation and documentation of internal controls, procedures, and processes. All ERP systems are designed to include an abundance of control features that can mirror an organization's business processes (e.g., controlling who has access to information and process steps, segregating duties across job functions, etc.). Such enterprise-wide capabilities provide organizations with tested solutions for developing and deploying a comprehensive compliance strategy. While the ERP system may not provide answers to all regulatory requirements, deploying an ERP has been a central strategy for many organizations struggling to adhere to the myriad legal, regulatory, and supply chain mandates that are common in today's highly regulated business environment.

Choosing an ERP System

When selecting an appropriate ERP system for an organization, management needs to take many factors into careful consideration. Although ERP systems come in a variety of shapes and sizes, each designed to accommodate certain transaction volumes, industries, and business processes,

KEY PLAYERS

The Titans of ERP

Titan: Noun. A person or thing of great size or power.
In the ERP world, the three largest and most powerful ERP providers are SAP, Oracle, and Microsoft. Founded in 1972, SAP is a German multinational software corporation that is the world's leader in enterprise software, particularly in the world's largest and most complex ERP implementations, capturing over 24 percent of the ERP market in 2012. In 2013, SAP had over 66,000 employees and revenues exceeding US$23.3 billion.

Oracle Corporation is an American multinational computer technology corporation that specializes in developing and marketing computer hardware systems and enterprise software products. Oracle is best known for its database systems, but has rapidly expanded its ERP market share through natural sales growth and several high-profile acquisitions of ERP applications, including JD Edwards, PeopleSoft, and Siebel CRM. Oracle targets mid-to-large organizations with ERP solutions that are highly customizable to a particular organization and industry, capturing about 13 percent of the ERP market in 2012. In 2013, Oracle employed approximately 115,000 people worldwide, with revenues exceeding US$37 billion.

Microsoft Corporation, also an American multinational corporation, is a very diverse company that develops, manufactures, licenses, and supports a wide range of products and services related to computing. Microsoft is the largest software corporation in the world, with over 99,000 employees and revenues exceeding US$77.8 billion in 2013. Microsoft entered the ERP marketplace in 2000 with the acquisition of Great Plains accounting software, and since acquired several other companies to expand its Dynamics ERP product line, which is targeted at small to mid-sized businesses desiring a simple, out-of-the-box ERP solution. In 2012, Microsoft captured about 5 percent of the ERP market.

The systems offered by SAP, Oracle, and Microsoft have different strengths, weaknesses, and trade-offs. Organizations interested in acquiring an ERP system typically work with consultants to find the right vendor and the right product to meet their different needs.

Based on:
Columbus, L. (2013, May 5). 2013 ERP market share update: SAP solidifies market leadership. *Forbes*. Retrieved May 3, 2014, from http://www.forbes.com/sites/louiscolumbus/2013/05/12/2013-erp-market-share-update-sap-solidifies-market-leadership.

they come as packaged software, which means that they are designed to appeal to many different companies. However, businesses have unique needs even within their own industries. In other words, like snowflakes, no two companies are exactly alike. Management must carefully select an ERP system that will meet the unique requirements of its particular company, and must consider a number of factors in the ERP selection. Among the most prevalent issues facing management are ERP control and ERP business requirements.

ERP CONTROL. ERP control refers to the locus of control over the computing systems and data contained in those systems, as well as decision-making authority. Companies typically either opt for centralized control or allow particular business units to govern themselves. In the context of ERP, these decisions are based on the level of detail in the information that must be provided to management. Some corporations want to have as much detail as possible made available at the executive level, whereas other companies do not require such access. For instance, an accountant in one company may want the ability to view costs down to the level of individual transactions, while an accountant in another company may want only summary information. Another area related to control involves the consistency of policies and procedures. Some companies prefer that policies and procedures remain consistent throughout an organization. Other companies want to allow each business unit to develop its own policies and procedures to accommodate the unique ways that they do business. ERP systems vary widely in their allowance for control, typically assuming either a corporate or a business-unit locus of control. Some ERP systems allow users to select or customize the locus of control. In either case, management must consider the ERP's stance on control to ensure that it will meet the business requirements of the company.

ERP BUSINESS REQUIREMENTS. When selecting an ERP system, organizations must choose which modules to implement from a large menu of options—most organizations adopt only a subset of the available ERP components. There are two major categories of ERP components—ERP *core* components and ERP *extended* components (Figure 7.16).

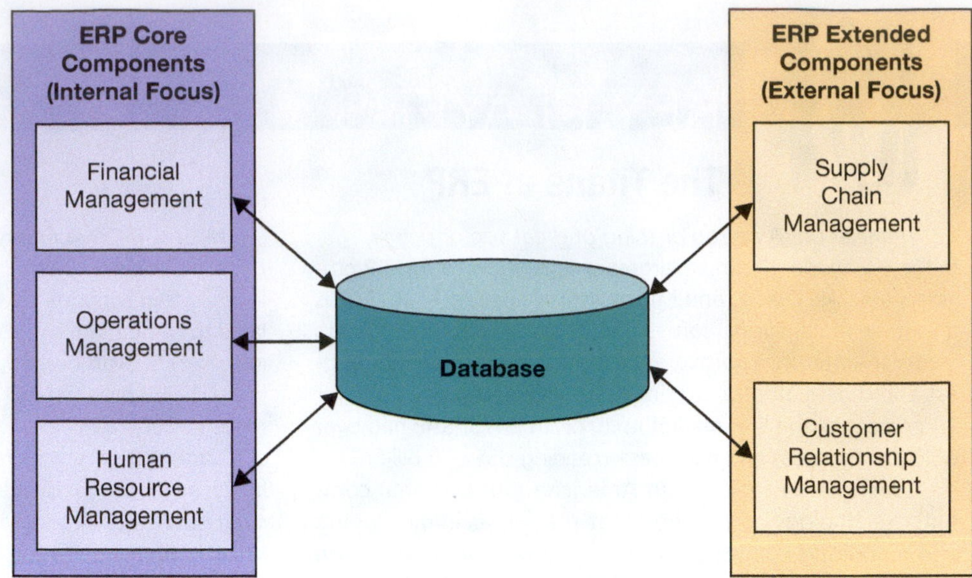

FIGURE 7.16

An ERP system consists of core and extended components.

ERP Core Components ERP **core components** support the important *internal* activities of the organization for producing its products and services. These components support internal operations such as the following:

1. ***Financial Management.*** Components to support accounting, financial reporting, performance management, and corporate governance
2. ***Operations Management.*** Components to simplify, standardize, and automate business processes related to inbound and outbound logistics, product development, manufacturing, and sales and service
3. ***Human Resource Management.*** Components to support employee recruitment, assignment tracking, performance reviews, payroll, and regulatory requirements

Whereas the operations management components enable the core activities of the value chain, financial management and human resources management are associated with activities supporting the core activities (Figure 7.17).

ERP Extended Components ERP **extended components** support the primary *external* activities of the organization for dealing with suppliers and customers. Specifically, ERP extended components focus primarily on supply chain management and customer relationship management. Both are discussed in detail in Chapter 8.

Enabling Business Processes Using ERP Core Components

To fit the needs of various businesses in different industries, an ERP system's core components are typically implemented using a building-block approach through a series of modules that support internally focused business processes. For example, Oracle's JD Edwards EnterpriseOne offers more than 70 different modules to support a variety of business processes. ERP vendors

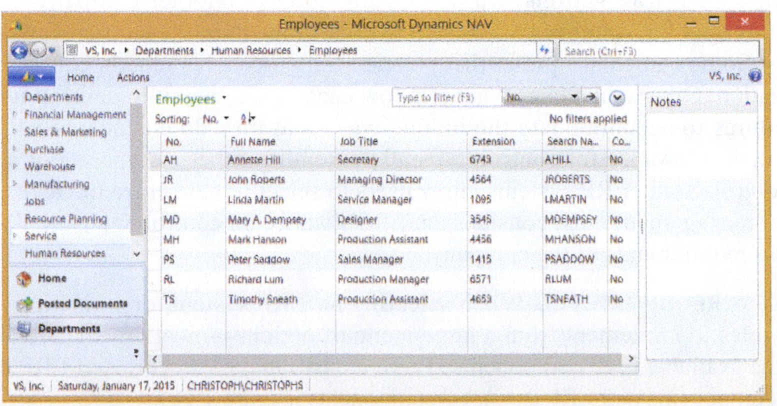

FIGURE 7.17

The human resources management component of an ERP enables core value chain activities to take place.

Source: Courtesy of Microsoft Corporation

TABLE 7.1 Industry-Specific Versions of the Microsoft Dynamics ERP System

Construction	Distribution
Education	Financial services
Government	Healthcare
Manufacturing	Not-for-profit
Professional services	Retail

typically package the various modules that enable industry-specific processes and offer such systems as "industry solutions." This way, organizations have to spend less effort in selecting the needed modules and can more easily implement the ERP system. For example, SAP's ERP application is built around modules that are modeled after the best practices for 25 different industries. Depending on the industries, the modules are localized for different countries: Whereas the modules for the automotive industry are localized for Japan or Germany, the modules for apparel and footwear industries are localized for China and India, the modules for the pharmaceutical industry are localized for Germany and the United States, and so on. Similarly, Microsoft offers its Dynamics ERP system for various industries, including construction, healthcare, manufacturing, retail, and others (Table 7.1). Depending on the way processes are typically performed in an industry, the modules within each industry-specific ERP system work together to enable the business processes needed to run a business efficiently and effectively. However, the modules provided by different vendors may vary in the specific business processes they support as well as in what they are called, and it is critical for managers to understand the vendors' naming conventions and software modules to gain an understanding of how these features can be implemented to support the company's business processes.

ORDER-TO-CASH. As discussed, the order-to-cash process entails the processes related to selling goods or services. Depending on the industry, the order-to-cash process can be very simple or extremely complex. In a retail environment, this process can be as simple as capturing product data, modifying the sale price (if needed), processing payment cards, and processing loyalty cards for customer profiling purposes. For a wholesale distributor, the order-to-cash process is more elaborate and consists of price quotation, stock allocation, credit limit check, picking, packing, shipping, billing, and receiving payment. For these processes to take place, different modules of the financial and operations management components work together. For example, the financial management component provides modules for checking credit limits, billing, and processing incoming payments. The operations management component provides modules related to sales and warehouse management operations, such as price quotation, stock allocation, picking, packing, and shipping (Figure 7.18).

PROCURE-TO-PAY. Recall that a generic procure-to-pay process entails negotiating price and terms, issuing purchase orders, receiving the goods, receiving the invoice, and settling the payment. As the order-to-cash process differs between industries, so does the procure-to-pay process. A grocery store, for example, typically orders a standard assortment of products, but also faces additional constraints such as having to optimize order quantities, taking into account not only demand and storage costs but also seasonality and perishability of products. In contrast, a construction company procures diverse materials, depending on the project at

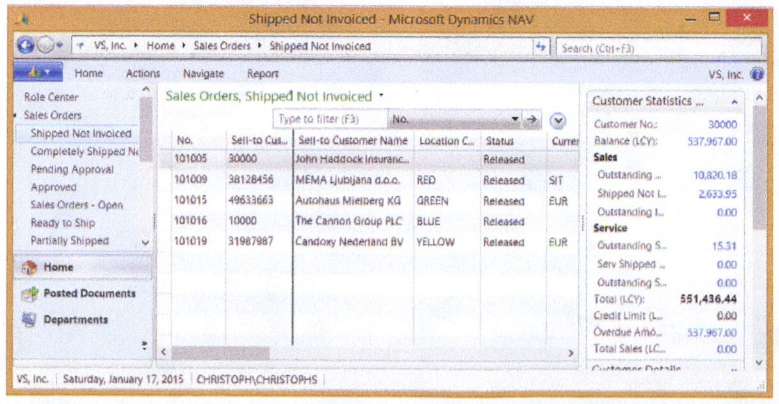

FIGURE 7.18

An ERP system can support all aspects of the order-to-cash process.

Source: Courtesy of Microsoft Corporation

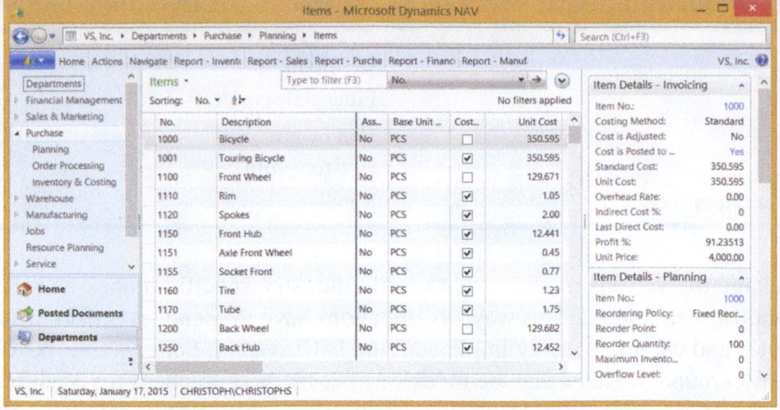

FIGURE 7.19

An ERP system can support all aspects of the procure-to-pay process.

Source: Courtesy of Microsoft Corporation

hand, and the procurement process could entail a lengthy sourcing process, including requests for quotations, a bidding process, reviewing of bids, awarding the contract, and thoroughly inspecting the delivered products or materials (see also Chapter 9 for the process of purchasing a new information system). Similar to the order-to-cash process, different modules of the financial management and operations management ERP components work together to enable the different activities related to the procure-to-pay process (Figure 7.19).

MAKE-TO-STOCK/MAKE-TO-ORDER. The processes related to producing goods differ widely between different industries. The biggest distinction is between the make-to-stock and make-to-order processes. As indicated, the make-to-stock process is typically used for commodities, whereas the make-to-order process is used for highly customizable goods or big-ticket items (such as aircraft or highway bridges). Many beverage companies, for instance, use a make-to-stock approach, involving production planning, manufacturing, and quality control. In contrast, an aerospace company has to start with planning the project and ordering subassemblies or raw materials with long lead times before planning and executing the production for each specific project, and finally checking quality and shipping the product. Many of the activities associated with the production process are supported by the operations management component of an ERP (Figure 7.20).

OTHER BUSINESS PROCESSES. In addition to these business processes, ERP systems typically enable a variety of other generic as well as industry-specific business processes. Any business needs to manage its workforce, including managing the hiring processes, scheduling the workforce, recording time and attendance, processing payroll, managing benefits, and so on. All these processes are supported by the human resources management component of an ERP. Similarly, the financial management component supports generic processes such as financial and managerial accounting, corporate governance, and the like. Industry-specific processes and the modules supporting these can vary widely. For example, the business of an aircraft manufacturer consists to a large extent of aftermarket support; a retail chain, in contrast, needs modules supporting retail space planning and price and markdown management; a commercial real estate company needs modules for managing assets, leases, and common spaces; and a large part of an airline's operations is related to maintenance, repair, overhaul, flight operations, catering, and customer care.

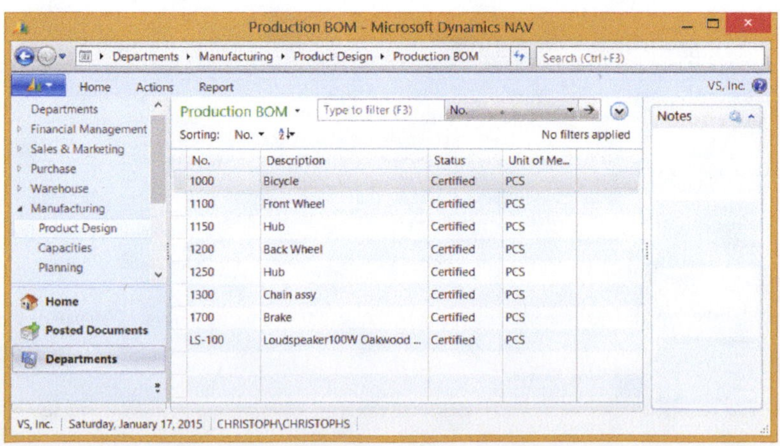

FIGURE 7.20

An ERP system can support all aspects of the production process.

Source: Courtesy of Microsoft Corporation

ERP Installation

Previously, we discussed how organizations can benefit from the integration of standalone systems; further, you learned how business processes can differ between industries. Thus, any organization considering the implementation of an ERP system has to carefully evaluate the different options available not only in terms of the overall systems offered by different vendors but also in terms of the industry-specific solutions offered by the software vendors. An evaluation should entail the assessment of how far the different modules can support existing business processes, which modules may have to be added, and the extent to which existing business processes have to be modified in order to fit the modules offered by the ERP system.

An activity that is widely underestimated, however, is the *configuration* of ERP systems. Whereas customization involves the programming of company-specific modules or changing how business processes are implemented within the system and is often discouraged, configuration is an activity to be performed during any ERP implementation. Specifically, the system must be configured to reflect the way an organization does business and the associated business rules. As one of the most important parts of an ERP system is the underlying company-wide database, setting up the database is key to a successful ERP implementation, and organizations have to make countless decisions on how to configure hundreds or thousands of database tables to fit the business's needs. Similarly, organizations have to make thousands of decisions related to the different business processes. For example, what should be the format of the unique identifier for a customer, when will a bill be considered overdue, what is considered the "standard" method of shipping, and so on? To make all these decisions, a good understanding of the way the company does its business is needed. Hence, many organizations hire experienced business analysts or outside consultants to assist with these configuration tasks.

WHO'S GOING MOBILE

Big ERP Systems Embracing Small Mobile Devices

As ERP technologies have transformed organizations of all sizes in all industries, mobile devices have transformed how people manage day-to-day activities and organizations. As a result, ERP vendors are rapidly evolving their systems to better support managers with a variety of mobile ERP applications, so that managers will be able to take advantage of the functionality, data, and benefits of their ERP application not only in the office, but also on the road, enabling real-time management. Mobile ERP applications can provide many benefits to an organization, including:

1. **Improving Service Quality**—Mobile ERP will allow remote workers access to relevant customer information, improving service quality and responsiveness.
2. **Improving Productivity**—Mobile ERP will allow remote workers to access key resources when commuting or waiting in airports, improving productivity and reducing downtime.
3. **Strengthening Customer Relationships**—Mobile ERP will allow remote workers to have key customer information when needed to strengthen customer relationships.
4. **Improving Competitive Advantage**—Mobile ERP can speed responsiveness to customer needs, improving competitive advantage.
5. **Improving Data Timeliness and Accuracy**—Mobile ERP allows for easier, less redundant, and more timely data capture, allowing workers in the field to capture critical data as they emerge without having to rekey the data into multiple systems where errors and inconsistencies can occur.

In 2014, SAP announced 6 new mobile applications, which will add to its nearly 300 mobile applications currently available via the SAP Store, where the company advertises the many mobile apps that have been developed for the SAP platform. Microsoft is also developing a suite of mobile applications for reporting and dashboarding for its Dynamics ERP system. As mobility is a megatrend that will only become more and more prevalent in the workplace, organizations should choose ERP systems that have the capability and flexibility to integrate with an expanding array of mobile devices and platforms.

Based on:

Anonymous. (2014, April 22). Synactive Inc. launches six new mobile apps for SAP ERP. *MarketWatch*. Retrieved May 3, 2014, from http://www.marketwatch.com/story/synactive-inc-launches-six-new-mobile-apps-for-sap-erp-2014-04-22.

Borek, R. (2011, July 22). 5 benefits to mobile ERP. *ERP Software-Blog*. Retrieved May 3, 2014, from http://www.erpsoftwareblog.com/2011/07/5-benefits-to-mobile-erp.

SAP Store. (2014, May 3). SAP Store. *SAP*. Retrieved May 3, 2014, from https://store.sap.com/sap/cpa/ui/resources/store/html/Solutions.html?pcntry=US&sap-language=EN&catID=MOB.

ERP Limitations

While ERP systems can help organizations streamline business processes, give personnel access to accurate, up-to-date information throughout the organization, and better respond to regulatory demands, they also pose limitations. In particular, ERP systems typically require organizations to modify various business processes; once an ERP system is implemented, the company is virtually locked in, and it is very difficult to make further changes, limiting organizations' flexibility and agility when facing new external challenges. Typically, even small changes to the way processes are implemented in the ERP system require programming changes, leading to higher costs for ongoing system maintenance.

ACHIEVING ENTERPRISE SYSTEM SUCCESS

To summarize, the main objective of enterprise systems is to help achieve competitive advantage by streamlining business activities within and outside a company. However, many implementations turn out to be more costly and time consuming than originally envisioned. It is not uncommon to have projects that run over budget, meaning that identifying common problems and devising methods for dealing with these issues can prove invaluable to management. Industry surveys have shown that over 90 percent of companies that undertake enterprise system implementations realize some benefits; around 50 percent realize about half of the expected benefits, and 6 percent report that they did not realize any benefits (Panorama, 2012).

Given these numbers, should businesses even attempt to tackle large IS projects? The answer is, in most cases, yes. Typically, organizations do not (or should not) start such projects for the sake of starting the projects; rather, organizations are trying to fix certain problems, such as inefficient or ineffective distribution, pricing, or logistics, or lack of compliance with government regulations. Further, businesses have realized that it is all but impossible to improve business processes without the support of information systems. Companies that have successfully installed enterprise systems are found to follow a basic set of recommendations related to enterprise system implementations. As with all large projects, governance and risk mitigation are critical to success, and companies should attempt to share both risks and rewards with the vendors. Although the following list is not meant to be comprehensive, these recommendations will provide an understanding of some of the challenges involved in implementing enterprise systems:

Recommendation 1. Secure executive sponsorship.

Recommendation 2. Get help from outside experts.

Recommendation 3. Thoroughly train users.

Recommendation 4. Take a multidisciplinary approach to implementations.

Recommendation 5. Evolve the implementation.

Secure Executive Sponsorship

The primary reason why enterprise system implementations fail is believed to be a lack of top-level management support. Although executives do not necessarily need to make decisions concerning the enterprise system, it is critical that they buy into the decisions made by project managers. Many problems can arise if projects fail to grab the attention of top-level management. In most companies, executives have the ultimate authority regarding the availability and distribution of resources within the organization. If executives do not understand the importance of the enterprise system, this will likely result in delays or stoppages because the necessary resources may not be available when they are needed.

A second problem that may arise deals with top-level management's ability to authorize changes in the way the company does business. When business processes need to be changed to incorporate best practices, these modifications need to be completed. Otherwise, the company will have a piece of software on its hands that does not fit the way people accomplish their business tasks. Lack of executive sponsorship can also have a trickle-down effect within the organization. As people, in general, are reluctant to change the way they are working, there is bound to be resistance to the implementation of an ERP system. If users and midlevel management perceive the enterprise system to be unimportant, they are not likely to view it as a priority. Enterprise systems require a concentrated effort, and executive sponsorship can propel or stifle the implementation. Executive sponsorship can obliterate many obstacles that arise.

Get Help from Outside Experts

Enterprise systems are complex. Even the most talented IS departments can struggle in coming to grips with ERP, customer relationship management, and supply chain management applications. Most vendors have trained project managers and experienced consultants to assist companies with installing enterprise systems. Outside consultants can prove invaluable when helping the organization to stick to the implementation schedule and resist changes in project scope. Using consultants tends to move companies through the implementation more quickly and tends to help companies train their personnel on the applications more effectively. However, companies should not rely too heavily on support from the vendors. The salespeople's job is, after all, selling a system, and they are unlikely to thoroughly understand the company's exact business needs. Thus, organizations should also draw on external consultants to help define the functionality *before* selecting a vendor, and to ensure that all requirements are incorporated in the contract with the vendor. In addition, companies should plan for the consultants leaving once the implementation is complete. When consultants are physically present, company personnel tend to rely on them for assistance. Once the application goes live and the consultants are no longer there, users have to do the job themselves. A key focus should therefore be facilitating user learning.

Thoroughly Train Users

Training is often the most overlooked, underestimated, and poorly budgeted expense involved in planning enterprise system implementations. Enterprise systems are much more complicated to learn than standalone systems. Learning a single application requires users to become accustomed to a new software interface, but enterprise system users typically need to learn a new set of business processes as well. Once enterprise systems go live, many companies initially experience a dramatic drop-off in productivity. This issue can potentially lead to heightened levels of dissatisfaction among users, as they prefer to accomplish their business activities in a familiar manner rather than doing things the new way. By training users before the system goes live and giving them sufficient opportunities to learn the new system, a company can allay fears and mitigate potential productivity issues.

WHEN THINGS GO WRONG

The Not-So-Beautiful ERP Implementation

Avon Products, Inc. is an international manufacturer of beauty and personal care products. Avon uses door-to-door and referral marketing to sell its products to generate its annual revenue of over US$10 billion in 2013; customers satisfied with the product can become a distributor themselves for discounts and extra income.

To support its business processes, Avon announced the "Promise" program in 2009, an initiative to develop and support a mobile application and Web site for local sales reps to use for entering product orders. After spending four years developing the ERP infrastructure and inventory management systems to support the program, Avon launched a pilot of the program in Canada in 2012, and sales reps were told to use the new system to enter all their orders, either via a browser or a newly developed iPad app.

Unfortunately, the pilot was a miserable failure. The mobile application and Web site were not simple enough to use for the average local sales rep to understand, and sales reps left the company in droves; at least one sales manager has reported that the Promise program annihilated the business in her area. After several months of difficulty and negative press, Avon cancelled the project, resulting in a write-off of US$125 million for the cost of the software and a decline in Avon's stock price of over 30 percent.

In the aftermath of the failure, the companies involved pointed the finger of blame at each other. SAP was involved in the development of the ERP backend, while a third party handled the development of the front-end ordering Web site and mobile application. Either of those companies may be somewhat at fault. Avon is also reported to have rushed the program into production before it was ready, so perhaps Avon is also to blame. In any case, though the original intention of the program was clearly attractive, the end result that users interact with appears to have been the deciding factor in the program's demise.

Based on:

Avon Products. (2014, April 26). In *Wikipedia, The Free Encyclopedia*. Retrieved May 3, 2014, from http://en.wikipedia.org/w/index.php?title=Avon_Products&oldid=605848949.

Henschen, D. (2013, December 12). Avon pulls plug on $125 million SAP project. *InformationWeek.com*. Retrieved May 3, 2014, from http://www.informationweek.com/software/enterprise-applications/avon-pulls-plug-on-$125-million-sap-project/d/d-id/1113061.

Take a Multidisciplinary Approach to Implementations

Enterprise systems affect the entire organization; thus, companies should include personnel from different levels and departments in the implementation project (Kumar & Crook, 1999). In customer relationship management and supply chain management environments in which other organizations are participating in the implementation, it is critical to enlist the support of personnel in their organizations as well. During implementation, project managers need to include personnel from midlevel management, the IS department, external consultants, and, most important, end users.

Failing to include the appropriate people in the day-to-day activities of the project can prove problematic in many areas. From a needs-analysis standpoint, it is critical that all the business requirements be sufficiently captured before selecting an enterprise solution. Since end users are involved in every aspect of daily business activities, their insights can be invaluable. For instance, an end user might make salient a feature that no one on the project team had thought of. Having an application that does not meet all of the business's requirements can result in poorly fitting software or customizations. Another peril in leaving out key personnel is the threat of alienation. Departments and/or personnel that do not feel included may develop a sense of animosity toward the new system and view it in a negative light. In extreme cases, users will refuse to use the new application, resulting in conflicts and inefficiencies within the organization.

Evolve the Implementation

As you can see, implementing ERP systems is a highly complex undertaking; although a successful implementation can have huge payoffs for an organization, some organizations fear losing the ability to quickly respond to changing business requirements, particularly since large ERP systems are difficult to install, maintain, and upgrade. In addition, the life cycle of a large ERP installation is typically 10 to 15 years. A recent trend, especially for small and mid-sized companies, is to move away from such large, comprehensive in-house systems toward cloud-based ERP solutions. As with other cloud-based solutions, companies implementing cloud-based ERP can benefit from scalability and agility. In addition, many companies extending into new markets or new market segments are extending their existing ERP systems with cloud-based solutions. Such two-tier ERP strategy can support operations at the corporate level, while providing the needed flexibility and agility at the subsidiary level. This can be especially beneficial when entering global markets, as the cloud-based solutions can be easily adapted to local needs and regulations, without having to make extensive changes to the core ERP system.

Another key trend is the ability to manage a business in real time. With the costs of sensors decreasing at a tremendous pace (see Chapter 1), organizations are now able to acquire data about various operational processes in real time. Being able to use this data for business decisions is regarded as critical for successfully competing in the digital world. Traditionally, organizations separated the processing of transactions from the analysis (see Chapter 6, "Enhancing Business Intelligence Using Information Systems"), so as to prevent the analytical applications from slowing down the transaction processing. Even then, batch transactions could take hours, and decision makers could not get quick answers to pressing business questions, as transactional data was loaded only periodically into the analytical systems, so that the data needed for real-time business intelligence was just not available. New technology using in-memory computing (see Chapter 3) can help to tremendously increase processing speed by reducing disk latency, while at the same time enabling the removal of the distinction between transactional and analytical systems. Paired with the continuing trend of mobile access to ERP systems, this enables managers to manage business in real time and quickly respond to changes as they occur.

Although expansive enterprise system implementations are often cumbersome and difficult, the potential payoff is huge. As a result, organizations are compelled to implement these systems. Further, given the popularity and necessity of integrating systems and processes on an organization-wide basis, you are likely to find yourself involved in the implementation and/or use of such a system. We are confident that after reading this chapter, you will be better able to understand and help with the development and use of such systems.

INDUSTRY ANALYSIS

The Automobile Industry

There are more than 800 million cars and light trucks on the road throughout the world. With almost 83 million vehicles sold worldwide in 2013, experts predict this number to climb to 100 million by 2018, with China alone accounting for 30 million vehicles sold. In addition, countries such as Brazil, Russia, and India, but also other emerging economies (especially in Southeast Asia), will significantly contribute to this growth.

Currently, there is growing global demand for small, energy-efficient vehicles. Since 2006, the "World Car of the Year" has been selected by a jury of 48 international automotive journalists from 22 countries. Cars nominated for this award need to have been sold in at least five countries and on at least two continents. In recent years, the Nissan Leaf (2011), Volkswagen Up! (2012), and Volkswagen Golf (2013), all small and highly efficient vehicles, have been chosen as winners.

In the meantime, the automobile industry continues to explore other ways of responding to global market demands. Many automobile manufacturers have dramatically evolved their global networks of suppliers (such as Bosch and Continental from Germany, Magna and Lear from the United States, and Yazaki from Japan), leveraging these broad supply chains to bring new innovations to market, ranging from USB ports to hard drives for storing music to mobile data connectivity. In addition, manufacturers and technology companies are finding interesting ways to make cars safer and more convenient. For several years, Google has famously been working on technology to support a self-driving car. The system drives the car at the speed limit it has stored from Google's mapping database and maintains distance from other vehicles using an array of sensors.

Beyond optimizing supply chains and adding new innovative features, automakers are trying to attract new customers by finding new ways to present their newest models. For example, to reach a broader audience, BMW recently opened a virtual showroom in an upscale shopping center in Paris, France, which includes five 3D car configurators so shoppers can design their dream car with all desired options. Audi built a similar store in Beijing, allowing customers to view their custom configuration on six wall-sized displays. Such stores provide a new way to attract customers, and help premium brands to differentiate their offerings.

Questions

1. How has globalization changed the business processes of auto manufacturers?
2. What innovative technologies may be included in the cars of the future?

Based on:

Google driverless car. (2014, May 3). In *Wikipedia, The Free Encyclopedia*. Retrieved May 3, 2014, from http://en.wikipedia.org/wiki/Google_driverless_car.

Gibbs, N. (2013, March 14). Audi, BMW, Mercedes look for edge with virtual showrooms. *Automotive News Europe*. Retrieved May 3, 2014, from http://europe.autonews.com/article/20130314/ANE/130309959/audi-bmw-mercedes-look-for-edge-with-virtual-showrooms.

LeBeau, P. (2014, January 9). Global auto sales hit record high of 82.8 million. *CNBC*. Retrieved May 3, 2014, from http://www.cnbc.com/id/101321938.

Key Points Review

1. ***Explain core business processes that are common in organizations.*** Most organizations are organized around distinct functional areas that work together to execute the core business processes order-to-cash, procure-to-pay, and make-to-stock/order. Together, these core business processes enable the creation of value chains that are involved in transforming raw materials into products sold to the end consumer. Value chains are composed of both core activities (inbound logistics, operations and manufacturing, outbound logistics, marketing and sales, and customer service) and support activities (administrative activities, infrastructure, human resources, technology development, and procurement). Companies connect their value chains with suppliers and customers, creating value systems such that information flows from one company's value chain to another company's value chain.
2. ***Describe what enterprise systems are and how they have evolved.*** Enterprise systems are information systems that span the entire organization and can be used to integrate business processes, activities, and information across all the functional areas of a firm. Enterprise systems evolved from legacy systems that supported distinct organizational activities by combining data and applications into a single comprehensive system, and can be either prepackaged software or custom-made applications. The implementation of enterprise systems often involves business process management, a systematic, structured improvement approach by all or part of an organization that critically examines, rethinks, and redesigns processes in order to achieve dramatic improvements in one or more performance measures, such as quality, cycle time, or cost.

3. ***Describe enterprise resource planning systems and how they help to improve internal business processes.*** ERP systems allow information to be shared throughout the organization through the use of a large database, helping to streamline business processes and improve customer service. When selecting an ERP system, organizations must choose which modules to implement from a large menu of options—most organizations adopt only a subset of the available ERP components. ERP core components support the major internal activities of the organization for producing its products and services, while ERP extended components support the primary external activities of the organization for dealing with suppliers and customers.
4. ***Understand and utilize the keys to successfully implementing enterprise systems.*** Experience with enterprise system implementations suggests that there are some common problems that can be avoided and/or should be managed carefully. Organizations can avoid common implementation problems by (1) securing executive sponsorship, (2) getting necessary help from outside experts, (3) thoroughly training users, (4) taking a multidisciplinary approach to implementations, and (5) keeping track of evolving ERP trends.

Key Terms

best practices 265
business process management (BPM) 265
business process reengineering (BPR) 265
core activities 255
custom software 263
customization 264
downstream information flow 259
enterprise resource planning (ERP) 267
enterprise system 260
enterprise-wide information system 260
ERP core components 270
ERP extended components 270
externally focused system 262
internally focused system 262
interorganizational system (IOS) 262
legacy system 260
make-to-order process 254
make-to-stock process 254
module 263
off-the-shelf software 263
order-to-cash process 253
packaged software 263
procure-to-pay process 253
standalone application 259
support activities 257
upstream information flow 258
value system 258
vanilla version 264

Go to **mymislab.com** to complete the problems marked with this icon.

Review Questions

7-1. What are core business processes?
7-2. What are the core and support activities of a value chain?
7-3. Give an example of upstream and downstream information flows in a value system.
 **7-4.** Describe what enterprise systems are and how they have evolved.
7-5. Compare and contrast customized and packaged software as well as vanilla versions versus best practices–based software.
7-6. What are the core components of an ERP system?
7-7. What are the keys to successfully implementing an ERP system?

Self-Study Questions

7-8. ______________ are information systems that allow companies to integrate information and support operations on a company-wide basis.
A. Customer relationship management systems
B. Enterprise systems
C. Wide area networks
D. Interorganizational systems

7-9. Which of the following is a core activity according to the value chain model?
A. firm infrastructure
B. customer service
C. human resources
D. procurement

7-10. According to the value chain model, which of the following is a support activity?
A. technology development
B. marketing and sales
C. inbound logistics
D. operations and manufacturing

7-11. All of the following are true about legacy systems except ______________.
A. they are standalone systems
B. they are older software systems
C. they are ERP systems
D. they may be difficult to integrate into other systems

7-12. The processes associated with obtaining goods from external vendors are referred to as ______________.
A. make-to-order processes
B. make-to-stock processes
C. procure-to-pay processes
D. order-to-cash processes

7-13. The processes associated with selling a product or service are referred to as ______________.
A. make-to-order processes
B. make-to-stock processes
C. procure-to-pay processes
D. order-to-cash processes

7-14. Which processes are most often associated with pull-based manufacturing of products?
A. make-to-order processes
B. make-to-stock processes
C. procure-to-pay processes
D. order-to-cash processes

7-15. Information systems that focus on supporting functional areas, business processes, and decision making within an organization are referred to as ______________.
A. legacy systems
B. enterprise-wide information systems
C. interorganizational systems
D. internally focused systems

7-16. An enterprise system that has not been customized is commonly referred to as ______________.
A. a vanilla version
B. a root version
C. a core version
D. none of the above

7-17. ______________ is a systematic, structured improvement approach by all or part of an organization that critically examines, rethinks, and redesigns processes in order to achieve dramatic improvements in one or more performance measures, such as quality, cycle time, or cost.
A. Systems analysis
B. Business process management
C. Customer relationship management
D. Total quality management

Answers are on page 280.

Problems and Exercises

7-18. Match the following terms with the appropriate definitions:

i. Enterprise systems
ii. Legacy systems
iii. Value system
iv. ERP extended components
v. Standalone applications
vi. Vanilla version
vii. Make-to-stock process
viii. Business process management
ix. Procure-to-pay process
x. Internally focused systems

a. Components that support the primary *external* activities of the organization for dealing with suppliers and customers
b. Systems that focus on the specific needs of individual departments
c. The processes associated with producing goods based on forecasted demand
d. Older systems that are not designed to communicate with other applications beyond departmental boundaries
e. Information systems that allow companies to integrate information on a company-wide basis
f. The features and modules that a packaged software system comes with out of the box
g. The processes associated with acquiring goods from suppliers
h. A systematic, structured improvement approach by all or part of an organization whereby people critically examine, rethink, and redesign business processes in order to achieve dramatic improvements in one or more performance measures, such as quality, cycle time, or cost
i. Information systems that support functional areas, business processes, and decision making within an organization
j. A collection of interlocking company value chains

7-19. Find an organization that you are familiar with and determine how many software applications it is utilizing concurrently. Are the company's information systems cohesive, or do they need updating and streamlining?

7-20. What part does training users in an ERP system play, and how important is it in job satisfaction? What productivity problems can result from an ERP implementation?

7-21. What are the payoffs from taking a multidisciplinary approach to an ERP implementation? What departments are affected, and what is the typical time frame? Research an organization that has recently implemented an ERP system. What could the company have done better, and what did it do right?

7-22. For a business or organization that you are familiar with, describe its order-to-cash process using the steps outlined in Figure 7.3; if the organization doesn't have a particular step, explain why this is so.

7-23. For a business or organization that you are familiar with, describe its procure-to-pay process using the steps outlined in Figure 7.4; if the organization doesn't have a particular step, explain why this is so.

7-24. For a business or organization that you are familiar with, describe either its make-to-stock or make-to-order process using the steps outlined in Figure 7.5; if the organization doesn't have a particular step, explain why this is so.

7-25. Using Figure 7.6 as a guide, develop a supply chain diagram for some other product.

7-26. Explain what is meant by upstream and downstream in the value chain and explain how Walmart influences both ends to control costs.

7-27. Based on your own experiences with applications, have you used customized or off-the-shelf applications? What is the difference, and how good was the system documentation?

7-28. Search the Web for the phrase "best practices," and you will find numerous sites that summarize the best practices for a variety of industries and professions. Choose one and summarize these best practices in a one-page report.

7-29. Examine and contrast the differences between packaged and custom software. When is one approach better or worse than the other?

7-30. Search the Web for recent articles on business process management and related approaches (e.g., business process reengineering) for improving organizations. What is the current state of the art for these approaches? To what extent are these "headlines" about IS implementations, especially regarding enterprise systems?

7-31. Search the Web for recent stories about the use of cloud-based ERP systems. To what extent does it appear that cloud-based ERP systems will be replacing traditional ERP systems?

Application Exercises

Note: The existing data files referenced in these exercises are available on the book's Web site: www.pearsonhighered.com/valacich.

Spreadsheet Application: Choosing an ERP System at Campus Travel

7-32. Campus Travel is interested in integrating its business processes to streamline processes such as purchasing, sales, human resource management, and customer relationship management. Because of your success in implementing the e-commerce infrastructure, the general manager asks you for advice on what to do to streamline operations at Campus Travel. Use the data provided in the file ERPSystems.csv to make a recommendation about which ERP system to purchase. The file includes ratings of the different modules of the systems and the weights assigned to these ratings. You are asked to do the following:

- Determine the product with the highest overall rating. (Hint: Use the SUMPRODUCT formula to multiply each vendor's scores with the respective weights and add the weighted scores.)
- Prepare the necessary graphs to compare the products on the different dimensions and the overall score.
- Be sure to professionally format the graphs before printing them out.

Database Application: Creating Forms at Campus Travel

7-33. After helping Campus Travel off to a good start with its databases, you have decided that it should enter data using forms rather than doing it from tables. From your experience, you know that employees have an easier time being able to browse, modify, and add records from a form view. As this can be implemented using your existing database, you decide to set up a form. You can accomplish this by doing the following:

- Open the database employeeData.mdb.
- Select the employee table in the database window.
- Create a form using the table. (Hint: This can be done by selecting "More Forms >> Form Wizard" under "Forms" in the "Create" tab.)
- Save the form as "employees."

Team Work Exercise

Net Stats: Should They Expect to Fail?

For years, broad surveys have reported surprisingly high rates of ERP project failures. In a survey exploring the nature of these failures, Panorama Consulting Solutions, an ERP systems integrator found that in 2013, over 50 percent of ERP projects experienced cost overruns, and over 60 percent experienced schedule overruns. Even worse, fully 60 percent of the survey respondents reported receiving under half of the expected benefit from their ERP implementation. Only about 8 percent reported receiving 80 percent or more of the expected benefit from their new ERP system. Clearly, ERP implementations are prone to difficulties and delays, but the reasons behind the problems are difficult to pinpoint.

Questions and Exercises

7-34. Search the Web to identify a story about a recent ERP implementation failure.

7-35. As a team, interpret this article. What caused the project to fail? What could have been done differently?

7-36. As a team, discuss how the Panorama survey might look in 5 years and 10 years. Will success rates improve? Get worse? Why?

7-37. Using your presentation software of choice, create two or three slides that summarize the findings you consider most important.

Based on:

Krigsman, M. (2013, February 22). 2013 ERP research: Compelling advice for the CFO. *ZDNet*. Retrieved May 3, 2014, from http://www.zdnet.com/2013-erp-research-compelling-advice-for-the-cfo-7000011619.

Answers to the Self-Study Questions

7-8. B, p. 260	**7-9.** B, p. 255	**7-10.** A, p. 257	**7-11.** C, p. 260	**7-12.** C, p. 253
7-13. D, p. 253	**7-14.** A, p. 254	**7-15.** D, p. 262	**7-16.** A, p. 264	**7-17.** B, p. 265

CASE 1 Software as a Service: ERP by the Hour

As you know by now, an organization's IS infrastructure is not simple to construct or maintain, but is a complex infrastructure of servers and databases useful for managing large amounts of information. A new model of IS infrastructure and software has appeared and is rapidly changing the way many organizations do business. Software as a service, or SaaS, is a way for organizations to use cloud-based Internet services to accomplish the goals that traditional IS infrastructure and software models have in the past. SaaS allows software application vendors to deploy their products over the Internet through Web-based services. SaaS customers pay to use applications on demand, giving them the freedom to access a software service only when needed. Applications and software are developed, hosted, and operated by SaaS vendors, and customers are charged on a pay-per-use basis. Once the customer's "license" expires, it no longer has to carry the cost of the software. If a future need for the software arises, the customer simply orders it again to have access. SaaS products can be licensed for single or multiple users within the organization, making them flexible and scalable.

Using the SaaS model has several advantages. Through SaaS applications, organizations can move their data storage into the cloud, reducing the cost of buying storage and diminishing the risk of catastrophic data loss, as it is in the vendor's financial interest to keep the services it provides running at peak performance, or the vendor risks losing customers to another vendor. In addition, SaaS allows for less resource expenditure on long-term software licensing because an organization can get what it needs when it needs it. SaaS utilization also allows organizations to become more productive outside the physical confines of their buildings. Since SaaS services are in the cloud, employees can access services in remote offices, on the road, or from their mobile device.

One of the main disadvantages of SaaS is that customers must give up some autonomy over their applications and data. Some organizations require specialized software solutions and are used to customizing software in-house to meet their needs. Although some SaaS vendors are beginning to offer customizable solutions, the problem is still a roadblock for some. Computing off-site also means that security may be an issue, as organizational operations and data are effectively running on someone else's computer. As it is virtually impossible for some types of organizations to keep their data—and their secrets—in the cloud, such concerns are another roadblock that organizations must overcome in order to use SaaS products.

These disadvantages aside, organizations are reaping the benefits of SaaS, utilizing them for human resources activities, e-mail services, collaboration efforts, storage solutions, and financial tasks such as billing, invoicing, and timekeeping. In addition to more general-purpose applications, many organizations are deploying ERP capabilities via SaaS vendors. And the growth of the SaaS industry doesn't appear to be slowing. In fact, a recent study by Gartner found that by 2016, SaaS revenues should reach US$232.8 billion.

Companies like Google, Amazon.com, and Microsoft have become well-known SaaS vendors offering a range of services to organizations, including shared-document management, communication services, cloud-based e-mail, calendaring, photo and video sharing, Web and intranet page management, and data storage services, just to name a few. Given the challenges and issues associated with implementing in-house enterprise systems, ERP vendors are increasingly offering their software as a service as well. For example, SAP offers SAP Business ByDesign, an integrated on-demand ERP solution for small and medium-sized enterprises. Similarly, Microsoft offers its Dynamics customer relationship management system as a service, and Oracle offers the subscription-based Oracle On-Demand customer relationship management solution.

As more organizations continue to adopt SaaS services as a way of carrying out their day-to-day activities, vendors will continue to upgrade and expand the available technologies for use. The question of whether organizations will adopt SaaS services has, for the most part, been answered. The question has now become how much of their business they will put in the cloud.

Questions

7-38. Would you trust an external provider with your organization's data? Why or why not? What would be needed to raise your trust in the reliability, security, and privacy of the data?

7-39. What are the potential drawbacks of using a relatively simple in-house database with limited capabilities versus a more robust, SaaS database solution? Do the benefits outweigh these limitations? Why or why not?

7-40. Are there any types of applications that should only be purchased rather than obtained through an SaaS relationship? If so, why or why not?

Based on:

Biddick, M. (2010, January 16). Why you need a SaaS strategy. *InformationWeek*. Retrieved May 3, 2012, from http://www.informationweek.com/news/services/saas/showArticle.jhtml?articleID=222301002.

Rosenfield, C. (2013, September 14). Gartner forecasts that the SaaS market will grow to $32.8 billion in 2016. *Qoints.com*. Retrieved May 3, 2014, from http://qoints.com/2013/09/14/market-insight/gartner-forecasts-that-the-saas-market-will-grow-to-32-8-billion-in-2016.

Software as a service. (2014, April 29). In *Wikipedia, The Free Encyclopedia*. Retrieved May 3, 2014, from http://en.wikipedia.org/w/index.php?title=Software_as_a_service&oldid=606295197.

CASE 2 Big Project, Big Failure

If you Google the phrase "ERP failure" you will find millions of search results. While most ERP industry experts know that far too many ERP projects run over budget and fail to live up to expected benefits, one recent project failure demonstrates just how bad a failure can be.

Bridgestone Americas, a large automobile tire manufacturer, receives approximately one tire order every second, eight hours a day, five days a week, requesting delivery to over 62,000 locations across North America. Prior to 2012, all of these orders were processed by an aging computer mainframe system, running a program written in the COBOL computer language. In 2007, Bridgestone contracted with IBM to design, install, and configure SAP software across the entire business to replace the legacy mainframe system. IBM promised "all of its best people, methodologies, tools, and design and management practices" to ensure a smooth transition. IBM also promised that they new ERP system would be ready for launch on July 30, 2011.

Six months after the promised deadline, and after Bridgestone had spent over US$75 million on the project, the system failed on launch day, disrupting many of the company's day-to-day activities. This disaster threw Bridgestone's tire and retail operations into chaos. Bridgestone had to turn off or disconnect automated systems, and the entire organization had to go into manual disaster recovery, with everyone, including management, working day and night to find creative ways to deliver products critical to their customers' businesses. Bridgestone even delivered tires to manufacturers without any purchase orders to keep customers' production lines running and to mitigate damages. As Bridgestone scrambled to recover, the company were forced to hire SAP directly for the first six months of 2012 to identify and resolve defects in IBM's SAP implementation.

Ultimately, Bridgestone filed a lawsuit against IBM for US$600 million, claiming $200 million in business losses and additional damages for fraud and breach of contract. IBM vigorously and publicly defended itself, claiming that Bridgestone "lacked leadership" and disrupted the design and implementation process by replacing its chief information officer six times in two years. According to IBM, after insisting that it have control over the design and final approval of the system, Bridgestone failed to timely approve those designs, failed to provide the necessary design documents for IBM to complete its work, and failed to conduct the required user testing necessary to understand how the system would work under real-world conditions. IBM further claimed that Bridgestone ignored IBM's suggestions to employ a more conservative, staggered rollout of the new system and instead insisted on a "big bang" go-live in which the entire system would be implemented overnight across all North American operations. Bridgestone continued to demand that the system be implemented in this manner and insisted on the scheduled go-live date, even after IBM had advised that the go-live date was premature and therefore fraught with business risk. Bridgestone elected to proceed regardless of the identified risks, even after acknowledging that the system would fail to meet the go-live criteria that Bridgestone itself had set. At go-live, the system experienced many of the errors that IBM had predicted.

These two companies have much to resolve in the legal courts, and it is unclear whether Bridgestone will be granted, or even deserves, its desired settlement amount. What is obvious from this example, however, is the clear risk involved with any large-scale IT project. Given most of ERP systems' level of integration with key business functions, companies have to carefully consider the risks and rewards inherent in such a large undertaking.

Questions:

7-41. Who was more at fault—IBM or Bridgestone? Why?

7-42. What could have been done, and at what stage, to help prevent the project failure? List and discuss two or three changes.

7-43. Should any large businesses attempt an ERP implementation of such a large scale? What factors should managers consider in making that kind of a decision?

Based on:

Bort, J. (2013, November 20). IBM rips into Bridgestone over $600 million lawsuit. *BusinessInsider.com.* Retrieved May 3, 2014, from http://www.businessinsider.com/ibm-rips-into-bridgestone-over-600-million-lawsuit-2013-11.

Bridgestone Americas, Inc. (2013, November 12). Bridgestone Americas, Inc. vs. IBM Corporation. *Nashville Post.* Retrieved May 3, 2014, from http://nashvillepost.com/sites/default/files/attachments/78417/BStoneIBM.pdf.

Krigsman, M. (2013, November 29). PR finger pointing: IBM and Bridgestone wrangle over failed ERP. *ZDNet.* Retrieved May 3, 2014, from http://www.zdnet.com/pr-finger-pointing-ibm-and-bridgestone-wrangle-over-failed-erp-7000023711.

Go to mymislab.com for auto-graded writing questions as well as the following assisted-graded writing questions:

7-44. Describe and contrast order-to-cash, procure-to-pay, make-to-stock, and make-to-order business processes.

7-45. Contrast internally and externally focused systems.

References

Brown, P. C. (2007). *Succeeding with SOA: Realizing business value through total architecture*. New York: Addison-Wesley.

Christensen, C. M. (1997). *The innovator's dilemma*. Boston: Harvard Business School Press.

Erl, T. (2008). *SOA principles of service design*. Upper Saddle River, NJ: Pearson Prentice Hall.

Hammer, M., & Champy, J. (1993). *Reengineering the corporation: A manifesto for business revolution*. New York: Harper Business Essentials.

Jacobs, F. R., & Whybark, D. C. (2000). *Why ERP? A primer on SAP implementation*. Boston: Irwin/McGraw-Hill.

Kumar, R. L., & Crook, C. W. (1999). A multi-disciplinary framework for the management of interorganizational systems. *Database for Advances in Information Systems, 30*(1), 22–36.

Langenwalter, G. A. (2000). *Enterprise resource planning and beyond*. Boca Raton, FL: St. Lucie Press.

Larson, P. D., & Rogers, D. S. (1998), Supply chain management: Definition, growth and approaches. *Journal of Marketing Theory and Practice*, *6*(4), 1–5.

Olson, D. (2004). *Managerial issues of enterprise resource planning systems*. Boston: McGraw-Hill/Irwin.

Panorama Consulting Solutions. (2012). 2012 ERP report. Retrieved June 1, 2014, from http://Panorama-Consulting.com/resource-center/2012-erp-report.

Porter, M. E., & Millar, V. E. (1985, July–August). How information gives you competitive advantage. *Harvard Business Review*, 149–160.

Taylor, F. W. (1911). *The principles of scientific management.* New York: Harper Bros.

Wagner, B., & Monk, E. (2013). *Concepts in enterprise resource planning* (4th ed.). Boston: Cengage.

Wailgum, T. (2008, January 29). Why ERP systems are more important than ever. *CIO.com.* Retrieved June 1, 2014, from http://www.cio.com/article/177300/Why_ERP_Systems_Are_More_Important_Than_Ever.

Wailgum, T. (2008, April 17). ERP definition and solutions. *CIO.com.* Retrieved June 1, 2014, from http://www.cio.com/article/40323/ERP_Definition_and_Solutions.

8 Strengthening Business-to-Business Relationships via Supply Chain and Customer Relationship Management

After reading this chapter, you will be able to do the following:

1. Describe supply chain management systems and how they help to improve business-to-business processes.
2. Describe customer relationship management systems and how they help to improve the activities involved in promoting and selling products to customers as well as providing customer service and nourishing long-term relationships.

Preview

This chapter extends the prior discussion regarding how companies are deploying enterprise-wide information systems to build and strengthen organizational partnerships. Enterprise systems help integrate various business activities, streamline and better manage interactions with customers, and better coordinate with suppliers in order to meet changing customer demands more efficiently and effectively. In this chapter, two additional powerful systems are introduced: supply chain management (SCM) systems supporting business-to-business (B2B) transactions and customer relationship management (CRM) systems for promoting and selling products and building and nourishing long-term customer relationships. When added to enterprise resource planning (ERP) systems, both of these systems tie the customer to the supply chain that includes the manufacturer and suppliers all the way back to the raw materials that ultimately become the product no matter where in the world they originate.

More and more companies find that they need systems that span their entire organization to tie everything together. As a result, an understanding of supply chain management and customer relationship management is critical to succeed in today's competitive and ever-changing digital world.

Managing in the Digital World: Walmart

As the world's largest retailer, Walmart is known for its relentless pursuit of lowering costs and passing those savings on to shoppers to undercut competitors' prices. Much of the company's success has been widely attributed to its effective use of technology to support its supply chain. Through a combination of distribution practices, truck fleet management, and technological innovations, Walmart became a model of supply chain efficiency. Being the largest retailer and private-sector employer in the world, Walmart employs over 2.2 million people worldwide and, in 2014, reported nearly US$500 billion in revenue.

One of Walmart's famous supply chain innovations is vendor-managed inventory, where manufacturers are responsible for monitoring inventory levels of their products in Walmart's warehouses, helping Walmart achieve close to 100 percent order fulfillment on merchandise, essentially eliminating the loss of sales due to out-of-stock items. Walmart further streamlined its supply chain by creating communication networks with suppliers to improve product flow and lower inventories. The network of global suppliers, warehouses, and retail stores has been described as behaving almost like a single firm. Walmart also developed the concept of "cross docking"—direct transfers from inbound to outbound truck trailers without extra storage (see Figure 8.1). The company's trucks continuously deliver goods to distribution, where they are stored, repackaged, and distributed without sitting in inventory.

FIGURE 8.1

Walmart uses cross docking to optimize its supply chain.
Source: Chris Fertnig/Getty Images, Inc.

Walmart's investments in technology to support its supply chain have also resulted in powerful customer relationship management capabilities. Walmart's information systems record every purchase in every store around the world, along with a host of other information (location, time of day, other items purchased in the same order, etc.). Its data warehouse containing all of this data is one of the largest in the world. As a result, Walmart can stock more of the most popular products, and cluster items that people tend to buy at the same time. These and other innovations have fueled Walmart's impressive growth.

Information systems are increasingly central to business operations in every industry and in all areas of the world. Businesses use technology to streamline their supply chain, to coordinate with suppliers and distributors, and to manage and leverage their relationships with their customers. Those organizations that develop advanced systems capabilities in these crucial areas of business will, like Walmart, gain a significant edge over competitors in the market.

After reading this chapter, you will be able to answer the following:

1. How has Walmart used its supply chain management systems to lower costs and outperform the competition?
2. How does Walmart use the retail data it gathers to improve its relationship with its customers?
3. How can companies like Walmart benefit from combining their SCM and CRM systems into one integrated information system?

Based on:

Rigby, D. (2003, April). Winning customer loyalty is the key to a winning CRM strategy. *Ivey Business Journal*. Retrieved May 6, 2014, from http://iveybusinessjournal.com/topics/social-responsibility/winning-customer-loyalty-is-the-key-to-a-winning-crm-strategy.

Traub, T. (2012, July 2). Wal-Mart used technology to become supply chain leader. *Arkansas Business*. Retrieved May 6, 2014, from http://www.arkansasbusiness.com/article/85508/wal-mart-used-technology-to-become-supply-chain-leader.

Walmart. (2014, May 5). In *Wikipedia, The Free Encyclopedia*. Retrieved May 6, 2014, from http://en.wikipedia.org/w/index.php?title=Walmart&oldid=607208628.

SUPPLY CHAIN MANAGEMENT

In the previous chapter, we discussed the need to share internal data in order to streamline business processes, improving coordination within the organization to improve efficiency and effectiveness. Let's now turn our attention to collaborating with partners along the supply chain. Getting the raw materials and components that a company uses in its daily operations is an important key to business success. When deliveries from suppliers are accurate and timely, companies can convert them to finished products more efficiently. Coordinating this effort with suppliers has become a central part of many companies' overall business strategy, as it can help them reduce costs associated with inventory levels and get new products to market more quickly. Ultimately, this helps companies drive profitability and improve their customer service since they can react to changing market conditions swiftly. Collaborating or sharing information with suppliers has become a strategic necessity for business success. In other words, by developing and maintaining stronger, more integrated relationships with suppliers, companies can more effectively compete in their markets through cost reductions and responsiveness to market demands.

What Is a Supply Chain?

The term **supply chain** is commonly used to refer to a collection of companies and processes involved in moving a product from the suppliers of raw materials to the suppliers of intermediate components, then to final production, and, ultimately, to the customer. Companies often procure specific raw materials and components from many different "upstream" suppliers. These suppliers, in turn, work with their own suppliers to obtain raw materials and components; their suppliers work with additional suppliers, and so forth. The further out in the supply chain one looks, the more suppliers are involved. As a result, the term "chain" becomes somewhat of a misnomer since it implies one-to-one relationships facilitating a chain of events flowing from the first supplier to the second to the third and so on. Similarly, on the "downstream" side, the products move to many different customers. The flow of materials from suppliers to customers can thus be more accurately described as a **supply network** because of the various interrelated parties involved in moving raw materials, intermediate components, and, finally, the end product within the production process (Figure 8.2).

Most companies are depending on a steady source of key supplies needed to produce their goods or services. For example, luxury restaurants require their produce to be consistently of high quality; similarly, car manufacturers need steel, paint, or electronic components in the right quantities, at the right quality and price, and at the right time. Thus, most companies are seeking long-term B2B relationships with a limited number of carefully selected suppliers—rather than one-time deals—and invest considerable efforts in selecting their suppliers or business partners; often, suppliers are assessed not only on product features such as price or quality but also on suppliers' characteristics, such as trustworthiness, commitment, or viability.

Business-to-Business Electronic Commerce: Exchanging Data in Supply Networks

Transactions conducted between different businesses in a supply network, not involving the end consumer, are referred to as business-to-business electronic commerce (EC). This type of commerce accounts for almost 90 percent of all EC in the United States (U.S. Census Bureau, 2014). B2B transactions require proprietary information (such as orders for parts) to be communicated to an organization's business partners. For many organizations, keeping such information private can be of strategic value; for example, Apple tries to keep news about potential new product launches to a minimum, and any information about orders for key components (such as touchscreens) could give away hints of what a new product may be. Prior to the introduction of the Internet and Web, the secure communication of proprietary information in B2B EC was facilitated using **Electronic Data Interchange (EDI)**. EDI refers to computer-to-computer communication (without human intervention) following certain standards as set by the UN Economic Commission (for Europe) or the American National Standards Institute. Traditionally, using EDI, the exchange of business documents and other information took place via dedicated telecommunication networks between suppliers and customers, and thus the use of EDI was generally limited to large corporations that could afford the associated expenses. Today, the Internet has become an economical medium over which this business-related information can be transmitted, enabling

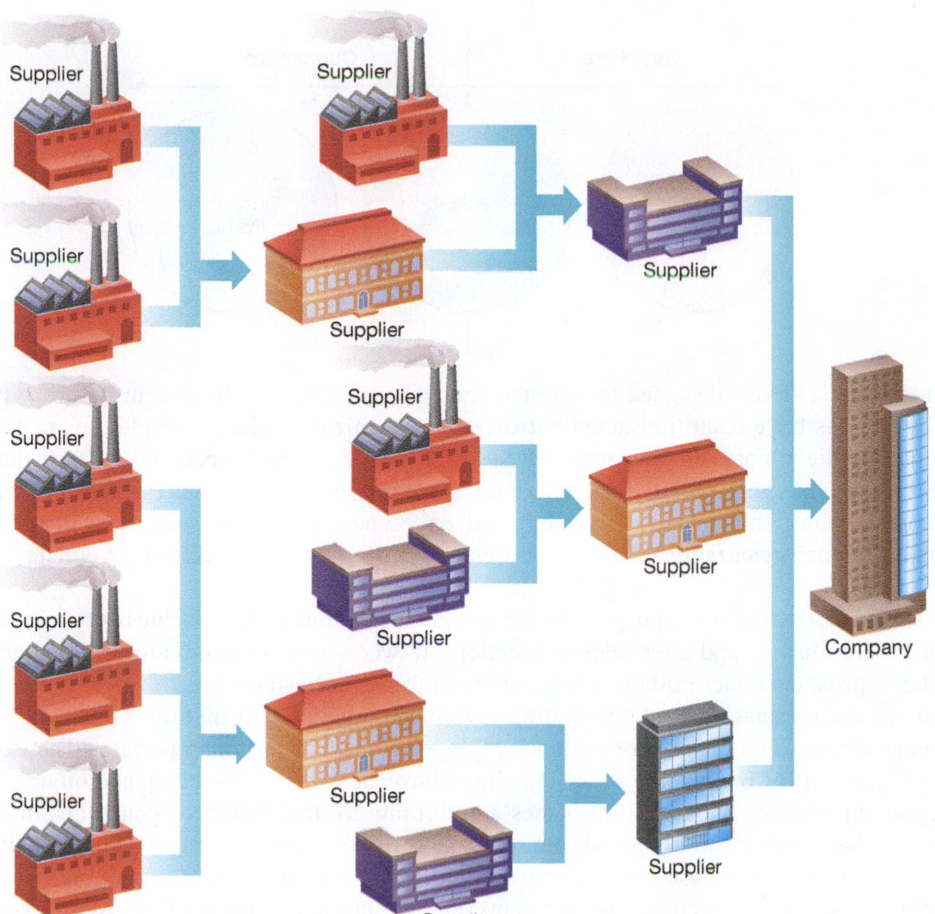

FIGURE 8.2

A typical supply network.

even small to mid-sized enterprises to use EDI; many large companies (such as the retail giant Walmart) require their suppliers to transmit information such as advance shipping notices using Web-based EDI protocols. Further, companies have devised a number of innovative ways to facilitate B2B transactions using Web-based technologies. Specifically, organizations increasingly use extranets (see Chapter 3, "Managing the Information Systems Infrastructure and Services") for exchanging data and handling transactions with their suppliers or organizational customers. Commonly, portals are used to interact with the business partners; these are discussed next.

PORTALS. **Portals**, in the context of B2B supply chain management, can be defined as access points (or front doors) through which a business partner accesses secured, proprietary information that may be dispersed throughout an organization (typically using extranets). By allowing direct access to critical information needed to conduct business, portals can thus provide substantial productivity gains and cost savings for B2B transactions.

In contrast to business-to-consumer (B2C) EC, where anyone can set up a customer account with a retailer, the suppliers or customers in B2B transactions are typically prescreened by the business, and access to the company's extranet will be given depending on the business relationship (typically, after a review of the supplier's or buyer's application). To support different types of business relationships, portals come in two basic forms: supplier portals and customer portals. Supplier portals are owned or managed by a "downstream" company, and automate the business processes involved in purchasing or procuring products from multiple suppliers; they connect a single buyer and multiple suppliers. On the other end of the spectrum, customer portals are owned or managed by an "upstream" company, and automate the business processes involved in selling or distributing products to multiple buyers; they connect a single supplier und multiple buyers. B2B marketplaces are typically run by separate entities and connect multiple buyers and multiple suppliers (Figure 8.3).

Supplier Portals Many companies that are dealing with large numbers of suppliers (e.g., The Boeing Company, Lilly, P&G, and Hewlett-Packard [HP]) set up **supplier portals** (sometimes referred to as sourcing portals or procurement portals). A supplier portal is a subset of an

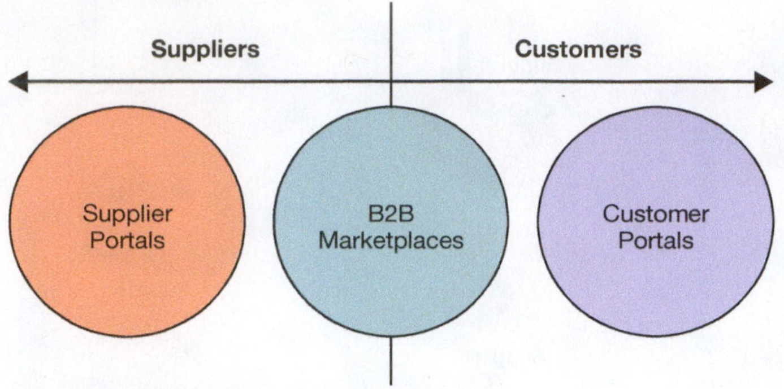

FIGURE 8.3

Supplier portals, B2B marketplaces, and customer portals.

organization's extranet designed to automate the business processes that occur before, during, and after sales have been transacted between the organization (i.e., a single buyer) and its multiple suppliers. For example, on the HP Supplier Portal, companies can register their interest in becoming a supplier for HP; access terms and conditions or guidelines (such as guidelines related to labeling, shipment, or packaging); and, once a business relationship is established with HP, manage interorganizational business processes associated with ordering and payment.

Customer Portals **Customer portals** are designed to automate the business processes that occur before, during, and after sales transactions between a supplier and multiple customers. In other words, customer portals provide efficient tools for business customers to manage all phases of the purchasing cycle, including reviewing product information, order entry, and customer service (Figure 8.4). For example, MyBoeingFleet, the customer portal of The Boeing Company, is part of Boeing's extranet and allows airplane owners, operators, and other parties to access information about their airplanes' configurations, maintenance documents, or spare parts. In other cases, customer portals are set up as B2B Web sites that provide custom-tailored offers or specific deals based on sales volume, as is the case with large office retailers such as OfficeMax (www.officemaxsolutions.com) or computer manufacturer Dell, which services business customers through its customer portal Dell Premier.

B2B MARKETPLACES. The purpose of supplier portals and customer portals is to enable interaction between a single company and its many suppliers or customers. Being owned/operated by a single organization, these portals can be considered a subset of the organization's extranet. However, setting up such portals tends to be beyond the reach of small to midsized businesses because of the costs involved in designing, developing, and maintaining this type of system. Many of these firms do not have the necessary monetary resources or skilled personnel to implement large-scale

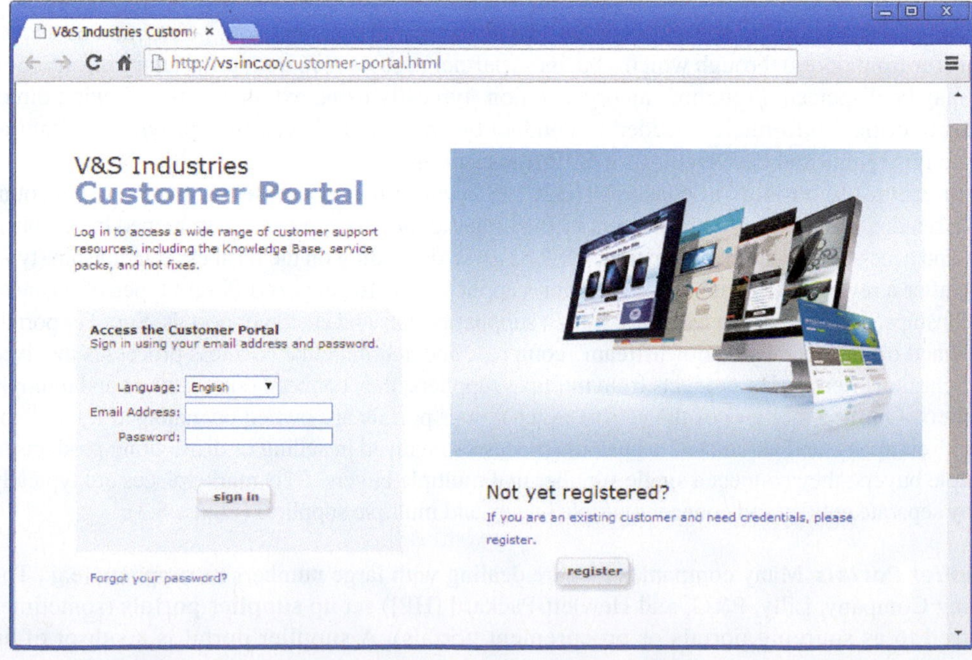

FIGURE 8.4

Customer portals automate business processes that occur before, during, and after sales transactions.

supply chain management applications on their own, and the transaction volume does not justify the expenses. To service this market, a number of **business-to-business marketplaces** have sprung up. B2B marketplaces are operated by third-party vendors, meaning they are built and maintained by a separate entity rather than being associated with a particular buyer or supplier. These marketplaces generate revenue by taking a small commission for each transaction that occurs, by charging usage fees, by charging association fees, and/or by generating advertising revenues. Unlike customer and supplier portals, B2B marketplaces allow many buyers and many sellers to come together, offering firms access to real-time trading with other companies in their **vertical markets** (i.e., markets comprised of firms operating within a certain industry sector). Such B2B marketplaces can create tremendous efficiencies for companies since they bring together numerous participants along the supply network. Some popular B2B marketplaces include www.steellink.com (steel), www.paperindex.com (paper), and www.fibre2fashion.com (textile and fashion supplies).

In contrast to B2B marketplaces serving vertical markets, other B2B marketplaces are not focused on any particular industry. One of the most successful examples is the Chinese marketplace Alibaba.com. Alibaba.com brings together buyers and suppliers from around the globe, from almost every industry, selling almost any product, ranging from fresh ginger to manufacturing machinery. Alibaba.com offers various services, such as posting item leads, displaying products, and contacting buyers or sellers, but also features such as trading tips or price watch for raw materials. Offering various trading tools including online storefronts, virtual factory tours, and real-time chat, such B2B marketplaces have enabled many small or little-known suppliers to engage in trade on a global basis.

Managing Complex Supply Networks

A prime example of a company having to manage extremely complex supply networks is Apple and its latest extremely successful mobile devices, such as the iPhone 5s or the iPad. Typically, Apple sells millions of these devices within the first few days following the product launch. How does Apple manage to produce such an incredible number of these products? If you take a close look at the devices, you will find a statement saying "Designed by Apple in California Assembled in China." Every time a new Apple device is launched, industry observers disassemble these devices to get a sneak peek into Apple's supply chain. The iPhone, like other Apple devices, is by no means *manufactured* by Apple. The components of the iPhone are sourced from dozens of companies located in various different countries. For example, according to market research firm IHS iSuppli, the iPhone's flash memory and central processing unit are produced by Korean Samsung; the display is sourced from Korean LG; the phone chips are made by German Infineon (manufactured in Germany or Southeast Asia); the Wi-Fi and global positioning system (GPS) chips are produced by U.S.-based Broadcom (but possibly assembled in China, Korea, Singapore, or Taiwan); the touchscreen controller is made by Texas Instruments; many other parts, such as the camera, are possibly made in Taiwan; and so on. The final product is assembled in a factory owned by Taiwanese electronics giant Foxconn, located in Shenzhen, China (a city of more than 10 million people, located just north of Hong Kong), from where the finished iPhones are shipped by air to the different countries where the iPhone is on sale (Figure 8.5). Although many have never heard of Foxconn, it is the largest electronics manufacturer in the world, producing components, cell phones, gaming consoles, and so on for various other companies, including Dell, HP, and Sony.

Coordinating such extensive supply network requires considerable expertise, especially when facing unexpected events such as shortages in touchscreen panels, other issues at suppliers' factories, or natural disasters. In 2010, for example, the eruption of a volcano in Iceland led to the closing of the northern European airspace for several days, causing delays in iPhone shipments to Europe; similarly, the earthquake and associated tsunami that devastated Japan in March 2011 disrupted the supply chains of electronics and automobile manufacturers that had to shut down plants around the world, as key components could not be produced in Japan and delivered to assembly lines. A limited pool of suppliers for critical components exacerbates such problems, as companies have fewer options to switch suppliers if necessary. It is thus important not only to monitor one's own direct suppliers but also to constantly monitor the company's extended supply chain so as to anticipate any issues that may have an impact on one's direct suppliers.

Benefits of Effectively Managing Supply Chains

Whereas effectively managing the supply chain can create various opportunities, many problems can arise when firms within the network do not collaborate effectively. For example,

FIGURE 8.5

The iPhone is assembled in China from globally sourced components.

collaboration within supply networks has enabled process innovations such as just-in-time manufacturing and vendor-managed inventory (discussed in the following sections). On the other hand, if firms do not collaborate effectively, information can easily become distorted as it moves through the supply network. Problems such as excessive inventories, inaccurate manufacturing capacity plans, and missed production schedules can run rampant, causing huge ripple effects that lead to degradations in profitability and poor customer service by everyone within the supply network. Further, effectively managing the supply chain is becoming increasingly important in terms of corporate social responsibility.

JUST-IN-TIME PRODUCTION. One of the most significant advances to production has been the use of **just-in-time (JIT)** strategies. Based on the notion that keeping inventory is costly (in terms of both storage costs and the capital that is tied up) and does not add value, companies using a JIT method are trying to optimize their ordering quantities such that parts or raw materials arrive just when they are needed for production. As the orders arrive in smaller quantities (but at higher frequency), the investment in storage space and inventory is minimized. Pioneered by Japanese automaker Toyota, many other businesses have now adopted a JIT approach. For example, computer maker Dell realized the problems with keeping large inventories, especially because of the fast rate of obsolescence of electronics components. To illustrate, recall our discussion of Moore's Law (see Chapter 3), which suggests that processor technology is doubling in performance approximately every 24 months. Because of this, successful computer manufacturers have learned that holding inventory that can quickly become obsolete or devalued is a poor strategy for success. In fact, Dell now only keeps about two hours of inventory in its factories. Obviously, using a JIT method is heavily dependent on tight cooperation between all partners in the supply network, not only including suppliers, but also other partners, such as shipping and logistics companies.

VENDOR-MANAGED INVENTORY. Under a traditional inventory model, the manufacturer or retailer would manage its own inventories, sending out requests for additional items as needed. In contrast, **vendor-managed inventory (VMI)** is a business model in which the suppliers to a manufacturer (or retailer) manage the manufacturer's (or retailer's) inventory based on negotiated service levels. To make VMI possible, the manufacturer (or retailer) allows the supplier to monitor stock levels and ongoing sales data. Such arrangements can help to optimize the manufacturer's (or retailer's) inventory, both saving costs and minimizing stockout situations (thus enhancing customer satisfaction); the supplier, in turn, benefits from the intense data sharing, which helps produce more accurate forecasts, reduces ordering errors, and helps prioritize the shipment of goods.

REDUCING THE BULLWHIP EFFECT. One major problem affecting supply chains are ripple effects referred to as the **bullwhip effect**. Each business forecasting demand typically includes a safety buffer in order to prevent possible stockouts. However, forecast errors and safety stocks multiply when moving up the supply chain, such that a small fluctuation in demand for an end product can lead to tremendous fluctuation in demand for parts or raw materials farther up the supply chain. Like someone cracking a bullwhip, a tiny "flick of the wrist" will create a big movement at the other end of the whip. Likewise, a small forecasting error at the end of the supply chain can cause massive forecasting errors farther up the supply chain. Implementing integrated business processes allows a company to better coordinate the entire supply network and reduce the impact of the bullwhip.

CORPORATE SOCIAL RESPONSIBILITY. Effectively managing the supply chain has also become tremendously important for aspects related to corporate social responsibility. Specifically, transparency and accountability within the supply chain can help organizations save costs and/or create a good image. Two related issues are product recalls and sustainable business practices; both are discussed next.

Product Recalls Given that a typical supply network comprises tens, hundreds, or sometimes thousands of players, many of which are dispersed across the globe, there are myriad possibilities where shortcuts are being taken or quality standards are not being met. Often, such issues are caught somewhere along the supply chain, but sometimes such incidents go unnoticed until the product reaches the end consumer. These problems can be exacerbated if companies are sourcing their products or raw materials globally, as more potential points of failure are added due to differences in quality or product safety regulations in the originating countries.

Hence, it is extremely important to have the necessary information to trace back the movement of products through the supply chain so as to be able to quickly identify the problematic link. Being able to single out the source of a problem can help a company to perform an appropriate response, helping to save goodwill and limiting the costs of a recall. Further, in many cases, only some batches of a product may be problematic (such as when certain raw materials or components are sourced from different suppliers). If a company is not able to clearly identify the affected batches, the recall will have to be much broader, costing the company much more (in both goodwill and money) than just having to recall the affected batches. Hence, companies need to have a clear picture of their supply chain, and also need to store these data in case of problems at a later point in time.

Sustainable Business Practices Another aspect related to corporate social responsibility is a growing emphasis on sustainable business practices. Particularly, organizations have come under increasing scrutiny for issues such as ethical treatment of workers (especially overseas) or environmental practices. For example, since 2010, more than 20 employees at Foxconn's Shenzhen plant have committed suicide. As the suicides happened at the plant manufacturing iPhones for Apple, many blamed Apple for the working conditions at the plant. Although Apple is certainly aware of the negative effects that a supplier's action can have on a company's reputation, it also faces a conundrum, as few (if any) companies besides Foxconn have sufficient production capacity to meet the demand for hugely popular products such as the iPhone.

Other companies are trying to portray a "green" image and attempt to minimize their carbon footprint. For example, HP takes a proactive approach, being the first major information technology company to publish its aggregate supply chain greenhouse gas emissions, restrict the use of hazardous materials, implement environmentally friendly packaging policies, and so on. In order to do that and to provide sound, convincing numbers to back a "green" image, a company such as HP needs to have a clear view of its entire supply chain. Similarly, U.S. regulations require 95 percent of computers purchased by the U.S. federal government to carry the EPEAT eco-label. To achieve this certification, a manufacturer has to possess and produce extensive evidence that the products meet EPEAT's strict requirements.

Optimizing the Supply Chain Through Supply Chain Management

Information systems focusing on improving supply chains have two main objectives: to accelerate product development and innovation and to reduce costs. These systems, called **supply chain**

WHEN THINGS GO WRONG

Switching Switches: Failure at a Global Scale

As supply chains become increasingly global, it is crucial for companies to carefully monitor their partnerships with other firms and implement effective controls to ensure product quality. Failure to do so can result in extensive product recalls harmful to the company's public image (and the bottom line), as was the case in a recent vehicle recall conducted by General Motors (GM). Faulty ignition switches used in several GM cars have been blamed for numerous vehicle accidents and at least 13 deaths. The faulty switches inadvertently turned off, shutting down the vehicles' systems and rendering the airbags useless. GM has recalled over 2.6 million affected vehicles to repair the issue. In addition to tremendous costs, the recall has severely damaged GM's public image.

Though the ignition switch supplier notified GM of the issue 10 years earlier, the company only reacted in 2014. In a recent U.S. congressional hearing investigating the issue, GM was questioned as to why it took over 10 years to identify the cause and implement the vehicle recall. It was discovered that an engineer, upon realizing his mistake in approving the faulty switches, authorized a replacement with functional switches, but attempted to cover the error by leaving the part number the same, making it close to impossible for GM to know which switches were faulty and which were not. Complex, global supply chains clearly require careful monitoring and control. In some cases, the repercussions of failure include the loss of human life.

Based on:

Bowman, R. (2014, April 1). Disaster looms: Why today's global supply chains are at risk. *Forbes.com*. Retrieved May 5, 2014, from http://www.forbes.com/sites/robertbowman/2014/04/01/disaster-looms-why-todays-global-supply-chains-are-at-risk.

Krisher, T. (2014, April 10). GM engineers suspended in ignition switch case. *CTV News*. Retrieved May 5, 2014, from http://www.ctvnews.ca/autos/gm-engineers-suspended-in-ignition-switch-case-1.1769751.

management (SCM), improve the coordination of suppliers, product or service production, and distribution. When executed successfully, SCM helps in not only reducing inventory costs, but also enhancing revenue through improved customer service. SCM is often integrated with ERP to leverage internal and external information in order to better collaborate with suppliers. Like ERP and customer relationship management applications, SCM packages are delivered in the form of modules (Table 8.1) that companies select and implement according to their differing business requirements.

TABLE 8.1 Functions That Optimize the Supply Network

Module	Key Uses
Demand planning and forecasting	Forecast and plan anticipated demand for products
Safety stock planning	Assign optimal safety stock and target stock levels in all inventories in the supply network
Distribution planning	Optimize the allocation of available supplies to meet demand
Supply network collaboration	Work with partners across the supply network to improve accuracy of demand forecasts, reduce inventory buffers, increase the velocity of materials flow, and improve customer service
Materials management	Ensure that the materials required for production are available where needed when needed
Manufacturing execution	Support production processes taking into account capacity and material constraints
Order promising	Provide answers to customer relationship management queries regarding product availability, costs, and delivery times
Transportation execution	Manage logistics between company locations or from company to customers, taking into account transportation modes and constraints
Warehouse management	Support receiving, storing, and picking of goods in a warehouse
Supply chain analytics	Monitor key performance indicators to assess performance across the supply chain

Source: Based on http://www.sap.com.

As discussed previously, ERP systems are primarily used to optimize business processes *within* the organization, whereas SCM is used to improve business processes that *span* organizational boundaries. Whereas some standalone SCM systems only automate the logistics aspects of the supply chain, organizations can reap the greatest benefits when the SCM system is tightly integrated with ERP and customer relationship management systems modules; this way, SCM systems can use data about customer orders or sales forecasts (from the customer relationship management system), data about payments (from the ERP system), and so on. Given its scope, SCM is adopted primarily by large organizations with a large and/or complex supplier network. At the same time, many smaller suppliers are interacting with the systems of large companies. To obtain the greatest benefits from the SCM processes and systems, organizations need to extend the system to include all trading partners regardless of size, providing a central location for information integration and common processes so that all partners benefit.

For an effective SCM strategy, several challenges have to be overcome. First and foremost, as with any information system, an SCM system is only as good as the data entered into it. This means that to benefit most from an SCM system, the organization's employees have to actually use the system and move away from traditional ways of managing the supply chain, as an order placed by fax or telephone will most likely not find its way into the system. Another challenge to overcome is distrust among partners in the supply chain; for many companies, sales and supply chain data are strategic assets, and no one wants to show his or her cards to other members in the supply chain. Further, many organizations (such as Apple) tend to be very clandestine about their suppliers, as such information could reveal their pricing strategies or give clues about new product development. In addition, more and more organizations are reluctant to share data along the supply chain because of an increase in intellectual property theft, especially in China, a major source of supplies for many companies. A final challenge is to get all partners within the supply chain to adopt an SCM system. Several years ago, the retail giant Walmart began mandating its suppliers use its RetailLink supply chain system, and refused to engage in a business relationship with any supplier who was not willing to use the system. Whereas large companies can force their suppliers or partners to use a system, smaller companies typically do not have this power.

Developing an SCM Strategy

When developing an SCM strategy, an organization must consider a variety of factors that will affect the efficiency and effectiveness of the supply chain. **Supply chain efficiency** is the extent to which a company's supply chain is focusing on minimizing procurement, production, and transportation costs, sometimes by sacrificing excellent customer service. In contrast, **supply chain effectiveness** is the extent to which a company's supply chain is focusing on maximizing customer service, with lesser focus on reducing procurement, production, and transportation costs (Figure 8.6). In other words, the design of the supply chain must consider natural trade-offs between a variety of factors and should reflect the organization's competitive strategy to reap the greatest benefits. For example, an organization utilizing a low-cost-provider competitive strategy would likely focus on supply chain efficiency. In contrast, an organization pursuing a superior customer service differentiation strategy would focus on supply chain effectiveness.

Supply Chain Strategy	Procurement	Production	Transportation
Effectiveness	More Inventory Multiple Inventory Sources ...	General-Purpose Facilities More Facilities Higher Excess Capacity ...	Fast Delivery Times More Warehouses ...
↕	↕	↕	↕
Efficiency	... Single Inventory Source Less Inventory	... Less Excess Capacity Fewer Facilities Special-Purpose Facilities	... Fewer Warehouses Longer Delivery Times

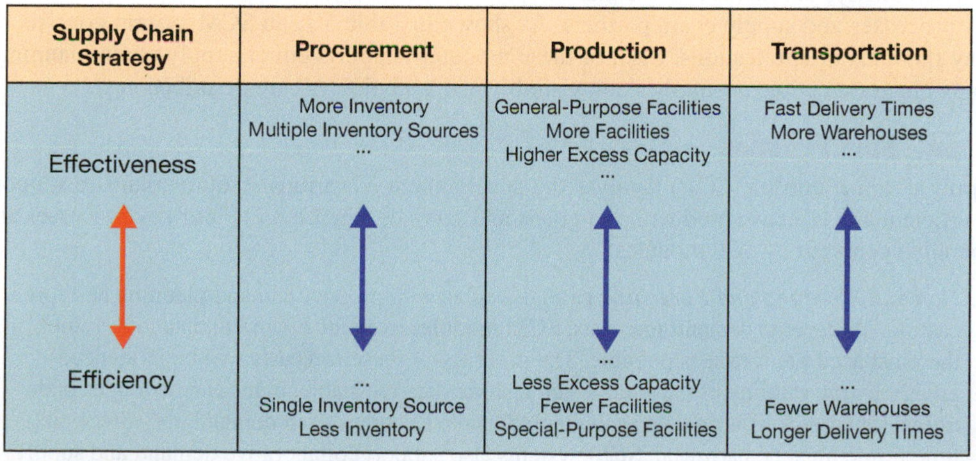

FIGURE 8.6

A supply chain strategy requires balancing supply chain efficiency and effectiveness.

BRIEF CASE The Formula for Success: Demand Media

Imagine Google, YouTube, and Wikipedia all merged into a single comprehensive system ready to help you answer any question you might have. You type in a typical question and receive an informative response, in the form of an instructional video, or a simple article focused on your exact question. Demand Media and its various sites on the Web provide such answers, offering intellectual nourishment to random inquiries that range from instructions for making banana pancakes to running a vintage clothing shop.

Demand Media, Inc., an American content and social media company, developed an algorithm that uses search engine query data and bids on advertising auctions to identify topics with high advertising potential. These topics are typically in the advice and how-to field. For example, the company has learned that the key words "best" and "how" tend to bring in high search traffic and click-through rates. Once the algorithm identifies a search query that is likely to draw traffic, Demand Media crowdsources the production of corresponding text or video content to answer the algorithm-generated search query (e.g., "Where can I donate a car in Dallas?"). The average writer earns US$15 per piece for articles containing a few hundred words, whereas a filmmaker receives US$20 per clip, both of which are paid on a weekly basis through PayPal. Demand Media also offers opportunities to copyedit, fact-check, approve the quality of a film, or transcribe. The content is then posted on the company's own sites such as eHow, Livestrong.com, Trails.com, GolfLink.com, and Cracked.com (as well as various other sites, such as YouTube), and Demand Media generates revenue through advertisements placed on these sites.

The volume and exposure that Demand Media creates and receives has been impressive; at one point, its total number of uploads to YouTube was twice the content of CBS, the Associated Press, Universal Music Group, CollegeHumor, Al Jazeera English, and Soulja Boy combined. Its network of 45 B-list sites managed to bring in more traffic than Web sites like ESPN and NBC Universal combined. It is no wonder that Internet giant Google has reached out to the company and is now working as Demand Media's top distribution partner, closely collaborating with Demand Media to generate more revenue from the algorithm of profiting from advertisers.

Questions

1. Would you be interested in working for Demand Media to produce content? Why or why not?
2. Does Demand Media have a competitive advantage? If so, what is it and how will the company sustain it? If not, why not?

Based on:

Anonymous. (n.d.). *Demand Media.* Retrieved May 6, 2014, from http://create.demandstudios.com.

Demand Media. (2014, April 15). In *Wikipedia, The Free Encyclopedia.* Retrieved May 6, 2014, from http://en.wikipedia.org/w/index.php?title=Demand_Media&oldid=604232028.

Roth, D. (2009, October 19). The answer factory: Demand Media and the fast, disposable, and profitable as hell media model. *Wired.* Retrieved May 6, 2014, from http://www.wired.com/magazine/2009/10/ff_demandmedia/all/1.

SCM systems typically allow for making trade-offs between efficiency and effectiveness for individual components or raw materials. For example, if a hurricane is likely to delay the arrival of a key component by sea, the company can perform simulations to evaluate the effect of the delay on production and can assess the feasibility of temporarily switching suppliers, switching modes of transportation (e.g., expediting the shipment via air freight), or substituting the component altogether. In such cases, making changes to the original plans may be more costly but can help the organization meet promised delivery deadlines, thus maintaining goodwill and avoiding possible contract penalties. On the other hand, companies can dynamically adjust schedules for noncritical components or raw materials so as to minimize costs while still meeting the targets set in the production schedule.

An SCM system includes more than simply hardware and software; it also integrates business processes and supply chain partners. As shown in Table 8.1, an SCM system consists of many modules or applications. Each of these modules supports either supply chain planning, supply chain execution, or supply chain visibility and analytics. All are described next.

Supply Chain Planning

Supply chain planning (SCP) involves the development of various resource plans to support the efficient and effective production of goods and services (Figure 8.7). Four key processes are generally supported by SCP modules:

1. ***Demand Planning and Forecasting.*** SCP begins with product demand planning and forecasting. To develop demand forecasts, SCM modules examine historical data to develop the most accurate forecasts possible. The accuracy of these forecasts will be influenced greatly by the stability of the data. When historic data are stable, plans can be longer in duration, whereas if historic data show unpredictable fluctuations in demand, the forecasting time frame must be narrowed. SCM systems also support collaborative demand and supply

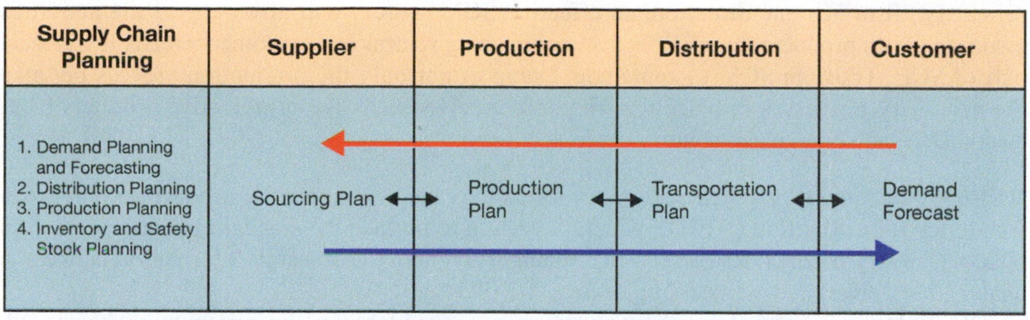

Supply Chain Planning	Supplier	Production	Distribution	Customer
1. Demand Planning and Forecasting 2. Distribution Planning 3. Production Planning 4. Inventory and Safety Stock Planning	Sourcing Plan ↔	Production Plan ↔	Transportation Plan ↔	Demand Forecast

FIGURE 8.7

SCP includes (customer) demand planning and forecasting, distribution planning, production planning, and (supplier) inventory and safety stock planning.

planning such that a sales representative can work together with the demand planner, taking into account information provided by the organization's point-of-sale system, promotions entered in the customer relationship management system, and other factors influencing demand. Demand planning and forecasting leads to the development of the overall *demand forecast.*

2. ***Distribution Planning.*** Once demand forecasts are finalized, plans for moving products to distributors can be developed. Specifically, distribution planning focuses on delivering products or services to consumers as well as warehousing, delivering, invoicing, and payment collection. Distribution planning leads to the development of the overall *transportation plan.*
3. ***Production Scheduling.*** Production scheduling focuses on the coordination of all activities needed to create the product or service. When developing this plan, analytical tools are used to optimally utilize materials, equipment, and labor. Production also involves product testing, packaging, and delivery preparation. Production scheduling leads to the development of the *production plan.*
4. ***Inventory and Safety Stock Planning.*** Inventory and safety stock planning focuses on the development of inventory estimates. Using inventory simulations and other analytical techniques, organizations can balance inventory costs and desired customer service levels to determine optimal inventory levels. Once inventory levels are estimated, suppliers are chosen who contractually agree to preestablished delivery and pricing terms. Inventory and safety stock planning leads to the development of a *sourcing plan.*

As suggested, various types of analytical tools—such as statistical analysis, simulation, and optimization—are used to forecast and visualize demand levels, distribution and warehouse locations, resource sequencing, and so on. Once these plans are developed, they are used to guide supply chain execution. Additionally, it is important to note that SCM planning is an ongoing process—as new data are obtained, plans are updated. For example, if shortages in the capacity for manufacturing touchscreen displays suddenly become evident, Apple has to dynamically adjust its plans so as to obtain the needed quantities to meet customer demand.

Supply Chain Execution

Supply chain execution (SCE) is the execution of SCP. Essentially, SCE puts the SCM planning into motion and reflects the processes involved in improving the collaboration of all members of the supply chain—suppliers, producers, distributors, and customers. SCE involves the management of three key elements of the supply chain: product flow, information flow, and financial flow (Figure 8.8). Each of these flows is discussed next.

PRODUCT FLOW. **Product flow** refers to the movement of goods from the supplier to production, from production to distribution, and from distribution to the consumer. Although products

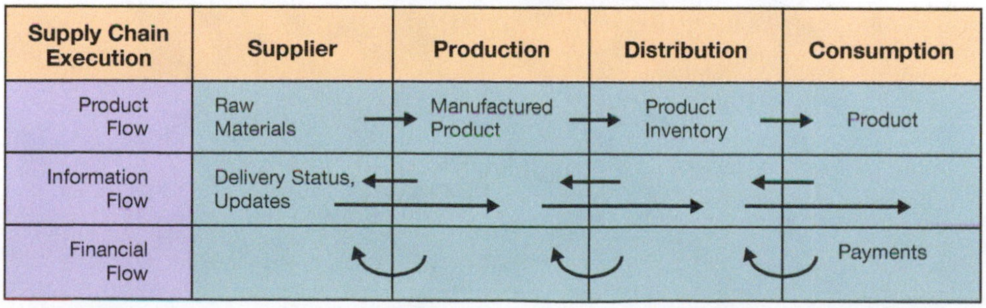

Supply Chain Execution	Supplier	Production	Distribution	Consumption
Product Flow	Raw Materials →	Manufactured Product →	Product Inventory →	Product
Information Flow	Delivery Status, Updates ↔	↔	↔	
Financial Flow				Payments

FIGURE 8.8

SCE focuses on the efficient and effective flow of products, information, and finances along the supply chain.

primarily "flow" in one direction, an effective SCM system will also support the activities associated with product returns. Effectively processing returns and customer refunds is a critical part of SCE. Thus, an SCM system should support not only the production process but also the necessary processes in place to efficiently receive excessive or defective products from customers (and ship replacements or credit accounts).

Radio Frequency Identification A key technology helping to monitor product flows is **radio frequency identification (RFID)**, which is starting to replace the standard bar codes you find on almost every product. RFID uses electromagnetic energy to transmit information between a reader (transceiver) and a processing device, or RFID tag.

RFID tags can be used just about anywhere a unique identification system might be needed, such as on clothing, pets, cars, keys, missiles, or manufactured parts. RFID tags can range in size from being a fraction of an inch, which can be inserted beneath an animal's skin, up to several inches across and affixed to a product or shipping container (Figure 8.9). The tag can carry information as simple as the name of the owner of a pet or as complex as how a product is to be manufactured on the shop floor.

RFID systems offer advantages over standard bar code technologies in that RFID eliminates the need for line-of-sight reading. RFID also does not require time-consuming hand scanning, and RFID information is readable regardless of the entity's position or whether the tag is plainly visible. RFID tags can also contain more information than bar codes. Further, a company can program any information that it wants or needs onto an RFID tag, enabling a vast array of potential uses. Thus, it is possible to retrieve information about an entity's version, origin, location, maintenance history, and other important information, and to manipulate that information on the tag. RFID scanning can also be done at greater distances than can bar code scanning. *Passive tags* are small and relatively inexpensive (starting from a few cents) and typically have a range up to several feet. *Active tags,* on the other hand, cost upward of US$5, include a battery, and can transmit hundreds of feet.

RFID systems offer great opportunities for managing supply chains, and virtually all major retailers are adopting RFID to better manage their supply chains, as are governments for tracking military supplies and weapons, drug shipments and ingredients (i.e., for eliminating counterfeit drugs), and citizens with RFID chips on passports.

INFORMATION FLOW. **Information flow** refers to the movement of information along the supply chain, such as order processing and delivery status updates. Like the product flow, information can also flow up or down the supply chain as needed. The key element to the information flow is the complete removal of paper documents. Specifically, all information about orders, fulfillment, billing, and consolidation is shared electronically. These paperless information flows save not only paperwork but also time and money. Additionally, because SCM systems use a central database to store information, all supply chain partners have at all times access to the most current information necessary for scheduling production, shipping orders, and so on.

Extensible Markup Language A key enabler for optimizing information flows is XML. **Extensible Markup Language (XML)** is a standard for exchanging structured information over

FIGURE 8.9

RFID tags can range in size from being a fraction of an inch up to several inches across.
Source: Albert Lozano-Nieto/Fotolia.

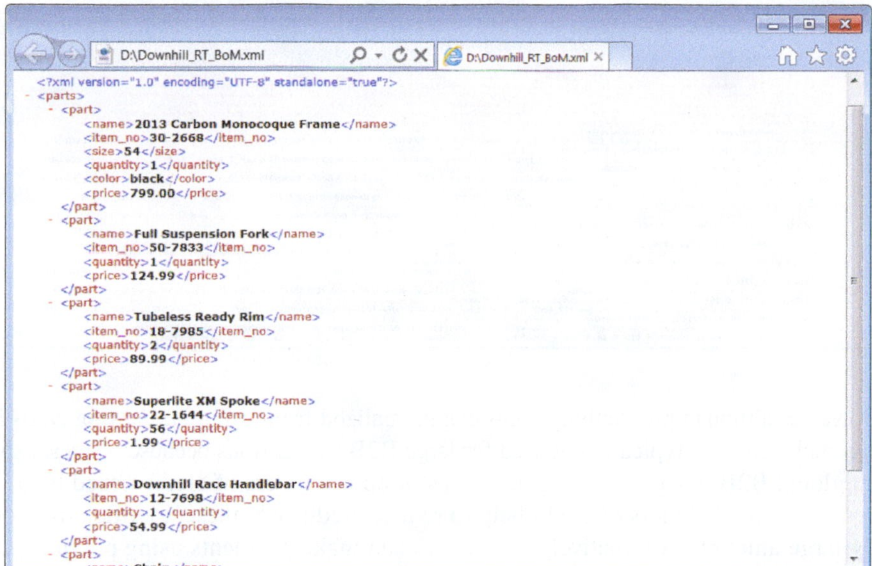
D:\Downhill_RT_BoM.xml
<?xml version="1.0" encoding="UTF-8" standalone="true"?>
- <parts>
- <part>
<name>2013 Carbon Monocoque Frame</name>
<item_no>30-2668</item_no>
<size>54</size>
<quantity>1</quantity>
<color>black</color>
<price>799.00</price>
</part>
- <part>
<name>Full Suspension Fork</name>
<item_no>50-7833</item_no>
<quantity>1</quantity>
<price>124.99</price>
</part>
- <part>
<name>Tubeless Ready Rim</name>
<item_no>18-7985</item_no>
<quantity>2</quantity>
<price>89.99</price>
</part>
- <part>
<name>Superlite XM Spoke</name>
<item_no>22-1644</item_no>
<quantity>56</quantity>
<price>1.99</price>
</part>
- <part>
<name>Downhill Race Handlebar</name>
<item_no>12-7698</item_no>
<quantity>1</quantity>
<price>54.99</price>
</part>
- <part>

FIGURE 8.10

An XML file for transmitting a bill of materials for a bicycle.
Source: Courtesy of Microsoft Corporation.

the Web. XML allows creating documents consisting of customized tags, enabling the definition, transmission, validation, and interpretation of data between applications and between organizations.

As described in Chapter 3, Hypertext Markup Language (HTML) uses tags to instruct a Web browser how data on a Web page should be presented by a user's browser. Much like HTML, XML also uses tags, but focuses on the content rather than the presentation. An **XML tag** is a label that is inserted into an XML document in order to specify how the data contained in the document or a portion of the document should be interpreted and/or used. For example, the tags <item_no> . . . </item_no> would instruct the application reading the XML file that the numbers enclosed in the tags should be interpreted as a product's item number (Figure 8.10). The application could use this information when displaying a product on a Web page or when updating inventory records. As a result, XML is a powerful tagging system that can be tailored to share similar data across applications over the Web. With these advanced data definition capabilities built into Web applications, organizations can then use the Web as the worldwide network for electronic commerce and SCM.

Many people think that XML is on its way to becoming the standard for automating data exchange between business information systems and may well replace all other formats for electronic data interchange. Companies can, for example, use XML to create applications for Web-based ordering, for checking on and managing inventory, for signaling to a supplier that more parts are needed, for alerting a third-party logistics company that a delivery is needed, and so on. All these various applications can work together using the common language of XML.

XML is customizable, and variations of XML have been developed. For example, **Extensible Business Reporting Language (XBRL)** is an XML-based specification for publishing financial information. XBRL makes it easier for public and private companies to share information with each other, with industry analysts, and with shareholders. XBRL includes tags for data such as annual and quarterly reports, Securities and Exchange Commission filings, general ledger information, and net revenue and accounting schedules (Figure 8.11).

FINANCIAL FLOW. **Financial flow** refers primarily to the movement of financial assets throughout the supply chain. Financial flows also include information related to payment schedules, consignment and ownership of products and materials, and other relevant information. Linkages to electronic banking and financial institutions allow payments to automatically flow into the accounts of all members within the supply chain.

Managing B2B Financial Transactions In B2C electronic commerce, most transactions are settled using credit cards or electronic payment services such as PayPal; in contrast, B2B payments are lagging far behind. In fact, according to some estimates, about 75 percent of all noncash B2B payments in the United States are made by check. While this may sound archaic, the time needed to process a check serves as a form of trade credit, which can amount to a significant part of an organization's working capital. For smaller purchases, organizations also often use purchasing

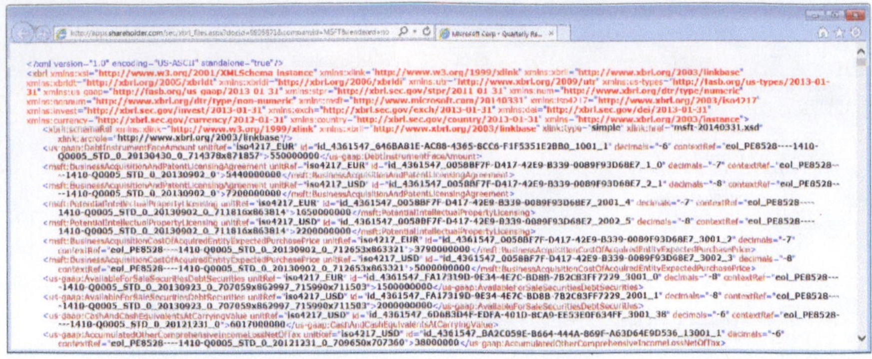

FIGURE 8.11

An XBRL file for sharing Securities and Exchange Commission filings.

Source: Courtesy of Microsoft Corporation.

cards. However, although productivity gains can be realized from using purchasing cards instead of checks, such cards are typically not used for large B2B transactions because of preset spending limits. In global B2B transactions, organizations often use letters of credit issued by a bank to make payments. While letters of credit help to reduce credit risk, these are often used only for relatively large amounts. Alternatively, businesses can make payments using providers such as Western Union. In any case, making a B2B payment is far from being as simple as making a purchase at Amazon.com using your credit card, and making B2B payments easier can greatly enhance efficiency as well as reduce costs for organizations. Thus, it is no wonder that businesses have started asking for payment methods as simple as PayPal for B2B transactions. When dealing with new, unknown suppliers, there is considerable fraud risk involved; this is especially of concern in global EC, so businesses often use third-party escrow services, which release payment only when the buyer has confirmed satisfactory delivery of the goods, reducing the risks for the buyer.

Supply Chain Visibility and Analytics

Supply chain visibility refers to the ability not only to track products as they move through the supply chain but also to foresee external events. Being able to see where a shipment is at any given time can be of tremendous help, especially when using JIT methods or when maintaining low inventory levels. For example, knowing where a shipment is and being able to expedite it can help in not losing a sale or help in taking away a sale from a competitor. Further, knowing where a supplier's facilities are located can help to anticipate and react to issues arising from adverse weather conditions, natural disasters, or political issues; if I don't know where in Taiwan my suppliers' factories are located, how will I know whether they might be affected by a fast-approaching typhoon? Similarly, some companies even want to know when labor contracts of key suppliers' workers expire in order to plan for potential labor disputes (Penfield, 2008). Needless to say, such levels of information sharing throughout the supply chain require tremendous trust among the partners.

Supply chain analytics refers to the use of key performance indicators to monitor performance of the entire supply chain, including sourcing, planning, production, and distribution. For example, a purchasing manager can identify the suppliers that are frequently unable to meet promised delivery dates. Being able to access key performance metrics can help to identify and remove bottlenecks, such as by switching suppliers, spreading orders over multiple suppliers, expediting shipping for critical goods, and so on.

CUSTOMER RELATIONSHIP MANAGEMENT

With the changes introduced by the Web, in most industries a company's competition is simply a mouse click away. It is increasingly important for companies not only to generate new business but also to attract repeat business from existing customers. This means that to remain competitive, companies must keep their customers satisfied. In today's highly competitive markets, customers hold the balance of power because, if they become dissatisfied with the levels of customer service they are receiving, they have many alternatives readily available. The global nature of the Web has affected companies worldwide in virtually all industries. An economic transformation is taking place, shifting the emphasis from conducting business transactions to managing relationships. If a company successfully manages its relationships with customers—satisfying them and solving their problems—then customers are less price sensitive. Hence, leveraging and managing customer relationships is equally as important as product development.

COMING ATTRACTIONS

Saving Lives Through 3D Bioprinting

When building prototypes or manufacturing parts, companies have traditionally used machine tools to drill, cut, or mill the part out of a solid piece of material. As you can imagine, such traditional forms of machining are not very efficient, often leaving up to 90 percent of a slab of material ready to go in the recycling or garbage bin. Recently, 3D printing has become a viable alternative for producing various parts using different materials. 3D printing works by adding successive layers of material onto a surface, thus building a 3D model out of myriad individual slices. In addition to being extremely precise, 3D printing creates significantly less waste. Successful applications of 3D printing range from Airbus using 3D printers to make lighter airplane parts to doctors and engineers collaborating to design custom-made prosthetics, benefitting people who have missing limbs by creating prosthetics that exactly fit their personal shape and size.

Three-dimensional printing is about to bring about another revolution; this time in the world of medicine, where this new technology could save lives where existing drugs cannot. Researchers in the Netherlands have successfully used 3D printing to completely replace a patient's skull with a custom version designed specifically for that individual. The patient suffered from a chronic disease that caused her skull to be too thick, which caused vision loss and would have led to her death. But three months after the surgery the patient regained her vision and was able to resume normal activities.

A UK-based company is using 3D printing to print up to 150 prosthetic eyes an hour, significantly decreasing costs of production, and allowing for slight variations in each eye, producing better aesthetic results. The company says that the more affordable eyes are intended to benefit those in developing countries who cannot typically afford conventional prosthetic eyes.

The development of 3D bioprinting continues making great strides, with researchers attempting to print complete organs for transplants. Statistics provided by Donate Life America show that every day, 18 people die from a lack of available organs for transplants and another name is added to the waiting list every 10 minutes, with more than 100,000 people already needing life-saving organ transplants in the United States alone. Then there is the other problem of the rejection of transplanted organs due to incompatibility. These printing technologies are expected to address both problems—literally printing and growing a heart for someone through the use of his or her own cells, just like in the movie *Star Trek*.

Based on:

3D printing. (2014, May 5). In *Wikipedia, The Free Encyclopedia*. Retrieved 16:17, May 6, 2014, from http://en.wikipedia.org/w/index.php?title=3D_printing&oldid=607145917.

Senthilingam, M. (2014, April 17). Artificial eyes, plastic skulls: 3D printing the human body. *CNN.com*. Retrieved May 6, 2014, from http://www.cnn.com/2014/04/17/tech/innovation/artificial-eyes-3d-printing-body.

Indeed, customer relationship management systems often collect data that can be mined to discover the next product line extension that consumers covet.

The megatrends mobile, social media, Big Data, cloud computing, and Internet of Things have tremendously changed the way organizations need to interact with their customers. Some researchers argue that we have moved from the Internet age to the "age of the customer" (Bernoff et al., 2011). The age of the customer is characterized by customers being part of social circles, and being increasingly empowered by social media (Figure 8.12). For example, customers have much more access to information from various sources; at the same time, customers' word of mouth can be spread anywhere, anytime using mobile devices, and has a much wider reach through social media such as blogs, Twitter, or Facebook. This can pose tremendous challenges for organizations trying to present and maintain a positive public image, as unmonitored information can have huge negative impacts, and monitoring and participating in ongoing conversations can be an important part of shaping public opinion. In addition, companies face significant changes in the competitive landscape. For example, the Internet has freed customers from having to purchase goods locally, and has thus lowered the barriers to entry for potential rivals. Similarly, many products have been replaced or marginalized by digital substitutes. The power of buyers has increased, as people can quickly and easily find information, reviews, or prices at a competitor's store. At the same time, employees, an important source of supply, have more mobility, and thus have higher power. Last but not least, not only other customers, but also one's competitors have tremendous amounts of information about one's products (and its strengths and weaknesses) available at their fingertips, and can more easily predict the one's next strategic move. Thus, businesses have to rethink their interactions with customers; rather than seeing customers as a passive audience, organizations need to engage in conversations with their

FIGURE 8.12

Today's empowered customers have many ways to obtain and spread information and opinions about companies.

customers. In their attempts to engage with customers and build long-lasting relationships, organizations are increasingly utilizing cloud-based systems and Big Data to better understand their customers and predict their needs and desires. Likewise, the Internet of Things serves as a source for additional data not only about the customers, but also about their usage of products, and can offer various opportunities to offer customers better value.

Many of the world's most successful corporations have realized the importance of developing and nurturing relationships with their customers. For example, Starbucks Coffee uses a variety of means to engage with its customers: Like many other businesses, Starbucks uses a loyalty card to entice people to return to its stores; further, Starbucks actively solicits feedback and new product ideas from its customers, not only within the stores but also via its open innovation platform mystarbucksidea.com, and it has one of the most successful fan pages on Facebook. Computer manufacturer Dell, in contrast, has different needs when interacting with its customers. For instance, when Dell sales representatives are dealing with large corporate clients that routinely make large computer purchases, issues of quantity pricing and delivery are likely to be paramount; whereas when dealing with less computer-savvy individuals ordering a new notebook for personal use, questions about compatibility with an older printer or the ability to run a specific program may be asked. No matter the customer, Dell attempts to provide all customers with a positive experience during both the presale and the ongoing support phases. Large banks and insurance companies, in contrast, are trying to widen and deepen relationships with customers so as to be able to sell more financial services and products, maximizing the lifetime value of each individual customer. Chase Card Services, for example, has more than 4,000 agents, handling 200 million customer calls a year. Being able to increase **first-call resolution**, that is, addressing the customers' issues during the first call, can help to save costs tremendously while increasing customer satisfaction.

Marketing researchers have found that the cost of trying to win back customers who have gone elsewhere can be up to 50 to 100 times as much as keeping a current one satisfied. Thus, companies are finding it imperative to develop and maintain customer satisfaction and widen (by attracting new customers), lengthen (by keeping existing profitable customers satisfied), and deepen (by transforming minor customers into profitable customers) the relationships with their customers in order to compete effectively in their markets (Figure 8.13). To achieve this, companies need to not only understand who their customers are but also determine the lifetime value of each customer. With the increasing popularity of social media such as social networks, blogs, and microblogs, companies have more ways than ever to learn about their customers.

To assist in deploying an organization-wide strategy for managing these increasingly complex customer relationships, organizations are deploying **customer relationship management (CRM)** systems. CRM is not simply a technology, but also a corporate-level strategy to create and maintain, through the introduction of reliable systems, processes, and procedures, lasting relationships with customers by concentrating on downstream information flows. Applications focusing on downstream information flows have three main objectives: to attract potential customers, to create customer loyalty, and to portray a positive corporate image. The appropriate CRM technology combined with the management of sales-related business processes can have tremendous benefits for an organization (Table 8.2). To pursue customer satisfaction as a basis for achieving

FIGURE 8.13

Companies search for ways to widen, lengthen, and deepen customer relationships.

competitive advantage, organizations must be able to access information and track customer interactions throughout the organization regardless of where, when, or how the interaction occurs. This means that companies need to have an integrated system that captures information from retail stores, Web sites, social networks, microblogs, call centers, and various other channels that organizations use to communicate downstream within their value chain. More important, managers need the capability to monitor and analyze factors that drive customer satisfaction (as well as dissatisfaction) as changes occur according to prevailing market conditions.

CRM applications come in the form of packaged software that is purchased from software vendors. CRM applications are commonly integrated with a comprehensive ERP implementation to leverage internal and external information to better serve customers. Thus, most large vendors of ERP packages, such as Oracle, SAP, and Microsoft, also offer CRM systems; further, specialized vendors, such as Salesforce.com or Sugar CRM, offer CRM solutions on a software-as-a-service basis. Like ERP, CRM applications come with various features and modules. Management must carefully select a CRM application that will meet the unique requirements of their business processes.

TABLE 8.2 Benefits of a CRM System

Benefit	Examples
24/7/365 operation	Web-based interfaces provide product information, sales status, support information, issue tracking, and so on.
Individualized service	Learn how each customer defines product and service quality so that customized product, pricing, and services can be designed or developed collaboratively.
Improved information	Integrate all information for all points of contact with the customers—marketing, sales, and service—so that all who interact with customers have the same view and understand current issues.
Improved problem identification/resolution	Improved record keeping and efficient methods of capturing customer complaints help to identify and solve problems faster.
Optimized processes	Integrated information removes information handoffs, speeding both sales and support processes.
Improved integration	Information from the CRM can be integrated with other systems to streamline business processes and gain business intelligence as well as make other cross-functional systems more efficient and effective.
Improved product development	Tracking customer behavior over time helps to identify future opportunities for product and service offerings.
Improved planning	This provides mechanisms for managing and scheduling sales follow-ups to assess satisfaction, repurchase probabilities, time frames, and frequencies.

KEY PLAYERS

Salesforce.com

Customer relationship management (CRM) is a critical component for the success of most medium to large organizations. More and more, CRM is becoming a necessity for many small organizations as well. To deploy a CRM system in the recent past, organizations would need to run one or more in-house servers and databases and have the necessary information technology (IT) admin skills to install and maintain the CRM system. Because of its investment cost, CRM remained a tool primarily used by larger organizations. However, given the ease with which systems can be adopted and deployed using a cloud-based software-as-a-service (SaaS) model, this is changing; organizations of any size can easily deploy CRM solutions. The benefits of a cloud-based SaaS deployment are notable, including quicker implementations, lower initial costs, and higher return on investment (ROI). The leader in cloud-based SaaS CRM is Salesforce.com, which provides a suite of tools to support all CRM-related needs. Some key capabilities of Salesforce.com's solutions include:

1. ***The Sales Cloud:*** This application provides sales representatives with a complete customer profile and account history; allows the user to manage marketing campaign spending and performance across a variety of channels; and tracks all opportunity-related data, including milestones, decision makers, customer communications, and any other information unique to the company's sales process.
2. ***The Service Cloud:*** This application allows organizations to create and track service cases coming in from every sales or communication channel, automatically routing and escalating cases as needed. A customer portal also provides customers with the ability to track their own cases 24 hours a day.
3. ***Chatter:*** This enterprise social network sends information proactively via a real-time news feed. Chatter helps organizations to communicate better, locate and share knowledge within the organization, and provide improved customer service.

All Salesforce.com applications are accessible on traditional computers and a variety of mobile devices. In addition, external developers can create add-on applications that can be integrated into the main Salesforce.com application or offered for sale on an online marketplace. These capabilities are transforming organizations of all sizes. Clearly, the advanced capabilities of CRM systems are not just for the big boys anymore.

Based on:
Salesforce.com. (n.d.). Retrieved May 6, 2014, from http://www.salesforce.com.

Salesforce.com. (2014, May 3). In *Wikipedia, The Free Encyclopedia*. Retrieved May 6, 2014, from http://en.wikipedia.org/w/index.php?title=Salesforce.com&oldid=606885708.

Companies that have successfully implemented CRM can experience greater customer satisfaction and increased productivity of their sales and service personnel, which can translate into dramatic enhancements to the company's profitability. CRM allows organizations to focus on driving revenue as well as on reducing costs, as opposed to emphasizing only cost cutting. Cost cutting tends to have a lower limit because there are only so many costs that companies can reduce, whereas revenue generation strategies are bound only by the size of the market itself. The importance of focusing on customer satisfaction is emphasized by findings from the National Quality Research Center, which estimates that increasing customer satisfaction by 1 percent can lead to a 3 percent increase in a company's market valuation (Fornell, 2001).

Developing a CRM Strategy

To develop a successful CRM strategy, organizations must do more than simply purchase and install CRM software. The first consideration is whether a comprehensive CRM system is even needed for a company; for example, the closer an organization is to the end customer, the more important CRM becomes. Further, companies have to realize that a successful CRM strategy must include enterprise-wide changes, including changes to:

- ***Policies and Business Processes.*** Organizational policies and procedures need to reflect a customer-focused culture.
- ***Customer Service.*** Key metrics for managing the business need to reflect customer-focused measures for quality and satisfaction as well as process changes to enhance the customer experience.
- ***Employee Training.*** Employees from all areas—marketing, sales, and support—must have a consistent focus that values customer service and satisfaction.
- ***Data Collection, Analysis, and Sharing.*** All aspects of the customer experience—prospecting, sales, support, and so on—must be tracked, analyzed, and shared to optimize the benefits of the CRM.

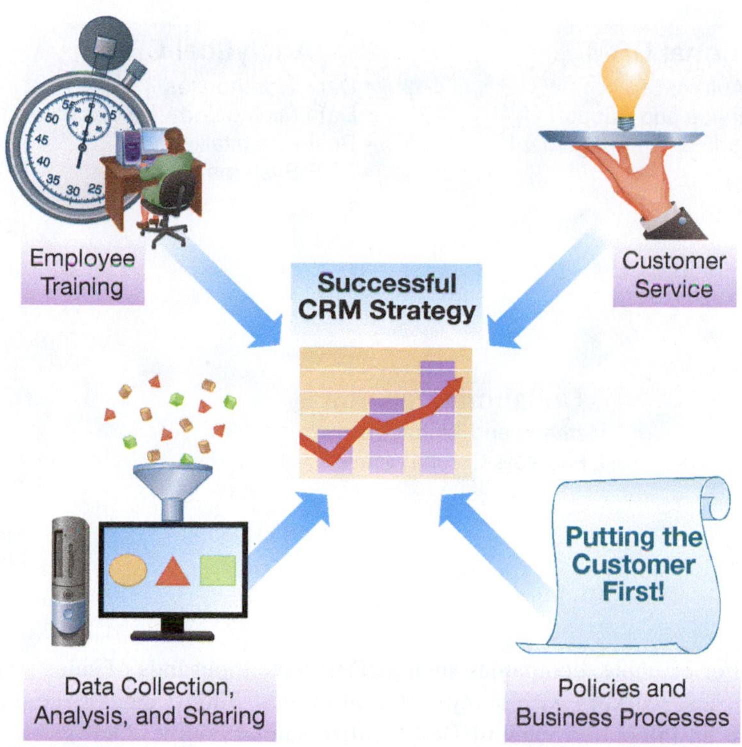

FIGURE 8.14

A successful CRM strategy requires enterprise-wide changes.

In sum, the organization must focus and organize its activities to provide the best customer service possible (Figure 8.14). Additionally, a successful CRM strategy must carefully consider the ethical and privacy concerns of customers' data (discussed later in this chapter).

Architecture of a CRM System

A comprehensive CRM system comprises three primary components:

1. ***Operational CRM.*** Systems for automating the fundamental business processes—marketing, sales, and support—for interacting with the customer
2. ***Analytical CRM.*** Systems for analyzing customer behavior and perceptions (e.g., quality, price, and overall satisfaction) in order to provide business intelligence
3. ***Collaborative CRM.*** Systems for providing effective and efficient communication with the customer from the entire organization

Operational CRM enables direct interaction with customers; in contrast, analytical CRM provides the analysis necessary to more effectively manage the sales, service, and marketing activities. Whereas analytical CRM aids in the development of a company's CRM strategy, operational CRM aids in the execution of CRM strategy; thus, either component alone provides no real benefit for a business. Finally, collaborative CRM provides the communication capabilities of the CRM environment (Figure 8.15). Next, we examine each of these components.

OPERATIONAL CRM. **Operational CRM** includes the systems used to enable customer interaction and service. For example, operational CRM systems help create the mass e-mail marketing campaigns wherein each consumer receives an individualized e-mail based on prior purchase history. With an effective operational CRM environment, organizations are able to provide personalized and highly efficient customer service. Customer-focused personnel are provided complete customer information—history, pending sales, and service requests—in order to optimize interaction and service. It is important to stress that the operational CRM environment provides *all* customer information regardless of the touch point (i.e., technical support, customer service, and in-store sales, as well as Web site interactions such as downloading content and e-commerce clickstream data). This means that marketing, sales, and support personnel see *all* prior and current interactions with the customer regardless of where it occurred within the organization. To facilitate the sharing of information and customer interaction, three separate modules are utilized (Figure 8.16).

Sales Force Automation The first component of an operational CRM is **sales force automation (SFA)**. SFA refers to modules that support the day-to-day sales activities of an

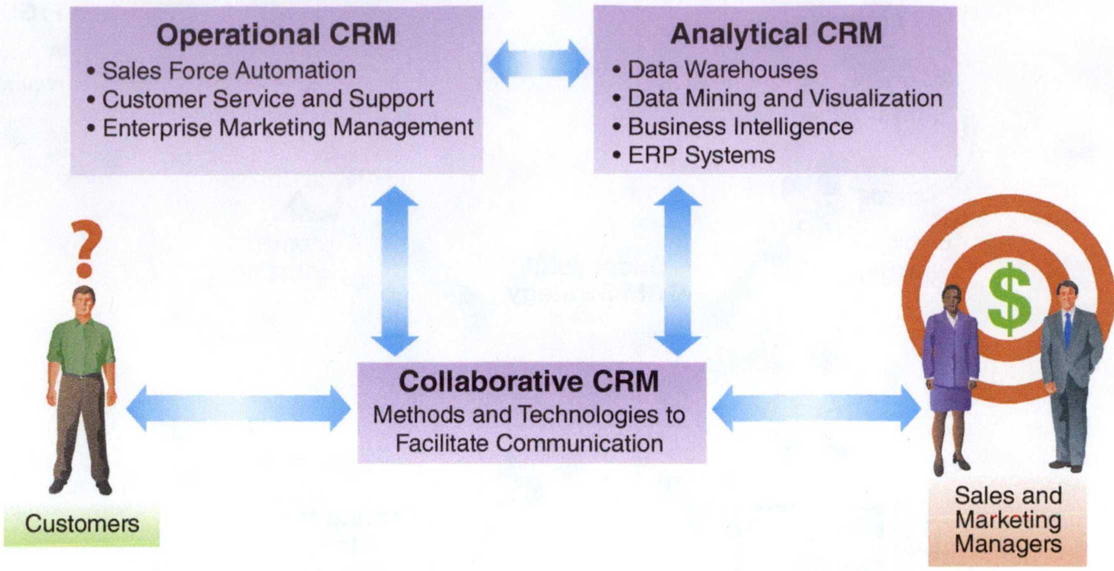

FIGURE 8.15

A comprehensive CRM environment includes operational, analytical, and collaborative components.

organization. For example, companies such as Dell have thousands of sales staff in various different countries, working with many different clients. Unless sales personnel and sales managers have an integrated view of Dell's entire sales pipeline, Dell sales staff may be competing with each other for the same contracts, unbeknownst to each other. SFA supports a broad range of sales-related business processes, such as order processing and tracking, managing accounts, contacts, opportunities, and sales, and tracking and managing customer history and preferences (both in terms of product and communication). Together, this can help in creating more accurate sales forecasts and analyzing sales performance.

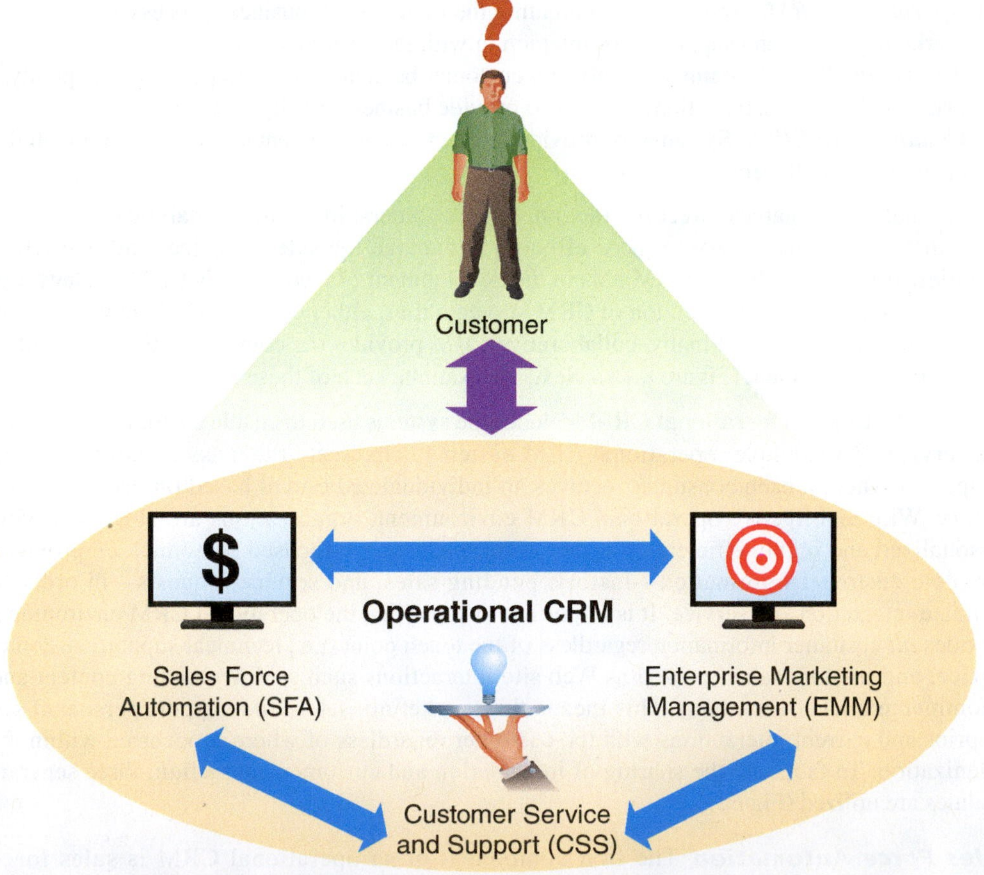

FIGURE 8.16

An operational CRM environment is used to enable customer interaction and service.

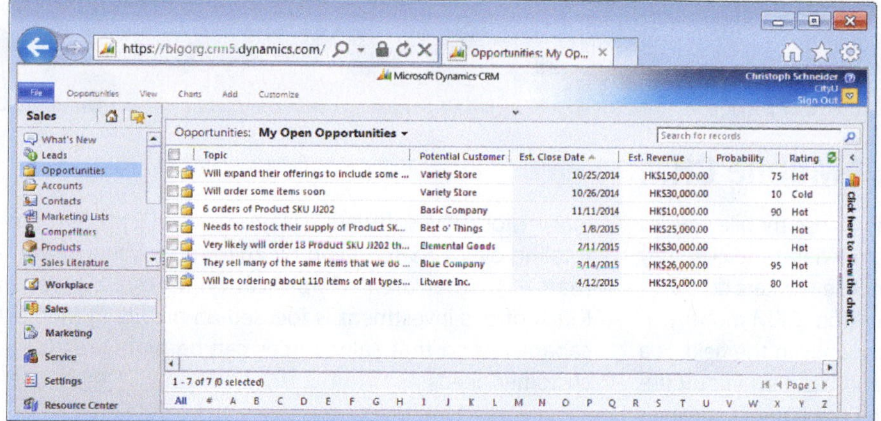

FIGURE 8.17

SFA allows sales managers to track sales performance.
Source: Courtesy of Microsoft Corporation.

SFA systems provide advantages for sales personnel, sales managers, and marketing managers. For sales personnel, SFA reduces the potentially error-prone paperwork associated with the selling process. Because all the information is within the system, personnel can more easily hand off work and collaborate; it is also easier to train new personnel. Sales personnel can then use their time more efficiently, and ultimately focus more on selling than on paperwork and other non-selling tasks. Likewise, for sales managers, the SFA system provides tremendous benefits, such as accurate, up-to-the-minute information on all customers, markets, and sales personnel. This improved information allows better planning, scheduling, and coordination. Ultimately, SFA provides better day-to-day management of the sales function. For example, SFA allows sales managers to track a plethora of sales performance measures, such as the sales pipeline for each salesperson, including rating and probability (Figure 8.17), revenue per salesperson, per territory, or as a percentage of sales quota, or number of calls per day, time spent per contact, revenue per call, cost per call, or ratio of orders to calls. Further, sales managers can obtain other useful information such as number of lost customers per period or cost of customer acquisition; product-related information such as margins by product category, customer segment, or customer; or percentage of goods returned, number of customer complaints, or number of overdue accounts. All of these measures aid in assessing sales performance and detecting potential problems in certain regions, or issues with product or service quality.

Finally, SFA improves the effectiveness of the marketing function by providing an improved understanding of market conditions, competitors, and products. This enhanced information will provide numerous advantages for the management and execution of the marketing function. Specifically, SFA aids in gaining a better understanding of markets, segments, and customers, as well as competitors and the overall economic structure of the industry. Such broad and deep understanding of the competitive landscape can help organizations assess their unique strengths and weaknesses, thereby facilitating new product development and improving strategic planning.

In sum, the primary goals of SFA are to better identify potential customers, streamline selling processes, and improve managerial information. Next, we examine systems for improving customer service and support.

Customer Service and Support The second component of an operational CRM system is **customer service and support (CSS)**. CSS refers to modules that automate service requests, complaints, product returns, and information requests. In the past, organizations had *help desks* and *call centers* to provide customer service and support. Today, organizations are deploying a **customer engagement center (CEC)**, using multiple communication channels to support the communication preferences of customers, such as the Web, the company's Facebook page, industry blogs, face-to-face contact, telephone, and so on (see the section "Collaborative CRM " later in this chapter). The CEC utilizes a variety of communication technologies for optimizing customers' communications with the organization. For example, automatic call distribution systems forward calls to the next available person; while waiting to connect, customers can be given the option to use the keypad or voice response technologies to check account status information. Southwest Airlines improves customer service by using "virtual hold technology," where customers can choose to stay on the line or be called back when the next agent is available; this helped to save

WHO'S GOING MOBILE

The Power of Mobile CRM

Mobile CRM allows employees on the go to use mobile devices to access, update, and interact with customer data wherever they are. The best mobile CRM solutions let mobile workers do everything they could do with CRM at their desktop. CRM mobility, in organizations where the sales staff is frequently in the field, is a critical component to the CRM solution and has a significant impact on sales performance for staff and the company. Companies using mobile CRM solutions reap many benefits, including:

- Better year-over-year revenue growth
- Increased customer renewals
- Increased deal size
- Increased CRM user adoption
- Higher sales team quota attainment
- Lower personnel turnover

CRM is one of the hottest software investments for organizations of all sizes. In 2013, Gartner predicted that the market for CRM software will grow over 15 percent per year, totaling over US$36 billion by 2017, and will increase faster than any other area of application software investment. Much of this investment is focused on providing mobile CRM capabilities so that sales forces can be highly responsive to customer needs.

Based on:

Aberdeen Group. (2010, December 9). Improving sales effectiveness through a mobile sales team. Retrieved May 6, 2014, from http://www.aberdeen.com/Press/Details/Sales-Mobility/100.aspx.

Anonymous. (n.d.). About mobile CRM. *Tendigits*. Retrieved May 6, 2014, from http://www.tendigits.com/about-mobile-crm.html.

Columbus, L. (2013, June 18). Gartner predicts CRM will be a $36B market by 2017. *Forbes*. Retrieved May 6, 2014, from http://www.forbes.com/sites/louiscolumbus/2013/06/18/gartner-predicts-crm-will-be-a-36b-market-by-2017.

almost 25 million toll minutes in 2009, and reduced the number of abandoned calls, which provides additional opportunities for ticket sales and signals increased customer satisfaction. In essence, the goal of CSS is to provide great customer service—anytime, anywhere, and through any channel—while keeping service and support costs low. For example, many CECs use powerful self-service diagnostic tools that guide consumers to their needed information. Customers can log service requests or gain updates to pending support requests using a variety of self-service or assisted technologies (Figure 8.18). Successful CSS systems enable faster response times, increased first-contact resolution rates, and improved productivity of service and support personnel. Managers can utilize digital dashboards to monitor key metrics such as first-contact resolution and service personnel utilization, which allows for improved management of the service and support functions (see Chapter 6, "Enhancing Business Intelligence Using Information Systems").

Enterprise Marketing Management The third component of an operational CRM system is **enterprise marketing management (EMM)**. EMM tools help a company in the execution of the CRM strategy by improving the management of promotional campaigns (Figure 8.19). Today, many companies use a variety of channels (such as e-mail, telephone, direct mail, Facebook pages and YouTube channels, Twitter status updates, and so on; see Chapter 4, "Enabling Business-to-Consumer Electronic Commerce," and Chapter 5, "Enhancing Organizational Communication and Collaboration Using Social Media") to reach potential customers and drive them to Web pages customized for their target market (based on demographics and lifestyle). Using EMM tools can help integrate those campaigns such that the right messages are sent to the right people through the right channels. This necessitates that customer lists are managed carefully to avoid targeting people who have opted out of receiving marketing communication and to be able to personalize messages that can deliver individualized attention to each potential customer. At the same time, EMM tools provide extensive analytical capabilities that can help to analyze the effectiveness of marketing campaigns and can help to efficiently route sales leads to the right salespeople, leading to higher conversion rates.

ANALYTICAL CRM. **Analytical CRM** focuses on analyzing customer behavior and perceptions in order to provide the business intelligence necessary to identify new opportunities and to provide superior customer service. Organizations that effectively utilize analytical CRM can more easily customize marketing campaigns from the segment level to even the individual customer. Such customized campaigns help to increase cross- or up-selling (i.e., selling more profitable products or identifying popular bundles of products and services tailored to different market segments)

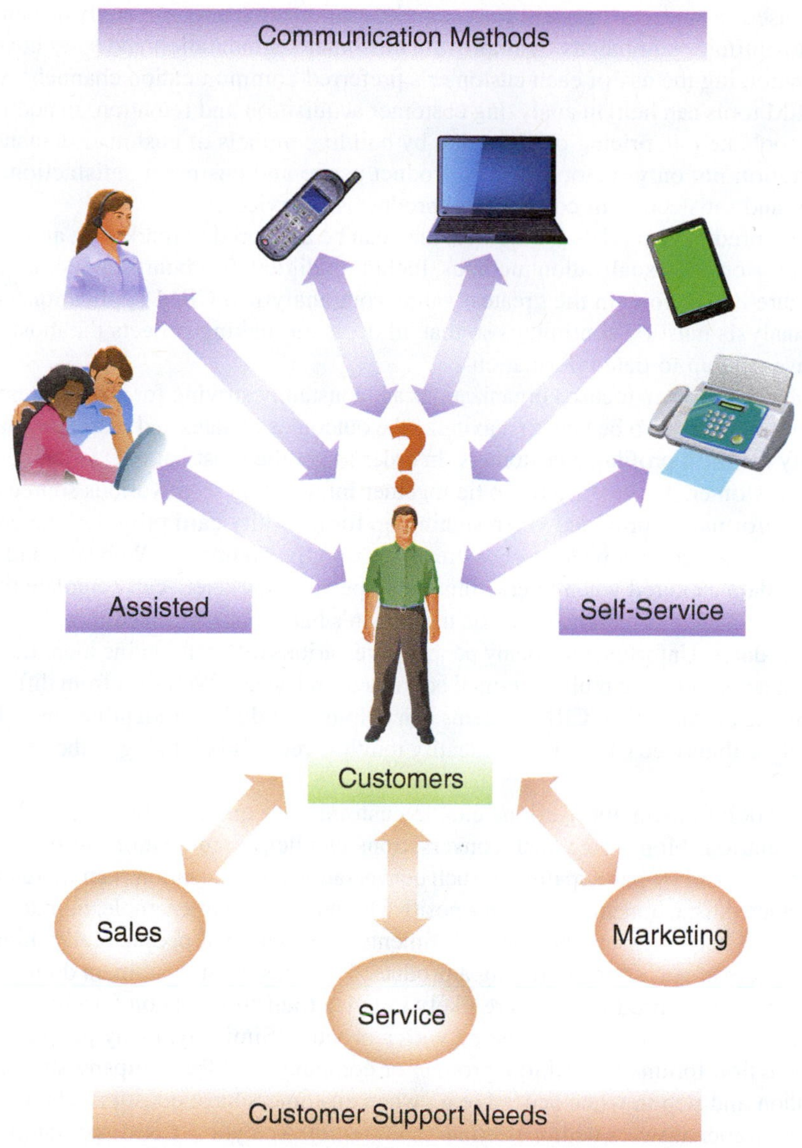

FIGURE 8.18

A CEC allows customers to use a variety of self-service and assisted technologies to interact with the organization.

as well as retain customers by having accurate, timely, and personalized information. Analytical CRM systems are also used to spot sales trends by ZIP code, state, and region as well as specific target markets within those areas.

Key technologies within analytical CRM systems include data mining, decision support, and other business intelligence technologies that attempt to create predictive models of various customer attributes (see Chapter 6). These analyses can focus on enhancing a broad range of

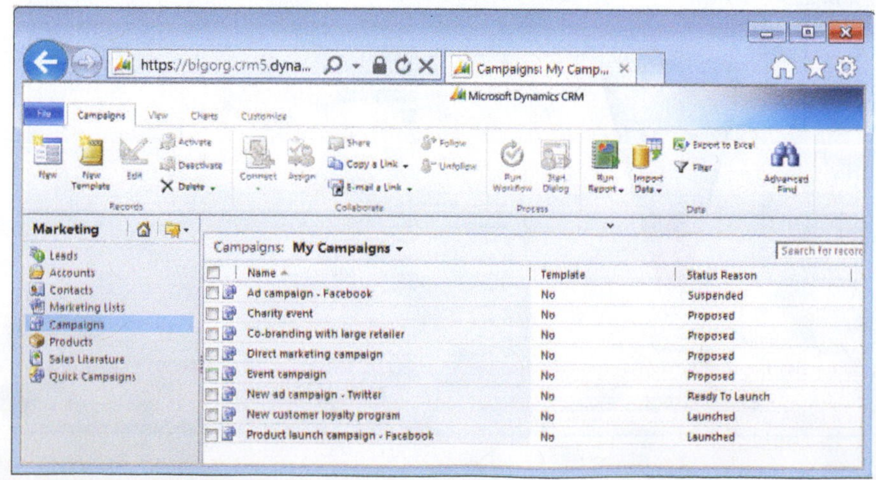

FIGURE 8.19

CRM systems allow for managing various types of promotional campaigns.

Source: Courtesy of Microsoft Corporation.

customer-focused business processes; for example, marketing campaign analysis can help organizations to optimize campaigns by improving customer segmentation and sales coverage, as well as by optimizing the use of each customer's preferred communication channels. Similarly, analytical CRM tools can help in analyzing customer acquisition and retention. In addition, analytical CRM tools help in pricing optimization by building models of customer demand, taking into consideration not only factors such as product usage and customer satisfaction, but also price, quality, and satisfaction of competitors' products or services.

Once these predictive models are created, they can be delivered to marketing and sales managers using a variety of visualization methods, including digital dashboards and other reporting methods (Figure 8.20). To gain the greatest value from analytical CRM applications, data collection and analysis must be continuous so that all decision making reflects the most accurate, comprehensive, and up-to-date information.

One goal that customer-focused organizations are constantly striving for is to get a 360-degree view of the customer so as to be able to maximize the outcomes of sales and marketing campaigns and to identify the most profitable customers. In order to get the most complete picture of a sales prospect or a customer, marketers have to tie together information from various sources, such as demographic information provided when signing up for a loyalty card program, the customer's address, purchase and contact history, clickstream data on the company's Web site, and so on. In addition to the data captured when interacting with a person, marketers can complete the picture with publicly available information posted on the person's Facebook or LinkedIn profile or the person's Twitter updates. Unfortunately, many people have various different online identities (e.g., for different social networks), use multiple e-mail addresses, and access Web sites from different computers (Figure 8.21). Analytical CRM systems can help merge different identities by using fuzzy logic–based algorithms (see Chapter 6) to identify multiple records belonging to the same person.

Social CRM Social media applications enable customers to quickly share both positive and negative information. Monitoring such conversations can help organizations to better measure public perceptions, and by participating in such conversations, organizations can more effectively manage customer satisfaction and maintain a positive brand image. For example, monitoring online conversations can help to assess customer sentiments, find out what people really think about a product, and discover ways for improving a product: Whereas most customers do not bother to fill out a survey about a product, they are likely to voice their thoughts on Facebook or Twitter if they are very satisfied or very dissatisfied with a product. Similarly, many people participate in online discussion forums related to a product or company, and the company should monitor the conversation and step in when needed (e.g., when customers have questions about a product, but no other customer answers within a certain time frame). Analytical CRM applications such as the Social Networking Accelerator add-on for Microsoft Dynamics CRM help in monitoring and

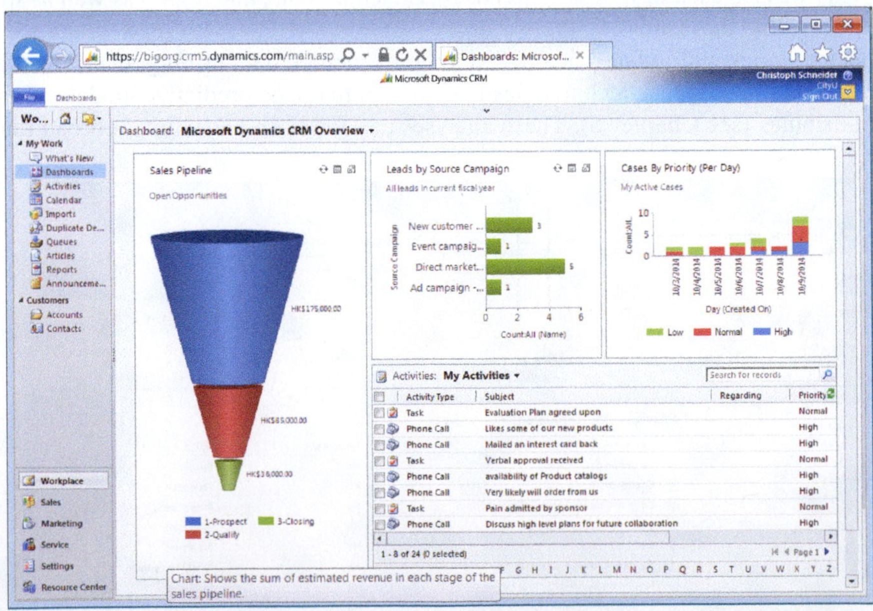

FIGURE 8.20

Digital dashboards help to visualize key CRM performance metrics.

Source: Courtesy of Microsoft Corporation.

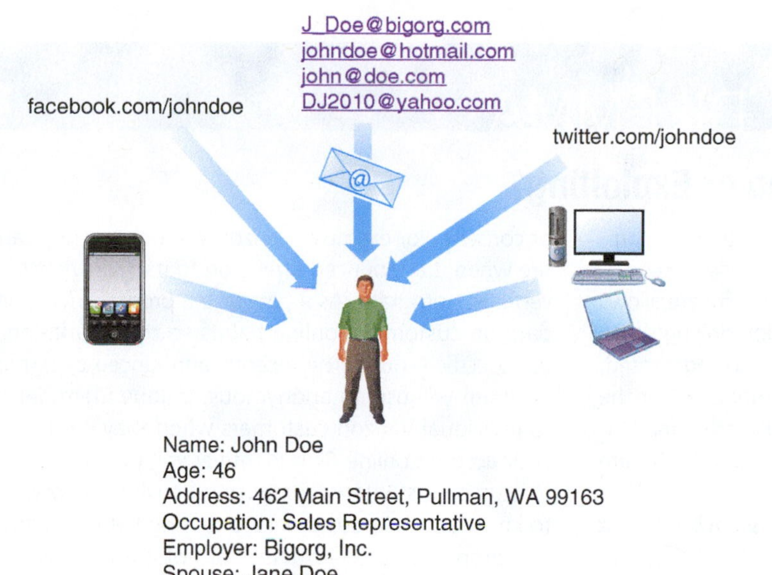

FIGURE 8.21

Many people interact with a company in many different ways using various online identities.

analyzing ongoing conversations on social media sites, helping to spot potential perception issues or to discover trends in customer sentiment (the use of social media for customer relationship management is often referred to as **social CRM**). Needless to say, an organization should have an appropriate social CRM strategy in place and should have clear policies, such as when to step into an online discussion, which (or how many) tweets to reply to, or how to strike a balance between grassroots marketing and deceiving people by posing as casual conversation partners.

Given the rise in importance of social media for reaching out and communicating with customers, many organizations are creating a formal organizational group to engage in social media monitoring. **Social media monitoring** is the process of identifying and assessing the volume and sentiment of what is being said about a company, individual, product, or brand. To collect this information, organizations utilize a variety of tools to track and aggregate social media content from blogs, wikis, news sites, microblogs such as Twitter, social networking sites like Facebook, video-/photo-sharing Web sites like YouTube and Flickr, forums, message boards, blogs, and user-generated content in general. Depending on the goal of the social media monitoring program, a simple tool like Google Alerts might be adequate; to gain deep and timely understanding of evolving customer sentiment, specialized applications that provide sophisticated analyses and full integration with existing CRM applications are available. As organizations increasingly rely on social media, social media monitoring will become a central part of analyzing and understanding evolving market trends and customer sentiments. In addition, social media monitoring helps in identifying the "influencers" who are most likely to share their views through social media. Even though social media allow anybody to voice opinions, not everyone does so. For example, while many people regularly read blogs, only a few people write their own blogs; yet, these blogs can be influential in swaying others' opinions. The importance of social media monitoring is exemplified by large companies such as Dell, which established a Social Media Listening Command Center, where a number of full-time staff monitor over 22,000 daily posts made about the company on various social media. Having a dedicated team helps to quickly react to customer complaints or changes in public sentiment about the company, enabling near-real-time communication with the customers through social media.

COLLABORATIVE CRM. **Collaborative CRM** refers to systems for providing effective and efficient communication with the customer from the entire organization. Collaborative CRM systems facilitate the sharing of information across the various departments of an organization in order to increase customer satisfaction and loyalty. Sharing useful customer information on a company-wide basis helps improve information quality and can be used to identify products or services a customer may be interested in. A collaborative CRM system supports customer communication and collaboration with the entire organization, thus providing more streamlined customer service with fewer handoffs. The CEC (as described previously) enables customers to utilize the communication method they prefer when interacting with the organization. In other words, collaborative CRM integrates the communication related to all aspects of the marketing,

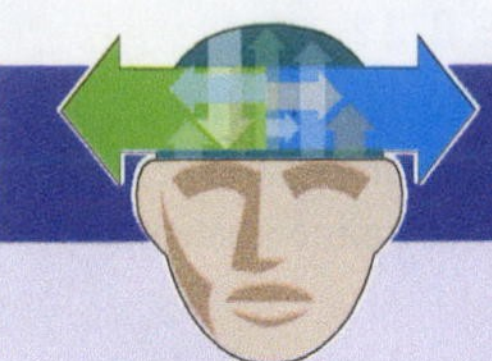

ETHICAL DILEMMA

CRM: Targeting or Exploiting?

Promising companies the ability to get to know their customers and maximize the benefit gained from each one, CRM systems could be called a marketer's dream. CRM software allows companies to look closely at customer behavior, drilling down to smaller and smaller market segments. Once so segmented, customers can be targeted with specific promotions. For the company, this process reaps the greatest returns from marketing efforts since only those customers are targeted who are likely to respond to the marketing campaign.

From a customer's perspective, CRM systems seem like a great idea. You finally stop receiving advertisements for things that don't interest you. But what if a company uses its CRM software in a more discriminating way? Where do companies draw the line between using CRM data to offer certain clients customized deals and unethically discriminating against other customers? For example, banks, which often segment their customers according to their creditworthiness, might use this credit risk data to target customers having a low credit rating. Although these customers are more risky for the banks, the higher fees and interest charged for credit make these customers especially lucrative.

Some companies go so far as selling customer data collected through CRM programs—without customer knowledge or consent. For example, Verizon wireless recently came under fire when it announced a revision to its "Relevant Mobile Advertising" program. As a part of the program, Verizon collects data on customers' online habits so that marketers can target specific groups. The recently announced expansion to the program will use an anonymous, unique identifier, assigned to individual Verizon customers when they log in to manage their account online. This identifier will then be used to monitor customers' Internet browsing activities, allowing Verizon to know about its customers' browsing habits on any desktop or laptop computer—whether or not it is accessing the Internet through a Verizon broadband connection. The company will then share that additional data with marketers. Such data sharing alliances benefit from the use of CRM programs, and they are legal—but are they ethical?

Based on:

Jourdier, A. (2002, May 1). Privacy & ethics: Is CRM too close for comfort? *CIO.com*. Retrieved May 6, 2014, from http://www.cio.com/article/31062/Privacy_Ethics_Is_CRM_Too_Close_for_Comfort_.

Lazarus, D. (2014, April 24). Verizon Wireless sells out customers with creepy new tactic. *Los Angeles Times*. Retrieved May 6, 2014, from http://www.latimes.com/business/la-fi-lazarus-20140425-column.html.

sales, and support processes in order to better serve and retain customers. Collaborative CRM enhances communication in the following ways:

- ***Greater Customer Focus.*** Understanding customer history and current needs helps to focus the communication on issues important to the customer.
- ***Lower Communication Barriers.*** Customers are more likely to communicate with the organization when personnel have complete information and when they utilize the communication methods and preferences of the customer.
- ***Increased Information Integration.*** All information about the customer as well as all prior and ongoing communication is given to all organizational personnel interacting with the customer; customers can get status updates from any organizational touch point.

In addition to these benefits, collaborative CRM environments are flexible such that they can support both routine and non-routine events.

Ethical Concerns with CRM

Although CRM has become a strategic enabler for developing and maintaining customer relationships, it is not viewed positively by those who feel that it invades customer privacy and facilitates coercive sales practices. Proponents of CRM warn that relying too much on the "systems" profile of a customer, based on statistical analysis of past behavior, may categorize customers in a way that they will take exception to. Additionally, given that a goal of CRM is to better meet the needs of customers by providing highly *personalized* communication and service (such as Amazon.com's recommendations), at what point does the communication get *too* personal? It is intuitive to conclude that when customers feel that the system knows too much about them, personalization could backfire on a company. Clearly, CRM raises several ethical concerns in the digital world (see Chapter 1, "Managing in the Digital World," for a comprehensive discussion of information privacy). Nevertheless, as competition continues to increase in the digital world, CRM will remain a key technology for attracting and retaining customers.

INDUSTRY ANALYSIS

Manufacturing

Regardless of whether you're thinking about a new computer, a TV, an automobile, or a toy for your baby brother, most of today's consumer products have undergone an elaborate design and manufacturing process, and few companies do not make heavy use of information systems in the process. Traditionally, designers and engineers used large drawing boards to sketch detailed drawings of each component of a product. Today, designers use computer-aided design (CAD) software for this task, allowing them to create drawings faster and more accurately, thus cutting down cycle time (i.e., the time from inception to the shipment of the first product) tremendously. Further, CAD allows easier sharing of designs and can be used to produce 3D drawings of a new product. However, while you can create realistic 3D drawings of a new product, people often still prefer holding a physical model in their hands to evaluate it. 3D printing, sometimes known as "fabbing," can greatly speed up the creation of models and an increasing range of finished products. In essence, 3D printers add successive layers of material onto a surface, thus building a 3D model out of myriad individual slices. In fact, some 3D printers even use materials such as titanium, allowing battleships to produce spare parts on an as-needed basis rather than carrying warehouses full of parts. 3D printing is rapidly evolving. In 2014 for example, engineers used 3D printing to create large satellite fuel tank simulators in order to test key satellite components. The simulator was required to test how best to assemble the fuel tanks, and 3D printing was the best choice to meet a tight deadline and contain costs.

The use of technology doesn't stop there. Inventory planning, job scheduling, or warehouse management are all supported by information systems, often in the form of ERP and SCM systems. Once a product leaves the manufacturer, information systems are used throughout the distribution of the product, from transportation scheduling to route optimization to improvement of a trucking company fleet's fuel efficiency. Clearly, information systems have changed and will continue to change the process of designing, manufacturing, and shipping products to you.

Based on:

3D printing. (2014, May 5). In *Wikipedia, The Free Encyclopedia*. Retrieved 20:17, May 6, 2014, from http://en.wikipedia.org/w/index.php?title=3D_printing&oldid=501858773.

Howell, E. (2014, May 6). Engineers build space fuel tank simulators with 3D printing. *Space.com*. Retrieved May 6, 2014, from http://www.space.com/25775-3d-printing-satellite-fuel-tank-video.html.

Key Points Review

1. ***Describe supply chain management systems and how they help to improve business-to-business processes.*** SCM focuses on improving interorganizational business processes in B2B relationships and has two main objectives: to accelerate product development and to reduce costs associated with procuring raw materials, components, and services from suppliers. Supplier and customer portals provide secure access points for established business partners. Smaller organizations often use B2B marketplaces for sourcing supplies. Organizations must match their overall supply chain strategy to their overall competitive strategy to reap the greatest benefits. SCM systems consist of SCP, SCE, and supply chain visibility and analytics components. SCP involves the development of various resource plans to support the efficient and effective production of goods and services. SCE involves the management of product flows, information flows, and financial flows. Supply chain visibility and analytics help in foreseeing the impacts of external events and monitoring the performance of the supply chain.

2. ***Describe customer relationship management systems and how they help to improve the activities involved in promoting and selling products to customers as well as providing customer service and nourishing long-term relationships.*** CRM is a corporate-level strategy to create and maintain lasting relationships with customers by concentrating on downstream information flows, to attract potential customers, to create customer loyalty, and to portray a positive corporate image. To develop a successful CRM strategy, organizations must make changes to policies and business processes, customer service, employee training, and data utilization. A CRM system consists of operational CRM, analytical CRM, and collaborative CRM. Operational CRM focuses on activities that deal directly with customers. Analytical CRM focuses on activities that aid managers in analyzing the sales and marketing functions as well as monitoring ongoing conversations in social media. Finally, collaborative CRM provides effective communication capabilities within the organization and externally with customers.

Key Terms

analytical CRM 306
bullwhip effect 291
business-to-business marketplace 289
collaborative CRM 309
customer engagement center (CEC) 305
customer portal 288
customer relationship management (CRM) 300
customer service and support (CSS) 305
Electronic Data Interchange (EDI) 286
enterprise marketing management (EMM) 306
Extensible Business Reporting Language (XBRL) 297
Extensible Markup Language (XML) 296
financial flow 297
first-call resolution 300
information flow 296
just-in-time (JIT) 290
operational CRM 303
portal 287
product flow 295
radio frequency identification (RFID) 296
RFID tag 296
sales force automation (SFA) 303
social CRM 309
social media monitoring 309
supplier portal 287
supply chain 286
supply chain analytics 298
supply chain effectiveness 293
supply chain efficiency 293
supply chain execution (SCE) 295
supply chain management (SCM) 291
supply chain planning (SCP) 294
supply chain visibility 298
supply network 286
vendor-managed inventory (VMI) 290
vertical market 289
XML tag 297

Go to **mymislab.com** to complete the problems marked with this icon .

Review Questions

8-1. Describe supply chains and explain why "supply network" may be a more accurate term.
8-2. Contrast B2B portals with B2B marketplaces.
8-3. What are two process innovations enabled by effective collaboration within supply networks?
8-4. How does SCP differ from SCE?
8-5. How does supply chain visibility help an organization react to external events?
8-6. Contrast supply chain effectiveness and supply chain efficiency.
8-7. What is XML, and what is its role in SCM?
8-8. What is RFID, and what is its role in SCM?
8-9. How does CRM differ from SCM?
8-10. What is a CRM system, and what are its primary components?
8-11. Contrast operational and analytical CRM.
8-12. How does analytical CRM help in monitoring social conversations?

Self-Study Questions

8-13. Which of the following is commonly used to refer to the producers of supplies that a company uses?
A. procurement
B. sales force
C. supply network
D. customers

8-14. Under a VMI model, ______________.
A. a manufacturer has to signal restocking quantities to the supplier
B. the suppliers to a manufacturer manage the manufacturer's inventory levels based on negotiated service levels
C. the vendor has access only to stock levels
D. stockout situations are more likely to occur

8-15. The bullwhip effect refers to ______________.
A. contract penalties resulting from a supplier's inability to deliver raw materials on time
B. small forecasting errors at the end of the supply chain causing massive forecasting errors farther up the supply chain
C. pressure to use a specific SCM system by a company in a supply chain
D. rising stock values due to effective SCM practices

8-16. Which type of flow does SCE not focus on?
A. procurement flow
B. product flow
C. information flow
D. financial flow

8-17. RFID tags can be used for ______________.
A. tracking military weapons
B. eliminating counterfeit drugs
C. tracking passports
D. all of the above

8-18. A comprehensive CRM system includes all but which of the following components?
A. operational CRM
B. analytical CRM
C. cooperative CRM
D. collaborative CRM

8-19. SFA is most closely associated with what?
A. operational CRM
B. analytical CRM
C. cooperative CRM
D. collaborative CRM

8-20. All the following are channels used for promotional campaigns except ______________.
A. Twitter
B. telephone
C. direct mail
D. all of the above are used

8-21. A metric for being able to quickly resolve customers' issues is called ______________.
A. customer satisfaction and complaint management
B. customer communication optimization
C. virtual-hold technology
D. first-call resolution

8-22. Categorizing customers based on statistical analysis of past behavior is ______________.
A. illegal
B. a common but sometimes ethically questionable business practice
C. ethical and a common business practice
D. technically impossible

Answers are on page 314.

Problems and Exercises

8-23. Match the following terms with the appropriate definitions:

i. JIT
ii. Supply chain efficiency
iii. Supply chain
iv. Supply chain visibility
v. CRM systems
vi. CEC
vii. SCM systems
viii. VMI
ix. vertical market
x. RFID

a. The ability not only to track products as they move through the supply chain but also to foresee external events
b. A market comprised of firms within a specific industry sector
c. The use of electromagnetic energy to transmit information between a reader (transceiver) and a processing device, used to replace bar codes and bar code readers
d. The extent to which a company's supply chain is focusing on minimizing procurement, production, and transportation costs
e. An SCM innovation that optimizes ordering quantities such that parts or raw materials arrive just when they are needed for production
f. Applications that help to create and maintain lasting relationships with customers by concentrating on the downstream information flows
g. Commonly used to refer to the collection of producers of supplies that a company uses
h. A business model in which the suppliers to a manufacturer (or retailer) manage the manufacturer's (or retailer's) inventory levels based on negotiated service levels
i. A part of operational CRM that provides a central point of contact for an organization's customers
j. Applications that help to improve interorganizational business processes to accelerate product development and innovation and to reduce costs

8-24. Find an organization that you are familiar with and determine how it manages its supply chain. Is the company effective in managing the supply chain, or does it need closer integration and collaboration with its suppliers?

8-25. Search the Web for a recent product recall. How did the company affected handle the recall? Were the actions appropriate, or could increased supply chain visibility have helped?

8-26. Search the Web for companies using sustainable SCM practices. Are those attempts convincing? Why or why not? Under what circumstances would such practices influence your purchasing decisions?

8-27. Analyze the supply chain of your favorite electronic gadget and compare this with the supply chain of your favorite pair of jeans. How do the supply chains differ? What are potential reasons for this?

8-28. When purchasing a product on the Web, how important is the visibility of *your* supply chain for this product? Why? Does the importance differ for different products?

8-29. Choose a company you are familiar with and examine how efficiently or effectively it has designed the procurement, production, and transportation aspects of its business.

8-30. What applications, other than those mentioned, are there for RFID tags? What must happen in order for the use of RFID to become more widespread?

8-31. Assume you are a sales manager. What sales performance measures would you want the CRM system to provide you in order to better manage your sales force? For each measure, describe how you would use it and at what interval you would need to update this information.

8-32. Find an organization that is utilizing CRM (visit vendor Web sites for case studies or industry journals such as *CIO Magazine* or *Computerworld*). Who within the organization is most involved in this process, and who benefits?

8-33. When you last contacted a company with a product or service request, which contact options did you have? Which option did you choose, and why?

8-34. Search the Web for recent articles on social CRM. What is the current state-of-the-art application for managing customer relationships in social media?

8-35. Use the Web to visit sites of three companies offering CRM systems. Do these companies sell only CRM systems? What do they have in common? What do they have that is unique?

8-36. Search on Facebook for your favorite company's page. How does this company present itself in the social media? How does it handle customer conversations? Is the organization's strategy effective?

8-37. Discuss the ethical trade-offs involved when using large databases that profile and categorize customers so that companies can more effectively market their products. Think about products that are "good" for the consumer versus those that are not.

Application Exercises

Note: The existing data files referenced in these exercises are available on the book's Web site: www.pearsonhighered.com/valacich.

Spreadsheet Application: Tracking Web Site Visits at Campus Travel

8-38. Campus Travel has recently started selling products on the Internet; the managers are eager to know how the company's Web site is accepted by the customers. The file CampusTravel.csv contains transaction information for the past three days, generated from the company's Web server, including IP addresses of the visitors, whether a transaction was completed, and the transaction amount. You are asked to present the current status of the e-commerce initiative. Use your spreadsheet program to prepare the following graphs:

- A graph highlighting the total number of site visits and the total number of transactions per day
- A graph highlighting the total sales per day

Make sure to format the graphs in a professional manner, including headers, footers, and the appropriate labels, and print each graph on a separate page. (Hint: To calculate the total number of site visits and the total number of transactions, use the "countif" function to count the number.)

Database Application: Managing Customer Relations at Campus Travel

8-39. Not all frequent fliers accumulate large amounts of miles. There are many who never travel for years but have frequent-flier accounts. As manager of sales and marketing, you want to find out how to target these individuals with promotions and special offers. To accomplish this task, you will need to create the following reports:

- A report displaying all frequent fliers, sorted by distance traveled
- A report displaying all frequent fliers, sorted by the total amount spent on air travel

In the file InfrequentFliers.mdb, you find travel data on the members of a frequent-flier program for the previous year. Prepare professionally formatted printouts of all reports, including headers, footers, dates, and so on. (Hint: Use the report wizard to create the reports; use queries to sum up the fares and distances for each traveler before creating the respective reports.)

Team Work Exercise

Net Stats: RFID on the Rise

The market for RFID tags, those high-tech devices that let businesses keep track of certain products via radio frequency readers and tags, has been steadily increasing for the past few years. According to a recent research report, the global RFID market in 2014 is worth US$9.2 billion, and is expected to grow to US$30.2 billion by 2024. As RFID becomes more mainstream in more industries, the software and services segment of this industry will play an increasingly larger role to help companies better utilize the data collected by these devices. While the adoption of RFID technology may require a large startup investment for organizations, it provides a strong long-term return on investment.

Questions and Exercises

8-40. Search the Web for the most up-to-date statistics on the forecast and use of RFID technology.

8-41. As a team, interpret these numbers (or stories). What is striking/important about these findings?

8-42. As a team, discuss what these findings will look like in 5 years and 10 years. How are things in the U.S. market the same or different across the world? Where are things moving faster/slower? Why?

8-43. Using your presentation software of choice, create a brief presentation about the findings you consider most important.

Based on:
Das, R., & Harrop, P. (2014, March). RFID forecasts, players, and opportunities 2014-2024. *IDTechEx*. Retrieved May 6, 2014, from http://www.idtechex.com/research/reports/rfid-forecasts-players-and-opportunities-2014-2024-000368.asp.

Answers to the Self-Study Questions

8-13. C, p. 286	**8-14.** B, p. 290	**8-15.** B, p. 291	**8-16.** A, p. 295	**8-17.** D, p. 296
8-18. C, p. 303	**8-19.** A, p. 304	**8-20.** D, p. 306	**8-21.** D, p. 300	**8-22.** B, p. 310

CASE 1 Supply Chain Havoc

Information systems have assisted in the creation of global supply networks that allow for the worldwide procurement of raw materials and components needed as inputs into production processes. For the purpose of achieving an optimal balance between quality and costs, manufacturers often have had to rely on a complicated and fragile supply chain. Imagine that you are the manufacturer of a trendy new gadget that is gaining popularity worldwide. Also imagine that a tsunami just rolled over the key manufacturer of a certain critical component in your device. At best, you may encounter long shipment delays and lost sales; at worst, your opportunity in the marketplace fades and you go out of business. Thus, shielding the delicate supply chain from negative impacts arising from external events is a tremendous challenge for many organizations, especially in a reality where disruptions can rarely be forecast and the results can be devastating.

One example of such external events is the serious flooding in Thailand during the 2011 monsoon season. The World Bank estimated US$47.5 billion in economic loss and a massive disruption in production within the country. This disruption was not limited to the country itself, but sent shockwaves through global supply chains. Thailand is the second biggest producer of computer hard drives in the world, as well as a critical supplier of key components; for instance, 70 percent of all hard drive motors are produced in the Southeast Asian country. Because the floods caused tremendous damage to concerned factories, hard drive production all around the world dropped about 30 percent compared to the previous quarter. The cost of this disruption was a surge in the price of hard drives; in some temporary yet exceptional cases, prices were up to 150 percent higher. In the quarter following the floods, hard drive prices were still about 5 to 15 percent higher than before the natural disaster. Consumers, producers, and organizations alike suffered from the natural disaster. In fact, over a year after the floods, huge shortages still lingered for some types of hard drives.

The flooding in Thailand shows a domino effect that can eventually disrupt entire global supply networks; the collapse of one piece of the network leads to the fall of another, until eventually the entire chain crumbles. The flooding started the dominoes toppling, leading to the shortage of hard drives, which triggered computer manufacturers to focus on building higher-margin, more expensive computers. Thus, manufacturers reduced production of lower-margin low-end PCs, netbooks, and the like, ultimately resulting in an increase in prices for these devices as well. Likewise, two other well-known consumer electronics companies experienced severe disruptions of their supply chains during and after the devastating floods. Nikon suffered greatly as the entire first floor of one of its primary factories assembling digital single-lens reflex (DSLR) cameras was submerged in water. The company subsequently announced that the production of 90 percent of its DSLR cameras—from low to mid-range—was affected by the flood and had reached a state of non-recovery. Similarly, Sony, 100 percent of whose DSLRs were made in a factory damaged by the flood, found itself scrambling to resume production. Both Nikon and Sony were unable to quickly bring production back to prior levels, and were even forced to postpone the release of various newly introduced camera models, resulting in net losses for both companies.

It is not just natural disasters that can wreak havoc on global supply networks. In 2013, a large clothing factory in Bangladesh with over 3,000 workers collapsed, tragically taking over 1,129 lives and injuring thousands more. The factory serviced 29 different clothing companies around the world, and the effects of the production loss rippled throughout these companies' supply chains. Perhaps more important, the building collapse has led to widespread discussions about corporate social responsibility across global supply chains.

In their quest to achieve sustainable competitive advantage, many companies face a dilemma when trying to maximize efficiency and effectiveness of their global supply chains. Without doubt, supply chain management systems have contributed tremendously to improving interorganizational business processes, such as by allowing to build highly efficient supply chains that minimize inventory levels. However, minimum inventory levels, short product cycles, and inadequate risk management all contribute to the fragile nature of many global supply networks, and the danger of unforeseen external events disrupting these supply networks always lingers. Furthermore, the question as to who among the many companies in a supply chain should be held responsible for things like working conditions or adherence to child labor laws remains under debate.

Questions

8-44. What are the benefits of a global supply network?

8-45. What are the trade-offs when developing a supply chain strategy?

8-46. Who do you think should be held accountable for worker conditions in overseas factories? The local governments? The factory owners? The U.S.-based businesses that purchase from the factories? The consumers who purchase the end products?

Based on:

2013 Savar building collapse. (2014, May 5). In *Wikipedia, The Free Encyclopedia*. Retrieved 21:17, May 6, 2014, from http://en.wikipedia.org/w/index.php?title=2013_Savar_building_collapse&oldid=607211199.

Fuller, T. (2011, November 6). Thailand flooding cripples hard-drive supply. *The New York Times*. Retrieved July 9, 2012, from http://www.nytimes.com/2011/11/07/business/global/07iht-floods07.html.

Grattan, E. (2013, May 1). Bangladesh disaster throws new light on supply chain management. *Edelmaneditions.com*. Retrieved May 6, 2014, from http://edelmaneditions.com/2013/05/bangladesh-disaster-throws-new-light-on-supply-chain-management.

CASE 2 CRM 2.0

Organizations are attempting to learn more about customers' needs and behaviors in order to widen, lengthen, and deepen their relationships with them. CRM is a broadly recognized and implemented methodology for managing an organization's interactions with its customers and potential clients. It involves the use of technology for organizing and automating a number of organizational activities, such as marketing, customer service, tech support, and, most often, sales.

Visualizing CRM as just technology, however, is the wrong way to think about it; technology is merely one of the tools that enable CRM. CRM is a customer-centric business philosophy that helps organizations bring together information about their products, services, customers, and the market forces that are driving them. Data are gathered and aggregated from as many internal and external sources as possible to give an actual, real-time picture of the customer base. CRM allows an organization to provide better customer service, discover new customers, sell products more effectively, and simplify marketing and sales processes. Although there are many facets, the following are some core CRM components:

- CRM helps an organization enable its marketing departments to identify and target their best customers, manage marketing campaigns, and generate quality leads for the sales team.
- CRM assists an organization in improving its customer accounts and sales management by optimizing information shared across the employee base and streamlining existing processes.
- CRM enables the formation of individualized relationships with an organization's customers, with the aim of improving customer satisfaction and maximizing profits.
- CRM provides employees with the information and processes necessary to build relationships between the company, its customer base, and distribution partners.
- Once the best and most profitable customers are identified through CRM, organizations can ensure that they are providing them the highest level of service.

In addition to these features, CRM environments support collaboration and communication within the organization. Just as Facebook, LinkedIn, Twitter, and other social media are becoming a preferred way to stay connected to friends and family members, CRM applications are also evolving to reflect the movement toward social media. In fact, CRM pioneer Salesforce.com provides a product called Salesforce Chatter, which provides a similar set of capabilities found on many of the popular social media sites, allowing individuals throughout an organization to collaborate more effectively using methods that have become extremely popular. For instance, with a Web-based interface that looks very similar to Facebook, Chatter allows individuals within organizations to post profiles, provide real-time status updates about themselves or activities, organize groups, monitor feeds, share documents, and so on. Clarence So, senior vice president for Salesforce.com, when talking about how individuals within organizations are working together, states, "Increasingly, instead of using the Web for search, they're using platforms such as Facebook and YouTube. Instead of communicating by e-mail, they're using instant messaging and texts. And instead of accessing the Web from a desktop, they're turning to smartphones and other mobile devices." Chatter is designed to bring the best collaboration features found on the most popular Web sites into a single collaboration environment, allowing people within an organization to collaborate more effectively. As So adds, "It's a Facebook-like feed interface that lets a user follow objects, which could be fellow employees, a customer record, a project, a document, anything that's an object within Salesforce.com. They can interact with and receive updates on the objects they follow in their Chatter feed." Chatter is also offered for mobile devices such as the iPad, helping to support a mobile CRM strategy.

Interacting with customers via social media, however, still presents many challenges for most organizations that are increasingly finding themselves being left out of conversations that customers are having about them. Traditional CRM communication channels have been built on the telephone and e-mail, but many customers are moving to social media. Strategies for understanding which customers to connect with through social media are still developing, but organizations are moving to embrace the technology via products like Chatter in order to keep pace with ever-changing communication styles. Social media are actually very synergistic with CRM tools, since social media are about interacting with someone on the other end. Organizations will do well to understand that social media are not just about pushing advertising or making announcements, but also about connecting with their customers and building relationships. Expect CRM tools and the sophistication of their use to continue to evolve, transforming CRM into an Enterprise 2.0 technology.

Questions

8-47. What role does technology play in CRM? Is CRM mostly about technology or mostly about relationships?

8-48. What types of communication (e.g., e-mail, texting, Facebook) methods would you want to have with a company you do business with? Explain.

8-49. If you were the chief executive officer of a Fortune 500 company, would you be comfortable using social media sites like Facebook or Twitter as part of your CRM strategy? Why or why not?

Based on:

Columbus, L. (2012, April 23). What's hot in CRM applications, 2012. *Forbes*. Retrieved May 6, 2014, from http://www.forbes.com/sites/louiscolumbus/2012/04/23/whats-hot-in-crm-applications-2012.

Customer relationship management. (2014, May 5). In *Wikipedia, The Free Encyclopedia*. Retrieved May 6, 2014, from http://en.wikipedia.org/w/index.php?title=Customer_relationship_management&oldid=607209742.

Salesforce.com. (n.d.). Salesforce Chatter. Retrieved May 6, 2014, from http://www.salesforce.com/chatter/overview.

Go to **mymislab.com** for auto-graded writing questions as well as the following assisted-graded writing questions:

8-50. Explain how effectively managing the supply chain can help an organization be a responsible social citizen.

8-51. Describe the enterprise-wide changes necessary for realizing a successful CRM strategy.

References

Anonymous. (2009). CRM and social networking: Engaging the social customer. *Techrepublic*. Retrieved June 1, 2014, from http://www.techrepublic.com/whitepapers/crm-and-social-networking-engaging-the-social-customer/1145249.

Anonymous. (2010). About vendor managed inventory. *Vendor Managed Inventory.com*. Retrieved June 1, 2014, from http://www.vendormanagedinventory.com/about.php.

Anonymous. (2014, May 29). Industry adoption updates. *CheckImage Central*. Retrieved May 29, 2014, from http://www.checkimagecentral.org/industryAdoptionUpdates.

Arano, N. (2010, July 21). Canadian university offers social CRM course. *CIO.com*. Retrieved June 1, 2014, from http://www.cio.com/article/600257/Canadian_University_Offers_Social_CRM_Course.

Barboza, D. (2010, July 5). Supply chain for iPhone highlights costs in China. *New York Times*. Retrieved June 1, 2014, from http://www.techrepublic.com/whitepapers/crm-and-social-networking-engaging-the-social-customer/1145249.

Benson, C. (2009, April 2). The problem with B2B payments. *Paymentsviews*. Retrieved May 29, 2014, from http://paymentsviews.com/2009/04/02/the-problem-with-b2b-payments.

Bernoff, J., Cooperstein, D., de Lussanet, M., & Madigan, C.J. (2011, June 6). *Competitive strategy in the age of the customer*. Cambridge, MA: Forrester Research.

Breen, B. (2004, November 1). Living in Dell time. *Fastcompany*. Retrieved June 1, 2014, from http://www.fastcompany.com/magazine/88/dell.html.

Dean, J. (2007, August 11). The forbidden city of Terry Gou. *Wall Street Journal*. Retrieved June 1, 2014, from http://online.wsj.com/article/NA_WSJ_PUB:SB118677584137994489.html.

Edwards, J. (2003, February 15). RFID creates fast asset identification and management. *CIO.com*. Retrieved June 1, 2014, from http://www.cio.com/article/31724/RFID_Creates_Fast_Asset_Identification_and_Management.

Firstdata. (2009, October 26). Why b2b payments need a "BizPal": An international perspective. Retrieved May 29, 2014, from http://www.firstdata.com/en_au/insights/b2b_payments_intl_marketinsights.

Fornell, C. (2001). The science of satisfaction. *Harvard Business Review, 79*(3), 120–121.

Gartner. (2014, February 12). Gartner says CRM will be at the heart of digital initiatives for years to come. *Gartner*. Retrieved May 28, 2014, from http://www.gartner.com/newsroom/id/2665215.

Harrison, A., & Van Hoek, R. (2011). *Logistics management and strategy: Competing through the supply chain* (4th ed.). Upper Saddle River, NJ: Pearson Prentice Hall.

Kanaracus, C. (2009, July 9). Microsoft ties Dynamics CRM to Twitter. *CIO.com*. Retrieved June 1, 2014, from http://www.cio.com/article/496978/Microsoft_Ties_Dynamics_CRM_to_Twitter.

Keller, K. (2010, June 28). iPhone 4 carries bill of materials of $187.51, according to iSuppli. *iSuppli.com*. Retrieved June 1, 2014, from http://www.isuppli.com/Teardowns-Manufacturing-and-Pricing/News/Pages/iPhone-4-Carries-Bill-of-Materials-of-187-51-According-to-iSuppli.aspx.

Keuky, R., & Clarke, S. (2011). Socializing CRM: Merits and approaches to deploying social CRM solutions. *Capgemini*. Retrieved June 1, 2014, from http://www.capgemini.com/discover/pdf/dilemma_4/Socializing%20CRM.pdf.

Lager, M. (2008, April). The 2008 CRM Service Awards: Elite—JPMorgan Chase Card Services. *destinationCRM.com*. Retrieved June 1, 2014, from http://www.destinationcrm.com/Articles/ReadArticle.aspx?ArticleID=46576.

Larson, P. D., & Rogers, D. S. (1998). Supply chain management: Definition, growth, and approaches. *Journal of Marketing Theory and Practice, 6*(4), 1–5.

Menchaca, L. (2010, December 8). Dell's next step: The Social Media Listening Command Center. *Dell.com*. Retrieved June 1, 2014, from http://en.community.dell.com/dell-blogs/direct2dell/b/direct2dell/archive/2010/12/08/dell-s-next-step-the-social-media-listening-command-center.aspx.

Nash, K. (2007, October 22). Beyond Peter Pan: How ConAgra's pot pie recall bakes in hard lessons for supply chain management. *CIO.com*. Retrieved June 1, 2014, from http://www.cio.com/article/148054/Beyond_Peter_Pan_How_ConAgra_s_Pot_Pie_Recall_Bakes_In_Hard_Lessons_for_Supply_Chain_Management.

Penfield, P. (2008, August 26). Visibility within the supply chain. *MHIA.org*. Retrieved June 1, 2014, from http://www.mhia.org/news/industry/7960/visibility-within-the-supply-chain.

Sebor, J. (2010, March). The 2010 CRM Service Awards: The service elite—Southwest Airlines. *destinationCRM.com*. Retrieved June 1, 2014, from http://www.destinationcrm.com/Articles/Editorial/Magazine-Features/The-2010-CRM-Service-Awards-The-Service-Elite—-Southwest-Airlines-61390.aspx.

Taber, D. (2009, September 28). Marketing automation: Unique kid on the CRM block. *CIO.com*. Retrieved June 1, 2014, from http://www.cio.com/article/503436/Marketing_Automation_Unique_Kid_on_the_CRM_Block.

Taber, D. (2010, February 22). CRM's identity crisis: Duplicate contacts, part 2. *CIO.com*. Retrieved June 1, 2014, from http://www.cio.com/article/551313/CRM_s_Identity_Crisis_Duplicate_Contacts_Part_2.

Taber, D. (2010, May 19). CRM problems come in threes. *CIO.com*. Retrieved June 1, 2014, from http://www.cio.com/article/594235/CRM_Problems_Come_in_Threes.

U.S. Census Bureau. (2014, May 22). E-stats 2012. Retrieved July 18, 2014, from http://www.census.gov/econ/estats/2012_e-stats_report.pdf.

Wagner, W., & Zubey, M. (2006). *Customer relationship management*. Boston: Course Technology.

Wailgum, T. (2008, November 20). Supply chain management definition and solutions. *CIO.com*. Retrieved June 1, 2014, from http://www.cio.com/article/40940/Supply_Chain_Management_Definition_and_Solutions.

9

Developing and Acquiring Information Systems

After reading this chapter, you will be able to do the following:

1. Describe how to formulate and present the business case for technology investments.
2. Describe the systems development life cycle and its various phases.
3. Explain how organizations acquire systems via external acquisition and outsourcing.

Preview

As you have read throughout this book and have experienced in your own life, information systems and technologies are of many different types, including high-speed Web servers to rapidly process customer requests, business intelligence systems to aid managerial decision making, and customer relationship management systems to provide improved customer service. Given this variety, when we refer to "systems" in this chapter, we are talking about a broad range of technologies, including hardware, software, and services. Just as there are different types of systems, there are different approaches for developing and acquiring them. If you are a business student majoring in areas such as marketing, finance, accounting, or management, you might be wondering why we have a discussion about developing and acquiring information systems. The answer is simple: No matter what area of an organization you are in, you will be involved in systems development or technology acquisition processes. In fact, research indicates that spending on systems in many organizations is controlled by the specific business functions rather than by the information systems (IS) department. What this means is that even if your career interests are in something other than information systems, it is very likely that you will be involved in the development and acquisition of systems, technologies, or services. Understanding this process is important to your future success.

Managing in the Digital World: **Microsoft Is "Kinecting" Its Ecosystem**

How useful would an iPhone or an Android smartphone be without the apps? How useful would a Blu-ray player be without a large selection of movies available in that format? The value of many devices or systems grows with the size of their ecosystems, including the users, application or content developers, sellers, and marketplaces. Like a tree standing still in a world without rain, birds, or flowers—a tree that would likely not be able to survive—the iPhone *sans* the "apps" would be much less useful, less exciting, and much less successful in the marketplace. Similarly, Google, Microsoft, and, not surprisingly, Amazon.com are trying to build large ecosystems around their products and services (Figure 9.1).

In the mobile device industry, these ecosystems are based on the products or services developed by the original creators, and are complemented by a pool of independent developers that expand the ecosystem's capabilities in the hope of developing the next killer app. This collective expansion in capabilities generates additional marketing buzz and market demand. To create such an expanded ecosystem, a cooperative development approach is the norm, as has been common in many successful software, hardware, and, more recently, consumer electronics marketplaces. This approach is characterized by systems development activities constantly shifting back and forth between the big, well-known product developers like Apple or Microsoft and small, virtually unknown independent app developers who build creative extensions that broaden the products' market appeal. One example of an ecosystem evolving around a device is Microsoft's Kinect, a US$150 body motion capture device for the Xbox, first launched in 2010. After initially barring individual developers from tinkering with the Kinect, Microsoft realized the power of ecosystems and released a software development kit (SDK), allowing anyone to build Kinect-related applications.

In 2013, Microsoft launched a much improved Kinect with its next generation game console, the Xbox One. The Kinect contains a collection of cameras, microphones, and sensors that enables users to control and interact with the game console using gestures and voice commands. For example, the newest Kinect can recognize faces so you don't have to manually log in, and can even read your lips to better understand your needs. Using these new capabilities, one group developed an easy method to create 3D scans of people and objects. Other applications are being developed to help people try on virtual clothing or help doctors manipulate images while performing surgery. Just as the iPhone and Android smartphones have gone beyond just being phones, the Kinect has become far more than a just gaming controller, thanks to the innovative ideas from the Kinect's ecosystem.

After reading this chapter, you will be able to answer the following:

1. How can a company make a business case for/against allowing access to an SDK?
2. What are potential pitfalls if established practices (such as the systems development life cycle) are not followed when developing third-party applications?
3. How is the "open sourcing" of systems development different from traditional outsourcing?

Based on:

Anonymous. (n.d.). The Microsoft Accelerator for Kinect. *Microsoft.com*. Retrieved March 20, 2014, from http://www.microsoft.com/bizspark/kinectaccelerator.

Greene, J. (2012, June 28). Turns out Kinect is for fashionistas and surgeons, too. *Cnet.com*. Retrieved March 20, 2014, from http://news.cnet.com/8301-10805_3-57463197-75/turns-out-kinect-is-for-fashionistas-and-surgeons-too.

Kinect. (2014, February 25). In *Wikipedia, The Free Encyclopedia*. Retrieved March 20, 2014, from http://en.wikipedia.org/w/index.php?title=Kinect&oldid=597143263.

The Digital Ecosystem

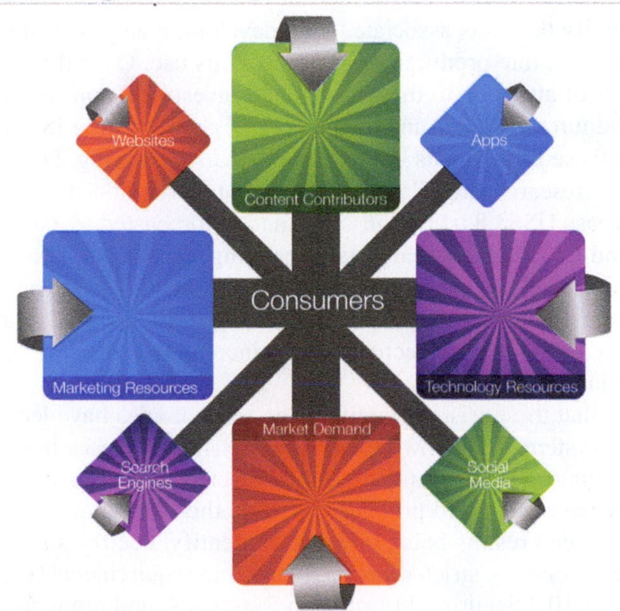

FIGURE 9.1

All parts of an ecosystem are interrelated.
Source: Fotolia.

MAKING THE BUSINESS CASE

Before people are willing to spend money to acquire or develop a new system, or spend more money on an existing one, they want to be convinced that this will be a good investment. **Making the business case** refers to the process of identifying, quantifying, and presenting the value provided by a system.

Business Case Objectives

What does making the business case mean? Think for a moment about what defense lawyers do in court trials. They carefully build a strong, integrated set of arguments and evidence to prove that their clients are innocent to those who will pass judgment on their clients. In much the same way, a manager has to build a strong, integrated set of arguments and evidence to prove that an information system (or any type of investment) is adding value to the organization or its constituents. This is, in business lingo, "making the business case" for a system.

As a business professional, you will be called on to make the business case for systems and other capital investments, or you will have to make the case for a new system or application you may need for your work to improve certain business processes. Thus, as a finance, accounting, marketing, or management professional, you are likely to be involved in this process and will therefore need to know how to effectively make the business case for a system (or other capital expenditures) and need to understand the relevant organizational issues involved. It will be in the organization's best interest—and in your own—to ferret out systems that are not adding value. In these cases, you will need to either improve the systems or replace them. Traditionally, business units turned to IS departments for new systems or applications. Today, business units often directly purchase applications from outside vendors, and expect these applications to function in the infrastructure provided by the IS departments. As more and more applications are purchased from external vendors, organizations have to make sure to go through a proper process in selecting the right applications.

Making the business case is as important for proposed systems as it is for the continued investment in an existing system. For a proposed system, the case will be used to determine whether the new system is a "go" or a "no-go." For an existing system, the case will be used to determine whether the company will continue to fund the system. Whether a new system or an existing one is being considered, your goal is to make sure that the investment adds value, that it helps the firm achieve its strategy and competitive advantage over its rivals, and that money is being spent wisely.

The Productivity Paradox

Unfortunately, while it is easy to quantify the costs associated with developing an information system, it is often difficult to quantify tangible productivity gains from its use. Over the past several years, the press has given a lot of attention to the impact of IS investments on worker productivity. In many cases, IS expenditures, salaries, and the number of people on the IS staff have all been rising, but results from these investments have often been disappointing. For instance, the information and technology research firm Gartner reports that worldwide spending on systems and technologies will surpass US$3.8 trillion in 2014, and is forecasted to exceed US$4.4 trillion by 2016. American and Canadian companies are spending, on average, around 4 percent of company revenues on system-related investments. As a result, justifying the costs for IS investments has been a hot topic among senior managers at many firms. In particular, "white-collar" productivity, especially in the service sector, has not increased at the rate one might expect, given the trillions of dollars spent.

Why has it been difficult to show that these vast expenditures on technologies have led to productivity gains? Have information systems somehow failed us, promising increases in performance and productivity and then failing to deliver on that promise? Determining the answer is not easy. Information systems may have increased productivity, but other forces may have simultaneously worked to reduce it, the end results being difficult to identify. Factors such as government regulations, more complex tax codes, stricter financial reporting requirements (such as the Sarbanes–Oxley Act; see Chapter 10, "Securing Information Systems"), and more complex products can all have major impacts on a firm's productivity.

It is also true that information systems introduced with the best intentions may have had unintended consequences. A paramount example is giving employees access to e-mail and the Internet—now employees are spending excessive amounts of time surfing the Web to check

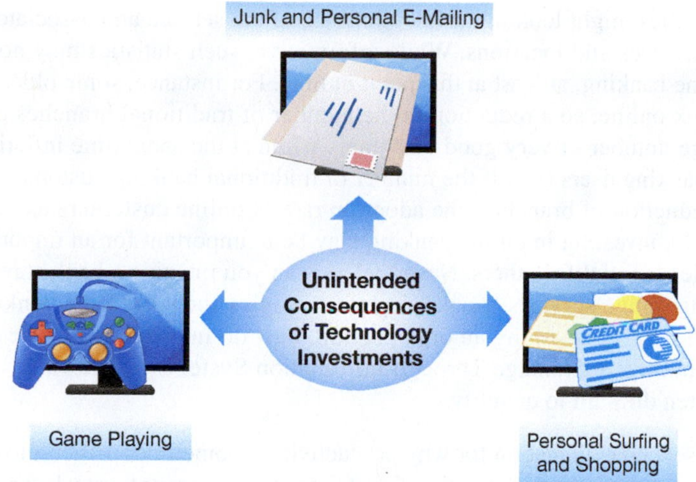

FIGURE 9.2

Unintended consequences can limit the productivity gains from IS investments.

sports scores on the ESPN Web site, read volumes of electronic junk mail received from Internet marketing companies or from personal friends, post status updates on social networking sites, or use company PCs to download and play software games (Figure 9.2); recently, it was reported that visits to social networking sites such as Facebook and Twitter cost U.K. firms alone approximately US$2.25 billion in lost productivity every year. In such situations, information systems can result in less efficient and less effective communication among employees and less productive uses of employee time than before the systems were implemented. Nevertheless, sound technology investments should increase organizational productivity. If this is so, why have organizations not been able to show larger productivity gains? A number of reasons have been given for the apparent **productivity paradox** of technology investments (Figure 9.3). This issue is examined next.

MEASUREMENT PROBLEMS. In many cases, the benefits of information systems are difficult to pinpoint because firms may be measuring the wrong things. Often, the biggest increases in productivity result from increased effectiveness (i.e., the extent to which goals or tasks are accomplished well). Unfortunately, many business metrics focus on efficiency (i.e., the extent to which goals are accomplished faster, at lower cost, or with relatively little time and effort).

A good example of measurement problems associated with a technology investment is the use of online banking. How much has online banking contributed to banking productivity?

FIGURE 9.3

Factors leading to the IS productivity paradox.

Traditional statistics might look at the adoption rate of the service and associated reductions in branch-based services and locations. While informative, such statistics may not work well for evaluating online banking, at least at this point in time. For instance, some older customers may not want to bank online, so a reduction in the number of traditional branches could threaten a potentially large number of very good customers while at the same time inflating the percentage of online banking users (i.e., if the number of traditional banking customers leave the bank because of a reduction of branches, the adoption rate of online customers as a percentage will be increased). So, investing in online banking may be unimportant for an important segment of customers while essential for others. Nevertheless, can you imagine a bank staying competitive without offering online services? Deploying technologies such as online banking has become a *strategic necessity*—something an organization must do in order to survive (see Chapter 2, "Gaining Competitive Advantage Through Information Systems"). The value of necessary investments is often difficult to quantify.

TIME LAGS. A second explanation for why productivity is sometimes difficult to demonstrate for some technology investments is that a significant time lag may occur from when a company makes the investment until that investment is translated into improvement in the bottom line. Let us return to our online banking example. In some markets, it may take years from the first implementation of this new system before the magnitude of benefits may be felt by the organization.

REDISTRIBUTION. A third possible explanation for why IS productivity figures are not always easy to define is that a new type of system may be beneficial for individual firms but not for a particular industry or the economy as a whole. Particularly in competitive situations, new innovations may be used to redistribute the pieces of the pie rather than making the whole pie bigger. The result for the industry or economy as a whole is a wash—that is, the same number of products are being sold, and the same number of dollars are being spread across all the firms.

MISMANAGEMENT. A fourth explanation is that the new system has not been implemented and managed well. Some believe that people often simply build bad systems, implement them poorly, and rely on technology fixes when the organization has problems that require a joint technology/process solution. Rather than increasing outputs or profits, IS investments might merely be a temporary bandage and may serve to mask or even increase organizational inefficiency. Also, as we mentioned in Chapter 1, "Managing in the Digital World," an information system can be only as effective as the business model that it serves. Bad business models can't be overcome by good information systems.

If it is so difficult to quantify the benefits of information systems for individual firms and for entire industries, why do managers continue to invest in information systems? The answer is that competitive pressures force managers to invest in information systems whether they like it or not. Also, for many organizations, information systems are an important source of competitive advantage. You might ask, then, so why waste time making the business case for a system? Why not just acquire or develop them? The answer: Given the vast number of potential systems and technologies that could be selected, a strong business case aids the decision-making process and helps direct resources in more strategic ways.

Making a Successful Business Case

People make a variety of arguments in their business cases for information systems. When managers make the business case for an information system, they typically base their arguments on faith, fear, and/or facts (Wheeler & Marakas, 1999). (Wheeler also adds a fourth "F" for "fiction," and notes that, unfortunately, managers sometimes base their arguments on pure fiction, which is not only bad for their careers but also not at all healthy for their firms.) Table 9.1 shows examples of these three types of arguments.

Do not assume that you must base your business case on facts only. It is entirely appropriate to base the business case on faith, fear, or facts (Figure 9.4). Indeed, the strongest and most convincing business case will include a little of each type of argument. In the following sections, we talk about each of these types of arguments for the business case.

BUSINESS CASE ARGUMENTS BASED ON FAITH. In some situations, arguments based on faith (or fear) can be the most compelling and can drive the decision to invest in an information system despite the lack of any hard data on system costs, or even in the face of some data that say that the

TABLE 9.1 Three Types of Arguments Commonly Made in the Business Case for an Information System

Type of Argument	Description	Example
Faith	Arguments based on beliefs about organizational strategy, competitive advantage, industry forces, customer perceptions, market share, and so on	"I know I don't have good data to back this up, but I'm convinced that having this customer relationship management system will enable us to serve our customers significantly better than our competitors do and, as a result, we'll beat the competition. . . You just have to take it on faith."
Fear	Arguments based on the notion that if the system is not implemented, the firm will lose out to the competition or, worse, go out of business	"If we don't implement this enterprise resource planning system, we'll get killed by our competitors because they're all implementing these kinds of systems . . . We either do this or we die."
Fact	Arguments based on data, quantitative analysis, and/or indisputable factors	"This analysis shows that implementing the inventory control system will help us reduce errors by 50 percent, reduce operating costs by 15 percent a year, increase production by 5 percent a year, and pay for itself within 18 months."

dollar cost for the system will be high. Arguments based on faith often hold that an information system must be implemented in order to achieve the organization's strategy effectively and to gain or sustain a competitive advantage over rivals.

For example, a firm has set as its strategy that it will be the dominant, global force in its industry. As a result, this firm must adopt a variety of collaboration technologies, such as desktop videoconferencing and groupware tools, in order to enable employees from different parts of the globe to work together effectively and efficiently. Similarly, a firm that has set as its strategy a broad scope—producing products and services across a wide range of consumer needs—may need to adopt some form of an enterprise resource planning system to better coordinate business activities across its diverse product lines.

In short, successful business case arguments based on faith should clearly describe the firm's mission and objectives, the strategy for achieving them, and the types of information systems that are needed in order to enact the strategy. A word of caution is warranted here. In today's business environment, cases based solely on strategic arguments, with no hard numbers demonstrating the value of the information system under consideration, are not likely to be funded.

FIGURE 9.4

A successful business case will be based on faith, fear, and fact.

BRIEF CASE Software Patent Wars

Have you ever used the slide-to-unlock feature on a smartphone? Apple has a patent on that. If your smartphone sends and receives data over a 4G network, well, Samsung has a patent for that. In the 1970s, when key technologies that made the Internet possible were being developed, intellectual property and patent claims were not much of a big deal. The idea then was to make the technology an international standard, and open it up for public use. Come the twenty-first century, things have changed, and battles over patents are constantly being fought, especially in the mobile market where companies are trying to protect clever technologies and applications and maintain or increase market share.

An overview of the mobile patent wars looks something like this: Microsoft sued Motorola for video encoding, Motorola counter-sued Microsoft's use of e-mail, instant messaging, and Wi-Fi; likewise, Google was sued by Oracle for its implementation of the Java programming language in its Android system. Google then acquired Motorola to gain access to its patent portfolio. Apple has made use of its patent rights to prevent Samsung Electronics from selling some products with features Apple argues violates its patents. In response, Samsung has retaliated by attempting to ban iPhone sales in some countries.

With the global smartphone market being estimated around $300 billion in 2014, the stakes are high. However, many feel that too much time, energy, and money are being wasted fighting these battles, and there is also a growing sense that the patent process itself is flawed. Considering that the U.S. patent system offers inventors a limited monopoly on their ideas for 20 years, consumers may actually find fewer choices in the market the next time they look for a new mobile handset.

Questions

1. With millions of software patents in existence, some claim that it is almost impossible to avoid infringing on someone else's patent. How does this affect innovation and small startups?
2. Many believe that the patent wars act to destroy small players in the mobile phone marketplace who cannot afford expensive and lengthy legal battles. What other impacts do the patent wars have on this industry?

Based on:

Holbrook, T. (2014, March 16). Is the Supreme Court about to rule that software is ineligible for patent protection? *Forbes*. Retrieved March 20, 2014, from http://www.forbes.com/sites/realspin/2014/03/16/is-the-supreme-court-about-to-rule-that-software-is-ineligible-for-patent-protection.

Nazer, D. (2014, March 17). Why is the patent office so bad at reviewing software patents? *Electronic Frontier Foundation*. Retrieved March 20, 2014, from https://www.eff.org/deeplinks/2014/03/why-patent-office-so-bad-reviewing-software-patents.

Phillips, M. (2013, November 22). Apple vs. Samsung: A patent war with few winners. *The New Yorker*. Retrieved March 20, 2014, from http://www.newyorker.com/online/blogs/elements/2013/11/a-patent-war-with-few-winners.html.

Software patent debate. (2014, March 18). In *Wikipedia, The Free Encyclopedia*. Retrieved March 20, 2014, from http://en.wikipedia.org/w/index.php?title=Software_patent_debate&oldid=600233238.

BUSINESS CASE ARGUMENTS BASED ON FEAR. There are several different factors to take into account when making a business case in which you will provide arguments based on fear. These include a number of factors involving competition and other elements of the industry in which the firm operates. For example, a mature industry, such as the automotive industry, may need systems simply to maintain the current pace of operations. While having the newest systems and technologies available may be nice, they may not be needed to stay in business. However, a company in a newer, expanding industry, such as the green technology industry, may find it more important to be on the leading edge of technology in order to compete effectively in the marketplace. Likewise, some industries are more highly regulated than others. In these cases, companies can use technology investments to better control processes and ensure compliance with appropriate regulations. The argument for the business case here would be something like, "If we do not implement this system, we run the risk of being sued or, worse, being thrown in jail" (see Chapter 10).

Probably the most important industry factor that can affect technology investments is the nature of competition or rivalry in the industry. For example, when competition in an industry is high and use of the newest technologies is rampant, as it is in the mobile phone industry, strategic necessity, more than anything else, forces firms to adopt new systems. Given how tight profit margins are in this industry, Apple, Samsung, and other manufacturers must use inventory control systems, business intelligence systems, and a host of other systems that help them to be more effective and efficient. If they do not adopt these systems, they will likely go out of business. As introduced in Chapter 2, a common way for assessing the level of competition within an industry is the five forces model (Porter, 1979). By assessing the various competitive forces, you can determine which specific technologies may be more or less useful. For instance, in a highly price-competitive market, where buyers have strong bargaining power, investments to reduce production costs might be advantageous. Business case arguments formulated this way sound something like, "If we do not implement this system, our competitors are going to beat us on price, we will lose market share, and we will go out of business."

BUSINESS CASE ARGUMENTS BASED ON FACT. Many people, including most chief financial officers, want to see the business case for an information system based on a convincing, quantitative analysis that proves beyond the shadow of a doubt that the benefits of the system will outweigh the costs. The most common way to prove this is to provide a detailed cost–benefit analysis of the information system. Although this step is critical, the manager must remember that there are inherent difficulties in, and limits to, cost–benefit analyses for information systems. To illustrate how a cost–benefit analysis could be used to build a fact-based business case, let us consider the development of a Web-based order entry system for a relatively small firm.

Identifying Costs One goal of a cost–benefit analysis is to accurately determine the **total cost of ownership (TCO)** for an investment. TCO is focused on understanding not only the total cost of *acquisition* but also all costs associated with ongoing *use and maintenance* of a system. Consequently, costs can usually be divided into two categories: **non-recurring costs** and **recurring costs**. Non-recurring costs are one-time costs that are not expected to continue after the system is implemented. These include costs for things such as site preparation and technology purchases. These one-time costs may also include the costs of attracting and training a webmaster or renovating some office space for new personnel or for hosting the Web servers.

Recurring costs are ongoing costs that occur throughout the life of the system. Recurring costs include the salary and benefits of the webmaster and any other personnel assigned to maintain the system, electricity, upgrades and maintenance of the system components, monthly fees paid to a local Internet service provider, and the continuing costs for the space in which the webmaster works or the data center where the servers reside. Personnel costs are usually the largest recurring costs, and the Web-based system is no exception in this regard. These recurring expenses can go well beyond the webmaster to include expenses for customer support, content management, ongoing maintenance, and more.

The sample costs described thus far are **tangible costs** that are relatively easy to quantify. Some **intangible costs** ought to be accounted for as well, even though they will not fit neatly into the quantitative analysis. These might include the costs of reduced traditional sales, losing some customers that are not "Web ready," or losing customers if the Web application is poorly designed or not on par with competitors' sites. You can choose to either quantify these in some way (i.e., determine the cost of losing a customer) or simply reserve these as important costs to consider outside of—but along with—the quantitative cost–benefit analysis.

Identifying Benefits Next, you determine both **tangible benefits** and **intangible benefits**. Some tangible benefits are relatively easy to determine. For example, you can estimate that the increased customer reach of the new Web-based system will result in at least a modest increase in sales. Based on evidence from similar projects, you might estimate, say, a 5 percent increase in sales the first year, a 10 percent increase the second year, and a 15 percent increase the third year. In addition, you might also include as tangible benefits the reduction of order entry errors because orders will now be tracked electronically and shipped automatically. You could calculate the money previously lost on faulty and lost orders, along with the salaries and wages of personnel assigned to find and fix these orders, and then consider the reduction of these costs as a quantifiable benefit of the new system. Cost avoidance is a legitimate, quantifiable benefit of many systems. Similarly, the new system may enable the company to use fewer order entry clerks or redeploy these personnel to other, more important functions within the company. You could consider these cost reductions as benefits of the new system.

A Web-based system may have intangible benefits as well. Some intangible benefits of this new system might include improvements in customer service resulting from faster turnaround on fulfilling orders. These are real benefits, but they might be hard to quantify with confidence. Perhaps an even more intangible benefit would be the overall improved perception of the firm. Customers might consider it more progressive and customer service–oriented than its rivals; in addition to attracting new customers, this might increase the value of the firm's stock if it is a publicly traded firm. Another intangible benefit might be simply that it was a strategic necessity to offer customers Web-based ordering to keep pace with rivals. While these intangibles are difficult to quantify, they must be considered along with the more quantitative analysis of benefits.

COMING ATTRACTIONS

IBM's 5 in 5

As its catchphrase goes, IBM is focused on building a smarter planet. As part of this campaign, IBM researchers have created the 5 in 5 forecast: five innovations that will transform our lives within the next five years. At the core of this forecast is Big Data and machine learning. Machine learning is a branch of artificial intelligence that allows systems to learn by processing massive amounts of data (see Chapter 6, "Enhancing Business Intelligence Using Information Systems"). Because Big Data and machine learning can help a company better understand customers and therefore better meet their needs, IBM believes that Big Data will help offline retail stores understand their customers as well as Amazon.com does, leading to a resurgence of offline retailing. Likewise, with the continued drop in costs for processing data, your doctor will rely more and more on your DNA to help keep you well.

IBM researchers also predict that a digital guardian will protect your online information from cyber criminals, by better understanding you, your friends, and your habits and activities. Similarly, the classroom will learn about students, helping students master the necessary skills by tailoring the educational experience to each individual student. Finally, cities will help you improve your day-to-day lifestyle, by suggesting events based on your prior behavior. Big Data is often viewed by many as potentially invasive and likened to Orwell's "Big Brother." IBM is hoping to make Big Data your big buddy.

Based on:

The 5 in 5. *IBM.com*. Retrieved on March 28, 2014, from http://www.ibm.com/smarterplanet/us/en/ibm_predictions_for_future/ideas.

In fact, the intangible benefits of this Web-based system might be so important that they could carry the day despite an inconclusive or even negative cost–benefit analysis.

Performing Cost–Benefit Analyses An example of a simplified **cost–benefit analysis** that contrasts the total expected tangible costs versus the tangible benefits is presented in Figure 9.5. Notice the fairly large investment up front, with another significant outlay in the fifth year for a system upgrade. You could now use the net costs/benefits for each year as the basis of your conclusion about this system. Alternatively, you could perform a **break-even analysis**—a type of cost–benefit analysis to identify at what point (if ever) tangible benefits equal tangible costs (note that break-even occurs early in the second year of the system's life in this example)—or a more formal **net-present-value analysis** of the relevant cash flow streams associated with the system at the organization's **discount rate** (i.e., the rate of return used by an organization to compute the present value of future cash flows). In any event, this cost–benefit analysis helps you make the business case for this proposed Web-based order fulfillment system. It clearly shows that the investment for this system is relatively small, and the company can fairly quickly recapture the investment. In addition, there appear to be intangible strategic benefits to deploying this system. This analysis—and the accompanying arguments and evidence—goes a long way toward convincing senior managers in the firm that this new system makes sense. For more on cost–benefit analyses, see any introductory finance or managerial accounting textbook.

Comparing Competing Investments One method for deciding among different IS investments or when considering alternative designs for a given system is **weighted multicriteria analysis**, as illustrated in Figure 9.6. For example, suppose that for a given application being considered for purchase, there are three alternatives that could be pursued—A, B, or C. Let's also suppose that early planning meetings identified three key system requirements and four key constraints that could be used to help make a decision on which alternative to pursue. In the left column of Figure 9.6, three system requirements and four constraints are listed. Because not all requirements and constraints are of equal importance, they are weighted on the basis of their relative importance. In other words, you do not have to weight requirements and constraints equally; it is certainly possible to make requirements more or less important than constraints. Weights are arrived at in discussions among the analysis team, users, and managers. Weights tend to be fairly subjective and, for that reason, should be determined through a process of open discussion to reveal underlying assumptions, followed by an attempt to reach consensus among stakeholders. Notice that the total of the weights for both the requirements and constraints is 100 percent.

	2014	2015	2016	2017	2018
Costs					
Non-recurring					
Hardware	$ 20,000				
Software	$ 7,500				
Networking	$ 4,500				
Infrastructure	$ 7,500				
Personnel	$100,000				
Recurring					
Hardware		$ 500	$ 1,000	$ 2,500	$ 15,000
Software		$ 500	$ 500	$ 1,000	$ 2,500
Networking		$ 250	$ 250	$ 500	$ 1,000
Service fees		$ 250	$ 250	$ 250	$ 500
Infrastructure			$ 250	$ 500	$ 1,500
Personnel		$ 60,000	$ 62,500	$ 70,000	$ 90,000
Total costs	$139,500	$ 61,500	$ 64,750	$ 74,750	$110,500
Benefits					
Increased sales	$ 20,000	$ 50,000	$ 80,000	$115,000	$175,000
Error reduction	$ 15,000	$ 15,000	$ 15,000	$ 15,000	$ 15,000
Cost reduction	$100,000	$100,000	$100,000	$100,000	$100,000
Total benefits	$135,000	$165,000	$195,000	$230,000	$290,000
Net costs/benefits	$ (4,500)	$103,500	$130,250	$155,250	$179,500

FIGURE 9.5

Worksheet showing a simplified cost–benefit analysis for the Web-based order fulfillment system.

Next, each requirement and constraint is rated on a scale of 1 to 5. A rating of 1 indicates that the alternative does not meet the requirement very well or that the alternative violates the constraint. A rating of 5 indicates that the alternative meets or exceeds the requirement or clearly abides by the constraint. Ratings are even more subjective than weights and should also be determined through open discussion among users, analysts, and managers. For each requirement and constraint, a score is calculated by multiplying the rating for each requirement and each

Criteria	Weight	Alternative A		Alternative B		Alternative C	
		Rating	Score	Rating	Score	Rating	Score
Requirements							
Web-based Interface	18	5	90	5	90	5	90
Security capabilities	18	1	18	5	90	5	90
BI capabilities	14	1	14	5	70	5	70
	50		122		250		250
Constraints							
Software Costs	15	4	60	5	75	3	45
Hardware Costs	15	4	60	4	60	3	45
Operating Costs	15	5	75	1	15	5	75
Ease of Training	5	5	25	3	15	3	15
	50		220		165		180
Total	100		342		415		430

FIGURE 9.6

Decisions about alternative projects or system design approaches can be assisted using a weighted multicriteria analysis.

TABLE 9.2 Characteristics of Different Stakeholders Involved in Making IS Investment Decisions

Stakeholder	Perspective	Focus/Project Characteristics
Management	Representatives or managers from each of the functional areas within the firm	Greater strategic focus; largest project sizes; longest project durations
Steering committee	Representatives from various interest groups within the organization (they may have their own agendas at stake when making investment decisions)	Cross-functional focus; greater organizational change; formal cost–benefit analysis; larger and riskier projects
User department	Representatives of the intended users of the system	Narrow, non-strategic focus; faster development
IS executive	Has overall responsibility for managing IS development, implementation, and maintenance of selected systems	Focus on integration with existing systems; fewer development delays; less concern with cost–benefit analysis

Source: Based on Hoffer, George, & Valacich (2014) and McKeen, Guimaraes, & Wetherbe (1994).

constraint by its weight. The final step is to add up the weighted scores for each alternative. Notice that we have included three sets of totals: for requirements, for constraints, and for overall totals. If you look at the totals for requirements, alternative B or C is the best choice because each meets or exceeds all requirements. However, if you look only at constraints, alternative A is the best choice because it does not violate any constraints. When we combine the totals for requirements and constraints, we see that the best choice is alternative C. Whether alternative C is actually chosen for development, however, is another issue. The decision makers may choose alternative A because it has the lowest cost, knowing that it does not meet two key requirements. In short, what may appear to be the best choice for a systems development project may not always be the one that ends up being developed or acquired. By conducting a thorough analysis, organizations can greatly improve their decision-making outcomes.

Presenting the Business Case

Up to this point, we have discussed the key issues to consider as you prepare to make the business case for a system. We have also shown you some tools for determining the value that a system adds to an organization. Now you are actually ready to make the case—to present your arguments and evidence to the decision makers in the firm.

KNOW THE AUDIENCE. Depending on the firm, a number of people from various areas of the firm might be involved in the decision-making process. People from different areas of the firm typically hold very different perspectives about what investments should be made and how those investments should be managed (Table 9.2). Consequently, presenting the business case for a new system investment can be quite challenging. Ultimately, a number of factors come into play in making investment decisions, and numerous outcomes can occur (Figure 9.7). For instance,

FIGURE 9.7

Investment selection decisions must consider numerous factors and can have numerous outcomes.

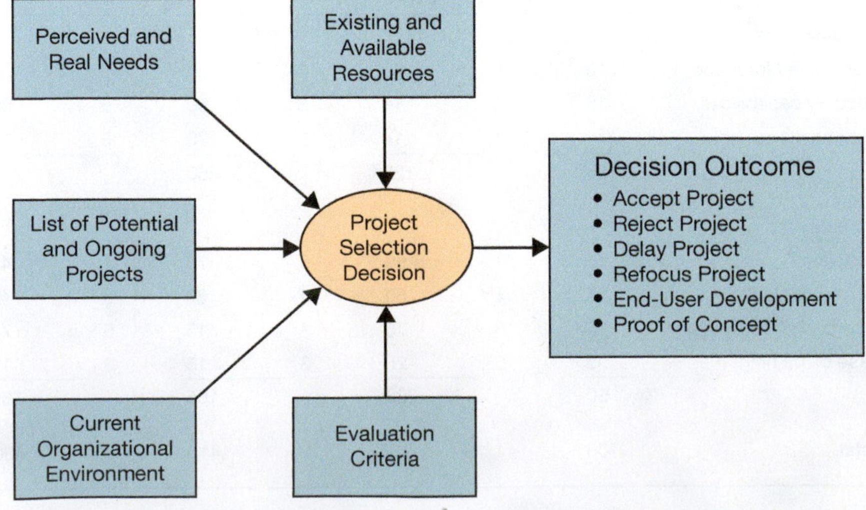

Benefit:

New system saves at least one hour per day for 12 mid-level managers.

Quantified as:

Manager's salary (per hour)	$30.00
Number of managers affected	12
Daily savings (one hour saved × 12 managers)	$360.00
Weekly savings (daily savings × 5)	$1,800.00
Annual savings (weekly savings × 50)	$90,000.00

FIGURE 9.8

Converting time savings into dollar figures.

decisions and choices are driven by perceived needs, resource availability, evaluation criteria, and so on. Numerous outcomes can occur from this decision process. Of course, the project can be accepted or rejected; often, projects can be conditionally accepted or asked to be revised in order to more carefully consider resource, time, or other constraints. Understanding the audience and the issues important to them is a first step in making an effective presentation. Various ways to improve the development of a business case are examined next.

CONVERT BENEFITS TO MONETARY TERMS. When making the case for an IS investment, it is desirable to translate all potential benefits into monetary terms. For example, if a new system saves department managers an hour per day, try to quantify that savings in terms of dollars. Figure 9.8 shows how you might convert time savings into dollar figures. While merely explaining this benefit as "saving managers' time" makes it sound useful, managers may not consider it a significant enough inducement to warrant spending a significant amount of money. Justifying a US$50,000 system because it will "save time" may not be persuasive enough. However, an annual savings of US$90,000 is more likely to capture the attention of decision makers and is more likely to result in project approval. Senior managers can easily rationalize a US$50,000 expense for a US$90,000 savings and can easily see why they should approve such a request. They can also more easily rationalize their decision later on if something goes wrong with the system.

DEVISE PROXY VARIABLES. The situation presented in Figure 9.8 is fairly straightforward. Anyone can see that a US$50,000 investment is a good idea because the return on that investment is US$90,000 the first year. Unfortunately, not all cases are this clear-cut. In cases in which it is not as easy to quantify the impact of an investment, you can come up with **proxy variables** (i.e., alternative measures of outcomes) to help clarify what the impact on the firm will be. Proxy variables can be used to measure changes in terms of their perceived value to the organization. For example, if mundane administrative tasks are seen as a low value (perhaps a 1 on a 5-point scale), but direct contact with customers is seen as a high value (a rating of 5), you can use these perceptions to indicate how new systems will add value to the organization. In this example, you can show that a new system will allow personnel to have more contact with customers while at the same time reducing the administrative workload. Senior managers can quickly see that individual workload is being shifted from low-value to high-value activities.

You can communicate these differences using percentages, increases or decreases, and so on—whatever best conveys the idea that the new system is creating changes in work, in performance, and in the way people think about their work. This gives decision makers some relatively solid data on which to base their decision.

MEASURE WHAT IS IMPORTANT TO MANAGEMENT. One of the most important things you can do to show the benefits of a system is one of the simplest: Measure what senior managers think is important. You may think this is trivial advice, but you would be surprised how often people calculate impressive-looking statistics in terms of downtime, reliability, and so on, only to find that senior managers disregard or only briefly skim over those figures. You should concentrate on the issues senior business managers care about. The "hot-button" issues with senior managers should be easy to discover, and they are not always financial reports. Hot issues with senior managers could include cycle time (how long it takes to process an order), regulatory or compliance issues, customer feedback, and employee morale. By focusing on what senior business managers believe to be important, you can make the business case for systems in a way

ETHICAL DILEMMA

Ethical App Development

In the past, systems development was in the hands of large software companies, with large development teams and legal departments that would scrutinize new functionalities for legal and ethical compliance. With the advent of the smartphone and social media came the promise of getting rich quick by developing the next Facebook, WhatsApp, Pinterest, or some other killer app. Nowadays, it's not only large companies building those apps, but individuals with a creative idea, aided by easy-to-use development tools.

However, with the hope of developing the next killer app, ethical implications are often overlooked or outright ignored, as evidenced by examples such as Facebook or Path. Throughout its history, Facebook has changed its privacy policies, at times grossly violating its users' privacy expectations. Similarly, in 2012 it became known that the iOS version of the social media app Path secretly sent the users' complete address book data to Path's servers. Not only was this not mentioned in the apps' Terms of Use, the data was also sent in an unencrypted way, potentially subjecting the app's users to security problems.

In addition, mobile devices offer various tempting ways of collecting user data, with many apps requesting access to functionalities such as your phone book, location, and so on. Given these vulnerabilities, a new code of conduct for app development is needed. "Just because you can collect data, should you?" Many argue that an app should only be allowed to collect and utilize information it needs, nothing more. Developers should also carefully consider the consequences of personal data being compromised. Who would be affected, and how serious might the consequences be? Given the high value of your personal data, the maxim of the app development industry should be: "Even though you can, maybe you shouldn't!"

Based on:

Allamsetty, T. (2013, March 19). User privacy and the ethics of app data collection. *[X]Cubelabs.* Retrieved March 27, 2014, from http://www.xcubelabs.com/blog/user-privacy-and-the-ethics-of-app-data-collection.

Grothaus, M. (2013, December 4). Do developers need a standardized code of ethics? *Co.LABS.* Retrieved March 27, 2014, from http://www.fastcolabs.com/3022968/do-developers-need-a-standardized-code-of-ethics.

Phillips, J. (2012, December 8). Path social media app uploads iOS address books to its servers. *Wired.* Retrieved March 27, 2014, from http://www.wired.com/gadgetlab/2012/02/path-social-media-app-uploads-ios-address-books-to-its-servers.

Siegel, E. (2014, February 5). Becoming an ethical app developer at Renaissance IO. *Apptentive.* Retrieved March 27, 2014, from http://www.apptentive.com/blog/ethical-app-developer-at-renaissance-io.

that is more meaningful for those managers, which makes selling systems to decision makers much easier. Managers are more likely to buy in to the importance of systems if they can see the impact on areas that are important to them. Now that you understand how to make the business case for new information systems, we now examine the development process.

THE SYSTEMS DEVELOPMENT PROCESS

No matter if a software company such as Microsoft is planning to build a new version of its popular Office software suite, or if a company such as Netflix is trying to build a system to improve its movie recommendations, companies follow a standardized approach. This process of designing, building, and maintaining information systems is often referred to as **systems analysis and design**. Likewise, the individual who performs this task is referred to as a **systems analyst**. Because few organizations can survive without effectively utilizing information and computing technology, the demand for skilled systems analysts is very strong. In 2014, *U.S. News* named being a systems analyst one of the top jobs; in fact, it was ranked as number 2, just behind software developer. Likewise, the U.S. Bureau of Labor Statistics ranks systems analysts near the top of all professions for job stability, income, and employment growth through 2016, with average growth exceeding 29 percent. Organizations want to hire systems analysts because they possess a unique blend of managerial and technical expertise—systems analysts are not just "techies." Systems analysts remain in demand precisely because of this unique blend of abilities.

Custom Versus Off-the-Shelf Software

When deciding to deploy new systems to support their operations in order to gain or sustain a competitive advantage, organizations can typically choose between custom and off-the-shelf software. For example, many types of application software (such as word processors, spreadsheet, or accounting software) can be used by a variety of businesses within and across industries. These types of general-purpose systems are typically purchased off the shelf. Often, however, organizations have very specific needs that cannot be met by generic technologies. This is especially true for companies trying to capitalize on a first-mover advantage, and therefore may not be able to purchase a preexisting system to meet their specific needs. For example, pioneers in online retailing (such as Amazon.com) or budget air travel (such as Southwest Airlines) needed entirely new systems and technologies to support their revolutionary business models and had to develop (or have someone else develop) custom solutions. The approaches to developing or acquiring custom and off-the-shelf software are quite different, but they also have many similarities. Before going into the details of developing or acquiring such systems, we'll first contrast these two types of systems.

CUSTOM SOFTWARE. Custom software is developed to meet the specifications of an organization (it is thus also sometimes called tailor-made, or bespoke, software). Such software may be developed (or configured) in-house by the company's own IS staff, or the development may be contracted, or outsourced, to a specialized vendor charged with developing the system to the company's contractual specifications. Custom software has two primary advantages over general purpose commercial technologies:

1. ***Customizability.*** The software can be tailored to meet unique organizational requirements. Such requirements, for example, can reflect a desire to achieve a competitive advantage through a specific type of system (e.g., Amazon.com's one-click ordering) or to better fit business operations, characteristics of the organizational culture, or proprietary security requirements, or to better interface with existing systems. Further, company- or industry-specific terms or acronyms can be included in a new software application, as can unique types of required reports. Such specificity is not typically possible in off-the-shelf systems that are targeted at a more general audience.
2. ***Problem Specificity.*** The company pays only for the features specifically required for its users. In contrast to software packages such as Microsoft Office, which include a wide range of individual programs (some of which may never be used), only those components that are really needed can be implemented.

Today, building a complete system from scratch is quite rare; most information systems that are developed within an organization for its internal use typically include a large number of preprogrammed, reusable modules as well as off-the-shelf hardware technologies that are purchased from development organizations or consultants.

OFF-THE-SHELF SOFTWARE. Although custom software has advantages, it is not automatically the best choice for an organization. Off-the-shelf software (or packaged software) is typically used to support common business processes that do not require any specific tailoring. In general, off-the-shelf systems, whether hardware or software, are less costly, faster to procure, of higher quality, and less risky than custom systems. Table 9.3 summarizes examples of off-the-shelf application software.

TABLE 9.3 Examples of Off-the-Shelf Application Software

Category	Application	Description	Examples
Business information systems	Payroll	Automation of payroll services, from the optical reading of time sheets to generating paychecks	ZPAY Intuit Payroll
	Inventory	Automation of inventory tracking, order processing, billing, and shipping	Intuit QuickBooks InventoryPower 5
Office automation	Personal productivity	Support for a wide range of tasks from word processing to graphics to e-mail	OpenOffice Corel Office Microsoft Office

Traditionally, the most common option for packaged software was so-called commercial off-the-shelf (COTS) software; this type of software is typically developed by software companies that spread the development costs over a large number of customers. An alternative to commercial off-the-shelf software is open source software.

Open Source Software

Open source is a philosophy that promotes developers' and users' access to the source of a product or idea. Particularly in the area of software development, the open source movement has taken off with the advent of the Internet; people around the world are contributing their time and expertise to develop or improve software, ranging from operating systems to application software. As the programs' source code is freely available for use and/or modification, this software is referred to as **open source software**. Open source software owes its success to the inputs from a large user base, helping to fix problems or improve the software. One of the great success stories of open source software is the Android operating system. In 2014, Android's share of the global smartphone shipment market—led by Samsung products—was over 80 percent! Android is based on another open source operating system called Linux, developed as a hobby by the Finnish university student Linus Torvalds in 1991. Linux has since become the operating system of choice for Web servers, embedded systems (such as TiVo boxes and network routers), and supercomputers alike (as of June 2014, 97 percent of the world's 500 fastest supercomputers ran Linux operating systems [Top 500, 2014]). In addition to the Linux operating system, other open source software has been gaining increasing popularity because of its stability and low cost. For example, in 2014, 38 percent of all Web sites were powered by the Apache Web server, another open source project (Netcraft, 2014). Other popular examples of open source application software include the Firefox Web browser and the office productivity suite Apache OpenOffice.

How do large open source projects such as Firefox work? Typically, most contributors can only *suggest* modifications for changes; for example, they can contribute to program code or provide new designs for the system's user interface, but only a small group of carefully selected "committers" can implement these modifications into the official releases of the software, which helps to ensure the quality and stability of the software.

While there are many benefits to open source software, vendors of proprietary software are still highlighting "hidden" costs of running open source software, such as obtaining reliable customer support. On the other hand, however, commercial open source vendors are providing customer support, installation, training, and so on to their paying customers. Men's Wearhouse, the State of Oregon, and many other large organizations are using a CRM system offered by SugarCRM, Inc., a commercial open source vendor that offers free "community editions" as well as other, more feature-rich paid editions of its software. Similarly, the popular MySQL database, which is used by Yahoo!, Facebook, the Associated Press, and many other companies, is provided under an open source license for personal use, but the company employs its own developers and offers commercial licenses (including dedicated 24/7 technical support, consulting, and indemnification clauses) to business users. Further, many open source projects are now backed by major information technology (IT) companies such as IBM, which give money and human resources to Linux projects, or Oracle, which donated the source code of the OpenOffice productivity suite to the Apache Software Foundation.

Combining Custom, Open Source, and Off-the-Shelf Systems

It is possible to combine the advantages of custom, open source, and off-the-shelf systems. Companies can purchase off-the-shelf technologies and add custom components for their specific needs. For example, an online retailer may want to purchase an off-the-shelf inventory management system and then add tailor-made modules it needs to conduct its day-to-day business. This system could be based on the open source database MySQL; further, the online retailer could use the open source Apache Web server to power its online shopping site. In some cases, for example, with large ERP systems, companies selling off-the-shelf software make customized changes for a fee. Other vendors, however, may not allow their software to be modified (as is the case with generic, all-purpose software, such as Microsoft Office).

Commercial, off-the-shelf systems are almost always acquired from an external vendor, whereas custom systems can be either developed in-house or developed by an outside vendor (Figure 9.9). Regardless of the source of the new system—custom, open source, or off-the-shelf—the primary role of managers and users in the organization is to make sure that it will meet the organization's

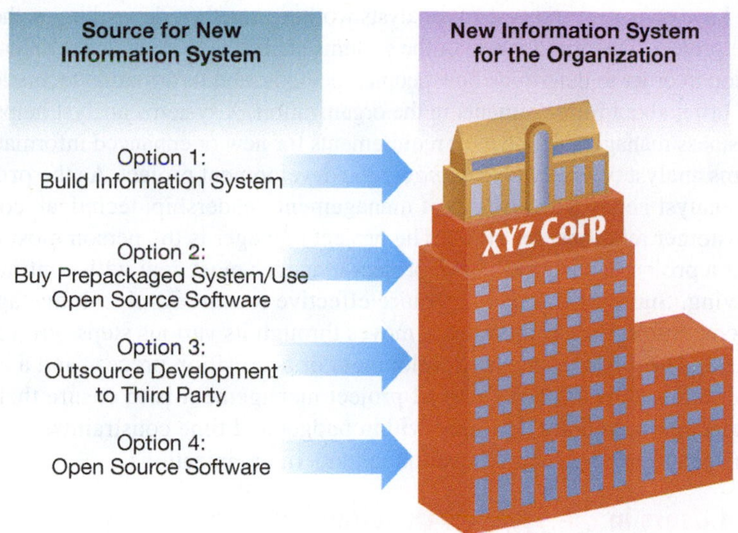

FIGURE 9.9

There are a variety of sources for information systems.

business needs. This may be especially important in the case of end users developing systems. End users typically do not program elaborate systems, but frequently use spreadsheet or database software to create solutions for accomplishing narrow, well-defined tasks; while such applications may be useful for accomplishing certain tasks, end user development may cause problems related to the adherence to standards, lack of documentation, security concerns, or a lack of continuity if the employee who built the spreadsheet or database leaves the organization.

IS Development in Action

The tools and techniques used to develop information systems are continually evolving with the rapid changes in IS hardware and software. As you will see, IS development is a fairly disciplined and structured process that moves from step to step. Systems analysts become adept at decomposing large, complex problems into many small, simple problems. The goal of the systems analyst is to design the final system by piecing together many small software modules and technologies into one comprehensive system (Figure 9.10). For example, think about using LEGO™ blocks for building a model of a space station. Each individual block is a small, simple piece that is nothing without the others. When put together, the blocks can create a large and very complex design (Google co-founder Larry Page had gained some notoriety for building a working printer out of LEGO bricks). When systems are built in this manner, they are much easier to design, build, and, most important, maintain.

Although many people in organizations, such as managers and users, are responsible and participate in a systems development project, the systems analyst has primary responsibility. Some

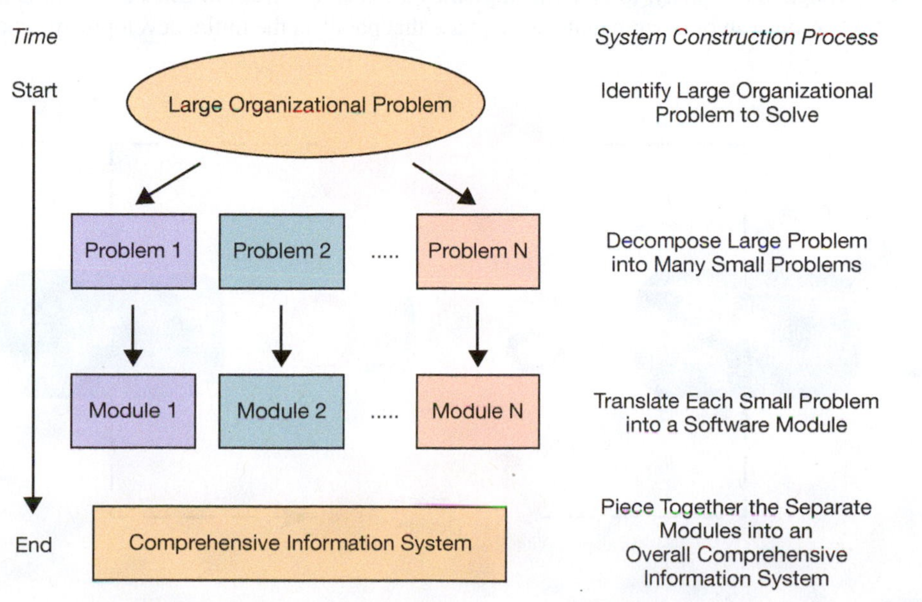

FIGURE 9.10

Problem decomposition makes solving large, complex problems easier.

projects may have one or several systems analysts working together, depending on the size and complexity of the project. The primary role of the systems analyst is to study the problems and needs of an organization in order to determine how people, methods, and information technology can best be combined to bring about improvements in the organization. A systems analyst helps systems users and other business managers define their requirements for new or enhanced information systems.

A systems analyst typically also *manages* the development project. As the **project manager**, the systems analyst needs a diverse set of management, leadership, technical, conflict management, and customer relationships skills. The project manager is the person most responsible for ensuring that a project is a success. The project manager must deal with continual change and problem solving. Successful projects require effective resource and task management as well as effective communication as the project moves through its various steps. Project management is an important aspect of the system development or acquisition process and a critical skill for successful systems analysts. The focus of project management is to ensure that projects meet customer expectations and are delivered within budget and time constraints. Clearly, a systems analyst is an agent of change and innovation in modern organizations.

The Role of Users in the Systems Development Process

Many organizations have a huge investment in transaction processing and management information systems. These systems are most often designed, constructed, and maintained by systems analysts within the organization, using a variety of methods. When building and maintaining information systems, systems analysts rely on information provided by system users, who are involved in all phases of the system's development process. To effectively participate in the process, it is important for all members of the organization to understand what is meant by systems development and what activities occur. A close, mutually respectful working relationship between analysts and users is key to project success.

Steps in the Systems Development Process

Just as the products that a firm produces and sells follow a life cycle, so do organizational information systems. For example, a new type of tennis shoe follows a life cycle of being designed, introduced to the market, being accepted into the market, maturing, declining in popularity, and ultimately being retired. The term **systems development life cycle (SDLC)** describes the life of an information system from conception to retirement (Hoffer et al., 2014). The SDLC has four primary phases:

1. Systems planning and selection
2. Systems analysis
3. Systems design
4. Systems implementation and operation

Figure 9.11 is a graphical representation of the SDLC containing four boxes connected by arrows. Within the SDLC, arrows flow from systems planning and selection, to systems analysis, to systems design, and, finally, to systems implementation and operation. Once a system is in operation, it moves into an ongoing maintenance phase that parallels the initial development process. For

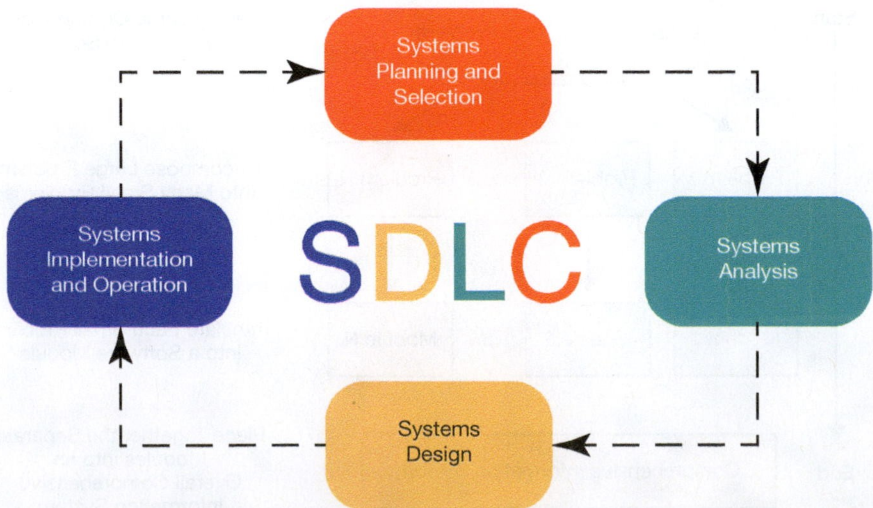

FIGURE 9.11

The SDLC defines the typical process for building systems.

WHO'S GOING MOBILE

Creating Mobile Apps

With the rapid rise of smartphone usage, various useful and entertaining apps are rapidly being developed, greatly enhancing the phones' capabilities. In 2013, both Google and Apple announced that they had over 1 million apps in their app stores, with many more apps appearing every day. The primary reason there are so many apps is that anyone can build and try to sell apps, from software companies focused on translating their existing products (such as Adobe Reader) onto mobile platforms, to individuals who have a clever idea for a game.

Owing to the intense competition between these apps, it is not surprising that only relatively few are highly successful. However, if you have the right idea, creating a winning app can be surprisingly easy. In fact, it is estimated that it took the maker of the widely successful game Flappy Bird a mere two to three days to create that game (alone, that is). At its peak, the game netted US$50,000 *per day* for the person who built the game. Given that games for popular consoles such as the PlayStation or the Xbox cost millions of dollars to develop, how did Flappy Bird's creator manage to pull that off?

In the past few years, a number of marketplaces have sprung up where anyone can purchase game templates for as low as US$199. These templates typically include certain game mechanics, which the buyer can modify to create a functioning game. Typically, there's not even a need to write a single line of code; all that is needed is a winning idea, coming up with a good story, game title, and key words, and the skills needed to create the graphics.

What if your idea is for an app other than a game, such as a productivity tool for students, or a better way to keep track of your passwords? There are tools to help develop these as well. Once the app is created, all that is needed is uploading the app to the various marketplaces, and watching the download count. Good luck!

Based on:

Anonymous. (2014). AppMachine. Retrieved March 27, 2014, from www.appmachine.com.

Rubens, P. (February 18, 2014). Flap happy: How you too can become a mobile games mogul. *BBC*. Retrieved March 27, 2014, from http://www.bbc.com/news/business-26224428.

example, when new features are added to an existing system, analysts must first plan and select which new features to add, then analyze the possible impact of adding these features to the existing system, then design how the new features will work, and, finally, implement these new features into the existing system. While some consider maintenance another SDLC phase, it is really a repeated application of the core SDLC phases. In this way, the SDLC becomes an ongoing *cycle*. During ongoing systems maintenance, the entire SDLC is followed to implement system repairs and enhancements.

Phase 1: Systems Planning and Selection

The first phase of the SDLC is **systems planning and selection** (see Figure 9.11). Understanding that it can work on only a limited number of projects at a given time because of limited resources, an organization must take care that only those projects that are critical to enabling the organization's mission, goals, and objectives are undertaken. Consequently, the goal of systems planning and selection is simply to identify, plan, and select a development project from all possible projects that could be performed. Organizations differ in how they identify, plan, and select projects. Some organizations have a formal **information systems planning** process whereby a senior manager, a business group, an IS manager, or a steering committee identifies and assesses all possible systems development projects that the organization could undertake. Project managers present the business case for the new system and it is accepted or rejected. Others follow a more ad hoc process for identifying potential projects. Nonetheless, after all possible projects are identified, those deemed most likely to yield significant organizational benefits, given available resources, are selected for subsequent development activities.

Just as there are often differences in the source of systems projects within organizations, there are often different evaluation criteria used within organizations when classifying and ranking potential projects, such as strategic alignment, costs and benefits, resource availability, project size and duration, or technical difficulties and risks. During project planning, the analyst works with the customers—the potential users of the system and their managers—to collect a broad range of information to gain an understanding of the project size, potential benefits and costs, and other relevant factors. After collecting and analyzing this information, the analyst builds the business case that can be reviewed and compared with other possible projects. If the organization accepts the project, systems analysis begins.

Phase 2: Systems Analysis

The second phase of the SDLC is called **systems analysis** (see Figure 9.11). One purpose of the systems analysis phase is for designers to gain a thorough understanding of an organization's current way of doing things in the area for which the new information system will be constructed. The process of conducting an analysis requires that many tasks, or subphases, be performed. The first subphase focuses on determining system requirements. To determine the requirements, an analyst works closely with users to determine what is needed from the proposed system. After collecting the requirements, analysts organize this information using data, process, and logic modeling tools.

COLLECTING REQUIREMENTS. The collection and structuring of requirements is arguably the most important activity in the systems development process because how well the IS requirements are defined influences all subsequent activities. The old saying "garbage in, garbage out" very much applies to the systems development process. **Requirements collection** is the process of gathering and organizing information from users, managers, customers, business processes, and documents to understand how a proposed information system should function. Systems analysts use a variety of techniques for collecting system requirements, including the following (Hoffer et al., 2014):

- ***Interviews.*** Analysts interview people informed about the operation and issues of the current or proposed system.
- ***Questionnaires.*** Analysts design and administer surveys to gather opinions from people informed about the operation and issues of the current or proposed system.
- ***Observations.*** Analysts observe system users at selected times to see how data are handled and what information people need to do their jobs.
- ***Document Analysis.*** Analysts study business documents to discover issues, policies, and rules, as well as concrete examples of the use of data and information in the organization.
- ***Joint Application Design.*** **Joint application design (JAD)** is a group meeting–based process for requirements collection (Figure 9.12). During this meeting, the users *jointly* define and agree on system requirements or designs. This process can result in dramatic reductions in the length of time needed to collect requirements or specify designs.

MODELING DATA. Data are facts that describe people, objects, or events. A lot of different facts can be used to describe a person: name, age, gender, race, and occupation, among others. To construct an information system, systems analysts must understand what data the information system needs in order to accomplish the intended tasks. To do this, they use data modeling tools to collect and describe the data to users to confirm that all needed data are known and presented to users as useful information. Figure 9.13 shows an *entity-relationship diagram,* a type of data model describing students, classes, majors, and classrooms at a university. Each box in the diagram is referred to as a data entity, and each entity is related to other entities. Data modeling tools enable the systems analyst to represent data in a form that is easy for users to understand and critique. For more information on databases and data modeling, see the Technology Briefing.

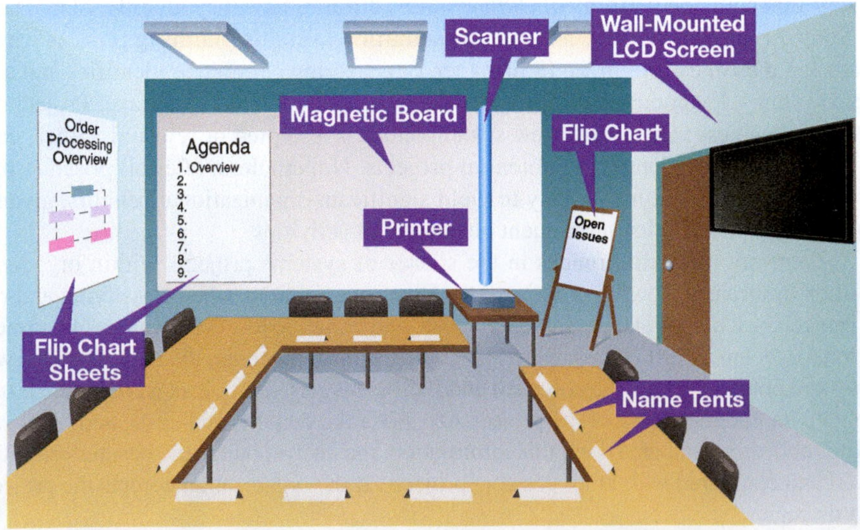

FIGURE 9.12

A JAD room.

Source: Based on Wood & Silver (1989); Hoffer et al. (2014).

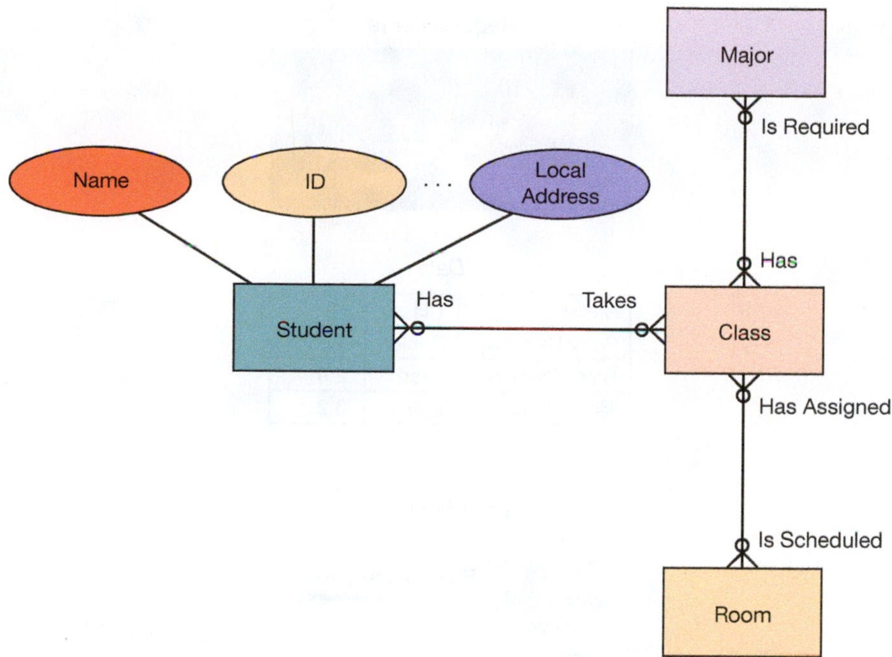

FIGURE 9.13

A sample entity-relationship diagram for students.

MODELING PROCESSES AND LOGIC. The next step in this phase is to model how data are being input, processed, and presented to the users. As the name implies, **data flows** represent the movement of data through an organization or within an information system. For example, your registration for a class may be captured in a registration form on paper or in an interactive form on the Web. After it is filled out, this form probably flows through several processes to validate and record the class registration, shown as "Data Flows" in Figure 9.14. After all students have been registered, a repository of all registration information can be processed for developing class rosters or for generating student billing information, which is shown as "Data" in Figure 9.14. **Processing logic** represents the way in which data are transformed. Processing logic is often expressed in **pseudocode**, which is a representation of the program's internal functioning, independent of the actual programming language being used. As there are no standards for pseudocode, the level of detail can vary. For example, pseudocode to calculate students' grade-point averages at the conclusion of a term is shown in the "Processing Logic" section in Figure 9.14.

After the data, data flow, and processing logic requirements for the proposed system have been identified, analysts develop one or many possible overall approaches—sometimes called designs—for the information system. For example, one approach for the system may possess only basic functionality but has the advantage of being relatively easy and inexpensive to build. An analyst might also propose a more elaborate approach for the system, but it may be more difficult and more costly to build. Analysts evaluate alternative system design approaches with the knowledge that different solutions yield different benefits and different costs. After a system approach is selected, details of that particular system approach can be defined.

Phase 3: Systems Design

The third phase of the SDLC is **systems design** (see Figure 9.11). As its name implies, it is during this phase that the proposed system is designed; that is, the details of the chosen approach are elaborated. As with analysis, many different activities must occur during systems design. The elements that must be designed when building an information system include the following:

- Processing and logic
- Databases and files
- Human–computer interface

DESIGNING PROCESSING AND LOGIC. The processing and logic operations of an information system are the steps and procedures that transform raw data inputs into new or modified information. There are typically different ways to complete each process, with some being more

FIGURE 9.14

Four key elements to the development of a system: requirements, data, data flows, and processing logic.

Requirements

Data

Name	Class	GPA
Patty Nicholls	Senior	3.7
Brett Williams	Grad	2.9
Mary Shide	Fresh	3.2

Data Flows

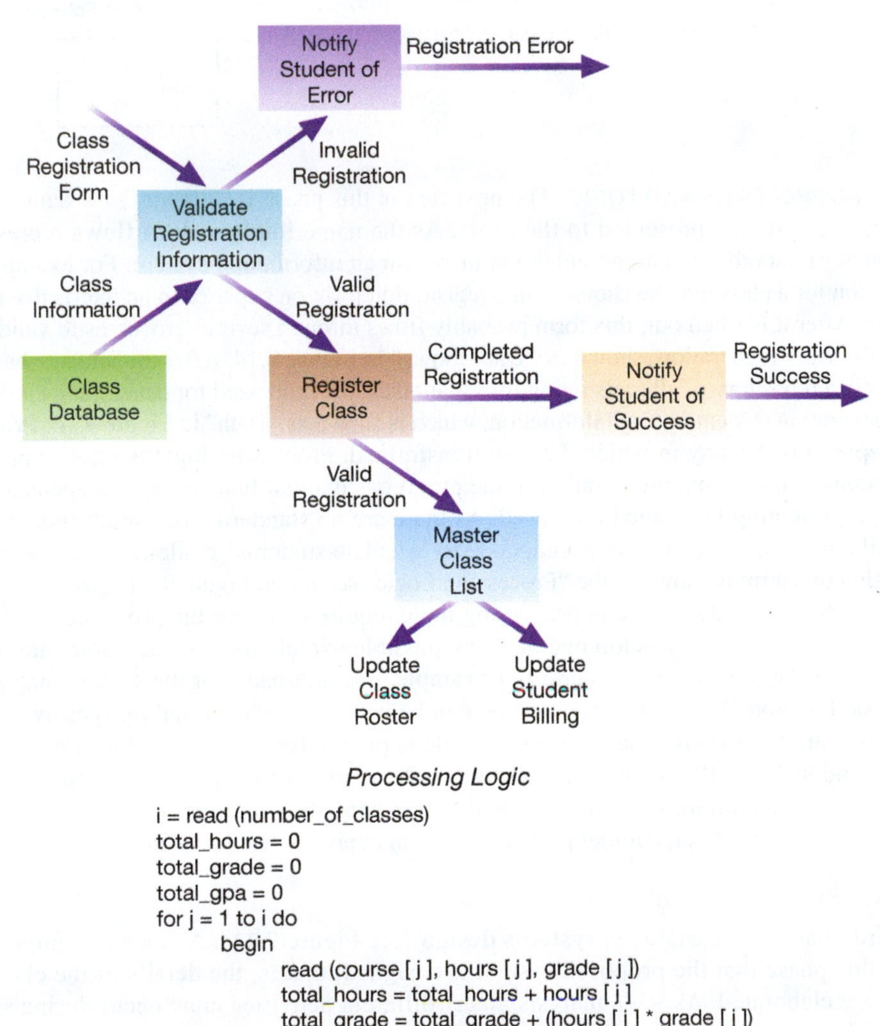

Processing Logic

```
i = read (number_of_classes)
total_hours = 0
total_grade = 0
total_gpa = 0
for j = 1 to i do
        begin
                read (course [ j ], hours [ j ], grade [ j ])
                total_hours = total_hours + hours [ j ]
                total_grade = total_grade + (hours [ j ] * grade [ j ])
        end
current_gpa = total_grade/total hours
```

efficient or effective than others. Modeling the processes thus includes not only specifying what is to be done, but also the specific algorithms, which outline the steps, or set of rules, to be followed (that is, how a certain process is accomplished). For example, when calculating your grade-point average, your school needs to perform the following steps:

1. Obtain the prior grade-point average, credit hours earned, and list of prior courses
2. Obtain the list of each current course, final grade, and course credit hours

3. Combine the prior and current credit hours into aggregate sums
4. Calculate the new grade-point average

The logic and steps needed to make this calculation can be represented in many ways, including structure charts, decision trees, pseudocode, programming code, and so on (see Figure 9.14). Regardless of how the logic is represented, the process of converting pseudocode, structure charts, or decision trees into actual program code during system implementation is a relatively straightforward process.

DESIGNING DATABASES AND FILES. To design databases and files, a systems analyst must have a thorough understanding of an organization's data and informational needs. For example, Figure 9.15 shows the database design to keep track of student information in a Microsoft Access database. The database design is more complete (shows each attribute of the student) and more detailed (shows how the information is formatted) than a conceptual data model built during systems analysis (as was shown in Figure 9.14).

DESIGNING THE HUMAN–COMPUTER INTERFACE. Just as people have different ways of interacting with other people, information systems can have different ways of interacting with people. A **human–computer interface (HCI)** is the point of contact between a system and users. With people being used to interacting with easy-to-use systems and Web sites like Facebook, Twitter, and Amazon.com, their expectations in terms of ease of use are ever increasing. In addition, increasing a system's **usability**—that is, whether the system is easy to use and aesthetically pleasing—can lower error rates, increase efficiency, or increase customer satisfaction (in the case of customer-facing systems). Thus, analysts also take great care in designing data entry forms and management reports. A form is a business document containing some predefined data, often including some areas where additional data can be filled in (Figure 9.16). Similarly, a report is a business document containing only predefined data for online viewing or printing (Figure 9.17). For more on forms and reports, see Chapter 6.

Phase 4: Systems Implementation and Operation

Many separate activities occur during **systems implementation**, the fourth phase of the SDLC (see Figure 9.11). One group of activities focuses on transforming the system design into a working information system. These activities include software programming and testing. A second group of activities focuses on preparing the organization for using the new information system. These activities include system conversion, documentation, user training, and support. This section briefly describes what occurs during systems implementation.

SOFTWARE PROGRAMMING AND TESTING. Programming is the process of transforming the system design into a working computer system. During this transformation, both programming

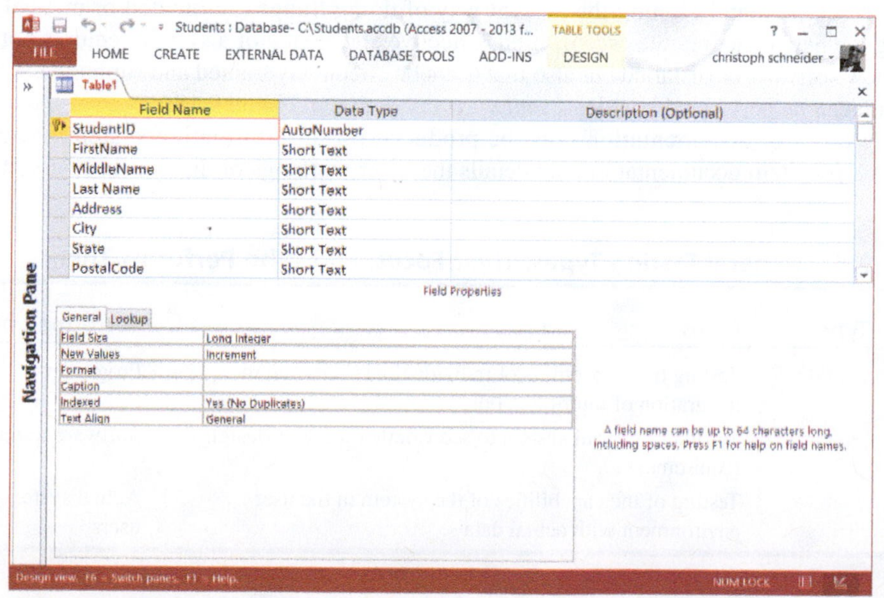

FIGURE 9.15

The database design for student information from an Access database.

Source: Courtesy of Microsoft Corporation.

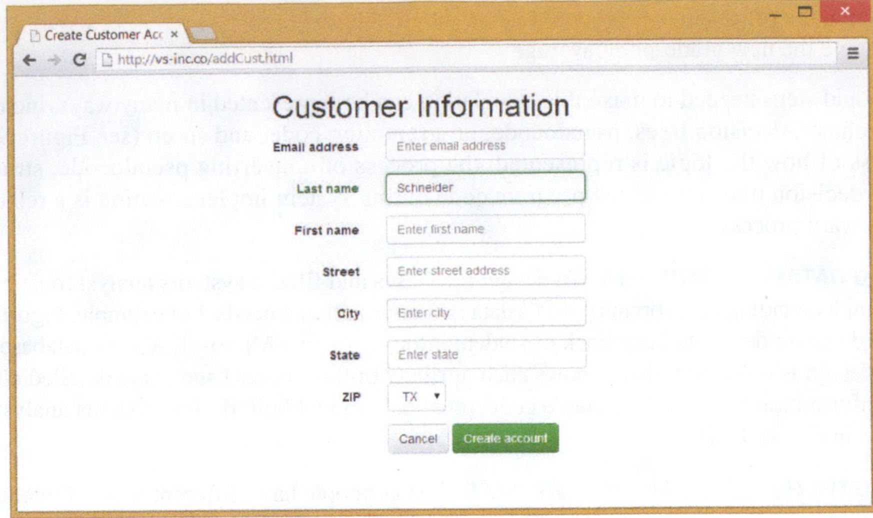

FIGURE 9.16
A data entry form.

FIGURE 9.17
Sales summary report.

Ascend Systems Incorporated
SALESPERSON ANNUAL SUMMARY REPORT 2016

REGION	SALESPERSON	SSN	QUARTERLY ACTUAL SALES FIRST	SECOND	THIRD	FOURTH
Northwest and Mountain						
	Wachter	999-99-0001	16,500	18,600	24,300	18,000
	Mennecke	999-99-0002	22,000	15,500	17,300	19,800
	Wheeler	999-99-0003	19,000	12,500	22,000	28,000
Midwest and Mid-Atlantic						
	Spurrier	999-99-0004	14,000	16,000	19,000	21,000
	Powell	999-99-0005	7,500	16,600	10,000	8,000
	Topi	999-99-0006	12,000	19,800	17,000	19,000
New England						
	Speier	999-99-0007	18,000	18,000	20,000	27,000
	Morris	999-99-0008	28,000	29,000	19,000	31,000

and testing should occur in parallel. As you might expect, a broad range of tests is conducted before a system is complete, including **developmental testing**, **alpha testing**, and **beta testing** (Table 9.4).

SYSTEM CONVERSION, DOCUMENTATION, TRAINING, AND SUPPORT. **System conversion** is the process of decommissioning the current way of doing things (automated or manual) and installing the new system in the organization. Effective conversion of a system requires not only that the new software be installed but also that users be effectively trained and supported. System conversion can be performed in at least four ways, as shown in Figure 9.18.

Many types of documentation must be produced for an information system. Programmers develop system documentation that details the inner workings of the system to ease future

TABLE 9.4 General Testing Types, Their Focus, and Who Performs Them

Testing Type	Focus	Performed by
Developmental	Testing the correctness of individual modules and the integration of multiple modules	Programmer
Alpha	Testing of overall system to see whether it meets design requirements	Software tester
Beta	Testing of the capabilities of the system in the user environment with actual data	Actual system users

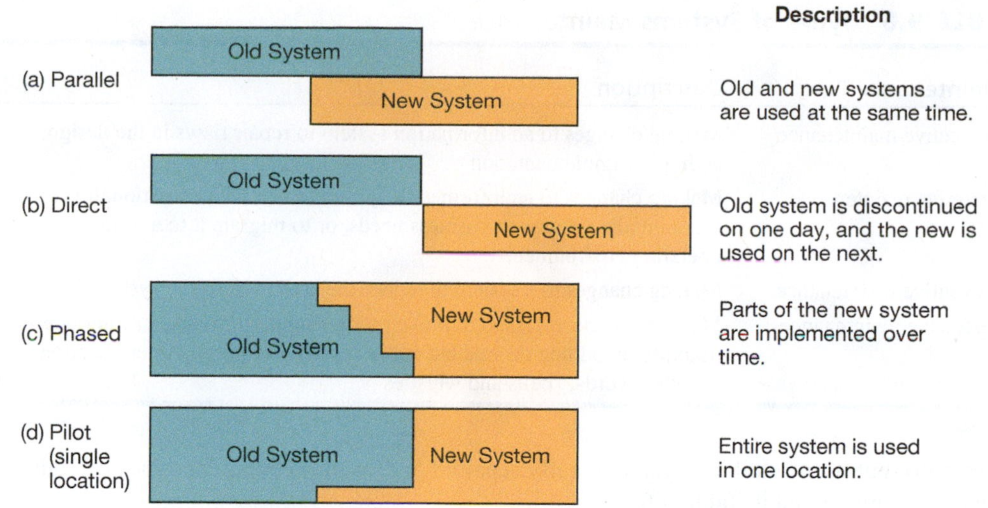
Description
(a) Parallel
Old System
New System
Old and new systems are used at the same time.
(b) Direct
Old System
New System
Old system is discontinued on one day, and the new is used on the next.
(c) Phased
New System
Old System
Parts of the new system are implemented over time.
(d) Pilot (single location)
Old System
New System
Entire system is used in one location.

FIGURE 9.18

Software conversion strategies.

maintenance and to ensure reliability of the system. A second type of documentation is user-related documentation, which is typically written not by programmers or analysts but by users or professional technical writers. The range of documents can include the following:

- User and reference guides
- User training manuals and tutorials
- Installation procedures and troubleshooting suggestions

In addition to documentation, users may also need training and ongoing support to use a new system effectively. Different types of training and support require different levels of investment by the organization. Self-paced training and tutorials are the least expensive options, and one-on-one training is the most expensive. Table 9.5 summarizes various user training options.

Besides training, providing ongoing education and problem-solving assistance for users may also be necessary. This is commonly referred to as system support, which is often provided by a special group of people in the organization who make up an information center or help desk. Support personnel must have strong communication skills and be good problem solvers in addition to being expert users of the system. An alternative option for a system not developed internally is to outsource support activities to a vendor specializing in technical system support and training. Regardless of how support is provided, it is an ongoing issue that must be managed effectively for the company to realize the maximum benefits of a system.

Repeating the SDLC: Systems Maintenance

After an information system is installed, it is essentially in the **systems maintenance** phase. A system does not wear out in the physical manner that cars, buildings, or other physical

TABLE 9.5 User Training Options

Training Option	Description
Tutorial	One person taught at a time
Course	Several people taught at a time
Computer-aided instruction	One person taught at a time by the computer system
Interactive training manuals	Combination of tutorials and computer-aided instruction
Resident expert	Expert on call to assist users as needed
Software help components	Built-in system components designed to train users and troubleshoot problems
External sources	Vendors and training providers offering tutorials, courses, and other training activities

TABLE 9.6 Types of Systems Maintenance

Maintenance Type	Description
Corrective maintenance	Making changes to an information system to repair flaws in the design, coding, or implementation
Adaptive maintenance	Making changes to an information system to evolve its functionality, to accommodate changing business needs, or to migrate it to a different operating environment
Preventive maintenance	Making changes to a system to reduce the chance of future system failure
Perfective maintenance	Making enhancements to improve processing performance or interface usability, or adding desired but not necessarily required system features (in other words, "bells and whistles")

objects do, but it must still be systematically repaired and/or improved. The types of maintenance are summarized in Table 9.6.

During systems maintenance, it is typical that one person within the systems development group is responsible for collecting maintenance requests from system users. Periodically, these requests are analyzed to evaluate how a proposed change might alter the system and what business benefits might result from such a change, and are prioritized accordingly (Figure 9.19). As with **adaptive maintenance**, both **perfective maintenance** and **preventive maintenance** are typically a much lower priority than **corrective maintenance**, which deals with repairing flaws in the system. Corrective maintenance is most likely to occur after initial system installation as well as over the life of a system after major system changes. This means that adaptive, perfective, and preventive maintenance activities can lead to corrective maintenance activities if they are not carefully designed and implemented.

As with developing or acquiring new systems, any changes to an existing system need to be carefully managed. Unmanaged change can have a variety of negative consequences, including system malfunction, system failure, increasing unreliability (as errors tend to build up over time, making the system more fragile), or opening the door for fraud or deliberate misuse (e.g., if a "backdoor" is introduced during changes to a system). If the change request is approved, a system change is designed and then implemented. As with the initial development of the system, implemented changes are formally reviewed and tested before being installed into operational systems. Thus, **change request management** is a formal process that ensures that any proposed system

FIGURE 9.19

Change request management is used during systems maintenance.

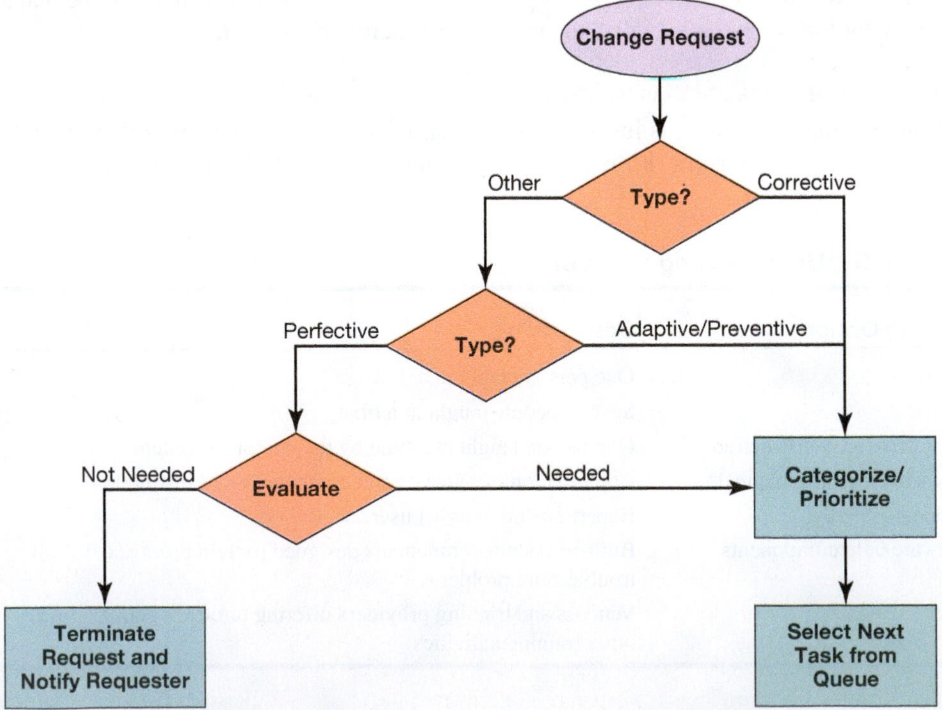

KEY PLAYERS

Game Development Studios

Have you ever wondered how and where tech companies generate so much money each year? For example, in 2012, some of the largest tech companies, including mainstays like IBM (US$104 billion in total revenue) and Apple (US$164 billion in total revenue), generated their massive revenues with a mix of hardware, services, and software sales. For these giants, however, software revenue was a relatively modest portion, amounting to 27.6 percent (US$29 billion) for IBM, and only 1.0 percent (US$1.6 billion) for Apple. In contrast, software giant Microsoft, with total revenue topping US$73 billion, generated about 80 percent (US$58 billion) of its revenue through software sales, making Microsoft the highest-grossing software company in the world.

A closer analysis of the sources of revenue of the largest "software companies" shows that most derive income from a variety of sources beyond software sales. Few software companies are capable of standing out solely by relying on software revenue—that is, with the exception of gaming. Top game developers such as CAPCOM (e.g., *Resident Evil*), and Rockstar North (*Grand Theft Auto*) generate nearly 100 percent of their revenue from software sales.

While all software development follows a methodology like the SDLC, game development has some unique characteristics given the high entertainment or educational goals of this type of software. In a normal SDLC, analysis and design activities are carried out by a relatively narrow group of system and business analysts, while programming and testing are carried out by programmers and software testers. Like any software project, game development begins with the establishment of a general project goal (such as to have a best-selling game or to produce a game associated with a certain sports event). From there, things change quite a bit. Designing a bestselling game more or less resembles the process of a heavily invested movie production. Like high-budget, blockbuster movies, games targeted for massive markets can be extremely expensive to create. In fact, leading games have been reported to cost more than US$100 million to develop. So, building a game that has low sales can literally bankrupt a game studio. Given the complexity, expense, and deep specialization required to develop top-selling games, it is easy to see why those companies focus their efforts solely on software sales to create the next bestseller.

Based on:

Anonymous. (n.d.). Global software top 100—edition 2013. *PWC.com.* Retrieved March 20, 2014, from http://www.pwc.com/gx/en/technology/publications/global-software-100-leaders/compare-results.jhtml.

Game development life cycle. (n.d.). Retrieved March 20, 2014, from http://personanonymous.wordpress.com/2013/01/06/game-development-lifecycle.

LaMothe, A. (n.d.). Designing video games. *Dummies.com.* Retrieved March 20, 2014, from http://www.dummies.com/how-to/content/designing-video-games.html.

changes are documented, reviewed for potential risks, appropriately authorized, prioritized, and carefully managed (to establish an audit trail; to be able to trace back who reviewed, authorized, implemented, or tested the changes). In other words, the systems maintenance process parallels the process used for the initial development of the information system, as shown in Figure 9.20. Interestingly, it is often during system maintenance that the largest part of the system development effort occurs.

Today, vendors of commercial off-the-shelf software packages incorporate **patch management systems** to facilitate the different forms of systems maintenance for the user; patch management systems use the Internet to check the software vendor's Web site for available patches and/or updates. If the software vendor offers a new patch, the application will download and install the patch in order to fix the software flaw. An example of a patch management system in wide use is the Windows Update Service, which automatically connects to a Microsoft Web service to download critical operating system patches for corrective maintenance (e.g., to fix bugs in the Windows operating system) or preventive maintenance (e.g., to fix security holes that could be exploited by malicious hackers).

As you can see, there is more to systems maintenance than you might think. Lots of time, effort, and money are spent in this final phase of a system's development, and it is important to follow prescribed, structured steps. In fact, the approach to systems development described here—from the initial phase of identifying, selecting, and planning for systems to the final phase of systems maintenance—is a very structured and systematic process. Each phase is fairly well prescribed and requires active involvement by systems people, users, and managers. It is likely that you will have numerous opportunities to participate in the acquisition or development of a

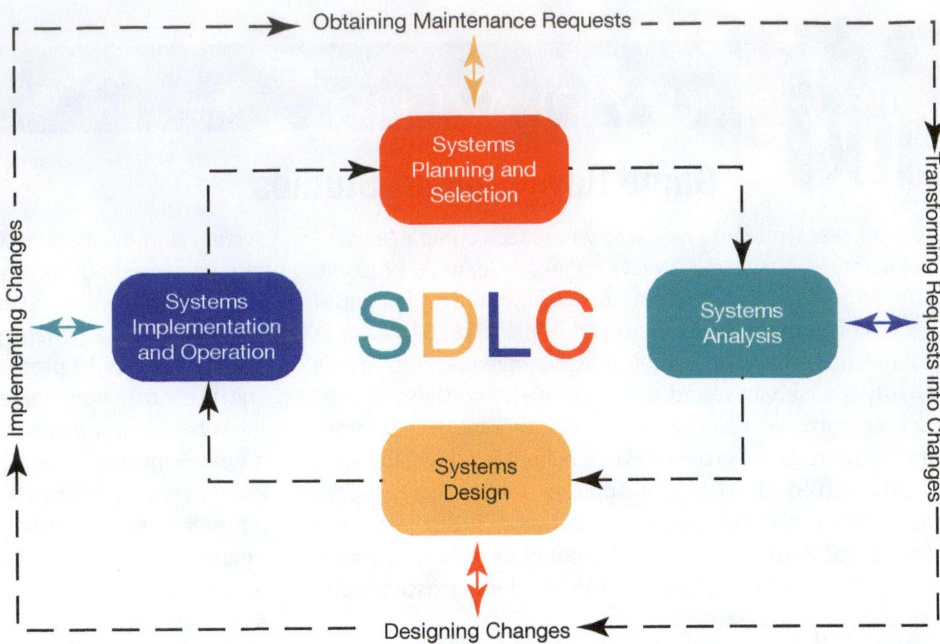

FIGURE 9.20

Mapping of system maintenance activities to the SDLC.

new system for an organization for which you currently work or will work in the future. Now that you have an understanding of the process, you should be better equipped to make a positive contribution to the success of any systems development project.

Other Approaches to Designing and Building Systems

The SDLC is one approach to managing the development process, and it is a very good approach to follow when the requirements for the information system are highly structured and straightforward—for example, for a payroll or inventory system. Today, in addition to "standard" systems such as payroll and inventory systems, organizations need a broad variety of company-specific information systems, for which requirements either are very hard to specify in advance or are constantly changing. For example, an organization's Web site is likely to evolve over time to keep pace with changing business requirements. How many Web sites have you visited in which the content or layout seemed to change almost every week? For this type of system, the SDLC might work as a development approach, but it would not be optimal.

A commonly used alternative to the SDLC is **prototyping**, which uses a trial-and-error approach for discovering how a system should operate. You may think that this does not sound like a process at all; however, you probably use prototyping all the time in many of your day-to-day activities, but you just do not know it. For example, when you buy new clothes, you likely use prototyping—that is, trial and error—by trying on several shirts before making a selection.

Figure 9.21 diagrams the prototyping process when applied to identifying/determining system requirements. To begin the process, the system designer interviews one or several users of the system, either individually or as a group, in a JAD session. After the designer gains a general understanding of what the users want, he or she develops a prototype of the new system as quickly as possible to share with the users. The users may like what they see or ask for changes. If the users request changes, the designer modifies the prototype and again shares it with them. This process of sharing and refinement continues until the users approve the functionality of the system.

FIGURE 9.21

The prototyping process uses a trial-and-error approach to discovering how a system should operate.

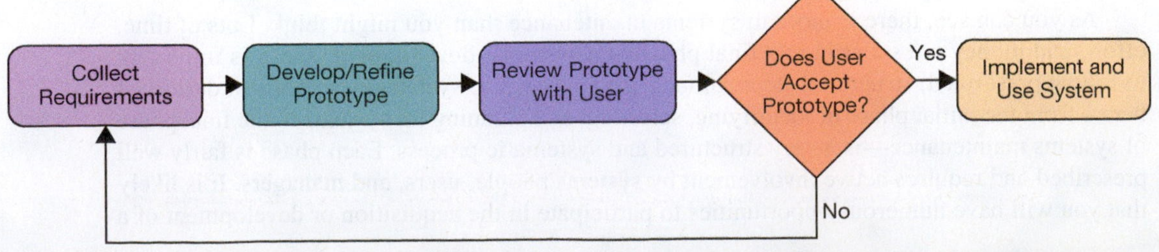

Beyond the SDLC and prototyping, there are many more approaches for designing and constructing information systems (e.g., Agile Methodologies, Extreme Programming, RAD [Rapid Application Development], object-oriented analysis and design, and so on). Each alternative approach has its strengths and weaknesses, providing a skilled systems analyst with a variety of tools to best meet the needs of a situation (for more, see Hoffer et al., 2014).

ACQUIRING INFORMATION SYSTEMS

We have now explained some of the general approaches that organizations follow when building systems in-house with their own IS staff. Many times, however, this is not a feasible solution. The following are four situations in which you might need to consider alternative development strategies.

- ***Situation 1: Limited IS Staff.*** Often, an organization does not have the capability to build a system itself. Perhaps its development staff is small or deployed on other activities and does not have the capability to take on an in-house development project.
- ***Situation 2: IS Staff Has Limited Skill Set.*** In other situations, the IS staff may not have the skills needed to develop a particular kind of system. This has been especially true with the explosive growth of the Web and mobile devices; many organizations are having outside groups develop and manage their Web sites and mobile apps.

WHEN THINGS GO WRONG

Conquering Computer Contagion

Blue Security, an Israel-based Internet security company startup, thought it had the answer to spammers. For every unwanted spam message that the half million clients of the company's e-mail service, Blue Frog, received, a message was returned to the advertiser. As a result, 6 of the top 10 spammers were inundated by the opt-out messages and were forced to eliminate Blue Frog's clients from their mailing list. One spamming company, however, decided to fight back. According to Blue Security, PharmaMaster responded by sending so many spam messages to Blue Frog's clients that several Internet service providers' servers crashed. Under PharmaMaster's threat of continuing and expanded attacks, Blue Security folded after a mere two weeks. "We cannot take the responsibility for an ever-escalating cyberwar through our continued operations," said Eran Reshef, chief executive officer (CEO) and founder of Blue Security.

Like PharmaMaster, all authors of malware have continued to flout efforts to cleanse the Internet of their disruptive and exasperating wares. As the Internet evolves, so have the approaches taken by attackers; Table 9.7 lists the top malware issues of 2014. Unfortunately, the battle against malware will probably rage as long as the Internet exists.

Based on:

Anonymous. (2014). Security threat report 2014: Smarter, shadier, stealthier malware. *Sophos.com*. Retrieved March 20, 2014, from http://www.sophos.com/en-us/medialibrary/PDFs/other/sophos-security-threat-report-2014.pdf.

Lemos, R. (2006, May 17). Blue Security folds under spammer's wrath. *SecurityFocus*. Retrieved March 20, 2014, from http://www.securityfocus.com/news/11392.

TABLE 9.7 Top Malware Issues for 2014

Rank	Issue	Description
1	Botnets Grow	Botnets are becoming more widespread, resilient, and camouflaged.
2	Android-Based Malware	Android malware continues to grow and evolve.
3	Linux Is Attracting Criminals	Linux is a targeted platform because it is widely used to run Web sites.
4	Mac OS X Attacks	Mostly ignored in the past, a steady stream of modest, creative, and diverse attacks are being launched.
5	Web-Based Malware Matures	Dangerous, difficult-to-detect Web server attacks, leading to more drive-by attacks against vulnerable Web clients.
6	Targeting Financial Accounts	More persistent attacks aimed at compromising financial accounts.
7	Windows XP	In 2014, Windows XP and Office 2003 were no longer updated, creating significant issues in specialized markets such as point-of-sale and medical equipment.
8	Spam Evolves	Spammers continue to reinvent their attacks to overcome blocking.

- ***Situation 3: IS Staff Is Overworked.*** In some organizations, the IS staff may simply not have the time to work on all the systems that the organization requires or wants.
- ***Situation 4: Problems with Performance of IS Staff.*** Earlier in this book, we discussed how and why systems development projects could sometimes be risky. Often, the efforts of IS departments are derailed because of staff turnover, changing requirements, shifts in technology, or budget constraints. Regardless of the reason, the result is the same: another failed (or flawed) system.

When it isn't possible or advantageous to develop a system in-house, organizations are pursuing two popular options:

1. External acquisition of a prepackaged system
2. Outsourcing systems development

These options are examined next.

External Acquisition

Purchasing an existing system from an outside vendor such as IBM, HP Enterprise Services, or Accenture is referred to as **external acquisition**. How does external acquisition of an information system work? Think about the process that you might use when buying a car. Do you simply walk into the first dealership you see, tell them you need a car, and see what they try to sell you? You had better not. Probably you have done some upfront analysis and know how much money you can afford to spend and what your needs are. If you have done your homework, you probably have an idea of what you want and which dealership can provide the type of car you desire.

This upfront analysis of your needs can be extremely helpful in narrowing your options and can save you a lot of time. Understanding your needs can also help you sift through the salespeople's hype that you are likely to encounter from one dealer to the next as each tries to sell you on why his or her model is perfect for you. After getting some information, you may want to take a couple of promising models for a test-drive, actually getting behind the wheel to see how well the car fits you and your driving habits. You might even talk to other people who have owned this type of car to see how they feel about it. Ultimately, you are the one who has to evaluate all the different cars to see which one is best for you. They may all be good cars; however, one may fit your needs just a little better than the others.

The external acquisition of an information system is very similar to the purchase of a car. When you acquire a new system, you should do some analysis of your specific needs. For example, how much can you afford to spend, what basic functionality is required, and approximately how many people will use the system? Next, you can begin to "shop" for the new system by asking potential vendors to provide information about the systems that they have to offer. After you evaluate this information, it may become clear that several vendors have systems that are worth considering. You may ask those vendors to come to your organization and set up their systems so that you and your colleagues are able to "test-drive" them (Figure 9.22). Seeing how people react to the systems and seeing how each system performs in the organizational environment can help you "see" exactly what you are buying. By seeing the actual system and how it performs with real users, with real or simulated data, you can get a much clearer idea of whether that system fits your needs. When you take a car for a test-drive, you learn how the car meets your needs. By seeing how the system meets your needs before you buy, you can greatly reduce the risk associated with acquiring that system.

STEPS IN EXTERNAL ACQUISITION. In many cases, your organization will use a competitive bid process for making an external acquisition. In the competitive bid process, vendors are given an opportunity to propose systems that meet the organization's needs. The goal of the competitive process is to help the organization ensure that it gets the best system at the lowest possible price. Most competitive external acquisition processes have at least five general steps:

1. Systems planning and selection
2. Systems analysis
3. Development of a request for proposal

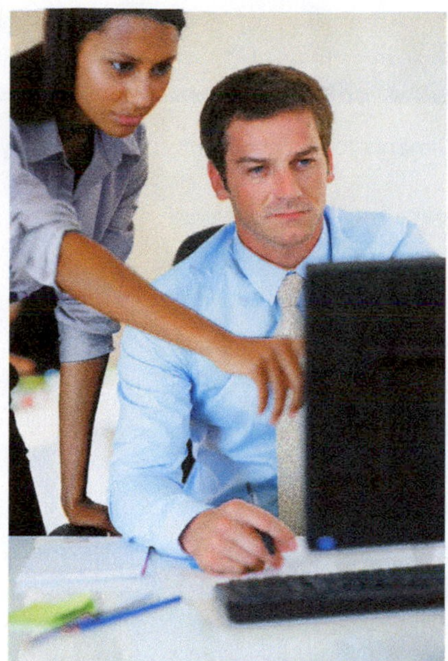

FIGURE 9.22

Taking software for a "test-drive" prior to purchase.
Source: Yuri Arcurs/Fotolia.

4. Proposal evaluation
5. Vendor selection

You have already learned about the first two steps because they apply when you build a system yourself as well as when you purchase a system through an external vendor. Step 3, development of a request for proposal, is where the external acquisition process differs significantly from in-house development.

DEVELOPMENT OF A REQUEST FOR PROPOSAL. A **request for proposal (RFP)** is simply a document that is used to tell vendors what your requirements are and to invite them to provide information about how they might be able to meet those requirements. An RFP is sent to vendors who might potentially be interested in providing hardware and/or software for the system.

Among the areas that may be covered in an RFP are the following:

- A summary of existing systems and applications
- Requirements for system performance and features
- Reliability, backup, and service requirements
- The criteria that will be used to evaluate proposals
- Timetable and budget constraints (how much you can spend)

The RFP is then sent to prospective vendors along with an invitation to present their bids for the project. Eventually, you will likely receive a number of proposals to evaluate. If, on the other hand, you do not receive many proposals, it may be necessary to rethink the requirements—perhaps the requirements are greater than the budget limitations or the time frame is too short. In some situations, you may first need to send out a preliminary request for information simply to gather information from prospective vendors. This will help you determine whether, indeed, the desired system is feasible or even possible. If you determine that it is, you can then send out an RFP. Often, rather than trying to identify all potential vendors and sending out RFPs, companies set up a project Web site, allowing potential bidders to find out more about the organization and its current and planned information systems (Figure 9.23).

PROPOSAL EVALUATION. The fourth step in external acquisition is to evaluate proposals received from vendors. This evaluation may include viewing system demonstrations, evaluating the performance of those systems, examining criteria important to the organization, and judging how the proposed systems "stack up" to those criteria. Demonstrations are a good way to get a feel for the different systems' capabilities. Just as you can go to the showroom to look at a new car and get a feel for whether it meets your needs, it is also possible to screen various

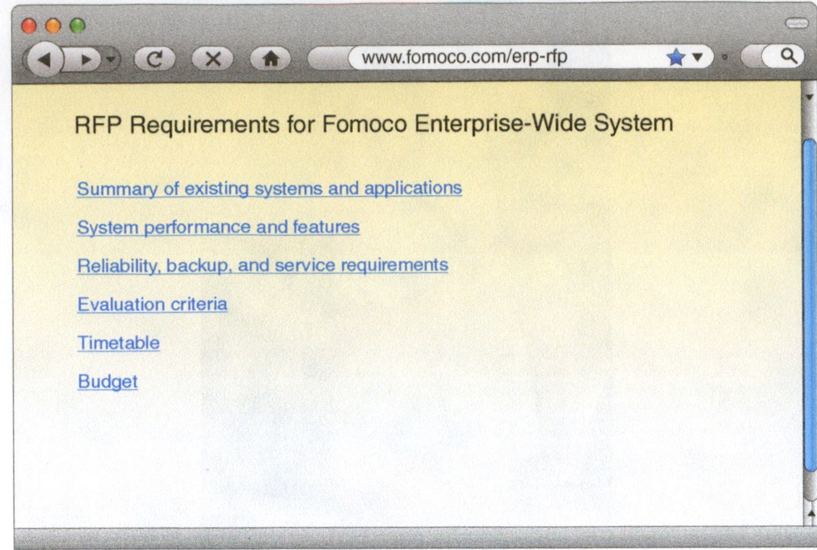

FIGURE 9.23
Sample RFP Web site for an information systems project.

systems through a demonstration from the vendor. During a demonstration, a sales team from the vendor gives an oral presentation about the system, its features and cost, followed by a demonstration of the actual system. Although such demonstrations are often useful in helping you understand the features of different systems being proposed, they are rarely enough in and of themselves to warrant purchasing the system without further evaluation.

One of the methods you can use to evaluate a proposed system is **systems benchmarking**, which is the use of standardized performance tests to facilitate comparison between systems. Benchmark programs are sample programs or jobs that simulate a system's workload. You can have benchmarks designed to test portions of the system that are most critical to your needs, based on your systems analysis. A benchmark might test how long it takes to calculate a set of numbers, how long it takes to access a set of records in a database, or how long it would take to access certain information given a certain number of concurrent users. Some common system benchmarks include the following:

- Response time given a specified number of users
- Time to sort records
- Time to retrieve a set of records
- Time to produce a given report
- Time to read in a set of data

In addition, vendors may also supply benchmarks that you can use, although you should not rely solely on vendor information. For popular systems, you may be able to rely on system benchmarks published in computer trade journals such as *PC Magazine* or on industry Web sites, such as www.cnet.com. However, in most cases, demos and benchmarks alone do not provide all the information you need to make a purchase. The systems analysis phase should have revealed some specific requirements for the new system. These requirements may be listed as criteria that the organization can use to further evaluate vendor proposals. Depending on what you are purchasing—hardware, software, or both—the criteria you use will change. Table 9.8 provides examples of commonly used evaluation criteria.

VENDOR SELECTION. In most cases, more than one system will meet your needs, just as more than one car will usually meet your needs. However, some probably "fit" better than others. In these cases, you should have a way of prioritizing or ranking competing proposals. One way of doing this is by devising a scoring system for each of the criteria and benchmarking results as described when making the business case.

Companies may use other, less formalized approaches to evaluate vendors. Sometimes they use simple checklists; other times they use a more subjective process. Regardless of the mechanism, eventually a company completes the evaluation stage and selects a vendor, ending the external acquisition process.

TABLE 9.8 Commonly Used Evaluation Criteria

Hardware Criteria	Software Criteria	Other Criteria
Clock speed of CPU	Memory requirements	Installation
Memory availability	Help features	Testing
Secondary storage (including capacity, access time, and so on)	Usability	Price
	Learnability	
Video display size	Number of features supported	
Printer speed	Training and documentation	
	Maintenance and repair	

MANAGING SOFTWARE LICENSING. When purchasing commercial, off-the-shelf software, companies usually have to agree to a license agreement. In general, software licenses can be classified based on their restrictiveness or the freedom they offer to use or modify the software. Software licensing has been a hot-button topic for software companies as they lose billions in piracy and mislicensed customers (see Chapter 10). Traditionally, software licensing is defined as the permissions and rights that are imposed on applications; the use of software without a proper license is illegal in most countries.

Most software licenses differ in terms of restrictiveness, ranging from no restrictions at all to completely restricted. Note that although freeware or shareware is freely available, the copyright owners often retain their rights and do not provide access to the program's source code. For organizations using proprietary software, two types of licenses are of special importance. The first type includes the **shrink-wrap licenses** and **click-wrap licenses** that accompany the software, which are used primarily for generic, off-the-shelf application and systems software. The shrink-wrapped contract has been named as such because the contract is activated when the shrink wrap on the packaging has been removed; similarly, a click-wrap license refers to a license primarily used for downloaded software that requires computer users to click on "I accept" before installing the software. The second type of license is an **enterprise license** (also known as a **volume license**). Enterprise licenses can vary greatly and are usually negotiated. In addition to rights and permissions, enterprise licenses usually contain limitations of liability and warranty disclaimers that protect the software vendor from being sued if its software does not operate as expected.

As shown in Table 9.9, there are a variety of software licenses. For different business needs, organizations often depend on a variety of software, each having different licenses, which can cause headaches for many organizations. For organizations, not knowing about the software installed can have a variety of consequences. For example, companies are not able to negotiate volume licensing options, unused licenses strain the organization's budget, or license violations can lead to fines or public embarrassment. **Software asset management** helps organizations to avoid such negative consequences. Usually, software asset management consists of a set of activities, such as performing a software inventory (either manually or using automated tools), matching the installed software with the licenses, reviewing software-related policies and procedures, and creating a software asset management plan. The results of these processes help organizations to better manage their software infrastructure by being able to consolidate and standardize their software titles, decide to retire unused software, or decide when to upgrade or replace software.

EXTERNAL ACQUISITION THROUGH THE CLOUD. Undoubtedly, managing the software infrastructure is a complex task, often resulting in high operating costs for organizations; further, many systems are not scalable in response to large increases in demand. To deal with these issues, business organizations increasingly use software as a service (SaaS)—that is, clients access applications in the cloud on an as-needed basis using standard Web-enabled interfaces (see Chapter 3, "Managing the Information Systems Infrastructure and Services"). For organizations, using SaaS provides a variety of benefits, such as a reduced need to maintain or upgrade software, variable costs based on the actual use of the services (rather

TABLE 9.9 Different Types of Software Licenses

Restrictiveness	Software Types	Rights	Restrictions	Examples
Full rights	Public domain software	Full rights	No restrictions; owner forsakes copyright	Different programs for outdated IBM mainframes
	Non-protective open source (e.g., Berkeley software development [BSD] license)	Freedom to copy, modify, and redistribute the software; can be incorporated into a commercial product	Creator retains copyright	Free BSD operating system; BSD components in (proprietary) Mac OS X operating system
	Protective open source (e.g., general public license [GPL])	Freedom to copy, modify, and redistribute the software	Modified or redistributed software must be made available under the same license; cannot be incorporated into commercial product	Linux operating system
	Proprietary software	Right to run the software (for licensed users)	Access to source code severely restricted; no rights to copy or modify software	Windows operating system
No rights	Trade secret	Software typically only used internally	Access to source code severely restricted; software is not distributed outside the organization	Google PageRank™ algorithm

than fixed IS costs), and the ability to rely on a provider that has gained considerable expertise because of a large number of clients.

Outsourcing Systems Development

Outsourcing systems development is a way to acquire new systems that closely resembles the process of in-house development. However, in the case of outsourcing, the responsibility for some or all of an organization's information systems development (and potentially the day-to-day management of its operation) is turned over to an outside firm. Information systems outsourcing includes a variety of working relationships. The outside firm, or service provider, may develop your information systems applications and house them within their organization; they may run your applications on their computers; or they may develop systems to run on existing computers within your organization. Anything is fair game in an outsourcing arrangement. Today, outsourcing has become a big business and is a very popular option for many organizations (see Chapter 1 for more information on outsourcing).

WHY OUTSOURCING? A firm might outsource some (or all) of its information systems services for varied reasons. Some of these are old reasons, but some are new to today's environment (Applegate, Austin, & Soule, 2009):

- ***Cost and Quality Concerns.*** In many cases it is possible to achieve higher-quality systems at a lower price through economies of scale, better management of hardware, lower labor costs, and better software licenses on the part of a service provider.
- ***Problems in IS Performance.*** IS departments may have problems meeting acceptable service standards because of cost overruns, delayed systems, underutilized systems, or poorly performing systems. In such cases, organizational management may attempt to increase reliability through outsourcing.
- ***Supplier Pressures.*** Perhaps not surprisingly, some of the largest service providers are also the largest suppliers of software or computer equipment (e.g., IBM or Hewlett-Packard). In some cases, the aggressive sales forces of these suppliers are able to convince senior managers at other organizations to outsource their IS functions.

- ***Simplifying, Downsizing, and Reengineering.*** Organizations under competitive pressure often attempt to focus on only their "core competencies." In many cases, organizations simply decide that running information systems is not one of their core competencies and decide to outsource this function to companies such as IBM and HP Enterprise Services, whose primary competency is developing and maintaining information systems.
- ***Financial Factors.*** When firms turn over their information systems to a service provider, they can sometimes strengthen their balance sheets by liquidating their IT assets. Also, if users perceive that they are actually paying for their IT services rather than simply having them provided by an in-house staff, they may use those services more wisely and perceive them to be of greater value.
- ***Organizational Culture.*** Political or organizational problems are often difficult for an IS group to overcome. However, an external service provider often brings enough clout, devoid of any organizational or functional ties, to streamline IS operations as needed.
- ***Internal Irritants.*** Tensions between end users and the IS staff are sometimes difficult to eliminate. At times this tension can intrude on the daily operations of the organization, and the idea of a remote, external, relatively neutral IS group can be appealing. Whether the tensions between users and the IS staff (or service provider) are really eliminated is open to question; however, simply having the IS group external to the organization can remove a lingering thorn in management's side.

MANAGING THE IS OUTSOURCING RELATIONSHIP. The ongoing management of an outsourcing alliance is the single most important aspect of the outsourcing project's success. Some advice includes the following:

1. A strong, active chief information officer (CIO) and staff should continually manage the legal and professional relationship with the outsourcing firm.
2. Clear, realistic performance measurements of the systems and of the outsourcing arrangement, such as tangible and intangible costs and benefits, should be developed.
3. The interface between the customer and the outsourcer should have multiple levels (e.g., links to deal with policy and relationship issues and links to deal with operational and tactical issues).

Managing outsourcing alliances in this way has important implications for the success of the relationship. For example, in addition to making sure a firm has a strong CIO and staff, McFarlan and Nolan (1995) recommend that firms assign full-time relationship managers and coordinating groups lower in the organization to "manage" the project. The structure and nature of the internal system activities change from exclusively building and managing systems to also including managing relationships with outside firms that build and manage systems under legal contract.

NOT ALL OUTSOURCING RELATIONSHIPS ARE THE SAME. Most organizations no longer enter into a strictly legal contract with an outsourcing vendor but rather into a mutually beneficial relationship with a strategic partner. In such a relationship, both the firm and the vendor are concerned with—and perhaps have a direct stake in—the success of the other. Yet other types of relationships exist, meaning that not all outsourcing agreements need to be structured the same way. In fact, at least three different types of outsourcing relationships can be identified:

- Basic relationship
- Preferred relationship
- Strategic relationship

A basic relationship can best be thought of as a "cash-and-carry" relationship in which you buy products and services on the basis of price and convenience. Organizations should try to have a few preferred relationships in which the buyer and the supplier set preferences and prices to the benefit of each other. For example, a supplier can provide preferred pricing to customers that do a specified volume of business. Most organizations have just a few strategic relationships in which both sides share risks and rewards.

INDUSTRY ANALYSIS

Broadcasting

Only a few years ago, radio and television were among the primary sources for satisfying the desire for both entertainment and up-to-date news and information. Over the past few years, this situation has changed dramatically, with many people turning to the Internet for both information and entertainment.

For many television news companies, the Internet has opened opportunities, as news features can be easily transmitted over the Internet, allowing easier connection between the newsrooms and the "action" on the field. At the same time, viewing habits have changed, and many viewers prefer to obtain their latest news via the Internet or while on the move. As a reaction, television stations (both focusing on news and entertainment) are increasingly using the Internet as a distribution medium for their content.

These changes force TV stations to adjust their revenue models. Whereas traditionally large revenues were derived from TV advertising, advertisers are now less willing to pay high advertising fees in light of dwindling viewership. On the other hand, TV stations can potentially charge more for advertising tied to online shows, as the Internet offers benefits such as advertising targeted at the individual viewer and provides detailed tracking metrics such as click-through rates, allowing the advertiser to directly assess the success of a campaign.

For radio stations, the situation is similar. With more and more people listening to various Internet radio stations, using music services like Pandora or Spotify, or downloading music, the number of listeners to traditional radio has dwindled and along with it advertising revenues. Online advertising now surpasses radio advertising spending. Facing competition from Internet radio, satellite radio, podcasting, and a plethora of other online diversions, many radio stations will have to find innovative ways to prosper in these times of profound change.

Questions

1. What is the effect of the Internet on television and radio content quality? With less advertising revenue, how can broadcasters continue to produce high-quality content?
2. Today there are thousands of AM/FM stations competing with Internet radio stations and music downloading. Forecast their future and provide a strategy for retaining and gaining market share.

Based on:

eMarketer. (2014, February 12). Music listeners pump up the volume on digital radio. *eMarketer.* Retrieved April 1, 2014, from http://www.emarketer.com/Article/Music-Listeners-Pump-Up-Volume-on-Digital-Radio/1010600.

Leggett, T. (2014, January 3). Is niche Internet television broadcasting the future? *BBC.com.* Retrieved April 1, 2014, from http://www.bbc.com/news/business-25457001.

Rose, A. (2013, May 1). Exploring the connected future of TV and the challenge to broadcasters. *The Guardian.* Retrieved April 1, 2014, from http://www.theguardian.com/media-network/2013/may/01/connected-tv-broadcasters.

Venturini, F., Marshall, C., & Di Alberto, E. (2011). The future of broadcasting III: Strategy delivers. *Accenture.* Retrieved April 1, 2014, from http://www.accenture.com/SiteCollectionDocuments/PDF/Accenture-Future-of-Broadcasting-III-Strategy-Delivers.pdf.

Key Points Review

1. ***Describe how to formulate and present the business case for technology investments.*** Making the business case is the process of building and presenting the set of arguments that show that an information system investment is adding value to an organization. In order to make a convincing presentation, you should be specific about the benefits this investment will provide for the organization. Choosing the wrong measures can yield a negative decision about a beneficial system.
2. ***Describe the systems development life cycle and its various phases.*** The development of information systems follows a process called the systems development life cycle. The SDLC is a process that first identifies the need for a system and then defines the processes for designing, developing, and maintaining an information system. The process is very structured and formal and requires the active involvement of managers and users. The SDLC has four phases: systems planning and selection, systems analysis, systems design, and systems implementation and operation. A variety of other approaches are available to enhance the development process for different types of systems and contexts.
3. ***Explain how organizations acquire systems via external acquisition and outsourcing.*** External acquisition is the process of purchasing an existing information system from an external organization or vendor. External acquisition is a five-step process. Steps 1 and 2 mirror the first two steps of the SDLC. Step 3 is the development of a request for proposal (RFP). Step 4 is proposal evaluation, which focuses on evaluating proposals received from vendors. Step 5 is vendor selection, which focuses on choosing the vendor to provide the system. Outsourcing refers to the turning over of partial or entire responsibility for information systems development and management to an outside organization.

Key Terms

adaptive maintenance 342
alpha testing 340
beta testing 340
break-even analysis 326
change request management 342
click-wrap license 349
corrective maintenance 342
cost–benefit analysis 326
data flows 337
developmental testing 340
discount rate 326
enterprise license 349
external acquisition 346
human–computer interface (HCI) 339
information systems planning 335
intangible benefit 325
intangible cost 325
joint application design (JAD) 336
making the business case 320
net-present-value analysis 326
non-recurring cost 325
open source software 332
patch management system 343
perfective maintenance 342
preventive maintenance 342
processing logic 337
productivity paradox 321
project manager 334
prototyping 344
proxy variable 329
pseudocode 337
recurring cost 325
request for proposal (RFP) 347
requirements collection 336
shrink-wrap license 349
software asset management 349
system conversion 340
systems analysis 336
systems analysis and design 330
systems analyst 330
systems benchmarking 348
systems design 337
systems development life cycle (SDLC) 334
systems implementation 340
systems maintenance 341
systems planning and selection 335
tangible benefit 325
tangible cost 325
total cost of ownership (TCO) 325
usability 339
volume license 349
weighted multicriteria analysis 326

Go to **mymislab.com** to complete the problems marked with this icon .

Review Questions

9-1. Describe the productivity paradox.

9-2. Describe how to make a successful business case, contrasting faith-, fear-, and fact-based arguments.

9-3. Compare and contrast tangible and intangible benefits and costs.

9-4. What are the four phases of the systems development life cycle (SDLC)?

9-5. List and describe five techniques used in requirements collection.

9-6. What are the three major components/tasks of the systems design phase of the SDLC?

9-7. What are the four options for system conversion? How do they differ from each other?

9-8. Compare and contrast the four types of systems maintenance.

9-9. Define outsourcing and list three general types of outsourcing relationships.

9-10. List and describe two main types of software licenses.

Self-Study Questions

9-11. Which of the following is not one of the four phases of the systems development life cycle?
A. systems analysis
B. systems implementation
C. systems design
D. systems resource acquisition

9-12. ______________ is the process of gathering and organizing information from users, managers, business processes, and documents to understand how a proposed information system should function.
A. Requirements collection
B. Systems collection
C. Systems analysis
D. Records archiving

9-13. Which of the following is the correct order of phases in the systems development life cycle?
A. analysis, planning, design, implementation
B. analysis, design, planning, implementation
C. planning, analysis, design, implementation
D. design, analysis, planning, implementation

9-14. In the systems design phase, the elements that must be designed when building an information system include all of the following except ______________.
A. the human–computer interface
B. questionnaires
C. databases and files
D. processing and logic

9-15. ______________ maintenance involves making enhancements to improve processing performance or interface usability or adding desired (but not necessarily required) system features (in other words, "bells and whistles").
A. preventive
B. perfective
C. corrective
D. adaptive

9-16. Which of the following is not one of the three types of arguments commonly made in the business case for an information system?
A. fear
B. fact
C. faith
D. fun

9-17. A ______________ is a document that an organization uses to tell vendors what its requirements are and to invite them to provide information about how they might be able to meet those requirements.
A. request letter
B. vendor request
C. request for proposal
D. requirements specification

9-18. Which of the following is not a type of outsourcing?
A. basic
B. elite
C. strategic
D. preferred

9-19. Which of the following factors is a good reason to outsource?
A. problems in IS performance
B. supplier pressures
C. financial factors
D. all of the above

9-20. Most competitive external acquisition processes have at least five general steps. Which of the following is not one of those steps?
A. vendor selection
B. proposal evaluation
C. development of a request for proposal
D. implementation

Answers are on page 356.

Problems and Exercises

9-21. Match the following terms with the appropriate definitions:

i. Request for proposal
ii. Systems benchmarking
iii. Alpha testing
iv. Systems development life cycle
v. Productivity paradox
vi. Prototyping
vii. Pilot conversion
viii. Systems analysis
ix. Outsourcing
x. External acquisition
xi. Data flows
xii. Requirements collection

a. The movement of data through an organization or within an information system
b. Term that describes the life of an information system from conception to retirement
c. The second phase of the systems development life cycle
d. The process of gathering and organizing information from users, managers, business processes, and documents to understand how a proposed information system should function
e. Testing performed by the development organization to assess whether the entire system meets the design requirements of the users
f. Using a new system in one location before rolling it out to the entire organization
g. A systems development methodology that uses a trial-and-error approach for discovering how a system should operate
h. The practice of turning over responsibility for some or all of an organization's information systems development and operations to an outside firm
i. The observation that productivity increases at a rate that is lower than expected when new technologies are introduced
j. The process of purchasing an existing system from an outside vendor
k. A way to evaluate a proposed system by testing a portion of it with the system workload
l. A report that is used to tell vendors what the requirements are and to invite them to provide information about how they might be able to meet those requirements

9-22. After reading this chapter, it should be fairly obvious why an IS professional should be able to make a business case for a given system. Why, however, is it just as important for non-IS professionals? How are they involved in this process? What is their role in making IS investment decisions?

9-23. Why can it be difficult to develop an accurate cost–benefit analysis? What factors may be difficult to quantify? How can this be handled? Is this something that should just be avoided altogether? What are the consequences of that approach?

9-24. Contrast the total cost of acquisition versus the total cost of ownership for the purchase of a new car. Demonstrate how the type of car, year, make, model, and so on change the values of various types of costs and benefits.

9-25. Identify and describe three different situations where fear, faith, or fact arguments would be most compelling when making an information systems investment decision.

9-26. Contrast the differing perspectives of different stakeholders involved in making information systems investment decisions.

9-27. Explain the differences between data and data flows. How might systems analysts obtain the information they need to generate the data flows of a system? How are these data flows and the accompanying processing logic used in the system design phase of the life cycle? What happens when the data and data flows are modeled incorrectly?

9-28. When Microsoft posts a new version of Internet Explorer on its Web site and states that this is a beta version, what does it mean? Is this a final working version of the software, or is it still being tested? Who is doing the testing? Search the Web to find other companies that have beta versions of their products available to the public. You might try Corel (www.corel.com) or Adobe (www.adobe.com). What other companies did you find?

9-29. Conduct a search on the Web for "systems development life cycle." Check out some of the hits. Compare them with the SDLC outlined in this discussion. Do all these life cycles follow the same general path? How many phases do the ones you found on the Web contain? Is the terminology the same or different? Prepare a 10-minute presentation to the class on your findings.

9-30. Choose an organization with which you are familiar that develops its own information systems. Does this organization follow an SDLC? If not, why not? If so, how many phases does it have? Who developed this life cycle? Was it someone within the company, or was the life cycle adopted from somewhere else?

9-31. Describe your experiences with information systems that were undergoing changes or updates. What kind of conversion procedure was being used? How did this affect your interaction with the system as a user? Who else was affected? If the system was down altogether, for how long was it down? Do you or any of your classmates have horror stories, or were the situations not that bad?

9-32. Find an organization on the Internet (e.g., at www.computerworld.com or www.infoworld.com) or a company you may want to work for in the future that outsources work. What are the managerial challenges of outsourcing, and why is this a popular alternative to hiring additional staff?

9-33. Imagine that you have just been hired by an organization, and you have been tasked with purchasing 10 tablet computers. Compile a list of at least three criteria you will use to evaluate at least three alternatives using weighted multicriteria analysis. Make a purchase recommendation based on your analysis.

Application Exercises

Note: The existing data files referenced in these exercises are available on the book's Web site: www.pearsonhighered.com/valacich.

Spreadsheet Application: Outsourcing Information Systems at Campus Travel

9-34. Campus Travel wants to increase its customer focus and wants to be able to better serve its most valued customers. Many members of the frequent flier program have requested the ability to check on the status of their membership online; furthermore, the frequent fliers would welcome the opportunity to book reward flights online. As you know that there are a number of companies specializing in building such transactional systems, you have decided to outsource the development of such a system. The following weights are assigned to evaluate the different vendors' systems:

- Online booking capability: 20 percent
- User friendliness: 25 percent
- Maximum number of concurrent users: 20 percent
- Integration with current systems: 10 percent
- Vendor support: 10 percent
- Price: 15 percent

To evaluate the different offers, you need to calculate a weighted score for each vendor using the data provided in the Outsourcing.csv spreadsheet. To calculate the total points for each vendor, do the following:

- Open the file Outsourcing.csv.
- Use the SUMPRODUCT formula to multiply each vendor's scores with the respective weights and add the weighted scores.
- Use conditional formatting to highlight all vendors falling below a total of 60 percent and above a total of 85 percent to facilitate the vendor selection.

Database Application: Building a Special Needs Database for Campus Travel

9-35. In addition to international travel, travel reservations for people with special needs is an area of specialty of Campus Travel. However, to be able to recommend travel destinations and travel activities, you should know what facilities are available at each destination. Therefore, you have been asked to create a database of the destinations and the type of facilities that are available for people with special needs. In order to make the system as useful as possible for all, you need to design reports for the users to retrieve information about each destination. Your manager would like to have a system that contains the following information about the destinations:

- Location
- Availability of facilities for the physically handicapped
- Distance to medical facilities
- Pet friendliness

Each location may have one or more handicap facility (e.g., hearing, walking, sight, and so on). A type of handicap facility can be present at multiple locations. Also, each location has to have one pet-friendly accommodation/activity and may also have accommodation for different types of pets (dogs, cats, and so on). After designing the database, please design three professionally formatted reports that (1) list the locations in alphabetical order, (2) list all locations that have the handicap facilities for those that find it difficult to walk, and (3) list all locations that have a cat-friendly policy.

Hint: In Microsoft Access, you can create queries before preparing the reports. Enter a few sample data sets and print out the reports.

Team Work Exercise

Net Stats: Moore's Law and the Laggards

The technology industry, laboring under Moore's law, depends on technology users to regularly adopt new hardware and software. Millions of users, however, accustomed to the tried and true, would rather stick with those products they know—at least as long as possible. Sometimes the reason for not rushing to replace the old with the new is familiarity with and an acquired expertise in using the older version of a product or service:

- In September 2013, 70 percent of U.S. households had broadband Internet access, but 3 percent still used dialup; that is over 2.5 million people.
- In January 2014, 10 percent of U.S. adults had not yet purchased a mobile phone.
- In March 2014, worldwide, hundreds of millions of people were still using Windows XP, even though Microsoft officially ended support for this product. By February 2014, Windows 7 had 47 percent of the desktop market share; Windows XP, initially released in 2001, still retained nearly 30 percent of the market share!

Individual computer users are free to opt to be tortoises or hares regarding the adoption of new technology. Information technology (IT) directors, however, must usually follow company culture and management preferences when opting whether to adopt new technology. If management is comfortable with risk and likes to be on the cutting edge, for example, IT directors can probably feel safe in adopting new technology early on. A staid, risk-averse management attitude, however, would probably not appreciate an IT director who rushes to adopt new technology. In any event, whether to adopt new technology immediately as it becomes available is a decision that will always be with us.

Questions and Exercises

9-36. In 2014, 58 percent of Americans owned a smartphone; search the Web for the most up-to-date statistics on this technology.

9-37. As a team, interpret the changes in numbers (or stories). What is striking/important about these findings?

9-38. As a team, discuss what these numbers will look like in 5 years and 10 years. How are things in the U.S. market the same or different across the world? Where are things moving faster/slower? Why?

9-39. Using your spreadsheet software of choice, create a graph/figure most effectively visualizing the finding you consider most important.

Based on:

Anonymous. (n.d.). Broadband technology fact sheet. *Pew Research.* Retrieved March 20, 2014, from http://www.pewinternet.org/fact-sheets/broadband-technology-fact-sheet.

Anonymous. (n.d.). Mobile technology fact sheet. *Pew Research.* Retrieved March 20, 2014, from http://www.pewinternet.org/fact-sheets/mobile-technology-fact-sheet.

Endler, M. (2014, March 17). Windows XP holdouts: 6 top excuses. *Information Week.com.* Retrieved on March 20, 2014, from http://www.informationweek.com/software/operating-systems/windows-xp-holdouts-6-top-excuses/d/d-id/1127666.

Kooser, A (2013, August 26). 3 percent of American adults still cling to dial-up Internet. *Cnet.com.* Retrieved on March 20, 2014, from http://news.cnet.com/8301-17938_105-57600112-1/3-percent-of-american-adults-still-cling-to-dial-up-internet.

Usage share of operating systems. (2014, March 18). In *Wikipedia, The Free Encyclopedia.* Retrieved March 20, 2014, from http://en.wikipedia.org/w/index.php?title=Usage_share_of_operating_systems&oldid=600217105.

Answers to the Self-Study Questions

9-11. D, p. 334	**9-12.** A, p. 336	**9-13.** C, p. 334	**9-14.** B, p. 337	**9-15.** B, p. 342
9-16. D, p. 322	**9-17.** C, p. 347	**9-18.** B, p. 351	**9-19.** D, p. 350	**9-20.** D, p. 346

CASE 1 Next Generation Identification: FBI, ICE Databases Expand and Join Forces

As crime-solving aids, first there was fingerprinting; decades later came DNA analysis. Next is the US$1.2 billion "Next Generation Identification" (NGI) database of the Federal Bureau of Investigation (FBI), used to store biometric identification ranging from palm prints to iris patterns, photos of scars and tattoos, and distinctive facial characteristics for criminal identification. In the past, fingerprints have been the most widely used means of uniquely identifying people, with the FBI keeping over 100 million sets of fingerprints in its current database dubbed "Integrated Automated Fingerprint Identification System" (IAFIS). The next step includes storing additional biometric characteristics. Unfortunately, taken alone, many of those have been proven to be rather unreliable (facial recognition accuracy in public places can be as low as 10 to 20 percent, depending on lighting conditions), such that a real increase in identification accuracy can come only from combining the results of multiple biometrics.

Similar to the FBI's IAFIS database, the Department of Homeland Security (DHS) maintains the massive "Automated Biometric Identification System" (IDENT) database. The Immigration and Customs Enforcement Agency (ICE), part of the DHS, uses this database in its "Secure Communities" initiative to aid in capturing criminal aliens. The Secure Communities program is a federal, state, and local government partnership that allows state and local law enforcement officials to quickly share information with ICE on captured suspects. The data forwarded to ICE are used to make immigration processing and removing more efficient if the suspect turns out to be a criminal alien. At the heart of the Secure Communities program is the automatic integration of the IAFIS and IDENT databases. When someone is arrested, local law enforcement puts the suspect's fingerprints into the FBI's database. However, the fingerprints are not only checked against the FBI's IAFIS system, but also against the DHS' IDENT database to see if the suspect is in the country legally. If the suspect isn't legal, ICE can immediately begin the deportation process. The system also prioritizes removal of criminal aliens based on their risk to national security and the local community. The prioritization helps ensure that serious criminals (aliens or otherwise) are not inadvertently released and cuts down on the time criminal aliens must be held in custody before being returned to their home country. Since its deployment (2009–2013), nearly 32 million queries into the database have been made, with 1.7 million matches, leading to more 300,000 deportations. The FBI's Next Generation Identification database will take this a step further, as it will not only be based on data from both existing databases, but will also include a host of other biometric identifiers.

Both the FBI and Secure Communities programs have been criticized by privacy advocates. Critics say that Secure Communities, for example, can lead to unnecessary or prolonged detention, make accessing a lawyer difficult, and prevent release on bail. There is also a fear that there is no complaint mechanism associated with the systems. Opponents believe that victims of system errors will have little redress if they are erroneously identified as a criminal or illegal alien. In addition, opponents to the Secure Communities program argue that the integration of databases undermines the trust between immigrant communities and local law enforcement agencies. Fearing that illegal immigrants may be dissuaded from reporting crimes or may not be willing to serve as witnesses, Washington, D.C., Mayor Vincent Gray announced in June 2012 that law enforcement officers would be prohibited from asking about people's immigration status.

While the FBI and ICE maintain that their programs are strictly limited to criminals and those in the country illegally, privacy and civil rights activists are watching the developments to ensure that the government respects the rights of its citizens.

Questions

9-40. List a set of tangible and intangible benefits as well as tangible and intangible costs for the FBI database system.

9-41. Develop a set of faith-, fear-, and fact-based arguments to support the continued and ongoing expansion of the FBI database. Which arguments do you think are the strongest? Why?

9-42. Some privacy advocates argue that biometric systems can become unreliable and single out innocent people, especially over time as these databases become less accurate because of a person's natural aging process, weight loss, weight gain, injury, or permanent disability. Discuss the problems associated with having these systems single out innocent people.

Based on:

American Immigration Council. (2011, November 29). Secure Communities: a fact sheet. *Immigrationpolicy.org*. Retrieved March 20, 2014, from http://www.immigrationpolicy.org/just-facts/secure-communities-fact-sheet.

Anonymous. (n.d.). Integrated Automated Fingerprint Identification System. *FBI.gov*. Retrieved on March 20, 2014, from http://www.fbi.gov/about-us/cjis/fingerprints_biometrics/iafis/iafis.

Howell, J. (2012, June 4). D.C. prepares to walk fine line on deportations. *The Washington Times*. Retrieved March 20, 2014, from http://www.washingtontimes.com/news/2012/jun/4/dc-prepares-to-walk-fine-line-on-deportations.

Integrated Automated Fingerprint Identification System. (2013, October 9). In *Wikipedia, The Free Encyclopedia*. Retrieved March 21, 2014, from http://en.wikipedia.org/w/index.php?title=Integrated_Automated_Fingerprint_Identification_System&oldid=576514800

Lynch, J. (2011, July 8). The FBI's Next Generation Identification: Bigger and faster but much worse for privacy. *Electronic Frontier Foundation*. Retrieved March 20, 2014, from https://www.eff.org/deeplinks/2011/07/fbis-next-generation-identification-database.

U.S. Immigrations and Customs Enforcement. (2012, June 5). Activated jurisdictions. Retrieved June 6, 2012, from http://www.ice.gov/doclib/secure-communities/pdf/sc-activated.pdf.

U.S. Immigrations and Customs Enforcement. (2013, September 30). Secure Communities IDENT/IAFIS interoperability monthly statistics through September 30, 2013. Retrieved March 20, 2014, from http://www.ice.gov/doclib/foia/sc-stats/nationwide_interop_stats-fy2013-to-date.pdf.

CASE 2 The Emergence of Open Source Software

You're probably well aware by now that some software, such as the Android mobile phone operating system and the Firefox browser, is *open source*. That is, creators of the programs made the source code available so that anyone could program changes to improve the software's performance.

Founded in 1998, the Open Source Initiative (OSI) is a non-profit organization dedicated to promoting open source software. The OSI formulated an *open source definition* to determine whether software can be considered for an open source license. An open source license is a copyright license for software that specifies that the source code is available for redistribution and modification without programmers having to pay the original author. Specifically, the open source definition includes the following:

- The software can be redistributed for free.
- Source code is freely available.
- Redistribution of modifications must be allowed.
- No one who wants to modify the code can be locked out.
- The use of the software cannot be restricted to certain uses.
- License may not be restricted to a specific product.

What has started as a communal, hacker-driven approach has matured, to a point where open source software is considered to be ready for prime time. Instead of merely being free or low-cost versions of proprietary software, many open source software projects are on the cutting edge, providing solutions that are secure and scalable enough for even the largest corporations. As a result, open source software is having an ever-expanding role in all areas of business. In part, the success of popular open source projects is based on the notion of a free ecosystem, where a large pool of contributors develops modifications, add-ons, or extensions, thus enhancing the value of the original project.

Open source, making use of the wisdom of the crowds, fuels some of the big IT megatrends, including cloud computing, mobile applications, and Big Data. For example, companies such as PayPal, Intel, and Comcast use OpenStack, an open source cloud computing platform, to host their private clouds.

Another megatrend fueled by open source is mobility; in particular, the Android operating system has made inroads into the mobile operating system market, now having the largest market share of all mobile phone operating systems. Building on the success of the Android operating system, Amazon even based Fire OS, the operating system for its popular Kindle Fire HDX tablet, on Android.

Finally, open source projects have become indispensable for Big Data initiatives ranging from storing and managing vast amounts of unstructured data to analyzing these data. Not only do open source applications provide the tools to deal with Big Data, the openness of the source code also helps instill confidence as to why and where the results come from. Today, many Big Data startups, but also established companies from Adobe to Yahoo!, use Hadoop, a framework for distributed processing of large-scale data sets. For example, recently, the oil company Chevron turned to the open source project Hadoop for storing and managing huge amounts of seismic data needed to locate oil or gas deposits on the ocean floor.

As with the Internet, servers, cloud computing, mobility, and Big Data, open source seems to have been at the forefront of many megatrends. What will be the next megatrend fueled by open source?

Questions

9-43. What are the pros and cons of depending on open source software?

9-44. For what types of applications do you think open source is better than proprietary software? When is it worse?

9-45. Find a for-profit company that is distributing open source software. What is the software? How does the company make money? Is its revenue model sustainable?

Based on:

Anonymous. (2014). The open source definition. *Opensource.org.* Retrieved March 27, 2014, from http://opensource.org/osd.

Bloom, B. (2012, May 29). The open-source answer to Big Data. *ITWorld.com.* Retrieved March 27, 2014, from http://www.itworld.com/open-source/279090/open-source-answer-big-data.

King, R. (2012, June 5). Chevron explores open source using Hadoop. *Wall Street Journal.* Retrieved March 27, 2014, from http://blogs.wsj.com/cio/2012/06/05/chevron-explores-open-source-using-hadoop.

Rooney, P. (2012, May 22). Open source driving cloud, Big Data, mobile, survey finds. *ZDNet.com.* Retrieved March 27, 2014, from http://www.zdnet.com/blog/open-source/open-source-driving-cloud-big-data-mobile-survey-finds/11015.

Volpi, M. (2014, March 25). A "perfect storm" moment for multibillion-dollar open source companies. *Re/code.* Retrieved March 27, 2014, from http://recode.net/2014/03/25/a-perfect-storm-moment-for-multibillion-dollar-open-source-companies.

MyMISLab™ | Go to **mymislab.com** for Auto-graded writing questions as well as the following Assisted-graded writing questions:

9-46. Contrast the perspectives of different stakeholders involved in making information systems investment decisions.

9-47. What are the advantages and disadvantages of prototyping?

References

Anonymous. (2009, October 26). Twitter "costs businesses £1.4bn." *BBC News*. Retrieved June 1, 2014, from http://news.bbc.co.uk/2/hi/business/8325865.stm.

Anonymous. (2014, April 15). The 10 best jobs of 2014. *Wall Street Journal.* Retrieved June 1, 2014, from http://blogs.wsj.com/atwork/2014/04/15/best-jobs-of-2014-congratulations-mathematicians.

Applegate, L. M., Austin, R. D., & Soule, D.L. (2009). *Corporate information strategy and management* (8th ed.). New York: McGraw-Hill.

Fuller, M. A., Valacich, J. S., & George, J. F. (2008). *Information systems project management: A process and team approach.* Upper Saddle River, NJ: Pearson Prentice Hall.

Hoffer, J. A., George, J. F., & Valacich, J. S. (2014). *Modern systems analysis and design* (7th ed.). Upper Saddle River, NJ: Pearson Prentice Hall.

McFarlan, F. W., & Nolan, R. L. (1995). How to manage an IT outsourcing alliance. *Sloan Management Review, 36*(2), 9–24.

McKeen, J. D., Guimaraes, T., & Wetherbe, J. C. (1994). A comparative analysis of MIS project selection mechanisms. *Database, 25*(2), 43–59.

Netcraft. (2014, June 1). May 2014 Web server survey. *Netcraft.com.* Retrieved June 1, 2014, from http://news.netcraft.com/archives/category/web-server-survey.

Porter, M. E. (1979, March–April). How competitive forces shape strategy. *Harvard Business Review, 57,* 137–145.

Top 500. (2014, June). Retrieved July 20, 2014, from http://www.top500.org/lists/2014/06/.

US News. (2014). The 100 best jobs. *USNews.com.* Retrieved May 28, 2014, from http://money.usnews.com/careers/best-jobs/rankings/the-100-best-jobs.

Valacich, J. S., George, J. F., & Hoffer, J. A. (2016). *Essentials of systems analysis and design* (6th ed.). Upper Saddle River, NJ: Pearson Prentice Hall.

Van der Meulen, R., & Pettey, C. (2012, July 9). Gartner says worldwide IT spending on pace to surpass $3.6 trillion in 2012. *Gartner.* Retrieved June 1, 2014, from http://www.gartner.com/it/page.jsp?id=2074815.

Walsh, D. C. (2014, March 18). Enemy ID: How DOD uses biodata in the field. *DefenseSystems.com.* Retrieved March 20, 2014, from http://defensesystems.com/articles/2014/03/18/dod-biometrics-ng-abis.aspx.

Wheeler, B. C., & Marakas, G. M. (1999). Making the business case for IT investments through facts, faith, and fear. Retrieved June 1, 2014, from https://scholarworks.iu.edu/dspace/handle/2022/15186?show=full.

Wood, J., & Silver, D. (1989). *Joint application design.* New York: Wiley.

10 Securing Information Systems

After reading this chapter, you will be able to do the following:

1. Define computer crime and describe several types of computer crime.
2. Describe and explain the differences between cyberwar and cyberterrorism.
3. Discuss the process of managing IS security and describe various IS controls that can help in ensuring IS security.

Preview

With the proliferation of computing technologies to every corner of the world, most people and organizations have become completely dependent upon their smartphone, tablet, or information system (IS) to support communication and commerce. With this increasing dependency on technology to work flawlessly, we have never been more vulnerable to catastrophic security disasters. Because of this, individuals and organizations are focusing more of their attention on information systems security. Here, we first examine computer crime and other threats to information systems security, followed by a discussion of various approaches for securing information systems and the critical information they hold.

Managing in the digital world requires careful attention to IS security. Having thorough plans and approaches for dealing with IS security attacks and natural disasters is critical for effectively managing IS resources within organizations and your personal life.

Managing in the Digital World: **Not So "Anonymous"—Activists, Hacktivists, or Just Plain Criminals?**

File-sharing sites like Megaupload.com, best known for its massive size and volume of downloaded content, are hotbeds of online piracy. After being shut down by U.S. authorities, Megaupload.com formally bade goodbye in 2012 as New Zealand police raided several homes and businesses linked to its founder Kim Dotcom (a name he took on after making a fortune during the dotcom bubble). With only a slight warning from a tweet reading, "One thing is certain: EXPECT US!," a hacktivist group called Anonymous launched "Operation Payback" (Figure 10.1); utilizing 5,635 *zombie computers* distributed throughout the Internet, Anonymous delivered a retaliatory attack resulting in a string of highly coordinated takedowns of Web sites managed by the U.S. Department of Justice and a number of other organizations that have publicly supported anti-piracy legislation, including the Recording Industry Association of America, the Motion Picture Association of America, and Universal Music.

Who is Anonymous? Having no formal organization and no formal leadership, Anonymous is often considered to be a loose collective of hacktivists—Internet users practicing civil disobedience by taking part in cyberattacks on Web sites. The group has participated in several cyberattacks; the best known concerned a vigilante movement against VISA, MasterCard, and PayPal as a protest for their freezing the accounts of the whistleblower site **WikiLeaks**. Anonymous is also politically active, launching attacks on Israeli government Web sites in response to Israeli military actions in the Gaza Strip. Not all of Anonymous's actions are controversial, however: Anonymous garnered much public sympathy with the 2011 "Operation Darknet," its attempt to battle child pornography. In 2012, Anonymous members defended a teen victim of cyberbullying. Following the devastation of Hurricane Sandy in 2012 and massive tornado damage in Oklahoma in 2013, Anonymous mobilized its online influence to support relief efforts. These efforts were considered by many to be more effective than those of government relief agencies.

Anonymous is well known for its Internet vigilantism. Although Anonymous claims to have good intentions, what the group does is sometimes illegal, and Anonymous and its supporters face a dilemma between pursuing (sometimes worthwhile) ideological goals and crossing the boundaries of legality.

After reading this chapter, you will be able to answer the following:

1. What is the difference between hacktivists, cyberterrorists, and other computer criminals?
2. What tools can hacktivists and other computer criminals use to attack information systems?
3. How can organizations and individuals protect themselves from attacks by hacktivists and other computer criminals?

Based on:

Anonymous (group). (2014, April 5). In *Wikipedia, The Free Encyclopedia*. Retrieved April 23, 2014, from http://en.wikipedia.org/w/index.php?title=Anonymous_(group)&oldid=602836811.

Gallagher, S. (2011, October 24). Anonymous takes down darknet child porn site on Tor network. *Arstechnica*. Retrieved April 22, 2014, from http://arstechnica.com/business/2011/10/anonymous-takes-down-darknet-child-porn-site-on-tor-network.

Gillmor, D. (2011, October 27). WikiLeaks payments blockade sets dangerous precedent. *The Guardian*. Retrieved April 22, 2014, from http://www.guardian.co.uk/commentisfree/cifamerica/2011/oct/27/wikileaks-payments-blockade-dangerous-precedent.

Murphy, L. (2012, November 14). How Anonymous helped prevent a teen's suicide. *The Daily Dot*. Retrieved April 22, 2014, from http://www.dailydot.com/news/anonymous-kylie-suicide-trolls-bully.

FIGURE 10.1

The symbol of the Anonymous group is a mask depicting the historical figure Guy Fawkes.
Source: dny3d/Shutterstock

COMPUTER CRIME

Computer crime is defined as the use of a computer to commit an illegal act. This broad definition of computer crime includes the following:

- Targeting a computer while committing an offense. For example, someone gains unauthorized entry to a computer system in order to cause damage to the computer system or to the data it contains.
- Using a computer to commit an offense. In such cases, computer criminals may steal credit card numbers from Web sites or a company's database, skim money from bank accounts, or make unauthorized electronic fund transfers from financial institutions.
- Using computers to support a criminal activity despite the fact that computers are not actually targeted. For example, drug dealers and other professional criminals may use computers to store records of their illegal transactions.

The global economic impact of cybercrime and cyber espionage is estimated to be around US$400 billion (McAfee, 2013). While this is a fraction of the estimated US$70 trillion global gross domestic product (GDP), its greater impact is its effect on trade, technology development, and competitiveness. Additionally, many organizations do not report incidents of computer crime because of fear that negative publicity could hurt stock value or provide advantages to competitors. Thus, experts believe that many incidents are never reported and that real losses exceed these estimates. It is clear, however, that computer crime is a fact of life. In this section, we briefly introduce this topic of growing importance.

Hacking and Cracking

Those individuals who are knowledgeable enough to gain access to computer systems without authorization have long been referred to as **hackers**. The name was first used in the 1960s to describe expert computer users and programmers who were students at the Massachusetts Institute of Technology. Based on curiosity and the desire to learn as much as possible about computers, they wrote programs for the mainframes they used that allowed them to roam freely through computer systems, and freely exchanged information about their "hacks"; however, they followed unwritten rules against damaging or stealing information belonging to others.

As computer crime became more prevalent and damaging, true hackers—those motivated by curiosity and not by a desire to do harm (sometimes referred to as "white hats")—objected to use of the term to describe computer criminals (Figure 10.2). Today, those who break into computer systems with the intention of doing damage or committing a crime are usually called **crackers** or "black hats." Some computer criminals attempt to break into systems or deface Web sites to promote political or ideological goals (such as free speech, human rights, and antiwar campaigns); these Web vandals are referred to as **hacktivists**.

Types of Computer Criminals and Crimes

Computer crimes are almost as varied as the users who commit them. Some involve the use of a computer to steal money or other assets or to perpetrate a deception for money, such as advertising merchandise for sale on a Web auction site, collecting orders and payment, and then sending either inferior merchandise or no merchandise at all. Other computer crimes involve stealing or altering information. Some of those thieves who steal information or disrupt a computer system have demanded a ransom from victims in exchange for returning the information or repairing the damage. Cyberterrorists have planted destructive programs in computer systems, and then threatened to activate them if a ransom is not paid (see upcoming discussion on cyberterrorism). Crimes in the form of electronic vandalism cause damage when offenders plant viruses, cause computer systems to crash, or deny service on a Web site.

Use of the Internet has fostered other types of criminal activity, such as the stalking of minors by sexual predators through newsgroups and chat rooms. Those who buy, sell, and distribute pornography have also found in the Internet a new medium for carrying out their activities.

FIGURE 10.2

Malicious hackers are referred to as black hats and those not motivated to do harm are referred to as white hats.

WHO COMMITS COMPUTER CRIMES? When you hear the term "cracker" or "computer criminal," you might imagine a techno-geek, someone who sits in front of his or her computer all day and night, attempting to break the ultra-super-secret security code of one of the most sophisticated computer systems in the world, perhaps a computer for the U.S. military, a Swiss bank, or the Central Intelligence Agency (CIA). While this fits the traditional profile for a computer criminal, there is no clear profile today. More and more people have the skills, the tools, and the motives to hack into a computer system. A modern-day computer criminal could be a disgruntled, middle-aged, white-collar worker sitting at a nice desk on the fourteenth floor of the headquarters building of a billion-dollar software manufacturer. Computer criminals have been around for decades. For the most part, we associate hackers and crackers with their pranks and crimes involving security systems and viruses. Nevertheless, hackers and crackers have caused the loss of billions of dollars' worth of stolen goods, repair bills, and lost goodwill with customers.

Studies attempting to categorize computer criminals show that they generally fall into one of four groups. These groups are listed next, from those who commit the most infractions to those who commit the fewest infractions:

1. Current or former employees who are in a position to steal or otherwise do damage to employers; most organizations report insider abuses as their most common crime (CSI, 2011)
2. People with technical knowledge who commit business or information sabotage for personal gain
3. Career criminals who use computers to assist in crimes
4. Outside crackers simply snooping or hoping to find information of value—crackers commit millions of intrusions per year, but most cause no harm (Estimates are that only around 10 percent of cracker attacks cause damage.)

Some crackers probe others' computer systems, electronically stored data, or Web sites for fun, for curiosity, or just to prove they can. Others have malicious or financial motives and intend to steal for gain or do other harm. Whatever the motives, discovery, prosecution, fines, and jail terms can result.

How do computer criminals gain access to computer systems? Frequently, computer criminals use sophisticated software such as **vulnerability scanners** that automatically test targeted systems for weaknesses, **packet sniffers** to analyze network traffic and capture unencrypted passwords, keyloggers (to be discussed) or tools to break passwords using a brute-force approach (note that vulnerability scanners and packet sniffers can also be used by organizations to test the effectiveness of controls; see the upcoming discussion of IS controls). Alternatively, crackers try to exploit human weaknesses by using methods such as phishing attacks (to be

ETHICAL DILEMMA

Industrial Espionage

Industrial espionage describes covert activities, such as the theft of trade secrets, bribery, blackmail, and technological surveillance to gain an advantage over rivals. Many notable companies have been victims of industrial espionage, including Procter & Gamble, IBM, DuPont, Gillette, Kodak, Starwood, and Microsoft. Industrial espionage is most commonly associated with technology-heavy industries, such as the computer hardware and software industries, but also with any other industry in which a significant amount of money is spent on research and development, such as the defense, automobile, and pharmaceutical industries. Often, competitors attempt to steal prototypes to gain access to new technological developments. Industrial espionage is also often carried out by compromising someone who works for a targeted company through bribery, coercion, or blackmail.

Insiders pose a particular threat for organizations. Recently laid-off or fired employees may be disgruntled and willing to trade their valuable secrets for a price, or people currently working within a targeted company may trade their secrets for a price. While earning money this way may seem lucrative for the people involved, penalties for a person giving confidential information away can include not only being fired, but also criminal charges if the employee signed a confidentiality agreement, or worked on projects that required a governmental security clearance.

The proliferation of the Internet and mobile devices is providing additional avenues for industrial espionage. Cracking into a company's computer system has become a fairly common practice, where criminals steal information and trade secrets that might be sold to others. Laptops, mobile devices, and USB drives can be stolen or accessed while left unattended in hotel rooms or can be stolen while in transit (e.g., stolen out of checked baggage when traveling). In the Information Age, critical information is always vulnerable to attacks, and the loss of strategic information may give an organization's rivals a competitive advantage and can have devastating impacts on the company's bottom line.

Imagine you were the owner of a company that fell victim to industrial espionage, and as a result, your company is on the verge of bankruptcy. At a trade show, a competitor's salesperson leaves a USB drive within your direct reach, and no one would notice it's missing until after the show. You suspect the competitor to have copied your products and ideas before, and the contents of the USB drive could save your company, as well as your employees' jobs. What would you do?

Based on:

Anonymous. (2011, April 25). 10 Most notorious acts of corporate espionage. Retrieved April 22, 2014, from http://www.businesspundit.com/10-most-notorious-acts-of-corporate-espionage.

Industrial espionage. (2014, April 22). In *Wikipedia, The Free Encyclopedia*. Retrieved April 22, 2014, from http://en.wikipedia.org/w/index.php?title=Industrial_espionage&oldid=605015730.

discussed), **social engineering** (misrepresenting oneself to trick others into revealing information), **shoulder surfing** (looking over one's shoulder while the person is keying in access information), or **dumpster diving** (scouring wastebaskets for potentially useful information).

UNAUTHORIZED ACCESS. **Unauthorized access** occurs whenever people who are not authorized to see, manipulate, or otherwise handle information look through electronically stored information for interesting or useful data, peek at monitors displaying proprietary or confidential information, or intercept electronic information on the way to its destination. Here are a few additional examples from recent media reports:

- Employees steal time on company computers to do personal business.
- Intruders break into government Web sites and change the information displayed.
- Thieves steal credit card numbers and Social Security numbers from electronic databases, and then use the stolen information to charge thousands of dollars in merchandise to victims.
- Competitors' employees posing as interns steal proprietary information about products or corporate strategies (i.e., engage in industrial espionage).

When computer information is shared by several users, as in an organization, in-house system administrators can prevent casual snooping or theft of information by requiring correct permissions. Further, administrators can log attempts of unauthorized individuals trying to obtain access. Determined attackers, however, will try to gain access by giving themselves system administrator status or otherwise elevating their permission level—sometimes by stealing passwords and logging on to a system as authorized users (Figure 10.3). Today, these malicious insiders, a top concern for government and corporate agencies, are referred to as an insider threat.

FIGURE 10.3

Unauthorized access can occur in many ways.

The term **insider threats** refers to "trusted adversaries" who operate within an organization's boundaries and are a significant danger to both private and public sectors. Insider threats include disgruntled employees or ex-employees, potential employees, contractors, business partners, or auditors. The damage caused by an insider threat can take many forms, including workplace violence; the introduction of malware into corporate networks; the theft of information, corporate secrets, or money; the corruption or deletion of data; and so on. Especially in very large organizations, identifying insider threats can be extremely difficult. For instance, identifying a small number of potential insider threats within an organization with thousands of employees is a literal "needle in the haystack" problem. In fact, in January 2014, James R. Clapper, director of National Intelligence, cited the malicious insider as the greatest threat to the United States, exceeding terrorism.

The most famous insider threat in recent history is Ed Snowden, an American computer professional who once worked for the CIA and was a contract worker for the National Security Agency (NSA). He came to international attention when he disclosed thousands of classified documents to several media outlets, which he had acquired while working for the American consulting firm Booz Allen Hamilton. In addition, software vendors may (intentionally or unintentionally) build **backdoors** (i.e., hidden access points allowing for unauthorized access) into their systems. Such backdoors might be exploited by malicious crackers, intelligence agencies, or one's competitors (for industrial espionage).

INFORMATION MODIFICATION. Often related to unauthorized access, **information modification** occurs when someone accesses electronic information and then changes the information in some way, such as when crackers hack into government Web sites and change information or when employees give themselves electronic raises and bonuses (Figure 10.4).

OTHER THREATS TO IS SECURITY. Many times, IS security is breached simply because organizations and individuals do not exercise proper care in safeguarding information. Some examples follow:

- Employees keep passwords or access codes on slips of paper in plain sight.
- Individuals have never bothered to install antivirus software, or they install the software but fail to keep it up to date.
- Computer users within an organization continue to use default network passwords after a network is set up instead of passwords that are more difficult to break.
- Employees are careless about letting outsiders view computer monitors, or they carelessly give out information over the telephone.

FIGURE 10.4
Information modification attack.

- Organizations fail to limit access to company files and system resources.
- Organizations fail to install effective firewalls or intrusion detection systems, or they install an intrusion detection system but fail to monitor it regularly.
- Proper background checks are not done on new hires.
- Employees are not properly monitored, and they steal company data or computer resources.
- Fired employees are resentful and install harmful code, such as computer viruses, when they leave the company.

With the popularity of mobile devices like smartphones and tablets, many additional security threats have emerged, including:

- Individuals lose their mobile devices and don't have capabilities to remotely wipe data from the device.
- Individuals keep sensitive data on mobile devices and do not use passcodes.
- Individuals **"jailbreaking"** their mobile phone—that is, modify the operating system to remove manufacturer or carrier restrictions—in order to run applications other than those from the official app store. Jailbreaking can allow unsecure applications to run on devices or make it difficult to upgrade devices that have been modified.
- Individuals use poorly designed mobile applications that can have security vulnerabilities.
- Individuals use unsecure wireless networks, leaving their devices vulnerable to different types of attacks.

While there are many threats to IS security, there are also ways to combat those threats. Later, we discuss safeguards organizations can use to improve IS security.

Computer Viruses and Other Destructive Code

Malware—short for "malicious software" such as viruses, worms, and Trojan horses—continues to have a tremendous economic impact on the world, costing organizations more than US$114 billion to respond to and to enact countermeasures (Brown, 2013). Accurate estimates of real costs to organizations and society are difficult to obtain, as many organizations choose not to report major incidents (CSI, 2011); most organizations do not want to alarm customers and shareholders of malware and other security breaches. Whatever the true costs are, antivirus Web vendors report thousands of new forms of malware each month.

COMPUTER VIRUSES. A **virus** is a destructive program that disrupts the normal functioning of computer systems. Viruses differ from other types of malicious code in that they can reproduce themselves. Some viruses are intended to be harmless pranks, but more often they do damage to a computer system by erasing files on the hard drive or by slowing computer processing or otherwise compromising the system. Viruses infect a single computer only, potentially spreading to other computers if infected files are shared. Viruses are planted in host computers in a number of ways (Figure 10.5), but are most often spread through malicious e-mail attachments, the sharing of removable media (such as USB sticks), or file downloads from malicious Web sites.

WHEN THINGS GO WRONG

The Bug That Almost Killed the Internet

On December 31, 2011, Stephen Henson reviewed a new section of code for inclusion into the OpenSSL Project. OpenSSL is a popular encryption framework used to secure many Internet-based transactions. Dr. Henson, one of the core developers of the software, apparently failed to notice a flaw in the code, and the bug was adopted into widespread use across the Internet, where it remained undetected for over two years. When the flaw was finally fixed in April 2014, an estimated 17 percent (about half a million) of Web servers were believed to be vulnerable to attack. *Forbes* magazine labeled the bug as the worst since commercial traffic began to flow on the Internet.

The security bug—popularly known as heartbleed—allows an attacker to read the active memory of systems with the vulnerability. This compromises various types of secure information, including encryption keys, user names and passwords, and the actual data that those encryption and authentication technologies are intended to protect.

Though many Internet companies were quick to update their sever software, we do not know the extent to which the vulnerability has been exploited. The vulnerability thus has repercussions for thousands of companies and millions of users. It serves as a cogent reminder of the potential dangers associated with transacting via the Internet.

Based on:

Heartbleed. (2014, April 23). In *Wikipedia, The Free Encyclopedia*. Retrieved April 23, 2014, from http://en.wikipedia.org/w/index.php?title=Heartbleed&oldid=605409069.

McMillan, R. (2014, April 11). How heartbleed broke the Internet—and why it can happen again. *Wired*. Retrieved April 22, 2014, from http://www.wired.com/2014/04/heartbleedslesson.

Steinberg, J. (2014, April 10). Massive Internet security vulnerability—here's what you need to do. *Forbes*. Retrieved April 22, 2014, from http://www.forbes.com/sites/josephsteinberg/2014/04/10/massive-internet-security-vulnerability-you-are-at-risk-what-you-need-to-do.

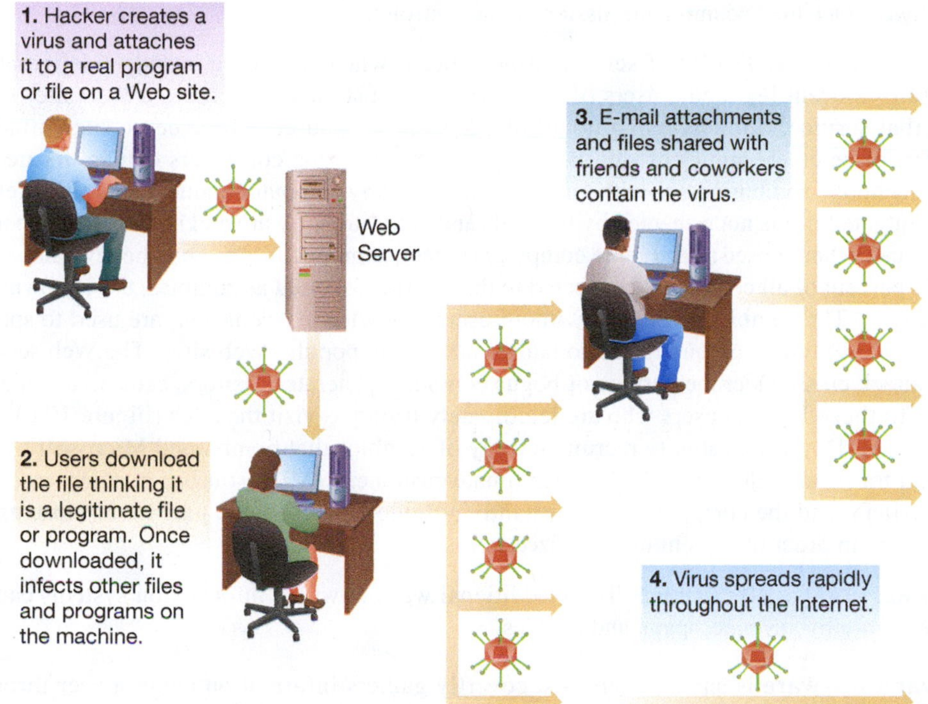
1. Hacker creates a virus and attaches it to a real program or file on a Web site.
Web Server
2. Users download the file thinking it is a legitimate file or program. Once downloaded, it infects other files and programs on the machine.
3. E-mail attachments and files shared with friends and coworkers contain the virus.
4. Virus spreads rapidly throughout the Internet.

FIGURE 10.5

How a computer virus is spread.

WORMS, TROJAN HORSES, AND OTHER SINISTER PROGRAMS. Viruses are among the most virulent forms of computer infections, but other destructive code can also be damaging. A **worm**, a variation of a virus that is targeted at networks, is designed to spread by itself, without the need for an infected host file to be shared. Worms take advantage of security holes in operating systems and other software to replicate endlessly across the Internet, thus causing servers to crash, which denies service to Internet users.

Another category of destructive programs is called **Trojan horses**. Like the Trojan horse in Greek mythology, Trojan horses appear to be legitimate, benign programs, but carry a destructive payload. Unlike viruses, Trojan horses typically do not replicate themselves, but, like viruses, can do much damage, such as by giving the creator unauthorized access to a system. When a Trojan horse is planted in a computer, its instructions remain hidden. The computer appears to function normally, but in fact it is performing underlying functions dictated by the intrusive code. For example, under the pretext of playing chess with an unsuspecting systems operator, a cracker group installed a Trojan horse in a Canadian mainframe. While the game appeared to be proceeding normally, the Trojan horse program was sneakily establishing a powerful unauthorized account for the future use of the intruders.

Logic bombs or **time bombs** are variations of Trojan horses. They also do not reproduce themselves, and are designed to operate without disrupting normal computer function. Instead, they lie in wait for unsuspecting computer users to perform a triggering operation. Time bombs are set off by specific dates, such as the birthday of a famous person. Logic bombs are set off by certain types of operations, such as entering a specific password or adding or deleting names and other information to and from certain computer files. Disgruntled employees have planted logic and time bombs on being fired, intending for the program to activate after they have left the company. In at least one instance in recent history, a former employee in Minnesota demanded money to deactivate the time bomb he had planted in company computers before it destroyed employee payroll records.

Recently, a new type of malware called **ransomware** has emerged. Ransomware holds a user's computer hostage by locking or taking control of the user's computer, or encrypting files or documents. Once infected, the scammers demand a ransom to be paid by a certain deadline in order to unlock the computers or decrypt the files. Alternatively, an official-looking message from a law enforcement agency (typically, the Federal Bureau of Investigation [FBI]) is displayed (complete with logos) that demands the payment of a fine to avoid being prosecuted for illegal activity/content detected on the computer. In either case, paying the ransom does not guarantee getting access to the files again, and having backups is the best safeguard against ransomware (see the upcoming discussion about controls).

DENIAL OF SERVICE. **Denial-of-service attacks** occur when electronic intruders deliberately attempt to prevent legitimate users of a service (e.g., customers accessing a Web site) from using that service, often by using up all of a system's resources. To execute such attacks, intruders often create armies of **zombie computers** by infecting computers that are located in homes, schools, and businesses with viruses or worms. Any computer connected to the Internet can be infected if it is not protected by firewalls and antivirus software and is, therefore, open to attacks and to being used as a zombie computer (in fact, some security experts believe that more than 10 percent of all computers connected to the Internet are used as zombies, unbeknownst to the owners). The zombie computers, without users' knowledge or consent, are used to spread the malware to other computers and to launch attacks on popular Web sites. The Web servers under attack crash under the barrage of bogus computer-generated visitors, causing a denial of service to those Internet users who are legitimately trying to visit the sites (Figure 10.6). For example, MyDoom was able to recruit an army of zombies that bombarded Microsoft's Web site with traffic and literally locked out legitimate customers. (Microsoft is a popular target for virus writers, and the company must constantly provide downloadable patches to those using its software in order to prevent unauthorized intrusion.)

SPYWARE, SPAM, AND COOKIES. Three additional ways in which information systems can be threatened are by spyware, spam, and cookies.

Spyware **Spyware** is any software that covertly gathers information about a user through an Internet connection without the user's knowledge. Spyware is sometimes hidden within freeware or shareware programs. In other instances, it is embedded within a Web site and is downloaded to the user's computer, without the user's knowledge, in order to track data about the user for marketing and advertisement purposes. Spyware can monitor your activity (such as Web site visits) and secretly transmit that information to someone else. **Keyloggers** can capture every keystroke and thus gather information such as e-mail addresses, passwords, and credit card numbers (note that keyloggers may be installed on companies' computers to monitor employees). Spyware presents problems because it uses your computer's memory resources; eats network bandwidth as it sends information back to the spyware's home base via your Internet connection; causes system instability or, worse, system crashes; and exposes

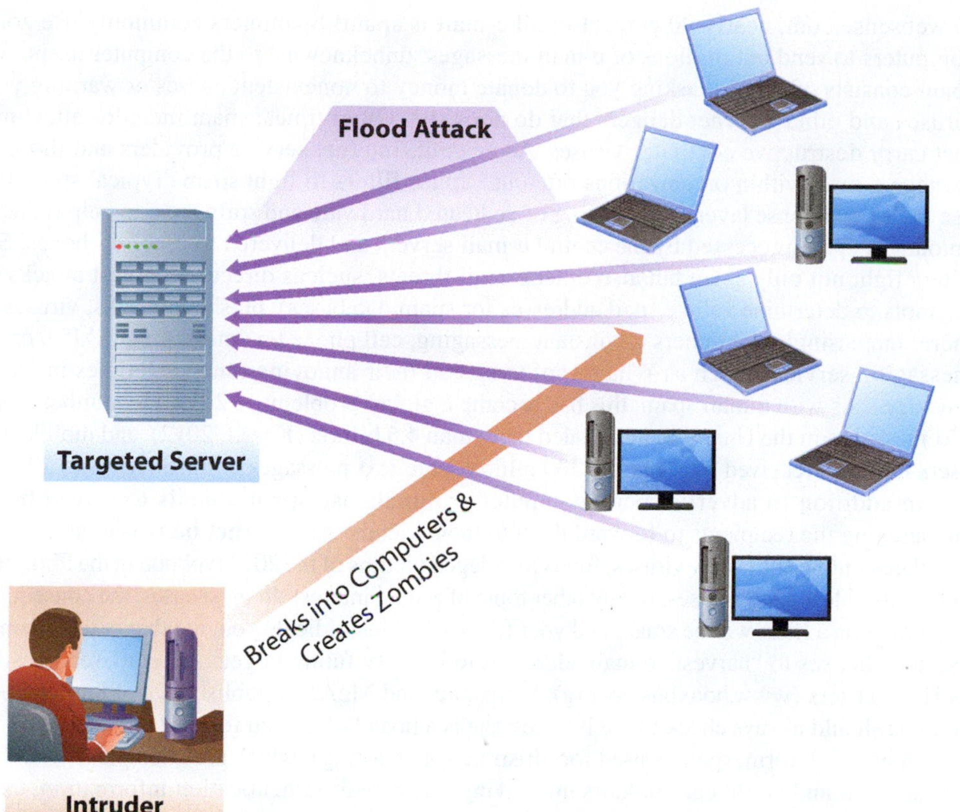

FIGURE 10.6

Denial-of-service attack.

users to identity theft, credit card fraud, and other types of crime. **Adware** (free software paid for by advertisements appearing during the use of the software) sometimes contains spyware that collects information about a person's Web surfing behavior in order to customize Web site banner advertisements. It is important to note that spyware is not currently illegal, although there is ongoing legislative hype about regulating it in some way. Fortunately, firewalls and spyware protection software can be used to scan for and block spyware.

Spam Another prevalent form of network traffic that invades our e-mail is spam. **Spam** is electronic junk mail or junk newsgroup postings, usually for the purpose of advertising for some product and/or service (Figure 10.7). In addition to being a nuisance and wasting our time, spam also eats up huge amounts of storage space and network bandwidth. Today, according

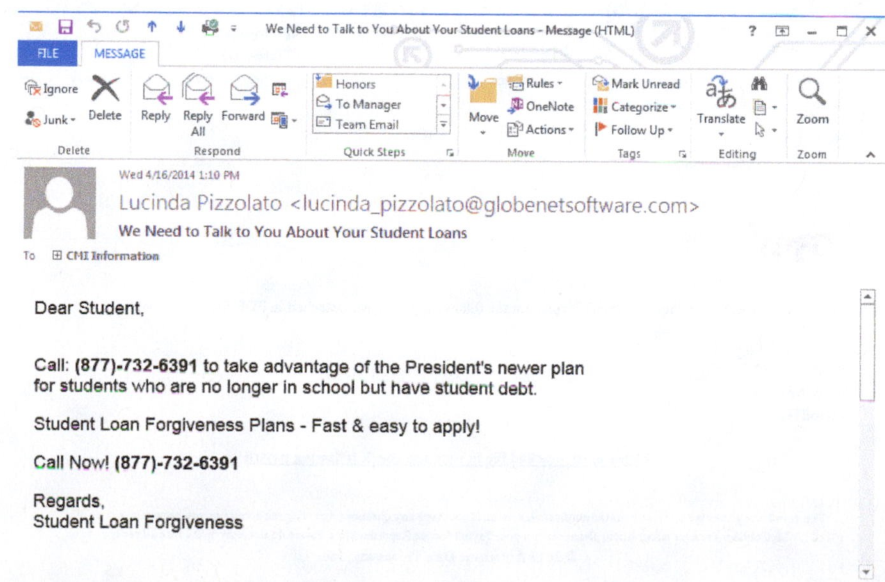

FIGURE 10.7

Spam is rampant and consumes an enormous amount of human and technology resources.

Source: Courtesy of Microsoft Corporation

to websense.com, nearly 90 percent of all e-mail is spam! Spammers commonly use zombie computers to send out millions of e-mail messages, unbeknownst to the computer users. Some spam consists of hoaxes, asking you to donate money to nonexistent causes or warning you of viruses and other Internet dangers that do not exist. Other times, spam includes attachments that carry destructive computer viruses. As a result, Internet service providers and those who manage e-mail within organizations often use **spam filters** to fight spam. Typical spam filters use multiple defense layers—consisting of dedicated hardware and software—to help reduce the amount of spam processed by the central e-mail servers and delivered to users' in-boxes. Spam filters fight not only spam but also other e-mail threats, such as directory harvest attacks (i.e., attempts to determine valid e-mail addresses for spam databases), phishing attacks, viruses, and more. Increasingly, spammers use instant messaging, cell phone text messaging (SMS), or other messaging services (such as WhatsApp) to spread their annoying (and sometimes malicious) messages. As with e-mail spam, this has become a global problem: In 2011, the number of spam text messages in the United States totaled more than 4.5 billion (Kharif, 2012), and mobile phone users in China received a staggering 300 billion spam text messages in 2013 (Xinhua, 2014).

In addition to advertisement, computer criminals use spam e-mails to spread hoaxes, encouraging the recipients to forward them to their friends. An **Internet hoax** is a false message circulated online about new viruses; funds for alleged victims of the 2013 typhoon in the Philippines; kids in trouble; cancer causes; or any other topic of public interest. In most cases, the consequences of passing on a hoax will be small, and your friends will just ridicule you; in other cases, spammers use such hoaxes to "harvest" e-mail addresses to identify future targets. Several Web sites, such as Hoaxbusters (www.hoaxbusters.org), Symantec, and McAfee, publish lists of known hoaxes, and you should always check to see if a message is a hoax before you forward it to others.

In its worst form, spam is used for **phishing** (or spoofing), which are attempts to trick financial account and credit card holders into giving away their authentication information, usually by sending spam messages to literally millions of e-mail accounts (i.e., attackers are "phishing" [fishing] for victims). These phony messages contain links to Web sites that duplicate legitimate sites to capture account information. For example, most e-mail users regularly receive phishing attempts from various spoofed banks, eBay, or PayPal (Figure 10.8). As people learn that generically addressed e-mail from a bank is not likely legitimate, criminals have turned to spear phishing. **Spear phishing** is a more sophisticated fraudulent e-mail attack that targets a specific person or organization by personalizing the message (phishing with a spear rather than a broad net) in order to make the message appear as if it is from a trusted source such as an individual within the recipient's company (often someone in a position of authority), a government entity, or a well-known company. While spear phishing can be very effective, the attacker needs some basic information in order to optimally target the phishing message. Many fear that social media

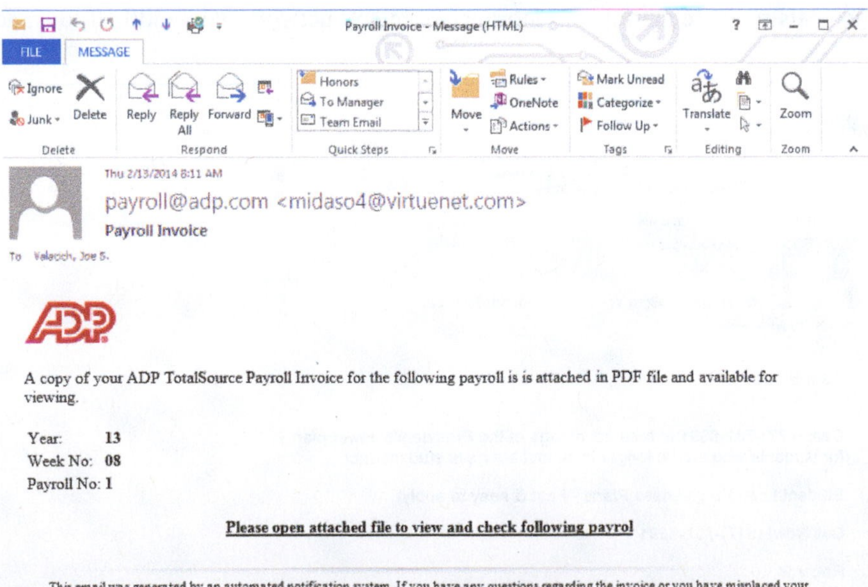

FIGURE 10.8

A phishing e-mail message.

Source: Courtesy of Microsoft Corporation

sites like Facebook will increasingly provide valuable information about potential victims to criminals designing spear phishing attacks.

Often, spammers post their spam messages in online forums, blogs, or wikis, or create thousands of e-mail accounts at free providers such as Yahoo! or Hotmail to send out their messages. Rather than manually going through such tedious tasks to set up these accounts or post thousands of messages, spammers use bots (i.e., software robots that work in the background to provide services to their owners; see Chapter 6, "Enhancing Business Intelligence Using Information Systems") to do this. Faced with this problem, e-mail providers and managers of online forums are attempting to prevent spammers from using bots to automatically submit online forms. One commonly used approach for preventing bots from submitting forms is the use of CAPTCHAs. A **CAPTCHA** (Completely Automated Public Turing Test to Tell Computers and Humans Apart) typically consists of a distorted image displaying a combination of letters and/or numbers that a user has to input into a form (in addition to other required information) before submitting it. As the image is distorted, (currently) only humans can interpret the letters/numbers, preventing the use of automated bots for creating accounts or posting spam to forums, blogs, or wikis. CAPTCHAs are also used to prevent bots from trying to break passwords using a brute force approach (Figure 10.9).

However, trying to stop spammers is a cat-and-mouse game, and increasingly, webmasters are using a combination of multiple techniques to stop spammers, such as detecting mouse movements (as automated agents do not use a mouse), detecting the rate at which text is entered into forms, or incorporating invisible fields (which would be "seen" and filled out by an automated agent but not a human user), together with CAPTCHAs in order to distinguish between malicious bots and legitimate users.

Cookies Another potential nuisance in Internet usage is cookies. A **cookie** is a small text file passed to a Web browser on a user's computer by a Web server. The browser then stores the message in a text file, and the message is sent back to the server each time the user's browser requests a page from that server.

Cookies are normally used for legitimate purposes, such as identifying a user in order to present a customized Web page or for authentication purposes. Although you can choose to not accept the storage of cookies, you may not be able to visit the site, or it may not function properly. For example, to read the *New York Times* online, you must register by entering your name and other information. When you go through the registration process, cookies are stored on your machine. If you don't accept cookies or you delete the stored cookies, you are not allowed to access the online newspaper without reregistering. Similarly, you will have to accept cookies when purchasing from many e-tailers, as most online shopping carts require cookies to function properly. In some cases, cookies may contain sensitive information (such as credit card numbers) and thus pose a security risk in case unauthorized persons gain access to the computer.

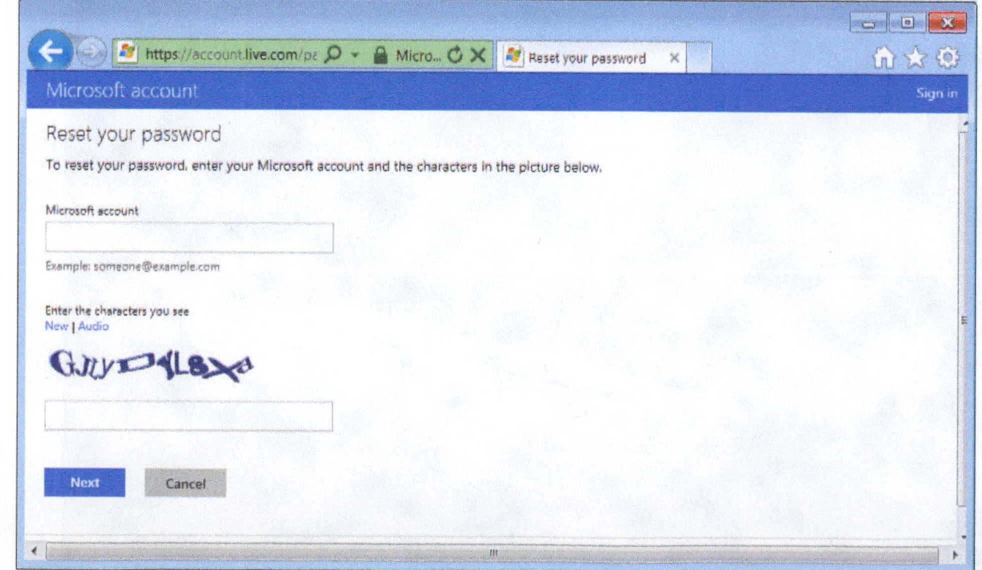

FIGURE 10.9

A CAPTCHA is used to prevent bots from submitting an online form.

Source: Courtesy of Microsoft Corporation

Specific cookie management or cookie killer software can be used to manage cookies, but an even simpler way to manage cookies is through the settings in your Web browser. In the settings for the Firefox Web browser, for example, you can set levels of restrictions on the use of cookies, you can block them altogether, and, if you do allow them, you can go in periodically and delete them from your computer.

THE RISE OF BOTNETS AND THE CYBERATTACK SUPPLY CHAIN. Destructive software robots called bots (see Chapter 6), working together on a collection of zombie computers via the Internet, called **botnets**, have become the standard method of operation for professional cybercriminals. For example, about 85 percent of all e-mail spam is sent out by only six major botnets. Attacks using botnets are emerging into a global supply chain of highly specialized criminals. For instance, a phishing attack can involve the following:

1. A *programmer* writes a phishing attack template and makes this available for purchase.
2. A *phisher* who wants to run an attack purchases the template and designs an attack (e.g., ask recipients of a spam e-mail to update their banking information at the Wells Fargo Bank).
3. The *phisher* contracts with a *cracker* to provide hosting space for the phishing Web sites.
4. The *phisher* contacts a bot herder—a criminal who has a botnet residing on a collection of zombie computers—to send out the spam e-mail that carries the attack to unsuspecting people.
5. After launching the attack and collecting information from those who responded to the phishing attack, the *phisher* provides the stolen personal information to a *collector* who specializes in removing funds from the affected financial institutions.
6. The *collector* works with a criminal called a *mule herder* who has a network of people who carry out the withdrawals from affected banks.

Each member of the supply chain has very specialized skills and can be located anywhere in the world. In fact, one of the difficulties in stopping this global crime syndicate is the difficulty of not only tracking the locations of these villains but also prosecuting criminals across international borders. Today, a would-be cybercriminal does not need highly specialized computer skills to build a botnet; rather, the criminal can easily "rent" space on a botnet (including technical support from the bot herder, tremendous resources, and bandwidth) starting at US$150, depending on the size of the botnet.

IDENTITY THEFT. One of the fastest-growing "information" crimes in recent years has been **identity theft** (Figure 10.10). Identity theft is the stealing of another person's Social Security

FIGURE 10.10

Identity theft is one of the fastest-growing information crimes.
Source: Henrik5000/Getty Images

number, credit card number, and other personal information for the purpose of using the victim's credit rating to borrow money, buy merchandise, and otherwise run up debts that are never repaid. In some cases, thieves even withdraw money directly from victims' bank accounts. Since many government and private organizations keep information about individuals in accessible databases, opportunities abound for thieves to retrieve it. Reclaiming one's identity and restoring a good credit rating can be frustrating and time consuming for victims.

The solution to identity theft lies in the government and private sector working together to change practices used to verify a person's identity. For example, a mother's maiden name and an individual's Social Security number are too easily obtained. Other methods of personal identification, such as biometrics and encryption, may need to be used if the problem is to be solved. Methods of information security, including biometrics and encryption, are presented later in our discussion.

Cyberharassment, Cyberstalking, and Cyberbullying

The Internet has become a place where people utilize its anonymity to harass, stalk, and bully others. **Cyberharassment**, a crime in many states and countries, broadly refers to the use of a computer to communicate obscene, vulgar, or threatening content that causes a reasonable person to endure distress. A single offensive message can be considered cyberharassment.

Repeated contacts with a victim are referred to as **cyberstalking**. Cyberstalking can take many forms, including the following:

- Making false accusations that damage the reputation of the victim on blogs, Web sites, chat rooms, or e-commerce sites (e.g., eBay)
- Gaining information about a victim by monitoring online activities, accessing databases, and so on
- Encouraging others to harass a victim by posting personal information about the victim on Web sites, chat rooms or social networking sites
- Attacking data and equipment of the victim by sending e-mail viruses and other destructive code
- Using the Internet to place false orders for goods and services, such as magazines, pornography, and other embarrassing items, as well as having such items delivered to work addresses
- Posting incriminating pictures on social networking sites

Many states, the U.S. government, and many countries have anti-cyberstalking laws. Unfortunately, law enforcement has a difficult time catching most cyberstalkers. While cyberstalking can take many forms and can go undetected by the victim, the intent of **cyberbullying** is to *deliberately* cause emotional distress in the victim. Cyberharassment, cyberstalking, and cyberbullying are typically targeted at a particular person or group as a means of taking revenge or expressing hatred. The widespread and increasing use of mobile devices has led to increases in cyberbullying, cyberharassment, and cyberstalking.

In contrast, **online predators** typically target vulnerable people, usually the young or old, for sexual or financial purposes. While typically online chat rooms and instant messaging systems have been the playground for online predators, these villains are also targeting many social networking sites like Facebook. To combat these online predators, parents must educate their children not to share personal information and possibly must use monitoring software to track online activity. Fortunately, most social networking and online chat sites also provide ways to report abuse by these predators.

Software Piracy

Software developers and marketers want you to buy as many copies of their products as you want, of course. But commercial software vendors do not want you or anyone else to buy one copy and then bootleg additional copies to sell or to give to others. Vendors also take a dim view of companies that buy one copy of a software application and then make many copies to distribute to employees. In fact, these practices are called **software piracy**, and are illegal.

Both patent and copyright laws can apply to software, which is a form of intellectual property—creations of the mind (e.g., music, software, and so on), inventions, names, images, designs, and other works used in commerce. Patents and copyrights are recognized and enforced by most countries, giving the creator exclusive rights to benefit from the creation for a limited period of time. **Patents** typically refer to process, machine, or material inventions. For example, Amazon.com's "one-click buying" process is protected by patent law, and Apple has patented its multitouch technology (including the "pinch" for shrinking and expanding items) used in the iPhone and iPad. **Copyrights** generally refer to creations of the mind such as music, literature, or software.

When you buy commercial software, it is typically legal for you to make one (1) backup copy for your own use (although the software vendor can make it very difficult to copy the software). It is also legal to offer shareware or public domain software for free on a Web site. But **warez** peddling—offering stolen proprietary software for free over the Internet—is a crime. ("Warez" is the slang term for such stolen software.)

Software piracy has become a problem because it is so widespread, costing the commercial software industry and the entire economy billions of dollars a year. A 2013 study conducted by the Business Software Alliance (BSA) suggested that reducing software piracy by only 1 percent globally would inject US$73 billion into the world's economy, producing hundreds of thousands new jobs and billions of dollars in tax revenue. The crime is difficult to trace, but many individuals and even companies have been successfully prosecuted for pirating software.

Many software vendors are trying to limit software piracy by requiring the users to enter license keys or verifying the key before allowing the customer to register or update the software. To discover and understand any protection mechanisms (such as registration or license keys) built into the software by its original developer, computer criminals typically disassemble the software, a practice referred to as **reverse engineering**. Once the crackers understand the inner workings of the protection mechanism, they can build a **key generator** that can be used to generate fake license keys to circumvent the protection mechanism. (Reverse engineering is not always destructive and may be legally used to improve a program, but use of the term here implies using the process for gaining unauthorized access to a program's internal structure.)

SOFTWARE PIRACY IS A GLOBAL BUSINESS. A major international issue that businesses deal with is the willingness (or unwillingness) of governments and individuals to recognize and enforce the ownership of intellectual property—in particular, software copyrights. Piracy of software and other technologies is widespread internationally (Figure 10.11). The BSA (2012) points to countries such as Georgia (91 percent), Zimbabwe (92 percent), and Bangladesh (90 percent) as those with the highest percentages of illegal software. Worldwide losses due to piracy exceeded US$63 billion in 2011. Countries with the lowest piracy rates include the United States (19 percent), Japan (21 percent), Luxembourg (20 percent), and New Zealand (22 percent). Because technology usage varies significantly by region, average piracy levels and dollar losses greatly differ across regions (Table 10.1). For instance, even though the United States has the lowest piracy rate, it also is the country where the greatest losses occur (more than US$9.7 billion) because of its high level of computer usage.

In addition to being a crime, is software piracy also an ethical problem? Perhaps in part, but businesspeople must acknowledge and deal with other perspectives as well. In part, the problem stems from other countries' differing concepts of ownership. Many of the ideas about intellectual property ownership stem from long-standing cultural traditions. For example, the concept

FIGURE 10.11

In many parts of the world, using pirated software is a common practice.

Source: Courtesy of Christoph Schneider.

TABLE 10.1 Software Piracy Levels and Dollar Losses by Region

Region	Piracy Level	Dollar Loss (in US$ millions)
North America	19%	10,958
Western Europe	32%	13,749
Asia/Pacific	60%	20,998
Latin America	61%	7,459
Middle East/Africa	58%	4,159
Eastern Europe	62%	6,133
Worldwide	42%	63,456

Source: Based on Business Software Alliance. (2012). Extracted from unnumbered tables on pages 8–9 from http://portal.bsa.org/globalpiracy2011/downloads/study_pdf/2011_BSA_Piracy_Study-Standard.pdf.

of individual ownership of knowledge is traditionally a strange one in many Middle Eastern countries, where knowledge is meant to be shared. Plagiarism does not exist in a country where words belong to everyone. By the same token, piracy does not exist either. This view is gradually changing; the Saudi Arabia Patent Office granted its first patents several years ago, and its piracy rates have plummeted from 79 percent in 1996 to 51 percent in 2011. Other factors leading to piracy or infringement of intellectual property agreements throughout the world include lack of public awareness about the issue and the increasingly high demand for computers and other technology products.

In other cases, there are political, social, and economic reasons for piracy. In many countries, software publishers are not catering to the needs of those consumers who simply may not have the funds to purchase software legitimately. This is true in many areas of South America, Africa, and other regions with low per capita income. It is particularly true of students and other members of university communities whose needs are critical in some areas. Recognizing these issues, many software manufacturers offer educational versions, or use differential pricing for different regions.

Cybersquatting

Another form of piracy is **cybersquatting**, the dubious practice of registering a domain name and then trying to sell the name for big bucks to the person, company, or organization most likely to want it. Domain names are one of the few scarce resources on the Internet, and victims of cybersquatting include Panasonic, Hertz, Avon, and numerous other companies and individuals. Fortunately, the U.S. government passed the Anti-Cybersquatting Consumer Protection Act in 1999, which made it a crime to register, traffic in, or use a domain name to profit from the goodwill of a trademark belonging to someone else. Fines for cybersquatting can reach as high as US$100,000, in addition to the forfeiture of the disputed domain name. As a result, recent court cases have not been kind to cybersquatters. Many feel, however, that it is often much easier simply to pay the cybersquatter because that will likely be much faster and cheaper than to hire a lawyer and go through a lengthy legal process. No matter how companies or individuals deal with this problem, valuable resources of time and money are wasted resolving these disputes.

Federal and State Laws

In the United States, there are two main federal laws against computer crime: the Computer Fraud and Abuse Act of 1986 and the Electronic Communications Privacy Act of 1986. The Computer Fraud and Abuse Act of 1986 prohibits the following:

- Stealing or compromising data about national defense, foreign relations, atomic energy, or other restricted information
- Gaining unauthorized access to computers owned by any agency or department of the U.S. government
- Violating data belonging to banks or other financial institutions
- Intercepting or otherwise intruding on communications between states or foreign countries

- Threatening to damage computer systems in order to extort money or other valuables from persons, businesses, or institutions
- Threatening the U.S. president, vice president, members of Congress, and other administrative members (even if it's just in a critical e-mail)

In 1996, the Computer Abuse Amendments Act expanded the Computer Fraud and Abuse Act of 1986 to prohibit the dissemination of computer viruses and other harmful code.

The Electronic Communications Privacy Act of 1986 makes it a crime to break into any electronic communications service, including telephone services. It prohibits the interception of any type of electronic communications. Interception, as defined by the law, includes listening in on communications without authorization and recording or otherwise taking the contents of communications. In 2002, however, the U.S. Congress passed the USA PATRIOT Act (Patriot Act) to extend the Computer Fraud and Abuse Act. Prior to the Patriot Act, investigators could not monitor voice communication—or stored voice communication—when investigating someone suspected of violating the Computer Fraud and Abuse Act. Under the Patriot Act, investigators can gain access to voice-related communications much more easily, and this makes it a very controversial law. Many civil libertarians feel that the Patriot Act greatly erodes many existing constitutional protections, and it is likely to be hotly debated long into the future.

In addition to the primary laws discussed here, other federal laws may apply to computer crime. Patent laws protect some software and computer hardware, and contract laws may protect trade secrets that are stored on computers. In 1980, the U.S. Copyright Act was amended to include computer software, making it a violation of this act to post online written compositions, photos, sound files, and software without the permission of the copyright holder. Other laws covering software include a 1992 act that made software piracy a felony, and the 1997 No Electronic Theft Act, which made copyright infringement a criminal act even when no profit was involved. Further, the CAN-SPAM (Controlling the Assault of Non-Solicited Pornography and Marketing) was introduced to limit spam, and a 2013 change to the Telephone Consumer Protection Act (TCPA) provided stricter regulations for cell phone spam. Nevertheless, very little can be done to stop a motivated spammer (see www.spamlaws.com for more information).

The FBI and the U.S. Secret Service jointly enforce federal computer crime laws. The FBI is in charge when crimes involve espionage, terrorism, banking, organized crime, and threats to national security. The Secret Service investigates crimes against U.S. Treasury Department computers and against computers that contain information protected by the Right to Financial Privacy Act. Information protected by the Financial Privacy Act includes credit card usage, credit reporting, and bank loan application data. In some federal computer crime cases, the U.S. Customs Department, the Commerce Department, or the military may have jurisdiction. In addition to federal laws against computer crime, all 50 states have passed laws prohibiting computer crime. Many foreign countries also have similar laws.

Some violations of state and federal computer crime laws are charged as misdemeanors. These violations are punishable by fines and by not more than one year in prison. Other violations are classified as felonies and are punishable by fines and by more than one year in prison. The Patriot Act converted many misdemeanors into felony-level offenses. Nevertheless, intent can often determine whether crimes are prosecuted as misdemeanors or felonies. If intruders breach computer systems with intent to do harm, they may be charged with a felony. If a break-in is classified as reckless disregard but causes no damage, the offense may be classified as a misdemeanor.

Some critics argue that laws do not go far enough to prosecute computer crimes, while others believe that they should not be invoked when systems are breached but no damage is done. Even the definition of "damage" is debatable. For instance, has damage occurred if someone gains unauthorized access to a computer system but does not steal or change information?

There are additional difficulties in legislating and enforcing laws that affect global networks. Since many countries can be involved when break-ins and other crimes occur, who has jurisdiction? Should e-mail messages be monitored for libelous or other illegal content, and, if so, who should have monitoring responsibility? Should e-mail be subject to the same laws as mail delivered by the U.S. Postal Service, or should it be more akin to telephone conversations and the laws that apply to them?

WHO'S GOING MOBILE

Mobile Security

The rise of smartphones and tablets has added a new dimension to potential security threats—mobile malware. Today's smartphone owners can download hundreds of thousands of apps from various sources; for example, there are over 1.1 million apps available on Google Play (Google's market for Android apps), and over 1 million apps on Apple's App Store. Yet, when installing apps on their devices, users may risk installing mobile malware at the same time. Such malware could be capable of issuing commands to an attacked device, could steal the user's contacts and photos, or worse, it could turn on the device's camera or send premium-rate text messages.

Other mobile malware is designed for snooping on a targeted smartphone. Such apps, once installed and activated, are capable of tracking the target's location in real time, recording phone calls, and saving and displaying chats and text messages, even if the user has deleted them. Spyware apps typically work by disguising themselves so that they never show up in the user's list of installed apps. Although such apps can be used for legitimate purposes (such as law enforcement, following a court order), in the wrong hands, these apps can cause tremendous damage.

Security companies are rising to the occasion and developing mobile security solutions. Popular applications such as Avast! Mobile security, Lookout Security and Antivirus, and 360 Mobile Security are designed to detect and remove known security threats, primarily on the Android smartphone platform.

In 2013, Security firm Kaspersky reported that mobile malware poses significant security threats, including mobile banking fraud, mobile botnets, and even using infected mobile devices to gain access to connected PCs. The Android platform accounts for the overwhelming majority (over 98 percent) of mobile malware, due to its leading market position and relatively open architecture (as compared to Apple's App Store, which is significantly more selective in its app approval process). Yet, Apple's iOS devices are not immune to security threats. The company recently rushed a security update to all iOS devices to fix a severe vulnerability that allowed potential attackers to eavesdrop on secure communications, including personal e-mail, Internet banking, and online social network activities. Further, many users who are frustrated with the closed nature of Apple's platform choose to "jailbreak" their phones, so as to be able to download apps from sources other than the official App Store; this, however, exposes them to various potential threats. Considering the rapid increase in malware, it is no surprise that even the U.S. Department of Defense has called for a search of innovative ways to protect mobile devices from malware.

Based on:

Barret, B. (2014, February 23). Why Apple's recent security flaw is so scary. Retrieved April 22, 2014, from http://gizmodo.com/why-apples-huge-security-flaw-is-so-scary-1529041062.

Raiu, C., & Emm, D. (2013, December 10). Kaspersky security bulletin 2013. Retrieved April 22, 2014, from https://www.securelist.com/en/analysis/204792318/Kaspersky_Security_Bulletin_2013_Overall_statistics_for_2013.

CYBERWAR AND CYBERTERRORISM

Over the past several years, individual computer criminals have caused billions of dollars in losses by spreading malware or through unauthorized access to computers. In the future, many believe that coordinated efforts by national governments or terrorist groups have the potential to cause hundreds of billions of dollars in damage as well as put the lives of countless people at stake (Boyle & Panko, 2013). Most experts believe that cyberwar and cyberterrorism are imminent threats to the United States and other technologically advanced countries. A major attack that cripples a country's information infrastructure or power grid or even the global Internet could have devastating implications for a country's (or the world's) economic system and make transportation systems, medical capabilities, and other key infrastructure extremely vulnerable to disaster, especially given the proliferation of cloud computing for many personal, commercial, and governmental applications.

Cyberwar

Cyberwar refers to an organized attempt by a country's military to disrupt or destroy the information and communication systems of another country. Cyberwar is often executed simultaneously with traditional methods to quickly dissipate the capabilities of an enemy, and intelligence agencies from countries around the world are secretly testing networks and looking for weaknesses in their potential enemies' computer systems. For example, the United States reportedly conducted its first cyberwar campaign during the 78-day Serbia/Kosovo war by establishing a team of information warriors to support its bombing campaign against Serbia. The U.S. information operation cell electronically attacked Serbia's critical networks and command-and-control systems. However, given that the United States and NATO alliance is the most technologically sophisticated war machine in the world—and also the most dependent on its networking and computing infrastructure—it is also the most vulnerable to cyberwar (or cyberterrorism) attacks.

CYBERWAR VULNERABILITIES. The goal of cyberwar is to turn the balance of information and knowledge in one's favor in order to enhance one's capabilities while diminishing those of an opponent. Cyberwar utilizes a diverse range of technologies, including software, hardware, and networking technologies, to gain an information advantage over an opponent. These technologies can be used to electronically blind, jam, deceive, overload, and intrude into an enemy's information systems infrastructure in order to diminish various capabilities, including the following:

- Command-and-control systems
- Intelligence collection, processing, and distribution systems
- Tactical communication systems and methods
- Troop and weapon positioning systems
- Friend-or-foe identification systems
- Smart weapons systems

Additionally, controlling the content and distribution of propaganda and information to an opponent's civilians, troops, and government is a key part of a cyberwar strategy. At the simplest level, **Web vandalism** can occur by simply defacing Web sites. Likewise, cyberpropaganda can be quickly and easily distributed through chat rooms, Web sites, and e-mail. Espionage—stealing of secrets or modifying information—can occur if data and systems are not adequately protected and secure.

While there are several known attacks, most governments deny involvement. Typically, governments accused of cyberwar activities blame uncontrolled **patriot hackers**—independent citizens or supporters of a country that perpetrate attacks on perceived or real enemies. A recent example of such attack was discovered in June 2010 when a Belarus-based computer security company discovered a computer worm called **Stuxnet** on a computer system belonging to an Iranian client. Stuxnet is a computer worm designed to find and infect a particular piece of industrial hardware inside Iranian nuclear plants. Once Stuxnet found its intended target, centrifuges within Iran's nuclear enrichment program, it was programmed to manipulate their motor speeds. The manipulation of the motor speeds beyond normal operating tolerances would ultimately destroy the equipment, slowing and degrading the nuclear program. Since its discovery, computer security experts around the globe have studied its design. Stuxnet is a very sophisticated and unprecedented method for attacking an adversary. While most experts agreed that Stuxnet was most likely designed by a nation state, from the time of its discovery, no country had come forward to admit involvement in its creation. This suspicion ended in June 2012, when it was revealed that both Israel and the United States worked together to design Stuxnet. It is one of the first examples where cyberwarfare was used to inflict physical damage to critical infrastructures of a nation state. Another (admittedly less damaging attack) on the Iranian nuclear program happened in 2012, when malware introduced into Iranian nuclear facilities caused computers to play AC/DC's "Thunderstruck" at full volume in the middle of the night. In traditional war, destroying equipment by dropping a bomb is an act of war. Time will tell how nation states will respond to cyberattacks that ultimately cause similar damage, and regardless of the source of these attacks, it is clear that one of the big challenges for governments moving forward will be to fully integrate a cyberwar strategy into their overall plans and capabilities.

Cyberterrorism

Unlike cyberwar, **cyberterrorism** is launched not by governments but by individuals and organized groups. Cyberterrorism is the use of computer and networking technologies against persons or property to intimidate or coerce governments, civilians, or any segment of society in order to attain political, religious, or ideological goals. One of the great fears about cyberterrorism is that an attack can be launched from a computer anywhere in the world—no borders have to be crossed, no bombs smuggled and placed, and no cyberterrorists' lives lost in carrying out the attack. Because computers and networking systems control power plants, telephone systems, and transportation systems, as well as water and oil pipelines, any disruption in these systems could

TABLE 10.2 Categories of Potential Cyberterrorist Attacks

Category	Description
Coordinated bomb attacks	To distribute a number of devices—from small explosive devices to large weapons of mass destruction—that communicate with each other through the Internet or cellular phone networks and are made to simultaneously detonate if one device stops communicating with the others
Manipulation of financial and banking information	To disrupt the flow of financial information with the objective of causing fear and lack of confidence in the world's or a country's financial system
Manipulation of the pharmaceutical industry	To make hard-to-detect changes in the formulas of medications in order to cause fear and lack of confidence in this important industry
Manipulation of transportation control systems	To disrupt airline and railroad transportation systems, possibly leading to disastrous collisions
Manipulation of the broader civilian infrastructures	To compromise the communication, broadcast media, gas lines, water systems, and electrical grids in order to cause panic and fear within the population
Manipulation of nuclear power plants	To disrupt cooling systems in order to cause a meltdown that would disperse radiation

cause loss of life or widespread chaos. Just as physical terrorist attacks have physical and psychological effects, so also do cyberattacks. Dealing with the unknown—where, when, and how—of an indiscriminant terrorist attack is what leads to "terror."

WHAT KINDS OF ATTACKS ARE CONSIDERED CYBERTERRORISM? Cyberterrorism could involve physical destruction of computer systems or acts that destroy economic stability or infrastructure. Cyberterrorist acts could likely damage the machines that control traffic lights, power plants, dams, or airline traffic in order to create fear and panic. Attacks launched in cyberspace could take many forms, such as viruses, denial of service, destruction of government computers, stealing classified files, altering Web page content, deleting or corrupting vital information, disrupting media broadcasts, and otherwise interrupting the flow of information. Table 10.2 summarizes several categories of attacks that experts believe cyberterrorists will try to deliver.

The goal of cyberterrorists is to cause fear, panic, and destruction. Through the power of computer technology and global networks, terrorists can gain access to critical parts of the world's infrastructure to produce both physical and virtual terror. Given the great potential for cyberterrorism, many experts believe that it will, unfortunately, become the weapon of choice for the world's most sophisticated terrorists.

HOW THE INTERNET IS CHANGING THE BUSINESS PROCESSES OF TERRORISTS. Virtually all modern terrorist groups utilize the Internet (Weimann, 2006). Beyond using the Internet to wage cyberattacks, the Internet is a powerful tool for improving and streamlining the business processes of the modern terrorist (Table 10.3). Just as the Internet has fueled globalization for organizations and societies, it too has fueled global terrorism. Clearly, the Internet is transforming the "business processes" of the modern terrorist.

ASSESSING THE CYBERTERRORISM THREAT. Some experts claim that because of the general openness of access, the Internet infrastructure is extremely vulnerable to cyberterrorism. Each year, cyberattacks on critical infrastructure such as nuclear power plants, dams, and power grids are increasing. While the majority of such attacks have not done damage at this point, a few have been alarmingly successful and concerning:

- In May 2003, Romanian crackers compromised systems that housed life-support control for 58 scientists and contractors in Antarctica. FBI agents assisted in the arrest of the crackers, who attempted to extort money from the research station.
- In May 2007, government networks and commercial banks within Estonia came under a very sophisticated cyberattack by cyberterrorists in retaliation for the removal of a Soviet-era memorial to fallen soldiers.
- In 2010–2013, "The Jester," believed to be a former U.S. soldier, claimed responsibility for attacks on WikiLeaks, Islamists' Web sites, and even the Web site of Iranian President Mahmoud Ahmadinejad. After a successful attack, The Jester broadcasts "TANGO DOWN"—a military term that means a target has been injured or killed—on Twitter.

TABLE 10.3 How Terrorists Are Using the Internet

Use	Description
Information dissemination	The use of Web sites to disseminate propaganda to current and potential supporters, to influence international public opinion, and to notify potential enemies of pending plans.
Data mining	The use of the vast amount of information available on the Internet regarding virtually any topic for planning, recruitment, and numerous other endeavors.
Fundraising	The use of Web sites for bogus charities and nongovernmental organizations to raise funds and transfer currencies around the world.
Recruiting and mobilization	The use of Web sites to provide information for recruiting new members as well as roaming online chat rooms, social media, and cybercafés for receptive individuals.
Networking	The use of the Internet to enable a less hierarchical, cell-based organizational structure that is difficult to combat; networking capabilities also allow different groups with common enemies to better share and coordinate information.
Information sharing	The use of the Internet as a powerful tool for announcing events as well as sharing best practices.
Training	The use of the Internet to disseminate training materials. For example, the official Hamas Web site details how to make homemade poisons and gases, and Syrian rebels use YouTube to disseminate weapons training videos.
Planning and coordinating	The use of communication and information dissemination capabilities to facilitate designing and executing plans.
Information gathering	The use of mapping software such as Google Earth to locate potential targets for terrorist attacks.
Location monitoring	The use of public Web cams to monitor and study potential attack sites (e.g., public places or civil infrastructure such as tunnels or power generation facilities).

While cyberterrorism obviously remains a threat to computer and network security, some experts point out that there are disadvantages to using acts of cyberterrorism as a weapon, including the following:

1. Computer systems and networks are complex, so cyberattacks are difficult to control and may not achieve the desired destruction as effectively as physical weapons.
2. Computer systems and networks change and security measures improve, so it requires an ever-increasing level of knowledge and expertise on the part of intruders for cyberattacks to be effective. This means that perpetrators will be required to continuously study and hone their skills as older methods of attack no longer work.
3. Cyberattacks rarely cause physical harm to victims; therefore, there is less drama and emotional appeal than for perpetrators using conventional weapons.

Some experts believe that the likelihood of a devastating attack that causes significant disruption in the major U.S. infrastructure systems is quite low because of the resources and intelligence needed carry out a sophisticated attack. Nevertheless, small attacks have been occurring for years and are likely to increase in frequency and severity—even a "small" attack, like an individual suicide bomber, can cause tremendous chaos to a society. While cyberterrorism and cyberwar may be methods of choice for future generations with advanced computer knowledge, experts are hopeful that the increasing sophistication of computer security measures will help reduce the number of such incidents.

RESPONDING TO GLOBAL CYBERTERRORISM THREATS. With the proliferation of and dependence on technology increasing at an astronomical rate, the threat of cyberterrorism will continue to increase. As has been true with virtually all governments and business organizations, fueled by the digitization of information and the Internet, terrorism has become a global business. To be adequately prepared, national governments along with industry partners must design coordinated responses to various attack scenarios. In addition to greater cooperation and preparedness, governments must improve their intelligence-gathering capabilities so that potential attacks are thwarted before they begin. Industry must also be given incentives to secure their information resources so that losses and disruptions in operations are minimized. International laws and treaties must rapidly evolve to reflect the realities of cyberterrorism, where attacks can be launched from anywhere in the world to anywhere in the world. Clearly, there are great challenges ahead.

BRIEF CASE 3D Crime Scenes

3D technology is now widely used for re-creating crime scenes, from comparing footprints to testing crime theories. For example, modern 3D forensic ballistics technologies help to re-create a crime scene for understanding the origination and path of bullets. These technologies are also capable of creating a 3D image of a bullet that has been fired and then finding a match from previous criminal cases. Likewise, the process of capturing every minute detail of a crime scene, including the location of bloodstains, has been enhanced by the use of laser scanning equipment. Once the crime scene is re-created, technology further allows detectives and/or police to revisit the scene in three dimensions, from any vantage point desired, in real time. 3D images of cities and buildings are also being stored to help police foil future terrorist attacks. 3D home security systems also play a role in protecting homes and belongings from fire or burglary, allowing users to check for potential loss and search for probable causes, the same way the police do at crime scenes. These advances, and their display in popular TV programs such as *CSI: Crime Scene Investigation* have become so pervasive that they have created the so-called CSI effect. The CSI effect refers to the belief that jurors demand more forensic evidence in criminal trials due to advances in forensic and investigative technology that are learned by watching modern police shows, thereby raising the effective standard of proof for prosecutors.

Questions

1. How does the rapid evolution of technology change the way crimes are investigated and cases are presented in court proceedings?
2. Will 3D crime scene capabilities increase or decrease the CSI effect? Why?

Based on:

CSI effect. (2014, March 27). In *Wikipedia, The Free Encyclopedia*. Retrieved April 22, 2014, from http://en.wikipedia.org/w/index.php?title=CSI_effect&oldid=601486187.

DeGood, J. (2014, April 10). WPD uses 3D scanner to document police involved shooting. *KWCH.com*. Retrieved April 22, 2014, from http://www.kwch.com/news/local-news/wpd-uses-3d-scanner-to-document-police-involved-shooting/25421540.

MANAGING INFORMATION SYSTEMS SECURITY

Everyone who uses an information system (IS) knows that disasters can happen to stored information or to entire systems. Some disasters are accidents caused by power outages, inexperienced computer users, or mistakes, while others are caused on purpose by malicious crackers. The primary threats to the security of information systems include the following (Figure 10.12):

- ***Natural Disasters*:** power outages, hurricanes, floods, and so on
- ***Accidents*:** inexperienced or careless computer operators (or cats walking across keyboards!)
- ***Employees and Consultants*:** people within an organization who have access to electronic files
- ***Links to Outside Business Contacts*:** electronic information that can be at risk when it travels between or among business affiliates as part of doing business
- ***Outsiders*:** hackers and crackers who penetrate networks and computer systems to snoop or to cause damage (Viruses, perpetually rampant on the Internet, are included in this category.)

For individuals as well as organizations, trying to recover from disasters carries high costs in terms of time and money; in addition, organizations can lose much goodwill if their systems are unavailable (no matter what the reason is) or are compromised by malicious crackers. How do you secure information systems from such dangers? How do you know what systems are at risk of being compromised? The rule of thumb for deciding whether an information system is at risk is simple: All systems connected to networks are vulnerable to security violations from outsiders as well as insiders as well as to virus infections and other forms of computer crime. Further, no information system is immune to intentional or unintentional physical harm. In short, threats to information systems can come from a variety of places internal and external to an organization. **Information systems security** refers to precautions taken to keep all aspects of information systems (e.g., all hardware, software, network equipment, and data) safe from destruction, manipulation, or unauthorized use or access, while providing the intended functionality to legitimate users. Specifically, organizations have to consider the following:

- ***Availability*:** ensuring that legitimate users can access the system
- ***Integrity*:** ensuring that unauthorized manipulations of data and systems (that may compromise accuracy, completeness, or reliability of data) are prevented

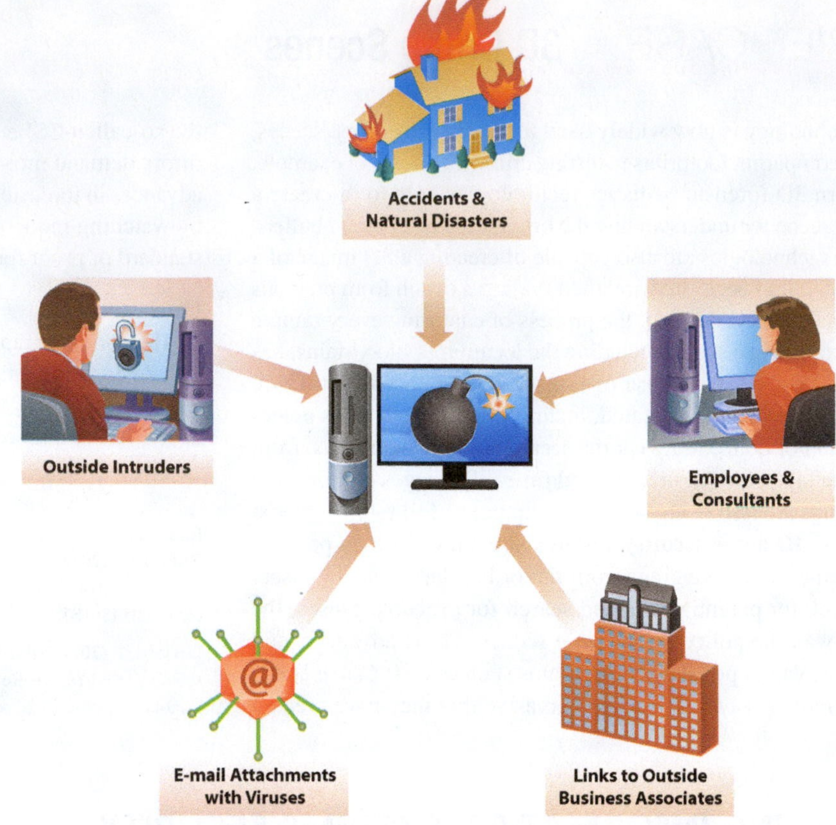

FIGURE 10.12
Threats to IS security.

- ***Confidentiality***: ensuring that data are protected from unauthorized access
- ***Accountability***: ensuring that actions can be traced

Hence, for organizations, it is essential to carefully manage IS risk and to ensure business continuity by securing their IS infrastructure. As use of the Internet and related telecommunications technologies and systems has become pervasive, use of these networks now creates a dangerous vulnerability for organizations. These networks can be infiltrated and/or subverted in a number of ways. As a result, the need for tight computer and network security has increased dramatically. Fortunately, there are a variety of managerial methods and security technologies that can be used to manage IS security effectively. However, as threats to information systems constantly evolve, information systems security is an ongoing process, consisting of (Figure 10.13):

1. Assessing risks
2. Developing a security strategy
3. Implementing controls and training
4. Monitoring security

In addition, organizations should continuously watch for emerging threats and vulnerabilities, as well as attacks (including attacks on other organizations), so as to update risk assessments and strategies, and implement additional controls.

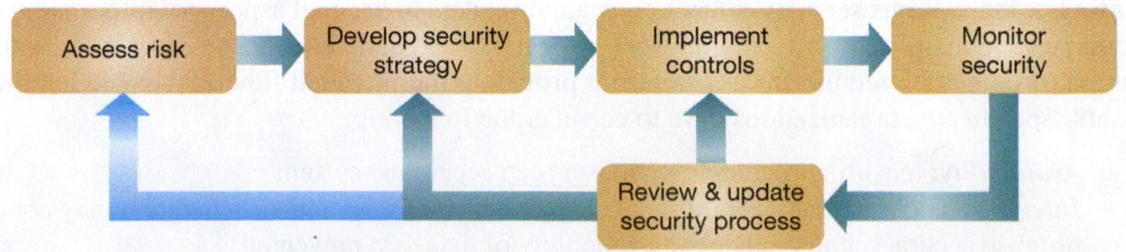

FIGURE 10.13
Information systems security is an ongoing process.

Assessing Risks

Maintaining customer confidence is essential for any organization, and any IS security-related incident can lead to reputation, operational, legal, and strategic risks. Consequently, any good approach to securing information systems begins first with a thorough **information systems risk assessment** to obtain an understanding of the risks to the availability, integrity, and confidentiality of data and systems. It would not make sense to spend literally millions of dollars a year to protect an asset the loss of which would cost the organization only a few thousand dollars. As a result, organizations attempt to identify and rank the risks in order to develop the most effective strategies. In other words, organizations assess the value of the assets being protected, determine their probability of being compromised, and compare the probable costs of their being compromised with the estimated costs of whatever protections they might have to take. Protecting an asset only makes economic sense if the cost of protecting the asset is less than (or equal to) the value of the asset (and the associated data that can be lost or damage that can be done) multiplied by the probability of a disaster. Thus, organizations perform risk assessments for their systems to ensure that IS security programs make sense economically (Stallings & Brown, 2012).

Such assessment should encompass all of an organization's systems, including hardware, software, data, networks, and any business processes that involve them, so as to identify threats and vulnerabilities, determine their probabilities of being exploited, and to assess the potential impact (i.e., the severity of the consequences if a threat indeed causes damage by exploiting a vulnerability) (Figure 10.14). **Threats** are typically defined as undesirable events that can cause harm, and can arise from actions performed by agents internal or external to an organization. In other words, threats can come from current or former insiders (such as employees, contractors, etc.) as well as criminals, competitors, terrorists, or the elements. In contrast, **vulnerabilities** are defined as weaknesses in an organization's systems or security policies that can be exploited to cause damage, and can encompass both known vulnerabilities (such as vulnerabilities discovered during audits) and expected vulnerabilities (such as unpatched software, new attack methodologies, or staff turnover).

By understanding and evaluating these factors, organizations can then design and implement a security strategy that makes the best use of the available resources in order to eliminate vulnerabilities or reduce impacts. In addition to an information systems risk assessment, organizations then periodically perform security audits to determine the effectiveness of the implemented measures. People within the IS department are usually responsible for implementing the security measures chosen, though people from throughout the organization should participate in the risk assessment.

In order to get a thorough understanding of risks, organizations need to consider both technical information (such as information about databases, hardware and software, and networks) and non-technical information (such as information about processes and procedures related to physical or personnel security) to determine and assess the threats and vulnerabilities. Typically, a thorough information systems risk assessment uses both quantitative data (such as value of the asset or implementation costs of security measures) and qualitative data (e.g., results from interviews or walkthroughs) to arrive at a risk rating that reflects the possible impact, likelihood, and ultimate risk level for each particular function or asset (Table 10.4).

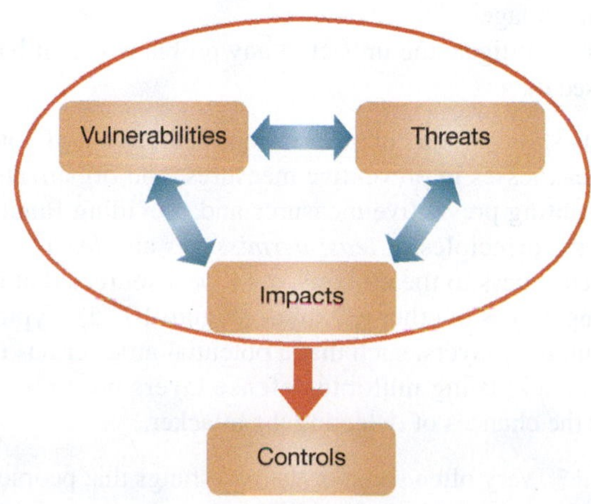

FIGURE 10.14

Organizations have to understand the interplay between threats, vulnerabilities, and impacts to plan and implement effective IS controls.

TABLE 10.4 Sample Risk Rating Matrix for a Customer Database

Risk Category	Impact	Likelihood	Risk Level (Impact × Likelihood)
Confidentiality	3	2	6
Integrity	2	3	6
Availability	3	1	3
Overall	*8*	*6*	*15*

TABLE 10.5 Options for Addressing IS Risks

Option	Description	Condition
Risk reduction	Taking active countermeasures to protect your systems	■ High risk cannot be accepted.
Risk acceptance	Implementing no countermeasures and simply absorbing any damages that occur	■ There exists a low likelihood/impact. ■ Other factors are more important than security.
Risk transference	Having someone else absorb the risk	■ Other parties may be better equipped to manage the risk.
Risk avoidance	Using alternate means, or not perform tasks that would cause risk	■ Risk is unmanageable. ■ Risk is too high.

This risk rating then enables the organization to determine what steps, if any, to take to secure systems. Large organizations typically use a balance of different approaches, taking steps in **risk reduction** for some systems, accepting risk and living with it in other cases (i.e., **risk acceptance**), and also insuring all or most of their systems activities (i.e., **risk transference**). A fourth category—**risk avoidance** (e.g., by not engaging in e-commerce, not having a Web site, or not using e-mail)—can often be impractical or even infeasible in today's networked environment. See Table 10.5 for a summary of these options.

Developing a Security Strategy

Once risks are assessed, a strategy should be formulated that details what **information systems controls** (in terms of technology, people, and policies) should be implemented. By ensuring the availability, integrity, and confidentiality of information, the controls help an organization to control costs, gain and protect trust, remain competitive, and comply with internal or external governance mandates (e.g., the Sarbanes–Oxley Act, discussed later in this section). Such controls can consist of a variety of different measures; to be most effective, an IS security strategy should focus on the following:

- **Preventive controls:** to prevent any potentially negative event from occurring, such as by preventing outside intruders from accessing a facility
- **Detective controls:** to assess whether anything went wrong, such as unauthorized access attempts, and to limit damage
- **Corrective controls:** to mitigate the impact of any problem after it has arisen, such as restoring compromised data

Whereas most efforts should focus on prevention, detection and correction are important to compensate for any weaknesses in preventive measures, and organizations have to strike the balance between implementing preventive measures and providing functionality for the users. Thus, organizations use the principles of *least permissions* and *least privileges*, meaning that users should only be given access to the systems, data, or resources that are needed to perform their duties, and restricting access to other resources (Figure 10.15). Typically, information systems controls comprise multiple layers, such that a potential attacker has to break several layers to conduct a successful attack; using multiple defense layers not only helps in thwarting the attack, but also increases the chances of detecting the attacker.

POLICIES AND PROCEDURES. Very often some of the best things that people can do to secure their information systems are not necessarily technical in nature. Instead, they may involve changes

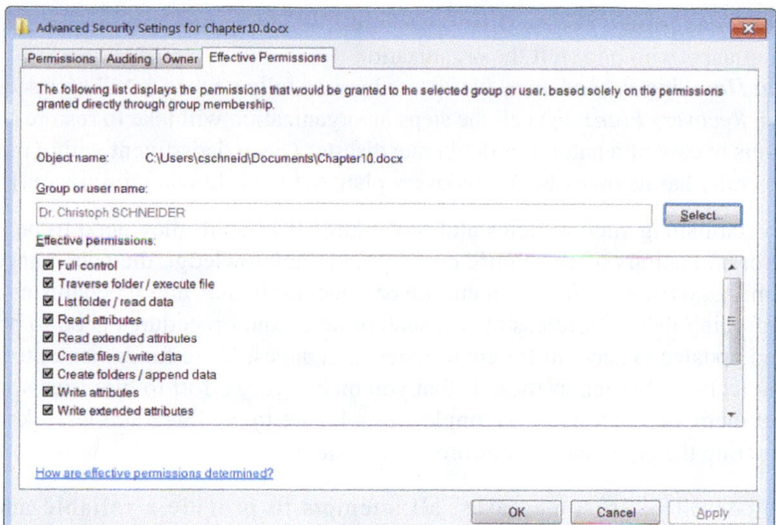

FIGURE 10.15

Following the principles of least permissions and least privileges, users should only be given access to the systems, data, or resources that are needed to perform their duties.
Source: Courtesy of Microsoft Corporation

within the organization and/or better management of people's use of information systems. For example, one of the outcomes of the risk assessment described here may well be a set of computer and/or Internet use policies (sometimes referred to as **acceptable use policies**) for people within the organization, with clearly spelled out penalties for noncompliance (Figure 10.16).

In general, policies and procedures that guide users' decisions and establish responsibilities include the following:

a. ***Information Policy:*** outlines how sensitive information will be handled, stored, transmitted, and destroyed
b. ***Security Policy:*** explains technical controls on all organizational computer systems, such as access limitations, audit-control software, firewalls, and so on
c. ***Use Policy:*** outlines the organization's policy regarding appropriate use of in-house computer systems; may mandate no Internet surfing, use of company computer systems only for employment-related purposes, restricted use of social networking and e-mail, and so on
d. ***Backup Policy:*** explains requirements for backing up information, so that critical data can be restored in case of data loss

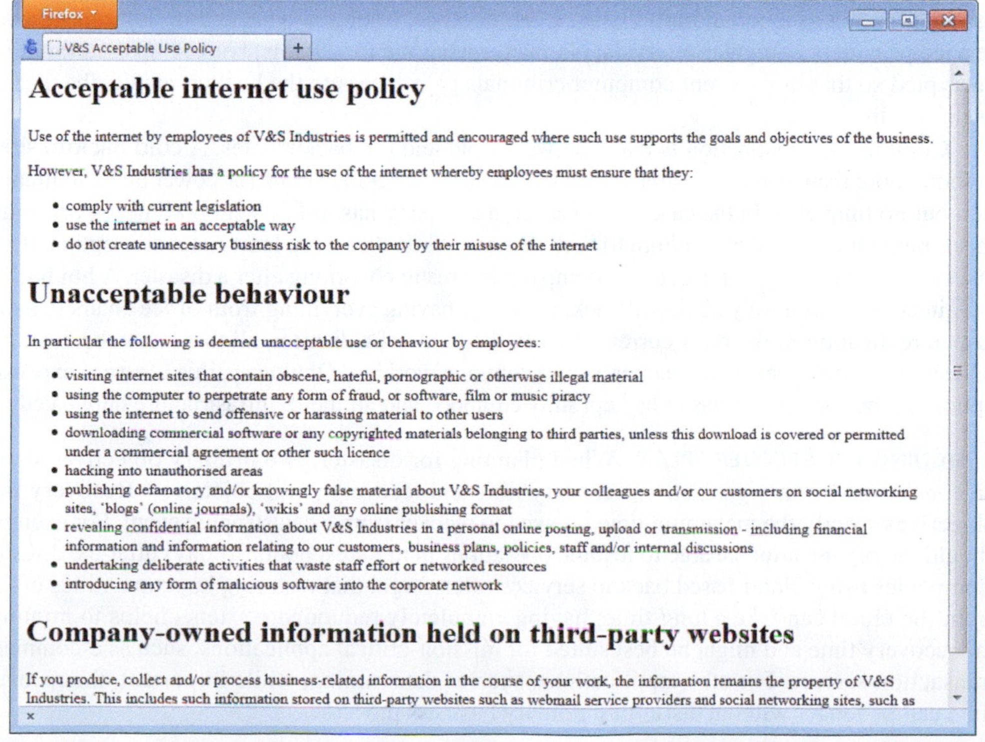

FIGURE 10.16

Most organizations provide employees or customers with an acceptable use policy.

e. ***Account Management Policy:*** lists procedures for adding new users to systems and removing users who have left the organization
f. ***Incident Handling Procedures:*** lists procedures to follow when handling a security breach
g. ***Disaster Recovery Plan:*** lists all the steps an organization will take to restore computer operations in case of a natural or deliberate disaster (Each department within the organization generally has its own disaster recovery plan; see the following discussion.)

While establishing such policies and procedures is crucial, they need to be clearly communicated; organizations often require employees to acknowledge the acceptance of policies in order to mitigate risks arising from employee noncompliance, and mechanisms should be in place for enforcing these. Needless to say, such policies and procedures need to be continually reviewed and updated to account for environmental changes. More fundamental to security than management techniques such as these is that you make every effort to hire trustworthy employees and treat them well. Trustworthy employees who are treated well are less likely to commit offenses affecting the organization's information systems.

DISASTER PLANNING. In some cases, all attempts to provide a reliable and secure IS infrastructure are in vain, and disasters cannot be avoided. Thus, organizations need to be prepared for potential impacts. A **business continuity plan** describes how a business continues operating after a disaster, before normal operations have been restored; relatedly, a **disaster recovery plan** spells out detailed procedures for recovering from systems-related disasters, such as virus infections and other disasters that might cripple the IS infrastructure. This way, even under the worst-case scenario, people will be able to replace or reconstruct critical files or data, or they will at least have a plan readily available to begin the recovery process. A typical disaster recovery plan includes information that answers the following questions:

- What events are considered a disaster?
- What should be done to prepare the backup site?
- What is the chain of command, and who can declare a disaster?
- What hardware and software are needed to recover from a disaster?
- Which personnel are needed for staffing the backup sites?
- What is the sequence for moving back to the original location after recovery?
- Which providers can be drawn on to aid in the disaster recovery process?

Backup sites are critical for business continuity in the event a disaster strikes; in other words, backup sites can be thought of as a company's office in a temporary location. In addition, organizations should have **backups** of important data in place. Typically, such backups use media such as external hard drives, CDs, or tapes, or data are backed up to online backup service providers at regular intervals. No matter what the medium is, backed up data should be encrypted so that in the event computer criminals gain access to the backup media, the data are useless to them.

Commonly, a distinction is made between cold and hot backup sites. A **cold backup site** is nothing more than an empty warehouse with all necessary connections for power and communication but nothing else. In the case of a disaster, a company has to first set up all necessary equipment, ranging from office furniture to Web servers. While this is the least expensive option, it also takes a relatively longer time before a company can resume working after a disaster. A **hot backup site**, in contrast, is a fully equipped backup facility, having everything from office chairs to a one-to-one replication of the most current data. In the event of a disaster, all that has to be done is to relocate the employees to the backup site to continue working. Obviously, this is a very expensive option, as the backup site has to be kept fully equipped and all the IS infrastructure duplicated.

DESIGNING THE RECOVERY PLAN. When planning for disaster, two primary objectives should be considered by an organization: recovery time and recovery point objectives. **Recovery time objectives** specify the maximum time allowed to recover from a catastrophic event. For example, should the organization be able to resume operations in minutes, hours, or days after the disaster? Companies using cloud-based backup services often forget that restoring large quantities of data from the cloud can take a long time; having completely redundant systems helps to minimize the recovery time and might be best suited for mission-critical applications, such as e-commerce transaction servers. For other applications, such as data mining, while important, the recovery time can be longer without disrupting primary business processes.

Recovery point objectives specify how current the backup data should be. Imagine that your computer's hard drive crashes while you are working on a term paper. Luckily, you recently backed up your data. Would you prefer the last backup to be a few days old, or would you rather have the last backup include your most recent changes to the term paper? Hot backup sites typically have a redundant backup of the data so that the business processes are interrupted as little as possible and data loss is minimized (or even avoided) in the event of a catastrophic failure. To achieve this redundancy, all data are **mirrored** on separate servers (i.e., everything is stored synchronously on two independent systems). This might seem expensive, but for a critical business application involving customers, it may be less expensive to run a redundant backup system in parallel than it would be to disrupt business or lose customers in the event of catastrophic system failure.

Often, companies choose to replicate their data centers in multiple locations. Thinking about the location of redundant systems is an important aspect of disaster planning. If a company relies on redundant systems, all of which are located within the same building, a single event can incapacitate all the systems. Similarly, events such as a hurricane can damage systems that are located across town from each other. Thus, even if the primary infrastructure is located in-house, it pays to have a backup located in a different geographic area to minimize the risk of a disaster happening to both systems.

Implementing Controls and Training

Once a comprehensive strategy has been formulated, organizations can decide which controls to implement and train personnel regarding security policies and measures. Such controls can encompass different measures, such as systems security policies and their physical implementation, access restrictions, or record keeping, to be able to trace actions and transactions and who is responsible for these. IS controls thus need to be applied throughout the entire IS infrastructure. There are two broad categories of approaches for reducing risk—technological- and human-based approaches—and any comprehensive security strategy will include both. Commonly used controls to safeguard information systems include:

- Physical access restrictions
- Firewalls
- Encryption
- Virus monitoring and prevention
- Secure data centers
- Systems development controls
- Human controls

Within any type of safeguard, there are a variety of ways in which it can be deployed. Next, we briefly review each of these methods.

PHYSICAL ACCESS RESTRICTIONS. Organizations can prevent unauthorized access to information systems by keeping stored information safe and allowing access only to those employees who need it to do their jobs. Of course, organizations can protect computers and data resources by physically securing computers to desks or requiring users to lock hard drives with keys when leaving a computer unattended. However, most organizations don't go to such lengths and control access only by requiring some form of **authentication** to confirm the identity of a user. The most common form of authentication is the use of passwords, which are effective only if chosen carefully and changed frequently (Figure 10.17). Besides passwords, employees may be asked to provide an ID combination, a security code sequence, or personal data, such as their mother's maiden name. Employees authorized to use computer systems may also be issued keys to physically unlock a computer, photo ID cards, smart cards with digital ID, and other physical devices allowing computer access. In sum, access is usually limited by making it dependent on one of the following:

- ***Something You Have.*** Keys, picture identification cards, smart cards, or smart badges that contain memory chips with authentication data on them (Figure 10.18)
- ***Something You Know.*** Passwords, code numbers, PIN numbers, lock combinations, or answers to secret questions (your pet's name, your mother's maiden name, and so on)
- ***Something You Are.*** Unique attributes, such as fingerprints, voice patterns, facial characteristics, or retinal patterns (collectively called *biometrics*)

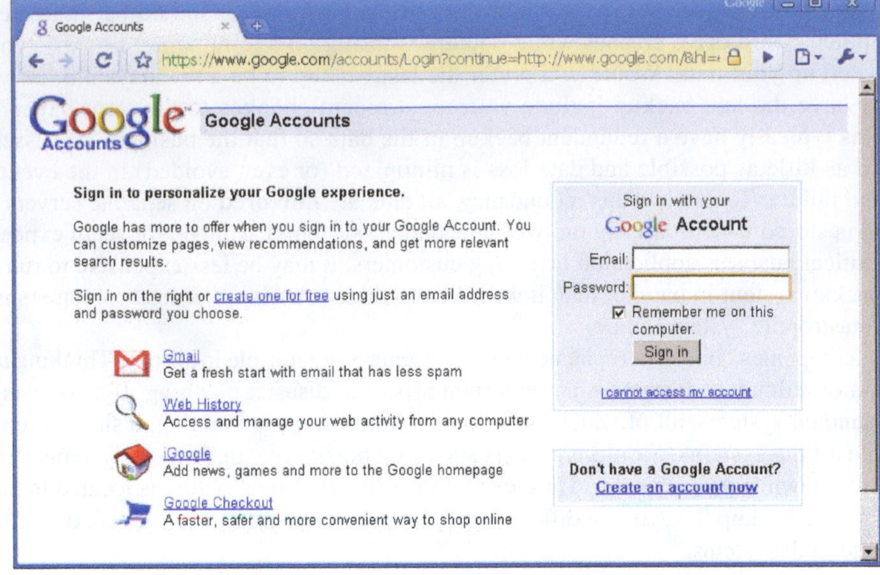

FIGURE 10.17

The most common form of authentication is through passwords.
Source: Courtesy of Google, Inc.

FIGURE 10.18

A smart card.
Source: al62/Fotolia

Some measures that limit access to information are more secure than others. For example, smart cards and smart badges, passwords, lock combinations, and code numbers can be stolen. Biometric devices are difficult to fool, but determined intruders may sometimes devise ways to bypass them. Any of the previously mentioned single items can be used, but it is safer to use combinations of safeguards, such as a password *and* a smart card. No matter what safeguards are used, organizations should have formal processes in place for enrolling new users, authorizing specific users to access systems or data, authenticating the users, and monitoring the access of resources. Needless to say, policies should be in place to revoke access for employees who are leaving the company, or who are taking on different roles or responsibilities. Next, we examine various methods for implementing physical access control.

Biometrics **Biometrics** is one of the most sophisticated forms of governing access to systems, data, and/or facilities. With biometrics, employees may be identified by fingerprints, retinal patterns in the eye, facial features, or other bodily characteristics before being granted access

COMING ATTRACTIONS

Speeding Security Screening

Just about everyone who uses airline travel today dreads the invasive and time-consuming airport security screening process. Researchers at the University of Arizona are developing an interactive screening kiosk called AVATAR to naturally interact with people, conduct interviews, and detect changes in arousal, behavior, and cognitive effort by using psychophysiological indicators (Figure 10.19). The kiosk uses embodied intelligent agents (avatars) to ask people questions and then has a variety of sensors to noninvasively monitor their responses. The AVATAR kiosk assesses cues through sensors in body movement, vocalics (e.g., voice pitch changes), pupillometry (e.g., pupil dilation and blinking), and eye tracking. The kiosk is an interactive screening technology designed to be on the front lines of border crossings and airports. It is envisioned that individuals will approach the AVATAR kiosk, scan their identification, answer a few simple questions, and then move on. Meanwhile, the AVATAR kiosk uses noninvasive sensor technology and artificial intelligence algorithms to gauge suspicious behavior. The AVATAR kiosk is envisioned to help border agents better utilize their valuable time. For instance, several AVATAR kiosks could be operated by a single officer who would step in to work directly with individuals whose behavior has been flagged as abnormal. In 2012, the AVATAR was tested for several months at the Nogales, Arizona, border crossing with Mexico, supporting agents in the U.S. Customs and Border Protection Trusted Travel program. With each test of the AVATAR kiosk, the researchers learn more and improve its design. Someday, you too may be interviewed by AVATAR before entering the restricted area of an airport or when crossing international borders.

Based on:
Higgenbotham, A. (2013, January 17). Deception is futile when Big Brother's lie detector turns its eyes on you. *Wired.* Retrieved April 22, 2014, from http://www.wired.com/2013/01/ff-lie-detector/all.

FIGURE 10.19

The AVATAR screening kiosk is designed to automate the screening process using noninvasive sensors to detect changes in arousal and cognitive effort.

Source: Borders Group, Inc.

to use a computer or to enter a facility (Figure 10.20). Biometrics has the promise of providing very high security while at the same time authenticating people extremely efficiently, so many governments and companies are investigating how best to use this technology. For example, many laptops and computer keyboards now incorporate fingerprint readers; similarly, residents of Hong Kong can quickly pass through immigration checkpoints by using a smart card and their thumbprints.

Access-Control Software Following the principles of least permissions and least privileges, access should only be granted to the resources needed to perform the work; anything beyond that potentially exposes the organization to vulnerabilities. **Access-control software** can reduce such vulnerabilities by allowing computer users access only to those files related to their work. The user might even be restricted to these resources only at certain times or for specified periods of time, and, depending on the access level, the user can be restricted to being able to only read a file, to read and edit the file, to add to the file, and/or to delete the file. Many common business systems applications now build in these kinds of security

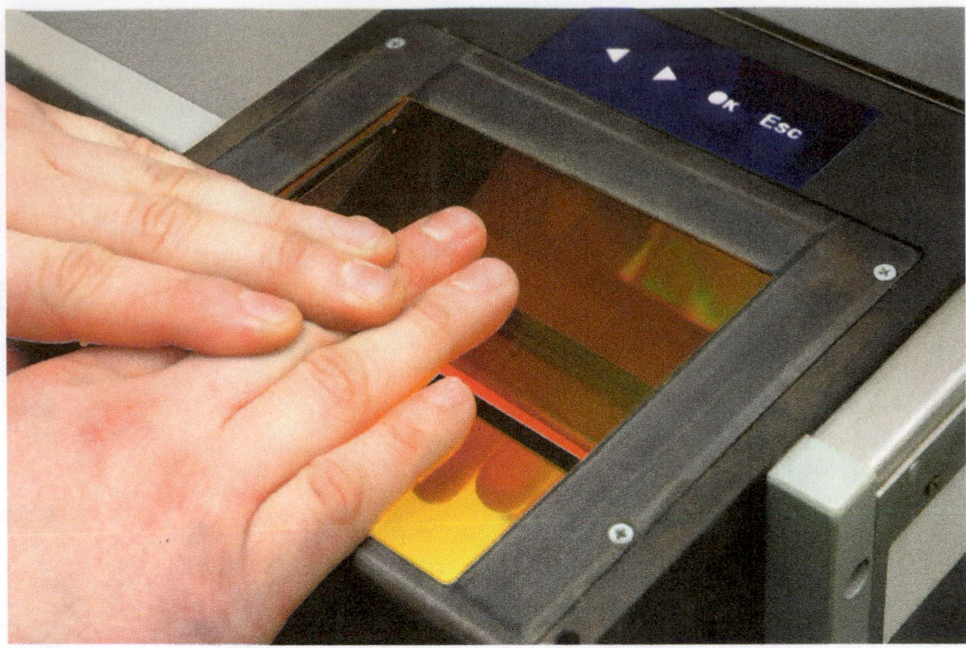

FIGURE 10.20

Biometric devices are used to verify a person's identity.
Source: Kilukilu/Dreamstime LLC

features so that you do not have to have additional, separate access-control software running on top of your applications software.

Wireless LAN Control Given how easy and inexpensive wireless local area networks (WLANs) are to install and use, their use has skyrocketed, leaving many systems open to attack. On an unsecured network, for instance, unauthorized people can thus easily "steal" company resources (e.g., by surfing the Web for free, which is illegal in many countries) or do considerable damage to the network. A new form of attack known as **drive-by hacking** has arisen, where an attacker accesses the network, intercepts data from it, and even uses network services and/or sends attack instructions to it without having to enter the home, office, or organization that owns the network (Figure 10.21). Wireless LAN control refers to methods of configuring the WLAN so that only authorized users can gain access.

Virtual Private Networks A **virtual private network (VPN)** is a network connection that is constructed dynamically within an existing network—often called a secure tunnel—in order to connect users or nodes (Figure 10.22). For example, a number of companies and software solutions enable you to create VPNs within the Internet as the medium for transporting

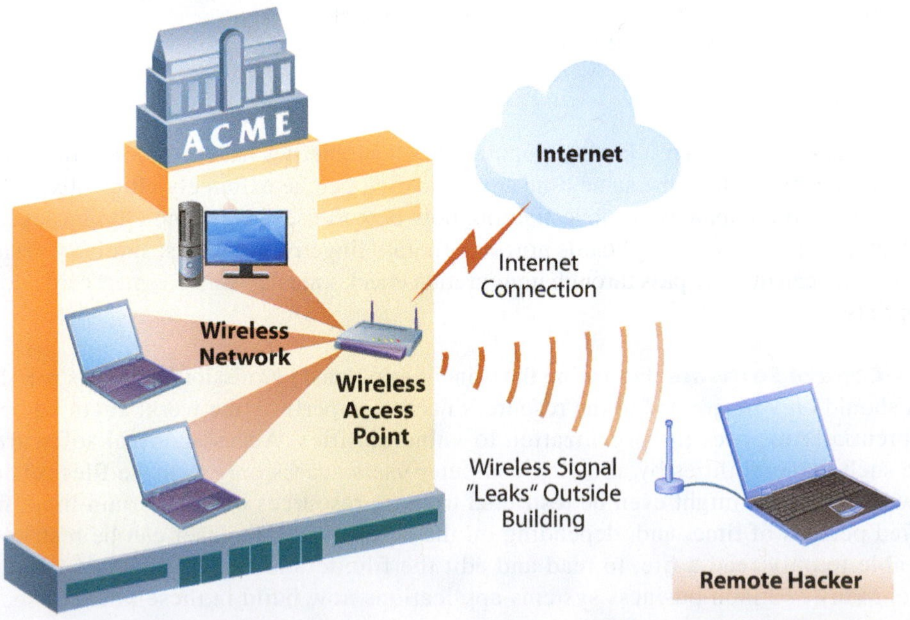

FIGURE 10.21

Drive-by hacking is on the rise given the proliferation of unsecured wireless LANs.

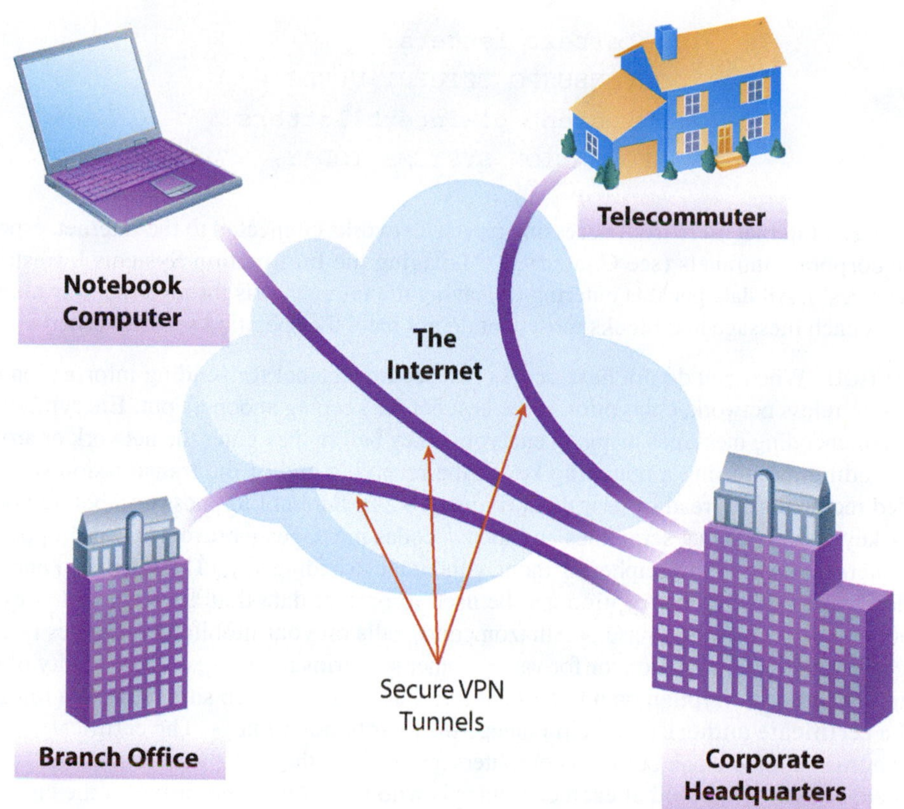

FIGURE 10.22

A virtual private network (VPN) allows remote sites and users to connect to organizational network resources using a secure tunnel.

data. These systems use authentication and encryption (discussed later) and other security mechanisms to ensure that only authorized users can access the VPN and that the data cannot be intercepted and compromised; this practice of creating an encrypted "tunnel" to send secure (private) data over the (public) Internet is known as **tunneling**. For example, The University of Arizona requires VPN software to be used when accessing some critical information resources from remote (off-campus) locations.

FIREWALLS. A **firewall** is a part of a computer system designed to detect intrusion and prevent unauthorized access to or from a private network (Figure 10.23). Think of a firewall essentially as a security fence around the perimeter of an organization's information systems that spots any intruders that try to penetrate the organization's outer defenses. Firewalls can be implemented in hardware, in software, or in a combination of both. Firewalls are frequently used to prevent

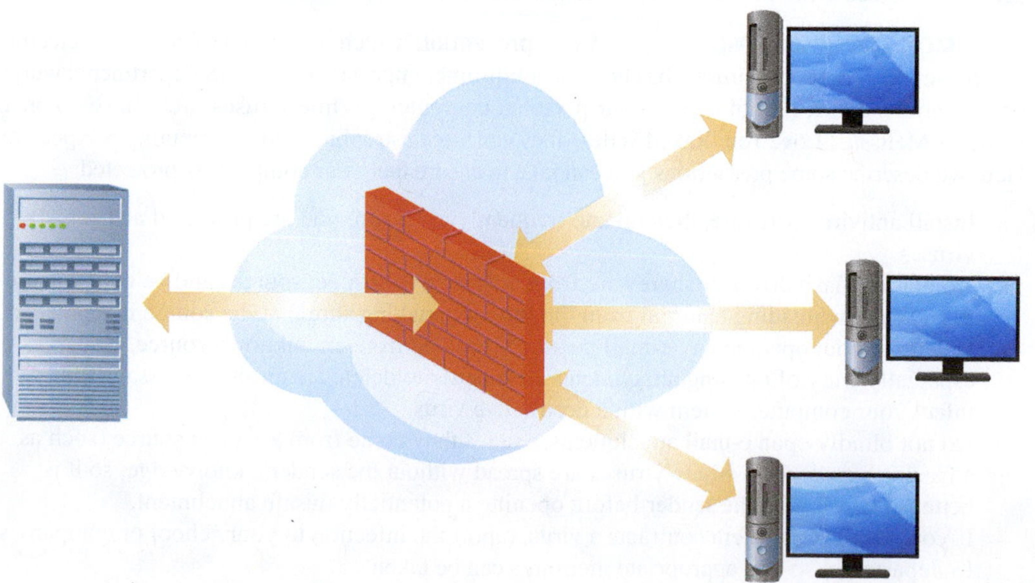

FIGURE 10.23

A firewall blocks unauthorized access to organizational systems and data, while permitting authorized communication to flow in and out of the organization to the broader Internet.

FIGURE 10.24

Encryption is used to encode information so that unauthorized people cannot understand it.

```
Ciphertext letters:
JOGPSNBUJPO TZTUFNT UPEBZ
Equivalent plaintext letters:
INFORMATION SYSTEMS TODAY
```

unauthorized Internet users from accessing private networks connected to the Internet, especially private corporate intranets (see Chapter 3, "Managing the Information Systems Infrastructure and Services"). All data packets entering or leaving the intranet pass through the firewall, which examines each message and blocks those that do not meet the specified security criteria.

ENCRYPTION. When you do not have access to a secure channel for sending information over a wired or wireless network, encryption is the best bet for keeping snoopers out. **Encryption** is the process of encoding messages using an encryption key before they enter the network or airwaves, then decoding them using a matching key at the receiving end of the transmission so that the intended recipients can read or hear them (Figure 10.24). Scrambling messages before you send using a key—the code that scrambles and then decodes messages—prevents eavesdroppers who might intercept them from deciphering them without the decoding key. (The science of encryption is called *cryptography*.) Encryption can be used to protect data that are transmitted over the Internet (e.g., your new purchase at Amazon.com), calls on your mobile phone, files or folders contacting sensitive information, or for various other scenarios requiring confidentiality of data.

Implementing encryption on a large scale, such as on a busy Web site, requires a third party, called a **certificate authority**, to help manage the distribution of keys. The certificate authority acts as a trusted middleman between computers and verifies that a Web site is a trusted site. The certificate authority knows that each computer is who it says it is and provides the encryption/decryption keys to each computer. **Secure Sockets Layer**, developed by Netscape, is a popular public key encryption method used on the Internet. There are many different encryption approaches for different types of data transmission.

Cloud Security With more and more data and applications being moved to the cloud, **cloud security** is becoming increasingly important; specifically, organizations not only need to secure data at rest (e.g., files or folders stored on a physical medium) and data in transit (i.e., data traveling across a network) but also data in use (i.e., data being processed by a computer). Regular encryption approaches can be utilized to secure data at rest and data in transit; securing data in use is more problematic, as encrypted data typically need to be decrypted before being processed, even for simple manipulations such as summing up a range of numbers. However, in such case, the cloud service provider would be able to access the decrypted data, potentially compromising the availability, integrity, and confidentiality of the data. Recently, researchers have developed new algorithms that allow for "encryption in use," such that the encrypted data can be processed without being accessible to a cloud service provider.

VIRUS MONITORING AND PREVENTION. **Virus prevention**, which is a set of activities for detecting and preventing computer viruses, has become a full-time, important task for IS departments within organizations and for all of us with our personal computers. While viruses often have colorful names—Melissa, I Love You, Naked Wife—they can be catastrophic from a computing perspective. Here we describe some precautions you can take to ensure that your computer is protected:

- Install antivirus software, then update frequently to be sure you are protected against new viruses.
- Do not use flash drives or shareware from unknown or suspect sources and be equally careful when downloading material from the Internet, making sure that the source is reputable.
- Delete without opening any e-mail message received from an unknown source. Be especially wary of opening attachments. It is better to delete a legitimate message than to infect your computer system with a destructive virus.
- Do not blindly open e-mail attachments, even if they come from a known source (such as a friend or coworker). Many viruses are spread without the sender's knowledge, so it is better to check with the sender before opening a potentially unsafe attachment.
- If your computer system contracts a virus, report the infection to your school or company's IS department so that appropriate measures can be taken.

KEY PLAYERS

White Knights of the Internet Age

Ever since organizational and personal computing became ubiquitous, computer criminals have attempted to infect computers with malicious software. Using malicious software to gain access to an unsuspecting computer user's password, or stealing the user's credit card data is a relatively "clean" and easy endeavor, and is less risky than most other forms of crime. Because every computer is vulnerable to an attack, computer criminals have many different ways to attack unsuspecting users. Users typically do not expect to become victims, and are thus not constantly on alert. As computer criminals think of new ways to exploit vulnerabilities, neither users nor virus protection software know what to look for, making protection from malware a cat-and-mouse game. A common recommendation is to install antivirus software, which attempts to protect users by finding, then deleting, quarantining, or repairing any files deemed malicious.

Given this cat-and-mouse contest, security software has become a lucrative business. Even with the global economy slowing, spending on security software hasn't slowed; according to research firm Gartner, the market for security software increased by 4.9 percent from 2012 to 2013, totaling more than US$19.9 billion in 2013. The biggest players in the market for security software include specialized computer security companies such as Symantec, McAfee, TrendMicro, IBM, AVG, and others. Many of these companies offer full suites of security software, including virus and malware detection, e-mail protection, and other safeguards.

There are plenty of different software products to choose from, and many are free for personal use. However, a worldwide survey conducted by Microsoft revealed that in 2013, 24 percent of PCs were not protected by up-to-date antivirus software, even though unprotected PCs are over five times more likely to be infected with malware. These figures show that even with frequent coverage of malware in the news, people seem to be unaware of the threats. As in many other situations, not only are technological safeguards needed, but user education seems to be key.

Based on:

Antivirus software. (2014, April 11). In *Wikipedia, The Free Encyclopedia*. Retrieved April 22, 2014, from http://en.wikipedia.org/w/index.php?title=Antivirus_software&oldid=603748580.

Rains, T. (2013, April 17). Latest security intelligence report shows 24 percent of PCs are unprotected. Retrieved April 22, 2014, from http://blogs.technet.com/b/microsoft_blog/archive/2013/04/17/latest-security-intelligence-report-shows-too-many-pcs-lack-antivirus-protection.aspx.

van der Meulen, R., & Rivera, J. (2014, June 10). Gartner says worldwide security software market grew 4.9 percent in 2013. *Gartner.* Retrieved July 21, 2014, from http://www.gartner.com/newsroom/id/2762918.

SECURE DATA CENTERS. Specialized facilities are an important component of creating a reliable and secure IS infrastructure. Data and the ability to process the data are the lifeblood for many of today's large organizations, such as Amazon.com, Travelocity.com, or Facebook. Consequently, organizations need to protect important equipment from both outside intruders and the elements, such as water or fire. The most prominent threats to an organization's IS facilities come from floods, seismic activity, rolling blackouts, hurricanes, and the potential of criminal activities (Figure 10.25). How can an organization reliably protect its facilities from such threats?

Ensuring Business Continuity As many potential causes of disasters cannot be avoided (there's no way to stop a hurricane), organizations should attempt to plan for the worst and implement necessary controls in their data centers. For companies operating in the digital world, the IS infrastructure is often critical for most business processes, so special care has to be taken to secure it. Whereas some applications can tolerate some downtime in case something malfunctions or disaster strikes, other applications (such as UPS's package tracking databases) can't tolerate any downtime—these companies need 24/7/365 reliability (Figure 10.26).

Securing the Facilities Infrastructure An organization's data centers always needs to be secured to protect it from outside intruders. Absolute protection against security breaches remains out of reach, but here are a few safeguards organizations can employ:

- ***Site Selection.*** Organizations should ensure that data centers are not built in areas that are prone to earthquakes, floods, hurricanes, or other damaging natural forces.
- ***Physical Access Restrictions.*** As with any valuable asset, data centers should be protected from intruders using measures such as fences, barriers, and security guards. Organizations should also strive to maintain information about data center locations confidential.

FIGURE 10.25

Potential threats to IS facilities include floods, hurricanes, terrorism, power outages, and seismic activity.

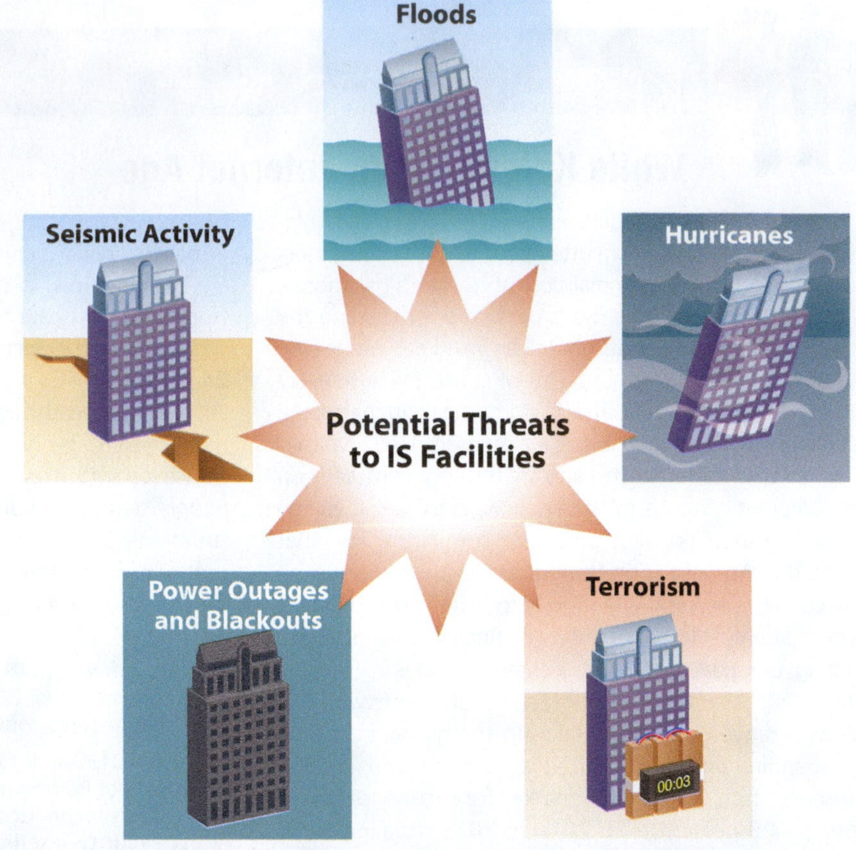

FIGURE 10.26

The UPS servers handle up to 20 million requests per day.
Source: Alejandro Mendoza R/ Shutterstock

- ***Intrusion Detection.*** Closed-circuit television (CCTV) systems should monitor the physical interior and/or exterior of a facility for physical intruders, allowing in-house security personnel or an outside security service to detect and immediately report suspicious activity. In addition, security alarm systems using motion, sound, and/or vibration detectors should be installed. Recording CCTV footage as well as all events from the security alarm systems can help investigate the causes of an intrusion.

FIGURE 10.27

Collocation facilities allow organizations to rent secure space for their infrastructure.
Source: Shutterstock

- ***Uninterruptible Power and Cooling.*** To ensure uninterrupted service, the data centers should be self-sufficient, and be able to operate for a pre-specified time period on self-generated power. In addition to implementing an uninterruptible power supply for powering the computers, the data center should provide for continuous cooling in case of a power interruption (some data centers store chilled water for such purposes).
- ***Protection from Environmental Threats.*** To protect the data centers from the elements, data centers should be built to withstand strong winds (depending on the location). Other measures include raised floors (to protect from floods) as well as heat sensors, smoke detectors, and fire suppression systems.

For reasons of business continuity, companies such as UPS maintain large data centers in different geographic areas. Many (especially smaller) organizations do not need facilities the size of one of the UPS data centers; instead, they may just need space for a few servers. For such needs, companies can turn to **collocation facilities**. Organizations can rent space (usually in the form of cabinets or shares of a cabinet; see Figure 10.27) for their servers in such collocation facilities, and the organizations managing collocation facilities provide the necessary infrastructure in terms of power, backups, connectivity, and security. Alternatively, organizations increasingly attempt to transfer risk by using cloud computing services.

SYSTEMS DEVELOPMENT CONTROLS. The final set of technological controls is related to ensuring that all systems (including hardware and software) are properly developed, acquired, and maintained. Following a structured systems development process helps to minimize threats arising from software bugs, security holes, or other issues (refer to Chapter 9 for a complete discussion). In general, these processes should ensure that the necessary security features are implemented and enabled, and that proper change management processes are followed. When acquiring systems from outside vendors, organizations face risks not only from software bugs, but also from backdoors that may exist in the system. Thus, organizations should exercise due diligence to ensure that the software is trustworthy, for example by reviewing the software's source code (if possible), and by performing background checks on the vendor's history and trustworthiness.

Clearly, there are a broad range of technology-based approaches for securing information systems, and a comprehensive security plan will include numerous technological controls. Next, we examine human-based controls.

HUMAN CONTROLS. In addition to the technological controls, various human safeguards can help to protect information systems, specifically ethics, laws, and effective management (Figure 10.28). *IS ethics*, discussed in Chapter 1, "Managing in the Digital World," relates to a broad range of standards of appropriate conduct by users. Educating potential users at an early age as to what

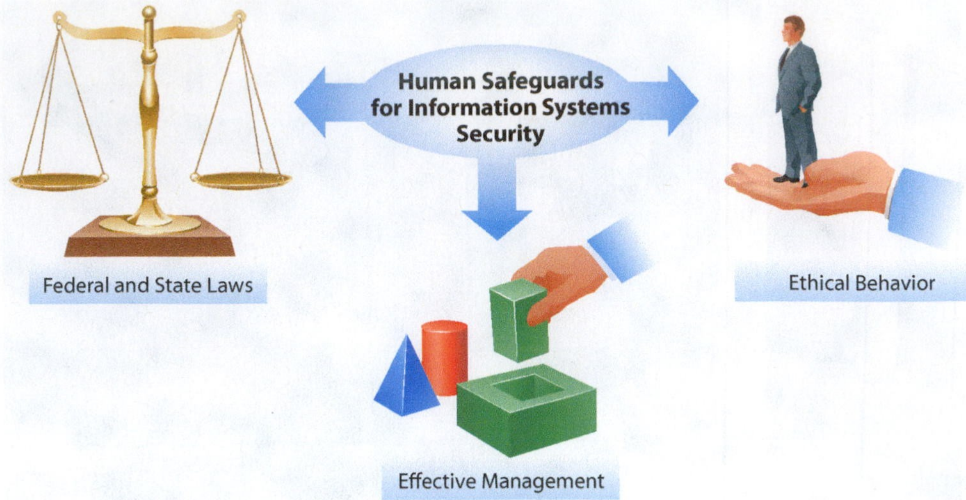

FIGURE 10.28

Human safeguards for IS security.

constitutes appropriate behavior can help, but unethical users will undoubtedly always remain a problem for those wanting to maintain IS security. Additionally, there are numerous federal and state laws against unauthorized use of networks and computer systems. Unfortunately, individuals who want unauthorized access to networks and computer systems usually find a way to exploit them; often, after the fact, laws are enacted to prohibit that activity in the future.

DEPLOYMENT AND TRAINING. Once the organization has decided on the necessary controls, network security mechanisms such as firewalls are deployed, as are intrusion detection systems, antivirus software, manual and automated log examination software, and host- and network-based intrusion detection software. Encryption information, passwords, and smart cards and smart badges are also disseminated and explained during this phase. The IS department is usually responsible for implementing these controls. At the same time, personnel throughout the organization should receive training about the security policies and plans for disaster recovery and be prepared to perform assigned tasks in that regard—both routinely on a daily basis and disaster related.

Monitoring Security

To minimize risk, organizations should continuously monitor the effectiveness of the controls. Any user—authorized or unauthorized—leaves electronic footprints that can be traced. Automated log examination software and host- and network-based intrusion detection software is used to keep track of computer activity in order to spot suspicious activity and take action. Using such software helps creating an audit trail, a record showing who has used a computer system and how it was used. For the software to effectively protect security, of course, auditors within the organization—most often someone in the IS department or information security department—must monitor and interpret the results. Needless to say, the level of monitoring should be based on an assessment of the potential impact of a certain asset being compromised; in other words, the most monitoring efforts should be focused on high-risk systems. In addition to monitoring internal events, organizations should also monitor external events, in order to obtain a full view of threats and vulnerabilities (Figure 10.29).

FIGURE 10.29

Organizations should monitor internal and external threats and vulnerabilities to ensure the effectiveness of their IS controls.

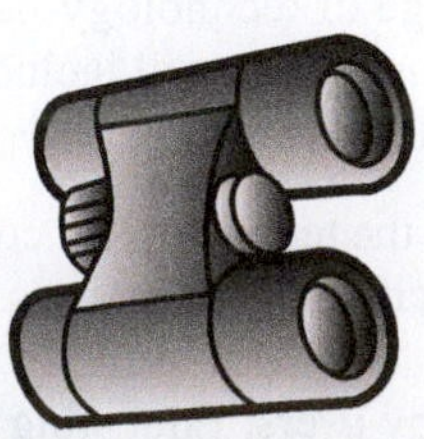

MONITORING EXTERNAL EVENTS. Several online organizations issue bulletins to alert organizations and individuals to possible software vulnerabilities or attacks based on reports from organizations that have experienced security breaches. Further, Information Sharing and Analysis Centers (ISAC, http://www.isaccouncil.org/) representing various industry sectors and the United States Computer Emergency Readiness Team (http://www.us-cert.gov/) provide additional resources for organizations by publishing security alerts or conducting and publishing research related to IS security.

IS AUDITING. Monitoring internal and external vulnerability information should be an ongoing process for organizations. However, it can also be beneficial for organizations to periodically have an external entity review the controls so as to uncover any potential problems. An **information systems audit**, often performed by external auditors, can help organizations assess the state of their IS controls to determine necessary changes and to help ensure the information systems' availability, integrity, and confidentiality. The response to the strengths and weaknesses identified in the IS audit is often determined by the potential risks an organization faces. In other words, the IS audit has to assess whether the IS controls in place are sufficient to address the potential risks. Thus, a major component of the IS audit is a risk assessment (discussed in prior sections), which aims at determining what type of risks the organization's IS infrastructure faces, the criticality of those risks to the infrastructure, and the level of risks the organization is willing to tolerate.

Once the risk has been assessed, auditors have to evaluate the organization's internal controls, trying to answer questions such as: Can the intrusion detection system detect attacks? Are incident response procedures effective? Can the network be penetrated? Is physical security adequate? Do employees know security policies and procedures? In other words, auditors assess aspects such as policy adherence, the security of new projects, and whether the organization's defense layers can be penetrated. During such audits, the auditor tries to gather evidence regarding the effectiveness of the controls. However, testing all controls under all possible conditions is very inefficient and often infeasible. Thus, auditors frequently rely on **computer-assisted audit tools** to test applications and data using test data or simulations, or tools such as vulnerability scanners or packet sniffers. In addition to using specific auditing tools, auditors use audit sampling procedures to assess the controls, enabling the audit to be conducted in the most cost-effective manner. Further, penetration tests are conducted in-house and/or by an outside contractor to see how well the organization's computer security measures are working. Once the audit has been performed and sufficient evidence has been gathered, reports are issued to the organization. Usually, such reports are followed up with a discussion of the results and potential courses of action.

THE SARBANES–OXLEY ACT. Performing an IS audit can help an organization reduce costs or remain competitive by identifying areas where IS controls are lacking and need improvement. Another major factor that has contributed to a high demand for IS auditors is the need to comply with government regulations, most notably the **Sarbanes–Oxley Act** of 2002 (hereafter S-OX). Formed as a reaction to large-scale accounting scandals that led to the downfall of corporations such as WorldCom and Enron, and to protect investors from fraudulent practices by organizations, S-OX mandates companies to demonstrate compliance with accounting standards and to establish controls and sound corporate governance. Commonly used controls include limiting a single employee's influence over transactions, such as by segregation of duties and establishing proper checks and balances. For example, if the employee who creates a purchase order also has the authority to approve the purchase order, this opens up a possibility for creating fraudulent orders; similarly, if the same employee is responsible for disbursing cash, recording the disbursements, and reconciling the related accounts, the employee can devise schemes to embezzle money. Implementing proper controls not only helps to reduce the potential for fraud, but also helps to prevent unintentional errors. To demonstrate S-OX compliance, public companies are required, among other things, to have external auditors assess the effectiveness of their internal controls, as well as audit their financial statements. While S-OX addresses primarily the accounting side of organizations, it is of major importance to include IS controls in compliance reviews, given the importance of an IS infrastructure and IS controls for an organization's financial applications.

According to S-OX, companies have to demonstrate that there are controls in place to prevent misuse or fraud, controls to detect any potential problems, and effective measures to correct any problems; S-OX goes so far that corporate executives face jail time and heavy fines if the appropriate controls are not in place or are ineffective. The IS architecture plays a key role in S-OX compliance, given that many controls are IS based, providing capabilities to detect exceptions and providing a management trail for tracing these. However, S-OX itself barely addresses IS controls specifically; rather, it addresses general processes and practices, leaving companies wondering how to comply with the guidelines put forth in the act. Further, it is often cumbersome and time consuming for organizations to identify the relevant systems to be audited for S-OX compliance. Thus, many organizations find it easier to review their entire IS infrastructure, following objectives set forth in guidelines such as the **control objectives for information and related technology (COBIT)**—a set of best practices that helps organizations both maximize the benefits from their IS infrastructure and establish appropriate controls.

Another issue faced by organizations because of S-OX is the requirement to preserve evidence to document compliance and for potential lawsuits. Since the inception of S-OX, e-mails and even instant messages have achieved the same status as regular business documents and thus need to be preserved for a period of time, typically up to seven years. Failure to present such documents in the case of litigious activity can lead to severe fines being imposed on companies and their executives, and courts usually will not accept the argument that a message could not be located. For example, the investment bank Morgan Stanley faced fines up to US$15 million for failing to retain e-mail messages. On the surface, it seems easiest for an organization to simply archive all the e-mail messages sent and received. However, such a "digital landfill," where everything is stored, can quickly grow to an unmanageable size, and companies cannot comply with the mandate to present evidence in a timely manner. Thus, many organizations turn to e-mail management software that archives and categorizes all incoming and outgoing e-mails based on key words. Even using such specialized software, finding e-mails related to a certain topic within the archive can pose a tremendous task: Some analysts estimate that a business with 25,000 employees generates over 4 billion e-mail messages over the course of seven years (not counting any increase in e-mail activity), which would be hard to handle for even the most sophisticated programs.

RESPONDING TO SECURITY INCIDENTS. Organizations that have developed a comprehensive IS security plan will have the ability to rapidly respond to any type of security breach to their IS resources or to a natural disaster. Typically, incident handling policies detail how the incident is classified in terms of severity, who has the authority to escalate the incident, and what incidents need to be internally or externally reported. Responses to a security breach include containing the security breach, restoring systems, and notifying or assisting customers (if needed). Further, when intruders are discovered, organizations can contact local law enforcement agencies and the FBI for assistance in locating and prosecuting the intruders. In addition, common responses to a security breach include performing a new risk audit and implementing a combination of additional (more secure) controls (as described previously).

COMPUTER FORENSICS. As computer crime has gone mainstream, law enforcement has had to become much more sophisticated in their computer crime investigations. **Computer forensics** is the use of formal investigative techniques to evaluate digital information for judicial review. Most often, computer forensics experts evaluate various types of storage devices to find traces of illegal activity or to gain evidence in related non-computer crimes. In fact, in most missing-person or murder cases today, investigators immediately want to examine the victim's computer for clues or evidence.

Organizations and governments are increasingly utilizing *honeypots* to proactively gather intelligence to improve their defenses or to catch cybercriminals. A **honeypot** is a computer, data, or network site that is designed to be enticing to crackers so as to detect, deflect, or counteract illegal activity. For instance, the FBI operated a cybercrime clearinghouse called "DarkMarket" where unsuspecting hackers, credit card swindlers, and identity thieves bought and sold products and information (Poulsen, 2008). Products for sale included electronic banking logins, stolen personal data, and even specialized hardware for producing counterfeit credit cards. The FBI operated DarkMarket for more than two years to collect information on the global marketplace for cybercriminals. In late 2008, DarkMarket was shut down because it had become known to the criminals. It is without question that countless other honeypots are being operated by governments and computer forensics experts to track criminals and gather information.

Although computer forensics experts are extremely skilled in investigating prior and on-going computer crime, many computer criminals are also experts, making the forensics process extremely difficult in some cases. Some criminals, for example, have special "booby-trap" programs running on computers to destroy evidence if someone other than the criminal uses the machine. Using special software tools, computer forensics experts can often restore data that have been deleted from a computer's hard drive. Clearly, computer forensics will continue to evolve as criminals utilize more sophisticated computer-based methods for committing and aiding criminal activities.

The State of Information Systems Security Management

We continue to hear and read about cases where a breach of computer security was catastrophic and/or had potentially dire consequences. For example, in late 2013, malware introduced into the point-of-sale system of retail giant Target captured credit card data of 40 million shoppers. Nevertheless, despite these highly publicized incidents and the fact that no one is immune from cybercrime, information systems security strategies are often lacking. Many of the over 500 U.S. respondents to the 2013 U.S. State of Cybercrime Survey do not have a good understanding of the threats they face, the capabilities of computer criminals, and the nature of their organizations' vulnerabilities. Key findings from the survey include the following:

- Of the C-level executives surveyed, 38 percent indicated they did not have a methodology that uses clear measures to assess the organization's security programs.
- The greatest security threats came from crackers (22 percent), insiders (21 percent), and foreign nation states (11 percent).
- For 34 percent of the organizations, insider attacks were more costly than attacks from outsiders (31 percent).
- Business executives primarily use free Internet sites (71 percent) and free subscription-based services (63 percent) as sources for information about threats and vulnerabilities; these sources may vary in accuracy, timeliness, or quality. Far fewer executives use government Web sites (47 percent), paid services (33 percent), or information sharing and analysis centers (23 percent).

Clearly, because malicious crackers won't become complacent anytime soon, organizations need to guard against attacks. The lesson learned here is that we need to continue to implement vigilant approaches to better manage information systems security in the digital world.

INDUSTRY ANALYSIS

Cybercops Track Cybercriminals

The *CSI* (*Crime Scene Investigation*) television shows have made "DNA testing" a household phrase. Virtually everyone knows that a criminal who leaves body cells or fluids—hair and skin cells, saliva, blood, semen, and so on—at the scene of a crime can be linked to the crime through DNA analysis. (DNA, or deoxyribonucleic acid, is present in all living tissue—plant or animal.) Just as a criminal leaves DNA traces, cybercriminals are leaving digital footprints. However, using computer forensics to track down cybercriminals requires sophisticated tools and methods.

Because technological advancement has been rapid, law enforcement has lagged behind cybercriminals, but is catching up. At the U.S. federal level, the Computer Crime and Intellectual Property Section within the Department of Justice is devoted to combating cybercrime. In addition, the FBI has created cyber squads in 56 field offices around the country specifically to investigate cybercrime, in addition to a cyber division at the FBI headquarters. Each federal judicial district has at least one assistant U.S. attorney who has received special training in how to investigate and prosecute cybercrime. Every state now has a computer crime investigation unit available as a resource to local law enforcement agencies, and many municipal police departments have their own computer crime investigative units.

Software tools available to law enforcement agencies have improved greatly in recent years. Programs such as the Software Forensic Tool Kit provide police with the ability to search and re-create deleted files on computers. Also digitized for law enforcement use are criminal identification systems, such as the Statewide Network of Agency Photos (SNAP). Law enforcement officers can search SNAP's digital database for mug shots that show a criminal's distinguishing marks, such as scars and tattoos, making criminal identification simpler. Similarly, the Classification System for Serial Criminal Patterns, developed by the Chicago Police Department, allows detectives to look for possible patterns connecting crimes.

It is unfortunate that criminals use the Internet and other technologies to their advantage. Clearly, however, law enforcement is keeping pace with them; officers use technological advances to track, arrest, and prosecute online and offline criminals.

Questions

1. Today, is it harder or easier to be a criminal? Why?
2. Provide an argument as to whether law enforcement can or cannot get ahead of criminals technologically.

Based on:

FBI Cyber Crime Division. (n.d.). Retrieved April 22, 2014, from http://www.fbi.gov/about-us/investigate/cyber.

Justice Technology Information Network. (n.d.). Retrieved April 22, 2014, from https://www.justnet.org.

Key Points Review

1. ***Define computer crime and describe several types of computer crime.*** Computer crime is defined as the use of a computer to commit an illegal act, such as targeting a computer while committing an offense, using a computer to commit an offense, or using computers in the course of a criminal activity. Those who break into computer systems with the intention of doing damage or committing a crime are usually called crackers. Crackers are associated with the making and distributing of computer viruses and other destructive codes. People are increasingly using information systems to aid in crimes against individuals, including identity theft, cyberharassment, cyberstalking, and cyberbullying. Finally, making illegal copies of software, a worldwide computer crime, is called software piracy.
2. ***Describe and explain the differences between cyberwar and cyberterrorism.*** Cyberwar refers to an organized attempt by a country's military to disrupt or destroy the information and communication systems of another country. The goal of cyberwar is to turn the balance of information and knowledge in one's favor in order to diminish an opponent's capabilities and also to enhance those of the attacker. Cyberterrorism is the use of computer and networking technologies by individuals and organized groups against persons or property to intimidate or coerce governments, civilians, or any segment of society to attain political, religious, or ideological goals. Now that terrorist groups are increasingly using the Internet for their purposes, one of the great fears about cyberterrorism is that an attack can be launched from a computer anywhere in the world.
3. ***Discuss the process of managing IS security and describe various IS controls that can help in ensuring IS security.*** Information systems security refers to precautions taken to keep all aspects of information systems (e.g., all hardware, software, network equipment, and data) safe from unauthorized use or access, to ensure availability, integrity, confidentiality, and accountability. IS security is an ongoing process, consisting of assessing risks, developing a security strategy, implementing controls and training, and monitoring security. An information systems risk assessment is performed to identify threats and vulnerabilities, determine their probabilities of being exploited, and to assess the potential impact. An IS security strategy details what controls should be implemented, as well as security-related policies and procedures. General categories of controls include: physical access restrictions, firewalls, encryption, virus monitoring and protection, secure data centers, systems development controls, and human controls. To ensure the effectiveness of the controls, organizations should continuously monitor internal and external events and periodically perform IS audits.

Key Terms

Go to **mymislab.com** to complete the problems marked with this icon ✪.

Review Questions

10-01. List and describe the primary threats to IS security.

✪ **10-02.** Define computer crime and list several examples of computer crime.

10-03. Explain the purpose of the Computer Fraud and Abuse Act of 1986 and the Electronic Communications Privacy Act of 1986.

10-04. Contrast hackers versus crackers.

✪ **10-05.** Why are insider threats particularly dangerous for organizations?

10-06. Define malware and give several examples.

10-07. Define and contrast cyberharassment, cyberstalking, and cyberbullying.

10-08. Define and contrast cyberwar and cyberterrorism.

10-09. What are physical access restrictions, and how do they make an information system more secure?

10-10. Describe several methods for preventing and/or managing the spread of computer viruses.

10-11. Describe three human-based controls for safeguarding information systems.

✪ **10-12.** Describe the process of managing IS security.

10-13. Describe how the Sarbanes–Oxley Act impacts the IS security of an organization.

Self-Study Questions

10-14. What is the common rule for deciding if an information system faces a security risk?

A. Only desktop computers are at risk.
B. Only network servers are at risk.
C. All systems connected to networks are vulnerable to security violations.
D. Networks have nothing to do with computer security.

10-15. Those individuals who break into computer systems with the intention of doing damage or committing a crime are usually called __________.

A. hackers
B. crackers
C. computer geniuses
D. computer operatives

10-16. Which of the following does not pose a threat to electronic information?

A. unauthorized access
B. jailbreaking one's mobile phone
C. unauthorized information modification
D. all of the above can compromise information

10-17. Information modification attacks occur when __________.

A. an authorized user changes a Web site address
B. a Web site crashes
C. the power is cut off
D. someone who is not authorized to do so changes electronic information

10-18. Technological controls used to protect information include ______________.
A. laws
B. effective management
C. firewalls and physical access restrictions
D. ethics

10-19. Limiting access to electronic information usually involves ______________.
A. something you have
B. something you know
C. something you are
D. all of the above

10-20. Which of the following is the process of determining the true, accurate identity of a user of an information system?
A. audit
B. authentication
C. firewall
D. virtual private network

10-21. The use of computer and networking technologies by individuals and organized groups against persons or property to intimidate or coerce governments, civilians, or any segment of society in order to attain political, religious, or ideological goals is known as ______________.
A. cyberwar
B. cybercrime
C. cyberterrorism
D. none of the above

10-22. A(n) ______________ is a system composed of hardware, software, or both that is designed to detect intrusion and prevent unauthorized access to or from a private network.
A. encryption
B. firewall
C. alarm
D. logic bomb

10-23. ______________ is the process of encoding messages before they enter the network or airwaves, then decoding them at the receiving end of the transmission so that recipients can read or hear them.
A. encryption
B. biometrics
C. authentication
D. disaster recovery

Answers are on page 405.

Problems and Exercises

10-24. Match the following terms to the appropriate definitions:

i. Acceptable use policy
ii. Authentication
iii. Cyberwar
iv. Biometrics
v. Firewall
vi. Phishing
vii. Information systems audit
viii. Spyware
ix. Unauthorized access
x. Zombie computer

a. Body characteristics such as fingerprints, retinal patterns in the eye, or facial characteristics that allow the unique identification of a person
b. Hardware or software designed to keep unauthorized users out of network systems
c. An organized attempt by a country's military to disrupt or destroy the information and communication systems of another country
d. The process of confirming the identity of a user who is attempting to access a restricted system or Web site, typically by requiring something that the user knows (e.g., a password) together with something that the user carries with him or her or has access to (e.g., an identification card or file)
e. Computer and/or Internet use policy for people within an organization, with clearly spelled-out penalties for noncompliance
f. An assessment of the state of an organization's information systems controls to determine necessary changes and to help ensure the information systems' availability, integrity, and confidentiality
g. Attempts to trick financial account and credit card holders into giving away their authorization information
h. A virus-infected computer that can be used to launch attacks on Web sites without the knowledge of the owner
i. Software that covertly gathers information about a user through an Internet connection without the user's knowledge
j. An IS security breach where an unauthorized individual sees, manipulates, or otherwise handles electronically stored information

10-25. Take a poll of classmates to determine who has had personal experience with computer virus infections, identity theft, or other computer/information system intrusions. How did victims handle the situation? What are classmates who have not been victimized doing to secure computers and personal information?

10-26. Research the statistics for the number of unauthorized intrusions into computer systems last year. Which type was most prevalent? Which groups committed the highest number of intrusions—hackers, employees, and so on?

10-27. Visit the Web site for the U.S. Computer Emergency Readiness Team at www.us-cert.gov/ncas/tips/ST04-015 and answer the following:

a. What is a distributed denial-of-service attack?
b. How can you spot a denial-of-service attack?
c. What devices or activities within an organization might be impacted by denial-of-service attacks?
d. Name three steps organizations might take to prevent denial-of-service attacks.

If the previously given URL is no longer active, conduct a Web search for "denial-of-service attacks." Other active links can provide answers to the questions.

10-28. Do you feel the media generate too much hype regarding hackers and crackers? Since prominent companies such as Microsoft are often hacked into, are you concerned about your bank account or other sensitive information?

10-29. Visit www.fraud.org to find ways to protect yourself from identity theft. Search the Internet for additional sources that provide information on identity theft and make a list of other ways to safeguard against it. What are some of the losses in addition to stolen documents and additional bills to pay that may result from identity theft?

10-30. Search the Internet for information about the damaging effects of software piracy and/or look at the following Web sites: www.bsa.org and www.microsoft.com/piracy. Is software piracy a global problem? What can you do to mitigate the problem? Prepare a short presentation to present to the class.

10-31. Check one or more of the following Web sites to see which hoaxes are currently circulating online: www.hoax-slayer.com, www.truthorfiction.com, or www.snopes.com/info/top25uls.asp. What are five popular hoaxes now circulating online?

10-32. What laws should be enacted to combat cyberterrorism? How could such laws be enforced?

10-33. Contrast cyberharassment, cyberstalking, and cyberbullying using real-world examples found from recent news stories.

10-34. There are many brands of software firewalls, with ZoneAlarm, Norton 360, and Comodo Firewall being three popular choices. Search for these products on the Web and learn more about how a firewall works and what it costs to give you this needed protection; prepare a one-page report that outlines what you have learned.

10-35. Search for further information on encryption. What is the difference between 128-bit and 40-bit encryption? What level of encryption is used in your Web browser? Why has the U.S. government been reluctant to release software with higher levels of encryption to other countries?

10-36. What levels of user authentication are used at your school and/or place of work? Do they seem to be effective? What if a higher level of authentication were necessary? Would it be worth it, or would the added steps cause you to be less productive?

10-37. Should the encryption issue be subject to ethical judgments? For instance, if an absolutely unbreakable code becomes feasible, should we use it with the knowledge that it may help terrorists and other criminals evade the law? Should governments regulate which encryption technology can be used so that government law enforcement agents can always read material generated by terrorists and other criminals? Explain your answer. Should the government continue to regulate the exportation of encryption technology to foreign countries, excluding those that support terrorism as it does now? Why or why not?

10-38. Assess and compare the security of the computers you use regularly at home, work, and/or school. What measures do you use at home to protect your computer? What measures are taken at work or school to protect computers? (If possible, interview IT/IS personnel at work and/or at school to determine how systems are protected in the workplace and in classrooms.) Describe any security vulnerabilities you find and explain how they might be patched.

10-39. In some cases, individuals engage in cybersquatting in the hope of being able to sell the domain names to companies at a high price; in other cases, companies engage in cybersquatting by registering domain names that are very similar to their competitors' product names in order to generate traffic from people misspelling Web addresses. Would you differentiate between these practices? Why or why not? If so, where would you draw the boundaries?

10-40. Find your school's guidelines for ethical computer use on the Internet and answer the following questions: Are there limitations as to the type of Web sites and material that can be viewed (e.g., pornography)? Are students allowed to change the programs on the hard drives of the lab computers or download software for their own use? Are there rules governing personal use of computers and e-mail?

10-41. To learn more about protecting your privacy, visit www.usa.gov/topics/family/privacy-protection/online.shtml and https://www.privacyrights.org/. Did you learn something that will help protect your privacy? Why is privacy more important now than ever?

10-42. Should tougher laws be passed to make spam a crime? If so, how should lawmakers deal with First Amendment rights? How would such laws be enforced?

10-43. Insider threats are not new. Use the Web and find two examples of insider threats throughout history that have had a big negative impact on their organization or government.

10-44. Microsoft and other software producers make free upgrades available to legitimate buyers of applications when security risks are exposed, but those using pirated copies are not eligible to receive security downloads. Should security patches for popular software be given for free to everyone, no questions asked? Why or why not?

Application Exercises

Note: The existing data files referenced in these exercises are available on the book's Web site: www.pearsonhighered.com/valacich.

Spreadsheet Application: Analyzing Ethical Concerns at Campus Travel

10-45. Because of the employees' increased use of IS resources for private purposes at Campus Travel, you have announced that a new acceptable use policy will be implemented. You have set up a Web site for the employees to provide feedback to the proposed changes; the results of this survey are stored in the file EthicsSurvey.csv. Your boss wants to use the survey results to find out what the greatest concerns in terms of ethical implications are for the employees, so you are asked to do the following:

- Complete the spreadsheet to include descriptive statistics (mean, standard deviation, mode, minimum, maximum, and range) for each survey item. Use formulas to calculate all statistics for the responses to the individual questions. (Hint: In Microsoft Excel, you can look up the necessary formulas in the category "Statistical"; you will have to calculate the ranges yourself.)
- Format the means using color scales to highlight the items needing attention.
- Make sure to professionally format the pages before printing them out.

Database Application: Tracking Software Licenses at Campus Travel

10-46. Recently, you have taken on the position of IS manager at Campus Travel. In your second week at work, you realize that many of the software licenses are about to expire or have already expired. As you know about the legal and ethical implications of unlicensed software, you have decided to set up a software asset management system that lets you keep track of the software licenses. You have already set up a database and stored some of the information, but you want to make the system more user friendly. Using the SWLicenses.mdb database, design a form to input the following information for new software products:

- Software title
- Installation location (office)
- License number
- Expiration date

Furthermore, design a report displaying all software licenses and expiration dates (sorted by expiration dates). (Hint: In Microsoft Access, use the form and report wizards to create the forms and reports; you will find the wizards under the "Create" tab.)

Team Work Exercise

Top Cyberthreats

Robert Morris's worm, a bug that crashed a record 6,000 computers (a statistic compiled from an estimate that there were 60,000 computers connected to the Internet at the time and the worm affected 10 percent of them), now seems as antiquated as the 1911 Stutz Bearcat automobile. Morris was a student at Cornell University in 1988 when he devised a program that he later insisted was intended simply to gauge how many computers were connected to the Internet. Errors in Morris's program turned it into a self-replicating monster that overloaded computers and threatened frightened Internet users. Dubbed simply the Internet Worm, Morris's program was the precursor for today's multitude of malevolent codes.

According to Kaspersky Lab, a leading developer of content management security solutions, attackers are having to continuously change their methods in response to the growing competition among the IT security companies that investigate and protect against targeted attacks. Increased public attention to security lapses will also force the attackers to search for new instruments. For example, conventional methods of attacks involving e-mail attachments will gradually become less effective, while browser attacks will gain in popularity. For 2014 and beyond, they expected to see the following:

- Mobile threats will continue to rise.
- Bitcoin (the virtual currency) will increasingly be under attack.
- Maintaining privacy will become increasingly difficult.
- Attacks on cloud storage facilities will increase.
- Attacks on software developers will increase.
- Cyber-mercenaries will be on the rise.
- Fragmentation of the Internet will continue to increase.

In addition to these various trends, an old favorite, the Windows operating system, will continue to be a popular target. Nevertheless, given some major security improvements within Windows 7 and Windows 8, many experts believe that this is driving criminals to other, easier targets.

Questions and Exercises

10-47. Search the Web for the most up-to-date statistics and events related to IS security.

10-48. As a team, interpret these numbers (or stories). What is striking/important about these findings?

10-49. As a team, discuss what these findings will look like in 5 years and 10 years. What will the changes mean for globalization? What issues/opportunities do you see arising?

10-50. Using your spreadsheet software of choice, create a graph/figure most effectively visualizing the findings you consider most important.

Based on:

Gosteff, Alexander. (2013). Kaspersky security bulletin 2013. Retrieved April 19, 2014, from http://report.kaspersky.com.

Markoff, J. (1990, May 5). Computer intruder is put on probation and fined $10,000. *The New York Times.* Retrieved April 19, 2014, from http://www.nytimes.com/1990/05/05/us/computer-intruder-is-put-on-probation-and-fined-10000.html.

Answers to the Self-Study Questions

10-14. C, p. 381 **10-15.** B, p. 362 **10-16.** D, p. 366 **10-17.** D, p. 365 **10-18.** C, p. 395
10-19. D, p. 387 **10-20.** B, p. 387 **10-21.** C, p. 378 **10-22.** B, p. 397 **10-23.** A, p. 392

CASE 1 Stopping Insider Threats: Edward Snowden and the NSA

Insider threats—trusted adversaries who operate within an organization's boundaries—are a significant danger to both private and public sectors, and are often cited as the greatest threat to an organization. Although insider threats such as disgruntled employees or ex-employees, contractors, business partners, or auditors can cause various threats to organizations, insider threats in the right places may even have serious diplomatic consequences.

In June 2013, major news agencies—including *The Guardian, The Washington Post,* and *The New York Times*—began publishing news articles about a global surveillance program being orchestrated by the U.S. National Security Agency (NSA) in cooperation with intelligence agencies from several other countries. The source of information for these news stories was Edward Snowden, a former employee of the Central Intelligence Agency (CIA) and former contractor for the NSA. Snowden provided these news agencies with hundreds of thousands of classified documents that he acquired during his contract work with the NSA. His motivation for leaking these documents was to reveal to the public the nature and extent of government surveillance of the everyday electronic activities of its citizens.

The leaked documents revealed a staggering amount of surveillance being executed. Individuals' personal e-mail and instant message contact lists were being harvested; e-mail content was being routinely searched; certain cell phone call records and location information was being tracked; even users of online games such as Second Life and World of Warcraft were being monitored and analyzed. Snowden claimed that the NSA's surveillance activities were not limited to protecting national security, but instead consisted of gratuitous surveillance of everyday citizens and businesses. In a 2013 letter, Snowden wrote, "there is a huge difference between legal programs, legitimate spying . . . and these programs of dragnet mass surveillance that put entire populations under an all-seeing eye and save copies forever . . . These programs were never about terrorism: they're about economic spying, social control, and diplomatic manipulation. They're about power."

The Snowden leaks, which reveal a great many U.S. intelligence secrets beyond the NSA's surveillance activities, have been called the most damaging breach of national security in history. The U.S. Department of Justice charged Snowden with espionage and he will face trial if he returns to the United States. Snowden currently resides in Russia, where he has been granted temporary political asylum. Snowden is variously called a hero, a whistle-blower, a dissident, a traitor, and a patriot.

Regardless of whether you support the NSA's surveillance activities, and regardless of whether you agree with Snowden's actions, the events described here were clearly the result of an exploited insider threat. Edward Snowden was a trusted contractor for the NSA and was granted wide access to classified data because of his role as a security administrator and analyst. While the Snowden revelations initiated widespread debate on the legality and morality of government electronic surveillance policies, these events have also sparked renewed interest from governments and companies regarding effective means of reducing insider threats.

Questions

10-51. Choose a large company that many people are familiar with. How could this company be damaged by insider threats?

10-52. How can companies reduce insider threats?

10-53. Research the Snowden leaks on the Web. How was Snowden able to gain access to so many classified documents?

Based on:

Edward Snowden. (2014, April 23). In *Wikipedia, The Free Encyclopedia.* Retrieved April 23, 2014, from http://en.wikipedia.org/w/index.php?title=Edward_Snowden&oldid=605421815.

Mazzetti, M., & Schmidt, M. (2013, June 9). Ex-worker at C.I.A. says he leaked data on surveillance. *The New York Times.* Retrieved April 22, 2014, from http://www.nytimes.com/2013/06/10/us/former-cia-worker-says-he-leaked-surveillance-data.html.

CASE 2 China's Great (Fire) Wall

Welcome to modern-day China, where the government blocks Web site access to the country's 618 million Internet users on such subjects as democracy, Tibet, Taiwan, health, education, news, entertainment, religion, and revolution. Various chat rooms, blogs, photo- and video-sharing sites, gaming and podcasting sites, and bulletin boards are also forbidden stops on the Web, and don't even think about googling "Tiananmen Square massacre" or anything remotely considered pornographic.

Building censorship into China's Internet infrastructure is the first step for the country's government in controlling access to politically sensitive material. To accomplish this, the Chinese government prevents Internet service providers (ISPs)—many of them privately held businesses, some with foreign investments—from hosting any material the government calls politically objectionable by holding the ISPs liable for content and imposing severe penalties for violations, including imprisonment.

In addition, the Chinese government targets Internet content providers (ICPs—organizations and individuals who post Web sites, both nonprofit and for profit), who are required to register for and post a license to operate legally, and like ISPs are held liable for politically incorrect content. To keep a license, ICPs must police sites for objectionable content and must take down those sites that violate regulations governing content. Yahoo!, Microsoft's MSN, and Google all act as ICPs in China and have been criticized for complying with China's strict Internet censorship policy.

Managing ISPs and ICPs is not the only tool China has for controlling what content its citizens can access. Beginning operations in 2003, China instituted the Golden Shield Project. More popularly known as "The Great Firewall of China," the system can automatically filter and block content that the government deems inappropriate. Through IP tracking, blocking, DNS/URL filtering, and redirection, the Golden Shield not only blocks and filters content but acts as a surveillance system as well. The Great Firewall also creates a sluggish and congested network infrastructure, though some believe this is intentional to discourage Internet use.

In 2014, a reported 2,600 popular Web sites were blocked in China, including Facebook, Twitter, Google+, and YouTube.

Historically, many foreign ICPs have cooperated with the Chinese government by censoring information in order to operate in the country. Yahoo!, the only non-Chinese company providing e-mail service in China, has even turned over e-mail content to the authorities, resulting in the prosecution and conviction of at least four persons for criticizing the government. In 2010, however, Google took a different course with China.

In late 2009, Google was hit with a sophisticated attack on its Gmail servers and some of its other corporate networks. Google believed that the attack was an attempt to access the Gmail accounts of human rights activists. Up until then, Google had been censoring content like other ICPs, tailoring results to remove topics deemed subversive or pornographic. However, after the network attack, tensions began to rise between Google and China, as it was widely believed that the attacks came from the Chinese government or were at least sponsored by them in an effort to root out political dissidents. As a result, Google threatened to end its practice of censoring search results or even completely pull its business out of China.

Early in 2010, Google made the decision to redirect all its search traffic in China to servers in Hong Kong, where greater civil liberties remain, effectively ending its practice of censoring results and opening unrestricted searches to the Chinese public. Within days of the move, China began filtering and blocking searches directed to the Hong Kong servers using the Golden Shield system, and even pulled out of lucrative agreements to use Google's Android operating system on a number of mobile platforms. In March 2010, Google's annual license to be an ICP in China expired. In summer 2010, China renewed Google's license, but it remains to be seen how this standoff between the search giant and China will end. Today, Google is "back to normal," operating in China with government-imposed limitations on its search results; several Google applications including Docs, Drive, and Picasa are also blocked.

As is true of most attempts to censor the Internet, tech-savvy users in China find ways to circumvent the government's firewall. One group of Chinese dissidents created Greatfire.org, which includes mirror duplicates of several blocked Web sites. The group also created Freeweibo.com, which collects and publishes posts deleted from China's popular social media service Sina Weibo. Another example is an iPhone app called FireChat, a mobile messaging app designed to allow anonymous group messaging through the iPhone's peer-to-peer and Bluetooth connections. The app was recently used as a part of a political protest in Taiwan, and protesters in Taiwan and China were able to communicate and encourage each other without censorship from the Chinese government.

Questions

10-54. Should foreign companies provide their technologies to China, knowing that the technologies are used to limit the individual freedom of Chinese citizens? Why or why not?

10-55. Given that China has the largest number of Internet users, do you think they can ultimately succeed in controlling information? Why or why not?

10-56. Should the rest of the world care if China limits information access within China? Why or why not? Now that Google has moved against censorship, do you think other companies will follow suit? Why or why not?

Based on:

August, O. (2007, October 23). The great firewall: China's misguided—and futile—attempt to control what happens online. *Wired.* Retrieved May 21, 2012, from http://www.wired.com/politics/security/magazine/15-11/ff_chinafirewall.

Chen, L. (2014, March 20). Breaking through China's Great Firewall. *Business Week.* Retrieved April 22, 2014, from http://www.businessweek.com/articles/2014-03-20/secretive-web-activists-give-chinese-a-way-around-censorship.

Horwitz, J. (2014, March 31). Unblockable? Unstoppable? FireChat messaging app unites China and Taiwan in free speech. . . and it's not pretty. *Tech in Asia.* Retrieved April 22, 2014, from http://www.techinasia.com/unblockable-unstoppable-firechat-messaging-app-unites-china-and-taiwan-in-free-speech-and-its-not-pretty.

Levin, D. (2014, June 2). China escalating attack on Google. *The New York Times.* Retrieved September 11, 2014, from http://www.nytimes.com/2014/06/03/business/chinas-battle-against-google-heats-up.html.

Online Censorship in China (2014). Retrieved September 11, 2014, from https://en.greatfire.org.

Go to **mymislab.com** for Auto-graded writing questions as well as the following Assisted-graded writing questions:

10-57. Describe information systems risk assessment and explain four ways to approach systems security risk.

10-58. Define and contrast spyware, spam, and cookies.

References

Ackerman, S. (2012, July 17). Syrian rebels use YouTube, Facebook for weapons training. *Wired.com*. Retrieved June 1, 2014, from http://www.wired.com/dangerroom/2012/07/syria-youtube-facebook.

Addison-Hewitt Associates. (2005). The Sarbanes–Oxley Act. Retrieved June 1, 2014, from http://www.soxlaw.com/index.htm.

Bielski, Z. (2008, June 21). World unprepared for coming catastrophes, warn experts. *National Post*. Retrieved June 1, 2014, from http://www2.canada.com/cars/story.html?id=602830.

Bocij, P. (2004). *Cyberstalking: Harassment in the Internet age and how to protect your family*. Westport, CT: Greenwood.

Boyle, R. E., & Panko, R. (2013). *Corporate computer security* (3rd ed.). Upper Saddle River, NJ: Pearson Prentice Hall.

Brown, S. (2013, September 25). An introduction to malware for lawyers. Retrieved July 22, 2014, from http://www.shannonbrownlaw.com/archives/1981.

Burgess-Proctor, A., Patchin, J. W., & Hinduja, S. (2008). Cyberbullying and online harassment: Reconceptualizing the victimization of adolescent girls. In V. Garcia & J. Clifford (Eds.), *Female crime victims: Reality reconsidered* (pp. 162–176). Upper Saddle River, NJ: Pearson Prentice Hall.

Business Software Alliance. (2007). The fight for cyber space. Retrieved May 20, 2012, from http://www.bsa.org/country/Research%20and%20Statistics/~/media/9CA4C9DFEDE24250AA16F16F0ED297A6.ashx.

Business Software Alliance. (2012). Ninth annual BSA global 2011 software piracy study. Retrieved June 2, 2014, from http://portal.bsa.org/globalpiracy2011/downloads/study_pdf/2011_BSA_Piracy_Study-Standard.pdf.

Business Software Alliance. (2013). Competitive advantage: The economic impact of properly licensed software. Retrieved May 28, 2014, from http://portal.bsa.org/insead/assets/studies/2013softwarevaluestudy_en.pdf

CAPTCHA. (2010). Telling humans and computers apart automatically. Retrieved June 1, 2014, from http://www.captcha.net.

Champlain, J. (2003). *Auditing information systems*. Hoboken, NJ: Wiley.

Chen, H., Reid, E., Sinai, J., Sike, A., & Ganor, B. (2008). *Terrorism informatics: Knowledge management and data mining for homeland security*. Berlin: Springer.

Clapper, J. R. (2014, January 29). Worldwide threat assessment of the US intelligence community. Retrieved May 28, 2014, from http://www.dni.gov/files/documents/Intelligence%20Reports/2014%20WWTA%20%20SFR_SSCI_29_Jan.pdf.

Cobb, M. (2012) Measuring risk: A security pro's guide. *InformationWeek*. Retrieved June 1, 2014, from http://reports.informationweek.com.

Computer Security Institute. (2011). 2010/2011: The 15th annual computer crime and security survey. Retrieved May 21, 2012, from http://gocsi.com/members/reports.

Federal Bureau of Investigation. (2008, October 16). FBI coordinates global effort to nab "Dark Market" cyber criminals. Retrieved June 1, 2014, from http://www.fbi.gov/news/pressrel/press-releases/fbi-coordinates-global-effort-to-nab-2018dark-market2019-cyber-criminals.

Federal Financial Institutions Examination Council. (2006). IT examination handbook: Information security. Retrieved June 1, 2014, from http://ithandbook.ffiec.gov/ITBooklets/FFIEC_ITBooklet_InformationSecurity.pdf.

Finneran, M. (2013). 2013 state of mobile security. *InformationWeek*. Retrieved June 1, 2014, from http://reports.informationweek.com.

Fisher, D. (2014, February 27). Cybersquatters rush to claim brands in the new GTLD territories. *Forbes*. Retrieved May 28, 2014, from http://www.forbes.com/sites/danielfisher/2014/02/27/cybersquatters-rush-to-claim-brands-in-the-new-gtld-territories.

Fitzgerald, T. (2008). The ocean is full of phish. *Information Systems Security*. Retrieved June 1, 2014, from http://www.infosectoday.com/Articles/Phishing.htm.

Geers, K. (2008). A new approach to cyber defense. *Internet Evolution*. Retrieved June 1, 2014, from http://www.internetevolution.com/author.asp?id=628&doc_id=151762.

Glenny, M. (2011, September 21). Cybercrime: Is it out of control? *The Guardian*. Retrieved June 1, 2014, from http://www.guardian.co.uk/technology/2011/sep/21/cybercrime-spam-phishing-viruses-malware.

Kabay, M. E. (2007). How far could cyberware go? *NetworkWorld*. Retrieved June 1, 2014, from http://www.networkworld.com/newsletters/sec/2007/0723sec2.html.

Keizer, G. (2010). Botnets "the Swiss Army knife of attack tools" (hacker militias can turn to botnets for instant cyberattacks). *Computerworld*. Retrieved June 1, 2014, from http://www.omputerworld.com/s/article/9174560/Botnets_the_Swiss_Army_knife_of_attack_tools.

Kharif, O. (2012, April 30). Mobile spam texts hit 4.5 billion raising consumer ire. *BusinessWeek*. Retrieved June 1, 2014, from http://www.businessweek.com/news/2012-04-30/mobile-spam-texts-hit-4-dot-5-billion-raising-consumer-ire.

Leyden, J. (2002, March 27). Drive-by hacking linked to cyberterror. *The Register*. Retrieved June 1, 2014, from http://www.theregister.co.uk/2002/03/27/driveby_hacking_linked_to_cyberterror.

McAfee. (2013, July). The economic impact of cybercrime and cyber espionage. Retrieved May 28, 2014, from http://www.mcafee.com/us/resources/reports/rp-economic-impact-cybercrime.pdf.

National Audit Office. (2004, February). Review of information systems controls. Retrieved June 1, 2014, from http://www.auditnet.org/Guides/NAOReviewofISWorkbook2004.pdf.

Poulsen, K. (2008, October 13). Cybercrime supersite "DarkMarket" was FBI sting, documents confirm. *Wired.com*. Retrieved June 1, 2014, from http://www.wired.com/threatlevel/2008/10/darkmarket-post.

PriceWaterhuoseCoopers. (2013, June). Key findings from the 2013 US State of Cybercrime Survey. *PWC.com*. Retrieved May 28, 2014, from https://www.pwc.com/en_US/us/increasing-it-effectiveness/publications/assets/us-state-of-cybercrime.pdf.

Reuters. (2006). Morgan Stanley offers $15M fine for e-mail violations. *Computerworld*. Retrieved June 1, 2014, from http://www.computerworld.com/hardwaretopics/storage/story/0,10801,108687,00.html.

Ruggiero, P., & Foote, J. (2011). Cyber threats to mobile phones. Retrieved May 28, 2014, from https://www.us-cert.gov/sites/default/files/publications/cyber_threats-to_mobile_phones.pdf.

Russon, M. (2014, March 27). China arrests 1,500 people for sending spam text messages from fake mobile base stations. *International Business Times*. Retrieved May 28, 2014, from http://www.ibtimes.co.uk/china-arrests-1500-people-sending-spam-text-messages-fake-mobile-base-stations-1442099.

Salek, N. (2008, June 24). Does cyberterrorism exist? *CRN.com.au*. Retrieved June 1, 2014, from http://www.crn.com.au/Feature/4652,does-cyberterrorism-exist.aspx.

SearchCIO. (2007). Business continuity and disaster recovery planning guide for CIOs. *SearchCIO.com*. Retrieved June 1, 2014, from http://searchcio.techtarget.com/generic/0,295582,sid182_gci1206807,00.html.

Stallings, W. (2011). *Network security essentials: Applications and standards* (4th ed.). Upper Saddle River, NJ: Pearson Prentice Hall.

Stallings, W., & Brown, L. (2012). *Computer security: Principles and practices* (2nd ed.). Upper Saddle River, NJ: Pearson Prentice Hall.

Stuxnet. (2014, May 24). In *Wikipedia, The Free Encyclopedia*. Retrieved June 2, 2014, from http://en.wikipedia.org/w/index.php?title=Stuxnet&oldid=609978568

The Jester. (2014, May 7). In *Wikipedia, The Free Encyclopedia*. Retrieved 02:26, June 2, 2014, from http://en.wikipedia.org/w/index.php?title=The_Jester&oldid=607416029

US-CERT. (2014). United States Computer Emergency Response Readiness Team. Retrieved June 1, 2014, from http://www.us-cert.gov.

Volonino, L., & Robinson, S. R. (2004). *Principles and practice of information security*. Upper Saddle River, NJ: Pearson Prentice Hall.

Websense. (2012). Websense 2012 threat report. Retrieved June 1, 2014, from http://www.websense.com/content/websense-2012-threat-report-download.aspx.

Wehner, M. (2012, July 24). Iran nuclear energy facility hit with malware that plays AC/DC at full volume. *Yahoo! News*. Retrieved June 1, 2014, from http://news.yahoo.com/blogs/technology-blog/iran-nuclear-energy-facility-hit-malware-plays-ac-203806981.html.

Weimann, G. (2006). *Terror on the Internet: The new arena, the new challenges*. Washington, DC: United States Institute of Peace Press.

Xinhua. (2014, April 12). Chinese bombed by 300 bln spam SMS in 2013. *Globaltimes.cn*. Retrieved May 28, 2014, from http://www.globaltimes.cn/content/854142.shtml.

Technology Briefing

Foundations of Information Systems Infrastructure

After reading this briefing, you will be able to do the following:

1. Discuss foundational information systems (IS) hardware concepts.
2. Describe foundational topics related to system software, programming languages, and application development environments.
3. Describe foundational networking and Internet concepts.
4. Explain foundational database management concepts.

Preview

In Chapter 3, "Managing the Information Systems Infrastructure and Services," you learned about the key components of a comprehensive information systems (IS) infrastructure and why its careful management is necessary. This Technology Briefing will expand that discussion, providing you with a deeper understanding of those topics. Each of the major sections within this briefing provides optional material that stands alone from the other sections as well as the entire book. Likewise, the end-of-chapter material is presented in separate sections to facilitate this independence.

FOUNDATIONAL TOPICS IN IS HARDWARE

IS hardware is an integral part of the IS infrastructure and is broadly classified into three types: input, processing, and output technologies. In this section, we examine foundational topics related to IS hardware.

Input Technologies

Input technologies are used to enter information into a computer, laptop, tablet, or smartphone (see Figure TB1). Well-known input devices include various types of keyboards or pointing devices like track pads and mice. Other, more specialized input devices include biometric fingerprint readers to authenticate people (for access control, such as for secure laboratories, or for border controls; see Chapter 10, "Securing Information Systems"), radio-frequency identification (RFID) scanners to track valuable inventory in a warehouse (see Chapter 8, "Strengthening Business-to-Business Relationships Via Supply Chain and Customer Relationship Management"), and eye-tracking devices, an innovative pointing device developed primarily for the disabled for help with operating computers.

ENTERING BATCH DATA. Large amounts of routine data, referred to as **batch data**, are often entered into the computer using scanners that convert printed text and images into digital data. Scanners range from small handheld devices to large desktop boxes that resemble personal photocopiers. Rather than duplicating the image on another piece of paper, the computer translates the image into digital data that can be stored or manipulated by the computer. Insurance companies, universities, and other organizations that routinely process a large number of forms and documents are typically using scanner technology to increase employee productivity; entering a large number of separate forms or documents into a computer system and then manipulating these data at a single time is referred to as **batch processing**.

Once a document is converted into digital format, **text recognition software** uses **optical character recognition** to convert typed, printed, or handwritten text into the computer-based characters that form the original letters and words. Other special-purpose scanning technologies include **optical mark recognition** devices, **bar code readers**, and **magnetic ink character recognition**, as summarized in Table TB1.

Other Input Technologies **Smart cards** are special credit card–sized cards containing a microprocessor chip, memory circuits, and often a magnetic stripe. Smart cards can be used for various applications, including identification, providing building access, or making payments

FIGURE TB1

All computing devices utilize input technologies.

Sources: (a) Nikolai Sorokin/Fotolia; (b) Aaron Amat/Fotolia; (c) Jan Engel/Fotolia

TABLE TB1 Specialized Scanners for Inputting Information

Scanner	Description
Optical mark recognition	Used to scan questionnaires and test answer forms ("bubble sheets") where answer choices are marked by filling in circles using pencil or pen
Optical character recognition	Used to read and digitize typewritten, computer-printed, and even handwritten characters such as on sales tags on department store merchandise, patient information in hospitals, or the address information on a piece of postal mail
Bar code reader	Used mostly in grocery stores and other retail businesses to read bar code data at the checkout counter; also used by libraries, banks, hospitals, utility companies, and so on
Magnetic ink character recognition	Used by the banking industry to read data, account numbers, bank codes, and check numbers on preprinted checks
Biometric scanner	Used to scan human body characteristics of users to enable everything from access control to payment authorization

(e.g., at vending machines or checkout counters). Some smart cards allow for contactless transmission of data using RFID technology (e.g., the Exxon Speedpass for purchasing gasoline). Biometric devices, discussed in more detail in Chapter 10, are being used primarily for identification and security purposes. These devices read certain body features, including irises, fingerprints, and hand or face geometry, and compare them with stored profiles. Biometric devices are now also being included in consumer products such as laptops or keyboards, allowing users to log on to the computer by scanning their fingerprints rather than typing their user names and passwords. Finally, most modern smartphones use various sensors to obtain data about the device's location (global positioning system [GPS] sensor), orientation (compass and gyroscope), acceleration (accelerometer), altitude (barometer), proximity to the user's body, or ambient light.

ENTERING AUDIO AND VIDEO. When entering **audio** (i.e., sound) or **video** (i.e., still and moving images) data into a computer, the data have to be digitized before they can be manipulated, stored, and played or displayed. In addition to the manipulation of music, audio input is helpful for operating a computer when a user's hands need to be free to do other tasks. Video is used for assisting in security-related applications, such as room monitoring and employee verification, as well as for videoconferencing and chatting on the Internet, using a PC and a webcam.

Voice Input Voice data are input into a computer system using microphones. A process called **speech recognition** also makes it possible for your computer or smartphone to understand speech. **Voice-to-text software** is an application that uses a microphone to monitor a person's speech and then converts the speech into text. Speech recognition technology can also be especially helpful for disabled computer users, physicians and other medical professionals, airplane pilots, factory workers whose hands get too dirty to use keyboards, mobile users who don't want to type while walking or driving, and computer users who cannot type and do not want to learn. Increasingly, **interactive voice response (IVR)**, based on speech recognition technology, is used for telephone surveys or to guide you through the various menu options when calling a company's customer service line.

Other Forms of Audio Input In addition to using a microphone, users can enter audio using electronic keyboards, or they can transfer audio from another device (such as an audio recorder). The users can then analyze and manipulate the sounds via sound editing software for output to speakers or storage to MP3 files, CDs, or other media.

Video Input Video data can be entered into a computer using digital cameras that record still images or video clips in digital form on small, removable memory cards. File size is primarily influenced by the resolution and file format you select for pictures or the length of the recording for video. Digital camera technology has become so portable that it is used in a variety of products, including cell phones and laptops. As webcams have become very popular with people wanting to use the Internet for chatting with friends and family using programs like

Skype, Google Talk, or Yahoo! Messenger, protocols to transmit data in a continuous fashion are used. In contrast to discrete files (such as audio or image files), which have to be completely downloaded before they can be opened, **streaming audio** and **streaming video** (together referred to as **streaming media**) are data streams transmitted using specific protocols that are available for immediate playback on the recipient's computer. Similarly, the video-sharing site YouTube, online radio stations, and Netflix use specific protocols to stream media content.

Processing: Transforming Inputs into Outputs

In this section we provide a brief overview of computer processing. **Processing technologies**, contained inside any computing device (including smartphones, tablets, or wireless routers), transform inputs into outputs.

HOW A COMPUTER WORKS. Inside any computing device, you will find the **motherboard**, a plastic or fiberglass circuit board that holds or connects to all of the computer's electronic components (see Figure TB2). The motherboard holds the **central processing unit (CPU)** or **microprocessor**, which is the main component of a computing device, and connects it to the power supply, primary and secondary storage, as well as to various peripherals (such as input and output devices, or expansion cards, such as dedicated sound or video cards). The CPU is often called the computer's brain, as it is responsible for performing all the operations of the computer (see Figure TB3). Its job includes loading the *operating system* (e.g., Windows 8, Mac OS X, or Ubuntu Linux) when the machine is first turned on and performing, coordinating, and managing all the calculations and instructions relayed to it while the computer is running. The CPU, a small device made of silicon, is composed of millions of tiny transistors arranged in complex patterns that allow it to interpret and manipulate data. In addition to the number of transistors on the CPU, three other factors greatly influence its speed—its system *clock speed* (the number of instructions a CPU can execute in a fixed amount of time), registers, and *cache memory* (described later). The CPU consists of two main sections: the **arithmetic logic unit (ALU)** and the **control unit**. The ALU performs calculations and logical operations, which involves comparing packets of data and then executing appropriate instructions. Combined in various ways, these functions allow the computer to perform complicated operations rapidly. The control unit works closely with the ALU, fetching and decoding instructions as well as retrieving and storing data.

Inside all computers, data are represented in the form of binary digits, or **bits** (i.e., the 0s and 1s a computer understands); a sequence of 8 bits is referred to as a **byte**. Different **binary codes** have been developed to represent characters or numbers as strings of bits. A widely used standard is the **American Standard Code for Information Interchange (ASCII)**, where, for example, the binary digits "01100001" represent the letter "a." Due to limitations in the number

FIGURE TB2

A computer's motherboard holds or connects to all of the computer's electronic components.
Source: Bretislav Horak/Shutterstock

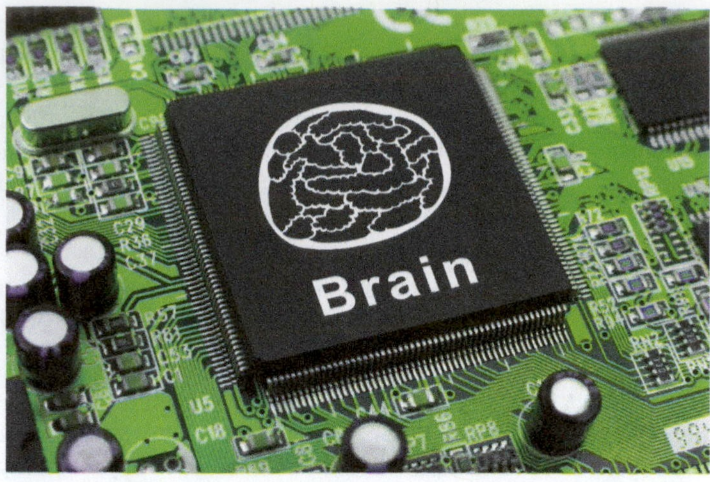

FIGURE TB3

A CPU performs all operations of a computer.

Source: Tatiana Popova/Shutterstock

of characters that can be represented, as well as for specialized applications, various other codes have been developed. For example, **Unicode** has gained widespread acceptance, as it allows for representing characters and scripts beyond the Latin alphabet, including Chinese, Cyrillic, Hebrew, and Arabic. Any input your computer receives (say, a keystroke or mouse movement) is **digitized**, or translated into binary code, and then processed by the CPU.

Within the computer, an electronic circuit generates pulses at a rapid rate, setting the pace for processing events to take place, just like a metronome marks time for a musician. This circuit is called the **system clock**. A single pulse is a **clock tick**, and a fixed number of clock ticks is required to execute a single instruction. In microcomputers, the processor's **clock speed** is measured in hertz (Hz) or multiples thereof. One megahertz (MHz) is 1 million clock ticks, or instruction cycles, per second. Personal computer speeds are most often indicated in gigahertz (GHz, or 1 billion hertz). Microprocessor speeds improve so quickly that faster chips are on the market about every six months. Today, most new PCs operate at more than 3 GHz. To give you an idea of how things have changed, the original IBM PC had a clock speed of 4.77 MHz.

As its inner workings are very complex, for most of us it is easiest to think of a CPU as being a "black box" where all the processing occurs. The CPU uses registers and cache memory (both located inside the CPU) and RAM (located outside the CPU) as *primary*, or temporary, storage space for data that are currently being processed. The CPU interacts with *secondary storage* (such as a *hard drive*, *optical disk*, or *flash drive*) for permanently storing data; as primary storage is considerably faster than secondary storage, the amount of primary storage greatly influences a computer's performance. The different types of storage are discussed next.

STORAGE. A computer has various different types of storage, each serving a specific purpose. The primary differences between different types of storage are capacity, volatility, and read/write speed (see Table TB2 for a comparison of different storage technologies).

Primary Storage **Primary storage** (such as **random-access memory [RAM]**), also called main memory, is located on the motherboard and is used to store the data and programs currently in use; primary storage uses memory chips (consisting of transistors and capacitators) to store data. Because instructions and work stored in RAM are lost when the power to the computer is turned off, it is referred to as **volatile memory**. Within the CPU itself, registers provide temporary storage locations where data must reside while being processed or manipulated. For example, if two numbers are to be added together, both must reside in registers, with the result placed in a register. Consequently, the number and size of the registers can also greatly influence the speed and power of a CPU.

A **cache** (pronounced "cash") is a small block of memory used by processors to store those instructions most recently or most often used. Just as you might keep file folders that you use most in a handy location on your desktop, cache memory is located within the CPU. Thanks to cache memory, before performing an operation, the processor does not have to go directly to main memory, which is slower, farther away from the microprocessor, and takes longer to reach. Instead, it can check first to see if needed data are contained in the cache. Cache memory is another way computer engineers have increased processing speed.

TABLE TB2 Different Storage Technologies

Name	Volatility	Speed	Access	Capacity	Usage
Register	Volatile	Extremely fast	Random	Less than 200 bytes	Data directly used by CPU
Cache	Volatile	Extremely fast	Random	Typically up to 8 MB	Data and instructions used by CPU
RAM	Volatile	Very fast	Random	Depends on configuration; typically up to 32 GB	Programs and data currently used
ROM	Nonvolatile	Fast	Random	Very low	Instructions used before the operating system is loaded
Hard drive	Nonvolatile	Relatively slow	Random	High	Storage of programs and data
SSD	Nonvolatile	Fast	Random	High	Storage of programs and data
Optical disks	Nonvolatile	Slow	Random	Medium	Backup and long-term storage; software distribution; music and movies
Tape	Nonvolatile	Very slow	Sequential	High	Archiving of data

Modern CPUs have a hierarchy of cache memory (level 1, level 2, or even level 3); the lower levels of cache memory are faster but also smaller and more expensive. The more cache available to a CPU, the better the overall system performs because more data are readily available (although at a certain size, factors such as heat emission and power consumption become prohibitive to increasing the CPU cache).

Read-only memory (ROM) is used to store programs and instructions that are automatically loaded when the computer is turned on (before the operating system is loaded), such as the **basic input/output system (BIOS)**. In contrast to other forms of primary storage, ROM is **nonvolatile memory**, which means that it retains the data when the power to the computer is shut off.

Secondary Storage **Secondary storage** refers to technologies for permanently storing data to a large-capacity, nonvolatile storage component, such as a **hard drive**. Most of the software run on a computer, including the operating system, is stored on the hard drive (or hard disk). Hard drives are usually installed internally but additional hard drives may be externally located and connected via cables.

The storage capacity of the hard drives for today's microcomputers is typically measured in gigabytes (GB, billions of bytes) or terabytes (TB, trillions of bytes). It is not unusual for PCs currently on the market to come equipped with hard drives with 1,000–2,000 GB (i.e., 1–2 TB) storage capacities. Modern supercomputers can have millions of terabytes of storage. To make sure critical data are not lost, some computers employ **redundant array of independent disks (RAID)** technology to store redundant copies of data on two or more hard drives. RAID is not typically used on an individual's computer, but it is very common for Web servers and many business applications. RAID is sometimes called a "redundant array of *inexpensive* disks" because it is typically less expensive to have multiple redundant disks than fewer highly reliable and expensive ones.

Hard drives consist of several magnetic disks, or platters, used for data storage (see Figure TB4). Each disk within a disk pack has an access arm with two **read/write heads**—one positioned close to the top surface of the disk and another positioned close to the bottom surface of the disk—to inscribe or retrieve data. When reading from or writing to the disks, the read/write heads are constantly repositioned to the desired storage location for the data while the disks are spinning at speeds of 5,400 to 15,000 revolutions per minute. The read/write heads do not actually touch either surface of the disks. In fact, a **head crash** occurs if the read/write head for some reason touches the disk, leading to a loss of data. Because of the mechanical action needed to position the read/write heads, hard drives are comparably slow; it takes a permanent storage device such as a hard disk about 3–10 milliseconds to access data. Within a CPU, however, a single transistor can be changed from a 0 to a 1 in about 10 picoseconds (10-trillionths

FIGURE TB4

A hard drive consists of several disks that are stacked on top of one another and read/write heads to read and write data.
Source: Alias Studiot Oy/Shutterstock

of a second). Changes inside the CPU occur about 1 billion times faster than they do in a hard drive because the CPU operates only on electronic impulses, whereas the hard drives perform both electronic and mechanical activities, such as spinning the disk and moving the read/write head. Mechanical activities are extremely slow relative to electronic activities; however, modern hard drives use cache memory to decrease the time needed to access frequently used data. A newer secondary storage technology called **solid-state drive (SSD)** uses nonvolatile memory chips (i.e., *flash memory*) to store data; as SSDs have no moving parts, they are typically faster (with access times of 0.1–0.5 millisecond), quieter, and more reliable, but also more expensive than traditional hard disk–based drives. Solid-state drives have become increasingly popular due to the rise of smartphones and tablets. Given their performance, weight, and reliability, they are also increasingly used for laptops and even high performance servers and supercomputers.

Removable Storage Media Today, there are different types of removable storage: flash memory, optical disks, and tapes. **Flash memory** is a memory-chip-based nonvolatile computer storage method that is used in USB flash drives, solid-state hard drives, and memory cards (such as SD cards) used for storing music and pictures in digital cameras and music players. A **flash drive** is a data storage device that includes flash memory with an integrated USB interface. Flash drives are a relatively inexpensive storage device typically having capacities of 16–128 GB; as of 2014, the highest-capacity flash drive could store 1 TB of data.

Optical disks (i.e., disks that are written/read using laser beam technology) are very inexpensive removable nonvolatile storage media used to store data (e.g., photos and videos) and distribute software, video games, and movies. Optical disks store binary data in the form of pits and flat areas on the disk's surface (where the pits and flats represent the 0s and 1s, respectively); an optical disk drive's laser beam can then read the data based on the reflection of the disk's surface. For many years, CD-ROMs (compact disc—read-only memory) were the standard for distributing data and software because of their low cost and their storage capacity of 700 MB. As CD-ROMs cannot be written to, most computers support another type of optical disk that data can be written to, the **CD-R (compact disc–recordable)**. Whereas a CD-R can be written onto only once, a **CD-RW (compact disc–rewritable)** can be written onto multiple times. The **DVD-ROM (digital versatile disc–read-only memory)** has more storage space than a CD-ROM, because DVD-ROM (or typically referred to as simply DVD) drives use a shorter-wavelength laser beam that allows more optical pits to be deposited on the disk. Like compact discs, there are recordable (DVD-R) and rewritable (DVD-RW) versions of this storage technology. DVDs used for the distribution of movies are also called **digital video disks**. The increasing demand for high-definition video content led to the creation of Blu-ray, a DVD format that provides up to 50 GB of storage.

Tapes are removable, high-capacity, secondary storage media; allowing only for sequential access, tapes are typically only used for archiving data and long-term storage. Tapes used for data storage consist of narrow plastic tape coated with a magnetic substance. Storage tapes are typically enclosed in a cartridge, similar to a music cassette, and must be inserted into a tape reader. As with other forms of magnetic storage, data are stored in tiny magnetic spots. The storage capacity of tapes is expressed as **density**, which equals the number of **characters per inch** or **bytes per inch** that can be stored on the tape.

Having a life span of several decades, magnetic tape is still used for backing up or archiving large amounts of computer data, but it is gradually being replaced by high-capacity disk storage, since disk storage is equally reliable. In fact, data stored on disks are easier and faster to locate, because computers do not have to scan an entire tape to find a specific data file when using disks.

PORTS AND POWER SUPPLY. To use the full functionality of a computer, you need to be able to connect various types of peripheral devices, such as mice, printers, and cameras, to the system unit. A **port** provides a hardware interface for connecting devices to computers. The characteristics of various types of ports are summarized in Table TB3. A final key component of any computing device is the **power supply**, which converts electricity from the wall socket to a lower voltage. Whereas typically power supplied by the utility companies can vary from 100 to 240 volts AC, depending on where you are in the world, a PC's components use lower voltages—3.3 to 12 volts DC. The power supply converts the power accordingly and also regulates the voltage to eliminate spikes and surges common in most electrical systems. For added protection against external power surges, many PC owners opt to connect their systems to a separately purchased voltage surge suppressor. The power supply includes one or several fans for air cooling the electronic components inside the system unit—that low humming noise you hear while the computer is running is the fan.

Now that you understand how data are input into a computer and how data can be processed and stored, we can turn our attention to the third category of hardware—output technologies.

Output Technologies

Output technologies, such as a computer monitor or printer, deliver information to you in a usable format. A **printer** is an output device that produces a paper copy of alphanumeric or graphic data from a computer. Printers vary in price, performance and capabilites (e.g., document size, color or black and white, technology, speed, resolution quality). Ink-jet, LED, or laser technology is used in most personal printers.

Monitors are used to display information from a computer and, like printers, can vary in price, performance, and capabilities (e.g., screen size, color, technology, resolution, and so on).

TABLE TB3 Common Computer Ports, Their Applications, and Description

Port Name	Used to Connect	Description
Serial	Modem, mouse, keyboard, terminal display, MIDI	■ Transfers one bit at a time ■ Slowest data transfer rates
USB	Printer, scanner, mouse, keyboard, digital camera and camcorders, external disk drives	■ Extremely high-speed data transfer method ■ Up to 10 Gbps using USB3.1 ■ Up to 127 devices simultaneously connected
IEEE 1394 ("Fire Wire")	Digital cameras and camcorders, external disk drives	■ Extremely high-speed data transfer method ■ Up to 3.2 Gbps ■ Up to 63 devices simultaneously connected
Thunderbolt	Simultaneous transmission of Display Port (video and audio), PCI Express (data), and power	■ Extremely high-speed data transfer method ■ Up to 20 Gbps ■ Up to 7 devices simultaneously connected to a single port
Ethernet	Network	■ Most common standard for local area networks
VGA (Video Graphics Array), DVI (Digital Visual Interface)	Monitors	■ VGA is designed for transmission of analog video signals ■ DVI allows for transmission of digital video signals
HDMI (High Definition Multimedia Interface)	Monitors, home theater	■ HDMI allows for simultaneous transmission of digital audio and video signals

Monitors can be color, black and white, or monochrome (meaning all one color, usually green or amber). Today, monochrome monitors are used primarily in cash registers and other point-of-sale applications. Most modern monitors use **liquid crystal display (LCD)** technology, because they are lighter and thinner than the bulky **cathode ray tubes** used in old computer displays and televisions. Because display monitors are embedded into a broad range of products and devices, such as cell phones, digital cameras, and automobiles (e.g., to display route maps and other relevant information), they must be sturdy, reliable, lightweight, energy efficient, and low in cost. Recent developments in monitor technologies have thus focused on other display technologies, such as **organic light-emitting diodes**, which require far less power and are much thinner than traditional LCD panels. Finally, projectors are often used for presentation to an audience (and by many as a way to project a large video image in a home theater).

In addition to traditional monitors, touchscreen displays have become extremely popular with the development of high-resolution smartphones, tablet computers like the iPad, and a variety of technology gadgets. A **touchscreen** is a display screen that is also an input device; a user interacts with the device by touching pictures or words on the screen with a finger or a stylus. In addition to your smartphone or tablet PC, touchscreens are used in ATM machines, retail point-of-sale terminals, car navigation, and industrial control computers. Touchscreens provide great flexibily in how an input device can look and operate.

Especially for mobile computing, monitor technology is still a challenge. In addition to screen size and power requirements of commonly used display technologies, glare is often an issue, and many laptop screens are hard to read in bright sunlight. Over the past decades, there has been a steady stream of enhancements related to improved resolution and reduced power consumption. It is forecasted that the next generation will be lightweight, thin, and flexible like paper, as well as be inexpensive and not require external power to retain an image. Recently, manufacturers have introduced flexible glass for touchscreens, which has allowed for new form factors of mobile devices.

Now that you have learned more about IS hardware, we will focus on software, another key component of the IS infrastructure.

FOUNDATIONAL TOPICS IN IS SOFTWARE

Software refers to programs, or sets of instructions, that allow all the hardware components in your computer system to speak to each other and to perform the desired tasks. Throughout the book, we have discussed a variety of application software, from large business systems (e.g., an enterprise resource planning system) to office automation and personal productivity tools. Without software, the biggest, fastest, most powerful computer in the world is nothing more than a fancy paperweight. Software is intertwined with all types of products and services—toys, music, appliances, health care, and countless other products. Here, we provide some background on this critical component to all computer-based products.

System Software

In Chapter 3, you learned about one type of system software, the operating system, and its many different tasks. More specifically, common tasks of an operating system include the following:

- Booting (or starting) your computer
- Reading programs into memory and managing memory allocation
- Managing where programs and files are located in secondary storage
- Maintaining the structure of directories and subdirectories
- Formatting disks
- Controlling the computer monitor
- Sending documents to the printer

Just as there are many kinds of computers, there are many different kinds of operating systems (see Table TB4). In general, operating systems—whether for large mainframe computers or for small notebook computers—perform similar operations. Obviously, large multiuser mainframes are more complex than small desktop systems; therefore, the operating system must account for and manage that complexity. However, the basic purpose of all operating systems is the same.

A second type of system software, **utilities** (or **utility programs**), is designed to manage computer resources and files. Some utilities are included in operating systems, while others

TABLE TB4 Common Operating Systems

Operating System	Description
z/OS	A proprietary operating system developed specifically for large IBM mainframe systems.
Unix	A multiuser, multitasking operating system that is available for a wide variety of computer platforms. Commonly used because of its superior security.
Windows	Currently, the Windows desktop operating system is by far the most popular in the world. Variations are also used to operate large servers, small handhelds, and cell phones.
Mac OS	The first commercial graphical-based operating system, making its debut in 1984. The operating system of Apple computers.
Linux	An open source operating system designed in 1991 by a Finnish student. Known as a secure, low-cost, multiplatform operating system. Linux powers about one-third of all Web servers. Linux users can choose between different "flavors" (or distributions) depending on their needs (such as the novice-friendly Ubuntu).
Android	Google's Linux-based operating system for mobile devices.
iOS	Apple's mobile operating system, previously named iPhone OS; also used on the iPod Touch and iPad.

must be purchased separately and installed on your computer. Table TB5 provides a sample of a few utility programs that are considered essential.

Programming Languages and Development Environments

Each piece of software is developed using some programming language. A programming language is the computer language the software vendor uses to write programs. For application software, such as spreadsheets, Web browsers, or accounting software, the underlying programming language is invisible to the user. However, programmers in an organization's IS group, and in some instances end users, can use programming languages to develop their own specialized applications. The **source code** (i.e., the program written in a programming language) must be translated into object code—called assembly or machine language—that the hardware can understand. Normally, the source code is translated into machine language using programs called *compilers* and *interpreters*.

COMPILERS AND INTERPRETERS. A **compiler** takes an entire program's source code written in a programming language and converts it into an **executable**, that is, a program in machine language that can be read and executed directly by the computer (see Figure TB5). Although the compilation process can take quite some time (especially for large programs), the resulting executables run very fast; thus, programs are usually compiled before they are sold as executables to the customers. The customers purchase only the executable but do not have access to the program's source code, thus, they can run the program but not make any modifications to it.

TABLE TB5 Common Types of Computer Software Utilities

Utility	Description
Backup	Archives files from the hard disk to tapes, flash drives, or other storage devices
File defragmentation	Converts fragmented files (i.e., files not stored contiguously) on your hard disk into contiguous files that will load and be manipulated more rapidly
Disk and data recovery	Allows the recovery of damaged or erased data from hard disks and flash drives
Data compression	Compresses data by substituting a short code for frequently repeated patterns of data, much like the machine shorthand used by court reporters, allowing more data to be stored on a storage medium
File conversion	Translates a file from one format to another so that it can be used by an application other than the one used to create it
Antivirus	Scans files for viruses and removes or quarantines any virus found
Device driver	Allows the computer to communicate with various different hardware devices
Spyware detection and removal	Scans a computer for spyware and disables or removes any spyware found
Media player	Allows listening to music or watching video on a computer

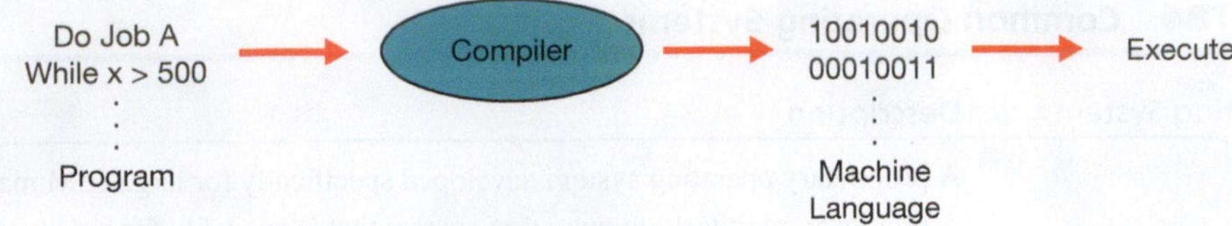

FIGURE TB5
A compiler translates the entire computer program into machine language, then the CPU executes the machine language program.

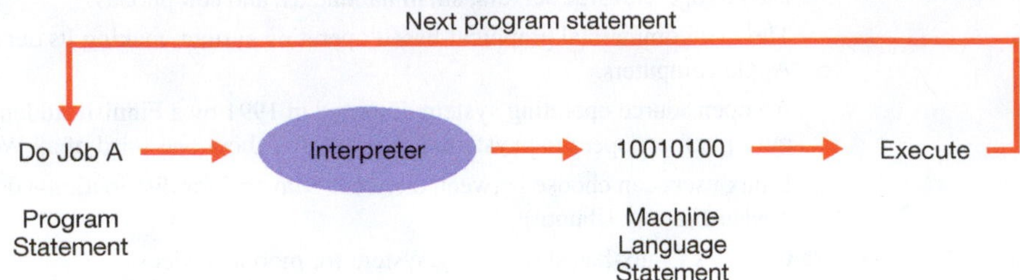

FIGURE TB6
Interpreters read, translate, and execute one line of source code at a time.

Some programming environments do not compile the entire program into machine language. Instead, each statement of the program is converted into machine language and executed "on the fly" (i.e., one statement at a time), as depicted in Figure TB6. The type of program that does the conversion and execution is called an **interpreter**. As the source code is translated each time the program is run, it is easy to quickly evaluate the effects of any changes made to the program's source code. However, this also causes interpreted programs to run much slower than compiled executables. Programming languages can be either compiled or interpreted.

PROGRAMMING LANGUAGES. Over the past few decades, software has evolved. As software has evolved, so have the programming languages. Each programming language has been designed at a particular time, for a particular use, and the first generations of programming languages were quite crude by today's standards. Some popular programming languages are listed in Table TB6.

TABLE TB6 Examples of Popular Programming Languages

Language	Application	Description
BASIC	General purpose	Beginner's All-Purpose Symbolic Interaction Code. An easy-to-learn language, BASIC works on almost all PCs.
C/C++	General purpose	C++ is a newer version of C. Developed at AT&T Bell Labs. Complex languages used for a wide range of applications.
COBOL	Business	COmmon Business-Oriented Language. Developed in the 1960s, it was the first language for developing business software. COBOL is still frequently used for many business transaction processing applications on mainframes.
FORTRAN	Scientific	FORmula TRANslator. The first commercial high-level language developed by IBM in the 1950s. Designed for scientific, mathematical, and engineering applications.
Java	World Wide Web	An object-oriented programming language developed by Sun Microsystems in the early 1990s. It is a popular programming language for the Internet because it is highly transportable from one computer to another. Java is also used for programing Android apps.
.NET Framework	World Wide Web	A variety of programming languages (e.g., ASP.NET and C#) offered by Microsoft that can easily be integrated into Web applications.
LISP	Artificial Intelligence	LISt Processor. Dates from the late 1950s. One of the main languages used to develop applications in artificial intelligence and high-speed arcade graphics.
PERL	World Wide Web	A dynamic programming language commonly used for writing scripts for Web sites, as well as for batch processing of large amounts of data.
Objective-C	App development	Evolved from C, Objective-C is used for developing apps for iPhones, iPads, and Apple computers.

TABLE TB7 Concepts Related to Object-Oriented Languages

Concept	Description	Examples
Class	A set of objects having the same properties and behaviors (but the values of the properties can differ for each individual object). Classes can be reused for different programs.	A "student" has an address and a grade-point average (GPA) (properties) and can enroll in courses (behavior).
Object	Instantiation of a class.	Student Jeff Smith has a GPA of 3.94, and enrolls in MIS250.
Encapsulation	Data and behavior of a class are hidden from other classes and are thus protected from unexpected changes.	The registrar doesn't need to know how the GPA is calculated within the "student" class; the registrar cares only that it is updated.
Inheritance	More specific classes include the properties and behaviors of the more general class.	Both "distance degree student" and "on-campus student" inherit properties (such as address and GPA) and behaviors (such as enroll in a course) from the general class "student."
Event-driven program execution	The programmer does not determine the sequence of execution for the program; the flow is determined by user input (e.g., mouse clicks) or messages from other applications.	A word processor reacts to your typing and clicking.

Of course, programming languages continue to evolve, with object-oriented languages, visual programming languages, and Web development languages rapidly gaining popularity. We discuss these next.

Object-Oriented Languages **Object-oriented languages** are the most recent in the progression of high-level programming languages and are extremely popular with application developers. Object-oriented languages use common modules (called objects), which combine properties and behaviors to define the relevant system components. An example of an object would be a specific student who has a name, an address, and a date of birth (i.e., the properties), but can also perform certain operations, such as register for a course (the behaviors). If an object-oriented programming language is being used, it enables the design and implementation of the objects to happen quickly and simultaneously, as oftentimes preexisting objects can be reused or adapted. For important concepts related to object-oriented languages, see Table TB7.

Visual Programming Languages Just as you may have found it easier to use a computer operating system with a **graphical user interface (GUI)**, such as Windows 8 or Mac OS X, programmers using **visual programming languages** may also take advantage of the GUI. For instance, programmers can easily add a command button to a screen with a few clicks of a mouse (see Figure TB7) instead of programming the button pixel by pixel and using many lines

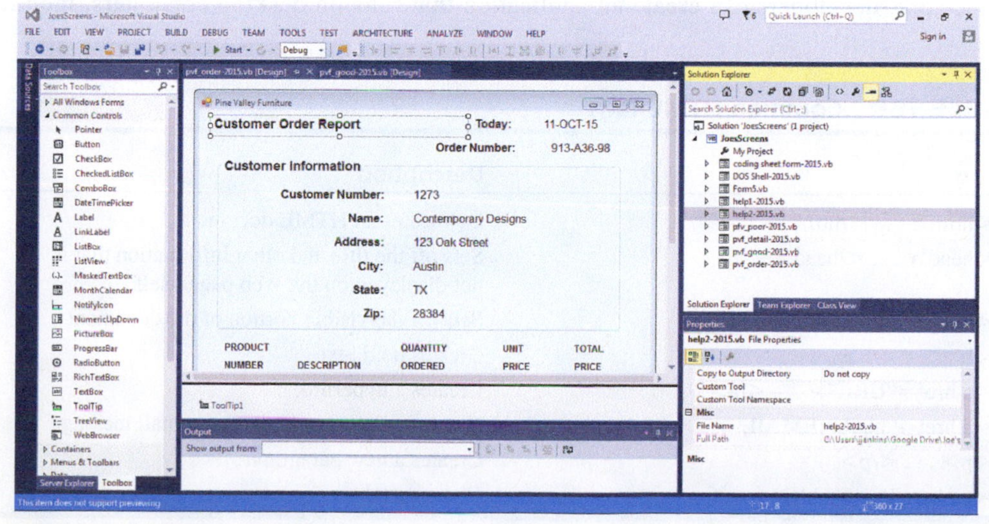

FIGURE TB7

Visual Basic.Net, a visual programming language, is used to create standard business forms.
Source: Courtesy of Microsoft Corporation

of code. Visual Basic.NET and Visual C# (pronounced as "C-sharp") are two popular examples of visual programming languages.

Web Development Languages If you have been surfing the Web for a while, you may have thought of creating a personal Web page or already have one. In that event, you have some experience with using a markup language. The markup language you used to create your Web page is called Hypertext Markup Language (HTML). HTML is a text-based file format that uses codes (i.e., tags) to specify the structure and content of a document; **HTML tags** are used to instruct the Web browser on how a document should be presented to the user. Because HTML editing programs are visually oriented and easy to use, you do not need to memorize the language to set up a Web page. Programs for creating Web pages (such as Brackets, Microsoft Visual Studio, and Adobe Dreamweaver) are called **Web page builders** or **HTML editors**.

In HTML, the tags used to identify different elements on a page are set apart from the text with angle brackets (<>). Specific tags are used to mark the beginning and the ending of an element or a formatting command. For example, if you want text to appear in bold type, the HTML tag to begin bolding is <b>. The tag to turn off bolding, at the end of the selected text, is </b>. The "a href" command sets up a hyperlink from a word or image on the page to another HTML document. Tags also denote document formatting commands, such as text to be used as the page title, levels of headings, the ends of paragraphs, underlining, italics, bolding, and places to insert pictures and sound (see Table TB8). Today, Web developers use **cascading style sheets (CSS)** to specify the formatting and layout of elements on a Web page.

A good way to understand how HTML works is to find a Web page you like, then use the "View Source" command on your browser to see the hypertext that created the page (see Figure TB8). Once you have created your own Web page and saved it to a disk, you can upload it to a Web space you have created through your Web site's host.

Markup languages such as HTML are for specifying the content and structure of Web pages. If you want to add dynamic content or have users interact with your Web page other than by clicking on hypertext links, then you will need to use special purpose programming languages such as Java or use Web services, scripting languages, and so on.

Java is a programming language that was developed by Sun Microsystems in the early 1990s to allow adding dynamic, interactive content to Web pages. For example, the chat feature in the Blackboard learning environment uses Java. You can add Java applications to a Web page in one of two ways: by learning Java or a similar language and programming the content you want, or by downloading free generalpurpose **applets** from the Web to provide the content you want on your Web page. Applets are small programs that are executed within another application, such as a Web page. When a user accesses your Web page, the applets you inserted are downloaded from the server along with your Web page to the user's browser, where they perform the desired action. Later, when the user leaves your Web page, the Web page and the applets disappear from his or her computer. Java is also frequently used to build Android apps.

Microsoft .NET is a programming platform that is used to develop applications that are highly interoperable across a variety of platforms and devices. For example, using the .NET framework, developers can create an application that runs on desktop computers, mobile

TABLE TB8 Common HTML Tags

Tag	Description
<html> . . . </html>	Delineates an HTML document
<head> . . . </head>	Sets off the title and other information that is not displayed on the Web page itself
<body> . . . </body>	Sets off the visible portion of the document
<b> . . . </b>	Creates bold text
<a href="URL"> . . . </a>	Creates a hyperlink
<a href="mailto:EMAIL"> . . . </a>	Creates a link creating a new e-mail message
<p> . . . </p>	Creates a new paragraph
<table> . . . </table>	Creates a table

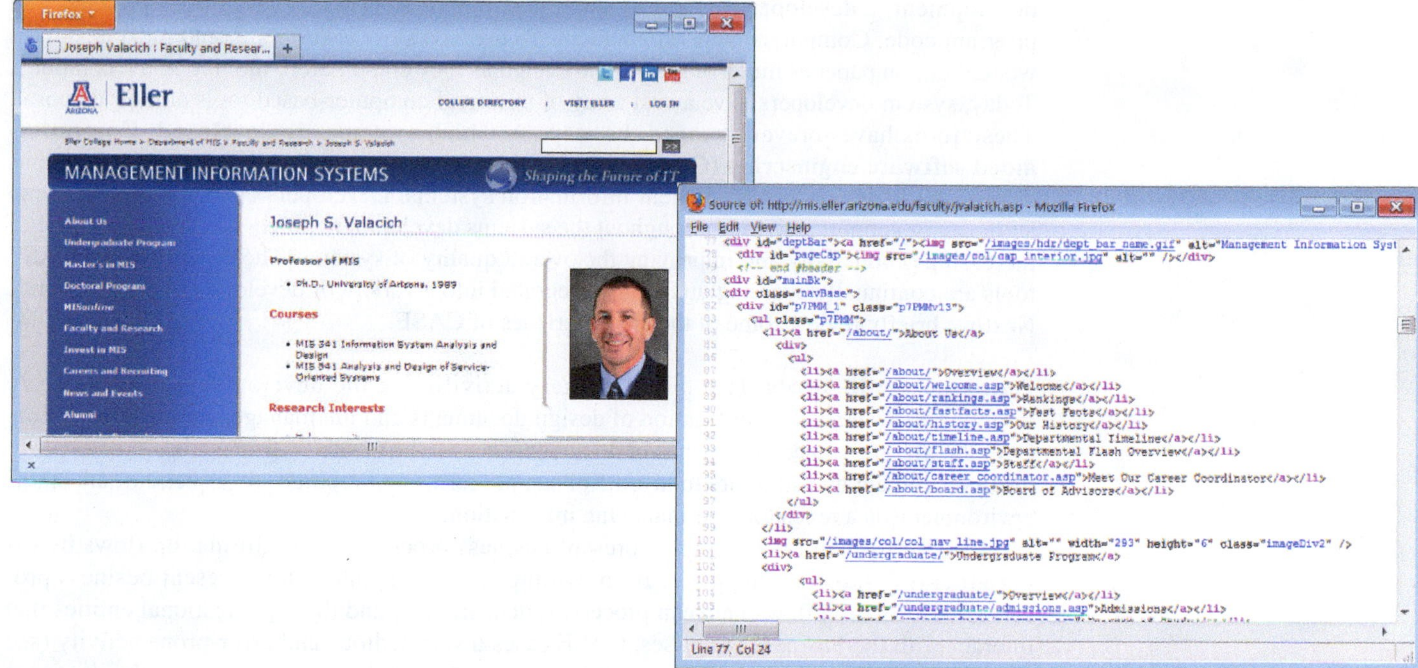

FIGURE TB8

A Web page and the HTML source code used to create it.

computers, or smartphones. A suite of visual programming languages including Visual C#, ASP .NET, and Visual Basic.NET can be used to construct .NET applications.

Scripting languages can also be used to supply interactive components and dynamic content to a Web page. These languages let you build programs or scripts directly into HTML page code. Web page designers frequently use them to check the accuracy of user-entered information, such as names, addresses, and credit card numbers. Two common scripting languages are Microsoft's VBScript and JavaScript.

JavaScript bears little resemblance to Java. The two are similar, however, in that both Java and JavaScript are useful component software tools for creating dynamic, interactive Web pages. That is, both allow users to add dynamic content to Web pages. Both are also cross-platform programs, meaning that they can typically be executed by computers running Windows, Linux, Mac OS, and other operating systems.

Another common way to add dynamic content to Web sites is Flash. Using the application development suite Adobe Flash, developers can create animation and video that can be compressed small enough for fast download speeds. When you browse the Web and see animation or complex data streams, this is often done in Flash. Flash animation is displayed on your screen using the Adobe Flash player. Flash can also allow data-driven animation. Some examples of data-driven flash animation on Web sites are the bag builder at Timbuk2 (www.timbuk2.com) and the live Major League Baseball game update at Yahoo!'s sports site (http://sports.yahoo.com/mlb/gamechannel). Yet, Flash content is not well suited for mobile devices, and in 2010, Apple announced that it would not support Flash on its iPhones and iPads, rather advocating the use of HTML5 (the newest standard of the HTML markup language), which allows for rich, interactive Web applications.

Along with commercial products, there are several open source tools in wide use today. The most common is PHP, originally designed as a high-level tool for producing dynamic Web content. The development of programming languages is an ongoing process of change and innovation, and these changes often result in more capable and complex systems for the user. The popularity of the Internet has further spurred the creation of innovative and evolving software. From the pace of change that is occurring, it is clear that many more innovations are on the horizon.

AUTOMATED DEVELOPMENT ENVIRONMENTS. Over the years, the tools for developing information systems have increased in both variety and power. In the early days of systems development, a developer was left to using pencil and paper to sketch out design ideas and program code. Computers were cumbersome to use and slow to program, and most designers worked out on paper as much of the system design as they could before moving to the computer. Today, system developers have a vast array of powerful computer-based tools at their disposal. These tools have forever changed the ways in which systems are developed. **Computer-aided software engineering (CASE)** refers to the use of automated software tools by systems developers to design and implement information systems. Developers can use CASE tools to automate or support activities throughout the systems development process with the objective of increasing productivity and improving the overall quality of systems. The capabilities of CASE tools are continually evolving and being integrated into a variety of development environments. Next we briefly review some of the characteristics of CASE.

Types of CASE Tools Two of the primary activities in the development of large-scale information systems are the creation of design documents and the management of information. Over the life of a project, thousands of documents need to be created—from screen prototypes to database content and structure to layouts of sample forms and reports. At the heart of all CASE environments is a repository for managing information.

CASE also helps developers represent business processes and information flows by using graphical diagramming tools. By providing standard symbols to represent business processes, information flows between processes, data storage, and the organizational entities that interact with the business processes, CASE eases a very tedious and error-prone activity (see Figure TB9). The tools not only ease the drawing process, but also ensure that the drawings conform to development standards and are consistent with other design documents created by other developers.

Another powerful capability of CASE is its ability to generate program source code automatically. CASE tools keep pace with contemporary programming languages and can automatically produce programming code directly from high-level designs in languages such as Java, Visual Basic.NET, and C#. In addition to diagramming tools and code generators, a broad range of other tools assists in the systems development process. The general types of CASE tools used throughout the development process are summarized in Table TB9.

Open Source Software

Open source software refers to systems software, applications, and programming languages in which the source code (i.e., the program code written in a programming language) is freely available to the general public for use and/or modification. Many large mainstream software

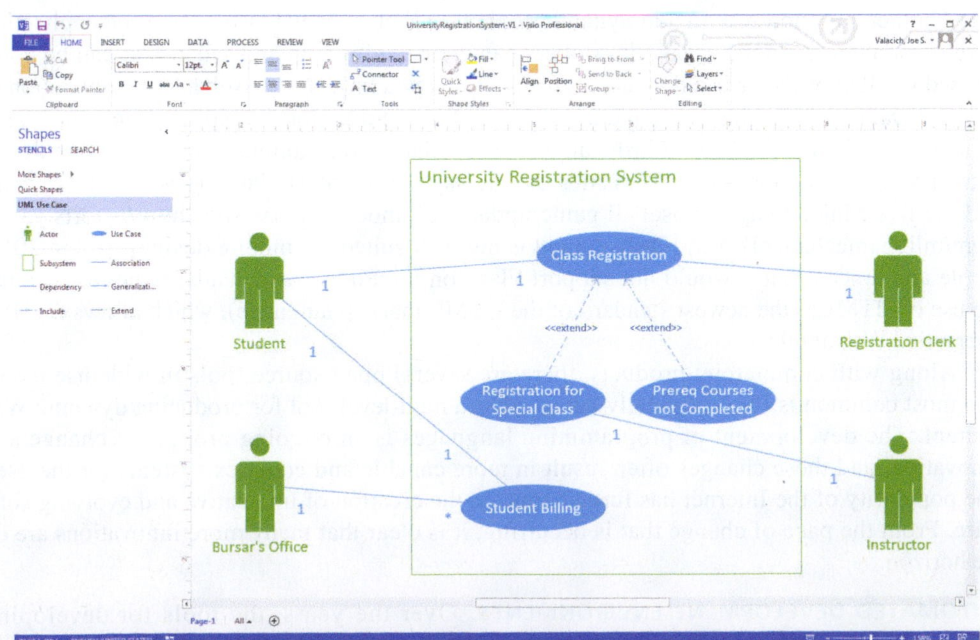

FIGURE TB9

System design diagram from Microsoft Visio.

Source: Courtesy of Microsoft Corporation

TABLE TB9 General Types of CASE Tools

CASE Tool	Description
Diagramming tools	Tools for graphically representing a system's processes, data, and control structures.
Screen and report generators	Tools that help model how systems look and feel to users. Screen and report generators also make it easier for the systems analyst to identify data requirements and relationships.
Analysis tools	Tools that automatically check for incomplete, inconsistent, or incorrect specifications in diagrams, screens, and reports.
Repositories	Tools that enable the integrated storage of specifications, diagrams, reports, and project management information.
Documentation generators	Tools that help produce both technical and user documentation in standard formats.
Code generators	Tools that enable the automatic generation of program and database definition code directly from the design documents, diagrams, screens, and reports.

Source: Hoffer, George, & Valacich (2014).

companies are actively involved in the open source community. For example, IBM is playing a leading role in evolving the Linux operating system. Likewise, Oracle was active in developing and extending the OpenOffice Productivity Suite before donating it to the Apache Foundation.

Open source is a philosophy that promotes developers' and users' access to the source of a product or idea. Particularly in the area of software development, the open source movement has taken off with the advent of the Internet; people around the world are contributing their time and expertise to develop or improve software, ranging from operating systems to applications software. Open source software owes its success to the inputs from a large user base, helping to fix problems or improve the software; however, with large open source projects, such as different variants of the operating system Linux, only a small group of contributors is ultimately responsible for ensuring the quality and stability of the software. Linux, one of the most prevalent examples of open source software, was developed as a hobby by Finnish university student Linus Torvalds in 1991. Having developed the first version himself, he made the source code of his operating system available to everyone who wanted to use it and improve on it. Since then, various Linux distributions (such as Ubuntu, Red Hat, and Debian) have been released; each distribution integrates the core part of the Linux operating system with different utilities and software applications, depending on the intended use (e.g., desktop computer, netbook, Web server, embedded system, and so on). With most distributions, users can only *suggest* modifications for official releases; for example, users can contribute to program code or provide new designs for the system's user interface, but only a small group of carefully selected "committers" can implement these modifications into the official releases of the software.

FOUNDATIONAL TOPICS IN NETWORKING

Telecommunications and networking technologies have become very important as almost all organizations rely on computer-based information systems to support various business processes. Understanding how the underlying networking technologies work and where these technologies are heading will help you better understand the potential of information systems. The discussion begins with a description of the evolution of computer networking.

Evolution of Computer Networking

Over the past decades, computer networking underwent an evolution from centralized computing to distributed computing to collaborative computing. These eras of computer networking are discussed next.

CENTRALIZED COMPUTING. **Centralized computing**, depicted in Figure TB10, remained largely unchanged through the 1970s. In this model, large centralized computers, called mainframes, were used to process and store data. During the mainframe era (beginning in the 1940s), people entered data on mainframes through the use of local input devices called **terminals**. These devices were called "dumb" terminals because they did not conduct any processing, or "smart," activities. The centralized computing model is not a true network because there is no sharing

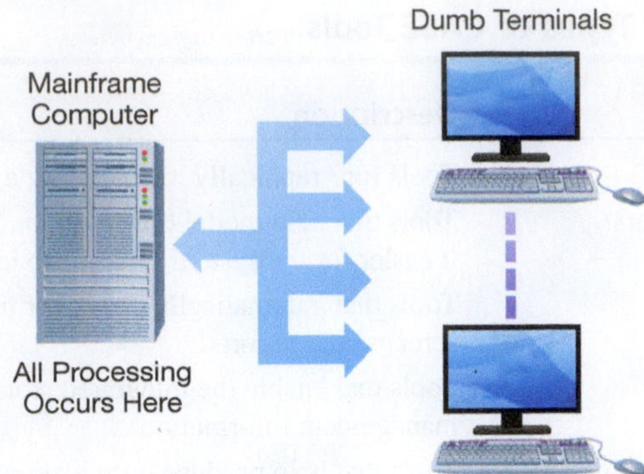

FIGURE TB10

In the centralized computing model, all processing occurs in one central mainframe.

of data and capabilities. The mainframe provides all the capabilities, and the terminals are only input/output devices. Computer networks evolved in the 1980s when organizations needed separate, independent computers to communicate with each other. Centralized computing has seen a renaissance as businesses turn to thin clients to reduce costs for support, energy, or software licenses, and to increase productivity and security.

DISTRIBUTED COMPUTING. The introduction of personal computers in the late 1970s and early 1980s gave individuals control over their own computing. Organizations also realized that they could use multiple small computers to achieve many of the same processing goals of a single large computer. People could work on subsets of tasks on separate computers rather than using one mainframe to perform all the processing. To achieve this goal, computer networks were needed so that data and services could be easily shared between these distributed computers. The 1980s were characterized by an evolution to a computing model called **distributed computing**, shown in Figure TB11, in which multiple types of computers are networked together to share data and services.

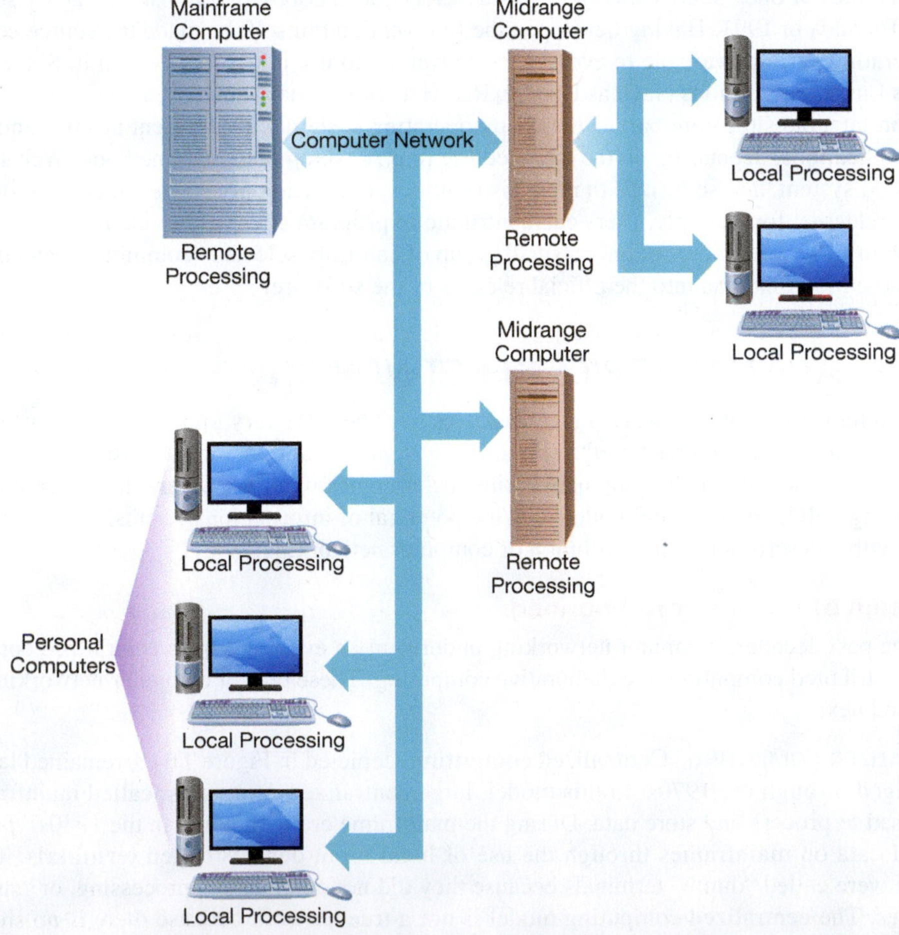

FIGURE TB11

In the distributed computing model, separate computers work on subsets of tasks and then pool their results by communicating over a network.

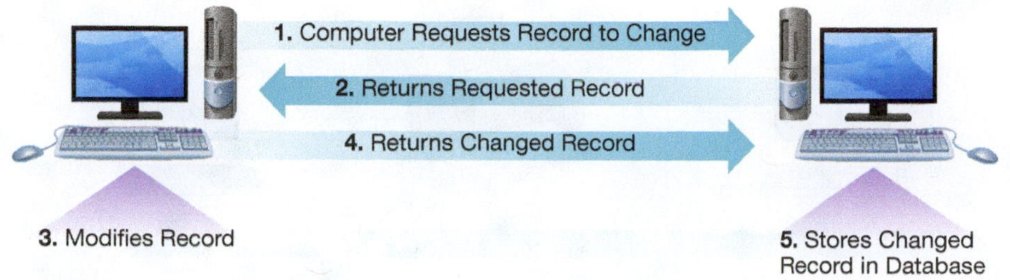
1. Computer Requests Record to Change
2. Returns Requested Record
4. Returns Changed Record
3. Modifies Record
5. Stores Changed Record in Database

FIGURE TB12

In the collaborative computing model, two or more networked computers work together to accomplish a common processing task.

COLLABORATIVE COMPUTING. In the 1990s, a new computing model, called **collaborative computing**, emerged. Collaborative computing is a synergistic form of distributed computing in which two or more networked computers work together to accomplish a common processing task. That is, in this model of computing, computers are not simply communicating data but are also sharing processing capabilities. For example, one computer may be used to store a large employee database. A second computer may be used to process and update individual employee records retrieved from this database. The two computers collaborate to keep the company's employee records current, as depicted in Figure TB12.

NETWORK SERVICES. Computer networks allow for sharing various capabilities between devices. For example, computer networks allow for efficiently storing, retrieving, and moving data between computers, or allow for accessing network printers and network-attached storage devices; similarly, e-mail, instant messaging, and the sending and receiving of pictures or video and audio data require the sender and recipient to be connected to a network. Finally, networks enable computers to share processing power, in that processing can be distributed between the client and server. Clients request data or services from the servers. The servers store data and application programs. For example, the physical search of database records may take place on the server, while the user interacts with a much smaller database application that runs on the client.

When an organization decides to network its computers and devices, it must decide what services will be provided; typically, different services on the network are offered by different servers, such as print servers, e-mail servers, and so on. In addition to those servers, networks typically have specialized systems for managing the network, its users, and its resources. These include computers providing **authentication services** for granting users and devices access rights to resources on a network, or **directory services**, which are repositories (or "address books") containing information about users, user groups, resources on a network, access rights, and so on.

Types of Networks

Computing networks today include all three computing models: centralized, distributed, and collaborative. The emergence of new computing models did not mean that organizations completely discarded older technologies. Rather, a typical organizational computer network includes mainframes, servers, personal computers, and a variety of other devices. Computer networks are commonly classified by size, distance covered, and structure. The most common are described next.

PRIVATE BRANCH EXCHANGE. A private branch exchange (PBX) is a telephone system that serves a particular location, such as a business. It connects telephone extensions within the system and connects internal extensions to the outside telephone network. It can also connect computers within the system to other PBX systems, to an outside network, or to various office devices, such as fax machines or photocopiers. Since they use ordinary telephone lines, PBX systems have limited bandwidth, preventing them from transmitting such forms of data as interactive video, digital music, or high-resolution photos. Using PBX technology, a business requires fewer outside phone lines, but has to purchase or lease the PBX equipment. Many organizations now use *Internet protocol*–based PBX systems, which make use of the organizations' data networks and allow for low-cost voice over IP calling.

LOCAL AREA NETWORK. A local area network (LAN), shown in Figure TB13, is a computer network that spans a relatively small area, allowing all computer users to connect with each other to share data and peripheral devices, such as printers. LAN-based communications may involve the sharing of data, software applications, or other resources between several users.

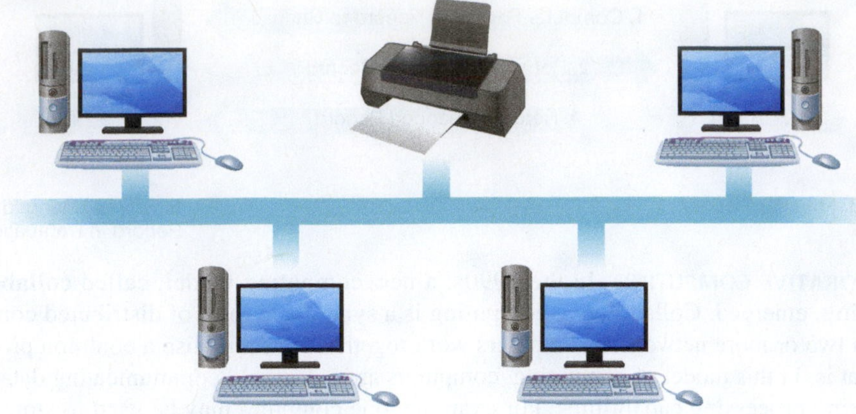

FIGURE TB13

A LAN allows multiple computers located near each other to communicate directly with each other and to share peripheral devices, such as a printer.

LANs typically do not exceed tens of kilometers in size and are typically contained within a single building or a limited geographical area.

WIDE AREA NETWORK. A wide area network (WAN) is a computer network that spans a relatively large geographical area. WANs are typically used to connect two or more LANs. Different hardware and transmission media are often used in WANs because they must cover large distances efficiently. Used by multinational companies, WANs transmit and receive data across cities and countries. A discussion follows of five specific types of WANs: campus area networks, metropolitan area networks, enterprise WANs, value-added networks, and global networks.

Campus Area Network A campus area network (CAN) is a computer network that is used (and owned or leased) by a single organization to connect multiple LANs. A CAN typically spans multiple buildings, such as at a corporate or university campus.

Metropolitan Area Network A metropolitan area network is a computer network of limited geographic scope, typically a citywide area, which combines both LAN and high-speed fiber-optic technologies. Such networks are attractive to organizations that need high-speed data transmission within a limited geographic area.

Enterprise WAN An **enterprise WAN** is a WAN connecting disparate local area networks of a single organization into a single network (see Figure TB14).

Value-Added Network **Value-added networks (VANs)** are private, third-party-managed WANs typically used for B2B communications. With much B2B data communication now happening over the Internet, VAN providers focus on offering services such as secure e-mail and translation of EDI standards to facilitate secure communication between businesses.

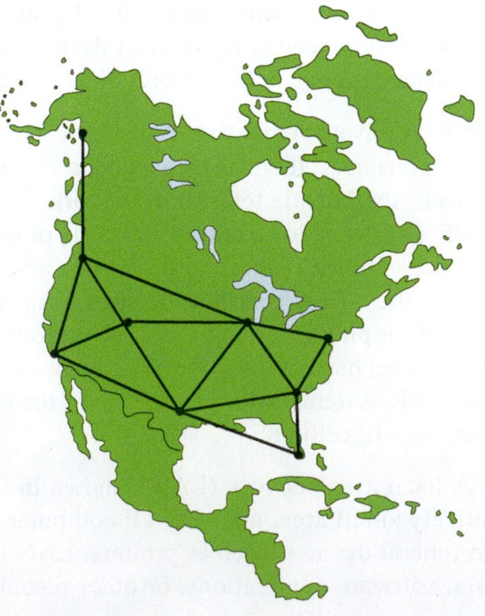

FIGURE TB14

An enterprise network allows an organization to connect distributed locations into a single network.

FIGURE TB15

Bluetooth is used by many to provide hands-free communication.

Source: Jupiterimages/Stockbyte/Getty Images

Global Networks A **global network** spans multiple countries and may include the networks of several organizations. The Internet is an example of a global network. The Internet is the world's largest computer network, consisting of thousands of individual networks connecting billions of computers, smartphones, and other devices in almost every country of the world.

PERSONAL AREA NETWORKS. A final type of computer network, called a personal area network (PAN), uses wireless communication to exchange data between computing devices using short-range radio communication, typically within an area of 10 meters (30 feet). The enabling technology for PAN is called **Bluetooth**, a specification for personal networking of desktop computers, peripheral devices, mobile phones, portable media players, and various other devices. Bluetooth is integrated into a variety of personal devices to ease interoperability and information sharing (see Figure TB15).

Now that you have an understanding of the general types of networks, the next sections examine some further fundamental concepts. After discussing packet switching as a concept for sharing communication channels, we will delve deeper into network standards and technologies. Together, these sections provide a foundation for understanding various types of networks.

Packet Switching

Telecommunications advances have enabled connecting individual computer networks—constructed with a variety of hardware and software—together in what appears to be a single network. Networks are increasingly being used to dynamically exchange relevant, value-added knowledge and information throughout global organizations and institutions. To enable rapid transmission of massive amounts of data, most data networks rely on packet switching. **Packet switching** is based on the concept of turn taking and enables millions of users to send large and small chunks of data across the network concurrently. To minimize delays, network technologies limit the amount of data that any computer can transfer on each turn. Consider a conveyor belt as a comparison. Suppose that the conveyor belt connects a warehouse and a retail store. When a customer places an order, it is sent from the store to the warehouse, where a clerk assembles the items in the order. The items are placed on the conveyor belt and delivered to the customer in the store. In most situations, clerks finish sending items from one order before proceeding to send items from another order. This process works well when orders are small, but when a large order with many items comes in, sharing a conveyor belt can introduce delays for others. Consider waiting in the store for your one item while another order with 50 items is being filled.

Local area networks (LANs), WANs, PANs, and the Internet all use packet-switching technologies so that users can share the communication channel and minimize delivery delays. Figure TB16 illustrates how computers use packet switching. Computer A wants to send

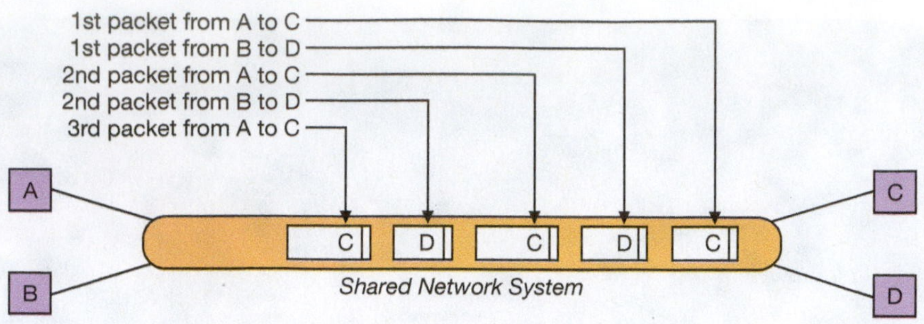

FIGURE TB16

Computers A and B use packet switching to send messages or files to computers C and D.

a message to computer C; similarly, computer B wants to send a message to computer D. For example, computer A is trying to send an e-mail message to computer C, while computer B is trying to send a word processing file to computer D. The outgoing messages are divided into smaller packets of data, and then each sending computer (A and B) takes turns sending the packets over the transmission medium. The incoming packets are reassembled at their respective destinations, using previously assigned packet sequence numbers.

For packet switching to work, each computer attached to a network must have a unique network address, and each packet being sent across a network must be labeled with a header containing the network address of the source (sending computer) and the network address of the destination (receiving computer). As packets are transmitted, network hardware detects whether a particular packet is destined for a local machine. Packet-switching systems adapt instantly to changes in network traffic. If only one computer needs to use the network, it can send data continuously. As soon as another computer needs to send data, packet switching, or turn taking, begins. Next, we explain the importance of network standards and protocols to enable data communication.

Network Standards and Protocols

Standards play a key role in creating networks. The physical elements of networks—adapters, cables, and connectors—are defined by a set of standards that have evolved since the early 1970s. Standards ensure the interoperability and compatibility of network devices, and each standard combines a media access control technique, network topology, and transmission media in different ways. The dominant standard for wired local area networks is 802.3, typically referred to as Ethernet; wireless local area networks are based on the 802.11 family of standards. As these standards are continuously evolving, other competing standards for local area networks have all but vanished. Software interacts with hardware to implement protocols that allow different types of computers and networks to communicate successfully.

PROTOCOLS. All networks employ protocols to make sure communication between computers is successful. Protocols are agreed-on formats for transmitting data between connected computers. They specify how computers should be connected to the network, how errors will be checked, what data compression method will be used, how a sending computer will signal that it has finished sending a message, and how a receiving computer will signal that it has received a message. Protocols allow packets to be correctly routed to and from their destinations. There are literally thousands of protocols to choose from, but a few are a lot more important than the others. In this section, we will first review the OSI model, the worldwide standard for implementing protocols. Next, we briefly review TCP/IP, the protocol used by the Internet, and Ethernet, a commonly used protocol for local area networks.

The OSI Model The need of organizations to interconnect computers and networks that use different protocols has driven the industry to an open systems architecture in which different protocols can communicate with each other. The International Organization for Standardization defined a networking model called Open Systems Interconnection (OSI), which divides computer-to-computer communications into seven connected layers. The **Open Systems Interconnection (OSI) model** represents a group of specific tasks (represented in Figure TB17) as successive layers that enable computers to communicate data. Each successively higher layer builds on the functions of the layers below. For example, suppose you are using a PC running Windows and are connected to the Internet, and you want to send a message to a friend who

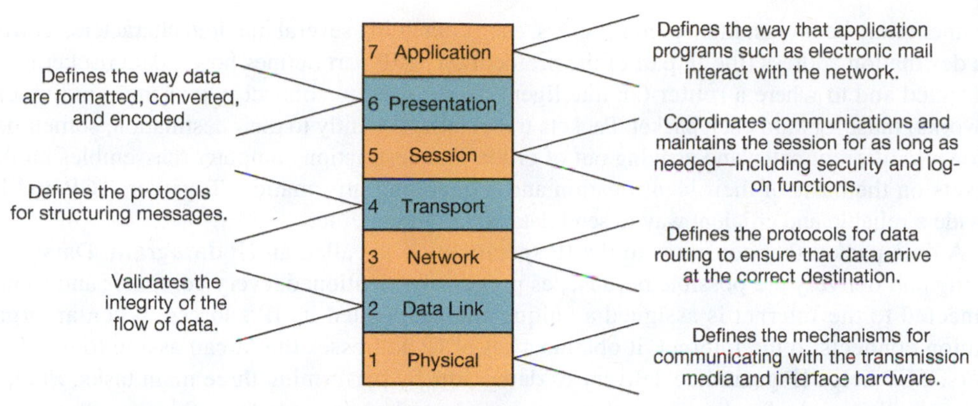

FIGURE TB17

The OSI model has seven layers and provides a framework for connecting different computers with different operating systems to a network.

uses a large workstation computer running Unix—two different computers and two different operating systems. When you transmit your message, it is passed down from layer to layer in the Windows protocol environment of your system. At each layer, special bookkeeping information specific to the layer, called a header, is added to the data. Eventually, the data and headers are transferred from the Windows layer 1 to Unix's layer 1 over some physical pathway. On receipt, the message is passed up through the layers in the Unix application. At each layer, the corresponding header information is stripped away, the requested task is performed, and the remaining data package is passed on until your message arrives as you sent it, as shown in Figure TB18. In other words, protocols represent an agreement between different parts of the network about how data are to be transferred.

Transmission Control Protocol/Internet Protocol (TCP/IP) Because so many different networks are interconnected throughout the world, they must have a common language, or protocol, to communicate. The protocol used by the Internet is called Transmission Control Protocol/Internet Protocol (TCP/IP). The first part, TCP, breaks data into small chunks and manages the transfer of those packets from computer to computer via packet switching. For example, a single

FIGURE TB18

Message passing between two different computers.

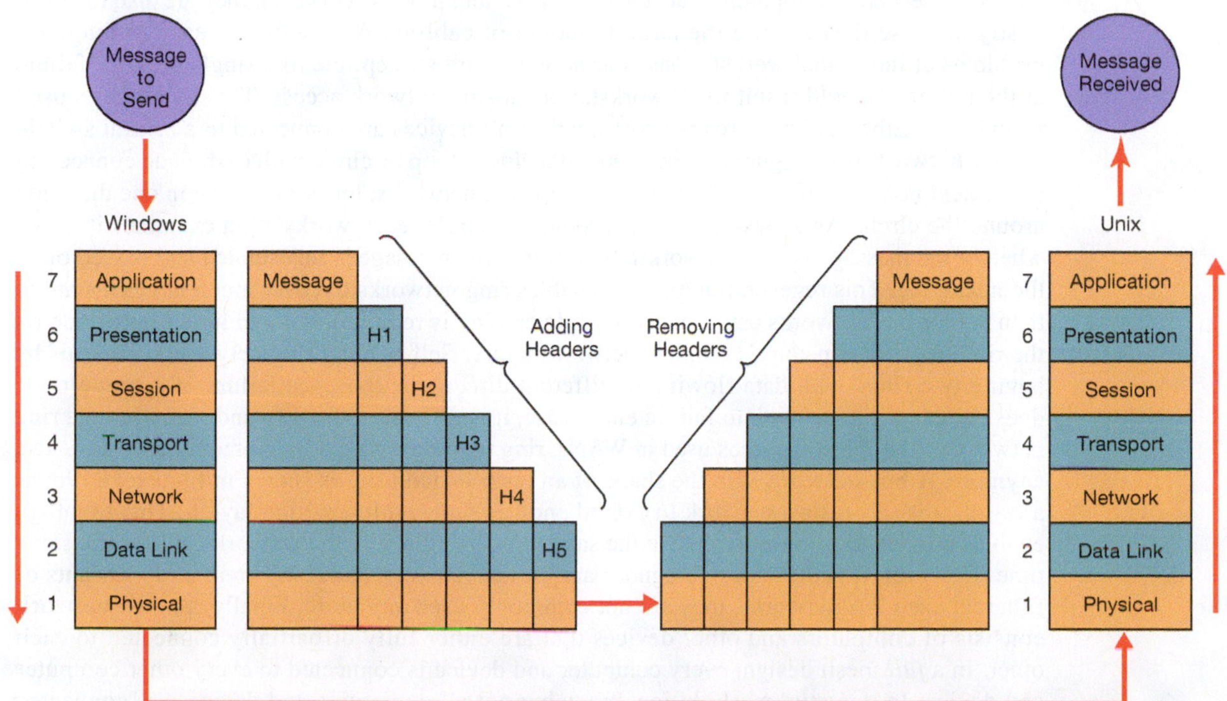

document may be broken into several packets, each containing several hundred characters, as well as a destination address (the IP part of the protocol). The IP part defines how a data packet must be formed and to where a **router** (an intelligent device used to connect two or more individual networks) must forward each packet. Packets travel independently to their destination, sometimes following different paths and arriving out of order. The destination computer reassembles all the packets on the basis of their identification and sequencing information. Together, TCP and IP provide a reliable and efficient way to send data across the Internet.

A data packet that conforms to the IP specification is called an **IP datagram**. Datagram routing and delivery are possible because, as previously mentioned, every computer and router connected to the Internet is assigned a unique address, called its IP address. When an organization connects to the Internet, it obtains a set of IP addresses that it can assign to its computers. TCP helps IP guarantee delivery of datagrams by performing three main tasks. First, it automatically checks for datagrams that may have been lost en route from their source to their destination. Second, TCP collects the incoming datagrams and puts them in the correct order to re-create the original message. Finally, TCP discards any duplicate copies of datagrams that may have been created by network hardware.

Ethernet **Ethernet** is a set of LAN protocols using packet switching developed by the Xerox Corporation in 1976. Different types of data (including IP datagrams) can travel on Ethernets by being enclosed in another set of headers to form packets called Ethernet frames. The original Ethernet protocol supports data transfer rates of 10 Mbps. A later version, called 100Base-T or Fast Ethernet, supports transfer rates of 100 Mbps; the latest version, called 100 Gb Ethernet, supports transfer rates of 100 Gbps, or 100,000 Mbps, over relatively large distances. Most new computers have a **network interface card (NIC)** (also known as network adapter or Ethernet card) installed, allowing you to use the Ethernet protocol to connect to broadband modems, home networks, or work networks. Each NIC has a unique identifier (called MAC address, assigned by the manufacturer) that is used to identify the computer on the network. The PC is then connected to other network components via transmission media, such as Ethernet cables. Increasingly, organizations use the Ethernet protocol for wide area networks, called Wide Area Ethernet or Ethernet WAN.

NETWORK TOPOLOGIES. **Network topology** refers to the shape of a network. The four basic network topologies are star, ring, bus, and mesh. A **star network** is configured, as you might expect, in the shape of a star, as shown in Figure TB19a. That is, all nodes or workstations are connected to a central hub through which all messages pass. The workstations represent the points of the star. Star topologies are easy to lay out and modify. However, they are also the most costly because they require the largest amount of cabling. Although it is easy to diagnose problems at individual workstations, star networks are susceptible to a single point of failure at the hub that would result in all workstations losing network access. This topology is used in switched Ethernet local area networks, where all devices are connected to a central switch. A **ring network** is configured in the shape of a closed loop or circle with each node connecting to the next node, as shown in Figure TB19b. In ring networks, messages move in one direction around the circle. As a message moves around the circle, each workstation examines it to see whether the message is for that workstation. If not, the message is regenerated and passed on to the next node. This regeneration process enables ring networks to cover much larger distances than star or bus networks can. Relatively little cabling is required, but a failure of any node on the ring network can cause complete network failure. Self-healing ring networks avoid this by having two rings with data flowing in different directions; thus, the failure of a single node does not cause the network to fail. In either case, it is difficult to modify and reconfigure a ring network. Although sometimes used in WANs, ring topologies are not commonly used in LANs anymore. A **bus network** is in the shape of an open-ended line, as shown in Figure TB19c; as a result, it is the easiest network to extend and has the simplest wiring layout. This topology enables all network nodes to receive the same message through the network cable at the same time. However, it is difficult to diagnose and isolate network faults. Whereas early variants of Ethernet used bus networks, they are not commonly used any more. Finally, a **mesh network** consists of computers and other devices that are either fully or partially connected to each other. In a *full* mesh design, every computer and device is connected to every other computer and device. In a *partial* mesh design, many but not all computers and devices are connected

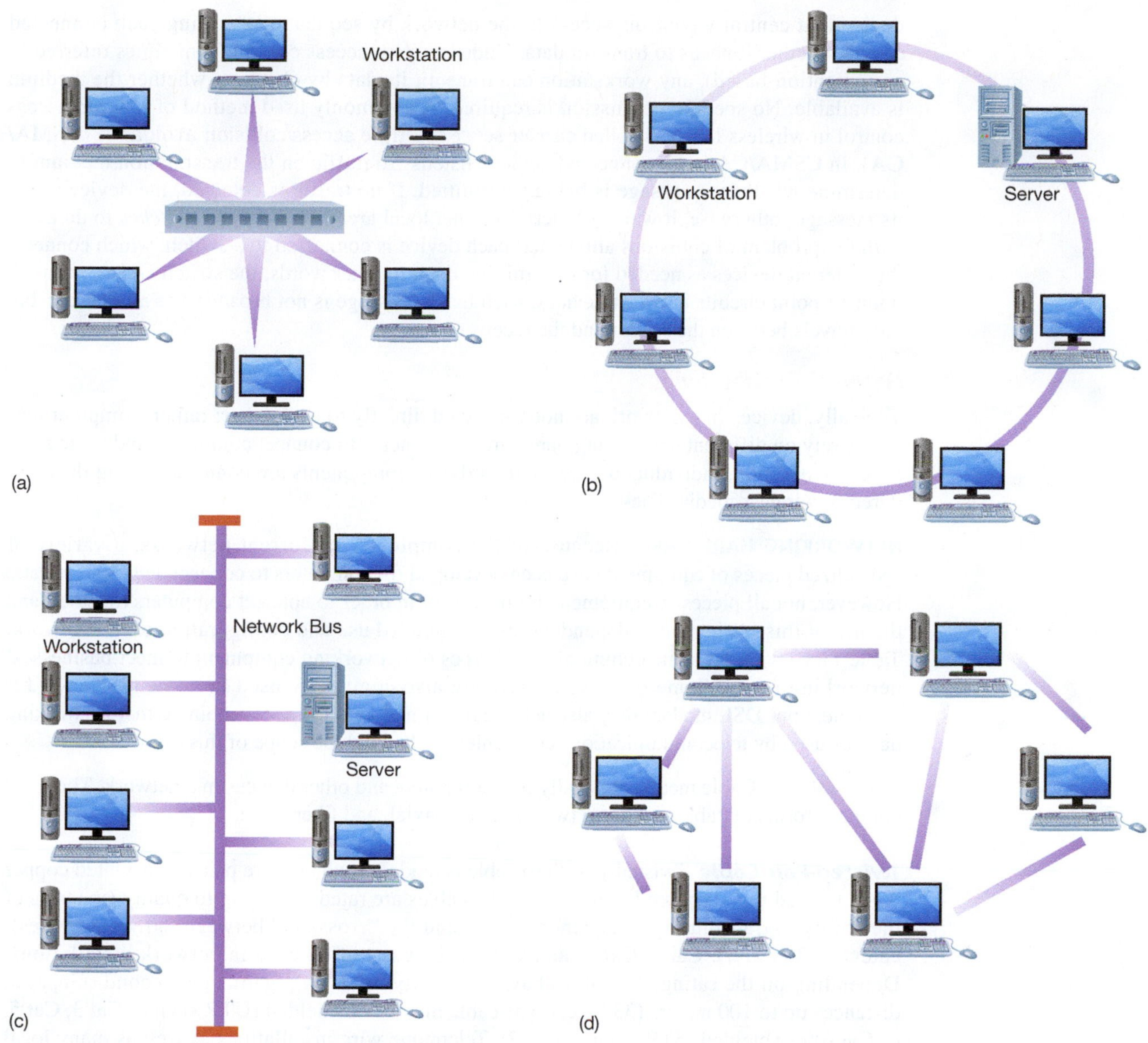

FIGURE TB19

(a) The star network has several workstations connected to a central hub. (b) The ring network is configured in a closed loop, with each workstation connected to another workstation. (c) The bus network is configured in the shape of an open-ended line where each workstation receives the same message simultaneously. (d) The mesh network consists of computers and other devices that are either fully or partially connected to each other.

(see Figure TB19d). Like a ring network, mesh networks provide relatively short routes from one node to another. Mesh networks also provide many possible routes through the network—a design that prevents one circuit or computer from becoming overloaded when traffic is heavy. Given these benefits, most WANs, including the Internet, use a partial mesh design.

MEDIA ACCESS CONTROL. **Media access control** is the set of rules that governs how a given node or workstation gains access to the network to send or receive data. Without access control, collisions are likely to happen if two or more workstations simultaneously transmit messages on the network. There are two general types of access control: distributed and random access. With distributed access control, only a single workstation at a time has authorization to transmit its data. One method of authorization is token passing, where authorization is transferred sequentially from workstation to workstation. Ring networks normally use a token-passing media access control method to regulate network traffic. Another method, polling, uses a master device that centrally controls access to the network by sequentially polling each connected device whether it needs to transmit data. Under random access control (sometimes referred to as contention-based), any workstation can transmit its data by checking whether the medium is available. No specific permission is required. A commonly used method of random access control in wireless LANs is called **carrier sense multiple access/collision avoidance (CSMA/CA)**. In CSMA/CA, each connected device "listens" to traffic on the transmission medium to determine whether a message is being transmitted. If no traffic is detected, the device sends its message; otherwise, it waits. Modern Ethernet local area networks use *switches* to do away with the problem of collisions altogether: each device is connected to a switch, which connects the different devices as needed for transmitting data; in other words, the switch creates separate point-to-point circuits between devices, such that a message is not broadcast to all devices, but only travels between the sender and the receiver.

Network Technologies

Typically, devices in a network are not connected directly to each other; rather, computer networks rely on different networking hardware components to connect computers and route messages. In addition, individual devices and hardware components are connected using different wired or wireless media. These are discussed next.

NETWORKING HARDWARE. Because of the complexity of current networks, a variety of specialized pieces of equipment have been developed for computers to connect and transfer data. However, not all pieces of equipment are necessary in order to connect computers together, and the use of this equipment is dependent on the intended use and configuration of the network. Table TB10 presents some commonly used types of networking equipment to meet businesses' networking needs. Some of these devices are also commonly used in home networks; for example, your DSL modem may also act as a router and wireless access point. Other networking devices used by telecommunications companies are beyond the scope of this discussion.

CABLE MEDIA. Cable media physically link computers and other devices in a network. The most common forms of cable media are twisted pair, coaxial, and fiber-optic.

Twisted-Pair Cable Twisted-pair (TP) cable is made of two or more pairs of insulated copper wires twisted together (see Figure TB20). TP cables are rated according to quality (in terms of the ability to transmit high frequency signals and the "crosstalk" between individual wires); category 3 (Cat 3), Cat 5, Cat 6, and Cat 7 cables are often used in network installations. Depending on the rating, TP cables have a capacity up to 10 gigabits per second (Gbps) at distances up to 100 meters (330 feet). The cable may be unshielded (UTP, such as Cat 3, Cat 5, or Cat 6) or shielded (STP, such as Cat 7). Telephone wire installations as well as many local

TABLE TB10 Networking Hardware

Networking Hardware	Description
Switch	A **switch** is used to connect multiple computers, servers, or printers to create a network. Switches typically inspect data packets received and forward them to the correct addressee.
Router	A router is an intelligent device used to connect two or more different networks. When a router receives a data packet, it looks at the network address and passes the packet on to the appropriate network. Routers are commonly used to connect a LAN to a WAN, such as the Internet.
Wireless access point	A **wireless access point** transmits and receives wireless (Wi-Fi) signals to allow wireless devices to connect to the network.
Wireless controller	A **wireless controller** manages multiple access points and can be used to manage transmission power and channel allocation to establish desired coverage throughout a building and minimize interference between individual access points. Further, wireless controllers can be used to manage authentication and other security features.

FIGURE TB20

(a) A cable spliced open showing several twisted pairs. (b) A sample network installation that utilizes many TP cables at once.

Sources: (a) Georgios Alexandris/Shutterstock; (b) Inara Prusakova/Shutterstock

(a)

(b)

area networks use UTP cabling, as it is cheap and easy to install. However, like all copper wiring, it has rapid attenuation and is very sensitive to electromagnetic interference (EMI) and eavesdropping—the undetected capturing of data transmitted over a network. STP uses wires wrapped in insulation, making it less prone to EMI and eavesdropping. STP cable is more expensive than unshielded TP cable, and it is more difficult to install because it requires special grounding connectors to drain EMI. Ethernet cables typically use RJ-45 connectors so that they can be plugged into an NIC or into other network components.

Coaxial Cable Coaxial (or coax) cable contains a solid inner copper conductor surrounded by plastic insulation and an outer braided copper or foil shield (see Figure TB21). Coax cable comes in a variety of thicknesses—thinnet coax and thicknet coax—based on resistance to EMI. Although less costly than TP, thinnet coax is not commonly used in networks anymore; thicknet coax is more expensive than TP. Coax cable is most commonly used for cable television installations and for networks operating at 10 to 100 megabits per second (Mbps). Its attenuation is lower than TP cable's, and it is moderately susceptible to EMI and eavesdropping.

FIGURE TB21

These coaxial cables are ready to be connected to a computer or other device.

Source: Kasia/Shutterstock

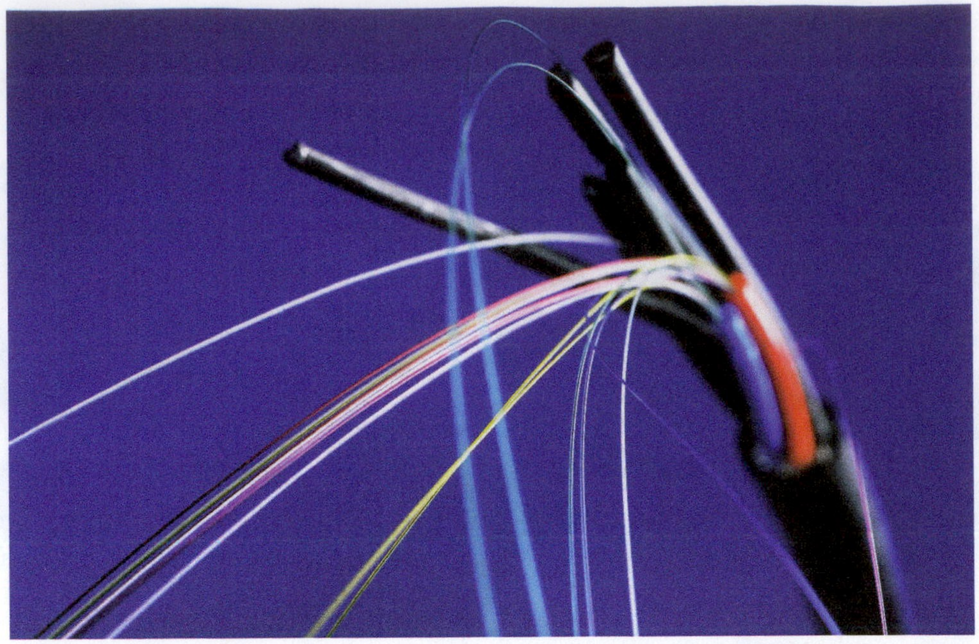

FIGURE TB22

Fiber-optic cable consists of a light-conducting glass or plastic core, surrounded by more glass, called cladding, and a tough outer sheath.

Source: Goodshoot/Thinkstock/Getty Images

Fiber-Optic Cable Fiber-optic cable is made of a light-conducting glass or plastic core surrounded by more glass, called cladding, and a tough outer sheath (see Figure TB22). The sheath protects the fiber from changes in temperature as well as from bending or breaking. This technology uses pulses of light sent along the optical cable to transmit data. Fiber-optic cable transmits clear and secure data because it is immune to EMI and eavesdropping. Transmission signals do not break up because fiber-optic cable has low attenuation. It can support bandwidths from 100 Mbps to greater than 2 Gbps and distances up to 25 kilometers (15 miles), with bandwidths increasing at an astonishing rate. Fiber-optic cable is more expensive than copper wire because the cost and difficulties of installation and repair are higher for fiber-optic. Fiber-optic cables are used for high-speed **backbones**—the high-speed central networks to which many smaller networks can be connected. A backbone may connect, for example, several different buildings in which other, smaller LANs reside. Submarine telecommunications cables (used for telephone and Internet traffic between continents) also use fiber-optic cable. In home environments, fiber-optic cable can be used to connect digital audio devices.

WIRELESS MEDIA. With the popularity of mobile devices such as laptops, tablets, and smartphones, wireless media are rapidly gaining popularity. Wireless media transmit and receive electromagnetic signals using methods such as infrared line of sight, high-frequency radio, and microwave systems.

Infrared Line of Sight Infrared line of sight uses high-frequency light waves to transmit signals on an unobstructed path between nodes. While commonly being used in remote controls for most audiovisual equipment, such as TVs, stereos, and other consumer electronics equipment, infrared systems are not well suited for rapidly transmitting large amounts of data; thus, this technology has since been surpassed by Wi-Fi and Bluetooth for data communication.

High-Frequency Radio High-frequency radio signals can transmit data at rates of up to several hundred Mbps to network nodes from 12.2 up to approximately 40 kilometers (7.5 to 25 miles) apart, depending on the nature of any obstructions between them. The flexibility of the signal path makes high-frequency radio ideal for mobile transmissions. For example, most police departments use high-frequency radio signals that enable police vehicles to communicate with each other as well as with the dispatch office. This medium is expensive because of the cost of antenna towers and high-output transceivers. Installation is complex and often dangerous because of the high voltages. Although attenuation is fairly low, this medium is very susceptible to EMI and eavesdropping.

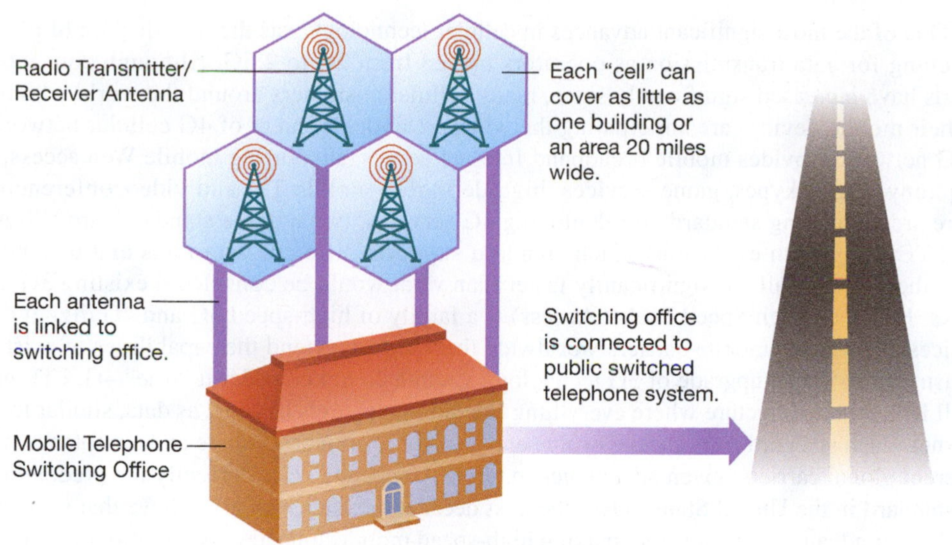
Radio Transmitter/
Receiver Antenna
Each "cell" can cover as little as one building or an area 20 miles wide.
Each antenna is linked to switching office.
Switching office is connected to public switched telephone system.
Mobile Telephone Switching Office

FIGURE TB23

A cellular network divides a geographic region into cells.

Two common applications of high-frequency radio communication are cellular phones and wireless networks. A **cellular phone** gets its name from how the signal is distributed. In a cellular system, a coverage area is divided into **cells** with a low-powered radio antenna/receiver in each cell; these cells are monitored and controlled by a central computer (see Figure TB23). Any given cellular network has a fixed number of radio frequencies. When a user initiates or receives a call, the mobile telephone switching office assigns the caller a unique frequency for the duration of the call. As a person travels within the network, the central computer at the switching office monitors the quality of the signal and automatically assigns the call to the closest cellular antenna. Cellular phones have gone through rapid changes since their first commercial use in the mid-1980s (see Table TB11). Because of the costs involved in setting up fixed telephone lines, cellular phones have become very popular in many African countries and are a key factor in bridging the digital divide.

TABLE TB11 Evolution of Cell Phone Technology

Generation	Description	Data Transfer	Advantages
0G	Preceded modern cellular mobile telephony and was usually mounted in cars or trucks; it was a closed circuit, so you could call only other radio telephone users.	Analog	Enabled communicating on the go.
1G	This technology, introduced in the 1980s, used circuit switching; it had poor voice quality, unreliable handoffs between towers, and nonexistent security.	Analog	Enabled users to communicate with other cell phones and land lines.
2G	The first all-digital signal that was divided into TDMA and CDMA standards. Allowed for SMS (text) messaging and e-mails to be sent/received.	Digital (up to 9.6 Kbps transfer)	Lower-powered radio signals allowed for longer battery life. Digital format allowed for clearer signal and reduced signal noise.
2.5G	Allows for faster data transmission via a packet-switched domain in addition to the circuit-switched domain.	Digital (up to 115 Kbps transfer)	Higher data speeds allow for more complex data to be transmitted (e.g., sports scores and news stories).
3G	Even faster. Requires a new cellular network, different from that already available in 2G systems.	Digital (minimum of 384 Kbps when moving and 2 Mbps when stationary)	Transfer full video and audio.
4G	Standards for high-speed mobile connectivity. Different standards on different networks and locations.	Digital (up to 100 Mbps when moving and 1 Gbps when stationary)	Data speeds similar to wired networks.

One of the most significant advances in cellular technology was the introduction of packet switching for data transmission as operators moved from 2G to 2.5G. Although connection speeds have increased significantly since, many cellular customers around the world who rely on their mobile devices are anticipating the widespread deployment of 4G cellular networks. A 4G network provides mobile broadband Internet access, supporting mobile Web access, IP telephony (e.g., Skype), game services, high-definition mobile TV, and videoconferencing. There are competing standards for deploying 4G services; two notable standards are HSPA+ and LTE (long-term evolution). Each standard supports different data rates and distances. Nevertheless, they all are significantly faster than what would be considered existing 3G networks. HSPA+ (High Speed Packet Access) is a family of high-speed 3G and 4G digital data services available to mobile carriers worldwide that helps to extend the capabilities of existing infrastructures; as an upgrade of 3G technologies, some do not consider it "true" 4G. LTE uses an all IP-based architecture where everything (including voice) is handled as data, similar to the Internet. Each standard continues to evolve and gain (or lose) market share and acceptance with different global carriers; given advantages in terms of speed, LTE is currently the predominant 4G standard in the United States. Over the next decade, industry insiders believe that standards will further advance and converge, making high-speed mobile connectivity a reality for much of the world.

High-frequency radio-wave technology is increasingly being used to support wireless local area networks (WLANs). WLANs based on a family of standards called 802.11 are also referred to as Wi-Fi (wireless fidelity). The 802.11 family of standards has been universally adopted and has transmission speeds up to 450 Mbps (using the 802.11n standard), with even faster standards being under development. The ease of installation has made WLANs popular for business and home use. For example, some homes and many buildings have (or want) multiple computers and need to share Internet access, files, and peripheral devices. Unfortunately, many older buildings and homes do not have a wired infrastructure to easily connect computers and devices, making wireless networking particularly attractive. Through the use of wireless technologies, many organizations are transforming their work environments into better team collaboration environments.

Microwave Transmission Microwave transmission uses high-frequency radio signals that are sent through the air using either terrestrial (earth-based) systems or satellite systems (microwaves are typically of shorter wavelength, and thus higher frequency than radio waves used by cellular or Wi-Fi networks). Terrestrial microwave, shown in Figure TB24, uses antennae that require an unobstructed path or line of sight between nodes. The cost of a terrestrial microwave system depends on the distance to be covered. Typically, businesses lease access to these microwave systems from service providers rather than invest in antenna equipment. Data may be transmitted at up to 274 Mbps. Over short distances, attenuation is not a problem, but signals can be disrupted over longer distances by environmental conditions such as high winds and heavy rain. EMI and eavesdropping are significant problems with microwave communications.

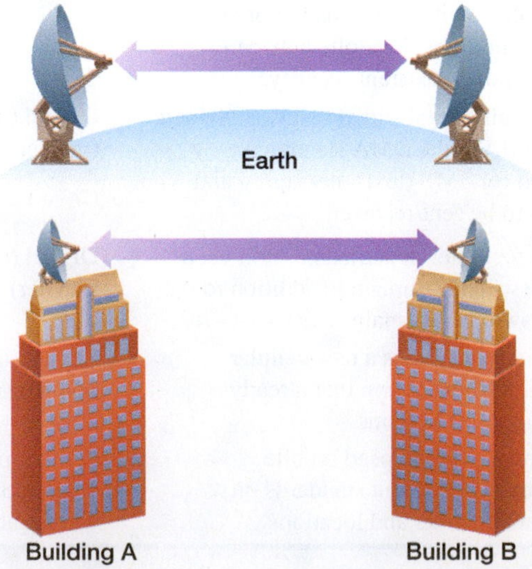

FIGURE TB24

Terrestrial microwave requires a line-of-sight path between a sender and a receiver.

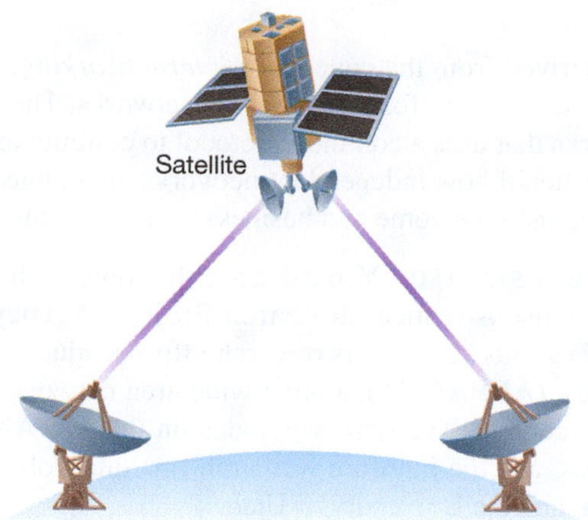

FIGURE TB25

Communications satellites are relay stations that receive signals from one earth station and rebroadcast them to another.

Satellite microwave, shown in Figure TB25, uses satellites orbiting the earth as relay stations to transfer signals between ground stations located on earth. Satellites orbit from 400 to 22,300 miles above the earth and have different uses and characteristics (see Table TB12). Because of the distance signals must travel, satellite transmissions are delayed (also known as **propagation delay**). Satellite transmission has become very viable for media such as TV and radio, including the digital radio stations XM and Sirius, both of which have their own satellites that send out scrambled signals to proprietary receivers.

Another strength of satellite communication is that it can be used to access very remote and undeveloped locations on the earth. Such systems are extremely costly because their use and installation depends on space technology. Companies such as AT&T sell satellite services with typical transmission rates ranging from less than 1 to 10 Mbps, but the rates can be as high as 90 Mbps. Like terrestrial microwave, satellite systems are prone to attenuation and are susceptible to EMI and eavesdropping. Table TB13 compares wireless media across several criteria.

TABLE TB12 Characteristics of Satellites with Different Orbits

Name	Distance from Earth	Characteristics/Common Application
Low Earth Orbit (LEO) Satellite	400–1,000 miles	■ Not fixed in space in relation to the rotation of the earth; circles the earth several times per day. ■ Photography for mapping and locating mineral deposits; monitoring ice caps, coastlines, volcanoes, and rain forests; researching plant and crop changes; monitoring wildlife habitats and changes; search and rescue for downed aircraft or ships that are in trouble; research projects in astronomy and physics.
Medium Earth Orbit (MEO)	1,000–22,300 miles	■ Not fixed in space in relation to the rotation of the earth; circles the earth more than one time per day. ■ Primarily used in geographical positioning systems (such as GPS) for navigation of ships at sea, spacecraft, airplanes, automobiles, and military weapons.
Geosynchronous Earth Orbit (GEO)	22,300 miles	■ Fixed in space in relation to the rotation of the earth; circles the earth one time per day. ■ Because it is fixed in space, transmission is simplified. ■ Transmission of high-speed data for television, weather information, remote Internet connections, digital satellite radio, and telecommunications (satellite phones).

TABLE TB13 Relative Comparison of Wireless Media

Medium	Expense	Speed	Attenuation	EMI	Eavesdropping
Infrared line of sight	Low	Up to 16 Mbps	High	High	High
High-frequency radio	Moderate	Up to 300 Mbps	Low	High	High
Terrestrial microwave	Moderate	Up to 274 Mbps	Low	High	High
Satellite microwave	High	Up to 90 Mbps	Moderate	High	High

The Internet

The name "Internet" is derived from the concept of *internetworking*, which means connecting host computers and their networks to form even larger networks. The Internet is a large worldwide collection of networks that uses a common protocol to communicate. In the following sections, we discuss in more detail how independent networks are connected to form the Internet, who manages the Internet, and how home and business users can connect to the Internet.

HOW DID THE INTERNET GET STARTED? You can trace the roots of the Internet back to the late 1960s, when the U.S. **Defense Advanced Research Projects Agency** began to study ways to interconnect networks of various kinds. This research effort produced the **Advanced Research Projects Agency Network (ARPANET)**, a large wide area network (WAN) that linked many universities and research centers. The first two nodes on the ARPANET were the University of California, Los Angeles, and the Stanford Research Institute, followed by the University of California, Santa Barbara, and the University of Utah.

ARPANET quickly evolved and was combined with other networks. For example, in 1986, the U.S. **National Science Foundation (NSF)** initiated the development of the **National Science Foundation Network (NSFNET)**, which became a major component of the Internet. Other networks throughout the United States and the rest of the world were interconnected and/or morphed into the growing "Internet." Throughout the world, support for the Internet has come from a combination of federal and state governments, universities, national and international research organizations, and industry.

CONNECTING INDEPENDENT NETWORKS. The Internet uses routers to interconnect independent networks. For example, Figure TB26 illustrates a router that connects Networks 1, 2, and 3. A router, like a conventional computer, has a central processor, memory, and network interfaces. However, routers do not use conventional software, nor are they used to run applications. Their only job is to interconnect networks and forward data packets from one network to another. As illustrated in Figure TB27, Computers A and F are connected to independent networks. If Computer A generates a data packet destined for Computer F, the packet is sent to the router that interconnects the two networks. The router forwards the packet on to Network 2, where it is delivered to its destination at Computer F.

Routers are the fundamental building blocks of the Internet because they connect thousands of LANs and WANs. LANs are connected to backbone WANs, as depicted in Figure TB28. A backbone network manages the bulk of network traffic and typically uses a higher-speed connection than the individual LAN segments. For example, a backbone network might use fiber-optic cabling, which can transfer data at a rate of 100 Gbps, whereas a LAN connected to the backbone may use Ethernet with TP cabling, transferring data at a rate of 10 Mbps to 10 Gbps.

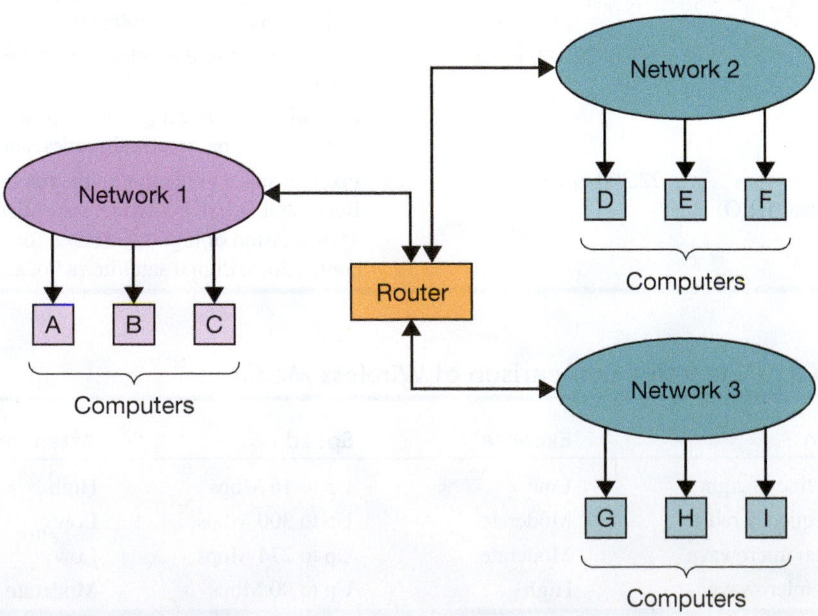

FIGURE TB26

Routers connect independent networks.

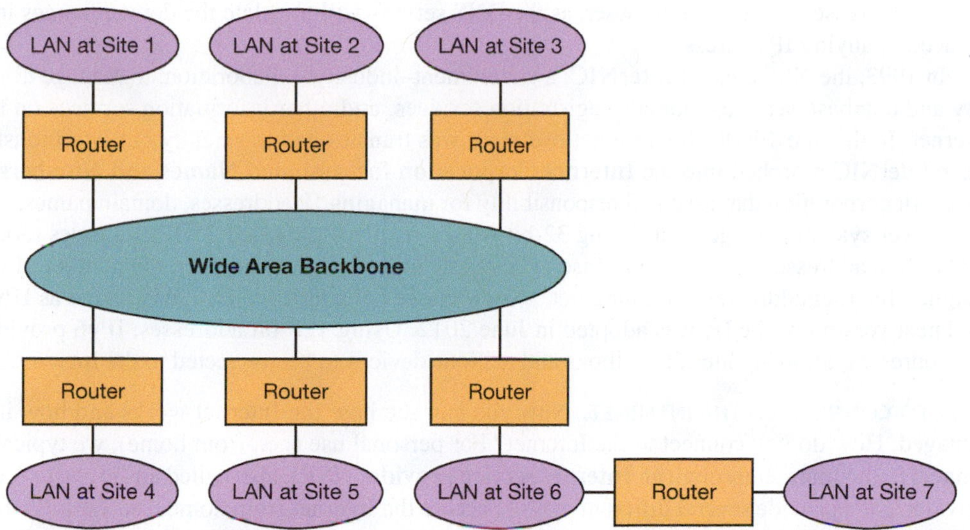

FIGURE TB27

LANs connect to wide area backbones.

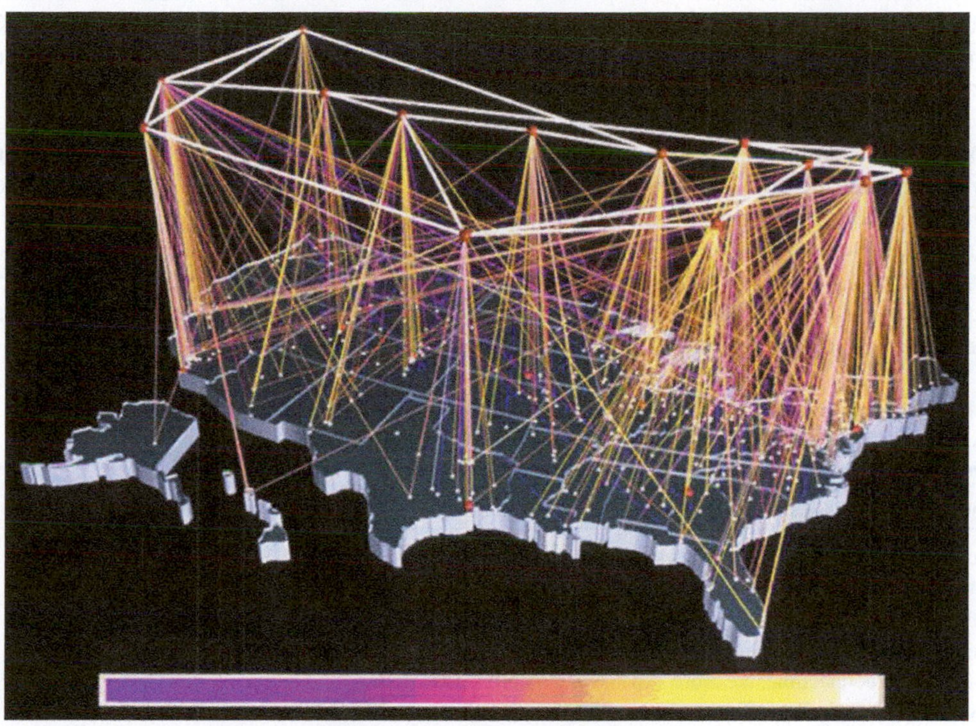

FIGURE TB28

The Internet backbone.

To gain access to the Internet, an organization installs a router between one of its own networks and the network of its Internet service provider. Business organizations typically connect to the Internet not only with personal computers but with Web servers as well.

WHO MANAGES THE INTERNET? Individual computers on the Internet are identified by their IP addresses. So who keeps track of these IP addresses on the Internet? A number of national and international standing committees and task forces have been used to manage the development and use of the Internet. Most notably, the Internet Assigned Numbers Authority is responsible for managing global and country code top-level domains, as well as global IP number space assignments. Similarly, the Internet Assigned Numbers Authority also provides central maintenance of the **Domain Name System (DNS)** root database, which points to distributed DNS servers replicated throughout the Internet. This database is used to associate Internet host names with their IP addresses. Users can access Web sites using domain name or IP addresses. The functionality of the DNS is to provide users easy-to-remember domain names to access Web sites. In other words, it is far easier to remember www.apple.com than it is to remember 17.178.96.59 (the IP address of a server mirroring Apple's content as of mid-2014), but both will work as addresses in any Web browser, as the DNS servers will translate the domain names into the accompanying IP address.

In 1993, the NSF created **InterNIC**, a government–industry collaboration, to manage directory and database services, domain registration services, and other information services on the Internet. In the late 1990s, this Internet oversight was transitioned more fully out into industry when InterNIC morphed into the **Internet Corporation for Assigned Names and Numbers**, a nonprofit corporation that assumed responsibility for managing IP addresses, domain names, and root server system management. Using 32-bit addresses, IPv4 provided 2^{32} IP addresses (about 4.29 billion addresses). With the increase of devices connected to the Internet, the number of unassigned Internet addresses is running out, so new classes of addresses are being added as **IPv6**, the latest version of the IP, was adopted in June 2012. Using 128-bit addresses, IPv6 provides 2^{128} addresses, allowing literally trillions and trillions devices to be connected to the Internet.

HOW TO CONNECT TO THE INTERNET. Now you can see how the Internet works and how it is managed. How do you connect to the Internet? For personal use (i.e., from home), we typically connect to the Internet through an **Internet service provider (ISP)**, also called an Internet access provider. ISPs provide several different ways to access the Internet from home (see Table TB14).

ISPs connect to one another through **Internet exchange points (IXPs)**. Much like railway stations, these IXPs serve as access points for ISPs and are an exchange point for Internet traffic. They determine how traffic is routed and are often the points of most Internet congestion. IXPs are a key component of the **Internet backbone**, which is the collection of main network connections and telecommunications lines that make up the Internet (see Figure TB28).

The Internet follows a hierarchical structure, similar to the interstate highway system. High-speed central network lines are like interstate highways, enabling traffic from midlevel networks to get on and off. Think of midlevel networks as city streets that, in turn, accept traffic from their neighborhood streets or member networks. However, you cannot get on an interstate or city street whenever you want to. You have to share the highway and follow traffic control signs to arrive safely at your destination. The same holds true for traffic on the Internet, and people can connect to the Internet in a number of ways. In the next section, we outline how typical home users connect to the Internet.

TABLE TB14 Methods for Connecting to the Internet

Service	Current Status and Future Outlook	Typical Bandwidth
Dial-up	Although still used in the United States, there are very few new dial-up customers. This market should dry up as broadband is moved to rural areas and developing nations.	52 Kbps
Integrated Services Digital Network	This technology has limited market share because of its expense. Typically, these connections are more expensive than broadband connections, although they offer less bandwidth.	128 Kbps
Cable	Coaxial cable used for cable TV provides much greater bandwidth than telephone lines and therefore is the market leader in broadband use for home users. Overselling of bandwidth that causes slower-than-average speeds tends to be a major problem for home users.	Upload: 2–10 Mbps Download: 12–50 Mbps
DSL	DSL technology has gained market share from cable. With many companies offering higher speeds at lower cost, DSL should continue to cut into cable's market share.	Upload: up to 16 Mbps Download: 1.5–50 Mbps
Satellite	Although satellite connectivity had a promising future, many users are moving away from this expensive technology in favor of faster and cheaper cable or DSL connections.	Upload: 50 Kbps Download: 5 Mbps
Wireless broadband	Wireless broadband offers the most promise of any of the current technologies, as the speeds are increasing while the coverage areas continue to grow.	Up to 54 Mbps
Fiber to the home	Fiber to the home has been adopted by several major players in the ISP industry. Although the technology typically can be placed only in new developments, the demand for fast connections is helping make this a significant technology for ISPs.	At least 100 Mbps, up to 1000 Mbps

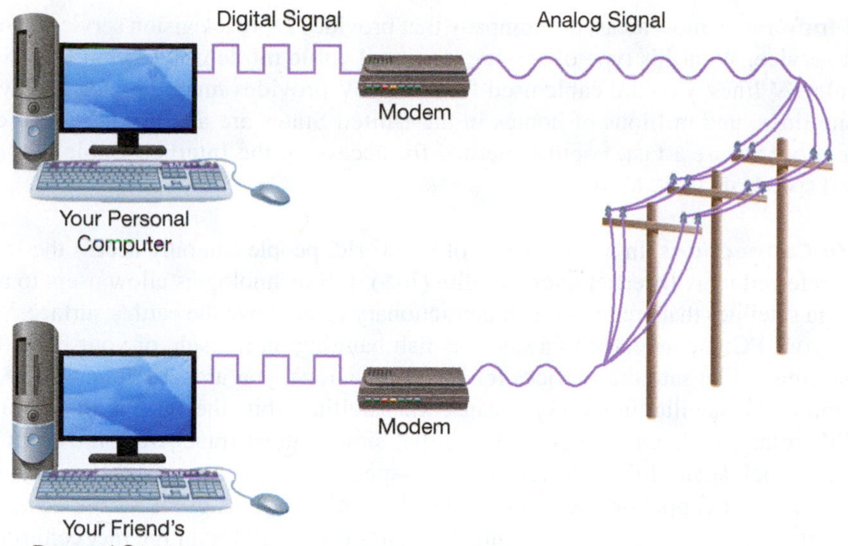

FIGURE TB29

Modems convert digital signals into analog and analog signals into digital.

Dial-Up Traditionally, most people connected to the Internet through a telephone line at home or work. The term we use for standard telephone lines is **plain old telephone service (POTS)** (the POTS system is also called the **public switched telephone network [PSTN]**). Because the dial-up telephone system was designed to pass sounds in the form of analog signals, it cannot pass the electrical pulses—**digital signals**—that computers use. The only way to pass digital data over conventional voice telephone lines is to convert it to audio tones—**analog signals**—that the telephone lines can carry. A **modem** (MOdulator/DEModulator) converts digital signals from a computer into analog signals so that telephone lines may be used as a transmission medium to send and receive electronic data, as shown in Figure TB29. As the speed, or bandwidth, of POTS is generally only about 52 Kbps (52,000 bits per second), today, most people connect to the Internet using some form of digital, high-speed connection.

Integrated Services Digital Network **Integrated services digital network (ISDN)** is a standard for worldwide digital communications. ISDN was designed in the 1980s to replace all analog systems, such as most telephone connections in the United States, with a completely digital transmission system. ISDN uses existing TP telephone wires to provide high-speed data service. ISDN systems can transmit voice, video, and data. Because ISDN is a purely digital network, you can connect your PC to the Internet without the use of a traditional modem. Removing the analog-to-digital conversion for sending data and the digital-to-analog conversion for receiving data and higher bandwidth greatly increase the data transfer rate. However, a small electronic box called an "ISDN modem" is typically required so that computers and older, analog-based devices such as telephones and fax machines can utilize and share the ISDN-based service. While ISDN has had moderate success in various parts of the world, it has largely been surpassed by DSL and cable modems.

Digital Subscriber Line **Digital subscriber line (DSL)** is a popular way of connecting to the Internet. DSL is referred to as a "last-mile" solution because it is used only for connections from a telephone switching station to a home or office and generally is not used between telephone switching stations.

The abbreviation DSL is used to refer collectively to **asymmetric digital subscriber line (ADSL)**, **symmetric digital subscriber line (SDSL)**, and other forms of DSL. DSL enables more data to be sent over existing copper telephone lines by sending digital pulses in the high-frequency area of telephone wires. Because these high frequencies are not used by normal voice communications, DSL enables your computer to operate simultaneously with voice connections over the same wires. ADSL speeds range from 1.5 to 50 Mbps downstream and up to 16 Mbps upstream. SDSL is said to be symmetric because it supports the same data rates for upstream and downstream traffic (up to 3 Mbps). Like ISDN, ADSL and SDSL require a special modem-like device. As most Internet users primarily download content, ADSL is most popular in consumer environments. SDSL is offered primarily to business customers.

Cable Modems In most areas, the company that provides cable television service also provides Internet service. With this type of service, a special **cable modem** is needed to transmit data over cable TV lines. Coaxial cable used for cable TV provides much greater bandwidth than telephone lines, and millions of homes in the United States are already wired for cable TV, so cable modems are a fast, popular method for accessing the Internet. Cable modems offer download speeds up to 50 Mbps.

Satellite Connections In many regions of the world, people can only access the Internet via satellite, referred to as **Internet over satellite (IoS)**. IoS technologies allow users to access the Internet via satellites that are placed in a geostationary orbit above the earth's surface. With these services, your PC is connected to a satellite dish hanging on the side of your home or placed on a pole (much like satellite services for your television); you are able to maintain a reliable connection to the satellite in the sky because the satellite orbits the earth at the exact speed of the earth's rotation. Given the vast distance that signals must travel from the earth up to the satellite and back again, IoS is slower than high-speed terrestrial (i.e., land-based) connections to the Internet over copper or fiber-optic cables. In remote regions of the world, however, IoS is the only option available because installing the cables necessary for an Internet connection is not economically feasible or, in many cases, is just not physically possible.

Wireless Broadband **Wireless broadband** is a technology that is usually found in rural areas where other connectivity options, such as DSL and cable, are not available. A common scenario is that the ISP will install an antenna at a high point, such as a large building or radio tower, and the consumer will mount a small dish to the roof and point it at the antenna. Wireless broadband offers speeds similar to DSL and cable and can bridge a distance of up to 50 kilometers (30 miles).

Mobile Wireless Access In addition to the fixed wireless approach, there are also many new **mobile wireless** approaches for connecting to the Internet. For example, with a subscription to a data plan, smartphones give you Internet access nearly anywhere. Also, special network adapter cards or USB "dongles" from a cellular service provider allow a notebook computer, tablet, or desktop computer to connect to cellular networks. The advantage of these systems is that as long as you are in the coverage area of that cell phone provider you have access to the Internet. Most mobile wireless service providers limit the amount of data that can be downloaded per month without incurring expensive fees, making this a relatively expensive option for a person's exclusive method for accessing the Internet.

Fiber to the Home **Fiber to the home (FTTH)**, also known as **fiber to the premises**, refers to connectivity technology that provides a superspeed connection to people's homes. This is usually done by fiber-optic cabling running directly into new homes. FTTH is currently available only in major metropolitan areas. The growth in FTTH is dependent on new home building, as it is currently cost prohibitive to distribute the technology to existing structures.

Until now, we have talked about ways that individuals typically access the Internet. In the following section, we talk more about ways that organizations typically access the Internet.

BUSINESS INTERNET CONNECTIVITY. Although home users have enjoyed a consistent increase in bandwidth availability, the demand for corporate use has increased at a greater pace; therefore, the need for faster speeds has become of great importance. In addition to the home connectivity options, business customers also have several high-speed options, described next.

Leased Lines To gain adequate access to the Internet, organizations are turning to long-distance carriers to lease dedicated **T1 lines** for digital transmissions. The T1 line was developed by AT&T as a dedicated digital transmission line that can carry 1.544 Mbps of data. In the United States, companies such as MCI that sell long-distance services are called **interexchange carriers** because their circuits carry service between the major telephone exchanges. A T1 line usually traverses hundreds or thousands of miles over leased long-distance facilities.

AT&T and other carriers charge as little as US$200 per month for a dedicated T1 circuit, and some providers will waive the installation fee if you sign up for some specified length of service. If you need an even faster link, you might choose a **T3 line**. T3 provides about 45 Mbps of service at about 10 times the cost of leasing a T1 line. Alternatively, organizations often choose to

TABLE TB15 Capacity of Telecommunication Lines

Type of Line	Data Rate
T1	1.544 Mbps
T3	44.736 Mbps
OC-1	51.85 Mbps
OC-3	155.52 Mbps
OC-12	622.08 Mbps
OC-24	1.244 Gbps
OC-48	2.488 Gbps

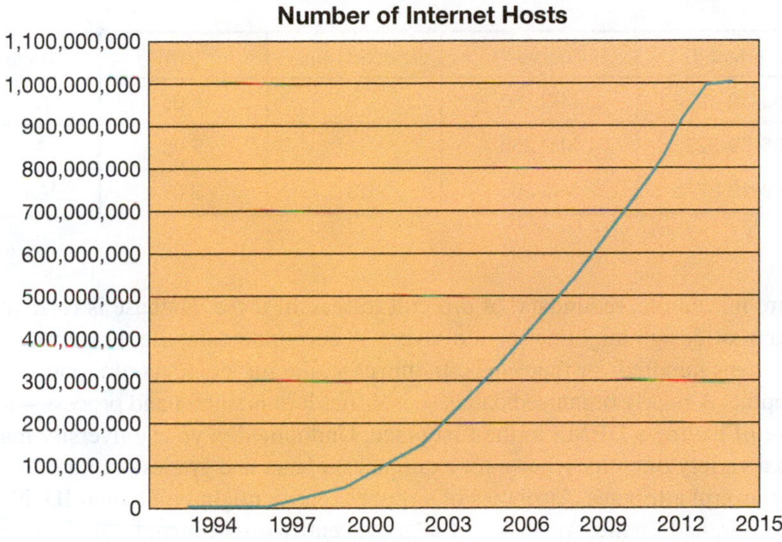

FIGURE TB30

Growth in Internet servers (hosts).

Source: Based on Internet Systems Consortium. http://www.isc.org/solutions/survey.

use two or more T1 lines simultaneously rather than jump to the more expensive T3 line. Higher speeds than the T3 are also available, but are not typically used for normal business activity. For example, fiber-optic networks offer speeds considerably faster than T3 lines. See Table TB15 for a summary of telecommunication line capacities, including optical carrier (OC) lines that use the Synchronous Optical Network standard.

THE CURRENT STATE OF INTERNET USAGE. The Internet is now the most prominent global network. Internet Live Stats (http://www.internetlivestats.com) reports that, as of 2014, over 2.9 billion people worldwide had access to the Internet. This means that over 40 percent of the world's population has Internet access at home, an increase of over 700 percent since 2000. In July 2014, almost 10 percent of the world's Internet users were located in the United States, with an Internet penetration of 87 percent.

One other way to measure the rapid growth of the Internet, in addition to the number of users, is to examine the growth in the number of **Internet hosts**—that is, computers working as servers on the Internet—as shown in Figure TB30.

FOUNDATIONAL TOPICS IN DATABASE MANAGEMENT

In Chapter 6, you were introduced to database concepts such as attributes, entities, and relationships, as well as managerial aspects related to databases. In the following sections, we delve deeper into the topic of relational database management to give you a better idea of the intricacies involved in designing a sound database. Note that the design of non-relational databases, such as NoSQL databases, are beyond the scope of this discussion.

Relational Database Design

Much of the work of creating an effective relational database is in the creation of the data model. If the model is not accurate, the database will not be effective. A poor data model will result in

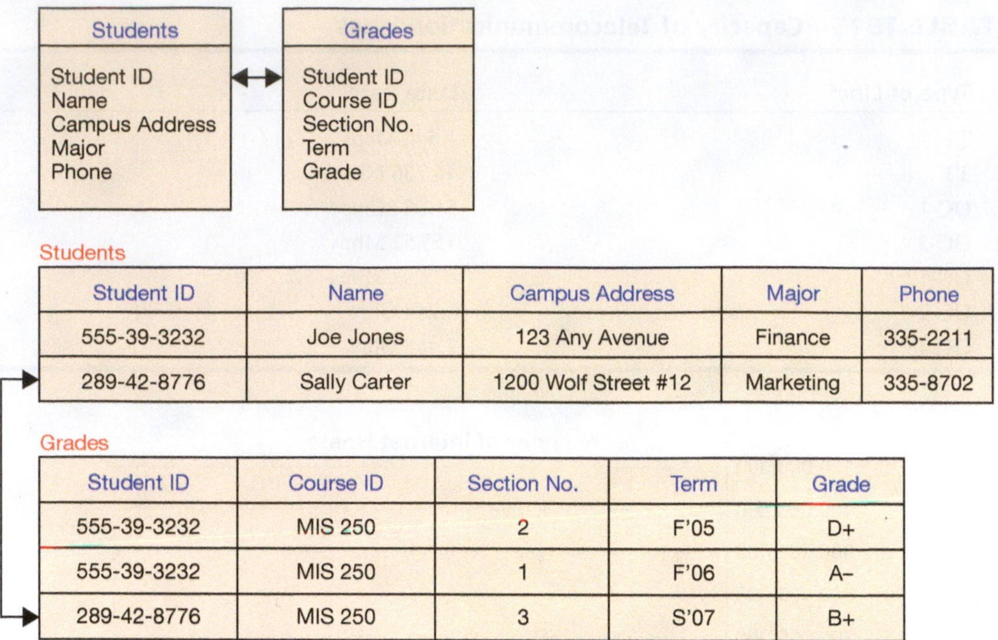

Students

Student ID	Name	Campus Address	Major	Phone
555-39-3232	Joe Jones	123 Any Avenue	Finance	335-2211
289-42-8776	Sally Carter	1200 Wolf Street #12	Marketing	335-8702

Grades

Student ID	Course ID	Section No.	Term	Grade
555-39-3232	MIS 250	2	F'05	D+
555-39-3232	MIS 250	1	F'06	A–
289-42-8776	MIS 250	3	S'07	B+

FIGURE TB31

The attributes for and links between two entities—students and grades.

data that are inaccurate, redundant, or difficult to search. If the database is relatively small, the effects of a poor design might not be too severe. A corporate database, however, contains many entities, perhaps hundreds or thousands. In this case, the implications of a poor data model can be catastrophic. A poorly organized database is difficult to maintain and process—thus defeating the purpose of having a DBMS in the first place. Undoubtedly, your university maintains databases with a variety of entity types—for example, students and grades—with both of these entities having several attributes. Attributes of a Student entity might be Student ID, Name, Campus Address, Major, and Phone. Attributes of a Grades entity might include Student ID, Course ID, Section Number, Term, and Grade (see Figure TB31).

For the DBMS to distinguish between records correctly, each instance of an entity must have one unique identifier. For example, each student has a unique Student ID. Note that using the student name (or most other attributes) would not be adequate because students may have the exact same name, live at the same address, or have the same phone number. Consequently, when designing a database, we must always create and use a unique identifier, called a **primary key**, for each type of entity in order to store and retrieve data accurately. In some instances, the primary key can also be a combination of two or more attributes, in which case it is called a **combination primary key**. An example of this is the Grades entity, shown in Figure TB31, where the combination of Student ID, Course ID, Section Number, and Term uniquely refers to the grade of an individual student in a particular class (section number) in a particular term. Attributes not used as the primary key can be referred to as **secondary keys** when they are used to identify one or more records within a table that share a common value. For example, a secondary key in the Student entity shown in Figure TB31 would be Major when used to find all students who share a particular major.

ASSOCIATIONS. To retrieve information from a relational database, it is necessary to associate or relate information from separate tables. The three types of **relationships** (or **associations**) among entities are one-to-one, one-to-many, and many-to-many. Table TB16 summarizes each of these three associations and shows how they should be handled in database design for a basketball league.

To understand how relationships work, consider Figure TB32, which shows four tables—Home Stadium, Team, Player, and Games—for keeping track of the information for a basketball league. The Home Stadium table lists the Stadium ID, Stadium Name, Capacity, and Location, with the primary key underlined. The Team table contains two attributes, Team ID and Team Name, but nothing about the stadium where the team plays. If we wanted to have such information, we could gain it only by creating a relationship between the Home Stadium and Team tables. For example, if each team has only one home stadium and each home stadium has only

TABLE TB16 Rules for Expressing Relationships Among Entities and Their Corresponding Data Structures

Relationship	Examples	Instructions
One-to-one	Each team has only one home stadium, and each home stadium has only one team.	Place the primary key from one table (e.g., Stadium) into the other (e.g., Team) as a foreign key.
One-to-many	Each player is on only one team, but each team has many players.	Place the primary key from the table on the "one" side of the relationship (e.g., Team) as a foreign key in the table on the "many" side of the relationship (e.g., Player).
Many-to-many	Each player participates in many games, and each game has many players.	Create a third table (e.g., Player Statistics) and place the primary keys from each of the original tables (e.g., Player and Team) together in the third as a combination primary key.

Home Stadium

Stadium ID	Stadium Name	Capacity	Location

Team

Team ID	Team Name

Player

Player ID	Player Name	Position

Games

Team ID (1)	Team ID (2)	Date	Final Score

FIGURE TB32

Tables used for storing information about several basketball teams, with no foreign key attributes added; thus, associations cannot be made.

one team, we have a one-to-one relationship between the Team and the Home Stadium entities. In situations in which we have one-to-one relationships between entities, we place the primary key from one table in the table for the other entity and refer to this attribute as a **foreign key**. In other words, a foreign key refers to an attribute that appears as a non–primary key attribute in one entity and as a primary key attribute (or part of a primary key) in another entity. By sharing this common—but unique—value, entities can be linked, or associated, together. We can choose in which of these tables to place the foreign key of the other. After adding the primary key of the Home Stadium entity to the Team entity, we can identify which stadium is the home for a particular team and then be able to find all the details about that stadium (see section A in Figure TB33).

When we find a one-to-many relationship—for example, each player plays for only one team, but each team has many players—we place the primary key from the entity on the "one"

A. One-to-one relationship: Each team has only one home stadium, and each home stadium has only one team.

Team

Team ID	Team Name	*Stadium ID*

B. One-to-many relationship: Each player is on only one team, but each team has many players.

Player

Player ID	Player Name	Position	*Team ID*

C. Many-to-many relationship: Each player participates in many games, and each game has many players.

Player Statistics

Team 1	*Team 2*	*Date*	*Player ID*	Points	Minutes	Fouls

FIGURE TB33

Tables used for storing information about several basketball teams, with foreign key attributes added in order to make associations.

side of the relationship, the Team entity, as a foreign key in the table for the entity on the "many" side of the relationship, the Player entity (see section B in Figure TB33). In essence, we take from the one and give to the many, a Robin Hood strategy.

When we find a many-to-many relationship (e.g., each player plays in many games, and each game has many players), we create a third (new) entity—in this case, the Player Statistics entity and corresponding table. We then place the primary keys from each of the original entities together into the third (new) table as a combination primary key (see section C in Figure TB33).

You may have noticed that by placing the primary key from one entity in the table of another entity, we are creating a bit of redundancy. We are repeating the data in different places. We are willing to live with this bit of redundancy, however, because it enables us to keep track of the interrelationships among the many pieces of important organizational data that are stored in different tables. By keeping track of these relationships, we can quickly answer questions such as "Which players on the SuperSonics played in the game on February 16 and scored more than 10 points?" In a business setting, the question might be "Which customers purchased a 2016 Toyota Prius from a salesperson named Jeff at the James Toyota dealership in Pullman, Washington, during the first quarter of 2016, and how much did each customer pay?" This kind of question would be useful in calculating the bonus money Jeff should receive for that quarter or in recalling those specific vehicles in the event of a recall by the manufacturer.

ENTITY-RELATIONSHIP DIAGRAMMING. A diagramming technique that creates an **entity-relationship diagram (ERD)** is commonly used when designing relational databases, especially when showing associations between entities. To create an ERD, you draw entities as boxes and draw lines between entities to show relationships. Each relationship can be labeled on the diagram to give it additional meaning. For example, Figure TB34 shows an ERD for the basketball league data previously discussed. From this diagram, you can see the following associations:

- Each Home Stadium has a Team.
- Each Team has Players.
- Each Team participates in Games.
- For each Player and Game, there are Game Statistics.

When you are designing a complex database, with numerous entities and relationships, ERDs are very useful. They allow the designer to talk with people throughout the organization to make sure that all entities and relationships have been found.

THE RELATIONAL MODEL. Now that we have discussed associations and data models, we need a mechanism for joining entities that have natural relationships with one another. For example, in the University database we described previously, there are several relationships among the four entities: students, instructors, classes, and grades. Students are enrolled in multiple classes. Likewise, instructors teach multiple classes and have many students in their classes in a semester. At the end of the semester, instructors assign a grade to each student, and each student earns grades in multiple classes. It is important to keep track of these relationships. We might, for example, want to know which courses a student is enrolled in so that we can notify her instructors that she will miss courses because of an illness. The primary DBMS approach, or model, for keeping track of these relationships among data entities is the relational model. Other models—the hierarchical, network, and object-oriented models—are also used to join entities within commercial DBMSs, but this is beyond the scope of our discussion (see Hoffer, Ramesh, & Topi, 2013).

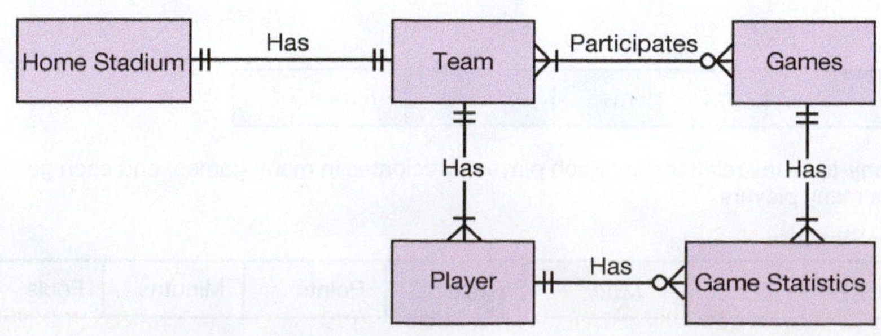

FIGURE TB34

An entity-relationship diagram showing the relationships between entities in a basketball league database.

Department Records

Dept No	Dept Name	Location	Dean
Dept A			
Dept B			
Dept C			

Instructor Records

Instructor No	Inst Name	Title	Salary	Dept No
Inst 1				
Inst 2				
Inst 3				
Inst 4				

FIGURE TB35

With the relational model, we represent these two entities, department and instructor, as two separate tables and capture the relationship between them with a common column in each table.

The most common DBMS approach in use today is the **relational database model**. A DBMS package using this approach is referred to as a relational DBMS. With this approach, the DBMS views and presents entities as two-dimensional tables, with records as rows and attributes as columns. Tables can be joined when there are common columns in the tables. The uniqueness of the primary key, as mentioned earlier, tells the DBMS which records should be joined with others in the corresponding tables. This structure supports very powerful data manipulation capabilities and linking of interrelated data. Database files in the relational model are three-dimensional: a table has rows (one dimension) and columns (a second dimension) and can contain rows of attributes in common with another table (a third dimension). This three-dimensional database is potentially much more powerful and useful than traditional, two-dimensional, "flat-file" databases (see Figure TB35).

A good relational database design eliminates unnecessary data duplications and is easy to maintain. To design a database with clear, non-redundant relationships, you perform a process called normalization.

NORMALIZATION. To be effective, databases must be efficient. Developed in the 1970s, **normalization** is a technique to make complex relational databases more efficient and more easily handled by the DBMS (Hoffer et al., 2013). Normalization makes sure that each table contains only attributes that are related to the entity; hence, normalization helps to eliminate data duplication. To understand the normalization process, let us return to the scenario in the beginning of this section. Think about your report card. It looks like nearly any other report or invoice. Your personal information is usually at the top, and each of your classes is listed, along with an instructor, a class day and time, the number of credit hours, and a location. Now think about how these data are stored in a relational database. Imagine that this database is organized so that in each row of the database, the student's identification number is listed on the far left. To the right of the student ID are the student's name, local address, major, phone number, course and instructor information, and a final course grade (see Figure TB36). Notice

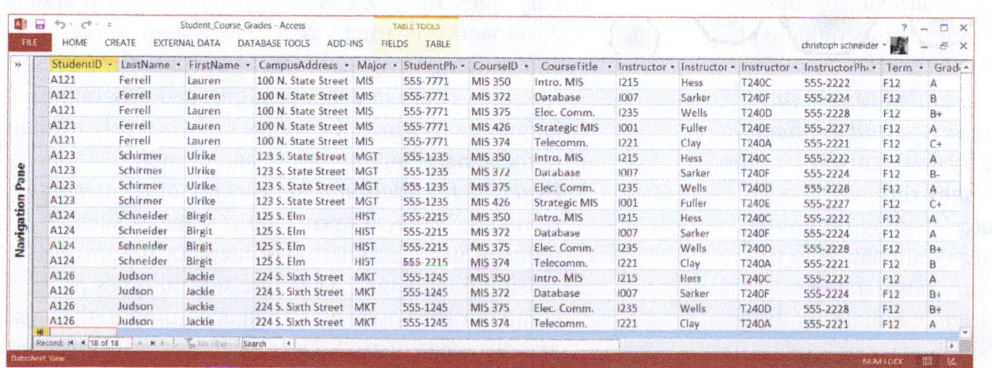

StudentID	LastName	FirstName	CampusAddress	Major	StudentPh	CourseID	CourseTitle	Instructor	Instructor	Instructor	InstructorPh	Term	Grad
A121	Ferrell	Lauren	100 N. State Street	MIS	555-7771	MIS 350	Intro. MIS	I215	Hess	T240C	555-2222	F12	A
A121	Ferrell	Lauren	100 N. State Street	MIS	555-7771	MIS 372	Database	I007	Sarker	T240F	555-2224	F12	B
A121	Ferrell	Lauren	100 N. State Street	MIS	555-7771	MIS 375	Elec. Comm.	I235	Wells	T240D	555-2228	F12	B+
A121	Ferrell	Lauren	100 N. State Street	MIS	555-7771	MIS 426	Strategic MIS	I001	Fuller	T240E	555-2227	F12	A
A121	Ferrell	Lauren	100 N. State Street	MIS	555-7771	MIS 374	Telecomm.	I221	Clay	T240A	555-2221	F12	C+
A123	Schirmer	Ulrike	123 S. State Street	MGT	555-1235	MIS 350	Intro. MIS	I215	Hess	T240C	555-2222	F12	A
A123	Schirmer	Ulrike	123 S. State Street	MGT	555-1235	MIS 372	Database	I007	Sarker	T240F	555-2224	F12	B-
A123	Schirmer	Ulrike	123 S. State Street	MGT	555-1235	MIS 375	Elec. Comm.	I235	Wells	T240D	555-2228	F12	A
A123	Schirmer	Ulrike	123 S. State Street	MGT	555-1235	MIS 426	Strategic MIS	I001	Fuller	T240E	555-2227	F12	C+
A124	Schneider	Birgit	125 S. Elm	HIST	555-2215	MIS 350	Intro. MIS	I215	Hess	T240C	555-2222	F12	A
A124	Schneider	Birgit	125 S. Elm	HIST	555-2215	MIS 372	Database	I007	Sarker	T240F	555-2224	F12	A
A124	Schneider	Birgit	125 S. Elm	HIST	555-2215	MIS 375	Elec. Comm.	I235	Wells	T240D	555-2228	F12	B+
A124	Schneider	Birgit	125 S. Elm	HIST	555-2215	MIS 374	Telecomm.	I221	Clay	T240A	555-2221	F12	B
A126	Judson	Jackie	224 S. Sixth Street	MKT	555-1245	MIS 350	Intro. MIS	I215	Hess	T240C	555-2222	F12	A
A126	Judson	Jackie	224 S. Sixth Street	MKT	555-1245	MIS 372	Database	I007	Sarker	T240F	555-2224	F12	B+
A126	Judson	Jackie	224 S. Sixth Street	MKT	555-1245	MIS 375	Elec. Comm.	I235	Wells	T240D	555-2228	F12	B+
A126	Judson	Jackie	224 S. Sixth Street	MKT	555-1245	MIS 374	Telecomm.	I221	Clay	T240A	555-2221	F12	A

FIGURE TB36

Database of students, courses, instructors, and grades with redundant data.

Source: Courtesy of Microsoft Corporation

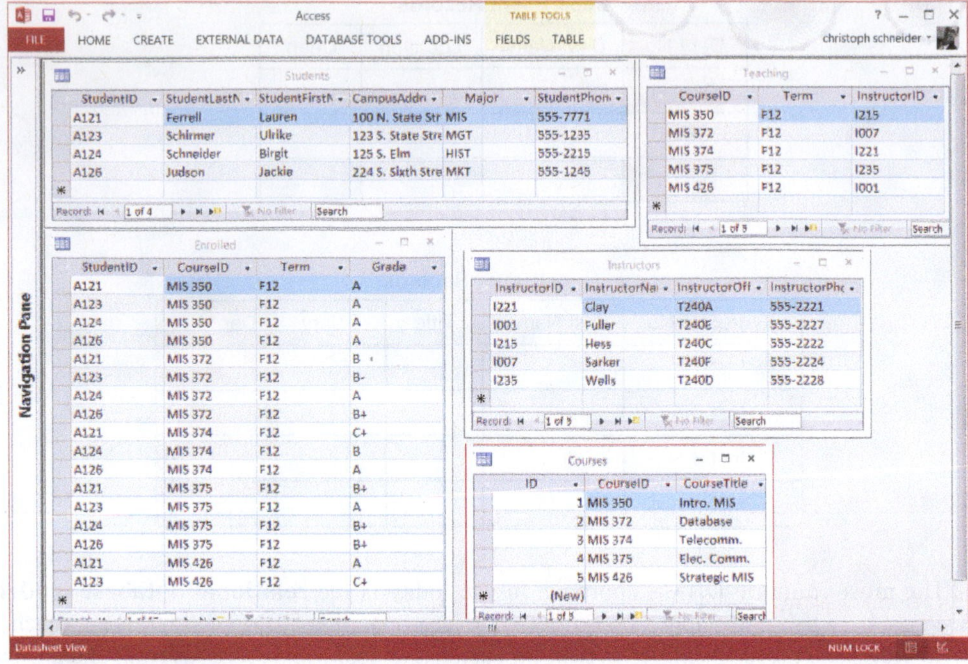

FIGURE TB37

Organization of information on students, courses, instructors, and grades after normalization.

Source: Courtesy of Microsoft Corporation

that there are redundant data for students, courses, and instructors in each row of this database. This redundancy means that this database is not well organized. If, for example, we want to change the phone number of an instructor who has hundreds of students, we have to change this number hundreds of times. In addition, this redundancy wastes storage space.

Elimination of data redundancy is a major goal and benefit of using data normalization techniques. After the normalization process, the student data are organized into five separate tables (see Figure TB37). This reorganization helps simplify the ongoing use and maintenance of the database and any associated analysis programs.

Key Points Review

1. ***Discuss foundational information systems (IS) hardware concepts.*** IS hardware is classified into three types: input, processing, and output technologies. Input hardware consists of devices used to enter data into a computer. Processing hardware transforms inputs into outputs. The CPU is the device that performs this transformation, with the help of several other closely related devices that store and recall data. Data are stored on primary and secondary storage devices. Finally, output-related hardware focuses on delivering information in a usable format to users.
2. ***Describe foundational topics related to system software, programming languages, and application development environments.*** System software, or the operating system, performs many different tasks, such as booting your computer, reading programs into memory, managing memory allocation to those programs, managing where programs and files are located in secondary storage, maintaining the structure of directories and subdirectories, and so on. A programming language is the computer language that programmers use to write application programs. In order to run on a computer, a programs' source code must be translated into binary machine language through special types of programs, called compilers and interpreters. Object-oriented programming, visual programming, and Web development languages are relatively new enhancements to programming languages. Finally, CASE environments help systems developers construct large-scale systems more rapidly and with higher quality. Open source software refers to systems software, applications, and programming languages in which the source code is freely available to the general public for use and/or modification.
3. ***Describe foundational networking and Internet concepts.*** Networks provide for services such as transmitting files, sharing printers, or sending and receiving messages. There are several types of computer networks, classified according to their use and distance covered. To enable rapid transmission

of massive amounts of data, most data networks rely on packet switching. Protocols are agreed-on formats for transmitting data between connected computers; the most prominent standards are TCP/IP and Ethernet. Networks exchange data by using cable or wireless transmission media, and media access control refers to the rules that govern how a given workstation gains access to the transmission media. The shape of a network can vary; the four most common topologies are star, ring, bus, and mesh configurations. The Internet is composed of networks that are developed and maintained by many different entities. It follows a hierarchical structure; high-speed central networks called backbones are like interstate highways, enabling traffic from midlevel networks to get on and off. Routers are used to interconnect independent networks.

4. ***Explain foundational database management concepts.*** In order to get the most of their data, organizations have to take care to create an accurate data model. Often, entity-relationship diagrams are used when designing relational databases. A primary key is used to uniquely identify records in a database. A foreign key is used to link entities together. A useful diagramming technique is entity-relationship diagramming, displaying entities and the associations between them. Normalization is used to reduce redundancy in a database.

Key Terms

Foundational Hardware Key Terms

American Standard Code for Information Interchange (ASCII) 413
arithmetic logic unit (ALU) 413
audio 412
bar code reader 411
basic input/output system (BIOS) 415
batch data 411
batch processing 411
binary code 413
bit 413
byte 413
bytes per inch 417
cache 414
cathode ray tube 418
CD-R (compact disc–recordable) 416
CD-RW (compact disc–rewritable) 416
central processing unit (CPU) 413
characters per inch 417
clock speed 414
clock tick 414
control unit 413
density 417
digital video disc 416
digitize 414
DVD-ROM (digital versatile disc–read-only memory) 416
flash drive 416
flash memory 416
hard drive 415
head crash 415
input technologies 411
interactive voice response 412
liquid crystal display (LCD) 418
magnetic ink character recognition 411
microprocessor 413
motherboard 413
nonvolatile memory 415
optical character recognition 411
optical disk 416
optical mark recognition 411
organic light-emitting diode 418
output technologies 417
port 417
power supply 417
primary storage 414
printer 417
processing technologies 413
random-access memory (RAM) 414
read-only memory (ROM) 415
read/write head 415
redundant array of independent disks (RAID) 415
secondary storage 415
smart card 411
solid-state drive (SSD) 416
speech recognition 412
streaming audio 413
streaming media 413
streaming video 413
system clock 414
tape 417
text recognition software 411
touch screen 418
Unicode 414
video 412
voice-to-text software 412
volatile memory 414

Foundational Software Key Terms

applet 422
cascading style sheets (CSS) 422
compiler 419
computer-aided software engineering (CASE) 424
executable 419
graphical user interface (GUI) 421
HTML editor 422
HTML tag 422
interpreter 420
Java 422
JavaScript 423
Microsoft.NET 422
object-oriented language 421
scripting language 423
source code 419
utilities 418
utility program 418
visual programming language 421
Web page builder 422

Foundational Networking Key Terms

Advanced Research Projects Agency Network (ARPANET) 440
analog signals 443
asymmetric digital subscriber line (ADSL) 443
authentication service 427
backbone 436
Bluetooth 429
bus network 432
cable modem 444
carrier sense multiple access/collision avoidance (CSMA/CA) 434
cell 437
cellular phone 437
centralized computing 425
collaborative computing 427
Defense Advanced Research Projects Agency 440
digital signals 443
digital subscriber line (DSL) 443
directory service 427
distributed computing 426
Domain Name System (DNS) 441
enterprise WAN 428
Ethernet 432

Foundational Database Key Terms

Go to **mymislab.com** to complete the problems marked with this icon ✪.

Review Questions

Foundational Hardware Review Questions

TB-1. IS hardware is classified into what three major types?
TB-2. Describe various methods for entering data into and interacting with a computer.
TB-3. How do computers represent data internally?
TB-4. Describe the role of a motherboard.
TB-5. What determines the speed of a CPU?
✪ **TB-6.** Compare and contrast the different types of secondary data storage.
TB-7. What are output devices? Describe various methods for providing computer output.

Foundational Software Review Questions

TB-8. Define the term *software* and list several software packages and their uses.
TB-9. Describe at least four different tasks performed by an operating system.
TB-10. Describe the similarities and differences between at least two major operating systems in use today.
TB-11. Name and describe four functions of utility programs.
✪ **TB-12.** What is HTML, and why is it important?
TB-13. Describe various options for adding dynamic content to a Web page.
TB-14. What is CASE, and how can it help in the development of information systems?
TB-15. What is open source software? Why would a business choose to implement open source software?

Foundational Networking Review Questions

TB-16. How are LANs, WANs, PANs, and global networks related to each other?
✪ **TB-17.** What are the roles of authentication services and directory services?
TB-18. What is packet switching, and why is it useful?
TB-19. What is the purpose of the OSI model?
TB-20. What is a network topology? Describe the four basic topologies.
TB-21. What are three common types of transmission media that use cabling?
TB-22. What are four common methods of wireless transmission media for networking, and how do they differ from each other?
TB-23. What is the Internet, and why was it created?
TB-24. Other than dialup, what are three alternatives for connecting to the Internet at home?

Foundational Database Review Questions

✪ **TB-25.** Describe why database design is important for modern organizations.
TB-26. Compare and contrast the primary key, combination key, and foreign key within an entity.
TB-27. Describe the three types of relationships in a relational database.
TB-28. What is the purpose of a secondary key?

TB-29. What is an entity-relationship diagram, and why is it useful?

TB-30. What is the relational model?

TB-31. Why is redundancy undesired?

Self-Study Questions

Foundational Hardware Self-Study Questions

TB-32. All of the following are considered primary storage except ______________.
A. SSDs
B. RAM
C. registers
D. cache

TB-33. Which of the following is not an input device?
A. biometric scanner
B. touchscreen
C. LCD screen
D. stylus

TB-34. Which of the following is an output device?
A. cathode ray tube
B. scanner
C. video camera
D. keyboard

TB-35. ______________ can convert handwritten text into computer-based characters.
A. scanners
B. bar code/optical character readers
C. text recognition software
D. audio/video

TB-36. A ______________ card is a special credit card with a microprocessor chip and memory circuits.
A. smart
B. master
C. universal
D. proprietary

Answers are on page 456.

Foundational Software Self-Study Questions

TB-37. An operating system performs which of the following tasks?
A. booting the computer
B. managing where programs and files are stored
C. sending documents to the printer
D. all of the above

TB-38. What is the name of the programming language developed by Sun Microsystems in the 1990s?
A. Latte
B. Java
C. Mocha
D. none of the above

TB-39. Which of the following programming languages would most likely not be used for building Web applications?
A. HTML
B. JavaScript
C. PHP
D. Fortran

TB-40. A utility program may provide ______________.
A. antivirus protection
B. file conversion capability
C. file compression and defragmentation
D. all of the above

TB-41. CASE tools support all of the following except: ______________.
A. diagramming
B. consistency checking
C. generating code
D. compiling code

Answers are on page 456.

Foundational Networking Self-Study Questions

TB-42. Which of the following is not a type of cable medium?
A. twisted pair
B. coaxial
C. fiber-optic
D. shielded pair

TB-43. All of the following are common applications of high-frequency radio communication except ______________.
A. police radios
B. cellular phones
C. microwave transmission
D. facsimiles

TB-44. Which of the following is the protocol of the Internet, allowing different interconnected networks to communicate using the same language?
A. Ethernet
B. C++
C. TCP/IP
D. router

TB-45. Which is the fastest connection available for home users?
A. dialup
B. DSL
C. wireless broadband
D. FTTH

TB-46. Which of the following is a typical way large corporations connect to the Internet?
A. satellite
B. cable
C. T1 lines
D. all of the above

Answers are on page 456.

Foundational Database Self-Study Questions

TB-47. A(n) _____________ is a unique identifier that can be a combination of one or more attributes.
A. secondary key
B. primary key
C. tertiary key
D. elementary key

TB-48. Which of the following is not true in regard to the relational database model?
A. Entities are viewed as tables, with records as rows and attributes as columns.
B. Databases use keys and redundant data in different tables in order to link interrelated data.
C. Entities are viewed as children of higher-level attributes.
D. A properly designed table has a unique identifier that may consist of one or more attributes.

TB-49. Each team has only one home stadium, and each home stadium has only one team. This is an example of which of the following relationships?
A. one-to-one
B. one-to-many
C. many-to-many
D. many-to-one

TB-50. A popular diagramming technique for designing databases is called _____________.
A. flowcharting
B. database diagramming
C. entity-relationship diagramming
D. none of the above

TB-51. _____________ is a technique to make a complex database more efficient by eliminating redundancy.
A. extraction, transformation, and loading
B. associating
C. normalization
D. standardization

Answers are on page 456.

Problems and Exercises

Foundational Hardware Problems and Exercises

TB-52. Match the following terms with the appropriate definitions:
i. Motherboard
ii. Audio
iii. DVD-ROM
iv. Smart card
v. Streaming video

a. Analog or digital sound data
b. A special credit card–sized card containing a microprocessor chip, memory circuits, and often a magnetic stripe
c. An optical storage device that has more storage space than a CD-ROM disk and uses a shorter-wavelength laser beam, which allows more optical pits to be deposited on the disk
d. A sequence of moving images, sent in a compressed form over the Internet and displayed on the receiver's screen as the images arrive
e. A large printed plastic or fiberglass circuit board that contains all the components that do the actual processing work of the computer and holds or connects to all the computer's electronic components

TB-53. Visit a computer shop or look on the Web for trackballs or touch pads. What is new about how these input devices look or how they are used? What are some of the advantages and disadvantages of each device?

TB-54. What types of printers are most common today? What is the cost of a color printer versus a black-and-white one? Compare and contrast laser and ink-jet printers in terms of speed, cost, and quality of output. What kind of printer would you buy or have you bought?

TB-55. Based on your experiences with different input devices, which do you like the best and least? Why? Are your preferences due to the devices' design or usability, or are they based on the integration of the device with the entire information system?

TB-56. Choose a few of the computer hardware vendors that sell computers to the general public. These include Dell, HP, Lenovo, Apple, and many lesser-known brands. Using each company's Web site, determine what options these vendors provide for input devices, processing devices, and output devices. Does it seem that this company has a broad range of choices for its customers? Is there something that you did not find available from this company? Present your findings in a 10-minute presentation to the rest of the class.

Foundational Software Problems and Exercises

TB-57. Match the following terms with the appropriate definitions:
i. Applet
ii. Visual programming language
iii. Scripting language
iv. Interpreter
v. Compiler

a. A software program that translates an entire program's source code into machine language that can be read and executed directly by the computer
b. Programming language that provides a graphical user interface and is generally easier to use than non-GUI languages

c. A program designed to be executed within another application (such as a Web page)
d. A software program that translates a programming language into machine language one statement at a time
e. A programming language for integrating interactive components into a Web page

TB-58. What are the implications for an organization of having more than one operating system? What might be the advantages? What are some of the disadvantages? Would you recommend such a situation? Prepare a 10-minute presentation to the rest of the class on your findings.

TB-59. Visit the Web site of your favorite online retailer. Which parts of the content are created dynamically? What interactive components do the different Web pages include? Do different types of pages (e.g., home page or payment and shipping page) need different types of interactive components?

TB-60. Based on your own experiences with computers and computer systems, what do you like and dislike about different operating systems that you have used? Were these uses on a professional or a personal level or both? Who made the decision to purchase that particular operating system? Did you have any say in the purchase decision?

TB-61. Imagine that you and a friend are at a local ATM getting some cash from your account to pay for a movie. The ATM does not seem to be working. It is giving you an error message every time you press any button. Is this most likely a software-related problem, a hardware-related problem, or a network-related problem? Why? Use the information in this and other briefings to help you make your decision.

Foundational Networking Problems and Exercises

TB-62. Match the following terms with the appropriate definitions:

i. Protocols
ii. Ethernet
iii. FTTH
iv. T1 line
v. Wireless access point

a. A dedicated digital transmission line that can carry 1.544 Mbps of information
b. A networking device that transmits and receives wireless signals to allow wireless devices to connect to the network
c. High-speed network connectivity to homes and offices that is implemented using fiber-optic cable
d. The most widely used local area network protocol, supporting data rates of up to 100 gigabits per second
e. The procedures that different computers follow when they transmit and receive data

TB-63. Discuss the difference between PBX networks and LANs. What are the advantages of each? What are possible disadvantages of each? When would you recommend one over the other?

TB-64. Personal area networks using Bluetooth are becoming increasingly popular. Visit www.bluetooth.com and investigate the types of products that this wireless technology is being used to enhance. Find three products that you find interesting and prepare a 10-minute presentation on what these products are and how Bluetooth is enhancing their operation and usage.

TB-65. Describe one of your experiences with a computer network. What type of topology was being used? Was the network connected to any other networks? How?

TB-66. Working in a group, have everyone describe what type of network would be most appropriate for a small office with about 10 computers, one printer, and one scanner, all within one floor in one building and relatively close to one another. Be sure to talk about transmission media, network topology, and hardware. Did all group members come up with the same option? Why or why not? What else would you need to know to make a good recommendation?

TB-67. Investigate the options for high-speed, broadband Internet access into your home. What options are available to you, and how much do they cost?

TB-68. You have probably experienced several different types of connection—from the university T1 connections to a home DSL or even dial-up connection. If you had to balance between cost and speed, which connection would you choose?

TB-69. Explain in simple language how the Internet works. Be sure to talk about backbones, packet switching, networks, routers, TCP/IP, and Internet services. What technologies, hardware, and software do you utilize when using the Internet? What would you like to use that isn't available to you?

Foundational Database Problems and Exercises

TB-70. Match the following terms with the appropriate definitions:

i. Primary key
ii. Foreign key
iii. Relational database model
iv. Relationship
v. Secondary key

a. Attributes not used as the primary key that can be used to identify one or more records within a table that share a common value
b. An attribute that appears as a nonprimary key attribute in one entity and as a primary key in another
c. A field included in a database table that ensures that each instance of an entity is stored or retrieved accurately
d. An association between entities in a database to enable data retrieval
e. A data management approach in which entities are presented as two-dimensional tables that can be joined together with common columns

TB-71. You see an announcement for a job as a database administrator for a large corporation but are unclear about what this title means. Research this on the Web and obtain a specific job announcement.

TB-72. Why would it matter what data type is used for the attributes within a database? How does this relate to programming? How does this relate to queries and calculations? Does the size of the database matter?

TB-73. Have several classmates interview database administrators within organizations with which they are familiar. To whom do these people report? How many employees report to these people? Is there a big variance in the responsibilities across organizations? Why or why not?

TB-74. Based on your understanding of a primary key and the information in the following sample grades table, determine the best choice of attribute(s) for a primary key.

Student ID	Course	Grade
100013	Visual Programming	A
000117	Telecommunications	A
000117	Introduction to MIS	A

TB-75. Search the Web for an organization with a Web page that utilizes a link between the Web page and the organization's own database. Describe the data that the browser enters and the organization's possible uses for these data. Can you retrieve company information, or can you only send information to the company? How are the data displayed on the Web page?

Answers to the Foundational Hardware Self-Study Questions

TB-34. A, p. 414 **TB-35.** C, p. 411 **TB-36.** A, p. 417 **TB-37.** C, p. 411 **TB-38.** A, p. 411

Answers to the Foundational Software Self-Study Questions

TB-39. D, p. 418 **TB-40.** B, p. 422 **TB-41.** D, p. 420 **TB-42.** D, p. 418 **TB-43.** D, p. 424

Answers to the Foundational Networking Self-Study Questions

TB-44. D, p. 434 **TB-45.** D, p. 436 **TB-46.** C, p. 431 **TB-47.** D, p. 442 **TB-48.** C, p. 444

Answers to the Foundational Database Self-Study Questions

TB-49. B, p. 446 **TB-50.** C, p. 448 **TB-51.** A, p. 447 **TB-52.** C, p. 448 **TB-53.** C, p. 449

Go to **mymislab.com** for Auto-graded writing questions as well as the following Assisted-graded writing questions.

TB-76. Compare and contrast centralized, distributed, and collaborative computing.

TB-77. What is the purpose of normalization?

References

Comer, D. E. (1997). *The Internet book* (2nd ed.). Upper Saddle River, NJ: Pearson Prentice Hall.

Hoffer, J. A., George, J. F., & Valacich, J. S. (2014). *Modern systems analysis and design* (7th ed.). Upper Saddle River, NJ: Pearson Prentice Hall.

Hoffer, J., Ramesh, V., & Topi, H. (2013). *Modern database management* (11th ed.). Upper Saddle River, NJ: Pearson Prentice Hall.

Laberta, C. (2012). *Computers are your future complete* (12th ed.). Upper Saddle River, NJ: Pearson Prentice Hall.

Panko, R., & Panko, J. (2013). *Business data networks and security* (9th ed.). Upper Saddle River, NJ: Pearson Prentice Hall.

Stallings, W. (2011). *Network security essentials: Applications and standards* (4th ed.). Upper Saddle River, NJ: Pearson Prentice Hall.

Te'eni, D., Carey, J. M., & Zhang, P. (2007). *Human-computer interaction: Developing effective organizational information systems.* New York: Wiley.

Acronyms

ADSL: Asymmetric Digital Subscriber Line
AI: Artificial Intelligence
ALU: Arithmetic Logic Unit
ARPANET: Advanced Research Projects Agency Network
ASCII: American Standard Code for Information Interchange
ATM: Automated Teller Machine
B2B: Business-to-Business
B2C: Business-to-Consumer
BI: Business Intelligence
BIOS: Basic Input-Output System
BPI: Bytes per Inch
BPM: Business Process Management
BPR: Business Process Reengineering
BYOD: Bring Your Own Device
C2B: Consumer-to-Business
C2C: Consumer-to-Consumer
CAN: Campus Area Network
CAPTCHA: Completely Automated Public Turing Test to Tell Computers and Humans Apart
CASE: Computer-Aided Software Engineering
CDN: Content Delivery Network
CDO: Chief Digital Officer
CD-R: Compact Disc–Recordable
CD-RW: Compact Disc–Rewritable
CEC: Customer Engagement Center
CIO: Chief Information Officer
COBIT: Control Objectives for Information and Related Technology
COPA: Child Online Protection Act
CPI: Characters per Inch
CPM: Cost per Mille
CPU: Central Processing Unit
CRM: Customer Relationship Management
CRT: Cathode Ray Tube
CSF: Critical Success Factor
CSMA/CA: Carrier Sense Multiple Access/Collision Avoidance
CSS: Cascading Style Sheet
CSS: Customer Service and Support
CVV2: Card Verification Value
DARPA: Defense Advanced Research Projects Agency
DBA: Database Administrator
DBMS: Database Management System
DNS: Domain Name System
DoS: Denial of Service
DRM: Digital Rights Management
DSL: Digital Subscriber Line
DSS: Decision Support System
DVD: Digital Video Disc
DVD-ROM: Digital Versatile Disc–Read-Only Memory
DVI: Digital Visual Interface
EC: Electronic Commerce
ECPA: Electronic Communications Privacy Act
EDI: Electronic Data Interchange
EEPROM: Electrically Erasable Programmable Read-Only Memory
EMI: Electromagnetic Interference
EMM: Enterprise Marketing Management
EMS: Electronic Meeting System
ERD: Entity-Relationship Diagram
ERP: Enterprise Resource Planning
ES: Expert System
ETL: Extraction, Transformation, and Loading
FTTH: Fiber to the Home
FTTP: Fiber to the Premises
G2B: Government-to-Business
G2C: Government-to-Citizens
G2G: Government-to-Government
GB: Gigabyte
Gbps: Gigabits per second
GEO: Geosynchronous Earth Orbit

GHz: Gigahertz
GIS: Geographic Information System
GPS: Global Positioning System
GTLD: Generic Top-Level Domain
GUI: Graphical User Interface
HCI: Human–Computer Interface
HDMI: High Definition Multimedia Interface
HIPAA: Health Insurance Portability and Accountability Act
HTML: Hypertext Markup Language
HTTP: Hypertext Transfer Protocol
Hz: Hertz
IaaS: Infrastructure as a Service
ICANN: Internet Corporation for Assigned Names and Numbers
IoS: Internet over Satellite
IOS: Interorganizational System
IP: Intellectual Property
IP: Internet Protocol
IS: Information System
ISDN: Integrated Services Digital Network
ISP: Internet Service Provider
IT: Information Technology
IVR: Interactive Voice Response
IXP: Internet Exchange Point
JAD: Joint Application Design
JIT: Just-in-Time
KB: Kilobyte
Kbps: Kilobits per second
KPI: Key Performance Indicator
LAN: Local Area Network
LCD: Liquid Crystal Display
LEO: Low Earth Orbit
LTE: Long-Term Evolution
MAN: Metropolitan Area Network
MB: Megabyte
Mbps: Megabits per second
MEO: Middle Earth Orbit
MHz: Megahertz
MICR: Magnetic Ink Character Recognition
MIS: Management Information System
NAT: Network Address Translation
NIC: Network Interface Card
NOS: Network Operating System
NoSQL: Not Only SQL
NPV: Net Present Value
NSF: National Science Foundation
NSFNET: National Science Foundation Network
OAS: Office Automation System
OCR: Optical Character Recognition
OLAP: Online Analytical Processing
OLED: Organic Light-Emitting Diode
OLPC: One Laptop Per Child
OLTP: Online Transaction Processing
OMR: Optical Mark Recognition
OSI: Open Systems Interconnection
P2P: Peer-to-Peer
PaaS: Platform as a Service
PAN: Personal Area Network
PBX: Private Branch Exchange
PC: Personal Computer
PDA: Personal Digital Assistant
PIN: Personal Identification Number
POTS: Plain Old Telephone Service
PSTN: Public Switched Telephone Network
RAD: Rapid Application Development
RAID: Redundant Array of Independent Disks
RAM: Random Access Memory
RDBMS: Relational Database Management System
RFID: Radio-Frequency Identification
RFP: Request for Proposal
ROM: Read-Only Memory
RSS: Real Simple Syndication
SaaS: Software as a Service
SAD: Systems Analysis and Design
SAM: Software Asset Management
SCE: Supply Chain Execution
SCM: Supply Chain Management
SCP: Supply Chain Planning
SDLC: Systems Development Life Cycle
SDSL: Symmetric Digital Subscriber Line
SEO: Search Engine Optimization
SFA: Sales Force Automation
SLA: Service-Level Agreement
SOA: Service-Oriented Architecture
SOX: Sarbanes–Oxley Act
SQL: Structured Query Language
SSD: Solid-State Drive
SSL: Secure Sockets Layer
STP: Shielded Twisted Pair
TB: Terabyte
TCO: Total Cost of Ownership

TCP/IP: Transmission Control Protocol/Internet Protocol

TP: Twisted Pair

TPS: Transaction Processing System

URL: Uniform Resource Locator

USB: Universal Serial Bus

UTP: Unshielded Twisted Pair

VAN: Value-Added Network

VGA: Video Graphics Array

VMI: Vendor Managed Inventory

VoIP: Voice over IP

VPN: Virtual Private Network

WAN: Wide Area Network

Wi-Fi: Wireless Fidelity

WiMax: Worldwide Interoperability for Microwave Access

WLAN: Wireless Local Area Network

WWW: World Wide Web

XBRL: Extensible Business Reporting Language

XML: Extensible Markup Language

Glossary

Acceptable use policies: Computer and/or Internet usage policies for people within an organization, with clearly spelled-out penalties for noncompliance.

Access-control software: Software for securing information systems that allows only specific users access to specific computers, applications, or data.

Ad hoc query: A request for information created due to unplanned information needs that is typically not saved for later use.

Adaptive maintenance: Making changes to an information system to make its functionality meet changing business needs or to migrate it to a different operating environment.

Advanced Research Projects Agency Network (ARPANET): A wide area network linking various universities and research centers; forerunner of the Internet.

Adware: Free software paid for by advertisements appearing during the use of the software.

Affiliate marketing: A type of marketing that allows individual Web site owners to earn commission by posting other companies' ads on their Web pages.

Algorithm: The step-by-step procedures used in a computer program to make a calculation or perform some type of computer-based process.

Alpha testing: Testing performed by the development organization to assess whether the entire system meets the design requirements of the users.

"Amateurization" of journalism: The replacement of professional journalism by amateur bloggers.

American Standard Code for Information Interchange (ASCII): Character encoding method for representing characters of the English alphabet that provides binary codes to represent symbols.

Analog signals: Audio tones used to transmit data over conventional voice telephone lines.

Analytical CRM: Systems for analyzing customer behavior and perceptions in order to provide business intelligence.

App: A software program (typically downloaded to mobile devices) that is designed to perform a particular, well-defined function.

Applet: A program designed to be executed within another application, such as a Web page.

Application software: Software used to perform a specific task that the user needs to accomplish.

Arithmetic logic unit (ALU): A part of the central processing unit (CPU) that performs mathematics and logical operations.

Artificial intelligence (AI): The science of enabling information technologies to simulate human intelligence as well as gain sensing capabilities.

Association: *See* Relationship.

Association discovery: A data mining technique used to find associations or correlations among sets of items.

Asymmetric digital subscriber line (ADSL): A variant of DSL offering faster download speeds than upload speeds.

Asynchronous: Not coordinated in time.

Attribute: An individual piece of information about an entity in a database.

Audio: Analog or digital sound data.

Augmented reality: The use of information systems to enhance a person's perception of reality by providing relevant information about the user's surroundings.

Authentication: The process of confirming the identity of a user who is attempting to access a restricted system or Web site.

Authentication service: A service on a network granting users and devices access rights to resources on the network.

Automating: Using information systems to do an activity faster, cheaper, and perhaps with more accuracy and/or consistency.

Backbone: A high-speed central network to which many smaller networks can be connected.

Backdoor: A hidden access point allowing for unauthorized access to a system.

Backup: A copy of critical data on a separate storage medium.

Backup site: A facility allowing businesses to continue functioning in the event a disaster strikes.

Bandwidth: The transmission capacity of a computer or communications channel.

Bar code reader: A specialized scanner used to read bar code data.

Basic input-output system (BIOS): Programs and instructions that are automatically loaded when the computer is turned on.

Batch data: Large amounts of routine data.

Batch processing: The processing of transactions after some quantity of transactions is collected; the transactions are processed together as a "batch" at some later time.

Best-cost provider strategy: A strategy to offer products or services of reasonably good quality at competitive prices.

Best practices: Procedures and processes used by business organizations that are widely accepted as being among the most effective and/or efficient.

Beta testing: Testing performed by actual system users with actual data in their work environment.

Big Data: Extremely large and complex datasets, typically characterized as being of high volume, variety, and velocity.

Binary code: The digital representation of data and information using sequences of zeroes and ones.

Biometrics: Body characteristics such as fingerprints, retinal patterns in the eye, or facial characteristics that allow the unique identification of a person.

Bit: A basic unit of data in computing. Short for "binary digit"; the individual ones and zeroes that make up a byte.

Blog: Short for "Web log." Chronological online text diary that can focus on anything the user desires.

Blogging: The creation and maintenance of a blog.

Bluetooth: A wireless specification for personal area networking (PAN) of desktop computers, peripheral devices (such as headsets, keyboards, mice, and printers), mobile phones, tablets, and various other devices.

Bot: Short for "software robot"; a program that works in the background to provide some service when a specific event occurs.

Botnet: A collection of zombie computers used for destructive activities or spamming.

Bounce rate: The percentage of single-page visits; reflecting the percentage of users for whom a particular page is the only page visited on the Web site during a session.

Breakeven analysis: A type of cost–benefit analysis to identify at what point (if ever) tangible benefits equal tangible costs.

Brick-and-mortar business strategy: A business approach exclusively utilizing physical locations, such as department stores, business offices, and manufacturing plants, without an online presence.

Bricks-and-clicks business strategy: *See* Click-and-mortar business strategy.

Bullwhip effect: Large fluctuations in suppliers' forecasts caused by small fluctuations in demand for the end product and the need to create safety buffers.

Bus network: A network in the shape of an open-ended line.

Business analytics: Applications that augment business intelligence by using statistical analysis and predictive modelling to build explanatory models, help understand the data, identify trends, or predict business outcomes.

Business continuity plan: A plan describing how a business continues operating after a disaster.

Business intelligence: The use of information systems to gather and analyze information from both external and internal sources to make better decisions, and the data derived from these processes.

Business model: The summary of a business's strategic direction, outlining how the objectives will be achieved; a business model specifies how a company will create, deliver, and capture value.

Business process: A set of related activities an organization performs in order to reach its business goals.

Business process management (BPM): A systematic, structured improvement approach by all or part of an organization, including a critical examination and redesign of business processes in order to achieve dramatic improvements in one or more performance measures such as quality, cycle time, or cost.

Business process reengineering (BPR): Legacy term for business process management (BPM).

Business rules: Policies by which a business runs.

Business/IT alignment: The alignment of information systems with a business's strategy.

Business-to-business (B2B): Electronic commerce transactions between business partners, such as suppliers and intermediaries.

Business-to-business marketplace: A trading exchange operated by a third-party vendor, not associated with a particular buyer or supplier.

Business-to-consumer (B2C): Electronic commerce transactions between businesses and consumers.

Buyer agent: An intelligent agent used to find the best price for a particular product a consumer wishes to purchase. Also known as a "shopping bot."

BYOD: Bring your own device; employees using their own devices for work-related purposes.

Byte: A unit of data typically containing 8 bits, or about one typed character.

Bytes per inch (BPI): The numbers of bytes that can be stored on 1 inch of magnetic tape.

Cable modem: A specialized piece of equipment that enables a computer to access Internet service via cable TV lines.

Cache: A small block of special high-speed memory used by processors to store those instructions most recently or most often used (pronounced "cash").

Campus area network (CAN): A type of network spanning multiple buildings, such as a university or business campus.

Capabilities: An organization's ability to leverage its resources.

CAPTCHA: Short for "Completely Automated Public Turing Test to Tell Computers and Humans Apart." A system designed to prevent automated mechanisms from repeatedly attempting to submit forms or gain access to a system. A CAPTCHA requires the user to enter letters or numbers that are presented in the form of a distorted image before submitting an online form.

Card Verification Value 2 (CVV2): A three-digit code located on the back of a credit card; used in transactions when the physical card is not present.

Carrier sense multiple access/collision avoidance (CSMA/CA): A random access control method in which each workstation "listens" to the traffic on the transmission medium to determine whether a message is being transmitted. If no traffic is detected, the workstation sends its message; otherwise, it waits. When a workstation gains access to the medium and sends data onto the network, messages are broadcast to all workstations on the network; however, only the destination with the proper address is able to "open" the message.

Cascading style sheets (CSS): Style language used to specify the formatting and layout of elements on a Web page.

Cathode ray tube (CRT): Display technology similar to a television monitor.

CD-R (compact disc–recordable): A type of optical disk that data can be written to.

CD-RW (compact disc–rewritable): A type of optical disk that can be written onto multiple times.

Cell: A geographic area containing a low-powered radio antenna/receiver for transmitting telecommunications signals within that area; monitored and controlled by a central computer.

Cellular phone: Mobile phone using a communications system that divides a geographic region into sections called cells.

Central processing unit (CPU): Responsible for performing all the operations of the computer. Also called a microprocessor, processor, or chip.

Centralized computing: A computing model utilizing large centralized computers, called mainframes, to process and store data and local input/output devices called "terminals"; no sharing of data and capabilities between mainframes and terminals.

Certificate authority: A trusted middleman between computers that verifies that a Web site is a trusted site and that provides large-scale public-key encryption.

Change request management: A formal process that ensures that any proposed system changes are documented, reviewed for potential risks, appropriately authorized, prioritized, and carefully managed.

Characters per inch (CPI): The number of characters that can be stored on 1 inch of magnetic tape.

Classification: A data mining technique used for grouping instances into predefined categories.

Click-and-mortar business strategy: A business approach utilizing both physical locations and virtual locations. Also referred to as "bricks-and-clicks."

Click fraud: The abuse of pay-per-click advertising models by repeatedly clicking on a link to inflate revenue to the host or increase costs for the advertiser.

Click-only business strategy: A business approach that exclusively utilizes an online presence. Companies using this strategy are also referred to as virtual companies.

Click-through rate: The number of surfers who click on an ad (i.e., clicks), divided by the number of times it was displayed (i.e., impressions).

Click-wrap license: A type of software license primarily used for downloaded software that requires computer users to accept the license terms by clicking a button before installing the software.

Clickstream data: A recording of the users' path through a Web site.

Client: Any computer or software application that requests and uses the services provided by a server.

Client-server network: A network in which servers and clients have defined roles.

Clock speed: The speed of the system clock, typically measured in hertz (Hz) or multiples thereof.

Clock tick: A single pulse of the system clock.

Cloud-based collaboration tools: Tools enabling teams to collaborate on projects using the Internet.

Cloud computing: A computing model enabling ubiquitous, convenient, on-demand network access to a shared pool of configurable computing resources (e.g., networks, servers, storage, applications, and services) that can be rapidly provisioned and released with minimal management effort or service provider interaction (NIST, 2011).

Cloud security: Security concerned with storing and processing data in the cloud; the need to secure data at rest, data in transit, and data in use.

Clustering: Data mining technique grouping related records on the basis of having similar attributes.

Cold backup site: A backup facility consisting of an empty warehouse with all the necessary connections for power and communication but nothing else.

Collaboration: Two or more people, teams, or organizations working together to achieve a common goal.

Collaborative computing: A synergistic form of distributed computing in which two or more networked computers are used to accomplish common processing tasks.

Collaborative CRM: Systems for providing effective and efficient communication with the customer from the entire organization.

Collective intelligence: A concept based on the notion that distributed groups of people with a divergent range of information and expertise will be able to outperform the capabilities of individual experts.

Collocation facility: A facility in which businesses can rent space for servers or other information systems equipment.

Combination primary key: A unique identifier consisting of two or more attributes.

Competitive advantage: A firm's ability to do something better, faster, cheaper, or uniquely as compared with rival firms in the market.

Competitive click fraud: A competitor's attempt to inflate an organization's online advertising costs by repeatedly clicking on an advertiser's link.

Competitive intelligence: Information about competitors, used to enhance a business's strategic position.

Compiler: A software program that translates an entire program's source code into machine language that can be read and executed directly by the computer.

Computer-aided software engineering (CASE): The use of software tools that provide automated support for some portion of the systems development process.

Computer-assisted auditing tool: Software used to test information systems controls.

Computer-based information system: A combination of hardware, software, and telecommunication networks that people build and use to collect, create, and distribute data.

Computer crime: The use of a computer to commit an illegal act.

Computer ethics: A broad range of issues and standards of conduct that have emerged through the use and proliferation of information systems.

Computer fluency: The ability to independently learn new technologies as they emerge and assess their impact on one's work and life.

Computer forensics: The use of formal investigative techniques to evaluate digital information for judicial review.

Computer literacy: The knowledge of how to operate a computer.

Computer networking: The sharing of data or services between computers using wireless or cable transmission media.

Consumer-to-business (C2B): Electronic commerce transactions in which consumers sell goods or services to businesses.

Consumer-to-consumer (C2C): Electronic commerce transactions taking place solely between consumers.

Consumerization of IT: The trend of technological innovations first being introduced in the consumer marketplace before being used by organizations.

Content delivery network: A network of servers in various physical locations that store copies of particular Web sites, so as to reduce latency.

Content management system: An information system enabling users to publish, edit, version track, and retrieve digital information (or content).

Continuous planning process: A strategic business planning process involving continuous monitoring and adjusting of business processes to enable rapid reaction to changing business conditions.

Control objectives for information and related technology (COBIT): A set of best practices that help organizations to both maximize the benefits from their information systems infrastructure and establish appropriate controls.

Control unit: Part of the central processing unit (CPU) that works closely with the ALU (arithmetic logic unit) by fetching and decoding instructions as well as retrieving and storing data.

Conversion rate: The percentage of visitors to a Web site who perform the desired action.

Cookie: A small text file (typically containing certain information collected from/about a user or data related to the user's browsing session) passed by a Web server to a Web browser to be stored on a user's computer; this message is then sent back to the server each time the user's browser requests a page from that server.

Copyright: A form of intellectual property, referring to creations of the mind such as music, literature, or software.

Core activities: The activities within a value chain that process inputs and produce outputs, including inbound logistics, operations and manufacturing, outbound logistics, marketing and sales, and customer service.

Corrective controls: Controls used to mitigate the impact of any problem after it has arisen, such as restoring compromised data.

Corrective maintenance: Making changes to an information system to repair flaws in its design, coding, or implementation.

Cost–benefit analysis: Techniques that contrast the total expected tangible costs versus the tangible benefits of an investment.

Cracker: An individual who breaks into computer systems with the intention of doing damage or committing a crime.

Crowdfunding: The securing of business financing from individuals in the marketplace—the "crowd"—to fund an initiative.

Crowdsourcing: The use of everyday people as cheap labor force, enabled by information technology.

Custom software: Software programs that are designed and developed for a company's specific needs as opposed to being bought off the shelf.

Customer engagement center (CEC): A part of operational CRM that provides a central point of contact for an organization's customers, employing multiple communication channels to support the communication preferences of customers.

Customer portal: An enterprise portal designed to automate the business processes that occur before, during, and after sales between a supplier and multiple customers.

Customer relationship management (CRM): A corporate-level strategy designed to create and maintain lasting relationships with customers by concentrating on the downstream information flows through the introduction of reliable systems, processes, and procedures.

Customer service and support (CSS): A part of operational CRM that automates service and information requests, complaints, and product returns.

Customization: Modifying software so that it better suits user needs.

Cyberbullying: The use of a computer to intentionally cause emotional distress to a person.

Cyberharassment: The use of a computer to communicate obscene, vulgar, or threatening content that causes a reasonable person to endure distress.

Cybersquatting: The dubious practice of registering a domain name, then trying to sell the name to the person, company, or organization most likely to want it.

Cyberstalking: The use of a computer to repeatedly engage in threatening or harassing behavior.

Cyberterrorism: The use of computer and networking technologies against persons or property to intimidate or coerce governments, individuals, or any segment of society to attain political, religious, or ideological goals.

Cyberwar: An organized attempt by a country's military to disrupt or destroy the information and communications systems of another country.

Data: Raw symbols, such as words and numbers, that have no meaning in and of themselves, and are of little value until processed.

Data cleansing: The process of detecting, correcting (e.g., standardizing the format), or removing corrupt or inaccurate data retrieved from different systems.

Data dictionary: A document prepared by database designers to describe the characteristics of all items in a database.

Data driven organizations: Organizations that make decisions that can be backed up with verifiable data.

Data flows: Data moving through an organization or within an information system.

Data mart: A data warehouse that is limited in scope and customized for the decision support applications of a particular end-user group.

Data mining: Methods used by companies to discover "hidden" predictive relationships in data to better understand their customers, products, markets, or any other phase of their business for which data have been captured.

Data mining agent: An intelligent agent that continuously analyzes large data warehouses to detect changes deemed important by a user, sending a notification when such changes occur.

Data model: A map or diagram that represents the entities of a database and their relationships.

Data privacy statement: A statement on a Web site containing information about what data are gathered, what they are used for, who will have access to the data, whether provision of the data is required or voluntary, and how confidentiality will be ensured.

Data reduction: A preparatory step to running data mining algorithms, performed by rolling up a data cube to the smallest level of aggregation needed, reducing the dimensionality, or dividing continuous measures into discrete intervals.

Data type: The type (e.g., text, number, or date) of an attribute in a database.

Data warehouse: A repository containing data from multiple large databases and other sources that is suitable for direct querying, analysis, or processing.

Database: A collection of related data organized in a way to facilitate data searches.

Database management system (DBMS): A software application used to create, store, organize, and retrieve data from a single database or several databases.

Decision support system (DSS): A special-purpose information system designed to support organizational decision making.

Dedicated grid: A grid computing architecture consisting of homogeneous computers that are dedicated to performing the grid's computing tasks.

Defense Advanced Research Projects Agency (DARPA): The U.S. governmental agency that began to study ways to interconnect networks of various kinds, leading to the development of the ARPANET (Advanced Research Projects Agency Network).

Denial of service attack: An attack by crackers—often using zombie computers—that makes a network resource (e.g., Web site) unavailable to users or available with only a poor degree of service.

Density: The storage capacity of magnetic tape; typically expressed in characters per inch (CPI) or bytes per inch (BPI).

Desktop videoconferencing: The use of integrated computer, telephone, video recording, and playback technologies—typically by two people—to remotely interact with each other using their desktop computers.

Desktop virtualization: The practice of providing workers with a virtual desktop environment (hosted on a central computer), helping to reduce costs for software licensing or maintenance, and to comply with stringent privacy and data protection laws.

Destructive agent: A malicious agent designed by spammers and other Internet attackers to farm e-mail addresses off Web sites or deposit spyware on machines.

Detective controls: Controls used to assess whether anything went wrong, such as unauthorized access attempts, and to limit damage.

Developmental testing: Testing performed by programmers to ensure that each module of a new program is error free.

Device driver: A computer program that allows the computer to communicate with various different hardware devices.

Differentiation strategy: A strategy in which an organization differentiates itself by providing better products or services than its competitors.

Digital dashboard: A display delivering summary information to managers and executives to provide warnings, action notices, and summaries of business conditions.

Digital divide: The gap between those individuals in our society who are computer literate and have access to information resources such as the Internet and those who do not.

Digital rights management (DRM): A technological solution that allows publishers to control their digital media (music, movies, and so on) to discourage, limit, or prevent illegal copying and distribution.

Digital signals: The electrical pulses that computers use to send bits of information.

Digital subscriber line (DSL): A high-speed data transmission method that uses special modulation schemes to fit more data onto traditional copper telephone wires.

Digital video disc: A DVD used for storing movies.

Digitize: To convert analog input into digital data.

Dimension: A way to summarize data, such as region, time, or product line.

Directory service: A repository (or "address book") containing information about users, user groups, resources, access rights, etc., on a network.

Disaster recovery plan: An organizational plan that spells out detailed procedures for recovering from systems-related disasters, such as virus infections and other disasters that might strike critical information systems.

Discount rate: The rate of return used by an organization to compute the present value of future cash flows.

Discussion forum: An electronic bulletin board that allows for threaded discussions among participants.

Disintermediation: The phenomenon of cutting out the "middleman" in transactions and reaching customers more directly and efficiently.

Disruptive innovation: A new technology, product, or service that eventually surpasses the existing dominant technology, product, or service in a market.

Disruptive innovation cycle: A model suggesting that the extent to which modern organizations use information technologies and systems in timely, innovative ways is the key to success.

Distinctive competency: Any unique strength possessed by an organization (e.g., innovation, agility, quality, or low cost) that helps to pursue an organizational strategy.

Distributed computing: Using separate computers to work on subsets of tasks and then pooling the results by communicating over a network.

Domain name: The part of a Uniform Resource Locator (URL) that identifies a source or host entity on the Internet.

Domain Name System (DNS): A collection of databases used to associate Internet host names with their IP addresses.

Domestic company: A company operating solely in its domestic market.

Downsizing: The practice of slashing costs and streamlining operations by laying off employees.

Downstream information flow: An information flow that relates to the information that is produced by a company and sent along to another organization, such as a distributor.

Drill down: To analyze data at more detailed levels of a specific dimension.

Drill-down report: A report that provides details behind the summary values on a key-indicator or exception report.

Drive-by hacking: A computer attack in which an attacker accesses a wireless computer network, intercepts data, uses network services, and/or sends attack instructions without entering the office or organization that owns the network.

Dumpster diving: Scouring wastebaskets for potentially useful information.

DVD-ROM (digital versatile disc–read-only memory): A DVD that can be read but not written to.

E-auction: An electronic auction.

E-business: A term used to refer to the use of a variety of types of information technologies and systems to support every part of the business.

Economic opportunities: Opportunities that a firm finds for making more money and/or making money in new ways.

Effectiveness: The extent to which goals or tasks are accomplished well.

Efficiency: The extent to which goals are accomplished faster, at lower cost, or with relatively little time and effort.

E-government: The use of information systems to provide citizens, organizations, and other governmental agencies with information about and access to public services.

Electronic bill pay: The use of online banking for bill paying.

Electronic commerce (EC): The exchange of goods and services via the Internet among and between customers, firms, employees, business partners, suppliers, and so on.

Electronic Data Interchange (EDI): The digital, or electronic, transmission of business documents and related data between organizations via dedicated telecommunications networks.

Electronic meeting system (EMS): A collection of personal computers networked together with sophisticated software tools to help group members solve problems and make decisions through interactive electronic idea generation, evaluation, and voting.

Embedded system: A microprocessor-based system optimized to perform a well-defined set of tasks.

Employee portal: An intranet portal used for communication and collaboration between an organization and its employees.

Employee self-service: Intranet-based applications that allow employees to manage human-resources-related tasks.

Enabling technology: An information technology that enables a firm to accomplish a task or goal or to gain or sustain a competitive advantage in some way.

Encryption: The process of encoding messages or files so that only intended recipients can decipher and understand them.

Enterprise 2.0: The use of social media within a company's boundaries or between a company and its customers or stakeholders.

Enterprise license: A type of software license that is usually negotiated and covers all users within an organization. Also known as a "volume license."

Enterprise marketing management (EMM): CRM tools used to integrate and analyze marketing campaigns.

Enterprise resource planning (ERP): An information system that integrates business activities across departmental boundaries, including planning, manufacturing, sales, marketing, and so on.

Enterprise system: An information system that spans the entire organization and can be used to integrate business processes, activities, and information across all functional areas of a firm.

Enterprise WAN: A WAN connecting disparate networks of a single organization into a single network.

Enterprise-wide information systems: *See* Enterprise system.

Entity: Something data are collected about, such as people or classes.

Entity-relationship diagram (ERD): A diagram used to display the structure of data and show associations between entities.

ERP core components: The components of an ERP that support the internal activities of an organization for producing products and services.

ERP extended components: The components of an ERP that support the primary external activities of an organization for dealing with suppliers and customers.

E-tailing: Electronic retailing; the online sales of goods and services.

Ethernet: The most widely used local area network protocol, supporting data rates of up to 100 gigabits per second.

Exception report: A report providing users with information about situations that are out of the normal operating range.

Executable: A program in machine language that can be read and executed directly by a computer.

Executive level: The top level of the organization, where executives focus on long-term strategic issues facing the organization.

Exit rate: The percentage of visitors who leave the Web site (terminate the session) after viewing a particular page.

Expert system (ES): A special-purpose information system designed to mimic human expertise by manipulating knowledge—understanding acquired through experience and extensive learning—rather than simply information.

Explicit knowledge asset: A knowledge asset that can be documented, archived, and codified.

Extensible Business Reporting Language (XBRL): An XML-based specification for publishing financial information.

Extensible Markup Language (XML): A data presentation standard that allows designers to create customized markup tags that enable data to be more easily shared between applications and organizations.

External acquisition: The process of purchasing an existing information system from an external organization or vendor.

Externally focused system: An information system that coordinates business activities with customers, suppliers, business partners, and others who operate outside an organization's boundaries.

Extraction, transformation, and loading (ETL): The process of consolidating, cleansing, and manipulating data before loading the data into a data warehouse.

Extranet: A private part of the Internet that is cordoned off from ordinary users, that enables two or more firms to use the Internet to do business together.

Fact: *See* Measure.

Fiber to the home (FTTH): *See* Fiber to the premises.

Fiber to the premises (FTTP): High-speed network connectivity to homes and offices that is implemented using fiber-optic cable. Also known as "fiber to the home."

Financial flow: The movement of financial assets throughout the supply chain.

Firewall: Hardware or software designed to keep unauthorized users out of network systems.

First-call resolution: Addressing the customers' issues during the first call.

First-mover advantage: Being the first to enter a market.

Flash drive: A portable, removable data storage device using flash memory.

Flash memory: A memory-chip-based non-volatile computer storage technology.

Folksonomy: A categorization system created by Internet users (as opposed to experts).

Foreign key: An attribute that appears as a non–primary key attribute in one entity and as a primary key attribute (or part of a primary key) in another entity.

Form: A business document that contains some predefined data and may include some areas where additional data are to be filled in, typically for modifying data related to a single record.

Freeconomics: The leveraging of digital technologies to provide *free* goods and services to customers as a business strategy for gaining a competitive advantage.

Freemium: Freeconomics-based revenue model where basic services are offered for free, but a premium is charged for special features.

Functional area information system: A cross-organizational-level information system designed to support a specific functional area.

Functional convenience: A Web page's characteristics that make the interaction with the site easier or more convenient.

Fuzzy logic: A type of logic used in intelligent systems that allows rules to be represented using approximations or subjective values in order to handle situations where information about a problem is incomplete.

Geographic information system (GIS): A system for creating, storing, analyzing, and managing geographically referenced information.

Geotagging: Adding geospatial metadata (such as latitude, longitude, or altitude) to digital media.

Global business strategy: An international business strategy employed to achieve economies of scale by producing identical products in large quantities for a variety of different markets.

Global network: A network spanning multiple countries that may include the networks of several organizations. The Internet is an example of a global network.

Globalization: The integration of economies throughout the world, enabled by innovation and technological progress.

Government-to-business (G2B): Electronic commerce that involves a country's government and businesses.

Government-to-citizen (G2C): Online interactions between federal, state, and local governments and their constituents.

Government-to-government (G2G): Electronic interactions that take place between countries or between different levels of government within a country.

Graphical user interface (GUI): A computer interface that enables the user to select or manipulate pictures, icons, and menus to send instructions to the computer.

Green computing: Attempts to use computing resources more efficiently to reduce environmental impacts, as well as the use of information systems to reduce negative environmental impacts.

Grid computing: A computing architecture that combines the computing power of a large number of smaller, independent, networked computers (often regular desktop PCs) into a cohesive system in order to solve large-scale computing problems.

Group buying: Special volume discounts negotiated with local businesses and offered to people in the form of "daily deals"; if enough people agree to purchase the product or service, everyone can purchase the product at the discounted price.

Groupware: Software that enables people to work together more effectively.

Hacker: An individual who gains unauthorized access to computer systems.

Hacktivist: A cybercriminal pursuing political, religious, or ideological goals.

Hard drive: A magnetic storage device used for secondary storage. Also called "hard disk."

Hardware: Physical computer equipment, such as the computer monitor, central processing unit, or keyboard.

Hashtag: A tag (pound sign) added to messages posted on microblogging services, allowing users to search for content related to a certain topic.

Head crash: A hard disk failure occurring when the read/write head touches the disk, resulting in the loss of the data and/or irreparable damage to the hard disk.

Home-replication strategy: An international business strategy that views the international business as an extension of the home business.

Honeypot: A computer, piece of data, or network site that is designed to be enticing to crackers so as to detect, deflect, or counteract illegal activity.

Hot backup site: A fully equipped backup facility, having everything from hardware, software, and current data to office equipment.

HTML editor: *See* Web page builder.

HTML tag: Markup that is inserted into the source document of a Web page to specify the structure and content of a document.

Human–computer interface (HCI): The point of contact between an information system and its users.

Hyperlink: A reference or link on a Web page to another document that contains related information.

Hypertext: Text in a Web document that is linked to other text or content.

Hypertext Markup Language (HTML): The standard method of specifying the structure and content of Web pages.

Hypertext Transfer Protocol (HTTP): The standard regulating how servers process user requests for Web pages.

Identity theft: Stealing another person's Social Security number, credit card number, and other personal information for the purpose of using the victim's credit rating to borrow money, buy merchandise, or run up debts that are never repaid.

Industrial espionage: Covert activities, such as the theft of trade secrets, bribery, blackmail, and technological surveillance to gain an advantage over rivals.

Inferencing: The matching of user questions and answers to information in a knowledge base within an expert system in order to make a recommendation.

Information: Data that have been formatted and/or organized in some way as to be useful to people.

Information Age: A period of time in society when information became a valuable or dominant currency.

Information flow: The movement of information along the supply chain.

Information modification: The intentional change of electronic information by unauthorized users.

Information privacy: An ethical issue that is concerned with what information an individual should have to reveal to others through the course of employment or through other transactions such as online shopping.

Information system (IS): System that uses information technology to collect, create, and distribute useful data.

Information systems audit: An assessment of the state of an organization's information systems controls to determine necessary changes and to help ensure the information systems' availability, confidentiality, and integrity.

Information systems controls: Controls helping to ensure the availability, integrity, and confidentiality of data and information systems.

Information systems infrastructure: The hardware, software, networks, data, facilities, human resources, and services used by organizations to support their decision making, business processes, and competitive strategy.

Information systems planning: A formal process for identifying and assessing all possible information systems development projects of an organization.

Information systems risk assessment: Assessment performed to obtain an understanding of the risks to the confidentiality, integrity, and availability of data and systems.

Information systems security: Precautions taken to keep all aspects of information systems safe from destruction, manipulation, or unauthorized use or access.

Information technology (IT): The hardware, software, and networking components of an information system.

Informational system: A system designed to support decision making based on stable point-in-time or historical data.

Infrastructure: The interconnection of various structural elements to support an overall entity, such as an organization, city, or country.

Infrastructure as a Service (IaaS): A cloud computing model in which only the basic capabilities of processing, storage, and networking are provided.

In-memory computing: Processing of analytical and transactional tasks where the data are stored in a computer's main memory, rather than on a comparatively slow hard drive, removing the bottlenecks associated with reading and writing data.

Innovator's dilemma: The notion that disruptive innovations can cause established firms or industries to lose market dominance, often leading to failure.

Input technologies: Hardware that is used to enter information into a computer.

Insider threat: A trusted adversary who operates within an organization's boundaries.

Instant messaging: Online chat emulating real-time written conversations.

Intangible benefit: A benefit of using a particular system or technology that is difficult to quantify.

Intangible cost: A cost of using a particular system or technology that is difficult to quantify.

Integrated Services Digital Network (ISDN): A standard for worldwide digital telecommunications that uses existing twisted-pair telephone wires to provide high-speed data service.

Intellectual property (IP): Creations of the mind that have commercial value.

Intelligent agent: A program that works in the background to provide some service when a specific event occurs.

Intelligent system: A system comprised of sensors, software, and computers embedded in machines and devices that emulates and enhances human capabilities.

Interactive voice response (IVR): A system using speech recognition technology to guide callers through online surveys or menu options.

Interexchange carrier (IXC): A company selling long-distance services with circuits that carry signals between the major telephone exchanges.

Internally focused system: An information system that supports functional areas, business processes, and decision making within an organization.

International business strategy: A set of strategies employed by organizations operating in different global markets.

Internet: A large worldwide collection of networks that use a common protocol to communicate with each other.

Internet backbone: The collection of primary network connections and telecommunications lines making up the Internet.

Internet Corporation for Assigned Names and Numbers (ICANN): A nonprofit corporation that is responsible for managing IP addresses, domain names, and the root server system.

Internet exchange point (IXP): An access point for ISPs and an exchange point for Internet traffic.

Internet hoax: A false message circulated online about any topic of public interest, typically asking the recipient to perform a certain action.

Internet host: A computer working as a server on the Internet.

Internet of Things: A broad range of physical objects (such as computer, sensors, or motors) that are interconnected and automatically share data over the Internet.

Internet over Satellite (IoS): A technology that allows users to access the Internet via satellites that are placed in a geostationary orbit.

Internet service provider (ISP): An organization that enables individuals and organizations to connect to the Internet.

Internet Tax Freedom Act: An act mandating a moratorium on electronic commerce taxation in order to stimulate electronic commerce.

Internetworking: Connecting host computers and their networks to form even larger networks.

InterNIC: A government–industry collaboration created by the NSF in 1993 to manage directory and database services, domain registration services, and other information services on the Internet.

Interorganizational system (IOS): An information system that communicates across organizational boundaries.

Interpreter: A software program that translates a program's source code into machine language one statement at a time.

Intranet: An internal, private network using Web technologies to facilitate the secured transmission of proprietary information within an organization, thereby limiting access to authorized users within the organization.

IP address: A numerical address assigned to every computer and router connected to the Internet that serves as the destination address of that computer or device and enables the network to route messages to the proper destination.

IP convergence: The use of the Internet protocol for transporting voice, video, fax, and data traffic.

IP datagram: A data packet that conforms to the Internet protocol specification.

IPv6: The latest version of the Internet protocol.

Jailbreaking: Modifying a mobile phone's operating system to remove manufacturer or carrier restrictions.

Java: An object-oriented programming language that is used for developing applications that can run on multiple computing platforms.

JavaScript: A scripting language that allows developers to add dynamic content to Web sites.

Joint application design (JAD): A special type of a group meeting in which all (or most) users meet with a systems analyst to jointly define and agree on system requirements or designs.

Just-in-time (JIT): A method to optimize ordering quantities so that parts or raw materials arrive just when they are needed for production.

Key generator: Software used to generate fake license or registration keys to circumvent a program's protection mechanism.

Key-indicator report: A report that provides a summary of critical information on a recurring schedule.

Key performance indicator (KPI): A metric deemed critical to assessing progress toward a certain organizational goal.

Keylogger: Software programs used to capture users' keystrokes.

Knowledge: A body of governing procedures such as guidelines or rules that are used to organize or manipulate data to make the data suitable for a given task.

Knowledge assets: The set of skills, routines, practices, principles, formulas, methods, heuristics, and intuitions (both explicit and tacit) used by organizations to improve efficiency, effectiveness, and profitability.

Knowledge management: The processes an organization uses to gain the greatest value from its knowledge assets.

Knowledge management system: A collection of technology-based tools that includes communications technologies and information storage and retrieval systems to enable the generation, storage, sharing, and management of tacit and explicit knowledge assets.

Knowledge portal: A specific portal used to share knowledge collected in a repository with employees (often using an intranet), with customers and suppliers (often using an extranet), or the general public (often using the Internet).

Knowledge society: A term coined by Peter Drucker to refer to a society in which education is the cornerstone of society and there is an increase in the importance of knowledge workers.

Knowledge worker: A term coined by Peter Drucker to refer to professionals who are relatively well educated and who create, modify, and/or synthesize knowledge as a fundamental part of their jobs.

Layer: In a GIS, related data can be made visible or invisible when viewing a map; each *layer* acts like a transparency that can be turned on or off and provides additional information, such as roads, utilities, ZIP code boundaries, floodplains, and so on.

Legacy system: Older standalone computer systems within an organization with older versions of applications that are either fast approaching or beyond the end of their useful life within the organization.

Liquid crystal display (LCD): A type of monitor used for most current notebook and desktop computers.

Local area network (LAN): A computer network that spans a relatively small area, allowing all computer users to connect with each other to share information and peripheral devices, such as printers.

Location-based services: Highly personalized mobile services based on a user's location.

Logic bomb: A type of computer virus that lies in wait for unsuspecting computer users to perform a triggering operation before executing its instructions.

Long Tail: The large parts of consumer demand that are outside the relatively small number of mainstream tastes.

Low-cost leadership strategy: A strategy to offer the best prices in the industry on goods or services.

Magnetic ink character recognition (MICR): Scanning technology used by the banking industry to read data, account numbers, bank codes, and check numbers on preprinted checks.

Mainframe: A very large computer typically used as the main, central computing system by major corporations and governmental agencies.

Make-to-order process: The set of processes associated with producing goods based on customers' orders.

Make-to-stock process: The set of processes associated with producing goods based on demand forecasts.

Making the business case: The process of identifying, quantifying, and presenting the value provided by an information system.

Malware: Malicious software, such as viruses, worms, or Trojan horses.

Management information system (MIS): An information system designed to support the management of organizational functions at the managerial level of the organization.

Managerial level: The middle level of the organization, where functional managers focus on monitoring and controlling operational-level activities and providing information to higher levels of the organization.

Machine learning: The branch of artificial intelligence that allows systems to learn by identifying meaningful patterns when processing massive amounts of data.

Mashup: A new application or Web site that uses data from one or more service providers.

Mass customization: Tailoring products and services to meet the particular needs of individual customers on a large scale.

Master data: The data that are deemed most important in the operation of a business; typically the "actors" in an organization's transactions.

Master data management: Consolidating master data so as to facilitate arriving at a single version of the truth.

M-commerce (mobile commerce): Any electronic transaction or information interaction conducted using a wireless, mobile device and mobile networks that leads to a transfer of real or perceived value in exchange for information, services, or goods.

Measure: The values and numbers a user wants to analyze. Also referred to as "facts."

Media access control: The rules that govern how a given node or workstation gains access to a network to send or receive information.

Menu-driven pricing: A pricing system in which companies set and present non-negotiable prices for products to consumers.

Mesh network: A network that consists of computers and other devices that are either fully or partially connected to each other.

Metadata: Data about data, describing data in terms of who, where, when, why, and so on.

Metropolitan area network (MAN): A computer network of limited geographic scope, typically a citywide area that combines both LAN and high-speed fiber-optic technologies.

Microblogging: Voicing thoughts through relatively short "status updates" using social presence tools.

Microblogging tools: Tools enabling people to voice thoughts through relatively short "status updates."

Microprocessor: *See* Central processing unit.

Microsoft.NET: A programming platform that is used to develop applications that are highly interoperable across a variety of platforms and devices.

Mirror: To store data synchronously on independent systems to achieve redundancy for purposes of reliability and/or performance.

Mobile banking: Conducting financial transactions using mobile devices.

Mobile wireless: The transfer of data to a moving computer or handheld device.

Model: A conceptual, mathematical, logical, or analytical formula used to represent or project business events or trends.

Modem: Short for "modulator-demodulator"; a device or program that enables a computer to transmit data over telephone or cable television lines.

Module: A component of a software application that can be selected and implemented as needed.

Monitoring and sensing agent: An intelligent agent that keeps track of key data, such as data provided by various sensors, meters, cameras, and the like, and notifies the user when conditions change.

Moore's law: The prediction that computer processing performance would double every 24 months.

Motherboard: A large printed plastic or fiberglass circuit board that holds or connects to all the computer's electronic components.

Multidomestic business strategy: A decentralized international business strategy using a federation of associated business units, employed to be flexible and responsive to the needs and demands of heterogeneous local markets.

National Science Foundation (NSF): A U.S. government agency responsible for promoting science and engineering; the NSF initiated the development of the National Science Foundation Network (NSFNET), which became a major component of the Internet.

National Science Foundation Network (NSFNET): A network developed by the United States in 1986 that became a major component of the Internet.

Net neutrality: The principle that all Internet traffic should be treated the same.

Net-present-value analysis: A type of cost–benefit analysis of the cash flow streams associated with an investment.

Network: A group of computers and associated peripheral devices connected by a communication channel capable of sharing data and other resources among users.

Network effect: The notion that the value of a network (or tool or application based on a network) is dependent on the number of other users.

Network interface card (NIC): An expansion board that plugs into a computer so that it can be connected to a network.

Network topology: The shape of a network; the four common network topologies are star, ring, bus, and mesh.

Neural network: An information system that attempts to approximate the functioning of the human brain.

Non-recurring cost: A one-time cost that is not expected to continue after a system is implemented.

Nonvolatile memory: Memory that does not lose its data after power is shut off.

Normalization: A technique for making complex relational databases more efficient and more easily handled by a database management system.

NoSQL: A variety of database technologies enabling highly scalable databases that do not conform to RDBMS schemas.

Object-oriented language: A programming language that groups together data and their corresponding instructions into manipulable objects.

Off-the-shelf software: Software designed and used to support general business processes that does not require any specific tailoring to meet an organization's needs.

Office automation system (OAS): A collection of software and hardware for developing documents, scheduling resources, and communicating.

OLAP cube: A data structure allowing for multiple dimensions to be added to a traditional two-dimensional table for detailed analysis.

OLAP server: The chief component of an OLAP system that understands how data are organized in the database and has special functions for analyzing the data.

Online analytical processing (OLAP): The process of quickly conducting complex analyses of data stored in a database, typically using graphical software tools.

Online banking: The use of the Internet to conduct financial transactions.

Online investing: The use of the Internet to obtain information about stock quotes and manage financial portfolios.

Online predator: A cybercriminal using the Internet to target vulnerable people, usually the young or old, for sexual or financial purposes.

Online transaction processing (OLTP): Immediate automated responses to the requests from multiple concurrent transactions of customers.

Open innovation: The process of integrating external stakeholders into an organization's innovation process.

Open source software: Software for which the source code is freely available for use and/or modification.

Open Systems Interconnection (OSI) model: A networking model that represents a group of specific communication tasks as successive layers.

Operating system: Software that coordinates the interaction between hardware devices, peripherals, application software, and users.

Operational CRM: Systems for automating the fundamental business processes—marketing, sales, and support—for interacting with the customer.

Operational level: The bottom level of an organization, where the routine, day-to-day business processes and interactions with customers occur.

Operational systems: The systems that are used to interact with customers and run a business in real time.

Opt-in: To signal agreement to the collection/further use of one's data (e.g., by checking a box).

Opt-out: To signal that data cannot be collected/used in other ways (e.g., by checking a box).

Optical character recognition (OCR): Scanning technology used to read and digitize typewritten, computer-printed, or handwritten characters.

Optical disk: A storage disk coated with a metallic substance that is written to (or read from) when a laser beam passes over the surface of the disk.

Optical mark recognition (OMR): Scanning technology used to scan questionnaires and test answer forms ("bubble sheets") where answer choices are marked by filling in circles using a pencil or pen.

Order-to-cash process: The set of processes associated with selling a product or service.

Organic light-emitting diode (OLED): A display technology using less power than LCD technology.

Organizational learning: The ability of an organization to learn from past behavior and information, improving as a result.

Organizational strategy: A firm's plan to accomplish its mission and goals as well as to gain or sustain competitive advantage over rivals.

Output technologies: Hardware devices that deliver information in a usable form.

Outsourcing: The moving of routine jobs and/or tasks to people in another firm.

Packaged software: A software program written by a third-party vendor for the needs of many different users and organizations.

Packet sniffer: Software program to capture and analyze network traffic.

Packet switching: The process of breaking information into small chunks called data packets and then transferring those packets from computer to computer via the Internet, based on the concept of turn taking.

Paid inclusion: The inclusion of a Web site in a search engine's listing after payment of a fee.

Patch management system: An online system that utilizes Web services to automatically check for software updates, downloading and installing these "patches" as they are made available.

Patent: A type of intellectual property typically referring to process, machine, or material inventions.

Patriot hacker: Independent citizens or supporters of a country that perpetrate computer attacks on perceived or real enemies.

Pay-per-click: A payment model used in online advertising where the advertiser pays the Web site owner a fee for visitors clicking on a certain link.

Peer: Any computer that may both request and provide services.

Peer production: The creation of goods or services by self-organizing communities.

Peer-to-peer networks: Networks that enable any computer or device on the network to provide and request services.

Perfective maintenance: Making enhancements to improve processing performance, to improve usability, or to add desired but not necessarily required system features.

Peripheral: An auxiliary device, such as mouse or keyboard, that is connected to a computer.

Personal area network (PAN): A wireless network used to exchange data between computing devices using short-range radio communication, typically within an area of 10 meters.

Personal computer (PC): A stationary computer used for personal computing and small business computing.

Phishing: Attempts to trick financial account and credit card holders into giving away their authorization information, usually by sending spam messages to literally millions of e-mail accounts. Also known as "spoofing."

Plain old telephone service (POTS): Standard analog telephone lines; also called "public switched telephone network (PSTN)."

Planned obsolescence: The design of a product so that it lasts for only a certain life span.

Platform as a service (PaaS): A cloud computing model in which the customer can run his or her own applications that are typically designed using tools provided by the service provider; the customer has limited or no control over the underlying infrastructure.

Podcast: *See* Webcast.

Podcasting: *See* Webcasting.

Port: A hardware interface by which a computer communicates with another device or system.

Portal: An access point (or front door) through which a business partner accesses secured, proprietary information from an organization (typically using extranets).

Post-PC era: An era characterized by the proliferation of new device form factors, such as tablets or smartphones, which complement or even replace traditional PCs and laptops.

Power supply: A device that converts electricity from the wall socket to a lower voltage appropriate for computer components and regulates the voltage to eliminate surges common in most electrical systems.

Predictive modelling: Business intelligence techniques focusing on identifying trends or predicting business outcomes.

Preventive controls: Controls used to prevent any potentially negative event from occurring, such as by preventing outside intruders from accessing a facility.

Preventive maintenance: Making changes to a system to reduce the chance of future system failure.

Primary key: A field included in a database table that contains a unique value for each instance of an entity to ensure that it is stored or retrieved accurately.

Primary storage: Temporary storage for data used in current calculations.

Printer: An output device that produces a paper copy of alphanumeric or graphic data from a computer.

Private branch exchange (PBX): A telephone system that serves a particular location, such as a business, connecting one telephone extension to another within the system and connecting the internal extensions to the outside telephone network.

Private cloud: Cloud infrastructure that is internal to an organization.

Processing logic: The steps by which data are transformed or moved, as well as a description of the events that trigger these steps.

Processing technologies: Computer hardware that transforms inputs into outputs.

Procure-to-pay process: The set of processes associated with procuring goods from external vendors.

Product flow: The movement of goods from the supplier to production, from production to distribution, and from distribution to the consumer.

Productivity paradox: The observation that productivity increases at a rate that is lower than expected when new technologies are introduced.

Project manager: The person most responsible for ensuring that a project is a success.

Propagation delay: The delay in the transmission of a satellite signal because of the distance the signal must travel.

Protocols: Procedures that different computers follow when they transmit and receive data.

Prototyping: An iterative systems development process in which requirements are converted into a working system that is continually revised through close work between analysts and users.

Proxy variable: An alternative measurement of outcomes; used when it is difficult to determine and measure direct effects.

Pseudocode: A way to express processing logic independent of the actual programming language being used.

Public cloud: Cloud infrastructure offered on a commercial basis by a cloud service provider.

Public switched telephone network: *See* Plain old telephone service (POTS).

QR code: A two-dimensional barcode with a high storage capacity.

Query: A method used to retrieve information from a database.

Radio-frequency identification (RFID): The use of electromagnetic energy to transmit information between a reader (transceiver) and a processing device; used to replace bar codes and bar code readers.

Random-access memory (RAM): A type of primary storage that is volatile and can be accessed randomly by the CPU.

Ransomware: Malicious software that holds a user's computer hostage by locking or taking control of the user's computer, or encrypting files or documents.

RDBMS: A database management system based on the relational database model.

Read-only memory (ROM): A type of nonvolatile primary storage that is used to store programs and instructions that are automatically loaded when the computer is turned on.

Read/write head: A device that inscribes data to or retrieves data from a hard disk or tape.

Real Simple Syndication (RSS): A set of standards for sharing updated Web content, such as news and sports scores, across sites.

Record: A collection of related attributes about a single entity.

Recovery point objective: An objective specifying how timely backup data should be preserved.

Recovery time objective: An objective specifying the maximum time allowed to recover from a catastrophic event.

Recurring cost: An ongoing cost that occurs throughout the life cycle of systems development, implementation, and maintenance.

Redundant array of independent disks (RAID): A secondary storage technology that makes redundant copies of data on two or more hard drives.

Reintermediation: The design of a business model that reintroduces middlemen in order to reduce the chaos brought on by disintermediation.

Relational database model: The most common DBMS approach; entities are presented as two-dimensional tables, with records as rows and attributes as columns.

Relationship: An association between entities in a database to enable data retrieval.

Report: A compilation of data from a database that is organized and produced in printed format.

Report generator: A software tool that helps users build reports quickly and describe the data in a useful format.

Representational delight: A Web page's characteristics that stimulate a consumer's senses.

Request for proposal (RFP): A communication tool indicating buyer requirements for a given system and requesting information or soliciting bids from potential vendors.

Requirements collection: The process of gathering and organizing information from users, managers, customers, business processes, and documents to understand how a proposed information system should function.

Resources: An organization's specific assets that are utilized to create cost or product differentiation from its competitors.

Revenue model: Part of a business model that describes how the organization will earn revenue, generate profits, and produce a superior return on invested capital.

Reverse engineering: Disassembling a piece of software in order to understand its functioning.

Reverse pricing: A pricing system in which customers specify the product they are looking for and how much they are willing to pay; this information is routed to appropriate companies that either accept or reject the customer's offer.

RFID tag: The processing device used in an RFID system that uniquely identifies an object.

Ring network: A network that is configured in the shape of a closed loop or circle, with each node connecting to the next node.

Risk acceptance: A computer system security policy in which no countermeasures are adopted and any damages that occur are simply absorbed.

Risk avoidance: A computer system security policy in which alternate means are used to perform a task that would cause risk, or the task is not performed at all.

Risk reduction: The process of taking active countermeasures to protect information systems.

Risk transference: A computer system security policy in which someone else absorbs the risk, as with insurance.

Roll up: To analyze data at less detailed levels of a certain dimension.

Router: An intelligent device used to connect and route data traffic across two or more individual networks.

Rule: A way of encoding knowledge, typically expressed using an "if–then" format, within an expert system.

Sales force automation (SFA): CRM systems to support the day-to-day sales activities of an organization.

Sarbanes–Oxley Act: A U.S. government regulation mandating companies to demonstrate compliance with accounting standards and establishing controls and corporate governance.

Scalability: The ability to adapt to increases or decreases in demand for processing or data storage.

Scheduled report: A report produced at predefined intervals—daily, weekly, or monthly—to support the routine informational needs of managerial-level decision making.

Scripting language: A programming language for integrating interactive components into a Web page.

Search advertising: Advertising that is listed in the sponsored search results for a specific search term.

Search engine optimization (SEO): Methods for improving a site's ranking in search engine results.

Secondary key: An attribute that can be used to identify two or more records within a table that share a common value.

Secondary storage: Methods for permanently storing data to a large-capacity storage component, such as a hard disk, CD-ROM disk, or tape.

Secure Sockets Layer (SSL): A popular public-key encryption method used on the Internet.

Semantic web: A set of design principles that will allow computers to be able to index Web sites, topics, and subjects, enabling computers to understand Web pages and search engines to provide richer and more accurate results.

Semistructured data: Data (such as clickstreams and sensor data) that do not fit neatly into relational database structures.

Semistructured decision: A decision where problems and solutions are not clear-cut and often require judgment and expertise.

Sentiment analysis: The analysis of semistructured and unstructured data to learn about customers' thoughts, feelings, and emotions.

Sequence discovery: A data mining technique used to discover associations over time.

Server: Any computer on the network that enables access to files, databases, communications, and other services available to users of the network.

Service: An individual software component designed to perform a specific task.

Service-level agreement: A contract specifying the level of service provided in terms of performance (e.g., as measured by uptime), warranties, disaster recovery, and so on.

Service-oriented architecture (SOA): A software architecture in which business processes are broken down into individual components (or services) that are designed to achieve the desired results for the service consumer (which can be either an application, another service, or a person).

Shopping bot: *See* Buyer agent.

Shoulder surfing: Looking over one's shoulder while the person is keying in access information.

Showrooming: Shoppers coming into a store to evaluate the look and feel of a product, and then purchasing it online or at a competitor's store.

Shrink-wrap license: A type of software license that is used primarily for consumer products; the contract is activated when the shrink wrap on the packaging has been removed.

Slicing and dicing: Analyzing data on subsets of certain dimensions.

Smart card: A special credit card–sized card containing a microprocessor chip, memory circuits, and often a magnetic stripe.

Social bookmarking: The sharing and categorization of Internet bookmarks by Internet users.

Social cataloging: The creation of categorizations by Internet users.

Social commerce: Leveraging visitors' social networks in e-commerce interactions to build lasting relationships, advertise products, or otherwise create value.

Social CRM: The use of social media for customer relationship management.

Social engineering: Misrepresenting oneself to trick others into revealing information.

Social media: Web-based applications embodying core Web 2.0 values such as collaboration and social sharing, allowing people to communicate, interact, and collaborate in various ways.

Social media monitoring: The process of identifying and assessing the volume and sentiment of what is being said in social media about a company, individual, product, or brand.

Social network analysis: A technique that maps people's contacts to discover connections or missing links (sometimes called structural holes) within the organization.

Social networking: Connecting to colleagues, family members, or friends for business or entertainment purposes.

Social online community: A community within a social network.

Social presence tools: *See* Microblogging tools.

Social search: A search functionality that attempts to increase the relevance of search results by including content from social networks, blogs, or microblogging services.

Social software: *See* Social media.

Software: A program (or set of programs) that tells the computer to perform certain processing functions.

Software as a service (SaaS): A cloud computing model in which a service provider offers applications via a cloud infrastructure.

Software asset management (SAM): A set of activities performed to better manage an organization's software infrastructure by helping to consolidate and standardize software titles, decide when to retire unused software, or decide when to upgrade or replace software.

Software piracy: A type of computer crime where individuals make illegal copies of software protected by copyright laws.

Solid-state drive (SSD): A secondary storage technology using flash memory to store data.

SoLoMo: The integration of social, local, and mobile services.

Source code: A computer program's code written in a programming language.

Spam: Electronic junk mail.

Spam filter: A hardware or software device used to fight spam and other e-mail threats, such as directory harvest attacks, phishing attacks, viruses, and more.

Spear phishing: A sophisticated fraudulent e-mail attack that targets a specific person or organization by personalizing the message in order to make the message appear as if it is from a trusted source, such as an individual within the recipient's company, a government entity, or a well-known company.

Speech recognition: The process of converting spoken words into commands and data.

Sponsored search: *See* Search advertising.

Spyware: Software that covertly gathers information about a user through an Internet connection without the user's knowledge.

Stand-alone application: A system that focuses on the specific needs of an individual department and is not designed to communicate with other systems in the organization.

Star network: A network with several workstations connected to a central hub.

Stickiness: A Web site's ability to attract and keep visitors.

Strategic: A way of thinking in which plans are made to accomplish specific long-term goals.

Strategic necessity: Something an organization must do in order to survive.

Strategic planning: The process of forming a vision of where the organization needs to head, converting that vision into measurable objectives and performance targets, and crafting a plan to achieve the desired results.

Streaming audio: Audio data streams, transmitted via specific protocols, that are available for immediate playback on the recipient's computer.

Streaming media: An umbrella term for streaming audio and streaming video; audio and video data streams, transmitted via specific protocols, that are available for immediate playback on the recipient's computer.

Streaming video: Video data streams, transmitted via specific protocols, that are available for immediate playback on the recipient's computer.

Structural firmness: A Web page's characteristics related to security and performance.

Structured data: Data (such as transaction data) that fit neatly into spreadsheets or databases.

Structured decision: A decision where the procedures to follow for a given situation can be specified in advance.

Structured Query Language (SQL): The most common language used to interface with databases.

Stuxnet: A computer worm designed to find and infect a particular piece of industrial hardware; used in an attack against Iranian nuclear plants.

Supercomputer: The most expensive and most powerful category of computers. It is primarily used to assist in solving massive research and scientific problems.

Supplier portal: A subset of an organization's extranet designed to automate the business processes that occur before, during, and after sales have been transacted between a single buyer and multiple suppliers. Also referred to as a "sourcing portal" or "procurement portal."

Supply chain: The collection of companies and processes involved in moving a product from the suppliers of raw materials, to the suppliers of intermediate components, to final production, and ultimately to the customer.

Supply chain analytics: The use of key performance indicators to monitor performance of the entire supply chain, including sourcing, planning, production, and distribution.

Supply chain effectiveness: The extent to which a company's supply chain is focusing on maximizing customer service, with lesser focus on reducing procurement, production, and transportation costs.

Supply chain efficiency: The extent to which a company's supply chain is focusing on minimizing procurement, production, and transportation costs, sometimes by reducing customer service.

Supply chain execution (SCE): The execution of supply chain planning, involving the management of product flows, information flows, and financial flows.

Supply chain management (SCM): Information systems focusing on improving upstream information flows with two main objectives—to accelerate product development and to reduce costs associated with procuring raw materials, components, and services from suppliers.

Supply chain planning (SCP): The process of developing various resource plans to support the efficient and effective production of goods and services.

Supply chain visibility: The ability to track products as they move through the supply chain and to foresee external events.

Supply network: The network of multiple (sometimes interrelated) producers of supplies that a company uses.

Support activities: Business activities that enable the primary activities to take place. Support activities include administrative activities, infrastructure, human resources, technology development, and procurement.

Switch: A device used to connect multiple computers, servers, or printers to create a network.

Symmetric digital subscriber line (SDSL): A variant of DSL that supports the same data rates for upstream and downstream traffic.

Synchronous: Coordinated in time.

System clock: An electronic circuit inside a computer that generates pulses at a rapid rate for setting the pace of processing events.

System conversion: The process of decommissioning the current system and installing a new system into the organization.

System software: The collection of programs that controls the basic operations of computer hardware.

Systems analysis: The second phase of the systems development life cycle, in which the current ways of doing business are studied and alternative replacement systems are proposed.

Systems analysis and design: The process of designing, building, and maintaining information systems.

Systems analyst: The primary person responsible for performing systems analysis and design activities.

Systems benchmarking: The use of standardized performance tests to compare different systems.

Systems design: The third phase of the systems development life cycle, in which details of the chosen approach are developed.

Systems development life cycle (SDLC): A model describing the life of an information system from conception to retirement.

Systems implementation: The fourth phase of the systems development life cycle in which the information system is programmed, tested, installed, and supported.

Systems integration: Connecting separate information systems and data to improve business processes and decision making.

Systems maintenance: The process of systematically repairing and/or improving an information system.

Systems planning and selection: The first phase of the systems development life cycle, in which potential projects are identified, selected, and planned.

T1 line: A dedicated digital transmission line that can carry 1.544 Mbps of data.

T3 line: A dedicated digital transmission line that can carry about 45 Mbps of data.

Table: A collection of related records in a database where each row is a record and each column is an attribute.

Tacit knowledge assets: Knowledge assets that reflect the processes and procedures located in employees' minds.

Tag cloud: A way to visualize user-generated tags or content on a site, where the size of a word represents its importance or frequency.

Tagging: Adding metadata to media or other content.

Tangible benefit: A benefit of using a particular system or technology that is quantifiable.

Tangible cost: A cost of using a particular system of technology that is quantifiable.

Tape: A removable, high-capacity, secondary storage medium allowing only for sequential access; typically used for archiving data.

Telecommunications network: A group of two or more computer systems linked together with communications equipment.

Terminal: A local input device used to enter data into mainframes in centralized computing systems.

Text mining: Analytical techniques for extracting information from textual documents.

Text recognition software: Software designed to convert handwritten text into computer-based characters.

Thin client: A microcomputer with minimal memory, storage, and processing capabilities, used for remotely accessing virtual desktops.

Threat: An undesirable event that can cause harm.

3D printing: Technology for creating physical three-dimensional objects from digital models.

Time bomb: A type of computer virus that lies in wait for a specific date before executing its instructions.

Top-level domain: A URL's suffix (i.e., .com, .edu, or .org) representing the highest level of Internet domain names in the domain name system.

Total cost of ownership (TCO): The cost of owning and operating a system, including the total cost of acquisition, as well as all costs associated with its ongoing use and maintenance.

Touchscreen: A touch-sensitive computer display used as an input device.

Transaction: Any event, such as the exchange of goods or services for money, that occurs as part of daily business of which an organization must keep a record.

Transaction processing system (TPS): An information system designed to process day-to-day business-event data at the operational level of the organization.

Transmission Control Protocol/Internet Protocol (TCP/IP): The protocol of the Internet, which allows different interconnected networks to communicate using the same language.

Transmission media: The physical pathways to send data and information between two or more entities on a network.

Transnational business strategy: An international business strategy that allows companies to leverage the flexibility offered by a decentralized organization (to be more responsive to local conditions) while at the same time reaping economies of scale enjoyed by centralization; characterized by a balance between centralization and decentralization and interdependent resources.

Trending: A word phrase or topic that is tagged at a greater rate than others.

Trojan horse: A program that appears to be a legitimate, benign program, but carries a destructive payload. Trojan horses typically do not replicate themselves.

Tunneling: A technology used by VPNs to encapsulate, encrypt, and securely transmit data over the public Internet infrastructure, enabling business partners to exchange confidential information in a secured, private manner between organizational networks.

Unauthorized access: An information systems security breach where an unauthorized individual sees, manipulates, or otherwise handles electronically stored information.

Unicode: Character encoding method for representing characters and scripts beyond the Latin alphabet, including Chinese, Cyrillic, Hebrew, and Arabic.

Uniform Resource Locator (URL): The unique Internet address for a Web site and specific Web pages within sites.

Unstructured data: Data (such as audio and video data, comments on social networks, and so on) that do not have any identifiable structure.

Unstructured decision: A decision where few or no procedures to follow for a given situation can be specified in advance.

Upstream information flow: An information flow consisting of information received from another organization, such as from a supplier.

Usability: A system's quality of being easy to use and aesthetically pleasing.

User agent: An intelligent agent that automatically performs specific tasks for a user, such as automatically sending a report at the first of the month, assembling customized news, or filling out a Web form with routine information.

Utilities: *See* Utility programs.

Utility computing: A form of on-demand computing where resources in terms of processing, data storage, or networking are rented on an as-needed basis. The organization only pays for the services used.

Utility program: Software designed to manage computer resources and files.

Value-added network (VAN): Private, third-party-managed WANs typically used for B2B communications, offering services such as secure e-mail and translation of EDI standards to facilitate secure communication between a business and its suppliers and/or customers.

Value chain: The set of primary and support activities in an organization where value is added to a product or service.

Value chain analysis: The process of analyzing an organization's activities to determine where value is added to products and/or services and the costs that are incurred for doing so.

Value creation: An organization providing products at a lower cost or with superior (differentiated) benefits to the customer.

Value proposition: The utility that the product/service has to offer to customers.

Value system: A collection of interlocking company value chains.

Vanilla version: The features and modules that a packaged software system comes with out of the box.

Vendor-managed inventory (VMI): A business model in which the suppliers to a manufacturer (or retailer) manage the manufacturer's (or retailer's) inventory levels based on negotiated service levels.

Vertical market: A market comprised of firms within a specific industry sector.

Video: Still and moving images that can be recorded, manipulated, and displayed on a computer.

Videoconferencing over IP: The use of Internet technologies for videoconferences.

Viral marketing: A type of marketing that resembles offline word-of-mouth communication in which advertising messages are spread similar to how real viruses are transmitted through offline social networks.

Virtual company: *See* Click-only business strategy.

Virtual meeting: A meeting taking place using an online environment.

Virtual private network (VPN): A network connection that is constructed dynamically within an existing network—often called a "secure tunnel"—in order to securely connect remote users or nodes to an organization's network.

Virtual team: A work team that is composed of members who may be from different organizations and different locations that forms and disbands as needed.

Virtual world: An online environment allowing people to communicate synchronously using 3D avatars.

Virus: A destructive program that disrupts the normal functioning of computer systems.

Virus prevention: A set of activities designed to detect and prevent computer viruses.

Visual analytics: The combination of various analysis techniques and interactive visualizations to solve complex problems.

Visual data discovery: *See* Visual analytics.

Visual programming language: A programming language that has a graphical user interface (GUI) for the programmer and is designed for programming applications that will have a GUI.

Visualization: The display of complex data relationships using a variety of graphical methods.

Voice over IP (VoIP): The use of Internet technologies for placing telephone calls.

Voice-to-text software: An application that uses a microphone to monitor a person's speech and then converts the speech into text.

Volatile memory: Memory that loses its contents when the power is turned off.

Volume license: *See* Enterprise license.

Vulnerability: A weaknesses in an organization's systems or security policies that can be exploited to cause damage.

Vulnerability scanners: Software programs that automatically test targeted systems for weaknesses.

Warez: A slang term for stolen proprietary software that is sold or shared for free over the Internet.

Watermark: A digital or physical mark that is difficult to reproduce; used to prevent counterfeiting or to trace illegal copies to the original purchaser.

Wearable technologies: Clothing or accessories, such as smart watches or fitness trackers, that incorporate electronic technologies.

Web 2.0: A term used to describe dynamic Web applications that allow people to collaborate and share information online.

Web analytics: The analysis of Web surfers' behavior in order to improve a site's performance.

Web browser: A software application that can be used to locate and display Web pages including text, graphics, and multimedia content.

Web content mining: Extracting textual information from Web documents.

Web crawler: An intelligent agent that continuously browses the Web for specific information (e.g., used by search engines). Also known as a "Web spider."

Web page: A hypertext document stored on a Web server that contains not only information, but also references or links to other documents that contain related information.

Web page builder: A program for assisting in the creation and maintenance of Web pages.

Web server: A computer used to host Web sites.

Web site: A collection of interlinked Web pages typically belonging to the same person or business organization.

Web spider: *See* Web crawler.

Web usage mining: An analysis of a Web site's usage patterns, such as navigational paths or time spent.

Web vandalism: The act of defacing Web sites.

Webcam: A small camera that is used to transmit real-time video images within desktop videoconferencing systems.

Webcast: A digital media stream that can be distributed to and played by digital media players.

Webcasting: The process of publishing webcasts.

Weighted multicriteria analysis: A method for deciding among different information systems investments or alternative designs for a given system in which requirements and constraints are weighted on the basis of their importance.

What-if analysis: An analysis of the effects hypothetical changes to data have on the results.

Wide area network (WAN): A computer network that spans a relatively large geographic area; typically used to connect two or more LANs.

Wi-Fi network (wireless fidelity): Wireless LAN, based on the 802.11 family of standards.

Wiki: A Web site allowing people to create, edit, or delete content, as well as discuss article content or suggested changes with other members of the community. A wiki is linked to a database keeping a history of all prior versions and changes; therefore, a wiki allows viewing prior versions of the pages as well as reverting any changes made to the content.

WikiLeaks: An information disclosure portal where volunteers submit and analyze classified and restricted material provided by whistleblowers.

Wikipedia: An online encyclopedia using wiki technology.

Wireless access point: A networking device that transmits and receives wireless (Wi-Fi) signals to allow wireless devices to connect to the network.

Wireless broadband: Wireless transmission technology with speeds similar to DSL and cable that requires line of sight between the sender and receiver.

Wireless controller: A networking device that manages multiple access points and can be used to manage transmission power and channel allocation to establish desired coverage throughout a building and minimize interference between individual access points.

Wireless local area network (WLAN): A local area network that uses a wireless transmission protocol.

Workstation: A high-performance computer that is designed for medical, engineering, or animation and graphics design uses, and is optimized for visualization and rendering of three-dimensional models.

World Wide Web (WWW): A system of Internet servers that support documents formatted in HTML, which supports links to other documents as well as graphics, audio, and video files.

Worm: A destructive computer code that is designed to copy and send itself throughout networked computers.

XML tag: Markup that is inserted into a document in order to specify how information should be interpreted and used.

Zombie computer: A virus-infected computer that can be used to launch attacks on Web sites.

Name Index

T

V

W

Y

Z

Organization Index

U

V

W

X

Y

Z

Subject Index

Key terms and the page numbers where they are defined appear in boldface.

C

D

E

N

O

P

Q

R

S